D0890102

THE MODERN LAW OF CONTRACTS

Second Edition

By

Bruce W. Frier
Henry King Ransom Professor of Law
University of Michigan Law School

James J. White
Robert A. Sullivan Professor of Law
University of Michigan Law School

AMERICAN CASEBOOK SERIES®

Mat #40585449

610 Opperman Drive
St. Paul, MN 55123
1–800–313–9378

Printed in the United States of America

ISBN: 978–0–314–18026–1

Introduction for the Student

Hey You. You, beginning law student, don't hurry by here on your way to Constitutional Law or Criminal Procedure. Don't think that you will make your living as a defender of persons wrongly accused of crime or that you will save your clients by asserting grand issues of constitutional law. Most of you will be "contract lawyers," not criminal defense lawyers or defenders of the First Amendment. And it's a good thing, too, because contract law is much more interesting than con law or criminal procedure. Studying contracts will carry you from the elegantly philosophical to the crudely practical. It will fill your hours in law school study with gloriously subtle issues and fill your years of practice in the office or in court with a grand array of questions.

Contracts and the legal questions that follow contracts are everywhere. Some contracts control transfer of enormous wealth. For example, does the lessee of the World Trade Center collect $7 billion from his insurer because there were two "occurrences" when two aircraft hit the towers, or only $3.5 billion because there was only one "occurrence?" Some contracts intrude deeply into our personal lives. Does the birth mother who has given her egg and has contracted to carry a baby for another couple get to keep the baby despite her promise to give it up? Some contracts rule our daily lives in ways we barely perceive. Does the subway motorman's labor contract keep him from striking? When the market turns sharply up or down, will the American buyers and Saudi sellers honor their contracts to sell oil—and so make gasoline widely available? Dozens of contracts for goods (paper, ink, delivery trucks), services (writers, printers, deliverymen, satellite transmission), and real estate (leases of offices and printing plants) are necessary for the production of a daily newspaper; will they be observed?

Understand how these legal questions ride into the lawyer's life on the back of contracts. First, the lawyer may be called upon to draft the contract, and then to negotiate it with the other party's lawyer. Yet later another lawyer must interpret the contract to tell a client whether it obliges the client to do something that he would rather not do. Finally a lawyer may have to try a lawsuit to uphold or challenge the contract, and if she loses, appeal the trial court's judgment by arguing from appellate cases on contract law.

What are these many legal questions? A contract is no more than a bunch of symbols put down on paper. What can be so hard about drafting, interpreting, or understanding the legal significance of a contract? We will try to give you a taste of the questions that you will face here.

1. What promises should the law enforce? All of them? Even a promise to make a gift? To honor and obey until death do us part?

2. What ritual should we require of the parties before we find a "contract?" Must one make a detailed "offer" and the other a clear "acceptance?" Or is it enough that each shares the same general notion and leaves some loose ends?

3. What formalities must a promise have before the law recognizes it? Must it be in writing? Could it be electronic or even oral?

4. What do these words mean? Are we looking for the meaning buried in the heads of the parties (or of one of them) or for the meaning that the common man would ascribe to these words? In the insurance contracts the word "occurrence" is frequently used and often interpreted by the courts. Do we look at cases that have interpreted that word in other contexts, or should we focus on the definitions and other terms in the insurance contract?

5. What terms will the law supply if the parties do not provide them? If a second year student offers to sell you his 190-page contracts outline from last year, and you agree to buy it for $50, do you have a right to inspect the outline to see if it is legible and if it in fact has 190 pages before you pay? In this case the law on the sale of goods supplies the term that you never thought of including; yes, you can look before you pay.

6. What should the law do with weird cases where, for example, the parties have made a deal to sell a Kentucky Derby winner at a low price in the belief that he was sterile (and so good only for some low level claiming races), and he turns out to be fertile (and so capable of producing a large cash flow in many years of stud service)?

7. What about contracts where one party has skinned the other? What if a seller charges a poorly informed buyer $700 in installment payments for a TV that can be bought for $150 at Circuit City? Should the law police these, or should it just stand aside and hope that the buyer learns his lesson?

8. What remedies for broken contracts? If paying money is what the breacher must do, how much and why? Should he pay what the other has paid out and so carry the plaintiff back to the economic beginning point? Or should he pay an approximation of what the contract would have done for the other and so carry the plaintiff forward to the economic place where he would have been had the contract been performed?

You can see how some of these questions are utterly practical (How do I convince the jury that one "occurrence" could include two aircraft hitting two buildings?). You can also see that some of them raise hard ethical issues (Can the birth mother keep the child?) and may even present important questions of public policy (Should courts be laissez faire or should they intrude to help the weak? What is gained and what lost with each choice?).

So count your lucky stars. You are about to embark on the study of the most magnificent subject in the legal curriculum. There will be no slogging through dismal search and seizure cases like you will see in criminal procedure, nor wrestling with fat and fatuous federal statutes like you have to do in tax and patent law, nor any need to deal with trivial questions like George Carlin's right to utter nasty words. Here—by looking at their contracts—you get to see commerce, industry and individual activity parading before you in kaleidoscopic splendor.

*

Introduction for the Contracts Teacher

This casebook is the indirect result of a curricular reform at the University of Michigan, which resulted in first-year Contracts being reduced from a five- or six-hour course to a four-hour course. Both of us had taught Contracts under the older schedule, but were now obliged to present the same material within a substantially briefer framework. We soon found that the standard Contracts casebooks (Farnsworth and Sanger; Knapp, Crystal, and Prince), although of unmatched quality, were difficult to abridge for a quicker course, at any rate if certain other important course goals were to be preserved. We decided that a new casebook could fill a useful niche. What resulted is the casebook you have before you.

The other course goals are significant. We wanted comprehensive coverage; that is, we were unwilling to forgo at least swift introductions to all the topics that constitute the standard course, and in particular we were adverse to abbreviating the curriculum by simply tossing out important subjects like the Statute of Frauds or third-party interests in contracts. This meant, of necessity, a casebook that would be markedly less exhaustive than the standards for the field. Subjects such as the doctrine of consideration, or the etiquette of offer-and-acceptance, are open to almost endless analysis, much of which is extremely fruitful for first-year students who are still struggling with basic structures of legal thinking. But we were required to hurry, hurry, if we were to provide a casebook with even the remotest hope that teachers could complete it entirely within a four-hour course.

At the same time, we wanted the casebook to be reasonably up to date. This is an era of change in Contracts law: the Convention on the International Sale of Goods and other international contract treaties or conventions are settling down as part of the day-to-day life of practicing commercial lawyers; and Article Two of the Uniform Commercial Code, the bedrock statute for sale of goods, has recently been revised, although its legislative future remains uncertain. At the same time, courts have forged onward in generating novel doctrines particularly in the areas of reliance and form contracts. In order to give due space to these considerable recent developments, we were forced to sideline some familiar war horses—cases that we ourselves had enjoyed teaching, but that are no longer of such urgency. And further simplification was required: a shorter casebook cannot remotely represent the complexity of contemporary contract law in the various American jurisdictions.

Any casebook is a product of such compromises. Inadequacies will undoubtedly obtrude. But the authors have test-taught this casebook in two law schools, and we are convinced that, if the proper drill-sergeant demeanor is maintained, it is possible to complete the book more or less entirely, with perhaps only minor omissions of a case here or there, during a single four-hour course.

One note on the reporting of judicial opinions: We have been relatively full, sometimes to the point of indulgence, so that students can observe the full panoply of prudential considerations that underlie (or undermine) a decision. We have, on the other hand, taken slight liberties. Where a judge (or a law clerk) makes minor and obvious errors of spelling or diction, we have simply corrected the text, rather than inserting an obtrusive and ugly *sic*. On a very few occasions we have also slightly adjusted the paragraphing in order to elucidate the flow of judicial reasoning. We omit many footnotes, and renumber those that remain within each chapter.

Throughout this casebook, we assume that students have access to a standard companion collection of pertinent statutes and Restatement selections, such as Burton and Eisenberg's Contract Law in its latest edition. In the text, we have often but not always quoted relevant statutory or Restatement language, so that students will not necessarily have to have a second book open in order to understand this one. Still, in many instances more context will be required.

* * * * *

In the preparation of the first and now the second editions, both editors are grateful for help received from the Cook Research Fund at the University of Michigan Law School, and also from their long suffering secretaries, Janis Weston, Eeva Joensuu, and Chris Killen. We would also like to thank our research assistants Sean Whalen, Jonathan Hanks, Larry Marcus, and Ryan Vlcko.

Summary of Contents

Table of Contents

Page

Table of Cases

The principal cases are in bold type. Cases cited or discussed in the text are roman type. References are to pages. Cases cited in principal cases and within other quoted materials are not included.

THE MODERN LAW OF CONTRACTS

Second Edition

*

Chapter 1

A ROADMAP FOR CONTRACT LAW

We begin with two cases that illustrate not only the general subject matter of Contracts, but also the legal methods most commonly used in handling contractual problems. The two cases are as different as they can be: one, a dispute between four private citizens over a contract concluded in the casual atmosphere of a bar, and the other, a dispute between two companies over a long-term contract for the sale of coal. We also come in on different stages of the contracting process: the first case concerns whether an enforceable contract has been concluded, while the second handles an apparent breach of contract by one party.

The two cases further illustrate the variety of legal materials that are typically used in solving contract disputes. The first case is a pure Common Law case, with the Virginia Supreme Court seeking additional counsel from the Restatement on Contracts and standard treatises. The second case, by contrast, concerns the sale of goods. Here, in American law, Article 2 of the Uniform Commercial Code (UCC) governs, a general statute that virtually all states have adopted with small variations; so the judge's decision starts, not from traditional case law, but from the wording and application of the UCC's statutory language. We will frequently return to the UCC throughout the book.

LUCY v. ZEHMER

Supreme Court of Virginia, 1954.
196 Va. 493, 84 S.E.2d 516.

BUCHANAN, J. This suit was instituted by W. O. Lucy and J. C. Lucy, complainants, against A. H. Zehmer and Ida S. Zehmer, his wife, defendants, to have specific performance of a contract by which it was alleged the Zehmers had sold to W. O. Lucy a tract of land owned by A. H. Zehmer in Dinwiddie county containing 471.6 acres, more or less, known as the Ferguson farm, for $50,000. J. C. Lucy, the other complainant, is a brother of W. O. Lucy, to whom W. O. Lucy transferred a half interest in his alleged purchase.

The instrument sought to be enforced was written by A. H. Zehmer on December 20, 1952, in these words: "We hereby agree to sell to W. O.

Lucy the Ferguson Farm complete for $50,000.00, title satisfactory to buyer," and signed by the defendants, A. H. Zehmer and Ida S. Zehmer.

DE LUXE CABINS STEAM HEATED HOTEL ROOMS
YE OLDE VIRGINNIE RESTAURANT
GARAGE - SERVICE STATION
25 MILES SOUTH OF PETERSBURG
U. S. No. 1 McKENNEY, VA.

SERVER	GUESTS	TABLE	CHECK
			25216

PLEASE PAY CASHIER

[Front]

[Back]

The answer of A. H. Zehmer admitted that at the time mentioned W. O. Lucy offered him $50,000 cash for the farm, but that he, Zehmer, considered that the offer was made in jest; that so thinking, and both he and Lucy having had several drinks, he wrote out "the memorandum" quoted above and induced his wife to sign it; that he did not deliver the memorandum to Lucy, but that Lucy picked it up, read it, put it in his pocket, attempted to offer Zehmer $5 to bind the bargain, which Zehmer refused to accept, and realizing for the first time that Lucy was serious, Zehmer assured him that he had no intention of selling the farm and that the whole matter was a joke. Lucy left the premises insisting that he had purchased the farm.

Depositions were taken and the decree appealed from was entered holding that the complainants had failed to establish their right to specific performance, and dismissing their bill. The assignment of error is to this action of the court.

W. O. Lucy, a lumberman and farmer, thus testified in substance: He had known Zehmer for fifteen or twenty years and had been familiar with the Ferguson farm for ten years. Seven or eight years ago he had offered Zehmer $20,000 for the farm which Zehmer had accepted, but the agreement was verbal and Zehmer backed out. On the night of December 20, 1952, around eight o'clock, he took an employee to McKenney, where Zehmer lived and operated a restaurant, filling station and motor court. While there he decided to see Zehmer and again try to buy the Ferguson farm. He entered the restaurant and talked to Mrs.

Zehmer until Zehmer came in. He asked Zehmer if he had sold the Ferguson farm. Zehmer replied that he had not. Lucy said, "I bet you wouldn't take $50,000.00 for that place." Zehmer replied, "Yes, I would too; you wouldn't give fifty." Lucy said he would and told Zehmer to write up an agreement to that effect. Zehmer took a restaurant check and wrote on the back of it, "I do hereby agree to sell to W. O. Lucy the Ferguson Farm for $50,000 complete." Lucy told him he had better change it to "We" because Mrs. Zehmer would have to sign it too. Zehmer then tore up what he had written, wrote the agreement quoted above and asked Mrs. Zehmer, who was at the other end of the counter ten or twelve feet away, to sign it. Mrs. Zehmer said she would for $50,000 and signed it. Zehmer brought it back and gave it to Lucy, who offered him $5 which Zehmer refused, saying, "You don't need to give me any money, you got the agreement there signed by both of us."

The discussion leading to the signing of the agreement, said Lucy, lasted thirty or forty minutes, during which Zehmer seemed to doubt that Lucy could raise $50,000. Lucy suggested the provision for having the title examined and Zehmer made the suggestion that he would sell it "complete, everything there," and stated that all he had on the farm was three heifers.

Lucy took a partly filled bottle of whiskey into the restaurant with him for the purpose of giving Zehmer a drink if he wanted it. Zehmer did, and he and Lucy had one or two drinks together. Lucy said that while he felt the drinks he took he was not intoxicated, and from the way Zehmer handled the transaction he did not think he was either.

December 20 was on Saturday. Next day Lucy telephoned to J. C. Lucy and arranged with the latter to take a half interest in the purchase and pay half of the consideration. On Monday he engaged an attorney to examine the title. The attorney reported favorably on December 31 and on January 2 Lucy wrote Zehmer stating that the title was satisfactory, that he was ready to pay the purchase price in cash and asking when Zehmer would be ready to close the deal. Zehmer replied by letter, mailed on January 13, asserting that he had never agreed or intended to sell.

Mr. and Mrs. Zehmer were called by the complainants as adverse witnesses. Zehmer testified in substance as follows: He bought this farm more than ten years ago for $11,000. He had had twenty-five offers, more or less, to buy it, including several from Lucy, who had never offered any specific sum of money. He had given them all the same answer, that he was not interested in selling it. On this Saturday night before Christmas it looked like everybody and his brother came by there to have a drink. He took a good many drinks during the afternoon and had a pint of his own. When he entered the restaurant around eight-thirty Lucy was there and he could see that he was "pretty high." He said to Lucy, "Boy, you got some good liquor, drinking, ain't you?" Lucy then offered him a drink. "I was already high as a Georgia pine, and didn't have any more better sense than to pour another great big slug out and gulp it down, and he took one too."

After they had talked a while Lucy asked whether he still had the Ferguson farm. He replied that he had not sold it and Lucy said, "I bet you wouldn't take $50,000.00 for it." Zehmer asked him if he would give $50,000 and Lucy said yes. Zehmer replied, "You haven't got $50,000 in cash." Lucy said he did and Zehmer replied that he did not believe it. They argued "pro and con for a long time," mainly about "whether he had $50,000 in cash that he could put up right then and buy that farm."

Finally, said Zehmer, Lucy told him if he didn't believe he had $50,000, "you sign that piece of paper here and say you will take $50,000.00 for the farm." He, Zehmer, "just grabbed the back off of a guest check there" and wrote on the back of it. At that point in his testimony Zehmer asked to see what he had written to "see if I recognize my own handwriting." He examined the paper and exclaimed, "Great balls of fire, I got 'Firgerson' for Ferguson. I have got satisfactory spelled wrong. I don't recognize that writing if I would see it, wouldn't know it was mine."

After Zehmer had, as he described it, "scribbled this thing off," Lucy said, "Get your wife to sign it." Zehmer walked over to where she was and she at first refused to sign but did so after he told her that he "was just needling him [Lucy], and didn't mean a thing in the world, that I was not selling the farm." Zehmer then "took it back over there * * * and I was still looking at the dern thing. I had the drink right there by my hand, and I reached over to get a drink, and he said, 'Let me see it.' He reached and picked it up, and when I looked back again he had it in his pocket and he dropped a five dollar bill over there, and he said, 'Here is five dollars payment on it.' * * * I said, 'Hell no, that is beer and liquor talking. I am not going to sell you the farm. I have told you that too many times before.' " . . . [Eds.: A summary of testimony to much the same effect from Ida Zehmer and from the waitress is omitted.]

The defendants insist that the evidence was ample to support their contention that the writing sought to be enforced was prepared as a bluff or dare to force Lucy to admit that he did not have $50,000; that the whole matter was a joke; that the writing was not delivered to Lucy and no binding contract was ever made between the parties.

It is an unusual, if not bizarre, defense. When made to the writing admittedly prepared by one of the defendants and signed by both, clear evidence is required to sustain it.

In his testimony Zehmer claimed that he "was high as a Georgia pine," and that the transaction "was just a bunch of two doggoned drunks bluffing to see who could talk the biggest and say the most." That claim is inconsistent with his attempt to testify in great detail as to what was said and what was done. It is contradicted by other evidence as to the condition of both parties, and rendered of no weight by the testimony of his wife that when Lucy left the restaurant she suggested that Zehmer drive him home. The record is convincing that Zehmer was not intoxicated to the extent of being unable to comprehend the nature and consequences of the instrument he executed, and hence that instrument is not to be invalidated on that ground. 17 C.J.S., Contracts, § 133 b., p. 483; *Taliaferro v. Emery*, 124 Va. 674, 98 S.E. 627. It was in fact conceded by defendants' counsel in oral argument that under the evidence Zehmer was not too drunk to make a valid contract.

The evidence is convincing also that Zehmer wrote two agreements, the first one beginning "I hereby agree to sell." Zehmer first said he could not remember about that, then that "I don't think I wrote but one out." Mrs. Zehmer said that what he wrote was "I hereby agree," but that the "I" was changed to "We" after that night. The agreement that was written and signed is in the record and indicates no such change. Neither are the mistakes in spelling that Zehmer sought to point out readily apparent.

The appearance of the contract, the fact that it was under discussion for forty minutes or more before it was signed; Lucy's objection to the first draft because it was written in the singular, and he wanted Mrs. Zehmer to sign it also; the rewriting to meet that objection and the signing by Mrs. Zehmer; the discussion of what was to be included in the sale, the provision for the examination of the title, the completeness of the instrument that was executed, the taking possession of it by Lucy with no request or suggestion by either of the defendants that he give it back, are facts which furnish persuasive evidence that the execution of the contract was a serious business transaction rather than a casual, jesting matter as defendants now contend....

If it be assumed, contrary to what we think the evidence shows, that Zehmer was jesting about selling his farm to Lucy and that the transaction was intended by him to be a joke, nevertheless the evidence shows that Lucy did not so understand it but considered it to be a serious business transaction and the contract to be binding on the Zehmers as well as on himself.

The very next day he arranged with his brother to put up half the money and take a half interest in the land. The day after that he employed an attorney to examine the title. The next night, Tuesday, he was back at Zehmer's place and there Zehmer told him for the first time, Lucy said, that he wasn't going to sell and he told Zehmer, "You know you sold that place fair and square." After receiving the report from his attorney that the title was good he wrote to Zehmer that he was ready to close the deal.

Not only did Lucy actually believe, but the evidence shows he was warranted in believing, that the contract represented a serious business transaction and a good faith sale and purchase of the farm.

In the field of contracts, as generally elsewhere, "We must look to the outward expression of a person as manifesting his intention rather than to his secret and unexpressed intention. 'The law imputes to a person an intention corresponding to the reasonable meaning of his words and acts.' " *First Nat. Bank v. Roanoke Oil Co.*, 169 Va. 99, 114, 192 S.E. 764, 770.

At no time prior to the execution of the contract had Zehmer indicated to Lucy by word or act that he was not in earnest about selling the farm. They had argued about it and discussed its terms, as Zehmer admitted, for a long time. Lucy testified that if there was any jesting it was about paying $50,000 that night. The contract and the evidence show that he was not expected to pay the money that night. Zehmer said that after the writing was signed he laid it down on the counter in front of Lucy. Lucy said Zehmer handed it to him. In any event there had been what appeared to be a good faith offer and a good faith acceptance, followed by the execution and apparent delivery of a written contract. Both said that Lucy put the writing in his pocket and then offered Zehmer $5 to seal the bargain. Not until then, even under the defendants' evidence, was anything said or done to indicate that the matter was a joke. Both of the Zehmers testified that when Zehmer asked his wife to sign he whispered that it was a joke so Lucy wouldn't hear and that it was not intended that he should hear.

The mental assent of the parties is not requisite for the formation of a contract. If the words or other acts of one of the parties have but one reasonable meaning, his undisclosed intention is immaterial except when an unreasonable meaning which he attaches to his manifestations is known to the other party. Restatement of the Law of Contracts, Vol. I, § 71, p. 74.

" * * * The law, therefore, judges of an agreement between two persons exclusively from those expressions of their intentions which are communicated between them. * * *." Clark on Contracts, 4 ed., § 3, p. 4.

An agreement or mutual assent is of course essential to a valid contract but the law imputes to a person an intention corresponding to the reasonable meaning of his words and acts. If his words and acts, judged by a reasonable standard, manifest an intention to agree, it is immaterial what may be the real but unexpressed state of his mind. 17 C.J.S., Contracts, § 32, p. 361; 12 Am. Jur., Contracts, § 19, p. 515.

So a person cannot set up that he was merely jesting when his conduct and words would warrant a reasonable person in believing that he intended a real agreement, 17 C.J.S., Contracts, § 47, p. 390; Clark on Contracts, 4 ed., § 27, at p. 54.

Whether the writing signed by the defendants and now sought to be enforced by the complainants was the result of a serious offer by Lucy and a serious acceptance by the defendants, or was a serious offer by Lucy and an acceptance in secret jest by the defendants, in either event it constituted a binding contract of sale between the parties.

Defendants contend further, however, that even though a contract was made, equity should decline to enforce it under the circumstances. These circumstances have been set forth in detail above. They disclose some drinking by the two parties but not to an extent that they were unable to understand fully what they were doing. There was no fraud, no misrepresentation, no sharp practice and no dealing between unequal parties. The farm had been bought for $11,000 and was assessed for taxation at $6,300. The purchase price was $50,000. Zehmer admitted that it was a good price. There is in fact present in this case none of the grounds usually urged against specific performance.

Specific performance, it is true, is not a matter of absolute or arbitrary right, but is addressed to the reasonable and sound discretion of the court. *First Nat. Bank v. Roanoke Oil Co.*, supra, 169 Va. at p. 116, 192 S.E. at p. 771. But it is likewise true that the discretion which may be exercised is not an arbitrary or capricious one, but one which is controlled by the established doctrines and settled principles of equity; and, generally, where a contract is in its nature and circumstances unobjectionable, it is as much a matter of course for courts of equity to decree a specific performance of it as it is for a court of law to give damages for a breach of it. *Bond v. Crawford,* 193 Va. 437, 444, 69 S.E.(2d) 470, 475.

The complainants are entitled to have specific performance of the contracts sued on. The decree appealed from is therefore reversed and the cause is remanded for the entry of a proper decree requiring the defendants to perform the contract in accordance with the prayer of the bill.

Reversed and remanded.

Notes and Discussion

1. Procedural Posture. The Lucy brothers originally sued in the Circuit Court of Dinwiddie County, Virginia, seeking to enforce the contract that they believed they had made with the Zehmers. They wanted "specific performance," a contractual remedy in the form of a judicial decree requiring the Zehmers to transfer to them the Ferguson farm's deed in exchange for their paying the $50,000 purchase price. The trial judge determined that the Lucys "had failed to establish their right to specific performance," and so dismissed their suit. As the appellate opinion notes, specific performance is a remedy in equity, meaning that the court can consider the background of the alleged deal, including its fairness in light of the circumstances in which it was made. (Specific performance is available only on an exceptional basis in Common Law, which generally prefers money damages for contract claims. See Chapter 6.) It is unclear from the appellate opinion why the judge below dismissed the Lucys' demand for specific performance. Perhaps the judge was not convinced that a contract existed at all; or perhaps the judge felt that there was a contract, but that "equity should decline to enforce it under the circumstances," as the Zehmers contended. If this second alternative were true, the Lucys would be denied specific performance but could still sue for monetary damages from the Zehmers.

In any case, the judge below heard testimony from all four litigants and from at least one witness to the purported deal (a waitress). The Virginia

Supreme Court, as an appellate court, reaches farther than seems appropriate when it finds, on its own and without benefit of testimony, that "the execution of the contract was a serious business transaction rather than a casual, jesting matter."

2. Capacity to Contract: Intoxication. There evidently had been a fair amount of pre-Christmas drinking in the Ye Olde Virginnie Restaurant. Indeed, W. O. Lucy testified that he took along some whiskey "for the purpose of giving Zehmer a drink if he wanted it." A. H. Zehmer described himself as "high as a Georgia pine" even before he drank some of Lucy's whiskey, and asserted also that Lucy himself was "pretty high." Even if Zehmer's claims are devalued as self-interested exaggeration, the Virginia Supreme Court sets a steep requirement for escaping a signed contract on grounds of intoxication (from alcohol or drugs): a party must be "unable to comprehend the nature and consequences of the instrument he executed."

If a party is not utterly disabled, the prevailing view is Restatement 2d, Contracts § 16, Comment b: "Where there is some understanding of the transaction despite intoxication, avoidance [of a contract] depends on a showing that the other party induced the drunkenness or that the consideration was inadequate or that the transaction departed from the normal pattern of similar transactions; if the particular transaction in its result is one which a reasonably competent person might have made, it cannot be avoided even though entirely executory" (as was true in this case; neither side had yet begun performance when Zehmer repudiated the deal). Lucy appears to have played some role in getting Zehmer intoxicated. If the Court had paid more attention to this fact, it might have reached a different outcome.

For adults, mental illness is the other main reason for lack of capacity. The modern standard is set by Restatement 2d § 15, which is somewhat more forgiving than § 16; a contract is voidable if a person with a mental illness "is unable to understand in a reasonable manner the nature and consequences of the transaction," or "is unable to act in a reasonable manner in relation to the transaction and the other party has reason to know of his condition."

The more general issue here is whether Zehmer had the legal capacity to conclude a contract. Restatement 2d § 12(1): "No one can be bound by contract who has not legal capacity to incur at least voidable contractual duties...." Besides the intoxicated and the mentally ill, so-called "infants" (minors below the age of 18) usually can make only voidable contracts, which means that they may avoid a contract even if it has already been executed. Legal capacity is a complex subject that we have chosen to omit.

3. Intent to Contract: "A Bluff Or Dare"; "A Joke." The Zehmers' main line of defense was that they had lacked the intent necessary to conclude a binding contract. Reconstruct what their attorney argued regarding their behavior. What is the difference between a bluff and a joke? The Zehmers might have been better advised to emphasize the jovial atmosphere in the restaurant, rather than their baiting response when Lucy insisted on buying the Ferguson farm. In retrospect, A. H. Zehmer should have made it crystal clear to Lucy that he had no intention to be legally bound by the words he was writing.

As this case suggests, when a person appears to be making a serious promise, the intent to contract is normally presumed, unless the more general social context of the promise clearly indicates otherwise. (For instance, a social invitation: "Thank you so much for asking me, and I promise to join you for dinner on Friday.") In modern contract law, difficulties in this area arise chiefly when two parties are negotiating over a contract, as for instance when one party comes to believe that a contract has already been formed, but the other disputes this. See Chapter 2.C.

4. The Objective Theory of Contract. The Virginia Supreme Court treats the Zehmers' argument as "an unusual, if not bizarre, defense." When the court states that: "The mental assent of the parties is not requisite for the formation of a contract," and that: "We must look to the outward expression of a person as manifesting his intention rather than to his secret and unexpressed intention," it is underscoring what a reasonable person in the Lucy's position would believe, not what Lucy actually believed. What if we turn the problem on its head? Assume that a reasonable person would have believed Zehmer was joking, but that Lucy, more gullible or insightful than most, believed him to be serious. Would an advocate of the objective theory of contract allow Lucy's belief to control?

The objective theory of contract received near classic articulation from Judge Learned Hand in 1911: "A contract has, strictly speaking, nothing to do with the personal, or individual, intent of the parties. A contract is an obligation attached by the mere force of law to certain acts of the parties, usually words, which ordinarily accompany and represent a known intent. If, however, it were proved by twenty bishops that either party when he used the words intended something else than the usual meaning which the law imposes on them, he would still be held, unless there were some mutual mistake or something else of the sort." *Hotchkiss v. National City Bank of N.Y.*, 200 F. 287, 293 (S.D.N.Y. 1911).

This theory has dominated American contract law since the late nineteenth century, and it has certain advantages in an impersonal modern economy. For one possible advantage, see UCC § 2–204(4)(b) (amended version 2003): "A contract may be formed by the interaction of an electronic agent and an individual acting on the individual's own behalf or for another person." This provision looks mainly to the formation of contracts on the internet, when a customer orders something by electronically pressing the "buy" button on a seller's website, and the site then "confirms" the order by e-mail; the seller can be bound even in the absence of any human intervention, much less human "intent."

Though there are good reasons for adopting an objective theory as the norm, there are limits. For example, suppose that (as is common) a party signs a form contract without fully reading it, and that the contract contains a singularly oppressive clause. Should the signatory be bound by the apparent manifestation of agreement? As we will see especially in Chapter 3, this is a major issue in modern contract law.

As you will see throughout this book, objective and subjective interpretations of contractual behavior are at war in judges' minds day by day. When a court or a commentator speaks of "manifestation of assent," it is usually impossible to know whether the speaker has in mind something that would be a manifestation of the subjective intention of a contracting party, or rather only that the act of the contracting party should have the meaning that an objective third party would normally ascribe to it whether or not that was truly the actor's intention. So we suspect that despite Judge Hand's bold statement of the objective theory in *Hotchkiss*, thousands of judges act each day in blessed ignorance of the tension between objective and subjective interpretations of the contract, and in equally blissful ignorance of the fact that prominent judges and the Restatement of Contracts have endorsed the objective theory.

5. The Contract/No Contract Dichotomy: Expectation, Reliance, and Restitution. The court concludes that W. O. Lucy and the Zehmers entered into a contract at the moment when the Zehmers signed the restaurant check. Lucy claims that he did not find out about the Zehmers' repudiation until several weeks later, after he had arranged for his brother to take a half interest in the purchase and had also retained an attorney to examine the title. By contrast, A.H. Zehmer alleges that almost immediately after signing he indicated to Lucy his intention not to carry out the contract ("I am not going to sell you the farm."). If the court had believed him, would it have made any difference?

In traditional contract theory, the concluding of a valid contract instantly alters the situation between the two parties. The formation process is over; an offer has been made and accepted, and (in the typical case where the parties exchange promises) both sides are now bound to their agreement. But in the moments after the Zehmers signed their promise, neither they nor Lucy had changed position in any substantial respect. To put it technically, both parties had no more than an **"expectation interest"** in performance by the other. Nonetheless, this interest, on Lucy's side, would have been legally sufficient to prevent the Zehmers from avoiding the contract without liability, even though their doing so would cause no loss to Lucy beyond his disappointment at not obtaining the Ferguson farm.

Although contract law today enforces "executory" deals where neither party has spent time and effort in reliance on the contract and there has been no performance by either party, it was slow to do so. Consider the different situation after Lucy had arranged for financing and a title search. Although he had still not executed his side of the bargain (by paying the Zehmers for their farm), Lucy had invested time and money. He now had what is called a **"reliance interest"** in the Zehmers' executing their promise, in the sense that he would lose materially if they could escape their contract without liability. The case for enforcing the Zehmers' promise is stronger than when Lucy had only an expectation interest.

This analysis helps in understanding what Lucy tried to accomplish by offering to pay the Zehmers five dollars "to bind the bargain." Had the Zehmers accepted, the payment would, of course, represent detrimental reliance by Lucy on the Zehmers' promise. But because the payment would also (however marginally) have enriched the Zehmers, it would also have provided him with an additional **"restitution interest"**: the Zehmers would have profited from their promise at Lucy's expense, and the moral case for enforcing their promise might seem even stronger. But although Lucy (like many laypersons) probably believed his legal position would be stronger if he made such a symbolic payment, in fact it was a legally superfluous act, except, perhaps, as further evidence of contractual intent to be bound. In the ordinary case where parties form a contract by exchanging promises, their contract is enforceable on the basis of their expectation interests alone.

Explaining why this is so, or why it should be so, has taxed the minds of many great legal scholars; perhaps the best treatment is Patrick Atiyah, Promises, Morals, and Law (1981). In any case, the respect given to the expectation interest tends to increase the contract/no contract dichotomy, since, in most instances, parties have only limited legal protection during the pre-contractual negotiating phase, but a full array of contractual protections the instant a contract has been formed. For this reason, the first question a court will usually ask is: Is there a binding contract between these parties? If so, only then will the court look to the appropriate remedy if a promise has not been carried out.

The interplay between expectation, reliance, and restitution interests is a central starting point of modern American contract law. However, as we will see, the contract/no contract dichotomy has tended to erode somewhat in recent law.[1] (Or at least so believes Frier. White is doubtful.)

6. Fairness. A. H. Zehmer conceded that $50,000 was "a good price" for the Ferguson farm. Suppose that the circumstances were otherwise similar, but that the price had been much less than the farm's value. It might have changed the court's mind about the seriousness of the contractual intent, not so? In the venerable case of *Keller v. Holderman*, 11 Mich. 248 (1863), a buyer paid for a $15 watch with a check for $300. The Michigan Supreme Court affirmed that "the whole transaction was a *frolic and a banter*, the plaintiff not expecting to sell, nor the defendant to buy the watch at the sum for which the check was drawn," and on this basis concluded that "no contract was ever made by the parties." Do not assume that this conclusion follows automatically from the exceedingly high price. What information in addition to the price would be helpful?

Modern law tends to approach the problem of inequality of exchange in a more direct manner, by vetting the formation process and the substance of the contract for unconscionability. See Chapter 5.C below. But the issue of fairness was directly relevant in *Lucy v. Zehmer* because gross inequality of exchange is one criterion that equity courts have long used in denying specific performance. A good example is *Bergstedt v. Bender*, 222 S.W. 547 (Tex. Comm'n App. 1920, judgm't approved), in which an elderly woman sold a home worth $4,900 for $1,500 plus the right to live in it for her life, but died soon thereafter, before conveying her property to the buyer. Specific performance in these circumstances was denied as "harsh and inequitable." We may wonder whether the woman actually made a bad deal, or whether it only turned out to be bad because of her untimely death.

7. The Written Contract. On his own testimony, W. O. Lucy went to great pains to get a written and signed promise from the Zehmers to sell the Ferguson farm. If Lucy had not obtained a written and signed promise, his

1. The classic article on this subject is Charles L. Knapp, *Enforcing the Contract to Bargain*, 44 N.Y.U.L. Rev. 673 (1969).

chance of prevailing would have been small. This is because of the **Statute of Frauds**, which for some types of contract (including "a contract for the sale of an interest in land") requires a writing signed by the party against whom a promise is to be enforced; see Chapter 3.F. Note, however, that Lucy did not sign a promise himself. If, the next day, the Zehmers had wanted to go through with the sale, but Lucy had not, the Zehmers could not have enforced the contract for want of a signature against the "party to be charged."

The writing itself is problematic in other ways. First, some of its terms are potentially ambiguous. For example, what is meant by "the Ferguson farm"? (Suppose that there were several farms of that name in Dinwiddie County.) What is "the Ferguson farm complete"? (Are the three heifers included?) More important, the title must be "satisfactory to buyer"; exactly how open-ended is this condition? Can Lucy use it in order to get out of the contract at will ("I'm *still* not satisfied")? This is the subject of rules on **interpreting contracts**; see Chapter 4.B.

Second, the writing in *Lucy v. Zehmer* is "bare bones," indeed about as bare as it could be. It says nothing about when the exchange is to be executed, whether Lucy must pay before the Zehmers transfer the farm, what form the payment should take, whether there are any warranties, and so on. If a contract is too vague, a court could elect not to enforce it at all; but if the contract is enforced, the omitted terms often have to be supplied from **default terms**, standard "off the shelf" contractual provisions. You will encounter many of these terms throughout this book. The problem of implied terms is dealt with especially in Chapter 4.C.

Third, had the contract been written out more fully, the opposite problem might have arisen, particularly when the written document was so full that it apparently embodies the entire agreement between the parties. Then the issue is often whether one party can introduce evidence to interpret the written contract or to add terms that were orally agreed to but are not in the written document. This is the subject of the **Parol Evidence Rule**; see Chapter 4.A.

All these issues are part of traditional contract law. In the modern world, writings raise many additional problems, particularly because standard form contracts are increasingly often used to conduct transactions. Standard form contracts are usually prepared by one party and presented to the other, who has no choice but to sign the form if it wishes to do business (what is called a **contract of adhesion**). A great deal of modern contract law centers on the difficulties that such form contracts occasion; see especially Chapters 3.E and 5.D. The writing in *Lucy v. Zehmer* is, of course, clearly not a standard form contract.

As should be evident, many serious legal problems can arise from the relationship between a contractual agreement and the reduction of that agreement to writing. This troubled relationship will be virtually a leit-motif of this course.

thematic passage

8. Third Parties. The day after the contract was concluded, W. O. Lucy sold half his interest in the Ferguson farm to his brother, J. C. Lucy, who was to pay $25,000 to the Zehmers. Although the brother had not participated in the transaction with the Zehmers, he then joined W. O. in bringing suit on the contract. Although contract law is often thought of in terms of an arrangement between two parties, third parties fairly frequently obtain rights through contracts, usually either because a contract was meant to benefit them (third-party beneficiaries) or because rights or duties are later transferred to them (through assignment or delegation). J. C. Lucy was an assignee and delegate under his brother's contract. This subject is considered in Chapter 8.

9. Sources of Contract Law: The Restatements. *Lucy v. Zehmer* is a Common Law case, and the Virginia Supreme Court relies mainly on its own previous decisions. But it also cites the Restatement of the Law of Contracts (commonly called the First Restatement) to back up its argument that an undisclosed intention is immaterial. The First Restatement, approved by the American Law Institute in 1932, was an attempt to capsulize existing American contract law, but in part also an effort to simplify and reform it. The Second Restatement (Restatement 2d) was published in 1981. The Restatements are not statutes and so judges are free to use their discretion in applying them, but they nonetheless have considerable influence on judicial decisions.

The two Restatements share many elements, but differ in their articulation. The first Restatement, heavily shaped by Profs. Samuel Williston of Harvard and Arthur Corbin of Yale, tended toward dogmatic clarity and rigor. The Second Restatement is considerably more relaxed, principally because of influence from the Uniform Commercial Code (see below).

Section 71 of the First Restatement says that "the undisclosed understanding of either party of the meaning of his own words and other acts, or of the other party's words and other acts," is immaterial except in unusual circumstances. The Second Restatement has no exact equivalent to this section, but in § 2(1) it defines a promise as "a manifestation of intention to act or refrain from acting in a specified way, so made as to justify a promisee in understanding that a commitment has been made." In Comment b on § 2, Restatement 2d says: "The phrase 'manifestation of intention' adopts an external or objective standard for interpreting conduct; it means the external expression of intention as distinguished from undisclosed intention."

Problem 1–1

In an advertising campaign, Pepsico, Inc., invited consumers to acquire merchandise ("Pepsi Stuff," including t-shirts, sunglasses, and leather jackets) in exchange for "Pepsi Points." These points could be obtained either by buying Pepsi or by purchasing points for ten cents each. One television ad describing the available Pepsi Stuff concluded with a smug young man sitting in the cockpit of a jet airplane; the caption said "HARRIER FIGHTER 7,000,000 PEPSI POINTS." John Leonard, a teenager, raised $700,000 from acquaintances and claimed his Harrier. Pepsico, which had no Harriers, rejected Leonard's claim, and Leonard then sued. What outcome? It may help to know that a Harrier costs $23 million.

NORTHERN INDIANA PUBLIC SERVICE CO. v. CARBON COUNTY COAL CO.

United States Court of Appeals, Seventh Circuit, 1986.
799 F.2d 265.

POSNER, J. These appeals bring before us various facets of a dispute between Northern Indiana Public Service Company (NIPSCO), an electric utility in Indiana, and Carbon County Coal Company, a partnership that until recently owned and operated a coal mine in Wyoming. In 1978 NIPSCO and Carbon County signed a contract whereby Carbon County agreed to sell and NIPSCO to buy approximately 1.5 million tons of coal every year for 20 years, at a price of $24 a ton subject to various provisions for escalation which by 1985 had driven the price up to $44 a ton.

NIPSCO's rates are regulated by the Indiana Public Service Commission. In 1983 NIPSCO requested permission to raise its rates to reflect increased fuel charges. Some customers of NIPSCO opposed the increase on the ground that NIPSCO could reduce its overall costs by buying more electrical power from neighboring utilities for resale to its customers and producing less of its own power. Although the Commission granted the requested increase, it directed NIPSCO, in orders issued in December 1983 and February 1984 (the "economy purchase orders"), to make a good faith effort to find, and wherever possible buy from, utilities that would sell electricity to it at prices lower than its costs of internal generation. The Commission added ominously that "the adverse effects of entering into long-term coal supply contracts which do not allow for renegotiation and are not requirement contracts, is a burden which must rest squarely on the shoulders of NIPSCO management." Actually the contract with Carbon County did provide for renegotiation of the contract price—but one-way renegotiation in favor of Carbon County; the price fixed in the contract (as adjusted from time to time in accordance with the escalator provisions) was a floor. And the contract was indeed not a requirements contract: it specified the exact amount of coal that NIPSCO must take over the 20 years during which the contract was to remain in effect. NIPSCO was eager to have an assured supply of low-sulphur coal and was therefore willing to guarantee both price and quantity.

Unfortunately for NIPSCO, however, as things turned out it was indeed able to buy electricity at prices below the costs of generating electricity from coal bought under the contract with Carbon County; and because of the "economy purchase orders," of which it had not sought judicial review, NIPSCO could not expect to be allowed by the Public Service Commission to recover in its electrical rates the costs of buying coal from Carbon County. NIPSCO therefore decided to stop accepting coal deliveries from Carbon County, at least for the time being; and on April 24, 1985, it brought this diversity suit against Carbon County in a federal district court in Indiana, seeking a declaration that it was excused from its obligations under the contract either permanently or at least until the economy purchase orders ceased preventing it from passing on the costs of the contract to its ratepayers. In support of this position it argued that ... NIPSCO's performance was excused or suspended—either under the contract's *force majeure* clause or under the doctrines of frustration or impossibility—by reason of the economy purchase orders.

On May 17, 1985, Carbon County counterclaimed for breach of contract and moved for a preliminary injunction requiring NIPSCO to continue taking delivery under the contract. On June 19, 1985, the district judge granted the preliminary injunction, from which NIPSCO has appealed. Also on June 19, rejecting NIPSCO's argument that it needed more time for pretrial discovery and other trial preparations, the judge scheduled the trial to begin on August 26, 1985. Trial did begin then, lasted for six weeks, and resulted in a jury verdict for Carbon County of $181 million. The judge entered judgment in accordance with the verdict, rejecting Carbon County's argument that in lieu of damages it should get an order of specific performance requiring NIPSCO to comply with the contract. Upon entering the final judgment the district judge dissolved the preliminary injunction, and shortly afterward the mine—whose only customer was NIPSCO—shut down. NIPSCO has appealed from the damage judgment ...

We are left with the following issues to decide: ... (3) whether NIPSCO's obligations under the contract were excused or suspended by virtue of either the *force majeure* clause or (4) the doctrines of frustration or impracticability, (5) whether Carbon County was entitled to specific performance of the contract, ... [Eds.: Discussion of other issues is omitted.]

3. The contract permits NIPSCO to stop taking delivery of coal "for any cause beyond [its] reasonable control ... including but not limited to ... orders or acts of civil ... authority ... which wholly or partly prevent ... the utilizing ... of the coal." This is what is known as a *force majeure* clause. See, e.g., *Northern Illinois Gas Co. v. Energy Coop.*, Inc., 122 Ill. App. 3d 940, 949–52, 461 N.E.2d 1049, 1057–58, 78 Ill. Dec. 215 (1984). NIPSCO argues that the Indiana Public Service Commission's "economy purchase orders" prevented it, in whole or part, from using the coal that it had agreed to buy, and it complains that the district judge instructed the jury incorrectly on the meaning and application of the clause. The complaint about the instructions is immaterial. The judge should not have put the issue of *force majeure* to the jury. It is evident that the clause was not triggered by the orders.

All that those orders do is tell NIPSCO it will not be allowed to pass on fuel costs to its ratepayers in the form of higher rates if it can buy electricity cheaper than it can generate electricity internally using Carbon County's coal. Such an order does not "prevent," whether wholly or in part, NIPSCO from using the coal; it just prevents NIPSCO from shifting the burden of its improvidence or bad luck in having incorrectly forecasted its fuel needs to the backs of the hapless ratepayers. The purpose of public utility regulation is to provide a substitute for competition in markets (such as the market for electricity) that are naturally monopolistic. Suppose the market for electricity were fully competitive, and unregulated. Then if NIPSCO signed a long-term fixed-price fixed-quantity contract to buy coal, and during the life of the contract competing electrical companies were able to produce and sell electricity at prices below the cost to NIPSCO of producing electricity from that coal, NIPSCO would have to swallow the excess cost of the coal. It could not raise its electricity prices in order to pass on the excess cost to its consumers, because if it did they would buy electricity at lower prices from NIPSCO's competitors. By signing the kind of contract it did, NIPSCO gambled that fuel costs would rise rather than fall over the life of the contract; for if they rose then the contract price would give it an advantage over its (hypothetical) competitors who would have to buy fuel at the current market price. If such a gamble fails, the result is not *force majeure*.

This is all the clearer when we consider that the contract price was actually fixed just on the downside; it put a floor under the price NIPSCO had to pay, but the escalator provisions allowed the actual contract prices to rise above the floor, and they did. This underscores the gamble NIPSCO took in signing the contract. It committed itself to paying a price at or above a fixed minimum and to taking a fixed quantity at that price. It was willing to make this commitment to secure an assured supply of low-sulphur coal, but the risk it took was that the market price of coal or substitute fuels would fall. A *force majeure* clause is not intended to buffer a party against the normal risks of a contract. The normal risk of a fixed-price contract is that the market price will change. If it rises, the buyer gains at the expense of the seller (except insofar as escalator provisions give the seller some protection); if it falls, as here, the seller gains at the expense of the buyer. The whole purpose of a fixed-price contract is to allocate risk in this way. A *force majeure* clause interpreted to excuse the buyer from the consequences of the risk he expressly assumed would nullify a central term of the contract....

If the Commission had ordered NIPSCO to close a plant because of a safety or pollution hazard, we would have a true case of *force majeure*. As a regulated firm NIPSCO is subject to more extensive controls than unregulated firms and it therefore wanted and got a broadly worded *force majeure* clause that would protect it fully (hence the reference to partial effects) against government actions that impeded its using the coal. But as the only thing the Commission did was prevent NIPSCO from using its monopoly position to make consumers bear the risk that NIPSCO assumed when it signed a long-term fixed-price fuel contract, NIPSCO cannot complain of *force majeure*; the risk that has come to pass was one that NIPSCO voluntarily assumed when it signed the contract.

4. The district judge refused to submit NIPSCO's defenses of impracticability and frustration to the jury, ruling that Indiana law does

not allow a buyer to claim impracticability and does not recognize the defense of frustration. Some background (on which see Farnsworth, Contracts §§ 9.5–9.7 (1982)) may help make these rulings intelligible. In the early common law a contractual undertaking unconditional in terms was not excused merely because something had happened (such as an invasion, the passage of a law, or a natural disaster) that prevented the undertaking. See *Paradine v. Jane*, Aleyn 26, 82 Eng. Rep. 897 (K.B. 1647). Excuses had to be written into the contract; this is the origin of *force majeure* clauses. Later it came to be recognized that negotiating parties cannot anticipate all the contingencies that may arise in the performance of the contract; a legitimate judicial function in contract cases is to interpolate terms to govern remote contingencies—terms the parties would have agreed on explicitly if they had had the time and foresight to make advance provision for every possible contingency in performance. Later still, it was recognized that physical impossibility was irrelevant, or at least inconclusive; a promisor might want his promise to be unconditional, not because he thought he had superhuman powers but because he could insure against the risk of nonperformance better than the promisee, or obtain a substitute performance more easily than the promisee. See *Field Container Corp. v. ICC,* 712 F.2d 250, 257 (7th Cir. 1983); Holmes, The Common Law 300 (1881). Thus the proper question in an "impossibility" case is not whether the promisor could not have performed his undertaking but whether his nonperformance should be excused because the parties, if they had thought about the matter, would have wanted to assign the risk of the contingency that made performance impossible or uneconomical to the promisor or to the promisee; if to the latter, the promisor is excused.

Section 2–615 of the Uniform Commercial Code takes this approach. It provides that "delay in delivery . . . by a seller . . . is not a breach of his duty under a contract for sale if performance as agreed has been made impracticable by the occurrence of a contingency the non-occurrence of which was a basic assumption on which the contract was made. . . ." Performance on schedule need not be impossible, only infeasible—provided that the event which made it infeasible was not a risk that the promisor had assumed. Notice, however, that the only type of promisor referred to is a seller; there is no suggestion that a buyer's performance might be excused by reason of impracticability. The reason is largely semantic. Ordinarily all the buyer has to do in order to perform his side of the bargain is pay, and while one can think of all sorts of reasons why, when the time came to pay, the buyer might not have the money, rarely would the seller have intended to assume the risk that the buyer might, whether through improvidence or bad luck, be unable to pay for the seller's goods or services. To deal with the rare case where the buyer or (more broadly) the paying party might have a good excuse based on some unforeseen change in circumstances, a new rubric was thought necessary, different from "impossibility" (the common law term) or "impracticability" (the Code term, picked up in Restatement (Second) of Contracts § 261 (1979)), and it received the name "frustration." Rarely is it impracticable or impossible for the payor to pay; but if something has happened to make the performance for which he would be paying worthless to him, an excuse for not paying, analogous to impracticability or impossibility, may be proper. See Restatement, supra, § 265, comment a.

The leading case on frustration remains *Krell v. Henry*, [1903] 2 K.B. 740 (C.A.). Krell rented Henry a suite of rooms for watching the coronation of Edward VII, but Edward came down with appendicitis and the coronation had to be postponed. Henry refused to pay the balance of the rent and the court held that he was excused from doing so because his purpose in renting had been frustrated by the postponement, a contingency outside the knowledge, or power to influence, of either party. The question was, to which party did the contract (implicitly) allocate the risk? Surely Henry had not intended to insure Krell against the possibility of the coronation's being postponed, since Krell could always relet the room, at the premium rental, for the coronation's new date. So Henry was excused.

NIPSCO is the buyer in the present case, and its defense is more properly frustration than impracticability; but the judge held that frustration is not a contract defense under the law of Indiana. He relied on an Indiana Appellate Court decision which indeed so states ..., but solely on the basis of an old decision of the Indiana Supreme Court ... that doesn't even discuss the defense of frustration and anyway precedes by years the recognition of the defense by American courts. At all events, the facts of the present case do not bring it within the scope of the frustration doctrine, so we need not decide whether the Indiana Supreme Court would embrace the doctrine in a suitable case....

Whether or not Indiana recognizes the doctrine of frustration, and whether or not a buyer can ever assert the defense of impracticability under section 2–615 of the Uniform Commercial Code, these doctrines, so closely related to each other and to *force majeure* as well, ... cannot help NIPSCO. All are doctrines for shifting risk to the party better able to bear it, either because he is in a better position to prevent the risk from materializing or because he can better reduce the disutility of the risk (as by insuring) if the risk does occur. Suppose a grower agrees before the growing season to sell his crop to a grain elevator, and the crop is destroyed by blight and the grain elevator sues. Discharge is ordinarily allowed in such cases. ...The grower has every incentive to avoid the blight; so if it occurs, it probably could not have been prevented; and the grain elevator, which buys from a variety of growers not all of whom will be hit by blight in the same growing season, is in a better position to buffer the risk of blight than the grower is.

Since impossibility and related doctrines are devices for shifting risk in accordance with the parties' presumed intentions, which are to minimize the costs of contract performance, one of which is the disutility created by risk, they have no place when the contract explicitly assigns a particular risk to one party or the other. As we have already noted, a fixed-price contract is an explicit assignment of the risk of market price increases to the seller and the risk of market price decreases to the buyer, and the assignment of the latter risk to the buyer is even clearer where, as in this case, the contract places a floor under price but allows for escalation. If, as is also the case here, the buyer forecasts the market incorrectly and therefore finds himself locked into a disadvantageous contract, he has only himself to blame and so cannot shift the risk back to the seller by invoking impossibility or related doctrines. See Farnsworth, supra, at 680 and n. 18; White & Summers, Handbook of the Law Under the Uniform Commercial Code 133 (2d ed. 1980). It does not matter that it is an act of government that may have made the contract less advantageous to one party.... Government these days is a pervasive factor in the economy and among the risks that a fixed-price contract allocates between the parties is that of a price change induced by one of government's manifold interventions in the economy. Since "the very purpose of a fixed price agreement is to place the risk of increased costs on the promisor (and the risk of decreased costs on the promisee)," the fact that costs decrease steeply (which is in effect what happened here—the cost of generating electricity turned out to be lower than NIPSCO thought when it signed the fixed-price contract with Carbon County) cannot allow the buyer to walk away from the contract. *In re Westinghouse Electric Corp. Uranium Contracts Litigation*, 517 F. Supp. 440, 453 (E.D. Va. 1981); ...

5. This completes our consideration of NIPSCO's attack on the damages judgment and we turn to Carbon County's cross-appeal, which seeks specific performance in lieu of the damages it got. Carbon County's counsel virtually abandoned the cross-appeal at oral argument, noting that the mine was closed and could not be reopened immediately—so that if specific performance (i.e., NIPSCO's resuming taking the coal) was ordered, Carbon County would not be able to resume its obligations under the contract without some grace period. In any event the request for specific performance has no merit. Like other equitable remedies, specific performance is available only if damages are not an adequate remedy, Farnsworth, supra, § 12.6, and there is no reason to suppose them inadequate here. The loss to Carbon County from the breach of contract is simply the difference between (1) the contract price (as escalated over the life of the contract in accordance with the contract's escalator provisions) times quantity, and (2) the cost of mining the coal over the life of the contract. Carbon County does not even argue that $181 million is not a reasonable estimate of the present value of the difference. Its complaint is that although the money will make the owners of Carbon County whole it will do nothing for the miners who have lost their jobs because the mine is closed and the satellite businesses that have closed for the same reason. Only specific performance will help them.

But since they are not parties to the contract their losses are irrelevant. Indeed, specific performance would be improper as well as unnecessary here, because it would force the continuation of production that has become uneconomical. Cf. Farnsworth, supra, at 817–18. No one wants coal from Carbon County's mine. With the collapse of oil prices, which has depressed the price of substitute fuels as well, this coal costs far more to get out of the ground than it is worth in the market. Continuing to produce it, under compulsion of an order for specific performance, would impose costs on society greater than the benefits. NIPSCO's breach, though it gave Carbon County a right to damages, was an efficient breach in the sense that it brought to a halt a production process that was no longer cost-justified.... The reason why NIPSCO must pay Carbon County's loss is not that it should have continued buying coal it didn't need but that the contract assigned to NIPSCO the risk of market changes that made continued deliveries uneconomical. The judgment for damages is the method by which that risk is being fixed on NIPSCO in accordance with its undertakings.

With continued production uneconomical, it is unlikely that an order of specific performance, if made, would ever actually be implemented. If, as a finding that the breach was efficient implies, the cost of substitute supply (whether of coal, or of electricity) to NIPSCO is less than the cost of producing coal from Carbon County's mine, NIPSCO and Carbon County can both be made better off by negotiating a cancellation of the contract and with it a dissolution of the order of specific performance. Suppose, by way of example, that Carbon County's coal costs $20 a ton to produce, that the contract price is $40, and that NIPSCO can buy coal elsewhere for $10. Then Carbon County would be making a profit of only $20 on each ton it sold to NIPSCO ($40–$20), while NIPSCO would be losing $30 on each ton it bought from Carbon County ($40–$10). Hence by offering Carbon County more than contract damages (i.e., more than Carbon County's lost profits), NIPSCO could induce Carbon County to discharge the contract and release NIPSCO to buy cheaper coal. For example, at $25, both parties would be better off than under specific performance, where Carbon County gains only $20 but NIPSCO loses $30. Probably, therefore, Carbon County is seeking specific performance in order to have bargaining leverage with NIPSCO, and we can think of no reason why the law should give it such leverage. We add that if Carbon County obtained and enforced an order for specific performance this would mean that society was spending $20 (in our hypothetical example) to produce coal that could be gotten elsewhere for $10—a waste of scarce resources.

As for possible hardships to workers and merchants in Hanna, Wyoming, where Carbon County's coal mine is located, we point out that none of these people were parties to the contract with NIPSCO or third-party beneficiaries. They have no legal interest in the contract.... Of course the consequences to third parties of granting an injunctive remedy, such as specific performance, must be considered, and in some cases may require that the remedy be withheld.... The frequent references to "public interest" as a factor in the grant or denial of preliminary injunction invariably are references to third-party effects.... But even though the formal statement of the judicial obligation to consider such effects extends to orders denying as well as granting injunctive relief ..., the actuality is somewhat different: when the question is whether third parties would be injured by an order denying an injunction, always they are persons having a legally recognized interest in the lawsuit, so that the issue really is the adequacy of relief if the injunction is denied. In *Mississippi Power & Light Co. v. United Gas Pipe Line Co.*, 760 F.2d 618 (5th Cir. 1985), for example, a public utility sought a preliminary injunction against alleged overcharges by a supplier. If the injunction was denied and later the utility got damages, its customers would be entitled to refunds; but for a variety of reasons explained in the opinion, refunds would not fully protect the customers' interests. The customers were the real parties in interest on the plaintiff side of the case, and their interests had therefore to be taken into account in deciding whether there would be irreparable harm (and how much) if the preliminary injunction was denied. See id. at 623–26. Carbon County does not stand in a representative relation to the workers and businesses of Hanna, Wyoming. Treating them as real parties in interest would evade the limitations on the concept of a third-party beneficiary and would place the promisor under obligations potentially far heavier than it had thought it was accepting when it signed the contract. Indeed, if we are right that an order of specific performance would probably not be carried out—that instead NIPSCO would pay an additional sum of money to Carbon County for an agreement not to enforce the order—it becomes transparent that granting specific performance would make NIPSCO liable in money damages for harms to nonparties to the contract, and it did not assume such liability by signing the contract....

Moreover, the workers and merchants in Hanna assumed the risk that the coal mine would have to close down if it turned out to be uneconomical. The contract with NIPSCO did not guarantee that the mine would operate throughout the life of the contract but only protected the owners of Carbon County against the financial consequences to them of a breach. As Carbon County itself emphasizes in its brief, the contract was a product of the international oil cartel, which by forcing up the price of substitute fuels such as coal made costly coal-mining operations economically attractive. The OPEC cartel is not a source of vested rights to produce substitute fuels at inflated prices.

... To summarize, ... we have turned down Carbon County's appeals as well as NIPSCO's.

SO ORDERED.

Notes and Discussion

1. **Sources of Contract Law: The UCC and the CISG.** Unlike *Lucy v. Zehmer*, this is not a Common Law case. In American law, a contract for the sale of goods (e.g., coal) is decided by applying Article 2 of the Uniform Commercial Code (UCC) if this statute is relevant. The UCC is a massive piece of legislation that has been adopted, with small but occasionally significant variations, in virtually all American jurisdictions. (The major

exception is Louisiana, which has adopted portions of the UCC but not Article 2.) The UCC was prepared jointly by the National Conference of Commissioners on Uniform State Laws (NCCUSL) and the American Law Institute (ALI); the first version was published in the 1950s, and the UCC has been periodically updated since then. A substantially revised version of Article 2 received final approval by NCCUSL and the ALI in 2003, but no State has yet adopted it.

According to § 1–102(1)–(2) (revised § 1–103(a)), the UCC's "underlying purposes and policies ... are (1) to simplify, clarify, and modernize the law governing commercial transactions; (2) to permit the continued expansion of commercial practices through custom, usage, and agreement of the parties, and (3) to make uniform the law among the various jurisdictions." Article 2 applies to all sales of goods, whether or not the parties are merchants. Nonetheless, many provisions are limited in their scope to merchants, or otherwise affected by one or both parties having merchant status. Article 2 also interacts with other portions of the UCC, especially Article 3 on commercial paper and Article 9 on secured transactions; these Articles are normally treated in a course on Commercial Transactions.

The United Nations Convention on Contracts for the International Sale of Goods (commonly abbreviated CISG) is a treaty that entered into force, for signatory nations, in 1988. The United States and most of its international trading partners (although not Japan or the United Kingdom) are now signatories. Unless the parties provide otherwise in their contract, the CISG usually applies when a non-consumer sale takes place "between parties whose places of business are in different [signatory] States." CISG art. 1. The CISG represents a broad compromise between Common Law and the Civil Law jurisdictions of Europe.

You should note that the UCC is a statute, and the CISG, as a self-executing treaty, also has status roughly equivalent to a statute. Therefore their use, when by their language they are applicable to particular contracts, is not optional. This is important because both the UCC and the CISG deviate significantly from Common Law. To be sure, even for contracts to which the UCC, in particular, does not apply, judges have often invoked its rules and principles by analogy in order to liberalize traditional contract law, a practice that was strengthened by the Second Restatement of Contracts. Nonetheless, significant differences remain between the UCC and Common Law, and it is always important to bear these differences in mind.

On cases interpreting the CISG, see Larry A. DiMatteo et al., *The Interpretive Turn in International Sales Law: An Analysis of Fifteen Years of CISG Jurisprudence*, 24 Nw. J. Int'l L. & Bus. 299 (2004). Modern cases are surveyed in John Spanogle et al., *Global Issues in Contract Law* (2007).

2. Background: The Energy Crisis. This contract was intended to last for 20 years, from 1978 until 1998. It was concluded against the backdrop of a severe energy crisis brought on by the OPEC oil embargo in 1973. The embargo led to a rapid rise in the price of other basic fuels. (This crisis provides a background to several other cases in this book as well.) The price of bituminous coal remained fairly steady from 1949 to 1973; in 1973 the average U. S. price was $8.71 per short ton. In 1974 the price nearly doubled, to about $16.01; in 1978, when NIPSCO made its contract, it had reached $22.64, and most predictions were for continued escalation. As you can imagine, this sudden increase was a serious blow to companies, like NIPSCO, that were heavily dependent on coal for energy production. (Ecological interests did not yet figure in the discussion.) Think about this background to the contract between NIPSCO and Carbon County Coal. Why did these two partners come together, and what was each seeking from such a very long-term commitment? Despite its name, Carbon County, located in south-central Wyoming, is not a big player in Wyoming coal production, although its coal is unusually cheap to mine.

As it turned out, however, the price of coal did not continue its inexorable rise. By 1984, when the Indiana Public Service Commission finally intervened, the nominal price of bituminous coal had stabilized around $31, far below the $44 price that NIPSCO was then paying; and in real terms, after adjusting for inflation, the price of coal was actually falling. On historical coal prices, see http://www.eia.doe.gov/emeu/aer/coal.html, the website of the Energy Information Administration of the Department of Energy.

This contract is very different from one-off contracts like the sale of a farm in *Lucy v. Zehmer*. Long-term contracts involve considerable risks resulting, among other things, from the insecurity of making economic projections into the distant future. This quandary is obviously of direct relevance to any commercial lawyer who attempts to bargain on behalf of a business client. If you are in this role, what warnings should you give your client? What protections should you insist on including within the contract? This is an issue that will arise in many other cases throughout this book.

3. Breach of Contract. In *NIPSCO*, unlike in *Lucy v. Zehmer*, no problem comes up about the existence of a contract; both sides accept that there is a contract between them, one that has, indeed, been functioning for some years. Rather, the legal questions that Judge Posner considers stem from NIPSCO's decision, in response to the Public Service Commission, "to stop accepting coal deliveries from Carbon County, at least for the time being." NIPSCO may well have felt that it could get off lightly, since it soon thereafter brought suit seeking "a declaration that it was excused from its obligations under the contract"; see below. As it turned out, however, Carbon County Coal was able to argue successfully that NIPSCO's refusal to accept deliveries amounted to a complete breach of contract, not just for any immediate deliveries of coal but also for the entire remainder of the contract.

What this part of the case illustrates is that great care is required not only in executing a contract, but also in attempting to escape from it. Carbon County Coal went out of business after NIPSCO's refusal to accept more coal. Were its executives entitled to take NIPSCO's money and run? Evidently yes, at any rate if they could not find another buyer. Did they have any obligation at least to try to persuade NIPSCO to remain with the contract? For more on the alternatives available to aggrieved parties, or to parties who think they are aggrieved, see Chapter 7.

4. Assessing the Damages for the Breach. The jury verdict on Carbon County Coal's counterclaim for damages was $181,000,000, a huge sum of money. How was this figure arrived at? This involves the UCC formulas for calculation of damages, which are the subject of Chapter 6.A, below. For now, though, take a look at UCC § 2–708(1), which describes the basic "market differential" measure: "the difference between the market price at the time and place for tender and the unpaid contract price together with any incidental damages provided in this Article (Section 2–710), but less expenses saved in consequence of the buyer's breach." Since, however, the NIPSCO contract had such a long time still to run, this measure would be difficult to apply, no?

Judge Posner indicates that the trial judge, confronted with this predicament, resorted to the substitute measure in § 2–108(2), available when the standard measure is "inadequate": "the profit (including reasonable overhead) which the seller would have made from full performance by the buyer . . ." Judge Posner describes the resulting calculation: "The loss to Carbon County from the breach of contract is simply the difference between (1) the contract price (as escalated over the life of the contract in accordance with the contract's escalator provisions) times quantity, and (2) the cost of mining the coal over the life of the contract." The resulting figure was presumably discounted to reflect the present value of future money, but does this measure nonetheless seem to you excessively generous? Is it at least good enough to fulfill one objective of the UCC (rev. § 1–305), that "remedies . . . be liberally administered to the end that the aggrieved party may be put in as good a position as if the other side had fully performed . . ."?

5. NIPSCO's Argument. Neither side was happy with the outcome in the trial court. NIPSCO argued, on appeal, that it was entitled to cancel its contract without becoming liable for a breach of contract. NIPSCO made two quite different arguments, both of which would lead to the desired result.

First, it argued that it was entitled to cancel because of the *force majeure* clause in its contract with Carbon County Coal. Such clauses vary somewhat in wording, but their usual purpose, particularly in long-term contracts, is to protect parties against some types of unpredictable and catastrophic events ("Acts of God") that may very adversely affect them. Here the written contract itself envisaged circumstances under which one party might quit without becoming liable for breach. Whether the clause helped NIPSCO is a matter of contractual interpretation; see below, Chapter 4, Part B. How does Judge Posner establish that the *force majeure* clause does NIPSCO no good whatsoever? Do you agree with his argument that there is a significant legal difference between allowing NIPSCO to buy the coal but not pass on the excess in price to its customers, and ordering NIPSCO to cease buying the coal altogether?

But second, outside the contract itself, there are also contractual doctrines that now and again allow courts to intervene when contracts go wildly wrong, in ways that the parties could not possibly have anticipated in their negotiations: because of events subsequent to the making of the contract, either performance becomes "impracticable" for one party, or one party's evident goals in making the contract are "frustrated." Judge Posner discusses these doctrines, which, so he contends, likewise give NIPSCO no traction. For the moment, ignore the differences between them (although you might want to take a peek at § 2–615, which the opinion cites); we will return to this issue in Chapter 7, Part C, when you should re-read the *NIPSCO* decision. For now, though, it suffices if you just think about the broader issue: how readily should courts intervene to save a party's bacon when it has not adequately provided for itself in negotiating a contract?

Judge Posner invokes the following principle: "the proper question in an 'impossibility' case is not whether the promisor could not have performed his undertaking but whether his nonperformance should be excused because the parties, if they had thought about the matter, would have wanted to assign the risk of the contingency that made performance impossible or uneconomical to the promisor or to the promisee; if to the latter, the promisor is excused." He then argues that under its contract, NIPSCO had in fact assumed the "risk" that coal prices would not continue to rise. Does this argument strike you as entirely fair? For instance, do you think the judge is right to compare NIPSCO to a gambler who made a losing bet?[2]

6. Carbon County Coal's Argument. For its part, Carbon County Coal was also unhappy with the verdict; it wanted specific performance of the contract, which would mean that NIPSCO would be obliged to continue accepting the coal. In principle, this is the analogue to specific performance in *Lucy v. Zehmer*, but unlike in that case, here specific performance is held to be unavailable. The UCC standard for specific performance is given in § 2–716(1): "Specific performance may be decreed where the goods are unique or in other proper circumstances." There is certainly no presumption of this remedy's availability for sale of goods (unlike for sale of land), although Official Comment 1 to § 2–716 does nudge courts toward "a more liberal attitude." Do the circumstances of this case strike you as possibly amounting to "other proper circumstances"? We will further examine the prevailing judicial reluctance to grant specific performance in Chapter 6.E.

Carbon County Coal's argument for specific performance was based on the adverse effects that the contract's cancellation allegedly had on its laid-off workers and on other residents of Carbon County. These persons were not, of course, participants in the contract itself, although they had come to have (we may assume) a very considerable stake in its execution; they are third-party beneficiaries, to whom we turn in Chapter 8.A. Nonetheless, so Judge Posner holds, their interests do not provide a basis for giving specific performance. Look closely at his argument. He makes two broad points, one practical ("it is unlikely than an order of specific performance, if made, would ever actually be implemented") and one dogmatic ("workers and merchants in Hanna, Wyoming, . . . have no legal interest in the contract"). How do these arguments interact?

Judge Posner was one of the earliest, and still is one of the foremost, advocates of an approach to legal reasoning based on economics; he was nominated to the Seventh Circuit in 1981, but continues as a Professor at the University of Chicago Law School. See esp. Richard A. Posner, Economic Analysis of the Law (7th ed. 2007). How does his way of thinking color his decision? If you feel that larger community interests should in fact have more force in this case, how would you try to argue against him? When, if ever, should third parties be encouraged to build their lives around contracts to which they are not a party? More specifically, under Judge Posner's

2. See Roy Kreitner, *Speculations of Contract, or How Contract Stopped Worrying and Learned to Love Risk*, 100 Colum. L. Rev. 1096 (2000).

criteria, how would the NIPSCO contract have to have been phrased in order to make the Carbon County workers and merchants intended third-party beneficiaries who would have an independent right to enforce the contract?

For further reading on law and economics in relation to contract, see also Steven Shavell, Foundations of Economic Analysis of Law 289–386 (2004); Michael J. Trebilcock, The Limits of Freedom of Contract (1993); Readings in the Economics of Contract Law (Victor P. Goldberg, ed., 1989). Louis Kaplow and Steven Shavell, in their book Fairness Versus Welfare (2002), argue vigorously, if rather abstractly, that general economic welfare, and not considerations of moral "fairness," should always be the basis for determining and evaluating public policy and law, including contract rules (pp. 155–224). As you read the cases in this book, try to determine whether, and to what extent, you agree.

7. What Happened to Fault? NIPSCO breached its contract because it could no longer pass the cost of the coal on to its customers; by its breach it became liable for the damages that flowed from its breach. But the Court has no interest in exploring the deeper reasons for this breach—whether because of unforeseeable circumstances or as a result of NIPSCO's own fault (if it caused the breach intentionally or through carelessness). This outcome would doubtless make intuitive sense if we were, for instance, dealing with the violation of a warranty; a party that invites another's reliance by affirming that a machine will have certain characteristics, cannot then escape liability by asserting that its assertion, while erroneous, was nonetheless honest and reasonable. However, as we shall see, in our contract law it is much more widely true that both in establishing whether a party has breached in the first place, and then in determining the amount of damages it must pay, courts are mainly concerned only with whether the party has in fact failed to keep its promise.

Fault does creep into the contractual argument at certain critical junctures—when, for example, a court must make a very difficult decision between two competing measures of damages (see *Peevyhouse v. Garland Coal Mining Co.* in Chapter 6.A), or between two competing ways to assess whether a party has performed (see *Jacob & Youngs, Inc. v. Kent* in Chapter 7.B). Further, professionals (doctors, lawyers, architects) are usually held contractually liable only on a negligence standard unless they make very specific promises about their performance, and courts are loath to find such promises; although this may be a matter of courtesy among the learned professions, more likely such a proffer of services is not correctly construed as "guaranteeing" results. More generally, either expressly or by implication, contract duties themselves are often cast in relativistic terms: to perform "in good faith" or to "use best efforts." Finally, a promisor may sometimes be excused from a performance that has, for instance, become impracticable owing to the occurrence of unforeseeable circumstances (Chapter 7.C), but courts are generally reluctant to grant such excuses.

Speaking very generally, however, our contract regime is one of strict liability. If your contractual promise is binding on you, then you are liable if you fail to keep your promise. As Judge Holmes put it with his customary fierceness: "The consequences of a binding promise at common law are not affected by the degree of power which the promisor possesses over the promised event." O.W. Holmes, Jr., *Lecture VII: Elements of Contract, in* The Common Law 289, 299 (Boston, Little Brown & Co., 1881). An example is *Laborers Combined Funds v. Mattei*, 359 Pa.Super. 399, 518 A.2d 1296 (1986). Officers of a corporation appealed from a judgment rendering them liable to a union for failing to deduct wage and pension benefits from employees' gross wages. The officers claimed they could not meet the obligation because of a bookkeeper's embezzlement. But the Pennsylvania Superior Court affirmed, stating that: "contract liability is strict liability. It is an accepted maxim that *pacta sunt servanda*, contracts are to be kept. In other words, the obligor is therefore liable for damages in breach of contract even if he is without fault and even if circumstances have made the contract more burdensome or less desirable than he had anticipated." Id. at 1300 n.4. Compare Restatement 2d § 235(2): "When performance of a duty under a contract is due any non-performance is a breach."

Why this should be so is hard to say. Other legal regimes than ours (e.g., the Civil Law systems of Europe) make far heavier use of fault in evaluating alleged breaches of contract. See G. H. Treitel, Remedies for Breach of Contract: A Comparative Account 7–42 (1988); Konrad Zweigert & Hein Kötz, Introduction to Comparative Law 486–515 (3d ed. 1998). But Common Law obviously sees the matter differently, although this difference is not easily encapsulated. For instance, Robert Cooter asks: "Why are fault rules more common in tort law than for breach of contract?" He observes that a strict liability rule keeps administrative costs low since courts do not need to make a determination of fault. In tort, however, a strict liability rule would reduce incentives for precaution on the part of potential victims; this is not so great a problem in contract. Cooter goes on to point out that the role played by negligence in tort is filled in contract law by such concepts as the duty to mitigate. Robert Cooter, *Unity in Tort, Contract, and Property: The Model of Precaution*, 73 Cal. L. Rev. 1, 31–32 (1985). It is clear, in any case, that the principle of strict liability is ancient in Common Law: Albert Kiralfy, *Absolute Liability in Contract*, 1 J. Legal Hist. 89 (1980).

More theoretical arguments are canvassed in Stephen A. Smith, Contract Theory 376–386 (2004); see also Ward Farnsworth, The Legal Analyst: A Toolkit for Thinking about the Law 51–53 (2007), on the promisor as "least cost avoider." But note E. Allan Farnsworth, *On Trying to Keep One's Promises: The Duty of Best Efforts in Contract Law*, 46 U. Pitt. L. Rev. 1 (1984), who argues that fault plays a larger role in contract law than is sometimes realized.

Note: Why People Make Contracts

Anyone arguing for the importance of contract faces the small embarrassment that the English made do without contract law—at least, contract law as we know it—until the beginning of the seventeenth century. In the King's courts in medieval England, where most of our law grew up, courts recognized claims that we would call torts (John killed my cow; he must pay me), suits to collect formally documented covenants (Ralph signed a bond; he must pay 50 pounds plus interest), and suits on the basis of unjustified enrichment in contract-like situations (Robert has received a benefit from me; he must repay me what he had promised me in return for this benefit).

But there was no suit for breach of an ordinary executory contract not documented by these uncommon formalities. Only with the famous *Slade's Case*[3] in 1602 did English courts conclude that the old action of *assumpsit* allowed one to collect the money promised in return for the sale (not just the delivery) of a commodity. If England could get by without contract for so long, what makes it so important now? If twenty-first century Americans find legally enforceable contracts to be an indispensable part of daily commercial and personal life, how could a sixteenth century Englishman do without? We ask this question as a way of getting you to think about why a person in modern society might want to make a contract and what sort (or sorts) of contract such a person might seek.

Part of the explanation for the remarkable change in contract law's position over the last four centuries is that life was more immediate then than now; part is that life was also more local, and part is that persons were less free to do as they wished, they were more closely tied to a landlord or a noble protector.

Life was more immediate then in the sense that most people had no need to contract for the manufacture of goods to be delivered in nine months, or for the sale of a corn crop in six months. The simple goods that the common man needed could be bought (if he had the money) by cash sale, the simultaneous exchange of coin for shoes or salt. The contract, if you call it that, was usually initiated and executed simultaneously.

In the twenty-first century, we are accustomed to contracting for things that take years to build (e.g., the World Trade Center replacement). Business people routinely sign contracts for computer or other services that may run for a year or longer; General Motors may typically have a five-year contract from a parts supplier. We plan further into the future, using contract in order to allay many of the future's uncertainties. Most modern contracts are like those in *Lucy v. Zehmer* and *NIPSCO*, with an exchange that will take place entirely or largely in the future. They are entered not just for purposes of convenience (Lucy doesn't have $50,000 at hand, and the Zehmers don't have the deed with them), but also to secure the future, under economic conditions where one or both parties fear that markets will not prove adequate in the future. Thus, W. O. Lucy needed a contract because he could not be sure that the Zehmers would remain willing to sell the Ferguson farm for $50,000; and this consideration would have become even more important to him if he had had reason to suspect, for instance, that the farm was likely to appreciate in value soon (for instance, if he had learned that WalMart was about to start buying up property in the area). NIPSCO also needed to nail down the delivery of coal so that it could organize its generation of electricity. In principle, its contract with Carbon County Coal secured its supply line.

In the sixteenth century, life was more local in the sense that goods, services, and real estate were bought close to home. So even if there was a time between agreement and performance, the aggrieved party might have self-help to insure performance. Self-help might take the form of shaming—I

3. 76 Eng. Rep. 1074 (K. B. 1602). For a short history of contract, together with reference to historical discussions, see E. Allan Farnsworth, Contracts 11–26 (4th student ed. 2004).

carry out my obligations because others will shame me if I do not. Of course, self-help might also involve the forcible or stealthy seizure of something sold or promised.

Today we frown on aggressive self-help; trashing a breacher's business or snatching back sold goods would be a crime. Sometimes a person has enough market power to threaten his contracting opposite with injury if he breaches, but those cases are not the rule. And in a national or global market, a party suffers no shame from breaking a contract with a faceless, distant party. Instead of calling upon social norms as the ultimate basis for enforcement, we rely much more heavily on the legal rules that gradually grew up around contracts, as well as on the courts that enforce these rules; but we have largely forgotten that these rules are of comparatively recent origin. (*Hadley v. Baxendale*, the earliest major Common Law case on damages, was decided only in 1854, a century and more after the beginning of the Industrial Revolution; we will examine this case in Chapter 6.)

Finally, in sixteenth century England I would not need a contract of employment if I were the serf of a wealthy landowner, nor even if I were his tenant farmer. In those cases both I and my master or landlord would know our duties from ancient practice that governed all who share our status. By contrast, when a modern American makes a contract with an Italian or a Chinese, there is no such common expectation about pay or performance, no practice that each understands as part of an "inevitable" social reality.

So in an economy where business people and consumers deal freely with people whom they have never met, in an economy where many complex transactions require assured performance far into the future, in an economy where competition is intense and efficiency critical, what do contracts do for us? To answer that question, think of Lucy, Zehmer, NIPSCO, and Carbon County Coal. What did they each expect from their contracts?

At least in theory each of the four wants to be able to invoke the power of the state to get performance (or money damages as a substitute). All four knew (though in the case of the Zehmers there could be some question) that they were entering a "legal" deal, and each probably vaguely appreciated that they or the opposite party could go to court. We describe this as a theoretical consideration because not only are most contracts performed without controversy, but few of the many disputes that arise over contracts result in court judgments. Still, the threat or possibility of suit doubtless changes parties' behavior even when there is no suit.

A second reason to contract, and particularly to contract in a written or electronic document, is to make sure that we agree on the terms of our deal. Writing things down may reveal a misunderstanding or disagreement even before the deal is closed, and, more important, it may remedy bad memories and inhibit fraud. But writing is also filled with traps; consider, from NIPSCO's viewpoint, what emerged as the inadequacies of its *force majeure* clause.

The contract also allocates and may protect against known risks. The buyer of real estate, for instance, is always concerned that the seller may lack good title. By requiring "title satisfactory to buyer," Lucy covered the possibility that the Zehmers' title might be clouded.

Note too how this power to allocate risk makes it possible to achieve a more efficient deal that could be had in sixteenth-century England. Back then the doctrine of *caveat emptor* prevailed and the law and practice allocated the risk of latent defects in a product sold (at least those not caused by the seller's negligence) to the buyer. But assume that the seller could prevent such defects or repair them for $2, whereas their avoidance or repair in buyer's hands would cost $5. If the parties can make a contract to allocate this risk to the seller through a warranty against latent defects, they gain $3 collectively and each can be better off.

The parties may also want to limit or shape the form of state intervention. For example, they might agree to settle any disputes through arbitration, not litigation. Or they might agree that damages should be limited to the purchase price, or that seller should have an opportunity to cure.

There are other, more remote reasons to contract. A coal mining company might want a long-term contract not because it doubted the buyer's willingness to buy coal for the term but because the contract could convince its banker of the buyer's interest and so induce the bank to lend to the mining company.

Return to the two cases in this chapter. What additional reasons for contracts can you find there?

Chapter 2

THE BARGAIN THEORY OF CONTRACT

All but a tiny fraction of the contracts you will see in law practice will be written documents containing the promises of two or more parties who have struck a deal. Usually one party will have promised to pay money to the other, and the other will have promised to sell or to work, or otherwise to perform. At the outset these contracts will be "executory"—that is, neither party will yet have performed. In the words of contract law, the "consideration" for each promise is the other's promise. I promise to pay, you promise to work; you promise to pay, I promise to transfer title to my car. Without consideration or some substitute, executory contracts are not enforceable in American law. With luck, you will be able to practice years without ever seeing a contract that lacks consideration, since nearly all commercial contracts and most non-commercial ones contain reciprocal, bargained-for promises.

Now look at the cases in this chapter. A pathological lot, not so? One deals with the promise to make a gift; another with a promise to pay for a greatly desired but unbargained-for act, the deflection of an ax wielded by an angry spouse. Yet another concerns the enforceability of promises that were relied upon but never responded to with a reciprocal promise. These are sports, the pathological cases of contract law; they are not the cases that you will see often, or, perhaps, at all.

Then why must we deal with this stuff? Is this just law school hazing? Is it law teachers' attempt to maintain the upper hand by forcing the learning of arcane and counterintuitive doctrine? We don't think so. One justification for the study of consideration and the like is to know what promises will be enforced by the courts as contracts. One might regard this chapter as a small venture into legal philosophy. Here we ask what promises should be enforced, and why those and not others. "I will always love you" is a promise but hardly an enforceable contract.

Second, this might be regarded as a small lesson in legal history. Early English law did not enforce bilateral executory promises, but their enforceability is today unquestioned. Nineteenth and twentieth century law has seen the rise of reliance as a basis for the enforcement of promises that generate no reciprocal promises, and this development probably continues under our noses.

The third justification concerns that tiny percentage of cases where even a commercial contract may be unenforceable for lack of consideration. For example, one of your editors was just presented with a television station's lease of space on a projection tower. The lease, for a large amount of money, was for fifteen years with options to extend the term twice. But the lease had no starting date; it started when the lessee commenced installing its equipment on the tower. More than a year after the lease had been concluded, the lessee had still made no move to install any equipment. Since the lessee made no express promise ever to install its equipment, is the deal lacking in consideration for want of a truly binding promise by the lessee? May the lessor now lease to another without fear of suit by the first lessee?

A. CONSIDERATION

Restatement 2d § 1 defines a contract as "a promise or a set of promises for the breach of which the law gives a remedy, or the performance of which the law in some way recognizes as a duty." This definition isolates two essential elements of contract in Common Law. First, our legal system focuses primarily on individual promises as the essential building blocks of contract law; it is therefore mainly oriented toward future performance. A different starting point was possible; the Civil Law jurisdictions of Europe, for instance, concentrate on the present agreement between two or more parties as the basis for contractual analysis.[1] Second, in Common Law a promise does not become enforceable simply by virtue of its being made. Rather, law must recognize the promise as resulting in legal duties and remedies.

On what basis is this recognition to occur? Consider two broad possibilities. First, we might adopt the position that all promises ought to be enforced unless there is some good reason for not enforcing them. Such a position accords well with the common moral claim that one who makes a promise has, as a general rule, a duty to carry it out, and that other persons are entitled to trust such promises; fidelity to one's word is a mark of character.[2] A position such as this also has some influence

1. In general, of course, this makes small difference; most enforceable American contracts would also be enforceable as contracts in France or Germany or Japan. But at the margins there are some differences. On the basis of party agreement, Civil Law treats as contracts not only many gratuitous arrangements, but also cash sales (with no immediate promissory element), that we usually do not. On the other hand, we regard offers of rewards as contractual because they are emphatically promissory; Civil Law treats such offers as non-contractual because they lack immediate agreement between the parties. See Konrad Zweigert & Hein Kötz, Introduction to Comparative Law 388–399 (trans. Tony Weir; 3rd ed. 1998); Hein Kötz, 1 European Contract Law 52–77 (1997).

2. "The obligation to keep a promise is grounded not in arguments of utility but in respect for individual autonomy and in trust.... An individual is morally bound to keep his promises because he has intentionally invoked a convention whose function it

within American contract law. For instance, courts usually try to avoid interpreting contracts in a way that renders them void.

On the other hand, we might start from the opposite position, that no promise ought to be enforced unless there is some good reason for enforcing it. This is a more skeptical position, and one that does not wholly jibe with our common moral perceptions. But it is a position that may represent a more realistic assessment of the seriousness with which promises are in fact characteristically made. If it is true that people commonly use the language of promising in order to make promises they may not wish to be bound by, and if it is also true that, by social convention, the recipients of these promises often understand them as undertaken without full commitment—that is, if there is a significant gap between common morality and the actual practice of promising—then judges will need to devise some sort of filter in order to separate serious promises from those that are more lightly given.

In general, Common Law has inclined toward the second and more skeptical of these two positions, with profound consequences for the general shape of our contract law. As we saw in *Lucy v. Zehmer*, intent to contract can stand on its own as one criterion in determining whether a promise is enforceable. But since intent is often difficult to establish under the stress of adversary proceedings, courts have also made use of more immediate interpretative devices.

Form. One traditional filter is for a legal system simply to specify a means whereby a promisor can make a promise legally binding: "If you want your promise to count, follow this procedure exactly." Such prescribed procedures can take almost any form: an oral question-and-answer in solemn words (Roman law), some sort of quasi-public registration (Civil Law countries), and so on. In Common Law, the long-standing procedure was a written statement of the promise to which the promisor affixed a seal before delivering it to the promisee. The contract under seal is an example of a **formal contract**, one that it is legally enforceable not, or not in the first instance, because of its content or because of the circumstances in which it was given, but chiefly because of way in which it was made.[3]

A formal contract has numerous advantages. In the famous old case of *Dougherty v. Salt*, 227 N.Y. 200, 125 N.E. 94 (1919), Aunt Tillie wanted to promise a gift of $3,000 to her orphaned eight-year-old

is to give grounds—moral grounds—for another to expect the promised performance. To renege is to abuse a confidence he was free to invite or not, and which he intentionally did invite." Charles Fried, Contract as Promise 16 (1981) (footnotes omitted). On promissory theories of contract, see Stephen A. Smith, Contract Theory 54–78 (2004).

3. A formal contract is distinct from a contract employing a standardized set of terms that one party supplies and the other party adheres to (often called a "form contract"). Such a standard form contract is obviously very frequent in modern law, and we will see many instances of standard form contracts in this Casebook. Standard form contracts are, however, not formal contracts in the sense that they acquire their validity from their form. On formalities in modern contract law, see Zweigert & Kötz, Introduction, supra, 365–379; Kötz, 1 European Contract Law, supra, 78–96.

nephew Charley, but the boy's guardian doubted her commitment. If the two parties had available to them a formal instrument such as a contract under seal, Aunt Tillie could have ended all doubt by expressing her promise in this final and irrevocable form. The formal contract brings with it evidence of her commitment, plus a clear indication that her negotiating with the guardian has ended. The document itself also serves as proof of the content of the promise.

On the other hand, there are some disadvantages. A contract under seal is socially obtrusive; for example, Aunt Tillie might well question why Charley's guardian does not accept her word as good enough. Further, to the extent that the form is "content-neutral," it places a burden on the parties to express the promise exactly—something that may be difficult when the promise is complex. Finally, and perhaps most importantly, a formal contract can be inflexible. What happens, for instance, if Aunt Tillie came to have legitimate reasons for regretting her promise, perhaps because Charley had turned out to be an ungrateful little brat, or because she had suffered severe financial setbacks that made her original promise improvident?[4]

Although the contract under seal survives as an independent basis for enforcing contracts in a few jurisdictions (most notably Massachusetts), in most states it is no longer effective. The UCC, for instance, specifically abolishes it for the sale of goods: § 2–203.

Formal elements do survive, however, in many areas of contract law. A good example is the Statute of Frauds, which requires that some types of contracts cannot be enforced against a promisor unless there is a written memorandum signed by the promisor; see Chapter 3.F. Indeed, the importance of form is today generally increasing. For example, consumer legislation now frequently requires that consumers cannot be bound by some provisions in standard contracts unless they have separately signed or initialed the provisions, in order to indicate that they are specifically aware of these provisions.

Consideration. This is the principal device that our law employs in order to determine whether a promise is worthy of legal protection. Restatement 2d § 71 defines the requirement of consideration in the following way:

> (1) To constitute consideration, a performance or a return promise must be bargained for.
>
> (2) A performance or return promise is bargained for if it is sought by the promisor in exchange for his promise and is given by the promisee in exchange for that promise.
>
> (3) The performance may consist of (a) an act other than a promise, or (b) a forbearance, or (c) the creation, modification, or destruction of a legal relation....

4. In the actual case, Aunt Tillie did not use a contract under seal, but instead signed a promissory note, which (in an opinion by Judge Benjamin Cardozo for the New York Court of Appeals) was held insufficient to bind her estate in the absence of consideration for the promise.

Section 71 defines consideration in terms of a bargain between the promisor and the promisee (or some third party). This is the "bargain theory" of consideration, the dominant modern view. It is premised on the idea that a promise is presumptively serious, and so worthy of legal enforcement, if and only if it is consciously given in return for something that is sought: in short, an exchange. However, Restatement 2d § 79 adds that: "If the requirement of consideration is met, there is no additional requirement of (a) a gain, advantage, or benefit to the promisor or a loss, disadvantage, or detriment to the promisee; or (b) equivalence in the values exchanged; or (c) 'mutuality of obligation.' " Section 79 is largely intended to clear away older conceptions of consideration, some of which can be found in the cases below.

HAMER v. SIDWAY

Court of Appeals of New York, 1891.
124 N.Y. 538, 27 N.E. 256.

PARKER, J. All concur. The question which provoked the most discussion by counsel on this appeal, and which lies at the foundation of plaintiff's asserted right of recovery, is whether by virtue of a contract defendant's testator William E. Story became indebted to his nephew William E. Story, 2d, on his twenty-first birthday in the sum of five thousand dollars. The trial court found as a fact that "on the 20th day of March, 1869, * * * William E. Story agreed to and with William E. Story, 2d, that if he would refrain from drinking liquor, using tobacco, swearing, and playing cards or billiards for money until he should become 21 years of age then he, the said William E. Story, would at that time pay him, the said William E. Story, 2d, the sum of $5,000 for such refraining, to which the said William E. Story, 2d, agreed," and that he "in all things fully performed his part of said agreement."

The defendant contends that the contract was without consideration to support it, and, therefore, invalid. He asserts that the promisee by refraining from the use of liquor and tobacco was not harmed but benefited; that that which he did was best for him to do independently of his uncle's promise, and insists that it follows that unless the promisor was benefited, the contract was without consideration. A contention, which if well founded, would seem to leave open for controversy in many cases whether that which the promisee did or omitted to do was, in fact, of such benefit to him as to leave no consideration to support the enforcement of the promisor's agreement. Such a rule could not be tolerated, and is without foundation in the law. The Exchequer Chamber, in 1875, defined consideration as follows: "A valuable consideration in the sense of the law may consist either in some right, interest, profit or benefit accruing to the one party, or some forbearance, detriment, loss or responsibility given, suffered or undertaken by the other." Courts "will not ask whether the thing which forms the consideration does in fact benefit the promisee or a third party, or is of any substantial value to anyone. It is enough that something is promised, done, forborne or suffered by the party to whom the promise is made as consideration for the promise made to him." (Anson's Prin. of Con. 63.) . . .

Now, applying this rule to the facts before us, the promisee used tobacco, occasionally drank liquor, and he had a legal right to do so. That right he abandoned for a period of years upon the strength of the promise of the testator that for such forbearance he would give him $5,000. We need not speculate on the effort which may have been required to give up the use of those stimulants. It is sufficient that he restricted his lawful freedom of action within certain prescribed limits upon the faith of his uncle's agreement, and now having fully performed the conditions imposed, it is of no moment whether such performance actually proved a benefit to the promisor, and the court will not inquire into it, but were it a proper subject of inquiry, we see nothing in this record that would permit a determination that the uncle was not benefited in a legal sense. Few cases have been found which may be said to be precisely in point, but such as have been support the position we have taken.

In *Shadwell v. Shadwell* (9 C. B. [N. S.] 159), an uncle wrote to his nephew as follows:

"My Dear Lancey—I am so glad to hear of your intended marriage with Ellen Nicholl, and as I promised to assist you at starting, I am happy to tell you that I will pay to you 150 pounds yearly during my life and until your annual income derived from your profession of a chancery barrister shall amount to 600 guineas, of which your own admission will be the only evidence that I shall require.

"Your affectionate uncle,

"CHARLES SHADWELL."

It was held that the promise was binding and made upon good consideration.

In *Lakota v. Newton*, an unreported case in the Superior Court of Worcester, Mass., the complaint averred defendant's promise that "if you (meaning plaintiff) will leave off drinking for a year I will give you $100," plaintiff's assent thereto, performance of the condition by him, and demanded judgment therefor. Defendant demurred on the ground, among others, that the plaintiff's declaration did not allege a valid and sufficient consideration for the agreement of the defendant. The demurrer was overruled. . . .

The cases cited by the defendant on this question are not in point. . . .

In further consideration of the questions presented, then, it must be deemed established for the purposes of this appeal, that on the 31st day of January, 1875, defendant's testator was indebted to William E. Story, 2d, in the sum of $5,000 . . .

[Eds.: Although the contractual claim had expired because of the Statute of Limitations, the plaintiff was nonetheless permitted to sue on the promise because, the court held, William Story had later established what was, in effect, an enforceable trust for the money.]

The order appealed from should be reversed and the judgment of the Special Term affirmed, with costs payable out of the estate.

Notes and Discussion

1. **Uncle William's Promise.** William Story promised $5,000 to his nephew Willie (as he is referred to elsewhere in the opinion) if Willie refrained from doing certain things until age 21. This is, of course, a very large sum of money—in modern terms, perhaps as much as $100,000. According to the findings of the trial court, Willie first agreed to refrain, and then "in all things fully performed his part of said agreement." Which did William want: Willie's promise to behave, or Willie's actual behavior? If Willie had then smoked or gambled before age 21, would *he* have breached a contract with William? Surely not, true?

When a promise is given in exchange for a future act, the contract is often referred to as a **unilateral contract**. The classic example is the offer of a reward, e.g., for the capture of an escaped criminal; what the reward's offeror (the promisor) clearly wants in return is not a promise ("I promise to capture the criminal"), but rather an act, the capture itself. Such promises can raise certain problems in formation, which are dealt with briefly in Chapter 3.B; but here no problems seem to have resulted. In an omitted portion of the opinion, the Court quotes a letter from Uncle William stating that Willie had performed to his uncle's satisfaction.

Most contracts are not unilateral, but rather **bilateral**: the exchange of a promise for a promise, with each promise serving as consideration for the other.

2. **Consideration as Benefit or Detriment.** The New York Court cites an English case for the proposition that: "A valuable consideration in the sense of the law may consist either in some right, interest, profit or benefit accruing to the one party [i.e., the promisor], or some forbearance, detriment, loss or responsibility given, suffered or undertaken by the other [i.e., the promisee]." This mode of analysis, once common, is still frequently found.

In arguing to the Court of Appeals, the defendant's lawyer asserted: "There is no consideration to support the promise to pay the nephew $5,000. If the nephew was required to do something that would injure him, or something that would benefit the uncle, and did so with the assent of his father, then there would be a consideration for the payment of the $5,000. Simply failing to play cards or billiards for money, or drink liquor, or use tobacco, would not benefit the uncle; would not, and did not injure the nephew." (The defendant's argument is summarized in the trial report.)

On the benefit side of the ledger, the Court believes that "nothing in this record" contradicts the view that Uncle William derived a benefit from his promise. That the Court calls this a benefit "in a legal sense" shows that it is talking about something other than a conventional or direct benefit to the uncle. The Court goes on to say that it is "of no moment whether such performance [by Willie] *actually* proved a benefit to the promisor" (emphasis supplied).

On the detriment side, many would say that Willie did not suffer any personal loss from his abstention from liquor, smoking, swearing, or gambling. Indeed, a staunch Baptist might claim that Willie clearly benefited by refraining from these things. Look at the opinion again and note how the Court dances around the common meaning of the words that it uses by describing certain benefits as benefits only "in a legal sense."

The Court explains that Willie "had a legal right" to drink and smoke. Presumably his refraining from those acts would not have been consideration if the law had prohibited him from doing such things. Why so? What of a contract to refrain from using heroin, or from robbing banks?

3. Uncle William's Promise as a Bargain. In the Second Restatement, the benefit/detriment test is dispensed with, and in its place is put the "bargain." The crucial element in a bargain is exchange. As Comment b to Restatement 2d § 71 puts it, "In the typical bargain, the consideration and the promise bear a reciprocal relation of motive or inducement: the consideration induces the making of the promise and the promise induces the furnishing of the consideration.... [I]t is not enough that the promise induces the conduct of the promisee or that the conduct of the promisee induces the making of the promise; both elements must be present, or there is no bargain."

In one sense Uncle William had bargained for Willie's abstention since he offered money in return for this conduct. But the "bargain" was unconventional, since Willie did not promise (at least, not in an effective legal fashion) to do any of the things that his uncle wanted. There need not be actual haggling over the terms in order for a bargain to be present, but it is an unusual bargain where one party promises to make a payment in return for another's act, especially when the act must occur over an extensive period of time, cannot be observed by the other party, and consists in *not*

doing something. (Ann Arbor folklore has it that Willie had attended the University of Michigan in the intervening time. It is just possible that he snuck into a billiard parlor or smoked a single cigar during his time there.)

4. Equivalence of Exchange. One characteristic of consideration theory, which often seems surprising, is that modern courts do not ordinarily use it to police an agreement for fairness. (There are some exceptions, which will be dealt with as they arise.) The Court quotes a treatise holding that it is immaterial whether what is given in consideration "is of *any substantial value to any one*. It is enough that something is promised, done, forborne or suffered by the party to whom the promise is made as consideration for the promise made to him." (Emphasis added.)

What does this mean in the context of *Hamer v. Sidway*? Some might interpret Uncle William's promise as primarily donative (like Aunt Tillie's in *Dougherty v. Salt*), and only hazily conditioned on Willie's future behavior. At issue is the rigor with which courts apply consideration theory in separating serious promises from casual social ones.

5. Background of the Lawsuit. The opinion from the General Term of the New York Supreme Court (*Hamer v. Sidway*, 11 N.Y.S. 182; 1890) gives many additional facts. Uncle William made his promise at his father's golden wedding anniversary in March, 1869. The lower court opinion, after analyzing the surrounding circumstances, concludes that the uncle's promise was "a mere promise to make a gift, . . . that he would give William $5,000 when he became 21 years of age, if he should prove himself worthy of it by abstaining from certain useless, evil, and expensive habits." The Court goes on to say that Uncle William had then basically fulfilled this promise during his lifetime, and that in any case Willie had formally renounced any additional claim as a result of the promise. Louisa Hamer, who allegedly acquired the claim by assignment, brought suit on the promise in 1887, almost twenty years after it was made and just after Uncle William had died, so that his testimony was no longer available. The General Term opinion strongly suggests that Hamer's lawsuit was fraudulent, a phony claim contrived by Willie and Hamer in the aftermath of Uncle William's death. This additional information may suggest to you why courts are often cautious in crediting gift-like promises.

Problem 2–1

Fortune Magazine sent a letter addressed to a three-year-old boy. The outside of the envelope stated: "I'll give you this versatile new calculator watch free Just for Opening this Envelope Before Feb. 15, 1985." The boy's mother opened the envelope for him and discovered that defendant's offer was also conditional on subscribing to the magazine. The boy's father and others then brought a class-action suit claiming that they were entitled to the calculator. The defendant responded that: "the mere act of opening the envelope was valueless and therefore did not constitute adequate consideration." Will this argument succeed?

LAKE LAND EMPLOYMENT GROUP OF AKRON, LLC v. COLUMBER

Supreme Court of Ohio, 2004.
101 Ohio St.3d 242, 2004 Ohio 786, 804 N.E.2d 27.

MOYER, C.J. Lake Land Employment Group of Akron, LLC ("Lake Land"), appellant, initiated this action by filing a complaint asserting that its ex-employee, appellee Lee Columber, had breached a noncompetition agreement the parties had executed. The agreement provided that for a period of three years after his termination of employment Columber would not engage in any business within a 50–mile radius of Akron, Ohio, that competed with the business of Lake Land. Lake Land further claimed that Columber's employment with Lake Land terminated in 2001 and that he thereafter violated the terms of the noncompetition agreement. Lake Land sought money damages and an order prohibiting Columber from engaging in any activities that violated the noncompetition agreement.

Columber answered and admitted that he had been employed by Lake Land from 1988 until 2001. He further admitted that he had signed the noncompetition agreement and that following his discharge from

Lake Land he had formed a corporation that is engaged in a business similar to that of Lake Land. Columber pled lack of consideration in his answer.

Columber moved for summary judgment, claiming that the noncompetition agreement was unenforceable. He asserted that the agreement was not supported by consideration and that the restrictions in the agreement were overly restrictive and imposed an undue hardship on him.

Columber could remember very little about the presentation or execution of the noncompetition agreement. He could not remember whether he had been told that his continued employment was dependent upon execution of the agreement or whether he had posed questions about the restrictions it contained. He testified that he vaguely remembered signing the agreement after his employer presented it to him and told him to read and sign it. He acknowledged that he had read the agreement, but had not talked to an attorney or anybody else about it. The at-will relationship of the parties continued for ten years thereafter.

The trial court granted summary judgment in Columber's favor. It found no dispute that Columber had been employed by Lake Land beginning in 1988 and that Columber signed the agreement in September 1991. It further found no dispute that there "was no increase of salary, benefits, or other remunerations given as consideration for Columber signing the non-competition agreement" and "no change in his employment status in connection with the signing of the noncompetition agreement." The trial court concluded that the noncompetition agreement lacked consideration, and was unenforceable. The trial court therefore found it unnecessary to determine the reasonableness of the temporal and geographical restrictions in the noncompetition agreement.

The court of appeals affirmed. It certified a conflict, however, between its decision and the judgments of the Eighth District Court of Appeals in *Swagelok Co. v. Young*, 8th Dist. No. 78976, 2002 Ohio 3416, 2002 WL 1454058, and the Twelfth District Court of Appeals in *Willis Refrigeration, Air Conditioning & Heating, Inc. v. Maynard* (Jan. 18, 2000), 12th Dist. No. CA99–05–047, 2000 Ohio App. LEXIS 102, 2000 WL 36102. The certified issue is "Is subsequent employment alone sufficient consideration to support a covenant-not-to-compete agreement with an at-will employee entered into after employment has already begun?"

I. Legal Background

Generally, courts look upon noncompetition agreements with some skepticism and have cautiously considered and carefully scrutinized them. Ingram, Covenants Not to Compete (2002), 36 Akron L.Rev. 49, 50. Under English common law, agreements in restraint of trade, including noncompetition agreements, were disfavored as being against public policy, although partial restraints supported by fair consideration were upheld.... In a society in which working men entered skilled trades only by serving apprenticeships, and mobility was minimal, restrictive covenants precluding an ex-employee from competing with his ex-employer "either destroyed a man's means of livelihood, or bound him to his master for life." *Raimonde v. Van Vlerah* (1975), 42 Ohio St.2d 21, 71 Ohio Op. 2d 12, 325 N.E.2d 544.

Modern economic realities, however, do not justify a strict prohibition of noncompetition agreements between employer and employee in an at-will relationship. "The law upholds these agreements because they allow the parties to work together to expand output and competition. If one party can trust the other with confidential information and secrets, then both parties are better positioned to compete with the rest of the world. * * * By protecting ancillary covenants not to compete, even after an employee has launched his own firm, the law 'makes it easier for people to cooperate productively in the first place.'" *KW Plastics v. United States Can Co.* (Feb. 2, 2001), M.D. Ala. Nos. Civ. A. 99–D–286–N and 99–D–878–N, 131 F. Supp. 2d 1289, 2001 U.S. Dist. LEXIS 1630, 2001 WL 135722, quoting *Polk Bros., Inc. v. Forest City Ent., Inc.* (C.A.7, 1985), 776 F.2d 185, 189.

Accordingly, this court has long recognized the validity of agreements that restrict competition by an ex-employee if they contain reasonable geographical and temporal restrictions. *Briggs v. Butler* (1942), 140 Ohio St. 499, 507, 24 O.O. 523, 45 N.E.2d 757. Such an agreement does not violate public policy, "being reasonably necessary for the protection of the employer's business, and not unreasonably restrictive upon the rights of the employee." Id. at 508, 24 O.O. 523, 45 N.E.2d 757.

In *Rogers v. Runfola & Assoc., Inc.* (1991), 57 Ohio St.3d 5, 565 N.E.2d 540, this court found valid a noncompetition clause in a written contract for a one-year term of employment that was subject to automatic renewal, in which the employer agreed to discharge the employee only for specified reasons. We rejected the argument of the ex-employee that her promise not to compete lacked consideration in light of the "the exchange of mutually beneficial promises," id. at 7, 565 N.E.2d 540, even though the agreement was signed well after the employment relationship had begun. The case at bar, however, is distinguishable, as it involves an at-will employee who had no express contractual expectation of, or legal entitlement to, continued employment.

Jurisdictions throughout the country are split on the issue presented by the certified question. See, generally, Annotation, Sufficiency of Consideration for Employee's Covenant Not to Compete, Entered into after Inception of Employment (1973), 51 A.L.R.3d 825. As summarized by the Supreme Court of Minnesota, "cases which have held that continued employment is not a sufficient consideration stress the fact that an employee frequently has no bargaining power once he is employed and can easily be coerced. By signing a noncompetition agreement, the employee gets no more from his employer than he already has,[5] and in such cases there is a danger that an employer does not need protection for his investment in the employee but instead seeks to impose barriers to prevent an employee from securing a better job elsewhere. Decisions in which continued employment has been deemed a sufficient consideration for a noncompetition agreement have focused on a variety of factors, including the possibility that the employee would otherwise have been discharged, the employee was actually employed for a substantial time after executing the contract, or the employee received additional compensation or training or was given confidential information after he signed the agreement." (Citations omitted.) *Davies & Davies Agency, Inc.* v. Davies (Minn.1980), 298 N.W.2d 127, 130.

More recently, some courts have found sufficient consideration in an at-will employment situation where a substantial period of employment ensues after a noncompetition covenant is executed, especially when the continued employment is accompanied by raises, promotion, or similar tangible benefits. 6 Lord, Williston on Contracts (4th Ed.1995), Section 13:13. These courts thereby implicitly find that the execution of a noncompetition agreement changes the prior employment relationship from one purely at will. Id. at 577–584. In effect, these courts infer a promise on the part of the employer to continue the employment of his previously at-will employee for an indefinite yet substantial term. Under this approach, however, neither party knows whether the agreement is enforceable until events occur after its execution.

This diversity of approach to the issue is reflected in opinions of the courts of appeals of this state....

II. Formation of Binding Contract

The elements of a contract include the following: an offer, an acceptance, contractual capacity, consideration (the bargained-for legal benefit or detriment), a manifestation of mutual assent, and legality of object and of consideration. *Kostelnik v. Helper*, 96 Ohio St.3d 1, 2002 Ohio 2985, 770 N.E.2d 58, P 16.

The certified question puts in issue only the element of consideration. It asks, "Is subsequent employment alone sufficient consideration to support a covenant-not-to-compete agreement with an at-will employee entered into after employment has already begun?" We conclude that forbearance on the part of an at-will employer from discharging an at-will employee serves as consideration to support a noncompetition agreement.

This court has long recognized the rule that a contract is not binding unless supported by consideration.... Consideration may consist of either a detriment to the promisee or a benefit to the promisor.... A benefit may consist of some right, interest, or profit accruing

5. Note, however, that an at-will employee does not already have a right to come to work in the future at all, let alone under past terms of employment. Although both parties may very well contemplate continuation of the relationship, either may terminate it at any time....

to the promisor, while a detriment may consist of some forbearance, loss, or responsibility given, suffered, or undertaken by the promisee....

At-will employment is contractual in nature.... In such a relationship, the employee agrees to perform work under the direction and control of the employer, and the employer agrees to pay the employee at an agreed rate. Moreover, either an employer or an employee in a pure at-will employment relationship may legally terminate the employment relationship at any time and for any reason.... In the event that an at-will employee quits or is fired, he or she provides no further services for the employer and is generally entitled only to wages and benefits already earned.

It follows that either an employer or an employee in an at-will relationship may propose to change the terms of their employment relationship at any time. If, for instance, an employer notifies an employee that the employee's compensation will be reduced, the employee's remedy, if dissatisfied, is to quit. Similarly, if the employee proposes to the employer that he deserves a raise and will no longer work at his current rate, the employer may either negotiate an increase or accept the loss of his employee. In either event the employee is entitled to be paid only for services already rendered pursuant to terms to which they both have agreed. Thus, mutual promises to employ and to be employed on an ongoing at-will basis, according to agreed terms, are supported by consideration: the promise of one serves as consideration for the promise of the other.

The presentation of a noncompetition agreement by an employer to an at-will employee is, in effect, a proposal to renegotiate the terms of the parties' at-will employment. Where an employer makes such a proposal by presenting his employee with a noncompetition agreement and the employee assents to it, thereby accepting continued employment on new terms, consideration supporting the noncompetition agreement exists. The employee's assent to the agreement is given in exchange for forbearance on the part of the employer from terminating the employee.

We therefore hold that consideration exists to support a noncompetition agreement when, in exchange for the assent of an at-will employee to a proffered noncompetition agreement, the employer continues an at-will employment relationship that could legally be terminated without cause.

III. Caveat

We concur in the view that in cases involving noncompetition agreements, "as in other cases, it is still believed to be good policy to let people make their own bargains and their own valuations." 15 Corbin on Contracts (Interim Ed.2002) 96–97, Section 1395. Professor Corbin suggests that courts should inquire into the sufficiency of consideration in cases involving noncompetition agreements by examining the extent and character of the consideration received by the promisor-employee, "even though we do not do so in ordinary contract cases." Id. at 94–95.

Our decision today does no more than recognize that consideration exists where an at-will employer and an at-will employee continue their employment relationship, rather than terminate it, after the employer imposes a new requirement for employment, i.e., execution of a noncompetition agreement by the employee. While we are not prepared to abandon our long-established precedent that courts may not inquire into the adequacy of consideration, we do not disagree with Corbin's conclusion that the validity of a restraining contract such as a noncompetition agreement should be "determined by weighing as best we can the sum-total of all factors standing together." Id. at 97. We simply recognize that weighing of these factors should not be performed in the context of an inquiry concerning the sufficiency of consideration. That balancing instead should occur in the context of our established precedent recognizing that only reasonable noncompetition agreements are enforceable. We reaffirm the law set forth in paragraphs one and two of the syllabus to *Raimonde*, as follows:

> "1. A covenant not to compete which imposes unreasonable restrictions upon an employee will be enforced to the extent necessary to protect an employer's legitimate interests. * * *
>
> "2. A covenant restraining an employee from competing with his former employer upon termination of employment is reasonable if the restraint is no greater than is required for the protection of the employer, does not impose undue hardship on the employee, and is not injurious to the public."

42 Ohio St.2d 21, 71 Ohio Op. 2d 12, 325 N.E.2d 544.

Our refusal to sanction judicial inquiry into the adequacy of consideration in cases similar to the one at bar does not exclude consideration of other requisites of a contract. It remains the law that noncompetition agreements, like other purported contractual arrangements, may be voidable or unenforceable for reasons other than lack of consideration.

IV. Disposition

Both Columber and his employer had a legal right to terminate their at-will employment relationship when Columber was presented with the noncompetition agreement in 1991. Neither party exercised that legal right to terminate the employment relationship, and, in fact, Columber continued working for the appellant for an additional ten years. Accordingly, the noncompetition agreement is not void for lack of consideration, and summary judgment in Columber's favor should not have been entered on that basis.

Although the trial court erred in entering summary judgment based on its determination that the noncompetition agreement lacked consideration, it must yet determine whether the noncompetition agreement is reasonable pursuant to controlling precedent. We therefore reverse the judgment of the court of appeals and remand the cause for further proceedings.

Judgment reversed and cause remanded.

ALICE ROBIE RESNICK, J., DISSENTING. Courts everywhere are sharply divided on the present certified issue. However, I adhere to the principle that continued employment in an at-will situation does not by itself constitute consideration. I respectfully dissent.

As the majority confirms, "a contract is not binding unless supported by consideration," which is generally defined as "a detriment to the promisee or a benefit to the promisor." Thus, in order for the September 1991 noncompetition agreement executed between appellant, Lake Land Employment Group of Akron, LLC, and appellee, Lee Columber, to be binding, either Lake Land must have given something for it or Columber must have received something in return. Yet, when all is said and done, the only difference in the parties' employment relationship before and after September 1991 is the noncompetition agreement.

The majority's holding that "consideration exists to support a noncompetition agreement when * * * the employer continues an at-will employment relationship * * *" belies itself. If the same at-will employment relationship continues, where is the consideration? The employer has relinquished nothing, since it retains exactly the same preexisting right it always had to discharge the employee at any time, for any reason, for no reason, with or without cause. The employee has gained nothing, for he has not been given or promised anything other than that which he already had, which is "employment which need not last longer than the ink is dry upon [his] signature." *Kadis v. Britt* (1944), 224 N.C. 154, 163, 29 S.E.2d 543. It is precisely because the same at-will employment relationship continues that there is no consideration.

In fact, the majority endeavors to transform this mutual exchange of nothing into consideration by formulating such artful euphemisms as "forbearance on the part of an at-will employer from discharging an at-will employee," "mutual promises to employ and to be employed on an ongoing at-will basis," and "a proposal to renegotiate the terms of the parties' at-will employment." But in the end, the employer simply winds up with both the noncompetition agreement and the continued right to discharge the employee at will, while the employee is left with the same preexisting "nonright" to be employed for so long as the employer decides not to fire him. The only actual "forbearance," "proposal," or "promise" made by the employer in this situation is declining to fire the employee until he executes the noncompetition agreement.

Moreover, the majority's holding and supporting rationale would allow the enforcement of a noncompetition agreement that was exacted from an employee who, at the time of execution, had already acquired all the knowledge his or her position affords and who was fired the day after affixing his or her signature to the document. In cryptic fashion, the majority is essentially holding that a restrictive covenant may henceforth be exacted from an at-will employee without any supporting consideration.

Thus, as well summarized in one analysis: " 'A contract by an employee not to divulge information obtained in the employment and not to engage in other employment in a similar business for two years after the cessation of his employment is not supported by a sufficient consideration where it [is] not executed until after he has been in the employment for several years, his position and duties and the nature of the business remain exactly the same as before, and the employer, reserving the right to discharge him at any time, does not assume any obligation which he does not already have.' " *Morgan Lumber Sales Co. v. Toth* (1974), 41 Ohio Misc. 17, 19, 70 Ohio Op. 2d 33, 321 N.E.2d 907, quoting Headnote 1 to *Kadis v. Britt*, supra, as reported in 224 N.C. 154, 29 S.E.2d 543, 152 A.L.R. 405.

Since the noncompetition agreement in this case lacked consideration and therefore was unenforceable, I would affirm the judgment of the court of appeals.

[Eds.: A second dissenting opinion is omitted.]

Notes and Discussion

1. Employment at Will and the Noncompetition Clause. Lee Columber was an at-will employee of Lake Land. This means that so long as Columber continued to work for Lake Land, he was paid as agreed between him and his employer; but he could quit at any time without having to give a reason, and likewise Lake Land could fire him at any time without having to give a reason. Their positions were, in this respect, symmetrical, although the employer inevitably enjoyed the upper hand in economic reality. This (it may surprise you to learn) is almost always the default position in our law, meaning that, with some important exceptions,[6] an employment relationship is presumed to be at will unless evidence can be found to suggest otherwise. In particular, most states do not require employers to show good cause in terminating at-will employees, although employers are, of course, obliged to obey nondiscrimination statutes and other laws and regulations that can act to restrict their freedom to fire.

As we will see in later cases, discharge of at-will employees remains a highly contested area of contract law. In recent decades many exceptions to the at-will doctrine have emerged, but *Lake Land*, of course, involved an employee who had already been discharged and is not contesting the discharge itself. On social aspects of the employment relationship in the United States, see especially H. J. Howell, The Right to Manage (1982). See also Theodore J. St. Antoine, *A Seed Germinates: Unjust Discharge Reform Heads Toward Full Flower*, 67 Neb. L. Rev. 56 (1988); Clyde W. Summers, *Effective Remedies for Employment Rights: Preliminary Guidelines and Proposals*, 141 U. Pa. L. Rev. 457 (1992); Michael Kittner and Thomas Kohler, *Conditioning Expectations: The Protection of the Employment Bond in German and American Law*, 21 Comp. Lab. L. & Pol'y J. 263 (2000).

6. For instance, in most states employment may not be at will if an employer promises, in an employee handbook or even orally, that it will not fire employees except for cause.

At some point during his employment, Columber signed the noncompetition agreement in question here. Had he signed it at the outset of his employment, it would almost certainly have been part of his contract with Lake Land. The problem arises because there was no such direct temporal relationship.

The decision in this case was closely divided, 4–3. Both sides express their positions well. As the majority notes, courts have traditionally treated noncompetition agreements with considerably skepticism, mainly because they can violate public policy on restraint of trade; we will return to this problem below in Chapter 5. In this case, though, the only issue was the consideration for Columber's promise. As you read this decision, try to figure out the problems with the reasoning on either side. Is the majority straining unduly in finding consideration simply in the acceptance of continued employment? On the other hand, is the minority actually just using the consideration argument to police against a contract term it finds disagreeable on other grounds?

2. **Some Problems.** Would the result in this case have been different if Columber was not an employee at will but an employee under a five-year term contract, and he had been presented with the noncompetition agreement in the middle of the term? Why or why not?

Assume that Columber, as an at-will employee, came to Lake Land with an offer from a third party, and that Lake Land then agreed to raise his wages by 10% if he did not quit. At the end of that month Lake Land informed Columber that it was revoking the 10% pay increase for the future and that it did not intend to pay the additional 10% for the previous month. Columber must have a claim, but for what? (You are beginning to appreciate the bedeviling intricacies of at-will employment contracts.)

3. **Forbearance as Consideration.** A person's forbearance from exercising a legal right has long been recognized as one form of consideration. Here the employer forbore from firing his at-will employee. That was enough for the majority but not for the dissent. We suspect that the division between the majority and the dissent reflects a difference of opinion about at will employment that we will see also in later cases.

There is much law on the question whether abandoning or promising to abandon a claim amounts to consideration for a contract. That topic has claimed an entire section, § 74, in the Second Restatement. You will note that § 74 recognizes the abandonment of even invalid claims as consideration—at least if the forbearing party "believes that the claim or defense may be fairly determined to be valid." Why does the Restatement go to such lengths to recognize the surrender of even potentially invalid claims as consideration? We suspect that the drafters feared that any other rule would lead to *ex post facto* challenges to routine lawsuit settlements.

For a nice example of the forbearance problem, see *Fiege v. Boehm*, 210 Md. 352, 123 A.2d 316 (Md. 1956). Hilda Boehm obtained a promise from Louis Fiege to pay expenses incident to the birth of her child, upon condition that she would not institute bastardy proceedings against him over the child. He paid for a time, then stopped; but when she instituted bastardy proceedings, it was determined through blood tests that he could not have been the child's father, and so he was acquitted of bastardy. She then sued him on the contract. Although the Maryland court was plainly influenced by a desire to secure support for the child, if possible, it ultimately holds more broadly for Boehm: "forbearance to sue for a lawful claim or demand is sufficient consideration to pay for the forbearance if the party forbearing had an honest intention to prosecute litigation which is not frivolous, vexatious, or unlawful, and which he believed to be well founded." 210 Md. at 361.

Problem 2–2

In a job-related accident, Dale Warren Dyer, an at-will employee, lost his right foot. His employer placed him on a paid leave of absence for a year, after which he returned to work as a foreman, the job he had held before the injury. A year later he was laid off. Dyer sues for breach of contract, claiming that he had believed he had a valid claim against his employer for his personal injury, and that he had forborne pursuing this claim because the employer had promised him "lifetime employment." In reply, the employer asserts that this promise, even if it had been made, would be unenforceable for lack of consideration, since the state workers' compensation act states that: "The rights and remedies provided in this chapter ... for an employee on account of injury ... for which benefits under this chapter ... are recoverable, shall be the exclusive and only rights and remedies of such employee ... at common law or otherwise, on account of such injury, against his or her employer." Both parties agree that the employee's injury is covered by this statute. Will the employer prevail?

PETROLEUM REFRACTIONATING CORP. v. KENDRICK OIL CO.

Circuit Court of Appeals, Tenth Circuit, 1933.
65 F.2d 997.

PHILLIPS, C. J. The Petroleum Corporation brought this action against the Kendrick Company to recover damages for breach of contract. After setting out the jurisdictional facts, the amended petition alleged that on January 15, 1932, the Kendrick Company gave an order to the Petroleum Corporation, the material portions of which read as follows:

"January 15th, 1932.

"To Petroleum Refractionating Company, Tulsa, Oklahoma.

"Ship to Metropolitan Utilities District, Gas Plant, 20th & Center Streets, Omaha, Nebraska. * * * Shipping date, February, March, April and May. Cars—1,500,000 gallons, 10% more or less. Commodity—35–37 straight run gas oil, meeting Metropolitan Utilities District specifications. Price—45 cent barrel. F.O.B.—Pampa, Texas.

"Terms–1–10. * * *

"Seller may cancel any unshipped portion of this order on five days' notice, if for any reason, he should discontinue making this grade of oil. * * *"

[Eds.: The amended petition also alleged:] That the Petroleum Corporation accepted such order and delivered thereunder 62,601 gallons of such oil; that on February 16, 1932, the Kendrick Company notified the Petroleum Corporation that it would not accept further deliveries under such order for the reason that the grade of oil being shipped was not of the standard stipulated in the order; that after notice to the Kendrick Company, and on February 21, 1932, the Petroleum Corporation resold the portion of the oil remaining undelivered under such contract at 25 cents a barrel. It sought damages for the difference between the contract price and the resale price of such oil.

The Kendrick Company demurred to the petition on the ground that it did not state facts sufficient to constitute a cause of action. The trial court held that there was no consideration for the promise of the Kendrick Company to purchase, and sustained the demurrer. The Petroleum Corporation elected to stand on its amended petition, and the trial court entered judgment for the Kendrick Company. This is an appeal therefrom.

Counsel for the Petroleum Corporation contend that the promise of the Kendrick Company to purchase was supported by the agreement of the Petroleum Corporation either to sell, which would be a benefit to the Kendrick Company, or, in the alternative, to discontinue making such grade of oil, which would be a detriment to the Petroleum Corporation. On the other hand, counsel for the Kendrick Company contend that whether the Petroleum Corporation should sell and deliver the oil was conditioned only by the will or wish of the Petroleum Corporation.

A benefit to the promisor or a detriment to the promisee is a sufficient consideration for a contract.... The detriment need not be real; it need not involve actual loss to the promisee. The word, as used in the definition, means legal detriment as distinguished from detriment in fact. It is the giving up by the promisee of a legal right; the refraining from doing what he has the legal right to do, or the doing of what he has the legal right not to do.... And where there is a detriment to the promisee, there need be no benefit to the promisor....

Under the terms of the contract, the Petroleum Corporation agreed either to sell and deliver the oil or to discontinue making the grade of oil contracted for, and to give five days' notice of cancellation of the contract.

Since alternative courses were open to the Petroleum Corporation, the contract was without consideration on its part, if any one of the courses standing alone would have been an insufficient consideration. Restatement, Contracts, § 79; Williston on Contracts, § 104, p. 219; *McManus v. Bark L.R.* 5 Exch. 65.

The question then is, Would a discontinuance by the Petroleum Corporation to manufacture the grade of oil contracted for result in such a detriment to it as would constitute a consideration for the promise of the Kendrick Company to purchase?

The giving up by the seller of the right to sell to others such goods as he should manufacture during a specified period has been held a sufficient consideration for the promise of the buyer to purchase such goods, although the seller was not obligated to manufacture any goods whatever. *Ramey Lumber Co. v. John Schroeder Lumber Co. (CCA. 7)*, 237 F. 39 [1916]; . . .

In *City of Marshall v. Kalman*, 153 Minn. 320, 190 N.W. 597 [1922], Kalman agreed to purchase all the street improvement certificates which the city should issue during a specified period, at par plus accrued interest. It was urged that the contract was without consideration on the part of the city because it was not obligated to issue any certificates. The Court held that, although the city had not agreed to issue any certificates, it had restricted its freedom to sell to others any certificates which it might issue, and that such restriction was a valid consideration for the promise of Kalman to purchase.

Should the Petroleum Corporation, under the alternative provision of the contract, discontinue to manufacture the grade of oil specified in the contract, it would refrain from doing that which it had the right to do; and it would thereby give up a legal right—the right to continue to make the grade of oil specified.

It follows that, under the principles above stated, the discontinuance by the Petroleum Corporation to manufacture the grade of oil specified in the contract would constitute a detriment to it, and the promise so to do would be a sufficient consideration for the promise of the Kendrick Company to purchase.

The judgment is reversed with instructions to overrule the demurrer.

Notes and Discussion

1. **Illusory Promises and Mutuality.** Arthur and Betty arrange that Arthur will work for Betty for five years, but Betty reserves the power to terminate their agreement whenever she wishes. Restatement 2d § 77, Comment a, holds that: "Words of promise which by their terms make performance entirely optional with the 'promisor' do not constitute a promise." This means that Betty's promise is not a real one, and so it cannot serve as consideration for Arthur's promise. In traditional doctrine, it is irrelevant both that Betty has not exercised her power to terminate and that she does not wish to exercise it; if the other is unwilling, neither Arthur nor Betty can enforce the arrangement.

Kendrick made a version of this argument, but lost. It is a good thing, too. If every contract that had a conditional "out" was rendered unenforceable in this way, modern commerce would be in big trouble.

Note that it is always the person who is not the beneficiary of the condition who claims freedom from a contractual obligation because the *other* party has made an illusory promise. Understand that the party that made the so-called illusory promise does not need the doctrine of mutuality in order to escape from the contract.

Mutuality, once treated as an independent requirement for valid contracts, is today usually considered just an aspect of consideration. "If the requirement of consideration is met, there is no additional requirement of . . . 'mutuality of obligation.' " Restatement 2d § 79(c). Mutuality applies, of course, only to so-called bilateral contracts, where parties exchange promises.

2. Conditional Contracts. The contract between the Petroleum Corporation and Kendrick stated that: "Seller [i.e., the Petroleum Corporation] may cancel any unshipped portion of this order on five days' notice, if for any reason, he should discontinue making this grade of oil." On alternative promises, see Restatement 2d § 77.

The Court seems to be saying that if there is enough pain in the condition, the promise has not been made illusory by the inclusion of that condition. Here is a place where the doctrine of consideration may actually intrude into commercial contracts, for many commercial contracts are conditional, and when one party is more powerful than the other, the condition may grant to that party a nearly unfettered right to get out of the contract.

3. Output and Requirements Contracts. A case that the opinion cites by analogy is *Ramey Lumber*, in which a seller agreed to sell all "such goods as he should manufacture during a specified period" to a buyer. This is called an output contract, and the precedent held it valid. The opposite situation is a requirements contract, in which a buyer agrees to buy all its requirements from a seller. Would the outcome be different if, for instance, the seller in *Ramey Lumber* had fixed a price for all its sales to the buyer, but had held open the possibility of selling to other buyers as well?

Courts once treated output and requirements contracts as suspect for want of mutuality. Today they are universally accepted. For sale of goods, such contracts are governed by UCC § 2–306(1). Problems associated with the enforcement of these contracts are considered below in Chapter 4.C.

4. Should the Requirement of Consideration Be Relaxed or Abolished? Evaluate the following argument: "The consideration doctrine prohibits the enforcement of gift promises not because of a policy against gift-giving but because courts want to encourage parties to be specific about the content of their exchanges in order to ease the judicial burden of interpretation. Similarly, in the past courts resisted enforcing firm offers and requirements contracts not because they were socially undesirable, but because, like gift exchanges, they were vague. But judicial convenience had to give way to commercial exigency. Courts gradually realized—or, at least, came to believe—that parties would prefer the uncertainty of judicial enforcement of vague terms to the certainty of non-enforcement, and over time courts yielded to entreaties to enforce vague contracts. Whether courts will treat gift promises in a similar way remains to be seen. They should only if the social value of enforcement of such promises exceeds the cost of fraud—an empirical question." Eric A. Posner, Law and Social Norms 64 (2000).

And what about the following argument: In the only place where the consideration has a significant bite in commercial transactions, namely promises regarded as illusory because they insufficiently bind one party, the doctrine is dubious. For example, it is clearly worth something to a supplier to be recognized as a potential seller to General Motors or Ford. By submitting its products and having them evaluated by GM or Ford, a supplier may become an authorized seller of a certain part. It might then be willing to enter into a contract to sell "as many gizmos (not to exceed 100,000 a year) as General Motors may wish to buy." By getting onto GM's recognized purchase list, the supplier will have accomplished something and may rightly regard itself as in a better economic position than if it had no writing signed by GM at all. If so, the contract should be enforceable, right? What possible argument, economic or otherwise, is there for declining to enforce such a contract? None, says White. (Frier concurs in the outcome.)

Problem 2–3

Donald agreed with Ivana that, within the United States and for the space of five years, he would have the exclusive right to market the fashionable clothing that she endorsed, and that they would split the profits from any sales. If Ivana then repudiates the agreement, can Donald successfully sue her? What exactly has he promised in return for her promise? This hypothetical is based on the famous old case of *Wood v. Lucy, Lady Duff-Gordon*, 222 N.Y. 88, 118 N.E. 214 (1917), in which Benjamin Cardozo upheld the contract by implying a counter-promise to "use reasonable efforts" in marketing. Such "exclusive dealing" contracts are now governed by UCC § 2–306(2), which speaks of "best efforts."

HARRINGTON v. TAYLOR

Supreme Court of North Carolina, 1945.
225 N.C. 690, 36 S.E.2d 227.

PER CURIAM. The plaintiff in this case sought to recover of the defendant upon a promise made by him under the following peculiar circumstances:

The defendant had assaulted his wife, who took refuge in plaintiff's house. The next day the defendant gained access to the house and began another assault upon his wife. The defendant's wife knocked him down with an axe, and was on the point of cutting his head open or decapitating him while he was laying on the floor, and the plaintiff intervened, caught the axe as it was descending, and the blow intended for defendant fell upon her hand, mutilating it badly, but saving defendant's life.

Subsequently, defendant orally promised to pay the plaintiff her damages; but, after paying a small sum, failed to pay anything more. So, substantially, states the complaint.

The defendant demurred to the complaint as not stating a cause of action, and the demurrer was sustained. Plaintiff appealed.

The question presented is whether there was a consideration recognized by our law as sufficient to support the promise. The Court is of the opinion that however much the defendant should be impelled by common gratitude to alleviate the plaintiff's misfortune, a humanitarian act of this kind, voluntarily performed, is not such consideration as would entitle her to recover at law.

The judgment sustaining the demurrer is: Affirmed.

Notes and Discussion

1. **Moral Consideration and Past Consideration.** This uncommonly brusque decision hardly seems a straightforward application of the bargain theory of consideration. There are two main circumstances in which a promise, although not bargained for, might still seem worthy of enforcement: if the promisor acts from a strong sense of duty toward the promisee (so-called moral consideration); or if the promisor is seeking to recompense the promisee for a benefit previously conferred (so-called past consideration). Lena Harrington could state her claim against Lee Taylor under either theory, but *Webb v. McGowin*, cited below, suggests that moral consideration is the stronger theory. Note that Taylor promised only to pay for Harrington's damages (medical expenses, lost work, and so on), not an additional reward.

At issue here is whether the bargain theory is underinclusive, in that it excludes enforcement of some promises that should be enforced. What arguments can be given on either side of this matter? Should it matter that promises based on moral or past consideration usually have no direct economic benefits?

2. **Material Benefit.** In 1925, Joe Webb, an employee in an Alabama lumber company, leaped onto a 75-pound block and diverted its fall, thereby preventing the death or serious injury of J. Greeley McGowin; but in the process Webb was crippled for life. In gratitude, McGowin promised, apparently orally, to care for and maintain Webb for the rest of Webb's life. McGowin kept up payments until his death in 1934. The executors of his estate then stopped them. Alabama appeals courts enforced the promise on that theory that: "a moral obligation is a sufficient consideration to support a subsequent promise to pay where the promisor has received a material benefit, although there was no original duty or liability resting on the promisor." *Webb v. McGowin,* 27 Ala.App. 82, 168 So. 196 (1935), *cert. denied* 232 Ala. 374, 168 So. 199 (1936). We can't distinguish *Harrington v. Taylor*. Can you?

Webb v. McGowin is the leading case for a narrow exception to the rule in *Harrington v. Taylor*. The exception is formalized in Restatement 2d § 86, but is hedged round with conditions: the benefit must have been "received by the promisor from the promisee"; the promise "is binding to the extent necessary to prevent injustice," and may be limited if "its value is disproportionate to the benefit"; and the promise is not binding if the promisor "conferred the benefit as a gift or for other reasons the promisor has not been unjustly enriched." These restrictions are quite rigid, and few courts seem to have followed the Restatement.

Statutes in some states make promises of this type enforceable provided that specified requirements are met. N.Y. Gen. Oblig. Law § 5–1105 (Consol.

2004) (promise must be written; consideration must be valid "but for the time when it was given or performed"); Cal. Civ. Code § 1606 (Deering 2004).

For further information relating to *Harrington* and *Webb*, see Richard Danzig and Geoffrey R. Watson, The Capability Problem in Contract Law 149–213 (2nd ed. 2004). Lena Harrington's complaint describes her injuries as follows: "[T]he plaintiff's fingers were cut to the bone by the aforesaid blow, and [she] suffered great pain and suffering thereby; . . . [her] hand is permanently injured and is practically useless." Further, "the plaintiff has spent considerable sums of money for treatment thereof." Danzig and Watson, at 188. They also reprint the brief of her appeal (pp. 205–208).

3. Exceptions. There are a few traditional exceptions to the rule that moral consideration is not enough. Most involve promises renewing obligations that would have been enforceable except for a legal "technicality." For instance, a debtor promises to pay a debt that had been barred by the statute of limitations; this promise is usually enforceable. So too if a minor's promise is voidable for lack of legal capacity, but the promisor then renews the promise upon reaching majority. More controversial is a debtor who has undergone bankruptcy and then promises to pay a pre-bankruptcy creditor; such a promise, if enforceable, arguably defeats the whole purpose of bankruptcy. In the 1978 revision of the Bankruptcy Law, Congress allowed and gave legal enforceability to reaffirmations by bankrupts in certain cases. A moment's thought will reveal that even a bankrupt might rationally wish to make a binding contract with one or more creditors. For example, I might want to kiss off all my creditors except for the one who has a security interest in my automobile. Since bankruptcy does not invalidate perfected security interests, I may be able to keep the car (and so my job) only by reaffirming. See generally § 524(c)-(f) of the Bankruptcy Code.

Another traditional exception, supported by Restatement 2d § 90(2), is promises made to charitable organizations or in the context of property settlements prior to marriage. Although the Restatement is probably right in just making an outright exception on the basis of a public policy favoring charitable organizations and marriage, most courts have tended instead to stretch orthodox concepts of consideration in order to cover particular cases. Judge Cardozo led the way in this respect: *Allegheny College v. National Chautauqua County Bank*, 246 N.Y. 369, 159 N.E. 173 (1927) (donation to a college); *De Cicco v. Schweizer*, 221 N.Y. 431, 117 N.E. 807 (1917) (pre-marriage settlement by bride's father on the groom).

BOARD OF CONTROL OF EASTERN MICHIGAN UNIVERSITY v. BURGESS

Court of Appeals of Michigan, 1973.
45 Mich.App. 183, 206 N.W.2d 256.

BURNS, J. On February 15, 1966, defendant signed a document which purported to grant to plaintiff a 60-day option to purchase defendant's home. That document, which was drafted by plaintiff's agent, acknowledged receipt by defendant of "One and no/100 ($1.00) Dollar and other valuable consideration." Plaintiff concedes that neither the one dollar nor any other consideration was ever paid or even tendered to defendant. On April 14, 1966, plaintiff delivered to defendant written notice of its intention to exercise the option. On the closing date defendant rejected plaintiff's tender of the purchase price. Thereupon, plaintiff commenced this action for specific performance.

At trial defendant claimed that the purported option was void for want of consideration, [and] that any underlying offer by defendant had been revoked prior to acceptance by plaintiff.... The trial judge ... held that defendant's acknowledgment of receipt of consideration bars any subsequent contention to the contrary. Accordingly, the trial judge entered judgment for plaintiff.

Defendant appeals. She claims that acknowledgment of receipt of consideration does not bar the defense of failure of consideration....

I.

Options for the purchase of land, if based on valid consideration, are contracts which may be specifically enforced.... *George v. Schuman*, 202 Mich 241, 250 (1918). Conversely, that which purports to be an option, but which is not based on valid consideration, is not a contract and will not be enforced. *Bailey v. Grover*, 237 Mich. 548 (1927); *George v. Schuman, supra*, at 248. One dollar is valid consideration for an option to purchase land, provided the dollar is paid or at least tendered.... In the instant case defendant received no consideration for the purported option of February 15, 1966.

A written acknowledgment of receipt of consideration merely creates a rebuttable presumption that consideration has, in fact, passed. Neither the parol evidence rule nor the doctrine of estoppel bars the presentation of evidence to contradict any such acknowledgment.[7] *Hagan v. Moch*, 249 Mich. 511, 517 (1930).

It is our opinion that the document signed by defendant on February 15, 1966, is not an enforceable option, and that defendant is not barred from so asserting.

The trial court premised its holding to the contrary on *Lawrence v. McCalmont*, 43 U.S. (2 How) 426, 452; 11 L. Ed. 326, 336 (1844). That case is significantly distinguishable from the instant case. Mr. Justice Story held that "[t]he guarantor acknowledged the receipt of one dollar, and is now estopped to deny it." However, in reliance upon the guaranty substantial credit had been extended to the guarantor's sons. The guarantor had received everything she bargained for, save one dollar.... In the instant case defendant claims that she never received any of the consideration promised her.

That which purports to be an option for the purchase of land, but which is not based on valid consideration, is a simple offer to sell the

7. [Eds.: This means that Burgess is not prevented by any standard legal means from presenting evidence that she never actually received the dollar, despite her signature on the writing.]

same land. *Bailey v. Grover, supra.* An option is a contract collateral to an offer to sell whereby the offer is made irrevocable for a specified period. *George v. Schuman, supra*, at 248. Ordinarily, an offer is revocable at the will of the offeror. Accordingly, a failure of consideration affects only the collateral contract to keep the offer open, not the underlying offer.

A simple offer may be revoked for any reason or for no reason by the offeror at any time prior to its acceptance by the offeree. *Weiden v. Woodruff*, 38 Mich 130, 131–132 (1878). Thus, the question in this case becomes, "Did defendant effectively revoke her offer to sell before plaintiff accepted that offer?" . . .

Defendant testified that within hours of signing the purported option she telephoned plaintiff's agent and informed him that she would not abide by the option unless the purchase price was increased. Defendant also testified that when plaintiff's agent delivered to her on April 14, 1966, plaintiff's notice of its intention to exercise the purported option, she told him that "the option was off."

Plaintiff's agent testified that defendant did not communicate to him any dissatisfaction until sometime in July, 1966.

If defendant is telling the truth, she effectively revoked her offer several weeks before plaintiff accepted that offer, and no contract of sale was created. If plaintiff's agent is telling the truth, defendant's offer was still open when plaintiff accepted that offer, and an enforceable contract was created. The trial judge thought it unnecessary to resolve this particular dispute. In light of our holding the dispute must be resolved.

An appellate court cannot assess the credibility of witnesses. We have neither seen nor heard them testify. . . . Accordingly, we remand this case to the trial court for additional findings of fact based on the record already before the court. . . .

Notes and Discussion

1. Nominal Consideration. If a promise must be supported by bargained-for consideration in order to be binding, can the pretense of a bargain suffice? Despite the general rule against using the requirement of consideration to evaluate fairness of exchange, courts may look suspiciously on "pseudo-bargains." In *Schnell v. Nell*, 17 Ind. 29 (1861), a widower signed a document promising $600 to three relatives of his wife, "in consideration of one cent." The Court held: "It is true, that as a general proposition, inadequacy of consideration will not vitiate an agreement. . . . But this doctrine does not apply to a mere exchange of sums of money, of coin, whose value is exactly fixed, but to the exchange of something of, in itself, indeterminate value, for money, or, perhaps, for some other thing of indeterminate value." The Court would not have been satisfied with a document that read: "in consideration of an old sweatshirt," would it? What is the underlying issue that the Court is concerned about?

Modern contract law has actually become increasingly disapproving of "pseudo-bargains." The First Restatement seems to permit them; see Illustration 1 to § 84 (in order to make binding A's promise to give property worth $5,000 to B, A and B agree that A will "sell" the property for $1; this is sufficient consideration). The Second Restatement apparently reverses this; see Illustration 5 to § 71 (in order to make binding A's promise to give $1,000 to B, A and B agree that B will "sell" to A a book worth $1; there is no consideration for A's promise).

2. **Option Contracts.** Burgess signed a writing that purportedly gave EMU 60 days within which to decide whether to purchase her home, in exchange for $1.00 and "other valuable consideration." Although the writing contained an offer looking forward to the possible conclusion of a sale, in external form it was, as the Court observes, a contract in its own right: an option contract. See Restatement 2d § 25. Options are a very common part of modern life, particularly for real estate, because they make an offer binding for a period of time during which the offeree can decide whether to accept the offer; the offeree can use this time in order to arrange financing, to inspect, and to price out prospective repairs and additions. Supposing that this was a valid option contract, what exactly did Ms. Burgess promise to EMU?

3. **Consideration for Option Contracts.** As the Michigan Court says, a promise that is in form an option requires consideration in order to be binding. This rule is traditional. It makes no difference how absolute the original language of the offer is. For example, in *Hill v. Corbett*, 33 Wash.2d 219, 204 P.2d 845 (1949), an offer was held to be revocable despite language that: "the first parties do hereby grant unto the second parties the option to extend the lease," where there was no consideration for the promise.

On the other hand, relatively small sums have been held to constitute consideration even for large potential deals. A good example is *Keaster v. Bozik*, 191 Mont. 293, 623 P.2d 1376 (1981), in which five dollars (combined with efforts to obtain an FHA loan) was deemed adequate consideration to make binding a one-year option to purchase 899 acres of land for $200,000.

What does the Michigan Court of Appeals insist on in order to satisfy the requirement of consideration? To what extent does it remain committed to the bargain requirement? To what extent has consideration become, in the context of an option contract, a mere formality? Lon Fuller's classic article on *Consideration and Form*, 41 Colum. L. Rev. 799 (1941), is still very helpful in sorting out the formalistic elements of consideration.

Perhaps the Court could have rescued EMU by implying a promise to pay the dollar to Burgess. Compare *Smith v. Wheeler*, 233 Ga. 166, 210 S.E.2d 702 (1974), where an option to purchase real estate contained a recital that one dollar had been paid as consideration; it was held that "the recital of the one dollar consideration gives rise to an implied promise to pay which can be enforced by the other party," and that failure to pay it did not void the option contract. Few courts have taken this position, however; why?

4. **Reform.** The rule requiring consideration for option contracts has often been criticized. Restatement 2d § 87(1)(a) makes an option binding if it "is in writing and signed by the offeror, recites a purported consideration for the making of the offer, and proposes an exchange on fair terms within a reasonable time." Burgess would be bound under this rule, no?

For sale of goods, UCC § 2–205 introduces the concept of a "firm offer," "[a]n offer by a merchant to buy or sell goods in a signed writing"; under certain conditions, it is valid "for a reasonable time" not to exceed three months. The CISG art. 16(2)(a), following European law, goes even further: "an offer cannot be revoked . . . if it indicates, whether by stating a fixed time for acceptance or otherwise, that it is irrevocable . . . "

Should the concept of a binding "firm offer" (in effect, an option binding without consideration) be extended more widely in Common Law? Think about this in relation to the *Burgess* case.

Problem 2–4

"[A] buyer begins her search for a car by taking a new Chevrolet for a test drive. After the test drive, the buyer plans to continue her search by visiting other car dealers. The seller wants to induce the buyer to consider carefully the purchase of the new Chevrolet. Consequently, the seller promises to sell the new Chevrolet to the buyer for a stated price, provided that the buyer accepts within one week. In other words, the seller makes a 'firm' offer and promises to 'keep it open' for one week. The buyer does not want to waste her time by considering the offer carefully and then finding that the seller has reneged. Consequently, the buyer wants the promise to be enforceable. The seller knows that the buyer is more likely to consider the offer carefully if the promise is enforceable, so the seller wants the promise to be enforceable. Thus, the promisor and the promisee want the promise to be enforceable." Robert Cooter and Thomas Ulen, Law and Economics 183 (3d. ed. 2000).

Under the bargain theory of consideration, is the seller's offer enforceable if the seller wishes to revoke it early? Should it be? As to this, Cooter and Ulen argue yes: "By enforcing the promise, the court can give both parties what they want. Giving them what they want promotes exchange and encourages cooperation by reducing uncertainty and risk." Id. at 185.

FISHER v. JACKSON

Supreme Court of Connecticut, 1955.
142 Conn. 734, 118 A.2d 316.

WYNNE, J. The plaintiff instituted this action to recover damages for the breach of an oral agreement of employment. The defendant has appealed from the judgment rendered upon a plaintiff's verdict. The questions presented are whether the court was in error in denying the defendant's motion to set the verdict aside on the ground that it is not supported on the issue of liability, and in denying the defendant's motion for judgment notwithstanding the verdict.

The substituted complaint alleged that the defendant, through his authorized agent, induced the plaintiff to give up his employment with a firm of bakers, where he was making $50 per week, and to enter upon employment as a reporter, for $40 per week, under an oral contract that the employment would be for the life of the plaintiff or until he was physically disabled for work, with a yearly increase in salary of $5 per week. The defendant's contention is that there was no evidence that the parties had agreed upon such a contract. The defendant's claim is that the job under discussion was a permanent one rather than for a definite term and was terminable at will by either party.

In the absence of a consideration in addition to the rendering of services incident to the employment, an agreement for a permanent employment is no more than an indefinite general hiring, terminable at the will of either party without liability to the other. *Carter v. Bartek*, 142 Conn. 448, 450, 114 A.2d 923, and cases there cited.

The plaintiff was hired by the defendant's managing editor in January, 1944, and went to work as a reporter for the New Haven Register, a newspaper owned by the defendant. He was discharged on or about January 7, 1949. The contact between the parties began with a notice which was put in a trade magazine by the defendant, just prior to the admitted hiring of the plaintiff. That advertisement set forth that a "permanent position" as a reporter awaited an "all-around male newsman with experience on several beats and educational background that [would stand] up in a University city." The plaintiff wrote a letter in response to the advertisement and as a result was interviewed by the defendant's managing editor for about ten minutes and was thereafter hired. Whether or not the plaintiff was an "all-around newsman" with experience on several beats and with an educational background, however nebulous, that would stand up in a university city nowhere appears. The managing editor, who was the only other party to the interview, was deceased at the time of the trial. The plaintiff, in his letter seeking an interview, had written that he was looking for a connection which, "in the event my services are satisfactory, will prove permanent." So it must be quite apparent that the significant thought expressed was in his mind during his brief interview with the defendant's managing editor. It seems clear to us that the negotiations amounted to nothing more than the hiring of a reporter for a job which was permanent in the sense that it was not a mere temporary place. The hiring was indefinite as to time and terminable by either party at his will.

There is no occasion to discuss at length the claim advanced by the plaintiff that special consideration moved to the defendant because the plaintiff gave up his job with the bakery firm. The plaintiff did no more than give up other activities and interests in order to enter into the service of the defendant. The mere giving up of a job by one who decides to accept a contract for alleged life employment is but an incident necessary on his part to place himself in a position to accept and perform the contract; it is not consideration for a contract of life employment. . . .

The plaintiff argues that he suffered a detriment by giving up his job. To constitute sufficient consideration for a promise, an act or promise not only must be a detriment to the promisee but must be bargained for and given in exchange for the promise . . . Restatement, 1

Contracts § 75. In the present case, the plaintiff's giving up of his job at the bakery was not something for which the defendant bargained in exchange for his promise of permanent employment. Nowhere in the plaintiff's testimony does it appear that the defendant's agent even suggested that the plaintiff give up the job he had with the bakery firm, much less that the agent induced him to do so. It would thus appear that there was not even a semblance of a claim that the giving up of the plaintiff's job was consideration for any promise that may have been made by the defendant's agent....

Inasmuch as the contract of employment which was proved would not in any event warrant a judgment in favor of the plaintiff, even though the case were retried, the court should have directed judgment for the defendant notwithstanding the verdict....

There is error, the judgment is set aside and the case is remanded with direction to render judgment for the defendant notwithstanding the verdict.

Notes and Discussion

1. **Employment at Will, Revisited.** According to the plaintiff's complaint, the defendant offered employment "for the life of the plaintiff or until he was physically disabled for work." The Court interprets this as an offer of "permanent employment," which is then described as "no more than an indefinite general hiring, terminable at the will of either party without liability to the other." This is a legal construction of what it was that the plaintiff was offered, although not necessarily the most persuasive construction of the word "permanent." Why doesn't it matter what the plaintiff thought he was being offered?

2. **Conditions and Consideration.** I promise you that I will treat you to lunch if you meet me at the Chez Paris restaurant at a specified time. You appear on time. Does your appearance constitute consideration for my promise of lunch, meaning that you now have a legal claim on me? How, if at all, is a promise of this form different from Uncle William's promise to pay his nephew Willie $5,000 if the boy grows up straight and true?

3. **Was There Additional Consideration?** In order to establish that his job was truly for life, the plaintiff in *Fisher v. Jackson* had to demonstrate "a consideration in addition to the rendering of services incident to the employment." Again, this view is traditional. It is not enough that the plaintiff had showed up at his new job and worked there for five years, since this work was paid for by the employer (or so the reasoning goes).

Why was the plaintiff's attorney unsuccessful in showing additional consideration? The Court lays much stress on the record, which gave no sign that the plaintiff's previous position in a bakery had been mentioned during the job interview. The outcome could have been different if this had been mentioned.

The Court could have paid more attention to the plaintiff's 20 percent reduction in pay as he moved from a blue collar to a white collar job. What do you make of the Court's suggestion that the plaintiff was unqualified when he was hired?

Problem 2–5

Ben Collins was a full professor with tenure at a state university. Another college recruited him by offering him tenure and a specified salary, with specified annual increments for five years. Subsequently, during the five-year period, Collins's new employer experienced financial difficulties and tried to lower his pay. When Collins refused to accept this, the college fired him. In response to Collins's lawsuit, the college asserts that there was no consideration for its promise of tenure, and also notes that Collins had not promised to serve permanently or even for the five years mentioned in Collins's contract. Is this case distinguishable from *Fisher v. Jackson*?

B. RELIANCE

RICKETTS v. SCOTHORN

Supreme Court of Nebraska, 1898.
57 Neb. 51, 77 N.W. 365.

SULLIVAN, J. In the district court of Lancaster county the plaintiff Katie Scothorn recovered judgment against the defendant Andrew D. Ricketts, as executor of the last will and testament of John C. Ricketts, deceased. The action was based upon a promissory note, of which the following is a copy:

"May the first, 1891. I promise to pay to Katie Scothorn on demand, $2,000, to be at 6 per cent per annum. J. C. RICKETTS."

In the petition the plaintiff alleges that the consideration for the execution of the note was that she should surrender her employment as bookkeeper for Mayer Bros. and cease to work for a living. She also alleges that the note was given to induce her to abandon her occupation, and that, relying on it, and on the annual interest, as a means of support, she gave up the employment in which she was then engaged. These allegations of the petition are denied by the executor. The material facts are undisputed. They are as follows: John C. Ricketts, the maker of the note, was the grandfather of the plaintiff. Early in May,—presumably on the day the note bears date,—he called on her at the store where she was working. What transpired between them is thus described by Mr. Flodene, one of the plaintiff's witnesses:

A. Well the old gentleman came in there one morning about 9 o'clock,—probably a little before or a little after, but early in the morning,—and he unbuttoned his vest and took out a piece of paper in the shape of a note; that is the way it looked to me; and he says to Miss Scothorn, "I have fixed out something that you have not got to work any more." He says, "None of my grandchildren work and you don't have to."

Q. Where was she?

A. She took the piece of paper and kissed him; and kissed the old gentleman and commenced to cry.

It seems Miss Scothorn immediately notified her employer of her intention to quit work and that she did soon after abandon her occupation. The mother of the plaintiff was a witness and testified that she had a conversation with her father, Mr. Ricketts, shortly after the note was executed in which he informed her that he had given the note to the plaintiff to enable her to quit work; that none of his grandchildren worked and he did not think she ought to.

For something more than a year the plaintiff was without an occupation; but in September, 1892, with the consent of her grandfather, and by his assistance, she secured a position as bookkeeper with Messrs. Funke & Ogden. On June 8, 1894, Mr. Ricketts died. He had paid one year's interest on the note, and a short time before his death expressed regret that he had not been able to pay the balance. In the summer or fall of 1892 he stated to his daughter, Mrs. Scothorn, that if he could sell his farm in Ohio he would pay the note out of the proceeds. He at no time repudiated the obligation. We quite agree with counsel for the defendant that upon this evidence there was nothing to submit to the jury, and that a verdict should have been directed peremptorily for one of the parties. The testimony of Flodene and Mrs. Scothorn, taken together, conclusively establishes the fact that the note was not given in consideration of the plaintiff pursuing, or agreeing to pursue, any particular line of conduct. There was no promise on the part of the plaintiff to do or refrain from doing anything. Her right to the money promised in the note was not made to depend upon an abandonment of her employment with Mayer Bros. and future abstention from like service. Mr. Ricketts made no condition, requirement, or request. He exacted no quid pro quo. He gave the note as a gratuity and looked for nothing in return. So far as the evidence discloses, it was his purpose to place the plaintiff in a position of independence where she could work or remain idle as she might choose. The abandonment by Miss Scothorn of her position as bookkeeper was altogether voluntary. It was not an act done in fulfillment of any contract obligation assumed when she accepted the note. The instrument in suit being given without any valuable consideration, was nothing more than a promise to make a gift in the future of the sum of money therein named. Ordinarily, such promises are not enforceable even when put in the form of a promissory note.... But it has often been held that an action on a note given to a church, college, or other like institution, upon the faith of which money has been expended or obligations incurred, could not be successfully defended on the ground of a want of consideration.... In this class of cases the note in suit is nearly always spoken of as a gift or donation, but the decision is generally put on the ground that the expenditure of money or assumption of liability by the donee, on the faith of the promise, constitutes a valuable and sufficient consideration. It seems to us that the true reason is the preclusion of the defendant, under the doctrine of estoppel, to deny the consideration....

Under the circumstances of this case is there an equitable estoppel which ought to preclude the defendant from alleging that the note in controversy is lacking in one of the essential elements of a valid contract? We think there is. An estoppel in pais is defined to be "a right arising from acts, admissions, or conduct which have induced a change of position in accordance with the real or apparent intention of the party against whom they are alleged." Mr. Pomeroy has formulated the following definition: "Equitable estoppel is the effect of the voluntary conduct of a party whereby he is absolutely precluded, both at law and in equity, from asserting rights which might, perhaps, have otherwise existed, either of property, of contract, or of remedy, as against another person who in good faith relied upon such conduct, and has been led thereby to change his position for the worse, and who on his part acquires some corresponding right, either of property, of contract, or of remedy." 2 Pom. Eq. Jur. 804.

According to the undisputed proof, as shown by the record before us, the plaintiff was a working girl, holding a position in which she earned a salary of $10 per week. Her grandfather, desiring to put her in a position of independence, gave her the note, accompanying it with the remark that his other grandchildren did not work, and that she would not be obliged to work any longer. In effect he suggested that she might abandon her employment and rely in the future upon the bounty which he promised. He, doubtless, desired that she should give up her occupation, but whether he did or not, it is entirely certain that he contemplated such action on her part as a reasonable and probable consequence of his gift. Having intentionally influenced the plaintiff to alter her position for the worse on the faith of the note being paid when due, it would be grossly inequitable to permit the maker, or his executor, to resist payment on the ground that the promise was given without consideration. The petition charges the elements of an equitable estoppel, and the evidence conclusively establishes them. If errors intervened at the trial they could not have been prejudicial. A verdict for the defendant would be unwarranted. The judgment is right and is

AFFIRMED.

Notes and Discussion

1. **Equitable Estoppel.** This traditional doctrine in procedural law (also called estoppel in pais) has wide application in contract law. Equitable estoppel is available when one party knowingly misrepresents material facts that are then predictably relied upon by the other. The misrepresenting party is "estopped" (precluded) from asserting facts that contradict its misrepresentations.

Equitable estoppel is easier to recognize in an example. In *American National Bank v. A.G. Sommerville, Inc.*, 191 Cal. 364, 216 P. 376 (1923), Richard Tomlinson signed two documents each of which stated that he had purchased and received an automobile for $3,900, and that he promised to pay the balance of the purchase price. A.G. Sommerville, the putative seller, then sold the contracts, and they ended up in the hands of American National Bank, which eventually brought suit on them. At trial, Tomlinson attempted to assert that, although in the documents he "acknowledges receipt of said property," in fact he had never received either vehicle; therefore, so he reasoned, there was a failure of consideration and he could not be held to his promise. But Tomlinson was prevented from mounting this defense by "[t]he doctrine of estoppel *in pais* [which] proceeds upon the theory that the party has, by his declarations or conduct, misled another to his prejudice, so that it would be a fraud upon the latter to allow the true state of facts to be proved." Id., 216 P. at 379. This, reasoned the Court, "is an application of the fundamental, equitable, and moral rule that a man may not be permitted to deny the truthfulness of an assurance which he has given to another for the purpose of having it acted upon by the latter, and which the latter has acted upon." Equitable estoppel is a widely used procedural device both within and outside of contract law. A good example is *Scholle Corp. v. Blackhawk Molding Co., Inc.*, 133 F.3d 1469 (Fed. Cir. 1998), a patent dispute; Blackhawk introduced a new valved cap for water bottles that arguably infringed on Scholle's patent, but Scholle declined for some years to object despite being repeatedly invited by Blackhawk to do so. Scholle was eventually estopped from suing for patent infringement.

See also *Lawrence v. McCalmont*, an 1844 case referred in *EMU v. Burgess* above, where a guarantor (a surety) acknowledged receipt of one dollar for her promise; after the creditor, relying on her guarantee, extended substantial credit to her sons, she was estopped from proving that the dollar had never been paid. The Michigan court's attempt to distinguish this case is not wholly persuasive, true?

2. Confusion in Nebraska: The Emergence of Promissory Estoppel. John Ricketts promised $2,000 to his granddaughter Katie Scothorn, and she then quit her job as a bookkeeper. As the Court makes clear, although Ricketts made it clear that he did not want Scothorn to work, he did not bargain for her quitting or for her promise to quit; therefore this case is unlike *Hamer v. Sidway.* The Court tries to fit the doctrine of equitable estoppel to this case. But Ricketts did not misrepresent a fact. What Scothorn relied on was not a fact but a promise, not a misrepresentation of some present reality but rather an (apparently honest) statement of future intent. Does that matter?

3. Section 90. From *Ricketts v. Scothorn* and a few cases like it, the First Restatement (of 1932) created § 90: "A promise which the promisor should reasonably expect to induce action or forbearance of a definite and substantial character on the part of the promisee and which does induce such action or forbearance is binding if injustice can be avoided only by enforcement of the promise." "Promissory estoppel" is not used in this definition, and the basic "estoppel" concept is actually superfluous, although some courts still refer to it. What § 90 provides is a new basis for enforcement of a promise: 1) that the promisor should anticipate "definite and substantial" reliance by the promisee; and 2) that such reliance then occurs. Reliance is now the explicit backbone of the theory. When the anticipatable reliance occurs, the promise becomes "binding if injustice can be avoided only by enforcement of the promise." (Why this grudging language?)

Section 90 was probably intended mainly for gratuitous promises, especially in a family context. But its application steadily increased, and in time § 90 was applied also in more commercial contexts. The original language of § 90 is generally preserved in Restatement 2d § 90, but a series of changes reflect the evolution of the doctrine: 1) the reliance no longer need be "definite and substantial"; 2) courts may consider reliance not only by the promisee but also by third parties, where appropriate; and 3), perhaps most significantly, "The remedy for breach may be limited as justice requires."

Apply these two versions of § 90 to *Ricketts v. Scothorn.* Katie Scothorn is more likely to prevail under the more recent § 90 than under the earlier one. On the other hand, the remedy she gets under the later § 90 may prove to be more limited. Do you see why?

4. Reliance and Consideration. Oliver Wendell Holmes famously argued that: "It would cut up the doctrine of consideration by the roots, if a promisee could make a gratuitous promise binding by subsequently acting in reliance on it." *Commonwealth by Comm'r of Sav. Banks v. Scituate Sav. Bank*, 137 Mass. 301, 302 (1884). Some scholarly commentators have argued that this prophecy has been borne out. Grant Gilmore, for instance, argued that: "[T]he promissory estoppel principle of [Restatement 2d] § 90 . . . has, in effect, swallowed up the bargain principle of § 75," as part of a larger process in which " 'contract' is being reabsorbed into the mainstream of 'tort.' " Grant Gilmore, The Death of Contract 72, 87 (1974).

John Dawson thought this view exaggerated and unconvincing. He argued that: "[B]argain consideration has been and will remain for a long time to come a central feature of our law of contract, central in the sense that it provides a strong affirmative reason for enforcing promises, the reason that is by a wide margin the most often used, though it is not the only one. The reason is persuasive: the promisor receives or is assured that he will receive the kind of advantage that he in fact desires and has expressly promised to pay for." John P. Dawson, Gifts and Promises 3 (1980). Dawson's view seems accurate still today at least as a representation of the dominant theory; wherever a reasonable case can be made for finding consideration in support of a promise, courts still strongly prefer it to reliance as a rationale for enforcement.

You will have to judge for yourself the long-term potential for reliance within contract law. At a minimum, it is always important for lawyers to note when justifiable reliance on a promise has occurred, because even though reliance may not be the primary reason for enforcing a promise, it at least makes the case for enforcement more compelling.

Problem 2–6

Anna Feinberg began working for the Pfeiffer Co. when she was 17. After 37 years of employment, she had attained a highly responsible post. In gratitude for her "many years of long and faithful service," the company's Board of Directors met and adopted a resolution that promised her a monthly pension if she elected to retire in the future, but that also stated it "sincerely hoped and desired that Mrs. Feinberg would continue in her present position for as long as she felt able." Feinberg continued to work for two more years and then retired. Pfeiffer paid the pension for seven years, but then reduced payments. Feinberg can show that she was still capable of working after her retirement, but that she did not do so because of the pension; now, however, she can no longer work because she has cancer. Will she succeed in a suit against Pfeiffer?

COHEN v. COWLES MEDIA CO.

Supreme Court of Minnesota, 1992.
479 N.W.2d 387.

SIMONETT, J. This case comes to us on remand from the United States Supreme Court. We previously held that plaintiff's verdict of $200,000 could not be sustained on a theory of breach of contract. On remand, we now conclude the verdict is sustainable on the theory of promissory estoppel and affirm the jury's award of damages.

The facts are set out in *Cohen v. Cowles Media Co.*, 457 N.W.2d 199, 200–02 (Minn. 1990),[8] and will be only briefly restated here. On October 28, 1982, the Minneapolis Star and Tribune (now the Star Tribune) and the St. Paul Pioneer Press each published a story on the gubernatorial election campaign, reporting that Marlene Johnson, the DFL nominee for lieutenant governor, had been charged in 1969 for three counts of unlawful assembly and in 1970 had been convicted of shoplifting. Both newspapers revealed that Dan Cohen had supplied this information to them. The Star Tribune identified Cohen as a political associate of the Independent-Republican gubernatorial candidate and named the advertising firm where Cohen was employed.

Cohen then commenced this lawsuit against defendants Cowles Media Company, publisher of the Minneapolis Star Tribune, and Northwest Publications, Inc., publisher of the St. Paul Pioneer Press Dispatch. It was undisputed that Cohen had given the information about Marlene Johnson's arrests and conviction to a reporter for each of the newspapers in return for the reporters' promises that Cohen's identity be kept confidential. The newspapers' editors overruled these promises. The disparaging information about the candidate leaked in the closing days of the election campaign was such, decided the editors, that the identity of the source of the information was as important, as newsworthy, as the information itself. Put another way, the real news story was one of political intrigue, and the information about the particular candidate was only a part, an incomplete part, of that story. Moreover, not to reveal the source, felt the editors, would be misleading, as it would cast suspicion on others; and, in any event, it was likely only a matter of time before competing news media would uncover Cohen's identity. Finally, the Star Tribune had endorsed the Perpich-Johnson ticket in its opinion section, and thus to withhold Cohen's identity might be construed as an effort by the newspaper to protect its favored candidates. On the same day as the newspaper stories were published, Cohen was fired.

8. [Eds.: The Minnesota Court hereafter refers to this decision as *Cohen I*.]

[Eds.: The Court then summarizes the subsequent history of the lawsuit. In its earlier decision, the Minnesota Supreme Court denied recovery to Cohen; it found no binding contract of traditional form, and it rejected liability based on promissory estoppel because this would involve an impermissible intrusion into the newspaper's First Amendment free press rights. Cohen then appealed to the United States Supreme Court, which held that in this case the doctrine of promissory estoppel does not implicate the First Amendment. *Cohen v. Cowles Media Co.*, 501 U.S. 663, 111 S.Ct. 2513, 115 L.Ed.2d 586 (1991). However, the Justices declined to reinstate the jury verdict for $200,000 in compensatory damages, instead remanding the case for consideration by the Minnesota Supreme Court.]

On remand, we must address four issues: (1) Does Cohen's failure to plead promissory estoppel bar him from pursuing that theory now; (2) does our state constitutional guarantee of a free press bar use of promissory estoppel to enforce promises of confidentiality; (3) does public policy bar Cohen from enforcing the newspapers' promises of confidentiality; and (4) if Cohen may proceed under promissory estoppel, should the case be remanded for retrial or should the jury's award of compensatory damages be reinstated?

I.

Generally, litigants are bound on appeal by the theory or theories upon which the case was tried. *Johnson v. Jensen*, 446 N.W.2d 664, 665 (Minn. 1989). Here, promissory estoppel was neither pled nor presented at the trial, and this court first raised the applicability of that theory during oral argument in *Cohen I*. See 457 N.W.2d at 204 n.5. Nevertheless, this court considered promissory estoppel and held that the First Amendment barred recovery under that theory.

The defendant newspapers argue it is too late for Cohen to proceed now under promissory estoppel, and this case should be at an end. We have, however, on rare occasions exercised our discretion to allow a party to proceed on a theory not raised at trial. See Minn. R. App. P. 103.04 (appellate courts "may review any * * * matter as the interest of justice may require."). Thus in *Christensen v. Minneapolis Mun. Employees Retirement Bd.*, 331 N.W.2d 740, 747 (Minn. 1983), we held that a public employee had a protectable interest in his pension based on a promissory estoppel theory, even though the plaintiff employee had raised only a contract theory at trial. Indeed, in *Cohen I* we relied on *Christensen*. 457 N.W.2d at 203. But see *W. H. Barber v. McNamara-Vivant Contracting Co., Inc.*, 293 N.W.2d 351, 357 (Minn. 1979) (refusing to consider promissory estoppel theory when not raised at trial).

We conclude it would be unfair not to allow Cohen to proceed under promissory estoppel. Throughout the litigation, the issue has been the legal enforceability of a promise of anonymity. Promissory estoppel is essentially a variation of contract theory, a theory on which plaintiff prevailed through the court of appeals. The evidence received at trial was as relevant to promissory estoppel as it was to contract, and the parties now have briefed the issue thoroughly. . . .

What we have here is a novel legal issue of first impression where this court has adopted an approach closely akin to the theory on which the case was originally pled and tried; under these unique circumstances we conclude it is not unfair to the defendants to allow the case to be decided under principles of promissory estoppel. . . .

II.

[The court holds that plaintiff's lawsuit is not barred by Minnesota's constitution.]

III.

What, then, should be the appropriate disposition of this case? We conclude a retrial is unnecessary.

Under promissory estoppel, a promise which is expected to induce definite action by the promisee, and does induce the action, is binding if injustice can be avoided only by enforcing the promise. *Cohen I*, 457 N.W.2d at 204; Restatement (Second) of Contracts § 90(1) (1981). First of all, the promise must be clear and definite. As a matter of law, such a promise was given here. *Cohen I*, 457 N.W.2d at 204 ("We have, without dispute, the reporters' unambiguous promise to treat Cohen as an anonymous source."). Secondly, the promisor must have intended to induce reliance on the part of the promisee, and such reliance must have occurred to the promisee's detriment. Here again, these facts appear as a matter of law. In reliance on the promise of anonymity, Cohen turned over the court records and, when the promises to keep his name confidential were broken, he lost his job. Id.

This leads to the third step in a promissory estoppel analysis: Must the promise be enforced to prevent an injustice? As the Wisconsin Supreme Court has held, this is a legal question for the court, as it involves a policy decision. *Hoffman v. Red Owl Stores, Inc.*, 26 Wis.2d 683, 698, 133 N.W.2d 267, 275 (1965); . . .

It is perhaps worth noting that the test is not whether the promise should be enforced to do justice, but whether enforcement is required to prevent an injustice. As has been observed elsewhere, it is easier to recognize an unjust result than a just one, particularly in a morally ambiguous situation. Cf. Edmond Cahn, The Sense of Injustice (1964). The newspapers argue it is unjust to be penalized for publishing the whole truth, but it is not clear this would result in an injustice in this case. For example, it would seem veiling Cohen's identity by publishing the source as someone close to the opposing gubernatorial ticket would have sufficed as a sufficient reporting of the "whole truth."

Cohen, on the other hand, argues that it would be unjust for the law to countenance, at least in this instance, the breaking of a promise. We agree that denying Cohen any recourse would be unjust. What is significant in this case is that the record shows the defendant newspapers themselves believed that they generally must keep promises of confidentiality given a news source. The reporters who actually gave the promises adamantly testified that their promises should have been honored. The editors who countermanded the promises conceded that never before or since have they reneged on a promise of confidentiality. A former Minneapolis Star managing editor testified that the newspapers had "hung Mr. Cohen out to dry because they didn't regard him very highly as a source." The Pioneer Press Dispatch editor stated nothing like this had happened in her 27 years in journalism. The Star Tribune's editor testified that protection of sources was "extremely important." Other experts, too, stressed the ethical importance, except on rare occasions, of keeping promises of confidentiality. It was this long-standing journalistic tradition that Cohen, who has worked in journalism, relied upon in asking for and receiving a promise of anonymity.

Neither side in this case clearly holds the higher moral ground, but in view of the defendants' concurrence in the importance of honoring promises of confidentiality, and absent the showing of any compelling need in this case to break that promise, we conclude that the resultant harm to Cohen requires a remedy here to avoid an injustice. In short, defendants are liable in damages to plaintiff for their broken promise.

This leaves, then, the issue of damages. For promissory estoppel, "the remedy granted for breach may be limited as justice requires." Restatement (Second) of Contracts § 90(1) (1981).... In this case the jury was instructed: "A party is entitled to recover for a breach of contract only those damages which: (a) arise directly and naturally in the usual course of things from the breach itself; or (b) are the consequences of special circumstances known to or reasonably supposed to have been contemplated by the parties when the contract was made."

This instruction, we think, provided an appropriate damages remedy for the defendants' broken promise, whether considered under a breach of contract or a promissory estoppel theory. There was evidence to support the jury's award of $200,000, and we see no reason to remand this case for a new trial on damages alone.

Our prior reversal of the verdict having been vacated, we now affirm the court of appeals' decision, but on promissory estoppel grounds. We affirm, therefore, plaintiff's verdict and judgment for $200,000 compensatory damages.

Affirmed on remand on different grounds.

Notes and Discussion

1. The Promise. *Cohen I* describes the promise in more detail: "Sturdevant and Salisbury were experienced reporters covering the gubernatorial election and knew Cohen as an active Republican associated with the Wheelock Whitney campaign. Cohen told Sturdevant that he would also be offering the documents to other news organizations. Neither reporter informed Cohen that their promises of confidentiality were subject to approval or revocation by their editors. Both reporters promised to keep Cohen's identity anonymous, and both intended to keep that promise. At trial Cohen testified he insisted on anonymity because he feared retaliation from the news media and politicians." *Cohen v. Cowles Media Co.*, 457 N.W.2d 199, 200 (Minn. 1990). In a footnote, the Court adds: "Cohen then met with reporters for the Associated Press and WCCO-TV. They, too, promised Cohen anonymity and received the court documents. The Associated Press published the story and honored its promise. WCCO-TV did not run the story." Id. at 200 n.1.

2. No Contract? In *Cohen I*, the Minnesota Supreme Court explains why it finds no contract between the reporter and Cohen:

"The law, however, does not create a contract where the parties intended none.... Nor does the law consider binding every exchange of promises. See, e.g., Minn. Stat. ch. 553 (1988) (abolishing breaches of contract to marry); see also Restatement (Second) of Contracts §§ 189–91 (1981) (promises impairing family relations are unenforceable). We are not persuaded that in the special milieu of media newsgathering a source and a reporter ordinarily believe they are engaged in making a legally binding contract. They are not thinking in terms of offers and acceptances in any commercial or business sense. The parties understand that the reporter's promise of anonymity is given as a moral commitment, but a moral obligation alone will not support a contract....

"In other words, contract law seems here an ill fit for a promise of news source confidentiality. To impose a contract theory on this arrangement puts an unwarranted legal rigidity on a special ethical relationship, precluding necessary consideration of factors underlying that ethical relationship. We conclude that a contract cause of action is inappropriate for these particular circumstances." *Cohen v. Cowles Media Co.*, 457 N.W.2d 199, 203 (Minn. 1990).

We are unpersuaded by the Court's reasoning. Absent reliance as a basis for contractual liability, the Minnesota Court might still have found a contract in the exchange of information for the newspaper's promise of confidentiality, not so?

3. Reliance. If the newspaper's promise represented only "a moral commitment," then why was Cohen justified in relying on it? (See Restatement 2d § 21: "Neither real nor apparent intention that a promise be legally binding is essential to the formation of a contract ... ")

Cohen evidently had been flogging his story to all available media. Suppose that the reporters had not given their promise in response to Cohen's specific insistence, but instead gave it spontaneously in the course of discussion. (E.g., "Oh, of course, rest assured, by the way, we'll see to it that your name stays out of this.") Would the outcome have been different?

4. Damages. How would you calculate Cohen's damages? No amount of money will restore him to "as good a position as if the other party had fully performed," true?

MIDWEST ENERGY, INC. v. ORION FOOD SYSTEMS, INC.

Court of Appeals of Missouri, Eastern District, Division Five, 2000.
14 S.W.3d 154.

BLACKMAR, J. The trial court granted summary judgment on all three counts of the plaintiff's petition and entered final judgment for both defendants. On this appeal we accept as true the facts appropriately established by the plaintiff in the manner prescribed by Rule 74.04 and afford the plaintiff all reasonable inferences from the facts adduced, disregarding defendants' contrary proffers except to the extent they are uncontradicted and unequivocal.... We state the facts from the plaintiff's point of view, without any intimation that court or jury has to find any of these facts.

The plaintiff Midwest, a Missouri corporation, operates a chain of service station convenience stores in Southeast Missouri. The defendant Orion, a South Dakota corporation, has developed recipes and equipment for several fast food systems for which it issues franchises to local outlets. Defendant Ted Ries at material times was the district sales manager for Orion in the area in which Midwest has facilities.

In early 1996 Midwest undertook the construction of a substantial building in Fruitland, Missouri, designed for the operation of a service station and convenience store and estimated to cost $800,000. Its president and sole stockholder, Laura Younghouse, inquired into the possibility of a franchise for some of Orion's product lines. On March 27, 1996, Ries visited Younghouse and delivered to her an offering circular required by the Federal Trade Commission accompanied by a specimen franchise agreement in which the blank spaces were not filled in. The circular contained a caution about taking any further action until Midwest had been notified in writing that its application had been approved. Younghouse receipted for these documents and read them.

Ries advised Younghouse he had to check with other Orion franchisees in the area to determine whether they had any contractual protection from nearby competition. He checked particularly with Rhodes Oil, which had Orion franchises at several nearby locations. On April 13, 1996 Ries again visited with Younghouse, advising her that Rhodes and other franchisees interposed no obstacle and that "we can go forward with the franchise." Younghouse had already filled out and delivered a franchise application on behalf of Midwest for the new location. Midwest's building contractor was present at this conference and discussed the proposed construction with Ries and Younghouse.

During the next several months Orion provided drawings and specifications setting forth its requirements for the area in which its franchised products would be prepared and dispensed. Ries was in touch with both the general contractor and the electrician. He pointed out the need to enlarge the convenience store area to 800 square feet to meet Orion's special requirements. This was a larger area than Younghouse had originally planned. The final store layout and design was provided by Orion to Midwest on July 2, 1996.

Ries reported his contacts with Midwest to his immediate supervisor, Keith Watts, who told him to "go ahead" at the Midwest location. Orion prepared orders for the equipment necessary to prepare and serve the franchised products.

Under date of September 4, 1996 Midwest received from Orion an unsigned franchise agreement specifying an opening date of November 8, 1996. On September 13, Ries called to advise Younghouse he would call on September 18, 1996 to "pick up the franchise agreement."[9] He did not appear on that date and did not respond to Younghouse's persistent attempts to get in touch with him. There is evidence that his superiors instructed him to "make himself scarce" while they reevaluated the franchise situation.

On September 30, 1996 Younghouse executed the franchise agreement on behalf of Midwest and mailed it to Orion. In the meantime a representative of Rhodes, Midwest's potential competitor, had called Orion to report that he had seen a notice of Midwest's opening date of November 8 for the new facility and was not pleased at the thought of competition. Orion's executives decided not to issue the franchise to Midwest, and one Schendel, an analyst, was instructed to write a letter to Midwest conveying this decision. For some reason the letter was not mailed until October 11, 1996. On October 1, however, Watts called Younghouse to advise her Orion was "withdrawing the franchise offer."[10]

The foregoing is an abbreviated summary of the bare facts that might be found. The record provided on summary judgment is voluminous, and other facts will be stated in the discussion of each of the several counts.

Midwest's petition declares in three counts as follows: (I) Breach of contract by Orion in failing to grant a franchise to Midwest; (II) Promissory estoppel against Orion in accordance with the provisions of Section 90 of the Restatement (2d) of Contracts; and (III) Fraud and deceit against Ries for willfully misstating the extent of his authority. We affirm the judgment on Count I, but find error in the entry of summary judgment on Counts II and III, and so remand this portion of the case for further proceedings.

Count I—Breach of Contract. Count I declares on the five-year franchise agreement submitted to Midwest on September 4, 1996 as a contract between Midwest and Orion. The contract, however, is not signed by Orion. It cannot be performed within one year of its stated

9. Younghouse testified that Ries said he would appear to sign the franchise agreement. For present purposes we disregard this statement because of questions about Ries's authority to sign not resolved by the cold record.

10. The record does not show whether Watts had received the franchise agreement signed by Younghouse and returned by mail to Orion when he made this call, but, for want of Orion's signature, the time of receipt is not legally significant.

effective date of November 8, 1996. This contract is clearly unenforceable under section 432.010 *RSMo* 1994, known as the "Statute of Frauds," and nothing short of Orion's signature can make it into an enforceable contract....

The parties clearly contemplated a written contract, and so neither was bound by the proposed franchise agreement until an authorized representative of each had affixed a signature.

There was no error in granting summary judgment on Count I.

Count II—Promissory Estoppel. Count II seeks to state a claim under Section 90, Restatement (2d) of Contracts which reads in pertinent part as follows:

Section 90. Promise Reasonably Inducing Action or Forbearance: "(1) A promise which the promisor should reasonably expect to induce action or forbearance on the part of the promisee or a third person and which does induce such action or forbearance is binding if injustice can be avoided only by enforcement of the promise. The remedy granted for breach may be limited as justice requires.... "

Promissory estoppel has been part of the law of Missouri for many years, and our courts have cited Section 90 of both the First and Second Restatements of Contracts.... Numerous cases, involving widely different fact situations, have considered the requirements for recovery under Section 90. In some the opinions seem overexpansive, seeking to lay down rules which are broader than required for the resolution of the immediate problem. We seek to apply the governing principle of the Restatement. We take note of several recent cases which have allowed recovery based on Section 90. See *Delmo, Inc. v. Maxima Elec. Sales, Inc.*, 878 S.W.2d 499 (Mo. App. 1994)....

We have found no case discussing the method of jury instruction in Section 90 cases, and there are no MAI patterns. Nor do we find discussion of the appropriate form for findings of fact. There is some variation in the manner of stating essential elements, but, as Judge Shrum observed in *Delmo,* all pertinent opinions list the elements as: (1) A promise; (2) foreseeability of reliance; (3) reliance; and (4) injustice absent enforcement. 878 S.W.2d at 504....

The sense of the cases, and especially the recent cases, is that a plaintiff who can point to evidence which, if believed, would permit a judge or jury to find each of these elements, is entitled to go to trial without prior judicial determination as to whether the case is "extreme." ... We conclude that Midwest's proffer is sufficient to establish fact questions as to all four essential elements.

We consider initially the scope of the authority of Ted Ries. Orion has argued strenuously that Ries had no authority to bind Orion to any kind of an agreement, and that any action predicated on a promise by him must fail. Almost all of the argument, however, has been directed to the question of his authority to sign franchise agreements. From the statements in the record a jury could find that Ries had the duty of promoting new franchises for his employer's product and of working with prospective franchisees to do what was necessary in order to ready new franchises for opening. . . .

We now consider whether the transactions between Ries, on behalf of Orion, are sufficient to provide a basis for the relief Midwest seeks.

(1) Promise. The record shows several promissory statements made by Ries. On April 13, 1996, Ries called on Younghouse and told her he had received clearance from other franchisees and that "[we can] go forward with the franchise." He repeated his assurances that all was in order, providing floor plans, lists of required equipment, and, on July 2, 1996, a definitive layout. On September 4, 1996 Orion mailed to Younghouse a franchise agreement providing for an opening date of November 8, 1996. This document was not signed by anyone purporting to act on behalf of Orion, but Ries advised Younghouse he would appear on September 18 to pick up the franchise agreement. Younghouse understood that Ries proposed to sign on behalf of Orion. From the facts just stated the trier of fact could find Ries promised Midwest that a franchise conforming to the specimen provided to Midwest in March would be issued as soon as Midwest was ready to operate, and that Midwest could make preparations based on those assurances.

We have held the Statute of Frauds precludes recovery of damages for failure to grant Midwest a five-year franchise. This holding does not necessarily preclude an action on the theory of promissory estoppel. The last sentence of Section 90(1) provides "The remedy granted for breach may be limited as justice requires." Damages are measured by the reliance and should be limited to those naturally flowing from the reliance. *Mahoney v. Delaware McDonald's Corp.*, 770 F.2d 123 (8th Cir. 1985). Thus, there are cases holding that partial relief may be accorded in cases in which the Statute of Frauds stands as a barrier to complete enforcement. See *Geisinger v. A & B Farms, Inc.*, 820 S.W.2d 96, 98–9 (Mo. App. 1991) (citing *Feinberg v. Pfeiffer Co.*, 322 S.W.2d 163, 168 (Mo. App. 1959) and *Katz v. Danny Dare, Inc.*, 610 S.W.2d 121, 126 (Mo. App. 1980)); see also *Chesus v. Watts*, 967 S.W.2d 97, 110 (Mo. App. 1998). Mahoney points out the difference between the full contractual enforcement of a promise which cannot be performed within one year, and provision of a remedy for inducing reliance on a promise, limited by the extent of the reliance. See Section 90, Restatement (2d) of Contracts, Illustration 8. The promises shown by the proffers are sufficient to establish the first element of promissory estoppel.

(2) Foreseeable Reliance. The trier of fact could certainly find that, between April 13 and September 4, Orion and Midwest wanted to do business with each other. Ries was Orion's authorized liaison with Midwest in order to further preparation for undertaking the franchise. He had every reason to believe Midwest would hasten to comply with his directions, for fear that the tender of the franchise would be withdrawn. To the extent that his requests, on behalf of Orion, required expenditure or forbearance, he could confidently expect these would be forthcoming.

Whatever authority Ries had with regard to executing franchise documents, he could surely forestall the granting of a franchise by expressing his disapproval.

(3) Reliance in Fact. The record shows, at the very least, that Midwest relied on Ries's promises by making changes in its plans for the fast food area and by forbearing attempts to interest other possible franchisors in its new facility. These, in and of themselves, are sufficient to demonstrate reliance and, when the reliance proved to be unjustified, damages. There may be other provable damages. There is no briefing of the issue, and argument did not focus on the quantitative scope of recovery. This trier of fact may be totally unimpressed with Midwest's evidence of damages, but enough has been shown to raise a factual issue.

Orion asserts emphatically that Midwest had no right to rely on anything Ries said as being binding on Orion. It is not necessary to show, however, that Ries had authority to determine that a franchise should be granted. As has been said earlier, it could be found that he had the authority to transmit Orion's instructions and requirements so as to assist Midwest in putting itself in a position to commence operations under an Orion franchise. He could also confirm Orion's continued interest in Midwest as a franchisee and advise Midwest as to further necessary steps.

Orion also points to the cautionary language in the offering circular required by the Federal Trade Commission and in the specimen franchise agreement delivered with the circular on the occasion of Ries's first visit. These documents confirm the franchise agreement as the sole agreement between the parties, strongly suggest that Midwest avail itself of legal counsel in examining the documents, and expressly warn Midwest that it should not take any other action in anticipation of receiving the franchise unless and until it should have an executed franchise agreement in hand. The promises on which Midwest relies to invoke Section 90, however, came after these documents were delivered, at a time when Orion was encouraging Midwest to make active preparation to undertake the franchise. Under Section 90 Orion is not necessarily free to encourage reliance by promises made in the expectation of reliance, simply by reason of a prior written warning that its promises mean nothing until both parties have signed a franchise agreement. . . .

(4) Injustice Absent Enforcement. This element is not cast with precision. Numerous writings on Section 90 make it clear it is designed to protect the reliance interest. Damages are measured by the degree of reliance. When the other elements of a Section 90 claim are present, the "injustice" element is not appropriate for determination in a summary judgment proceeding. The parties will have to work with the trial court in determining the appropriate manner of submission.

We again caution that our somewhat detailed expostulation of the fact governing Count II represents only our conception of the permissible findings the trier of fact might make. We do not suggest in any respect that the fact-finder should make any particular finding, or that any particular conclusion is preferable. The record is voluminous, and we simply say we perceive genuine issues of material fact on each of the essential elements of an action under Section 90 sufficient to withstand a motion for summary judgment.

Count III—Fraud and Deceit against Ries. [Eds.: The Court also permits the plaintiff to seek, in the alternative, actual and punitive damages on account of Ries's alleged misrepresentation of his authority to act for Orion.]

The judgment for Orion on Count I is affirmed. The judgments on Counts II and III are reversed, and the case is remanded for appropriate proceedings consistent with this opinion.

CRAHAN, J., CONCURRING IN PART AND DISSENTING IN PART. I concur in the disposition of the breach of contract claim. I would affirm the judgment on the remaining counts as well.

[Eds.: Judge Crahan reviews the evidence, laying particular stress on written materials that warned Midwest against reliance. For example, Orion's Uniform Franchise Offering Circular, which Younghouse admitted having read, stated, in capital letters: "Caution. Any fact, information, promise, assurance, representation or circumstance communicated to you that is not contained in the attached agreement or this offering circular is unauthorized by Orion and should not be relied upon by you in deciding whether to purchase an Orion franchise." The Judge then turns to consider promissory estoppel.]

The recognized elements of promissory estoppel in Missouri are: (1) a promise, (2) on which the party relies to his detriment; (3) in a way the promisor expected or should have expected; and (4) resulting in injustice which only enforcement of the promise can cure. *Response Oncology, Inc. v. Blue Cross and Blue Shield of Missouri*, 941 S.W.2d 771, 778 (Mo.App. 1997). On the record before the court on summary judgment, there is no genuine issue of material fact that Midwest cannot establish any of these elements.

Ries' statement to Younghouse in April that "We can proceed with the franchise" was not a promise that a franchise has been or would be granted. It was a truthful statement of Orion's intent to work with Midwest to process its application, provide Midwest with the necessary information and, upon completion of that process, and assuming both parties were satisfied that the other was prepared to do what the franchise agreement would require it to do, to enter into a written franchise agreement. Although Younghouse claims to have interpreted Ries' statement to constitute an oral contract, such interpretation is unreasonable as a matter of law and inconsistent with her own actions. If Younghouse truly believed she had an oral contract in April, she would not have felt free to drop the Cinnamon Street Bakery products unilaterally in August. Younghouse does not claim that Ries ever told her she could dispense with a written agreement or any of the other requirements and still have a franchise.

The cases further establish that a party seeking to enforce a "promise" under the doctrine of promissory estoppel must show that his or her reliance was reasonable. *Delmo, Inc. v. Maxima Elec. Sales, Inc.*, 878 S.W.2d 499, 505 (Mo. App. 1994) (citing *Otten v. Otten*, 632 S.W.2d 45, 49 (Mo. App. 1982)). As a matter of law, Younghouse's alleged reliance on Ries' alleged oral promise was unreasonable because she concedes that she was specifically apprised in writing, twice, that she should refrain from taking any action or making any commitments until and unless she was notified in writing by Orion that the application for a franchise had been approved and an Orion franchise had been issued in her name. I can find nothing in Ries' conduct or statements that could conceivably be construed as waiving that requirement. To take action in reliance on Ries' oral statement of intent to proceed with the franchise, having been previously and repeatedly apprised of Orion's explicit admonition to refrain from such reliance is, as a matter of law, unreasonable.

Nor does the record reflect any actual reliance in the form of any material change of position by Midwest. Contrary to the suggestion by Midwest that it built a building 800 sq. ft. larger than it would have in anticipation of obtaining the franchise, Ms. Younghouse conceded that Midwest probably would not have constructed a smaller building if she had known she would not be awarded an Orion franchise. Indeed, the space that would have been used for the Orion products proved readily adaptable to a competitor's similar products. Although it is true that if Midwest had been apprised sooner that Orion wasn't going through with the deal it could have pursued other alternatives, this is true of any business relationship that remains unconsummated for whatever reason. Such failure to pursue alternatives cannot properly be characterized as "reliance" on the hoped for relationship; it is a well recognized risk of pursuing business opportunities that may not come to fruition.

Based on the very same language in the UFOC set forth above, Midwest likewise cannot establish that Orion should reasonably have expected reliance by Midwest prior to obtaining a signed agreement. Orion was entitled to assume that Midwest would heed its explicit and unambiguous warning. Even attributing Ries' knowledge to Orion, there was nothing to indicate any material change in Midwest's position in reliance on any alleged promise of a franchise.

Finally, there is no evidence that there is any injustice to Midwest that can be avoided only by enforcement of the alleged promise.[11] Although they were to be featured, Orion's products would have been but a few of hundreds, if not thousands, offered at Midwest's convenience store. Having failed to obtain an Orion franchise, Midwest promptly obtained a substitute from a competing firm. Ironically, if Midwest had heeded Orion's admonition and not jumped the gun with its radio advertising, it very likely would have secured the Orion franchise it

11. The majority does not, in fact, enforce any identifiable promise to any degree. The fact that some as yet unspecified measure of damages must be substituted for enforcement of a "promise" is but a further indication why the doctrine is inapplicable.

sought. Rhodes Oil had no contractual right to prevent a new franchise in Fruitland and but for Midwest's premature advertising probably wouldn't have voiced any objections before an agreement had been signed. All of the evidence before the trial court indicates that Orion had every intention of awarding Midwest a franchise if Rhodes Oil had not objected.

Application of the doctrine of promissory estoppel is to be used with caution, sparingly and only in extreme cases to avoid unjust results. *Meinhold v. Huang*, 687 S.W.2d 596, 599 (Mo. App. 1985). This is not an extreme case. This is a garden variety business negotiation that didn't pan out, at least in part because Midwest disregarded Orion's explicit instructions not to do anything until the deal was consummated in writing. I find no injustice warranting application of the doctrine of promissory estoppel. If Midwest's claim is allowed, should Orion have a counterclaim for whatever it expended in drawing plans for the display of Cinnamon Street Bakery products? I would hope not, but the question illustrates the absence of mutuality that underscores the need to apply the doctrine sparingly.

It is also appropriate to note that the manner in which franchises are offered is heavily regulated. 16 *C.F.R.* Sec. 436.1 et seq. These rules require extensive disclosures that would have afforded Midwest ample protection if it had heeded the information provided. As required by the regulations, Midwest was provided with the names of Orion's officers, who could readily have cleared up any confusion Younghouse may have had about Ries' authority. If Midwest felt it necessary to materially change its position to accommodate the planned franchise, it could have insisted Orion expedite negotiation of a signed agreement. Midwest was specifically advised to consult with legal counsel but failed to do so. Given the substantial protections already enacted into law, it seems to me unreasonable to stretch a disfavored doctrine in an effort to protect those who ignore the many protections they already have. I would affirm summary judgment on the promissory estoppel count.

I would also affirm the judgment in favor of Ries on Midwest's fraudulent misrepresentation claim. All of the evidence provided to the trial court on summary judgment establishes that Ries' statement to Younghouse in April that "We can proceed with the franchise" was a truthful representation of Orion's present intent. Thus, it was not actionable. See *Trotter's Corp. v. Ringleader Restaurants, Inc.*, 929 S.W.2d 935, 940 (Mo. App. 1996).

For the foregoing reasons, I would affirm the judgment in its entirety.

Notes and Discussion

1. ***Hoffman v. Red Owl.*** This historic case was decided by the Supreme Court of Wisconsin in 1965. The Hoffmans operated a bakery in northern Wisconsin, but were interested in obtaining a franchise from Red

Owl, a chain of grocery supermarkets. Over more than two years they dealt with Red Owl's agents, who involved the Hoffmans in numerous business deals (including the sale of their original bakery and the purchase of a grocery store in another city) while repeatedly assuring them that the franchise would eventually be granted. Typical of the agents' statements was this one: "[E]verything is ready to go. Get your money together and we are set." However, no actual agreement on a franchise was ever reached, and many terms were still not fixed, including the rent and the size and design of the store. The Hoffmans finally withdrew from further negotiations after they rejected an additional Red Owl request.

The Court affirmed a jury verdict for the Hoffmans, but limited their recovery to losses they had clearly sustained in reliance on the agents' promises. *Hoffman v. Red Owl Stores, Inc.*, 26 Wis.2d 683, 133 N.W.2d 267 (1965). This decision is usually regarded as the most far-reaching example of the doctrine of detrimental reliance as a basis for liability. A critic of the decision might challenge it as follows: "must the law save every fool, however gullible?"

How would you compare the *Hoffman* case to *Midwest Energy*?

2. No Contract, But Liability for Reliance? As in *Cohen v. Cowles Media*, the Court found no enforceable contract between the two parties; but here the explanation is technical: the plaintiff did not have a franchise agreement signed by the defendant as franchisor, and so could not enforce a contract because of the Statute of Frauds (see Chapter 3.F). This means, in essence, that during a short period Orion could hold Midwest to the contract, but Midwest could not hold Orion.

Set out the argument between the majority and the dissent. Which side seems to have the better of it?

There are still some States that do not recognize promissory estoppel as a cognizable cause of action. One such is Virginia; see *W.J. Schafer Assocs., Inc. v. Cordant, Inc.*, 254 Va. 514, 493 S.E.2d 512, 516 (Va. 1997). Therefore when a plaintiff (associated with the investigation of President Clinton) raised a claim quite similar to Cohen's, a federal court, deciding under Virginia law, rejected her argument that she had relied on a reporter's broken promise to keep her revelations "off the record." *Steele v. Isikoff*, 130 F. Supp. 2d 23, 33 (D. D. C. 2000).

Problem 2–7

General Motors operated two plants in Ypsilanti, Michigan, with a total of about 11,000 employees. In order to keep the plants from being moved, the city granted significant tax abatements; but eventually GM decided to move its production to Arlington, Texas. During the course of negotiations for the abatements, a GM plant manager had stated in a public meeting, "Upon completion of this project and favorable market demand, it will allow Willow Run to continue production and maintain continuous employment for our employees"; and other closely similar remarks were made by other GM officials. Can Ypsilanti successfully seek an injunction preventing GM from closing the plants?

C. THE RESTITUTION INTEREST

"Restitution" is like "equity," "condition," and many other legal terms. From your lay experience you probably have a general idea about its meaning, but are not confident of that meaning. You may suspect that it has multiple legal meanings, all of which are known only to others. You imagine that the smart ass just down the row knows those meanings, but fear that you, not he, will be called upon to stumble through them.

In this instance we can alleviate your fear. In law the word restitution identifies both a cause of action (He sued in restitution.) and a measure of damages (She recovered restitution damages, not expectation damages.). Our colleague George Palmer described the essence of the cause of action as follows: "The term 'restitution' appears in early decisions, but general recognition probably began with the publication of the *Restatement of Restitution* [in 1937]. The term is not wholly apt since it suggests restoration to the successful party of some benefit obtained from him. Usually this will be the case where relief is given, but by no means always. There are cases in which the successful party obtains restitution of something he did not have before, for example a benefit received by the defendant from a third person which justly should go to the plaintiff." 1 George E. Palmer, The Law of Restitution § 1.1, at 4 (1978) (footnotes omitted).

This cause of action is similar to a contract cause of action but not the same. It is often used by a plaintiff whose contract with the defendant was unenforceable for some reason, and it may also be used by a party that has not even had a contract-like interchange with another. The essence of the cause of action is to get the thing or the value of the thing that belongs to the plaintiff and is now (or was) in the hands of the defendant.

Damages for breach of contract are said to be justified under the theory of restitution when the plaintiff's recovery is measured by the benefit that his act conferred on the defendant. So use your words carefully here; there are restitution causes of action and there are damages recovered for breach of contract that are labeled "restitution."

BAILEY v. WEST

Supreme Court of Rhode Island, 1969.
105 R.I. 61, 249 A.2d 414.

PAOLINO, J. This is a civil action wherein the plaintiff alleges that the defendant is indebted to him for the reasonable value of his services rendered in connection with the feeding, care and maintenance of a certain race horse named "Bascom's Folly" from May 3, 1962 through July 3, 1966. The case was tried before a justice of the superior court sitting without a jury, and resulted in a decision for the plaintiff for his cost of boarding the horse for the five months immediately subsequent to May 3, 1962, and for certain expenses incurred by him in trimming its hoofs. The cause is now before us on the plaintiff's appeal and defendant's cross appeal from the judgment entered pursuant to such decision.

The facts material to a resolution of the precise issues raised herein are as follows. In late April 1962, defendant, accompanied by his horse trainer, went to Belmont Park in New York to buy race horses. On April 27, 1962, defendant purchased "Bascom's Folly" from a Dr. Strauss and arranged to have the horse shipped to Suffolk Downs in East Boston, Massachusetts. Upon its arrival defendant's trainer discovered that the horse was lame, and so notified defendant, who ordered him to reship the horse by van to the seller at Belmont Park. The seller refused to accept delivery at Belmont on May 3, 1962, and thereupon, the van driver, one Kelly, called defendant's trainer and asked for further instructions. Although the trial testimony is in conflict as to what the trainer told him, it is not disputed that on the same day Kelly brought "Bascom's Folly" to plaintiff's farm where the horse remained until July 3, 1966, when it was sold by plaintiff to a third party.

While "Bascom's Folly" was residing at his horse farm, plaintiff sent bills for its feed and board to defendant at regular intervals. According to testimony elicited from defendant at the trial, the first such bill was received by him some two or three months after "Bascom's Folly" was placed on plaintiff's farm. He also stated that he immediately returned the bill to plaintiff with the notation that he was not the owner of the horse nor was it sent to plaintiff's farm at his request. The plaintiff testified that he sent bills monthly to defendant and that the first notice he received from him disclaiming ownership was "* * * maybe after a month or two or so" subsequent to the time when the horse was left in plaintiff's care.

In his decision the trial judge found that defendant's trainer had informed Kelly during their telephone conversation of May 3, 1962, that "* * * he would have to do whatever he wanted to do with the horse, that he wouldn't be on any farm at the defendant's expense * * *." He also found, however, that when "Bascom's Folly" was brought to his farm, plaintiff was not aware of the telephone conversation between Kelly and defendant's trainer, and hence, even though he knew there was a controversy surrounding the ownership of the horse, he was entitled to assume that "* * * there is an implication here that, 'I am to take care of this horse.'" Continuing his decision, the trial justice stated that in view of the result reached by this court in a recent opinion[12] wherein we held that the instant defendant was liable to the original seller, Dr. Strauss, for the purchase price of this horse, there was a contract "implied in fact" between the plaintiff and defendant to board "Bascom's Folly" and that this contract continued until plaintiff received notification from defendant that he would not be responsible for the horse's board. The trial justice further stated that "* * * I think

12. See *Strauss v. West*, 100 R. I. 388, 216 A.2d 366. [Eds.: This case found that Bascom's Folly was sound as warranted when originally delivered to the buyer West in New York, and that the horse's subsequent lameness was at the buyer's risk.]

there was notice given at least at the end of the four months, and I think we must add another month on there for a reasonable disposition of his property."

In view of the conclusion we reach with respect to defendant's first two contentions, we shall confine ourselves solely to a discussion and resolution of the issues necessarily implicit therein, and shall not examine other subsidiary arguments advanced by plaintiff and defendant.

I.

The defendant alleges in his brief and oral argument that the trial judge erred in finding a contract "implied in fact" between the parties. We agree. . . .

The source of the obligation in a contract "implied in fact," as in express contracts, is in the intention of the parties. We hold that there was no mutual agreement and "intent to promise" between the plaintiff and defendant so as to establish a contract "implied in fact" for defendant to pay plaintiff for the maintenance of this horse. From the time Kelly delivered the horse to him plaintiff knew there was a dispute as to its ownership, and his subsequent actions indicated he did not know with whom, if anyone, he had a contract. After he had accepted the horse, he made inquiries as to its ownership and, initially, and for some time thereafter, sent his bills to both defendant and Dr. Strauss, the original seller.

There is also uncontroverted testimony in the record that prior to the assertion of the claim which is the subject of this suit neither defendant nor his trainer had ever had any business transactions with plaintiff, and had never used his farm to board horses. Additionally, there is uncontradicted evidence that this horse, when found to be lame, was shipped by defendant's trainer not to plaintiff's farm, but back to the seller at Belmont Park. What is most important, the trial justice expressly stated that he believed the testimony of defendant's trainer that he had instructed Kelly that defendant would not be responsible for boarding the horse on any farm.

From our examination of the record we are constrained to conclude that the trial justice overlooked and misconceived material evidence which establishes beyond question that there never existed between the parties an element essential to the formulation of any true contract, namely, an "intent to contract." . . .

II.

The defendant's second contention is that, even assuming the trial justice was in essence predicating defendant's liability upon a quasi-contractual theory, his decision is still unsupported by competent evidence and is clearly erroneous.

The following discussion of quasi-contracts appears in 12 Am. Jur., Contracts, § 6 (1938) at pp. 503 to 504:

"* * * A quasi contract has no reference to the intentions or expressions of the parties. The obligation is imposed despite, and frequently in frustration of, their intention. For a quasi contract neither promise nor privity, real or imagined, is necessary. In quasi contracts the obligation arises, not from consent of the parties, as in the case of contracts, express or implied in fact, but from the law of natural immutable justice and equity. The act, or acts, from which the law implies the contract must, however, be voluntary. Where a case shows that it is the duty of the defendant to pay, the law imputes to him a promise to fulfil that obligation. The duty, which thus forms the foundation of a quasi-contractual obligation, is frequently based on the doctrine of unjust enrichment. * * *

"* * * The law will not imply a promise against the express declaration of the party to be charged, made at the time of the supposed undertaking, unless such party is under legal obligation paramount to his will to perform some duty, and he is not under such legal obligation unless there is a demand in equity and good conscience that he should perform the duty."

Therefore, the essential elements of a quasi-contract are a benefit conferred upon defendant by plaintiff, appreciation by defendant of such benefit, and acceptance and retention by defendant of such benefit under such circumstances that it would be inequitable to retain the benefit without payment of the value thereof. *Home Savings Bank v. General Finance Corp.*, 10 Wis.2d 417, 103 N.W.2d 117.

The key question raised by this appeal with respect to the establishment of a quasi-contract is whether or not plaintiff was acting as a "volunteer" at the time he accepted the horse for boarding at his farm. There is a long line of authority which has clearly enunciated the general rule that "* * * if a performance is rendered by one person without any request by another, it is very unlikely that this person will be under a legal duty to pay compensation." 1 A. Corbin, Contracts § 234.

The Restatement of Restitution, § 2 (1937) provides: "A person who officiously confers a benefit upon another is not entitled to restitution therefor." Comment a in the above-mentioned section states in part as follows: "* * * Policy ordinarily requires that a person who has conferred a benefit * * * by way of giving another services * * * should not be permitted to require the other to pay therefor, unless the one conferring the benefit had a valid reason for so doing. A person is not required to deal with another unless he so desires and, ordinarily, a person should not be required to become an obligor unless he so desires."

Applying those principles to the facts in the case at bar it is clear that plaintiff cannot recover. The plaintiff's testimony on cross-examination is the only evidence in the record relating to what transpired between Kelly and him at the time the horse was accepted for boarding. The defendant's attorney asked plaintiff if he had any conversation with Kelly at that time, and plaintiff answered in substance that he had noticed that the horse was very lame and that Kelly had told him: "That's why they wouldn't accept him at Belmont Track." The plaintiff also testified that he had inquired of Kelly as to the ownership of "Bascom's Folly," and had been told that "Dr. Strauss made a deal and that's all I know." It further appears from the record that plaintiff acknowledged receipt of the horse by signing a uniform livestock bill of lading, which clearly indicated on its face that the horse in question had been consigned by defendant's trainer not to plaintiff, but to Dr. Strauss's trainer at Belmont Park. Knowing at the time he accepted the horse for boarding that a controversy surrounded its ownership, plaintiff could not reasonably expect remuneration from defendant, nor can it be said that defendant acquiesced in the conferment of a benefit upon him. The undisputed testimony was that defendant, upon receipt of plaintiff's first bill, immediately notified him that he was not the owner of "Bascom's Folly" and would not be responsible for its keep.

It is our judgment that the plaintiff was a mere volunteer who boarded and maintained "Bascom's Folly" at his own risk and with full knowledge that he might not be reimbursed for expenses he incurred incident thereto.

The plaintiff's appeal is denied and dismissed, the defendant's cross appeal is sustained, and the cause is remanded to the superior court for entry of judgment for the defendant.

Notes and Discussion

1. The Plaintiff's Theories of Liability. When Howard Bailey took in Bascom's Folly, he surely anticipated being paid for his care. Yet he made no effort to contact Richard West, who, the Court observes, also had had no prior dealings with him. Why did Bailey act as he did?

Bailey's attorneys asserted two distinct theories of liability. The first is that there was a contract "implied in fact" between Bailey and West. A contract implied in fact is an ordinary contract that is simply not "express," not arranged in words but rather inferred from social circumstances, such as when a person drops off laundry that the attendant accepts without further inquiry beyond the customer's name; it is not hard to understand that the laundry is tacitly agreeing to wash the clothing and the customer is agreeing to pay, although all other details will have to be supplied by a court if a dispute arises. Why does Bailey lose on this theory?

The plaintiff's second theory is non-contractual, but analogous to contract: that despite the absence of a contract, West owes Bailey for the care that was given. Why does Bailey also lose on this theory? To understand the issues better, suppose that the van driver Kelly had simply dumped the lame horse onto the road, and that Bailey had then taken in Bascom's Folly and fed it while attempting to discover its owner. Would his chances of recovery on a "quasi-contractual" theory be greater?

Although Bailey's two theories differ in that one supposes a tacit agreement while the other is based on restitution of a benefit conferred, you should note that if Bailey had prevailed on either theory, he would probably have recovered about the same amount. Non-contractual theories of restitution often act to supplement, and to some extent also to mitigate, contract law.

2. Law and the Economics of Restitution. Consider two situations. In the first, a doctor discovers a stranger lying unconscious on a street; the doctor administers first aid, and later demands a fee. In the second, a street musician plays a violin while a woman stands waiting for a bus; she listens to the music with obvious enjoyment, and he then demands a fee. In Common Law, the doctor would usually have a legal claim, while the musician would not. What explains the difference?

Richard Posner, from a law and economics perspective, argues as follows: "In the case of the doctor, the costs of a voluntary transaction would be prohibitive. The reason is incapacity. In other cases it might be time (e.g., the stranger is conscious but bleeding profusely and there is no time to discuss terms). In such cases, the law considers whether, had transaction costs not been prohibitive, the parties would have come to terms and if so what (approximately) the terms would have been." By contrast, the musician "conferred an unbargained-for benefit in circumstances in which the costs of a voluntary bargain would have been low. In such cases, the law insists that the voluntary route be followed—and is on firm economic grounds in doing so." Richard. A. Posner, Economic Analysis of Law 135 (7th ed. 2007) (footnote omitted).

Although Posner's discussion throws broader light on the assumptions that underlie contract law, his analysis does not persuade Frier. What additional economic factors might be worth considering? Which of Posner's examples is closest to the situation in *Bailey v. West*?

Chapter 3

NEGOTIATION AND FORMATION OF THE CONTRACT

A. INTRODUCTION: THE ROLE OF THE COURTS

This chapter addresses the human ritual that produces an enforceable deal, a contract. In the minds of "objective" contract believers it is this ritual that counts, not the ideas or unmanifested intentions. Like the groom who cannot avoid the contractual consequences of his public statement "I do" by crossing his fingers, a person responding to an offer cannot say that her statement "I accept" had no legal consequence just because she intended none (recall *Lucy v. Zehmer*).

There is no vigilant Bishop to ensure the unwavering performance of these rituals. Unlike the stupid goose or simple wolf who can count on its unconscious mind to direct repeated perfect performance of a mating or hierarchical ritual, human intelligence insinuates error. Parties make offers that are misunderstood; parties send responses that conflict with offerors' proposals—sometimes they send responses that conflict even with their own statements. Parties make preliminary deals that are to be followed up by formal documents, but neglect ever to prepare or execute the formal documents. Most of all, parties focus on the deal and its performance, while ignoring the pathological possibility that the deal will abort or that someone will not perform as agreed, and so they pay little attention to the legal rituals until it is too late.

The traditional contract formation ritual that we inherited from the British is for one party (the offeror) to make an offer of a contract to the other (the offeree). The offeree may either extend the negotiation by giving a counteroffer or conclude the deal by an acceptance. Originally deals were made face to face, then by mail or on the telephone, and now sometimes by e-mail. Each new medium brings its problems, as does each new practice.

Parts C, D, and E deal with problematic practices and with difficulties in the rituals that are now well known by their frequent recurrence in the reported cases. Often parties "agree in principle" but expect that their lawyers will draft and negotiate a more extensive agreement. When the agreement in principle is documented but the detailed agreement is not, what to do? If the agreement in principle has no legal effect, then why did they negotiate it and even write it down and sign it? Perhaps in these cases of aborted negotiations the duty of good faith requires the parties to continue to negotiate in good faith? And if they do not, what liability? Some of the cases in C and D deal with that issue.

Part E introduces you to a widespread business practice, sometimes called the battle of the forms. It is common for a purchasing manager from one commercial company to negotiate orally with the salesperson from another company for the purchase of some commodity. Typically the buyer will send a document known as a purchase order. A purchase order has talismanic significance in the commercial sales trade; it means that the buyer's agent has authority, and that he is ready to go ahead. Typically the buyer's agent does not issue a purchase order until done negotiating and satisfied with the deal.

Translated into legal language for this chapter, the purchase order might be an offer. But what if the parties had reached an oral agreement over the telephone before the purchase order was sent? Then it would be an acknowledgment, not an offer, for the offer and the acceptance would already have occurred in the telephone conversation. Commonly the seller will send a responsive document that might be labeled as an acknowledgment (or maybe even as an offer if the counsel for the seller has had a hand in its drafting). As this game is usually played, both parties will have entered the same information on the face of their documents (description of goods, price, number of pieces and, maybe, time and mode of delivery). But the reverse of each document will be a printed form in small, faint type that was drafted by each party's lawyer. These forms often differ radically. The buyer's will say that you give me the moon, warranties beyond imagination, rights to reject, and so on. The seller's will disclaim all warranties, limit the buyer to a remedy of two Kleenex for his tearful despair, foreclose damages, and so on.

Do these differences in the language on the reverse of the parties' documents mean that there is no contract? Maybe yes at common law, but probably no under § 2–207 of the UCC, and certainly no in the stereotypical case. In that case no trouble will have arisen until the seller has delivered and the buyer has paid. Clearly there is a contract then, for each has performed. In the sale of goods the lawyers and the parties will turn to § 2–207 (in cases outside of Article 2 of the UCC to the law of contract formation) not to see if there is a contract, but to find its terms. If my purchase order has an arbitration clause and your acknowledgement does not, the contract requires arbitration only if my document is the contract and yours isn't, and vice versa. So the parties here usually concede the presence of a contract; they are looking for the upper hand in the litigation by getting a term from one or the other document. In effect Section 2–207 is being used as a device for interpretation of the contract, not as a contract formation tool.

Part F covers a particular ritual, the requirement that certain deals be written down and signed to be effective. This requirement is called the Statute of Frauds after the English rule of the same name. Considering this ritual to be no longer necessary in modern law, the English abolished most of it fifty years ago. It is sometimes said that the Statute does not prevent but, in fact, facilitates fraud by allowing those who have made deals to weasel out when they were not written down. Many law professors share that view, but practicing lawyers do not.

One of your editors was part of a committee for the revision of Article 2. Believing—as any good professor should—that the Statute facilitated fraud and not otherwise, he agreed to the proposed excision of the Statute from Article 2. After the first draft hit the street, the Statute was put back almost verbatim. The lawyers' cries about ill-informed and impractical academics still ring in his ears.

In this chapter, as in the last, you will find pathological cases. But these cases are not the same as those; these are like cases that you will see in practice. Now we are down at the feed store shoveling feed; we are not up at the university studying philosophy.

We begin the Chapter with a case that illustrates some basic problems that courts face in handling contract formation, as well as the choices that judges make in tackling these problems.

SUN PRINTING & PUBLISHING ASSOCIATION v. REMINGTON PAPER & POWER CO.

Court of Appeals of New York, 1923.
235 N.Y. 338, 139 N.E. 470.

CARDOZO, J. Plaintiff agreed to buy and defendant to sell 1,000 tons of paper per month during the months of September, 1919, to December, 1920, inclusive, 16,000 tons in all. Sizes and quality were adequately described. Payment was to be made on the 20th of each month for all paper shipped the previous month. The price for shipments in September, 1919, was to be $3.73 3/4 per 100 pounds, and for shipments in October, November and December, 1919, $4 per 100 pounds. "For the balance of the period of this agreement the price of the paper and length of terms for which such price shall apply shall be agreed upon by and between the parties hereto fifteen days prior to the expiration of each period for which the price and length of term thereof have been previously agreed upon, said price in no event to be higher than the contract price for newsprint charged by the Canadian Export Paper Company to the large consumers, the seller to receive the benefit of any differentials in freight rates."

Between September, 1919, and December of that year, inclusive, shipments were made and paid for as required by the contract. The time then arrived when there was to be an agreement upon a new price and upon the term of its duration. The defendant in advance of that time gave notice that the contract was imperfect, and disclaimed for the future an obligation to deliver. Upon this, the plaintiff took the ground that the price was to be ascertained by resort to an established standard. It made demand that during each month of 1920 the defendant deliver 1,000 tons of paper at the contract price for newsprint charged by the Canadian Export Paper Company to the large consumers, the defendant to receive the benefit of any differentials in freight rates. The demand was renewed month by month till the expiration of the year. This action has been brought to recover the ensuing damage.

Seller and buyer left two subjects to be settled in the middle of December and at unstated intervals thereafter. One was the price to be paid. The other was the length of time during which such price was to govern. Agreement as to the one was insufficient without agreement as to the other. If price and nothing more had been left open for adjustment, there might be force in the contention that the buyer would be viewed, in the light of later provisions, as the holder of an option (*Cohen & Sons v. Lurie Woolen Co.*, 232 N. Y. 112). This would mean that in default of an agreement for a lower price, the plaintiff would have the privilege of calling for delivery in accordance with a price established as a maximum. The price to be agreed upon might be less, but could not be more than "the contract price for newsprint charged by the Canadian Export Paper Company to the large consumers." The difficulty is, however, that ascertainment of this price does not dispense with the necessity for agreement in respect of the term during which the price is to apply. Agreement upon a maximum payable this month or to-day is not the same as an agreement that it shall continue to be payable next month or tomorrow....

The argument is made that there was no need of an agreement as to time unless the price to be paid was lower than the maximum. We find no evidence of this intention in the language of the contract. The result would then be that the defendant would never know where it stood. The plaintiff was under no duty to accept the Canadian standard. It does not assert that it was. What it asserts is that the contract amounted to the concession of an option. Without an agreement as to time, however, there would be not one option, but a dozen. The Canadian price today might be less than the Canadian price tomorrow. Election by the buyer to proceed with performance at the price prevailing in one month would not bind it to proceed at the price prevailing in another. Successive options to be exercised every month would thus be read into the contract. Nothing in the wording discloses the intention of the seller to place itself to that extent at the mercy of the buyer. Even if, however, we were to interpolate the restriction that the option, if exercised at all, must be exercised only once, and for the entire quantity permitted, the difficulty would not be ended. Market prices in 1920 happened to rise. The importance of the time element becomes apparent when we ask ourselves what the seller's position would be if they had happened to fall. Without an agreement as to time, the maximum would be lowered from one shipment to another with every reduction of the standard. With such an agreement, on the other hand, there would be stability and certainty.

The parties attempted to guard against the contingency of failing to come together as to price. They did not guard against the contingency of failing to come together as to time. Very likely they thought the latter contingency so remote that it could safely be disregarded. In any event, whether through design or through inadvertence, they left the gap unfilled. The result was nothing more than "an agreement to agree." ... Defendant "exercised its legal right when it insisted that there was need of something more." ... The right is not affected by our appraisal of the motive....

We are told that the defendant was under a duty, in default of an agreement, to accept a term that would be reasonable in view of the nature of the transaction and the practice of the business. To hold it to such a standard is to make the contract over. The defendant reserved the privilege of doing its business in its own way, and did not undertake to conform to the practice and beliefs of others (*United Press v. New York Press Co.*, 164 N. Y. 406, 413). We are told again that there was a duty, in default of other agreement, to act as if the successive terms were to expire every month. The contract says they are to expire at such intervals as the agreement may prescribe. There is need, it is true, of no high degree of ingenuity to show how the parties, with little change of language, could have framed a form of contract to which obligation would attach. The difficulty is that they framed another. We are not at liberty to revise while professing to construe....

The order of the Appellate Division should be reversed and that of the Special Term affirmed, with costs in the Appellate Division and in this court, and the question certified answered in the negative.

CRANE, J., DISSENTING. I cannot take the view of this contract that has been adopted by the majority. The parties to this transaction beyond question thought they were making a contract for the purchase and sale of 16,000 tons rolls news print. The contract was upon a form used by the defendant in its business, and we must suppose that it was intended to be what it states to be, and not a trick or device to defraud merchants....

I not only think it possible, but think the paper itself clearly states a contract recognized under all the rules at law. It is said that the one essential element of price is lacking; that the provision above quoted is an agreement to agree to a price, and that the defendant had the privilege of agreeing or not, as it pleased; that if it failed to agree to a price there was no standard by which to measure the amount the plaintiff would have to pay. The contract does state, however, just this very thing. Fifteen days before the first of January, 1920, the parties were to agree upon the price of the paper to be delivered thereafter, and the length of the period for which such price should apply. However, the price to be fixed was not "to be higher than the contract price for newsprint charged by the Canadian Export Paper Company to large consumers." Here surely was something definite. The 15th day of December arrived. The defendant refused to deliver. At that time there was a price for newsprint charged by the Canadian Export Paper Company. If the plaintiff offered to pay this price, which was the highest price the defendant could demand, the defendant was bound to deliver. This seems to be very clear.

But while all agree that the price on the 15th day of December could be fixed, the further objection is made that the period during which that price should continue was not agreed upon. There are many answers to this.

We have reason to believe that the parties supposed they were making a binding contract; that they had fixed the terms by which one was required to take and the other to deliver; that the Canadian Export Paper Company price was to be the highest that could be charged in any event. These things being so, the court should be very reluctant to permit a defendant to avoid its contract. (*Wakeman v. Wheeler & Wilson Mfg. Co.*, 101 N. Y. 205.)

On the 15th of the fourth month, the time when the price was to be fixed for subsequent deliveries, there was a price charged by the Canadian Export Paper Company to large consumers. As the defendant failed to agree upon a price, made no attempt to agree upon a price and deliberately broke its contract, it could readily be held to deliver the rest of the paper, a thousand rolls a month, at this Canadian price. There is nothing in the complaint which indicates that this is a fluctuating price, or that the price of paper as it was on December 15th was not the same for the remaining twelve months.

Or we can deal with this contract, month by month. The deliveries were to be made 1,000 tons per month. On December 15th 1,000 tons could have been demanded. The price charged by the Canadian Export Paper Company on the 15th of each month on and after December 15th, 1919, would be the price for the thousand ton delivery for that month.

Or again, the word as used in the miscellaneous provision quoted is not "price," but "contract price"—"in no event to be higher than the contract price." Contract implies a term or period and if the evidence should show that the Canadian contract price was for a certain period of weeks or months, then this period could be applied to the contract in question.

Failing any other alternative, the law should do here what it has done in so many other cases, apply the rule of reason and compel parties to contract in the light of fair dealing. It could hold this defendant to deliver its paper as it agreed to do, and take for a price the Canadian Export Paper Company contract price for a period which is reasonable under all the circumstances and conditions as applied in the paper trade.

To let this defendant escape from its formal obligations when any one of these rulings as applied to this contract would give a practical and just result is to give the sanction of law to a deliberate breach. (*Wood v. Duff-Gordon*, 222 N. Y. 88; *Moran v. Standard Oil Co.*, 211 N. Y. 187; *United States Rubber Co. v. Silverstein*, 229 N. Y. 168.)

For these reasons I am for the affirmance of the courts below.

Notes and Discussion

1. Two Judicial Approaches. The vote in the New York Court of Appeals was 5 to 2. What is the most basic point of disagreement between the majority and the dissenters? What additional reasons can you give in support of either side's argument? Put differently, how does each side conceive the judicial role in relation to contracts?

2. Cardozo on *Sun Printing*. Shortly after writing this opinion, Benjamin Cardozo commented on it: "Here was a case where advantage had been taken of the strict letter of a contract to avoid an onerous engagement. Not inconceivably a sensitive conscience would have rejected such an outlet of escape. We thought this immaterial. The court subordinated the equity of a particular situation to the overmastering need of certainty in the transactions of commercial life.... The loss to business would in the long run be greater than the gain if judges were clothed with the power to revise as well as to interpret. Perhaps, with a higher conception of business and its needs, the time will come when even revision will be permitted if it is revision in consonance with established standards of fair dealing, but the time is not yet." Benjamin N. Cardozo, The Growth of the Law 110–111 (1924).

Cardozo concedes that the defendant Remington took advantage of a legal loophole in order to escape from its contract with Sun. Yet he still maintains that there would be a "loss to business" if courts intervened in such a situation. Why do commercial transactions have an "overmastering need of [legal] certainty," and why exactly does Cardozo believe that "the equity of a particular situation" should be subordinated to that need? He has some underlying assumptions about how judicial decisions are likely to influence commerce, and he might not be right.

B. OFFER AND ACCEPTANCE

FORD MOTOR CREDIT CO. v. RUSSELL

Court of Appeals of Minnesota, 1994.
519 N.W.2d 460.

HUSPENI, J. Appellants Dawn Russell and David Russell challenge entry of summary judgment in favor of respondents Ford Motor Credit Company and Monticello Ford and Mercury, Inc. on appellants' claims for breach of contract, violation of the Minnesota Motor Vehicle Retail Installment Sales Act, the Federal Truth in Lending Act, and the Federal Equal Credit Opportunity Act. Because we find that the automobile advertisement did not constitute an offer to the general public, and that Ford Credit complied with the various Acts in question and resold the automobile in a commercially reasonable manner, we affirm.

FACTS

During March 1988, Monticello Ford and Mercury, Inc. (Monticello Ford) advertised a 1988 Ford Escort Pony in The Monticello Shopper for a sale price of $7,826. The publication advertised monthly payments of $159.29, based on a 60-month loan at 11% A.P.R. On March 15, 1988, Dawn Russell sought to purchase a 1988 Escort at the advertised sales price. Monticello Ford contacted three finance companies in an attempt to obtain 11% financing for Ms. Russell. Two companies refused to extend credit due to Ms. Russell's limited credit history. Ford Motor Credit Company (Ford Credit) offered to finance the purchase at a 13.75% A.P.R. under a special retail plan for persons with limited or poor credit. Ford Credit also required Ms. Russell to provide a cosigner on the loan.

Monticello Ford drew up the contract, which Ms. Russell signed, providing for the sale of the automobile at a cash price of $7,826. Ms. Russell also purchased optional credit disability insurance and an extended service contract, which she financed. The total amount financed was $8,275.60, to be paid in 60 monthly installments of $192.63, based upon an A.P.R. of 13.75%. Ms. Russell's father cosigned the loan.

Monticello Ford subsequently assigned to Ford Credit its rights under the contract. The contract provided that, upon default, Ford Credit could accelerate the balance due and repossess the vehicle. On April 19, 1989, Ms. Russell cancelled her credit life insurance, as well as the extended service contract. The unused premiums were applied to the balance of her loan, reducing her monthly payments as a result.

In 1990, Ms. Russell defaulted on numerous payments. After several failed attempts to work out a payment schedule, Ford Credit sent the Russells a notice of default and intent to repossess. Ford Credit repossessed the automobile on February 13, 1991, and mailed the Russells a notice of repossession and right to redeem and a notice of private sale that same day. Neither Ms. nor Mr. Russell attempted to redeem the automobile. Ford Credit sold the automobile for $2,200 to a used car dealer at the Minneapolis Auto Auction.

When Ford Credit sought a deficiency judgment against the Russells, they counterclaimed, alleging breach of contract and violation of the Minnesota Motor Vehicle Retail Installment Sales Act, the Federal Truth in Lending Act and the Federal Equal Credit Opportunity Act, and named Monticello Ford as a third-party defendant. The district court granted Ford Credit's motion for summary judgment on its deficiency claim, and Monticello Ford's motion for summary judgment on the Russells' third-party complaint. . . .

ANALYSIS

On appeal from summary judgment, this court must decide whether genuine issues of material fact exist, and whether the district court correctly applied the law.... The evidence must be viewed in the light most favorable to the nonmoving party. . . .

I. Deceptive trade practices

Appellants contend that the advertisement in The Monticello Shopper constituted an offer that Ms. Russell accepted, and therefore Ford

Credit breached its contract to sell her a 1988 Ford Escort at 11% A.P.R. We disagree. Generally, if goods are advertised for sale at a certain price, it is not an offer and no contract is formed; such an advertisement is merely an invitation to bargain rather than an offer. 1 Samuel Williston, A Treatise on the Law of Contracts § 4:7 (4th ed. 1990); Restatement (Second) of Contracts § 26 (1981). The test of whether a binding obligation may originate in advertisements addressed to the general public is "whether the facts show that some performance was promised in positive terms in return for something requested." *Lefkowitz v. Great Minneapolis Surplus Store, Inc.*, 251 Minn.188, 191, 86 N.W.2d 689, 691 (1957) (quoting 1 Samuel Williston, A Treatise on the Law of Contracts § 27) (3rd ed. 1957).

We conclude that the advertisement here did not constitute an offer of sale to the general public. See id. (an advertisement may constitute an offer where it is clear, definite, explicit, and leaves nothing open for negotiation). Because not everyone qualifies for financing and Monticello Ford does not have an unlimited number of Ford Escorts to sell, it was unreasonable for appellants to believe that the advertisement was an offer binding the advertiser.

Appellants further contend that Monticello Ford falsely represented that financing would be provided at 11%, then changed the rate when it reduced the parties' agreement to writing. There is no evidence, however, that either Ford Credit or Monticello Ford induced Ms. Russell to enter into the contract by promising her an 11% A.P.R. The written contract clearly and conspicuously stated that a 13.75% A.P.R. applied to the financing. Ms. Russell admits that she had ample opportunity to hold the contract in her hands without any obstruction and read it before signing it.

Appellants also assert that Ford Credit participated in a "bait and switch" operation. See Minn. Stat. § 325D.44, subd. 1(9) (1992) (the advertising of goods or services with intent not to sell them as advertised is prohibited). We disagree. Monticello Ford did sell 1988 Ford Escorts at an 11% A.P.R. to those who qualified for the rate. Ms. Russell received the same sale price and the same rebate as the other customers; she merely did not qualify for the same interest rate....

Decision

The automobile advertisement did not constitute an offer to the general public so as to bind the advertiser.... [S]ummary judgment was proper. Affirmed.

Notes and Discussion

1. **Offers.** Restatement 2d § 24 defines an offer as "the manifestation of willingness to enter into a bargain, so made as to justify another person in understanding that his assent to that bargain is invited and will conclude it." This wording closely resembles the definition of a promise in § 2(1): "a manifestation of intention to act or refrain from acting in a specified way, so

made as to justify a promisee in understanding that a commitment has been made." In both cases, the definition is from an objective standpoint: the justified reaction of a reasonable person who is the recipient of the offer or promise. But it is also true that an offer contains within it a promissory element, so what is the promise that an offer contains?

2. Advertisements and Quotations. As the *Ford Motor Credit Co.* case indicates, ads are not usually regarded as legal offers even when they refer to fairly specific items ("This '88 Ford Escort Pony is yours for $7,826"). That is, a contract usually cannot be concluded simply by calling the advertiser and saying, "I accept your offer." What practical reasons underlie this legal position?

If Monticello Ford did not make an offer through its ad, then who did make the offer? Suppose that Dawn Russell had walked in off the street and said: "That Ford Escort Pony in the window, I'll pay you $7,826 for it." That would be an offer, obviously. Does the Court treat what actually happened in this case as equivalent to this hypothetical? In other words, does the Court treat the ad as effectively irrelevant to the transaction that resulted?

A similar rule is applied to price quotations by sellers. Restatement 2d § 26 gives the following example (Illustration 3): "A writes to B, 'I can quote you flour at $5 a barrel in carload lots.' " The Restatement comments: "This is not an offer, in view of the word 'quote' and the incompleteness of the terms. The same words, in response to an inquiry specifying detailed terms, would probably be an offer; and if A added 'for immediate acceptance' the intent to make an offer would be unmistakable."

3. Deceptive Advertising. The standard legal view of offers necessarily opens the way to some abuse. Dawn Russell saw an advertisement with an 11% A.P.R. financing rate. The contract she then signed "clearly and conspicuously stated" a 13.75% rate, and she also had the opportunity to read it before signing. The Court here is obviously referring to a general "duty to read," which is a common theme in contract law. As we will see in subsequent cases, courts have often had occasion to question the realism of the assumptions that underlie this duty.

The *Lefkowitz* case, referred to by the Court, is a classic example of an advertiser who overreached. In a newspaper, the surplus store advertised: "1 Black Lapin Stole / Beautiful, worth $139.50.... $1.00 / First Come First Served." When the plaintiff showed up at the head of the line, the store refused to sell him the stole. In this case, the ad was held to be an offer. *Lefkowitz*, 86 N.W.2d at 690–691. It can be conjectured that the decision was influenced by the whiff of fraudulent advertising. Today, problems of deceptive advertising (such as "bait and switch" tactics) are more commonly handled through consumer legislation, as the Court indicates.

Problem 3–1

Robert Steinberg applied to medical school after receiving a school brochure that stated: "Students are selected on the basis of scholarship, character, and motivation without regard to race, creed, or sex," and other criteria. The school rejected his application allegedly because of his inability to pledge large sums of money to the school. Steinberg then brought suit for, among other things, breach of contract. He claimed that the brochure constituted an invitation for an offer to apply, that the filing of his application constituted an offer to have his credentials appraised under the terms described by the school, and that the school's voluntary reception of the application along with his application fee constituted an acceptance, the final act necessary for the creation of a binding contract. Will he succeed in this claim?

DAVIS v. SATROM

Supreme Court of North Dakota, 1986.
383 N.W.2d 831.

ERICKSTAD, C. J. Dwight W. Davis appeals from a district court summary judgment dismissing his complaint against Gayle E. Satrom and D. C. Blair for specific performance of an alleged contract for the sale and purchase of a mobile home park or damages for breach of the contract. We affirm.

After negotiating to buy a mobile home park from Satrom and Blair, Davis sent to David Wisdom, a real estate agent, a "letter of intent" dated July 24, 1984, to purchase the park. The letter, which contained various terms and conditions, provided:

> "If this proposal is acceptable, please have owner sign below and return the signed copy to us. We will then deposit $10,000 into a trust account at the Bank of America and will prepare an agreement of purchase and sale.... "

Blair changed some of the terms contained in the letter and returned it to Davis.

After further negotiations, Davis submitted an unsigned "commercial purchase agreement and deposit receipt" containing terms not present in the letter of intent. Blair signed the commercial purchase agreement and deposit receipt, after inserting several additional handwritten conditions, including one making the agreement subject to the approval of the sellers' attorney. Davis received a copy of the agreement as altered and signed by Blair.

By letter dated September 7, 1984, Blair told Wisdom that they would "pass" Davis' offer and terms. Wisdom forwarded Blair's letter to Davis and by letter dated September 17, 1984, informed Davis that Satrom and Blair "have indicated to me that they are unwilling to negotiate further or close this transaction."

In a September 25, 1984 letter to Satrom, Davis stated "I am ready to fully perform under the terms of the purchase agreement that you and Mr. Blair signed," and enclosed a check in the amount of $10,000, which Satrom returned uncashed.

Davis sued for specific performance or damages, and the trial court entered summary judgment dismissing the action. The sole issue on appeal is whether or not summary judgment was properly granted.... The purpose of summary judgment is to promote expeditious disposition of cases without trial when there is no dispute as to material facts or inferences to be drawn from undisputed facts, or when only a question of law is involved....

In *Greenberg v. Stewart*, 236 N.W.2d 862 (N.D. 1975), a series of letters were exchanged between a property owner and a prospective purchaser. The trial court granted summary judgment dismissing the prospective purchaser's action for specific performance, holding as a matter of law that the letters exchanged "did not constitute acceptances, but were counter offers." *Id.*, at 868. We affirmed, stating in the Syllabus that:

> "3. In order to form a contract for the sale of real property there must be a meeting of the minds between the parties with respect to all of the terms and conditions of the sale and there must be an unqualified and absolute acceptance of an offer by either party.
>
> "4. A conditional or qualified acceptance is itself a counter offer and rejects the original offer so that no valid contract is made.
>
> "5. Whenever a modification of the terms of a proposal, made in response to a proposal, changes the terms of the original proposal, the modification is a new proposal or counter offer."

Davis' letter of July 24 was an offer. Blair's modifications of that offer constituted a counteroffer. The commercial purchase agreement submitted by Davis was another counteroffer. Blair's acceptance of the commercial purchase agreement after inserting several additional handwritten conditions also constituted a counteroffer. Consequently, there was no contract at that point because there had never been an unqualified acceptance of an offer without the introduction of additional terms and conditions. *Greenberg v. Stewart*, supra....

Assuming that Davis accepted the commercial purchase agreement as modified by Blair, as he contends (although he did not sign it), he accepted it with the conditions imposed by Blair. One of those conditions was that the agreement be approved by the sellers' attorney, Mr. Ruemmele. Ruemmele did not approve the agreement because, among other things, it reserved to Davis the right to allocate the purchase price among the land, improvements, and personal property, which could have resulted in unfavorable tax consequences to Blair and Satrom.

The formation of a contract may be conditioned upon the act of a third person.... *Lilly v. Haynes Co-op. Coal Mining Co.*, 50 N.D. 465, 196 N.W. 556 (1923). *In Lilly v. Haynes*, supra, we specifically held in Syllabus para. 1: "Where one of the parties to a contract stipulates for the approval of his attorney, in the absence of fraud in withholding the approval, the contract, made conditional on such approval, is not effective or operative unless it be obtained."

The trial court determined that "Ruemmele's disapproval of the agreement was reasonable and was not fraudulently obtained." Therefore, the contract never became effective because the condition precedent, Ruemmele's approval, never occurred. Davis' unsupported assertion that Ruemmele's "review was merely one as to form and not as to substance," is without merit.

For the reasons stated, we conclude that, as a matter of law, there was no enforceable contract. When viewed in a light most favorable to Davis, the information available to the trial court precluded the existence of a genuine issue as to any material fact and entitled Satrom and Blair to summary judgment.

Notes and Discussion

1. **When an Offer Terminates.** An offer creates, in the offeree, a legal power of acceptance. When does that power expire? Restatement 2d § 36 ("Methods of Termination of the Power of Acceptance") lists five possibilities: the offer is terminated 1) if the offeree rejects the offer or makes a counteroffer (note that, somewhat counterintuitively, these actions are treated as equivalent for this purpose; see §§ 38–39); 2) at the time specified in the contract, or, failing that, at the end of a reasonable time after the offer is made (see § 41); 3) if the offeror revokes the offer (see § 42, and also in the case just below); 4) if either the offeror or the offeree dies or becomes incapacitated (§ 48); and 5) if the terms of the offer include a condition for acceptance and the condition fails to occur.

Apply these rules to *Davis v. Satrom*. Why is Davis' letter of July 24 described as an offer, despite his description of it as "a letter of intent"? Suppose that, after Davis received Blair's counteroffer, he had rejected it, and Blair had then said, "Okay, then I accept the terms in the July 24 letter"; no contract would have been formed, right? From a legal perspective, what would such a statement be: a "counteroffer"?

Why does the Court emphasize Blair's attorney's reasons for not approving the agreement?

MERCED COUNTY SHERIFF'S EMPLOYEES' ASS'N v. COUNTY OF MERCED

Court of Appeal of California, 1987.
188 Cal.App.3d 662, 233 Cal.Rptr. 519.

FRANSON, ACTING P. J.

STATEMENT OF THE CASE

This appeal turns on the interpretation of two "memoranda of understanding" (MOU), one between respondent Merced County (the County) and petitioner Merced County Sheriff's Employees' Association (the Sheriff's Association), the other between the County and petitioner Merced County Professional Firefighters' Association Local 1396 (the Firefighters' Association), pertaining to salary increases to petitioners' members for a three-year period commencing July 1, 1985. Petitioners sought a writ of mandate in the superior court ordering the County to follow the agreements according to petitioners' interpretation.

The trial court ruled that the salary increase formula in the Sheriff's Association MOU was ambiguous, and that the parties' consent to that formula was based on a mutual good faith mistake in its meaning; it ordered the paragraph rescinded and renegotiated. The Firefighters' Association salary formula, however, with additional explanatory language, was found by the court to be unambiguous and binding on the parties "in accordance with its express terms." This appeal and cross-appeal followed.

For the reasons to be explained, we hold the Sheriff's Association agreement to be enforceable according to the interpretation placed on it by the Sheriff's Association. However, we hold the Firefighters' Association agreement to be unenforceable because of its irreconcilable ambiguity and the failure of the parties to reach a meeting of the minds. We reverse the judgment.

STATEMENT OF THE FACTS

In the summer of 1983, representatives of the County entered into separate negotiations with representatives of the Sheriff's Association and the Firefighters' Association. The negotiations were to discuss the implementation of successor MOUs to replace those due to expire in 1983. Negotiations were interrupted by court proceedings brought by petitioners challenging a 5 percent reduction in wages and benefits by the County. Having won that lawsuit, petitioners resumed separate negotiations with the County in January 1984.

On or about February 17, 1984, during one of the negotiating sessions between the County and the Sheriff's Association, the parties believed they had achieved an agreement on future salaries. This agreement was memorialized as paragraph 7 of a new MOU, executed February 24. The meaning of subparagraphs a, b, and e of paragraph 7 is undisputed. The Sheriff's Association and the County were jointly to conduct a nine-county survey of "Deputy II" salaries. The salaries included in the survey were to be determined by averaging the bottom and top salary for deputy II positions in each of the nine counties. Then the highest and lowest of the nine average salaries would be discarded, and the average of the remaining seven salaries taken.

Subparagraph c of paragraph 7 is the problem. The Sheriff's Association, whose representative, Barry J. Bennett, drafted the MOU, maintains that subparagraph c functions as follows. In July 1985, deputy II positions were to be paid their prior salary plus 90 percent of the differential between that salary and the survey average. In 1986 and 1987, multipliers of 95 and 100 percent respectively would be employed. On the other hand, the County argues that the paragraph means that in July 1985 the deputy II position pay would be no less than 90 percent of the survey average; in 1986, no less than 95 percent of such average; and in 1987, no less than 100 percent of such average. (Precise percentages could not be provided for, as the County required all pay raises to be rounded off to the nearest 2.5 percent.) Thus, the distinction: the

Sheriff's Association understood the percentages would apply to the differential between the existing salary and the survey average, while the County understood the percentages would apply to the survey average itself.

The trial court received the following extrinsic evidence in support of the parties' respective interpretations of the meaning of paragraph 7c. Kenneth Thurman, a deputy sheriff and member of the Sheriff's Association executive committee, testified that at the negotiating session on February 14, 1984, a proposal was made to the County's representatives (William Gnass, county counsel, and Gregory Wellman, deputy county administrative officer) that a salary increase be structured on 90, 95 and 100 percent of the differential between the nine-county salary average and the Merced County salary, the nine-county survey to be conducted on a yearly basis. Wellman and Gnass said they would discuss the proposal with the County Board of Supervisors (Board) and "come back again with us." According to Thurman, at the next meeting, on February 17, Mr. Wellman said that he and Gnass had discussed the matter with the Board, and the Board "was giving them guidelines to go ahead with the proposal." Wellman said his office had done a preliminary survey of the nine counties and had prepared a document (petitioners' exhibit No. 2) showing the salary range for each county and a percentage difference between the nine-county average and the Merced County average of 13.66 percent. Thurman testified that he then asked, "I see a lot of salaries and comparisons, ... but for practical purposes if we were to initiate this [increase] today, where would we stand?" Wellman and his secretary Lou Ann Parsons then made some calculations, and Wellman stated that taking 90 percent of the 13.66 differential would give 12.294 percent and rounding to the nearest 2 1/2 percent would produce a figure of 12.5 percent which, according to Thurman, he understood would be the basis of a salary increase if the increase were effective immediately. Because the County had already agreed to reinstate a 5 percent salary cut previously instituted, Thurman understood that the 12 1/2 percent would be reduced by 5 percent for a net 7 1/2 percent salary increase if instituted immediately. Mr. Wellman then wrote in pencil at the bottom of petitioners' exhibit No. 2 opposite the words "% Difference (13.66)" the following: "X .90 = 12.294 = 12.5%."

Thurman denied hearing any reference to or mention by the County representatives at the February 17 meeting of an increase of salary based on a percentage of the nine-county salary average.

Barry Bennett, legal counsel for the Sheriff's Association who was present at all of the negotiating sessions and who drafted the contract, testified that an agreement was reached on February 17 whereby the deputies would receive a salary increase on July 1, 1985, based on a "formula." The formula was to be arrived at by summarizing nine counties, throwing out the highest and lowest counties, averaging the top and bottom range of each county, comparing that average with the Merced County salary "to determine how high, if at all, it was above the Merced Deputy II salary. [para.] During the first year, as of July 1,

1985, the increase ... was to be 90 percent of *that difference*. That is, the difference between Merced and the average salary of the other counties." (Italics added.) The same formula would apply in 1986, "the increase ... to be based on ninety-five percent of the difference. And then—as of July 1, 1987, the Deputies would be brought to one hundred percent of parity."

After an agreement was supposedly reached on February 17, Bennett prepared a written draft which he testified "embodied my understanding of the agreement" and delivered it along with an accompanying letter dated February 22, 1984, to Mr. Gnass, the county counsel, for his review. Bennett met with Gnass on February 23 and they went over the draft, made some revisions not pertinent to this litigation, and agreed that Gnass was to type the final document for signature by the parties. The final contract as approved by both Bennett and Gnass was signed on February 24, 1984, by Jorge Perez, president of the Sheriff's Association and Albert Goman, chairman of the Board.

Within a few days, a dispute surfaced over the meaning of paragraph 7c. According to Mr. Bennett, he brought the dispute to Mr. Gnass's attention, and Gnass became very angry; he said that Bennett's interpretation of the meaning of paragraph 7c was not the proposal that Gnass had presented to the Board in getting their approval. At this point, Bennett asked Gnass to read the "last two phrases" of paragraph 7c. After doing this, Gnass replied, "I should have read it more carefully."

Bennett, like Thurman, at no time could recall any proposal or comments by the County to the effect that the salary increase would be based on a percentage of the average survey salary.

Gregory Wellman testified for the County. He had been the chief spokesperson for the County during the Sheriff's Association negotiation. Mr. Wellman testified that he did not recall any proposal by the Sheriff's Association reflecting a salary increase based on a specified percentage of the difference between the survey average and the Merced salary. Based on what he understood had been proposed by the deputies at the February 14 meeting, Wellman had presented to the Board in closed session a proposed wage increase that would "Bring deputy II benchmark to 90%, 95% and 100% of the *average salary* in the 9–county survey over a 3 year period...." (Italics added.) This proposal to the Board was written in large colored print on butcher paper and was received in evidence below as respondents' exhibit E. The Board authorized Wellman and Gnass to accept this proposal and, according to Wellman, on February 17 he orally presented the proposal to the Sheriff's Association's representatives as per the guidelines laid down by the Board. Respondents' exhibit E, however, was not shown to the sheriff's representatives at this meeting.

Wellman recalled being asked about the 13.66 percentage difference. He said it was a "theoretical ... or hypothetical question" by Mr. Thurman as to "where the County [was] in ... taking the salary difference or differential and applying a ninety percent figure to that differential, then what would the practical results be, according to the County's current rules of rounding?" The discussion on this point, according to Wellman, resulted in his writing the mathematical calculation at the bottom of petitioner's exhibit No. 2.

William Gnass, county counsel, testified to his part in the negotiations. He understood the structural increases would be based on a specified percentage of "the average in the survey area" for each of three years commencing July 1, 1985. He also did not recall any conversations about applying the percentage to the differential between Merced County salary and the nine-county survey. Gnass, however, did recall some questions being asked about the difference "in regard to rounding, the rounding rules, and I know the dialogue went [on] between Mr. Wellman in that regard."

Gnass substantiated Wellman's testimony about their meeting privately with the Board and getting its authority to present the proposal contained in respondents' exhibit E to the Sheriff's Association representatives at the February 17 meeting. "[That's] ... the sole direction, that Mr. Wellman and I—that we were given, ... " However, Mr. Gnass acknowledged that respondents' exhibit E was not shown to Bennett or Thurman or anyone representing the Sheriff's Association at the February 17 meeting.

Gnass also testified that he reviewed the proposed contract drafted by Bennett "page by page, paragraph by paragraph with Mr. Channing, the CAO, and Mr. Goman [chairman of the Board] ... went over it pagewise in his office."

Albert Goman, chairman of the Board who signed the final contract on behalf of the County, testified that the Board had authorized Mr. Wellman to negotiate a three-year agreement with the deputies whereby they were to receive a raise based on 90, 95 and 100 percent of the nine-county average salary as specified in respondents' exhibit E. Mr. Goman stated that when the final contract was presented to him by Mr. Gnass he read it and signed it. "Other individual Board members had seen it prior to my signing it also." Mr. Goman understood the contract to "contain terms similar to that listed on [respondents' exhibit E] on the board." Goman, of course, never attended any of the negotiating sessions between the County and the Sheriff's Association.

The extrinsic evidence pertaining to the firefighters' agreement can be summarized as follows. Gnass testified about his last negotiating session with the Firefighters' Association which took place on March 9, 1984, after the dispute had arisen between Bennett and Gnass over the meaning of the Sheriff's Association agreement. On direct examination, Gnass testified that he had added the three extra sentences at the end of paragraph 7d which express the intent that the engineer's salary would approximate a specified percentage (85, 90, 95) "of said Deputy Sheriff II average in the survey area." Gnass told the firefighters the practical effect of the formula, as set forth in paragraph 7d of the firefighters' agreement, "[very] carefully." He "explained to them we were talking [about] salary averages." He did this because he had received Bennett's letter and "I wanted to make sure that there was no dispute, that what we were talking about was salary average, wasn't talking about any differential, or anything, but salary averages."

On cross-examination, however, Gnass seemed to contradict his direct testimony. In response to a question as to whether he discussed paragraph 7d with the firefighters, he stated, "I don't recall saying anything about it." Nor did Gnass recall being asked about the purpose of the language which he had added to the firefighters' contract. Gnass did acknowledge that he did not tell the firefighters the nature of the dispute that had arisen with the Sheriff's Association over their contract; he simply told them that he and Mr. Bennett were not getting along. Finally, Gnass acknowledged that "[staying] five percent behind the Sheriffs was something that was discussed."

Mark Johnson, a firefighter and member of the negotiating team, testified that he was at the March 9 meeting with Mr. Gnass. He said Gnass presented the salary proposal to the firefighters. "[He] presented what was in the contract as we signed it. We did have a contract before us of the Sheriff's Department, and we reviewed them and compared them, not line-by-line, but we compared it more or less page by page. . . ."

Johnson testified that he asked Mr. Gnass specifically "why there was an additional [*sic*] addition to the [salary] paragraph, compared to the Sheriff's contract." Gnass responded that it "was to make clear to us that we were to stay five percent behind the Sheriff's Deputy [salary]." Johnson also verified that when Gnass was asked about a problem with the Sheriff's Association he responded, " ... Mr. Bennett and I are having a disagreement." Mr. Gnass gave the firefighters no explanation of the County's salary proposal. "He said, ... this is it."

Discussion

I. The Sheriff's Association agreement.

Without mutual assent, there is no contract (Civ. Code, § 1550, subd. 2; *Chakmak v. H. J. Lucas Masonry, Inc.* (1976) 55 Cal.App.3d 124, 129 [127 Cal.Rptr. 404]). "The existence of mutual consent is determined by objective rather than subjective criteria, the test being what the outward manifestations of consent would lead a reasonable person to believe. [Citation.] Accordingly, the primary focus in determining the existence of mutual consent is upon the acts of the parties involved." (*Meyer v. Benko* (1976) 55 Cal.App.3d 937, 942–943 [127 Cal.Rptr. 846].) The manifestation of assent to a contractual provision may be "wholly or partly by written or spoken words or by other acts or by failure to act." (Rest.2d Contracts, § 19.)

Nevertheless, as expressed in the Restatement Second of Contracts section 20, subdivision (1), "There is no manifestation of mutual assent to an exchange if the parties attach materially different meanings to their manifestations and [para.] (a) neither party knows or has reason to know the meaning attached by the other; or [para.] (b) each party knows or each party has reason to know the meaning attached by the other." Under these rules no contract is formed if neither party is at fault or if both parties are equally at fault. (Rest.2d Contracts, § 20, com. d; see also Rest.2d Contracts, § 201.)

Conversely, "The manifestations of the parties are operative in accordance with the meaning attached to them by one of the parties if ... that party has no reason to know of any different meaning attached by the other, and the other has reason to know the meaning attached by the first party." (Rest.2d Contracts, § 20, subd. (2)(b); see also Rest.2d Contracts, § 201, subd. (2).) Thus, under this rule, a party may be bound by a negligent manifestation of assent, provided the other party is not negligent. (Rest.2d Contracts, § 20, com. d.)

In the present case, the trial court found there was no contract between the County and the Sheriff's Association because the parties each had a mistaken belief as to the meaning of paragraph 7c even though the representatives of both parties "acted in good faith, based upon a reasonable and justifiable interpretation of Paragraph 7(c)." This finding of good faith is sound since no one argues that the parties subjectively acted otherwise when they negotiated the contract; however, a serious question arises as to whether the County acted reasonably and justifiably in formulating its understanding of the meaning of the language of paragraph 7c. In making our analysis of this issue, we assume that the County is bound by the manifestations of assent as well as the knowledge of its agents Mr. Wellman and Mr. Gnass in the negotiating process.

First, we turn to the pertinent language of paragraph 7: A7. The parties agree that, effective the first pay period following July 1, 1985, July 1, 1986, and July 1, 1987, the wages of employees in the unit represented by Association shall be determined as follows:

> "a. The survey shall jointly be conducted by the parties comparing the wages of a Deputy II (top step) in Merced County to the wages of a Deputy II (top step, or comparable classification) in nine (9) designated counties, to wit: the Counties of Butte, Fresno, Humboldt, Madera, San Joaquin, Solano, Stanislaus, Tulare, and Yolo;
>
> "b. In determining the *average top step pay* for said positions, the *percentage differentials* between first step and top step of Deputy II shall be determined, then averaged;
>
> "c. Wage increases, if any, shall be those approximating ninety percent (90%) of *said average* (July 1985), ninety-five percent (95%) of *said average* (July 1986), and one hundred percent (100%) of *said average* (July 1987), said percentages to be *applied to the actual differential determined by the survey*, then rounded off to the nearest two and one-half percent (2.5%); ...

"e. The increases, if any, to be effective in July of 1985–87 shall be determined, to the greatest extent possible, by March 31, of each of the enumerated years, except that the salaries to be determined by said inquiry shall be those which would be effective on July 1 of each of those years. Should any of the enumerated counties not have reached agreement by July 1 of each of the enumerated years, the parties agree that the salary in effect as of July 1 of that particular year shall be the one to be used in determining the average. In determining the nine county averages as described above, the highest and lowest wage level paid by said counties shall not be used;

"f. It is understood that under no circumstances will the implementation of this provision result in a wage decrease for any employee represented by Association." (Italics added.)

It is obvious that the phrase "said average" as used in the first clause of subparagraph 7c has reference to the "average" determined by the formula provided in subparagraph 7b, but which "average" in subparagraph 7b does it refer to—the "average top step pay" for the nine-county deputy II position or the average of the "percentage differential" between Merced County and the survey salaries? Both concepts are used in subparagraph 7b. The first clause of subparagraph 7c can probably be read in either way. But Mr. Bennett was careful in his drafting B he added a second clause to subparagraph 7c which made clear what he intended: "Said percentages [90, 95 and 100 percent] to be applied to the *actual differential* determined by the survey, . . . " (Italics added.) Thus, the reasonable interpretation of subparagraph 7c is that the salary increases were to be geared to a specified percentage of the *difference* between the average survey salary and the Merced County salary rather than to a percentage of the average survey salary.[1]

Our holding does not mean that the County did not entertain a contrary subjective meaning but, as we have previously explained, the existence of mutual assent is determined by an objective rather than a subjective standard, i.e., what a reasonable person would believe from the outward manifestations of consent. Here, we have a written integrated contract which reasonably can be interpreted as meaning exactly what the Sheriff's Association intended it to mean. Ordinarily, absent fraud or mistake of fact, the outward manifestations or expression of consent in such a contract is controlling, i.e., mutual assent is gathered from the reasonable meaning of words and the acts of the parties, not from their unexpressed intentions or understanding. (1 Witkin, Summary of Cal. Law (8th ed. 1973) Contracts, § 88, p. 92.)

1. It is "solely a judicial function to interpret a written instrument unless the interpretation turns upon the credibility of extrinsic evidence," (*Parsons v. Bristol Development Co.* (1965) 62 Cal.2d 861, 865 [44 Cal.Rptr. 767, 402 P.2d 839].) We find no credibility conflict in the extrinsic evidence below. Each party's subjective "understanding" of the meaning of the written contract as well as what was agreed to at the negotiating sessions does not present a credibility question nor does each party's failure to "recall" conversations or statements by the other party at the negotiating sessions raise such a question. Thus, as an appellate court we are required to independently determine the meaning of the contract. (Id. at p. 866.)

Furthermore, even if we should conclude that the provisions of paragraph 7c are so ambiguous that either party's intended meaning reasonably can be derived from the language used, the contract should nevertheless be enforced according to the meaning asserted by the Sheriff's Association. The guiding principle in this situation is articulated in Restatement Second of Contracts, section 20, subdivision (2)(b). "The manifestations of the parties are operative in accordance with the meaning attached to them *by one of the parties* if . . . that party has no reason to know of any different meaning attached by the other, and *the other has reason to know* the meaning attached by the first party." (Italics added; cf. Rest.2d Contracts, § 201, subd. (2) and com. d.) A party may thus be bound by a negligent manifestation of assent if the other party is not equally negligent. (Rest.2d Contracts, § 20, com. d.)

The evidence shows that the County had "reason to know" the meaning intended by the Sheriff's Association. At the last negotiating session on February 17 Deputy Sheriff Thurman asked Mr. Wellman, the County's representative, what the practical effect of the wage increase would be if it went into effect immediately. Wellman responded by calculating the projected raise at the specified percentage (90 percent) of the 13.66 differential in pay between the nine-county average and the Merced average as shown by petitioners' exhibit No. 2. Wellman's handwritten notes on petitioners' exhibit No. 2 corroborate Thurman's testimony. Wellman's attempted explanation that the calculations were intended only to illustrate the County's "rounding [off] process" is not convincing; it does not explain his application of the 90 percent standard to the 13.66 differential. At the very least, Wellman's conduct reasonably should be deemed to have placed the County on notice of the intended meaning of the Sheriff's Association, i.e., that the pay raise was to be based on the percentage difference between the Merced County deputies' salaries and the average survey salary.

Further, Mr. Bennett's insertion of the second clause in paragraph 7c—"said percentages to be applied to the *actual differential* determined by the survey, . . . " (italics added) should have put Mr. Gnass, the county counsel, as well as Mr. Wellman, on notice of the meaning intended by the Sheriff's Association. If Mr. Gnass had read the contract carefully, he would have realized that the Sheriff's Association had a different understanding of the pay raise than did Gnass and Wellman. Thus, the County through its negotiating agents had ample reason to know of the intended meaning of the Sheriff's Association.

The next question is whether the Sheriff's Association had reason to know the meaning attached to paragraph 7c by the County. If the Sheriff's Association had reason to know of the County's interpretation, then the Sheriff's Association would be deemed to be equally negligent with the County in misinterpreting paragraph 7c, and the result would be no contract. (Rest.2d Contracts, § 20, subd. (1).) We find no evidence to support a finding that the Sheriff's Association was negligent in negotiating the contract with the County. The County's argument that the deputies could not reasonably have believed their asserted meaning because the deputies understood they would not achieve parity the first year and that conceivably under their interpretation parity could be achieved the first year because of the process of rounding off to the nearest 2 1/2 percent is not convincing. The fact that under some conceivable hypothesis the deputies could achieve parity the first year does not foreclose a reasonable belief by the deputies that "pragmatically" they were to receive a pay increase based on a percentage of the salary differential.

Also the County's argument that subparagraph f of paragraph 7, which prohibits decreases in salaries during the term of the contract, would be redundant if the deputies' interpretation were accepted—hence, the deputies could not have intended their interpretation—does not wash. Paragraph 7f can be viewed simply as an expression of a bargain already made, i.e., no wage decreases during the three-year salary adjustment period. In short, the redundancy of paragraph 7f does not foreclose the reasonableness of the deputies' understanding of the meaning of paragraph 7c.

We conclude, therefore, that subparagraph 7c should be interpreted to mean that the percentages apply to the differential between the nine-county average and the Merced County salaries, the interpretation espoused by the Sheriff's Association.

II. Firefighters' MOU.

Subparagraph 7d of the Firefighters agreement reads as follows: "Wage increases, if any, shall be those approximating eighty-five percent (85%) of said average (July 1985), ninety percent (90%) of said average (July 1986), and ninety-five percent (95%) of said average (July 1987), *said percentages to be applied to the actual differential determined by the survey*, then rounded off to the nearest two and one half percent (2.5%). It is the intent of the parties that as of July 1, 1985, that the Engineers' salary range will approximate eighty-five percent (85%) of said *Deputy Sheriff II average in the survey area.* It is intent of the parties that as of July 1, 1986, the Engineers' salary range will approximate ninety percent (90%) of said *Deputy Sheriff II average in the survey area.* It is intent of the parties that as of July 1, 1987, that the Engineers' salary range will approximate ninety-five percent (95%) of said *Deputy Sheriff II average in the survey area.*" (Italics added.)

The first sentence of paragraph 7d other than the specified percentages is identical to the language in paragraph 7c of the Sheriff's Association agreement. As we have explained, this sentence means that the percentages shall be applied to the difference between the survey salaries and the Merced County deputy II salary. However, Mr. Gnass added to the firefighters' contract the three additional sentences found in paragraph 7d. According to Gnass, he did this to make sure the firefighters understood that they were talking about salary averages and not salary differential. Gnass testified on direct examination that he carefully explained this point to the firefighters at the March 9, 1984, negotiating session before the contract was signed. This additional language, of course, makes paragraph 7d ambiguous on its face – the addition directly contradicts the clear meaning of the first sentence of the paragraph.

As we have already explained, Mr. Gnass seems to contradict himself on cross-examination. He was unable to recall the specifics of any discussion at the March 9 meeting about his addition to paragraph 7d, he did not recall being asked by anyone about the purpose of the additional language, he did not disclose to the firefighters the substance of the County's dispute with the Sheriff's Association over the meaning of the language incorporated in the first sentence of paragraph 7d but he did acknowledge some discussion about the firefighters' remaining 5 percent behind the deputies in the salary adjustment formula.

Mark Johnson, the firefighters' representative, testified that he specifically asked Mr. Gnass at the March 9 meeting why there was an addition to their contract as compared with the Sheriff's Association contract, and Gnass only responded that it was "to make clear to us that we were to stay five percent behind the sheriff's deputy."

It should be emphasized at this point that the trial court did not rely on the testimony of either Gnass or Johnson in reaching its decision on the firefighters' contract. Rather, the trial court looked only to the terms of the written contract and found "there is no ambiguity in the language . . . of the contract;" it is "clear and unambiguous" and ordered it enforced "in accordance with its express terms."

We respectfully disagree with the trial court's holding that the language of paragraph 7d of the firefighters' contract is unambiguous. The language added by Gnass to the formula derived from the Sheriff's Association contract directly conflicts with the Sheriff's Association's formula and renders the entire paragraph 7d contradictory on its face.

Examining the extrinsic evidence as to what was said at the March 9 meeting sheds little, if any, light on the meaning of paragraph 7d. Gnass obviously intended by the additional language to make clear that any salary increase would be based on a percentage of the survey salaries rather than any differential. But what did the firefighters reasonably understand the language of paragraph 7d to mean?—they do not recall any discussion about the formula other than that it would keep them 5 percent behind the deputies. Gnass acknowledges this was discussed.

If the sheriff's deputies are to get a percentage raise based on the differential in pay with the nine-county average but the firefighters are to get a percentage raise based only on the survey average, then it is quite apparent that the firefighters would receive far less than 5 percent below the sheriff's deputies, at least during the first and second years. This obviously was not contemplated by the parties.

We defy any rational person to make sense of the language contained in paragraph 7d of the firefighters' contract. This is particularly so in light of our determination of the meaning of the language contained in paragraph 7c of the Sheriff's Association contract which becomes tangentially relevant in determining the meaning of the firefighters' paragraph 7d because of the uncontradicted testimony that the firefighters were to stay within 5 percent of the deputies' salaries.

"There is no manifestation of mutual assent to an exchange if the parties attach materially different meanings to their manifestations and [para.] (a) neither party knows or has reason to know the meaning attached by the other; or [para.] (b) each knows or each party has reason to know the meaning attached by the other." (Rest.2d Contracts, § 20; see also *Rovegno v. Defferari* (1871) 40 Cal. 459, 462–463.) The basic principle governing material misunderstanding is thus: no contract is formed if neither party is at fault or if both parties are equally at fault. We conclude that both parties are at fault in their understanding of the meaning of the firefighters' agreement. The County, by Mr. Gnass, improperly advised the firefighters that the purpose of the language added to paragraph 7d was to insure that the firefighters would remain 5 percent below the deputies' salary. The firefighters were equally at fault in light of Mr. Gnass's testimony that he told them their percentages would apply to the survey salaries and not to a differential between salaries, and the firefighters' failure to appreciate the import of the words added to paragraph 7d by Mr. Gnass. In short, the County and the firefighters were so intent on their own subjective understanding of the meaning of paragraph 7d that they passed each other like two ships on a stormy sea—neither aware of the other's presence insofar as understanding the other's intended meaning of the contract. We therefore have no alternative but to declare that the parties failed to reach a meeting of the minds; there was no objective manifestation of assent, and the parties will have to renegotiate the salary increase.

The judgment is reversed. The trial court is ordered to issue a writ of mandate directing the County to follow the contract with the Sheriff's Association according to the interpretation espoused by the Sheriff's Association and to direct the parties to renegotiate paragraph 7d of the Firefighters' Association. In all other respects, the judgment is affirmed. The Sheriff's Association and the Firefighters' Association to recover their respective costs on appeal.

Notes and Discussion

1. **Misunderstanding: Two Ships Named "Peerless."** In the famous old case of *Raffles v. Wichelhaus*, 159 Eng. Rep. 375 (Ex. 1864), plaintiff sold to defendant 125 bales of cotton "to arrive ex 'Peerless' from Bombay" at Liverpool. As it emerged, the defendants believed that the "Peerless" was a ship that would set sail in October, while the plaintiffs were thinking of a different ship "Peerless" that would sail in December. The Court of Exchequer upheld the argument that: "there is a latent ambiguity, and parol evidence may be given for the purpose of shewing that the defendant meant one 'Peerless' and the plaintiff another. That being so, there was no *consensus ad idem* [agreement on the same thing, i.e., the object of sale], and therefore no binding contract."

The Court of Exchequer appears to have held that there was no subjective agreement between the parties. That is, their ostensible contract was not binding because each party was thinking of a different ship, even though, to an external observer, they might seem to be agreeing. They had gone through the process of offer and acceptance, but had really just "talked past" one another. An external observer, confronted with the reality of multiple ships named Peerless, might have later concluded that this agreement was ambiguous, and the Court does acknowledge the possibility of "latent ambiguity." But, or so the Court saw it, the real issue in *Raffles v. Wichelhaus* was not that the word "Peerless" could refer to more than one ship (with the result that a court may have to decide which ship was intended—a problem of contract interpretation), but that the parties themselves did not both mentally agree on a ship and so never formed a contract in the first place. To this extent, the English court required a real "meeting of the minds" before a contract can exist.

Brian Simpson has a wonderful essay on the historical background of this case: *The Beauty of Obscurity: Raffles v. Wichelhaus and Busch*, in Leading Cases in the Common Law 135–162 (1995).

2. Restatement 2d § 20 (Effect of Misunderstanding). Misunderstanding as a barrier to contract formation survives, but has been modified to reflect objective theories of contract formation. Section 20 takes the position that: "There is no manifestation of mutual assent to an exchange [which is a requirement for a valid contract: § 17] if the parties attach materially different meanings to their manifestations and (a) neither party knows or has reason to know the meaning attached by the other . . . " Restatement 2d § 20(1). However, when the parties attach different meanings to their manifestations, and one party is unaware of the discrepancy while the other party either knows or (much more important) has reason to know of the other party's meaning, then the first party's meaning controls.

The manifestations of the parties need not entirely concur, of course. The Restatement comments, "Almost never are all the connotations of a bargain exactly identical for both parties; it is enough that there is a core of common meaning sufficient to determine their performances with reasonable certainty or to give a reasonably certain basis for an appropriate legal remedy." Restatement 2d § 20 Comment b.

Still, § 20 seems to conflict with the objective theory of contract, not so? Does § 20 require courts to examine additional aspects of situations like that in *Raffles v. Wichelhaus*?

3. Ships That Pass in the Night. *Merced County* amalgamates two distinct cases, both concerning the interpretation of an important contract clause (paragraph 7.c.) governing pay increases. In the case of the Sheriff's Association, both the union and Merced County agreed that the clause was intended, over three years, to bring deputy II salaries into alignment with the current average salary of nine nearby counties; but they disagreed on how swiftly this re-alignment was to occur during the first two years, with, as would be expected, the union arguing that the language established a more accelerated schedule, and the county, that it favored a much slower one. The language may at first seem utterly opaque to you, but try to parse it out and see how each side understood the wording. Judge Franson is at pains to describe the tortured process that led to this language. He then applies § 20 and determines that the county probably knew of the union's meaning, while the union did not know of the county's meaning. So the union wins, right?

The Firefighters' agreement had much the same language, but with some additional gobbledygook that Judge Franson finds incomprehensible to "any rational person." The court might have concluded that neither party was at fault for the resulting confusion (as seems to have been the case in *Raffles v. Wichelhaus*); instead, it finds both at fault. But the result, under § 20, is the same: "they passed each other like two ships on a stormy sea—neither aware of the other's presence insofar as understanding the other's intended meaning of the contract."

It is not easy to distinguish misunderstandings, where there is often no contract, from mere ambiguity and uncertainty, where a court must interpret the contract. In this case the appellate court comes to exactly the opposite conclusion of the trial court. With which court do you agree? Why, do you suppose, were these memoranda left so unclear? (We suspect that one of the negotiating parties in each case may have appreciated the uncertainty and may have intentionally failed to disclose it to the other side. A negotiator who does that is too clever by a half, true?)

4. **"What Is Chicken?"** In 1957, two contracts were concluded for the sale of 150,000 pounds of "Frozen Chicken, Grade A, Government Inspected." The seller was a New Jersey firm, the buyer a Swiss importer of foodstuffs. After the first shipment arrived in Switzerland, a dispute broke out, the seller asserting that all chickens, no matter their age, were included in the designation "chicken," while the buyer believed that only young chicken (suitable for broiling or frying) were meant. The Judge treated this dispute as a matter of interpretation, but, after examining every possible angle, concluded that neither side had sufficient evidence to prevail over the other if it bore the burden of proof as the plaintiff. *Frigaliment Importing Co. v. B.N.S. Intern. Sales Corp.*, 190 F.Supp. 116 (S.D.N.Y. 1960) (Friendly, J.) (famously beginning: "The issue is, what is chicken?").

What may seem odd about this case is that it is not treated as one of misunderstanding, even though it seems clear that both parties had attached different meanings to the word "chicken" from the outset of their negotiations. Indeed, in an opinion written the following year, the Judge admitted that this might have been the better course. *Dadourian Export Corp. v. United States*, 291 F.2d 178, 187 n.4 (2d Cir. 1961) (Friendly, J., dissenting). Why, then, did both parties and the Judge pursue the interpretive route? The legal consequences may be different if the case is analyzed as misunderstanding rather than as an issue of interpretation. How?

Problem 3–2

Frederick Hamann was employed as a teacher, without tenure, at a junior college. He took a leave of absence for a year. The college's regulations provided that: "Professional employees granted leaves will, if possible, be reinstated in positions that are similar to the position held when granted the leave." Hamann interpreted this sentence to mean that he had an absolute right to reinstatement, and "if possible," in a position similar to that previously held. The college, however, interpreted "if possible" as meaning that Hamann would be reinstated only if a position was available. If, at the time he requested his leave, Hamann was aware of the college's interpretation, can he force the college to reinstate him?

ARDENTE v. HORAN

Supreme Court of Rhode Island, 1976.
117 R.I. 254, 366 A.2d 162.

DORIS, J. Ernest P. Ardente, the plaintiff, brought this civil action in Superior Court to specifically enforce an agreement between himself and William A. and Katherine L. Horan, the defendants, to sell certain real property. The defendants filed an answer together with a motion for summary judgment pursuant to Super. R. Civ. P. 56. Following the submission of affidavits by both the plaintiff and the defendants and a hearing on the motion, judgment was entered by a Superior Court justice for the defendants. The plaintiff now appeals.

In August 1975, certain residential property in the city of Newport was offered for sale by defendants. The plaintiff made a bid of $250,000 for the property which was communicated to defendants by their attorney. After defendants' attorney advised plaintiff that the bid was acceptable to defendants, he prepared a purchase and sale agreement at the direction of defendants and forwarded it to plaintiff's attorney for plaintiff's signature. After investigating certain title conditions, plaintiff executed the agreement. Thereafter plaintiff's attorney returned the document to defendants along with a check in the amount of $20,000 and a letter dated September 8, 1975, which read in relevant part as follows:

> "My clients are concerned that the following items remain with the real estate: a) dining room set and tapestry wall covering in dining room; b) fireplace fixtures throughout; c) the sun parlor furniture. I would appreciate your confirming that these items are a part of the transaction, as they would be difficult to replace."

The defendants refused to agree to sell the enumerated items and did not sign the purchase and sale agreement. They directed their attorney to return the agreement and the deposit check to plaintiff and subsequently refused to sell the property to plaintiff. This action for specific performance followed.

In Superior Court, defendants moved for summary judgment on the ground that the facts were not in dispute and no contract had been formed as a matter of law.[2] The trial justice ruled that the letter quoted above constituted a conditional acceptance of defendants' offer to sell the property and consequently must be construed as a counteroffer. Since

2. Although the contract would appear to be within the statute of frauds, defendants did not raise this defense in the trial court, nor do they raise it here. Where a party makes no claim to the benefit of the statute, the court *sua sponte* will not interpose it for him. . . .

defendants never accepted the counteroffer, it followed that no contract was formed, and summary judgment was granted.

Summary judgment is a drastic remedy and should be cautiously applied; nevertheless, where there is no genuine issue as to any material fact and the moving party is entitled to judgment as a matter of law, summary judgment properly issues. . . .

The plaintiff assigns several grounds for appeal in his brief. . . . The plaintiff's second contention is that the trial justice incorrectly applied the principles of contract law in deciding that the facts did not disclose a valid acceptance of defendants' offer. Again we cannot agree.

The trial justice proceeded on the theory that the delivery of the purchase and sale agreement to plaintiff constituted an offer by defendants to sell the property. Because we must view the evidence in the light most favorable to the party against whom summary judgment was entered, in this case plaintiff, we assume as the trial justice did that the delivery of the agreement was in fact an offer.[3]

The question we must answer next is whether there was an acceptance of that offer. The general rule is that where, as here, there is an offer to form a bilateral contract, the offeree must communicate his acceptance to the offeror before any contractual obligation can come into being. A mere mental intent to accept the offer, no matter how carefully formed, is not sufficient. The acceptance must be transmitted to the offeror in some overt manner. . . . 1 Restatement Contracts § 20 (1932). See generally 1 Corbin, Contracts § 67 (1963). A review of the record shows that the only expression of acceptance which was communicated to defendants was the delivery of the executed purchase and sale agreement accompanied by the letter of September 8. Therefore it is solely on the basis of the language used in these two documents that we must determine whether there was a valid acceptance. Whatever plaintiff's unexpressed intention may have been in sending the documents is irrelevant. We must be concerned only with the language actually used, not the language plaintiff thought he was using or intended to use.

There is no doubt that the execution and delivery of the purchase and sale agreement by plaintiff, without more, would have operated as an acceptance. The terms of the accompanying letter, however, apparently conditioned the acceptance upon the inclusion of various items of personalty. In assessing the effect of the terms of that letter we must keep in mind certain generally accepted rules. To be effective, an acceptance must be definite and unequivocal. "An offeror is entitled to know in clear terms whether the offeree accepts his proposal. It is not enough that the words of a reply justify a probable inference of assent." 1 Restatement Contracts § 58, comment a (1932). The acceptance may

3. The conclusion that the delivery of the agreement was an offer is not unassailable in view of the fact that defendants did not sign the agreement before sending it to plaintiff, and the fact that plaintiff told defendants' attorney after the agreement was received that he would have to investigate certain conditions of title before signing the agreement. If it was not an offer, plaintiff's execution of the agreement could itself be no more than an offer, which defendants never accepted.

not impose additional conditions on the offer, nor may it add limitations. "An acceptance which is equivocal or upon condition or with a limitation is a counteroffer and requires acceptance by the original offeror before a contractual relationship can exist." *John Hancock Mut. Life Ins. Co. v. Dietlin*, 97 R.I. 515, 518, 199 A.2d 311, 313 (1964)....

However, an acceptance may be valid despite conditional language if the acceptance is clearly independent of the condition. Many cases have so held. Williston states the rule as follows:

> "Frequently an offeree, while making a positive acceptance of the offer, also makes a request or suggestion that some addition or modification be made. So long as it is clear that the meaning of the acceptance is positively and unequivocally to accept the offer whether such request is granted or not, a contract is formed." 1 Williston, Contracts § 79 at 261–62 (3d ed. 1957). Corbin is in agreement with the above view. 1 Corbin, supra § 84 at 363–65. Thus our task is to decide whether plaintiff's letter is more reasonably interpreted as a qualified acceptance or as an absolute acceptance together with a mere inquiry concerning a collateral matter.

In making our decision we recognize that, as one text states, "The question whether a communication by an offeree is a conditional acceptance or counter-offer is not always easy to answer. It must be determined by the same common-sense process of interpretation that must be applied in so many other cases." 1 Corbin, supra § 82 at 353. In our opinion, the language used in plaintiff's letter of September 8 is not consistent with an absolute acceptance accompanied by a request for a gratuitous benefit. We interpret the letter to impose a condition on plaintiff's acceptance of defendants' offer. The letter does not unequivocally state that even without the enumerated items plaintiff is willing to complete the contract. In fact, the letter seeks "confirmation" that the listed items "are a part of the transaction." Thus, far from being an independent, collateral request, the sale of the items in question is explicitly referred to as a part of the real estate transaction. Moreover, the letter goes on to stress the difficulty of finding replacements for these items. This is a further indication that plaintiff did not view the inclusion of the listed items as merely collateral or incidental to the real estate transaction.

A review of the relevant case law discloses that those cases in which an acceptance was found valid despite an accompanying conditional term generally involved a more definite expression of acceptance than the one in the case at bar....

Accordingly, we hold that since the plaintiff's letter of acceptance dated September 8 was conditional, it operated as a rejection of the defendants' offer and no contractual obligation was created.

The plaintiff's appeal is denied and dismissed, the judgment appealed from is affirmed and the case is remanded to the Superior Court.

Notes and Discussion

1. **Why Did This Contract Fall Apart?** It's often worth the effort to conjecture about the motives of the parties. Ernest Ardente, acting evidently on the advice of his attorney, signed the Horans' sale agreement without altering it, and also tendered a check for $20,000. Why did he take care to put his proposal in a separately signed letter? He could have redrafted the acceptance and included his proposals in the redrafted document.

2. **The "Mirror Image" Rule.** Restatement 2d § 59 states: "A reply to an offer which purports to accept it but is conditional on the offeror's assent to terms additional to or different from those offered is not an acceptance but is a counteroffer." See also § 61: an "acceptance which requests a change or addition to the terms of the offer" is not invalid "unless the acceptance is made to depend on an assent" to the new terms.

This is the core of the "mirror image" rule. As one court has put it, "Unless an acceptance mirrors the offeror's terms, neither omitting nor adding terms, it has no legal effect as an acceptance and operates as a rejection and a counter offer." *Safeco Ins. Co. of Am. v. City of White House*, 36 F.3d 540, 546 (6th Cir. 1994).

The Court could have given a different reading to Ardente's letter. For instance, the Horans might have treated the letter as an acceptance rather than a counteroffer, perhaps by responding: "Good, we have a deal, but the sun parlor furniture is not included." Or would this be itself a counteroffer?

3. **The Realism of the Rule.** Here and elsewhere, in assessing the traditional Common Law rules for offer and acceptance, it is worth querying whether they demand too much of human nature. As we will see, the UCC has significantly moderated some of the more stringent requirements, and the CISG also is substantially more liberal.

Problem 3–3

James Price was a tenured Professor in a medical school. Each year the school sent him a letter outlining his terms of employment for the following year and asking him to indicate his acceptance by signing the letter; Price regularly did so, but often with a note giving his reasons for signing "under protest." The notes occasioned little difficulty until one year when the school sent him a reply stating that because of his "non-acceptance," his employment was being terminated. Does Price have a legal basis for suing?

Note: Contracts Concluded by Exchange of Letters

Today, parties who are not dealing face-to-face often make use of virtually instantaneous e-mail or internet communications in order to negotiate and reach contracts. Concluding contracts by mail is nonetheless still quite common, though less prevalent than formerly. Posted correspondence requires special rules, particularly because of the delay in communications that it entails. Traditional Common Law has some special rules designed to deal chiefly (but usually not exclusively) with posted offers and acceptances.

The Offeror is Master of the Offer. As Restatement 2d § 30(1) states, "An offer may invite or require acceptance to be made by an affirmative answer in words, or by performing or refraining from performing a specified act, or may empower the offeree to make a selection of terms in his acceptance." What this means is that the offeror can control the form in which acceptance occurs. Illustration 1 to § 30 has A sending a letter to B "stating the terms of a proposed contract. At the end he writes, 'You can accept this offer only by signing on the dotted line below my own signature.' B replies by telegram, 'I accept your offer.' There is no contract." It is irrelevant that A may actually be indifferent to the mode of communication.

In most cases, in fact, the offeror does not expressly require a particular mode of acceptance. When this happens, some older legal rules tried to limit the proper modes of acceptance, but the UCC took a different tack; § 2–206(1): "Unless otherwise unambiguously indicated by the language or circumstances (a) an offer to make a contract shall be construed as inviting acceptance in any manner and by any medium reasonable in the circumstances; . . . " Restatement 2d § 30(2) follows this language virtually verbatim.

This rule is not confined to contracts concluded by writings, of course, but it is particularly appropriate for them, since an offeror has a strong interest in being able to recognize an acceptance when it occurs.

The Mailbox Rule. Ordinarily, posted communications take effect when they reach the person for whom they are destined. This includes, for instance, offers, rejections, and revocations of offers. Acceptances, however, are different. Here Common Law follows the rule in *Adams v. Lindsell*, 106 Eng. Rep. 250 (K.B. 1818), whereby an acceptance becomes effective when and where it is dispatched. As Restatement 2d § 63 puts it, "Unless the offer provides otherwise, (a) an acceptance made in a manner and by a medium invited by an offer is operative and completes the manifestation of mutual assent as soon as put out of the offeree's possession, without regard to whether it ever reaches the offeror; . . . " Dispatch of a valid acceptance therefore creates a contract immediately, with nothing further. (Note, however, two exceptions. Restatement 2d § 63(b) makes an acceptance under an option contract effective only upon receipt. CISG art. 18(2), for international sale of goods between merchants, with some qualification follows the Civil Law rule that acceptance of an offer is effective upon receipt. See Konrad Zweigert and Hein Kötz, Introduction to Comparative Law 358–359 (Tony Weir trans.; 3rd ed. 1998).)

The usual modern rationale for the mailbox rule is that, since both parties are now taken as committed, the rule prevents the offeror from speculating during the period after acceptance is mailed and before it arrives; but a better explanation may be just that some dispositive rule is needed, and this rule, although somewhat counterintuitive, is not demonstrably inferior to alternatives.

A large number of legal problems flowing from the mailbox rule can occasionally be significant even today. Here are some illustrations.

1. The Overtaking Rejection. By letter, A offers to sell B a drill-press for $5,000. B posts acceptance and then, before A receives this letter, B telephones to reject the offer. Is the rejection effective? What if, relying on the rejection, A sells to a third party before receiving B's acceptance?

2. The Overtaking Acceptance. By letter, A offers to sell B a racehorse for $3,000. B sends A a letter rejecting the offer, but then, before A receives the rejection, B posts an acceptance. Is B's acceptance effective? Does it matter whether A receives the rejection before the acceptance? Whether A relies on the rejection?

3. The Overtaking Revocation. Corporation A sends corporation B a letter offering to sell an airplane for $10,000,000. A short time later, A mails a revocation of its offer; but before B receives A's revocation, it mails its acceptance. Is the acceptance effective?

Note, finally, that the offeror, as master of the offer, can require receipt before an acceptance becomes effective. Also, the offeree, in dispatching an acceptance, is expected to take normal precautions to assure that the letter reaches its destination.

Silence as Acceptance. It is commonly said, even by courts, that offers cannot be accepted by silence (an acceptance is "a *manifestation* of assent," Restatement 2d § 50(1) (emphasis added)), and also that although the offeror is master of the offer, he or she cannot frame the offer so as to make a contract binding unless the offeree expressly rejects the offer. Although this may be generally true, under certain exceptional circumstances the offeree may have a duty to respond; the most common situation is when the parties' previous dealings create a reasonable expectation that the offeree will give notice of any intention not to accept. See Restatement 2d § 69.

This issue is of considerable importance in relation to modern standard form contracts.

Problem 3–4: An Exchange of E-Mails

Having been out of town for 10 days, White returned to Ann Arbor on June 17, 2004 and commenced to go through approximately 75 e-mails that had accumulated. Early in the list was a June 13 e-mail from an enterprising Columbia student, Ben Trachtenberg (in the fall of 2004 White was to be a visiting professor at Columbia).

Date: **Sun, 13 Jun 2004, 194933**
From: Ben Trachtenberg <blt2006@columbia.edu>
To: jjwhite@umich.edu
Subject: Contracts at Columbia

Professor White

My name is Ben Trachtenberg, and I'm in the Columbia Law School class of 2005. I'm writing to see if you might need a teaching assistant for your fall Contracts course. I did pretty well in that class, winning the Class of 1912 Prize given to the 1L "most proficient" in Contracts.

Because I'm considering pursuing a career in legal scholarship, I'm excited to try my hand at teaching while still in law school.

Attached please find a resume and transcript. You can reach me at this e-mail address and at the phone number and address listed on my resume. Please let me know if there is any more information I can provide.

White responded:

Date: **Thu, 17 Jun 2004, 072614**
To: Ben Trachtenberg <blt2006@columbia.edu>
From: "James J. White" <jjwhite@umich.edu>
Subject: Re: Contracts at Columbia

Ben, barring some evidence that you have been convicted of a felony (other than service on a student college newspaper), you're hired. I assume that Columbia has a fund on which I can draw for research assistance, but we can work that out. I will be at Columbia the day after Labor Day. I look forward to seeing you then or in the following couple of days. jjw

Two minutes and a dozen e-mails later, White came upon a second e-mail that Ben had sent on June 14.

Date: **Mon, 14 Jun 2004, 084108**
From: Ben Trachtenberg <blt2006@columbia.edu>
To: jjwhite@umich.edu
Subject: Contracts at Columbia Update

I feel foolish doing this, but I must withdraw my offer to work as a TA for you this fall. It turns out that my own Contracts professor, Mel Eisenberg, has decided to have TAs this year and has invited me to be one. In the past he has not used TAs, so I did not anticipate this turn of events. I apologize for the confusion.

Good luck at Columbia this fall. If you do end up in the market for TAs, I'd be happy to recommend a candidate or two.

White responded:

Date: **Thu, 17 Jun 2004, 072831**
To: Ben Trachtenberg <blt2006@columbia.edu>
From: "James J. White" <jjwhite@umich.edu>
Subject: Re: Contracts at Columbia Update

Ben, since I responded before your withdrawal was received by me, we might just have a contract that you will have to perform. Mel surely needs no more than eight hours a day and that leaves at least ten for me. jjw

Does Ben have a contract to work for White or did he successfully revoke his offer before White's acceptance?

MID-SOUTH PACKERS, INC. v. SHONEY'S, INC.

United States Court of Appeals, Fifth Circuit, 1985.
761 F.2d 1117.

PER CURIAM: This diversity action on a Mississippi contract is before us following the district court's entry of summary judgment in favor of plaintiff Mid-South Packers, Inc., (Mid-South) and against defendant Shoney's, Inc., (Shoney's). We affirm.

I.

The facts, as viewed in the light most favorable to Shoney's, are as follows. In the spring of 1982, Mid-South and Shoney's engaged in negotiations for the sale by Mid-South to Shoney's of various pork products including bacon and ham. A business meeting was held between representatives of the two companies on April 17, 1982, at the offices of Mid-South in Tupelo, Mississippi. The discussion concerned prices and terms at which Mid-South could supply bacon and ham to Shoney's. At this meeting, Mid-South submitted a letter styled "Proposal" that set forth prices and terms at which Mid-South would supply Shoney's with various types of meat. The letter also provided that Shoney's would be informed forty-five days prior to any adjustment in price. The letter contained neither quantity nor durational terms. Shoney's expressed neither assent to nor rejection of the prices outlined in the letter. Shoney's estimated its needs from Mid-South at 80,000 pounds of meat per week. The legal effect of the letter proposal is the center of the controversy.

In July 1982, Shoney's began purchasing goods from Mid-South. The transactions were initiated by Shoney's, either through purchase orders or through telephone calls. On the day following each shipment, Mid-South sent invoices to Shoney's containing additional provisions for payment of both fifteen percent per annum interest on accounts not paid within seven days and reasonable collection costs, including attorney's fees. Shoney's bought vast quantities of bacon from Mid-South until August 12, 1982. On that date, Mid-South informed Shoney's at a meeting of their representatives that the price for future orders of bacon would be raised by $0.10 per pound, due to a previous error in computation by Mid-South. Shoney's objected to the price modification, apparently in reliance on the forty-five day notice provision contained in the disputed letter proposal. After negotiations, Mid-South agreed to increase the price by only $0.07 per pound. Shoney's neither agreed nor refused to purchase at the new price. Mid-South's new proposal was never reduced to writing.

On the first Shoney's purchase order sent after the August 12 meeting, Shoney's requested shipment at the old lower price. When Mid-South received the purchase order its representative, Morris Ates, called Shoney's representative, Ray Harmon, and advised Harmon that Mid-South would only deliver at the new higher price. The uncontradicted testimony of Ates is that Harmon told Ates to ship the bacon and to note the higher price on Shoney's purchase order. The bacon was shipped, and an invoice at the new price followed as did Shoney's payment, also at the new price.

From August 18 until October 5, 1982, Shoney's placed numerous orders for goods, including bacon, with Mid-South. Some if not all of these orders involved telephone conversations between representatives of the two companies, at which time Mid-South again quoted its increased selling price. The telephone conversations were followed by written purchase orders from Shoney's which quoted both the new price from Mid-South and a price computed at the original amount of $0.07 less per pound. In all cases, the orders were filled by Mid-South and invoiced at the new price. These invoices also included the additional terms providing for interest on delinquent accounts and reasonable collection costs. Shoney's paid Mid-South's quoted prices in all instances except the final order. On the final order before Shoney's began purchasing from another supplier, Shoney's offset the amount due on the invoice by $26,208, the amount allegedly overcharged on prior orders as a result of the $0.07 price increase.

Mid-South then brought this action to recover the amount offset plus interest and reasonable collection costs, including attorney's fees, as provided in the invoices. Shoney's admits that it owes $8,064.00 of the offset to Mid-South, inasmuch as this amount is attributable to orders placed after the expiration of the forty-five day notice period which, Shoney's contends, commenced on August 12 when Mid-South asked for the price increase.

II.

Shoney's contends that it accepted the proposal of Mid-South to supply it meat by placing orders with Mid-South, thereby forming a binding contract between the parties. Shoney's characterizes the contract as a "requirements contract" and asserts that the quantity term under the contract was that amount it reasonably and in good faith required. Accordingly, Shoney's argues that the notice provision contained in the letter proposal contractually bound Mid-South to notify Shoney's forty-five days before increasing its prices.

Mid-South asserts that the proposal was at most a "firm offer." Mid-South argues that under Miss.Code Ann. § 75–2–205 (1972), Uniform Commercial Code § 2–205, (hereinafter referred to as U.C.C. or the Code), a firm offer is irrevocable despite a lack of consideration "during the time stated or if no time is stated for a reasonable time; but in no event may such period of irrevocability exceed three (3) months." Thus, Mid-South contends that under any construction of the document, the offer must have expired three months after April 17, 1982, the date of the letter proposal, or on approximately July 17, 1982; therefore, it asserts the right on August 12, 1982, to increase the selling price without notice.

The district court, on consideration of cross summary judgment motions, adopted Mid-South's theory, holding that no long-term requirements contract was created and that each purchase order constituted a separate contract for the amount stated at the price required by Mid-South.

Requirements contracts are recognized in Mississippi and are not void for indefiniteness. Miss.Code Ann. § 75–2–306(1). However, an essential element of a requirements contract is the promise of the buyer to purchase exclusively from the seller either the buyer's entire requirements or up to a specified amount.... 1 S. Williston, Contracts § 104A, at 406–07 (3d ed. 1957); 1A A. Corbin, Contracts § 157, at 48–49 (2d ed. 1963 & Supp.1971); Restatement (Second) of Contracts § 77 comment d, illustration 8 (1981). Absent such a commitment, the requirements contract fails for want of consideration.... 1 S. Williston, Contracts § 105A, at 423; 1A A. Corbin, Contracts § 152 at 8–10, § 157 at 40–41; Restatement (Second) of Contracts §§ 71, 79 comment F.

Ray Harmon, Shoney's agent in the transaction, maintained that Shoney's at all times had the right to purchase goods from suppliers other than Mid–South, that Shoney's continued to purchase from Mid-South because it was satisfied with its service and the quality of its goods, and that the purchase orders sent by Shoney's to Mid-South beginning in July 1982 "would have been the only commitment (Shoney's) would have made." Mid-South agrees that Shoney's had the right to change suppliers. Thus, by Shoney's own admission, no requirements contract could have arisen from the April 17 letter proposal and the meeting at which it was discussed.

Under the Code, the letter proposal and surrounding negotiations constituted, at most, a "firm offer" which was irrevocable, without consideration, only for a period of three months commencing on April 17 and ending on July 17, 1982. Miss.Code Ann. § 75–2–205. Thus, Mid–South had the right, after July 17, to raise its offered price as it did and the district court was correct in so holding.

The district court was also correct in holding that each purchase order stood on its own as a contract between Shoney's and Mid-South. More specifically, Mid-South's letter proposal was its offer in the sense that it was a promise to sell at the listed prices, justifying Shoney's in understanding that its assent, i.e., its purchase orders or telephone calls, would close the bargain.... 1 A. Corbin, Contracts § 11 at 25 (1963); 1 S. Williston, Contracts § 24A (3d ed. 1957); Restatement (Second) of Contracts § 24 (1981) (offer as promise). Thus, each time Shoney's manifested its assent, in telephone calls or purchase orders to Mid-South, a new and independent contract between the parties was created. See ... 1A A. Corbin, Contracts § 157 at 40–46 (where the theory here espoused is discussed at length).

Mid-South's offer, held open in its discretion at least after July 17, was properly revoked and replaced by the offer of a seven-cent price increase at the August 12 meeting. Cf. 1A A. Corbin § 157 at 46. Shoney's accepted this new offer for the first time on August 18 when Harmon, having been informed by Ates that Mid-South would not sell except at the new price, ordered shipment. Thereafter, Shoney's created separate contracts and obligated itself to pay the new price each time it mailed purchase orders with that price noted on them. Shoney's practice of also noting the old price on the purchase orders had no contractual significance since Harmon admitted that the practice was "a tracking procedure" used by Shoney's internally in order to determine the difference between the old price and the new. Ates' testimony is uncontradicted that Harmon also told him this.

In addition, Harmon admitted that Shoney's ordered at and paid the new price with the intention of causing Mid-South to believe that Shoney's had accepted the new price so that the shipments would continue; and Mid-South attached precisely that significance to Shoney's conduct. Shoney's secretly harbored intent to later deduct the difference between the old and new price could not bind Mid-South. See, e.g., *Hotchkiss v. National City Bank*, 200 Fed. 287, 293 (S.D.N.Y.1911) (Hand, J.), aff'd 231 U.S. 50, 34 S.Ct. 20, 58 L.Ed. 115 (1913) (only manifested assent is binding); Restatement (Second) of Contracts §§ 20(2)(a), 201(2)(a) (1981) (same). Conduct may bind a party to a contract if it "show[s] agreement." Miss.Code Ann. § 75–2–204(1); § 75–2–207(3). "Agreement" of the parties must be manifested either in language or conduct in the circumstances. Miss.Code Ann. § 75–1–201(3). The only manifestations Shoney's made were those consistent with assent to Mid-South's new offer. Finally, the parties' "course of performance" is consistent only with Mid-South's expressed offer and Shoney's expressed acceptance of the new price. Miss.Code Ann. § 75–1–205(3)-(4); cf. Miss.Code Ann. § 75–2–202(a).

Shoney's remedy under the circumstances was either to reserve whatever right it might have had to the old price by sending its purchase orders with an "explicit reservation," Miss.Code Ann. § 75–1–207, or to find a supplier who would sell at an acceptable price. No rational theory of the law of contracts could permit Shoney's to manifest acceptance of Mid-South's new offer, thus inducing performance, and then revoke that acceptance and demand compliance with the terms of the prior, withdrawn offer. See Miss.Code Ann. § 75–2–606(1)(b); § 75–2–607(1). Hence, the entire $26,208 offset by Shoney's is due and owing Mid-South and the district court's judgment, to this extent, was proper.... [Eds.: Discussion of other issues is omitted.]

Notes and Discussion

1. The Revocability of Offers; Options. Ordinarily the power to accept an offer "is terminated at the time specified in the offer, or, if no time is specified, at the end of a reasonable time." Restatement 2d § 41(1). But can the offeror withdraw it in the meantime? Usually, yes; see § 42. Indeed, even if the offeree "acquires reliable information" that the offeror has taken "definite action inconsistent with an intention to enter into the proposed contract," the offeree's power of acceptance is terminated; see § 43. The classic case is *Dickinson v. Dodds*, 2 Ch. D. 463 (Ch. App. 1876), where the offeree futilely attempted to accept after he had been told by the offeror's agent that the offer was no longer valid.

Why this rule? In Common Law, the standard explanation is that since the offeror's promise to keep the offer open is not supported by consideration, it may be revoked at will, the major limitation being that the offeree retains the right to accept until directly or indirectly informed of the revocation. A sharp line is drawn between ordinary offers (which are unsupported by consideration and can be withdrawn at will) and so-called option contracts: offers that are accompanied by an independent promise to keep the offer open, where this promise is supported by consideration. See Restatement 2d § 25.

Restatement 2d § 87(1)(a) makes an offer binding as an option contract if it 1) "is in writing and signed by the offeror"; 2) "*recites* a purported consideration for the making of the offer"; and 3) "proposes an exchange on fair terms within a reasonable time." (Emphasis added.) No actual payment of the consideration is required. Case law offers some support for this Restatement position; e.g., *Real Estate Co. of Pittsburgh v. Rudolph*, 301 Pa. 502, 153 A. 438 (1930) (offeror who acknowledges receipt of consideration is estopped from denying receipt). But most courts hold that there must be consideration for the option, and that the consideration must be paid; see *Bd. of Control of E. Mich. Univ. v. Burgess*, in Chapter 2.A.

Although traditional Common Law applies the ordinary consideration analysis to option contracts, in one respect this analysis is awkward. When a valid option contract exists, the offeree is entitled to accept it during the option period, and this right is, in effect, specifically enforced against the offeror, contrary to the usual contract rule; therefore the offeror cannot revoke (thereby breaching the option contract) in the hope of paying only monetary damages for lost expectation on the value of the option. Furthermore, until the term of the option expires, does the offeree retain the right to accept it even after having first rejected it? Most courts have held that an option contract is not automatically terminated by rejection or by a counter-offer, unless the offeror then justifiably relies. See, e.g., *Ryder v. Wescoat*, 535 S.W.2d 269 (Mo. Ct. App. 1976); *Humble Oil & Refining Co. v. Westside Investment Corp.*, 428 S.W.2d 92 (Tex. 1968); Restatement 2d § 37.

2. **Firm Offers.** The formalism of traditional Common Law has led to much inconvenience. The UCC takes a more forthright approach in § 2–205, which applies only to a merchant who in a signed writing makes an offer and assures that it will be held open. Such an offer is "not revocable, for lack of consideration, during the time stated or if no time is stated for a reasonable time, but in no event may such period of irrevocability exceed three months ... " What balance of considerations is reflected in this wording? The section goes on to note that if the offeror's assurance is on the offeree's form, it "must be separately signed by the offeror."

Mid-South argued that its April 17 proposal "was *at most* a 'firm offer.' " (Emphasis added.) Is it clear that the proposal should be regarded as an offer at all, much less a firm offer? Why should the proposal be regarded as different from an advertisement or a price quotation?

Assuming Mid-South's proposal was at least an offer, what more is required in order to make it a firm offer under the UCC? For example, what if an offer that otherwise meets the requirements of § 2–205 states the date at which it will end, but does not also give assurance that the offer will be irrevocable until that date? Will a court imply irrevocability? See *Ivey's Plumbing & Elec. Co. v. Petrochem Maint., Inc.*, 463 F.Supp. 543 (N.D. Miss. 1978) (no). If Mid-South's proposal was a firm offer, could the Court have been more creative in handling the three-month limit from § 2–205?

For offers in the international sale of goods between merchants, the CISG art. 16(2) goes further than the UCC: "[A]n offer cannot be revoked: (a) if it indicates, whether by stating a fixed time for acceptance or otherwise, that it is irrevocable; . . . " As it appears, there is no time limit, nor does the CISG require a signed record of the offer.

Is a firm offer terminated if the offeree rejects it?

Note: Contracts Accepted by the Offeree's Performance

The offeror, as master of the offer, can mandate that an offer is accepted not by a promise of future performance, but rather by some specified act. In *Hamer v. Sidway*, for instance, Uncle William promised his nephew Willie $5,000 if the boy abstained from certain forms of vice until he reached age 21. It seems very doubtful that Uncle William was interested in obtaining a promise of good conduct from Willie; rather, what he was interested in was Willie's actions (or, more exactly, his forbearance from actions), i.e., that Willie live in the manner Uncle William had envisaged. If, before age 21, Willie had begun smoking like a chimney, he would not have been violating a contractual duty not to smoke. He would just have made himself ineligible for the $5,000. This contract can be compared to the offer of a reward for the capture of a bank robber or the return of a pet, except that such an offer is made to the entire world, not to a single person; but what is bargained for is a specific act, which recipients of the offer may or may not choose to carry out. See Restatement 2d § 30.

Although the Second Restatement avoids this terminology, such contracts are traditionally described as "unilateral contracts," in the sense that, so long as the offer remains open and until it is accepted, the offeror is bound to it, but the offeree is not obligated. Contracts of this type raise certain unusual problems, which the Restatement attempts to address.

Acceptance by Part Performance. Suppose that Willie had followed Uncle William's prescriptions from age 18 to age 20, and then, two weeks before his twenty-first birthday, Uncle William had suddenly withdrawn the offer. It seems unfair that Willie have no recourse. This problem is met by Restatement 2d § 45(1), which states that when an offer clearly envisages a unilateral contract, "an option contract is created when the offeree tenders or begins the invited performance or tenders a beginning of it." The option lies with the offeree, who can choose whether or not to complete the performance; but the promise in the offer is not enforceable until the offeree has finished performance. Id. (2).

Note that only actual performance triggers § 45. Suppose that Harriet offers a million dollars to the first person who crosses the North Pole in a balloon, and that Gwen decides to try for this reward. She would obviously need substantial preparations for the journey, all made in reliance on Harriet's offer: purchase of a balloon and other supplies, assemblage of a ground team, and so on. But these preparation costs are not enough. Not until she actually is airborne on the Arctic trip does Harriet's offer become irrevocable as to Gwen.

The consequence of § 45 is that, for a certain time, one party is bound to the offer while the other is not—a lack of symmetry that is no longer regarded as troubling. To this extent, § 45 undermines the contract/no contract dichotomy.

Offers Ambiguous As to Manner of Acceptance. Uncle William's promise is fairly clearly unilateral, but many offers are not. Traditionally, courts had tried to divide all contracts into those accepted by performance (unilateral) and those accepted by a return promise (bilateral); but today this effort has largely been abandoned, since even though offerors can specify the manner of acceptance more closely, most seem indifferent to the issue.

Take, for example, a firm that sends an order for a machine to a seller company, but does not specify the manner of acceptance. How should the seller respond? By sending a confirmation that, essentially, promises performance, or by sending the machine itself? Under many circumstances the buyer may not care. UCC § 2–206(1) provides that: "Unless otherwise unambiguously indicated by the language or circumstances (a) an offer to make a contract shall be construed as inviting acceptance in any manner and by any medium reasonable in the circumstances; ... " Subsection (b) goes on to state specifically that an offer to buy goods, if it is ambiguous, can be accepted "either by a prompt promise to ship or by the prompt or current shipment of conforming or non-conforming goods ... "[4]

The UCC language is picked up by Restatement 2d § 30, and also by § 32, which provides that: "In case of doubt an offer is interpreted as inviting the offeree to accept either by promising to perform what the offer requests or by rendering the performance, as the offeree chooses." Restatement 2d § 62 completes the picture: When an offer is ambiguous as to whether a promise or a performance constitutes acceptance, not only is the beginning or tender of performance "an acceptance by performance," but this acceptance "operates as a promise to render complete performance."

Thus, in the case of an offer that invites acceptance by performance only, the offeree who starts performance has the option not to continue; but when the offer is ambiguous as to the manner of acceptance, the offeree who starts performance becomes legally obliged to complete it.

Issues related to unilateral contracts figure also in the *Arango* case just below.

ARANGO CONSTRUCTION CO. v. SUCCESS ROOFING, INC.

Court of Appeals of Washington, 1986.
730 P.2d 720, 46 Wash.App. 314.

COLEMAN, J. Arango Construction Co., a general contractor, appeals a denial of its motion for reconsideration after the trial court

4. This subsection is subject to the proviso that shipment of non-conforming goods is not an acceptance "if the seller seasonably notifies the buyer that the shipment is offered only as an accommodation to the buyer." UCC § 2–206(1)(b). An example of how this proviso is applied is *Corinthian Pharmaceutical Systems, Inc. v. Lederle Laboratories*, 724 F.Supp. 605 (S.D. Ind. 1989), where Lederle, having learned of an impending price increase in a Corinthian drug, placed a huge order at the previous price. Corinthian shipped a small amount at that price, but indicated that future orders would be at the new price. Because the shipment was less than ordered, the goods were non-conforming, and Corinthian was not accepting Lederle's offer.

granted summary judgment to Success Roofing, Inc., the defendant subcontractor, in a claim for breach of contract. We reverse and remand for entry of judgment in favor of Arango Construction Co.

On December 6, 1983, Success Roofing, Inc. submitted a telephone bid to Arango Construction Co. to install a "built-up" roof on additions to the tactical equipment shops at Fort Lewis, Washington. The bid had been prepared by Estimates, Inc. in the employ of Success. The bid included work in only two sections of the project (7A and 7B) and amounted to $34,659. On December 6, Arango included the Success bid in its prime bid to the United States Army Corps of Engineers for the Fort Lewis project. The Army Corps of Engineers postponed the bid opening until December 21, 1983. On December 8, 1983, Arango informed Success of this delay and asked that their bid be confirmed as accurate and current. Success confirmed the bid made for sections 7A and 7B at $34,659.

Arango had received another bid for sections 7A and 7B of $38,500 from Tin Benders, but that bid was expressly contingent on the award to that subcontractor of sections 7C, 7E, and 7F as well. Arango chose to use the Success bid for 7A and 7B with a bid for work on 7C, 7E, and 7F from Cleo Roofing because these combined subcontracting bids made Arango's bid the lowest price for the roofing work. Thus, Arango resubmitted its prime bid and the bids were opened on December 21, 1983.

On January 12, 1984, the Corps of Engineers awarded the Fort Lewis contract to Arango. Arango notified Success on January 30, 1984 by sending its standard subcontract form for signature. On February 6, 1984, Cleo Roofing's subcontract was fully executed. Upon receipt of Arango's contract, Success requested and received a set of prints and specifications for the project. In reviewing the plans and the bid that had been developed for Success by Estimates, Inc., Success discovered an error in the contract bid amount. The bid suggested by Estimates, Inc. for Success was 50 percent less than it should have been because Estimates, Inc. had failed to note that the drawings and specifications they used to compute the bid were reduced 50 percent. It is undisputed that this error was made by Estimates, Inc. After confirming the mistake with Estimates, Inc., Success phoned Arango on February 13, 1984, informed Arango of the error, and stated that they would not perform at the original bid price. On February 16, 1984, Success wrote Arango, withdrawing its original bid and explaining its error. On May 7, 1984, because Success refused to perform, Arango awarded the contract for sections 7A and 7B to Cleo Roofing (the contractor that was already committed to do the work on sections 7C, 7E, and 7F). The price at which Cleo agreed to perform the work on the two sections was $54,733.

On April 30, 1984, Arango filed this action for breach of contract against Success. On November 5, 1984, Arango filed a motion for summary judgment based on the doctrine of promissory estoppel. Success then moved to add Estimates, Inc. as a third party defendant in the action and filed a cross motion for summary judgment based on application of the Uniform Commercial Code, article 2 statute of frauds, RCW 62A.2–201. The trial court held that the statute of frauds provision (RCW 62A.2–201) applied, rendering the oral bid unenforceable. Arango's complaint was dismissed with prejudice. Following denial of Arango's motion for reconsideration, this appeal was timely filed.

We first determine whether the provisions of RCW 62A.2–201 apply in this case.[5]

Arango contends that since this is not a contract for goods, it is not subject to the provisions of article 2 of the U.C.C. The scope of article 2 is described in RCW 62A.2–102: "Unless the context otherwise requires, this Article applies to transactions in goods; it does not apply to any transaction which although in the form of an unconditional contract to sell or present sale is intended to operate only as a security transaction nor does this Article impair or repeal any statute regulating sales to consumers, farmers or other specified classes of buyers." RCW 62A.2–102.

The comments to RCW 62A.2–102 indicate that construction contracts are not within the scope of this statute: "This section rephrases the coverage stated in USA 75 (RCW 63.04.750), implicitly continuing exclusion of construction, service and real property transactions." RCWA 62A.2–102, at 95.

In interpreting this statute, Washington courts have held in accordance with the comment. In *Crystal Rec., Inc. v. Seattle Ass'n of Credit Men*, 34 Wash.2d 553, 209 P.2d 358 (1949), the court stated that the Uniform Sales Act (precursor of RCW 62A.2) did not apply to a contract for work, labor, and materials: "[W]e must first determine whether the agreement was a contract for the sale of goods to be manufactured or a contract for the manufacture of goods. If it be held the former, then the various provisions of the uniform sales act will apply in construing this contract. If it be held the latter, then it is in the nature of the common-law contract for work, labor, and materials, and the uniform sales act will not be applicable. In such a case, we must interpret the agreement according to the general principles of the law of contracts." *Crystal*, at 558, 209 P.2d 358.

The principle that contracts for work, labor, and materials are governed by common law principles of contract, while contracts for goods are governed by the Uniform Sales Act, was again stated in *Whatcom Builders Supply Co. v. H.D. Fowler, Inc.*, 1 Wash.App. 665, 463 P.2d 232

5. [Eds.: The UCC Statute of Frauds, § 2–201, provides, although with many qualifications, that "a contract for the sale of goods for the price of $500 or more is not enforceable by way of action or defense unless there is some writing sufficient to indicate that a contract for sale has been made between the parties and signed by the party against whom enforcement is sought or by his authorized agent or broker." § 2–201(1). The UCC Statute of Frauds is further discussed in Section F below. In order to determine whether it applied, the trial judge first had to determine whether or not the transaction between Arango and Success was a sale of goods—an important issue in itself.]

(1969). There, Whatcom Builders had a construction contract with the City of Blaine to construct a sewage treatment plant. Whatcom also had a subcontract with Fowler to supply a pump for the plant. *Whatcom*, at 666, 463 P.2d 232. The court held that the Whatcom/Fowler contract was a contract for the sale of goods to be manufactured; therefore, that contract was within the scope of the Uniform Sales Act. The Whatcom/Blaine contract, however, was a contract for work, labor, and materials. Therefore, the general principles of contract law, not the Uniform Sales Act, applied to that contract. *Whatcom*, at 668, 463 P.2d 232....

The Success contract is not a contract for materials only; it is a construction contract for work, labor, and materials. Therefore, RCW 62A.2 does not apply, and RCW 62A.2–201 does not govern in this case.

Success further contends that there was no meeting of the minds on the terms of the contract, so there was no contract. Success states that the terms of the standard form contract it received from Arango had not been discussed and were not agreed upon. Success's examples of terms in dispute are of sections that require submission of disputes to arbitration, that include an attorney's fees clause, and that waive contractor responsibility for the conduct of its officers or agents prior to execution of the contract. The only issue presented by this case, however, is the enforceability of the oral bid. The letter of withdrawal sent by Success to Arango on February 16, 1984 states that the only term in dispute was the price, due to an error in computing the bid. The evidence indicates that the oral bid was given; Success and Arango believed it to be correct; Arango used that bid in its prime bid; Arango then accepted the bid when it was granted the contract and sent Success a standard form contract including that bid amount. Upon receipt of the contract form, Success determined that the bid amount was 50 percent less than it should have been. Success then withdrew its original bid and did not make an offer or contest the contract terms. Success's argument that contract terms were in dispute is without merit.

Success also alleges that the failure of a condition precedent rendered the bid unenforceable. Success argues that its bid to Arango was conditioned upon a written confirmation. Since its bid was never confirmed in writing, there was no contract. Further, it posits that oral subcontractor bids are traditionally so conditioned. Success then cites *Corbit v. J.I. Case Co.*, 70 Wash.2d 522, 539–540, 424 P.2d 290 (1967), for the proposition that a conditioned contract is unenforceable until that condition is met.

The *Corbit* case, however, did not involve a construction bid, but a contract for the execution of a deed conditioned upon payment. In contract law, construction bidding is treated as a unique category. Since construction bidding deadlines make the drafting of written agreements impossible, contractors must rely on oral bids. Therefore, the courts consider the subcontractor's oral bid an irrevocable offer until the general contractor has been awarded the prime contract; then the courts apply promissory estoppel to ensure that the subcontractor does not raise the bid.

This concept was explained in J. Feinman, Promissory Estoppel and Judicial Method, 97 Harv.L.Rev. 678 (1984). "A recurrent example of the flexible approach to promise is found in the courts' treatment of construction bidding cases, which have repeatedly generated important promissory estoppel decisions. In the typical case, a general contractor preparing to bid on a construction project receives bids on parts of the job from subcontractors and suppliers. The general then prepares its own bid on the basis of the lowest reliable subcontract bids. Subcontractors occasionally miscalculate, in part because they often compute their bids and telephone them to the general only hours before the general's bid is due. A subcontractor may also intentionally submit a low bid in the hope of receiving the contract and renegotiating the price. Conflict typically arises when, after the general has calculated and submitted its own bid and won the contract, a subcontractor notifies the general that the subcontractor has made an error or an intentionally low bid and refuses to perform.

"Under traditional contract analysis, the subcontractor could withdraw with impunity, because its bid was regarded as an offer, revocable until accepted, to enter into a bilateral contract. In the leading case of *Drennan v. Star Paving Co.*, [51 Cal.2d 409, 333 P.2d 757 (1958),] however, Justice Traynor held that the business context of the bid required that promissory estoppel apply to make the subcontractor's offer irrevocable until the general contractor had an opportunity to accept after being awarded the prime contract. The general's acceptance of the subcontractor's bid then created a traditional bilateral contract, for breach of which the subcontractor was required to pay as damages the difference between its bid and the higher price the general had to pay another subcontractor to perform the work. Cases since *Drennan* have held that promissory estoppel normally binds a subcontractor to the terms of its bid. Although the subcontractor does not make an explicit promise to keep its bid open, the court infers such a promise." (Footnotes omitted.) J. Feinman at 692–94. See also Restatement of Contracts 2d § 87(2) comment e (1979).

This court has accepted the *Drennan* rationale in *Ferrer v. Taft Structurals, Inc.*, 21 Wash.App. 832, 587 P.2d 177 (1978): "This concept [promissory estoppel] applies readily to the unique situation of a subcontractor and a general contractor, as exists here. A subcontractor submits a bid to the general contractor, knowing the general cannot accept the bid as an offer immediately, but must first incorporate it into the general's offer to the prospective employer. The general contractor incorporates the bid in reliance upon the subcontractor to perform as promised, should the prospective employer accept the general's offer. Thus, the elements of predictable and justifiable reliance and change of position are satisfied. Numerous courts and authorities have opined that a subcontractor's bid upon which a general contractor relies should be deemed irrevocable for a reasonable time pursuant to the doctrine of promissory estoppel. *Drennan v. Star Paving Co.*, 51 Cal.2d 409, 333 P.2d 757 (1958).

"Thus, had Taft refused to perform following the award of the contract to Halvorson, a breach of contract action based on Taft's original bid would have been appropriate." (Citations omitted.) *Ferrer*, at 835, 587 P.2d 177.

Thus, as a matter of law, a subcontractor's bid is considered an irrevocable offer until the award of the prime contract; then, the general contractor's acceptance of the bid results in a bilateral contract. Further, there is nothing in the record to indicate that Success imposed the condition of a written confirmation on its quote. In short, the record does not support a conclusion that there was a failure to formulate an enforceable contract.

Finally, we consider Arango's contention that its motion for summary judgment should have been granted.

Arango's motion for summary judgment is based on the *Ferrer/Drennan* rationale that once a general contractor has incorporated a subcontractor's bid, he has justifiably relied and changed position. Thus, if the subcontractor refuses to perform following the award of the contract, the general contractor may recover damages under the doctrine of promissory estoppel. *Ferrer*, at 835, 587 P.2d 177.

The *Ferrer* court listed the five elements of promissory estoppel: "The prerequisites for an action based on promissory estoppel, a doctrine well recognized in this jurisdiction, have been stated as follows: '(1) A promise which (2) the promisor should reasonably expect to cause the promisee to change his position and (3) which does cause the promisee to change his position (4) justifiably relying upon the promise, in such a manner that (5) injustice can be avoided only by enforcement of the promise.' *Corbit v. J.I. Case Co.*, 70 Wn.2d 522, 539, 424 P.2d 290 (1967)." (Citation omitted.) *Ferrer,* at 834, 587 P.2d 177.

Elements (1) through (3) are met in this case. Success's bid was a promise. Success could reasonably expect that promise to cause Arango to change position by including the Success bid in Arango's prime bid. Success confirmed its bid 2 days after it was given, and Arango informed Success that it would be including that bid in its prime bid to be submitted 13 days later. Arango did include Success's bid in its prime bid, thereby changing its position.

The only element of promissory estoppel in dispute is whether Arango justifiably relied on Success's bid. Success contends that as a prudent and experienced general contractor, Arango should have known that Success's bid was too low for the job involved. To avoid Arango's summary judgment, Success had to present evidence supporting this assertion. See *Boardman v. Dorsett*, 38 Wash.App. 338, 340, 685 P.2d 615 (1984). Success, however, has submitted no evidence that Arango should have known. The only other bid found in the record was from Tin Benders. Its bid was for $38,500 for sections 7A and 7B as compared to the $34,659 bid by Success.[6] There is nothing in the record to support an inference that Arango knew or should have known that Success had made a mistake.

Success raises the ultimate cover price that Arango had to pay as evidence that Arango should have known Success's bid was in error. But this bid was received after the award of the prime contract. Arango relied on Success's bid before the award of the prime contract; so the price Arango had to pay after the prime contract was granted is not evidence of Arango's knowledge at the time it relied on Success's bid. Therefore, the cover price does not support the proposition that Arango was not justified in relying on Success's bid. On the state of this record, Arango's motion for summary judgment should have been granted.

The judgment of the trial court is reversed and the cause remanded with instruction to enter judgment in favor of Arango on its complaint for damages.

Notes and Discussion

1. **The Construction Industry.** Construction contracts typically involve at least three parties: a customer, who gives the job to a general contractor (the general), who in turn doles out pieces of the job to subcontractors (the subs). The bidding process runs first from subs to generals, and then from generals to customers. Legal problems arising out of construction contracts are frequent, chiefly because performance usually occurs over a considerable time and because more than two parties are directly involved.

In this case, how did the discord begin? Success Roofing had ample opportunity to check that its bid was accurate, but more commonly subcontractors telephone in their bids at the last possible instant. Why do they delay so long?

Success mistakenly bid $34,659 on the contract. Arango eventually paid the substitute subcontractor $54,733, although the subcontractor had earlier bid $38,500 for the same work. Should Arango have been aware of Success's error before submitting its own bid? One issue in this case is whether Success, having made a mistake, was able to retrieve its error once Arango had relied on the offer. Courts are usually unforgiving of such unilateral errors; see below, Chapter 5.A.

2. **Can an Offer Become Irrevocable If the Offeree Relies on It? *Hand v. Traynor*.** The problem that arose in this case has long been a judicial headache. The best outcome to it famously pits against one another two of the most influential twentieth-century judges: Learned Hand (2d Cir.) and Roger Traynor (Cal. S. Ct.), who had sharply different intuitions about how to handle the problem of sub-contractor bids.

The conflict between Hand and Traynor is lucidly described in *Pavel Enterprises, Inc. v. A.S. Johnson Co., Inc.*, 342 Md. 143, 152–156, 674 A.2d 521, 526–527 (Ct. App. 1996):

6. While it is true that this bid was conditioned on Tin Benders receiving the bid for sections 7C, 7E, and 7F of the project, it is nevertheless a comparable bid and without more, does not put Arango on notice that Success's bid was unusually low.

"The problem the construction bidding process poses is the determination of the precise points on the timeline that the various parties become bound to each other. The early landmark case was *James Baird Co. v. Gimbel Bros., Inc.*, 64 F.2d 344 (2d Cir. 1933). The plaintiff, James Baird Co., ['Baird'] was a general contractor from Washington, D.C., bidding to construct a government building in Harrisburg, Pennsylvania. Gimbel Bros., Inc., ['Gimbel'], the famous New York department store, sent its bid to supply linoleum to a number of bidding general contractors on December 24, and Baird received Gimbel's bid on December 28. Gimbel realized its bid was based on an incorrect computation and notified Baird of its withdrawal on December 28. The letting authority awarded Baird the job on December 30. Baird formally accepted the Gimbel bid on January 2. When Gimbel refused to perform, Baird sued for the additional cost of a substitute linoleum supplier. The Second Circuit Court of Appeals held that Gimbel's initial bid was an offer to contract and, under traditional contract law, remained open only until accepted or withdrawn. Because the offer was withdrawn before it was accepted there was no contract. Judge Learned Hand, speaking for the court, also rejected two alternative theories of the case: unilateral contract and promissory estoppel. He held that Gimbel's bid was not an offer of a unilateral contract[7] that Baird could accept by performing, i.e., submitting the bid as part of the general bid; and second, he held that the theory of promissory estoppel was limited to cases involving charitable pledges.

"Judge Hand's opinion was widely criticized, see Note, *Contracts-Promissory Estoppel*, 20 Va. L. Rev. 214 (1933) [hereinafter, 'Promissory Estoppel'] . . , but also widely influential. The effect of the *James Baird* line of cases, however, is an 'obvious injustice without relief of any description.' Promissory Estoppel, at 215. The general contractor is bound to the price submitted to the letting party, but the subcontractors are not bound, and are free to withdraw.[8]

"As one commentator described it, 'If the subcontractor revokes his bid before it is accepted by the general, any loss which results is a deduction from the general's profit and conceivably may transform overnight a profitable contract into a losing deal.' Franklin M. Schultz, *The Firm Offer Puzzle: A Study of Business Practice in the Construction Industry*, 19 U. CHI. L. REV. 237, 239 (1952).

"The unfairness of this regime to the general contractor was addressed in *Drennan v. Star Paving*, 333 P.2d 757, 51 Cal.2d 409 (1958). Like *James Baird*, the *Drennan* case arose in the context of a bid mistake.[9] Justice Traynor, writing for the Supreme Court of California, relied upon § 90 of the Restatement (First) of Contracts: 'A promise

7. A unilateral contract is a contract which is accepted, not by traditional acceptance, but by performance. 2 Williston on contracts § 6:2 (4th ed.).

8. Note that under the *Baird* line of cases, the general contractor, while bound by his offer to the letting party, is not bound to any specific subcontractor, and is free to "bid shop" prior to awarding the subcontract. . . .

9. Commentators have suggested that the very fact that many of these cases have arisen from bid mistake, an unusual subspecies, rather than from more typical cases, has distorted the legal system's understanding of these cases. . . .

which the promisor should reasonably expect to induce action or forbearance of a definite and substantial character on the part of the promisee and which does induce such action or forbearance is binding if injustice can be avoided only by enforcement of the promise.' Restatement (First) of Contracts § 90 (1932).[10]

"Justice Traynor reasoned that the subcontractor's bid contained an implied subsidiary promise not to revoke the bid. As the court stated: 'When plaintiff [, a General Contractor,] used defendant's offer in computing his own bid, he bound himself to perform in reliance on defendant's terms. Though defendant did not bargain for the use of its bid neither did defendant make it idly, indifferent to whether it would be used or not. On the contrary it is reasonable to suppose that defendant submitted its bid to obtain the subcontract. It was bound to realize the substantial possibility that its bid would be the lowest, and that it would be included by plaintiff in his bid. It was to its own interest that the contractor be awarded the general contract; the lower the subcontract bid, the lower the general contractor's bid was likely to be and the greater its chance of acceptance and hence the greater defendant's chance of getting the paving subcontract. Defendant had reason not only to expect plaintiff to rely on its bid but to want him to. Clearly defendant had a stake in plaintiff's reliance on its bid. Given this interest and the fact that plaintiff is bound by his own bid, it is only fair that plaintiff should have at least an opportunity to accept defendant's bid after the general contract has been awarded to him.' *Drennan*, 51 Cal.2d at 415, 333 P.2d at 760.

"The *Drennan* court however did not use 'promissory estoppel' as a substitute for the entire contract, as is the doctrine's usual function. Instead, the Drennan court, applying the principle of § 90, interpreted the subcontractor's bid to be irrevocable. Justice Traynor's analysis used promissory estoppel as consideration for an implied promise to keep the bid open for a reasonable time. Recovery was then predicated on traditional bilateral contract, with the sub-bid as the offer and promissory estoppel serving to replace acceptance.

"The *Drennan* decision has been very influential. Many states have adopted the reasoning used by Justice Traynor.... "

Despite Hand's defeat on this issue, his opinion in *James Baird* is well remembered for a famous dictum: "The contractors had a ready escape from their difficulty by insisting upon a contract before they used the figures; and in commercial transactions it does not in the end promote justice to seek strained interpretations in aid of those who do not protect themselves." 64 F.2d at 346. Here you see Hand's view as to the proper role of courts in dealing with commercial transactions.

Traynor took a different, far more activist stance; he wanted to use judicial decisions in order to shape not only commerce, but human interaction generally. As the Maryland Court observes, Traynor made heavy use of reliance theory, as advanced in the First Restatement § 90. But Traynor

10. This section of the Restatement has been supplanted by the Restatement (Second) of Contracts § 90(1) (1979)....

blended his reliance analysis with themes from Restatement § 45, which broadly resembles Restatement 2d § 45 ("Option Contract Created by Part Performance or Tender"). How different are these two modes of approaching the subcontractor problem? Do they involved "strained interpretations" of the underlying business relationship?

Traynor's view is explicitly endorsed in Restatement 2d § 87(2), which provides that: "An offer which the offeror should reasonably expect to induce action or forbearance of a substantial character on the part of the offeree before acceptance and which does induce such action or forbearance is binding as an option contract to the extent necessary to avoid injustice." Note that this language generally tracks § 90, but with some important differences. In discussing the construction bid situation, courts have often scouted § 87(2), and the Court in *Arango* is no exception. Why this reluctance, do you think? It is not as easy to reconcile § 87(2) with § 45, for instance. The reasoning in *Drennan* has seldom prevailed except in construction cases.

The CISG art. 16(2)(b) holds even more sweepingly than § 87(2) that an offer is irrevocable "if it was reasonable for the offeree to rely on the offer as being irrevocable and the offeree has acted in reliance on the offer." What problems would you predict in implementing this rule? The CISG rule is heavily influenced by European Civil Law, in which offers are commonly construed as firm; see Zweigert and Kötz, Introduction to Comparative Law, supra, 359–362.

3. Protecting the Subs. Under the *Drennan* line of reasoning, the general can hold the sub to its bid after relying on the bid in submitting its own bid to the customer, but the winning general is not obliged to give the contract to the sub. This may seem unfair. Here some might say that Justice Traynor's judicial activism crept up and bit him in the rear. By fearlessly proclaiming a general rule, he further weakened the position of the subcontractor, already at the mercy of a general contractor. The most common dangers are bid-shopping (using the lowest subcontractor's bid as a tool in negotiating lower bids from other subs) and bid-chopping (pressuring subs to lower their bids).

Consider the following comment on *Drennan*: "Bid shopping and peddling have long been recognized as unethical by construction trade organizations. These 'unethical,' but common practices have several detrimental results. First, as bid shopping becomes common within a particular trade, the subcontractors will pad their initial bids in order to make further reductions during post-award negotiations. This artificial inflation of subcontractor's offers makes the bid process less effective. Second, subcontractors who are forced into post-award negotiations with the general often must reduce their sub-bids in order to avoid losing the award. Thus, they will be faced with a Hobson's choice between doing the job at a loss or doing a less than adequate job. Third, bid shopping and peddling tend to increase the risk of loss of the time and money used in preparing a bid. This occurs because generals and subcontractors who engage in these practices use, without expense, the bid estimates prepared by others. Fourth, it is often impossible for a general to obtain bids far enough in advance to have sufficient time to properly prepare his own bid because of the practice, common among many subcontractors, of holding sub-bids until the last possible moment in order to avoid pre-award bid shopping by the general. Fifth, many subcontractors refuse to submit bids for jobs on which they expect bid shopping. As a result, competition is reduced, and, consequently, construction prices are increased. Sixth, any price reductions gained through the use of post-award bid shopping by the general will be of no benefit to the awarding authority, to whom these price reductions would normally accrue as a result of open competition before the award of the prime contract. Free competition in an open market is therefore perverted because of the use of post-award bid shopping." Thomas P. Lambert, *Bid Shopping and Peddling in the Subcontract Construction Industry*, 18 UCLA L. Rev. 389, 394–96 (1970) (citations omitted).

How can the sub be protected against bid-shopping and bid-chopping? In *Drennan*, Justice Traynor observed: "It bears noting that a general contractor is not free to delay acceptance after he has been awarded the general contract in the hope of getting a better price. Nor can he reopen bargaining with the subcontractor and at the same time claim a continuing right to accept the original offer." *Drennan*, 333 P.2d at 760. Big deal.

Particularly in the area of public contracting, statutes in some states provide additional protection for subs. Typical is Cal. Gov. Code §§ 4100–10, which requires generals to include the names of anticipated subcontractors in their bids and then restricts their power to change if they win.

4. Alternatives. Note that Arango and Success could have agreed that Arango's use of Success's bid would constitute acceptance, so that if Arango received the contract, it would be obliged to use Success as the subcontractor. Such agreements seem to be uncommon, however. Why?

Other possibilities are canvassed in *Loranger Construction Corp. v. E.F. Hauserman Co.*, 376 Mass. 757, 384 N.E.2d 176 (1978), an opinion written by Robert Braucher (the original Reporter for the Second Restatement). In that case, which resembled *Arango*, Judge Braucher avoided the term promissory estoppel as "tend[ing] to confusion rather than clarity," and preferred instead to use a bargain theory. As he reasoned, "review of the cases suggests that many decisions based on reliance might have been based on bargain. See Henderson, *Promissory Estoppel and Traditional Contract Doctrine*, 78 Yale L.J. 343, 368–371 (1969). Once consideration and bargain are found, there is no need to apply § 90 of the Restatement, dealing with the legal effect of reliance in the absence of consideration." *Loranger*, 384 N.E.2d at 180. Would this line of argument work in *Arango*?

C. NEGOTIATION AND CLOSURE

The ordinary "legal template" of offer and acceptance works well enough for most contracts, but is often strained when applied to complex business agreements. As Allan Farnsworth has observed, "Major contractual commitments are typically set out in a lengthy document, or in a set of documents, signed by the parties in multiple copies and exchanged more or less simultaneously at a closing. The terms are reached by negotiations, usually face-to-face over a considerable period of time and often involving corporate officers, bankers, engineers, accountants, lawyers, and others. The negotiations are a far cry from the simple bargaining envisioned by the classic rules of offer and acceptance, which evoke an image of single-issue, adversarial, zero-sum bargaining as opposed to multi-issue, problem-solving, gain-maximizing negotiation." E. Allan Farnsworth, Contracts § 3.5 at 113 (4th student ed. 2004) (footnotes omitted.)

The three cases in this section illustrate types of legal problems that typically arise during the passage from negotiating a complex contract to closing it. First, in actual cases it can be very difficult to tell when parties have moved from negotiating to closure: many issues may be "on the table," the parties may regard some of them as crucial and others as peripheral and easily settled at some later date, and they may have widely discordant impressions of the progress that they are making. Although they usually assume that their negotiations will culminate in a written document, and although each party may believe that it is not committed to the deal until the writing is fully agreed upon, in some circumstances a court may find that a contract exists even though there is not yet a definitive signed record of it. The issue here is whether the parties regard the final document as only a formality, whether instead they consider it as affording a last opportunity to decide on whether to commit, or something in between.

Second, during the course of negotiations the parties may signal their growing commitment to a bargain by preparing "intermediate documents" such as Letters of Intent, Memoranda of Agreement, and so on. These documents may describe their consensus on parts of the final contract, or on it in its entirety but without the full detail yet filled in. What is the status of such documents? If the parties seem to have reached virtual agreement on a contract, but one of them then wants to back away, can the intermediate document serve to prevent this by demonstrating a mature contractual intent? Here the objective theory of contract formation, with its emphasis not on what the parties each believe is happening but rather on what a reasonable observer would infer, can lead courts to discover the existence of a contract despite the absence of final formalities.

Finally, it is also possible that the parties, in the higher interest of obtaining a final contract, may deliberately leave certain matters unsettled, even though these matters are likely eventually to arise in the course of the contract's execution. As courts put it, the parties may include within their contract certain "agreements to agree." At one time, courts looked skeptically upon such agreements, for reasons similar to those outlined by Judge Cardozo in *Sun Printing*. Today the judicial attitude is more differentiated, and under proper circumstances courts may imply a contractual duty to negotiate in good faith on remaining differences.

It should be stressed that the parties execute many, and perhaps the vast majority, of these complex contracts without appreciable difficulty, simply relying on subsequent talks in order to solve problems as they occur. Indeed, parties may proceed into performance without having settled the issues on which they are divided. Litigation often becomes relevant only when informal processes subsequently break down; thus courts are often attempting to put Humpty Dumpty together again, without an adequate guide as to the original assembly.

SITUATION MANAGEMENT SYSTEMS, INC. v. MALOUF, INC.

Supreme Judicial Court of Massachusetts, 2000.
430 Mass. 875, 724 N.E.2d 699.

IRELAND, J. Situation Management Systems, Inc. (SMS), filed suit against Malouf, Inc., doing business as LMA, Inc. (LMA), following the dissolution of a seventeen-year business relationship. In response, LMA filed several counterclaims, including a breach of contract claim based on an oral agreement between the parties. The case was tried before a jury, which returned a verdict in favor of LMA and awarded damages of $3.8 million. SMS's motion for judgment notwithstanding the verdict, or, alternatively, a new trial or *remittitur*, was denied and SMS appealed. We granted SMS's application for direct appellate review. We conclude that there was sufficient evidence from which a jury reasonably could have found the existence of an enforceable agreement between these parties, and accordingly affirm the judgment.

In considering a motion for a judgment notwithstanding the verdict, we view the evidence in the light most favorable to the nonmoving party.... During the relevant time period, SMS was in the business of developing and selling training materials and conducting seminars and workshops on topics such as communication and negotiation skills. LMA was in a similar business, primarily using materials it purchased from SMS. LeRoy Malouf, the founder of LMA, began his career as an employee of SMS before founding LMA, and LMA was an independent agent of SMS from 1976 to 1992.

The parties had three agency contracts over the years. The terms of each were substantially the same, except that the duration of the contracts varied between two and three years. The last written contract between the parties was executed in May 1989, and had a two-year initial term beginning January 1, 1989. The contract also had a single two-year option to renew. Before the execution of the 1989 agency agreement, the parties' previous agreement had expired on July 1, 1988. During that time, LMA and SMS continued to do business together. All of the agency contracts provided that the contract would not be renewable unless LMA met a certain sales goal. LMA always met its assigned goals.

In 1989, one of the independent agents selling SMS products, The Kasten Company (Kasten), was for sale. SMS considered buying Kasten in order to retain the clients who bought SMS products, but it did not or could not meet the asking price. Malouf learned of the opportunity to purchase Kasten and had a discussion with Earl Rose, the president of SMS, about the possibility of LMA making the purchase. In early 1990, they had a second discussion about the prospective purchase. Rose encouraged the purchase during these conversations and stated that if anyone was going to buy Kasten, he preferred it to be LMA because of its long-established course of dealing with SMS. Malouf repeatedly told Rose, during their conversations and meetings, that he would need at least a five-year agreement with SMS before LMA could afford to commit to the purchase of Kasten.

On February 20, 1990, there were two meetings between LMA and SMS. In the morning, there was a meeting at LMA's offices where its marketing team discussed LMA's future projections regarding business with SMS. There was also a later meeting at Logan Airport to talk about LMA's possible purchase of Kasten. Present at that meeting were Malouf, William LeClere, executive vice-president of LMA, and Alex Moore, chairman of SMS. At the airport meeting, Malouf told Moore that LMA would not purchase Kasten without a commitment from SMS that it would enter into a long-term agreement. Moore assured Malouf of that commitment, agreeing to change the existing contract to a five-year term. Based on this statement, Malouf negotiated an agreement to purchase Kasten.

By June, 1990, LMA had not received a written contract from SMS. Malouf telephoned Rose and told him that the closing date with Kasten was approaching and that he needed confirmation that a five-year agreement was forthcoming. During that conversation, Rose expressed to Malouf his assurance of both a long-term agreement of at least five years and his "enthusiastic support" of LMA's purchase of Kasten. Immediately after the conversation with Rose, Malouf telephoned the owner of Kasten to confirm that a five-year agreement with SMS was in place and that LMA would proceed with the purchase.

In August, 1990, SMS sent a proposed renewal contract to LMA. The proposed contract contained significant changes from past contracts, including a term stating that LMA had to increase its sales of SMS products by twelve per cent every year or face termination. Negotiations regarding the new terms stretched out over many months, and in February, 1991, SMS terminated the negotiations and advised LMA that it would allow the existing contract to expire in December, 1992. Following the expiration of that contract, LMA's sales declined from $2,700,000 in 1992 to $500,000 in 1993.

Subsequent to the expiration of the contract, SMS sued LMA for payment of seminar materials and LMA filed a counterclaim for breach of contract. The parties eventually stipulated to the amount LMA owed SMS on the original claim for payment of seminar materials, and the only issue remaining at trial was LMA's breach of contract counterclaim.

At trial, an economist testifying for LMA estimated lost profits over the three-year period, 1993-1995, totaling $3,834,000. The judge instructed the jury, without objection, that in order to prove a contract, LMA had to show that it "was more probable than not" that there was an offer, an acceptance of that offer, and an agreement between LMA and SMS as to the essential elements of the contract. The jury were instructed that, while it was not necessary for LMA to show that every detail of the contract was agreed to, LMA must have shown that all the essential or material terms were agreed to before the agreement could become enforceable. The judge further instructed the jury that promises made with an "understood intention" that they were not to be binding did not create a contract; that evidence that the parties intended to execute a formal agreement is evidence that the parties did not intend to be bound until the execution of that agreement; and that agreements to agree or agreements which do not adequately specify essential terms are unenforceable. The jury returned a special verdict finding that SMS promised a five-year commitment to LMA and that LMA suffered $3.8 million in damages as a result of SMS's breach of contract.

1. Existence Of An Enforceable Agreement

SMS argues that the evidence at trial did not warrant a finding that the parties had entered into an enforceable contract because there was no "meeting of the minds"—that is, that significant, material terms were still to be negotiated.

It is axiomatic that to create an enforceable contract, there must be agreement between the parties on the material terms of that contract, and the parties must have a present intention to be bound by that agreement. See *McCarthy v. Tobin,* 429 Mass. 84, 87, 706 N.E.2d 629 (1999); *Rosenfield v. United States Trust Co.*, 290 Mass. 210, 216, 195 N.E. 323 (1935) (failure to agree on material terms may be evidence that parties do not intend to be presently bound).... It is not required that all terms of the agreement be precisely specified, and the presence of undefined or unspecified terms will not necessarily preclude the formation of a binding contract.... The parties must, however, have progressed beyond the stage of "imperfect negotiation." ...

We conclude that there was evidence introduced at trial from which a jury could reasonably determine that when either Moore or Rose assured Malouf of SMS's commitment to LMA for five years, in return for LMA's commitment to purchase Kasten, the parties created an enforceable contract on the same or substantially similar terms as their three prior agreements, even if certain terms of the agreement were yet to be negotiated.... The evidence showed that, by 1990, LMA and SMS had continuously been doing business together for fifteen years; that the terms of the parties' prior agency agreements had been substantially the same over the entire course of their business dealings; that the principals of the respective companies, Rose and Malouf, had a personal relationship in addition to their trusting business relationship; that previous agency contract negotiations between the parties had been mostly perfunctory; that the parties at one time had continued to do business together for almost one year without an executed contract; and that SMS was well aware that LMA was purchasing Kasten in reliance on the five-year commitment and with an expectation that the terms of the agency agreement would remain substantially the same. Although SMS introduced evidence to the contrary, particularly evidence that, after SMS gave the oral assurances, there were material terms yet to be negotiated, resolution of such fact questions are generally reserved for the jury, and were properly left to the jury's determination in this case. See *Gleason v. Mann*, 312 Mass. 420, 423, 45 N.E.2d 280 (1942), and cases cited (where existence and terms of agreement rested on oral evidence, it is for jury to determine existence of agreement and its provisions); ...

SMS further argues that the oral agreement was not binding because the parties intended to execute a written contract. While it is true that the parties' intention to execute a final written agreement "justifies a strong inference that the parties do not intend to be bound" until the agreement is executed, it is also true that if "all the material terms ... have been agreed upon, it may be inferred that the writing to be drafted and delivered is a mere memorial of the contract." *Rosenfield v. United States Trust Co.*, supra at 216. See *Kilham v. O'Connell*, 315 Mass. 721, 724–725, 54 N.E.2d 181 (1944) (where jury could find sufficient evidence that oral contract existed, parties' intention to memorialize contract in writing did not defeat existence of contract). Here, there was sufficient evidence to support either inference. The jury were therefore warranted in reaching their verdict.[11]

2. Measure Of Damages

SMS also argues that the damage award was improper because (1) it should have been limited to the amount LMA paid for Kasten; and (2) the amount of the award was erroneously based on LMA's gross revenue instead of net revenue.

The usual rule for damages in a breach of contract case is that the injured party should be put in the position they would have been in had the contact been performed.... An award of "expectancy" damages may include lost profits. As such, the jury were warranted in awarding lost profits to LMA. Further, we find nothing in the record to suggest that the damage award was based on gross revenue rather than net revenue. SMS did not challenge the expert testimony.

11. SMS also argues, citing *Rhode Island Hosp. Trust Nat'l Bank v. Varadian*, 419 Mass. 841, 647 N.E.2d 1174 (1995), that LMA cannot recover under a reliance theory because, to the extent it relied on SMS's verbal commitments to a five-year relationship, such reliance was unreasonable. In that case, we determined that a bank's oral promise to provide a multi-million dollar construction loan did not create an enforceable agreement. See id. at 850. We concluded that any reliance on the bank's oral commitment to provide the loan was unreasonable as a matter of law, because the jury had specifically found that both the bank and the intended loan recipient intended only to be bound by a written agreement. See id. at 842–843, 850. In this case, we decide the existence of a contract under traditional contract law.

Based on the above considerations, we conclude that there was sufficient evidence presented at trial from which a reasonable inference could be drawn that an enforceable contract between SMS and LMA had been formed, and that the damages awarded were proper.

Judgment affirmed.

Notes and Discussion

1. **What Went Wrong?** The Court does not speculate on why SMS decided not to finalize a long-term contract with LMA. If the cited evidence is correct, its change of heart came between the airport meeting on February 20, 1990, when SMS's chairman assured Malouf that a contract would be forthcoming, and February, 1991, when SMS terminated the negotiations. During this period a major economic recession was taking place. This may help explain why SMS got cold feet.

2. **Breach of Contract.** As it appears, both parties had intended to execute a written contract. However, they were unable to agree on the final version, or even on all its main terms. In the meantime, LMA, acting on assurances from SMS, had purchased Kasten. At exactly what point did SMS breach its contract, and how?

This contract was potentially worth millions to LMA. It seems unreasonable that business people would enter a binding agreement on a deal of this size without having some written or other memorial of their transaction. LMA could have waited to purchase Kasten until it secured something more than oral assurances from the chairman of SMS, true?

With this case, compare *Michigan Broadcasting Co. v. Shawd*, 352 Mich. 453, 90 N.W.2d 451 (1958), concerning the alleged sale of the stock of a radio corporation for $230,000. The plaintiff claimed that an oral agreement should be enforced despite the parties' failure to sign a written agreement, but the Court rejected that argument: "The negotiations were complex, as were the necessitous requirements of attaining the goal of such negotiations. A written agreement was proposed, referred to and suggested as the parties talked and a draft was ultimately ordered and prepared. The involved value and amount was something out of the ordinary, and the agreement toward which the parties were proceeding was 'of that class which are usually found to be in writing.' While these factors are by no means conclusive, they unitedly stand as 'some evidence that the parties intended it (a writing) to be the final closing of the contract . . . '" 90 N.W.2d at 456. How do you distinguish this case from *Situation Mgmt.*?

It is important to the outcome in *Situation Mgmt.* that Rose (the SMS Chairman) and Malouf had a long-standing personal and business relationship, and that for nearly a year the parties continued doing business despite the lapse of their contract, right? Should LMA's acquisition of Kasten be regarded as the start of performance under the contract between SMS and LMA?

ARNOLD PALMER GOLF CO. v. FUQUA INDUSTRIES, INC.

United States Court of Appeals, Sixth Circuit, 1976.
541 F.2d 584.

McCREE, J. This is an appeal from the district court's grant of summary judgment in favor of defendant Fuqua Industries, Inc. (Fuqua) in an action for breach of contract. The district court determined that a document captioned "Memorandum of Intent" and signed by both parties was not a contract because it evidenced the intent of the parties not to be contractually bound. We reverse and remand for trial.

Arnold Palmer Golf Company (Palmer) was incorporated under Ohio law in 1961, and has been primarily engaged in designing and marketing various lines of golf clubs, balls, bags, gloves, and other golf accessories. Palmer did none of its own manufacturing, but engaged other companies to produce its products. In the late 1960's, Palmer's management concluded that it was essential for future growth and profitability to acquire manufacturing facilities.

To that end, in January, 1969, Mark McCormack, Palmer's Executive Vice-President, and E. D. Kenna, Fuqua's President, met in New York City to consider a possible business relationship between the two corporations. The parties' interest in establishing a business relationship continued and they held several more meetings and discussions where the general outline of the proposed relationship was defined. In November 1969, Fuqua, with Palmer's assistance and approval, acquired Fernquest and Johnson, a California manufacturer of golf clubs. The minutes of the Fuqua Board of Directors meeting on November 3, 1969, reveal that Fuqua: "proposed that this Corporation participate in the golf equipment industry in association with Arnold Palmer Golf Co. and Arnold Palmer Enterprises, Inc. The business would be conducted in two parts. One part would be composed of a corporation engaged in the manufacture and sale of golf clubs and equipment directly related to the playing of the game of golf. This Corporation would be owned to the extent of 25% by Fuqua and 75% by the Arnold Palmer interests. Fuqua would transfer the Fernquest & Johnson business to the new corporation as Fuqua's contribution."

In November and December of 1969 further discussions and negotiations occurred and revised drafts of a memorandum of intent were distributed.

The culmination of the discussions was a six page document denominated as a Memorandum of Intent. It provided in the first paragraph that: "This memorandum will serve to confirm the general understanding which has been reached regarding the acquisition of 25% of the stock of Arnold Palmer Golf Company ('Palmer') by Fuqua Industries, Inc. ('Fuqua') in exchange for all of the outstanding stock of Fernquest and Johnson Golf Company, Inc. ('F & J'), a wholly-owned California subsidiary of Fuqua, and money in the amount of $700,000; and for the rendition of management services by Fuqua."

The Memorandum of Intent contained detailed statements concerning, inter alia, the form of the combination, the manner in which the business would be conducted, the loans that Fuqua agreed to make to Palmer, and the warranties and covenants to be contained in the definitive agreement.

Paragraph 10 of the Memorandum of Intent stated: "(10) Preparation of Definitive Agreement. Counsel for Palmer and counsel for Fuqua will proceed as promptly as possible to prepare an agreement acceptable to Palmer and Fuqua for the proposed combination of businesses. Such agreement will contain the representations, warranties, covenants and conditions, as generally outlined in the example submitted by Fuqua to Palmer.... "

In the last paragraph of the Memorandum of Intent, the parties indicated that: "(11) Conditions. The obligations of Palmer and Fuqua shall be subject to fulfillment of the following conditions: (i) preparation of the definitive agreement for the proposed combination in form and content satisfactory to both parties and their respective counsel; (ii) approval of such definitive agreement by the Board of Directors of Fuqua;.... "

The Memorandum of Intent was signed by Palmer and by the President of Fuqua. Fuqua had earlier released a statement to the press upon Palmer's signing that "Fuqua Industries, Inc., and The Arnold Palmer Golf Co. have agreed to cooperate in an enterprise that will serve the golfing industry, from the golfer to the greens keeper."

In February, 1970, the Chairman of Fuqua's Board of Directors, J. B. Fuqua, told Douglas Kenna, Fuqua's President, that he did not want to go through with the Palmer deal. Shortly thereafter Kenna informed one of Palmer's corporate officers that the transaction was terminated.

Palmer filed the complaint in this case on July 24, 1970. Nearly three and one-half years later, on January 14, 1974, the defendant filed a motion for summary judgment. More than one year after the briefs had been filed by the parties, on May 30, 1975, the district court granted defendant's motion.

The district court determined that: "The parties were not to be subject to any obligations until a definitive agreement satisfactory to the parties and their counsel had been prepared. The fact that this agreement had to be 'satisfactory' implies necessarily that such an agreement might be unsatisfactory.... The parties by the terms they used elected not to be bound by this memorandum and the Court finds that they were not bound."

The primary issue in this case is whether the parties intended to enter into a binding agreement when they signed the Memorandum of Intent, and the primary issue in this appeal is whether the district court erred in determining this question on a motion for summary judgment. The substantive law of Ohio applies.

We agree with the district court that both parties must have a clear understanding of the terms of an agreement and an intention to be bound by its terms before an enforceable contract is created.[12] As Professor Corbin has observed: "The courts are quite agreed upon general principles. The parties have power to contract as they please. They can bind themselves orally or by informal letters or telegrams if they like. On the other hand, they can maintain complete immunity from all obligation, even though they have expressed agreement orally or informally upon every detail of a complex transaction. The matter is merely one of expressed intention. If their expressions convince the court that they intended to be bound without a formal document, their contract is consummated, and the expected formal document will be nothing more than a memorial of that contract." 1 Corbin on Contracts, § 30 (1963). [Footnote omitted.]

The decision whether the parties intended to enter a contract must be based upon an evaluation of the circumstances surrounding the parties' discussions. The introduction of extrinsic evidence does not violate the parol evidence rule because that rule applies only after an integrated or a partially integrated agreement has been found.... As Judge Kalbfleisch observed in *New York Central Railroad Co. v. General Motors Corp.*, 182 F. Supp. 273, 285 (N.D. Ohio 1960): "The greatest latitude should be given in developing the surrounding situations and conditions attending the negotiations for the consummation of a contract, and the language employed in a contract should be construed in the light of circumstances surrounding the contracting parties at the time. *Circumstantial evidence is as competent to prove a contract as it is to prove a crime.*" [Emphasis added.]

12. See, e.g., *McMillen v. Willys Sales Corp.*, 118 Ohio App. 20, 193 N.E.2d 160 (1962).

Section 26 of the Restatement of Contracts states the general rule that Ohio follows: "Mutual manifestations of assent that are in themselves sufficient to make a contract will not be prevented from so operating by the mere fact that the parties also manifest an intention to prepare and adopt a written memorial thereof; but other facts may show that the manifestations are merely preliminary expressions as stated in Section 25."

Comment a to Section 26 of the Restatement explains the considerations that enter into a determination whether a binding contract exists: "Parties who plan to make a final written instrument as the expression of their contract, necessarily discuss the proposed terms of the contract before they enter into it and often, before the final writing is made, agree upon all the terms which they plan to incorporate therein. This they may do orally or by exchange of several writings. It is possible thus to make a contract to execute subsequently a final writing which shall contain certain provisions. If parties have definitely agreed that they will do so, and that the final writing shall contain these provisions and no others, they have then fulfilled all the requisites for the formation of a contract. On the other hand, if the preliminary agreement is incomplete, it being apparent that the determination of certain details is deferred until the writing is made out; or if an intention is manifested in any way that legal obligations between the parties shall be deferred until the writing is made, the preliminary negotiations and agreements do not constitute a contract."

At bottom, the question whether the parties intended a contract is a factual one, not a legal one, and, except in the clearest cases, the question is for the finder of fact to resolve....

We held in *S. J. Groves & Sons Co. v. Ohio Turnpike Comm'n*, 315 F.2d 235 (6th Cir.), cert. denied, 375 U.S. 824, 11 L. Ed. 2d 57, 84 S. Ct. 65 (1963), also a case governed by the substantive law of Ohio, that summary judgment was inappropriate in a breach of contract case that involved "complex facts and issues." Judge Shackelford Miller, writing for the court, stated: "It is often the case that although the basic facts are not in dispute, the parties in good faith may nevertheless disagree about the inferences to be drawn from these facts, what the intention of the parties was as shown by the facts, or whether an estoppel or a waiver of certain rights admitted to exist should be drawn from such facts. Under such circumstances the case is not one to be decided by the Trial Judge on a motion for summary judgment." 315 F.2d at 237–38....

Considering this appeal in the light of these authorities, we determine that our proper course is to remand this case to the district court for trial because we believe that the issue of the parties' intention to be bound is a proper one for resolution by the trier of fact. Upon first blush it may appear that the Memorandum of Intent is no more than preliminary negotiation between the parties. A cursory reading of the conditions contained in paragraph 11, by themselves, may suggest that the parties did not intend to be bound by the Memorandum of Intent.

Nevertheless, the memorandum recited that a "general understanding [had] been reached." And, as the *Itek* court noted, the entire document and relevant circumstances surrounding its adoption must be considered in making a determination of the parties' intention.[13] In this case we find an extensive document that appears to reflect all essential terms concerning the transfer of Arnold Palmer stock to Fuqua in exchange for all outstanding stock in Fernquest and Johnson. The form of combination, the location of the principal office of Palmer, the license rights, employment contracts of Palmer personnel and the financial obligations of Fuqua are a few of the many areas covered in the Memorandum of Intent, and they are all described in unqualified terms. The Memorandum states, for instance, that "Fuqua *will* transfer all of the ... stock," that the "principal office of Palmer will be moved to Atlanta," that "Palmer ... *shall* possess an exclusive license," and that "Fuqua agrees to advance to Palmer up to an aggregate of $700,000.... " [Emphasis added.]

Paragraph 10 of the Memorandum states, also in unqualified language, that counsel for the parties "will proceed as promptly as possible to prepare an agreement acceptable to [the parties].... " We believe that this paragraph may be read merely to impose an obligation upon the

13. Parties may orally or by informal memoranda, or by both, agree upon all essential terms of the contract and effectively bind themselves, if that is their intention, even though they contemplate the execution, at a later time, of a formal document to memorialize their undertaking. *Comerata v. Chaumont, Inc.*, 52 N.J. Super. 299, 145 A.2d 471 (1958).

parties to memorialize their agreement. We do not mean to suggest that this is the correct interpretation. The provision is also susceptible to an interpretation that the parties did not intend to be bound.

As we have indicated above, it is permissible to refer to extrinsic evidence to determine whether the parties intended to be bound by the Memorandum of Intent. In this regard, we observe that Fuqua circulated a press release in January 1970 that would tend to sustain Palmer's claim that the two parties intended to be bound by the Memorandum of Intent. Fuqua's statement said that the two companies "have agreed to cooperate in an enterprise that will serve the golfing industry."

Upon a review of the evidence submitted in connection with the motion for summary judgment, we believe that there is presented a factual issue whether the parties contractually obligated themselves to prepare a definitive agreement in accordance with the understanding of the parties contained in the Memorandum of Intent. Just as in *S. J. Groves, supra*, we believe that the parties may properly "disagree about the inferences to be drawn from [the basic facts that are not in dispute or] what the intention of the parties was as shown by the facts." 315 F.2d at 237. Because the facts and the inferences from the facts in this case indicate that the parties may have intended to be bound by the Memorandum of Intent, we hold that the district court erred in determining that no contract existed as a matter of law.

We reject appellee's argument that summary judgment was appropriate because the obligations of the parties were subject to an express condition that was not met. We believe a question of fact is presented whether the parties intended the conditions in paragraph 11 to operate only if the definitive agreement was not in conformity with the general understanding contained in the Memorandum of Intent. See *Frank Horton & Co. v. Cook Electricity Co.*, 356 F.2d 485, 490 (7th Cir.), cert. denied, 384 U.S. 952, 16 L. Ed. 2d 548, 86 S. Ct. 1572 (1966). The parties may well have intended that there should be no binding obligation until the definitive agreement was signed, but we regard this question as one for the fact finder to determine after a consideration of the relevant evidence. . . .

Accordingly, the judgment of the district court is reversed and the case is remanded for proceedings not inconsistent with this opinion.

Notes and Discussion

1. Contemplation of a Writing. In this case, unlike in *Situation Management Systems*, the parties clearly intended a final written version of their deal. Indeed, in their Memorandum of Intent they expressly made their respective "obligations . . . subject to fulfillment of the following conditions: (i) preparation of the definitive agreement . . [and] (ii) approval of such definitive agreement by the Board of Directors of Fuqua . . . " Why is this language not decisive?

If Fuqua wished to reserve its right to change its mind up till the last possible moment, what steps should it have taken to prevent the possibility of misinterpretation? Is it possible that Fuqua wanted to have it both ways: to crow about an impending deal and to be able to withhold its final approval?

On remand, the trial court will have to consider Fuqua's press release, the apparent completeness of the Memorandum, and a variety of other things that are suggested as follows by Restatement 2d § 27, Cmt. c: "the extent to which express agreement has been reached on all the terms to be included, whether the contract is of a type usually put in writing, whether it needs a formal writing for its full expression, whether it has few or many details, whether the amount involved is large or small, whether it is a common or unusual contract, whether a standard form of contract is widely used in similar transactions, and whether either party takes any action in preparation for performance during the negotiations."

In some cases these criteria may be helpful, but it seems unlikely they will be helpful in this case. To avoid the kind of problem faced in *Fuqua*, lawyers routinely insert clauses that say: "Except for paragraph X, this agreement is not legally binding." See, for example, the letter of intent set out below in Problem 3–5. One suspects that some parties intentionally avoid clarity. They may believe that their interests are served by intentionally leaving the enforceability of a letter of intent unclear.

2. An Eleven Billion Dollar Error. One of the most spectacular cases in this area arose from negotiations between the Pennzoil Company and Getty Oil. The two, along with some Getty shareholders, reached an "agreement in principle" for Getty's merger into Pennzoil, and Getty trumpeted the news in a press release. While lawyers worked on a final text of this agreement, the Getty shareholders opened parallel negotiations with Texaco, and these quickly led to a second merger agreement at a higher price per share. Pennzoil brought suit on a theory of tortious interference with contractual relations, arguing that the "agreement in principle" was meant to be binding even before the details had been fully worked out. A Texas jury awarded Pennzoil nearly $11 billion, including $3 billion in punitive damages and pre-judgment interest; an appeals court affirmed but reduced the punitive damages considerably. *Texaco, Inc. v. Pennzoil Co.*, 729 S.W.2d 768 (Tex. App. 1987). The Supreme Court later upheld the constitutionality of the Texas proceedings: *Pennzoil Co. v. Texaco, Inc.*, 481 U.S. 1, 107 S.Ct. 1519, 95 L.Ed.2d 1 (1987). See Thomas Patzinger, Jr., Oil and Honor (1987).

EMPRO MANUFACTURING CO., INC. v. BALL-CO MANUFACTURING, INC.

United States Court of Appeals, Seventh Circuit, 1989.
870 F.2d 423.

EASTERBROOK, J. We have a pattern common in commercial life. Two firms reach concord on the general terms of their transaction. They sign a document, captioned "agreement in principle" or "letter of intent," memorializing these terms but anticipating further negotiations and decisions—an appraisal of the assets, the clearing of a title, the list is endless. One of these terms proves divisive, and the deal collapses. The party that perceives itself the loser then claims that the preliminary document has legal force independent of the definitive contract. Ours is such a dispute.

Ball-Co Manufacturing, a maker of specialty valve components, floated its assets on the market. Empro Manufacturing showed interest. After some preliminary negotiations, Empro sent Ball-Co a three-page "letter of intent" to purchase the assets of Ball-Co and S.B. Leasing, a partnership holding title to the land under Ball-Co's plant. Empro proposed a price of $2.4 million, with $650,000 to be paid on closing and a 10-year promissory note for the remainder, the note to be secured by the "inventory and equipment of Ballco." The letter stated "[t]he general terms and conditions of such proposal (which will be subject to and incorporated in a formal, definitive Asset Purchase Agreement signed by both parties)." Just in case Ball-Co might suppose that Empro had committed itself to buy the assets, paragraph four of the letter stated that "Empro's purchase shall be subject to the satisfaction of certain conditions precedent to closing including, but not limited to" the definitive Asset Purchase Agreement and, among five other conditions, "[t]he approval of the shareholders and board of directors of Empro."

Although Empro left itself escape hatches, as things turned out Ball-Co was the one who balked. The parties signed the letter of intent in November 1987 and negotiated through March 1988 about many terms. Security for the note proved to be the sticking point. Ball-Co wanted a security interest in the land under the plant; Empro refused to yield.

When Empro learned that Ball-Co was negotiating with someone else, it filed this diversity suit. Contending that the letter of intent obliges Ball-Co to sell only to it, Empro asked for a temporary restraining order. The district judge set the case for a prompt hearing and, after getting a look at the letter of intent, dismissed the complaint under Fed.R.Civ.P. 12(b)(6) for failure to state a claim on which relief may be granted. Relying on *Interway, Inc. v. Alagna*, 85 Ill.App.3d 1094, 41 Ill.Dec. 117, 407 N.E.2d 615 (1st Dist.1980), the district judge concluded that the statement, appearing twice in the letter, that the agreement is "subject to" the execution of a definitive contract meant that the letter has no independent force.

Empro insists on appeal that the binding effect of a document depends on the parties' intent, which means that the case may not be dismissed—for Empro says that the parties intended to be bound, a factual issue. Empro treats "intent to be bound" as a matter of the parties' states of mind, but if intent were wholly subjective there would be no parol evidence rule, no contract case could be decided without a jury trial, and no one could know the effect of a commercial transaction until years after the documents were inked. That would be a devastating blow to business. Contract law gives effect to the parties' wishes, but they must express these openly. Put differently, "intent" in contract law is objective rather than subjective—a point Interway makes by holding that as a matter of law parties who make their pact "subject to" a later definitive agreement have manifested an (objective) intent not to be bound, which under the parol evidence rule becomes the definitive intent even if one party later says that the true intent was different. As the Supreme Court of Illinois said in *Schek v. Chicago Transit Authority*, 42 Ill.2d 362, 364, 247 N.E.2d 886, 888 (1969), "intent must be determined solely from the language used when no ambiguity in its terms exists." See also *Feldman v. Allegheny International, Inc.*, 850 F.2d 1217 (7th Cir. 1988) (Illinois law); . . . Parties may decide for themselves whether the results of preliminary negotiations bind them, *Chicago Investment Corp. v. Dolins*, 89 Ill.Dec. 869, 871, 481 N.E.2d 712, 715 (1985), but they do this through their words.

Because letters of intent are written without the care that will be lavished on the definitive agreement, it may be a bit much to put dispositive weight on "subject to" in every case, and we do not read *Interway* as giving these the status of magic words. They might have been used carelessly, and if the full agreement showed that the formal contract was to be nothing but a memorial of an agreement already reached, the letter of intent would be enforceable. *Borg-Warner Corp. v. Anchor Coupling Co.*, 16 Ill.2d 234, 156 N.E.2d 513 (1958). Conversely, Empro cannot claim comfort from the fact that the letter of intent does not contain a flat disclaimer, such as the one in *Feldman* pronouncing that the letter creates no obligations at all. The text and structure of the letter—the objective manifestations of intent—might show that the parties agreed to bind themselves to some extent immediately. *Borg-Warner* is such a case. One party issued an option, which called itself "firm and binding"; the other party accepted; the court found this a binding contract even though some terms remained open. After all, an option to purchase is nothing if not binding in advance of the definitive contract. The parties to *Borg-Warner* conceded that the option and acceptance usually would bind; the only argument in the case concerned whether the open terms were so important that a contract could not arise even if the parties wished to be bound, a subject that divided the court. See 156 N.E.2d at 930–36 (Schaefer, J., dissenting).

A canvass of the terms of the letter Empro sent does not assist it, however. "Subject to" a definitive agreement appears twice. The letter also recites, twice, that it contains the "general terms and conditions," implying that each side retained the right to make (and stand on) additional demands. Empro insulated itself from binding effect by listing, among the conditions to which the deal was "subject," the "approval of the shareholders and board of directors of Empro." The board could veto a deal negotiated by the firm's agents for a reason such as the belief that Ball-Co had been offered too much (otherwise the officers, not the board, would be the firm's final decisionmakers, yet state law vests major decisions in the board). The shareholders could decline to give their assent for any reason (such as distrust of new business ventures) and could not even be required to look at the documents, let alone consider the merits of the deal. . . . Empro even took care to require the return of its $5,000 in earnest money "without set off, in the event this transaction is not closed," although the seller usually gets to keep the earnest money if the buyer changes its mind. So Empro made clear that it was free to walk.

Neither the text nor the structure of the letter suggests that it was to be a one-sided commitment, an option in Empro's favor binding only Ball-Co. From the beginning Ball-Co assumed that it could negotiate terms in addition to, or different from, those in the letter of intent. The cover letter from Ball-Co's lawyer returning the signed letter of intent to Empro stated that the "terms and conditions are generally acceptable" but that "some clarifications are needed in Paragraph 3(c) (last sentence)", the provision concerning Ball-Co's security interest. "Some clarifications are needed" is an ominous noise in a negotiation, foreboding many a stalemate. Although we do not know what "clarifications" counsel had in mind, the specifics are not important. It is enough that even on signing the letter of intent Ball-Co proposed to change the bargain, conduct consistent with the purport of the letter's text and structure.

The shoals that wrecked this deal are common hazards in business negotiations. Letters of intent and agreements in principle often, and here, do no more than set the stage for negotiations on details. Sometimes the details can be ironed out; sometimes they can't. Illinois, as *Chicago Investment*, *Interway*, and *Feldman* show, allows parties to approach agreement in stages, without fear that by reaching a preliminary understanding they have bargained away their privilege to disagree on the specifics. Approaching agreement by stages is a valuable method of doing business. So long as Illinois preserves the availability of this device, a federal court in a diversity case must send the disappointed party home empty-handed. Empro claims that it is entitled at least to recover its "reliance expenditures," but the only expenditures it has identified are those normally associated with pre-contractual efforts: its complaint mentions the expenses "in negotiating with defendants, in investigating and reviewing defendants' business, and in preparing to acquire defendants' business." Outlays of this sort cannot bind the other side any more than paying an expert to tell you whether the painting at the auction is a genuine Rembrandt compels the auctioneer to accept your bid.

AFFIRMED.

Notes and Discussion

1. Distinction Without a Difference? How, if at all, can the holding in this case be distinguished from that in *Arnold Palmer*?

Problem 3–5: A Letter of Intent

You are a lawyer for BBI. Recently, on November 10, the Presidents of both BBI and Jackson Broadcasting signed a letter of intent (reproduced below) for the sale of two Arizona TV stations. BBI acknowledges that the parties never entered into a formal purchase agreement, but notes that all of the relevant terms had been agreed upon. At the conclusion of a meeting on January 10, the principals "embraced" and stated orally that they had a deal and would instruct their lawyers to put together the final document no later than February 1. At the end of the January 10 meeting, BBI asked if anything remained to be agreed upon. Jackson's principal shook his head "no." During the week of January 15, BBI's lawyers prepared a draft final agreement and sent it to Jackson, who returned a completely different document that had new payment terms and other terms contrary to those agreed upon on January 10 and before. At that point negotiations broke off.

By its terms, the letter of intent expired on January 21. Only two weeks after its expiration, Jackson Broadcasting entered into a contract of sale for the two television stations with a third party for approximately $30 million more than the price stated in the letter of intent. Furthermore, BBI believes that Jackson actually solicited other bids for the two stations and used BBI's bid as a basis for these solicitations after the November 10 letter was signed.

Letter of Intent

November 10 Mr. James Esch Jackson Broadcasting 275 Park Ave. New York, NY 10152

Dear Gentlemen:

This letter incorporates the terms of our October 19, 1999 letter to you, as modified by your October 28 and November 5, 1999 responses; relating to the proposed purchase of the assets of the television stations owned by Jackson Broadcasting, Inc. and Jackson Broadcasting of Tucson, Inc. (collectively, the "Seller").

BBI Holdings, Inc., a California corporation, or a direct or indirect wholly-owned subsidiary corporation ("BBI"), is interested in acquiring from Seller all the respective assets and properties of television station KNTS-TV, Channel 41, in Phoenix, Texas (the "Phoenix Station") and television station KDLT-TV, Channel 45, in Tucson, Texas (the "Tucson Station"), including in each case an assignment of licenses, permits and other authorizations issued by the FCC, all leases, all properties, real and personal, tangible and intangible, and all equipment, inventory and other assets (excluding only the cash and accounts receivable) associated with the Phoenix Station and the Tucson Station.

The following information is provided in response to your September 20, 1999 letter soliciting bids:

(1) The purchase price of the Phoenix Station will be $55 million cash, payable to Seller at the closing, less any accrued liabilities agreed to be assumed by BBI in connection with the transaction. It is expected that Seller will retain all accrued liabilities related to the Phoenix Station, except those liabilities that BBI specifically agrees to assume. BBI will assume the studio and tower leases. For purposes of the foregoing, lease or contract payments attributable to periods after the closing of the transaction will not be "accrued liabilities."

(2) Should BBI's digital plans include leasing excess channel space on the Phoenix Station, BBI understand that Seller is interested in

leasing a channel for broadcast use in the Phoenix market. The term of the lease would run until the channel needs to returned to digital use.

(3) The purchase price for the Tucson Station will be $30 million, with $15 million payable in cash ay the closing and the balance of $15 million represented by BBI's promissory note bearing interest at the prime rate, adjusted annually. Interest only will be paid quarterly and the principal will be paid in full at the end of the 30th month following the closing. It is expecting that Seller will retain all accrued liabilities related to the Tucson Station, except those accrued liabilities that BBI specifically agreed to assume. BBI will assume the studio and tower leases.

(4) Should BBI's digital plans include leasing excess channel space on the Tucson Station, BBI understands that Seller would be interested in leasing a channel for broadcast use in the Tucson market. The term of the lease would run until the channel needs to be returned for digital use.

(5) If, during the 30-month period following the closing of the transaction, BBI sells the Tucson Station to an unrelated third party, BBI's promissory note will become due and payable at the closing of such resale transaction and the principal and all accrued and unpaid interest will be paid to Seller.

(6) BBI shall make an escrow deposit to be negotiated as part of the definitive asset purchase agreement.

(7) The purchaser will be BBI. The sole shareholder of BBI's parent corporation are Josh Beal and Larry Beal. BBI is not aware of any requirement of regulatory approval other than by the FCC.

(8) In order to complete its due diligence investigation, BBI would expect to receive and approve a list and a description of the respective assets of the Phoenix Station and the Tucson Station, copies of all contracts to be assumed by BBI and information regarding Seller's employees engaged in activities on behalf of the Phoenix Station and the Tucson Station.

(9) Transnational Bank of California will provide the financing for the transaction.

In order to induce BBI to proceed with its due diligence and prepare a definitive asset purchase agreement, Seller agrees that between the date this letter is signed by Seller and January 31, 2000, neither Seller nor it owners will engage, directly or indirectly through others in negotiations with any other party for the sale of the Phoenix Station and that BBI and seller will keep all information acquired from the other confidential. However, it is understood and agreed that until a definitive asset purchase agreement is signed by BBI and Seller, Seller shall have the right to solicit offers and engage in negotiations for the sale of the Tucson Station, and if it is successful, Seller shall have the right to exclude the Tucson Station from the asset purchase agreement with BBI.

Except for this paragraph and the immediately preceding paragraph, which will be binding and enforceable agreements between BBI and Seller, this letter is not intended to be, and shall not constitute, a binding or enforceable agreement or commitment by BBI to purchase the Phoenix Station and the Tucson Station. Instead, it is intended to set forth the basis on which a definitive agreement between the parties might be negotiated. BBI's purchase of the Phoenix Station and the Tucson Station will be subject to the satisfactory completion of BBI's due diligence investigation and the successful negotiations and execution of a definitive asset purchase agreement.

This letter shall terminate and have no further force or effect if a definitive asset purchase agreement is not signed by January 21, 2000, unless extended by mutual written agreement.

Should you or Seller have any questions regarding this letter, please contact the undersigned or their representatives.

Sincerely,

Josh Beal
President, Beal Broadcasting, Inc.

Accepted and Agreed:

Jackson Broadcasting, Inc.

By:______________ (President)

You have commenced suit in the Federal District Court in Tucson against Jackson. You claim that the letter of intent, coupled with the actions at the end of the January 10 meeting, constituted an agreement to sell the station, and you have sued for breach of that agreement.

Jackson has moved for summary judgment. It argues that any such agreement is unenforceable because of the explicit terms of the third to the last paragraph in the letter.

How do you respond and what outcome do you expect?

CITY OF KENAI v. FERGUSON

Supreme Court of Alaska, 1987.
732 P.2d 184.

RABINOWITZ, C. J. This case arose out of a dispute over a provision in a fifty-five year lease entered into by the City of Kenai and Edward A. Ferguson. The provision was an agreement to agree to future rental terms at five-year intervals. The core of the dispute here is whether such a provision is valid and, if so, what standard should be used to determine the rental. Also at issue in this appeal are the superior court's rulings permitting withdrawal of admissions, awarding of attorney's fees, and continuing jurisdiction over the case.

I. Background

In May 1970, Edward A. Ferguson (Ferguson) bid for the right to lease Tract G2, Airport Lands, Gusty Subdivision, Lots 1, 2, 3, from the City of Kenai (City). Ferguson was the sole bidder. His bid was accepted by the City and a lease agreement with the City was signed by Ferguson and his partner in August 1970. The lease has a fifty-five year term. Through a series of assignments Ferguson became the sole lessee of Lot 1 of the Gusty Subdivision, and the City remains the lessor. Paragraph 10 of the lease agreement is the subject of the instant dispute:

"10. Rent Escalation: Every Five Years or Less: In the event this lease is for a term in excess of five years, the amount of rents or fees specified herein shall be subject to re-negotiation for increase or decrease at intervals of EVERY FIVE YEARS from the 1st day of July preceding the effective date of this lease." [Emphasis in original.]

Subsequent to entering into the lease Ferguson built a service station on Lot 1 with knowledge of the City. In May 1980, the City sent Ferguson a letter and asked him to sign an "Amendment to Lease" (amendment) which would have increased his rent from $1,140.80 to $7,017.00. This was purportedly done under paragraph 10. The amount of the new rent was determined by applying a formula adopted by City ordinance. The formula called for a six percent return on the appraised value of Airport Lands. The letter asking Ferguson to sign the amendment termed the new rental rate as "the rate we are proposing for the period July 1, 1980 through June 30, 1985." It then requested Ferguson to: "Please execute and notarize the enclosed 'Amendment to Lease' and return it to this office.... You will be receiving an adjusted billing at a later date."

Over the next two years the City and Ferguson communicated but failed to resolve the rent renewal issue.[14] The City then contacted Ferguson's counsel and advised him that renegotiation of the lease was more than three years overdue, and that unless Ferguson paid the amount due according to the City's appraisal (including retroactive payment to 1980) within 30 days, the City would proceed to terminate the lease and collect all sums due. Ferguson responded that he was willing to negotiate the rental rate but was not willing to accept a rate dictated by City appraisal and formula.

The City then filed suit seeking forfeiture and termination of the lease, possession of the property, all rents due, costs and attorney's fees. Ferguson denied the City's right to relief and counterclaimed that the City breached its covenant of quiet possession, that paragraph 10 of the lease either was invalid or did not give the City the right to demand

14. On June 18, 1980 the City again requested Ferguson to execute and return the amendment. Ferguson responded that he was not advised of any negotiations and found the appraisal used by the City to determine the new rental rate "completely out of reason" because it was much higher than the property's current assessment. He informed the City that he could not sign the amendment as it stood. Ferguson continued paying his rent according to the old rate.

Based on this newly calculated rental, the City informed Ferguson that his rent was delinquent and that if it remained unpaid his lease would be cancelled in May 1981. Ferguson, through counsel, responded that the City had no grounds to cancel his lease until a rent agreement was reached, and asked the City to propose a procedure for negotiating the matter. The City then suggested to Ferguson's counsel that, since Ferguson objected to the market value appraisal obtained by the City, Ferguson should obtain his own professionally conducted appraisal. If there was a difference in the appraisals, then the difference could be negotiated. Ferguson never responded.

additional rent without Ferguson's concurrence, and that Ferguson was entitled to a declaration of rights to that effect.

The parties filed cross-motions for summary judgment, and the superior court ruled in favor of Ferguson. The court dismissed the City's claim for rent based upon the "alleged" negotiation of the rent under paragraph 10. The court interpreted paragraph 10 to mean that either party could negotiate for the rental amount for any five-year period beginning July 1, 1985. If the parties could not agree, either party could seek a judicial determination of the "fair rental rate;" the rent would remain at $1,140.80 until a new rate was established under paragraph 10. The court further interpreted paragraph 10 as permitting but not mandating renegotiation of the rent every five years. If one party sought negotiations, then the other party was obligated to negotiate in good faith. In fixing a fair rental rate, the court directed the parties to another provision of the lease for factors to consider in adjusting the rent, and found simply arriving at the appraised highest and best use value was not contemplated under paragraph 10.

This appeal and cross-appeal followed.

II. The Superior Court's Grant Of Ferguson's Cross-Motion For Summary Judgment And Dismissal Of The City's Complaint

A. *Enforceability of Paragraph 10 of the Lease*

The superior court concluded that paragraph 10 is enforceable as a matter of law and that a fair rental value should be implied as the rental for the five-year periods for which the parties are unable to negotiate an agreement. The validity of the superior court's summary judgment decision turns on this conclusion of law.[15] We sustain the superior court's holding that paragraph 10 is enforceable.

Good faith is a term implied in every contract.[16] In this context, good faith requires the parties to attempt to reach agreement as to rent for the property for the five-year period in question. Forcing Ferguson to quit the property after his substantial reliance on the fifty-five-year length of the lease would be inequitable, as would be allowing Ferguson to continue using the property without reasonably compensating the City.

The City had notice that Ferguson intended to use the property to build a filling station. Ferguson constructed a filling station on the property and subleased the station for an original term of ten years with renewal options for two successive five-year terms. Under the terms of the lease Ferguson could neither sublet the premises nor construct a

15. There is a split of opinion throughout state courts on the validity of a lease provision which agrees to a future determination of a rental term without specifying either a prescribed method or standard to be used in ascertaining the new rental rate. See generally D. Feld, Validity and Enforceability of Provision for Renewal of Lease at Rental to Be Fixed by Subsequent Agreement of Parties, 58 A.L.R.3d 500 (1974); 2 M. Friedman, Friedman on Leases § 14.1, at 703–808 (1983); . . .

16. *Guin v. Ha*, 591 P.2d 1281, 1291 (Alaska 1979); see also 3 A. Corbin, Corbin on Contracts § 541, at 95 (1960).

filling station without the City's prior consent. He expended substantial sums in constructing the filling station. On the other hand, Ferguson should not benefit from a lease provision which he asserts is unenforceable, in order to obtain a better bargain than the parties intended when they entered into this long-term lease.

Courts are no longer reluctant to supply lease terms when parties who, at the time of contracting agreed to set or renegotiate particular terms in the future, are unable to reach agreement. This is particularly true when the amount of rental is the term left to future agreement. *Chaney v. Schneider*, 92 Cal. App. 2d 88, 206 P.2d 669, 669 (Cal. Dist. App. 1949). In concluding that paragraph 10 of the lease is enforceable in the factual circumstances just outlined, we find the reasoning of *Chaney* persuasive. Therein the court wrote in part: "Intent is to be determined from a view of the instrument as a whole, and a consideration of all of the facts in the case. If the agreement to renew was the essence of the contract, and the terms of the lease or the rental to be paid thereunder were to be fixed by agreement, or in some other way, at the time of the extension of the lease, then failure of the parties to so agree, or to fix particular terms does not avoid the lease. In such a case the courts will declare the terms upon which the parties fail to agree."[17] 206 P.2d at 671.

Based on this reasoning the court was willing to declare a missing rental term in order to effect the reasonable expectations of the parties, where the renewal option was "the essence of the contract." There is even greater reason to declare a rental term when, as here, parties under a long term lease are unable to reach agreement, since there are correspondingly greater reliance expectations created in the continuing use of the property.[18]

Our opinion in *Altman v. Alaska Truss & Mfg. Co.*, 677 P.2d 1215 (Alaska 1983), indicates our willingness under the proper circumstances to supply a fair market rental term and is in accord with the approach of the Chaney court.[19] In *Altman*, this court suggested that where a lessor

17. Similarly, in *Moolenaar v. Co-Build Cos.*, 354 F. Supp. 980, 982–83 (D. V.I. 1973) the court stated: "First, it will probably effectuate the intent of the parties better than would striking out the clause altogether. A document should be construed where possible to give effect to every term, on the theory that the signatories inserted each for a reason and if one party had agreed to the clause only in the secret belief that it would prove unenforceable, he should be discouraged from such paths. Secondly, a renewal option has a more sympathetic claim to enforcement than do most vague contractual terms, since valuable consideration will often have already been paid for it. The option of renewal is one factor inducing the tenant to enter into the lease, or to pay as high a rent as he did during the initial period. To this extent the landlord benefitted from the tenant's reliance on the clause, and so the tenant has a stronger claim to receive the reciprocal benefit of the option." ...

18. In determining the validity of agreements to agree, the lessee's reliance on the length of the term is a significant factor. "The fact that the lessee had acted in reliance on the option may be of controlling importance; he may have made valuable improvements.... " 1 A. Corbin, Corbin on Contracts § 97, at 432–33 (1960)....

19. In *Altman*, the agreement to agree to a future rental term prescribed arbitration as the method of resolution if agreement could not be reached. 677 P.2d at 1224.

had done everything possible to have the rental rate established by arbitration or appraisal, then the lessee would be obligated to pay the fair market rental value of the premises. Id. at 1224.

In this case, the "essence of the contract" is the fifty-five-year term of the lease. This is evidenced by the substantial long term investment made by the lessee in constructing the service station. It is clear that the parties contemplated that the rent over this fifty-five-year term would be adjusted to fluctuations in market conditions. Paragraph 10 provided in part that rents "shall be subject to renegotiation for increase or decrease" every five years. We therefore find no error in the superior court's decision to find paragraph 10 enforceable and to imply a reasonable fair market rent if necessary to give effect to the reasonable expectations of the parties.

B. The Standard for Determining Reasonable Fair Market Rent Under Paragraph 10 of the Lease

In ruling on the summary judgment motions, the superior court held in part that in deciding what is a reasonable rent under paragraph 10 of the lease "simply arriving at the highest and best use of the property is not contemplated. . . . " We hold that the court was correct in rejecting the highest and best use criterion as the applicable standard for the determination of reasonable rent under paragraph 10 and in holding that actual use of the premises is to be considered in ascertaining the fair market rental value of the premises.

Here Ferguson constructed a filling station. This improvement was required to be approved by the City under paragraph 7 of the lease. Under paragraph 4 of the lease no sublease could be entered into by Ferguson without the written consent of the City. Given that the City had notice of Ferguson's intended use at the time of leasing and consented to the construction of a service station and subleasing of the property, it is apparent that the parties contemplated that the premises would be used for the purpose of operating a gas station. Thus, we conclude that the superior court did not err in its adoption of the fair market value of equivalently used property as the standard to be employed in determining fair market rental value under paragraph 10 of the lease. . . .

AFFIRMED in part, REVERSED in part, and REMANDED for further proceedings consistent with this opinion.

Notes and Discussion

1. **A Contract with Terms Left Open.** The Court describes the 55-year term as the "essence of the contract" even though that term exceeded by ten times the time for which they were able to agree about rent. It seems as though the City should have anticipated Ferguson's construction of a structure (such as a service station) on the lot, and the Court may have been moved by a belief that the City's request for a rent increase was in bad faith. How would you explain the City's request for such a large increase in 1980 (from $1,140.80 to $7,017.00, or a 515% increase)?

2. An Agreement to Agree. In some ways, this case presents the opposite problem from *Arnold Palmer*. Here the parties deliberately left open an important term, and later turned to a court when they were unable to agree on the terms. Compare the results here with *Sun Printing*; the two cases display a different attitude toward the underlying problem of incomplete contracts. The result in *City of Kenai* may have been affected by the fact that the agreement to agree was an element within the larger lease, and also by Ferguson's reliance on the lease.

Would the result have been different if, for instance, the parties had not initially agreed on a rent, but had concluded a contract subject to later agreement on this? If the lot had been leased for only ten years, with an option of an additional ten-year renewal at a rent to be agreed upon? This latter situation resembles that in *Walker v. Keith*, 382 S.W.2d 198, 199 (Ky. 1964), in which the contract defined the rent for the additional period as follows: "rental will be fixed in such amount as shall actually be agreed upon by the lessors and the lessee with the monthly rental fixed on the comparative basis of rental values as of the date of the renewal with rental values at this time reflected by the comparative business conditions of the two periods." The Court held that this language was "ambiguous and indefinite.... If 'comparative business conditions' afforded sufficient certainty, we might possibly surmount the obstacle of the unenforceable agreement to agree. This term, however is very broad indeed. Did the parties have in mind local conditions, national conditions, or conditions affecting the lessee's particular business?" Id. at 199–203. The renewal condition was held to be: "fatally defective in failing to specify either an agreed rental or an agreed method by which it could be fixed with certainty." Id. at 205. Was the agreement in *City of Kenai* more precise than that in *Walker*?

3. The UCC on Open Terms. The UCC takes a broader view of the parties' ability to leave terms open. Section 2–204(3) specifies that: "Even though one or more terms are left open a contract for sale [of goods] does not fail for indefiniteness if the parties have intended to make a contract and there is a reasonably certain basis for giving an appropriate remedy." Note that the parties must have intended a contract, however—a fact that would need proving. A contract can be valid even though the price term is left open, or is subject to determination by one party or by a third party: § 2–305. Subsection 4 provides that: "Where, however, the parties intend not to be bound unless the price be fixed or agreed and it is not fixed or agreed there is no contract."

We wonder whether real estate or service transactions, not covered by the Code, call for greater precision and a more conservative approach. What do you think? Restatement 2d § 33 requires that "the terms of the contract [be] reasonably certain," by which is meant that "they provide a basis for determining the existence of a breach and for giving an appropriate remedy."

Problem 3–6

After prolonged negotiations, Litton Industries agreed to construct an innovative self-loading ore vessel for Bethlehem Steel Corporation. The parties also agreed that Bethlehem would have the option to require Litton to construct up to five more similar vessels at a base price of about $20 million each, with an escalation on terms that both parties were to agree upon. Litton pressed Bethlehem to exercise its option, but Bethlehem refused to do so; however, after Litton then closed its shipyard, Bethlehem attempted to exercise its option for three vessels. The parties tried to reach agreement on the escalated price, but failed despite good faith efforts. Bethlehem then sued Litton for $95 million in damages, claiming that the parties had intended to contract for three vessels and the court should set a reasonable, escalated price. Should Bethlehem prevail?

D. GOOD FAITH IN CONTRACT FORMATION

Most Civil Law systems recognize that persons who enter into negotiations have already at least limited obligations of good faith toward one another. Typical of Code provisions is the Italian Civil Code, § 1337: "The parties, in the conduct of negotiations and in the formation of the contract, shall conduct themselves according to good faith." The Italian Civil Code (Beltramo trans., 2001). Pre-contractual obligations arise from a legally imposed duty of care; since negotiation can often involve substantial expenditure, each party is expected to avoid deliberate or negligent conduct that might induce reliance and result in the other party wasting resources. Liability is usually limited to reliance damages. (See also UNIDROIT Principles art. 2.15(2)-(3): "[A] party who negotiates or breaks off negotiations in bad faith is liable for the losses caused to the other party. It is bad faith, in particular, for a party to enter into or continue negotiations when intending not to reach an agreement with the other party." The UNIDROIT Principles, prepared by the International Institute for the Unification of Private Law, are intended to state general rules for international commercial contracts, but have only persuasive force in the United States. The CISG, which does have legal force here, contains no parallel provision.)

Common law, by contrast, has generally rejected this position, although some academics have urged otherwise. Our system therefore lays more stress on parties looking out for themselves during the delicate period before a contract comes into existence. A duty of good faith arises only after the contract is concluded. In this respect, the wording of UCC § 1–203 (revised edition: § 1–304) is precise: "Every contract or duty within this Act imposes an obligation of good faith *in its performance or enforcement*." (Emphasis added.) Closely comparable is Restatement 2d § 205.

Why are our courts so reticent? Doubtless part of the reason is the enduring influence of the contract/no contract dichotomy: contractual liability begins only when a contract actually exists. But the result seems perverse in some respects. If, for instance, one party suffers damages because of the other's misrepresentations, why should liability be dependent on first proving the existence of a contract? In a contractual setting, even though no contract has yet been concluded, shouldn't misrepresentation be deterred? And, in fact, partially through the use of allied tort liabilities, courts have established a few avenues for preventing misconduct during the pre-contractual stage. The cases below describe some of these avenues. What remains unclear is whether these avenues are sufficient in the rough-and-tumble of the modern market.

Frier is sympathetic to the idea that contract liability should arise gradually and should often exist even before there has been a formal agreement between the parties. White is skeptical. He believes that our courts generally (both here and in torts) find too much liability, and that the world might be better served by courts turning away larger numbers of plaintiffs. To some extent this disagreement is an extension of the formalist/anti-formalist debate. The same people who favor writing and other formal requirements doubtless also favor the postponement of contract liability until the parties have fully performed the ritual of contract formation.

RACINE & LARAMIE, LTD., INC. v. DEPARTMENT OF PARKS AND RECREATION

Court of Appeal of California, 1992.
11 Cal.App.4th 1026, 14 Cal.Rptr.2d 335.

FROEHLICH, J. Racine & Laramie, Ltd., Inc. (Racine) is a concessionaire occupying and operating premises in Old Town San Diego State Historic Park under a contract, which bears many attributes of a long-term lease, with the California Department of Parks and Recreation (Department). The contract was executed in 1974 for a term of 40 years, thus extending until the year 2014. Over a period of several years in the 1980's Racine negotiated with the Department for modifications in the concession contract which would permit expanded operations of the premises. Originally limited to the operation of a tobacco shop and wine tasting facility, the negotiations contemplated operation of a restaurant and the on-premises sale of alcoholic beverages.

When negotiations broke down in 1988, Racine brought suit against the Department. Of the several initial causes of action, only one survived demurrers: a cause of action denominated "Breach of Implied Covenant of Good Faith and Fair Dealing." Tried to a jury, the case was submitted on special verdicts. The jury found that the Department was guilty of "breach [of] the covenant of good faith and fair dealing in its negotiations of an amendment/new contract to the concession agreement with the plaintiff" and that as a result of such breach Racine had been damaged in the sum of $592,110.

Department appeals the judgment on two grounds: (1) there can be no breach of the covenant of good faith by a refusal to enter into a new contract, and (2) the damage award is speculative and excessive. Since we rule in favor of Department as to its first contention, we do not reach the damage issue.

Controlling Facts

A very detailed examination of the parties' relationship and negotiations was presented to the jury. Since we are bound to accept the jury's determination of fact, assuming it to be supported by substantial evidence, we have no need of close focus on the history of the case. We therefore review the factual background summarily. Modification of a concession contract such as that here involved requires action by several state entities. The concessionaire deals with employees of the Department: Racine commenced doing this as early as 1980. Any contract which would permit on-premises sale of alcoholic beverages must, however, receive approval by the State Park and Recreation Commission (Commission) (Pub. Resources Code, § 5080.20), which is an entity vested with power to establish general policies to guide the Department. (Pub. Resources Code, § 530.539).

An "impact study" was presented by the Department to the Commission in 1983 which reflected Racine's efforts to establish a restaurant and on-premises liquor sales. On March 31, 1983, the Commission passed a resolution authorizing the Department to permit the expansion of Racine's concession, provided the concession contract be amended to conform to other contracts which had been negotiated with other Old Town concessionaires and include "such other terms as may be required."

Public Resources Code section 5080.20 requires that concession contracts involving certain floor figures of either investment or estimated gross sales, as included in this proposed contract modification, be submitted for review by the Legislature. On July 19, 1983, the Legislature authorized the renegotiation of the existing contract, directing that the Department "attempt to renegotiate the existing rent for the sale of pipes and tobacco products." Although Racine leans heavily on the actions of the Commission and the Legislature as somehow enhancing subsequent relations between Racine and the Department to a higher status than mere negotiations, it is clear that neither action binds the Department in any way.

The parties thereafter met at various times from 1983 through August 1985 and circulated various drafts of proposed amendments to the concession contract, but achieved no final agreement. After a hiatus of some 32 months, the parties renewed negotiations, resulting in a new written proposal from Racine, dated June 9, 1988. This proposal was quite different from that contained in the 1983 draft. For instance, instead of a 45- to 70-seat restaurant a 300-seat restaurant was proposed. Also, Racine sought to close the tobacco store operation completely. The Department replied by letter dated August 3, 1988, rejecting the proposal on several grounds. One ground, for instance, was that the Department felt the members of the then constituted Commission would probably not accept full alcoholic sale privileges. Another illustrative difference of approach was that the Department now favored only a "quick food" operation, as opposed to a full-service restaurant.

The instant lawsuit was then filed by Racine, without further negotiations. No negotiations have since taken place, although the Department in subsequent correspondence professed willingness to reopen the negotiations.

Racine's position is that having embarked upon lengthy negotiations over a period of several years, which negotiations resulted in tentative agreement as to some of the prospective changes in the concession contract, the Department was precluded arbitrarily and unilaterally from retreating from such positions. Racine emphasizes the fact that it was in an existing contractual relationship with the Department, and that this relationship explicitly contemplated future negotiations for contract modification. Paragraph 25 of the concession contract provided: "Notwithstanding any of the provisions of this contract, the parties may hereafter, by mutual consent, agree to modifications thereof or additions thereto in writing which are not forbidden by law. The State shall have the right to grant reasonable extensions of time to Concessionaire for any purpose or for the performance of any obligation of Concessionaire hereunder."

Once having entered into negotiations for a change in the contract, in accordance with paragraph 25 thereof, Racine takes the position that the bargaining had to be conducted in good faith. The Department's alleged reversal of its position on such matters as the full liquor sales privilege and the full restaurant service is characterized by Racine as arbitrary and capricious, and a violation of the covenant of good faith and fair dealing contained by implication in the concession contract.

We do not know exactly what it was in the facts of the case which led the jury to conclude, in its special verdict, that the Department had exhibited bad faith in its negotiations. We do know, however, that the jury was instructed generally on the law of the implied covenant of good faith and fair dealing, deemed to exist in every contract. We also know that counsel for Racine in argument contended that the sudden and arguably arbitrary reversal of negotiating stance taken by the Department constituted a violation of the covenant. We must assume that the jury so found.

We reverse because we conclude that the Department had no obligation to negotiate new terms of the concession contract, that its commencement and continuance of negotiations over a long period of time had no effect upon this lack of obligation, and that its assumption of an arbitrary stance at some point in the negotiations cannot therefore be a breach of any contract term, including implied contract terms of good faith and fair dealing, even though such conduct might be found by a jury to be unreasonable, unfair, or otherwise bad faith negotiation tactics.

Our conclusion in this regard is based, we believe, on rather simple and unassailable contract law principles. The implied covenant of good faith and fair dealing rests upon the existence of some specific contractual obligation. (*Foley v. Interactive Data Corp.* (1988) 47 Cal.3d 654, 683–684, 689–690 [254 Cal.Rptr. 211, 765 P.2d 373].) "The covenant of good faith is read into contracts in order to protect the express covenants or promises of the contract, not to protect some general public policy interest not directly tied to the contract's purpose." (at p. 690.) As we stated in *Love v. Fire Ins. Exchange* (1990) 221 Cal.App.3d 1136 at page 1153 [271 Cal.Rptr. 246]: "In essence, the covenant is implied as a supplement to the express contractual covenants, to prevent a contracting party from engaging in conduct which (while not technically transgressing the express covenants) frustrates the other party's rights to the benefits of the contract."

There existed no express contractual obligation here to negotiate a modification of the concession contract. The provision closest to a possible obligation is that contained in paragraph 25 of the contract, which falls far short of the imposition of any obligation on either party to even participate in activity leading to a modification of the concession. Similarly, the actions taken by the Commission and by the Legislature imposed upon the Department no obligation to enter into either contract negotiations or a contract amendment, but simply removed statutory conditions precedent to the Department's doing so if it should so elect.

There is no obligation to deal fairly or in good faith absent an existing contract.... If there exists a contractual relationship between the parties, as was the case here, the implied covenant is limited to assuring compliance with the express terms of the contract, and cannot be extended to create obligations not contemplated in the contract....

Racine attempts to avoid these accepted principles of law by asserting that, either in general or as related to this specific case, once a negotiation has been undertaken there is an obligation implied in law to negotiate in good faith. Racine relies heavily on a scholarly analysis of this concept set forth in Kessler and Fine, *Culpa in Contrahendo*, Bargaining in Good Faith, and Freedom of Contract: A Comparative Study (1964) 77 Harv.L.Rev. 401 (Kessler & Fine). This article reviewed and expanded upon a thesis first propounded in German legal philosophy in 1861, characterized by Kessler & Fine as "the thesis that damages should be recoverable against the party whose blameworthy conduct during negotiations for a contract brought about its invalidity or prevented its perfection." (Ibid.)

The difficulty with Racine's reliance on this thesis is that it has never been accepted in Anglo-American jurisprudence. Indeed, the authors' summation of the concept flatly states that "The common law appears to have no counterpart to the German doctrine of *culpa in contrahendo*."[20] Racine contends that the doctrine has been accepted by

20. Even were we to find that, somehow, this doctrine either existed or should be declared to exist in the common law, it would not support Racine's claim in this case. The *culpa in contrahendo* concept is one of repairing the damage done by bad faith negotiations, rather than awarding the damaged party the benefits or profits he would have gained had the negotiations succeeded. (Kessler & Fine, supra, at p. 405.) The evidence in this case disclosed no particular or specific damage incurred by Racine as a result of the flawed negotiations (such as having commenced work on the new restaurant, spent money for a liquor license, or the like). The damage testimony which resulted in the very large verdict reflected estimates of lost profits Racine

American jurisprudence, citing principally *Channel Home Centers, Grace Retail v. Grossman* (3d Cir. 1986) 795 F.2d 291. This reliance is, however, misplaced. *Channel* was a case in which negotiations for a lease led to the execution of a "letter of intent." Adhering to the law we have previously referenced, the *Channel* court first stated that "It is hornbook law that evidence of preliminary negotiations or an agreement to enter into a binding contract in the future does not alone constitute a contract." (at p. 298.) The court went on, however, to find that the terms of the letter of intent constituted an agreement to negotiate in good faith. "[S]uch an agreement, if otherwise meeting the requisites of a contract, is an enforceable contract." (at p. 299.) Citing and quoting from *Thompson v. Liquichimica of America, Inc.* (E.D.N.Y. 1979) 481 F.Supp. 365, 366, the court explained that " 'Unlike an agreement to agree, which does not constitute a closed proposition, an agreement to use best efforts [or to negotiate in good faith] is a closed proposition, discrete and actionable.' " (*Channel*, supra, at p. 299.) The court then found, as a matter of fact, that the letter of intent before it was an agreement to negotiate in good faith, and hence a failure to do so was actionable. The case does not stand for the proposition that failure to bargain in good faith is actionable absent an agreement imposing such obligation.

Racine also cites as supportive of its position Justice Traynor's opinion in *Drennan v. Star Paving Co.* (1958) 51 Cal.2d 409 [333 P.2d 757]. *Drennan* was a case of revocation of a construction bid before acceptance of the bid, but after the owner of the project had altered its position in reliance upon the bid. Finding no contract, but holding the bid nevertheless enforceable, the opinion relies upon traditional concepts of promissory estoppel....

Racine's claim was neither pleaded nor tried as promissory estoppel; moreover, the facts do not fit such theory. At no time was any promise made by the Department, and nothing the Department did resulted (insofar as the evidence adduced at trial indicated) in any action or forbearance of action on the part of Racine.

Finally, Racine attempts to find support for its position in the line of cases dealing with discretionary powers vested in one party to a contract to take action which affects the interests of the other party. Such discretionary powers must be exercised in good faith; in other words, when discretionary powers are vested in one party, an implied term of the contract provides that such powers will not be exercised arbitrarily or in disregard of the purposes of the contract and the interests of the other party.... These cases are inapposite to our situation. With respect to its concessionaire, at least in terms of modification of the concession contract, the Department had no discretionary powers which could be exercised unilaterally.

To recapitulate: The fact that parties commence negotiations looking to a contract, or to the amendment of an existing contract, does not

would have made over the balance of the 40-year lease had the negotiations succeeded—upon the terms Racine sought, of course.

by itself impose any duty on either party not to be unreasonable or not to break off negotiations, for any reason or for no reason. During the course of negotiations things may be done which do then impose a duty of continued bargaining only in good faith.[21]

For instance, a preexisting agreement may impose an obligation of good faith bargaining with respect to the modification of some term of the agreement. The preexisting agreement which vests a discretionary power of alteration of the terms of the agreement may impliedly require that such be done in good faith. Or, in anticipation of an agreement the parties may, by letter of intent or otherwise, agree that they will bargain in good faith for the purpose of reaching an agreement. Finally, in the course of negotiations it is possible for a party to so mislead another by promises or representations, upon which the second party detrimentally relies, as to bring into play the concept of promissory estoppel.

Absent the existence of such special circumstances or conditions, however, there is no obligation in California to bargain for a new or amended contract in good faith. None of the enumerated special circumstances existed in this case. The fact that bargaining took place over a period of many years and that the parties reached tentative agreement from time to time on some of the points at issue does not detract from this conclusion. There was in this case simply no contractual basis upon which to extract implied conditions of good faith bargaining.

Disposition

The judgment in favor of plaintiff is reversed, and the trial court is directed to enter judgment notwithstanding the verdict in favor of the Department. Defendant is entitled to costs on appeal.

Notes and Discussion

1. **What Was Racine Claiming?** Racine had a 40-year lease from the defendant, and was negotiating for a modification, as provided for in the lease. They argued that the long-term contract obligated the Department to negotiate with them in good faith. What is the relationship between the Court's view (quoting an earlier decision) that the covenant of good faith "protect[s] the express covenants or promises of the contract," and its further statement that: "There is no obligation to deal fairly or in good faith absent an existing contract"? Arguably the contractual paragraph on modification is not adequately protected by this decision.

Racine argued that when "lengthy negotiations ... resulted in tentative agreement as to some of the prospective changes in the concession contract, the Department was precluded arbitrarily and unilaterally from retreating from such positions"—in sum, "that the bargaining had to be conducted in good faith."

21. Of course, obligations of good faith bargaining may arise not by contractual agreement of the parties but by statutory imposition. (See, e.g., Lab. Code, § 1153, subd. (e), which imposes an obligation to conduct labor negotiations in good faith.) No such statutory obligation is presented in this case.

It is not easy to say, however, what "in good faith" means. What is fair in one bargain in one setting may be completely unfair and inappropriate in another. In some bargains there is a common understanding that no point is agreed upon until all points are agreed upon and therefore any party can revisit an issue to which he has apparently agreed. In other cases the convention may be the opposite. That is one of the reasons why White, at least, is instinctively put on edge by any invocation of the doctrine of good faith.

The trial jury awarded Racine almost $600,000 in damages. Is it likely that Racine had relied to this extent on the outcome of the negotiations, e.g., in preparing the "impact study," the drafts of proposed amendments to the concession contract, and other documents associated with the process? What obstacles would there be to Racine also claiming, for instance, its lost profits from the proposed restaurant?

Here and in *City of Kenai*, we have a long-term contract that expressly envisages future modification, yet the outcomes differ. The Court in *Racine* notes that the modification paragraph "falls far short of the imposition of any obligation on either party to even participate in activity leading to a modification of the concession." We wonder if the decision would have been different had the contract language imposed such an obligation.

2. *Culpa in Contrahendo.* The Court briefly discusses the Civil Law doctrine, which is now widespread in European-influenced law. If the Court had "received" this doctrine, how would this decision have been affected? The Department's case would not necessarily have collapsed; do you see why?

On precontractual liability, see especially E. Allan Farnsworth, *Precontractual Liability and Preliminary Agreements: Fair Dealing and Failed Negotiations*, 87 Colum. L. Rev. 217 (1987); Steven J. Burton & Eric F. Andersen, Contractual Good Faith 327–389 (1995).

NEW ENGLAND INSULATION CO. v. GENERAL DYNAMICS CORP.

Appeals Court of Massachusetts, 1988.
26 Mass.App.Ct. 28, 522 N.E.2d 997.

DREBEN, J. The plaintiff appeals from the dismissal of its action as against General Dynamics Corporation (General Dynamics) under Mass. R.Civ.P. 12(b)(6), 365 Mass. 754 (1974). We reverse in view of the generous reading which must be accorded to a complaint in passing on a motion to dismiss.

In numerous counts asserting various legal theories, . . . the plaintiff's allegations include: that General Dynamics invited the plaintiff to submit bids for the insulation of spherical tanks ("spheres") to hold liquified natural gas at sub-zero temperatures and for insulation of the holds of marine tanker vessels which would contain the spheres; that in its solicitations General Dynamics made representations that submissions would be retained in a locked file and would only be opened after the bid closing dates; that the plaintiff made its bids relying on these representations; that, contrary to published representations, prior to the bid closing dates, officers of General Dynamics (two of the individual defendants) made available to Frigitemp Corporation (Frigitemp) the previous bids submitted by the plaintiff; that such officers provided Frigitemp with the benefit of the plaintiff's confidential engineering and design work; that General Dynamics knew or should have known that its officers were engaged in a "kickback" scheme with officers (the other individual defendants) of Frigitemp so that Frigitemp would and did obtain the contracts; that General Dynamics authorized or permitted additional bids to be solicited from the plaintiff at a time when it knew or should have known that the contracts in question had been or would be awarded to Frigitemp without consideration of the price or the qualifications of the bidders; and that General Dynamics intended to induce the plaintiff to participate in a sham bidding procedure under which the plaintiff had no reasonable prospect of being awarded any contracts. The plaintiff sought damages including lost profits. . . .

General Dynamics quite rightly asserts that "[r]equests for bids are usually nonbinding invitations for offers," *Weinstein v. Green*, 347 Mass. 580, 582 (1964); *Chase Theaters, Inc. v. Paramount Pictures Corp.*, 25 Mass. App. Ct. 474, 478 (1988), and that it retained discretion to choose the insulation company with which it would contract. It was not bound to accept the plaintiff's bid, or indeed any bid. . . . It does not necessarily follow, however, that General Dynamics could not limit its freedom to act by making representations in its invitations to bid which it knew or should have known would be reasonably relied upon by the plaintiff.

Where the bid solicitor is a governmental entity, numerous cases impose liability on an implied contract theory. In the public contracting domain, an invitation to bid upon certain conditions followed by the submission of a bid on those conditions creates an implied contract obligating the bid solicitor to those conditions. Thus, for example, in *Heyer Prod. Co. v. United States*, 140 F. Supp. 409, 413 (Ct. Cl. 1956), the court pointed out that the contracting authority "knew it would involve considerable expense. . . . to comply with the invitation, and so, when it invited plaintiff to incur this expense, it must necessarily be implied that it promised to give fair and impartial consideration to its bid. . . . If . . . the [contracting authorities] knew from the beginning they were going to give [a certain company] the contract [and] [t]he advertisement for bids was a sham, . . . they practiced a fraud on plaintiff and on all other innocent bidders. They induced them to spend their money to prepare their bids on the false representation that their bids would be honestly considered. This implied contract has been broken and [the] plaintiff may maintain an action for damages for its breach."

The court allowed recovery of bid preparation costs. We reached the same result in *Paul Sardella Constr. Co. v. Braintree Housing Authy.* 3 Mass. App. Ct. 326, 333 (1975), S.C., 371 Mass. 235 (1976). . . .

We recognize that in public bidding cases the bidding process is governed by statute and that the legislative objectives of obtaining the lowest prices and establishing an honest and open procedure for competition for public contracts, see *Interstate Engr. Corp. v. Fitchburg*, 367 Mass. 751, 758 (1975), are furthered by allowing the award of reasonable bid preparation costs for "the failure to give fair consideration to a bidder in accordance with the statutory procedure." *Sardella*, 3 Mass. App. Ct. at 334. To the extent that the decisions are based on an implied contract or on promissory estoppel, however, those bases for recovery may be equally applicable to private solicitations for bids.... There is surely no policy which would be served by allowing solicitors of bids in the private sector to ignore the conditions they themselves set and ask others to rely upon.

Assuming, without deciding, that a promise to give fair and impartial consideration to all bids cannot be implied, that does not mean that, as matter of law, a promise not to divulge engineering and design work is not binding. Indeed, in *McNeil v. Boston Chamber of Commerce*, 154 Mass. 277, 279–281 (1891), the defendants, private solicitors of bids, were held bound by the terms of their notice as modified by an oral agreement with the bidders. Although the holding related to the condition requiring the defendants to accept the low bid from the invited bidders, the discussion suggests that the agreed upon terms, e.g., the opening of bids in the presence of all bidders, were also binding on the solicitor of bids.... See generally Restatement (Second) of Contracts § 28 comments c and d & illustration 5; 1 Williston, Contracts §§ 30 and 31 (3d ed. 1957); 1 Corbin, Contracts § 108 (1963).

The complaint also alleges misrepresentation. The misrepresentation cases involving bidding also arise primarily in the public sector, but there seems to be no reason in principle why they should not apply to private contractors. In fact, a number of cases which hold the governmental entity immune from tort liability point out that private persons might be held liable for the same actions....

In view of the foregoing authorities we think the allegations in the complaint suffice to warrant analysis of the actual facts to see if the plaintiff may recover under the theories discussed or perhaps under the broader aegis of c. 93A[22]....

The judgment dismissing the complaint against General Dynamics is reversed, and the matter is remanded for further proceedings consistent with this opinion.

Notes and Discussion

1. **The Plaintiff's Theories.** Although the Court runs them together, New England had several distinct reasons for dissatisfaction with the General Dynamics auction. These reasons included the collusive nature of the

22. We do not mean to imply that there must be a trial. It is possible that the matter can be resolved on motion for summary judgment.

"auction" and the disclosure of New England's confidential engineering and design work to Frigitemp before the bid closing dates. What larger issue underlies New England's grievances?

Of the auction of public contracts, the Court says that: "[A]n invitation to bid upon certain conditions followed by the submission of a bid on those conditions creates an implied contract obligating the bid solicitor to those conditions." What are the terms of this implied contract? What drawbacks are there to relying instead on promissory estoppel? Compare the outcome in *Midwest Energy, Inc. v. Orion Food Systems, Inc.*, considered in Chapter 2 as a reliance case.

New England had sought lost profits, but the Court apparently supports only "the award of reasonable bid preparation costs." Why?

2. The *Heyer* Case. As the Court indicates, most auction cases have involved public contracting. The archetype here is *Heyer Products Co. v. United States*, 135 Ct.Cl. 63, 140 F.Supp. 409 (1956), in which a U.S. Army ordnance unit solicited bids from Heyer and others on 5,500 low-voltage circuit testers. Heyer argued that the auction was rigged in favor of another manufacturer, who received the contract despite having bid twice as much. The *Heyer* decision denied the defendant's motion to dismiss, finding that the plaintiff had stated a cause of action to claim its expenses in preparing the bid. However, in the subsequent trial Heyer was unable to prove its claim: *Heyer Prod. Co. v. United States*, 147 Ct.Cl. 256, 177 F.Supp. 251 (1959). See also *B.K. Instrument, Inc. v. United States*, 715 F.2d 713 (2nd Cir. 1983; Friendly, J.).

The *New England* decision deals with the argument that a requirement of honesty in contracting should be restricted to public auctions only, but its counterargument is not entirely convincing.

3. Misrepresentation. The Court also briefly considers an alternative theory, that General Dynamics should be liable because it misrepresented its auction, thereby causing loss to New England. Since no contract resulted, the Court's reference is to the tort of fraudulent misrepresentation. But misrepresentation can also, in some circumstances, give rise to a contract claim for rescission and restitution; see below, Chapter 5.A.

An example of a case involving the tort of misrepresentation is *Markov v. ABC Transfer & Storage Co.*, 76 Wash.2d 388, 457 P.2d 535 (1969). A partnership leased warehouses to ABC for three years. As this lease neared its end, ABC sought to get the partners to extend the lease, explaining that its business with its principal customer depended on the renewal; and the partners, through their agents, repeatedly assured ABC that renewal would be granted. In the meantime, however, the partners were negotiating with a third party who sought to buy the warehouses; the partners did not inform ABC of these negotiations, apparently because they wanted the premises occupied during the negotiations and also wanted a fallback in case the sale did not go through. Ultimately the sale was successful, and ABC's renewal attempt then collapsed, resulting in substantial losses. The trial court judgment for ABC was $114,934.92.

The Supreme Court of Washington affirmed, observing: "There are times when the law demands of one an honest declaration of future intentions. If, instead of merely predicting future events, he promises to pursue a course of action, the law in all probability will oblige the promisor to keep his word. Even the failure to keep a promise one did not have to make may be as actionable as overt deceit and misrepresentation and in legal effect the equivalent of both." Id.

4. The Argument Against *Culpa in Contrahendo*. Prof. Allan Farnsworth takes note of "the common law's 'aleatory view' of negotiations: a party that enters negotiations in the hope of the gain that will result from ultimate agreement bears the risk of whatever loss results if the other party breaks off the negotiations." E. Allan Farnsworth, Contracts § 3.26 at 190 (4th student ed. 2004).

In his view, this position is felicitous. "[T]here is ample justification for judicial reluctance to impose a general obligation of fair dealing on parties to precontractual negotiations.... Although it is in society's interest to provide a regime under which the parties are free to negotiate ordinary contracts, the outcome of any particular negotiation is a matter of indifference. There is no reason to believe that imposition of a general obligation of fair dealing would improve the regime under which such negotiations take place. The difficulty of determining a point in the negotiations at which the obligation of fair dealing arises would create uncertainty. An obligation of fair dealing might have an undesirable chilling effect, discouraging parties from entering into negotiations if chances of success were slight. The obligation might also have an undesirable accelerating effect, increasing the pressure on parties to bring negotiations to a final if hasty conclusion. With no clear advantages to counter these disadvantages, there is little reason to abandon the present aleatory view." Id. at 199.

One of us is taken with this argument; the other is not. What do you think?

Problem 3–7

Falstaff & Co., a large firm of accountants, enters protracted negotiations with the owner of an office block, Hal & Sons, with the view to renting space for their new office in Everdale. In the course of these negotiations, Falstaff asks for various work to be done on the premises, including the installation of the wiring necessary for their computer and communications systems. Just before an appointment fixed by the parties for signing the contract, Falstaff finds equally suitable premises on offer at a lesser rent and refuses to go any further with Hal & Sons. What claim or claims do Hal & Sons have?

For a comparative law analysis of this problem, see Reinhard Zimmermann & Simon Whittaker, Good Faith in European Contract Law 236–257 (2000).

E. PROBLEMS WITH STANDARD FORM CONTRACTS

Standard contracts, usually with lengthy columns of terms, are a ubiquitous feature of modern commercial life, and the reasons are easy to understand. "When businesses become large enough to engage in numerous transactions of a kind, they can reduce their transaction costs by making their contracts in standard form. Businesses incur the costs of drafting a standard contract only once and spread them over as many transactions as they use the contracts. Standard contracts also make a business's legal risks more manageable by making them more uniform, also effecting a cost saving. These savings ultimately benefit consumers, because producers' cost savings are largely passed on in the form of lower prices in a competitive economy." W. David Slawson, Binding Promises: The Late 20th-Century Reformation of Contract Law 30 (1996).

Unfortunately, as Prof. Slawson goes on to point out, these undoubted benefits do not entirely offset some less positive aspects of standard contracts. Above all, they tend to facilitate efforts by one party to construct the contract according to its own wishes. Nor is this simply a matter of consumer protection, although consumers, as end-users, are certainly often at risk if they acquiesce in the intricate documents with which they are presented (in typical "contracts of adhesion"); and, after all, who among us actually does read such long and complicated contracts, other than when we are actually forced by circumstances to do so? But even in relations between large corporations, seller-producers can use standard contracts in order to take advantage because of their acquired experience with potential problems in their goods; warranties can be structured to their advantage, damages can be limited, choice of law problems can be favorably arranged, and so on. In short, standard contracts can accentuate inequities of bargaining power—where what is meant is less inequities of economic power than the unequal resources parties may have in entering into contracts. When it purchases "smart goods," General Motors may find itself as much at a disadvantage as you and I are.

American law has been forced to deal with the problems of standard form contracts. To some extent, the traditional template of contract law can still be used; but courts, and the legal community more generally, have also experimented with alternative ways of looking at contract.

We begin with UCC § 2–207. Recall the "mirror image" rule in *Ardente v. Horan*, in which a court interpreted a buyer's quibbling acceptance as a counteroffer that the seller was then free to refuse. Now suppose a situation like the following: a would-be buyer (whether a consumer or a firm) sends in an order for a computer, specifying only the model and price. The seller responds with an "acceptance" form that nominally accepts the order, but also contains a long list of contract terms favorable to it. At this stage, under traditional theory, the seller's "acceptance" is actually a counteroffer, and so there is no contract, of course. But what happens if the two parties then proceed as if they had a binding contract: the seller ships, the buyer takes delivery, and six months later a dispute arises over the computer's quality? Unless (what is exceedingly unlikely) the buyer has objected to the seller's terms, the "mirror image" rule holds that their contract was formed on the seller's terms. The seller fired the "last shot," and only the last shot counts.

Section 2–207 was designed, in part, to provide what was hoped would be a better outcome. In general, the UCC accepts the ordinary rules for contract formation; see especially §§ 2–204 and 206. Thus, for example, if the buyer sends in an order accompanied with a list of terms favorable to itself, the seller may expressly accept the buyer's offer, or in many cases it may tacitly do so by shipping the ordered goods (§ 2–206(1)(b)); but in either case the contract is ordinarily formed on the buyer's terms, and the same is true if the seller's terms are accepted by the buyer. But § 2–207 deals with situations that are less clear-cut, and it tries to reach a conclusion that avoids the inequities of the "last shot" rule. Unfortunately, the section does so in a manner that is so confusing as to cast more shadow than light.

It helps to begin by distinguishing three situations. First, suppose that two parties orally arrange a sale of goods—say, by telephone. Their agreement is a contract forthwith, although it may exist only in the barest outline. But what if one party then sends a written "confirmation" of the contract, and this confirmation contains a long list of terms? In many cases, these terms may be innocent, simply serving to fill out the initial agreement; but some terms may be more overtly partial to the drafting party. Section 2–207(1)-(2) in theory provides a sort of filter allowing the former, but not the latter, into the contract despite their arrival after the contract was made.

More difficult is the second case, where (typically) one party sends an order for goods, and the seller then sends what purports to be an acceptance but with terms that either add to or vary from the terms of the order. Again, § 2–207(1) and (2) were supposed to deal with this situation, but here the interpretative problems are far more dire; the subsections were, as all concede, poorly drafted, and courts have had to show dexterity in achieving equitable results. The *Gardner Zemke* case is a good illustration.

Subsections (1) and (2) also open the way for a third case, in which the exchange of documents between the parties does not lead to a contract between them (usually because each is insisting on its own terms exclusively), but they then proceed to "recognize[] the existence of a contract" through their conduct: the seller ships, the buyer pays, and so on. This is the domain of § 2–207(3), which allows the exchanged documents to influence the content of the contract even though the documents themselves do not establish a contract.

Section 2–207 is all about the intersection between the process of contract formation and contract interpretation in the Age of Standard Contracts. However, you should be warned that the many, many problems arising under this section almost never concern whether (à la *Ardente v. Horan*) a contract exists between seller and buyer. In virtually all instances, things have progressed too far for such a question to be taken seriously; both parties readily concede the existence of a contract, but sharply dispute what the terms of their contract are. On this ground the Battle of the Forms is fought.

This section concludes with two cases that represent additional ways of approaching the Battle. *Hill v. Gateway* introduces the concept of a "rolling contract" that may allow a seller to slip its terms past an unwary buyer; while *C & J Fertilizer* uses the concept of a consumer's "reasonable expectations" to avoid restrictions in standard form insurance contracts.

Note: Understanding § 2–207

Karl Llewellyn's § 2–207 had only two subsections, the present (1) and (2). As Prof. Grant Gilmore tells the story (in a letter to Prof. Summers), someone else added subsection (3) as an afterthought. This history explains much about the current section. Put yourself in the shoes of Llewellyn. As a teacher of sales and contracts, Llewellyn knew more than he needed to know about contract formation and he might have given that topic too much weight in the draft.

Look at subsection (1). It deals only with forming a contract; it insures that an exchange of documents that do not exactly match still may form a contract. Put differently, it abrogates the mirror image rule. Look at subsection (2); it does different work. Subsection (2) assumes the existence of a contract (found in (1)) and tells which of the offeree's proposals is part of that contract. So, subsection (1) deals with formation and subsection (2) deals with interpretation.

Now look at the two first subsections (which Llewellyn drafted) through the eyes of one who has just read *Ardente v. Horan*. Recall that Mr. Ardente had offered to buy the Horans' fancy house in Newport. In his acceptance, Mr. Ardente's agent stated that he was "concerned" that certain items like the dining room set and the sun parlor furniture go with the house. The court affirmed a finding that Mr. Ardente had made a counteroffer, not an acceptance. The decision allowed the Horans to sell to another and left Mr. Ardente without a house.

Applying § 2–207 to the *Ardente* facts (and pretending that real estate is covered by Article 2), Llewellyn would say that Ardente's response was an acceptance under subsection (1) because the acceptance was not "expressly ... conditional on assent to the additional terms ... " So a contract for sale was formed. One then goes to subsection (2) to decide the lesser question, whether the dining room set and parlor furniture are so valuable that they "materially" alter the offer. If so, there is a contract for sale of the house without the dining room set and furniture; if not, there is a contract with the set and furniture.

Reading Llewellyn's mind, we see him visualizing *Ardente v. Horan* and other formation cases as he drafts 2–207. He is interested in abolishing the obnoxious mirror image rule that he conceives to be inconsistent with normal business expectations. He wishes to bar welshers from using the mirror image rule to avoid contracts that they have made. For this purpose the Section is perfect; it fits *Ardente* like a glove.

Regrettably Llewellyn misread the legal landscape. In commerce, *Ardente* is a sport; business people rarely take up arms when a contract is aborted before birth. Instead of litigating at that early stage, they modify or buy or sell elsewhere. More than forty years of cases under 2–207 have shown that the Section is invariably called upon to answer the question "What are the terms of this contract that the parties acknowledge and have been performing?" and almost never to answer the question "Is there a contract?" As one of us once wrote, Section 2–207 is like a tank designed for the swamps that is made to fight in the desert.

Of course there were other mistakes too. Section 2–207(3), belatedly added to deal with the real cases, is awkward and seems to apply only where no contract has been formed by the writings. There is confusion about subsection (1)'s reference to "additional or different" followed by subsection (2)'s "additional" only. (Though perhaps that variation can be explained by looking to *Ardente*; there no one would say that "different" terms become part of the contract even if a document might be an acceptance of all of the offeror's terms despite its inclusion of some terms that contradict the terms in the offer.) Section 2–207 is also too respectful of the common law's distinction between offers and acceptances. In modern contracting, where a contract often evolves from a mess of phone calls, e-mails, and written forms, it is often hard to identify the offer and the acceptance; in that setting, it makes little sense to give greater rights to one party just because its message happens to be the first form or first e-mail.

When you have absorbed Section 2–207 in its current form, turn to Amended 2–207. You will see that it addresses some of the questions that we raise here.

Problem 3–8

As you wrestle with UCC 2–207, it's very important to think about the more general issue of when it is applicable and when not. Consider these three problems:

1) Buyer Buzz sends an order form for machinery to Seller Sally. The forms contain numerous terms highly favorable to Buzz, such as an extended seller warranty, a convenient choice of judicial forum, etc. Sally responds by shipping the machinery to Buzz, with no additional paperwork except for a bare invoice. Do Buzz's terms become part of the contract?

2) Buzz sends Sally an order form for 100 window frames @ $100. Sally sends back an acknowledgement that says: "We are happy to accept your order for 120 window frames @ $100." If only these two forms have thusfar been exchanged, is there a contract, and, if so, on what terms? If not, where are we?

3) Buzz sends Sally an order form for 100 window frames @ $100. Sally sends back an acknowledgement that says: "We are happy to accept your order for 100 window frames @ $100." Sally's acknowledgement also contains numerous additional clauses favorable to Sally, and it makes Sally's acceptance expressly conditional on Buzz's assent to these terms. If only these two forms have thusfar been exchanged, is

there a contract, and, if so, on what terms? If not, where are we, especially if Buzz and Sally proceed to implement the "contract"?

GARDNER ZEMKE CO. v. DUNHAM BUSH, INC.

Supreme Court of New Mexico, 1993.
115 N.M. 260, 850 P.2d 319.

FRANCHINI, J. This case involves a contract for the sale of goods and accordingly the governing law is the Uniform Commercial Code-Sales, as adopted in New Mexico. NMSA 1978, §§ 55–2–101 to –2–725 (Orig. Pamp. & Cum. Supp.1992) (Article 2). In the course of our discussion, we will also refer to pertinent general definitions and principles of construction found in NMSA 1978, Sections 55–1–101 to –1–209 (Orig. Pamp. & Cum. Supp.1992). Section 55–2–103(4). The case presents us with our first opportunity to consider a classic "battle of the forms" scenario arising under Section 55–2–207. Appellant Gardner Zemke challenges the trial court's judgment that a Customer's Acknowledgment (Acknowledgment) sent by appellee manufacturer Dunham Bush, in response to a Gardner Zemke Purchase Order (Order), operated as a counteroffer, thereby providing controlling warranty terms under the contract formed by the parties. We find merit in appellants' argument and remand for the trial court's reconsideration.

I.

Acting as the general contractor on a Department of Energy (DOE) project, Gardner Zemke issued its Order to Dunham Bush for air-conditioning equipment, known as chillers, to be used in connection with the project. The Order contained a one-year manufacturer's warranty provision and the requirement that the chillers comply with specifications attached to the Order. Dunham Bush responded with its preprinted Acknowledgment containing extensive warranty disclaimers, a statement that the terms of the Acknowledgment controlled the parties' agreement, and a provision deeming silence to be acquiescence to the terms of the Acknowledgment.

The parties did not address the discrepancies in the forms exchanged and proceeded with the transaction. Dunham Bush delivered the chillers, and Gardner Zemke paid for them. Gardner Zemke alleges that the chillers provided did not comply with their specifications and that they incurred additional costs to install the nonconforming goods. Approximately five or six months after start up of the chillers, a DOE representative notified Gardner Zemke of problems with two of the chillers. In a series of letters, Gardner Zemke requested on-site warranty repairs. Through its manufacturer's representative, Dunham Bush offered to send its mechanic to the job site to inspect the chillers and absorb the cost of the service call only if problems discovered were within any component parts it provided. Further, Dunham Bush required that prior to the service call a purchase order be issued from the DOE, to be executed by Dunham Bush for payment for their services in the event their mechanic discovered problems not caused by manufacturing defects. Gardner Zemke rejected the proposal on the basis that the DOE had a warranty still in effect for the goods and would not issue a separate purchase order for warranty repairs.

Ultimately, the DOE hired an independent contractor to repair the two chillers. The DOE paid $24,245.00 for the repairs and withheld $20,000.00 from its contract with Gardner Zemke. This breach of contract action then ensued, with Gardner Zemke alleging failure by Dunham Bush to provide equipment in accordance with the project plans and specifications and failure to provide warranty service.

II.

On cross-motions for summary judgment, the trial court granted partial summary judgment in favor of Dunham Bush, ruling that its Acknowledgment was a counteroffer to the Gardner Zemke Order and that the Acknowledgment's warranty limitations and disclaimers were controlling. Gardner Zemke filed an application for interlocutory appeal from the partial summary judgment in this Court, which was denied. A bench trial was held in December 1991, and the trial court again ruled the Acknowledgment was a counteroffer which Gardner Zemke accepted by silence and that under the warranty provisions of the Acknowledgment, Gardner Zemke was not entitled to damages.

On appeal, Gardner Zemke raises two issues: (1) the trial court erred as a matter of law in ruling that the Acknowledgment was a counteroffer; and (2) Gardner Zemke proved breach of contract and contract warranty, breach of code warranties, and damages.

III.

Karl N. Llewellyn, the principal draftsman of Article 2, described it as "[t]he heart of the Code." Karl N. Llewellyn, Why We Need the Uniform Commercial Code, 10 U.Fla.L.Rev. 367, 378 (1957). Section 2–207 is characterized by commentators as a "crucial section of Article 2" and an "iconoclastic Code section." Bender's Uniform Commercial Code Service (Vol. 3, Richard W. Duesenberg & Lawrence P. King, Sales & Bulk Transfers Under The Uniform Commercial Code) § 3.01 at 3–2 (1992). Recognizing its innovative purpose and complex structure Duesenberg and King further observe Section 2–207 "is one of the most important, subtle, and difficult in the entire Code, and well it may be said that the product as it finally reads is not altogether satisfactory." Id. § 3.02 at 3–13.

Section 55–2–207 provides:

> (1) A definite and seasonable expression of acceptance or a written confirmation which is sent within a reasonable time operates as an acceptance even though it states terms additional to or different from those offered or agreed upon, unless acceptance is expressly made conditional on assent to the additional or different terms.

(2) The additional terms are to be construed as proposals for addition to the contract. Between merchants such terms become part of the contract unless:

(a) the offer expressly limits acceptance to the terms of the offer;

(b) they materially alter it; or

(c) notification of objection to them has already been given or is given within a reasonable time after notice of them is received.

(3) Conduct by both parties which recognizes the existence of a contract is sufficient to establish a contract for sale although the writings of the parties do not otherwise establish a contract. In such case the terms of the particular contract consist of those terms on which the writings of the parties agree, together with any supplementary terms incorporated under any other provisions of this act [this chapter].

Relying on Section 2–207(1), Gardner Zemke argues that the trial court erred in concluding that the Dunham Bush Acknowledgment was a counteroffer rather than an acceptance. Gardner Zemke asserts that even though the Acknowledgment contained terms different from or in addition to the terms of their Order, it did not make acceptance expressly conditional on assent to the different or additional terms and therefore should operate as an acceptance rather than a counteroffer.

At common law, the "mirror image" rule applied to the formation of contracts, and the terms of the acceptance had to exactly imitate or "mirror" the terms of the offer.... If the accepting terms were different from or additional to those in the offer, the result was a counteroffer, not an acceptance.... Thus, from a common law perspective, the trial court's conclusion that the Dunham Bush Acknowledgment was a counteroffer was correct.

However, the drafters of the Code "intended to change the common law in an attempt to conform contract law to modern day business transactions." *Leonard Pevar Co. v. Evans Prods. Co.*, 524 F.Supp. 546, 551 (D.Del.1981). As Professors White and Summers explain: "The rigidity of the common law rule ignored the modern realities of commerce. Where preprinted forms are used to structure deals, they rarely mirror each other, yet the parties usually assume they have a binding contract and act accordingly. Section 2–207 rejects the common law mirror image rule and converts many common law counteroffers into acceptances under 2–207(1)." James J. White & Robert S. Summers, Handbook of the Law Under the Uniform Commercial Code § 1–3 at 29–30 (3d ed. 1988) (footnotes omitted).

On its face, Section 2–207(1) provides that a document responding to an offer and purporting to be an acceptance will be an acceptance, despite the presence of additional and different terms. Where merchants exchange preprinted forms and the essential contract terms agree, a contract is formed under Section 2–207(1). Duesenberg & King, § 3.04 at 3–47 to –49. A responding document will fall outside of the provisions of Section 2–207(1) and convey a counteroffer, only when its terms differ radically from the offer, or when "acceptance is expressly made conditional on assent to the additional or different terms"—whether a contract is formed under Section 2–207(1) here turns on the meaning given this phrase.

Dunham Bush argues that the language in its Acknowledgment makes acceptance expressly conditional on assent to the additional or different terms set forth in the Acknowledgment. The face of the Acknowledgment states:

> "IT IS UNDERSTOOD THAT OUR ACCEPTANCE OF THIS ORDER IS SUBJECT TO THE TERMS AND CONDITIONS ENUMERATED ON THE REVERSE SIDE HEREOF, IT BEING STRICTLY UNDERSTOOD THAT THESE TERMS AND CONDITIONS BECOME A PART OF THIS ORDER AND THE ACKNOWLEDGMENT THEREOF."

The following was among the terms and conditions on the reverse side of the Acknowledgment. "Failure of the Buyer to object in writing within five (5) days of receipt thereof to Terms of Sale contained in the Seller's acceptance and/or acknowledgment, or other communications, shall be deemed an acceptance of such Terms of Sale by Buyer."

In support of its contention that the above language falls within the "expressly conditional" provision of Section 2–207, Dunham Bush urges that we adopt the view taken by the First Circuit in *Roto-Lith, Ltd. v. F.P. Bartlett & Co.*, 297 F.2d 497 (1st Cir. 1962). There, Roto-Lith sent an order for goods to Bartlett, which responded with an acknowledgment containing warranty disclaimers, a statement that the acknowledgment reflected the terms of the sale, and a provision that if the terms were unacceptable Roto-Lith should notify Bartlett at once. Id. at 498–99. Roto-Lith did not protest the terms of the acknowledgment and accepted and paid for the goods. The court held the Bartlett acknowledgment was a counteroffer that became binding on Roto-Lith with its acceptance of the goods, reasoning that "a response which states a condition materially altering the obligation solely to the disadvantage of the offeror" falls within the "expressly conditional" language of 2–207(1). Id. at 500....

We have never adopted *Roto-Lith* in the context of the Code and decline to do so now. While ostensibly interpreting Section 2–207(1), the First Circuit's analysis imposes the common law doctrine of offer and acceptance on language designed to avoid the common law result. Roto-Lith has been almost uniformly criticized by the courts and commentators as an aberration in Article 2 jurisprudence. *Leonard Pevar Co.*, 524 F.Supp. at 551 (and cases cited therein); Duesenberg & King, § 3.05[1] at 3–61 to –62; White & Summers, § 1–3 at 36–37.

Mindful of the purpose of Section 2–207 and the spirit of Article 2, we find the better approach suggested in *Dorton v. Collins & Aikman Corp.*, 453 F.2d 1161 (6th Cir. 1972). In *Dorton*, the Sixth Circuit considered terms in acknowledgment forms sent by Collins & Aikman similar to the terms in the Dunham Bush Acknowledgment. The Collins & Aikman acknowledgments provided that acceptance of orders was subject to the terms and conditions of their form, together with at least seven methods in which a buyer might acquiesce to their terms, including receipt and retention of their form for ten days without objection. Id. at 1167–68.

Concentrating its analysis on the concept of the offeror's "assent," the Court reasoned that it was not enough to make acceptance expressly conditional on additional or different terms; instead, the expressly conditional nature of the acceptance must be predicated on the offeror's "assent" to those terms. Id. at 1168. The Court concluded that the "expressly conditional" provision of Section 2–207(1) "was intended to apply only to an acceptance which clearly reveals that the offeree is unwilling to proceed with the transaction unless he is assured of the offeror's assent to the additional or different terms therein." Id. This approach has been widely accepted. . . .

We agree with the court in *Dorton* that the inquiry focuses on whether the offeree clearly and unequivocally communicated to the offeror that its willingness to enter into a bargain was conditioned on the offerors "assent" to additional or different terms. An exchange of forms containing identical dickered terms, such as the identity, price, and quantity of goods, and conflicting undickered boilerplate provisions, such as warranty terms and a provision making the bargain subject to the terms and conditions of the offeree's document, however worded, will not propel the transaction into the "expressly conditional" language of Section 2–207(1) and confer the status of counteroffer on the responsive document.

While *Dorton* articulates a laudable rule, it fails to provide a means for the determination of when a responsive document becomes a counteroffer. We adopt the rule in *Dorton* and add that whether an acceptance is made expressly conditional on assent to different or additional terms is dependent on the commercial context of the transaction. Official Comment 2 to Section 55–2–207 suggests that "[u]nder this article a proposed deal which in commercial understanding has in fact been closed is recognized as a contract." While the comment applies broadly and envisions recognition of contracts formed under a variety of circumstances, it guides us to application of the concept of "commercial understanding" to the question of formation. See 2 William D. Hawkland, Uniform Commercial Code Series § 2–207:02 at 160 (1992) ("The basic question is whether, in commercial understanding, the proposed deal has been closed.").

Discerning whether "commercial understanding" dictates the existence of a contract requires consideration of the objective manifestations of the parties' understanding of the bargain. It requires consideration of the parties' activities and interaction during the making of the bargain; and when available, relevant evidence of course of performance, Section

55–2–208; and course of dealing and usage of the trade, Section 55–1–205. The question guiding the inquiry should be whether the offeror could reasonably believe that in the context of the commercial setting in which the parties were acting, a contract had been formed. This determination requires a very fact specific inquiry....

Our analysis does not yield an iron clad rule conducive to perfunctory application. However, it does remain true to the spirit of Article 2, as it calls the trial court to consider the commercial setting of each transaction and the reasonable expectations and beliefs of the parties acting in that setting....

The trial court's treatment of this issue did not encompass the scope of the inquiry we envision. We will not attempt to make the factual determination necessary to characterize this transaction on the record before us. Not satisfied that the trial court adequately considered all of the relevant factors in determining that the Dunham Bush Acknowledgment functioned as a counteroffer, we remand for reconsideration of the question.

In the event the trial court concludes that the Dunham Bush Acknowledgment constituted an acceptance, it will face the question of which terms will control in the exchange of forms. In the interest of judicial economy, and because this determination is a question of law, we proceed with our analysis.

IV.

The Gardner Zemke Order provides that the "[m]anufacturer shall replace or repair all parts found to be defective during initial year of use at no additional cost." Because the Order does not include any warranty terms, Article 2 express and implied warranties arise by operation of law. Section 55–2–313 (express warranties), § 55–2–314 (implied warranty of merchantability), § 55–2–315 (implied warranty of fitness for a particular purpose). The Dunham Bush Acknowledgment contains the following warranty terms:

> "WARRANTY: We agree that the apparatus manufactured by the Seller will be free from defects in material and workmanship for a period of one year under normal use and service and when properly installed: and our obligation under this agreement is limited solely to repair or replacement at our option, at our factories, of any part or parts thereof which shall within one year from date of original installation or 18 months from date of shipment from factory to the original purchaser, whichever date may first occur be returned to us with transportation charges prepaid which our examination shall disclose to our satisfaction to have been defective. THIS AGREEMENT TO REPAIR OR REPLACE DEFECTIVE PARTS IS EXPRESSLY IN LIEU OF AND IS HEREBY DISCLAIMER OF ALL OTHER EXPRESS WARRANTIES, AND IS IN LIEU OF AND IN DISCLAIMER AND EXCLUSION OF ANY IMPLIED WARRANTIES OF MERCHANTABILITY AND FITNESS FOR A

PARTICULAR PURPOSE, AS WELL AS ALL OTHER IMPLIED WARRANTIES, IN LAW OR EQUITY, AND OF ALL OTHER OBLIGATIONS OR LIABILITIES ON OUR PART. THERE ARE NO WARRANTIES WHICH EXTEND BEYOND THE DESCRIPTION HEREOF.... Our obligation to repair or replace shall not apply to any apparatus which shall have been repaired or altered outside our factory in any way.... "

The one proposition on which most courts and commentators agree at this point in the construction of the statute is that Section 2–207(3) applies only if a contract is not found under Section 2–207(1)....

The language of the statute makes it clear that "additional" terms are subject to the provisions of Section 2–207(2). However, a continuing controversy rages among courts and commentators concerning the treatment of "different" terms in a Section 2–207 analysis. While Section 2–207(1) refers to both "additional or different" terms, Section 2–207(2) refers only to "additional" terms. The omission of the word "different" from Section 55–2–207(2) gives rise to the questions of whether "different" terms are to be dealt with under the provisions of Section 2–207(2), and if not, how they are to be treated. That the terms in the Acknowledgment are "different" rather than "additional" guides the remainder of our inquiry and requires that we join the fray. Initially, we briefly survey the critical and judicial approaches to the problem posed by "different" terms.

One view is that, in spite of the omission, "different" terms are to be analyzed under Section 2–207(2). 2 Hawkland, § 2–207:03 at 168. The foundation for this position is found in Comment 3, which provides "[w]hether or not additional or different terms will become part of the agreement depends upon the provisions of Subsection (2)." Armed with this statement in Comment 3, proponents point to the ambiguity in the distinction between "different" and "additional" terms and argue that the distinction serves no clear purpose.... Following this rationale in this case, and relying on the observation in Comment 4 that a clause negating implied warranties would "materially alter" the contract, the Dunham Bush warranty terms would not become a part of the contract, and the Gardner Zemke warranty provision, together with the Article 2 warranties would control. § 55–2–207(2)(b).

Another approach is suggested by Duesenberg and King who comment that the ambiguity found in the treatment of "different" and "additional" terms is more judicially created than statutorily supported. While conceding that Comment 3 "contributes to the confusion," they also admonish that "the Official Comments do not happen to be the statute." Duesenberg & King, § 3.05 at 3–52. Observing that "the drafters knew what they were doing, and that they did not sloppily fail to include the term 'different' when drafting subsection (2)," Duesenberg and King postulate that a "different" term in a responsive document operating as an acceptance can never become a part of the parties' contract under the plain language of the statute. Id. § 3.03[1] at 3–38.

The reasoning supporting this position is that once an offeror addresses a subject it implicitly objects to variance of that subject by the offeree, thereby preventing the "different" term from becoming a part of the contract by prior objection and obviating the need to refer to "different" terms in Section 55–2–207(2). Id. § 3.05[1] at 3–77; ...

Professor Summers lends support to this position. White & Summers, § 1–3 at 34. Although indulging a different analysis, following this view in the case before us creates a result identical to that flowing from application of the provisions of Section 2–207(2) as discussed above—the Dunham Bush warranty provisions fall out, and the stated Gardner Zemke and Article 2 warranty provisions apply.

Yet a third analysis arises from Comment 6, which in pertinent part states: "Where clauses on confirming forms sent by both parties conflict each party must be assumed to object to a clause of the other conflicting with one on the confirmation sent by himself. As a result the requirement that there be notice of objection which is found in Subsection (2) is satisfied and the conflicting terms do not become a part of the contract. The contract then consists of the terms originally expressly agreed to, terms on which the confirmations agree, and terms supplied by this act, including Subsection (2)."

The import of Comment 6 is that "different" terms cancel each other out and that existing applicable code provisions stand in their place. The obvious flaws in Comment 6 are the use of the words "confirming forms," suggesting the Comment applies only to variant confirmation forms and not variant offer and acceptance forms, and the reference to Subsection 55–2–207(2)—arguably dealing only with "additional" terms—in the context of "different" terms. Of course, Duesenberg and King remind us that Comment 6 "is only a comment, and a poorly drawn one at that." Duesenberg & King, § 3.05[1] at 3–79.

The analysis arising from Comment 6, however, has found acceptance in numerous jurisdictions including the Tenth Circuit. *Daitom, Inc. v. Pennwalt Corp.*, 741 F.2d 1569, 1578–79 (10th Cir. 1984). Following a discussion similar to the one we have just indulged, the court found this the preferable approach. Id. at 1579; ... Professor White also finds merit in this analysis. White & Summers, § 1–3 at 33–35. Application of this approach here cancels out the parties' conflicting warranty terms and allows the warranty provisions of Article 2 to control.

We are unable to find comfort or refuge in concluding that any one of the three paths drawn through the contours of Section 2–207 is more consistent with or true to the language of the statute. We do find that the analysis relying on Comment 6 is the most consistent with the purpose and spirit of the Code in general and Article 2 in particular. We are mindful that the overriding goal of Article 2 is to discern the bargain struck by the contracting parties. However, there are times where the conduct of the parties makes realizing that goal impossible. In such cases, we find guidance in the Code's commitment to fairness, Section

55–1–102(3); good faith, Sections 55–1–203 & –2–103(1)(b); and conscionable conduct, Section 55–2–302.

While Section 2–207 was designed to avoid the common law result that gave the advantage to the party sending the last form, we cannot conclude that the statute was intended to shift that advantage to the party sending the first form. Such a result will generally follow from the first two analyses discussed. We adopt the third analysis as the most even-handed resolution of a difficult problem. We are also aware that under this analysis even though the conflicting terms cancel out, the Code may provide a term similar to one rejected. We agree with Professor White that "[a]t least a term so supplied has the merit of being a term that the draftsmen considered fair." White & Summers, § 1–3 at 35.

Due to our disposition of this case, we do not address the second issue raised by Gardner Zemke. On remand, should the trial court conclude a contract was formed under Section 2–207(1), the conflicting warranty provisions in the parties' forms will cancel out, and the warranty provisions of Article 2 will control.

IT IS SO ORDERED.

Notes and Discussion

1. **The Controversy.** Gardner Zemke ordered chillers that have already been delivered, installed, and paid for, but that turned out, so it appears, to be inadequate; because they "did not comply with their specifications," Gardner Zemke "incurred additional costs to install nonconforming goods," and in operation two of the chillers had additional problems requiring expensive repairs. As in virtually all § 2–207 cases, the issue between Gardner Zemke and seller Dunham Bush is not whether there is a contract, but rather what the terms of their contract are, particularly with respect to Dunham Bush's remedy provisions. What would the outcome of this case have been under the "mirror image rule"? On a "last shot" theory, how would the contract have been formed?

In most but not all sale of goods cases involving a "battle of the forms," the exchange of forms begins with the buyer's order, so that the seller's acknowledgment (whatever it is nominally called), if it varies significantly from the order, constitutes, in the pre-UCC theory of *Ardente v. Horan*, a counteroffer that the buyer then accepts essentially by acquiescence in delivery. Note that the "mirror image" rule is still largely preserved in the CISG, art. 19 (for the sale of goods between international merchants).

Suppose that after it received Gardner Zemke's order form, Dunham Bush had responded by simply shipping the chillers, without either sending an Acknowledgment or enclosing an invoice that stated its warranty disclaimers. Gardner Zemke's warranty provision would then have been part of the contract, true? See UCC § 2–206(1)(b) and Restatement 2d §§ 32, 62.

The *Roto-Lith* decision, discussed by the Court, encountered heavy criticism for its attempt to reintroduce the "mirror image" rule. Suitably chastened, the First Circuit finally overruled it in 1997: *Ionics, Inc. v. Elmwood Sensors, Inc.*, 110 F.3d 184, 187–189 (1st Cir. 1997).

2. Handling the Warranties. The New Mexico Supreme Court proceeds step-by-step in determining whether Dunham Bush's "extensive warranty disclaimers" make it into the contract with Gardner Zemke. The first step, under § 2–207(1), is to determine whether the exchange of documents resulted in a contract despite the discordant terms of the offer and acknowledgment and Dunham Bush's express attempt to limit the contract to its own terms. The Court concludes that there is a contract. Is there an ostensible justification for believing that during the formation process Dunham Bush, despite the language of its form, is unlikely to have been sufficiently keen on its terms to have insisted on them even if the disclaimers were deal breakers?

If (and only if) investigation under subsection 1 leads to a positive outcome, the Court proceeds to determine whether "additional or different" terms become part of the contract. "Additional" terms are expressly governed by the rules of § 2–207(2). If Gardner Zemke's order had not contained a remedy provision, Dunham Bush's disclaimers would have been additional terms. Look closely at the wording of subsection 2. The most difficult test is determining whether the additional terms "materially alter" the contract. Official Comments 4 and 5 give examples of clauses that are material and not material. The main criterion is whether the clauses would "result in surprise or hardship if incorporated without express awareness by the other party." UCC § 2–207 cmt. 4. Is that likely to be the case for a warranty disclaimer?

However, since the order did contain a seller's remedy provision, Dunham Bush's disclaimers and remedy limitations are "different" terms. The Court outlines the controversy about how to handle such terms. The solution it prefers—the "knock-out" rule whereby the conflicting terms cancel each other out and the default UCC warranties are used instead—is also the result that most courts have preferred. Which party (seller or buyer) is likeliest to benefit from this outcome? On the UCC implied warranties of merchantability and fitness for particular purpose, see Chapter 4.D.

3. An Oral Contract with Subsequent Written Confirmations. Suppose, now, that Gardner Zemke and Dunham Bush had arranged for the sale by telephone, and that one or both had then sent forms identical to those in this case, as "confirmations" of their contract. The difference here is that now a contract (albeit an oral one) would already exist before the "confirmations" were mailed. Therefore any terms in the "confirmations" would be additional. Would the outcome under § 2–207(1)-(2) be different than in this case?

Step-Saver Data Systems v. Wyse Technology, the case that follows, is an example of an oral contract with subsequent written confirmations.

4. The Battle Continues. Back to the original case. The drafters of boilerplate forms have in no wise been deterred by the rebuffs that their forms may receive under § 2–207(1)-(2). Suppose that the facts are as in the *Gardner Zemke* opinion, except that Gardner Zemke's order form states explicitly that it is willing to enter a contract only on its own terms; in the wording of § 2–207(2)(a), "the offer expressly limits acceptance to the terms of the offer.'' Alternatively, suppose that the facts are as in *Gardner Zemke*, except that—as § 2–207(1) puts it—Dunham Bush's ''acceptance is expressly made conditional on assent to the additional or different terms.'' Finally, suppose that the standardized forms of each party state its willingness to enter a contract only on its own terms.

In these circumstances, if the parties then act as if a contract exists between them (the seller ships the goods, the buyer pays, etc.), a court could well be justified in concluding that no contract was formed by the documents themselves, but that a contract exists under § 2–207(3). That subsection will be no more favorable to Dunham Bush's warranty disclaimers.

Although § 2–207 obscures the outcome, both sections here are bimodal. That is, there are only two outcomes: either warranty or no warranty, either disclaimer or no disclaimer. It makes little difference to the seller or the buyer whether the seller's disclaimer is ''knocked out'' or whether there is no disclaimer not because of a knockout but because no written contract is ever formed and because the implied contract has no disclaimer.

5. Can the Illness Be Diagnosed and Cured? The ''battle of the forms'' continues, and there seems also to be general agreement that § 2–207 has not been successful. The legal issue stems from conflict between three types of clauses: the terms that the parties negotiate explicitly (sometimes little more than the price and the object of sale); the terms that the parties do not negotiate but each still hopes to insert into the contract, usually through standardized forms; and the default terms supplied by the UCC or on the basis of course of performance, course of dealing, or trade usage. Terms in the second class, presumptively less worthy of respect, range from the innocuous to the highly partial. Lurking in the discussion of them is the following question: should it be presumed, as a strong rule, that regular default terms are likely to be fairer to both parties unless they expressly negotiate away from them?

The situation is substantially altered by the amended Article 2. See the new language of §§ 2–206 and 207.

STEP-SAVER DATA SYSTEMS, INC. v. WYSE TECHNOLOGY

United States Court of Appeals, Third Circuit, 1991.
939 F.2d 91.

WISDOM, J. The ''Limited Use License Agreement'' printed on a package containing a copy of a computer program raises the central issue in this appeal. The trial judge held that the terms of the Limited Use License Agreement governed the purchase of the package, and, therefore, granted the software producer, The Software Link, Inc. (''TSL''), a directed verdict on claims of breach of warranty brought by a disgruntled purchaser, Step-Saver Data Systems, Inc. We disagree with the district court's determination of the legal effect of the license, and reverse and remand the warranty claims for further consideration.

Step-Saver raises several other issues, but we do not find these issues warrant reversal. We, therefore, affirm in all other respects.

I. Factual And Procedural Background

[Eds.: Step-Saver marketed to the offices of physicians and lawyers a multi-user computer system in which terminals are attached by cable to a main computer. For this product, it selected terminals manufactured by Wyse and an operating system developed by TSL (the Multilink Advanced program). It began marketing the system in November, 1986, but almost immediately faced complaints from some customers. Step-Saver terminated sales in March, 1987.

[Step-Saver eventually brought suit alleging breach of warranties by both TSL and Wyse and intentional misrepresentations by TSL. As excerpted, the opinion below concerns only the TSL portion of the lawsuit. Both Step-Saver and TSL agreed that the operating system were "goods" within the meaning of UCC §§ 2–102 and 105. The district court agreed with TSL's contention that the form language printed on the packages for each operating system ("the box-top license") was the complete and exclusive agreement between Step-Saver and TSL. Based on § 2–316 of the UCC, the district court held that the box-top license disclaimed all express and implied warranties otherwise made by TSL. The court therefore granted TSL's motion *in limine* to exclude all evidence of the earlier oral and written express warranties made by TSL. On the misrepresentation claim the district court also granted a directed verdict in favor of TSL.

[Step-Saver appealed, arguing, among other things, that Step-Saver and TSL did not intend the box-top license to be a complete and final expression of the terms of their agreement.]

II. The Effect Of The Box-Top License

The relationship between Step-Saver and TSL began in the fall of 1984 when Step-Saver asked TSL for information on an early version of the Multilink program. TSL provided Step-Saver with a copy of the early program, known simply as Multilink, without charge to permit Step-Saver to test the program to see what it could accomplish. Step-Saver performed some tests with the early program, but did not market a system based on it.

In the summer of 1985, Step-Saver noticed some advertisements in Byte magazine for a more powerful version of the Multilink program, known as Multilink Advanced. Step-Saver requested information from TSL concerning this new version of the program, and allegedly was assured by sales representatives that the new version was compatible with ninety percent of the programs available "off-the-shelf" for computers using MS-DOS. The sales representatives allegedly made a number of additional specific representations of fact concerning the capabilities of the Multilink Advanced program.

Based on these representations, Step-Saver obtained several copies of the Multilink Advanced program in the spring of 1986, and conducted tests with the program. After these tests, Step-Saver decided to market a multi-user system which used the Multilink Advanced program. From

August of 1986 through March of 1987, Step-Saver purchased and resold 142 copies of the Multilink Advanced program. Step-Saver would typically purchase copies of the program in the following manner. First, Step-Saver would telephone TSL and place an order. (Step-Saver would typically order twenty copies of the program at a time.) TSL would accept the order and promise, while on the telephone, to ship the goods promptly. After the telephone order, Step-Saver would send a purchase order, detailing the items to be purchased, their price, and shipping and payment terms. TSL would ship the order promptly, along with an invoice. The invoice would contain terms essentially identical with those on Step-Saver's purchase order: price, quantity, and shipping and payment terms. No reference was made during the telephone calls, or on either the purchase orders or the invoices with regard to a disclaimer of any warranties.

Printed on the package of each copy of the program, however, would be a copy of the box-top license. The box-top license contains five terms relevant to this action:

(1) The box-top license provides that the customer has not purchased the software itself, but has merely obtained a personal, non-transferable license to use the program.

(2) The box-top license, in detail and at some length, disclaims all express and implied warranties except for a warranty that the disks contained in the box are free from defects.

(3) The box-top license provides that the sole remedy available to a purchaser of the program is to return a defective disk for replacement; the license excludes any liability for damages, direct or consequential, caused by the use of the program.

(4) The box-top license contains an integration clause, which provides that the box-top license is the final and complete expression of the terms of the parties's agreement.

(5) The box-top license states: "Opening this package indicates your acceptance of these terms and conditions. If you do not agree with them, you should promptly return the package unopened to the person from whom you purchased it within fifteen days from date of purchase and your money will be refunded to you by that person."

The district court, without much discussion, held, as a matter of law, that the box-top license was the final and complete expression of the terms of the parties's agreement. Because the district court decided the questions of contract formation and interpretation as issues of law, we review the district court's resolution of these questions de novo.

Step-Saver contends that the contract for each copy of the program was formed when TSL agreed, on the telephone, to ship the copy at the agreed price.[23] The box-top license, argues Step-Saver, was a material

23. See UCC § 2–206(1)(b) and comment 2....

alteration to the parties's contract which did not become a part of the contract under UCC § 2–207....

TSL argues that the contract between TSL and Step-Saver did not come into existence until Step-Saver received the program, saw the terms of the license, and opened the program packaging. TSL contends that too many material terms were omitted from the telephone discussion for that discussion to establish a contract for the software. Second, TSL contends that its acceptance of Step-Saver's telephone offer was conditioned on Step-Saver's acceptance of the terms of the box-top license. Therefore, TSL argues, it did not accept Step-Saver's telephone offer, but made a counteroffer represented by the terms of the box-top license, which was accepted when Step-Saver opened each package. Third, TSL argues that, however the contract was formed, Step-Saver was aware of the warranty disclaimer, and that Step-Saver, by continuing to order and accept the product with knowledge of the disclaimer, assented to the disclaimer.

In analyzing these competing arguments, we first consider whether the license should be treated as an integrated writing under UCC § 2–202, as a proposed modification under UCC § 2–209, or as a written confirmation under UCC § 2–207. Finding that UCC § 2–207 best governs our resolution of the effect of the box-top license, we then consider whether, under UCC § 2–207, the terms of the box-top license were incorporated into the parties's agreement.

A. *Does UCC § 2–207 Govern the Analysis?*

As a basic principle, we agree with Step-Saver that UCC § 2–207 governs our analysis. We see no need to parse the parties's various actions to decide exactly when the parties formed a contract. TSL has shipped the product, and Step-Saver has accepted and paid for each copy of the program. The parties's performance demonstrates the existence of a contract. The dispute is, therefore, not over the existence of a contract, but the nature of its terms. When the parties's conduct establishes a contract, but the parties have failed to adopt expressly a particular writing as the terms of their agreement, and the writings exchanged by the parties do not agree, UCC § 2–207 determines the terms of the contract....

Although UCC § 2–202 permits the parties to reduce an oral agreement to writing, and UCC § 2–209 permits the parties to modify an existing contract without additional consideration, a writing will be a final expression of, or a binding modification to, an earlier agreement only if the parties so intend. It is undisputed that Step-Saver never expressly agreed to the terms of the box-top license, either as a final expression of, or a modification to, the parties's agreement. In fact, Barry Greebel, the President of Step-Saver, testified without dispute that he objected to the terms of the box-top license as applied to Step-Saver. In the absence of evidence demonstrating an express intent to adopt a writing as a final expression of, or a modification to, an earlier agreement, we find UCC § 2–207 to provide the appropriate legal rules for determining whether such an intent can be inferred from continuing with the contract after receiving a writing containing additional or different terms. . . .

The UCC, in § 2–207, . . . recognized that, while a party may desire the terms detailed in its form if a dispute, in fact, arises, most parties do not expect a dispute to arise when they first enter into a contract. As a result, most parties will proceed with the transaction even if they know that the terms of their form would not be enforced. The insight behind the rejection of the last shot rule is that it would be unfair to bind the buyer of goods to the standard terms of the seller, when neither party cared sufficiently to establish expressly the terms of their agreement, simply because the seller sent the last form. Thus, UCC § 2–207 establishes a legal rule that proceeding with a contract after receiving a writing that purports to define the terms of the parties's contract is not sufficient to establish the party's consent to the terms of the writing to the extent that the terms of the writing either add to, or differ from, the terms detailed in the parties's earlier writings or discussions. In the absence of a party's express assent to the additional or different terms of the writing, section 2–207 provides a default rule that the parties intended, as the terms of their agreement, those terms to which both parties have agreed, along with any terms implied by the provisions of the UCC.

The reasons that led to the rejection of the last shot rule, and the adoption of section 2–207, apply fully in this case. TSL never mentioned during the parties's negotiations leading to the purchase of the programs, nor did it, at any time, obtain Step-Saver's express assent to, the terms of the box-top license. Instead, TSL contented itself with attaching the terms to the packaging of the software, even though those terms differed substantially from those previously discussed by the parties. Thus, the box-top license, in this case, is best seen as one more form in a battle of forms, and the question of whether Step-Saver has agreed to be bound by the terms of the box-top license is best resolved by applying the legal principles detailed in section 2–207.

B. Application of § 2–207

TSL advances several reasons why the terms of the box-top license should be incorporated into the parties's agreement under a § 2–207 analysis. First, TSL argues that the parties's contract was not formed until Step-Saver received the package, saw the terms of the box-top license, and opened the package, thereby consenting to the terms of the license. TSL argues that a contract defined without reference to the specific terms provided by the box-top license would necessarily fail for indefiniteness. Second, TSL argues that the box-top license was a conditional acceptance and counter-offer under § 2–207(1). Third, TSL argues that Step-Saver, by continuing to order and use the product with notice of the terms of the box-top license, consented to the terms of the box-top license.

1. Was the contract sufficiently definite?

TSL argues that the parties intended to license the copies of the program, and that several critical terms could only be determined by referring to the box-top license. Pressing the point, TSL argues that it is impossible to tell, without referring to the box-top license, whether the parties intended a sale of a copy of the program or a license to use a copy....

From the evidence, it appears that the following terms, at the least, were discussed and agreed to, apart from the box-top license: (1) the specific goods involved; (2) the quantity; and (3) the price. TSL argues that the following terms were only defined in the box-top license: (1) the nature of the transaction, sale or license; and (2) the warranties, if any, available. TSL argues that these two terms are essential to creating a sufficiently definite contract. We disagree.

As stated by the official comment to § 2–207: "1. This section is intended to deal with two typical situations. The one is the written confirmation, where an agreement has been reached either orally or by informal correspondence between the parties and is followed by one or more of the parties sending formal memoranda embodying the terms so far as agreed upon and adding terms not discussed....

"2. Under this Article a proposed deal which in commercial understanding has in fact been closed is recognized as a contract. Therefore any additional matter contained in the confirmation or in the acceptance falls within subsection (2) and must be regarded as a proposal for an added term unless the acceptance is made conditional on the acceptance of the additional or different terms."

First, the rights of the respective parties under the federal copyright law if the transaction is characterized as a sale of a copy of the program are nearly identical to the parties's respective rights under the terms of the box-top license. Second, the UCC provides for express and implied warranties if the seller fails to disclaim expressly those warranties. Thus, even though warranties are an important term left blank by the parties, the default rules of the UCC fill in that blank.

We hold that contract was sufficiently definite without the terms provided by the box-top license.

2. The box-top license as a counter-offer?

TSL advances two reasons why its box-top license should be considered a conditional acceptance under UCC § 2–207(1). First, TSL argues that the express language of the box-top license, including the integration clause and the phrase "opening this product indicates your acceptance of these terms," made TSL's acceptance "expressly conditional on assent to the additional or different terms." Second, TSL argues that the box-top license, by permitting return of the product within fifteen days if the purchaser does not agree to the terms stated in the license (the "refund offer"), establishes that TSL's acceptance was conditioned on Step-Saver's assent to the terms of the box-top license, citing *Monsanto Agricultural Products Co. v. Edenfield*. While we are not certain that a conditional acceptance analysis applies when a contract is established by performance, we assume that it does and consider TSL's arguments.

[Eds.: After protracted discussion, the Court concludes that TSL could make a conditional acceptance only if it clearly and unequivocally indicated that it was "unwilling[] to proceed with the transaction unless [its] additional or different terms are included in the contract.... [I]t is apparent that the integration clause and the 'consent by opening' language is not sufficient to render TSL's acceptance conditional. As other courts have recognized, this type of language provides no real indication that the party is willing to forgo the transaction if the additional language is not included in the contract."]

The second provision provides a more substantial indication that TSL was willing to forgo the contract if the terms of the box-top license were not accepted by Step-Saver. On its face, the box-top license states that TSL will refund the purchase price if the purchaser does not agree to the terms of the license. Even with such a refund term, however, the offeree/counterofferor may be relying on the purchaser's investment in time and energy in reaching this point in the transaction to prevent the purchaser from returning the item. Because a purchaser has made a decision to buy a particular product and has actually obtained the product, the purchaser may use it despite the refund offer, regardless of the additional terms specified after the contract formed.... We see no basis in the terms of the box-top license for inferring that a reasonable offeror would understand from the refund offer that certain terms of the box-top license, such as the warranty disclaimers, were essential to TSL, while others such as the non-transferability provision were not.

Based on these facts, we conclude that TSL did not clearly express its unwillingness to proceed with the transactions unless its additional terms were incorporated into the parties's agreement. The box-top license did not, therefore, constitute a conditional acceptance under UCC § 2–207(1).

3. Did the parties's course of dealing establish that the parties had excluded any express or implied warranties associated with the software program?

TSL argues that because Step-Saver placed its orders for copies of the Multilink Advanced program with notice of the terms of the box-top license, Step-Saver is bound by the terms of the box-top license. Essentially, TSL is arguing that, even if the terms of the box-top license would not become part of the contract if the case involved only a single transaction, the repeated expression of those terms by TSL eventually incorporates them within the contract.

Ordinarily, a "course of dealing" or "course of performance" analysis focuses on the actions of the parties with respect to a particular issue.[24] If, for example, a supplier of asphaltic paving material on two occasions gives a paving contractor price protection, a jury may infer that the parties have incorporated such a term in their agreement by their course of performance. Because this is the parties's first serious dispute, the parties have not previously taken any action with respect to the matters addressed by the warranty disclaimer and limitation of liability terms of the box-top license. Nevertheless, TSL seeks to extend the course of dealing analysis to this case where the only action has been the repeated sending of a particular form by TSL. While one court has concluded that terms repeated in a number of written confirmations eventually become part of the contract even though neither party ever takes any action with respect to the issue addressed by those terms, most courts have rejected such reasoning.

For two reasons, we hold that the repeated sending of a writing which contains certain standard terms, without any action with respect to the issues addressed by those terms, cannot constitute a course of dealing which would incorporate a term of the writing otherwise excluded under § 2–207. First, the repeated exchange of forms by the parties only tells Step-Saver that TSL desires certain terms. Given TSL's failure to obtain Step-Saver's express assent to these terms before it will ship the program, Step-Saver can reasonably believe that, while TSL desires certain terms, it has agreed to do business on other terms—those terms expressly agreed upon by the parties. Thus, even though Step-Saver would not be surprised to learn that TSL desires the terms of the box-top license, Step-Saver might well be surprised to learn that the terms of the box-top license have been incorporated into the parties's agreement.

Second, the seller in these multiple transaction cases will typically have the opportunity to negotiate the precise terms of the parties's agreement, as TSL sought to do in this case. The seller's unwillingness or inability to obtain a negotiated agreement reflecting its terms strongly suggests that, while the seller would like a court to incorporate its terms if a dispute were to arise, those terms are not a part of the parties's commercial bargain. For these reasons, we are not convinced that TSL's unilateral act of repeatedly sending copies of the box-top license with its product can establish a course of dealing between TSL and Step-Saver that resulted in the adoption of the terms of the box-top license.

With regard to more specific evidence as to the parties's course of dealing or performance, it appears that the parties have not incorporated the warranty disclaimer into their agreement. First, there is the evidence that TSL tried to obtain Step-Saver's express consent to the disclaimer and limitation of damages provision of the box-top license. Step-Saver refused to sign the proposed agreements. Second, when first notified of

24. A "course of performance" refers to actions with respect to the contract taken after the contract has formed. UCC § 2–208(1). "A course of dealing is a sequence of previous conduct between the parties to a particular transaction which is fairly to be regarded as establishing a common basis of understanding for interpreting their expressions and other conduct." UCC § 1–205. [Eds.: See, in the revised Article One, § 1–303(b), (c).]

the problems with the program, TSL spent considerable time and energy attempting to solve the problems identified by Step-Saver.

Course of conduct is ordinarily a factual issue. But we hold that the actions of TSL in repeatedly sending a writing, whose terms would otherwise be excluded under UCC § 2–207, cannot establish a course of conduct between TSL and Step-Saver that adopted the terms of the writing.

4. Public policy concerns

TSL has raised a number of public policy arguments focusing on the effect on the software industry of an adverse holding concerning the enforceability of the box-top license. We are not persuaded that requiring software companies to stand behind representations concerning their products will inevitably destroy the software industry. We emphasize, however, that we are following the well-established distinction between conspicuous disclaimers made available before the contract is formed and disclaimers made available only after the contract is formed.[25] When a disclaimer is not expressed until after the contract is formed, UCC § 2–207 governs the interpretation of the contract, and, between merchants, such disclaimers, to the extent they materially alter the parties's agreement, are not incorporated into the parties's agreement.

If TSL wants relief for its business operations from this well-established rule, their arguments are better addressed to a legislature than a court. . . .

C. The Terms of the Contract

Under section 2–207, an additional term detailed in the box-top license will not be incorporated into the parties's contract if the term's addition to the contract would materially alter the parties's agreement. Step-Saver alleges that several representations made by TSL constitute express warranties, and that valid implied warranties were also a part of the parties's agreement. Because the district court considered the box-top license to exclude all of these warranties, the district court did not consider whether other factors may act to exclude these warranties. The existence and nature of the warranties is primarily a factual question that we leave for the district court,[26] but assuming that these warranties

25. Compare *Hill v. BASF Wyandotte Corp.*, 696 F.2d 287, 290–91 (4th Cir. 1982). In that case, a farmer purchased seventy-three five gallon cans of a herbicide from a retailer. Because the disclaimer was printed conspicuously on each can, the farmer had constructive knowledge of the terms of the disclaimer before the contract formed. As a result, when he selected each can of the herbicide from the shelf and purchased it, the law implies his assent to the terms of the disclaimer. See also *Bowdoin v. Showell Growers, Inc.*, 817 F.2d 1543, 1545 (11th Cir. 1987) (disclaimers that were conspicuous before the contract for sale has formed are effective; post-sale disclaimers are ineffective); *Monsanto Agricultural Prods. Co. v. Edenfield*, 426 So. 2d at 575–76.

26. For example, questions exist as to: (1) whether the statements by TSL were representations of fact, or mere statements of opinion; (2) whether the custom in the trade is to exclude warranties and limit remedies in contracts between a software producer and its dealer; (3) whether Step-Saver relied on TSL's alleged representations, or whether these warranties became a basis of the parties's bargain; and (4) whether Step-Saver's testing excluded some

were included within the parties's original agreement, we must conclude that adding the disclaimer of warranty and limitation of remedies provisions from the box-top license would, as a matter of law, substantially alter the distribution of risk between Step-Saver and TSL. Therefore, under UCC § 2–207(2)(b), the disclaimer of warranty and limitation of remedies terms of the box-top license did not become a part of the parties's agreement.

Based on these considerations, we reverse the trial court's holding that the parties intended the box-top license to be a final and complete expression of the terms of their agreement. Despite the presence of an integration clause in the box-top license, the box-top license should have been treated as a written confirmation containing additional terms. Because the warranty disclaimer and limitation of remedies terms would materially alter the parties's agreement, these terms did not become a part of the parties's agreement. We remand for further consideration the express and implied warranty claims against TSL. . . .

VI.

We will reverse the holding of the district court that the parties intended to adopt the box-top license as the complete and final expression of the terms of their agreement. We will remand for further consideration of Step-Saver's express and implied warranty claims against TSL. Finding a sufficient basis for the other decisions of the district court, we will affirm in all other respects.

Notes and Discussion

1. **Step-Saver's Contracts.** According to Judge Wisdom, Step-Saver "typically" purchased the TSL programs through a telephone call in which it placed an order and TSL then accepted the order and promised to ship promptly. There followed an exchange of documents: Step-Saver's purchase order, and then TSL's shipment with the invoice containing the warranty disclaimers. (Judge Wisdom does not indicate what happened in the non-typical sales.)

How does the judge understand these transactions? Does he believe that the parties already had a contract—albeit an oral one—as of their telephone call, so that the subsequent documents acted only as "confirmations" within the meaning of § 2–207(1)? Or does he treat at least TSL's invoice also as an "acceptance" of Step-Saver's offer? If the latter, is Judge Wisdom implying that TSL still could have forced its terms onto Step-Saver if it had clearly stated in the invoice that it was unwilling to proceed with the transaction unless Step-Saver assented? In short, when does the judge think that the contracts came into existence? Is it possible that his abbreviated citation of Official Comments 1 and 2 on § 2–207 led him into confusion?

The judge never fully answers TSL's assertion that the contracts were incomplete and indefinite as of the telephone calls, and that the box-top

or all of these warranties. From the record, it appears that most of these issues are factual determinations that will require a trial, as did the warranty claims against Wyse. But we leave these issues open to the district court on remand.

licenses were necessary in order to understand what had been arranged. Why did it make no difference that TSL had sent the warranty disclaimers in transaction after transaction? Under § 2–207, a term does not enter a contract through sheer force of repetition, right?

The *Step-Saver* logic is somewhat improved in *Arizona Retail Systems, Inc. v. Software Link, Inc.*, 831 F.Supp. 759 (D. Ariz. 1993).

2. **The Contract/No Contract Dichotomy Revisited.** A deeper issue in *Step-Saver* is traditional contract law's emphasis on the moment of a contract's creation. It is very likely that a seller such as TSL will have strong policies about the warranties that it is prepared to extend to buyers; these policies are related to its business planning, particularly with regard to risk.

Note that the UCC does not necessarily accept the importance of exactly determining when a contract is made. See § 2–204(2): "An agreement sufficient to constitute a contract for sale may be found even though the moment of its making is undetermined." As the Official Comment notes, this subsection "is directed primarily to the situation where the interchanged correspondence does not disclose the exact point at which the deal was closed, but the actions of the parties indicate that a binding obligation has been undertaken."

This issue will reoccur in the next two cases.

3. **Does the UCC Apply?** Both parties agreed that Article Two applied to these transactions. That is not necessarily true. Look at the definition of "goods" in § 2–105(1). It is not absolutely clear that computer software should be regarded as "goods," true? This subject has been very controversial in the Article Two revision process.

The proposed amendments of Article Two tackle the problem. Section 2–103(k) defines "goods," following the earlier version, as "all things that are movable at the time of identification to a contract for sale." It then adds: "The term does not include information ... " The Comment adds: "The definition of 'goods' in this article has been amended to exclude information not associated with goods. Thus, this article does not directly apply to an electronic transfer of information, such as the transaction involved in *Specht v. Netscape*, 150 F. Supp. 2d 585 (S.D.N.Y. 2001). [Eds.: In *Specht*, an offeror provided free downloadable software on the web, but sought to limit its use through a license agreement that offerees accepted by clicking a box.] However, transactions often include both goods and information: some are transactions in goods as that term is used in Section 2–102, and some are not. For example, the sale of 'smart goods' such as an automobile is a transaction in goods fully within this article even though the automobile contains many computer programs. On the other hand, an architect's provision of architectural plans on a computer disk would not be a transaction in goods. When a transaction includes both the sale of goods and the transfer of rights in information, it is up to the courts to determine whether the transaction is entirely within or outside of this article, or whether or to what extent this article should be applied to a portion of the transaction." Am. Law Inst., Uniform Commercial Code Proposed Amendments to Article 2 Sales 8 (2003).

What would happen to TSL's transactions if they were not within amended Article Two? There are two main possibilities. First, by default, ordinary Common Law could apply. Second, in two states (Virginia and Maryland) the transactions could be determined by the Uniform Computer Information Transaction Act (UCITA), which has rules much more favorable to software manufacturers like TSL. However, UCITA has run into substantial consumer resistance and is unlikely to be adopted in other states. Could UCITA be used by analogy to find Common Law rules?

CARNIVAL CRUISE LINES, INC. v. SHUTE

Supreme Court of the United States, 1991.
499 U.S. 585, 111 S.Ct. 1522, 113 L.Ed.2d 622.

BLACKMUN, J. In this admiralty case we primarily consider whether the United States Court of Appeals for the Ninth Circuit correctly refused to enforce a forum-selection clause contained in tickets issued by petitioner Carnival Cruise Lines, Inc., to respondents Eulala and Russel Shute.

I.

The Shutes, through an Arlington, Wash., travel agent, purchased passage for a 7-day cruise on petitioner's ship, the Tropicale. Respondents paid the fare to the agent who forwarded the payment to petitioner's headquarters in Miami, Fla. Petitioner [Eds.: Carnival Cruise Lines] then prepared the tickets and sent them to respondents in the State of Washington. The face of each ticket, at its left-hand lower corner, contained this admonition:

> "SUBJECT TO CONDITIONS OF CONTRACT ON LAST PAGES IMPORTANT! PLEASE READ CONTRACT—ON LAST PAGES 1, 2, 3" App. 15.

The following appeared on "contract page 1" of each ticket:

> "TERMS AND CONDITIONS OF PASSAGE CONTRACT TICKET . . .
>
> "3. (a) The acceptance of this ticket by the person or persons named hereon as passengers shall be deemed to be an acceptance and agreement by each of them of all of the terms and conditions of this Passage Contract Ticket. . . .
>
> "8. It is agreed by and between the passenger and the Carrier that all disputes and matters whatsoever arising under, in connection with or incident to this Contract shall be litigated, if at all, in and before a Court located in the State of Florida, U. S. A., to the exclusion of the Courts of any other state or country." Id., at 16.

The last quoted paragraph is the forum-selection clause at issue.

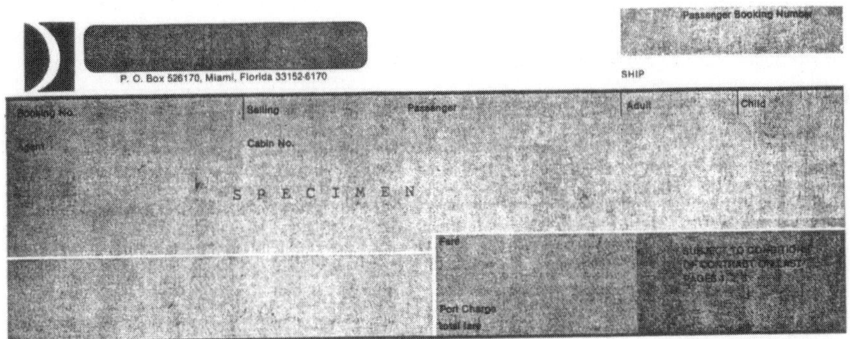

Passenger Booking Number

P. O. Box 526170, Miami, Florida 33152-6170

SHIP

Booking No. | Sailing | Passenger | Adult | Child

Agent | Cabin No.

S P E C I M E N

Fare

Port Charge

Total fare

Passenger Ticket - To Be Presented For Passage

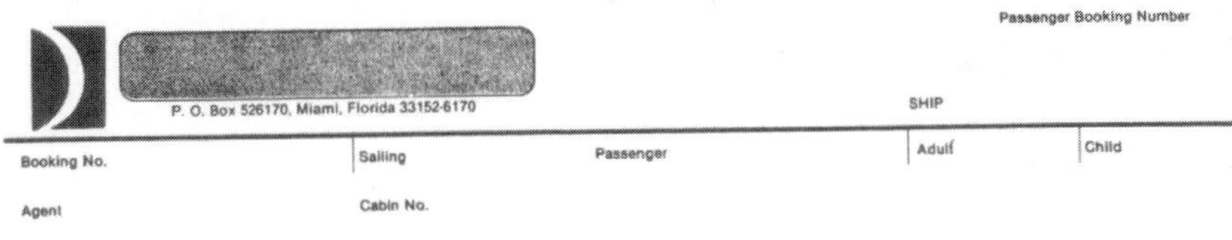

Passenger Booking Number

P. O. Box 526170, Miami, Florida 33152-6170

SHIP

Booking No. | Sailing | Passenger | Adult | Child

Agent | Cabin No.

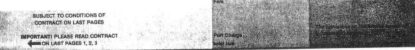

SUBJECT TO CONDITIONS OF CONTRACT ON LAST PAGES

IMPORTANT! PLEASE READ CONTRACT ON LAST PAGES 1, 2, 3

Fare

Port Charge

Total fare

Passenger's Copy - Not Good For Passage

PASSENGER TICKET

Paster — #1 — Back — 298-077 (QL 3)

TERMS AND CONDITIONS OF PASSAGE CONTRACT TICKET

1 (a) Whenever the word "Carrier" is used in this Contract it shall mean and include, jointly and severally, the Vessel, its owners, operators, charterers and tenders. The term "Passenger" shall include, the plural where appropriate, and all persons engaging to and/or traveling under this Contract. The masculine includes the feminine.

(b) The Master, Officers and Crew of the Vessel shall have the benefit of all of the terms and conditions of this contract.

2. This ticket is valid only for the person or persons named hereon as the passenger or passengers and cannot be transferred without the Carrier's consent written hereon. Passage money shall be deemed to be earned when paid and not refundable.

3 (a) The acceptance of this ticket by the person or persons named hereon as passengers shall be deemed to be an acceptance and agreement by each of them of all of the terms and conditions of this Passage Contract Ticket.

(b) The passenger admits a full understanding of the character of the Vessel and assumes all risk incident to travel and transportation and handling of passengers and cargo. The Vessel may or may not carry a ship's physician at the election of the Carrier. The fare includes full board, ordinary ship's food during the voyage, but no spirits, wine, beer or mineral waters.

4 The Carrier shall not be liable for any loss of life or personal injury or delay whatsoever wheresoever arising and howsoever caused even though the same may have been caused by the negligence or default of the Carrier or its servants or agents. No undertaking or warranty is given or shall be implied respecting the seaworthiness, fitness or condition of the Vessel. This exemption from liability shall extend to the employees, servants and agents of the Carrier and for this purpose this exemption shall be deemed to constitute a Contract entered into between the passenger and the Carrier on behalf of all persons who are or become from time to time its employees, servants or agents and all such persons shall to this extent be deemed to be parties to this Contract.

5 The Carrier shall not be liable for losses of valuables unless stored in the Vessel's safety depository and then not exceeding $500 in any event.

6 If the Vessel carries a surgeon, physician, masseuse, barber, hair dresser or manicurist, it is done solely for the convenience of the passenger and any such person in dealing with the passenger is not and shall not be considered in any respect whatsoever, as the employee, servant or agent of the Carrier and the Carrier shall not be liable for any act or omission of such person or those under his orders or assisting him with respect to treatment, advice or care of any kind given to any passenger.

The surgeon, physician, masseuse, barber, hair dresser or manicurist shall be entitled to make a proper charge for any service performed with respect to a passenger and the Carrier shall not be concerned in any way whatsoever in any such arrangement.

7. The Carrier shall not be liable for any claims whatsoever of the passenger unless full particulars thereof in writing be given to the Carrier or their agents within 185 days after the passenger shall be landed from the Vessel or in the case the voyage is abandoned within 185 days thereafter. Suit to recover any claim shall not be maintainable in any event unless commenced within one year after the date of the loss, injury or death.

8. It is agreed by and between the passenger and the Carrier that all disputes and matters whatsoever arising under, in connection with or incident to this Contract shall be litigated, if at all, in and before a Court located in the State of Florida, U.S.A., to the exclusion of the Courts of any other state or country.

9. The Carrier, in arranging for the service called for by all shore feature coupons or shore excursion tickets, acts only as agent for the holder thereof and assumes no responsibility and in no event shall be liable for any loss, damage, injury or delay to or of said person and/or baggage, property or effects in connection with said services, nor does Carrier guarantee the performance of any such service.

CONTRACT PAGE 1

10 Each fully paid adult passenger will be allowed an unlimited amount of baggage free of charge. Baggage means only trunks, valises, satchels, bags, hangers and bundles with their contents consisting of only such wearing apparel, toilet articles and similar personal effects as are necessary and appropriate for the station in life of the passenger and for the purpose of the journey.

11 No tools of trade, household goods, presents and/or property of others, jewelry, money, documents, valuables of any description including but not limited to such articles as are described in Section 4281 Revised Statute of the U S A (46 USCA § 181) shall be carried except under and subject to the terms of a special written contract or Bill of Lading entered into with the Carrier prior to embarkation upon application of the passenger and the passenger hereby warrants that no such articles are contained in any receptacle or container presented by him as baggage hereunder, and if any such article or articles are shipped and the passenger's baggage in breach of this warranty no liability for negligence, gross or ordinary, shall attach to the Carrier for any loss or damage thereto.

12. It is stipulated and agreed that the aggregate value of each passenger's property under the Adult ticket does not exceed $100.00 (half ticket: $50.00) and any liability of the Carrier for any cause whatsoever with respect to said property shall not exceed such sum, unless the passenger shall in writing, delivered to the Carrier prior to embarkation, declare the true value thereof and pay to the Carrier prior to embarkation a sum (in U S Dollars) equal to 5% of the excess of such value, in which event the Carrier's liability shall be limited to the actual damages sustained to the property but not in excess of the declared value.

13. The Vessel shall be entitled to leave and enter ports with or without pilots or tugs, to tow and assist other vessels in any circumstances to return to or enter any port at the Master's discretion and for any purpose and to deviate in any direction or for any purpose from the direct or usual course, all such deviations being considered as forming part of and included in the proposed voyage.

14 If the performance of the proposed voyage is hindered or prevented) or in the opinion of the Carrier or the Master is likely to be hindered or prevented) by war, hostilities, blockade, ice, labor conflicts, strikes on board or ashore, Restraint of Rulers or Princes, breakdown of the Vessel, congestion, docking difficulties, or any other cause whatsoever, or if the Carrier or the Master considers that for any reason whatsoever, proceeding to, attempting to enter, or entering or remaining at the port of passenger's destination may expose the Vessel to risk or loss or damage or be likely to delay her, the passenger and his baggage may be landed at the port of embarkation or at any port or place at which the Vessel may call when the responsibility of the Carrier shall cease and this contract shall be deemed to have been fully performed, or if the passenger has not embarked the Carrier may cancel the proposed voyage without liability to refund passage money or fares paid in advance.

15. The Carrier and the Master shall have liberty to comply with any orders, recommendations or directions whatsoever given by the Government of any nation or by any Department thereof or by any person acting or purporting to act with the authority of such Government or Department or by any Committee or person having under the terms of the War Risks Insuranace on the Vessel the right to give such orders, recommendations or directions, and if by reason of and in compliance with any such orders, recommendations or directions anything is done or is not done the same shall not be deemed a deviation or a breach of this Contract. Disembarkation of any passenger or discharge of his baggage in accordance with such orders, recommendations or directions shall constitute due and proper fulfillment of the obligations of the Carrier under this Contract.

16. (a) The Carrier shall not be liable to make any refund to passengers in respect of lost tickets or in respect of tickets wholly or partly not used by a passenger.

(b) If for any reason whatsoever the passenger is refused permission to land at the port of disembarkation or such other ports as is provided for in Clauses 14 and 15 hereof, the passenger and his baggage may be landed at any port or place at which the Vessel calls or be carried back to the port of embarkation and shall pay the Carrier full fare according to its tariff in use at such time for such further carriage, which shall be upon the terms herein contained.

CONTRACT PAGE 2

17. The Carrier and the Vessel shall have a lien upon all baggage, money, motor cars and other property whatsoever accompanying the passenger and the right to sell the same by public auction or otherwise for all sums whatsoever due from the passenger under this contract and for the costs and expenses of enforcing such lien and of such sale.

18. The passenger or if a minor his parent or guardian shall be liable to the Carrier and to the Master for any fines or penalties imposed on the Carrier by the authorities for his failure to observe or comply with local requirements in respect of immigration, Customs and Excise or any other Government regulations whatsoever.

19. No passenger shall be allowed to bring on board the Vessel Weapons, Firearms, Ammunition, Explosives or other dangerous goods without written permission from the Carrier.

20 The Carrier shall have liberty without previous notice to cancel at the port of embarkation or at any port this Contract and shall thereupon return to the passenger, if the Contract is cancelled at the port of embarkation, his passage money, or, if the Contract is cancelled later, a proportionate part thereof.

21. The passenger warrants that he and those traveling with him are physically fit at the time of embarkation. The Carrier and Master each reserves the right to refuse passage to anyone whose health or welfare would be considered a risk to his own well-being or that of any other passenger.

22. Should the Vessel deviate from its course due to passenger's negligence, said passenger or his estate shall be liable for any related costs incurred.

23. The Carrier reserves the right to increase published fares without prior notice. In the event of an increase, the passenger has the option of accepting the increased fare or cancelling reservations without penalty.

24. In addition to all of the restrictions and exemptions from liability provided in this Contract, the Carrier shall have the benefit of all Statutes of the United States of America providing for limitation and exoneration from liability and the procedures provided thereby, including but not limited to Sections 4282, 4282A, 4283, 4284, 4285 and 4286 of the Revised Statutes of the United States of America (46 USCA Sections 182, 183, 183b, 184, 185 and 186); nothing in this Contract is intended to nor shall it operate to limit or deprive the Carrier of any such statutory limitation of or exoneration from liability.

25. Should any provision of this Contract be contrary to or invalid by virtue of the law of any jurisdiction or be so held by a Court of competent jurisdiction, such provision shall be deemed to be severed from the Contract and of no effect and all remaining provisions herein shall be in full force and effect and constitute the Contract of Carriage.

CONTRACT PAGE 3

II.

Respondents boarded the Tropicale in Los Angeles, Cal. The ship sailed to Puerto Vallarta, Mexico, and then returned to Los Angeles. While the ship was in international waters off the Mexican coast, respondent Eulala Shute was injured when she slipped on a deck mat during a guided tour of the ship's galley. Respondents filed suit against petitioner in the United States District Court for the Western District of

Washington, claiming that Mrs. Shute's injuries had been caused by the negligence of Carnival Cruise Lines and its employees. Id., at 4.

Petitioner moved for summary judgment, contending that the forum clause in respondents' tickets required the Shutes to bring their suit against petitioner in a court in the State of Florida. [Eds.: Carnival Cruise also urged that the Washington District Court lacked personal jurisdiction; the District Court ruled for Carnival Cruise on this ground, but was reversed by the Ninth Circuit Court of Appeals.]

Turning to the forum-selection clause, the Court of Appeals acknowledged that a court concerned with the enforceability of such a clause must begin its analysis with *The Bremen v. Zapata Off-Shore Co.*, 407 U.S. 1 (1972), where this Court held that forum-selection clauses, although not "historically . . . favored," are "prima facie valid." Id., at 9–10. . . . The appellate court concluded that the forum clause should not be enforced because it "was not freely bargained for." . . . As an "independent justification" for refusing to enforce the clause, the Court of Appeals noted that there was evidence in the record to indicate that "the Shutes are physically and financially incapable of pursuing this litigation in Florida" and that the enforcement of the clause would operate to deprive them of their day in court and thereby contravene this Court's holding in *The Bremen*. 897 F.2d, at 389.

We granted certiorari to address the question whether the Court of Appeals was correct in holding that the District Court should hear respondents' tort claim against petitioner. 498 U.S. 807–808 (1990). . . .

III.

We begin by noting the boundaries of our inquiry. First, this is a case in admiralty, and federal law governs the enforceability of the forum-selection clause we scrutinize. . . . Second, we do not address the question whether respondents had sufficient notice of the forum clause before entering the contract for passage. Respondents essentially have conceded that they had notice of the forum-selection provision. Brief for Respondents 26 ("The respondents do not contest the incorporation of the provisions nor [sic] that the forum selection clause was reasonably communicated to the respondents, as much as three pages of fine print can be communicated"). Additionally, the Court of Appeals evaluated the enforceability of the forum clause under the assumption, although "doubtful," that respondents could be deemed to have had knowledge of the clause. . . .

Within this context, respondents urge that the forum clause should not be enforced because, contrary to this Court's teachings in *The Bremen*, the clause was not the product of negotiation, and enforcement effectively would deprive respondents of their day in court. . . .

IV.

A.

Both petitioner and respondents argue vigorously that the Court's opinion in *The Bremen* governs this case, and each side purports to find ample support for its position in that opinion's broad-ranging language. This seeming paradox derives in large part from key factual differences between this case and *The Bremen*, differences that preclude an automatic and simple application of *The Bremen's* general principles to the facts here.

In *The Bremen*, this Court addressed the enforceability of a forum-selection clause in a contract between two business corporations. An American corporation, Zapata, made a contract with Unterweser, a German corporation, for the towage of Zapata's oceangoing drilling rig from Louisiana to a point in the Adriatic Sea off the coast of Italy. The agreement provided that any dispute arising under the contract was to be resolved in the London Court of Justice. After a storm in the Gulf of Mexico seriously damaged the rig, Zapata ordered Unterweser's ship to tow the rig to Tampa, Fla., the nearest point of refuge. Thereafter, Zapata sued Unterweser in admiralty in federal court at Tampa. Citing the forum clause, Unterweser moved to dismiss. The District Court denied Unterweser's motion, and the Court of Appeals for the Fifth Circuit, sitting en banc on rehearing, and by a sharply divided vote, affirmed. *In re Complaint of Unterweser Reederei, Gm-H*, 446 F.2d 907 (1971).

This Court vacated and remanded, stating that, in general, "a freely negotiated private international agreement, unaffected by fraud, undue influence, or overweening bargaining power, such as that involved here, should be given full effect." 407 U.S., at 12–13 (footnote omitted). The Court further generalized that "in the light of present-day commercial realities and expanding international trade we conclude that the forum clause should control absent a strong showing that it should be set aside." Id., at 15. The Court did not define precisely the circumstances that would make it unreasonable for a court to enforce a forum clause. Instead, the Court discussed a number of factors that made it reasonable to enforce the clause at issue in *The Bremen* and that, presumably, would be pertinent in any determination whether to enforce a similar clause.

In this respect, the Court noted that there was "strong evidence that the forum clause was a vital part of the agreement, and [that] it would be unrealistic to think that the parties did not conduct their negotiations, including fixing the monetary terms, with the consequences of the forum clause figuring prominently in their calculations." Id., at 14 (footnote omitted). Further, the Court observed that it was not "dealing with an agreement between two Americans to resolve their essentially local disputes in a remote alien forum," and that in such a case, "the serious inconvenience of the contractual forum to one or both of the parties might carry greater weight in determining the reasonableness of the forum clause." Id., at 17. The Court stated that even where the forum clause establishes a remote forum for resolution of conflicts, "the party claiming [unfairness] should bear a heavy burden of proof." Ibid.

In applying *The Bremen*, the Court of Appeals in the present litigation took note of the foregoing "reasonableness" factors and rather automatically decided that the forum-selection clause was unenforceable because, unlike the parties in *The Bremen*, respondents are not business persons and did not negotiate the terms of the clause with petitioner. Alternatively, the Court of Appeals ruled that the clause should not be enforced because enforcement effectively would deprive respondents of an opportunity to litigate their claim against petitioner.

The Bremen concerned a "far from routine transaction between companies of two different nations contemplating the tow of an extremely costly piece of equipment from Louisiana across the Gulf of Mexico and the Atlantic Ocean, through the Mediterranean Sea to its final destination in the Adriatic Sea." Id., at 13. These facts suggest that, even apart from the evidence of negotiation regarding the forum clause, it was entirely reasonable for the Court in *The Bremen* to have expected Unterweser and Zapata to have negotiated with care in selecting a forum for the resolution of disputes arising from their special towing contract.

In contrast, respondents' passage contract was purely routine and doubtless nearly identical to every commercial passage contract issued by petitioner and most other cruise lines. See, e. g., *Hodes v. S. N. C. Achille Lauro ed Altri-Gestione*, 858 F.2d 905, 910 (CA3 1988), cert. dism'd, 490 U.S. 1001 (1989). In this context, it would be entirely unreasonable for us to assume that respondents—or any other cruise passenger—would negotiate with petitioner the terms of a forum-selection clause in an ordinary commercial cruise ticket. Common sense dictates that a ticket of this kind will be a form contract the terms of which are not subject to negotiation, and that an individual purchasing the ticket will not have bargaining parity with the cruise line. But by ignoring the crucial differences in the business contexts in which the respective contracts were executed, the Court of Appeals' analysis seems to us to have distorted somewhat this Court's holding in *The Bremen*.

In evaluating the reasonableness of the forum clause at issue in this case, we must refine the analysis of *The Bremen* to account for the realities of form passage contracts. As an initial matter, we do not adopt the Court of Appeals' determination that a nonnegotiated forum-selection clause in a form ticket contract is never enforceable simply because it is not the subject of bargaining. Including a reasonable forum clause in a form contract of this kind well may be permissible for several reasons: First, a cruise line has a special interest in limiting the fora in which it potentially could be subject to suit. Because a cruise ship typically carries passengers from many locales, it is not unlikely that a mishap on a cruise could subject the cruise line to litigation in several different fora. See *The Bremen*, 407 U.S., at 13, and n. 15; *Hodes*, 858 F.2d, at 913. Additionally, a clause establishing *ex ante* the forum for dispute resolution has the salutary effect of dispelling any confusion about where suits arising from the contract must be brought and defended, sparing litigants the time and expense of pretrial motions to determine the correct forum and conserving judicial resources that otherwise would be devoted to deciding those motions.... Finally, it stands to reason that passengers who purchase tickets containing a forum clause like that at issue in this case benefit in the form of reduced fares reflecting the savings that the cruise line enjoys by limiting the fora in which it may be sued....

We also do not accept the Court of Appeals' "independent justification" for its conclusion that *The Bremen* dictates that the clause should not be enforced because "there is evidence in the record to indicate that the Shutes are physically and financially incapable of pursuing this litigation in Florida." 897 F.2d, at 389. We do not defer to the Court of Appeals' findings of fact. In dismissing the case for lack of personal jurisdiction over petitioner, the District Court made no finding regarding the physical and financial impediments to the Shutes' pursuing their case in Florida. The Court of Appeals' conclusory reference to the record provides no basis for this Court to validate the finding of inconvenience. Furthermore, the Court of Appeals did not place in proper context this Court's statement in *The Bremen* that "the serious inconvenience of the contractual forum to one or both of the parties might carry greater weight in determining the reasonableness of the forum clause." 407 U.S., at 17. The Court made this statement in evaluating a hypothetical "agreement between two Americans to resolve their essentially local disputes in a remote alien forum." Ibid. In the present case, Florida is not a "remote alien forum," nor—given the fact that Mrs. Shute's accident occurred off the coast of Mexico—is this dispute an essentially local one inherently more suited to resolution in the State of Washington than in Florida. In light of these distinctions, and because respondents do not claim lack of notice of the forum clause, we conclude that they have not satisfied the "heavy burden of proof," ibid., required to set aside the clause on grounds of inconvenience.

It bears emphasis that forum-selection clauses contained in form passage contracts are subject to judicial scrutiny for fundamental fairness. In this case, there is no indication that petitioner set Florida as the forum in which disputes were to be resolved as a means of discouraging cruise passengers from pursuing legitimate claims. Any suggestion of such a bad-faith motive is belied by two facts: Petitioner has its principal place of business in Florida, and many of its cruises depart from and return to Florida ports. Similarly, there is no evidence that petitioner obtained respondents' accession to the forum clause by fraud or overreaching. Finally, respondents have conceded that they were given notice of the forum provision and, therefore, presumably retained the option of rejecting the contract with impunity. In the case before us, therefore, we conclude that the Court of Appeals erred in refusing to enforce the forum-selection clause. [Eds.: The Court also finds the forum-selection clause in accord with Federal statute.]

V.

The judgment of the Court of Appeals is reversed. It is so ordered.

STEVENS, J., DISSENTING. The Court prefaces its legal analysis with a factual statement that implies that a purchaser of a Carnival Cruise Lines passenger ticket is fully and fairly notified about the existence of the choice of forum clause in the fine print on the back of the ticket.... Even if this implication were accurate, I would disagree with the Court's analysis....

Of course, many passengers, like the respondents in this case, ... will not have an opportunity to read paragraph 8 until they have actually purchased their tickets. By this point, the passengers will already have accepted the condition set forth in paragraph 16(a), which provides that "the Carrier shall not be liable to make any refund to passengers in respect of ... tickets wholly or partly not used by a passenger." Not knowing whether or not that provision is legally enforceable, I assume that the average passenger would accept the risk of having to file suit in Florida in the event of an injury, rather than canceling—without a refund—a planned vacation at the last minute. The fact that the cruise line can reduce its litigation costs, and therefore its liability insurance premiums, by forcing this choice on its passengers does not, in my opinion, suffice to render the provision reasonable....

[C]ourts traditionally have reviewed with heightened scrutiny the terms of contracts of adhesion, form contracts offered on a take-or-leave basis by a party with stronger bargaining power to a party with weaker power. Some commentators have questioned whether contracts of adhesion can justifiably be enforced at all under traditional contract theory because the adhering party generally enters into them without manifesting knowing and voluntary consent to all their terms....

I respectfully dissent.

Notes and Discussion

1. **Notice of the Forum-Selection Provision.** As to the enforceability of the forum-selection provision, the Ninth Circuit panel had ruled in favor of the Shutes on the following rationale: "[I]n our view the evidence in this case suggests the sort of disparity in bargaining power that justifies setting aside the forum selection provision. First, there is no evidence that the provision was freely bargained for. To the contrary, the provision is printed on the ticket, and presented to the purchaser on a take-it-or-leave-it basis.... Even if we assume that the Shutes had notice of the provision, there is nothing in the record to suggest that the Shutes could have bargained over this language. Because this provision was not freely bargained for, we hold that it does not represent the expressed intent of the parties, and should not receive the deference generally accorded to such provisions." *Shute v. Carnival Cruise Lines,* 897 F.2d 377, 388–389 (1990).

On the issue of notice, it holds in a footnote: "This [notice] itself is doubtful, as the Shutes apparently did not have an opportunity to review the terms and conditions printed on the ticket until after the ticket was printed in Florida and mailed to them in Washington. Thus, the transaction was completed before the Shutes ever saw the ticket's terms and conditions." Id. at 389 n.11.

Writing for a 7-2 majority, Justice Blackmun states: "Respondents essentially have conceded that they had notice of the forum-selection provision. Brief for Respondents 26 ('The respondents do not contest the incorporation of the provisions nor [sic] that the forum selection clause was reasonably communicated to the respondents, as much as three pages of fine print can be communicated')." *Carnival Cruise Lines*, 499 U.S. at 590. In what sense is it true that the Shutes "essentially . . . conceded" that they had "sufficient notice"? What presumptions are the majority making about what the Shutes did or should have done after receiving the tickets? How is the dissent's view different?

What alternatives were open to the Shutes if they had read the ticket and found its terms unsatisfactory?

2. How Was the Contract Formed? In the majority's view, "Common sense dictates that a ticket of this kind will be a form contract the terms of which are not subject to negotiation, and that an individual purchasing the ticket will not have bargaining parity with the cruise line." Distinguish this case from *The Bremen*, the precedent that the Court discusses at some length.

When exactly, in the Court's opinion, did the Carnival Cruise contract come into existence? Should the ticket that Carnival Cruise mailed to the Shutes be regarded as an acceptance of their offer, or as a counteroffer that the Shutes accepted by retaining and using the ticket?

The Court discusses at some length the possible advantages both to Carnival Cruise and to its passengers from having standardized contractual terms. Of course, the vast majority of passengers would not suffer injuries severe enough to merit litigation. What protects consumers against overreaching by airlines and other corporations that deal with the general public?

3. Reasonableness and "Fundamental Fairness." The majority finds that this was "a reasonable forum clause," and it also notes the absence of findings that the Shutes were physically and financially unable to sue in Florida. Would the outcome be different if, for instance, the Carnival Cruise ticket had required the Shutes to litigate in Ankara, Turkey, or had required arbitration of any disputes?

As to "fundamental fairness," the majority says that: "[T]here is no indication that petitioner set Florida as the forum in which disputes were to be resolved as a means of discouraging cruise passengers from pursuing legitimate claims. Any suggestion of such a bad-faith motive is belied by two facts: Petitioner has its principal place of business in Florida, and many of its cruises depart from and return to Florida ports." Does this argument cohere?

Is the majority influenced by a sense that cruise tickets are luxury items?

4. Does Ordinary Contract Analysis Help or Hinder? On cases such as *Carnival Cruise*, Prof. Hillman has written: "Although courts and commentators focus on the time of contract formation, this analysis actually yields little fruit. First, the formation analysis is supposed to depend on when the parties intended to form their contract, but few parties think about this technical question, so the issue has little real-world relevance. Second, even if the time of contract formation is accessible, it does not tell us very much. Assuming contract formation occurs at the time of payment and shipment, the postponed terms could still become part of the contract, for example, if the consumer agreed, at this time, to delegate the duty of providing reasonable terms to the seller. The terms could also become part of the contract if the consumer, after having an opportunity to read the terms, accepted them as a contract modification agreement. Assuming contract formation occurs after the time for return has expired, courts could still bar the terms, for example, based on the theory that the consumer never expressly agreed to them." Robert A. Hillman, *Rolling Contracts*, 71 Fordham L. Rev. 743, 744–745 (2002). Do you agree?

HILL v. GATEWAY 2000, INC.

United States Court of Appeals, Seventh Circuit, 1997.
105 F.3d 1147.

EASTERBROOK, J. A customer picks up the phone, orders a computer, and gives a credit card number. Presently a box arrives, containing the computer and a list of terms, said to govern unless the customer returns the computer within 30 days. Are these terms effective as the parties' contract, or is the contract term-free because the order-taker did not read any terms over the phone and elicit the customer's assent?

One of the terms in the box containing a Gateway 2000 system was an arbitration clause. Rich and Enza Hill, the customers, kept the computer more than 30 days before complaining about its components and performance. They filed suit in federal court arguing, among other things, that the product's shortcomings make Gateway a racketeer (mail and wire fraud are said to be the predicate offenses), leading to treble damages under RICO for the Hills and a class of all other purchasers. Gateway asked the district court to enforce the arbitration clause; the judge refused, writing that "the present record is insufficient to support a finding of a valid arbitration agreement between the parties or that the plaintiffs were given adequate notice of the arbitration clause." Gateway took an immediate appeal, as is its right. 9 U.S.C. § 16(a)(1)(A).

The Hills say that the arbitration clause did not stand out: they concede noticing the statement of terms but deny reading it closely enough to discover the agreement to arbitrate, and they ask us to conclude that they therefore may go to court. Yet an agreement to arbitrate must be enforced "save upon such grounds as exist at law or in equity for the revocation of any contract." 9 U.S.C. § 2. *Doctor's Associates, Inc. v. Casarotto*, 134 L. Ed. 2d 902, 116 S. Ct. 1652 (1996), holds that this provision of the Federal Arbitration Act is inconsistent with any requirement that an arbitration clause be prominent. A contract need not be read to be effective; people who accept take the risk that the unread terms may in retrospect prove unwelcome.... Terms inside

Gateway's box stand or fall together. If they constitute the parties' contract because the Hills had an opportunity to return the computer after reading them, then all must be enforced.

ProCD, Inc. v. Zeidenberg, 86 F.3d 1447 (7th Cir. 1996), holds that terms inside a box of software bind consumers who use the software after an opportunity to read the terms and to reject them by returning the product. Likewise, *Carnival Cruise Lines, Inc. v. Shute*, 499 U.S. 585, 113 L. Ed. 2d 622, 111 S. Ct. 1522 (1991), enforces a forum-selection clause that was included among three pages of terms attached to a cruise ship ticket. *ProCD* and *Carnival Cruise Lines* exemplify the many commercial transactions in which people pay for products with terms to follow; *ProCD* discusses others. 86 F.3d at 1451–52. The district court concluded in *ProCD* that the contract is formed when the consumer pays for the software; as a result, the court held, only terms known to the consumer at that moment are part of the contract, and provisos inside the box do not count. Although this is one way a contract could be formed, it is not the only way: "A vendor, as master of the offer, may invite acceptance by conduct, and may propose limitations on the kind of conduct that constitutes acceptance. A buyer may accept by performing the acts the vendor proposes to treat as acceptance." Id. at 1452. Gateway shipped computers with the same sort of accept-or-return offer ProCD made to users of its software. *ProCD* relied on the Uniform Commercial Code rather than any peculiarities of Wisconsin law; both Illinois and South Dakota, the two states whose law might govern relations between Gateway and the Hills, have adopted the UCC; neither side has pointed us to any atypical doctrines in those states that might be pertinent; *ProCD* therefore applies to this dispute.

Plaintiffs ask us to limit *ProCD* to software, but where's the sense in that? *ProCD* is about the law of contract, not the law of software. Payment preceding the revelation of full terms is common for air transportation, insurance, and many other endeavors. Practical considerations support allowing vendors to enclose the full legal terms with their products. Cashiers cannot be expected to read legal documents to customers before ringing up sales. If the staff at the other end of the phone for direct-sales operations such as Gateway's had to read the four-page statement of terms before taking the buyer's credit card number, the droning voice would anesthetize rather than enlighten many potential buyers. Others would hang up in a rage over the waste of their time. And oral recitation would not avoid customers' assertions (whether true or feigned) that the clerk did not read term X to them, or that they did not remember or understand it. Writing provides benefits for both sides of commercial transactions. Customers as a group are better off when vendors skip costly and ineffectual steps such as telephonic recitation, and use instead a simple approve-or-return device. Competent adults are bound by such documents, read or unread....

For their second sally, the Hills contend that *ProCD* should be limited to executory contracts (to licenses in particular), and therefore does not apply because both parties' performance of this contract was complete when the box arrived at their home. This is legally and factually wrong: legally because the question at hand concerns the formation of the contract rather than its performance, and factually because both contracts were incompletely performed. *ProCD* did not depend on the fact that the seller characterized the transaction as a license rather than as a contract; we treated it as a contract for the sale of goods and reserved the question whether for other purposes a "license" characterization might be preferable. 86 F.3d at 1450. All debates about characterization to one side, the transaction in *ProCD* was no more executory than the one here: Zeidenberg paid for the software and walked out of the store with a box under his arm, so if arrival of the box with the product ends the time for revelation of contractual terms, then the time ended in *ProCD* before Zeidenberg opened the box. But of course ProCD had not completed performance with delivery of the box, and neither had Gateway. One element of the transaction was the warranty, which obliges sellers to fix defects in their products. The Hills have invoked Gateway's warranty and are not satisfied with its response, so they are not well positioned to say that Gateway's obligations were fulfilled when the motor carrier unloaded the box. What is more, both ProCD and Gateway promised to help customers to use their products. Long-term service and information obligations are common in the computer business, on both hardware and software sides. Gateway offers "lifetime service" and has a round-the-clock telephone hotline to fulfil this promise. Some vendors spend more money helping customers use their products than on developing and manufacturing them. The document in Gateway's box includes promises of future performance that some consumers value highly; these promises bind Gateway just as the arbitration clause binds the Hills.

Next the Hills insist that *ProCD* is irrelevant because Zeidenberg was a "merchant" and they are not. Section 2–207(2) of the UCC, the infamous battle-of-the-forms section, states that "additional terms [following acceptance of an offer] are to be construed as proposals for addition to a contract. Between merchants such terms become part of the contract unless . . . ". Plaintiffs tell us that *ProCD* came out as it did only because Zeidenberg was a "merchant" and the terms inside ProCD's box were not excluded by the "unless" clause. This argument pays scant attention to the opinion in *ProCD*, which concluded that, when there is only one form, " § 2–207 is irrelevant." 86 F.3d at 1452. The question in *ProCD* was not whether terms were added to a contract after its formation, but how and when the contract was formed—in particular, whether a vendor may propose that a contract of sale be formed, not in the store (or over the phone) with the payment of money or a general "send me the product," but after the customer has had a chance to inspect both the item and the terms. *ProCD* answers "yes," for merchants and consumers alike. Yet again, for what little it is worth we observe that the Hills misunderstand the setting of *ProCD*. A "merchant" under the UCC "means a person who deals in goods of the kind or otherwise by his occupation holds himself out as having knowledge or skill peculiar to the practices or goods involved in the transaction", § 2–104(1). Zeidenberg bought the product at a retail store, an uncommon place for merchants to acquire inventory. His corporation put ProCD's database on the Internet for anyone to browse, which led to the litigation but did not make Zeidenberg a software merchant.

At oral argument the Hills propounded still another distinction: the box containing ProCD's software displayed a notice that additional terms were within, while the box containing Gateway's computer did not. The difference is functional, not legal. Consumers browsing the aisles of a store can look at the box, and if they are unwilling to deal with the prospect of additional terms can leave the box alone, avoiding the transactions costs of returning the package after reviewing its contents. Gateway's box, by contrast, is just a shipping carton; it is not on display anywhere. Its function is to protect the product during transit, and the information on its sides is for the use of handlers ("Fragile!" "This Side Up!") rather than would-be purchasers.

Perhaps the Hills would have had a better argument if they were first alerted to the bundling of hardware and legal-ware after opening the box and wanted to return the computer in order to avoid disagreeable terms, but were dissuaded by the expense of shipping. What the remedy would be in such a case—could it exceed the shipping charges?—is an interesting question, but one that need not detain us because the Hills knew before they ordered the computer that the carton would include some important terms, and they did not seek to discover these in advance. Gateway's ads state that their products come with limited warranties and lifetime support. How limited was the warranty–30 days, with service contingent on shipping the computer back, or five years, with free onsite service? What sort of support was offered? Shoppers have three principal ways to discover these things. First, they can ask the vendor to send a copy before deciding whether to buy. The Magnuson-Moss Warranty Act requires firms to distribute their warranty terms on request, 15 U.S.C. § 2302 (b)(1)(A); the Hills do not contend that Gateway would have refused to enclose the remaining terms too. Concealment would be bad for business, scaring some customers away and leading to excess returns from others. Second, shoppers can consult public sources (computer magazines, the Web sites of vendors) that may contain this information. Third, they may inspect the documents after the product's delivery. Like Zeidenberg, the Hills took the third option. By keeping the computer beyond 30 days, the Hills accepted Gateway's offer, including the arbitration clause. . . .

The decision of the district court is vacated, and this case is remanded with instructions to compel the Hills to submit their dispute to arbitration.

Notes and Discussion

1. The *ProCD* Decision. Judge Easterbrook also wrote the decision in *ProCD*. At a cost of $10 million, ProCD compiled information from more than 3,000 phone directories onto a computer database, which it then offered for sale at a low price ($150) to the general public and at a higher price to trade customers. Matthew Zeidenberg purchased the lower-priced package at a retail outlet and then formed a corporation to resell the information on the Internet. ProCD sought to enjoin this resale, citing a restrictive "shrinkwrap license" that was found inside the box containing ProCD's disks and that also appeared on the user's screen whenever the software was run. This license limited use of the disks to non-commercial purposes.

Although Zeidenberg could not have seen the license before paying for the box in which the disks came, the Seventh Circuit, reversing the trial court, held that he was bound by it. Judge Easterbrook analyzed the process of contract formation as follows: "ProCD proposed a contract that a buyer would accept by *using* the software after having an opportunity to read the license at leisure. This Zeidenberg did. He had no choice, because the software splashed the license on the screen and would not let him proceed without indicating acceptance. So although the district judge was right to say that a contract can be, and often is, formed simply by paying the price and walking out of the store, the UCC permits contracts to be formed in other ways. ProCD proposed such a different way, and without protest Zeidenberg agreed." *ProCD*, 86 F.3d at 1452. The UCC surely so "permits," but it is far from clear that ProCD's behavior successfully caused the contract to be formed as the judge finds.

The opinion notes that Zeidenberg retained the right to return the opened box for a full refund if he found the license oppressive. Is *ProCD* easier or harder than *Hill v. Gateway*?

2. Is UCC § 2–207 Relevant? In both *ProCD* and *Hill*, Judge Easterbrook states that § 2–207 is "irrelevant." In *ProCD*, he distinguishes *Step-Saver* as follows: "*Step-Saver* is a battle-of-the-forms case, in which the parties exchange incompatible forms and a court must decide which prevails. . . . Our case has only one form; UCC § 2–207 is irrelevant." 86 F.3d at 1452. This observation is inaccurate; see the Comment to § 2–207.

A better reasoned argument for taking a contract like this one out of § 2–207 is given in *Brower v. Gateway 2000*, 676 N.Y.S.2d 569, 571, 246 A.D.2d 246, 250 (App. Div. 1998), rejecting "appellants' argument that the arbitration clause was invalid under UCC 2–207. Appellants claim that when they placed their order they did not bargain for, much less accept, arbitration of any dispute, and therefore the arbitration clause in the agreement that accompanied the merchandise shipment was a 'material alteration' of a pre-existing oral agreement. Under UCC 2–207(2), such a material alteration constitutes 'proposals for addition to the contract' that become part of the contract only upon appellants' express acceptance. However, as the [trial] court correctly concluded, the clause was not a 'material alteration' of an oral agreement, but, rather, simply one provision of the sole contract that existed between the parties. That contract, the court explained, was formed and acceptance was manifested not when the order was placed but only with the retention of the merchandise beyond the 30 days specified in the Agreement enclosed in the shipment of merchandise. Accordingly, the contract was outside the scope of UCC 2–207." Note, however, that this solution depends on a somewhat strained view of when the contract finally arises between the two parties; see below.

Under the amended form of Article Two, the *ProCD* contract would presumably not be within the UCC since it involves the sale of information (the compiled phone numbers), while the *Gateway* contract definitely would be within it. What arguments can be given for and against applying § 2–207? Comment 5 to § 2–207 states that: "The section omits any specific treatment of terms on or in the container in which the goods are delivered. This Article takes no position on whether a court should follow the reasoning in *Hill v. Gateway* . . . or the contrary reasoning in *Step-Saver* . . . "

3. Rolling Contracts. Contracts such as this one have been described as "rolling contracts," in which "a consumer orders and pays for goods before seeing most of the terms, which are contained on or in the packaging of the goods. Upon receipt, the buyer enjoys the right to return the goods for a limited period of time. Rolling contracts therefore involve the following contentious issue: Are terms that arrive after payment and shipment, such as an arbitration clause, enforceable?" Robert A. Hillman, *Rolling Contracts*, 71 Fordham L. Rev. 743, 744 (2002) (footnote omitted).

Prof. Hillman argues that the problems with such contracts are exaggerated. "Let's go back to Llewellyn's view that people fail to read their form contracts and that bargained-for terms and conscionable terms should constitute the contract." Id. at 745. As applied to *Hill v. Gateway*, "this approach would require courts to focus on whether the [arbitration clause] was . . . unconscionable," unduly oppressive (see Chapter 5.C). Id. at 755. In Hillman's opinion, Judge Easterbrook properly emphasized "the senselessness and wastefulness of requiring Gateway's agents to read the terms over the phone because of the great unlikelihood that the Hills or anyone else would understand the terms or even listen. Further, other seller alternatives, such as shipping only after receipt of a signed contract, are also cumbersome and wasteful of time, especially in light of the failure of consumers to read their form contracts. Put simply, consumers clearly desire the convenience of ordering goods over the telephone, or this method of marketing would not exist." Id. (But the seller could make the terms available by e-mail or on a web site.)

In this view, how significant is it that the Hills had the right to return the computer if they were dissatisfied with it? How important is it that courts now usually favor arbitration clauses as a dispute settlement device? It is worth contrasting *Brower*, in which the court followed Judge Easterbrook's analysis in *Hill*, but concluded that an arbitration provision requiring a New York plaintiff to pursue arbitration before the ICC in Chicago involved "excessive costs" and was unenforceable. 676 N.Y.S.2d at 574.

4. Does the Market Help? Judge Easterbrook suggests that consumers who fear being abused can defend themselves by seeking additional information through the Magnuson-Moss Warranty Act, public sources, or close inspection of documents. Are such defenses likely to be adequate? He also argues that sellers will not be shy about disclosure: "Concealment would be bad for business, scaring some customers away and leading to excess returns from others." We do not share his optimism, but the "market"—peeking through courts, class actions, and even actions of state and federal agencies—may affect the terms even if individual consumers do not themselves avoid products that come with undesirable contract terms.

5. Criticism. The *ProCD* and *Hill* decisions have also received heavy censure, not least because of Judge Easterbrook's eccentric view of § 2–207. *Klocek v. Gateway, Inc.*, 104 F. Supp.2d 1332 (D. Kan. 2000; Vratil, J.) (holding that a consumer had not accepted an arbitration clause enclosed in the box containing a scanner), is probably the strongest attack. E.g., "Disputes under § 2–207 often arise in the context of a 'battle of forms,' see, e.g., *Daitom, Inc. v. Pennwalt Corp.*, 741 F.2d 1569, 1574 (10th Cir. 1984), but nothing in its language precludes application in a case which involves only one form.... By its terms, § 2–207 applies to an acceptance or written confirmation. It states nothing which requires another form before the provision becomes effective. In fact, the official comment to the section specifically provides that §§ 2–207(1) and (2) apply 'where an agreement has been reached orally ... and is followed by one or both of the parties sending formal memoranda embodying the terms so far agreed and adding terms not discussed.' " *Klocek*, supra, at 1339—and quite correctly!

Among academic commentators, see especially John Edward Murray, Murray on Contracts § 50(I) at 763 (4th ed. 2001). Murray observes: "The United States Court of Appeals for the Seventh Circuit has provided particularly valuable insights in the interpretation of various provisions of UCC Article 2, many of which are cited elsewhere in this volume. The most charitable statement that can be made concerning the *ProCD/Hill* analysis, however, is that, even Homer nods." Also critical is Roger C. Bern, *"Terms Later" Contracting: Bad Economics, Bad Morals, and a Bad Idea for a Uniform Law, Judge Easterbrook Notwithstanding*, 12 J. Law & Policy 641 (2004).

Problem 3–9

Margo and Robert Rebar entered into a one-year renewable contract for termite protection with Cook's Pest Control, whose standard form contract contained a binding arbitration clause. When the initial term was about to expire, Cook's notified the Rebars that they could renew the contract by paying the annual renewal fee. The Rebars sent back a check for the fee along with an enclosed "Addendum to Customer Agreement" that read, in part:

> "Please read this addendum to your Customer Agreement carefully as it explains changes to some of the terms shown in the Agreement. Keep this document with the original Customer Agreement....
>
> "**Arbitration.** Cook's agrees that any prior amendment to the Customer Agreement shall be subject to written consent before arbitration is required. In the event that a dispute arises between Cook's and Customer, Cook's agrees to propose arbitration if so desired, estimate the cost thereof, and describe the process (venue, selection of arbitrator, etc.). Notwithstanding prior amendments, nothing herein shall limit Customer's right to seek court enforcement (including injunctive or class relief in appropriate cases) nor shall anything herein abrogate

Customer's right to trial by jury. Arbitration shall not be required for any prior or future dealings between Cook's and Customer. . . .

"**Acceptance by Continued Use.** Continued honoring of this account by you acknowledges agreement to these terms. If you do not agree with all of the terms of this contract, as amended, you must immediately notify me of that fact."

Cook's cashed the Rebars' check and continued its services. A few days after the beginning of the renewal year, the Rebars sued Cook's, alleging its failure to treat and control a termite infestation in the Rebars' home and to repair the damage to the home caused by the termites. Will Cook's move to compel arbitration succeed? One issue worth considering is whether the Cook's employee who opened the letter is likely to have had authority to accept a counteroffer on Cook's behalf. See UCC § 3–311 (on accord and satisfaction).

C & J FERTILIZER, INC. v. ALLIED MUTUAL INSURANCE CO.

Supreme Court of Iowa, 1975.
227 N.W.2d 169.

REYNOLDSON, J. This action to recover for burglary loss under two separate insurance policies was tried to the court, resulting in a finding plaintiff had failed to establish a burglary within the policy definitions. Plaintiff appeals from judgment entered for defendant. We reverse and remand.

Trial court made certain findings of fact in support of its conclusion reached. Plaintiff operated a fertilizer plant in Olds, Iowa. At time of loss, plaintiff was insured under policies issued by defendant and titled "BROAD FORM STOREKEEPERS POLICY" and "MERCANTILE BURGLARY AND ROBBERY POLICY." Each policy defined "burglary" as meaning, "* * * the felonious abstraction of insured property (1) from within the premises by a person making felonious entry therein by actual force and violence, of which force and violence there are visible marks made by tools, explosives, electricity or chemicals upon, or physical damage to, the exterior of the premises at the place of such entry * * *."

On Saturday, April 18, 1970, all exterior doors to the building were locked when plaintiff's employees left the premises at the end of the business day. The following day, Sunday, April 19, 1970, one of plaintiff's employees was at the plant and found all doors locked and secure. On Monday, April 20, 1970, when the employees reported for work, the exterior doors were locked, but the front office door was unlocked.

There were truck tire tread marks visible in the mud in the driveway leading to and from the plexiglass door entrance to the warehouse. It was demonstrated this door could be forced open without leaving visible marks or physical damage. There were no visible marks on the exterior of the building made by tools, explosives, electricity or chemicals, and there was no physical damage to the exterior of the building to evidence felonious entry into the building by force and violence.

Chemicals had been stored in an interior room of the warehouse. The door to this room, which had been locked, was physically damaged and carried visible marks made by tools. Chemicals had been taken at a net loss to plaintiff in the sum of $9,582. Office and shop equipment valued at $400.30 was also taken from the building.

Trial court held the policy definition of "burglary" was unambiguous, there was nothing in the record "upon which to base a finding that the door to plaintiff's place of business was entered feloniously, by actual force and violence," and, applying the policy language, found for defendant.

Certain other facts in the record were apparently deemed irrelevant by trial court because of its view the applicable law required it to enforce the policy provision. Because we conclude different rules of law apply, we also consider those facts.

The "BROAD FORM STOREKEEPERS POLICY" was issued April 14, 1969; the "MERCANTILE BURGLARY AND ROBBERY POLICY" on April 14, 1970. Those policies are in evidence. Prior policies apparently were first purchased in 1968. The agent, who had power to bind insurance coverage for defendant, was told plaintiff would be handling farm chemicals. After inspecting the building then used by plaintiff for storage he made certain suggestions regarding security. There ensued a conversation in which he pointed out there had to be visible evidence of burglary. There was no testimony by anyone that plaintiff was then or thereafter informed the policy to be delivered would define burglary to require "visible marks made by tools, explosives, electricity or chemicals upon, or physical damage to, the exterior of the premises at the place of * * * entry."

The import of this conversation with defendant's agent when the coverage was sold is best confirmed by the agent's complete and vocally-expressed surprise when defendant denied coverage. From what the agent saw (tire tracks and marks on the interior of the building) and his contacts with the investigating officers "* * * the thought didn't enter my mind that it wasn't covered * * *." From the trial testimony it was obvious the only understanding was that there should be some hard evidence of a third-party burglary vis-a-vis an "inside job." The latter was in this instance effectively ruled out when the thief was required to break an interior door lock to gain access to the chemicals.

The agent testified the insurance was purchased and "the policy was sent out afterwards." The president of plaintiff corporation, a 37-year-old farmer with a high school education, looked at that portion of the policy setting out coverages, including coverage for burglary loss, the amounts of insurance, and the "location and description." He could not recall reading the fine print defining "burglary" on page three of the policy....

There is nothing about trial court's factual findings which precludes this court from construing said contract to arrive at a proper determination of its legal operation as between these parties, or from considering whether the decision appealed from resulted from the application of an erroneous rule of law. And if the definition of "burglary" in defendant's policy is not enforceable here, then trial court's finding there was no evidence of forcible entry through an outside door is not controlling in the disposition of this case.

Plaintiff's theories of recovery based on "reasonable expectations," implied warranty and unconscionability must be viewed in light of accelerating change in the field of contracts.

I. Revolution In Formation Of Contractual Relationships

Many of our principles for resolving conflicts relating to written contracts were formulated at an early time when parties of equal strength negotiated in the historical sequence of offer, acceptance, and reduction to writing. The concept that both parties assented to the resulting document had solid footing in fact.

Only recently has the sweeping change in the inception of the document received widespread recognition: "Standard form contracts probably account for more than ninety-nine percent of all contracts now made. Most persons have difficulty remembering the last time they contracted other than by standard form; except for casual oral agreements, they probably never have. But if they are active, they contract by standard form several times a day. Parking lot and theater tickets, package receipts, department store charge slips, and gas station credit card purchase slips are all standard form contracts. * * * The contracting still imagined by courts and law teachers as typical, in which both parties participate in choosing the language of their entire agreement, is no longer of much more than historical importance." W. Slawson, *Standard Form Contracts and Democratic Control of Lawmaking Power*, 84 Harv. L. Rev. 529 (1971).

With respect to those interested in buying insurance, it has been observed that: "His chances of successfully negotiating with the company for any substantial change in the proposed contract are just about zero. The insurance company tenders the insurance upon a 'take it or leave it' basis.

"'* * * Few persons solicited to take policies understand the subject of insurance or the rules of law governing the negotiations, and they have no voice in dictating the terms of what is called the contract. They are clear upon two or three points which the agent promises to protect, and for everything else they must sign ready-made applications and accept ready-made policies carefully concocted to conserve the interests of the company. * * * The subject, therefore, is sui generis, and the rules of a legal system devised to govern the formation of ordinary contracts between man and man cannot be mechanically applied to it.'" 7 Williston on Contracts § 900, pp. 29–30 (3d Ed. 1963)....

The statutory requirement that the form of policies be approved by the commissioner of insurance, § 515.109, The Code, neither resolves the issue whether the fine-print provisions nullify the insurance bargained for in a given case nor ousts the court from necessary jurisdiction.... In this connection it has been pertinently stated: "Insurance contracts continue to be contracts of adhesion, under which the insured is left little choice beyond electing among standardized provisions offered to him, even when the standard forms are prescribed by public officials rather than insurers. Moreover, although statutory and administrative regulations have made increasing inroads on the insurer's autonomy by prescribing some kinds of provisions and proscribing others, most insurance policy provisions are still drafted by insurers. Regulation is relatively weak in most instances, and even the provisions prescribed or approved by legislative or administrative action ordinarily are in essence adoptions, outright or slightly modified, of proposals made by insurers' draftsmen.

"Under such circumstances as these, judicial regulation of contracts of adhesion, whether concerning insurance or some other kind of transaction, remains appropriate." R. Keeton, [*Insurance Law Rights at Variance with Policy Provisions*, 83 Harv. L. Rev. 961 (1970),] at 966–67. See also 3 Corbin on Contracts § 559, p. 267.

The mass-produced boiler-plate "contracts," necessitated and spawned by the explosive growth of complex business transactions in a burgeoning population left courts frequently frustrated in attempting to arrive at just results by applying many of the traditional contract-construing stratagems. As long as fifteen years ago Professor Llewellyn, reflecting on this situation in his book "The Common Law Tradition–Deciding Appeals," pp. 362–71 wrote, "What the story shows thus far is first, scholars persistently off-base while judges grope over well-nigh a century in irregular but dogged fashion for escape from a recurring discomfort of imbalance that rests on what is in fact substantial nonagreement despite perfect semblance of agreement." (pp. 367–368).

"* * * The answer, I suggest, is this: Instead of thinking about 'assent' to boiler-plate clauses, we can recognize that so far as concerns the specific, there is no assent at all. What has in fact been assented to, specifically, are the few dickered terms, and the broad type of transaction, and but one thing more. That one thing more is a blanket assent (not a specific assent) to any not unreasonable or indecent terms the seller may have on his form, which do not alter or eviscerate the reasonable meaning of the dickered terms. The fine print which has not been read has no business to cut under the reasonable meaning of those dickered terms which constitute the dominant and only real expression of agreement, but much of it commonly belongs in." (p. 370)....

Plaintiff's claim it should be granted relief under the legal doctrines of reasonable expectations, implied warranty and unconscionability should be viewed against the above backdrop.

II. Reasonable Expectations

This court adopted the doctrine of reasonable expectations in *Rodman v. State Farm Mutual Ins. Co.*, 208 N.W.2d 903, 905–908 (Iowa 1973). The *Rodman* court approved the following articulation of that concept: " 'The objectively reasonable expectations of applicants and intended beneficiaries regarding the terms of insurance contracts will be honored even though painstaking study of the policy provisions would have negated those expectations.' " 208 N.W.2d at 906. See ... 7 Williston on Contracts § 900, pp. 33–34 ("Some courts, recognizing that very few insureds even try to read and understand the policy or application, have declared that the insured is justified in assuming that the policy which is delivered to him has been faithfully prepared by the company to provide the protection against the risk which he had asked for. * * * Obviously this judicial attitude is a far cry from the old motto 'caveat emptor.' ").

At comment f to [§ 211] of Restatement (Second) of Contracts, ... we find the following analysis of the reasonable expectations doctrine: "Although customers typically adhere to standardized agreements and are bound by them without even appearing to know the standard terms in detail, they are not bound to unknown terms which are beyond the range of reasonable expectation. A debtor who delivers a check to his creditor with the amount blank does not authorize the insertion of an infinite figure. Similarly, a party who adheres to the other party's standard terms does not assent to a term if the other party has reason to believe that the adhering party would not have accepted the agreement if he had known that the agreement contained the particular term. Such a belief or assumption may be shown by the prior negotiations or inferred from the circumstances. Reason to believe may be inferred from the fact that the term is bizarre or oppressive, from the fact that it eviscerates the non-standard terms explicitly agreed to, or from the fact that it eliminates the dominant purpose of the transaction. The inference is reinforced if the adhering party never had an opportunity to read the term, or if it is illegible or otherwise hidden from view. This rule is closely related to the policy against unconscionable terms and the rule of interpretation against the draftsman."

Nor can it be asserted the above doctrine does not apply here because plaintiff knew the policy contained the provision now complained of and cannot be heard to say it reasonably expected what it knew was not there. A search of the record discloses no such knowledge.

The evidence does show, as above noted, a "dicker" for burglary insurance coverage on chemicals and equipment. The negotiation was for what was actually expressed in the policies' "Insuring Agreements" the insurer's promise "To pay for loss by burglary or by robbery of a watchman, while the premises are not open for business, of merchandise, furniture, fixtures and equipment within the premises * * *."

In addition, the conversation included statements from which the plaintiff should have understood defendant's obligation to pay would not arise where the burglary was an "inside job." Thus the following exclusion should have been reasonably anticipated:

> "Exclusions. This policy does not apply: * * * (b) to loss due to any fraudulent, dishonest or criminal act by any Insured, a partner therein, or an officer, employee, director, trustee or authorized representative thereof * * *."

But there was nothing relating to the negotiations with defendant's agent which would have led plaintiff to reasonably anticipate defendant would bury within the definition of "burglary" another exclusion denying coverage when, no matter how extensive the proof of a third-party burglary, no marks were left on the exterior of the premises. This escape clause, here triggered by the burglar's talent (an investigating law officer, apparently acquainted with the current modus operandi, gained access to the steel building without leaving any marks by leaning on the overhead plexiglas door while simultaneously turning the locked handle), was never read to or by plaintiff's personnel, nor was the substance explained by defendant's agent.

Moreover, the burglary "definition" which crept into this policy comports neither with the concept a layman might have of that crime, nor with a legal interpretation. See . . . *State v. Ferguson*, 149 Iowa 476, 478–479, 128 N.W. 840, 841–842 (1910) ("It need not appear that this office was an independent building, for it is well known that it is burglary for one to break and enter an inner door or window, although the culprit entered through an open outer door * * * "); . . .

The most plaintiff might have reasonably anticipated was a policy requirement of visual evidence (abundant here) indicating the burglary was an "outside" not an "inside" job. The exclusion in issue, masking as a definition, makes insurer's obligation to pay turn on the skill of the burglar, not on the event the parties bargained for: a bona-fide third party burglary resulting in loss of plaintiff's chemicals and equipment.

. . . . Appropriately applied to this case, the doctrine demands reversal and judgment for plaintiff. [Eds.: The Court also finds for the plaintiff on theories of implied warranty of fitness for its intended purpose and unconscionability.]

We reverse and remand for judgment in conformance herewith.

LeGRAND, J., DISSENTING. I dissent from the result reached by the majority because it ignores virtually every rule by which we have heretofore adjudicated such cases and affords plaintiff ex post facto insurance coverage which it not only did not buy but which it knew it did not buy.

The majority revokes, at least for this case, the principle that in law cases tried to the court the findings are binding on us if supported by substantial evidence and that we view the evidence in its most favorable light to sustain rather than defeat those findings. . . .

In the present case "burglary" is clearly and unambiguously defined; but now the majority complains because it's in the wrong place and in the wrong size type—this despite the universal rule of construction that a policy of insurance must be read and construed in its entirety....

While it may be very well to talk in grand terms about "mass advertising" by insurance companies and "incessant" assurances as to coverage which mislead the "unwary," particularly about "fine-print" provisions, such discussion should somehow be related to the case under review. Our primary duty, after all, is to resolve this dispute for these litigants under this record.

There is total silence in this case concerning any of the practices the majority finds offensive; nor is there any claim plaintiff was beguiled by such conduct into believing it had more protection than it actually did.

The record is even stronger against the majority's fine-print argument, the stereotype accusation which serves as a coup de grace in all insurance cases. Except for larger type on the face sheet and black (but not larger) print to designate divisions and sub-headings, the entire policies are of one size and style of print. To compare the face sheet with the body of the policy is like comparing a book's jacket cover with the narrative content; and the use of black type or other means of emphasis to separate one part of an instrument from another is an approved editorial expedient which serves to assist, not hinder, readability. In fact many of our opinions, including that of the majority in the instant case, resort to that device.

Tested by any objective standard, the size and style of type used cannot be fairly described as "fine print." The majority's description, right or wrong, of the plight of consumers generally should not be the basis for resolving the case now before us.

Like all other appeals, this one should be decided on what the record discloses—a fact which the majority concedes but promptly disregards.

Crucial to a correct determination of this appeal is the disputed provision of each policy defining burglary as "the felonious abstraction of insured property * * * by a person making felonious entry * * * by actual force and violence, of which force and violence there are visible marks made by tools, explosives, electricity or chemicals upon, or physical damage to, the exterior of the premises at the place of such entry * * *." The starting point of any consideration of that definition is a determination whether it is ambiguous. Yet the majority does not even mention ambiguity.

The purpose of such a provision, of course, is to omit from coverage "inside jobs" or those resulting from fraud or complicity by the assured. The overwhelming weight of authority upholds such provisions as legitimate in purpose and unambiguous in application....

Once this indisputable fact is recognized, plaintiff's arguments virtually collapse. We may not—at least we should not—by any accepted standard of construction meddle with contracts which clearly and plainly state their meaning simply because we dislike that meaning, even in the case of insurance policies....

Nor can the doctrine of reasonable expectations be applied here. We adopted that rule in *Rodman v. State Farm Mutual Automobile Insurance Company*, 208 N.W.2d 903, 906, 907 (Iowa 1973). We refused, however, to apply it in that case, where we said: "The real question here is whether the principle of reasonable expectations should be extended to cases where an ordinary layman would not misunderstand his coverage from a reading of the policy and where there are no circumstances attributable to the insurer which foster coverage expectations. Plaintiff does not contend he misunderstood the policy. He did not read it. He now asserts in retrospect that if he had read it he would not have understood it. He does not say he was misled by conduct or representations of the insurer. He simply asked trial court to rewrite the policy to cover his loss because if he had purchased his automobile insurance from another company the loss would have been covered, he did not know it was not covered, and if he had known it was not covered he would have purchased a different policy. Trial court declined to do so. We believe trial court correctly refused in these circumstances to extend the principle of reasonable expectations to impose liability."

Yet here the majority would extend the doctrine far beyond the point of refusal in *Rodman*. Here we have affirmative and unequivocal testimony from an officer and director of the plaintiff corporation that he knew the disputed provision was in the policies because "it was just like the insurance policy I have on my farm."

I cannot agree plaintiff may now assert it reasonably expected from these policies something it knew was not there.... [Eds.: The judge also rejects the plaintiff's other theories.]

For these several reasons—the principal one being that the findings of the trial court have substantial evidentiary support—I would affirm the judgment.

Notes and Discussion

1. **Visible Marks of Entry.** The Allied policy required "visible marks made by tools, explosives, electricity or chemicals upon, or physical damage to, the exterior of the premises at the place of ... entry." From Allied's perspective, what was the reason for this requirement? If Allied's agent had explained the policy provision to C & J at the time the policy was taken out, would the provision have been objectionable? C & J's plexiglass door entrance "could be forced open without leaving visible marks or physical damage." Should C & J have been advised either to alter their door or to take out a more comprehensive (and more expensive) policy?

At issue here is what viewpoint the Iowa Supreme Court takes in deciding that the contractual limitation should not be determinative of the case. Does the Court simply assume, on the basis of general experience, that C & J gave uninformed consent to Allied's insurance document? Does it impose any duty to read upon C & J?

2. **Reasonable Expectations.** This method of dealing with standard form contracts is largely confined to insurance cases, but is potentially of much wider application. The Court describes the doctrine; Robert Keeton's article, which the Court cites, was central in isolating the judicial trend. See also Robert C. Henderson, *The Doctrine of Reasonable Expectations in Insurance Law after Two Decades,* 51 Ohio St. L. J. 823 (1990); W. David Slawson, Binding Promises: The Late 20th-Century Reformation of Contract Law 44–73 (1996).

Traditionally, courts have interpreted insurance contracts against the drafter (*contra proferentem*), which in practice always means against the insurance company. The judicial motive, of course, was to make insurance policies as extensive as possible, since otherwise loss was borne by the victim. But this practice has the drawback that it may simply provide incentive to drafters to express themselves in ever more explicit language. Does the quoted passage from Allied's policy give evidence of this process?

The reasonable expectations doctrine goes a step further by departing from the actual contractual language and enforcing instead what the insured "should have reasonably anticipated" as the contents of the contract. What dangers are there in doing this? What limits should be imposed on such judicial activism, particularly in contractual areas outside of insurance?

3. **Restatement 2d § 211.** This section specifically deals with "Standardized Agreements." Of particular importance is § 211(3): "Where the other party has reason to believe that the party manifesting such assent would not do so if he knew that the writing contained a particular term, the term is not part of the agreement." Comment f., which the Court quotes at length, fills out what is meant by "reason to believe." To what extent does the decision in *C & J Fertilizer* go beyond the Restatement? Is the Iowa Court actually concerned with whether Allied had "reason to believe" that C & J would not have entered the contract had it known of the limitation?

With § 211(3), compare UNIDROIT § 2.20(1): "No term contained in standard terms which is of such a character that the other party could not reasonably have expected it, is effective unless it has been expressly accepted by that party."

4. **Continuing Controversy.** There is no end in sight to the disputes about this doctrine. "[T]he reasonable expectations idea has steadily gathered force. It has spread to become a key principle governing insurance policy interpretation in many, though by no means all, jurisdictions. At the same time, however, judicial recognition of this concept has sparked persistent controversy regarding just how far the reasonable expectations idea should be carried, particularly in situations where honoring the insured's expectations would run contrary to the intent and clear import of policy language.

"Although controversy has not prevented the reasonable expectations concept from gaining ground, it has not subsided, and it has deterred several courts from embracing Professor Keeton's thesis. Some courts have rejected the concept outright; others have vacillated between acceptance and rejection; still others have placed limitations on implementation of the concept that have prevented its full development. Many judges still regard the reasonable expectations doctrine as little more than an excuse for improper judicial rewriting of the policy." Mark C. Rahdert, *Reasonable Expectations Revisited*, 5 Conn. Ins. L. J. 107, 109 (1998) (footnotes omitted).

An example of judicial decisions rejecting the doctrine is *Deni Associates of Florida, Inc. v. State Farm Fire & Casualty Insurance Co.*, 711 So.2d 1135 (Fla. 1998), which resulted from personal injuries sustained after an accidental ammonia spill in an architectural engineering firm. Deni carried a State Farm comprehensive general liability policy that excluded any personal injury "arising out of the actual, alleged or threatened discharge, dispersal, release or escape of pollutants." Id. at 1137. The Supreme Court of Florida refused to depart from the contractual language on a theory of rational expectations because to do so "would be to rewrite the contract and the basis upon which the premiums are charged." Id. at 1140.

5. And Now, a Rant from Professor White. Where did this case come from? This is the IOWA Supreme Court. There are no flower children in Iowa. Iowa judges are cautious, serious Midwesterners, respectful of precedent. They do not write flamboyant opinions; they are not contemptuous of earlier decisions or dismissive of awkward facts. Perhaps the title is wrong; perhaps the case is really from California. In the heyday of Chief Justice Bird (or maybe even of Roger Traynor), the California Supreme Court could have done this, but . . . IOWA?

Yes, it is from Iowa. Maybe Justice Reynoldson was carried away by the times. The case follows on the heels of the student demonstrations of the late '60's and early '70's and on the publication of things like Professor Reich's book The Greening of America and Professor David Slawson's article on the evils of form contracts. Charles A. Reich, The Greening of America: How the Youth Revolution Is Trying to Make America Livable (1970); W. David Slawson, *Standard Form Contracts and the Democratic Control of Lawmaking Power,* 84 Harv. L. Rev. 529 (1971). No one filled with the spirit of that time could want an insurance company to win just because its form contract clearly excluded the recovery.

Look at what is omitted or disregarded. The insured admitted to reading the policy but could not "recall" reading the burglary exclusion; that weak denial might cause one to suppose that he did read the exclusion. And Justice LeGrand tells us that the policy was not in "fine print." Moreover the insured may have consciously chosen this policy over others with larger or smaller coverage and with larger or smaller premiums. But forget reading, aren't we all bound by the form contracts that we sign, for auto rentals, health care, credit cards and even insurance—whether we read them or not? Note too that this theft may have been by an employee who had a key to the front door but none to the chemical shed, not so?

The good news is that the Iowa Court reverted to its roots only 3 years later when the Court distinguished *C & J Fertilizer* in *Chipokas v. Travelers Indemnity Co.*, 267 N.W.2d 393 (Iowa 1978). In *Chipokas* the Court indorsed the outcome in *Rodman v. State Farm Mutual Automobile Ins. Co.*, 208 N.W.2d 903 (Iowa 1973), a case that preceded *C & J*. The Court reaffirms the proposition from *Rodman* that the doctrine of reasonable expectations does not "extend . . . to cases where an ordinary layman would not misunderstand his coverage from a reading of the policy and where no circumstances appear attributable to the insurer which would foster coverage expectations." *Chipokas*, 267 N.W.2d at 396. Is this approval, of an earlier and contrary case, a tacit reversal of the holding in *C & J*? We hope so.

The Iowa Supreme Court itself set further limits in *Weber v. IMT Insurance Co.*, 462 N.W.2d 283 (Iowa 1990). Ralph Newman grew sweet corn that was allegedly rendered unmarketable by hog manure from the Webers' farm. Newman brought suit, and the Webers looked to IMT to defend them on the basis of a comprehensive personal liability policy and an umbrella policy. IMT refused, citing the policies' exclusion of "bodily injury or discharge arising out of the discharge ... of ... waste material." The Court found for IMT and refused to apply the doctrine of reasonable expectations to this case. "[T]he pollution exclusion is not bizarre or oppressive, and does not eviscerate terms explicitly agreed to or eliminate the dominant purpose of the transaction. The dominant purpose of the liability policy was to insure Webers against a wide range of farm accidents which can cause serious personal injury or property damage. The pollution exclusion does not eliminate this purpose. It only denies coverage when specific materials are discharged by Webers, and, the discharge is not sudden or accidental. The insureds' reasonable expectations were not frustrated and, therefore, the doctrine of reasonable expectations is not applicable to this case." Id. at 288.

For further criticism of the judicial application of § 211(3), see James J. White, *Form Contracts under Revised Article 2*, 75 Wash. U. L.Q. 315 (1997).

Problem 3–10

Melinda Kay Broemmer entered a Phoenix clinic to obtain an abortion. While she was in a visibly disturbed emotional state prior to the abortion, she signed three standard forms, one of which required that any dispute with the clinic be subject to binding arbitration by "licensed medical doctors who specialize in obstetrics/gynecology." During the abortion, she suffered a punctured uterus that required medical treatment. If Broemmer brings a malpractice lawsuit, will the clinic be able to use the form to compel arbitration?

F. THE STATUTE OF FRAUDS

As a general rule (and contrary to widespread lay perception), Common Law does not require that contracts be in writing; oral contracts are as acceptable as written ones, although writing is obviously quite routine and is widely thought to provide parties with an added level of protection. For certain types of promises, however, a signed writing is of considerable importance for the enforcement of contracts. This requirement starts with the Statute of Frauds enacted by the Parliament of Charles II in 1677, and then incorporated into American law through colonization. For England and Wales the Statute was largely repealed in 1954, but in the United States it survives and has shown remarkable durability despite vastly changed circumstances and incessant academic and judicial criticism.

The original statutory list of particular types of contracts that must be in a signed writing is hard to make sense of today, but seems to go off on two main ideas. First, some promises are so important that they should be evidenced in a writing. Instances of this type, from the original Statute, are still frozen in place in Restatement 2d § 110: contracts for the sale of an interest in land (including not just the sale of land itself, but also, for instance, a long-term lease), and contracts that are not to be performed within one calendar year from their making. Both these contract types are intrinsically likely to be of social and economic importance, although not today for the same reasons or to the same extent as in 1677. Separately regulated both by the original Statute and in subsequent legislation are contracts for the sale of goods above a certain price. This provision is now UCC § 2–201(1), which sets a floor price of $500; the amended version of Article Two raises this to $5,000.

Rather different is a second class: promises that are potentially dangerous for promisors, usually because they are more or less unilateral and may be entered into without sufficient thought. Again, the original Statute's list is frozen in Restatement 2d § 110, but the one that is still of major significance is a contract to answer for the duty of another (suretyship), when one person promises to pay a debt owed by another. Here the danger is that, for instance, one spouse might too casually promise on behalf of another, or that a parent might too casually undertake the debt of a child. The list of promises that fall into this category has been expanding in recent decades, beyond the original Statute, largely because modern consumer legislation often requires this; however, the list varies widely in details from state to state.

Beyond the question of which contracts must be evidenced by a writing, there is the further vexed issue of what form such a writing must have, and in particular whether the writing must state at least the main terms of the contract, whether multiple writings can be pieced together to make a single document, and what satisfies the requirement of a signature. These difficult questions are related to an underlying issue: what is the purpose of the Statute of Frauds? Is it mainly concerned with the bare existence of a contract (did A and B actually make a contract?), or is it also concerned with proof of the contents of a contract? In general, the UCC takes a "minimalist" view of the Statute of Frauds: it is concerned mainly with the possibility that someone might fraudulently assert the existence of a contract that was never made. By contrast, non-Code cases often are more demanding.

Finally, you should be warned against the impression given by appellate cases on the Statute of Frauds, namely that its application is riddled with exceptions so large that you can drive an SUV through most of them. The reality at the trial court level is, in our experience, quite different. Trial judges tend to like the Statute, probably because it provides a ready mechanical aid ("Is this contract within the Statute? If yes, then is there a signed writing? If no, the case is over."). For this reason, the requirement of a writing looms larger in our law than may at first appear.

C.R. KLEWIN, INC. v. FLAGSHIP PROPERTIES, INC.

Supreme Court of Connecticut, 1991.
220 Conn. 569, 600 A.2d 772.

PETERS, C.J. The sole question before us in this certified appeal is whether the provision of the statute of frauds, General Statutes § 52–550 (a) (5),[27] requiring a writing for an "agreement that is not to be performed within one year from the making thereof," renders unenforceable an oral contract that fails to specify explicitly the time for performance when performance of that contract within one year of its making is exceedingly unlikely....

The plaintiff, C. R. Klewin, Inc. (Klewin), is a Connecticut based corporation that provides general construction contracting and construction management services. The defendants, Flagship Properties and DKM Properties (collectively Flagship), are engaged in the business of real estate development; although located outside Connecticut, they do business together in Connecticut under the trade name ConnTech.

Flagship became the developer of a major project (ConnTech Project) in Mansfield, near the University of Connecticut's main campus. The master plan for the project included the construction of twenty industrial buildings, a 280 room hotel and convention center, and housing for 592 graduate students and professors. The estimated total cost of the project was $120 million.

In March, 1986, Flagship representatives held a dinner meeting with Klewin representatives. Flagship was considering whether to engage Klewin to serve as construction manager on the ConnTech Project. During the discussions, Klewin advised that its fee would be 4 percent of the cost of construction plus 4 percent for its overhead and profit. This fee structure was, however, subject to change depending on when different phases of the project were to be constructed. The meeting ended with Flagship's representative shaking hands with Klewin's agent and saying, "You've got the job. We've got a deal." No other specific terms or conditions were conclusively established at trial. The parties publicized the fact that an agreement had been reached and held a press conference, which was videotaped. Additionally, they ceremoniously signed, without filling in any of the blanks, an American Institute of Architects Standard Form of Agreement between Owner and Construction Manager.

Construction began May 4, 1987, on the first phase of the ConnTech Project, called Celeron Square. The parties entered into a written agreement regarding the construction of this one part of the project.

27. General Statutes § 52–550 provides in pertinent part: "(a) No civil action may be maintained in the following cases unless the agreement, or a memorandum of the agreement, is made in writing and signed by the party, or the agent of the party, to be charged ... (5) upon any agreement that is not to be performed within one year from the making thereof.... "

Construction was fully completed by the middle of October, 1987. By that time, because Flagship had become dissatisfied with Klewin's work, it began negotiating with other contractors for the job as construction manager on the next stage of the ConnTech Project. In March, 1988, Flagship contracted with another contractor to perform the sitework for Celeron Square II, the next phase of the project.

After having been replaced as construction manager, Klewin filed suit in the United States District Court for the District of Connecticut, claiming (1) breach of an oral contract to perform as construction manager on all phases of the project; (2) *quantum meruit* recovery for services performed in anticipation of future stages of the project; and (3) detrimental reliance on Flagship's promise to pay for preconstruction services. Flagship moved for summary judgment, claiming, inter alia, that enforcement of the alleged oral contract was barred by the statute of frauds. The district court granted summary judgment, reasoning that (1) "the contract was not of an indefinite duration or open-ended" because full performance would take place when all phases of the ConnTech Project were completed, and (2) the contract "as a matter of law" could not possibly have been performed within one year. In drawing this second conclusion, the court focused on the sheer scope of the project and Klewin's own admission that the entire project was intended to be constructed in three to ten years.

Klewin appealed to the United States Court of Appeals for the Second Circuit. The Court of Appeals held that "the issues presented involve substantial legal questions for which there is no clear precedent under the decisions of the Connecticut Supreme Court"; . . . and certified to this court the following questions:[28]

> "A. Whether under the Connecticut Statute of Frauds, Conn. Gen. Stat. § 52–550 (a) (5), an oral contract that fails to specify explicitly the time for performance is a contract of 'indefinite duration,' as that term has been used in the applicable Connecticut precedent, and therefore outside of the Statute's proscriptions?
>
> "B. Whether an oral contract is unenforceable when the method of performance called for by the contract contemplates performance to be completed over a period of time that exceeds one year, yet the contract itself does not explicitly negate the possibility of performance within one year?" . . .

I.

The Connecticut statute of frauds has its origins in a 1677 English statute entitled "An Act for the prevention of Fraud and Perjuries." See 6 W. Holdsworth, A History of English Law (1927) pp. 379–84. The statute appears to have been enacted in response to developments in the common law arising out of the advent of the writ of assumpsit, which changed the general rule precluding enforcement of oral promises in the

28. These certified questions do not involve the question, which these facts raise, of whether the alleged oral contract was too vague to be enforceable. . . .

King's courts. Thereafter, perjury and the subornation of perjury became a widespread and serious problem. Furthermore, because juries at that time decided cases on their own personal knowledge of the facts, rather than on the evidence introduced at trial, a requirement, in specified transactions, of "some memorandum or note . . . in writing, and signed by the party to be charged" placed a limitation on the uncontrolled discretion of the jury. See 2 A. Corbin, Contracts (1950) § 275, pp. 2–3; 6 W. Holdsworth, supra, pp. 387–89; An Act for Prevention of Fraud and Perjuries, 29 Car. 2, c. 3, § 4 (1677), quoted in J. Perillo, "The Statute of Frauds in the Light of the Functions and Dysfunctions of Form," 43 Fordham L. Rev. 39, 39 n.2 (1974). Although the British Parliament repealed most provisions of the statute, including the one-year provision, in 1954; see The Law Reform (Enforcement of Contracts) Act, 2 & 3 Eliz. 2, c. 34 (1954); the statute nonetheless remains the law virtually everywhere in the United States.[29]

Modern scholarly commentary has found much to criticize about the continued viability of the statute of frauds. The statute has been found wanting because it serves none of its purported functions very well; see J. Perillo, supra; and because it permits or compels economically wasteful behavior; see M. Braunstein, "Remedy, Reason, and the Statute of Frauds: A Critical Economic Analysis," 1989 Utah L. Rev. 383. It is, however, the one-year provision that is at issue in this case that has caused the greatest puzzlement among commentators. As Professor Farnsworth observes, "of all the provisions of the statute, it is the most difficult to rationalize.

"If the one-year provision is based on the tendency of memory to fail and of evidence to go stale with the passage of time, it is ill-contrived because the one-year period does not run from the making of the contract to the proof of the making, but from the making of the contract to the completion of performance. If an oral contract that cannot be performed within a year is broken the day after its making, the provision applies though the terms of the contract are fresh in the minds of the parties. But if an oral contract that can be performed within a year is broken and suit is not brought until nearly six years (the usual statute of limitations for contract actions) after the breach, the provision does not apply, even though the terms of the contract are no longer fresh in the minds of the parties.

"If the one-year provision is an attempt to separate significant contracts of long duration, for which writings should be required, from less significant contracts of short duration, for which writings are unnecessary, it is equally ill-contrived because the one-year period does not run from the commencement of performance to the completion of performance, but from the making of the contract to the completion of performance. If an oral contract to work for one day, 13 months from now, is broken, the provision applies, even though the duration of

29. "The one-year provision has been omitted in North Carolina and Pennsylvania." 2 E. Farnsworth, Contracts (2d Ed. 1990) § 6.4, p. 110 n5.

performance is only one day. But if an oral contract to work for a year beginning today is broken, the provision does not apply, even though the duration of performance is a full year." 2 E. Farnsworth, Contracts (2d Ed. 1990) § 6.4, pp. 110–11; see also ... 1 Restatement (Second), Contracts (1979) § 130, comment a; J. Calamari & J. Perillo, Contracts (3d Ed. 1987) § 19–18, p. 807.

Historians have had difficulty accounting for the original inclusion of the one-year provision. Some years after the statute's enactment, one English judge stated that "the design of the statute was, not to trust to the memory of witnesses for a longer time than one year." Smith v. Westall, 1 Ld. Raym. 316, 317, 91 Eng. Rep. 1106, 1107 (1697). That explanation is, however, unpersuasive, since, as Farnsworth notes, the language of the statute is ill suited to this purpose. One eminent historian suggested that because such contracts are continuing contracts, it might be very difficult to give evidence of their formation, inasmuch as the rules of evidence of that time prohibited testimony by the parties to an action or any person who had an interest in the litigation. 6 W. Holdsworth, supra, p. 392. That argument, however, proves too much, since it would apply equally to all oral contracts regardless of the duration of their performance. The most extensive recent study of the history of English contract law offers plausible explanations for all of the other provisions, but acknowledges that this one is "curious." A. Simpson, A History of the Common Law of Contract (1975) p. 612. More recently, it has been suggested that the provision "may have been intended to prevent oral perjury in actions of assumpsit against customers who had forgotten the details of their purchases." P. Hamburger, "The Conveyancing Purposes of the Statute of Frauds," 27 Am. J. Leg. Hist. 354, 376 n.85 (1983).

In any case, the one-year provision no longer seems to serve any purpose very well, and today its only remaining effect is arbitrarily to forestall the adjudication of possibly meritorious claims. For this reason, the courts have for many years looked on the provision with disfavor, and have sought constructions that limited its application. See, e.g., *Landes Construction Co. v. Royal Bank of Canada*, 833 F.2d 1365, 1370 (9th Cir. 1987) (noting policy of California courts "of restricting the application of the statute to those situations precisely covered by its language"); *Cunningham v. Healthco, Inc.*, 824 F.2d 1448, 1455 (5th Cir. 1987) (one-year provision does not apply if the contract "conceivably" can be performed within one year); . . .

II.

Our case law in Connecticut, like that in other jurisdictions, has taken a narrow view of the one-year provision of the statute of frauds now codified as § 52–550 (a) (5). In *Russell v. Slade*, 12 Conn. 455, 460 (1838), this court held that "it has been repeatedly adjudged, that unless it appear *from the agreement itself*, that it is *not* to be performed within a year, the statute does not apply. . . . The statute of frauds plainly means an agreement not to be performed within the space of a year, and

expressly and *specifically* so agreed. A *contingency* is not within it; nor any case that *depends upon contingency.* It does *not* extend to cases where the thing only *may* be performed within the year." (Emphases in original; citation and internal quotation marks omitted.)

A few years later, in *Clark v. Pendleton,* 20 Conn. 495, 508 (1850), the statute was held not to apply to a contract that was to be performed following a voyage that both parties expected to take one and one-half years. "It is not alleged in any form, that it was made with reference to, or that its performance was to depend on the termination of a voyage which would necessarily occupy that time. It is only alleged, that it was expected by the parties, that the defendant would be absent for the period of eighteen months. But this expectation, which was only an opinion or belief of the parties, and the mental result of their private thoughts, *constituted no part of the agreement itself*; nor was it connected with it, so as to explain or give a construction to it, although it naturally would, and probably did, form one of the motives which induced them to make the agreement. The thing thus anticipated did not enter into the contract, *as one of its terms*; and according to it, as stated, the defendant, whenever he should have returned, after having embarked on the voyage, whether before or after the time during which it was thus expected to continue, would be under an obligation to perform his contract with the plaintiff. As it does not therefore *appear, by its terms, as stated,* that it was not to be performed within a year from the time when it was made, it is not within the statute." (Emphases added.)

In this century, in *Appleby v. Noble,* 101 Conn. 54, 57, 124 A. 717 (1924), this court held that " '[a] contract is not within this clause of the statute unless *its terms are so drawn* that it cannot by any possibility be performed fully within one year.' " (Emphasis added.) In *Burkle v. Superflow Mfg. Co.,* 137 Conn. 488, 492–93, 78 A.2d 698 (1951), we delineated the line that separates contracts that are within the one-year provision from those that are excluded from it. "*Where the time for performance is definitely fixed at more than one year,* the contract is, of course, within the statute.... If no time is definitely fixed but full performance *may* occur within one year through the happening of a contingency upon which the contract depends, it is not within the statute." (Emphases added; citations omitted.)

More recently, in *Finley v. Aetna Life & Casualty Co.,* 202 Conn. 190, 197, 520 A.2d 208 (1987), we stated that " '[u]nder the prevailing interpretation, the enforceability of a contract under the one-year provision does not turn on the actual course of subsequent events, nor on the expectations of the parties as to the probabilities. Contracts of uncertain duration are simply excluded; the provision covers *only* those contracts whose performance *cannot possibly* be completed within a year.' (Emphasis added.) 1 Restatement (Second), Contracts, [§ 130, comment a].... "

In light of this unbroken line of authority, the legislature's decision repeatedly to reenact the provision in language virtually identical to that of the 1677 statute suggests legislative approval of the restrictive interpretation that this court has given to the one-year provision....

III.

Bearing this history in mind, we turn to the questions certified to us by the federal court. Our case law makes no distinction, with respect to exclusion from the statute of frauds, between contracts of uncertain or indefinite duration and contracts that contain no express terms defining the time for performance. The two certified questions therefore raise only one substantive issue. That issue can be framed as follows: in the exclusion from the statute of frauds of all contracts except those "whose performance cannot possibly be completed within a year"; (emphasis omitted) *Finley v. Aetna Life & Casualty Co.*, supra, 197; what meaning should be attributed to the word "possibly"? One construction of "possibly" would only contracts whose completion within a year would be inconsistent with the express terms of the contract. An alternate construction would include as well contracts such as the one involved in this case, in which, while no time period is expressly specified, it is (as the district court found) realistically impossible for performance to be completed within a year. We now hold that the former and not the latter is the correct interpretation. "The critical test ... is whether 'by its terms' the agreement is not to be performed within a year," so that the statute will not apply where "the alleged agreement contain[s] [no] provision which directly or indirectly regulated the time for performance." *Freedman v. Chemical Construction Corporation*, 43 N.Y.2d 260, 265, 372 N.E.2d 12, 401 N.Y.S.2d 176 (1977). "It is the law of this state, as it is elsewhere, that a contract is not within this clause of the statute unless *its terms are so drawn* that it cannot by any possibility be performed fully within one year." (Emphasis added.) *Burkle v. Superflow Mfg. Co.*, supra, 492.

Flagship contends, to the contrary, that the possibility to which this court referred in *Burkle* must be a reasonable possibility rather than a theoretical possibility. It is true that in *Burkle* this court rejected the argument that "since all the members of a partnership [that was a party to the contract] may possibly die within a year, the contract is not within the statute." We noted that "[n]o case has come to our attention where the rule that the possibility of death within a year removes a contract from the statute has been extended to apply to the possibility of the death of more than one individual." Id., 494. In *Burkle*, however, we merely refused to extend further yet another of the rules by which the effect of the provision has been limited. *Burkle* did not purport to change the well established rule of narrow construction of the underlying one-year provision.

Most other jurisdictions follow a similar rule requiring an express contractual provision specifying that performance will extend for more than one year. Only "[a] few jurisdictions, contrary to the great weight of authority ... hold that the intention of the parties may put their oral agreement within the operation of the Statute." 3 S. Williston, Contracts

(3d Ed. W. Jaeger 1960) § 495, pp. 584–85. In "the leading case on this section of the Statute"; id., p. 578; the Supreme Court of the United States undertook an extensive survey of the case law up to that time and concluded that "[i]t ... appears to have been the settled construction of this clause of the statute in England, before the Declaration of Independence, that an oral agreement which, according to the intention of the parties, *as shown by the terms of the contract*, might be fully performed within a year from the time it was made, was not within the statute, although the time of its performance was uncertain, and might probably extend, and be expected by the parties to extend, and did in fact extend, beyond the year. The several States of the Union, in reenacting this provision of the statute of frauds in its original words, must be taken to have adopted the known and settled construction which it had received by judicial decisions in England." (Emphasis added.) *Warner v. Texas & Pacific R. Co.*, 164 U.S. 418, 422–23, 17 S. Ct. 147, 41 L. Ed. 495 (1896). The agreement at issue was one in which a lumbermill agreed to provide grading and ties and the railway agreed to construct rails and a switch and maintain the switch as long as the lumbermill needed it for shipping purposes. Although the land adjoining the lumbermill contained enough lumber to run a mill for thirty years, and the lumbermill used the switch for thirteen years, the court held that the contract was not within the statute. "The parties may well have expected that the contract would continue in force for more than one year; it may have been very improbable that it would not do so; and it did in fact continue in force for a much longer time. But they made no stipulation which in terms, or by reasonable inference, required that result. The question is not what the probable, or expected, or actual performance of the contract was; but whether the contract, *according to the reasonable interpretation of its terms*, required that it should not be performed within the year." (Emphasis added.) Id., 434; ...

Because the one-year provision "is an anachronism in modern life ... we are not disposed to expand its destructive force." *Farmer v. Arabian American Oil Co.*, 277 F.2d 46, 51 (2d Cir. 1960). When a contract contains no express terms about the time for performance, no sound reason of policy commends judicial pursuit of a collateral inquiry into whether, at the time of the making of the contract, it was realistically possible that performance of the contract would be completed within a year. Such a collateral inquiry would not only expand the "destructive force" of the statute by extending it to contracts not plainly within its terms, but would also inevitably waste judicial resources on the resolution of an issue that has nothing to do with the merits of the case or the attainment of a just outcome. See 2 A. Corbin, supra, § 275, p. 14 (the statute "has been in part the cause of an immense amount of litigation as to whether a promise is within the statute or can by any remote possibility be taken out of it. This latter fact is fully evidenced by the space necessary to be devoted to the subject in this volume and by the vast number of cases to be cited").

We therefore hold that an oral contract that does not say, in express terms, that performance is to have a specific duration beyond one year is, as a matter of law, the functional equivalent of a contract of indefinite duration for the purposes of the statute of frauds. Like a contract of indefinite duration, such a contract is enforceable because it is outside the proscriptive force of the statute regardless of how long completion of performance will actually take.

The first certified question is answered "yes." The second certified question is answered "no." No costs will be taxed in this court to either party.

Notes and Discussion

1. **Why the Hostility?** Chief Justice Peters gives a quick but informative history of the Statute and its tangled judicial history. If we assume that the legislators singled out contracts not to be performed within a year as singularly important ones that therefore required a signed writing, the judicial manipulations of this category in Connecticut and elsewhere might strike one as unwarranted. In any case, what do you make of the general failure of legislatures to repeal the one-year rule?

There seems to have been little doubt in this case that an oral contract had been concluded; the videotaped press conference, for instance, would seem to be conclusive. What policy considerations justify Flagship's position? Flagship apparently was dissatisfied with Klewin's performance, but this does not figure as an issue in the case. Why?

Clearly, as the opinion concedes, when the contract was made no one believed that the job would be completed, or even could be completed, within one year. What interpretative devices does Chief Justice Peters use in order to take the contract out of the statute? In particular, her interpretation of "possibly" is not persuasive, true?

Finally, quite apart from the Statute of Frauds, one may be surprised that experienced business persons would conclude a contract of this magnitude without putting the contract into writing. What might have prompted them?

2. **The International Sale of Goods.** The CISG has no Statute of Frauds. Article 11 provides: "A contract of sale need not be concluded in or evidenced by writing and is not subject to any other requirement as to form. It may be proved by any means, including witnesses." If this is the rule for international commerce in which communication may be hampered by language barriers, why does American law cling so desperately to the Statute?

3. **Signed Writings.** The various statutes of frauds, whether in the common law, in the general state statutes or in § 2–201 of the UCC, require a "writing, signed" by the party to be charged. Courts have sometimes stretched to find a "signature" in words or symbols that are far short of a conventional manual signature, and they have been willing to tie pieces of paper together to make a writing or memorandum that shows the contract. So, in life, the statute has never been as formidable as it seems at first

reading, but even in a generous court's hands any statute of frauds would bar a form of contract that is now commonplace in commerce—the so called electronic contract. Offers and acceptances by e-mail must now be frequent in commercial sales transactions. These and similar electronic transactions have a permanence and reliability that often surpasses the permanence and reliability of written and signed contracts, for they are easier to catalogue and retrieve and harder to discard by inadvertence.

Three statutes now recognize these facts and, by various means, modify Statutes of Frauds to accommodate them. First is the Uniform Electronic Transactions Act (UETA). That act was promulgated by NCCUSL in 1999; it has since been adopted by 46 states (but not in Georgia, Illinois, New York, and Washington). In 2000 Congress adopted the Electronic Signatures in Global and National Commerce Act (e-Sign). E-Sign is a backup for UETA; it applies only where a state has not adopted UETA in its standard format. The third statute is Amended Article 2 which proposes "record" for "writing" in Section 2–201 and a change in the definition of "Sign" in Section 2–103(1)(p) that will recognize electronic symbols as signatures.

Section 7 of UETA states the new law with clarity: "1. A record or signature may not be denied legal effect or enforceability solely because it is in electronic form. 2. If a law requires a record to be in writing, an electronic record satisfies the law."

Of course, the law is never that easy. Buried in UETA are questions of scope (can one make a valid electronic will? No, see Section 3 Scope) and of definition (Are optical scanners and printers using electronic-like, but not properly electronic, technology still "electronic" for this statute? Yes, see Section 2 Definitions). Note too that UETA (and the other two statutes) do not abolish the Statute of Frauds, for there still must be a "record," i.e. the information must be in tangible form or be "stored in an electronic or other medium and [be] retrievable in perceivable form."

Problem 3–11

In order to prevent an "at-will" employee from taking a job offer elsewhere, an employer, in front of several witnesses, makes an oral promise to her that she will have "a permanent job." Can the employer later use the Statute of Frauds in order to prevent enforcement of the promise? Would the outcome be the same if it had promised "a lifetime job"? "A job for ten years if she lives that long"? "A job for ten years unless she dies first"? "A job for ten years unless she is fired with cause"? Be warned that problems of this type are trickier than they may seem.

Look back at *Hamer v. Sidway* in Chapter 2.A. Uncle William's original promise was within the Statute of Frauds, right? But after Willie performed, Uncle William acknowledged his promise in a letter to his nephew. Even though this letter was written long after the making of the promise, it would have satisfied the Statute; there is no requirement that the writing be contemporaneous with the promise.

MIGEROBE, INC. v. CERTINA USA, INC.

United States Court of Appeals, Fifth Circuit, 1991.
924 F.2d 1330.

THORNBERRY, J. A watch manufacturer appeals a jury verdict which held that it had breached an oral contract to deliver an order of watches to a retail operator. The jury held that the manufacturer was liable to the retailer for $157,133.00 in damages as a result of the breach. Finding that the retail operator presented sufficient evidence to support a finding of breach and sufficient evidence to justify the damage award, we AFFIRM.

Facts And Procedural History

Appellant, Certina USA, is a watch manufacturer located in Lancaster, Pennsylvania. Appellee, Migerobe Inc., is a Mississippi corporation that owns and operates jewelry counters in McRae's department stores, which are located throughout the Southeast. This suit is based on the breach of an alleged oral contract that the two companies entered into in October 1987.

Certina sells its watches through the efforts of traveling salesmen, who are either salaried employees of Certina or independent representatives paid on a commission basis. Gerald Murff was one such representative, and his sales territory included Mississippi. Migerobe had purchased watches through Murff before, and, during the summer of 1987, Migerobe contacted Murff to notify him that Migerobe would be interested in buying Certina watches if the company decided to sell a large portion of its inventory at reduced prices. Migerobe suspected that Certina might make such an offer because another retailer recently had decided to stop carrying the Certina line of watches, and Migerobe believed that this would create a backlog of inventory for the manufacturer. In fact, Certina had decided to institute a special promotion to eliminate its inventory as a result of a corporate decision to withdraw its watches from the United States market.

Migerobe was hoping to acquire the Certina watches so that they could be used as "door-busters" for an After-Thanksgiving sales promotion. Doorbusters or "loss leaders" are items offered at a low price, which are designed to increase the traffic flow through a store and, thereby, increase corollary sales (the sale of non-advertised items). Murff later became aware that Migerobe was planning to use the watches in this special After-Thanksgiving promotion.

In a letter dated September 14, 1987, Murff responded to Migerobe's request, saying that he was "pursuing a special price on the Certina inventories on [Migerobe's] behalf" and that he would keep the company informed of his progress. Migerobe Record Excerpts at 5 (Plaintiff's Exhibit 64).  At the time, Murff was attempting to negotiate a special discounted price with Certina's vice president of retail sales, William

Wolfe. On October 21, 1987, Wolfe provided Murff with a list of watches from Certina's inventory that Murff could offer to Migerobe at a price of forty-five dollars each. Murff scheduled an October 29 meeting with Migerobe to present the offer. Prior to this meeting, Murff requested and received an additional list of watches from Wolfe, which were to be included in the offer to Migerobe.

Murff kept his October 29 appointment with Migerobe. During the course of the day, Murff made several phone calls to Certina's home office in Lancaster, Pennsylvania to verify the number of watches in Certina's inventory, and to secure specific payment terms. After a full day of negotiating for particular quantities and styles as well as payment terms and a shipping date, Migerobe agreed to purchase over 2,000 Certina watches at a price of forty-five dollars each. Murff phoned Certina's Lancaster office one final time to report the sale, and Wolfe's administrative assistant recorded it onto a Certina order form. On November 4, 1987, Certina's national accounts manager, Don Olivett, called Migerobe to say that Certina would not ship the watches that had been ordered on October 29. The president of Certina, John Gelson, later explained that the order was being rejected because the offered price was lower than that offered to other customers, and he feared that the offer might constitute a violation of the Robinson-Patman Act. Migerobe brought suit in district court for repudiation of the contract and, after a five-day trial, a jury awarded it $157,133.

After the district court denied its motion for judgment notwithstanding the verdict and for a new trial or remittitur, Certina filed a timely appeal. Certina urges us to reverse the district court based on several alleged errors. First, it argues that Migerobe failed to submit writings sufficient to satisfy the statute of frauds.... [Eds.: Other issues are omitted.]

Discussion

I. Statute of Frauds

A writing must meet three requirements to satisfy the statute of frauds: 1) the writing must be "sufficient to indicate that a contract for sale has been made between the parties," 2) the writing must be "signed by the party against whom enforcement is sought," and 3) the writing must specify a quantity. Miss. Code Ann. § 75–2–201 (1972); ... The statute of frauds can be met through the integration of several documents, each of which alone might not be sufficient to meet these three requirements.

A "writing" for the purposes of the statute of frauds may consist of separate writings, connected together by express reference to each other or internal evidence of their unity, connection, or relation; by so connecting the writings, otherwise separate documents may incorporate by reference the terms of each document. *Hunt Oil Co. v. FERC*, 853 F.2d 1226, 1248 (5th Cir. 1988).... The signed writing need not refer explicitly to the unsigned writing; a Mississippi court would consider them to be integrated if the signed writing "makes at least an implied reference to the other writing." . . .

In the case before us, the integration of two signed documents and one unsigned document tends to show that the parties had made a contract for sale. The two signed writings include an internal memorandum from Wolfe to Certina's chief financial officer, R.B. Oliver, see Record, vol. 2 at 305, and an internal memorandum from Charles Westhaeffer, a clerical employee in charge of inventory control, to several other employees, see Record, vol. 2 at 309. The unsigned writing includes a Certina order form, see Record, vol. 2 at 307.

Of the two signed writings, the memorandum from Wolfe to Oliver, dated October 29, 1987, is the most enlightening. In relevant part, the memo states that "Jerry Murff *has been authorized* to sell" Certina watches to Migerobe at a special forty-five dollar price. (Emphasis added.) Wolfe goes on to explain that "Murff's commission on *this sale has been set* at 3% so that our net selling price is $43.65." (Emphasis added.) Certina claims that the purpose of this memorandum was to solicit authorization from Oliver so that Wolfe could go ahead with the Migerobe offer. But Gelson, the president of the company, ultimately determined that the sale should be rejected, not Oliver. Moreover, the language used in the memorandum does not support Certina's interpretation that the memorandum was simply a request for authorization. On the contrary, the only mention of authorization occurs in the past tense, indicating that Murff had already been authorized to make the sale.

The second signed writing is a memorandum to several Certina employees from Charles Westhaeffer, the person in charge of inventory control. The handwritten note announces that a new "promotion code has been set up to cover a special order from Migerobe." The note serves as further confirmation that a transaction had taken place between Certina and Migerobe. Additionally, the note contains the same promotion code, "03," that is found on the Certina order form that was completed by Wolfe's administrative assistant in Lancaster.

The pertinent unsigned writing, the Certina order form, lists, among other things, the quantity, styles, and prices of watches ordered. The form includes other information which tends to connect it with the Wolfe and Westhaeffer memos as well, such as the customer name, "Migerobe," the promotion code, "03," the name of the salesman, "Murff," and the initials of Charles Westhaeffer, dated "10/30," the same date on which he sent out the signed memo described above. The connection among these three documents was sufficiently strong to justify their integration into a writing that would satisfy the statute of frauds under Mississippi case law.

In its brief to this court, Certina alternatively argues that section 75–2–201(2) of the Mississippi Uniform Commercial Code allowed it to reject the Migerobe offer within ten days after it received a copy of the Migerobe purchase order. Section 75–2–201(2) of the Code provides for an alternate method of satisfying the writing requirement of section 75–

2–201(1) of the Code and provides that: "Between merchants if within a reasonable time a writing in confirmation of the contract and sufficient against the sender is received and the party receiving it has reason to know its contents, it satisfies the requirements of [the statute of frauds] against such party unless written notice of objection to its contents is given within ten (10) days after it is received."

But the issue whether the Migerobe purchase order served as a confirmatory writing under this section of the Mississippi Code was never presented to the lower court. See Migerobe Brief at 23. As a general rule, this court will not consider issues that are raised for the first time on appeal.... Moreover, section 75–2–201(2) does not apply to the situation now before us. Section 75–2–201(2) provides merchants with a method of satisfying the statute of frauds when an oral contract has been formed, but the signature of the party to be charged is lacking. See *Perdue Farms Inc. v. Motts, Inc.*, 459 F. Supp. 7, 13–14 (N.D.Miss. 1978). In this case, we have two writings signed by Certina representatives, which, together with the unsigned Certina order form, are sufficient to establish a written contract. Section 75–2–201(2) cannot be invoked to excuse a breach of that contract.

Wolfe's memorandum shows that Murff was authorized to offer Migerobe a discounted price on Certina watches, and the Certina order form and the Westhaeffer memorandum evidence Migerobe's acceptance of that offer. Taken together, these documents provide sufficient evidence to satisfy the statute of frauds....

CONCLUSION

For the foregoing reasons, we AFFIRM the jury's finding of a contractual breach by Certina as well as the jury's award of damages to Migerobe in the amount of $157,133.00.

Notes and Discussion

1. **Piecing Together Documents.** It has long been possible to satisfy the Statute of Frauds through several linked documents. See Restatement 2d § 132: "The memorandum may consist of several writings if one of the writings is signed and the writings in the circumstances clearly indicate that they relate to the same transaction." A good example of how courts can stitch writings together is *Crabtree v. Elizabeth Arden Sales Corp.*, 305 N.Y. 48, 110 N.E.2d 551 (1953), in which the New York Court of Appeals found a two-year employment contract in the unsigned notes that a personal secretary had taken during the plaintiff's job interview (the notes outlined the broad terms of the contract, stated the plaintiff's salary, and gave him "2 years to make good"), plus a payroll change card subsequently prepared by the company's executive vice president (it was initialed and gave his pay in accord with the notes) and two payroll cards initialed either by the company's general manager or its comptroller.

Follow through the parallel process in *Migerobe*. How much importance attaches to the Mississippi rule that: "The signed writing need not refer explicitly to the unsigned writing; . . . "? Note especially that the writing need not be a complete or final statement of the contract; it is sufficient if it is an adequate memorandum. Nor need the writing be prepared specifically for the purpose of satisfying the Statute.

2. Completeness. The Common Law rule is stated by Restatement 2d § 131, which requires, in particular, that the writing must "(c) state[] with reasonable certainty the essential terms of the unperformed promises in the contract." Comment c. explains: "The primary purpose of the Statute is evidentiary, to require reliable evidence of the existence and terms of the contract and to prevent enforcement through fraud or perjury of contracts never in fact made." How much wiggle room does this standard leave to courts?

For sale of goods, § 2–201 considerably narrows the evidentiary purpose of the Statute. As Comment 1 observes, "The required writing need not contain all the material terms of the contract and such material terms as are stated need not be precisely stated. All that is required is that the writing afford a basis for believing that the offered oral evidence rests on a real transaction." The one exception is the quantity term, since "the contract is not enforceable under this paragraph beyond the quantity of goods shown in such writing." UCC § 2–201(1).

How does this narrower purpose play out both in the instant case and in the more general drafting of the UCC Statute of Frauds?

3. Failure to Plead the Statute. The UCC Statute provides several methods to satisfy the Statute of Frauds even though no adequate writing is available. On appeal, Certina tried to plead one of these methods, based on § 2–201(2); this method is discussed more fully in the case that follows. What is more important here is the brusque reception they received. In general, a defense under the Statute of Frauds is lost if it is not advanced at trial.

CONAGRA, INC. v. NIERENBERG

Supreme Court of Montana, 2000.
301 Mont. 55, 7 P.3d 369.

NELSON, J. ConAgra, Inc., d/b/a Peavey Company (ConAgra) appeals from a judgment issued by the Ninth Judicial District Court, Toole County, in favor of Ralph and Dennis Nierenberg (Nierenbergs), following a non-jury trial. We reverse. . . .

Factual And Procedural Background

This matter concerns whether an enforceable oral contract bound the respective parties to the purchase and sale of 12,500 bushels of wheat in the spring of 1996. It is undisputed that the Nierenbergs, who operate a wheat farm near Shelby, Montana, were never bound by a written contract bearing one of their signatures. ConAgra, which operates a grain elevator in Shelby and regularly buys and sells grain, brought suit claiming that the oral agreement between the two parties entitled it to recover $14,125 in expectation damages after the Nierenbergs failed to sell their wheat as promised.

A critical factor in this dispute is the fact that during that spring the price of wheat was steadily rising on a daily basis by as much as 20 cents per-bushel.

Following a non-jury trial on September 25, 1998, the District Court entered judgment for the Nierenbergs, on December 10, 1998. The court, in its Findings of Fact and Conclusions of Law, determined that ConAgra had failed to sufficiently establish that an enforceable oral agreement existed between the parties, and thus the Nierenbergs prevailed on their statute of frauds defense.

The origins of this dispute can be traced to a phone call placed by Dennis Nierenberg (hereinafter Dennis), on April 9, 1996, which was a Tuesday. On that day, Dennis, acting for himself and his father, Ralph Nierenberg, discussed the sale of the Nierenbergs' number-one, dark northern spring wheat with Marcus Raba (Raba), who at the time managed ConAgra's Shelby, Montana, grain elevator.

According to ConAgra's version of the conversation, the parties agreed that 12,500 bushels of wheat would be sold by the Nierenbergs and purchased by ConAgra for $5.01 a bushel. At that time, Raba filled out a customary order sheet memorializing the terms discussed during the phone call. ConAgra contends that such an oral agreement by phone is routine, as a matter of its own course of dealing with the Nierenbergs and other area farmers, as well as within the trade of grain purchase and sales by other area grain elevators.

Dennis, on the other hand, maintains that he was doing nothing more than checking the market price that day, and that it was understood that unless he signed a contract no enforceable agreement was reached. He alleges that he has never consummated a grain sale with ConAgra without first signing a written contract. It is undisputed that he requested that a written contract be prepared for his signature, and that Raba followed this instruction. In dispute is whether Dennis requested that the contract be mailed to his residence (which he contends), or whether he stated that he would stop by the elevator at some later time and sign the contract (which ConAgra contends).

Following the phone call, Raba instructed Eve Jacobson (Jacobson), another ConAgra employee, to prepare what ConAgra characterizes as a written "confirmation" contract based on the order sheet. ConAgra asserts that "Marcus signed it and held it for Dennis to come in and sign." According to ConAgra, when Dennis failed to show up at the elevator and sign the contract within the next few days, Raba "sent the original contract he signed to Dennis's Shelby address on April 17," which was the following Wednesday.

It is undisputed that Dennis received the confirmation contract on April 19, 1996, a Friday, and that this contract expressly provided the terms discussed on April 9, 1996: 12,500 bushels of wheat at $5.01 per bushel. The contract also provided a time of shipment: April 9, 1996 to May 31, 1996, and provided discount information, which pertains to reductions in the sales price determined by the actual quality of the grain, including protein, moisture content, and "waste." The District Court would find that the parties never discussed such discounts during the phone conversation. Also, the confirmation form provided no printed signature line for the seller, Dennis. Instead, a handwritten line was drawn in above the printed signature line, where Raba had signed. Raba would explain at trial that whether a farmer actually signs and returns such a confirmation contract is a formality that has no bearing on the formation of such an agreement; rather, the farmer's receipt confirms the existing oral agreement. He asserted that such oral contracts account for more than 90 percent of ConAgra's grain purchases.

[Eds.: Dennis Nierenberg continued dickering with ConAgra, neither acknowledging the existence of a contract nor clearly asserting that none had been formed.]

The Nierenbergs ultimately sold the 12,500 bushels to another grain elevator, Harvest States, for $5.85 per bushel the following Tuesday, April 23, 1996. Believing that he had no obligation to sell wheat to ConAgra—based on the advice of counsel—Dennis did not notify Raba or any other ConAgra agent of his sale to Harvest States. Raba called him some time later, apparently in early or mid-May. Again, Dennis did not indicate that he did not believe he was obligated to perform under an oral agreement. Instead, Dennis "put him off" by telling Raba that he would deliver the wheat "one of these days."

After independently learning of the Nierenbergs' sale to Harvest States, ConAgra, in a May 24, 1996 letter, advised the Nierenbergs that it would assert its contractual rights, and demand payment of the difference between the contract price ($5.01 per bushel), and the current market price ($6.14 per bushel) it had incurred in purchasing other grain to fulfill its sale obligations pursuant to its purchase of the Nierenbergs' wheat. Thus, ConAgra pursued this matter in order to recoup the $1.13 per-bushel price on 12,500 bushels for a total of $14,125.

In their Answer, the Nierenbergs denied that the parties entered into a contract, and asserted, as an affirmative defense, the signed-writing requirement under the statute of frauds, pursuant to the Uniform Commercial Code governing sales under § 30–2–201(1), MCA. Thus, any alleged oral contract between the parties was unenforceable, because the sale of goods price exceeded $500, and it is undisputed that Dennis never signed a contract. . . .

Following the trial on September 25, 1998, the District Court concluded that Dennis Nierenberg never "admitted" in his pleadings or testimony that a contract for the sale and purchase of his grain was made with ConAgra. . . .

Next, the court concluded that, although both parties were merchants, the confirmation received within 10 days by Dennis on April 19, 1996, was not within a reasonable time. This conclusion was reached in light of the "upwardly changing price at the time" of the phone conversation between ConAgra and Dennis. "Considering the fluctuation in price occurring at the time Dennis Nierenberg and Plaintiff had their telephone conversation, and considering that Plaintiff simply had to forward to Dennis Nierenberg a copy of the already prepared memorandum to satisfy Section 30–2–201(2)," the court concluded that ConAgra did not give Dennis Nierenberg written confirmation within a reasonable time.

The District Court entered a judgment on December 10, 1998, in favor of the Nierenbergs on all "unresolved counts of Plaintiff's complaint," and awarded the Nierenbergs costs. ConAgra appealed....

Discussion

This case presents a request for a straightforward, legal determination as to the respective rights of the parties as buyers and sellers of grain in Montana under a number of issues. Although we ultimately conclude that one issue is dispositive, it is necessary that we resolve the apparent uncertainty concerning the U.C.C. statute of frauds governing sales under the fairly common factual scenario set forth here.

First, we disagree with the Nierenbergs that the dispositive issue in this case is "whether or not the parties made an oral agreement." Rather, more precisely, the dispositive issue is whether the parties formed an enforceable oral agreement....

[A]s a starting point, the parties here could have discussed the purchase and sale of grain on April 9, 1996, and Dennis could have offered to sell 12,500 bushels of wheat, and Raba, as an agent of ConAgra, could have accepted.... Both parties could have even concluded the phone call with such language as "fine and dandy, you have a deal." ... Under § 30–2–201(1), MCA, however, such an oral contract simply is not enforceable unless it is reduced to writing and signed by the party against whom enforcement is sought.

The U.C.C. statute of frauds, however, provides alternatives, or exceptions, to the signed writing requirement of § 30–2–201(1), MCA, which effectively prevent a party from asserting the affirmative defense. Under § 30–2–201(3)(b), MCA, for example, if a party admits that an oral contract for sale was made by way of his pleadings, testimony, or "otherwise in court," then he can no longer assert a statute of frauds defense. Alternatively, under § 30–2–201(2), MCA, if both parties are "merchants," one party may send written confirmation of an oral contract to the other which, if received within a "reasonable time," provides that the receiving party has 10 days to object in writing. Should the receiving party subsequently fail to object as required, he too can no longer assert a statute of frauds defense....

In light of the fact that much of the foregoing turns on the question of formation, it is imperative to our discussion that we recognize that the U.C.C. rules governing sales agreements are far more permissive in this respect than the general common law rules governing contract formation....

Accordingly, we must expel certain unnecessary chaff from the parties' arguments regarding the terms of the alleged contract here, namely the Nierenbergs' contention that there was no "meeting of the minds" as to all material terms of the contract. As the foregoing indicates, the parties obviously reached accord on the quantity of the grain, namely 12,500 bushels, as well as the price at $5.01 per bushel, sufficient for a U.C.C. sales contract to be formed. Therefore, as a preliminary matter, we hold that the District Court, in determining that Dennis did not admit that a contract was formed because he did not unambiguously testify to the "necessary elements of a contract" is incorrect. That the parties did not discuss, according to the court's findings, the "reduction in per bushel price ... due to variance in protein, moisture content, or waste in the grain" is wholly immaterial under these facts in determining whether an enforceable sales contract was formed.

Far more critical to our discussion here is whether there is substantial evidence that Dennis's statements and conduct at the time indicate he was contractually bound as of April 9, 1996, pursuant to his discussion of contract terms with Raba, or whether the evidence instead reveals the statements and conduct of a person who would not be bound until the oral "discussion" or "contract" was reduced to writing and signed at a later time.

Generally, it is the duty of the court to enforce a contract if the parties intended that one exist....

Issue 1. Did the District Court err by finding and concluding that Dennis Nierenberg, as an agent for the Nierenbergs, did not admit making a contract to sell wheat to ConAgra?

The District Court concluded that Dennis Nierenberg did not admit in his pleadings or testimony that a contract for the sale and purchase of his grain was made with ConAgra, and thus the Nierenbergs could rely on their statute of frauds defense. As indicated, the District Court incorrectly reached its legal determination by narrowly focussing on whether the parties discussed certain terms that the court deemed material. However, we may nevertheless affirm a district court decision which is correct regardless of the district court's reasoning in reaching its decision.... We conclude that the District Court correctly determined that Dennis's "admissions" were ambiguous, and therefore ConAgra's reliance on § 30–2–201(3)(b), MCA, must fail.

On appeal, ConAgra points to numerous passages from Dennis's trial testimony that, once pieced together, allegedly show he intended to make a sales contract with ConAgra by phone on April 9, 1996, and therefore contends that the District Court erred in reaching its findings and conclusions. For example:

Q: Well, actually you ended up selling more than 10,000 didn't you? You sold 12,500.

A: Yeah, the discussion was it got to the point where I'd talked to him about 12,500.

* * *

Q: And when you spoke with Marcus and talked to him about selling that grain, that was over the phone, correct?

A: Yeah, it was to verify the price and tell him to send me a contract.

* * *

[P]rodding a party while on the witness stand or while testifying during a deposition to say certain magical legal words that may indicate a contract was formed must be viewed with disfavor. Thus, in accordance with Montana law, determining whether a party has admitted that a contract for sale was made sufficient to remove an oral contract from the signed-writing requirements of § 30–2–201(1), MCA, may be guided by those courts that have followed a "deliberate, clear and unequivocal" standard....

... Dennis provided several statements of fact regarding his conduct following the phone call, which ConAgra suggests are inferentially those of a person who is bound by an agreement. Primarily, ConAgra looks to the fact provided in Dennis's testimony that once he received the confirmation contract, and visited the elevator, he did not inform Raba, on April 19, 1996, that a contract had not been formed. Yet, the fact that Dennis was willing to further negotiate the quantity—10,000 bushels rather than the discussed 12,500 bushels—is not necessarily the objective conduct of person who is contractually bound without a signed writing. Dennis also testified to the fact that Raba had to explain to him that he was contractually obligated pursuant to their earlier phone conversation, as well as other fundamentals of how the grain elevator conducted its business. He testified that he then left the elevator that day planning to seek legal counsel concerning this new uncertainty regarding his unsigned confirmation contract. On the whole, the testimonial facts provided by Dennis concerning his post-phone conversation conduct are, as the District Court concluded, ambiguous.

We therefore hold that, pursuant to § 30–2–201(3)(b), MCA, Dennis did not deliberately, clearly, and unequivocally admit in his testimony that a contract for sale was made by phone with ConAgra on April 9, 1996. Accordingly, we hold that the decision of the District Court, that Dennis Nierenberg did not "admit in his pleadings or testimony that a contract for the sale and purchase of his grain was made with Plaintiff" is affirmed....

Issue 2. Did the District Court err by concluding that the Nierenbergs did not receive written confirmation of the sale and purchase of their grain within a reasonable time?

In relying on a 1976 Utah court decision, the District Court concluded that a written confirmation sent by ConAgra following the April 9, 1996 telephone discussion at issue was not received by Dennis Nierenberg within a "reasonable time," and therefore could not bar the Nierenbergs' statute of frauds defense. The court determined that receipt of the confirmation in this instance within 10 days was unreasonable.

The court's conclusion under this issue was premised on the court's earlier determination that Dennis Nierenberg was a "merchant" as defined under § 30–2–104, MCA, and related case law. Although farmers are not merchants as a matter of law in Montana., whether Dennis is a merchant was not cross-appealed by the Nierenbergs, and is therefore not at issue....

The ... "merchant" exception to § 30–2–201(1), MCA's writing requirement is one born from the coupling of custom and efficiency in the market place. Wheat, for example, must pass through numerous sales transactions on its journey from field to bakery, a process that simply does not permit the time-consuming enterprise of carefully drafted and executed written agreements stating all material terms. In theory, it is essential to the wheat farmer merchant, as well as to the merchant-buyer, that prices can be contractually fixed orally, by phone, given the constraints of both time and physical proximity. Subsection (2) assumes, therefore, that no written contract is necessary between two seasoned merchants because they prefer to transact business via a telephonic handshake....

As a preliminary matter, we observe that the District Court found and concluded that had Dennis accepted the confirmation "document," he would have been bound to its terms, indicating that the confirmation contract was enforceable once signed. The court concluded, therefore, that if the confirmation was received within a reasonable time, "the writing necessary to comply with § 30–2–201(1), MCA, is present." Further, the court, in issuing partial summary judgment in favor of ConAgra, concluded that Dennis generally sold grain "pursuant to an initial oral agreement, memorializing such agreement in a written contract signed when he received payment for the grain sold."

We conclude that, in view of the substantial evidence as a whole—notwithstanding Dennis's adamant denial which was the subject of the first issue—the court correctly reached its determinations in this regard.... Here, it is undisputed that Dennis never objected in writing to the written confirmation he received within 10 days. Further, Dennis has not once objected to any of the terms found within the signed confirmation contract. Quantity, price, time of delivery, date of formation all accord with Dennis's recollection of his discussion with Raba. His only contention is that "discounts" were not discussed—not that the discounts were unreasonable or inaccurate.

[W]e proceed to the focal issue of whether the confirmation here was received within a reasonable time. Once again, this Court is faced with little authority from its own case law upon which a rule, let alone a conclusion, can be drawn....

[W]e cannot establish a bright line rule for what is a reasonable time as between a merchant-farmer and merchant-buyer of grain. Nevertheless, we hold that it makes little sense to shorten what is "reasonable" under these circumstances to a term shorter than that offered the recipient, which is precisely what the District Court achieved in determining that 10 days was unreasonable.

Although a court must look at the broad "nature, purpose and circumstances" in determining whether written confirmation was received within a reasonable time, two specific factors may be examined: (1) the merchant's usual practice or policy for such transactions, and (2) the merchant's excuse for not following its practice or policy....

Here, ConAgra's "usual" practice was to either hold the confirmation contract until the farmer came in, or mail it to the farmer, depending on the farmer's preference. No definite time period was offered into evidence or otherwise established in this respect....

[A]ssuming but not deciding that it would be reasonable for ConAgra to mail the confirmation within one or two working days, the slight delay in Dennis's receipt of the confirmation due to an apparent misunderstanding would not be an unreasonable deviation from ConAgra's usual practice under the circumstances. We thus hold that the District Court did not rely on the substantial evidence of this case in determining that Dennis did not receive confirmation of the oral contract within a reasonable time, but instead relied on authority that we conclude is not persuasive on this issue....

This Court has often stated that each party to a contract has a justified expectation that the other will act in a reasonable manner and not outside of "accepted commercial practices" in not only its performance of a contract but in its "efficient breach" as well....

... Dennis Nierenberg chose to simply not honor his contractual obligation without notifying ConAgra of his true intentions. His mistake, therefore, was to not give ConAgra prompt notice of his breach so that his obligation for expectancy damages would be fixed; i.e., he acted outside of "accepted commercial practices." It is apparent that Dennis established his dubious position on the advice of legal counsel—meaning, had he received advice to the contrary, he may have indeed chosen a much different course of action. The testimonial record shows that after receiving this advice—at the latest, on the same day he sold the grain to Harvest States—he gave his obligation to ConAgra not a second thought, and that he was in fact deceptive about his sale to Harvest States when Raba called some time in May to determine when the grain would be delivered. Such a breach cannot, and should not, be excused or encouraged under any theory, due to the nature of the market place in which the Nierenbergs have chosen to make their living.

In this instance, the "Confirmation of Grain Purchase Contract," which the District Court determined would have contractually bound the Nierenbergs had Dennis accepted it, expressly provided that "unless you promptly notify us in writing with any objections" the confirmation would become enforceable. Thus, as a "merchant," Dennis simply failed to follow the ordinary course of business practices employed by the market in which he sold grain.

As this issue is dispositive, ... the conclusion by the District Court that the agreement between the Nierenbergs and ConAgra cannot be enforced is reversed and this matter is remanded for further proceedings consistent with this opinion.

Notes and Discussion

1. **Admissions.** UCC § 2–201(3) establishes three different ways in which a contract can be enforceable despite the absence of a record under subsections (1)-(2). The method discussed in this case is relevant when "the party against whom enforcement is sought admits in his pleading, testimony or otherwise in court" the existence of the contract; but note the statutory limit on the extent of enforceability. (For another of the sub-subsection (3) exceptions, see *Brookside Farms v. Mama Rizzo's, Inc.* in Chapter 4.E.)

As might be anticipated, plaintiffs have frequently sought to "elicit" such an admission by dogged questioning during deposition or in trials. Dennis Nierenberg successfully fought off an assault of this type. Had there been no other evidence of the contract, could he have escaped closer examination by simply submitting an affidavit asserting that no oral contract had been made? Authority is divided, but for a strong case supporting the conclusiveness of such an affidavit, see *DF Activities Corp. v. Brown*, 851 F.2d 920 (7th Cir. 1988) (Posner, J.).

2. **Are Farmers Merchants?** Article Two applies to all sales of goods, including those between ordinary persons (e.g., lawn sales), but it establishes many special rules that apply only to merchants. Section 2–104(1) defines a "merchant" as "a person who deals in goods of the kind or otherwise by his occupation holds himself out as having knowledge or skill peculiar to the practices or goods involved in the transaction or to whom such knowledge or skill may be attributed ... " This legal definition is substantially broader than in ordinary English usage. For instance, a person who regularly sells something may be a merchant even though the bulk of his work is elsewhere; see *Vince v. Broome*, 443 So.2d 23 (Miss. 1983) (a seller who annually sold a thousand cows is a merchant even though upwards of four-fifths of his time is spent in construction). The results are sometimes controversial. *Cook v. Downing*, 891 P.2d 611 (Okla. Ct. App. 1994), concerns a patient who sued her dentist over ill-fitting dentures; the plaintiff alleged a violation of UCC implied warranties. But is a dentist accurately described as a merchant who sells dentures? The court held no, over a vigorous dissent. Do lawyers sell the wills and contracts that they prepare?

Farmers, who trade extensively with their crops but lack commercial sophistication (or at least claim to lack it), have caused some difficulty, but are usually classed as merchants unless exceptional circumstances are present. An example is *Dixon v. Roberts*, 853 P.2d 235 (Okla. Ct. App. 1993), holding that amateur entrepreneurs who had little experience in the ostrich business were not merchants.

3. **A Confirmation.** The Statute of Frauds usually requires that the memorandum of a contract be signed by the party to be charged. For the sale of goods, UCC § 2–201(2) provides another, rather more curious means to satisfy the Statute: in a sale between merchants, a confirmation sent within a reasonable time, *if it is signed by and is sufficient to bind the sender*, and if the other party does not then object within ten days after receipt. The *ConAgra* decision suggests the commercial rationale that underlies this subsection. What does the Court mean when it says: "we disagree with the Nierenbergs that the dispositive issue in this case is 'whether or not the parties made an oral agreement.' Rather, more precisely, the dispositive issue is whether the parties formed an enforceable oral agreement"?

The Montana Supreme Court disagrees with the trial court's finding that, in a rapidly rising market, a delay of ten days in sending a confirmation was not a "reasonable time."

What is the point of the Court's further observation: "Dennis Nierenberg chose to simply not honor his contractual obligation without notifying ConAgra of his true intentions"? How is this relevant to the application of § 2–201?

LIGE DICKSON CO. v. UNION OIL CO. OF CALIFORNIA

Supreme Court of Washington, 1981.
96 Wash.2d 291, 635 P.2d 103.

DORE, J. The Ninth Circuit Court of Appeals certified the following question to us: "Under the law of the State of Washington, may an oral promise otherwise within the statute of frauds, Wash. Rev. Code § 62A.2–201, nevertheless be enforceable on the basis of promissory estoppel? See Restatement (Second) of Contracts § 217A. See generally *Klinke v. Famous Recipe Fried Chicken, Inc.*, 94 Wash.2d 255, 616 P.2d 644 (1980)." Our answer to this question is "no." Analysis and elaboration follow.

The business relationship between plaintiff Lige Dickson Company (or its predecessor partnership) and defendant Union Oil Company of California is long standing, dating from 1937. Plaintiff was a general contractor and purchased its oil-based products from defendant. In 1964, defendant encouraged and aided plaintiff in entering the asphalt paving business. From 1964 through 1973, with one exception, plaintiff purchased all its liquid asphalt from defendant. In the ordinary course of business, plaintiff telephoned orders to defendant, plaintiff was invoiced, and all bills were paid. Plaintiff and defendant never executed a written contract providing for the sale and purchase of liquid asphalt.

From 1964 until late 1970, the defendant's price for liquid asphalt remained constant. In December 1970, all of the suppliers of liquid asphalt in the Tacoma area raised their prices. Responding to this in May or June of 1971, plaintiff requested, and defendant provided, an oral guaranty against further increases insofar as would affect those contracts which committed the plaintiff to manufacture and sell asphalt paving at fixed, agreed sums. A list was made of the plaintiff's contracts and the parties computed the amount of liquid asphalt needed to fulfill them. At the same time, defendant promised plaintiff that any upward change in price would be applicable only to contracts which plaintiff entered into after the price increase.

At trial, an official of defendant conceded that by November 1973 there was an unwritten custom in the liquid asphalt business in the Tacoma area, well known and acted upon by suppliers and users, that any increase in price of liquid asphalt would not be applicable to manufacturers' then-existing contracts. From mid-1971 until November 1973, defendant's sales representatives visited plaintiff and ascertained tonnage of liquid asphalt needed for plaintiff to fulfill existing paving contracts and also promised plaintiff that the price for that liquid tonnage would be protected.

Nevertheless, in November 1973 defendant wrote to plaintiff that the price of liquid asphalt was rising by $3 per ton and plaintiff was informed on December 6 and 13, 1973 of further increases. The new prices were to be applicable to all purchases made after December 31, 1973. This was plaintiff's first notification that defendant was abandoning the parties' price protection agreement. In addition, the new prices were on a "verbal, indefinite basis ... subject to change" with or without notice.

Without a firm supplier, plaintiff was unable to seek new paving contracts during the first part of 1974. What liquid asphalt was available was used by plaintiff to complete existing contracts. Plaintiff incurred a total increased out-of-pocket cost of $39,006.50 in acquiring liquid asphalt to perform existing contracts.

Plaintiff brought suit against defendant in the United States District Court for Western Washington for breach of contract. The trial court found that there was an oral contract between the parties, but the statute of frauds, RCW 62A.2–201, rendered the contract unenforceable. The cause was appealed to the Ninth Circuit which certified the question quoted above to this court....

The Restatement (Second) of Contracts § [139][30] authorizes enforcement of a promise which induced action or forbearance by a promisee notwithstanding the statute of frauds. Adoption of § [139] was before this court in *Klinke v. Famous Recipe Fried Chicken, Inc.*, 94 Wn.2d 255, 616 P.2d 644 (1980).

In *Klinke*, the plaintiff had been induced by defendant to leave his employ in Alaska and to move to Washington to establish a food franchise. Defendant had promised plaintiff that defendant would qualify and register in Washington as a dealer in franchises. After plaintiff's move, defendant failed to secure the proper dealer registration and later abandoned its efforts to do so. The plaintiff claimed $200,000 in lost time

30. [Eds.: The Court refers to § 217A in the Tentative Draft; here and below we have replaced this reference with the section number in the final version.]

and wages and other damages. On summary judgment, the trial court dismissed the case because RCW 19.36.010(1)[31] voids unwritten contracts which cannot be performed in 1 year. The Court of Appeals reversed the trial court based on two theories. *Klinke v. Famous Recipe Fried Chicken, Inc.*, 24 Wn. App. 202, 600 P.2d 1034 (1979). First, defendant's failure to reduce the agreement with plaintiff to a writing, and plaintiff's reliance on such promise, estopped defendant from asserting the statute of frauds as a defense. Restatement of Contracts §§ 90, 178, comment f (1932). Second, the Court of Appeals adopted § [139]. On review of that decision, we refused to adopt § [139] but affirmed the court's reversal on its first theory. We stated: "The unforeseen application of section [139] to areas of law outside the scope of the facts of this case convinces us that it would be unwise to adopt that section now unless necessary to effectuate justice. That is not mandated by the facts of this case." *Klinke v. Famous Recipe Fried Chicken, Inc.*, 94 Wn.2d 255, 262, 616 P.2d 644 (1980).

Plaintiff in the subject case urges us to now adopt § [139] as being "necessary to effectuate justice." Plaintiff focuses on the parties' long-standing relationship and defendant's responsibility "in great part" for introducing plaintiff into the asphalt paving business. Plaintiff also asserts that defendant's price protection agreement and assurances encouraged (i.e., induced?) plaintiff to make bids and enter into contracts.

Defendant asks this court to distinguish the statute of frauds at issue in *Klinke* from the statute of frauds contained within the Uniform Commercial Code (U.C.C.) at issue here. Such distinction has been recognized. "The statute of frauds requirements may vary as to the nature of the agreements involved, and a close examination of the subject matter of the oral promise in question is therefore warranted. For example, if the oral promise in question concerned the sale of goods, the attorney would want to be aware of the requirements set out in UCC § 2–201(3) which states the circumstances under which a contract for the sale of goods may be enforceable notwithstanding the statute of frauds. . . . It should be pointed out that where there exists, in statute or in case law, clearly established means under which a contract dealing with a particular subject matter may be rendered enforceable notwithstanding the statute of frauds, the courts may be hesitant to apply promissory estoppel in such a manner as to enlarge upon those means of avoiding the statute." (Footnotes omitted.) Annot., Comment Note.—Promissory Estoppel as Basis for Avoidance of Statute of Frauds, 56 A.L.R.3d 1037, 1045 (1974).

31. RCW 19.36.010 states, in part: "In the following cases, specified in this section, any agreement, contract and promise shall be void, unless such agreement, contract or promise, or some note or memorandum thereof, be in writing, and signed by the party to be charged therewith, or by some person thereunto by him lawfully authorized, that is to say: (1) Every agreement that by its terms is not to be performed in one year from the making thereof . . . "

The Ninth Circuit Court of Appeals has held, in interpreting and applying California law, that U.C.C. § 2–201 cannot be overcome through the application of the doctrine of promissory estoppel. *C.R. Fedrick, Inc. v. Borg-Warner Corp.*, 552 F.2d 852 (9th Cir. 1977). The Kentucky Supreme Court reached the same conclusion based upon the U.C.C.'s internal method of avoiding § 2–201's hardship. *C.G. Campbell & Son, Inc. v. Comdeq Corp.*, 586 S.W.2d 40 (Ky. Ct. App. 1979). It reasoned that the statutory avoidance of § 2–201 found in § 2–201(3) was as far as the legislature was willing to go and "any attempt by the courts to judicially amend this statute which is plain on its face would contravene the separation of powers mandated by the Constitution." *Campbell*, at 41.

On the other hand, the Iowa Supreme Court reached the opposite result in *Warder & Lee Elevator, Inc. v. Britten*, 274 N.W.2d 339 (Iowa 1979). That court found that U.C.C. § 1–103 provided the authority for the use of promissory estoppel to defeat the statute of frauds. That section provides, *inter alia*, that "unless displaced by the particular provision of this chapter" estoppel and other validating or invalidating doctrines shall supplement the U.C.C. The court reasoned that the exceptions to the statute of frauds found at § 2–201(3)(a)-(c) are "definitional" and were not meant to displace equitable and legal principles otherwise applicable to contract actions. "If [2–201] were construed as displacing principles otherwise preserved in [1–103], it would mean that an oral contract coming within its terms would be unenforceable despite fraud, deceit, misrepresentation, dishonesty or any other form of unconscionable conduct by the party relying upon the statute. No court has taken such an extreme position. Nor would we be justified in doing so. Despite differences relating to the availability of an estoppel defense, courts uniformly hold 'that the Statute of Frauds, having been enacted for the purpose of preventing fraud, shall not be made the instrument of shielding[,] protecting, or aiding the party who relies upon it in the perpetration of a fraud or in the consummation of a fraudulent scheme.' 3 Williston on Contracts § 553A at 796 (Third Ed. Jaeger, 1960)." *Warder & Lee Elevator, Inc. v. Britten*, supra at 342.

Defendant asks us to adopt the view of the dissent in *Warder & Lee Elevator, Inc. v. Britten*, supra. The thrust of the dissent is that § 1–103 allows estoppel to supplement the U.C.C. "*unless displaced by the particular provisions of this chapter*"; and § 2–201 contains its own limiting language in that the statute of frauds applies "*except as otherwise provided in this section.*" (Italics ours.) Further, the dissent noted that a party to an oral contract who has been defrauded has available the equitable remedy of restitution. In such a case, the recovery is based on the wrong, not on a contract.

From the limited record before us in the subject case, it appears that equitable estoppel is not available to the plaintiff. There seems to be neither allegation nor proof of fraud or deceit. Plaintiff's only remedy may be based upon breach of the oral contract. Nonetheless, we must hold that promissory estoppel cannot be used to overcome the statute of frauds in a case which involves the sale of goods.

The Uniform Commercial Code was adopted to regulate commercial dealings. Uniformity among different jurisdictions in decisions concerning commerce was a major motivation behind development of the U.C.C. By so doing, it was hoped that this area of the law would become clearer and disputes would be more readily resolved. These policies are enunciated in the U.C.C., in part, as follows: "62A.1–102 Purposes; rules of construction; variation by agreement ... (2) Underlying purposes and policies of this Title are (a) to simplify, clarify and modernize the law governing commercial transactions; ... (c) to make uniform the law among the various jurisdictions." It was hoped that commercial transactions could take place across state boundaries without the stultifying effect caused by differences in states' laws. "The Uniform Commercial Code, hammered out by lawyers, judges and law teachers dedicated to clarity and good business sense in commercial law, has brought together into one coherent statement the best laws and practices prevalent in the United States." American Bar Ass'n, Uniform Commercial Code Handbook, "The Uniform Commercial Code," at 1 (1964). "Because of the federal system, the American lawyer, probably more than any other, has been conscious of the disadvantages of differing laws. Internally he has tried to do something about it." American Bar Ass'n, Uniform Commercial Code Handbook, "The Uniform Commercial Code," at 19 (1964).

If we were to adopt § [139] as applicable in the context of the sale of goods, we would allow parties to circumvent the U.C.C. See *Warder & Lee Elevator, Inc. v. Britten*, supra (Reynoldson, C.J., dissenting). For example, to prove justifiable reliance (an element of promissory estoppel), the promisee may offer evidence of course of dealing between the parties, as plaintiff did in this case. The Official Comments to RCWA 62A.1–205(4) state that the statute of frauds "restrict[s] the actions of the parties, and ... cannot be abrogated by agreement, or by a usage of trade ... " (Italics ours.) RCWA 62A.1–205, at 71.

Notwithstanding our appreciation of plaintiff's dilemma, we cannot help but foresee increased litigation and confusion as being the necessary result of the eroding of the U.C.C. if § [139] is adopted in this case. We join the other courts which limit the doctrine of promissory estoppel from overcoming a valid defense based on the statute of frauds contained within the Uniform Commercial Code. By so doing, we make no comment on the applicability of § [139] to defeat the raising of the statute of frauds as a defense under RCW 19.36.010.

[Eds.: A concurring opinion is omitted.]

Notes and Discussion

1. **The Price of Asphalt.** This case originated from the OPEC oil embargo of 1973, which sent the price of petroleum-related products soaring. Why is it that Lige Dickson was so concerned about price protection for its

existing contracts? Why had it and Union Oil kept their contracts unwritten for so many years?

For a contemporary case in which an asphalt manufacturer succeeded in obtaining price protection, see *Nanakuli Paving & Rock Co. v. Shell Oil Co., Inc.* below in Chapter 4.B.

2. The *Klinke* Case and Restatement 2d § 139. The year before *Lige Dickson* was decided, the Washington Supreme Court in the *Klinke* case had rejected an opportunity to use detrimental reliance as a broad means to circumvent the Statute of Frauds, by holding to a narrower rule: a party that promises to reduce a contract to a signed writing, but then fails to do so, may be estopped from pleading the absence of a writing if the other party relies on the promise. This rule, an early exception to the Statute of Frauds, courts once described as equitable estoppel on the theory that the first party was misrepresenting its intention, e.g., *Seymour v. Oelrichs*, 156 Cal. 782, 106 P. 88 (1909); the *Klinke* decision, however, more correctly preferred promissory estoppel. However, usually, as in *Lige Dickson*, there is no such promise, so this escape hatch is unavailable and the larger question must be confronted.

It may seem odd, at first, that when a contract within the Statute of Frauds is not evidenced by a written document satisfying the Statute, a party can nonetheless make the contract enforceable by relying on it. After all, in what sense can the party's reliance be regarded as justified? And doesn't permitting reliance as a means to circumvent the Statute make it a mockery? The traditional rule, therefore, was that promissory estoppel was inapplicable to the Statute of Frauds.

However, the gradual infusion of reliance thinking into Common Law led to a reconsideration of the older view. As usual, Roger Traynor was in the vanguard. *Monarco v. Lo Greco*, 35 Cal.2d 621, 220 P.2d 737 (1950; in bank), arose out of a disputed inheritance. Christie Lo Greco's mother and stepfather had promised him that if he remained on and ran the family farm, they would leave him most of their property. He did so for twenty years, but when the stepfather died it was discovered that he had left his property to his grandson. Since Lo Greco's was a contract for the sale of an interest in land, it fell afoul of the Statute of Frauds. But Justice Traynor rode to his rescue, holding that Lo Greco would be seriously prejudiced, and the defendants unjustly enriched, if this contract was not enforced. As Traynor reasoned, it is "the promise that the contract will be performed that a party relies upon when he changes his position because of it," and this promise, when so relied on, should be enforced. 220 P.2d at 741. The California decision has been widely followed and was generalized for Common Law in Restatement 2d § 139.

The rule has not been universally accepted, however. Some courts still feel that a reliance rationale is too defiant of statute. Others have tried to limit the rationale. An example is *Whiteco Indus., Inc. v. Kopani*, 514 N.E.2d 840 (Ind. Ct. App. 1987), in which several employees, who had been orally promised a full year's work, were terminated prematurely and then sued seeking application of Restatement 2d § 139. The Indiana Court refused, preferring to stick to its established rule that enforcement is available only when: " 'the other party's refusal to carry out the terms of the agreement has resulted not merely in a denial of the rights which the agreement was intended to confer, but the infliction of an unjust and unconscionable injury and loss.' " Id. at 845, citing an earlier case. This is a substantially higher standard than in the Restatement. For the rest, the Court felt that: "Whether the Statute of Frauds in general, or that section relating to contracts not to be performed within one year, in particular, have become outmoded is a question more properly addressed to the General Assembly." Id. at 844. Other courts have been more negative still.

Sort through the possible arguments on either side of this issue. Does it matter which type of contracts are in question?

3. **Reliance and § 2–201.** As *Lige Dickson* indicates, the same arguments have continued after the adoption of the UCC, and the underlying issue also remains the same. However, at least in the first instance the dispute has been over the UCC's text, with proponents of the rationale pointing to § 1–103 (§ 1–103(b) in the revised version; the "particular provisions" of the UCC are to be supplemented by "the principles of law and equity, including ... estoppel," unless the principles are "displaced by the [UCC's] particular provisions"), and opponents pointing to the opening seven words of § 2–201(1) itself ("Except as otherwise provided in this section," a phrase that appears to exclude exceptions other than those listed). State courts have come out variously and are about evenly divided. Does the *Lige Dickson* Court's little paean to the UCC do any real work either in this decision or in helping to determine the larger question?

For what it's worth, amended Article Two drops the first seven words of § 2–201(1). Preliminary Official Comment 2 notes that: "This change was made to provide that the statement of the three statutory exceptions in subsection (3) should not be read as limiting under subsection (1) the possibility that a promisor will be estopped to raise the statute-of-frauds defense in appropriate cases." Am. Law Inst., supra, at 21. If adopted, will the amendment settle the debate?

An addition to § 2–201 is subsection 4, which states: "A contract that is enforceable under this section is not unenforceable merely because it is not capable of being performed within one year or any other period after its making." This subsection deals with the situation in which a contract for the sale of goods satisfies the UCC Statute of Frauds, but is arguably still subject to the ordinary Statute of Frauds because it requires more than one year to perform.

Chapter 4

THE CONTENTS OF THE CONTRACT

The content of a beer bottle is beer; the content of a contract is words. Must we belabor that point? Would you be happier if we called it "Finding the Legal Meaning of Contracts" or "Interpretation, Implication, Modification etc.?" You should cut us some slack; it is hard to find a good name for all of the things that we think logically fit here, but we are sure that they are important things, things even more complicated than a Belgian beer.

The content of contracts is words but words are often ambiguous. If a contract called for the sale of 100,000 chickens, would the seller conform to the contract if he delivered 100,000 stewing chickens (tough old hens that are over the hill as egg layers and are being sent on to the dinner table)? Or capons (castrated males)? Roosters? Or would the seller need to ship broilers (succulent young females)? You see the problem. Justice Holmes once noted that "words" are merely the "skin of an idea." Words, sentences and whole documents need to be interpreted; ambiguity and uncertainty are everywhere. Here you start your life long education as an interpreter of words in a contract.

Even after the words are well and clearly understood, there is more contract "content" to consider. This content comes from at least three sources: 1) "gap-fillers," terms supplied by law to fill gaps that have been left in the contract (If the chickens arrive rotten in Rotterdam, who loses? see § 2–509; if they have feasted on genetically altered American feed, do the picky Dutch have a claim? see § 2–314); 2) oral or written terms that were part of the negotiation but never made it into the final document ("Your salesman assured me that this coat was waterproof and I spent 10 miserable, wet days fishing in it"); 3) oral or written terms that come after the contract was signed ("Your technical representative and I agreed to substitute number 10 steel for number 12 steel").

Even though this chapter may be a hotchpot of tasks that do not fit smoothly together, you must bear down here. Learning to interpret contracts is the opposite of knowing the doctrine of consideration; the former skill will be called on daily, even unconsciously, the latter, only rarely.

A. THE PAROL EVIDENCE RULE

The parol evidence rule deals with yet another aspect of writings and other records in relation to the act of making a contract. A written contract is often intended to create a sense of finality, not just as to the existence of a contract, but more particularly as to its contents: this document *is* the contract between us, so to speak, the written standard against which we each will measure our subsequent performances. Common law has a traditional body of techniques for dealing with this exclusive aspect of contractual records; these techniques go under the heading of the (somewhat ineptly named) parol evidence rule.

The parol evidence rule is not actually a procedural rule of evidence; that is, in no important way is it based on the belief that a writing is necessarily the best evidence of the contents of a contract. Rather, it is a rule of substantive contract law, which, under certain conditions, permits the parties to begin their performances with confidence that the written wording of their agreement is controlling and cannot be called into question by subsequent conflicting evidence. More specifically, when the rule is employed, it prevents the introduction at trial of *any* evidence (not just, as the word "parol" implies, the testimony of witnesses) that would contradict or, in many cases, would merely add to the terms of the contract in the writing. The great advantage of this rule is that it strips away all the back-and-forth of the negotiation process, allowing the parties to concentrate their attention henceforth on the written contract alone. This is also the rule's greatest danger, since the parties must take care, in completing the document, that their reciprocal undertakings are fully and accurately expressed.

When is the parol evidence rule employed? The answer is a bit complex. The helpful concept here is "integration": courts look to determine whether the parties intended their record to be the final statement of their contract, either in its entirety (complete integration) or to some extent (partial integration). But how, in turn, is this determination to be made? At one time courts commonly decided by inspecting the "four corners" of the document itself: does it appear to be integrated? If so, then the parol evidence rule applies. But the process has widened considerably in recent years, as the cases below should suggest.

Three final points need to be made. First, as with the Statute of Frauds (to which the parol evidence rule is otherwise unrelated), trial courts often give this rule more play than appellate decisions suggest, since the parol evidence rule offers the illusory refuge of mechanical simplicity: once the rule is applicable, the tiresome business of hearing evidence is considerably alleviated. Second, the parol evidence rule has, if anything, become even more significant in recent decades, in tandem with the ascent of standard form contracts. Such contracts very frequently contain "integration" or "merger clauses" stating that the written terms are the entire and final agreement between the parties; but because such standardized terms are often effectively dictated by one party, courts have at times been challenged to call these clauses into question.

Third, the parol evidence rule is in some respects yet another manifestation of the contract/no contract dichotomy, since the rule proceeds on the model of a "no contract" negotiation phase that culminates in a single conclusive writing, the contract itself, the "final expression of their agreement." As we shall see in the following section, this model has been gradually relaxed in recent decades, particularly under the influence of the UCC.

BAKER v. BAILEY

Supreme Court of Montana, 1989.
240 Mont. 139, 782 P.2d 1286.

McDONOUGH, J. Grant and Norma Baker (Bakers) appeal from a judgment of the District Court of the Fourth Judicial District, Missoula County. The District Court, sitting without a jury, found the Bakers liable for breach of the covenant of good faith and fair dealing and further found their claims for damages arising out of breach of contract should not be fully granted. We reverse in part and affirm in part....

In June of 1976, Arthur and Elma Bailey moved a mobile home onto property owned by their daughter and son-in-law. With their permission, the Baileys hooked onto the water line which serviced their daughter's home and installed a pipeline which would provide water for their trailer.

Approximately six years later, in the spring of 1982, the Bailey's daughter and son-in-law made the decision to sell their residence and the surrounding property. Because they were concerned about taking care of their parents, however, they transferred one acre of the property to the Baileys. This one acre surrounded the mobile home. The remaining property, consisting of forty-five acres, was sold to the Bakers.

In order to insure that the Bailey's continued to have access to water, a Water Well Use Agreement was prepared. Mrs. Baker was concerned about future ownership of the one-acre plot. In particular, she was worried that "a bunch of hippies" would move in next to her and consequently she wanted some control over the type of person who may, in the future, buy the Bailey's land. In order to address this concern, the well agreement specifically provided that the right to use water would only extend to the Baileys. In the event the Baileys conveyed the property, the Bakers were under no obligation to provide the new owners with water.

Despite the plain language used in the agreement, the Baileys believed that although not specifically set forth, the Bakers would transfer the right to use the water well to a subsequent "reasonable purchaser" of the Bailey property. The language of the agreement, according to testimony of both the Baileys and the Bakers, was included for the purpose of addressing Mrs. Baker's concern over potentially undesirable neighbors. This purpose was not, however, articulated within the contract.

In addition to the water well use agreement, the Bakers, at the time of purchase, asked for and received a right of first refusal in the event the Baileys received an offer to purchase their property. If an offer was received, the Baileys were to notify the Bakers of the offer in writing. The Bakers would then have the opportunity to exercise their "right of first refusal" within fifteen days of the offer.

Following sale of the land, the Bakers and Baileys lived next to one another and in fact became friends. The Baileys, however, decided to move to Butte, Montana, in the spring of 1984. On June 30, 1984, they executed a standard form listing contract with a local realty company. Under the terms of the listing, the Baileys represented that the property would be sold with "shared well water." Based upon the realtor's valuation of the property with water, it was listed for $47,500.00.

Shortly after the decision was made to sell the property, the water system developed several problems. As a result of these problems pressure in the line was reduced and the Baileys were unable to obtain sufficient water to meet their needs. As a result, they found it necessary to bring water to their residence in plastic jugs.

The Bakers were not as significantly affected by the problems. The Bakers always had sufficient water. In fact, during the entire period the Baileys were deprived of water, the Bakers had enough water to irrigate their lawn. Despite the fact this use adversely affected the Baileys' water supply, the Bakers refused to reduce their consumption. This problem persisted until August when the water system was finally repaired.

After the problems with the water well surfaced, the Bakers informed the Baileys that they would not share the water supply with any new purchaser. Consequently, the property would have to be sold without access to water from the well.

The Baileys searched for alternative sources of water, but unfortunately none was available. They approached the Bakers and offered to purchase joint use of the well. This offer was refused.

Recognizing that they would not be able to provide water for the property, the Baileys realized that the property was virtually without value. They, therefore, agreed to sell it for $8,000.00, which was the fair market value of the trailer and other improvements on the land.

After the Baileys made the decision to accept the $8,000.00 offer, they gave the Bakers notice of its terms in compliance with the right of first refusal provisions in the contract. On August 20, 1984, the Bakers exercised their option and purchased the property for $8,000.00. The transaction was closed on September 10, 1984. At that time, the Bakers acquired the Baileys' one-acre parcel which, if supplied with water, allegedly could be marketed for $40,000.00–$47,500.00.

The Bakers then filed a lawsuit to recover for the value of a refrigerator and certain unpaid expenses which they felt were owed by the Baileys. The Baileys, on the other hand, counterclaimed and sought damages for breach of the Water Well Use Agreement. The District Court found the Bakers in breach of contract and in breach of the implied covenant of good faith and fair dealing. It also found the Baileys liable for less than one-half of the electrical expenses of the well. Following this judgment, the Bakers appealed the lower court's findings in regard to their liability for breach of contract and the Baileys' limited liability for expenses incurred on the water well.

I.

The facts of this case present a classic parol evidence problem. The parol evidence rule, briefly stated, requires that in the absence of fraud, duress, or mutual mistake, all extrinsic evidence must be excluded if the parties have reduced their agreement to an integrated writing. Under this rule, all prior and contemporaneous negotiations or understandings of the contract are merged, once that contract is reduced to writing. Williston on Contracts, Third Edition § 631.

As this case illustrates, application of the rule can work to create harsh results. However, the policies behind the rule compel its consistent, uniform application. Commercial stability requires that parties to a contract may rely upon its express terms without worrying that the law will allow the other party to change the terms of the agreement at a later date.

The Baileys maintain that all of the parties to the Water Well Use Agreement, shared a common understanding that the Bakers would continue to share the well water with subsequent purchasers provided that the purchasers were acceptable to the Bakers. This contention may be true; however, it is not found within the terms of the contract.

The Water Well Use Agreement is very explicit concerning the rights and obligations of the parties. Its terms provide: "it being specifically understood that this Agreement is solely for the benefit of [the Baileys] and shall terminate in the event [the Baileys] no longer occupy [the land]." It further provides that "it is the intent of the parties to fully set forth their understanding concerning the utilization of the domestic water supplies for the respective tracts ..." There are no terms within the contract which state that the Bakers will provide water to subsequent "reasonable" purchasers.

Therefore, the fact there may have been further oral understandings between the parties is not admissible. The language of the Water Well Use Agreement is clear. Where the language of a written contract is clear and unambiguous, there is nothing for the court to construe. Rather, the duty of the court is simply to apply the language as written to the facts of the case and decide the case accordingly. The lower court's reliance upon evidence of the parties' oral negotiations was therefore in error, and there was no breach of contract.

In order to prove that a party acted unreasonably in violation of the implied covenant of good faith and fair dealing, one must show as an element there was a breach of the express terms of the contract. *Nordlund v. School District* (1987), 227 Mont. 402, 44 St.Rep. 1183, 738 P.2d 1299, [6 Ed. Law 179]. We have concluded that the Bakers did not breach the terms of the Water Well Use Agreement and accordingly, there was no violation of the covenant of good faith and fair dealing even if all other elements of the violation were met.

[Eds.: After affirming other aspects of the District Court decision, the Court reversed and remanded the case.]

Notes and Discussion

1. **Harsh Results and Commercial Stability.** The Court says: "As this case illustrates, application of the rule can work to create harsh results." According to the opinion, "the Baileys believed" that the Bakers would transfer water rights to a "subsequent 'reasonable purchaser.' " According to the Bakers, why wasn't this side agreement included in the Water Well Use Agreement? Assuming that the side agreement had been made, why didn't the Bakers ultimately carry it out?

The Court justifies the parol evidence rule by arguing that: "Commercial stability requires that parties to a contract may rely upon its express terms without worrying that the law will allow the other party to change the terms of the agreement at a later date." In the present case, had the Bakers actually relied on the Agreement's written terms, or, more to the point, on the absence of the oral agreement from the written terms? Should their reliance have been required? It is not quite fair to say that the Baileys were seeking "to change the terms of the agreement at a later date," true?

The real issue here is what legal function the parol evidence rule plays, particularly in cases where the evidence for a side agreement seems strong. In the *MCC-Marble Ceramic Center* case, in the next section, it will emerge that this rule is not recognized by the CISG (for international sale of goods between merchants), and, indeed, most non-Common Law systems do not have such a restriction on admitting extrinsic evidence. Is our rule sufficiently justified by the danger that juries (prevalent in American civil cases but not in most other countries) might be misled?

2. **Integration.** The Court summarizes the parol evidence rule as follows: "[I]n the absence of fraud, duress, or mutual mistake, all extrinsic evidence must be excluded if the parties have reduced their agreement to an integrated writing." Does the Court make a specific finding that the Water Well Use Agreement was integrated, or does it just assume this?

Restatement 2d § 210 distinguishes between a completely integrated agreement (one "adopted by the parties as a *complete and exclusive* statement of the terms of the agreement"; § 210(1), emphasis added), and a less than completely integrated agreement. Comment c. states: "It is often clear from the face of a writing that it is incomplete and cannot be more than a partially integrated agreement. Incompleteness may also be shown by other writings ... Or it may be shown by any relevant evidence, oral or written, that an apparently complete writing never became fully effective, or that it was modified after initial adoption."

This distinction between complete and less than complete integration is of no importance, however, if the alleged side agreement is inconsistent with the terms of an integrated writing. "Whether a binding agreement is completely integrated or partially integrated, it supersedes inconsistent terms of prior agreements." Restatement 2d § 213, Cmt. b. The matter is otherwise if the side agreement would be an addition to the contract. "Where the parties have adopted a writing as a complete and exclusive statement of the terms of the agreement, even consistent additional terms are superseded." Id., Cmt. c. But when the contract is less than completely integrated in a writing, proof of additional terms can be shown.

However, the boundary lines here are hard to maintain. Should the side agreement in this case be regarded as inconsistent with the writing, or as an addition? How much weight should be given to the merger clause ("it is the intent of the parties to fully set forth their understanding concerning the utilization of the domestic water supplies for the respective tracts ... ") in determining whether the writing was completely integrated?

Problem 4–1

Charles and Fred Lath owned a farm that they sold, through a written contract, to Catherine Mitchill. Directly across the road from the farm, on land belonging to a third party, the Laths had an ugly ice house to which Mitchill objected. As part of the sale, the Laths orally agreed to remove the ice house, but this agreement was not included in the written sale document. If the Laths later decline to remove the ice house, can Mitchill bring suit? See *Mitchill v. Lath*, 247 N.Y. 377, 381–382, 160 N.E. 646, 647 (1928), holding that: "[A]n inspection of this contract shows a full and complete agreement, setting forth in detail the obligations of each party. On reading it one would conclude that the reciprocal obligations of the parties were fully detailed.... Were such an agreement made [as that concerning the ice house] it would seem most natural that the inquirer should find it in the contract."

This famous old case displays the parol evidence rule at its most restrictive; more modern decisions are sharply to the contrary. Even though the result in this case is unappealing, it is worth reconstructing what a Court must determine in order to hold that no parol evidence is admissible on the ice house side-agreement.

MASTERSON v. SINE

Supreme Court of California, 1968.
68 Cal.2d 222, 65 Cal.Rptr. 545, 436 P.2d 561.

TRAYNOR, C.J. Dallas Masterson and his wife Rebecca owned a ranch as tenants in common. On February 25, 1958, they conveyed it to

Medora and Lu Sine by a grant deed "Reserving unto the Grantors herein an option to purchase the above described property on or before February 25, 1968" for the "same consideration as being paid heretofore plus their depreciation value of any improvements Grantees may add to the property from and after two and a half years from this date." Medora is Dallas' sister and Lu's wife. Since the conveyance Dallas has been adjudged bankrupt. His trustee in bankruptcy and Rebecca brought this declaratory relief action to establish their right to enforce the option.

The case was tried without a jury. Over defendants' objection the trial court admitted extrinsic evidence that by "the same consideration as being paid heretofore" both the grantors and the grantees meant the sum of $50,000 and by "depreciation value of any improvements" they meant the depreciation value of improvements to be computed by deducting from the total amount of any capital expenditures made by defendants grantees the amount of depreciation allowable to them under United States income tax regulations as of the time of the exercise of the option.

The court also determined that the parol evidence rule precluded admission of extrinsic evidence offered by defendants to show that the parties wanted the property kept in the Masterson family and that the option was therefore personal to the grantors and could not be exercised by the trustee in bankruptcy.

The court entered judgment for plaintiffs, declaring their right to exercise the option . . .

Defendants appeal. They contend that the option provision is too uncertain to be enforced and that extrinsic evidence as to its meaning should not have been admitted. The trial court properly refused to frustrate the obviously declared intention of the grantors to reserve an option to repurchase by an overly meticulous insistence on completeness and clarity of written expression. . . . It properly admitted extrinsic evidence to explain the language of the deed . . . The trial court erred, however, in excluding the extrinsic evidence that the option was personal to the grantors and therefore nonassignable.

When the parties to a written contract have agreed to it as an "integration"—a complete and final embodiment of the terms of an agreement—parol evidence cannot be used to add to or vary its terms. . . . When only part of the agreement is integrated, the same rule applies to that part, but parol evidence may be used to prove elements of the agreement not reduced to writing. . . .

The crucial issue in determining whether there has been an integration is whether the parties intended their writing to serve as the exclusive embodiment of their agreement. The instrument itself may help to resolve that issue. It may state, for example, that "there are no previous understandings or agreements not contained in the writing," and thus express the parties' "intention to nullify antecedent understandings or agreements." (See 3 Corbin, Contracts (1960) § 578, p.

411.) Any such collateral agreement itself must be examined, however, to determine whether the parties intended the subjects of negotiation it deals with to be included in, excluded from, or otherwise affected by the writing. Circumstances at the time of the writing may also aid in the determination of such integration. (See 3 Corbin, Contracts (1960) §§ 582–584; . . .).

California cases have stated that whether there was an integration is to be determined solely from the face of the instrument . . . and that the question for the court is whether it "appears to be a complete . . . agreement. . . ." (See *Ferguson v. Koch* (1928) 204 Cal. 342, 346 [268 P. 342, 58 A.L.R. 1176] . . .) Neither of these strict formulations of the rule, however, has been consistently applied. The requirement that the writing must appear incomplete on its face has been repudiated in many cases where parol evidence was admitted "to prove the existence of a separate oral agreement as to any matter on which the document is silent and which is not inconsistent with its terms"—even though the instrument appeared to state a complete agreement. . . . Even under the rule that the writing alone is to be consulted, it was found necessary to examine the alleged collateral agreement before concluding that proof of it was precluded by the writing alone. (See 3 Corbin, Contracts (1960) § 582, pp. 444–446.) It is therefore evident that "The conception of a writing as wholly and intrinsically self-determinative of the parties' intent to make it a sole memorial of one or seven or twenty-seven subjects of negotiation is an impossible one." (9 Wigmore, Evidence (3d ed. 1940) § 2431, p. 103.) For example, a promissory note given by a debtor to his creditor may integrate all their present contractual rights and obligations, or it may be only a minor part of an underlying executory contract that would never be discovered by examining the face of the note.

In formulating the rule governing parol evidence, several policies must be accommodated. One policy is based on the assumption that written evidence is more accurate than human memory. . . . This policy, however, can be adequately served by excluding parol evidence of agreements that directly contradict the writing. Another policy is based on the fear that fraud or unintentional invention by witnesses interested in the outcome of the litigation will mislead the finder of facts. (. . . *Mitchill v. Lath* (1928) 247 N.Y. 377, 388, 160 N.E. 646, 68 A.L.R. 239 . . .) . . . McCormick has suggested that the party urging the spoken as against the written word is most often the economic underdog, threatened by severe hardship if the writing is enforced. In his view the parol evidence rule arose to allow the court to control the tendency of the jury to find through sympathy and without a dispassionate assessment of the probability of fraud or faulty memory that the parties made an oral agreement collateral to the written contract, or that preliminary tentative agreements were not abandoned when omitted from the writing. (See McCormick, Evidence (1954) § 210.) He recognizes, however, that if this theory were adopted in disregard of all other considerations, it would lead to the exclusion of testimony concerning oral agreements whenever there is a writing and thereby often defeat the true intent of the parties. (See McCormick, op. cit. supra, § 216, p. 441.)

Evidence of oral collateral agreements should be excluded only when the fact finder is likely to be misled. The rule must therefore be based on the credibility of the evidence. One such standard, adopted by section 240(1)(b) of the Restatement of Contracts, permits proof of a collateral agreement if it "is such an agreement as might *naturally* be made as a separate agreement by parties situated as were the parties to the written contract." (Italics added; . . .) The draftsmen of the Uniform Commercial Code would exclude the evidence in still fewer instances: "If the additional terms are such that, if agreed upon, they would *certainly* have been included in the document in the view of the court, then evidence of their alleged making must be kept from the trier of fact." (Com. 3, § 2-202, italics added.)

The option clause in the deed in the present case does not explicitly provide that it contains the complete agreement, and the deed is silent on the question of assignability. Moreover, the difficulty of accommodating the formalized structure of a deed to the insertion of collateral agreements makes it less likely that all the terms of such an agreement were included. . . . The statement of the reservation of the option might well have been placed in the recorded deed solely to preserve the grantors' rights against any possible future purchasers, and this function could well be served without any mention of the parties' agreement that the option was personal. There is nothing in the record to indicate that the parties to this family transaction, through experience in land transactions or otherwise, had any warning of the disadvantages of failing to put the whole agreement in the deed. This case is one, therefore, in which it can be said that a collateral agreement such as that alleged "might naturally be made as a separate agreement." A fortiori, the case is not one in which the parties "would certainly" have included the collateral agreement in the deed.

It is contended, however, that an option agreement is ordinarily presumed to be assignable if it contains no provisions forbidding its transfer or indicating that its performance involves elements personal to the parties. . . . The fact that there is a written memorandum, however, does not necessarily preclude parol evidence rebutting a term that the law would otherwise presume. In *American Industrial Sales Corp. v. Airscope, Inc.*, supra, 44 Cal.2d 393, 397–398, we held it proper to admit parol evidence of a contemporaneous collateral agreement as to the place of payment of a note, even though it contradicted the presumption that a note, silent as to the place of payment, is payable where the creditor resides. . . . Of course a statute may preclude parol evidence to rebut a statutory presumption. . . . Here, however, there is no such statute. In the absence of a controlling statute the parties may provide that a contract right or duty is nontransferable. . . . Moreover, even when there is no explicit agreement—written or oral—that contractual duties shall be personal, courts will effectuate a presumed intent to that effect if the circumstances indicate that performance by a substituted person would be different from that contracted for....

In the present case defendants offered evidence that the parties agreed that the option was not assignable in order to keep the property in the Masterson family. The trial court erred in excluding that evidence.

The judgment is reversed.

BURKE, J., DISSENTING. I dissent. The majority opinion:

(1) Undermines the parol evidence rule as we have known it in this state since at least 1872 by declaring that parol evidence should have been admitted by the trial court to show that a written option, absolute and unrestricted in form, was intended to be limited and nonassignable;

(2) Renders suspect instruments of conveyance absolute on their face;

(3) Materially lessens the reliance which may be placed upon written instruments affecting the title to real estate; and

(4) Opens the door, albeit unintentionally, to a new technique for the defrauding of creditors.

The opinion permits defendants to establish by parol testimony that their grant to their brother (and brother-in-law) of a written option, absolute in terms, was nevertheless agreed to be nonassignable by the grantee (now a bankrupt), and that therefore the right to exercise it did not pass, by operation of the bankruptcy laws, to the trustee for the benefit of the grantee's creditors. And how was this to be shown? By the proffered testimony of the bankrupt optionee himself! Thereby one of his assets (the option to purchase defendants' California ranch) would be withheld from the trustee in bankruptcy and from the bankrupt's creditors. Understandably the trial court, as required by the parol evidence rule, did not allow the bankrupt by parol to so contradict the unqualified language of the written option.

The court properly admitted parol evidence to explain the intended meaning of the "same consideration" and "depreciation value" phrases of the written option to purchase defendants' land, as the intended meaning of those phrases was not clear. However, there was nothing ambiguous about the granting language of the option and not the slightest suggestion in the document that the option was to be nonassignable. Thus, to permit such words of limitation to be added by parol is to contradict the absolute nature of the grant, and to directly violate the parol evidence rule....

Comment hardly seems necessary on the convenience to a bankrupt of such a device to defeat his creditors. He need only produce parol testimony that any options (or other property, for that matter) which he holds are subject to an oral "collateral agreement" with family members (or with friends) that the property is nontransferable "in order to keep the property in the family" or in the friendly group. In the present case the value of the ranch which the bankrupt and his wife held an option to purchase has doubtless increased substantially during the years since they acquired the option. The initiation of this litigation by the trustee in bankruptcy to establish his right to enforce the option indicates his belief that there is substantial value to be gained for the creditors from this asset of the bankrupt. Yet the majority opinion permits defeat of the trustee and of the creditors through the device of an asserted collateral oral agreement that the option was "personal" to the bankrupt and nonassignable "in order to keep the property in the family"! . . .

I would hold that the trial court ruled correctly on the proffered parol evidence, and would affirm the judgment.

Notes and Discussion

1. **The Issue.** Dallas Masterson's trustee in bankruptcy, who was protecting the financial interests of Dallas's creditors, wanted to know whether Dallas's estate included a half-option to purchase the ranch at a determined price. This being California in the 1960s, we can safely assume that the ranch's market value had escalated rapidly since Dallas and Rebecca Masterson conveyed it to Medora and Lu Sine, with the reservation of the option to re-purchase; therefore the option was probably an asset of considerable value. At issue is whether the court may hear evidence that the option was also subject to an agreement whereby the ranch had to remain in the Masterson family, so that it (or its value) could not be part of the assets divided among Dallas's creditors.

2. **Chief Justice Traynor's Opinion.** If the proffered evidence as to the side agreement was heard, would it tend to contradict the written contract, or would it add to its terms? Was the written contract completely integrated, or only partially integrated, or not integrated at all, and how is this to be determined?

The Court sharply distinguishes between the admissibility of evidence as to the meaning of the phrases "the same consideration as being paid heretofore" and "depreciation value of any improvements," on the one hand, and the disputed reservation clause, on the other. What is the basis of the distinction, and do you find it persuasive?

The majority does not adequately answer the dissent's argument that this decision "[m]aterially lessens the reliance which may be placed upon written instruments affecting the title to real estate; and . . . [o]pens the door, albeit unintentionally, to a new technique for the defrauding of creditors." The dissenting opinion should open your eyes to a very important aspect of the parol evidence rule for the sale of real estate. In particular, the majority does not fully consider the interests of third parties; but does the dissent exaggerate?

Try to reconcile this decision with *Baker v. Bailey*.

In the wake of *Masterson*, how much survives of the parol evidence rule in California?

3. The Restatement 2d Position. "Whether an agreement is completely or partially integrated is to be determined by the court as a question preliminary to determination of a question of interpretation or to application of the parol evidence rule." Restatement 2d § 210(3).

The *Masterson* decision is used as the basis for § 204, Illustration 1. Comment e. to that section states: "The fact that an essential term is omitted may indicate that the agreement is not integrated or that there is partial rather than complete integration.... But omission of a term does not show conclusively that integration was not complete and a completely integrated agreement, if binding, discharges prior agreements within its scope." So where are we?

4. Merger Clauses. One aspect of *Masterson* that still gives parties some ability to put their written agreement beyond the reach of judicial inspection is the merger clause similar to the one in *Baker v. Bailey*; the Masterson/Sine contract seems to have lacked one. But is even this tamper-proof? In *L.S. Heath & Son v. AT & T Information Systems*, 9 F.3d 561 (1993), a panel of the Seventh Circuit found a contract not completely integrated despite such a term. In this case, the written contract lacked many important terms. The Court argued: "We find initially that the parties did not necessarily intend the Master Agreement to reflect the complete agreement between the parties simply because they included the merger clause. To be sure, the presence of a merger clause is strong evidence that the parties intended the writing to be the complete and exclusive agreement between them, but such a clause is not dispositive.... In order to determine whether the parties intended a writing to be the complete and exclusive agreement between them, a court must compare the writing with the prior negotiations.... If the allegedly integrated writing does not, without reference to another document or other coordinating information, reveal what the basic transaction entailed, then the writing is not integrated." Id. at 569.

This suggests that a merger clause will normally establish a strong, but still rebuttable, presumption that a document is completely integrated. Compare Restatement 2d § 209, Cmt. b.: "[S]uch a declaration may not be conclusive" as to integration.

Another possible line of attack, but one that courts rarely use in the absence of evidence of duress or fraud, is to find a merger clause unconscionable. See, e.g., *Smith v. Central Soya of Athens, Inc.*, 604 F.Supp. 518 (E.D.N.C. 1985). But it may matter if the merger clause is part of a long standardized form. See Restatement 2d § 216, Cmt. e (emphasis added): "Such a [merger] clause ... *if agreed to* is likely to conclude the issue whether the agreement is completely integrated." What is meant by the italicized phrase?

Note: The UCC Parol Evidence Rule

"Consistent." The UCC's parol evidence rule is § 2–202, a brief but complex section. In the usual case, analysis under this section begins with "a writing intended by the parties as a final expression of their agreement";

normally a trial judge will determine whether such a writing exists. If it does, the writing "may not be contradicted by evidence of any prior agreement or of a contemporaneous oral agreement but may be explained or supplemented" by two sorts of parol information: first, "by course of performance, course of dealing, or usage of trade," which the UCC treats as always admissible, although interpretive preference is given to the express terms of the agreement (see § 1–205(4); this is § 1–303(e) in revised Article 1); second, "by evidence of consistent additional terms unless the court finds the writing to have been intended also as a complete and exclusive statement of the terms of the agreement." Parol evidence of this second sort is obviously admissible only after a separate judicial finding that the writing, although a "final expression," is not "a complete and exclusive statement"—an integration clause normally creating a presumption to the contrary.

When the writing is not "complete and exclusive," parol evidence is admissible only if it tends to establish "consistent additional terms." What is meant by "consistent"? In *Hunt Foods & Industries, Inc. v. Doliner*, 26 A.D.2d 41, 270 N.Y.S.2d 937 (1966), the Appellate Division of the New York Supreme Court dealt with a case in which Hunt had a signed option to purchase stock for just under $6,000,000 from George M. Doliner. The writing appeared to establish an absolute option, but Doliner sought to introduce parol evidence of the parties' agreement that Hunt would only exercise the option if Doliner tried to solicit higher outside offers. The court held not only that the alleged condition did not contradict the writing (so far, the case resembles *Masterson v. Sine*), but that it was also "consistent" with the writing. As the Court reasoned, "In a sense any oral provision which would prevent the ripening of the obligations of a writing is inconsistent with the writing. But that obviously is not the sense in which the word is used (*Hicks v. Bush*, 10 N.Y.2d 488, 491, 225 N.Y.S.2d 34, 180 N.E.2d 425). To be inconsistent the term must contradict or negate a term of the writing. A term or condition which has a lesser effect is provable."

The reasoning in *Hunt* has attracted substantial negative comment. See *Luria Bros. & Co. v. Pielet Bros. Scrap Iron & Metal*, 600 F.2d 103, 111 (7 Cir. 1979): "The narrow view of inconsistency espoused in [*Hunt* and cases following it] has been criticized. In *Snyder v. Herbert Greenbaum & Assoc., Inc.*, 38 Md.App. 144, 380 A.2d 618 (1977), the court held that parol evidence of a contractual right to unilateral rescission was inconsistent with a written agreement for the sale and installation of carpeting. The court defined 'inconsistency' as used in § 2–202(b) as 'the absence of reasonable harmony in terms of the language and respective obligations of the parties.' Id. at 623 ... (citing U.C.C. § 1–205(4)).... We adopt this latter view of inconsistency and reject the view expressed in *Hunt*. Where writings intended by the parties to be a final expression of their agreement call for an unconditional sale of goods, parol evidence that the seller's obligations are conditioned upon receiving the goods from a particular supplier is inconsistent and must be excluded." See also James J. White and Robert S. Summers, Uniform Commercial Code § 2–10 (5th ed. 2000).

Alternative Theories. However, the *Hunt* court could probably have arrived at the same outcome by a different route. For example, it did not clearly rule on whether the signed option was "intended by the parties as a final expression of their agreement with respect to such terms as are included therein." This would, of course, have required the Court to take evidence on the formation process.

There was also another alternative. Traditionally, even an integrated written document may be subject to an oral condition that forestalls its enforceability, and parol evidence is admissible to prove that condition. For example, in *Smith v. Rosenthal Toyota, Inc.*, 83 Md.App. 55, 573 A.2d 418 (Ct. Spec. App. 1990), an over-eager husband traded in his Chevette for a Toyota truck; he signed several documents, including financing arrangements, one of which contained an integration clause. But the deal was subject to an oral condition: his wife had to approve, and she most certainly did not. Quoting an earlier decision, the Maryland Court held that, notwithstanding the integration clause, "the parol evidence rule does not prevent the introduction of parol evidence indicating that the written instrument was not to become *effective as an instrument,* until a prior condition or event had occurred." (See also Restatement 2d § 217.) The *Hunt* court might have adopted this same line of argument.

"Certainly . . . Included." One final wrinkle comes from Comment 3 to § 2–202, which states that "If the additional terms are such that, if agreed upon, they would certainly have been included in the document in the view of the court, then evidence of their alleged making must be kept from the trier of fact." This test is not clear. J.J. White and R.S. Summers, Uniform Commercial Code § 2–10 (5th ed. 2000) (footnotes omitted), suggest: "The word 'certainly' is not self-defining, nor can judges rationally apply it in the dark. Sometimes a judge, knowing the claim of the party wishing to add a term, can resolve the issue without evidence (this fifty-page document negotiated by New York lawyers would have included that term if it had been agreed upon). In other cases, the judge may need evidence explaining the offered term, the relevant practice on comprehensiveness of writings, and the reasons for the exclusion of the term from the writing."

THOMPSON v. ESTATE OF COFFIELD

Supreme Court of Oklahoma, 1995.
894 P.2d 1065.

SUMMERS, J. This is a lawsuit between the Seller and Buyers of land over the right to royalty proceeds from unrecorded coal mining leases. The parties had earlier exchanged a deed. Certain language in the deed supported Buyers' position. The trial court refused to consider Seller's offer of parol evidence which was at variance with the language in the deed. The court then denied Seller's counterclaim to reform the deed, instead quieting title to the disputed mineral interest in favor of the Buyers. Seller appeals. We reverse and remand.

Here are the basic facts. The estate of H. H. Coffield owned the Leflore County property. The executors executed several coal leases in favor of Heatherly Mining, Inc. Although the leases were confirmed by the probate court, they were not recorded with the County Clerk. (The leases provided they would not be recorded, in order to keep confidential the terms of the leases.)

Months later the estate, referred to as Seller, through its executors, commenced negotiations to sell the Leflore County land, some 4000 acres, to Thompson, Roberts, and Roberts, referred to as Buyers. In December of 1989 an agreement was reached, and the property was sold subject to several mineral interest reservations. The deed reserved in Seller a non-participating royalty interest in one-half the minerals. The deed also stated that all mineral interests covered by a "valid, recorded lease" shall not vest in the Buyers until the expiration or termination of such lease. The deed further stated that as for top leases, validly recorded or confirmed by the probate court, the mineral interest covered shall not vest in the Buyers until the expiration or termination of the leases.

It was the argument of the Buyers, both at trial and on appeal, that because the coal leases in question were not recorded, one-half the mineral interests affected by those leases were transferred to the Buyers at the time of the sale rather than at the expiration of the leases. Buyer thus claims one-half the coal royalty due under the unrecorded leases, a sum in excess of $40,000 at trial time. Seller, on the other hand, claims it was understood that Seller would retain 100% of the royalty interest under all existing leases until the leases expired. Buyer urges that any knowledge of the unrecorded leases, as well as evidence of oral agreements between the parties regarding these leases, cannot be considered by the trial court, since parol evidence may not be introduced to show that the parties intended something other than the exact words set forth in the written contract.

Seller urges that reformation of the deed is required because the deed did not conform to the negotiations, intent and knowledge of the parties. It claims that during negotiations, and at the confirmation of the deed before the probate court, the parties discussed the coal leases which had not been recorded, but had been confirmed by the probate court. Seller urges that it was always the intent that the mineral interests covered by these leases remain vested in Seller until the expiration or termination of the leases. Seller also claims that Buyer was aware and had full knowledge that the leases had not been recorded, and was aware that Seller intended for the minerals covered by the leases to remain with Seller until the leases expired or terminated.

The trial court overruled Buyer's motion for summary judgment, but sustained Buyer's motion *in limine* denying admissibility to any evidence regarding the negotiations and knowledge of the parties. The excluded evidence included District Court proceedings on confirmation of the sale on February 20, 1990. The transcript of this proceeding contains several statements consistent with Seller's version of the deal, including this statement by Seller's attorney, explaining to the judge the terms of the sale the judge was being asked to confirm: "Now, for all of the existing leases, including some leases I'm going to describe in a minute, if there is production under the existing leases, then the estate and its beneficiaries would retain the right to receive 100 percent of all the monies paid on account of oil, gas, or coal production, on account of any lease in current force and effect...." Buyer Thompson was personally present at that hearing, representing himself and Buyer Vernon Roberts.

Because this evidence was outside the four corners of the deed the trial court ruled it inadmissible. The case was then presented to the trial judge under written stipulations and offers of proof. The court held in favor of the Buyers. Seller appealed and the Court of Appeals affirmed. We have granted certiorari.

Seller urges that the trial court erred in failing to find that (1) the deed was ambiguous, and (2) that parol evidence is admissible in an action for reformation of a deed. Buyers defend by stating that (1) there is no ambiguity in the deed and (2) that the Sellers could not meet their burden of "clear and convincing evidence" to show that reformation is warranted, so parol evidence is inadmissible. The Court of Appeals affirmed, agreeing that the deed was not ambiguous, but did not address the Seller's counterclaim for reformation. We do so now.

Seller, in its counterclaim, asserts that the deed should be reformed to reflect the true intent of both parties. Title 15 O.S.1991 § 156 provides that a written agreement may be reformed when through "fraud, mistake, or accident" the agreement does not express the real intentions of the parties.... Even if the contract is free from ambiguity, reformation may be proper if it is shown there existed fraud or mutual mistake....

"Reformation of a written instrument will be decreed when the words that it contains do not correctly express the meaning that the parties agreed upon, as the court finds to be convincingly proved." Corbin on Contracts, § 614 (1960). Reformation is a remedy to make a written contract conform to the antecedent expressions on which the parties based their agreement, and insofar as the written document differs from these antecedent agreements, it will be reformed. Id. To obtain reformation, Seller must show an (1) instrument representing an antecedent agreement which should be reformed, (2) mutual mistake or mistake by one party and inequitable conduct on the part of the other, which results in an instrument that does not reflect what either party intended,[1] and (3) proof of these elements by clear and convincing evidence.... In the absence of mutual mistake or unilateral mistake plus inequitable conduct, the equitable remedy of reformation will not stand....

In an action for reformation of a contract, "parol evidence is admissible to show the parties' intent and a mutual mistake." ... The parol evidence rule is not applicable in suits for rescission or reformation of contracts. Williston on Contracts, § 631 (3d Ed. 1961). The extrinsic evidence is not admitted to contradict the written instrument, but to show that the final writing did not reflect the true agreement of the parties. Id.... The evidence needed to sustain an action for reformation must be clear and unequivocal, but need not be uncontradicted....

1. One party's mistake is not sufficient to warrant reformation....

Supreme Ct Finding

In the present case, the trial court excluded all extrinsic evidence relating to the prior discussions or agreements and court proceedings between the parties, even though the Seller sought reformation. Seller points out that in one court proceeding Seller's interpretation of the deed was explained to the probate court in the presence of Buyers, and Buyers apparently acquiesced in Seller's interpretation. Buyers urge that this is irrelevant.

Without making a determination as to whether the evidence Seller might present is sufficient to meet the high burden of proof required to obtain reformation, we hold that the trial court erred in failing to consider such evidence. Regardless of whether the evidence is conflicting, it should, according to Oklahoma law, be considered when the equitable remedy of reformation is sought.... Buyers urge that the Seller's evidence does not meet the high burden of proof required for reformation. This argument is one to be presented to the trial court after Seller has had the opportunity to present its case.

The Court of Appeals' opinion is vacated. This cause is reversed and remanded to the trial court for further proceedings consistent with the views expressed herein.

Reversed & Remanded

Notes and Discussion

1. **The Process of Reformation.** Restatement 2d § 155 makes reformation available as an equitable remedy "[w]here a writing that evidences or embodies an agreement in whole or in part fails to express the agreement because of a mistake *of both parties* as to the contents or effect of the writing." (Emphasis added.) Here the writing fails to capture the actual agreement, but usually it is one party, rather than both, that seeks reformation; note that the court's intervention is directed toward the document, not toward the underlying contractual agreement, which, at least in theory, is actually given better expression through the reformed writing. "Since the remedy of reformation is equitable in nature, a court has the discretion to withhold it, even if it would otherwise be appropriate, on grounds that have traditionally justified courts of equity in withholding relief." Id., Cmt. d. One ground could be that a third party has in good faith relied to its detriment on the erroneous writing.

The other possibility, acknowledged by the Court, is that only one party has subscribed to the erroneous document; here reformation is possible if it can be shown that the other party induced assent by misrepresenting the writing. Restatement 2d § 166. Failure to read is usually not enough in itself, however, to bar reformation unless it is more than merely negligent and "amounts to a failure to act in good faith and in accord with reasonable standards of fair dealing." Restatement 2d §§ 157, 172.

In either case, the party seeking reformation is held to a fairly high standard of proof: "clear and convincing evidence." Why is this?

2. **Parol Evidence and Reformation.** As the Court notes, parol evidence can be used to prove a case for reformation. Does this make possible an end-run around the parol evidence rule? Suppose that neither

party is mistaken about the contents of the writing, but the parties wish to keep an oral term secret and so do not include it in the writing; will one party succeed if it later seeks reformation and the other party stands on the writing? See, for instance, *Grombach v. Oerlikon Tool & Arms Corp.*, 276 F.2d 155 (4th Cir. 1960) (no).

B. INTERPRETING THE TERMS OF THE CONTRACT

A critical contract lawyer's skill is the interpretation of contracts; on some estimates, better than a quarter of all contracts cases turn on problems of interpretation. Common law has developed a variety of techniques for handling interpretation. Some are traditional and rather mechanical (these techniques usually have Latin names); others, more flexible and discretionary. Flexibility may seem a good thing in itself, but remember that a clever lawyer, if permitted to introduce extrinsic evidence to aid in "interpreting," may soon discover a convenient backdoor means to circumvent the parol evidence rule.

It is commonly said that the primary goal of interpretation is to get at what the parties themselves meant by their promises, but this turns out to be a bit misleading. In the first place, the objective theory of contract requires that courts be concerned less with what the parties subjectively intended their words to mean than with what each might reasonably have understood the other party to have meant. To be sure, the objective standpoint can be taken to extremes, as it was by Judge Learned Hand: "It makes not the least difference whether a promisor actually intends that meaning which the law will impose upon his words. The whole House of Bishops might satisfy us that he had intended something else, and it would make not a particle of difference in his obligation. That obligation the law attaches to his act of using certain words, provided, of course, the actor be under no disability. The scope of those words will, in the absence of some convention to the contrary, be settled, it is true, by what the law supposes men would generally mean when they used them; but the promisor's conformity to type is not a factor in his obligation. Hence it follows that no declaration of the promisor as to his meaning when he used the words is of the slightest relevancy, however formally competent it may be as an admission." *Eustis Mining Co. v. Beer, Sondheimer & Co.*, 239 F. 976, 984–985 (S.D.N.Y. 1917). Such an extreme position is untenable especially because, quite wisely, courts will rarely if ever bestow a meaning on a contract that neither party wants.

But further interpretive difficulties are endemic in a contracting process. First, there is the inherent haziness of language itself, its persistent ambiguity and vagueness; the net of words never quite succeeds, and never can succeed, in capturing its quarry. Unintentional ambiguities, myriad in the annals of contract law, have often led to later disputes. For example, the seller of a photo studio agrees not to compete with the buyer for business in any county "school"; is a local college included in the word "school"? See *Lawrence v. Cain*, 144 Ind.App. 210, 245 N.E.2d 663 (1969). Second, although through greater diligence contracting parties often might have succeeded in expressing themselves more exactly, there are clear transaction costs in nailing down every remote contingency, and so parties may often prefer, either through studied inattention or even deliberately, to leave such byroads unexplored, rather than confront the possibility of the deal's collapsing. Third, in fact the unexpected not all that infrequently does occur, sending adversely affected parties back to puzzle through their words in the hope of procuring refuge from the storm; the result is a strong incentive to ingenious construction and protracted disputes.

None of this is unanticipated, to be sure. But judges, confronted with litigation, must act to settle the problems before them. One of the central problems they then face is whether to force an interpretation onto the disputed words (often through resort to the "plain meaning" as it appears to the judges), or rather to accept the guidance of additional evidence provided by the parties themselves. The general modern trend, still resisted in some quarters, has been in the latter direction, and this more relaxed approach has been notably propelled by the UCC, which has also broadened the concept of a contract itself in other important ways.

RANDOM HOUSE, INC. v. ROSETTA BOOKS LLC

United States District Court, Southern District N.Y., 2001.
150 F. Supp. 2d 613, aff'd 283 F.3d 490 (2nd Cir. N.Y. 2002).

STEIN, J. In this copyright infringement action, Random House, Inc. seeks to enjoin Rosetta Books LLC and its Chief Executive Officer from selling in digital format eight specific works on the grounds that the authors of the works had previously granted Random House—not Rosetta Books—the right to "print, publish and sell the work[s] in book form." Rosetta Books, on the other hand, claims it is not infringing upon the rights those authors gave Random House because the licensing agreements between the publisher and the author do not include a grant of digital or electronic rights. Relying on the language of the contracts and basic principles of contract interpretation, this Court finds that the right to "print, publish and sell the work[s] in book form" in the contracts at issue does not include the right to publish the works in the format that has come to be known as the "ebook." Accordingly, Random House's motion for a preliminary injunction is denied.[2]

BACKGROUND

In the year 2000 and the beginning of 2001, Rosetta Books contracted with several authors to publish certain of their works—including *The Confessions of Nat Turner* and *Sophie's Choice* by William Styron; *Slaughterhouse-Five*, *Breakfast of Champions*, *The Sirens of Titan*, *Cat's Cradle*, and *Player Piano* by Kurt Vonnegut; and *Promised Land* by

2. [Eds.: References to the court records have regularly been omitted throughout.]

Robert B. Parker—in digital format over the internet. On February 26, 2001 Rosetta Books launched its ebook business, offering those titles and others for sale in digital format. The next day, Random House filed this complaint accusing Rosetta Books of committing copyright infringement and tortiously interfering with the contracts Random House had with Messrs. Parker, Styron and Vonnegut by selling its ebooks. It simultaneously moved for a preliminary injunction prohibiting Rosetta from infringing plaintiff's copyrights.

A. *Ebooks*

Ebooks are "digital book[s] that you can read on a computer screen or an electronic device." Ebooks are created by converting digitized text into a format readable by computer software. The text can be viewed on a desktop or laptop computer, personal digital assistant or handheld dedicated ebook reading device. Rosetta's ebooks can only be read after they are downloaded into a computer that contains either Microsoft Reader, Adobe Acrobat Reader, or Adobe Acrobat eBook Reader software.

Included in a Rosetta ebook is a book cover, title page, copyright page and "eforward" all created by Rosetta Books. Although the text of the ebook is exactly the same as the text of the original work, the ebook contains various features that take advantage of its digital format. For example, ebook users can search the work electronically to find specific words and phrases. They can electronically "highlight" and "bookmark" certain text, which can then be automatically indexed and accessed through hyperlinks. They can use hyperlinks in the table of contents to jump to specific chapters.

Users can also type electronic notes which are stored with the related text. These notes can be automatically indexed, sorted and filed. Users can also change the font size and style of the text to accommodate personal preferences; thus, an electronic screen of text may contain more words, fewer words, or the same number of words as a page of the original published book. In addition, users can have displayed the definition of any word in the text. In one version of the software, the word can also be pronounced aloud.

Rosetta's ebooks contain certain security features to prevent users from printing, emailing or otherwise distributing the text. Although it is technologically possible to foil these security features, anyone who does so would be violating the licensing agreement accompanying the software.

B. *Random House's licensing agreements*

While each agreement between the author and Random House differs in some respects, each uses the phrase "print, publish and sell the work in book form" to convey rights from the author to the publisher.

1. *Styron Agreements*

Forty years ago, in 1961, William Styron granted Random House the right to publish *The Confessions of Nat Turner*. Besides granting Random House an exclusive license to "print, publish and sell the work in book form," Styron also gave it the right to "license publication of the work by book clubs," "license publication of a reprint edition," "license after book publication the publication of the work, in whole or in part, in anthologies, school books," and other shortened forms, "license without charge publication of the work in Braille, or photographing, recording, and microfilming the work for the physically handicapped," and "publish or permit others to publish or broadcast by radio or television ... selections from the work, for publicity purposes...." Styron demonstrated that he was not granting Random House the rights to license publication in the British Commonwealth or in foreign languages by crossing out these clauses on the form contract supplied by Random House.

The publisher agreed in the contract to "publish the work at its own expense and in such style and manner and at such a price as it deems suitable." The contract also contains a non-compete clause that provides, in relevant part, that "the Author agrees that during the term of this agreement he will not, without the written permission of the Publisher, publish or permit to be published any material in book or pamphlet form, based on the material in the work, or which is reasonably likely to injure its sale." Styron's contract with Random House for the right to publish *Sophie's Choice*, executed in 1977, is virtually identical to his 1961 contract to publish *The Confessions of Nat Turner*....

[Eds.: The contracts with Kurt Vonnegut and Robert B. Parker were similar.]

DISCUSSION

A. *Preliminary Injunction Standard for Copyright Infringement*

Random House seeks a preliminary injunction against Rosetta Book's alleged infringing activity pursuant to 17 U.S.C. § 502(a) of the Copyright Act. In order to obtain a preliminary injunction, Random House must demonstrate "(1) irreparable harm and (2) either (a) a likelihood of success on the merits or (b) sufficiently serious questions about the merits to make them a fair ground for litigation and a balance of hardships tipping decidedly toward the party requesting relief." *Abkco Music, Inc. v. Stellar Records, Inc.*, 96 F.3d 60, 64 (2d Cir. 1996); ...

B. *Ownership of a Valid Copyright*

Two elements must be proven in order to establish a prima facie case of infringement: "(1) ownership of a valid copyright, and (2) copying of constituent elements of the work that are original." *Feist Publications, Inc. v. Rural Tel. Serv. Co.*, 499 U.S. 340, 361, 113 L. Ed. 2d 358, 111 S. Ct. 1282 (1991); see also *Abkco Music*, 96 F.3d at 64; ... In this case, only the first element—ownership of a valid copyright—is at issue, since all parties concede that the text of the ebook is identical to the text of the book published by Random House.

It is well settled that although the authors own the copyrights to their works, "the legal or beneficial owner of an exclusive right under a copyright is entitled ... to institute an action for any infringement of that particular right committed while he or she is the owner of it." 17 U.S.C. P 501 (b); ... The question for resolution, therefore, is whether Random House is the beneficial owner of the right to publish these works as ebooks.

1. Contract Interpretation of Licensing Agreements—Legal Standards

Random House claims to own the rights in question through its licensing agreements with the authors. Interpretation of an agreement purporting to grant a copyright license is a matter of state contract law. ...

In New York, a written contract is to be interpreted so as to give effect to the intention of the parties as expressed in the contract's language. See *Terwilliger v. Terwilliger*, 206 F.3d 240, 245 (2d. Cir. 2000) (citing *Breed v. Insurance Co. of N. Am.*, 46 N.Y.2d 351, 355, 385 N.E.2d 1280, 1283, 413 N.Y.S.2d 352, 355 (1978)). The court must consider the entire contract and reconcile all parts, if possible, to avoid an inconsistency. See *Terwilliger*, 206 F.3d at 245; ...

Determining whether a contract provision is ambiguous is a question of law to be decided by the court. ...Pursuant to New York law, "contract language is ambiguous if it is capable of more than one meaning when viewed objectively by a reasonably intelligent person who has examined the context of the entire integrated agreement and who is cognizant of the customs, practices, usages and terminology as generally understood in the particular trade or business." *Sayers v. Rochester Tel. Corp. Supplemental Management Pension Plan*, 7 F.3d 1091, 1095 (2d Cir. N.Y. 1993) (internal quotations and citation omitted); ... "No ambiguity exists when contract language has a 'definite and precise meaning, unattended by danger of misconception in the purport of the [contract] itself, and concerning which there is no reasonable basis for a difference of opinion.' " *Sayers*, 7 F.3d at 1095 (quoting *Breed*, 46 N.Y.2d at 355, 385 N.E.2d at 1283, 413 N.Y.S.2d at 355).

If the language of a contract is ambiguous, interpretation of the contract becomes a question of fact for the finder of fact and extrinsic evidence is admissible. ...

These principles are in accord with the approach the U.S. Court of Appeals for the Second Circuit uses in analyzing contractual language in disputes, such as this one, "about whether licensees may exploit licensed works through new marketing channels made possible by technologies developed after the licensing contract—often called 'new use' problems." *Boosey & Hawkes Music Publishers, Ltd. v. Walt Disney Co.*, 145 F.3d 481, 486 (2d Cir. 1998). The two leading cases in this Circuit on how to determine whether "new uses" come within prior grants of rights are *Boosey* and *Bartsch v. Metro-Goldwyn-Mayer, Inc.*, 391 F.2d 150 (2d Cir. 1968), decided three decades apart.

In *Bartsch*, the author of the play "Maytime" granted Harry Bartsch in 1930 "the motion picture rights [to 'Maytime'] throughout the world," including the right to "copyright, vend, license and exhibit such motion picture photoplays throughout the world; together with the further sole and exclusive rights by mechanical and/or electrical means to record, reproduce and transmit sound, including spoken words...." 391 F.2d at 150. He in turn assigned those rights to Warner Bros. Pictures, which transferred them to MGM. In 1958 MGM licensed its motion picture "Maytime" for viewing on television. Bartsch sued, claiming the right to transmit the play over television had not been given to MGM.

Judge Henry Friendly, for the Second Circuit, wrote in 1968 that "any effort to reconstruct what the parties actually intended nearly forty years ago is doomed to failure." Id. at 155. He added that the words of the grant by Bartsch "were well designed to give the assignee [i.e., MGM] the broadest rights with respect to its copyrighted property." Id. at 154. The words of the grant were broad enough to cover the new use—i.e. viewing on television—and Judge Friendly interpreted them to do so. This interpretation, he wrote, permitted the licensee to "properly pursue any uses which may reasonably be said to fall within the medium as described in the license." Id. at 155. That interpretation also avoided the risk "that a deadlock between the grantor and the grantee might prevent the work's being shown over the new medium at all." Id.

In *Boosey*, the plaintiff was the assignee of Igor Stravinsky's copyrights in the musical composition, "The Rite of Spring." In 1939, Stravinsky had licensed Disney's use of "The Rite of Spring" in the motion picture "Fantasia." Fifty-two years later, in 1991, Disney released "Fantasia" in video format and Boosey brought an action seeking, among other relief, a declaration that the grant of rights did not include the right to use the Stravinsky work in video format. In *Boosey*, just as in *Bartsch*, the language of the grant was broad, enabling the licensee "to record in any manner, medium or form, and to license the performance of, the musical composition [for use] in a motion picture." 145 F.3d at 484.

At the Second Circuit, a unanimous panel focused on "neutral principles of contract interpretation rather than solicitude for either party." Id. at 487. "What governs," Judge Pierre Leval wrote, "is the language of the contract. If the contract is more reasonably read to convey one meaning, the party benefitted by that reading should be able to rely on it; the party seeking exception or deviation from the meaning reasonably conveyed by the words of the contract should bear the burden of negotiating for language that would express the limitation or deviation. This principle favors neither licensors nor licensees. It follows simply from the words of the contract." Id.

The Second Circuit's neutral approach was specifically influenced by policy considerations on both sides. On the one hand, the approach seeks to encourage licensees—here, the publishers—to develop new technologies that will enable all to enjoy the creative work in a new way. On the other hand, it seeks to fulfill the purpose underlying federal copyright law—to encourage authors to create literary works. See *Boosey*, 145 F.3d at 487, 488 n.4.

2. *Application of Legal Standards*

Relying on "the language of the license contract and basic principles of interpretation," *Boosey*, 145 F.3d at 487 n.3, as instructed to do so by *Boosey* and *Bartsch*, this Court finds that the most reasonable interpretation of the grant in the contracts at issue to "print, publish and sell the work in book form" does not include the right to publish the work as an ebook. At the outset, the phrase itself distinguishes between the pure content—i.e. "the work"—and the format of display—"in book form." The Random House Webster's Unabridged Dictionary defines a "book" as "a written or printed work of fiction or nonfiction, usually on sheets of paper fastened or bound together within covers" and defines "form" as "external appearance of a clearly defined area, as distinguished from color or material; the shape of a thing or person." Random House Webster's Unabridged Dictionary (2001), . . .

Manifestly, paragraph #1 of each contract—entitled either "grant of rights" or "exclusive publication right"—conveys certain rights from the author to the publisher. In that paragraph, separate grant language is used to convey the rights to publish book club editions, reprint editions, abridged forms, and editions in Braille. This language would not be necessary if the phrase "in book form" encompassed all types of books. That paragraph specifies exactly which rights were being granted by the author to the publisher. Indeed, many of the rights set forth in the publisher's form contracts were in fact not granted to the publisher, but rather were reserved by the authors to themselves. For example, each of the authors specifically reserved certain rights for themselves by striking out phrases, sentences, and paragraphs of the publisher's form contract. This evidences an intent by these authors not to grant the publisher the broadest rights in their works.

Random House contends that the phrase "in book form" means to faithfully reproduce the author's text in its complete form as a reading experience and that, since ebooks concededly contain the complete text of the work, Rosetta cannot also possess those rights. While Random House's definition distinguishes "book form" from other formats that require separate contractual language—such as audio books and serialization rights—it does not distinguish other formats specifically mentioned in paragraph #1 of the contracts, such as book club editions and reprint editions. Because the Court must, if possible, give effect to all contractual language in order to "safeguard against adopting an interpretation that would render any individual provision superfluous," *Sayers*, 7 F.3d at 1095, Random House's definition cannot be adopted.

Random House points specifically to the clause requiring it to "publish the work at its own expense and in such a style and manner and at such a price as [Random House] deems suitable" as support for its position. However, plaintiff takes this clause out of context. It appears in paragraph #2, captioned "Style, Price and Date of Publication," not paragraph #1, which includes all the grants of rights. In context, the phrase simply means that Random House has control over the appearance of the formats granted to Random House in the first paragraph; i.e., control over the style of the book.

Random House also cites the non-compete clauses as evidence that the authors granted it broad, exclusive rights in their work. Random House reasons that because the authors could not permit any material that would injure the sale of the work to be published without Random House's consent, the authors must have granted the right to publish ebooks to Random House. This reasoning turns the analysis on its head. First, the grant of rights follows from the grant language alone. See *Boosey*, 145 F.3d at 488. Second, non-compete clauses must be limited in scope in order to be enforceable in New York. . . . Third, even if the authors did violate this provision of their Random House agreements by contracting with Rosetta Books—a point on which this Court does not opine—the remedy is a breach of contract action against the authors, not a copyright infringement action against Rosetta Books. . . .

The photocopy clause—giving Random House the right to "Xerox and other forms of copying, either now in use or hereafter developed"—similarly does not bolster Random House's position. Although the clause does appear in the grant language paragraph, taken in context, it clearly refers only to new developments in xerography and other forms of photocopying. Stretching it to include new forms of publishing, such as ebooks, would make the rest of the contract superfluous because there would be no reason for authors to reserve rights to forms of publishing "now in use." This interpretation also comports with the publishing industry's trade usage of the phrase. . . .

Not only does the language of the contract itself lead almost ineluctably to the conclusion that Random House does not own the right to publish the works as ebooks, but also a reasonable person "cognizant of the customs, practices, usages and terminology as generally understood in the particular trade or business," *Sayers*, 7 F.3d at 1095, would conclude that the grant language does not include ebooks.[3] "To print, publish and sell the work in book form" is understood in the publishing

3. Although *Boosey* recognizes that extrinsic evidence of industry custom is not likely to be helpful in analyzing the intent of the parties, it does not prohibit considering trade usage in understanding specific terms of the contract. See 145 F.3d at 488, 489 (acknowledging that evidence of industry custom will not likely illuminate the intent of the parties, but nonetheless taking into account industry custom in interpreting the meaning of a specific clause).

Even were this Court to find the contracts ambiguous, thus allowing consideration of extrinsic evidence other than trade usage to determine whether Random House has a likelihood of success on the merits, a review of that evidence leads to the conclusion that it is unhelpful to either party.

industry to be a "limited" grant. See *Field v. True Comics*, 89 F. Supp. 611, 613–14 (S.D.N.Y. 1950); . . .

In *Field v. True Comics*, the court held that "the sole and exclusive right to publish, print and market *in book form*"—especially when the author had specifically reserved rights for himself—was "much more limited" than "the sole and exclusive right to publish, print and market *the book*." 89 F. Supp. at 612 (emphasis added). In fact, the publishing industry generally interprets the phrase "in book form" as granting the publisher "the exclusive right to publish a hardcover trade book in English for distribution in North America." 1 Lindey on Entertainment, Publishing and the Arts Form 1.01–1 (2d ed. 2000) (using the Random House form contract to explain the meaning of each clause); . . .

3. Comparison to Prior "New Use" Caselaw

The finding that the five licensing agreements at issue do not convey the right to publish the works as ebooks accords with Second Circuit and New York case law. Indeed, the two leading cases limned above that found that a particular new use was included within the grant language—*Boosey*, 145 F.3d 481 (2d Cir. 1998), and *Bartsch*, 391 F.2d 150 (2d Cir. 1968)—can be distinguished from this case on four grounds.

First, the language conveying the rights in *Boosey* and *Bartsch* was far broader than here. . . . Second, the "new use" in those cases—i.e. display of a motion picture on television or videocassette—fell squarely within the same medium as the original grant. See *Boosey*, 145 F.3d at 486 (describing videocassettes and laser discs as "subsequently developed methods of distribution of a motion picture"); . . .

In this case, the "new use"—electronic digital signals sent over the internet—is a separate medium from the original use—printed words on paper. Random House's own expert concludes that the media are distinct because information stored digitally can be manipulated in ways that analog information cannot. Ebooks take advantage of the digital medium's ability to manipulate data by allowing ebook users to electronically search the text for specific words and phrases, change the font size and style, type notes into the text and electronically organize them, highlight and bookmark, hyperlink to specific parts of the text, and, in the future, to other sites on related topics as well, and access a dictionary that pronounces words in the ebook aloud. The need for a software program to interact with the data in order to make it usable, as well as the need for a piece of hardware to enable the reader to view the text, also distinguishes analog formats from digital formats. See *Greenberg v. National Geographic Soc'y*, 244 F.3d 1267, 1273 n.12 (11th Cir. 2001) (Digital format is not analogous to reproducing the magazine in microfilm or microfiche because it "requires the interaction of a computer program in order to accomplish the useful reproduction involved with the new medium.").

Therefore, *Boosey* and *Bartsch*, which apply to new uses within the same medium, do not control this case. See, e.g., . . . *Tele-Pac, Inc. v. Grainger*, 168 A.D.2d 11, 570 N.Y.S.2d 521 (1st Dep't 1991) (distinguishing Second Circuit "new use" doctrine by holding that right to "broadcast[] by television or any other similar device now known or hereafter to be made known" was so dissimilar from display on videocassette and videodisc "as to preclude consideration of video rights as even falling within the 'ambiguous penumbra' of the terms used in the agreement").

The third significant difference between the licensee in the motion picture cases cited above and the book publisher in this action is that the licensees in the motion picture cases have actually created a new work based on the material from the licensor. Therefore, the right to display that new work—whether on television or video—is derivative of the right to create that work. In the book publishing context, the publishers, although they participate in the editorial process, display the words written by the author, not themselves.

Fourth, the courts in *Boosey* and *Bartsch* were concerned that any approach to new use problems that "tilts against licensees [here, Random House] gives rise to antiprogressive incentives" insofar as licensees "would be reluctant to explore and utilize innovative technologies." *Boosey*, 145 F.3d at 488, n.4; see also *Bartsch*, 391 F.2d at 155. However, in this action, the policy rationale of encouraging development in new technology is at least as well served by finding that the licensors—i.e., the authors—retain these rights to their works. In the 21st century, it cannot be said that licensees such as book publishers and movie producers are ipso facto more likely to make advances in digital technology than start-up companies.

Other case law interpreting the scope of book publishing licensing agreements is similarly unhelpful to Random House. . . . [F]ederal courts applying New York law have interpreted publishing licensing agreements . . . narrowly. See *Werbungs Und Commerz Union Austalt v. Collectors' Guild, Ltd.*, 930 F.2d 1021, 1026 (2d Cir. 1991) (finding contract which conveys "right, title and interest in said two editions and all earnings therefrom" ambiguous as to whether it conveyed rights in the illustrations contained in those editions as well); *Field*, 89 F. Supp. at 613 (finding right to "publish, print and market in book form . . . the work" is limited right and does not include publication of cartoon strip in a magazine).

C. *Balance of Hardships*

Because Random House cannot establish a prima facie case of copyright infringement, it is not likely to succeed on the merits and is not entitled to a presumption of irreparable harm. Random House has made no showing of irreparable harm; therefore, it cannot meet the test for obtaining a preliminary injunction. Even if it could show such harm, and could be considered to have presented sufficiently serious questions about the merits to make them a fair ground for litigation, the balance of hardships does not tip decidedly in Random House's favor. Random House fears that Rosetta's ebooks will harm its goodwill with its customers and cause direct competition in Random House's own efforts to establish its ebook business. Rosetta worries that a preliminary injunction will effectively put its new company out of business because it will impede its ability to publish any works previously licensed to other publishers. While both parties present valid concerns, Random House has not demonstrated that its concerns decidedly outweigh Rosetta's.

III. CONCLUSION

Employing the most important tool in the armamentarium of contract interpretation—the language of the contract itself—this Court has concluded that Random House is not the beneficial owner of the right to publish the eight works at issue as ebooks. This is neither a victory for technophiles nor a defeat for Luddites. It is merely a determination, relying on neutral principles of contract interpretation, that because Random House is not likely to succeed on the merits of its copyright infringement claim and cannot demonstrate irreparable harm, its motion for a preliminary injunction should be denied.

Notes and Discussion

1. **Coast-to-Coast Interpretation.** This case and the two that follow deal, in varying ways, with the weight that is to be given to the parties' writing. Some judges (Henry Friendly is one) pay great attention to the writing and regard oral testimony—given after the fact and supporting one side's interpretation—with deep skepticism. Other judges (Roger Traynor is one) are suspicious of writings; these judges seem to regard the writing as a weapon that is constructed, and used by the stronger party to subjugate the weaker.

To a considerable extent, the cases presented here, two from New York and one from California, represent the divergent views of the judges in those two important states. We believe that a random draw among state and federal judges in New York is more likely to draw a judge who will worm his way into the language of the contract and turn a deaf ear to oral testimony than would be the case with the judge randomly drawn from the California state and federal courts. Is this a reflection of the culture wars?

2. **Salvation Through Writing?** Consider some of the ways that Judge Stein uses to elevate the writing. First, he quotes Judge Friendly's statement about the difficulty of finding "what the parties actually intended nearly forty years ago." Second, he notes that a party should be able to "rely" on the language of a contract and suggests that substantial deviation from the apparent meaning of the writing would undermine that reliance. Does he also imply that courts' respect for the writing may train parties and lawyers to be more careful drafters and negotiators, and so minimize disputes and judicial heartburn?

Pay very close attention to how Judge Stein establishes the "plain meaning" of the Random House agreement. To what extent does he draw on precedent and doctrine, to what extent on simple aids like household dictionaries? Is he justified in excluding testimony from the parties themselves as to their intent? What problems to you see with interpreting a contract "so as to give effect to the intention of the parties *as expressed in the contract's language*"? (Italics added.)

3. Unknown Unknowns. At the time of the drafting of the Random House contract, ebooks were certainly an "unknown." Were they, in the modern parlance, a "known unknown" or an "unknown unknown"? The former, of course, are things on the edge of our consciousness; we appreciate their importance, and we understand our ignorance. The latter are things so far from our consciousness that we do not even understand our ignorance. How would you deal with these unknowns if you were drafting a contract for Random House or an author today? The problem is more or less proportionate to the length of the contract: short-term contracts, small unknowns; long-term contracts, big unknowns.

Issues such as these come in many forms. In a long-term contract for the sale of natural gas or coal or any other commodity, a known unknown will be the market price at a remote time. In a contract for the license of a novel or for long-term purchase of ethanol or electricity, the known unknowns of price are, of course, present. But, in addition, there are unknowns that only some will perceive, having to do with exotic new forms of technology or leaps in our ability to produce, save, and transmit energy.

As you read this book, catalog the ways drafters have dealt with these issues. Sometimes parties use short-term contracts instead of long-term ones. Sometimes parties exploit formulas to measure price in long-term contracts. Sometimes parties resort to arbitration, or even to "agreements to agree." All of these are merely palliatives; none is a cure, and none is a substitute for a lawyer's carefully cultivated foresight.

W.W.W. ASSOCIATES, INC. v. GIANCONTIERI

Court of Appeals of New York, 1990.
77 N.Y.2d 157, 566 N.E.2d 639, 565 N.Y.S.2d 440.

KAYE, J. In this action for specific performance of a contract to sell real property, the issue is whether an unambiguous reciprocal cancellation provision should be read in light of extrinsic evidence, as a contingency clause for the sole benefit of plaintiff purchaser, subject to its unilateral waiver. Applying the principle that clear, complete writings should generally be enforced according to their terms, we reject plaintiff's reading of the contract and dismiss its complaint.

Defendants, owners of a two-acre parcel in Suffolk County, on October 16, 1986 contracted for the sale of the property to plaintiff, a real estate investor and developer. The purchase price was fixed at $750,000–$25,000 payable on contract execution, $225,000 to be paid in cash on closing (to take place "on or about December 1, 1986"), and the $500,000 balance secured by a purchase-money mortgage payable two years later.

The parties signed a printed form Contract of Sale, supplemented by several of their own paragraphs. Two provisions of the contract have particular relevance to the present dispute—a reciprocal cancellation provision (para 31) and a merger clause (para 19). Paragraph 31, one of the provisions the parties added to the contract form, reads: "The parties acknowledge that Sellers have been served with process instituting an action concerned with the real property which is the subject of this agreement. In the event the closing of title is delayed by reason of such litigation it is agreed that closing of title will in a like manner be adjourned until after the conclusion of such litigation provided, *in the event such litigation is not concluded, by or before 6–1–87 either party shall have the right to cancel this contract whereupon the down payment shall be returned and there shall be no further rights hereunder.*" (Emphasis supplied.) Paragraph 19 is the form merger provision, reading: "All prior understandings and agreements between seller and purchaser are merged in this contract [and it] completely expresses their full agreement. It has been entered into after full investigation, neither party relying upon any statements made by anyone else that are not set forth in this contract."

The Contract of Sale, in other paragraphs the parties added to the printed form, provided that the purchaser alone had the unconditional right to cancel the contract within 10 days of signing (para 32), and that the purchaser alone had the option to cancel if, at closing, the seller was unable to deliver building permits for 50 senior citizen housing units (para 29).

The contract in fact did not close on December 1, 1986, as originally contemplated. As June 1, 1987 neared, with the litigation still unresolved, plaintiff on May 13 wrote defendants that it was prepared to close and would appear for closing on May 28; plaintiff also instituted the present action for specific performance. On June 2, 1987, defendants canceled the contract and returned the down payment, which plaintiff refused. Defendants thereafter sought summary judgment dismissing the specific performance action, on the ground that the contract gave them the absolute right to cancel.

Plaintiff's claim to specific performance rests upon its recitation of how paragraph 31 originated. Those facts are set forth in the affidavit of plaintiff's vice-president, submitted in opposition to defendants' summary judgment motion.

As plaintiff explains, during contract negotiations it learned that, as a result of unrelated litigation against defendants, a *lis pendens* had been filed against the property.[4] Although assured by defendants that the suit was meritless, plaintiff anticipated difficulty obtaining a construction loan (including title insurance for the loan) needed to implement its plans to build senior citizen housing units. According to the affidavit, it was therefore agreed that paragraph 31 would be added for plaintiff's sole benefit, as contract vendee. As it developed, plaintiff's fears proved groundless—the *lis pendens* did not impede its ability to secure construction financing. However, around March 1987, plaintiff

4. [Eds.: A *lis pendens*, by giving notice of an imminent lawsuit, warns any interested party to be aware of the proceedings.]

claims it learned from the broker on the transaction that one of the defendants had told him they were doing nothing to defend the litigation, awaiting June 2, 1987 to cancel the contract and suggesting the broker might get a higher price.

Defendants made no response to these factual assertions. Rather, its summary judgment motion rested entirely on the language of the Contract of Sale, which it argued was, under the law, determinative of its right to cancel.

The trial court granted defendants' motion and dismissed the complaint, holding that the agreement unambiguously conferred the right to cancel on defendants as well as plaintiff. The Appellate Division, however, reversed and, after searching the record and adopting the facts alleged by plaintiff in its affidavit, granted summary judgment to plaintiff directing specific performance of the contract. We now reverse and dismiss the complaint.

Critical to the success of plaintiff's position is consideration of the extrinsic evidence that paragraph 31 was added to the contract solely for its benefit. The Appellate Division made clear that this evidence was at the heart of its decision: "review of the record reveals that under the circumstances of this case the language of clause 31 was intended to protect the plaintiff from having to purchase the property burdened by a notice of pendency filed as a result of the underlying action which could prevent the plaintiff from obtaining clear title and would impair its ability to obtain subsequent construction financing." (152 A.D.2d 333, 336.) In that a party for whose sole benefit a condition is included in a contract may waive the condition prior to expiration of the time period set forth in the contract and accept the subject property "as is," ... plaintiff's undisputed factual assertions—if material—would defeat defendants' summary judgment motion.

We conclude, however, that the extrinsic evidence tendered by plaintiff is not material. In its reliance on extrinsic evidence to bring itself within the "party benefitted" cases, plaintiff ignores a vital first step in the analysis: before looking to evidence of what was in the parties' minds, a court must give due weight to what was in their contract.

A familiar and eminently sensible proposition of law is that, when parties set down their agreement in a clear, complete document, their writing should as a rule be enforced according to its terms. Evidence outside the four corners of the document as to what was really intended but unstated or misstated is generally inadmissible to add to or vary the writing ... That rule imparts "stability to commercial transactions by safeguarding against fraudulent claims, perjury, death of witnesses * * * infirmity of memory * * * [and] the fear that the jury will improperly evaluate the extrinsic evidence." (Fisch, New York Evidence § 42, at 22 [2d ed].) Such considerations are all the more compelling in the context of real property transactions, where commercial certainty is a paramount concern.

Whether or not a writing is ambiguous is a question of law to be resolved by the courts ... In the present case, the contract, read as a whole to determine its purpose and intent ..., plainly manifests the intention that defendants, as well as plaintiff, should have the right to cancel after June 1, 1987 if the litigation had not concluded by that date; and it further plainly manifests the intention that all prior understandings be merged into the contract, which expresses the parties' full agreement (see, 3 Corbin, Contracts § 578, at 402–403). Moreover, the face of the contract reveals a "logical reason" ... for the explicit provision that the cancellation right contained in paragraph 31 should run to the seller as well as the purchaser. A seller taking back a purchase-money mortgage for two thirds of the purchase price might well wish to reserve its option to sell the property for cash on an "as is" basis if third-party litigation affecting the property remained unresolved past a certain date.

Thus, we conclude there is no ambiguity as to the cancellation clause in issue, read in the context of the entire agreement, and that it confers a reciprocal right on both parties to the contract.

The question next raised is whether extrinsic evidence should be considered in order to create an ambiguity in the agreement. That question must be answered in the negative. It is well settled that "extrinsic and parol evidence is not admissible to create an ambiguity in a written agreement which is complete and clear and unambiguous upon its face." (*Intercontinental Planning v. Daystrom, Inc.*, 24 N.Y.2d 372, 379 ...)

Plaintiff's rejoinder—that defendants indeed had the specified absolute right to cancel the contract, but it was subject to plaintiff's absolute prior right of waiver—suffers from a logical inconsistency that is evident in a mere statement of the argument. But there is an even greater problem. Here, sophisticated businessmen reduced their negotiations to a clear, complete writing. In the paragraphs immediately surrounding paragraph 31, they expressly bestowed certain options on the purchaser alone, but in paragraph 31 they chose otherwise, explicitly allowing both buyer and seller to cancel in the event the litigation was unresolved by June 1, 1987. By ignoring the plain language of the contract, plaintiff effectively rewrites the bargain that was struck. An analysis that begins with consideration of extrinsic evidence of what the parties meant, instead of looking first to what they said and reaching extrinsic evidence only when required to do so because of some identified ambiguity, unnecessarily denigrates the contract and unsettles the law ...

Accordingly, the Appellate Division order should be reversed, with costs, defendants' motion for summary judgment granted, and the complaint dismissed.

Notes and Discussion

1. **Partially Standardized Contracts.** The contract here is not unusual particularly in real estate transactions: Some of the terms are standardized, some are dickered. What if dickered terms are inconsistent with the standard ones? In general, where possible, courts interpret terms as consistent with each other: Restatement 2d § 202(5). Where this is not possible, "separately negotiated or added terms are given greater weight than standardized terms or other terms not separately negotiated." Restatement 2d § 203(d).

In this case, the reciprocal cancellation clause was a dickered term, while the merger clause was standard. They are not in conflict with one another. But how much weight should the merger clause receive in deciding whether to exclude parol evidence as to the reciprocal cancellation clause?

What other portions of the written contract does the Court use in interpreting the reciprocal cancellation clause, and how are they worked into its argument?

2. **Principles of Construction.** When interpreting documents, courts have developed a laundry list of standard principles. Typical is the list given by the Pennsylvania Supreme Court in *City of Philadelphia v. Philadelphia Transportation Co.*, 345 Pa. 244, 250–251, 26 A.2d 909, 912 (1942) (citations omitted): "In interpreting the foregoing provision, five principles of construction should be kept in mind. The first is that the entire contract should be read as a whole and every part interpreted with reference to the whole, so as to give effect to its true purpose The second is that 'the contract itself must be read in the light of the circumstances under which it was made' and that it is necessary to 'consider the situation of the parties at that time, the necessities for which they naturally provided, the advantages each probably sought to secure and the relation of the properties and rights in regard to which they negotiated.' The third is that where a public interest is affected, an interpretation is preferred which favors the public. The fourth is that specific provisions ordinarily will be regarded as qualifying the meaning of broad general words in relation to a particular subject. And the fifth is that, unless contrary to the plain meaning of the contract, an interpretation given by the parties themselves will be favored." (Citations omitted.)

Which of these principles figures in *W.W.W. Associates*? It is possible that they might conflict. For example, an interpretation favored by the public interest might be difficult to reconcile with the "true purpose" of the parties themselves (as private individuals).

Perhaps the most difficult principle is the fifth, "that, unless contrary to the plain meaning of the contract, an interpretation given by the parties themselves will be favored." Suppose that one party argues for what a judge is willing to accept as the "plain meaning" of a contract term, while the other favors a less apparent meaning but can present convincing evidence that both parties actually had originally adopted this meaning. What would justify excluding this evidence?

Other principles can easily be added to the list above; you will see some of them in the cases that follow. One of the most important is in Restatement 2d § 203(a): "[A]n interpretation which gives a reasonable, lawful, and effective meaning to all the terms is preferred to an interpretation which leaves a part unreasonable, unlawful, or of no effect." An example is *Goddard v. South Bay Union High School Dist.*, 79 Cal.App.3d 98, 144 Cal.Rptr. 701 (1978), in which a social studies teacher sought credit toward salary increases on the basis of courses he took at a law school. The school board's regulations stated: "All units accepted for placement on the salary schedule must be from a *duly accredited college or university. In California, an accredited institution would be one accredited by Western Association of Schools and Colleges*." The board denied the credit because the law school was accredited not by the Western Association but by the American Bar Association. What outcome?

3. **The Four Corners.** The central holding of *W.W.W. Associates* is manifest: "[W]hen parties set down their agreement in a clear, complete document, their writing should as a rule be enforced according to its terms. Evidence outside the four corners of the document as to what was really intended but unstated or misstated is generally inadmissible to add to or vary the writing." Quoting an earlier opinion, the Court argues that the rule "imparts 'stability to commercial transactions.' "

So the Court claims, "An analysis that begins with consideration of extrinsic evidence of what the parties meant, instead of looking first to what they said and reaching extrinsic evidence only when required to do so because of some identified ambiguity, unnecessarily denigrates the contract and unsettles the law." Consider this claim in light of the following case. One of us (the elder, wiser, but more forgetful) believes that fraud and mistake are common, and that oral testimony needs to be tightly reined in. The other (younger, smarter, but less wise) disagrees. It will be no surprise that White finds Justice Traynor's opinions anathema and Frier believes that the judge sings sweet reason.

4. **A Comma Worth $2 Million (Canadian).** In 2002, Rogers Cable Communications entered into an agreement with Aliant Telecom, whereby Rogers received the right to use Aliant's poles for a set (and favorable) annual fee per pole. The agreement was to run for five years, with possible renewal thereafter. However, the contract contained a termination clause phrased as follows: "[This agreement] shall be effective from the date it is made and shall continue in force for a period of five (5) years from the date it is made, and thereafter for successive five (5) year terms, unless and until terminated by one year prior notice in writing by either party."

In early 2005, Aliant notified Rogers that it intended to terminate the contract in accord with the language given above. Aliant based its argument on the clear and unambiguous meaning of the clause: since a comma closed the clause "and thereafter for successive five (5) year terms," the subsequent qualifier "unless and until terminated by one year prior notice in writing by either party" applied to all of the preceding section, including the initial five year period. Rogers protested that this interpretation was contrary both to the parties' intent and to common sense; if Aliant could terminate at any time upon one year's notice to Rogers, then the express agreement by the parties to a five-year term was effectively meaningless.

Assume that Rogers had to make substantial initial capital investments in order to string cable lines for its business, and that if Aliant can terminate now, the annual fee per pole will rise from $9.60 to as high as $28.05, with total additional costs to Rogers of approximately $2.13 million. Who wins? In 2006 the case was decided in Aliant's favor by the Canadian Radio–Television and Telecommunications Commission; see Telecom Decision CRTC 2006–45 (holding that "the comma placed before the phrase 'unless and until terminated by one year prior notice in writing by either party' means that the [following] phrase qualifies both the [preceding] phrases"). The Commission felt that this "interpretation does not bring about an unrealistic result or a result that would not be contemplated in a commercial environment." Do you agree?

According to a report in the Toronto Globe and Mail from August 21, 2007, Rogers eventually succeeded in getting this decision reversed by pointing to the French version of the contract, where the wording was unambiguously in its favor.

PACIFIC GAS & ELECTRIC CO. v. G.W. THOMAS DRAYAGE & RIGGING CO.

Supreme Court of California, 1968.
69 Cal.2d 33, 69 Cal.Rptr. 561, 442 P.2d 641.

TRAYNOR, C.J. Defendant appeals from a judgment for plaintiff in an action for damages for injury to property under an indemnity clause of a contract.

In 1960 defendant entered into a contract with plaintiff to furnish the labor and equipment necessary to remove and replace the upper metal cover of plaintiff's steam turbine. Defendant agreed to perform the work "at [its] own risk and expense" and to "indemnify" plaintiff "against all loss, damage, expense and liability resulting from . . . injury to property, arising out of or in any way connected with the performance of this contract." Defendant also agreed to procure not less than $50,000 insurance to cover liability for injury to property. Plaintiff was to be an additional named insured, but the policy was to contain a cross-liability clause extending the coverage to plaintiff's property.

During the work the cover fell and injured the exposed rotor of the turbine. Plaintiff brought this action to recover $25,144.51, the amount it subsequently spent on repairs. During the trial it dismissed a count based on negligence and thereafter secured judgment on the theory that the indemnity provision covered injury to all property regardless of ownership.

Defendant offered to prove by admissions of plaintiff's agents, by defendant's conduct under similar contracts entered into with plaintiff, and by other proof that in the indemnity clause the parties meant to cover injury to property of third parties only and not to plaintiff's property. Although the trial court observed that the language used was "the classic language for a third party indemnity provision" and that "one could very easily conclude that . . . its whole intendment is to indemnify third parties," it nevertheless held that the "plain language" of the agreement also required defendant to indemnify plaintiff for injuries to plaintiff's property. Having determined that the contract had a plain meaning, the court refused to admit any extrinsic evidence that would contradict its interpretation.

When the court interprets a contract on this basis, it determines the meaning of the instrument in accordance with the " . . . extrinsic evidence of the judge's own linguistic education and experience." (3 Corbin on Contracts (1960 ed.) [1964 Supp. § 579, p. 225, fn. 56].) The exclusion of testimony that might contradict the linguistic background of the judge reflects a judicial belief in the possibility of perfect verbal expression. (9 Wigmore on Evidence (3d ed. 1940) § 2461, p. 187.) This belief is a remnant of a primitive faith in the inherent potency[5] and inherent meaning of words.

The test of admissibility of extrinsic evidence to explain the meaning of a written instrument is not whether it appears to the court to be plain and unambiguous on its face, but whether the offered evidence is relevant to prove a meaning to which the language of the instrument is reasonably susceptible. . . .

A rule that would limit the determination of the meaning of a written instrument to its four-corners merely because it seems to the court to be clear and unambiguous, would either deny the relevance of the intention of the parties or presuppose a degree of verbal precision and stability our language has not attained.

Some courts have expressed the opinion that contractual obligations are created by the mere use of certain words, whether or not there was any intention to incur such obligations. Under this view, contractual obligations flow, not from the intention of the parties but from the fact that they used certain magic words. Evidence of the parties' intention therefore becomes irrelevant.

In this state, however, the intention of the parties as expressed in the contract is the source of contractual rights and duties.[6] A court must ascertain and give effect to this intention by determining what the parties meant by the words they used. Accordingly, the exclusion of relevant, extrinsic, evidence to explain the meaning of a written instrument could be justified only if it were feasible to determine the meaning the parties gave to the words from the instrument alone.

5. E.g., "The elaborate system of taboo and verbal prohibitions in primitive groups; the ancient Egyptian myth of Khern, the apotheosis of the words, and of Thoth, the Scribe of Truth, the Giver of Words and Script, the Master of Incantations; the avoidance of the name of God in Brahmanism, Judaism and Islam; totemistic and protective names in mediaeval Turkish and Finno–Ugrian languages; the misplaced verbal scruples of the 'Precieuses'; the Swedish peasant custom of curing sick cattle smitten by witchcraft, by making them swallow a page torn out of the psalter and put in dough. . . ." from Ullman, The Principles of Semantics (1963 ed.) 43. (See also Ogden and Richards, The Meaning of Meaning (rev. ed. 1956) pp. 24–47.)

6. "A contract must be so interpreted as to give effect to the mutual intention of the parties as it existed at the time of contracting, so far as the same is ascertainable and lawful." (Civ. Code, § 1636; . . .)

If words had absolute and constant referents, it might be possible to discover contractual intention in the words themselves and in the manner in which they were arranged. Words, however, do not have absolute and constant referents. "A word is a symbol of thought but has no arbitrary and fixed meaning like a symbol of algebra or chemistry, ..." (*Pearson v. State Social Welfare Board* (1960) 54 Cal.2d 184, 195 [5 Cal.Rptr. 553, 353 P.2d 33].) The meaning of particular words or groups of words varies with the "... verbal context and surrounding circumstances and purposes in view of the linguistic education and experience of their users and their hearers or readers (not excluding judges). ... A word has no meaning apart from these factors; much less does it have an objective meaning, one true meaning." (Corbin, The Interpretation of Words and the Parol Evidence Rule (1965) 50 Cornell L.Q. 161, 187.) Accordingly, the meaning of a writing "... can only be found by interpretation in the light of all the circumstances that reveal the sense in which the writer used the words. The exclusion of parol evidence regarding such circumstances merely because the words do not appear ambiguous to the reader can easily lead to the attribution to a written instrument of a meaning that was never intended. [Citations omitted.]" (*Universal Sales Corp. v. California Press Mfg. Co.*, supra, 20 Cal.2d 751, 776 (concurring opinion)); ...

Although extrinsic evidence is not admissible to add to, detract from, or vary the terms of a written contract, these terms must first be determined before it can be decided whether or not extrinsic evidence is being offered for a prohibited purpose. The fact that the terms of an instrument appear clear to a judge does not preclude the possibility that the parties chose the language of the instrument to express different terms. That possibility is not limited to contracts whose terms have acquired a particular meaning by trade usage,[7] but exists whenever the parties' understanding of the words used may have differed from the judge's understanding.

Accordingly, rational interpretation requires at least a preliminary consideration of all credible evidence offered to prove the intention of the parties. (Civ. Code, § 1647; Code Civ. Proc., § 1860; see also 9 Wigmore on Evidence, op. cit. supra, § 2470, fn. 11, p. 227.) Such evidence includes testimony as to the "circumstances surrounding the making of the agreement ... including the object, nature and subject matter of the writing ..." so that the court can "place itself in the same situation in which the parties found themselves at the time of contracting." (*Universal Sales Corp. v. California Press Mfg. Co.*, supra, 20 Cal.2d 751, 761; ...) If the court decides, after considering this evidence, that the language of a contract, in the light of all the circumstances, "is fairly susceptible of either one of the two interpretations contended for ..."

7. Extrinsic evidence of trade usage or custom has been admitted to show that the term "United Kingdom" in a motion picture distribution contract included Ireland (*Ermolieff v. R.K.O. Radio Pictures, Inc.* (1942) 19 Cal.2d 543, 549–552 [122 P.2d 3]); that the word "ton" in a lease meant a long ton or 2,240 pounds and not the statutory ton of 2,000 pounds (*Higgins v. California Petroleum etc. Co.* (1898) 120 Cal. 629, 630–632 [52 P. 1080]); ...

. . . extrinsic evidence relevant to prove either of such meanings is admissible.

In the present case the court erroneously refused to consider extrinsic evidence offered to show that the indemnity clause in the contract was not intended to cover injuries to plaintiff's property. Although that evidence was not necessary to show that the indemnity clause was reasonably susceptible of the meaning contended for by defendant, it was nevertheless relevant and admissible on that issue. Moreover, since that clause was reasonably susceptible of that meaning, the offered evidence was also admissible to prove that the clause had that meaning and did not cover injuries to plaintiff's property. Accordingly, the judgment must be reversed. . . .

Notes and Discussion

1. **Is Meaning Ever Plain?** Separate the actual decision in this case from Chief Justice Traynor's *dicta* about interpretation. The decision may not be as radical as it first appears. What is Traynor concerned about when he urges that courts not exclude parol evidence "merely because the words [of a contract] do not appear ambiguous"? Would he necessarily have come to a different outcome in *W.W.W. Associates*?

Try to locate Judges Stein, Kaye, and Traynor in relation to the two approaches to interpretation that are summarized in *Interform Co. v. Mitchell*, 575 F.2d 1270, 1275 (9th Cir. 1978) (some citations omitted), noting "a fundamental difference concerning the manner in which integration and interpretation should be approached. That difference relates to how a writing is to be viewed and the respective roles of the judge and jury.

"One view is to treat the writing as having a unique and quite compelling force. Under that approach a writing 'supersedes all previous undertakings' when the writing taken as a whole appears complete and the alleged additional terms ordinarily and naturally would have been included in the writing by reasonable parties situated as were the parties to the writing. See Calamari and Perillo, Contracts, 103–111 (1977) . . . Also a writing which so supersedes all previous undertakings, i.e., which is integrated, means what a reasonably intelligent person, 'acquainted with all the operative usages and knowing all the circumstances prior to and contemporaneous with the making of the integration, other than the oral statements made by the parties to each other as to what they intended it to mean,' would understand it to mean. Id. at 118. 4 Williston on Contracts §§ 607, 631 (1961) . . . The writing becomes the focus of attention and the judge by assuming the function of a reasonable person determines whether the writing did supersede all previous undertakings and, if so, its meaning to a reasonable person situated as described above. Williston §§ 616–17. An integrated writing clear in meaning to the reasonable person constitutes the contract between the parties. In this manner the judge can fix the legal relations of the parties without aid of a jury and provide a measure of security to written agreements.

"Another, and opposing view, imparts to the writing no unique or compelling force. A writing is integrated when the parties intend it to be and it means what they intended it to mean. Corbin on Contracts § 581 at 442, § 582 at 448–57, § 583 at 485 (1960) [hereinafter Corbin]. In theory, therefore, integration may be lacking even if the additional terms ordinarily and naturally would have been included in the writing and an integrated writing can have a meaning to which a reasonably intelligent person, situated as described above, could not subscribe. Corbin § 544 at 145–46. Again, in theory, this view accords the jury, when the trial employs one, a potentially larger role in the process of fixing contractual relations and provides somewhat less security to written agreements."

Which of these two approaches seems preferable? On the jury's role here, see *FDIC v. W.R. Grace & Co.*, 877 F.2d 614, 621 (7th Cir. 1989) (Posner, J.), observing, in defense of the "older view": "Parties to contracts may prefer, ex ante (that is, when negotiating the contract, and therefore before an interpretive dispute has arisen), to avoid the expense and uncertainty of having a jury resolve a dispute between them, even at the cost of some inflexibility in interpretation."

Can parties who accept Posner's argument insert a clause into their contract in order to prevent courts from considering extrinsic evidence when interpreting it? See *Garden State Plaza Corp. v. S.S. Kresge Co.*, 78 N.J.Super. 485, 189 A.2d 448 (App. Div. 1963) (no; void as against public policy).

2. **The Restatement View.** "It is sometimes said that extrinsic evidence cannot change the plain meaning of a writing, but meaning can almost never be plain except in a context.... Any determination of meaning or ambiguity should only be made in the light of the relevant evidence of the situation and relations of the parties, the subject matter of the transactions, preliminary negotiations and statements made therein, usages of trade, and the course of dealing between the parties.... But after the transaction has been shown in all its length and breadth, the words of an integrated agreement remain the most important evidence of intention." Restatement 2d § 212, Cmt. b. Has the Restatement adopted Traynor's view?

Illustration 4 to § 212 gives the following test case: "A and B are engaged in buying and selling shares of stock from each other, and agree orally to conceal the nature of their dealings by using the word 'sell' to mean 'buy' and using the word 'buy' to mean 'sell.' A sends a written offer to B to 'sell' certain shares, and B accepts. The parties are bound in accordance with the oral agreement." This reverses the result in Illustration 2 to § 231 of the First Restatement, where Williston's view had prevailed.

3. **Criticism of *Pacific Gas*.** Some of the negative reaction has been virulent. One of the foremost examples comes from Judge Alex Kozinski of the Ninth Circuit, who argues that: "*Pacific Gas* casts a long shadow of uncertainty over all transactions negotiated under the law of California. As this case illustrates, even when the transaction is very sizeable, even if it involves only sophisticated parties, even if it was negotiated with the aid of counsel, even if it results in contract language that is devoid of ambiguity, costly and protracted litigation cannot be avoided if one party has a strong enough motive for challenging the contract. While this rule creates much business for lawyers and an occasional windfall to some clients, it leads only to frustration and delay for most litigants and clogs already overburdened courts." *Trident Ctr. v. Connecticut General Life Ins. Co.*, 847 F.2d 564, 569

(9th Cir. 1988). (It should be observed that Judge Kozinski nonetheless has no choice but to apply California law when it is pertinent.)

Judge Kozinski's view has its adherents, but some scholars consider it overdrawn. See Harry G. Prince, *Contract Interpretation in California: Plain Meaning, Parol Evidence and Use of the "Just Result" Principle*, 31 Loy. L.A. L. Rev. 557 (1998). See also *Bank v. Truck Ins. Exch.*, 51 F.3d 736, 737 (7th Cir. 1995) (Posner, J.), noting "the exaggerated concern expressed by the Ninth Circuit in the *Trident* case with the [*Pacific Gas*] doctrine's corrosive effect.... [T]he California decisions since *Trident* have declined to endorse that decision's interpretation of California law."

4. **"Reasonably Susceptible."** In *Pacific Gas*, parol evidence can be introduced to clarify the meaning of contract terms when "the offered evidence is relevant to prove a meaning to which the language of the instrument is reasonably susceptible." How wide is "reasonably susceptible"?

In *Dore v. Arnold Worldwide, Inc.*, 39 Cal.4th 384, 46 Cal.Rptr.3d 668, 139 P.3d 56 (Cal. 2006), Brook Dore, who had been fired, sued his former employer. His original employment letter contained the following language: "Brook, please know that as with all of our company employees, your employment with Arnold Communications, Inc. is at will. This simply means that Arnold Communications has the right to terminate your employment at any time just as you have the right to terminate your employment with Arnold Communications, Inc. at any time." Dore sought to introduce extrinsic evidence proving that this language was ambiguous and that he could not be demoted or discharged except for good cause; but the California Supreme Court unanimously held that the letter's language was not reasonably susceptible to this meaning. In a concurring opinion, two Justices suggested that the time had come to reverse *Pacific Gas*: "Read in its broadest sense, *Pacific Gas* ... stretched the unremarkable principle that extrinsic evidence is admissible to resolve a contractual ambiguity into a rule that parol evidence is *always* admissible to *demonstrate* ambiguity *despite* facial clarity. The effect is that, despite their best efforts to produce a clear written agreement, parties can never confidently conduct their affairs on the basis of the language they have drafted." 39 Cal.4th at 395.

Is Roger Traynor rolling over in his grave?

Z.R.L. CORP. v. GREAT CENTRAL INSURANCE CO.

Appellate Court of Illinois, 1987.
156 Ill.App.3d 856, 510 N.E.2d 102, 109 Ill.Dec. 481.

SCARIANO, J. Z.R.L. Corporation d/b/a The Greenbay Shipping Company (hereinafter insured) filed a declaratory judgment action against Great Central Insurance Company (hereinafter insurer) to determine the rights and responsibilities of the parties under a liability insurance policy. The circuit court granted summary judgment to the insured holding that the insurer had an obligation to defend the insured in a lawsuit being prosecuted against it in Federal district court. We affirm.

The subject policy of insurance, entitled "Restaurant Package Policy," was issued by the insurer to cover the insured's restaurant business, which it operated as a private club, known as "Arthur's Club." The insured was designated "named insured," and the owners of the building in which the club was located were listed as "additional insureds." Under the personal injury liability provisions of the policy, coverage was provided as follows:

> "1. Personal Injury Liability: Great Central will pay on behalf of the Insured all sums which the Insured shall become legally obligated to pay as damages because of injury (herein called "personal injury") sustained by any person or organization and arising out of an occurrence involving one or more of the following offenses:
>
> "False arrest, malicious prosecution, detention, imprisonment, libel, slander, defamation of character, invasion of privacy, wrongful eviction or wrongful entry,
>
> "if such offense is committed in the conduct of the named Insured's business * * *."

The underlying lawsuit, filed in Federal court, involved claims for racial discrimination brought by William Terry (Terry), Tom Banks (Banks) and Allan May (May), who alleged that on December 7, 1984, May, a club member, brought his guests Banks and Terry, who were black, into Arthur's Club. The gravamen of the complaint was that Banks and Terry were forced to leave Arthur's Club on the pretext that they were not members of the club, while at the same time other guests of May, who also were not members but who were white, were allowed to remain in the club.

The insured asked the insurer to undertake the defense of the underlying action, but the insurer refused, contending that it was not obligated to defend the insured in this instance. The insured disagreed, arguing that the underlying action arose from an allegedly "wrongful eviction," and thus the insured brought this declaratory action asking the court to construe the insurance policy provision regarding "wrongful eviction."

At the outset, it should be noted that the "construction of an insurance policy presents only a question of law." (*Hartford Accident & Indemnity Co. v. Case Foundation Co.* (1973), 10 Ill. App. 3d 115, 121, 294 N.E.2d 7; . . .) Therefore, interpreting an insurance contract provision "is an appropriate issue for determination by means of summary judgment." (*State Farm Mutual Automobile Insurance Co. v. Schmitt* (1981), 94 Ill. App. 3d 1062, 1063, 419 N.E.2d 601; . . .).

The insurer cites *Puritan Insurance Co. v. 1330 Nineteenth Street Corp.* (D.D.C. March 19, 1984), 1984 CCH Insurance Fire & Casualty Cases 1149, Nos. 83–2228, 83–1754, in which the underlying lawsuit also was predicated on alleged racial discrimination by a restaurant. The policy required the insurer to defend the insured in a civil action arising from a variety of offenses, the third category of which included "wrongful entry or eviction, or other invasion of the right of private occupancy." The court held that the insurance policy used the phrase "wrongful eviction" in its legal sense as meaning to turn a tenant out of possession, and thus the insurer had no duty to defend the insured in the underlying action.

Puritan is distinguishable from the instant case for the reason that in *Puritan* "wrongful eviction" was included in a series of terms relating to invasions "of the right of private occupancy," while in the instant case the term was included in a group of torts which involve patrons. In such instances, words or phrases should be defined in the context of associated words or phrases in accordance with the maxim *noscitur a sociis*: "it is known from its associates." (Black's Law Dictionary 956 (5th ed. 1979).) The United States Supreme Court has roughly translated this Latin phrase as "a word is known by the company it keeps" (*Jarecki v. G.D. Searle & Co.* (1961), 367 U.S. 303, 307, 6 L. Ed. 2d 859, 862–63, 81 S. Ct. 1579, 1582), and Illinois also recognizes the doctrine ...

Although *noscitur a sociis* is a rule of statutory construction, the principle of analyzing words in context is also utilized by our courts when interpreting insurance contracts.... Accordingly, "wrongful eviction" includes making a patron leave a restaurant. Moreover, in response to a question propounded by the court in oral argument, the insurer conceded that the phrase "wrongful eviction" would include a situation in which the insured removed a rowdy patron from the premises. We cannot distinguish the scenario of the rowdy patron from one involving racial discrimination.

Finally, even assuming *arguendo* that the meaning of the phrase "wrongful eviction" in this insurance policy is ambiguous, the insured should be deemed covered.... In *Dora Township v. Indiana Insurance Co.* (1980), 78 Ill. 2d 376, 379, 400 N.E.2d 921, our supreme court held that "where language in an insurance policy is subject to different interpretations such ambiguity is to be construed in favor of the insured, and not the insurance company, which drafted the contract of insurance."

Accordingly, this court construes the phrase "wrongful eviction" in this particular insurance policy to include removing prospective clients from a business establishment on the basis of racial discrimination; therefore we affirm the circuit court.

Notes and Discussion

1. Interpreting Standard Form Contracts. Form contracts, almost invariably prepared by one party's lawyers, are intended to shape a transaction to the desires of that party, which not infrequently (but by no means always) results in their having a one-sided character. These contracts also tend to involve close and careful draftsmanship so as to insulate the wording of the contract, insofar as possible, from later judicial interpretation.

This case suggests the traditional judicial desire to interpret insurance contracts—which are archetypal contracts of adhesion—as broadly as possible, to the detriment of insurance companies. Compare the technique used here with that in *C & J Fertilizer, Inc. v. Allied Mutual Insurance Co.*, the "reasonable expectations" case from Chapter 3.E. There the Court simply read past the offending language. Would the Court in this case have been better advised to do the same? What grounds did Great Central Insurance have for not wanting to defend against the impending lawsuit?

2. ***Contra Proferentem.*** The Court, quoting an earlier opinion, notes that ambiguity in insurance contracts "is to be construed in favor of the insured, and not the insurance company, which drafted the contract of insurance." The rule here is a very old one, stretching back at least to Roman law, but it was perhaps dubious in an era when few contracts were prepared by skilled advisors with special knowledge. Today, by contrast, the rule has come fully into its own especially in relation to insurance and other standard form contracts. As the Ninth Circuit observes in *Kunin v. Benefit Trust Life Insurance Co.*, 910 F.2d 534, 539 (9th Cir. 1990), "This rule of *contra proferentem* has been called 'the most familiar expression in the reports of insurance cases.' " See Restatement 2d § 206.

In *Kunin*, the plaintiff's son suffered from autism and incurred medical bills for 1986 in excess of $50,000. Plaintiff's health insurance policy limited medical benefits for "mental illness or nervous disorders" to $10,000 per calendar year; and the defendant insurer determined that autism was a mental illness. What result would you anticipate?

3. **Limitations on Preferential Interpretation.** As the *Z.R.L.* Court notes, a different result had been reached in the *Puritan* case, but the cases are hard to distinguish, not so?

In any event, despite the general judicial tendency to interpret against insurers, the "plain meaning" of insurance contracts is often upheld. A good example is *National Insurance Underwriters v. Carter*, 17 Cal.3d 380, 551 P.2d 362, 131 Cal.Rptr. 42 (1976) (in Bank). The case concerned an airplane crash; the Thelens, who owned the plane, had purchased insurance from National. At the time of the crash, Pavitt, with the Thelen's permission, was the plane's pilot. The policy defined the word "insured" to include "... not only the Named Insured but also any person while using or riding in the aircraft ... provided the actual use is with the permission of the Named Insured." However, other sections of the contract provided that coverage was available only while Mr. or Mrs. Thelen (or a pilot employed by a "fixed base operator") was operating the plane. The Court found that this language was conspicuous and that the limitation was reasonable since: "In view of the relatively few persons qualified to fly a plane, and the obvious hazard to the occupants and to the aircraft from flights by unqualified pilots, it is understandable that an insurer would insist on knowing who the proposed pilots were, evaluating their qualifications, and making its policy inapplicable to accidents involving pilots not disclosed to, nor approved by, the insurer." Id. at 367.

NANAKULI PAVING & ROCK CO. v. SHELL OIL CO., INC.

United States Court of Appeals, Ninth Circuit, 1981.
664 F.2d 772.

HOFFMAN, J. Appellant Nanakuli Paving and Rock Company (Nanakuli) initially filed this breach of contract action against appellee Shell Oil Company (Shell) in Hawaiian State Court in February, 1976. Nanakuli, the second largest asphaltic paving contractor in Hawaii, had bought all its asphalt requirements from 1963 to 1974 from Shell under two long-term supply contracts; its suit charged Shell with breach of the later 1969 contract. The jury returned a verdict of $220,800 for Nanakuli on its first claim, which is that Shell breached the 1969 contract in January, 1974, by failing to price protect Nanakuli on 7200 tons of asphalt at the time Shell raised the price for asphalt from $44 to $76. Nanakuli's theory is that price-protection, as a usage of the asphaltic paving trade in Hawaii, was incorporated into the 1969 agreement between the parties, as demonstrated by the routine use of price protection by suppliers to that trade, and reinforced by the way in which Shell actually performed the 1969 contract up until 1974. Price protection, appellant claims, required that Shell hold the price on the tonnage Nanakuli had already committed because Nanakuli had incorporated that price into bids put out to or contracts awarded by general contractors and government agencies. The District Judge set aside the verdict and granted Shell's motion for judgment n. o. v., which decision we vacate. We reinstate the jury verdict because we find that, viewing the evidence as a whole, there was substantial evidence to support a finding by reasonable jurors that Shell breached its contract by failing to provide protection for Nanakuli in 1974. . . .

Nanakuli offers two theories for why Shell's failure to offer price protection in 1974 was a breach of the 1969 contract. First, it argues, all material suppliers to the asphaltic paving trade in Hawaii followed the trade usage of price protection and thus it should be assumed, under the U.C.C., that the parties intended to incorporate price protection into their 1969 agreement. This is so, Nanakuli continues, even though the written contract provided for price to be "Shell's Posted Price at time of delivery," F.O.B. Honolulu. Its proof of a usage that was incorporated into the contract is reinforced by evidence of the commercial context, which under the U.C.C. should form the background for viewing a particular contract. . . .

Nanakuli's second theory for price protection is that Shell was obliged to price protect Nanakuli, even if price protection was not incorporated into their contract, because price protection was the commercially reasonable standard for fair dealing in the asphaltic paving trade in Hawaii in 1974. Observance of those standards is part of the good-faith requirement that the Code imposes on merchants in performing a sales contract. Shell was obliged to price protect Nanakuli in order to act in good faith, Nanakuli argues, because such a practice was universal in that trade in that locality....

II. Trade Usage Before And After 1969

The key to price protection being so prevalent in 1969 that both parties would intend to incorporate it into their contract is found in one reality of the Oahu asphaltic paving market: the largest paving contracts were let by government agencies and none of the three levels of government—local, state, or federal—allowed escalation clauses for paving materials. If a paver bid at one price and another went into effect before the award was made, the paving company would lose a great deal of money, since it could not pass on increases to any government agency or to most general contractors. Extensive evidence was presented that, as a consequence, aggregate suppliers routinely price protected paving contractors in the 1960s and 1970s, as did the largest asphaltic supplier in Oahu, Chevron. Nanakuli presented documentary evidence of routine price protection by aggregate suppliers as well as two witnesses ... Both testified that price protection to their knowledge had always been practiced ... Such protection consisted of advance notices of increases, coupled with charging the old price for work committed at that price or for enough time to order the tonnage committed. The smallness of the Oahu market led to complete trust among suppliers and pavers....

III. Shell's Course Of Performance Of The 1969 Contract

The Code considers actual performance of a contract as the most relevant evidence of how the parties interpreted the terms of that contract. In 1970 and 1971, the only points at which Shell raised prices between 1969 and 1974, it price protected Nanakuli by holding its old price for four and three months, respectively, after announcing a price increase....

IV. Shell-Nanakuli Relations, 1973–74

Two important factors form the backdrop for the 1974 failure by Shell to price protect Nanakuli: the Arab oil embargo and a complete change of command and policy in Shell's asphalt management. The jury was read a page or so from the World Book about the events and effect of the partial oil embargo, which shortened supplies and increased the price of petroleum, of which asphalt is a byproduct. The federal government imposed direct price controls on petroleum, but not on asphalt. Despite the international importance of those events, the jury may have viewed the second factor as of more direct significance to this case. The structural changes at Shell offered a possible explanation for why Shell in 1974 acted out of step with, not only the trade usage and commercially reasonable practices of all suppliers to the asphaltic paving trade on Oahu, but also with its previous agreement with, or at least treatment of, Nanakuli.

Bohner [Eds.: the Hawaiian representative for Shell] testified to a big organizational change at Shell in 1973 when asphalt sales were moved from the construction sales to the commercial sales department. In addition, by 1973 the top echelon of Shell's asphalt sales had retired. Lewis and Blee, who had negotiated the 1969 contract with Nanakuli, were both gone. Their duties were taken over by three men: Fuller in San Mateo, California, District Manager for Shell Sales, Lawson, and Chippendale, who was Shell's regional asphalt manager in Houston. When the philosophy toward asphalt pricing changed, apparently no one was left who was knowledgeable about the peculiarities of the Hawaiian market or about Shell's long-time relations with Nanakuli or its 1969 agreement, beyond the printed contract. . . .

We conclude that the decision to deny Nanakuli price protection was made by new Houston management without a full understanding of Shell's 1969 agreement with Nanakuli or any knowledge of its past pricing practices toward Nanakuli. If Shell did commit itself in 1969 to price protect Nanakuli, the Shell officials who made the decisions affecting Nanakuli in 1974 knew nothing about that commitment. Nor did they make any effective effort to find out. They acted instead solely in reliance on the 1969 contract's express price term, devoid of the commercial context that the Code says is necessary to an understanding of the meaning of the written word. Whatever the legal enforceability of Nanakuli's right, Nanakuli officials seem to have acted in good faith reliance on its right, as they understood it, to price protection and rightfully felt betrayed by Shell's failure to act with any understanding of its past practices toward Nanakuli.

V. Scope Of Trade Usage

The validity of the jury verdict in this case depends on four legal questions. First, how broad was the trade to whose usages Shell was bound under its 1969 agreement with Nanakuli: did it extend to the Hawaiian asphaltic paving trade or was it limited merely to the purchase and sale of asphalt, which would only include evidence of practices by Shell and Chevron? Second, were the two instances of price protection of Nanakuli by Shell in 1970 and 1971 waivers of the 1969 contract as a matter of law or was the jury entitled to find that they constituted a course of performance of the contract? Third, could the jury have construed an express contract term of Shell's posted price at delivery as reasonably consistent with a trade usage and Shell's course of performance of the 1969 contract of price protection, which consisted of charging the old price at times of price increases, either for a period of time or for specific tonnage committed at a fixed price in non-escalating contracts? Fourth, could the jury have found that good faith obliged Shell to at least give advance notice of a $32 increase in 1974, that is, could they have found that the commercially reasonable standards of fair dealing in the trade in Hawaii in 1974 were to give some form of price protection?

We approach the first issue in this case mindful that an underlying purpose of the U.C.C. as enacted in Hawaii is to allow for liberal interpretation of commercial usages. The Code provides, "This chapter shall be liberally construed and applied to promote its underlying purposes and policies." Haw.Rev.Stat. § 490:1–102(1). Only three purposes are listed, one of which is "(t)o permit the continued expansion of commercial practices through custom, usage and agreement of the parties;. . . ." Id. § 490:1–102(2)(b). . . . We read that to mean that courts should not stand in the way of new commercial practices and usages by insisting on maintaining the narrow and inflexible old rules of interpretation. We seek the definition of trade usage not only in the express language of the Code but also in its underlying purposes, defining it liberally to fit the facts of the particular commercial context here.

The Code defines usage of trade as "any practice or method of dealing having such regularity of observance in a *place, vocation or trade* as to justify an expectation that it will be observed with respect to the transaction in question." Id. § 490:1–205(2) (emphasis supplied). This language indicates that Shell would be bound not only by usages of sellers of asphalt but by more general usages on Oahu, as long as those usages were so regular in their observance that Shell should have been aware of them. This reading of the Code, in our opinion, achieves an equitable result. A party is always held to conduct generally observed by members of his chosen trade because the other party is justified in so assuming unless he indicates otherwise. He is held to more general business practices to the extent of his actual knowledge of those practices or to the degree his ignorance of those practices is not excusable: they were so generally practiced he should have been aware of them.

No U.C.C. cases have been found on this point, but the court's reading of the Code language is similar to that of two of the best-known commentators on the U.C.C.: "Under pre-Code law, a trade usage was not operative against a party who *was not a member of the trade* unless he actually knew of it or *the other party could reasonably believe he knew of it.*" J. White & R. Summers, Uniform Commercial Code, § 12–6 at 371 (1972) (emphasis supplied) ... White and Summers add (emphasis supplied): "This view has been carried forward by 1–205(3), ... (U)sage of the trade is only binding on *members of the trade* involved or *persons* who know or *should know about it.* Persons who should be aware of the trade usage doubtless *include those who regularly deal with members of the relevant trade*, and also members of a second trade that commonly deals with members of a relevant trade (for example, farmers should know something of seed selling)." White & Summers, supra, § 12–6 at 371.

Using that analogy, even if Shell did not "regularly deal" with aggregate supplies, it did deal constantly and almost exclusively on Oahu with one asphalt paver. It therefore should have been aware of the usage of Nanakuli and other asphaltic pavers to bid at fixed prices and therefore receive price protection from their materials suppliers due to the refusal by government agencies to accept escalation clauses. Therefore, we do not find the lower court abused its discretion or misread the Code as applied to the peculiar facts of this case in ruling that the applicable trade was the asphaltic paving trade in Hawaii. An asphalt seller should be held to the usages of trade in general as well as those of asphalt sellers and common usages of those to whom they sell. Certainly, under the unusual facts of this case it was not unreasonable for the judge to extend trade usages to include practices of other material suppliers toward Shell's primary and perhaps only customer on Oahu. He did exclude, on Shell's motion *in limine*, evidence of cement suppliers. He only held Shell to routine practices in Hawaii by the suppliers of the two major ingredients of asphaltic paving, that is, asphalt and aggregate. . . .

Shell argued not only that the definition of trade was too broad, but also that the practice itself was not sufficiently regular to reach the level of a usage and that Nanakuli failed to show with enough precision how the usage was carried out in order for a jury to calculate damages. The extent of a usage is ultimately a jury question. The Code provides, "The existence and scope of such a usage are to be proved as facts." Haw.Rev. Stat. § 490:1–205(2). The practice must have "such regularity of observance ... as to justify an expectation that it will be observed. . . ." Id. The Comment explains: "The ancient English tests for 'custom' are abandoned in this connection. Therefore, it is not required that a usage of trade be 'ancient or immemorial,' 'universal' or the like ... (Full) recognition is thus available for new usages and for usages currently observed by the great majority of decent dealers, even though dissidents ready to cut corners do not agree." Id., Comment 5. The Comment's demand that "not universality but only the described 'regularity of observance' " is required reinforces the provision only giving "effect to usages of which the parties 'are or should be aware'. . . ." Id., Comment 7. A "regularly observed" practice of protection, of which Shell "should have been aware," was enough to constitute a usage that Nanakuli had reason to believe was incorporated into the agreement.

Nanakuli went beyond proof of a regular observance. It proved and offered to prove that price protection was probably a universal practice by suppliers to the asphaltic paving trade in 1969. It had been practiced by H.C. & D. since at least 1962, by P.C. & A. since well before 1960, and by Chevron routinely for years, with the last specific instance before the contract being March, 1969, as shown by documentary evidence. The only usage evidence missing was the behavior by Shell, the only other asphalt supplier in Hawaii, prior to 1969. That was because its only major customer was Nanakuli and the judge ruled prior course of dealings between Shell and Nanakuli inadmissible. Shell did not point in rebuttal to one instance of failure to price protect by any supplier to an asphalt paver in Hawaii before its own 1974 refusal to price protect Nanakuli. Thus, there clearly was enough proof for a jury to find that the practice of price protection in the asphaltic paving trade existed in Hawaii in 1969 and was regular enough in its observance to rise to the level of a usage that would be binding on Nanakuli and Shell.

Shell next argues that, even if such a usage existed, its outlines were not precise enough to determine whether Shell would have extended the old price for Nanakuli for several months or would have charged the old price on the volume of tonnage committed at that price. The jury awarded Nanakuli damages based on the specific tonnage committed before the price increase of 1974. Shell says the jury could not have ascertained with enough certainty how price protection was carried out to calculate such an award for Nanakuli. The argument is not persuasive.... The manner in which the usage of price protection was carried out was presented with sufficient precision to allow the jury to calculate damages at $220,800.

VI. Waiver Or Course Of Performance

Course of performance under the Code is the action of the parties in carrying out the contract at issue, whereas course of dealing consists of relations between the parties prior to signing that contract. Evidence of the latter was excluded by the District Judge; evidence of the former consisted of Shell's price protection of Nanakuli in 1970 and 1971. Shell protested that the jury could not have found that those two instances of price protection amounted to a course of performance of its 1969 contract, relying on two Code comments. First, one instance does not constitute a course of performance. "A single occasion of conduct does not fall within the language of this section...." Haw.Rev.Stat. § 490:2–208, Comment 4. Although the Comment rules out one instance, it does not further delineate how many acts are needed to form a course of performance. The prior occasions here were only two, but they constituted the only occasions before 1974 that would call for such conduct....

Shell's second defense is that the Comment expresses a preference for an interpretation of waiver.... [Eds.: The Court rejects this interpretation.]

VII. Express Terms As Reasonably Consistent With Usage In Course Of Performance

Perhaps one of the most fundamental departures of the Code from prior contract law is found in the parol evidence rule and the definition of an agreement between two parties. Under the U.C.C., an agreement goes beyond the written words on a piece of paper. " 'Agreement' means the bargain of the parties in fact as found in their language or by implication from other circumstances including course of dealing or usage of trade or course of performance as provided in this chapter (sections 490:1–205 and 490:2–208)." Id. § 490:1–201(3). Express terms, then, do not constitute the entire agreement, which must be sought also in evidence of usages, dealings, and performance of the contract itself. The purpose of evidence of usages, which are defined in the previous section, is to help to understand the entire agreement.... Course of dealings is more important than usages of the trade, being specific usages between the two parties to the contract. "(Course) of dealing controls usage of trade." Id. § 490:1–205(4)....

A commercial agreement, then, is broader than the written paper and its meaning is to be determined not just by the language used by them in the written contract but "by their action, read and interpreted in the light of commercial practices and other surrounding circumstances. The measure and background for interpretation are set by the commercial context, which may explain and supplement even the language of a formal or final writing." Id., Comment 1. Performance, usages, and prior dealings are important enough to be admitted always, even for a final and complete agreement; only if they cannot be reasonably reconciled with the express terms of the contract are they not binding on the parties. "The express terms of an agreement and an applicable course of dealing or usage of trade shall be construed wherever reasonable as consistent with each other; but when such construction is unreasonable express terms control both course of dealing and usage of trade and course of dealing controls usage of trade." Id. § 490:1–205(4). . . .

Our study of the Code provisions and Comments, then, form the first basis of our holding that a trade usage to price protect pavers at times of price increases for work committed on non-escalating contracts could reasonably be construed as consistent with an express term of seller's posted price at delivery. Since the agreement of the parties is broader than the express terms and includes usages, which may even add terms to the agreement, and since the commercial background provided by those usages is vital to an understanding of the agreement, we follow the Code's mandate to proceed on the assumption that the parties have included those usages unless they cannot reasonably be construed as consistent with the express terms.

Federal courts usually have been lenient in not ruling out consistent additional terms or trade usage for apparent inconsistency with express terms. The leading case on the subject is *Columbia Nitrogen Corp. v. Royster Co.*, 451 F.2d 3 (4th Cir. 1971). Columbia, the buyer, had in the past primarily produced and sold nitrogen to Royster. When Royster opened a new plant that produced more phosphate than it needed, the parties reversed roles and signed a sales contract for Royster to sell excess phosphate to Columbia. The contract terms set out the price that would be charged by Royster and the amount to be sold. It provided for the price to go up if certain events occurred but did not provide for price declines. When the price of nitrogen fell precipitously, Columbia refused to accept the full amount of nitrogen specified in the contract after Royster refused to renegotiate the contract price. The District Judge's exclusion of usage of the trade and course of dealing to explain the express quantity term in the contract was reversed. Columbia had offered to prove that the quantity set out in the contract was a mere projection to be adjusted according to market forces. Ambiguity was not necessary for the admission of evidence of usage and prior dealings. Even though the lengthy contract was the result of long and careful negotiations and apparently covered every contingency, the appellate court ruled that "the test of admissibility is not whether the contract appears on its face to be complete in every detail, but whether the proffered evidence of course of dealing and trade usage reasonably can be construed as consistent with the express terms of the agreement." Id. at 9. The express quantity term could be reasonably construed as consistent with a usage that such terms would be mere projections for several reasons: (1) the contract did not expressly state that usage and dealings evidence would be excluded; (2) the contract was silent on the adjustment of price or quantities in a declining market; (3) the minimum tonnage was expressed in the contract as Products Supplied, not Products Purchased; (4) the default clause of the contract did not state a penalty for failure to take delivery; and (5) apparently most important in the court's view, the parties had deviated from similar express terms in earlier contracts in times of declining market. Id. at 9–10. As here, the contract's merger clause said that there were no oral agreements. The court explained that its ruling "reflects the reality of the marketplace and avoids the overly legalistic interpretations which the Code seeks to abolish." Id. at 10. The Code assigns dealing and usage evidence "unique and important roles" and therefore "overly simplistic and overly legalistic interpretation of a contract should be shunned." Id. at 11....

Some guidelines can be offered as to how usage evidence can be allowed to modify a contract. First, the court must allow a check on usage evidence by demanding that it be sufficiently definite and widespread to prevent unilateral post-hoc revision of contract terms by one party. The Code's intent is to put usage evidence on an objective basis.... *Columbia Nitrogen*, supra, has been criticized as allowing the introduction of evidence of a usage that was not proved to be sufficiently well-established and that was not clearly applicable to the particular facts of the detailed contract between Royster and Columbia Nitrogen.... In *Columbia Nitrogen*, supra, the court should have examined the relationship of the usage to the facts of the case, for example, by determining whether any of the contracts that had been treated as only "fair estimates" in the past were the detailed result of long negotiations, as was the contract in Columbia Nitrogen....

Here the evidence was overwhelming that all suppliers to the asphaltic paving trade price protected customers under the same types of circumstances. Chevron's contract with H.B. was a similar long-term supply contract between a buyer and seller with very close relations, on a form supplied by the seller, covering sales of asphalt, and setting the price at seller's posted price, with no mention of price protection.... Levie, [*Trade Usage and Custom under the Common Law and the Uniform Commercial Law*, 40 N.Y.U. L. Rev. 1101 (1965)], at 1112, writes, "Astonishing as it will seem to most practicing attorneys, under the Code it will be possible in some cases to use custom to contradict the written agreement ... Therefore usage may be used to 'qualify' the agreement, which presumably means to 'cut down' express terms although not to negate them entirely." Here, the express price term was "Shell's Posted Price at time of delivery." A total negation of that term would be that the buyer was to set the price. It is a less than complete negation of the term that an unstated exception exists at times of price increases, at which times the old price is to be charged, for a certain period or for a specified tonnage, on work already committed at the lower price on non-escalating contracts. Such a usage forms a broad and important exception to the express term, but does not swallow it entirely. Therefore, we hold that, under these particular facts, a reasonable jury could have found that price protection was incorporated into the 1969 agreement between Nanakuli and Shell and that price protection was reasonably consistent with the express term of seller's posted price at delivery.

VIII. Good Faith In Setting Price

Nanakuli offers an alternative theory why Shell should have offered price protection at the time of the price increases of 1974. Even if price protection was not a term of the agreement, Shell could not have exercised good faith in carrying out its 1969 contract with Nanakuli when it raised its price by $32 effective January 1 in a letter written December 31st and only received on January 4, given the universal practice of advance notice of such an increase in the asphaltic paving trade. The Code provides, "A price to be fixed by the seller or by the buyer means a price for him to fix in good faith," Haw.Rev.Stat. § 490:2–305(2). For a merchant good faith means "the observance of reasonable commercial standards of fair dealing in the trade." Id. 490:2–103(1)(b). The comment to Section 2–305 explains, "(I)n the normal case a 'posted price' ... satisfies the good faith requirement." Id., Comment 3. However, the words "in the normal case" mean that, although a posted price will usually be satisfactory, it will not be so under all circumstances. In addition, the dispute here was not over the amount of the increase—that is, the price that the seller fixed—but over the manner in which that increase was put into effect. It is true that Shell, in order to observe the good faith standards of the trade in 1974, was not bound by the practices of aggregate companies, which did not labor under the same disabilities as did asphalt suppliers in 1974. However, Nanakuli presented evidence that Chevron, in raising its price to $76, gave at least six weeks' advance notice, in accord with the long-time usage of the asphaltic paving trade. Shell, on the other hand, gave absolutely no notice, from which the jury could have concluded that Shell's manner of carrying out the price increase of 1974 did not conform to commercially reasonable standards. In both the timing of the announcement and its refusal to protect work already bid at the old price, Shell could be found to have breached the obligation of good faith imposed by the Code on all merchants. "Every contract or duty within this chapter imposes an obligation of good faith in its performance or enforcement," id. § 490:1–203, which for merchants entails the observance of commercially reasonable standards of fair dealing in the trade.

The Comment to 1–203 reads: "This section sets forth a basic principle running throughout this Act. The principle involved is that in commercial transactions good faith is required in the performance and enforcement of all agreements or duties. Particular applications of this general principle appear in specific provisions of the Act ... It is further implemented by Section 1–205 on course of dealing and usage of trade." Id. § 490:1–203, Comment. Chevron's conduct in 1974 offered enough relevant evidence of commercially reasonable standards of fair dealing in the asphalt trade in Hawaii in 1974 for the jury to find that Shell's failure to give sufficient advance notice and price protect Nanakuli after the imposition of the new price did not conform to good faith dealings in Hawaii at that time.

Because the jury could have found for Nanakuli on its price protection claim under either theory, we reverse the judgment of the District Court and reinstate the jury verdict for Nanakuli in the amount of $220,800, plus interest according to law.

KENNEDY, J., CONCURRING. The case involves specific pricing practices, not an allegation of unfair dealing generally. Our opinion should not be interpreted to permit juries to import price protection or a similarly specific contract term from a concept of good faith that is not based on well-established custom and usage or other objective standards of which the parties had clear notice. Here, evidence of custom and usage regarding price protection in the asphaltic paving trade was not contradicted in major respects, and the jury could find that the parties knew or should have known of the practice at the time of making the contract. In my view, these are necessary predicates for either theory of the case, namely, interpretation of the contract based on the course of its performance or a finding that good faith required the seller to hold the price. With these observations, I concur.

Notes and Discussion

1. Once More § 2–202. Re-read § 2–202, this time concentrating on subsection (a). Note that course of performance, course of dealing, and usage of trade can all be used to "explain[] or supplement[]," but not to contradict, the terms "set forth in a writing intended by the parties as a final expression of their agreement"; and this remains true even if (to quote the language of subsection (b)) the writing was "intended also as a complete and exclusive statement of the terms of the agreement." For the definitions of course of performance, course of dealing, and usage of trade, see revised § 1–303, which gathers together many of the important rules once scattered through the UCC. Note especially revised § 1–303(e), which requires courts to interpret express terms as in accord with party practices, but establishes a hierarchy where there is inconsistency: "(1) express terms prevail over course of performance, course of dealing, and usage of trade; (2) course of performance prevails over course of dealing and usage of trade; and (3) course of dealing prevails over usage of trade." Further, the definitions of the three customary standards in revised § 1–303(a)–(c) are substantially wider than the pre-Code concepts.

Courts have widely recognized, as the *Nanakuli* Court does, that § 2–202(a) effects a profound transformation of traditional contract law. This is because it further undermines the contract/no contract dichotomy by not focusing so intensely on the language of writings, but instead opening up the boundaries of "the contract" to substantive influences from more general commercial practices (trade usage), the prior interactions of the parties (course of dealing), and even their interactions within the contract after the written document is executed (course of performance).

2. The Posted Price. Nanakuli's contract with Shell set the contract price as "Shell's Posted Price at time of delivery" in Honolulu. This price term is subject to the "good faith" in § 2–305(2): "A price to be fixed by the seller ... means a price for him to fix in good faith." By late 1973, Shell Oil's pricing structure came under substantial economic pressure as a result of the OPEC oil embargo; the 1973 reorganization of Shell's asphalt sales, which the Court discusses (for what purpose?), may well be associated with this pressure.

In any case, Nanakuli's second theory against Shell was not that its sudden price increases were in themselves a violation of good faith (what Comment 3 describes as the "observance of reasonable commercial standards of fair dealing in the trade"), but that this price increase could not in good faith be imposed without price protection for existing contracts; see the following section on the duty of good faith under § 1–203 (revised: § 1–304). Since Nanakuli defined "commercially reasonable" in terms of "the asphaltic paving trade in Hawaii in 1974," this theory basically restates its first and more important theory.

3. *Nanakuli* and the Problem of Consistency. In view of the clear and apparently unambiguous price in the written contract, how does the Court derive a contractual requirement of price protection?

What is the relevant trade whose usage is to govern? Is it the paving trade, or all the suppliers to the paving trade (including the suppliers of aggregate), or just the suppliers of asphalt? Is it reasonable to expect Shell to be aware of practices in the supply of aggregate? How regular must a practice be before it qualifies as "trade usage"?

Consider the course of performance under the 1969 contract. Would it be relevant if the price increases in 1970 and 1971 had been modest (as they almost certainly were) compared with the dramatic increase from $44 to $76 in 1974? (The trial court's exclusion of evidence of the prior course of dealings between Shell and Nanakuli is problematic, particularly inasmuch as Shell's only major customer in Hawaii was Nanakuli.) It is worth stressing that course of performance has the potential to alter what the parties intended when the contract was made. How can this possibility be explained?

Finally, and perhaps most significantly, how does the Court get round the plain injunction of revised § 1–303(e)(1) that, in the event of inconsistency, "express terms prevail over course of performance, course of dealing, and usage of trade"? You may well be reminded here of *Hunt Foods & Industries, Inc. v. Doliner*, which raises broadly similar problems. Is it enough to establish consistency that a proposed customary term is not a "total negation" of a written term? The *Nanakuli* Court does not adequately distinguish this decision from *Columbia Nitrogen*, which it criticizes.

The *Nanakuli* decision's treatment of consistency has been widely criticized. White and Summers, supra § 2–10 at 100 (5th ed. 2000), suggest: "In response to Shell's argument that this result impermissibly allowed trade usage to control 'express terms' ..., the court stated that 'Such a usage forms a broad and important exception to the express term but does not swallow it entirely.' The court would have done better to have ... held that the usage established a 'common basis of understanding for interpreting' the contract language 'Shell's Posted Price,' i.e., an understanding that changes in posted price would not be retroactive as above. So interpreted, no conflict would arise ... between express term and trade usage."

4. Is *Nanakuli* Right? Consider this argument from the economist Victor Goldberg: "[I]nterpretation can be enhanced by an understanding of the context of a transaction. But that does not mean that anything that might be labeled a course of dealing or a custom should be incorporated into the contract. The danger of a *Nanakuli-Columbia Nitrogen* interpretative strategy is that parties will be frustrated in trying to devise the terms of their agreement, and that they will have little confidence in their ability to predict the outcomes if their disputes do end up in litigation." Victor P. Goldberg, Framing Contract Law: An Economic Perspective 162 (2006). Are you persuaded?

MCC-MARBLE CERAMIC CENTER, INC. v. CERAMICA NUOVA D'AGOSTINO, S.P.A.

United States Court of Appeals, Eleventh Circuit, 1998.
144 F.3d 1384.

BIRCH, J. This case requires us to determine whether a court must consider parol evidence in a contract dispute governed by the United Nations Convention on Contracts for the International Sale of Goods ("CISG"). The district court granted summary judgment on behalf of the defendant-appellee, relying on certain terms and provisions that appeared on the reverse of a pre-printed form contract for the sale of ceramic tiles. The plaintiff-appellant sought to rely on a number of affidavits that tended to show both that the parties had arrived at an oral contract before memorializing their agreement in writing and that they subjectively intended not to apply the terms on the reverse of the contract to their agreements. The magistrate judge held that the affidavits did not raise an issue of material fact and recommended that the district court grant summary judgment based on the terms of the contract. The district court agreed with the magistrate judge's reasoning and entered summary judgment in the defendant-appellee's favor. We REVERSE.

Background

The plaintiff-appellant, MCC-Marble Ceramic, Inc. ("MCC"), is a Florida corporation engaged in the retail sale of tiles, and the defendant-appellee, Ceramica Nuova d'Agostino S.p.A. ("D'Agostino") is an Italian corporation engaged in the manufacture of ceramic tiles. In October 1990, MCC's president, Juan Carlos Mozon, met representatives of D'Agostino at a trade fair in Bologna, Italy and negotiated an agreement to purchase ceramic tiles from D'Agostino based on samples he examined at the trade fair. Monzon, who spoke no Italian, communicated with

Gianni Silingardi, then D'Agostino's commercial director, through a translator, Gianfranco Copelli, who was himself an agent of D'Agostino. The parties apparently arrived at an oral agreement on the crucial terms of price, quality, quantity, delivery and payment. The parties then recorded these terms on one of D'Agostino's standard, pre-printed order forms and Monzon signed the contract on MCC's behalf. According to MCC, the parties also entered into a requirements contract in February 1991, subject to which D'Agostino agreed to supply MCC with high grade ceramic tile at specific discounts as long as MCC purchased sufficient quantities of tile. MCC completed a number of additional order forms requesting tile deliveries pursuant to that agreement.

MCC brought suit against D'Agostino claiming a breach of the February 1991 requirements contract when D'Agostino failed to satisfy orders in April, May, and August of 1991. In addition to other defenses, D'Agostino responded that it was under no obligation to fill MCC's orders because MCC had defaulted on payment for previous shipments. In support of its position, D'Agostino relied on the pre-printed terms of the contracts that MCC had executed. The executed forms were printed in Italian and contained terms and conditions on both the front and reverse. According to an English translation of the October 1990 contract, the front of the order form contained the following language directly beneath Monzon's signature: "The buyer hereby states that he is aware of the sales conditions stated on the reverse and that he expressly approves of them with special reference to those numbered 1–2–3–4–5–6–7–8." R2–126, Exh. 3 P 5 ("Maselli Aff."). Clause 6(b), printed on the back of the form states: "Default or delay in payment within the time agreed upon gives D'Agostino the right to ... suspend or cancel the contract itself and to cancel possible other pending contracts and the buyer does not have the right to indemnification or damages." Id. P 6.

D'Agostino also brought a number of counterclaims against MCC, seeking damages for MCC's alleged nonpayment for deliveries of tile that D'Agostino had made between February 28, 1991 and July 4, 1991. MCC responded that the tile it had received was of a lower quality than contracted for, and that, pursuant to the CISG, MCC was entitled to reduce payment in proportion to the defects.[8] D'Agostino, however, noted that clause 4 on the reverse of the contract states, in pertinent part: "Possible complaints for defects of the merchandise must be made in writing by means of a certified letter within and not later than 10 days after receipt of the merchandise...." Maselli Aff. P 6. Although there is evidence to support MCC's claims that it complained about the quality of the deliveries it received, MCC never submitted any written complaints.

MCC did not dispute these underlying facts before the district court, but argued that the parties never intended the terms and conditions printed on the reverse of the order form to apply to their agreements. As

8. Article 50 of the CISG permits a buyer to reduce payment for nonconforming goods in proportion to the nonconformity under certain conditions. See CISG, art. 50.

evidence for this assertion, MCC submitted Monzon's affidavit, which claims that MCC had no subjective intent to be bound by those terms and that D'Agostino was aware of this intent. MCC also filed affidavits from Silingardi and Copelli, D'Agostino's representatives at the trade fair, which support Monzon's claim that the parties subjectively intended not to be bound by the terms on the reverse of the order form. The magistrate judge held that the affidavits, even if true, did not raise an issue of material fact regarding the interpretation or applicability of the terms of the written contracts and the district court accepted his recommendation to award summary judgment in D'Agostino's favor. MCC then filed this timely appeal.

DISCUSSION

We review a district court's grant of summary judgment *de novo* and apply the same standards as the district court.... Summary judgment is appropriate when the pleadings, depositions, and affidavits reveal that no genuine issue of material fact exists and the moving party is entitled to judgment as a matter of law. See Fed. R. Civ. P. 56(c).

The parties to this case agree that the CISG governs their dispute because the United States, where MCC has its place of business, and Italy, where D'Agostino has its place of business, are both States Party to the Convention. See CISG, art. 1. Article 8 of the CISG governs the interpretation of international contracts for the sale of goods and forms the basis of MCC's appeal from the district court's grant of summary judgment in D'Agostino's favor. MCC argues that the magistrate judge and the district court improperly ignored evidence that MCC submitted regarding the parties' subjective intent when they memorialized the terms of their agreement on D'Agostino's pre-printed form contract, and that the magistrate judge erred by applying the parol evidence rule in derogation of the CISG.

I. Subjective Intent Under the CISG

Contrary to what is familiar practice in United States courts, the CISG appears to permit a substantial inquiry into the parties' subjective intent, even if the parties did not engage in any objectively ascertainable means of registering this intent.[9] Article 8(1) of the CISG instructs courts to interpret the "statements ... and other conduct of a party ...

9. In the United States, the legislatures, courts, and the legal academy have voiced a preference for relying on objective manifestations of the parties' intentions. For example, Article Two of the Uniform Commercial Code, which most states have enacted in some form or another to govern contracts for the sale of goods, is replete with references to standards of commercial reasonableness. See e.g., U.C.C. § 2–206 (referring to reasonable means of accepting an offer); see also also *Lucy v. Zehmer*, 196 Va. 493, 503, 84 S.E.2d 516, 522 (1954) ("Whether the writing signed ... was the result of a serious offer ... and a serious acceptance ..., or was a serious offer ... and an acceptance in secret jest ..., in either event it constituted a binding contract of sale between the parties."). Justice Holmes expressed the philosophy behind this focus on the objective in forceful terms: "The law has nothing to do with the actual state of the parties' minds. In contract, as elsewhere, it must go by externals, and judge parties by their conduct." Oliver W. Holmes, The Common Law 242 (Howe ed. 1963) ...

according to his intent" as long as the other party "knew or could not have been unaware" of that intent. The plain language of the Convention, therefore, requires an inquiry into a party's subjective intent as long as the other party to the contract was aware of that intent.

In this case, MCC has submitted three affidavits that discuss the purported subjective intent of the parties to the initial agreement concluded between MCC and D'Agostino in October 1990. All three affidavits discuss the preliminary negotiations and report that the parties arrived at an oral agreement for D'Agostino to supply quantities of a specific grade of ceramic tile to MCC at an agreed upon price. The affidavits state that the "oral agreement established the essential terms of quality, quantity, description of goods, delivery, price and payment." See R3–133 P 9 ("Silingardi Aff."); R1–51 P 7 ("Copelli Aff."); R1–47 P 7 ("Monzon Aff."). The affidavits also note that the parties memorialized the terms of their oral agreement on a standard D'Agostino order form, but all three affiants contend that the parties subjectively intended not to be bound by the terms on the reverse of that form despite a provision directly below the signature line that expressly and specifically incorporated those terms.[10]

The terms on the reverse of the contract give D'Agostino the right to suspend or cancel all contracts in the event of a buyer's non-payment and require a buyer to make a written report of all defects within ten days. As the magistrate judge's report and recommendation makes clear, if these terms applied to the agreements between MCC and D'Agostino, summary judgment would be appropriate because MCC failed to make any written complaints about the quality of tile it received and D'Agostino has established MCC's non-payment of a number of invoices amounting to $108,389.40 and 102,053,846.00 Italian lira.

Article 8(1) of the CISG requires a court to consider this evidence of the parties' subjective intent. Contrary to the magistrate judge's report, which the district court endorsed and adopted, article 8(1) does not focus on interpreting the parties' statements alone. Although we agree with the magistrate judge's conclusion that no "interpretation" of the contract's terms could support MCC's position, article 8(1) also requires a court to consider subjective intent while interpreting the conduct of the parties. The CISG's language, therefore, requires courts to consider evidence of a party's subjective intent when signing a contract if the other party to the contract was aware of that intent at the time. This is precisely the type of evidence that MCC has provided through the Silingardi, Copelli, and Monzon affidavits, which discuss not only Mon-

10. MCC makes much of the fact that the written order form is entirely in Italian and that Monzon, who signed the contract on MCC's behalf directly below this provision incorporating the terms on the reverse of the form, neither spoke nor read Italian. This fact is of no assistance to MCC's position.... See e.g., *Samson Plastic Conduit and Pipe Corp. v. Battenfeld Extrusionstechnik GMBH*, 718 F. Supp. 886, 890 (M.D. Ala. 1989) ("A good and recurring illustration of the problem ... involves a person who is ... unfamiliar with the language in which a contract is written and who has signed a document which was not read to him. There is all but unanimous agreement that he is bound.... ")

zon's intent as MCC's representative but also discuss the intent of D'Agostino's representatives and their knowledge that Monzon did not intend to agree to the terms on the reverse of the form contract. This acknowledgment that D'Agostino's representatives were aware of Monzon's subjective intent puts this case squarely within article 8(1) of the CISG, and therefore requires the court to consider MCC's evidence as it interprets the parties' conduct.[11]

II. Parol Evidence and the CISG

Given our determination that the magistrate judge and the district court should have considered MCC's affidavits regarding the parties' subjective intentions, we must address a question of first impression in this circuit: whether the parol evidence rule, which bars evidence of an earlier oral contract that contradicts or varies the terms of a subsequent or contemporaneous written contract, plays any role in cases involving the CISG. We begin by observing that the parol evidence rule, contrary to its title, is a substantive rule of law, not a rule of evidence. See II E. Allen Farnsworth, Farnsworth on Contracts, § 7.2 at 194 (1990). The rule does not purport to exclude a particular type of evidence as an "untrustworthy or undesirable" way of proving a fact, but prevents a litigant from attempting to show "the fact itself—the fact that the terms of the agreement are other than those in the writing." Id. As such, a federal district court cannot simply apply the parol evidence rule as a procedural matter—as it might if excluding a particular type of evidence under the Federal Rules of Evidence, which apply in federal court regardless of the source of the substantive rule of decision. Cf. id. § 7.2 at 196.[12]

The CISG itself contains no express statement on the role of parol evidence. See Honnold, Uniform Law § 110 at 170. It is clear, however, that the drafters of the CISG were comfortable with the concept of permitting parties to rely on oral contracts because they eschewed any statutes of fraud provision and expressly provided for the enforcement of oral contracts. Compare CISG, art. 11 (a contract of sale need not be concluded or evidenced in writing) with U.C.C. § 2–201 (precluding the enforcement of oral contracts for the sale of goods involving more than

11. Without this crucial acknowledgment, we would interpret the contract and the parties' actions according to article 8(2), which directs courts to rely on objective evidence of the parties' intent. On the facts of this case it seems readily apparent that MCC's affidavits provide no evidence that Monzon's actions would have made his alleged subjective intent not to be bound by the terms of the contract known to "the understanding that a reasonable person ... would have had in the same circumstances." CISG, art 8(2).

12. An example demonstrates this point. The CISG provides that a contract for the sale of goods need not be in writing and that the parties may prove the contract "by any means, including witnesses." CISG, art. 11. Nevertheless, a party seeking to prove a contract in such a manner in federal court could not do so in a way that violated in the rule against hearsay. See Fed. R. Evid. 802 (barring hearsay evidence). A federal district court applies the Federal Rules of Evidence because these rules are considered procedural, regardless of the source of the law that governs the substantive decision. Cf. Farnsworth on Contracts § 7.2 at 196 & n. 16 (citing cases).

$500). Moreover, article 8(3) of the CISG expressly directs courts to give "due consideration ... to all relevant circumstances of the case including the negotiations ... " to determine the intent of the parties. Given article 8(1)'s directive to use the intent of the parties to interpret their statements and conduct, article 8(3) is a clear instruction to admit and consider parol evidence regarding the negotiations to the extent they reveal the parties' subjective intent....

As one scholar has explained: "The language of Article 8(3) that 'due consideration is to be given to all relevant circumstances of the case' seems adequate to override any domestic rule that would bar a tribunal from considering the relevance of other agreements.... Article 8(3) relieves tribunals from domestic rules that might bar them from 'considering' any evidence between the parties that is relevant. This added flexibility for interpretation is consistent with a growing body of opinion that the 'parol evidence rule' has been an embarrassment for the administration of modern transactions." Honnnold, Uniform Law § 110 at 170–71....

This is not to say that parties to an international contract for the sale of goods cannot depend on written contracts or that parol evidence regarding subjective contractual intent need always prevent a party relying on a written agreement from securing summary judgment. To the contrary, most cases will not present a situation (as exists in this case) in which both parties to the contract acknowledge a subjective intent not to be bound by the terms of a pre-printed writing. In most cases, therefore, article 8(2) of the CISG will apply, and objective evidence will provide the basis for the court's decision. See Honnold, Uniform Law § 107 at 164–65. Consequently, a party to a contract governed by the CISG will not be able to avoid the terms of a contract and force a jury trial simply by submitting an affidavit which states that he or she did not have the subjective intent to be bound by the contract's terms. Cf. *Klopfenstein v. Pargeter*, 597 F.2d 150, 152 (9th Cir. 1979) (affirming summary judgment despite the appellant's submission of his own affidavit regarding his subjective intent: "Undisclosed, subjective intentions are immaterial in [a] commercial transaction, especially when contradicted by objective conduct. Thus, the affidavit has no legal effect even if its averments are accepted as wholly truthful."). Moreover, to the extent parties wish to avoid parol evidence problems they can do so by including a merger clause in their agreement that extinguishes any and all prior agreements and understandings not expressed in the writing.

Considering MCC's affidavits in this case, however, we conclude that the magistrate judge and the district court improperly granted summary judgment in favor of D'Agostino. Although the affidavits are, as D'Agostino observes, relatively conclusory and unsupported by facts that would objectively establish MCC's intent not to be bound by the conditions on the reverse of the form, article 8(1) requires a court to consider evidence of a party's subjective intent when the other party was aware of it, and the Silingardi and Copelli affidavits provide that evidence. This is not to say that the affidavits are conclusive proof of what the parties intended.

A reasonable finder of fact, for example, could disregard testimony that purportedly sophisticated international merchants signed a contract without intending to be bound as simply too incredible to believe and hold MCC to the conditions printed on the reverse of the contract. Nevertheless, the affidavits raise an issue of material fact regarding the parties' intent to incorporate the provisions on the reverse of the form contract. If the finder of fact determines that the parties did not intend to rely on those provisions, then the more general provisions of the CISG will govern the outcome of the dispute.

MCC's affidavits, however, do not discuss all of the transactions and orders that MCC placed with D'Agostino. Each of the affidavits discusses the parties' subjective intent surrounding the initial order MCC placed with D'Agostino in October 1990. The Copelli affidavit also discusses a February 1991 requirements contract between the parties and reports that the parties subjectively did not intend the terms on the reverse of the D'Agostino order form to apply to that contract either. See Copelli Aff. P 12. D'Agostino, however, submitted the affidavit of its chairman, Vincenzo Maselli, which describes at least three other orders from MCC on form contracts dated January 15, 1991, April 27, 1991, and May 4, 1991, in addition to the October 1990 contract. See Maselli Aff. P 2, 25. MCC's affidavits do not discuss the subjective intent of the parties to be bound by language in those contracts, and D'Agostino, therefore, argues that we should affirm summary judgment to the extent damages can be traced to those order forms. It is unclear from the record, however, whether all of these contracts contained the terms that appeared in the October 1990 contract. Moreover, because article 8 requires a court to consider any "practices which the parties have established between themselves, usages and any subsequent conduct of the parties" in interpreting contracts, CISG, art. 8(3), whether the parties intended to adhere to the ten day limit for complaints, as stated on the reverse of the initial contract, will have an impact on whether MCC was bound to adhere to the limit on subsequent deliveries. Since material issues of fact remain regarding the interpretation of the remaining contracts between MCC and D'Agostino, we cannot affirm any portion of the district court's summary judgment in D'Agostino's favor.

Conclusion

MCC asks us to reverse the district court's grant of summary judgment in favor of D'Agostino. The district court's decision rests on pre-printed contractual terms and conditions incorporated on the reverse of a standard order form that MCC's president signed on the company's behalf. Nevertheless, we conclude that the CISG, which governs international contracts for the sale of goods, precludes summary judgment in this case because MCC has raised an issue of material fact concerning the parties' subjective intent to be bound by the terms on the reverse of the pre-printed contract. The CISG also precludes the application of the parol evidence rule, which would otherwise bar the consideration of evidence concerning a prior or contemporaneously negotiated oral agreement. Accordingly, we REVERSE the district court's grant of summary judgment and REMAND this case for further proceedings consistent with this opinion.

Notes and Discussion

1. **Parol Evidence under the CISG.** The trial judge had applied the ordinary Common Law rule. The appellate decision, by contrast, delves more deeply into the implications of the CISG.

What are the practical consequences of this decision? Is it worth considering whether the rule of this case should be extended more generally in American law? One obstacle to doing so stems from the role played in our law by juries, who, it is feared, might mishandle evidence as to side agreements.

2. **The CISG and the Restatement.** The CISG may not be all that different from Common Law. With art. 8(1), compare Restatement 2d § 201(2): "Where the parties have attached different meanings to a promise or agreement or a term thereof, it is interpreted in accordance with the meaning attached by one of them if at the time the agreement was made (a) that party did not know of any different meaning attached by the other, and the other knew the meaning attached by the first party; or (b) that party had no reason to know of any different meaning attached by the other, and the other had reason to know the meaning attached by the first party." A party's "intent" scarcely differs from the meaning it attaches to its promise. Is the "could not have been unaware" standard in the CISG more or less stringent than the Restatement's "had reason to know"?

With art. 8(3), compare Restatement 2d § 202(5): "Wherever reasonable, the manifestations of intention of the parties to a promise or agreement are interpreted as consistent with each other and with any relevant course of performance, course of dealing, or usage of trade."

C. IMPLIED TERMS AND THE IMPLIED COVENANT OF GOOD FAITH

Although it is theoretically possible for parties to create contracts containing every single promise between them, this is rare even with written contracts. Usually courts are called upon to supplement express contracts with terms of their own devising. This urgency becomes especially acute when what otherwise the parties clearly intended as a binding contract lacks some crucial term, as in *Haines v. City of New York* (the case that follows); in that event, as Restatement 2d § 204 puts it, "a term which is reasonable in the circumstances is supplied by the court," even though one party or the other may not wish that term to be present.

From this pattern of judicial supplementation there gradually grew up a list of "default terms" or "gap fillers," terms that are available "off the shelf," so to speak, when the parties fail to provide. For sale of goods, many of these terms are codified into statute. Within wide limits the parties may depart from them, if they wish, by providing expressly; but if they fail to do so, then the UCC terms apply. We have already seen these default terms as providing a background for "the battle of the forms" in § 2–207 (above, Chapter 3.E). A good example is § 2–504, which states what happens "[w]here the seller is required or authorized to send the goods to the buyer and the contract does not require him to deliver them at a particular destination."

Some implied terms, however, are much less neutral in their framing, and represent positive policy decisions about contractual interrelationships; depending on their seriousness, such implied terms can be difficult for parties to alter. For sale of goods, examples are § 2–312, the implied warranty of title, which can be "excluded or modified only by specific language or by circumstances which give the buyer reason to know that the person selling does not claim title"; or § 2–719(3), which sharply restricts the right of parties to limit liability for consequential damages for injury to the person. (The implied warranties of merchantability and fitness for a particular purpose are considered in the following section.) Other areas of contract law have similar restrictions on contractual freedom; one obvious example is the warranty of habitability in leases, which was originally judicially imposed and is now mainly statutory.

The implied obligation of good faith and fair dealing originates in case law, but was given a major boost by its adoption in the UCC (§ 1–203; revised § 1–304); this obligation was then generalized for all contracts by Restatement 2d § 205. The content of the good faith obligation remains, however, controversial. The obligation becomes particularly salient in "exclusivity" contracts, such as output and requirements contracts, where § 2–306(1) defines exclusivity in terms of "good faith."

HAINES v. CITY OF NEW YORK

Court of Appeals of New York, 1977.
41 N.Y.2d 769, 364 N.E.2d 820, 396 N.Y.S.2d 155.

GABRIELLI, J. In the early 1920's, respondent City of New York and intervenors Town of Hunter and Village of Tannersville embarked upon negotiations for the construction of a sewage system to serve the village and a portion of the town. These negotiations were prompted by the city's need and desire to prevent the discharge of untreated sewage by residents of the area into Gooseberry Creek, a stream which fed a reservoir of the city's water supply system in the Schoharie watershed.

In 1923, the Legislature enacted enabling legislation authorizing the city to enter into contracts with municipalities in the watershed area "for the purpose of providing, maintaining (and) operating systems and plants for the collection and disposal of sewage" (L.1923, ch. 630, § 1). The statute further provided that any such contracts would be subject to the approval of the New York City Board of Estimate and Apportionment.

The negotiations culminated in an agreement in 1924 between the city and intervenors. By this agreement, the city assumed the obligation of constructing a sewage system consisting of a sewage disposal plant and sewer mains and laterals, and agreed that "all costs of construction and subsequent operation, maintenance and repair of said sewerage system with the house connections thereof and said disposal works shall be at the expense" of the city. The agreement also required the city to extend the sewer lines when "necessitated by future growth and building constructions of the respective communities." The village and town were obligated to and did obtain the necessary easements for the construction of the system and sewage lines.

The Board of Estimate, on December 9, 1926, approved the agreement and authorized the issuance of $500,000 of "corporate stock" of the City of New York for construction of the system by appropriate resolution. It is interesting to here note that a modification of the original agreement occurred in 1925 wherein the village agreed to reimburse the city for a specified amount representing the expense of changing the location of certain sewer lines. The plant was completed and commenced operation in 1928. The city has continued to maintain the plant through the ensuing years and in 1958 expended $193,000 to rehabilitate and expand the treatment plant and facilities.

Presently, the average flow of the plant has increased from an initial figure of 118,000 gallons per day to over 600,000 gallons daily and the trial court found that the plant "was operating substantially in excess of design capacity." The city asserts, and it is not disputed by any of the parties in this action, that the system cannot bear any significant additional "loadings" because this would result in inadequate treatment of all the sewage and consequently harm the city's water supply. The instant controversy arose when plaintiff, who is the owner of a tract of unimproved land which he seeks to develop into 50 residential lots, applied to the city for permission to connect houses, which he intends to construct on the lots, to existing sewer lines. The city refused permission on the ground that it had no obligation to further expand the plant, which is presently operating at full capacity, to accommodate this new construction.

Plaintiff then commenced this action for declaratory and injunctive relief, in which intervenors town and village joined as plaintiffs, maintaining that the 1924 agreement is perpetual in duration and obligates the city to expend additional capital funds to enlarge the existing plant or build a new one to accommodate the present and future needs of the municipalities. Both the trial court and the Appellate Division, by a divided court, held in favor of plaintiff and intervenors concluding, that, while the contract did not call for perpetual performance, the city was bound to construct additional facilities to meet increased demand until such time as the village or town is legally obligated to maintain a sewage disposal system. Two members of the court dissented in part stating that the agreement should not be construed as requiring the city to construct new or additional facilities.

We conclude that the city is presently obligated to maintain the existing plant but is not required to expand that plant or construct any new facilities to accommodate plaintiff's substantial, or any other, increased demands on the sewage system. The initial problem encountered in ascertaining the nature and extent of the city's obligation pursuant to the 1924 agreement, is its duration. We reject, as did the courts below, the plaintiff's contention that the city is perpetually bound under the agreement. The contract did not expressly provide for perpetual performance and both the trial court and the Appellate Division found that the parties did not so intend. Under these circumstances, the law will not imply that a contract calling for continuing performance is perpetual in duration (. . . 1 Williston, Contracts (3d ed.), § 38, p. 113).

On the other hand, the city's contention that the contract is terminable at will because it provides for no express duration should also be rejected. In the absence of an express term fixing the duration of a contract, the courts may inquire into the intent of the parties and supply the missing term if a duration may be fairly and reasonably fixed by the surrounding circumstances and the parties' intent . . . It is generally agreed that where a duration may be fairly and reasonably supplied by implication, a contract is not terminable at will (1 Williston, op. cit., p. 112; . . . see, also, Restatement, Contracts 2d (Tent. Draft No. 7), § 230).

While we have not previously had occasion to apply it, the weight of authority supports the related rule that where the parties have not clearly expressed the duration of a contract, the courts will imply that they intended performance to continue for a reasonable time (. . . 1 Williston, op. cit., pp. 116–117; . . .). For compelling policy reasons, this rule has not been, and should not be, applied to contracts of employment or exclusive agency, distributorship, or requirements contracts which have been analogized to employment contracts . . . The considerations relevant to such contracts do not obtain here. Thus, we hold that it is reasonable to infer from the circumstances of the 1924 agreement that the parties intended the city to maintain the sewage disposal facility until such time as the city no longer needed or desired the water, the purity of which the plant was designed to insure. The city argues that it is no longer obligated to maintain the plant because State law now prohibits persons from discharging raw sewage into streams such as Gooseberry Creek. However, the parties did not contemplate the passage of environmental control laws which would prohibit individuals or municipalities from discharging raw, untreated sewage into certain streams. Thus, the city agreed to assume the obligation of assuring that its water supply remained unpolluted and it may not now avoid that obligation for reasons not contemplated by the parties when the agreement was executed, and not within the purview of their intent, expressed or implied.

Having determined the duration of the city's obligation, the scope of its duty remains to be defined. By the agreement, the city obligated itself to build a specifically described disposal facility and to extend the lines of that facility to meet future increased demand. At the present time, the extension of those lines would result in the overloading of the system. Plaintiff claims that the city is required to build a new plant or expand the existing facility to overcome the problem. We disagree. The city should not be required to extend the lines to plaintiffs' property if to do so would overload the system and result in its inability to properly treat sewage. In providing for the extension of sewer lines, the contract does not obligate the city to provide sewage disposal services for properties in areas of the municipalities not presently served or even to new properties in areas which are presently served where to do so could reasonably be expected to significantly increase the demand on present plant facilities.

Thus, those paragraphs of the judgment which provide that the city is obligated to construct any additional facilities required to meet increased demand and that plaintiff is entitled to full use of the sewer lines should be stricken.

Accordingly, the order of the Appellate Division should be modified and the case remitted to Supreme Court, Greene County, for the entry of judgment in accordance with the opinion herein and, as so modified, affirmed, with costs to appellants against plaintiffs-respondents only.

Notes and Discussion

1. **The Omissions.** The 1924 contract between New York City and the two municipalities had many omissions, all related to when or under what circumstances the contract would terminate. It was unclear what the effects of urban growth would be; there was no provision as to what would happen if New York City no longer needed protection against the discharge of raw sewage into its water supply; nor was there any definite ending to contractual obligations (perhaps with options for renewal).

Were the drafters unable to foresee these eventualities, or did they deliberately choose not to include such provisions? It seems unlikely that they were consciously leaving future disputes to be settled by judicial decisions as these disputes arose.

2. **Filling Gaps.** Note particularly the difference in the Court's handling of the duration of this contract, on the one hand, and the contract's scope, on the other. Why does it first examine the interpretations of the parties before proceeding to imply terms?

As to duration (is the contract permanent, or terminable at will, or something intermediate?), the Court turns to a default rule: the contract will continue for a "reasonable time." How does the Court go about determining what is reasonable? As it notes, the parties probably did not contemplate environmental laws forbidding the discharge of raw sewage; but why shouldn't the fact of such laws be at least relevant? Can't we presume that if the parties had thought about this possibility, New York City would have insisted on the contract terminating when such legislation was passed? In any case, under the Court's holding, how long into the future will New York City now be obligated?

As to scope, the issue centers around the original plaintiff's attempt to get his subdivision linked up to existing sewer lines, which would thereby be overstrained. The court takes a narrow view of the City's duties with respect to new hook-ups. It could be argued that the City's 1958 rehabilitation and expansion of its plant indicate that the City understood itself as obliged to meet urban growth, true?

3. Default Rules. The Court notes that while a "reasonable time" standard is used for most contracts without express duration, "[f]or compelling policy reasons, this rule has not been, and should not be, applied to contracts of employment ... " We have already met this rule in *Fisher v. Jackson* (Chapter 2.A). What are the compelling policy reasons? Default rules should be flexibly developed in response to different contractual situations, not so?

Problem 4–2

Between 1991 and 1994, the health insurance fund for the public school teachers in Coffeyville accumulated a surplus of about $140,000 because of lower than anticipated use of benefits. The teachers had a union contract with the Coffeyville School District. The District maintained it was entitled to the entire refund because it paid the insurance premiums under the contract with BCBS for the benefit of the teachers. The Union contended that the subscribers are entitled to the entire refund because they, not the District, paid the premiums that created the surplus; health and medical insurance had been bargained for in the negotiated agreements between its members and the district. The Union contract described any surplus as "divisible" and continued: "Any part of the Divisible Surplus that is paid in cash and is in excess of the Contract Holder's share of the dues shall be applied for the sole benefit of the Subscribers. Distribution of any Divisible Surplus in accordance with this provision shall completely discharge the Plan from liability with respect to the adjustment of dues so distributed." However, the contract said nothing as to who the recipients should be. What outcome?

CENTRONICS CORP. v. GENICOM CORP.

Supreme Court of New Hampshire, 1989.
132 N.H. 133, 562 A.2d 187.

SOUTER, J. A contract between the buyer and seller of business assets provided for arbitration of any dispute about the value of the property transferred, to which the purchase price was pegged, and required an escrow deposit of a portion of the price claimed by the seller pending final valuation. The seller has charged the buyer with breach of an implied covenant of good faith in refusing, during arbitration, to release a portion of the escrow fund claimed to be free from "dispute." The Superior Court (Hollman, J.) granted summary judgment to the buyer, which we affirm.

The agreement between the plaintiff-seller, Centronics Corporation and corporations related to it (Centronics), and the defendant-buyer,

Genicom Corporation (Genicom), sets the purchase price at the consolidated closing net book value (CCNBV) of the assets plus four million dollars.... The parties agreed that any timely dispute about the consolidated closing balance sheet or the computations based upon it would be referred to a New York accounting firm for final and binding "determination in accordance with the terms of [the] Agreement," a process that each party now describes as arbitration.

Although the parties agreed to use their best efforts to promote the resolution of disputed issues within fifteen days of their submission to the arbitrator, even on the optimistic assumption that arbitration would conclude that soon the parties faced a potential delay of more than one hundred days between closing and final calculation of the purchase price. Instead of deferring all payment for such a time or longer, they agreed that upon closing Genicom would pay Centronics an amount equal to the purchase price based on the September balance sheet, less $5,000,000 to be placed in escrow. They also agreed that if Centronics proposed revisions to the September balance sheet indicating a higher purchase price Genicom would promptly increase the escrow deposit by the difference, to be known as the Adjustment Amount.

Distribution from the escrow fund was to be governed by two sets of provisions. Insofar as the escrow agreement relates to the issue before us, it simply provided that "[i]n accordance with Section 2.07 of the Purchase Agreement, the Escrow Agent shall hold the Escrow Fund in its possession until instructed in writing" by respective New York counsel for Centronics and Genicom "to distribute the same or some portion thereof to Centronics or [Genicom] as the case may be," whereupon the escrow agent was to make the distribution as ordered. Section 2.07 of the Purchase Agreement, entitled "Final Payment of Purchase Price," began with a provision that "[f]inal settlement and payment of the Purchase Price shall be made not later than ten days after determination of [CCNBV] and computation of the Purchase Price," whether by agreement of the parties or decision of the arbitrator. There followed detailed instructions for payment out of escrow and final settlement between the parties, which are of no significance in the matter before us, being intended to provide for the payment to Centronics of whatever balance it might be owed on the purchase price, and the distribution to Genicom of any amount it might be found to have overpaid....

The arbitration had begun to drag by the summer of 1987, when Centronics sought a distribution of $5,653,836 from the escrow fund, being the difference between the total fund of $15,867,000 and the $10,213,164 in downward adjustments Genicom had proposed. Centronics described the amount requested as free from dispute and complained of a loss of economic opportunity to use the funds for its corporate purposes. Genicom replied that the purchase agreement provided for no distribution from escrow prior to determination of CCNBV and the final purchase price, which, as it turned out, would presumably be at the close of arbitration.

Centronics responded by bringing this two-count action to recover the amount in question and consequential damages.... Genicom moved for summary judgment on the theory that, given the dispute over CCNBV, the terms of the parties' agreements required payments out of escrow only upon completion of arbitration, thus barring the implication of any duty to authorize a distribution before that event. Centronics objected and sought its own summary judgment, grounded on affidavits said to indicate that Genicom's refusal was meant to pressure Centronics into conceding a disputed item worth a substantial amount.

The trial court ruled for Genicom, after construing the contract to provide that the "only way funds can be released is upon final determination of the purchase price, which, as the parties agree, is in the hands of the arbitrator. The instant suit is no more than [an] attempt on the part of [Centronics] to rewrite the contract. Essentially, [Centronics] asks this Court to read between the lines of § 2.07 and insert therein a provision regarding partial disbursal of funds from escrow in light of the protracted arbitration. While it is true that the parties contemplated a short time period for resolution of disputes through binding arbitration, the Court cannot insert a provision in the contract for partial payments where such provision does not exist.

"[Centronics] should have demanded a mechanism for partial payments from the Escrow Fund if the arbitration process lagged, or if the factual situation regarding adjustments to the final purchase price occurred as it did. The Court will not renegotiate the contract between the parties to obtain this result. To the extent [Centronics] made a less advantageous contract, it must now abide by the terms of that contract as originally agreed."

Centronics reads the foregoing order as denying that any obligation of good faith is implied in the parties' contract. We read it differently, as concluding that the express terms of the contract are inconsistent with the claim that an obligation of good faith and fair dealing, or any other sort of implied obligation, either requires Genicom to agree to an interim distribution or bars Genicom from refusing to agree except in return for Centronics's concession on a disputed item. We consequently view this appeal as raising the related questions of whether the trial judge misunderstood the implied obligation of good faith or misconstrued the contract. We conclude that he did neither.

Although an obligation of good faith is imposed by statute in the performance and enforcement of every contract or duty subject to the Uniform Commercial Code, see RSA 382–A:1–203, :1–201(19), the parties before us have addressed the implied contractual obligation of good faith at common law ...

Our own common law of good faith contractual obligation is not, however, as easily stated as we might wish, there being not merely one rule of implied good faith duty in New Hampshire's law of contract, but a series of doctrines, each of them speaking in terms of an obligation of good faith but serving markedly different functions. Since the time of our first contract decision couched in terms of good faith, *Griswold v. Heat Corporation*, 108 N.H. 119, 229 A.2d 183 (1967), we have relied on such an implied duty in three distinct categories of contract cases: those dealing with standards of conduct in contract formation, with termination of at-will employment contracts, and with limits on discretion in contractual performance, which is at issue in the instant case. Although decisions in the first and second categories are not directly relevant here, a short detour through their cases will serve clarity by indicating the categorical distinctions.

In our decisions setting standards of conduct in contract formation, the implied good faith obligations of a contracting party are tantamount to the traditional duties of care to refrain from misrepresentation and to correct subsequently discovered error, insofar as any representation is intended to induce, and is material to, another party's decision to enter into a contract in justifiable reliance upon it. See *Bursey v. Clement*, 118 N.H. 412, 414, 387 A.2d 346, 348 (1978).... In *Bursey* ..., the continuing good faith bar to misrepresentation is antecedent to the agreement itself ... Cf. Restatement (Second) of Contracts § 205, comment e.

By way of contrast, the good faith enforced in the second category of our cases is an obligation implied in the contract itself, where it fulfills the distinctly different function of limiting the power of an employer to terminate a wage contract by discharging an at-will employee. Under the rule evolved from *Monge v. Beebe Rubber Co.*, 114 N.H. 130, 316 A.2d 549 (1974) ..., an employer violates an implied term of a contract for employment at-will by firing an employee out of malice or bad faith in retaliation for action taken or refused by the employee in consonance with public policy ... Although good faith in this context has not been rigorously defined, bad faith has been spoken of as equivalent to malice ... and treated virtually as a subject of equitable estoppel in labor relations ... Indeed, the concepts of good and bad faith applied in these cases are best understood not as elements of general contract law as such, but as expressions of labor policy. See *Monge*, supra at 133, 316 A.2d at 551.

The differences between the obligations of good faith exemplified even in these first two groups of cases are enough to explain why the commentators despair of articulating any single concept of contractual good faith, even after the more than fifty years of litigation following in the wake of the American common law's first explicit recognition of an implied good faith contractual obligation in *Kirke La Shelle Co. v. Paul Armstrong Co.*, 263 N.Y. 79, 87, 188 N.E. 163, 167 (1933). See Summers, "Good Faith" in General Contract Law and the Sales Provisions of the Uniform Commercial Code, 54 Va. L. Rev. 195, 196 (1968); Summers, The General Duty of Good Faith—Its Recognition and Conceptualization, 67 Cornell L. Rev. 810, 819 (1982); Burton, More on Good Faith Performance of a Contract: A Reply to Professor Summers, 69 Iowa L. Rev. 497, 511 (1984); Restatement, supra at § 205, comments a, d, e.

Even within the narrower confines of the third category of cases, those governing discretion in contractual performance, the one notable attempt to conceptualize implied good faith in a single, general definition, Burton, Breach of Contract and the Common Law Duty to Perform in Good Faith, 94 Harv. L. Rev. 369 (1980), discussed infra, is opposed by the view that the obligation of good faith performance is better understood simply as excluding behavior inconsistent with common standards of decency, fairness, and reasonableness, and with the parties' agreed-upon common purposes and justified expectations, see Summers, 67 Cornell L. Rev. at 820, 826; Restatement, supra at § 205, comment a. This view is consonant with our own cases in the third category, a canvass of which should inform our consideration of what good faith may or may not demand of Genicom in the circumstances before us.

New Hampshire's seminal case on the implied obligation of good faith performance, *Griswold v. Heat Corporation*, 108 N.H. 119, 229 A.2d 183, held that a contract to pay $200 a month for " 'such [personal] services as [the plaintiff], in his sole discretion, may render' " required the plaintiff to provide a level of services consistent with good faith, id. at 124, 229 A.2d at 187. The court sought out the inadequately articulated objectives of the contracting parties by examining their contractual language, their prior dealings, and the commercial context in which they dealt, and found a mutual intention to be bound by a contract for actual services. Id. at 123–24, 229 A.2d at 186–87. The court then indicated its readiness to vindicate what it inferred to have been the parties' reasonable expectations, and so saved the agreement from the unenforceability that would have followed from finding the plaintiff's undertaking to have been as illusory as the contract literally gave him the discretion to make it. Id. at 124, 229 A.2d at 187. Thus, a contracting party with expressly conferred discretion to do nothing at all was denied the right to frustrate the other party's expectation of receiving some reasonable level of performance.

The discretion to refrain from acting, articulated in the *Griswold* contract, had been left unexpressed in the agreement litigated in the next case, where it resulted simply from the parties' failure to address any standard of enforceable performance on the point at issue. In *Seaward Construction Co. v. City of Rochester*, 118 N.H. 128, 383 A.2d 707 (1978), the city was obliged to pay for construction work only to the extent it received federal funds for that purpose, and the contract expressed no duty on the city's part to seek the funds, id. at 129, 383 A.2d at 708. When, however, the parties fell into dispute over amounts due, and the city blocked what it believed was the contractor's demand for excessive payment by the simple expedient of refusing to ask for any federal money, id., this court held that the city could not rely on a lack of federal funds in defending against the contractor's claim for payment, without also proving it had honored an implied obligation to make a good faith effort to obtain the money, id. at 130, 383 A.2d at 708. Thus, once again, the court imposed a limitation on one party's apparent discretion to thwart a reasonable expectation of the other party, going to the essence of the contract.... [Eds.: Other New Hampshire cases along this same line are also discussed.]

Despite the variety of their fact patterns, these cases illustrate a common rule: under an agreement that appears by word or silence to invest one party with a degree of discretion in performance sufficient to deprive another party of a substantial proportion of the agreement's value, the parties' intent to be bound by an enforceable contract raises an implied obligation of good faith to observe reasonable limits in exercising that discretion, consistent with the parties' purpose or purposes in contracting. A claim for relief from a violation of the implied covenant of good faith contractual performance therefore potentially raises four questions:

1. Does the agreement ostensibly allow to or confer upon the defendant a degree of discretion in performance tantamount to a power to deprive the plaintiff of a substantial proportion of the agreement's value? Contracts may be broken in a multitude of ways and theories of relief are correspondingly numerous, but the concept of good faith in performance addresses the particular problem raised by a promise subject to such a degree of discretion that its practical benefit could seemingly be withheld.

2. If the ostensible discretion is of that requisite scope, does competent evidence indicate that the parties intended by their agreement to make a legally enforceable contract? In many cases, such as ... *Seaward*, this question will not pose a serious issue, and it surely would not call for any extended consideration in the case before us. *Griswold*, however, illustrates why the question must at least be recognized, for the very breadth of discretion necessary to predicate a claim of bad faith can also raise doubt about the parties' intent to be bound.

3. Assuming an intent to be bound, has the defendant's exercise of discretion exceeded the limits of reasonableness? The answer to this question depends on identifying the common purpose or purposes of the contract, against which the reasonableness of the complaining party's expectations may be measured, and in furtherance of which community standards of honesty, decency and reasonableness can be applied.

4. Is the cause of the damage complained of the defendant's abuse of discretion, or does it result from events beyond the control of either party, against which the defendant has no obligation to protect the plaintiff? Although this question is cast in the language of causation, it may be seen simply as the other face of question three. Suffice it to say here that its point is to emphasize that the good faith requirement is not a fail-safe device barring a defendant from the fruits of every plaintiff's bad bargain, or empowering courts to rewrite an agreement even when a defendant's discretion is consistent with the agreement's legally contractual character.

Applying this analytical sequence to the instant case takes us no further than the first of the four questions, whether the agreement effectively confers such discretion on Genicom over the timing of distributions from the escrow fund that, in the absence of some good faith limitation, Genicom could deny Centronics a substantial proportion of the contract's benefit. Was Genicom, that is, given authority to deprive Centronics indefinitely of a portion of the agreed consideration for the business assets previously transferred? The answer is obviously no.... [This contract] contains express and unequivocal provisions governing the timing of payment, which must occur no later than ten days after final resolution of the purchase price, presumably on conclusion of the mandatory arbitration.... Genicom has no discretion to withhold approval for pay-out beyond that time, or to affect the timing of the arbitration itself. If, indeed, either party were dragging its heels in the conduct of the arbitration, it should go without saying that the dilatory conduct would be seen as a breach of contract, whether expressed in the language of bad faith or in traditional terms of the obligation to act within a reasonable time. See Restatement, supra at § 205, comment d. In short, because contractual provisions mandating payment on conclusion of the valuation process determine the date on which Centronics will get its due, it is clear that what Centronics claims to be Genicom's discretion over the timing of distribution is in reality a power that each party may exercise, but only jointly with the other, to agree to remove some or all of the escrowed funds from the ambit of the otherwise mandatory pay-out provisions.

Although this discussion reflects the analytical structure of the prior good faith performance cases cited by Centronics and followed here, we should also note that the same result would obtain from applying an alternative analysis proposed by Professor Burton, referred to above, which Centronics has also urged us to employ. Burton's functional analysis of the obligation to observe good faith in discretionary contract performance applies objective criteria, see Burton, 94 Harv. L. Rev. at 390–91, to identify the unstated economic opportunities intended to be bargained away by a promisor as a cost of performance, and it identifies bad faith as a promisor's discretionary action subjectively intended, id. at 386, 389, to recapture such an opportunity, thereby refusing to pay an expected performance cost, id. at 373. Centronics argues that its uncontradicted summary judgment affidavits establish that Genicom showed bad faith in Burton's sense, because its refusal to authorize distribution of the so-called undisputed amounts was an "attempt to recapture [the] degree of control concerning the amount of the final purchase price [which] it had agreed to place ... in the arbitrator's hands ... and thereby unjustifiably attain funds to which it was not entitled."

Genicom, of course, denies the uncontradicted evidentiary force that Centronics claims for its affidavits. But even assuming, *arguendo*, that the affidavits are uncontradicted and tend to prove what Centronics asserts, there are two respects in which the facts would fail the Burton test of bad faith as an exercise of discretion meant to recapture an opportunity foregone at the creation of the contract.

It is significant, first, that Genicom's refusal to consent to the distribution from escrow neither recaptures nor gains Genicom anything. In and of itself, the refusal removes no issue from the contingencies of arbitration and gives Genicom no present or future right to the money it wishes to obtain. Genicom's behavior thus contrasts sharply with examples of bad faith given by Burton, in which the discretionary delay preserved the actual use of funds or other valuable resources to the party exercising the discretion. See Burton, 94 Harv. L. Rev. at 394–402. The point is that only when the discretionary act recaptures an economic opportunity does the exercise of discretion pass from the realm of applying leverage for the sake of inducing further agreement into the sphere of bad faith, in which no agreement is necessary to realize the offending party's advantage.

The contrast is equally stark between the result of Genicom's decision and the beneficial results obtained by defendants in the cases Centronics specifically relies upon.... In each of these cases, the defendant's discretionary act of bad faith kept money in its pocket, with the attendant opportunities to use that money as it saw fit. On the contrary, by Genicom's refusal, standing alone, it neither retains nor obtains a penny of the money it wishes to receive.

A second and more fundamental flaw infects Centronics's reliance on the Burton analysis, however. It will be recalled that Burton's conception of bad faith in performance is the exercise of discretion for the purpose of recapturing opportunities forgone or bargained away at the time of contracting, with the identification of such forgone opportunities depending on objective analysis of the parties' "[e]xpectations [as they] may be inferred from the express contract terms in light of the ordinary course of business and customary practice...." Burton, 94 Harv. L. Rev. at 389. Hence, if an objective basis exists to infer that the parties never bargained away the right of either of them to condition any distribution on completing the arbitration of any disputes, then Genicom cannot be guilty of bad faith by so insisting, whatever its subjective motive may be. We infer that the opportunity for such insistence never was bargained away.

Although the contract documents do not concisely state there will be no interim distribution, the texts come very close to such a provision. We have previously quoted the language of the escrow agreement that "[i]n accordance with Section 2.07 of the Purchase Agreement," the escrow agent shall hold the fund until instructed by the buyer's and seller's counsel to make a distribution. Section 2.07 was also quoted above. Its topic heading is "Final Payment of Purchase Price," and it provides that final payment and settlement shall be made within ten days of the final determination of net book value and purchase price, which will presumably be at the close of arbitration. "Final Payment ... " is apparently so called to distinguish it from the "Payment to Sellers on Closing Date," required by § 2.03 of the agreement, since there is no other provision calling for any payment or distribution. The text thus supports the claim that the parties intended the escrow agent to leave the fund intact until the point of the final payment, if any, that would be due to Centronics ten days after the final price determination.

This reading is confirmed by an understanding of the evident business purposes to be served by such a restriction on pay-out. We explained above that the original escrow of $5,000,000 was to be increased by Genicom's deposit of an Adjustment Amount, which in effect was equal to the amount of Centronics's proposed revision of the final purchase price in excess of the preliminary purchase price. Although Centronics was obligated to follow accepted accounting procedures when it revised the balance sheet to calculate any adjustment, the revision was to be unaudited and Genicom had no control over the setting of this amount.

Genicom, however, was not left entirely subject to Centronics's natural temptation to state a higher, rather than a lower, Adjustment Amount. It is reasonable to suppose each party appreciated that the extent of disagreement and the resulting duration of arbitration would be roughly proportional to the size of the Adjustment Amount. If Centronics had to wait upon the outcome of arbitration before it received any escrowed funds, then Genicom would be able to rely on Centronics's own self-interest to limit the probable length of arbitration by limiting the amount of the adjustment potentially subject to arbitration.

It is also reasonable to assume that neither party expected the other to emerge from arbitration with the whole escrow fund. Each therefore had reason to seek some mechanism for inducing the other side to promote speedy arbitration and the prompt distribution of escrowed money. Such a mechanism would be provided by a scheme conditioning any distribution on completing arbitration, since each would thus be induced to hasten the process for their common benefit.

The probability is, therefore, that each party expected the escrow to remain intact throughout arbitration, as the reason for Genicom's agreement that Centronics would have discretion to state the amount of the adjustment, and as the inducement to a prompt effectuation of their common object of obtaining whatever would be due to each from the fund so escrowed. Whether, therefore, we rely on the analysis underlying our own prior cases, or on the rule as espoused by Burton, we affirm the trial judge's conclusion that Centronics is seeking a revision of the contract, not the enforcement of good faith in its performance.

Affirmed.

Notes and Discussion

1. ***Summers v. Burton.*** Judge Souter (writing before his elevation) describes two main theories of "good faith." The first is that of Robert Summers, who argues that good faith is not a unified concept, but rather a

covering word for the absence of a number of forms of bad faith. In his article he lists some specific forms of bad faith: evading the spirit of the bargain; failing to be sufficiently diligent; willfully shirking obligations; abusing the power to specify terms; abusing the power to determine compliance; and interfering with the other party's performance. Robert S. Summers, *"Good Faith" in General Contract Law and the Sales Provisions of the Uniform Commercial Code*, 54 Va. L. Rev. 195, 200–207 (1968).

Steven Burton, by contrast, attempts to identify a unified theory of good faith. He concentrates on discouraging (as the Court phrases it) "the exercise of discretion for the purpose of recapturing opportunities forgone or bargained away at the time of contracting." Steven J. Burton, *Breach of Contract and the Common Law Duty to Perform in Good Faith*, 94 Harv. L. Rev. 369 (1980). (Beware! The rule promises more than it delivers. In a given case, what has been "forgone" or "bargained away" will be hotly debated.)

Judge Souter argues that New Hampshire precedents are more in accord with Summers' view, but that Genicom would also prevail under Burton's conception. Examine the case carefully and see whether you agree. The dispute has continued, but Burton claims victory: "It can safely be said that the common law of good faith in contract performance now is focused on the obligations of a discretion-exercising party, consistent with the early history of the doctrine." S. Burton and E. Andersen, Contractual Good Faith 39 (1995) (citing *Centronics* among other cases). This book is in any case a good summary of the issues at stake.

2. Discretion. "[D]iscretion in contract performance arises in two ways. The parties may find it to their mutual advantage at formation to defer decision on a particular term and to confer decisionmaking authority on one of them as to that term. Thus, one party may be entitled to set terms of quantity, quality, price, or time to control the occurrence of a contractual condition. Discretion also may arise, with similar effect as things turn out, from a lack of clarity or an omission in the express contract. In either case, one party may be in control of its own or the other party's obligation under the contract. Since the agreed terms are indeterminate, the dependent party must rely on the good faith of the party in control. The law then *implies* an obligation of good faith in contract performance." S. Burton and E. Andersen, Contractual Good Faith 46 (1995). Apply this passage to *Centronics.*

3. Centronics' Position. While arbitration continued, the escrow fund forced Centronics to tie up almost $6 million that was not in dispute. This was a considerable hardship. It seems evident that Genicom could have acquiesced in the release of this sum, and this might well have been the "friendly" thing to do; and the Court also concedes that the parties had contemplated a relatively brief arbitration process. On the other hand, the contract did not expressly oblige Genicom to make a partial disbursal of funds from escrow.

Granted this position, why does Judge Souter come to the view that a generalized obligation of "good faith" cannot serve as a legal basis for requiring Genicom to release the money? Quite apart from the academic dispute between Summers and Burton, what can be said on either side of this argument? Do you agree with the outcome in this case? Should it make any difference if Centronics is right in alleging that "Genicom's refusal was meant to pressure Centronics into conceding a disputed item worth a substantial amount"? How much depends on the Court's finding of no evidence that "either party [was] dragging its heels in the conduct of the arbitration"?

4. Restatement 2d § 205. "Every contract imposes upon each party a duty of good faith and fair dealing in its performance and its enforcement." Comment a. glosses: "The phrase 'good faith' is used in a variety of contexts, and its meaning varies somewhat with the context. Good faith performance or enforcement of a contract emphasizes faithfulness to an agreed common purpose and consistency with the justified expectations of the other party; it excludes a variety of types of conduct characterized as involving 'bad faith' because they violate community standards of decency." Does this sound like Summers or Burton or both or neither?

Illustration 2, based on *Daitch Crystal Dairies, Inc. v. Neisloss*, 8 A.D.2d 965, 190 N.Y.S.2d 737 (App. Div. 1959), sets the following situation: "A, owner of a shopping center, leases part of it to B, giving B the exclusive right to conduct a supermarket, the rent to be a percentage of B's gross receipts. During the term of the lease A acquires adjoining land, expands the shopping center, and leases part of the adjoining land to C for a competing supermarket." What outcome?

5. European Codes. The CISG contains no clause requiring good faith in the international sale of goods by merchants, but most European codes have clauses closely similar to § 205. Their fate has varied depending on the willingness of judges to treat them expansively. The French Civil Code art. 1134 ("Legally formed agreements ... must be executed in good faith.") is invoked fairly rarely, perhaps because "French courts ... are reluctant to set loose such a wide-ranging principle." Barry Nicholas, The French Law of Contract 154 (2nd ed. 1992) (footnote omitted). By contrast, the German Civil Code § 242 ("The debtor is obliged to perform in such a manner as good faith requires, regard being paid to general practice.") has become, in the hands of German judges, "a 'super control norm' for the whole [Civil Code], and indeed for large parts of German law outside it." Norbert Horn et al., German Private and Commercial Law: An Introduction 135 (Tony Weir trans., 1982). This should suggest another dimension of analysis for cases like *Centronics*.

SHELL OIL CO. v. HRN, INC.

Supreme Court of Texas, 2004.
144 S.W.3d 429.

PHILLIPS, C.J. In this case, we must decide whether the price fixed by a refiner for the sale of its gasoline under an open-price-term contract with its dealers was in good faith as required by section 2.305(b) of the Texas Business and Commerce Code. The dealers claim that the refiner's pricing practices are forcing them out of business and therefore are not in good faith. The trial court concluded that the refiner had established its good faith as a matter of law, but the court of appeals reversed the summary judgment, concluding that circumstantial evidence raised a fact issue about the refiner's good faith. 102 S.W.3d 205. Although the refiner's price was commercially reasonable when compared to the prices of other refiners in the relevant market, the court found some evidence in the record to suggest that the refiner's price might have been influenced by improper subjective motives such as the desire to force some of its dealers out of business. Because we conclude that the refiner established as a matter of law that its price was fixed in good faith as defined in the Code, we reverse the judgment of the court of appeals and render judgment that plaintiffs take nothing.

I.

Plaintiffs are several hundred lessee dealers in seventeen different states who lease service stations and buy gasoline from Shell, operating those stations as independent businesses. Each dealer and Shell enter into two agreements: a Lease and a Dealer Agreement. Shell's relationship with its lessee dealers is also governed by the federal Petroleum Marketing Practices Act ("PMPA"), which regulates the grounds for termination and nonrenewal of petroleum franchise relationships. 15 U.S.C. §§ 2801–2806.

In the Dealer Agreement, each dealer agrees to buy Shell-branded gasoline from Shell at the "dealer prices ... in effect" at the time of purchase. Shell's price to its dealers is referred to as the DTW ("dealer tank wagon") price because it includes delivery to the dealer's station by a Shell tanker truck. The DTW pricing provision is an "open price term" governed by section 2.305(b) of the Texas Business and Commerce Code (which corresponds to section 2–305(2) of the Uniform Commercial Code). Open-price-term contracts are commonly used in the gasoline refining and marketing industry due to price volatility.

Shell markets gasoline to the public through a retail network that includes not only lessee dealers, but open dealers and company-operated stations as well. First, Shell acts as a franchisor, leasing service stations to franchisees such as the Dealers here that sell Shell-branded gasoline. Second, Shell sells Shell-branded gasoline directly to the public through company-operated stations. Finally, Shell sells branded and unbranded gasoline to jobbers. Some jobbers are wholesale distributors, selling Shell-branded and unbranded gasoline to stations operated by independent business owners. Other jobbers are also independent retail dealers, selling Shell-branded and unbranded gasoline directly to the public.

Jobbers operate fleets of trucks to pick up gasoline at refiners' terminals and distribute it to their own stations or to independent ones. Jobbers may have distribution agreements with several refiners simultaneously. Jobbers pay a "rack" price that is available for gasoline bought and picked up at Shell's terminals. The DTW price is typically higher than the rack price, although Shell does not set either price in relation to the other.

Shell's agreements with the Dealers prohibit them from selling any gasoline except Shell-branded gasoline. Although the contracts with the Dealers do not require them to buy Shell gasoline exclusively from Shell itself, agreements between Shell and its jobbers effectively eliminate the only major alternative source for Shell-branded gasoline. When a jobber sells gasoline to a Dealer, the jobber is retroactively charged the DTW price for that product, not the lower rack price it otherwise would pay.

The Dealers claim that Shell's pricing practices are forcing them out of business. Although Shell has the right under the Dealer Agreement to fix the DTW price at which the Dealers must buy its gasoline, all parties agree that it must exercise this right in good faith. See Tex. Bus. & Com. Code § 2.305(b). Dealers claim that Shell's DTW prices cannot be set in good faith because they are so high that they put Dealers at a competitive disadvantage. Dealers further assert that Shell's DTW pricing is part of a plan to replace them with company-operated outlets which are more profitable for Shell.

Shell moved for summary judgment on Dealers' good-faith pricing claims, contending that it was entitled to judgment as a matter of law because it charged a posted price applied uniformly to all Dealers and was a commercially reasonable price as well. Rather than contest the commercial reasonableness of Shell's DTW prices, Dealers argued that fact issues existed as to whether Shell had acted in bad faith by setting its DTW price with the subjectively improper motive of running Dealers out of business.

The trial court granted Shell's motion for summary judgment. The court of appeals reversed and remanded the case for trial, concluding that the Dealers had raised fact issues about Shell's subjective good faith when setting its DTW price. 102 S.W.3d 205.

II.

Most contracts for the sale of goods specify a price, but some do not because either the parties fail to consider the issue directly or purposefully leave it for later determination. When a contract for the sale of goods does not specify a price, section 2.305 of the Uniform Commercial Code supplies default rules for determining whether a contract exists and what the price should be. This section is one of a series of provisions in Article 2 of the Code that fill common "gaps" in commercial contracts.

In this instance, the Code imposes on Shell the obligation of good faith when fixing its DTW price under the Dealer Agreement, providing that "[a] price to be fixed by the seller or by the buyer means a price for him to fix in good faith." Tex. Bus. & Com. Code § 2.305(b). Good faith is defined elsewhere in the Code to mean "honesty in fact and the observance of reasonable commercial standards of fair dealing." Id. § 1.201(b)(20).[13] Official Comment 3 to section 2.305(b) further elaborates on the good faith requirement, creating a presumption in the

13. This definition was formerly limited to merchants, like Shell, but recent amendments to the Code have "brought the Article 2 merchant concept of good faith (subjective honesty and objective commercial reasonableness) into other Articles." See Tex. Bus. & Com. Code § 1.201(b)(20) cmt. 20.

normal case that a seller's posted price or price in effect is also a good faith price:

> 3. Subsection [b], dealing with the situation where the price is to be fixed by one party rejects the uncommercial idea that an agreement that the seller may fix the price means that he may fix any price he may wish by the express qualification that the price so fixed must be fixed in good faith. Good faith includes observance of reasonable commercial standards of fair dealing in the trade if the party is a merchant. (Section 2–103). But in the normal case a "posted price" or a future seller's or buyer's "given price," "price in effect," "market price," or the like satisfies the good faith requirement.

Tex. Bus. & Com. Code § 2.305 cmt. 3 (emphasis added). Despite this definition and comment, or perhaps because of them, Shell and the Dealers urge conflicting ideas about what good faith should mean in this case.

Shell argues that a good faith price, as section 2.305(b) requires, is one that is commercially reasonable and non-discriminatory. Because its DTW price fell within the range of DTW prices charged by other refiners in the relevant geographic markets (was commercially reasonable) and was applied uniformly among similarly-situated dealers (was non-discriminatory), Shell submits that summary judgment was appropriate. According to Shell, the chief concern of the drafters in adopting section 2.305(b) was to prevent suppliers from charging two buyers with identical pricing provisions different prices for arbitrary or discriminatory reasons. The drafters, however, also wished to minimize judicial intrusion into the setting of prices under open-price-term contracts. To balance these concerns, the drafters created a presumption under Official Comment 3 that a "posted price" or "price in effect" is a good faith price that may be rebutted only by evidence of discrimination. Shell asserts that because the Dealers brought forth no such evidence here, this is a normal case where the posted price or a price in effect is a good faith price under section 2.305.

The Dealers respond that Shell's concept of good faith and the "normal case" under section 2.305 is too narrow. They reject the notion that discriminatory pricing is the only way to rebut Comment 3's posted price presumption. Instead, the Dealers submit that the definition of good faith incorporates two elements: a subjective element, "honesty in fact," and an objective element, "the observance of reasonable commercial standards of fair dealing." See Tex. Bus. & Com. Code § 1.201(b)(20). They conclude that both elements must be satisfied before a case is considered normal and before the posted price presumption can apply.

III.

The Dealers rely extensively on the Fifth Circuit Court of Appeals' recent decision in *Mathis v. Exxon Corp.*, 302 F.3d 448 (5th Cir. 2002), which also involved open-price contracts between an oil refiner and its dealer/franchisees. Those dealers similarly complained that the refiner had breached its duty of good faith by purposefully setting its dealer price for gasoline at uncompetitively high levels to run them out of business. The *Mathis* court identified the central issue to be whether good faith required observance of both subjective and objective good faith in light of the apparent "safe harbor" described in Official Comment 3. Id. at 454–55. The refiner contended that a price fixed according to an established price schedule was within the safe harbor described in Comment 3. The court reasoned, however, that this safe harbor was not absolute because it applied only to "normal cases," or those cases in which an open price term was set with subjective good faith. Thus, the court placed the following limitation on Comment 3's safe harbor: "[Comment 3] avoids challenges to prices set according to an open price term unless that challenge is outside the normal type of case. Although price discrimination was the type of aberrant case on the minds of the drafters, price discrimination is merely a subset of what constitutes such an aberrant case. Any lack of subjective, honesty-in-fact good faith is abnormal; price discrimination is only the most obvious way a price-setter acts in bad faith B by treating similarly-situated buyers differently." Id. at 457. In support of its interpretation, the court cited *Nanakuli Paving & Rock Co. v. Shell Oil Co.*, 664 F.2d 772, 806 (9th Cir. 1981), and *Allapattah Serv., Inc v. Exxon Corp.*, 61 F. Supp. 2d 1308, 1322 (S.D. Fla. 1999), aff'd, 333 F.3d 1248 (11th Cir. 2003).

The court of appeals in this case adopted the reasoning in *Mathis*, concluding that good faith under section 2.305 encompasses both subjective and objective elements. 102 S.W.3d at 214. Although a commercially reasonable price might establish the oil company's objective good faith, it would not alone be sufficient if there were also evidence that the company's price might have been influenced by its desire to replace franchisees with more profitable company-owned stores (a lack of subjective good faith). Id. at 214–15. Because the court concluded that the Dealers had presented sufficient circumstantial evidence on Shell's subjective intent to drive them out of business, it reversed the summary judgment. Id. at 215.

IV.

Most courts have rejected the approach of the Fifth Circuit and the court below in interpreting the good faith requirement of section 2.305. Instead, the majority of decisions suggest that a commercially reasonable DTW price, that is, one within the range of DTW prices charged by other refiners in the market, is a good faith price under section 2.305 absent some evidence that the refiner used pricing to discriminate among its purchasers. See, e.g., ... *Wayman v. Amoco Oil Co.*, 923 F. Supp. 1322, 1332 (D. Kan. 1996) aff'd mem., 145 F.3d 1347 (10th Cir. 1998); ... As the court in *Wayman* observed, "[i]t is abundantly clear ... that the chief concern of the UCC Drafting Committee in adopting § 2–305(2) was to prevent discriminatory pricing—i.e., to prevent suppliers from charging two buyers with identical pricing provisions in their respective contracts different prices for arbitrary or discriminatory reasons." *Wayman*, 923 F. Supp. at 1346–47.

The Dealers themselves concede that Shell is not obligated to price its gasoline with their interests in mind or to protect them from competition. They further explain that their theory in this case does not turn on the DTW price set by Shell but rather on the reason why Shell chose to charge that price. Likewise, the court of appeals concludes that this is not the normal case because the price, although commercially in line with that charged by other refiners to their lessee dealers, may have been motivated by an improper underlying purpose to eliminate some dealerships.

It is not apparent, however, why the intent behind a commercially reasonable, non-discriminatory price should matter for purposes of a breach of contract claim under section 2.305(b). Dealers do not contend that they are entitled to any particular price and do not disagree that Shell's DTW price is within the range charged by other refiners to their dealers. Thus, if these Dealers were charged the same DTW price by another refiner who did not have a similar plan to thin their ranks, presumably the price would pass muster under the Dealers' view of section 2.305. Premising a breach of contract claim solely on assumed subjective motives injects uncertainty into the law of contracts and undermines one of the UCC's primary goal—to "promot[e] certainty and predictability in commercial transactions." *Am. Airlines Employees Fed. Credit Union v. Martin*, 29 S.W.3d 86, 92 (Tex. 2000).

Beyond prohibiting discriminatory pricing, the drafters wished to minimize judicial intrusion into the setting of prices under open-price-term contracts. They understood that requiring sellers in open-price industries, such as the oil and gas industry, to justify the reasonableness their prices in order to satisfy section 2.305 would "mean[] that in every case the seller is going to be in a lawsuit" and that every sales contract would become "a public utility rate case." Walter D. Malcolm, *The Proposed Commercial Code: A Report on Developments from May 1950 through February 1951*, 6 Bus. Law. 113, 186 (1951). The drafters reasonably foresaw that almost any price could be attacked unless it benefitted from a strong presumption. Thus, they adopted a safe harbor, Comment 3's posted price presumption, to preserve the practice of using "sellers' standard prices" while seeking "to avoid discriminatory prices." Id.; see also Tex. Bus. & Comm. Code § 2.305 cmt. 3.

The reasoning in *Mathis* and the court of appeals in this case negates the effect of Comment 3's "safe harbor" by concluding that circumstantial evidence of "[a]ny lack of subjective, honesty-in-fact good faith" is sufficient to create an "abnormal" case in which the posted-price presumption no longer applies. See *Mathis*, 302 F.3d at 457. The effect is to allow a jury to determine in every section 2.305(b) case whether there was any "improper motive animating the price-setter," even if the prices ultimately charged were undisputedly within the range of those charged throughout the industry. Id. at 454. This result appears to conflict with the drafters' desire to eliminate litigation over prices that are nondiscriminatory and set in accordance with industry standards. Although the subjective element of good faith may have a place elsewhere in the Code, see, e.g., *La Sara Grain Co. v. First Nat'l Bank*, 673 S.W.2d 558, 562–63 (Tex. 1984) (applying subjective good faith to a negotiable instrument), we do not believe this subjective element was intended to stand alone as a basis for a claim of bad faith under section 2.305. Rather we conclude that allegations of dishonesty under this section must also have some basis in objective fact which at a minimum requires some connection to the commercial realities of the case. See 2 James J. White & Robert S. Summers, Uniform Commercial Code § 17.6 at 167 (4th ed. 1995) (noting that "the subjective rule never prevailed in Article 2 with respect to merchants" and that in "various other articles of the Code there has been a movement from subjective to objective definitions of good faith").

The two cases relied on by *Mathis* appear to make a similar connection. In *Nanakuli*, a buyer of asphalt under an open-price-term contract asserted that the seller had breached its section 2.305 duty of good faith by failing to follow industry custom when changing its price. 664 F.2d at 778. The buyer established that by trade custom and usage the sellers of asphalt on the island of Oahu, Hawaii price protected their buyers by providing notice of price increases and an opportunity for the buyer to complete projects bid under the old price. The seller, however, abandoned this practice, raising the price without notice. The buyer complained that the price increase was not in good faith because the seller had not observed "reasonable commercial standards of fair dealing in the trade." *Nanakuli*, 664 F.2d at 805. Disregarding the posted-price presumption, the court concluded that this was not a normal case because the dispute was "not over the amount of the increase—that is, the price that the seller fixed—but over the manner in which that increase was put into effect." Id. The price increase failed to conform to commercially reasonable standards both in "the timing of the announcement and [the seller's] refusal to protect work already bid at the old price." Id. at 806.

In *Allapattah*, another case involving a refiner and its dealer network, the dispute concerned the calculation of a discount that was to be applied to the refiner's posted price. *Allapattah*, 61 F. Supp. 2d at 1312–13. The refiner implemented a discount for cash program to offset the costs of credit card processing which the dealers alleged resulted in their being charged twice for the cost of credit. The court concluded that these allegations were not the normal case contemplated under section 2.305 if there was evidence that the refiner double charged to recover its costs of credit while representing to its buyers that its price was net of credit costs. Id. at 1322. The posted-price presumption did not apply, according to the court, because the dispute was not about price but rather the "manner in which the wholesale price was calculated without considering the doubled charge for credit card processing." Id.

Both of these cases recognize that a price, commercially reasonable on its face, may nevertheless be applied in a dishonest fashion. But in both of these cases, the allegation of bad faith resulted in a commercial injury distinct from the price increase itself. Here the Dealers' claim of bad faith appears to be inextricably tied to the amount of the price set by Shell. We agree with those decisions that have upheld the posted price presumption against similar attacks. Applying that presumption, these courts have generally rendered judgment as a matter of law on similar claims under section 2–305 where the refiner used a posted price which it fairly applied to similarly-situated purchasers. See, e.g., ... *Wayman*, 923 F. Supp. at 1332; ...

V.

The Dealers maintain, however, that even though Shell used a posted price it nevertheless violated its duty of good faith by setting its DTW price too high with the conscious intention of driving some of its franchisees out of business. And the court of appeals agreed that there was enough circumstantial evidence to raise a fact issue about Shell's subjective motives and therefore its good faith. According to the court, this evidence generally included: (1) the DTW price itself, which was on the high end of the wholesale pricing spectrum, (2) the "captive" nature of relationship between Shell and its franchisees, and (3) the general decline in the business fortunes of Shell franchisees. 102 S.W.3d at 214–15.

Shell argues that these circumstantial factors are either irrelevant, unrelated to Shell's pricing, or unsupported by the record. Shell submits that there is no evidence that its DTW price caused any particular Dealer to fail or be uncompetitive in the market. And even if there were evidence of this, Shell submits it would not raise a fact issue about its good faith because section 2.305 does not require a competitive price or the lowest price available. Moreover, Shell argues that the fact that some franchisees have experienced declining sales, lost money, or gone out of business does not raise a fact issue about whether Shell had a bad-faith plan to price them out of business. Instead, Shell suggests that market forces beyond its control are at the root of these problems. Shell points out that the Dealers' own expert agreed that the lessee dealer is "a class of trade whose economic viability is dying" due to broader market forces, including the entry of mass merchandisers into gasoline retailing.

We agree with Shell that the court of appeals' list of circumstantial factors are not evidence that Shell lacked good faith when fixing its DTW price. The DTW price, the captive nature of the franchisee relationship, and the business losses suffered by the Dealers are variations of the same theme: Shell's DTW price is too high for the Dealers to compete with other gasoline retailers. But good faith under section 2.305(b) does not mandate a competitive price for each individual Dealer, nor could it. The competitive circumstances of each Dealer in the same pricing zone may vary from station to station, and yet Shell must treat them all the same.

The court of appeals, however, suggests that because the Dealers paid more than most of the other gasoline retailers in Houston, the DTW price itself is some evidence of Shell's subjective bad faith. 102 S.W.3d at 214 ("73-80% of [the Dealers'] Houston competition paid rack price—or lower—for gas. . . ."). We cannot agree that a relatively high, yet commercially reasonable, price is evidence of bad faith. A good-faith price under section 2.305 is not synonymous with a fair market price or the lowest price available. *TCP Indus., Inc. v. Uniroyal, Inc.*, 661 F.2d 542, 548 (6th Cir. 1981); *Harvey v. Fearless Farris Wholesale, Inc.*, 589 F.2d 451, 461 (9th Cir. 1979); see also 1 James J. White & Robert S. Summers, Uniform Commercial Code § 3–8, at 150 (4th ed. 1995) ("Note that the section says 'a reasonable price' and not 'fair market value of the goods.' These two would not be identical.").

Each Dealer contractually agreed to buy gasoline at the DTW price applicable only to Shell-branded lessee-dealers. The court of appeals' wholesale cost analysis indiscriminately compares Shell's DTW price to prices available to other classes of trade, with different contractual buying arrangements. Included in the comparison are branded and unbranded jobbers who pick up their gasoline at terminals, open dealers who own their own premises, and company-owned stores operated by other refiners. Evidence that different prices are available to different classes of trade is not evidence of bad faith under section 2.305. See *Ajir v. Exxon Corp.*, No. C 93–20830, 1995 WL 261412, at *4 (N.D. Cal. May 2, 1995) ("The existence of different prices for different classes of trade is not sufficient to demonstrate that [a refiner] is overcharging plaintiffs for gasoline."), aff'd, 185 F.3d 865 (table), 1999 WL 393666 (9th Cir. 1999); *Exxon Corp. v. Superior Court of Santa Clara County*, 60 Cal. Rptr. 2d 195, 205 (Cal. Ct. App. 1997) (same).

Moreover, the court's description of the Dealers as " 'captive buyers' required to purchase Shell-branded gas at Shell's price" is not evidence of bad faith or an abnormal case within the meaning of Comment 3. 102 S.W.3d at 214. Dealers are only "captive" as a result of their own choice to become Shell-branded lessee dealers, which involved their agreement to buy gasoline from Shell at the DTW price, rather than at rack or some other price. That is the nature of a long-term franchise. Such "captivity" is therefore the "normal" case.

Because the summary judgment evidence establishes that Shell's posted price was both commercially reasonable and fairly applied to the Dealers, we reverse the judgment of the court of appeals and render judgment that the plaintiffs take nothing.

Notes and Discussion

1. Good Faith in the UCC. This case depends in part on the UCC definition of good faith where recent revisions (not yet generally adopted in American jurisdictions) may possibly affect the law. Under the previous statutory standard, § 1–201(19) states that: " 'Good faith' means honesty in fact in the conduct or transaction concerned," while § 2–103(1)(b) states:

" 'Good faith' in the case of a merchant means honesty in fact and the observance of reasonable commercial standards." These two provisions appear to establish higher standards of good faith for merchants. What is this difference?

Revised Article 1 replaces both these sections with § 1–201(20): " 'Good faith,' except as otherwise provided in Article 5, means honesty in fact and the observance of reasonable commercial standards of fair dealing." In light of this change, § 2–103(1)(b) has been removed. Thereby the double standard is eliminated. Why was this change made?

Parties have a general duty to perform and enforce contracts in accord with good faith under § 1–203 (substantially identical to § 1–304 in the revised version). Contractual parties cannot disclaim UCC-based obligations of good faith, diligence, reasonableness, and care, but they "may by agreement determine the standards by which the performance of such obligations is to be measured if such standards are not manifestly unreasonable": § 1–102(3) (cf. § 1–302(b) revised). The good faith standard is also used in many other UCC sections, including § 2–305(2) which is discussed in this case.

2. Violating Good Faith. In rejecting summary judgment in favor of Shell, the Texas Court of Appeals determined that: "Although the refiner's price was commercially reasonable when compared to the prices of other refiners in the relevant market, ... some evidence in the record ... suggest[ed] that the refiner's price might have been influenced by improper subjective motives such as the desire to force some of its dealers out of business."

Suppose (purely hypothetically) that plaintiff dealers had obtained internal company documents indicating that Shell researchers have determined that, in the long-term, franchising is economically unviable in the Houston area. Accordingly, the company has revised its business strategy so as to keep its gasoline prices to dealers at the high end of the current price range, even though it is clear that many dealerships will be driven out of business as a result; Shell's business strategy is to move away from franchise dealerships. Why might the plaintiffs believe that documents of this type were relevant, under the UCC, in proving Shell's lack of good faith?

How does the Texas Supreme Court differ from the Court of Appeals (along the Fifth Circuit in the *Mathis* decision, on almost identical facts) in assessing what Shell can legitimately do within the UCC? Which interpretation of the UCC provisions seems to you more plausible? Look closely at the text of § 2–305 and its comments. Why might Shell have believed that so long as its pricing policy remained within market parameters, the UCC afforded it a "safe harbor" from complaints about lack of good faith?

Problem 4–3

As a result of sharply increasing gasoline prices, American Bakeries entered into a contract with Empire Gas whereby American Bakeries would purchase propane conversion units from Empire Gas and then purchase propane on an exclusive basis from Empire Gas for a period of eight years. The contract contained an estimate of the number of vehicles involved, "more or less depending upon requirements" of American Bakeries. Ultimately, however, American Bakeries decided not to convert its trucks and never ordered any conversion units or propane from Empire Gas, which has now sued for damages.

Look closely at the text of UCC § 2–306(1), on output and requirements contracts, and also at Official Comments 2 and 3. How clear is the distinction between "such actual ... requirements as may occur in good faith" and a "quantity unreasonably disproportionate to any stated estimate"? Can American Bakeries escape from the argument that the purchase of *no* conversion units is perforce "disproportionate to [the] stated estimate"? How can American Bakeries meet the burden of proof placed on it under § 2–306(1)? American Bakeries would prefer, of course, to provide no explanation for its decision not to convert its fleet. Would it meet its burden if it could show that it had obtained conversion units more cheaply elsewhere? That it had decided it was not in fact economical to convert its fleet to propane? That a new report from OSHA had documented the danger of propane-fueled vehicles? That after a management shake-up it had decided to eliminate its delivery fleet and lease vehicles from a third party?

In *Empire Gas Corp. v. American Bakeries Co.*, 840 F.2d 1333, 1340–1341 (7th Cir. 1988), Judge Posner, in affirming a decision for Empire Gas, held that: "The essential ingredient of good faith in the case of the buyer's reducing his estimated requirements is that he not merely have had second thoughts about the terms of the contract and want to get out of it.... Whether the buyer has any greater obligation is unclear, ... but need not be decided here. Once it is decided (as we have) that a buyer cannot arbitrarily declare his requirements to be zero, this becomes an easy case, because American Bakeries has never given any reason for its change of heart." See also, e.g., *Orange & Rockland Utilities v. Amerada Hess Corp.*, 59 A.D.2d 110, 397 N.Y.S.2d 814 (App. Div. 1977), and *Brewster of Lynchburg, Inc. v. Dial Corp.*, 33 F.3d 355 (4th Cir. 1994). How helpful in fact is the concept of good faith in solving a case such as *Empire Gas*?

DONAHUE v. FEDERAL EXPRESS CORP.

Superior Court of Pennsylvania, 2000.
753 A.2d 238.

LALLY–GREEN, J.: In this employment case, Appellant Brion O. Donahue appeals from the order dated April 29, 1999, granting preliminary objections in the nature of a demurrer filed by Defendants/Appellees Federal Express Corporation ("FedEx") and Robert W. Marshall and entering judgment in Appellees' favor. We affirm.

On January 22, 1999, Appellant filed a complaint against FedEx and Marshall, alleging the following. Appellant was a FedEx employee from November 1979 until January 1997.[14] Appellant's final position was Commercial MX Service Administrator. Marshall was Appellant's immediate supervisor.

14. [Eds.: We have omitted many page references to the parties' briefs and complaints.]

Appellant questioned numerous invoices which did not comport with repair orders in his department. Appellant also called FedEx's attention to other improprieties, such as FedEx's failure to pay invoices and Marshall's practice of directing auto body work to a Cleveland auto body shop owned by a person with whom Marshall vacationed. After Appellant complained to Marshall about the invoice-discrepancy issue, Marshall accused Appellant of gross misconduct. Specifically, Appellant was accused of making a racial remark in front of another FedEx employee, and was accused of making derogatory remarks about Marshall to vendors and others. In the months leading to his discharge, FedEx management denied Appellant the clerical assistance that he requested, gave Appellant additional duties of tire purchasing and file maintenance, and ordered Appellant to falsify data to meet administrative requirements.

FedEx has a Guaranteed Fair Treatment Procedure ("GFTP") for employee grievances. Appellant appealed his termination through Step 1 of the GFTP. FedEx management upheld the termination, concluding that Appellant violated FedEx's Acceptable Conduct Policy. Appellant appealed through Step 2 of the GFTP, alleging that Marshall was seeking retribution for exposing the vendor non-payment issue.

FedEx management again upheld the termination. Finally, Appellant appealed through Step 3 of the GFTP, alleging that FedEx accused him of making unprofessional remarks, "but did not identify the purported comments, nor give [Appellant] the opportunity to deny the same." Again, FedEx management upheld the termination.

In Count 1 of his complaint, labeled "Wrongful Termination," Appellant alleges: (1) FedEx breached the implied covenant of good faith and fair dealing in at-will employment contracts; (2) FedEx violated public policy insofar as the termination violates the Pennsylvania Human Relations Act ("PHRA"), 43 P.S. § 951 et seq.; (3) Appellant supplied sufficient additional consideration to remove his status from that of an at-will employee; and (4) FedEx violated public policy by retaliating against him for lodging complaints against Marshall. [Eds.: On appeal, Donahue did not challenge dismissal of his other counts.]

On March 17, 1999, FedEx and Marshall filed preliminary objections in the nature of a demurrer. Appellant filed a responsive brief. On April 29, 1999, the esteemed trial court, the Honorable Eugene Strassburger, granted the preliminary objections and entered judgment in favor of FedEx and Marshall. This appeal followed.

Appellant raises four issues on appeal . . .

First, Appellant argues that the trial court erred by dismissing his claim for breach of the implied duty of good faith and fair dealing. Specifically, Appellant claims that FedEx breached this duty "by terminating him in contravention of its GFTP and engaging in a sham review of his conduct in the GFTP."

Every contract in Pennsylvania imposes on each party a duty of good faith and fair dealing in its performance and its enforcement. *Kaplan v. Cablevision of Pa., Inc.*, 448 Pa. Super. 306, 671 A.2d 716, 722 (Pa. Super. 1996), appeal denied, 546 Pa. 645, 683 A.2d 883 (1996), citing, *inter alia*, *Somers v. Somers*, 418 Pa. Super. 131, 613 A.2d 1211, 1213 (Pa. Super. 1992), appeal denied, 533 Pa. 652, 624 A.2d 111 (1993). Good faith has been defined as "honesty in fact in the conduct or transaction concerned." *Kaplan*, 671 A.2d at 722. Appellant relies on *Somers* for the proposition that the implied duty of good faith and fair dealing applies to at-will employment relationships.

In that case, plaintiff Somers entered into an at-will employment relationship (as a consultant) with a corporation. The consulting contract further provided that if net profits were realized from a particular project, Somers would receive 50% of the profits. *Somers*, 613 A.2d at 1212. In order for profits to be realized, it was necessary for the corporation to resolve a claim with a third party. Id. Somers and the corporation disagreed as to how to handle this claim; as a result, Somers was fired. Id. Moreover, Somers alleged that the corporation showed a lack of good faith and due diligence in resolving its dispute with the third party, and in settling the claim for significantly less than was owed, thereby depriving him of approximately $3 million as his share of the proceeds. Id. at 1215. The trial court dismissed Somers' claim for breach of the implied duty of good faith and fair dealing.

This Court reversed, stating that "the duty to perform contractual obligations in good faith does not evaporate merely because the contract is an employment contract, and the employee has been held to be an employee at will." Id. at 1213, citing *Baker v. Lafayette College*, 350 Pa. Super. 68, 504 A.2d 247 (Pa. Super. 1986), affirmed, 516 Pa. 291, 532 A.2d 399 (1987), and *Jacobs v. Kraft Cheese Co.*, 310 Pa. 75, 164 A. 774 (1933).[15] We concluded that Somers should have the opportunity to establish that the corporation acted in bad faith when it settled the claim in such a manner as to deprive him of his fair share of the profits related to the project. *Somers*, 613 A.2d at 1215.

Somers and the cases cited therein provide that, in an at-will employment relationship, the duty of good faith and fair dealing applies to those contractual terms that exist beyond the at-will employment relationship. For example, the plaintiff in *Somers* could recover for breach of implied duties connected to the profit sharing provision, but could not recover for the termination *per se*.

15. In *Jacobs*, plaintiff Jacobs approached Kraft with a new method for making cream cheese. Kraft hired Jacobs for a fixed term of 78 weeks. The employment contract expressly stated that Jacobs' employment was conditioned on his producing a cream cheese "satisfactory to the market," as measured by sales. After nine weeks, Kraft fired Jacobs, declaring that the cheese was unmarketable. Kraft had not attempted to market the product. A jury found in Jacobs' favor. Our Supreme Court affirmed the verdict, holding that, under the circumstances, Kraft had an implied duty to attempt to market the cheese before firing Jacobs.

Baker involved a two-year employment contract between a college and a professor. The college's faculty handbook, which was explicitly made part of the contract itself, obliged the college to conduct an honest and meaningful evaluation of the professor's performance before deciding whether or not to extend the contract beyond its original term. *Baker*, 504 A.2d at 255.

The Court affirmed the grant of summary judgment in favor of the college and held that the implied duty of good faith and fair dealing applied to this reevaluation provision.[16] Id. Thus, the college was contractually obligated "to render a sincere and substantial performance of these contractual undertakings, complying with the spirit as well as the letter of the contract." Id. The *Baker* Court stressed that its holding was narrowly tailored to the facts of that case: "We emphasize that our holding is a narrow one. This case does not present the more difficult issue whether an obligation of good faith and fair dealing should be implied into any employer-employee relationship, including at-will employment. Consequently, we do not decide that issue. We hold only that when an employer such as the College here expressly provides in an employment contract for a comprehensive evaluation and review process, we may look to the employer's good faith to determine whether the employer has in fact performed those contractual obligations." Id. In the years since *Baker* was decided, it appears that no Pennsylvania appellate court has held that an implied duty of good faith and fair dealing applies to termination of a pure at-will employment relationship. Indeed, our Supreme Court has held that "an at will employee has no cause of action against his employer for termination of the at-will relationship except where that termination threatens clear mandates of public policy." *Pipkin v. Pennsylvania State Police*, 548 Pa. 1, 5, 693 A.2d 190, 191 (1997).... In keeping with the above authority, we hold that Appellant cannot as a matter of law maintain an action for breach of the implied duty of good faith and fair dealing, insofar as the underlying claim is for termination of an at-will employment relationship.

Appellant suggests that he can maintain a cause of action for breach of the implied duty of good faith and fair dealing arising out of his claim that he was not treated fairly under the GFTP. If the GFTP were expressly incorporated into Appellant's employment contract, his claim would be analogous to *Baker*, which held that such a claim is viable. Appellant's complaint, however, points to no specific provision of the GFTP indicating that its provisions imposed separate contractual duties on FedEx.[17] In fact, the GFTP expressly states that "the policies and

16. In *Baker*, the trial court had granted summary judgment to Lafayette College on Baker's breach of contract/bad faith claim. We affirmed, holding that the record contained no evidence tending to establish that the College's review procedures were a sham or otherwise undertaken in bad faith. *Baker*, 504 A.2d at 256. Our Supreme Court affirmed. *Baker*, 516 Pa. 291, 532 A.2d 399 (1987).

17. In this respect, Appellant's claim is more analogous to *Banas v. Matthews Int'l Corp.*, 348 Pa. Super. 464, 502 A.2d 637, 647–648 (Pa. Super. 1985) (*en banc*). In that case, Banas was fired for using company materials for personal projects without permission. Banas alleged that he had permis-

procedures set forth by the Company provide guidelines for management and other employees during employment but do not create contractual rights regarding termination or otherwise." Because Appellant has failed to allege facts indicating that the GFTP imposes any additional contractual duties on FedEx, Appellant's first claim lacks merit.

Appellant also argues that his termination violates public policy because he was fired for "blowing the whistle" on FedEx's failure to pay invoices and other unscrupulous practices. Generally, as noted above, no cause of action exists for termination of an at-will employment relationship unless the termination violates public policy. See *Pipkin,* supra. For example, "an employer (1) cannot require an employee to commit a crime, (2) cannot prevent an employee from complying with a statutorily imposed duty, and (3) cannot discharge an employee when specially prohibited from doing so by statute." *Spierling v. First Am. Home Health Servs, Inc.*, 1999 PA Super 222, 737 A.2d 1250, 1252 (Pa. Super. 1999), quoting *Hennessy v. Santiago*, 708 A.2d 1269, 1273 (Pa. Super. 1998). In an appropriate case, the courts may announce that a particular practice violates public policy, even in the absence of a legislative pronouncement to that effect. *Shick v. Shirey*, 552 Pa. 590, 602, 716 A.2d 1231, 1237 (1998). On the other hand, a court's power to announce public policy is limited: "public policy is to be ascertained by reference to the laws and legal precedents and not from general considerations of supposed public interest." Id. (citations omitted).

Our Courts have repeatedly rejected claims that a private employer violated public policy by firing an employee for whistleblowing, when the employee was under no legal duty to report the acts at issue. See *Geary v. United States Steel Corp.*, 456 Pa. 171, 183, 319 A.2d 174, 180 (1974) (no wrongful discharge claim where employee complained to superiors about substandard and potentially unsafe quality of employer's product); *Spierling*, 737 A.2d at 1254 (no wrongful discharge claim where employee was fired after searching discarded files for evidence of Medicare fraud and reporting such fraud to investigators); *Hennessy*, 708 A.2d at 1274 (no wrongful discharge claim where counselor alerted authorities to rape of one patient by another); . . .

Appellant contends that employees should not be fired from private companies for reporting unscrupulous practices.[18] Appellant has failed to identify any relevant statutes or legal precedents indicating that such retaliation violates public policy. Accordingly, Appellant's claim for wrongful discharge under the public policy exception cannot stand. . . .

Next, Appellant argues that he furnished sufficient additional consideration to overcome the presumption that he is an at-will employee.

sion, and pointed to sections of the employee handbook which stated that employees could use company materials for certain personal projects so long as they had permission. We found that the handbook was immaterial to the case, and that Banas could be fired at will regardless of the handbook because it did not create any contractual promise of job security.

18. Unlike Appellant, public employees are protected by Pennsylvania's Whistleblower Law. . . .

An employee can defeat the at-will presumption by establishing that he gave his employer additional consideration other than the services for which he was hired. *Cashdollar v. Mercy Hosp. of Pittsburgh*, 406 Pa. Super. 606, 595 A.2d 70, 72–73 (Pa. Super. 1991). Additional consideration exists "when an employee affords his employer a substantial benefit other than the services which the employee is hired to perform, or when the employee undergoes a substantial hardship other than the services which he is hired to perform." 595 A.2d at 73 (citation omitted). For example, in *Cashdollar*, we found sufficient additional consideration where the employee, in response to the employer's persistent recruitment efforts, gave up a stable position in another state, sold his house, and relocated to a new city with his pregnant wife, only to be fired after sixteen days on the job. Id. On the other hand, our Courts have found no additional consideration where the employee "has suffered detriments, in the course of his or her employment, that are 'commensurate with those incurred by all manner of salaried professionals.' " Id., citing *Veno v. Meredith*, 357 Pa. Super. 85, 515 A.2d 571, 580 (Pa. Super. 1986) (no additional consideration when employee was fired after eight years over a difference of opinion with his employer, even though employee had originally moved from Newark to Pennsylvania and had foregone other employment opportunities over the years), appeal denied, 532 Pa. 665, 616 A.2d 986 (1992).

Appellant argues that he gave additional consideration by conferring "substantial, superior job performance." A general allegation of superior work performance is insufficient to establish additional consideration. First, performing well on the job does not generally confer a substantial benefit on his employer beyond that which the employee is paid to do. Moreover, performing well on the job does not generally constitute a detriment beyond that which is incurred by all manner of salaried professionals. After reviewing Appellant's complaint as a whole, we conclude that Appellant has alleged no facts tending to establish that he conferred additional consideration. This claim fails. . . .

Order affirmed. McEwen, J.: Concurs in the Result.

Notes and Discussion

1. **Good Faith and At-Will Employment.** Re-read *Fisher v. Jackson* in Chapter 2, another at-will employment case. Employees like Brion Donahue, who are fired for what they consider to be improper reasons, have sought damages under many related theories, which are illustrated here. How did Donahue seek to use *Somers* to support his claim, and why does the court reject the *Somers* analogy?

2. **Whistle-Blowers and Public Policy.** Donahue believed that he had been fired in large part because he insisted on reporting a discrepancy in FedEx invoices. Most jurisdictions recognize a "public policy" exception to the usual rule on at-will contracts, but, as this case suggests, the exception is fairly narrow: there must be a public duty involved. A leading case is *Petermann v. International Brotherhood of Teamsters, Local 396*, 174 Cal.

App.2d 184, 344 P.2d 25 (1959), in which a fired at-will employee sued his employer, a labor union. His work had been judged "highly satisfactory," but he was fired after he was subpoenaed to testify before a California legislative committee; allegedly, the union told him to commit perjury, but he testified truthfully. The Court held that he was entitled to relief on the basis of "public policy," by which "is intended that principle of law which holds that no citizen can lawfully do that which has a tendency to be injurious to the public or against the public good." Id. at 27 (citations omitted). Another definition the Court suggests is that: "whatever contravenes good morals or any established interests of society is *against* public policy." Id. (emphasis added).

Such definitions may be too broad. For instance, in a recent Connecticut case, *Thibodeau v. Design Group One Architects, LLC*, 260 Conn. 691, 802 A.2d 731 (2002), a woman who became pregnant was fired from an architectural firm consisting of three principals and two employees. Connecticut statute forbade companies with three or more employees from discharging an employee who becomes pregnant. The Supreme Court overturned a Court of Appeals decision for the employee, arguing: "Although we acknowledge that there exists a general public policy in this state to eliminate all forms of invidious discrimination, including sex discrimination, we nevertheless disagree with the Appellate Court that the plaintiff therefore is entitled to maintain a discriminatory discharge claim against this defendant. Our disagreement arises from the fact that the exemption contained in the act for employers with fewer than three employees is, itself, an expression of public policy that cannot be separated from the policy reflected in the act's ban on discriminatory employment practices." Id. at 706.

When the circumstances are sufficiently severe, should there be a tort of wrongful discharge independent of stated public policy? See Lawrence E. Blades, *Employment at Will v. Individual Freedom: On Limiting the Abusive Exercise of Employer Power*, 67 Colum. L.Rev. 1404 (1967), arguing in favor of such a tort. What problems might a tort of this kind create?

Problem 4–4

In order to pay her college expenses, Olga Monge, a legal immigrant from Costa Rica, was working the night shift as an at-will employee in the Beebe Rubber Company. Allegedly, her foreman made repeated sexual advances, and he also treated her adversely when she refused. After a series of disputes, she was fired for failure to show up to work. Is it likely that she has any recourse? See *Monge v. Beebe Rubber Co.*, 114 N.H. 130, 316 A.2d 549 (1974), referred to also in the *Centronics*.

Problem 4–5

Twenty years ago Market Street Associates sold a small shopping center to General Electric Pension Trust under a "sale and leaseback" arrangement. Essentially, Market Street conveyed title to the Trust for four hundred thousand dollars, in exchange for cash and a long-term lease. Paragraph 34 in the contract provided that if in the future Market Street sought additional capital from the Trust and the Trust declined to make the loan, then Market Price would be entitled to buy back the property for the original price plus a modest annual adjustment to reflect inflation.

Today, the property is worth about $3 million dollars on the market, while the repurchase price, adjusted on the basis of Paragraph 34, is about $1 million. Market Street is now in need of several million dollars in additional capital and has applied to the Trust for a loan. The Trust has curtly rejected the application, but there is good reason to believe that its officers are unaware of the existence of Paragraph 34, much less of its implications.

You are a lawyer on retainer to Market Street, whose president has asked you whether Market Street, before it invokes its right to repurchase, has a legal or at least an ethical duty to inform the Trust about the consequences of its rejection in light of Paragraph 34. An Associate in your firm, fresh out of law school, suggests the following response: Market Street has no duty of any kind to inform the Trust about its own contractual rights, since the Trust, a sophisticated operation, is obliged to protect itself; so if its lawyers fail to read the contract, it has only itself to blame for the result. Should you adopt this response? If not, what advice would you give, and why?

Problems of this type are discussed in Melvin A. Eisenberg, *The Duty to Rescue in Contract Law*, 71 Fordham L. Rev. 647 (2002).

D. EXPRESS AND IMPLIED WARRANTIES

As a result of contacting an electrical wire, a boy named George Hawkins was afflicted with a severe scar on the palm of his right hand. Dr. Edward McGee undertook to cure the affliction through a skin graft. The operation, however, was a failure, and George's hand was left unuseable, covered by a matted, unsightly growth. A jury found that Dr. McGee had not been negligent, so tort liability was precluded. However, it also found that Dr. McGee had made an oral promise in approximately the following language: "I will guarantee to make the hand a hundred per cent perfect hand"; and these words were held to constitute a warranty giving rise to contractual liability if the promise was not carried out. In making a contract, Dr. McGee had promised not only to do the job and to do it in a skillful manner, but also to bring about a specific result; and since that result was not obtained, the doctor was liable. *Hawkins v. McGee*, 84 N.H. 114, 146 A. 641 (1929). Would the outcome have been similar if George's hand had been substantially improved, but had not become "a hundred per cent perfect"?

Express warranties of this type—oral or written promises or affirmations of fact made by one party to the other during the formation of the contract—can and frequently do enter the final bargain, particularly if there is reason to believe that the other party would not have agreed unless such a promise had been given. (It's different if the promise is just "puffery" that is unlikely to be taken seriously.)

However, warranties can also arise through implication. The UCC contains three major implied warranties: that "the title conveyed shall be good," § 2–312(1)(a); that "the goods shall be merchantable," § 2–314(1); and that "the goods shall be fit for [a particular] purpose," § 2–315. All three warranties are default terms of contracts for the sale of goods, and all three can be avoided by sellers who follow specified procedures; indeed, a considerable amount of modern contract litigation is concerned with the avoidance of warranties. As Comment 1 to § 2–313 puts it, " 'Implied' warranties rest so clearly on a common factual situation or set of conditions that no particular language or action is necessary to evidence them and they will arise in such a situation unless unmistakably negated."

CARPENTER v. CHRYSLER CORP.

Missouri Court of Appeals, 1993.
853 S.W.2d 346.

STEPHAN, J. Brian and Kendra Carpenter appeal from the judgment of the trial court ordering a new trial in favor of Chrysler Corporation ("Chrysler") and Scott Auto Sales and Finance Company d/b/a Chrysler-Plymouth West ("CPW"). This case arises out of the Carpenters' dissatisfaction with a new 1986 Chrysler LeBaron automobile they purchased at CPW in August 1986. The Carpenters subsequently learned that, prior to their purchase, their car had been driven some distance with a disconnected odometer. The Carpenters then sued Chrysler and CPW.... [Eds.: The jury awarded the Carpenters $7,200 for breach of warranty and $3,400 actual and $17,000 punitive damages for fraudulent misrepresentation against CPW, and $3,400 on statutory odometer altering and $3,400 actual and $1.19 million punitive damages on fraudulent misrepresentation counts against Chrysler. The excerpt below is confined to the CPW issues.]

The facts, despite protracted litigation spanning nearly four years and resulting in a voluminous record of more than 1500 pages in the legal file and over 900 pages of transcript, are fairly straightforward. CPW, an automobile dealer in west St. Louis County, Missouri, had received the car at issue here, a 1986 Chrysler LeBaron, from Chrysler's Detroit, Michigan plant in February 1986. In March 1986 CPW discovered a leak in the power steering system of the LeBaron while it was sitting on CPW's sales lot. CPW replaced a seal in the power steering unit and refilled the car's power steering fluid. In April 1986 Chrysler sent CPW a recall notice and repairs kit to correct a wiring harness defect causing intermittent failure to start. However, CPW did not make the repair.

On August 25, 1986, Brian Carpenter ("Carpenter") went to CPW to buy two cars, one for himself and another automobile primarily for the use of his older daughter Kendra, then sixteen, as well as his fifteen year old daughter Kerry. He told the salesman he wanted a reliable car for his daughters. The salesman directed Carpenter's attention to the Chrysler LeBaron stating it was a reliable car. Carpenter did not test-drive the car because it would not start. The salesman attributed the difficulty to a dead battery. Nevertheless, Carpenter signed a sales contract that day to buy the LeBaron. The salesman told him the car would be taken care of and would be ready in two days. Carpenter left.

The next day, on August 26, 1986, CPW noted a "powerless steering" problem on the LeBaron and made repairs adjusting a valve and some belts and putting power steering fluid in the car. A mechanic at CPW inspected the car and prepared a vehicle inspection certificate on August 26 indicating that the odometer recorded sixteen miles and that the car was in good mechanical order. CPW also replaced the steering gear on August 28, 1986.

Later that same day Carpenter returned to the dealer for his new car. CPW told him the LeBaron had needed alignment and was available at Firestone. Carpenter handled some paperwork and then picked up the LeBaron at Firestone. In order to finance his purchase, Carpenter traded in his Plymouth Reliant for a $2,000 credit and financed the balance of $17,268 under a retail installment contract. Carpenter also paid a $690 premium to purchase credit life insurance; $1,072.84 for credit disability insurance and $497 for an extended warranty or service contract. Carpenter began experiencing problems with the car almost immediately after his purchase. He returned the car to CPW on September 1, 1986, complaining of problems with the power steering, ignition, leaky oil and the electronic dash display. CPW replaced the power steering pump and ignition switch. Carpenter picked up the car September 4. He returned it one week later on September 11, 1986, because of persistent oil leaks. CPW replaced seven items.

Carpenter continued to experience problems with the car's power steering, oil leaking and digital dash display. He returned the car a third time to CPW on September 17. CPW removed the transmission and replaced the torque converter with a rebuilt assembly, replaced the oil pump and sent the car again to Firestone for realignment. Carpenter retrieved the car September 25.

The car's digital display gauges remained erratic, the steering "pulled" and, frequently, the car would not start in park, but would have to be started in neutral. On several occasions the car failed to start at all. Carpenter complained repeatedly to CPW and asked that the car be replaced. He took the car in for repairs several times in October and November, but no further work was done by CPW on those occasions.

In November Carpenter received notice of the recall for the defective wiring harness. He took the car to CPW in December for repairs for difficulties with the transmission, the steering, the radio and oil leaking. The car was in the shop from December 1 through December 9. CPW again replaced the torque converter, the speed sensor switch and the entire transaxle. However, CPW did not repair the defective wiring harness.

Despite Carpenter's continued complaints with the car's steering, CPW made no further repairs after those repairs of December 11, 1986, at 4,000 miles. Carpenter's recourse to other dealers provided no satisfaction because they refused to honor the mechanical breakdown protection extended warranty that Carpenter had purchased through CPW. In April 1987 Carpenter notified Mercantile, the assignee of the installment contract on the car, that he intended to make no further car payments because of the car's numerous defects.

In July 1987 Carpenter also received a letter from Lee Iacocca, Chrysler's chairman, informing Carpenter that Carpenter's LeBaron automobile had been utilized in Chrysler's overnight evaluation program while still at the manufacturer's site in Detroit, Michigan, before the car had been shipped to CPW. The Overnight Evaluation Program ("OEP") was a program Chrysler designed to provide an assessment of the function, performance, appearance, safety and quality of its vehicles. A Chrysler employee testified the program had been in effect since at least 1969. Under the program, Chrysler employees drove new Chrysler cars, ready to be shipped, from work to home and back to work in order to evaluate the vehicle's quality. During these test drives the odometers were disconnected. Upon learning of his car's use in the OEP program, Carpenter quit driving the LeBaron sometime in July or August 1987. . . .

The car was eventually repossessed while sitting in Carpenter's driveway by CPW which had repurchased the installment car contract from Mercantile Bank. CPW resold the car at a wholesale auction to a used car dealer for $2500. Another customer ultimately bought the car in July 1990 for $5200. . . .

CPW has also attacked the submissibility of the Carpenters' case against it on claims of breach of warranty and of fraudulent misrepresentation. . . . The Uniform Commercial Code, in Section 400.2–313 (1)(a), RSMo 1986, provides that an express warranty is created by an affirmation of fact or promise made by the seller to the buyer which relates to the goods and becomes part of the basis of the bargain. When such a warranty is made, the goods shall conform to the affirmation or promise. Id. It is not necessary to the creation of an express warranty that the seller use formal words such as "warrant" or "guarantee." Section 400.2–313 (2), RSMo 1986. The seller need not have a specific intention to make a warranty. Id. An affirmation merely of the value of the goods or a statement purporting to be merely the seller's opinion or commendation of the goods does not create a warranty. Id. Thus, construing MAI 25.07 and Section 400.2–313 together, in order to make a submissible case of breach of express warranty, a plaintiff must plead and prove the following elements: 1) defendant's sale of the goods to plaintiff; 2) defendant's representation to plaintiff that the goods were of certain kind or quality; 3) defendant's representation induced plaintiff's purchase of, or was a material factor in plaintiff's decision to purchase, the goods; 4) nonconformity of the goods to the representations made; 5) plaintiff's notice to defendant, within a reasonable time of discovery of the goods' nonconformity, of such failure to conform; and 6) plaintiff's damages.

The Carpenters submitted to the jury that CPW had represented the LeBaron was reliable and in good, safe and roadworthy condition. CPW contends that the Carpenters failed to show that CPW made any representations of fact, not merely opinions, or that any representations constituted a material factor in the Carpenters' decision to purchase the Chrysler LeBaron automobile. Thus, CPW disputes that the Carpenters established the second and third elements of a prima facie case for breach of warranty.

In detailing his discussions with the car salesman at CPW, Carpenter testified that he had two daughters and that he and his daughters needed two cars in order for them to get to work and to school and that both he and his daughters would need reliable transportation. He was looking for "something that you could count on." Carpenter testified that when the CPW salesman showed him the LeBaron, the salesman said, "it was a good car, reliable, brand new. This might be what you're looking for. This is the kind of car to have." In response to whether the salesman had talked "about success they had had with that type of model of car," Carpenter answered as follows: "He didn't elaborate on any success; just made the insinuations to me this was a new car, reliable, I can count on it. It was the kind of car I wanted to have for the deal I was trying to make."

When asked what the salesman said about his knowledge of customer satisfaction of other similar cars, Carpenter stated: "Yeah, it was a good car, reliable car, that people were satisfied with it." He testified that he told the salesman he intended the car to be used not only by himself but also by his sixteen year old daughter and, eventually, by his fifteen year old daughter as well. The dealer picked this particular car out for him as suitable, told him it was a new car and that it ran right. The salesman, however, never disclosed that the car had any prior mechanical problems. For example, when the car would not start for the test drive the salesman attributed the problem to a dead battery. Carpenter, instead, only test-drove the other car he purchased for himself. CPW also certified the Missouri Motor Vehicle Inspection Report listing the car's mileage. CPW never mentioned to Carpenter that CPW had repaired a leak in the car's power steering earlier that March or that a recall notice for a wiring harness defect had been sent. This testimony capsulizes the Carpenters' evidence against CPW concerning representations or warranties made by CPW when it sold the LeBaron to the Carpenters.

CPW is correct that a seller may exaggerate the quality or value of goods without becoming liable under a theory of breach of express warranty. See e.g. *Guess v. Lorenz*, 612 S.W.2d 831 (Mo. App. 1981). A seller may puff his wares or express his opinion about the quality and value of his goods even to the point of exaggeration without incurring warranty obligation. Id. at 833. On the other hand, if the representation is a statement of fact, a petition alleging such a misrepresentation may sufficiently state a claim for breach of express warranty or fraudulent misrepresentation. *Clark v. Olson*, 726 S.W.2d 718, 719–720 (Mo. banc

1987); *Lowther v. Hays*, 225 S.W.2d 708, 714 (Mo. 1950). A given representation can be an expression of opinion or a statement of fact depending upon the circumstances surrounding the representation. *Clark*, 726 S.W.2d at 720.

We believe that the Carpenters' petition alleged, and their evidence supported, that the representations made by CPW were statements of fact. CPW's salesman referred specifically to this particular car in attesting to its soundness, its reliability. The statements conveyed sufficient definite information about the quality of the LeBaron for that representation to be considered material. Accord, id. (seller's representation to prospective home buyer that house was "in good condition" held to be a material statement of fact.)

In *Guess v. Lorenz*, 612 S.W.2d 831 (Mo. App. 1981), we held the representation that the car was in good condition was an expression of opinion. Id. at 833. In *Guess*, the seller of a used car forthrightly pointed out its defects known to her, although her lack of mechanical knowledge was readily apparent. We concluded considering all the circumstances, it would not be reasonable to find that the seller's remarks about the car's condition were statements of fact and not purely opinion. Id.

Unlike *Guess* where buyer and seller were on equal footing, the seller here was an experienced car dealer. CPW enjoyed an additional advantage over the Carpenters because they had purchased an automobile from CPW in the past. Through his prior course of dealing with CPW, Carpenter was thereby rendered "disarmed and made credulous" in relying on the salesman's expertise. See *Shechter v. Brewer*, 344 S.W.2d 784, 788–89 [4] (Mo. App. 1961). More importantly, CPW (despite its knowledge to the contrary) failed to disclose that this new car had problems with leaks in its steering system and had already been subject to a recall notice for a wiring harness defect. The evidence sufficiently established that CPW made a material misrepresentation of a statement of fact to the Carpenters to permit submission to the jury of the Carpenters' claim for breach of express warranty.

CPW asserts the same two shortcomings—proof of CPW's making a representation of fact and proof that no such representation was material—are lacking as elements in the Carpenters' fraud claim. Having analyzed these two elements in our determination whether the Carpenters made a submissible case for breach of express warranty, we need not reiterate our earlier discussion. The same evidence deemed sufficient to establish a material representation of fact to support the Carpenters' claim for breach of express warranty also supports their claim for fraudulent misrepresentation. . . .

[The Court went on to discuss the Chrysler issues.]

The judgment of the trial court granting Chrysler a new trial is affirmed. The judgment of the trial court granting CPW a new trial is reversed and remanded with directions that the jury verdict in favor of the Carpenters be reinstated.

Notes and Discussion

1. **What Did CPW Promise?** According to the facts, "Brian Carpenter ... told the salesman he wanted a reliable car for his daughters. The salesman directed Carpenter's attention to the Chrysler LeBaron stating it was a reliable car." This is clearly based on Carpenter's testimony that the salesman had said, "[I]t was a good car, reliable, brand new. This might be what you're looking for. This is the kind of car you're looking for. This is the kind of car to have." Are these statements substantially different from the sorts of claims made in advertisements?

One problem that often arises in warranty cases is whether the seller's words of praise should be understood as more than vague and general exaggerations ("puffery") that no reasonable person would rely on in making a purchase. A non-contract case that raises this issue nicely is *Pizza Hut, Inc. v. Papa John's International, Inc.*, 227 F.3d 489 (5th Cir. 2000). Papa John's ran advertisements with the slogan "Better Ingredients. Better Pizza."—obviously, although tacitly, by comparison with the competition. Pizza Hut sued alleging that this was a false statement of fact actionable under § 43(a) of the Lanham Act (15 U.S.C. § 1125). The Fifth Circuit, reversing a jury verdict for Pizza Hut, held that: "Each half of the slogan amounts to little more than an exaggerated opinion of superiority that no consumer would be justified in relying upon. It has not been explained convincingly to us how the combination of the two phrases, without more, changes the essential nature of each phrase so as to make it actionable." Id. at 499. How is this different from what the salesman told Brian Carpenter?

In any case, provided the statement is sufficiently specific, the UCC requires "no particular reliance" on an affirmation by the buyer. "Rather, any fact which is to take such affirmations, once made, out of the agreement requires clear affirmative proof." Cmt. 3 on § 2–313. Must the buyer at least know of the affirmation?

How likely is it that the salesman would have been able to recall this specific conversation in any detail? The issue here (as also in *Hawkins v. McGee*) is what may happen when a jury is confronted with relatively detailed testimony from one party, and only vague remembrance from the other. It does not matter, in creating an express warranty, whether the promisor intended the warrant to arise.

2. **How Could CPW Have Protected Itself?** This case should give you a new appreciation of the possible uses for the parol evidence rule. Suppose that the signed contract between CPW and Carpenter had contained an integration clause disavowing all terms not contained in the final document. Would CPW have been entirely protected? See § 2–302. Note that express warranties once given cannot be "disclaimed"; see § 2–316(1) and Comment 1, which says that the section "seeks to protect a buyer from unexpected and unbargained language of disclaimer by denying effect to such language when inconsistent with language of express warranty."

Amended Article 2 contains two new and important sections, §§ 2–313A and 313B, that extend a seller's obligations to "remote purchasers." The situation envisaged in § 2–313A is where a manufacturer (say, Dell Inc.)

includes in its packaging a warranty that is, by its design, a "pass through" warranty, intended not for the immediate purchaser (say, a computer retailer) but for a consumer end user; it is the remote purchaser that acquires the warranty from the manufacturer. Section 2–313B creates similar remote obligations through advertising. Both sections are plainly intended to deal with the ordinary transactions of modern commerce.

3. Warranties by Description. Traditional express warranties arose from affirmations of fact or promises. But a warranty may also arise not from actual statements, but from specifications furnished during the formation of the contract. Section 2–313(1)(b) states that an express warranty is created by "[a]ny description of the goods which is made part of the basis of the bargain." This means that almost every description on any seller's acknowledgment of a contract for the sale of goods will be an express warranty that the goods conform to that description.

VLASES v. MONTGOMERY WARD & CO.

United States Court of Appeals, Third Circuit, 1967.
377 F.2d 846.

McLAUGHLIN, J. This case revolves around the charge that defendant-appellant, Montgomery Ward, was liable for the breach of implied warranties in the sale of one day old chickens to the plaintiff-appellee, Paul Vlases. The latter came to this country from Greece when he was sixteen and until 1954 his primary occupation was that of a coal miner. He had always raised chickens but because of his job as a miner his flocks were small, ranging from between twenty-five to one hundred chicks. In 1958 plaintiff began the construction of a two story chicken coop large enough to house 4,000 chickens and a smaller side building where he could wash, grade and sell the eggs. Vlases worked alone on the coop, twelve hours a day, fifty-two weeks a year, until its completion in 1961. In November of 1961 plaintiff placed an order at defendant's outlet store in Brownsville, Pennsylvania for the purchase of 2,000 one day old chicks. The chickens selected by the plaintiff from Ward's catalogue were hybrid Leghorns and were noted for their excellent egg production. On December 21, 1961 plaintiff received the 2,200 chickens and placed them on the first floor of the coop which had been equipped with new brooders, feeders and within a short time, waterers. As a further hygienic precaution wire and sugar cane were placed on the ground so the chickens would not come in contact with the dirt floor. For the first six months Vlases slept in the coop in order to give the new chicks his undivided attention.

During the first few weeks after delivery the chickens appeared to be in good health but by the third week plaintiff noticed that their feathers were beginning to fall off. This condition was brought to the attention of Mr. Howard Hamilton who represented the Agway Corporation which was supplying the plaintiff with feed on credit. In February of 1962 Mr. Hamilton took five chickens to the Bureau of Animal Industry Diagnostic Laboratory where they were examined by Dr. Daniel P. Ehlers. The examination revealed signs of drug intoxication and hemorrhagic disease involving the weakening of blood vessels. Four chicks were brought to Dr. Ehlers in May of 1962 and were found to be suffering from fatigue. On the 14th of August 1962 Mr. Hamilton brought three chickens to the laboratory where Dr. Ehlers' report noted that two of the chicks were affected with visceral leukosis, one with ocular leukosis, one had bumble foot and one had been picked. Visceral and ocular leukosis are two types of avian leukosis complex or bird cancer which disease infected plaintiff's flock either killing the chicks or causing those remaining to be destroyed.

Plaintiff in this two count suit in assumpsit charged negligence and breach of warranty with jurisdiction resting on the diversity provisions of 28 U.S.C.A. § 1332. After the second day of trial the negligence claim was dropped leaving the breach of warranty as the sole problem for the jury's consideration. A verdict was returned in favor of the plaintiff in the amount of $23,028.77. Montgomery Ward appeals from the resultant judgment.

I.

Appellant takes the position that an action for breach of implied warranties will not lie for the sale of one day old chicks where there is no human skill, knowledge or foresight which would enable the producer or supplier to prevent the occurrence of this disease, to detect its presence or to care for the sickness if it was present. The jury was instructed by the court that recovery on behalf of the plaintiff required a finding that the chickens were afflicted with leukosis at the time defendant made delivery. The expert testimony for both sides indicated that there was no way of determining whether newly hatched chicks have leukosis and that there is no medication available to prevent the disease from occurring. Assuming the chickens were diseased upon their arrival the thrust of appellant's argument questions the sufficiency of the law to support a finding that Ward is liable under Pennsylvania law for the breach of implied warranties.

The two implied warranties before us are the implied warranty of merchantability, 12A P.S. § 2–314, and the implied warranty of fitness for a particular purpose, 12A P.S. § 2–315. Both of these are designed to protect the buyer of goods from bearing the burden of loss where merchandise, though not violating a promise expressly guaranteed, does not conform to the normal commercial standards or meeting the buyer's particular purpose, a condition upon which he had the right to rely.

Were it to be assumed that the sale of 2,000 chickens infected with avian leukosis transgressed the norm of acceptable goods under both warranties, appellant's position is that the action will not lie in a situation where the seller is unable to discover the defect or cure the damage if it could be ascertained. That theory does not eliminate the consequences imposed by the Code upon the seller of commercially inferior goods. It is without merit.

The fact that avian leukosis is nondetectable could be an important issue but only as bearing on the charge of negligence, which is no longer in this suit. The Pennsylvania decision in *Vandenberg & Sons, N.V. v. Siter*, 204 Pa. Super. 392, 204 A.2d 494 (1964), buttresses our conclusion in upholding the implied warranties. There latent defects in certain tulip and hyacinth bulbs went undetected in the face of two inspections and the court, though aware that the imperfections could only be uncovered after growth, limited its concern to the question of whether the seller's express provision that notice of any breach be communicated within a certain time, was reasonable. The entire purpose behind the implied warranty sections of the Code is to hold the seller responsible when inferior goods are passed along to the unsuspecting buyer. What the Code requires is not evidence that the defects should or could have been uncovered by the seller but only that the goods upon delivery were not of a merchantable quality or fit for their particular purpose. If those requisite proofs are established the only exculpatory relief afforded by the Code is a showing that the implied warranties were modified or excluded by specific language under Section 2–316. Lack of skill or foresight on the part of the seller in discovering the product's flaw was never meant to bar liability. The gravamen here is not so much with what precautions were taken by the seller but rather with the quality of the goods contracted for by the buyer. Even a provision specifically disclaiming any warrant against avian leukosis would not necessarily call for the defendant's freedom from liability. Section 1–102(3) of the Code's General Provisions states that standards which are manifestly unreasonable may not be disclaimed and prevents the enforcement of unconscionable sales where, as in this instance, the goods exchanged are found to be totally worthless.

[Eds.: The Court goes on to discuss the evidence for the defect, concluding that the plaintiff had met his burden.]

The judgment of the District Court will be affirmed.

Notes and Discussion

1. **Section 2–314.** Look closely at the text of this section (which is left virtually unchanged in amended Article 2) to see what Paul Vlases had to prove in order to obtain contractual relief. Vlases also sued on the basis of negligence, but dropped that claim. Why might breach of the UCC warranty of merchantability have been preferable to him?

The implied warranty arises only "if the seller is a merchant with respect to goods of that kind." Montgomery Ward qualifies automatically, true?

Section 2–314(1) also permits exclusion or modification of the implied warranty. How to do this is described in § 2–316(2): "the language must mention merchantability and in case of a writing must be conspicuous." (This subsection is, however, qualified by subsection 3, which permits, in particular, warrantless sales "as is.") One other possibility for sellers is to limit the remedies available for breach of the implied warranty; see § 2–718 and especially § 2–719, where there is no requirement that the limitation be conspicuous. In light of this case, would you have advised Montgomery Ward to disclaim the implied warranty or to limit the buyer's remedies?

The CISG, art. 35(2)(a), also contains an implied warranty that goods "are fit for the purposes for which goods of the same description would ordinarily be used."

2. Merchantability. When exactly is an object of sale not "fit for the ordinary purposes for which such goods are used"? Chicks that die from an undetectable disease shortly after the buyer takes delivery—this is a pretty easy case. And so usually for goods that don't work properly or that cause unexpected harm, as with an insecticide that kills not only its intended target (weevils), but also the farmer's livestock; see *Holowka v. York Farm Bureau Cooperative Ass'n*, 2 UCC Rep. Serv. 445 (Pa. Ct. Comm. Pl. 1963).

But the many cases can present more complex problems. In *Zirpola v. Adam Hat Stores, Inc.* 122 N.J.L. 21, 4 A.2d 73 (1939), a pre-Code case that would doubtless be decided the same way today, the plaintiff purchased a hat that, after a few wearings, turned his hair red and caused skin eruptions on his forehead. It turned out that he was having an allergic reaction to a dye, but also that such a reaction was fairly rare, occurring only among four to five percent of all persons. The Court upheld liability. But the outcome might not be the same if only one person in ten thousand would have had this reaction. Where should the line be drawn? For another pre-Code case that deals with remote probabilities, see *Ray v. J.C. Penney Co.*, 274 F.2d 519 (10th Cir. 1959) (plaintiff's "one in a million" allergic reaction to a dye in gloves she purchased).

How far beyond this point should one press? Is butter unmerchantable because the cholesterol it contains can cause heart disease? Are cigarettes unmerchantable because they cause cancer? The latter issue has been heavily litigated; see especially *Green v. American Tobacco Co.*, 391 F.2d 97 (5th Cir. 1968), rev'd *per curiam* 409 F.2d 1166 (5th Cir. 1969) (en banc); and *Semowich v. R.J. Reynolds Tobacco Co.*, 8 UCC Rep. Serv. 2d 976 (N.D.N.Y. 1988). What outcome would you anticipate?

3. Strict Liability. Liability for breach of the contractual warranty of merchantability is much like strict products liability in tort. "One engaged in the business of selling or otherwise distributing products who sells or distributes a defective product is subject to liability for harm to persons or property caused by the defect." Restatement 3d, Torts, Products Liability (1998) § 1. How tort differs from warranty liability can be of considerable practical importance for plaintiffs' and defendants' lawyers. If *Vlases* were litigated today, is it likely that the plaintiff would invoke this tort theory? What of the plaintiff in *Holowka*? What advantages could using tort have?

MASSEY–FERGUSON, INC. v. UTLEY

Court of Appeals of Kentucky, 1969.
439 S.W.2d 57.

CULLEN, J. Appellant Massey-Ferguson, Inc., is a manufacturer of farming machinery. Farmers Implement Sales Company in Henderson, Kentucky, is a dealer for such equipment, buying the machines wholesale from Massey-Ferguson and selling them at retail. Appellee F. X. Utley is a farmer.

In October 1960 Utley purchased from Farmers Implement Sales Company a Massey-Ferguson No. 20, 2-row, cornhead combine attachment, being a device which, when attached to a combine harvester machine, will cut corn, separate and husk the ears, and shell the kernels. Utley made a down payment of $675 and executed an installment sales contract for the balance of $1,603.56, calling for three equal payments of $534.52 in November of 1961, 1962 and 1963. The contract immediately was assigned to Massey-Ferguson. Utley defaulted in the first payment due under the contract and Massey-Ferguson brought the instant action to recover the full amount of the deferred payments. Utley defended on the ground of breach of implied warranties of fitness. The case was submitted to a jury which found for the defendant. Judgment was entered accordingly, dismissing the action. Massey-Ferguson moved for an appeal to this court, which was granted. We now have before us the merits of the appeal.

Massey-Ferguson's principal argument is that the defense of breach of implied warranties could not be asserted against Massey-Ferguson because (1) the contract between the dealer and Utley expressly excluded any implied warranties, and (2) Utley had expressly covenanted in the contract that he would not assert against the assignee any defense he might have against the seller.

The arguments bring into consideration several provisions of the Uniform Commercial Code, particularly KRS 355.2–316, relating to exclusion of warranties, and KRS 355.9–206, relating to assertion of defenses against an assignee.

The contract in the instant case contained language expressly excluding implied warranties (as is authorized by KRS 355.2–314 and 355.2–315). However, it was on the back of the contract form, with a number of other provisions which substantially filled the back page. The paragraph containing the exclusionary language was headed "WARRANTY AND AGREEMENT" in bold-face capital letters, but the exclusionary language itself was in type of the same size and face as were the general contents of the contract. The circuit court ruled that the attempted exclusion was not valid or effective because it was not conspicuous within the requirement of KRS 355.2–316(2) that such an exclusion "must be by a writing and conspicuous."

In KRS 355.1–201(10) the word "conspicuous" is defined as follows: "(10) 'Conspicuous': A term or clause is conspicuous when it is so written that a reasonable person against whom it is to operate ought to have noticed it. A printed heading in capitals (as: NONNEGOTIABLE BILL OF LADING) is conspicuous. Language in the body of a form is 'conspicuous' if it is in larger or other contrasting type or color. But in a telegram any stated term is 'conspicuous.' Whether a term or clause is 'conspicuous' or not is for decision by the court."

The few cases that have interpreted this definition are annotated in 17 A.L.R.3rd 1010 at 1078 and 1079. They indicate a tendency to be strict in measuring what constitutes conspicuousness.

In the instant case the exclusionary language was not in "larger or other contrasting type or color" as contemplated by the statutory definition. It is true that the heading was in large, bold-face type, but there was nothing in the heading to suggest that an exclusion was being made; on the contrary, the words of the heading indicated a making of warranties rather than a disclaimer. Besides being in ordinary type, the exclusion was on the back of the instrument, with nothing on the front, except some words likewise in ordinary type, to direct attention to it. Such a location alone has been held to put the exclusion out of the conspicuous class. See *Hunt v. Perkins Machinery Co.*, 352 Mass. 535, 226 N.E.2d 228.

We concur in the decision of the trial court that the language excluding implied warranties was not "conspicuous." Accordingly, the dealer must be considered to have made implied warranties (1) that the machine was "fit for the ordinary purpose for which such goods are used," KRS 355.2–314(2)(c), and (2) that the machine was fit for the purpose for which the buyer required it (there being a showing that the dealer knew of such purpose and the buyer relied on the dealer's skill and judgment to select and furnish a suitable machine), KRS 355.2–315.

However, Massey-Ferguson maintains that a breach of any implied warranty made by the dealer cannot be asserted against Massey-Ferguson as assignee of the sales contract, because Utley expressly covenanted in the contract that he would "not set up any claim, which he may have against the seller as defense * * * in any action upon the debt or for possession brought by the seller's assignee." It appears that the circuit court held that this covenant was not enforceable because the dealer was the agent of Massey-Ferguson and the latter was therefore primarily a "seller" rather than an "assignee." That reason may not have been entirely valid, but in our opinion a valid reason of a similar nature does exist to justify the holding.

Covenants or agreements of the nature here involved, not to assert against an assignee any claim or defense the buyer may have against the seller, are by KRS 355.9–206(1) made enforceable only by an assignee who takes his assignment for value, in good faith and without notice of a claim or defense. This in substance simply expresses the long-established holder-in-due-course rule applicable to commercial paper.

In a substantial number of cases, annotated in 44 A.L.R.2d 8 at 157 to161, it was held that a manufacturer to whom a dealer had assigned commercial paper was not a holder in due course. As indicated in the annotation, it appears that in most of the cases the circumstances were held to warrant a conclusion that the manufacturer was the real vendor in the transaction. The circumstances most frequently held to be significant were (1) a manufacturer's representative assisted or participated in the sale by the dealer, and (2) the manufacturer's course of dealing was for it to furnish blank sales contracts to its dealer, and for the dealer to immediately and routinely assign the contract to the manufacturer as soon as a sale was made.

In the instant case the evidence was that a factory representative visited Utley with the dealer and participated in making the sale. Also, that Massey-Ferguson followed the course of dealing above described as to supplying blank forms and receiving immediate and routine assignments. So we have present here the two circumstances most frequently relied upon by other courts as a basis for holding the manufacturer-assignee not to be a holder in due course.

It is our opinion that under the circumstances of this case Massey-Ferguson cannot be considered to be within the class of those who are protected by the covenant against assertion of defenses, at least as to the defense of breach of an implied warranty of fitness. We base our conclusion on the proposition that Massey-Ferguson's conduct put it in the status of a "seller" and that its status as a "seller" outweighs its status as an "assignee," as those terms are used in KRS 355.9–206 and were used in the contract. It should not be accorded the protection of an assignee against defenses that derived from its actions as a seller.

We consider it to be the policy of the Uniform Commercial Code to encourage the supplying of credit for the buying of goods by insulating the lender from lawsuits over the quality of the goods. But we conceive that the insulation was intended primarily for financial institutions rather than the manufacturer who finances his own sales. He needs no inducement to supply credit for the purchase of his goods because the whole object of his business is to sell his goods.

Massey-Ferguson argues that the decision in *Root v. John Deere Company*, Ky., 413 S.W.2d 901, establishes its right to enforce the covenant against assertion of defenses. There the assignee, whom we presume was the manufacturer although the opinion does not so state, was held to be within the protection of the covenant. However, it does not appear that the assignee-manufacturer in that case had engaged in such course of dealings, or had so participated in the sale, as to put him in the category of a "seller." So the case is not controlling here....

In this opinion we have not indicated what the evidence was with respect to the alleged unfitness of the cornheader. That is because Massey-Ferguson has not questioned the sufficiency of the evidence. In neither of its two motions in the trial court for a directed verdict did Massey-Ferguson state as a ground the insufficiency of proof of breach of warranty, nor was any such ground included in the statement of questions presented in the brief on appeal.

The judgment is affirmed.

Notes and Discussion

1. Disclaimer of Warranties. In this rather complicated case, the immediate seller was Farmers Implement, which, however, had then assigned its contractual rights to Massey-Ferguson, the manufacturer of the cornhead combine attachment. Farmers Implement was not a party to the immediate lawsuit, which Massey-Ferguson brought in order to recover the balance of the price. The Court assumes that the cornheader was unfit under § 2–315.

Two separate issues therefore arise. First, under § 2–316 did either or both of the implied UCC warranties survive the disclaimer in the contract between Utley and Farmers Implement? Second, if they did survive, can they also be used against Massey-Ferguson as the assignee, particularly in light of the contract clause limiting the buyer's defenses? The latter question involves legal rules that you have not yet studied, but you should be able to piece together why a clause of this type is often used in financing arrangements.

What would be the consequences for Utley if it was unable to assert the implied warranty against Massey-Ferguson?

Note: UCC Warranties and the Magnuson-Moss Act

The UCC implied warranties are often supplemented or affected by state and federal consumer legislation, of which there is a very large quantity. Typical of the federal legislation is a disclosure statute called the Magnuson-Moss Act, which Congress enacted in 1975 (15 USCA §§ 2301–2312). The general aim of this legislation is to help consumers deal with confusing or misleading warranty language. Where this law applies, it supercedes the UCC. For example, provisions of the Magnuson-Moss Act require suppliers of most goods to clearly name and describe their warranties.

Section 108 of the Magnuson-Moss Act (15 USCA § 2308) explicitly negates the legal effect of § 2–316 of the Uniform Commercial Code, whereby a seller of goods is free to disclaim the warranties of merchantability and fitness for a particular purpose. To comply with 2–316 the seller need only use certain words (such as "MERCHANTABILITY") and make the message conspicuous. But if the seller makes a written warranty of a product—as almost all sellers of new goods do—the Magnuson-Moss renders the 2–316 disclaimer invalid. Section 108 states the rule as follows: "No supplier may disclaim or modify (except as provided in subsection (b)) any implied warranty to a consumer with respect to such consumer product if (1) such supplier makes any written warranty to the consumer with respect to such consumer product, or (2) at the time of sale, or within 90 days thereafter, such supplier enters into a service contract with the consumer which applies to such consumer product."

Several cases illustrate the operation of § 108. In *Felde v. Chrysler Credit Corp.*, 219 Ill.App.3d 530, 162 Ill.Dec. 565, 580 N.E.2d 191 (1991), a new car dealer issued an invoice stating that no warranties had been made by the dealer or the manufacturer "excepting only Chrysler Corporation's current printed warranty applicable to such vehicle or vehicle chassis which warranty is incorporated herein and made a part hereof and a copy of which will be delivered to buyer at the time of delivery of the new motor vehicle or motor vehicle chassis." This incorporation of the manufacturer's warranty into the dealer invoice was a written warranty within the meaning of

Magnuson-Moss. Therefore the court held that the dealer's disclaimer of the implied warranty of merchantability was invalid, and that seller made an implied warranty that the goods would be merchantable. Despite the disclaimer, the consumer recovered for breach of the express and implied warranties.

Likewise, in *Ventura v. Ford Motor Corp.*, 180 N.J.Super. 45, 433 A.2d 801 (App. Div. 1981), the court held that "having furnished a written warranty to the consumer, the dealer as a supplier may not 'disclaim or modify (except to limit in duration) any implied warranty to a consumer ....'" 433 A.2d at 810. The court invalidated the disclaimer by the dealer. Bound by the implied warranties arising under the UCC, the defendant dealer was liable to the consumer plaintiff for breach. Thus, the plaintiff could revoke his acceptance and claim a refund of the purchase price.

E. MODIFICATIONS

We now suppose that two parties have entered into a contract, and that for whatever reason one or both of them have come to regret the contract's terms. Under what circumstances is it possible for the parties to change their deal?

There are definite dangers here, which are illustrated by a venerable old case: *Lingenfelder v. Wainwright Brewery Co.*, 103 Mo. 578, 15 S.W. 844 (1890). Edmund Jungenfeld, an architect, had agreed to design brewery buildings and then superintend their erection. As the work was proceeding, Jungenfeld learned that the brewery had awarded the contract for its refrigerating plant to a third-party competitor. At that point he quit work. The brewery had to complete its facilities as swiftly as possible, so it promised to give Jungenfeld five percent on the cost of the refrigerating plant if he would resume work. Jungenfeld did so and completed his portion of the project. A dispute then arose about whether the brewery's promise of extra pay was enforceable.

Plainly, Jungenfeld's conduct raises questions, since he was using the pressure of breach in order to gain more pay from the brewery. The Court decides in the brewery's favor, using censorious language: "No amount of metaphysical reasoning can change the plain fact that Jungenfeld took advantage of Wainwright's necessities, and extorted the promise of 5 per cent on the refrigerator plant as the condition of his complying with his contract already entered into." 15 S.W. at 848. This might seem, in itself, adequate grounds for refusing to enforce the modification. However, in the end the Court advanced a different and more formalistic rationale: "[W]hen a party merely does what he has already obligated himself to do, he cannot demand an additional compensation therefor, and although by taking advantage of any necessities of his adversary, he obtains a promise for more, the law will regard it as *nudum pactum*, and will not lend its process to aid in the wrong." Id.

In short, the modification was held unenforceable not because it was improperly obtained, but because it lacked consideration; the doctrine of consideration was used to filter out an improper modification. Stated in a more general form, this principle seems simple and fair: a pre-existing duty cannot serve as consideration. This rule still survives today, in Restatement 2d § 73: "Performance of a legal duty owed to a promisor which is neither doubtful nor the subject of honest dispute is not consideration; . . ." The pre-existing duty rule has a tendency to pop up in odd and unexpected places. Suppose, for example, that a bank posts a reward for the capture of robbers, and employees of the bank then give information that aids in capturing the robbers; can the employees claim the reward? A Kentucky Court thought not: "They were under duty to protect and conserve the resources and moneys of the bank, and safeguard every interest of the institution furnishing them employment. Each of these employees exhibited great courage, and cool bravery, in a time of stress and danger. The community and the county have recompensed them in commendation, admiration and high praise, and the world looks on them as heroes. But in making known the robbery and assisting in acquainting the public and the officers with details of the crime and with identification of the robbers, they performed a duty to the bank and the public, for which they cannot claim a reward." *Denney v. Reppert*, 432 S.W.2d 647, 649 (Ky. Ct. App. 1968).

But in many instances the generalized principle turns out to be very doubtful, and specific applications of the principle can often be explained on other, more plausible grounds. In any case, it is also not clear that the doctrine of consideration, whatever its utility in judicial supervision of the formation of contracts, is also necessarily relevant to their subsequent modification.

ANGEL v. MURRAY

Supreme Court of Rhode Island, 1974.
113 R.I. 482, 322 A.2d 630.

ROBERTS, C.J. This is a civil action brought by Alfred L. Angel and others against John E. Murray, Jr., Director of Finance of the City of Newport, the city of Newport, and James L. Maher, alleging that Maher had illegally been paid the sum of $20,000 by the Director of Finance and praying that the defendant Maher be ordered to repay the city such sum. The case was heard by a justice of the Superior Court, sitting without a jury, who entered a judgment ordering Maher to repay the sum of $20,000 to the city of Newport. Maher is now before this court prosecuting an appeal.

The record discloses that Maher has provided the city of Newport with a refuse-collection service under a series of five-year contracts beginning in 1946. On March 12, 1964, Maher and the city entered into another such contract for a period of five years commencing on July 1, 1964, and terminating on June 30, 1969. The contract provided, among other things, that Maher would receive $137,000 per year in return for collecting and removing all combustible and noncombustible waste materials generated within the city.

In June of 1967 Maher requested an additional $10,000 per year from the city council because there had been a substantial increase in the cost of collection due to an unexpected and unanticipated increase of 400 new dwelling units. Maher's testimony, which is uncontradicted, indicates the 1964 contract had been predicated on the fact that since 1946 there had been an average increase of 20 to 25 new dwelling units per year. After a public meeting of the city council where Maher explained in detail the reasons for his request and was questioned by members of the city council, the city council agreed to pay him an additional $10,000 for the year ending on June 30, 1968. Maher made a similar request again in June of 1968 for the same reasons, and the city council again agreed to pay an additional $10,000 for the year ending on June 30, 1969.

The trial justice found that each such $10,000 payment was made in violation of law. His decision, as we understand it, is premised on two independent grounds. First, he found that the additional payments were unlawful because they had not been recommended in writing to the city council by the city manager. Second, he found that Maher was not entitled to extra compensation because the original contract already required him to collect all refuse generated within the city and, therefore, included the 400 additional units. The trial justice further found that these 400 additional units were within the contemplation of the parties when they entered into the contract. It appears that he based this portion of the decision upon the rule that Maher had a preexisting duty to collect the refuse generated by the 400 additional units, and thus there was no consideration for the two additional payments....

II.

Having found that the city council had the power to modify the 1964 contract without the written recommendation of the city manager, we are still confronted with the question of whether the additional payments were illegal because they were not supported by consideration.

A.

As previously stated, the city council made two $10,000 payments. The first was made in June of 1967 for the year beginning on July 1, 1967, and ending on June 30, 1968. Thus, by the time this action was commenced in October of 1968, the modification was completely executed. That is, the money had been paid by the city council, and Maher had collected all of the refuse. Since consideration is only a test of the enforceability of executory promises, the presence or absence of consideration for the first payment is unimportant because the city council's agreement to make the first payment was fully executed at the time of the commencement of this action.... However, since both payments were made under similar circumstances, our decision regarding the second payment (Part B, infra) is fully applicable to the first payment.

B.

It is generally held that a modification of a contract is itself a contract, which is unenforceable unless supported by consideration. See Simpson, [Contracts (2d ed. 1965) at] 93. In *Rose v. Daniels*, 8 R. I. 381 (1866), this court held that an agreement by a debtor with a creditor to discharge a debt for a sum of money less than the amount due is unenforceable because it was not supported by consideration.

Rose is a perfect example of the preexisting duty rule. Under this rule an agreement modifying a contract is not supported by consideration if one of the parties to the agreement does or promises to do something that he is legally obligated to do or refrains or promises to refrain from doing something he is not legally privileged to do. See Calamari & Perillo, Contracts § 60 (1970); 1A Corbin, Contracts §§ 171–72 (1963); 1 Williston, supra, § 130; Annot., 12 A.L.R.2d 78 (1950). In *Rose* there was no consideration for the new agreement because the debtor was already legally obligated to repay the full amount of the debt....

The primary purpose of the preexisting duty rule is to prevent what has been referred to as the "hold-up game." See 1A Corbin, supra, § 171. A classic example of the "hold-up game" is found in *Alaska Packers' Ass'n v. Domenico*, 117 F. 99 (9th Cir. 1902). There 21 seamen entered into a written contract with Domenico to sail from San Francisco to Pyramid Harbor, Alaska. They were to work as sailors and fishermen out of Pyramid Harbor during the fishing season of 1900. The contract specified that each man would be paid $50 plus two cents for each red salmon he caught. Subsequent to their arrival at Pyramid Harbor, the men stopped work and demanded an additional $50. They threatened to return to San Francisco if Domenico did not agree to their demand. Since it was impossible for Domenico to find other men, he agreed to pay the men an additional $50. After they returned to San Francisco, Domenico refused to pay the men an additional $50. The court found that the subsequent agreement to pay the men an additional $50 was not supported by consideration because the men had a preexisting duty to work on the ship under the original contract, and thus the subsequent agreement was unenforceable.

Another example of the "hold-up game" is found in the area of construction contracts. Frequently, a contractor will refuse to complete work under an unprofitable contract unless he is awarded additional compensation. The courts have generally held that a subsequent agreement to award additional compensation is unenforceable if the contractor is only performing work which would have been required of him under the original contract. See, e.g., *Lingenfelder v. Wainwright Brewing Co.*, 103 Mo. 578, 15 S.W. 844 (1890), which is a leading case in this area....

These examples clearly illustrate that the courts will not enforce an agreement that has been procured by coercion or duress and will hold the parties to their original contract regardless of whether it is profitable or unprofitable. However, the courts have been reluctant to apply the pre-existing duty rule when a party to a contract encounters unanticipated difficulties and the other party, not influenced by coercion or duress, voluntarily agrees to pay additional compensation for work already required to be performed under the contract. For example, the courts have found that the original contract was rescinded, *Linz v. Schuck*, 106 Md. 220, 67 A. 286 (1907); abandoned, *Connelly v. Devoe*, 37 Conn. 570 (1871); or waived, *Michaud v. MacGregor*, 61 Minn. 198, 63 N.W. 479 (1895).

Although the preexisting duty rule has served a useful purpose insofar as it deters parties from using coercion and duress to obtain additional compensation, it has been widely criticized as a general rule of law. With regard to the preexisting duty rule, one legal scholar has stated: "There has been a growing doubt as to the soundness of this doctrine as a matter of social policy. * * * In certain classes of cases, this doubt has influenced courts to refuse to apply the rule, or to ignore it, in their actual decisions. Like other legal rules, this rule is in process of growth and change, the process being more active here than in most instances. The result of this is that a court should no longer accept this rule as fully established. It should never use it as the major premise of a decision, at least without giving careful thought to the circumstances of the particular case, to the moral deserts of the parties, and to the social feelings and interests that are involved. It is certain that the rule, stated in general and all-inclusive terms, is no longer so well-settled that a court must apply it though the heavens fall." 1A Corbin, supra, § 171; see also Calamari & Perillo, supra, § 61.

The modern trend appears to recognize the necessity that courts should enforce agreements modifying contracts when unexpected or unanticipated difficulties arise during the course of the performance of a contract, even though there is no consideration for the modification, as long as the parties agree voluntarily.

Under the Uniform Commercial Code, § 2–209(1), which has been adopted by 49 states, "[an] agreement modifying a contract [for the sale of goods] needs no consideration to be binding." See G. L. 1956 (1969 Reenactment) § 6A–2–209(1). Although at first blush this section appears to validate modifications obtained by coercion and duress, the comments to this section indicate that a modification under this section must meet the test of good faith imposed by the Code, and a modification obtained by extortion without a legitimate commercial reason is unenforceable.

The modern trend away from a rigid application of the preexisting duty rule is reflected by § 89D(a) of the American Law Institute's Restatement Second of the Law of Contracts, which provides: "A promise modifying a duty under a contract not fully performed on either side is binding (a) if the modification is fair and equitable in view of circumstances not anticipated by the parties when the contract was made * * *."

We believe that § 89D(a) is the proper rule of law and find it applicable to the facts of this case. It not only prohibits modifications obtained by coercion, duress, or extortion but also fulfills society's expectation that agreements entered into voluntarily will be enforced by the courts. See generally Horwitz, The Historical Foundations of Modern Contract Law, 87 Harv. L. Rev. 917 (1974). Section 89D(a), of course, does not compel a modification of an unprofitable or unfair contract; it only enforces a modification if the parties voluntarily agree and if (1) the promise modifying the original contract was made before the contract was fully performed on either side, (2) the underlying circumstances which prompted the modification were unanticipated by the parties, and (3) the modification is fair and equitable.

The evidence, which is uncontradicted, reveals that in June of 1968 Maher requested the city council to pay him an additional $10,000 for the year beginning on July 1, 1968, and ending on June 30, 1969. This request was made at a public meeting of the city council, where Maher explained in detail his reasons for making the request. Thereafter, the city council voted to authorize the Mayor to sign an amendment to the 1954 contract which provided that Maher would receive an additional $10,000 per year for the duration of the contract. Under such circumstances we have no doubt that the city voluntarily agreed to modify the 1964 contract.

Having determined the voluntariness of this agreement, we turn our attention to the three criteria delineated above. First, the modification was made in June of 1968 at a time when the five-year contract which was made in 1964 had not been fully performed by either party. Second, although the 1964 contract provided that Maher collect all refuse generated within the city, it appears this contract was premised on Maher's past experience that the number of refuse-generating units would increase at a rate of 20 to 25 per year. Furthermore, the evidence is uncontradicted that the 1967–1968 increase of 400 units "went beyond any previous expectation." Clearly, the circumstances which prompted the city council to modify the 1964 contract were unanticipated. Third, although the evidence does not indicate what proportion of the total this increase comprised, the evidence does indicate that it was a "substantial" increase. In light of this, we cannot say that the council's agreement to pay Maher the $10,000 increase was not fair and equitable in the circumstances.

The judgment appealed from is reversed, and the cause is remanded to the Superior Court for entry of judgment for the defendants.

Notes and Discussion

1. **Maher's Contract.** In making his five-year contract with Newport, Maher must have accepted the risk that the volume of refuse might increase, and the $137,000 annual payment reflected this assumption of risk. Who was better placed, Maher or Newport, to determine whether the city was likely to grow substantially during the five-year period?

At issue here is how this case can be distinguished from earlier cases like *Lingenfelder* and *Alaska Packers*. In those cases, one party, having become dissatisfied with its bargain, also sought an increased payment from the other side. It is not easy for a court to distinguish between the "hold-up game" and what happened in Newport.

2. Modification Etiquette. Pointing to Restatement 2d § 89(a), the Rhode Island Supreme Court holds that the modification in this case is acceptable. Maher's refuse collection service was presumably in a bad state. How far could Maher go in petitioning the city council for a modification? Could he threaten breach? Could he threaten to declare bankruptcy?

At some point, his actions would probably become duress, as in *Lingenfelder*. Restatement 2d § 175(1) provides that: "If a party's manifestation of assent is induced by an improper threat by the other party that leaves the victim no reasonable alternative, the contract is voidable by the victim." An "improper threat" is defined in § 176. Physical violence ("an offer you can't refuse") is the easy case. Harder are other forms dealt with by this section, including a bad faith threat of prosecution or of civil process. However, as Comment e observes, "A threat by a party to a contract not to perform his contractual duty is not, of itself, improper.... [T]he threat is improper if it amounts to a breach of the duty of good faith and fair dealing imposed by the contract."

Official Comment 2 to UCC § 2–209 tries to clarify the law for merchants: "The test of 'good faith' ... may in some situations require an objectively demonstrable reason for seeking a modification. But such matters as a market shift which makes performance come to involve a loss may provide such a reason even though there is no such unforeseen difficulty as would make out a legal excuse from performance under Sections 2–615 and 2–616."

Try out this test on the following situation, from Illustration 8 to Restatement § 176: "A contracts to excavate a cellar for B at a stated price. A unexpectedly encounters solid rock and threatens not to finish the excavation unless B modifies the contract to state a new price that is reasonable but is nine times the original price. B, having no reasonable alternative, is induced by A's threat to make the modification by a signed writing that is enforceable by statute without consideration." Can B later void the modification? This illustration is based on *Watkins & Son v. Carrig*, 91 N.H. 459, 21 A.2d 591 (1941).

3. Standing Firm. Suppose that the Newport City Council had rejected Maher's petition; would he have had any recourse short of breaching the contract and paying damages? To what extent does the law now anticipate that, within very wide limits, a contractual party will be able to resist pressure from the other party when negotiating over modifications?

If the city council was unwilling to modify but felt constrained to do so by Maher's pressure, must it indicate its unwilling acquiescence to Maher in order to reserve its right to void the modification? See, for instance, *United States v. Progressive Enterprises*, 418 F.Supp. 662, 665 (E.D.Va. 1976), holding that a buyer who is coerced into executing a modification must "at least display some protest against the higher price in order to put the seller on notice that the modification is not freely entered into."

Problem 4–6

1. You represent a rookie running back in the National Football League. His contract calls for him to be paid $400,000 per year for three years. Since he has just been named Rookie of the Year, he is now quite dissatisfied with his pay. The team is willing to pay him more in order to keep him happy, but you're concerned about the potential implications of the pre-existing duty rule. What is the best way to handle this problem in drafting a contract modification?

2. Abner is constructing a home for Bernice, with an anticipated payment of $150,000. Bernice decides that she wants her kitchen window moved three feet to the right in order to accommodate her walk-in freezer; and Abner and Bernice agree in writing to the change. Abner, however, fails to execute the change. Can Bernice obtain damages? Look closely at the pre-existing duty rule in Restatement 2d § 73, and also at the three alternatives in § 89.

Problem 4–7: Jury Instructions

In the early 1990s, Boeing entered into a long-term contract with Aircraft Gear, a manufacturer of flap motor assemblies. The contract specified a range for the number of flap assemblies that Boeing would order each month, and also the price for each unit, with step-up prices at specified intervals. Several years into the contract, Aircraft Gear found that it was not meeting its profit forecasts for each assembly. It requested that Boeing renegotiate the contract under more favorable terms to Aircraft Gear, and Boeing granted the request

In March, 1999, Aircraft Gear requested another price increase, but this time Boeing refused. Aircraft Gear then threatened not to ship any assemblies until Boeing granted the price increase. Since such a stoppage would potentially have shut down Boeing's assembly lines, Boeing complied with Aircraft Gear's request. It then increased the number of assemblies it was ordering each month so as to stockpile them as a safeguard against future threats by Aircraft Gear. Simultaneously it began looking for another supplier. Since flap motor assemblies are complex systems, it took Boeing nearly a year to find one, but in the meantime it continued buying Aircraft Gear assemblies at the higher price.

When Boeing finally located another supplier and had a reasonable stockpile of assemblies, it notified Aircraft Gear that it was no longer honoring the March, 1999, agreement. Aircraft Gear then sued Boeing for damages related to Boeing's alleged breach. Boeing counter-sued claiming that it had entered the March, 1999, agreement under duress and that, therefore, it was entitled to rescind it.

What law governs this dispute? Look closely at Restatement §§ 175(1) and 176(1)(d). The UCC does not contain a section on duress, but § 1–203 (§ 1–304 in the revised edition) states that: "Every contract or duty within this Act imposes an obligation of good faith in its performance or enforcement."

After a jury trial, Judge Robert S. Lasnik of the U.S. District Court (W.D. Washington) gave the jury the following instructions:

Members of the jury, now that you have heard all the evidence, it is my duty to instruct you on the law which applies to this case. A copy of these instructions will be available in the jury room for you to consult if you find it necessary.

It is your duty to find the facts from all the evidence in the case. To those facts you will apply the law as I give it to you. You must follow the law as I give it to you whether you agree with it or not. You must not be influenced by any personal likes or dislikes, opinions, prejudices, or sympathy. That means that you must decide the case solely on the evidence before you. You will recall that you took an oath promising to do so at the beginning of the case.

In following my instructions, you must follow all of them and not single out some and ignore others; they are all equally important. You must not read into these instructions or into anything the court may have said or done any suggestion as to what verdict you should return—that is a matter entirely up to you.

The evidence from which you are to decide what the facts are consists of:

(1) the sworn testimony of any witness;

(2) the exhibits which have been received into evidence; and

(3) any facts to which the lawyers have agreed or stipulated.

In reaching your verdict, you may consider only the testimony and exhibits received into evidence. Certain things are not evidence, and you may not consider them in deciding what the facts are. I will list them for you:

(1) Arguments and statements by lawyers are not evidence. The lawyers are not witnesses. What they have said in their opening statements, will say in their closing arguments, and at other times is intended to help you interpret the evidence, but it is not evidence. If the facts as you remember them differ from the way the lawyers have stated them, your memory of them controls.

(2) Questions and objections by lawyers are not evidence. Attorneys have a duty to their clients to object when they believe a question is improper under the rules of evidence. You should not be influenced by the objection or by the court's ruling on it.

(3) Testimony that has been excluded or stricken, or that you have been instructed to disregard, is not evidence and must not be considered. In addition some testimony and exhibits have been received only for a limited purpose; where I have given a limiting instruction, you must follow it.

(4) Anything you may have seen or heard when the court was not in session is not evidence. You are to decide the case solely on the evidence received at the trial.

Evidence may be direct or circumstantial. Direct evidence is direct proof of a fact, such as testimony by a witness about what the witness personally saw or heard or did. Circumstantial evidence is proof of one or more facts from which you could find another fact. You should consider both kinds of evidence. The law makes no distinction between the weight to be given to either direct or circumstantial evidence. It is for you to decide how much weight to give to any evidence.

In deciding the facts in this case, you may have to decide which testimony to believe and which testimony not to believe. You may believe everything a witness says, or part of it, or none of it.

In considering the testimony of any witness, you may take into account:

(1) the opportunity and ability of the witness to see or hear or know the things attested to;

(2) the witness' memory;

(3) the witness' manner while testifying;

(4) the witness' interest in the outcome of the case and any bias or prejudice;

(5) whether other evidence contradicted the witness' testimony;

(6) the reasonableness of the witness' testimony in light of all the evidence; and

(7) any other factors that bear on believability.

The weight of the evidence as to a fact does not necessarily depend on the number of witnesses who testify.

You have heard testimony from persons who, because of education or experience, are permitted to state opinions and the reasons for those opinions. Opinion testimony should be judged just like any other testimony. You may accept it or reject it, and give it as much weight as you think it deserves, considering the witness' education and experience, the reasons given for the opinion, and all the other evidence in the case.

Certain charts and summaries have been received into evidence to illustrate information brought out in the trial. Charts and summaries are only as good as the underlying evidence that supports them. You should, therefore, give them only such weight as you think the underlying evidence deserves.

Certain charts and summaries that have not been received in evidence have been shown to you in order to help explain the contents of books, records, documents, or other evidence in the case. They are not themselves evidence or proof of any facts. If they do not correctly reflect the facts or figures shown by the evidence in the case, you should disregard these charges and summaries and determine the facts from the underlying evidence.

Some of you have taken notes during the trial. Whether or not you took notes, you should rely on your own memory of what was said. Notes are only to assist your memory. You should not be overly influenced by the notes.

Under the law, a corporation is considered to be a person. It can only act through its employees, agents, directors or officers. Therefore, a corporation is responsible for the acts of its employees, agents, directors, and officers performed within the scope of authority. All parties are equal before the law and a corporation is entitled to the same fair and conscientious consideration by you as any party.

When a party has the burden of proof on any claim or defense by a preponderance of the evidence, it means you must be persuaded by the evidence that the claim or defense is more probably true than not true.

One of the defenses in this case requires a different burden of proof of clear, cogent and convincing evidence. When a party has the burden of proof on a defense by clear, cogent and convincing evidence, it means that the proposition must be proven by evidence which carries greater weight and is more convincing than a preponderance of evidence. However, it does not mean that the proposition must be proven by evidence which is convincing beyond a reasonable doubt. You should base your decision on all of the evidence, regardless of which party presented it.

You should decide the case as to each party separately. Unless otherwise stated, the instructions apply to all parties.

Aircraft Gear is suing Boeing for damages related to Boeing's alleged breach of a March 1999 agreement between them. Boeing claims that it entered into the March 1999 agreement under duress and that, therefore, it was entitled to rescind it. Boeing has the burden to prove that it entered into the March 1999 agreement under duress by clear, convincing and cogent evidence.

Aircraft Gear denies that Boeing entered the March 1999 agreement under duress and claims that even if Boeing was under duress in March 1999, Boeing waived its duress defense by its subsequent behavior. Aircraft Gear has the burden to prove waiver by a preponderance of the evidence. Boeing denies that it waived its duress defense.

This is merely a summary of the claims.

A contract is a legally enforceable promise or set of promises. In order for a promise or set of promises to be legally enforceable, there must be mutual assent. A promise is an expression that justifies the person to whom it is made in reasonably believing that a commitment has been made that something specific shall happen or not happen in the future. A promise may be expressed orally, in writing, or by conduct.

In order for there to be mutual assent, the parties must agree on the essential terms of the contract, and must express to each other their agreement to the same essential terms.

Once a contract has been entered into, mutual assent of the contracting parties is essential for any modification of the contract. To constitute a modification, it must be shown through the words or conduct of the parties that there was an agreement of the parties on all essential terms of the contract modification, and that the parties intended the new terms to alter the contract.

A contract for sale imposes an obligation on each party that the other's expectation of receiving due performance will not be impaired. A duty of good faith and fair dealing is implied in every contract. This duty requires the parties to cooperate with each other so that each may obtain the full benefit of performance. However, this duty does not require a party to accept a material change in the terms of its contract.

The failure to perform fully a contractual duty when it is due is a breach of contract.

A party may rescind a contract on the ground of duress if the party proves by clear, cogent and convincing evidence that it agreed to the contract because of an improper threat by the other party which left no reasonable alternative.

Either party to a contract may waive a defense. A waiver is the intentional giving up of a known right.

Boeing may rescind the March 1999 agreement on the ground of duress. In order to rescind the agreement, Boeing must prove by clear, cogent and convincing evidence that it entered into it because of an improper threat by Aircraft Gear which left no reasonable alternative.

In this case, Aircraft Gear made an improper threat to Boeing when it threatened to discontinue shipments in March 1999. In order to rescind the agreement, Boeing must therefore prove by clear, cogent and convincing evidence that:

(a) it agreed to the March 1999 contract because of this improper threat; and

(b) it had no reasonable alternative.

If you find that Boeing has met its burden in showing duress, your verdict should be "yes" for Boeing's defense of duress. However, if you find that Boeing was unable to meet its burden in showing duress your verdict should be "no" on Boeing's defense of duress.

Aircraft Gear denies that Boeing acted under duress. It also claims that even if Boeing did act under duress, it waived this claim of duress. A party that desires to rescind a contract on the ground of duress is required to act to rescind with reasonable promptness upon removal of duress. Unreasonable delay in making an election to rescind constitutes a waiver of the claim of duress.

If Boeing meets its burden in showing duress, it is Aircraft Gear's burden to prove by a preponderance of the evidence that Boeing waived the defense of duress. If you find that Aircraft Gear has met its burden in showing the Boeing waived it defense of duress, your verdict should be "yes" on its claim that Boeing waived its defense of duress.

If you find that Aircraft Gear has not met its burden in showing that Boeing waived its defense of duress, your verdict should be "no" on its claim that Boeing waived its defense of duress.

It is the duty of the Court to instruct you about the measure of damages. By instructing you on damages, the Court does not mean to suggest for which party your verdict should be rendered.

Aircraft Gear claims the amounts set forth in Exhibit 293 as its claimed damages, including interest. Boeing claims the amounts set forth in Exhibit 294 are its claimed damages including interest. Depending upon your verdict, it is for you, the Jury, to determine what amount, if any, of the amounts claimed by either party have been proved and to which they are entitled.

If you find that Boeing has met its burden by showing by clear, convincing and cogent evidence that it acted under duress when it signed the March 1999 agreement and that Aircraft Gear has not shown that Boeing waived its duress defense by a preponderance of the evidence, then the March 1999 agreement cannot be enforced against Boeing. Boeing would then be entitled to get Aircraft Gear's parts at the price agreed on before March 19, 1999. Boeing's damages would then be equal to the amount it paid in excess of this price.

The burden of proving damages rests with Boeing and it is for you to determine, based upon the evidence, whether any particular element has been proved by a preponderance of the evidence. You must be governed by your own judgment, by the evidence in the case, and by these instructions, rather than by mere speculation, guess or conjecture.

If you find that Boeing has not met its burden of proving duress or that Aircraft Gear has met its burden in proving that Boeing waived its duress defense, then you must award damages for Boeing's breach of the March 1999 agreement.

In order to recover actual damages, Aircraft Gear has the burden of proving the following by a preponderance of the evidence:

(a) Aircraft Gear incurred actual economic damages as a result of Boeing's breach; and

(b) the amount of those damages.

If you find that Aircraft Gear has met its burden as to each of these elements, you shall award Aircraft Gear actual damages. Actual damages are those losses that were reasonably foreseeable, at the time the contract was made, as a probable result of a breach. A loss may be foreseeable as a probable result of a breach because it follows from the breach either:

(a) in the ordinary course of events, or

(b) as a result of special circumstances, beyond the ordinary course of events, that the party in breach had reason to know.

In calculating Aircraft Gear's actual damages, you should determine the sum of money that will put it in as good a position as it would have been in if both Aircraft Gear and Boeing had performed all of their promises under the March 1999 agreement. Damages available to Aircraft Gear in this case may include any lost net profits which Aircraft Gear can prove with reasonable certainty would have been earned, but were not, because of Boeing's breach.

The burden of proving damages rests with Aircraft Gear and it is for you to determine, based upon the evidence, whether any particular element has been proved by a preponderance of the evidence. You must be governed by your own judgment, by the evidence in the case, and by these instructions, rather than by mere speculation, guess or conjecture.

When you begin your deliberations, you should elect one member of the jury as your presiding juror. That person will preside over the deliberations and speak for you here in court. You will then discuss the case with your fellow jurors to reach agreement if you can do so. Your verdict must be unanimous. Each of you must decide the case for yourself, but you should do so only after you have considered all of the evidence, discussed it fully with the other jurors, and listened to the views of your fellow jurors. Do not be afraid to change your opinion if the discussion persuades you that you should. Do not come to a decision simply because other jurors think it is right. It is important that you attempt to reach a unanimous verdict but, of course, only if each of you can do so after having made your own conscientious decision. Do not change an honest belief about the weight and effect of the evidence simply to reach a verdict.

If it becomes necessary during your deliberations to communicate with me, you may send a note through the in-court deputy, signed by your presiding juror or by one or more members of the jury. No member of the jury should ever attempt to communicate with me except by a signed writing; and I will communicate with any member of the jury on anything concerning the case only in writing, or here in open court. If you send out a question, I will consult with the parties before answering it, which may take some time. You may continue your deliberations while waiting for the answer to any question. Remember that you are not to tell anyone—including me—how the jury stands, numerically or otherwise, until after you have reached a unanimous verdict or have been discharged. Do not disclose any vote count in any note to the court.

You will be provided with a special verdict form which consists of several questions for you to answer. When all jurors have unanimously agreed upon an answer to a question, you should proceed to the next question. It is necessary that you answer each of the questions unless the questions themselves specifically provide otherwise. You should answer the questions in the order in which they are asked as your answers to some questions will determine whether you are to answer all, some, or none of the remaining questions. Accordingly, it is important that you read the questions carefully and that you follow the directions set forth.

After you have reached unanimous agreement on a verdict, your presiding juror will fill in the form that has been given to you, sign and date it, and advise the court that you are ready to return to the courtroom.

This is a fairly good example of jury instructions in a complex contracts case that is potentially worth millions. How likely is it that the jury would fully understand these instructions? What findings of fact does the judge make, and what does he leave for the jury to consider? In particular, why does the judge state unequivocally that: "Aircraft Gear made an improper threat to Boeing when it threatened to discontinue shipments in March 1999"?

The jury made these findings of fact on the special verdict form:

WE, THE JURY make the following answers to the questions submitted by the Court:

1. Do you find that Boeing has proved by clear, convincing and cogent evidence that it acted under duress when it signed the March 1999 modification? (**Yes.**)

If you answered "Yes" to Question No. 1, continue to Question No. 2.

If you answered "No" to Question No. 1, please proceed to Question No. 3.

2. Do you find that Aircraft Gear proved by a preponderance of the evidence that Boeing waived its defense of duress by its conduct after March 1999? (**No.**)

If you answered "Yes" to Question No. 2, continue to Question No. 3.

If you answered "No" to Question No. 2, please proceed to Question No. 4.

3. What is the amount of damages, if any, that Aircraft Gear proved by a preponderance of the evidence?

$______

Please stop. Do not enter answers to any more questions. The presiding juror must sign and return the verdict form.

4. What is the amount of damages, if any, that Boeing proved by a preponderance of the evidence?

$______**1,830,000**

Please stop. The presiding juror must sign and return the verdict form.

What aspects of this decision do you regard as potentially problematic?

BROOKSIDE FARMS v. MAMA RIZZO'S, INC.

United States District Court for the Southern District of Texas, 1995.
873 F.Supp. 1029.

KENT, J. This is a breach of contract dispute in which plaintiff Brookside Farms ("Brookside") alleges that Defendant Mama Rizzo's Inc. ("MRI") breached its contract with Brookside to purchase 91,000 pounds of fresh basil leaves. Before the Court now are Plaintiff's Motion for partial Summary Judgment and Defendant's Motion for Summary Judgment. For the reasons discussed below, the Court finds that Defendant's Motion is DENIED and Plaintiff's Motion is GRANTED IN PART and DENIED IN PART.

Background

On October 13, 1993, Brookside Farms and MRI entered into a requirements contract for the sale of fresh basil leaves from Brookside to

MRI. Under the contract, MRI agreed to buy a minimum of 91,000 pounds of fresh basil leaves for a one-year term. Delivery was to be made daily, five days per week, in lots ranging from a minimum of 350 pounds to a maximum of 800 pounds. MRI agreed to pay for the basil it accepted within fifteen days of delivery date.

The price for the basil leaves under the contract was seasonally based, with one price applicable during the domestic growing season, and a higher price applicable during the non-growing season, when Brookside would look to Mexican growers to supply the basil it would need to fulfill its obligations under the contract. The original price for basil delivered during the domestic growing season—between June 1 and September 30—was $3.80 per pound; the original price for basil delivered during the non-growing season—October 1 to May 31—was $5.00 per pound.

It is undisputed that Mike Franklin, the vice-president of MRI, requested Wayde Burt, Brookside's general partner, to remove additional parts of the stems of the basil leaves, a task not specifically required under the original contract. Brookside agreed to do this work in exchange for a $0.50 per pound increase for the remainder of the contract term. The undisputed testimony shows that, because the original contract contained a clause forbidding oral modification, Franklin promised to make a notation of future price changes on MRI's copy of the original contract. The new price terms were also reflected on MRI's internally-generated purchase orders, Brookside's and MRI's payment checks. Between October 27, 1993, and November 16, 1993, MRI issued twelve separate purchase orders for shipments of basil at $5.50 per pound, and Brookside filled each order and invoiced MRI at the new price.

Between November 17, 1993, and January 9, 1994, MRI discontinued its order of basil leaves, and Brookside reduced its purchase of basil from its Mexican suppliers as a result. Consequently, Brookside was forced to pay higher prices for its supply of Mexican basil leaves when MRI resumed its orders under the contract. Two price modifications in the contract then followed in close sequence. Initially, Franklin and Burt agreed that MRI would pay $6.23 per pound for imported basil. Between January 10 and January 21, 1994, MRI issued fifteen separate purchase orders for shipments of basil at $6.25 per pound, and Brookside filled each order and invoiced MRI at that price. MRI paid all these invoices at the higher price. In mid-January, MRI agreed to pay $6.75 per pound for the basil Brookside imported from Mexico and issued sixty-seven separate purchase orders for shipments at that price. Each of these shipments was filled and paid without protest.

Between March 14, 1994, and May 17, 1994, MRI issued twenty-one purchase orders for basil at $6.75 per pound and issued a check to Brookside for $10,260 in payment for eight of those invoices. Unfortunately for both parties, this check was dishonored by MRI's bank for insufficient funds. Brookside has brought this suit on the claims that Defendant has breached the executory portion of the contract by refusing to accept the minimum amount of basil it agreed to and that

Defendant is also liable to Plaintiff for the 3,041 pounds of basil it accepted but did not pay for. MRI contends that no payment is due because Brookside itself breached the contract by raising prices in violation of the contract's express language that no modification would be binding unless it was reduced to written form....

ANALYSIS

The Price Modification Issue

The parties in this case vigorously dispute the question of whether they entered into a valid modification of the price of fresh basil leaves. Plaintiff has submitted undisputed affidavit testimony that several oral agreements to modify the original contract price for basil occurred. Within one week of the contract's formation, MRI discovered that the stems on the basil leaves would need to be removed before they could be properly used—a task not required by the original contract. As stated above, MRI's vice-president contacted Plaintiff's general partner, and both parties agreed that plaintiff would remove the basil stems before shipping the leaves and increase the purchase price by $0.50 per pound.

Both parties were aware that the contract contained a clause forbidding oral modifications of the contract's terms. Section 19 of the contract states: "This Agreement may be modified only by a writing signed by the party against whom or against whose successors and assigns enforcement of the modification is sought." Consequently, MRI's vice-president agreed to make a notation of the price change on MRI's copy of the original contract. (See Burt Affidavit, Instrument #7, at 2). Several subsequent price hikes were also agreed to by the parties, and MRI accepted and paid for 21,389 pounds of basil at purchase prices ranging from the original price to $6.75 per pound and accepted, but refused to pay for, an additional 3,041 pounds. Plaintiff currently seeks payment on this 3,041 pounds of basil at the purchase price of $6.75 per pound. MRI contends that no payment is due because Plaintiff itself breached the contract by raising prices in violation of the contract's express language that no modification would be binding unless it was reduced to written form. The Court disagrees.

Neither party in this case has properly pointed out that the contract in dispute falls within the Statute of Frauds under § 2.201 of the Texas Business and Commerce Code. That statute provides that "a contract for the sale of goods for the price of $500 or more is not enforceable by way of action or defense unless there is some writing sufficient to indicate that a contract for sale has been made between the parties and signed by the party against whom enforcement is sought." Clearly, the original contract between MRI and Brookside meets these requirements.

It is a general rule of Texas law that oral agreements that materially modify a written agreement within the Statute of Frauds are not enforceable. Tex.Bus. & Comm.Code Ann. § 26.01; ... However, not all modifications are prohibited. If the oral changes do not materially alter the underlying obligations, for example, they are not barred.... Second, the Texas Supreme Court has adopted the doctrine of promissory estoppel in some cases to forbid reliance on the Statute of Frauds as a defense to the validity of oral agreements. In specific, the Court has held that where one party reasonably relies on the oral promise of another to reduce an oral agreement to writing, the failure to create such a writing will not prevent the relying party from taking the modification out of the Statute of Frauds.[19] *"Moore" Burger, Inc. v. Phillips Petroleum Co.*, 492 S.W.2d 934, 937 (Tex. 1972); . . .

Finally, both parties in this case have also failed to note that Texas has adopted an exception to the Statute of Frauds contained in the Uniform Commercial Code. Sections 2.201(c) & (c)(3) of the Tex.Bus. & Comm.Code state in part that: "(c) A contract which does not satisfy the requirements of Subsection (a) [the general Statute of Frauds provision] but which is valid in other respects is enforceable. . . . (3) with respect to goods for which payment has been made and accepted or which have been received and accepted."

Thus, an oral modification that would itself form a binding contract in the absence of Statute of Frauds considerations can be binding on the parties to a sale of goods over $500 insofar as specific goods have been received and accepted. See Tex.Bus. & Comm.Code § 2.209.

The Court finds that a valid oral modification of the contract between MRI and Brookside occurred on both estoppel and statutory grounds. As stated above, it is undisputed that the parties agreed to alter the purchase price of the basil leaves. On each occasion, MRI issued separate purchase orders and Brookside filled each order and invoiced MRI on the price. In each case, MRI paid the invoiced price without protest. At the time the first price modification occurred, MRI's vice-president and Brookside's general partner discussed whether or not they needed to redraw the contract to account for the price changes in light of the fact that the contract did not allow for oral modifications. It is undisputed that MRI's vice-president assured Plaintiff that he would make a notation of price changes on MRI's copy of the contract and that this notation would be sufficient. . . .

The Court finds that such behavior clearly brings these parties within the estoppel theory adopted by the Texas Supreme Court in *"Moore" Burger*, 492 S.W.2d at 937. The promised notation would have constituted a valid written modification of the contract's terms. A valid writing under the Statute of Frauds requires only "some writing" signed by the party against whom it is to be enforced, namely, MRI. Tex.Bus. & Comm.Code § 2.201(a). In addition, given that the intent of the oral agreement to modify the written form of the contract was clearly

19. The Court specifically invoked both §§ 90 and 178, comment F of the Restatement, Contracts. Section 178, comment F reads: "Though there has been no satisfaction of the Statute, an estoppel may preclude objection on that ground in the same way that objection to the nonexistence of other facts essential for the establishment of a right or a defence may be precluded. A misrepresentation that there has been such satisfaction if substantial action is taken in reliance on the representation, precludes proof by the party who made the representation that it was false."

designed to bring it within the controlling language of the contract, Plaintiff could have reasonably relied on Defendant's implied promise to initial or sign the price change to indicate its intent to adopt the change; without such an implied promise, MRI's agreement to alter the written price terms would have been a mere fraud on the Plaintiff. Comment 6 to § 2.201(a) makes clear that such a writing need not be delivered to any other party; MRI could have made the notation on its signed copy of the contract and retained possession of it. It is also clear that MRI's promise to do so induced Brookside Farms to continue shipping basil leaves at the agreed price changes.[20]

Based on these actions, the Court finds that MRI cannot now invoke the no-oral-modification clause of the contract to bar Plaintiff's claim that a valid modification occurred in this case. To do so would be to reach the inequitable result that thousands of dollars could change hands over an extended period of commercial dealings between the parties, during which the Defendant knowingly and wilfully refrained from acting on the promise that induced the Plaintiff to continue shipments and then object to the course of dealing only when it has issued a bad check. The Court notes that the Uniform Commercial Code, which governs the transaction in question, has codified the contractual duty of good faith and fair dealing in commercial settings like the one presently before the Court. Tex.Bus. & Com.Code § 1.203 provides that "every contract or duty within this title imposes an obligation of good faith in its performance or enforcement." Where the party is a merchant, its standard of good faith performance requires honesty in fact and the observance of reasonable commercial standards of fair dealing in the trade. *Adolph Coors Co. v. Rodriguez*, 780 S.W.2d 477, 481 (Tx. App.—Corpus Christi, 1989, writ denied).[21] For the Court to allow Defendant to invoke the no-oral-modification clause after MRI itself induced and participated in the extended course of action it now complains of would be to convert the sale of basil leaves into a "basil sale carcinoma" that would devour all reasonable commercial standards of behavior between merchants.

The Court also finds that a valid modification of the contract's price terms occurred on statutory grounds. As stated above, oral modifications to contracts within the Statute of Frauds are generally forbidden. In addition, the Texas Business and Commerce Code specifically provides that signed contracts that exclude modifications that are not in the form

20. Mr. Burt's affidavit states that MRI promised to make the price change notations in regards to the first $0.50 per pound price increase. The Court notes that Burt does not specifically state that the parties agreed to alter the contract with each subsequent price change. Nevertheless, given the sophistication of the parties involved in this case and their extended course of conduct with one another, it is entirely reasonable to expect that, once having promised to make such changes, and having acted on these changes by shipment and subsequent payment, Plaintiff could have relied on MRI's initial promise to make a written notation to allow their commercial dealings to go forward.

21. The Court realizes, of course, that the duty of good faith and fair dealing under § 1.203 does not state an independent cause of action. Rather, it is designed to make an agreement's promises effective and defines other duties which grow out of specific contractual obligations. See id. at 482.

of signed writings are valid in this state. Tex.Bus. & Comm.Code § 2.209(b). Nevertheless, comment 4 to § 2.209 clearly states that such provisions do not limit the "actual later conduct" of parties that have entered into non-written modifications, despite a contract's provision that all modifications must be in writing. In this case, it is undisputed that the "actual later conduct" of these parties involved the order, shipment, and acceptance of 24,430 pounds of basil leaves, 3,041 pounds of which were paid for by a bad check on MRI's part.

Nevertheless, MRI argues that under the contract's "no waiver" clause, it did not waive its right to insist on the contract's initial terms and that, therefore, it now continues to have the right to demand that all modifications to this contract have been in writing to be valid. The Court disagrees.

Section 21 of the contract in question states: "The failure of either party to this Agreement to demand full performance of any of its provisions by the other party shall not constitute a waiver of performance unless the party failing to demand performance states in a writing signed by party that the party is waiving that performance. The waiver of any breach of any of the provisions of this Agreement by the parties shall not constitute a continuing waiver or a waiver of any subsequent breach by either party of the same or any other provision of this Agreement." (Defendant's Motion for Summary Judgment, Instrument #12, Exhibit A, at 4). The Court agrees with MRI that this "no-waiver" clause protects Defendant from a waiver of the "no-oral-modification" clause of the contract. Indeed, comment 4 of § 2.209, quoted above, explicitly relies on the theory that "later conduct" of the parties to a contract "waives" contractual obligations. By agreeing that a failure to demand full performance does not give rise to a waiver, the parties in this case have effectively agreed to their own private Statute of Frauds for modifying the contract. As comment 3 of Tex.Bus. & Com.Code § 2.209 states, agreements to modify a contract's terms only in written form "permits the parties in effect to make their own Statute of Frauds as regards any future modification of the contract. . . . " Like the general Statute of Frauds, § 2.209(b) is designed "to protect against false allegations of oral modifications." Id.

However, this does not protect MRI under these facts. Indeed, in one sense it destroys MRI's entire case, for if the failure to object to full performance reserves the right to demand such performance, then Brookside's failure to object to MRI's initial request for de-stemmed leaves reserves plaintiff's right to demand full performance of the original contract's terms, which apparently allowed basil to be shipped with stems still attached. More importantly, however, the private Statute of Frauds provision of the contract must be analyzed under the rules otherwise applicable to general Statute of Frauds issues, and under this analysis, the Court finds that the parties have entered into an effective agreement for those items Brookside shipped and MRI received and accepted.

Sections 2.201(c) and (c)(3) of the Texas Business and Commerce Code provide: "(c) A contract which does not satisfy the requirements of Subsection (a) [governing the Statute of Frauds] but which is valid in other respects is enforceable ... (3) with respect to goods for which payment has been made and accepted or which have been received and accepted."

This provision also governs the private Statute of Frauds contained in the contract before the Court. Assuming *arguendo* that the agreement between MRI and Brookside to modify the contract's terms did not meet the writing requirements of § 2.201(a), § 2.201(c) operates to bring the oral agreement within the Statute with respect to those goods MRI actually received and accepted, that is, the 24,430 pounds of basil Brookside shipped, including the 3,041 pounds of unpaid-for basil leaves. See *Bagby Land and Cattle Co. v. California Livestock Commission Co.*, 439 F.2d 315, 317 (5th Cir. 1971) ("receipt and acceptance either of goods or of the price constitutes an unambiguous overt admission by both parties that a contract actually exists."). Under the specific language of § 2.201(c), the new contractual price terms were not made enforceable as to future shipments of basil by Brookside, but they are enforceable as to the 3,041 pounds shipped under the agreed price of $6.75 per pound.[22]

For all these reasons, the Court finds that Plaintiff's Motion for Partial Summary Judgment is GRANTED on the claim that MRI is liable to Brookside for $20,526.75 in payment for the 3,041 pounds of basil accepted but not paid for.

Plaintiff also claims that MRI's refusal to accept and pay for the minimum amount of basil it agreed to buy in its requirements contract with Plaintiff constitutes a breach of contract, with the resulting damages to be determined at trial at a later date. In response, MRI claims that it was relieved of any obligation to purchase basil by Brookside's demand for higher prices than provided for in the contract. Having already decided that Plaintiff's price increases were legally justified, the Court now finds that for the same reasons articulated above, Brookside did not breach its contractual obligations and that MRI is liable for a material breach of its obligation to purchase a total of 91,000 pounds of basil from Plaintiff. Consequently, Plaintiff's Motion for Partial Summary Judgment is GRANTED on this point....

Conclusion

For all of the reasons stated above the Court finds that Plaintiff's Motion for Partial Summary Judgment is DENIED as to any claim for

22. Because of the general paucity of relevant Texas authority presented in the instant Motions, the Court does not rule on the question of whether sufficient written materials are present in this case to bring the oral agreements out of the Statute of Frauds. The Court notes, however, that purchase orders and invoices were generated for every shipment of basil made and that other courts have found such materials sufficient to satisfy the Statute of Frauds. See *Brochsteins, Inc. v. Whittaker Corp.*, 791 F. Supp. 660, 661 (S.D. Tex. 1992).

attorney's fees and is GRANTED as to the claims that MRI breached the executory portion of the parties' contract, is liable in the amount of $20,526.75 for the payment of 3,041 pounds of basil accepted but not paid for, and that MRI is liable under the Perishable Agricultural and Commodities Act. For the same reasons, Defendant's Motion for Summary Judgment is DENIED on all counts, including its counterclaim that MRI is entitled to recover overpayments from Plaintiff for the amounts it paid for basil. Defendant's counterclaim for overpayment is also hereby DISMISSED WITH PREJUDICE. All relief not specifically granted herein is also DENIED. All parties are to bear their own taxable costs incurred in this case to date. It is further ORDERED that the parties file no further pleadings in the matters determined in this Order, including motions to reconsider and the like. Instead, they are instructed to seek any further relief to which they feel themselves entitled in the United States Court of Appeals for the Fifth Circuit, as may be appropriate in due course.

Notes and Discussion

1. The Chaos of Contract Execution. The modification in *Angel v. Murray* was a stately affair: in a public meeting Maher presented his case for a modification, and the Newport City Council then voted to grant him an additional $10,000. This case is far messier, and not just because of the tons of basil leaves that seem to be piling up. Alas, it is also typical of many actual business interrelationships in long-term contracts.

First of all, the contract between Brookside and MRI falls under the UCC (as, for some reason, the litigating attorneys failed to appreciate), and hence the trial judge resorts first to § 2–209 ("Modification, Rescission and Waiver"), and later to § 2–201, the UCC Statute of Frauds, which is applicable since the original contract was within the Statute (§ 2–209(3)). Section 2–209 was clearly intended to ease the traditional restrictions on modification. Comment 1: "This section seeks to protect and make effective all necessary and desirable modifications of sales contracts without regard to the technicalities which at present hamper such adjustments." Who gets to decide what is "necessary and desirable"?

Second, the drafters of the original contract, perhaps aware of the UCC view on modification, expressly precluded non-written modifications (see § 2–209(2)) and also tried to limit the effectiveness of waivers (see § 2–209(4)-(5)). Why did the parties include these contract provisions? It is worth noting, in this connection, § 2–208(1), which provides that: "[A]ny course of performance accepted or acquiesced in without objection shall be relevant to determining the meaning of the agreement"; see also § 2–202(a) (the terms of an integrated contract "may be explained or supplemented ... by course of performance"). There is a danger here that a long-term contract might morph into new being through laxity in enforcement.

In any case, why is it that MRI found no safe harbor in the express terms of its original contract? Will Mama Rizzo be displeased with her lawyers? How much importance does the Court attach to the "undisputed testimony" from Brookside's general partner that MRI's vice-president had promised to put the first price modification into writing?

2. Modifications and Waivers. Your apartment lease provides that you will pay your monthly rent on the first business day of each month. However, the monthly paycheck from your student job is deposited on the first Friday of each month, usually after the first business day. Two things might happen. You might go to your landlord and explain the difficulty, and she might agree that you can pay on the first Friday; this agreement would modify the original lease, and, if valid and in proper form (the Statute of Frauds is relevant, for instance; see Restatement 2d § 149), would in effect create a new contract in place of the original one. If your landlord then wanted to return to the original payment term, she would have to seek a modification from you, which you would be entitled to refuse.

Alternatively, you might just start paying on the first Friday. If your landlord accepts without objection, she would very likely be waiving her right to enforce the contract at least for that payment; and, particularly if this waiver is repeated, she would also be creating in you a justified expectation that late payment would be acceptable in the future. But the terms of the original contract are not modified by a waiver. So your landlord, by giving you reasonable notice, can reinstate her original contractual right to timely payment.

Waivers are common in commercial transactions, as we will see in Chapter 7. In the present case, MRI's lawyers contended that the "no-waiver" clause of their original contract prevented the enforceability of modifications that violated the contractual requirement of writing. Reconstruct their reasoning and explain why it failed.

3. The Common Law Position. Edward J. Wagner entered into a contract with Graziano Construction Company to paint and supply materials for a shopping center that Graziano was building. The agreement between Wagner and Graziano provided, *inter alia*: "Without invalidating this contract the Contractor may add to or reduce the work to be performed hereunder. No extra work or changes from plans and specifications under this contract will be recognized or paid for, unless agreed to in writing before the extra work is started or the changes made, in which written order shall be specified in detail the extra work or changes desired, the price to be paid or the amount to be deducted should said change decrease the amount to be paid hereunder." *Wagner v. Graziano Constr. Co.*, 390 Pa. 445, 136 A.2d 82 (1957) (Musmanno, J.).

Wagner was then orally requested by Graziano's superintendent to perform extra work and supply additional material; the superintendent assured him that there was no need for a writing. But Graziano then declined to pay for the extras. Can Wagner recover?

In Common Law, the answer is clearly yes, despite the "no oral modifications" clause; there is no need even to resort to estoppel doctrines. "The most ironclad written contract can always be cut into by the acetylene torch of parol modification supported by adequate proof.... Even where the contract specifically states that no non-written modification will be recognized, the parties may yet alter their agreement by parol negotiation. The hand that pens a writing may not gag the mouths of the assenting parties.

The pen may be more precise in permanently recording what is to be done, but it may not still the tongues which bespeak an improvement in or modification of what has been written." Id. at 83–84. In simpler words, the original contract simply cannot be insulated against subsequent oral modifications. This rule, which remains largely valid today, becomes a bit more explicable if it is recognized that, as in *Wagner*, the party seeking to avoid the original contract clause usually has relied to its detriment on the subsequent modification. Should reliance be a requirement for avoidance?

Compare CISG art. 29(2): "A contract in writing which contains a provision requiring any modification or termination by agreement to be in writing may not be otherwise modified or terminated by agreement. However, a party may be precluded by his conduct from asserting such a provision to the extent that the other party has relied on that conduct."

ASMUS v. PACIFIC BELL

Supreme Court of California, 2000.
23 Cal.4th 1, 999 P.2d 71, 96 Cal.Rptr.2d 179.

CHIN, J. We granted the request of the United States Court of Appeals for the Ninth Circuit for an answer to the following certified question of law under rule 29.5 of the California Rules of Court: "Once an employer's unilaterally adopted policy—which requires employees to be retained so long as a specified condition does not occur—has become a part of the employment contract, may the employer thereafter unilaterally [terminate][23] the policy, even though the specified condition has not occurred?" We conclude the answer to the certified question is yes. An employer may unilaterally terminate a policy that contains a specified condition, if the condition is one of indefinite duration, and the employer effects the change after a reasonable time, on reasonable notice, and without interfering with the employees' vested benefits.

I. Background . . .

B. Facts

In 1986, Pacific Bell issued the following "Management Employment Security Policy" (MESP): "It will be Pacific Bell's policy to offer all management employees who continue to meet our changing business expectations employment security through reassignment to and retraining for other management positions, even if their present jobs are eliminated. [&] This policy will be maintained so long as there is no

23. Pursuant to our authority under rule 29.5(g) to restate or clarify "[a]t any time" the Ninth Circuit's certified question, we have substituted the word "terminate" for the Ninth Circuit's word "rescind" in the question certified to this court. The reason for the substitution is that the courts below and the parties discuss this action in terms of Pacific Bell's ability to terminate, or otherwise change, its policy, rather than "rescind" it as that term is legally defined. A contract rescission is a statutorily governed event that extinguishes a contract as if it never existed. Rescission is effected by the parties' mutual consent or mistake, failure of consideration, illegality, or other public purpose. (Civ. Code, §§ 1688, 1689.) The word substitution best reflects the decisions below and does not in any way affect the parties' legal analysis.

change that will materially affect Pacific Bell's business plan achievement."

In January 1990, Pacific Bell notified its managers that industry conditions could force it to discontinue its MESP. In a letter to managers, the company's chief executive officer wrote: "[W]e intend to do everything possible to preserve our Management Employment Security policy. However, given the reality of the marketplace, changing demographics of the workforce and the continued need for cost reduction, the prospects for continuing this policy are diminishing—perhaps, even unlikely. We will monitor the situation continuously; if we determine that business conditions no longer allow us to keep this commitment, we will inform you immediately."

Nearly two years later, in October 1991, Pacific Bell announced it would terminate its MESP on April 1, 1992, so that it could achieve more flexibility in conducting its business and compete more successfully in the marketplace. That same day, Pacific Bell announced it was adopting a new layoff policy (the Management Force Adjustment Program) that replaced the MESP but provided a generous severance program designed to decrease management through job reassignments and voluntary and involuntary terminations. Employees who chose to continue working for Pacific Bell would receive enhanced pension benefits. Those employees who opted to retire in December 1991 would receive additional enhanced pension benefits, including increases in monthly pension and annuity options. Employees who chose to resign in November 1991 would receive these additional enhanced pension benefits as well as outplacement services, medical and life insurance for one year, and severance pay equaling the employee's salary and bonus multiplied by a percentage of the employee's years of service.

Plaintiffs are 60 former Pacific Bell management employees who were affected by the MESP cancellation. They chose to remain with the company for several years after the policy termination and received increased pension benefits for their continued employment while working under the new Management Force Adjustment Program. All but eight of them signed releases waiving their right to assert claims arising from their employment under the MESP or its termination.

Plaintiffs filed an action in federal district court against Pacific Bell and its parent company, Pacific Telesis Group, seeking declaratory and injunctive relief, as well as damages for breach of contract, breach of fiduciary duty, fraud, and violations of the Employee Retirement Income Security Act (ERISA) (29 U.S.C. § 1000 et seq.). The parties filed countermotions for partial summary judgment before conducting discovery. The district court granted summary judgment in Pacific Bell's favor against the 52 plaintiffs who signed releases. In an unpublished opinion, the Ninth Circuit affirmed the district court's judgment in this respect.

The district court granted summary judgment on the breach of contract claim in favor of the eight plaintiffs who did not sign releases. It held that even if an employer had the right unilaterally to terminate a personnel policy creating a contractual obligation, that right would not apply in cases where the original employment policy incorporated a term for duration or conditions for rescission, absent stronger evidence of the employees' assent to the policy modification than their continued employment. The court concluded that Pacific Bell could not terminate its MESP unless it first demonstrated (paraphrasing the words of the MESP) "a change that will materially alter Pacific Bell's business plan achievement."

Thereafter, the parties entered into a stipulation providing in part that Pacific Bell "elected not to present any further evidence in this action with respect to the question of whether there has been 'a change that will materially alter Pacific Bell's business plan achievement' . . . and agreed that summary judgment may be entered in favor of the eight remaining Plaintiffs on the issue of liability for their claims of breach of contract by breach of the MES policy. . . ." On May 5, 1997, the district court entered an order approving the stipulation and entered judgment in plaintiffs' favor on the issue.

Pursuant to the parties' agreement, the court certified for interlocutory appeal the issue whether Pacific Bell breached the MESP, and the Ninth Circuit accepted the interlocutory appeal. In a published opinion, the Ninth Circuit stated its certification request and noted that our answer to the certified question would determine the remaining portion of the case pending before it. . . .

II. Discussion

A. *California Employment Law*

We held in *Foley v. Interactive Data Corp.* (1988) 47 Cal.3d 654, 254 Cal.Rptr. 211, 765 P.2d 373 (*Foley*), that an implied-in-fact contract term not to terminate an employee without good cause will rebut the statutory presumption of Labor Code section 2922 that employment for an indefinite period is terminable at will. (47 Cal.3d at p. 677, 254 Cal.Rptr. 211, 765 P.2d 373.) The *Foley* court observed that the trier of fact can infer an agreement to limit grounds for an employee's termination based on the employee's reasonable reliance on company policy manuals. (Id. at pp. 681–682, 254 Cal.Rptr. 211, 765 P.2d 373.) In *Scott*,[24] we stated that, in light of *Foley*, we could find "no rational reason why an employer's policy that its employees will not be demoted except for good cause, like a policy restricting termination or providing for severance pay, cannot become an implied term of an employment contract. In each of these instances, an employer promises to confer a significant benefit on the employee, and it is a question of fact whether that promise was reasonably understood by the employee to create a contractual obligation."

24. [Eds.: *Scott v. Pacific Gas & Electric. Co.*, 11 Cal.4th 454, 46 Cal.Rptr.2d 427, 904 P.2d 834 (1995), which held that unilaterally created employment policies are enforceable, but also concluded that "employers have the capacity to alter their policies and practices so as not to create unwanted contractual obligations." This decision left open the question how employers can terminate or modify an existing policy, which is the focus of this opinion.]

(*Scott*, supra, 11 Cal.4th at p. 464, 46 Cal.Rptr.2d 427, 904 P.2d 834.) Both *Scott* and *Foley* emphasized that employment policies, manuals, and offers were not exempt from the rules governing contract interpretation. (*Scott*, supra, 11 Cal.4th at p. 469, 46 Cal.Rptr.2d 427, 904 P.2d 834; *Foley*, supra, 47 Cal.3d at p. 681, 254 Cal.Rptr. 211, 765 P.2d 373.)

In some cases, an employer adopts a no-layoff policy or provides employees with an employment security policy in order to earn the employees' loyalty in exchange for granting them job security. This exchange is fair and it may, depending on the facts, provide the basis for an enforceable unilateral contract, i.e., one in which the promisor does not receive a promise in return as consideration....

In a unilateral contract, there is only one promisor, who is under an enforceable legal duty. (1 Corbin on Contracts (1993) § 1.23, p. 87.) The promise is given in consideration of the promisee's act or forbearance. As to the promisee, in general, any act or forbearance, including continuing to work in response to the unilateral promise, may constitute consideration for the promise. ...[25]

As a Court of Appeal observed, "Of late years the attitude of the courts (as well as of employers in general) is to consider [employment security agreements] which offer additional advantages to employees as being in effect offers of a unilateral contract which offer is accepted if the employee continues in the employment, and not as being mere offers of gifts. They make the employees more content and happier in their jobs, cause the employees to forego their rights to seek other employment, assist in avoiding labor turnover, and are considered of advantage to both the employer and the employees." (*Chinn v. China Nat. Aviation Corp.* (1955) 138 Cal.App.2d 98, 99–100, 291 P.2d 91 (*Chinn*) [employer's agreement to pay severance benefits becomes enforceable unilateral contract if employee accepts benefit offer by continuing employment]; ...)

The parties agree that California law permits employers to implement policies that may become unilateral implied-in-fact contracts when employees accept them by continuing their employment. We do not further explore the issue in the context here, although we note that

25. An employment contract in which the employer promises to pay an employee a wage in return for the employee's work is typically described as a unilateral contract. Scholars observe, however, that it is not always easy to determine whether an offer creates a unilateral or bilateral contract. (1 Corbin on Contracts, supra, § 1.23, pp. 93–94.) Indeed, the distinction between the contract types often exaggerates the importance of the particular bargain compelling performance without commitment. "In response to these concerns, the Restatement (Second) of Contracts has abandoned the terms 'unilateral' and 'bilateral,' without, however, abandoning the concepts behind them." (Id. at § 1.23, p. 94.) In the Restatement Second of Contracts, the unilateral contract is preserved in the phrase, "Where an offer invites an offeree to accept by rendering a performance and does not invite a promissory acceptance...." (Rest.2d Contracts, § 45(1).)

Most legal scholars, however, prefer to rely on the traditional terminology to distinguish between the two types of offers and promises because the use of unilateral contract analysis has been growing in recent years, particularly in employment cases. (1 Corbin on Contracts, supra, § 1.23, p. 95.) ... In this case, we retain the distinction between unilateral and bilateral contracts.

whether employment policies create unilateral contracts will be a factual question in each case. (*Chinn*, supra, 138 Cal.App.2d at pp. 99–100, 291 P.2d 91.) The parties here disagree on how employers may terminate or modify a unilateral contract that has been accepted by the employees' performance. Plaintiffs assert that Pacific Bell was not entitled to terminate its MESP until it could demonstrate a change materially affecting its business plan, i.e., until the time referred to in a clause in the contract. Pacific Bell asserts that because it formed the contract unilaterally, it could terminate or modify that contract as long as it did so after a reasonable time, gave affected employees reasonable notice, and did not interfere with the employees' vested benefits (e.g., pension and other retirement benefits). Even if we were to require additional consideration, Pacific Bell contends it gave that consideration by offering enhanced pension benefits to those employees who chose to remain with the company after the modification took effect. Both parties rely on cases from other jurisdictions to support their respective positions.

B. Other Jurisdictions

Because there is no case in point on the present question in this state, the parties each rely on the rule as stated in other jurisdictions to support their particular views.

Pacific Bell points to the rule in the majority of jurisdictions that have addressed the question whether and how an employer may terminate or modify an employment security policy that has become an implied-in-fact unilateral contract. Regardless of the legal theory employed, the majority of other jurisdictions that have addressed the question conclude that an employer may terminate or modify a contract with no fixed duration period after a reasonable time period, if it provides employees with reasonable notice, and the modification does not interfere with vested employee benefits. (See, e.g., ... *Fleming v. Borden, Inc.* (1994) 316 S.C. 452, 450 S.E.2d 589, 595 (*Fleming*); ...)

Most of these courts refer to general contract law in deciding whether an employer may terminate or modify an employment contract. They reason that because the employer created the policy's terms unilaterally, the employer may terminate or modify them unilaterally with reasonable notice. (See, e.g., ... *Fleming*, supra, 450 S.E.2d at p. 595; ...)

Fleming indicated that of the three possible approaches to the termination question, it favored the majority approach as the one most consistent with unilateral contract principles. (*Fleming*, supra, 450 S.E.2d at pp. 594–595.) The first approach—to allow termination without notice at any time before completion of the contract—struck the *Fleming* court as too harsh. (Ibid.) That approach is now considered obsolete in California. (*Drennan v. Star Paving Co.* (1958) 51 Cal.2d 409, 414, 333 P.2d 757.) *Fleming* also rejected an alternative minority model that would impose bilateral concepts on a unilateral contract to require mutual assent and additional consideration to support the termination.

(*Fleming*, supra, 450 S.E.2d at p. 595.) The court settled on the majority approach after recognizing that the employer-employee relationship is not static. *Fleming* stated that "[e]mployers must have a mechanism which allows them to alter the employee handbook to meet the changing needs of both business and employees." (Ibid.)

As plaintiffs observe, a minority of jurisdictions today hold that an employer cannot terminate or modify a unilateral employment contract without the employees' express knowledge and consent.... Like the dissent, they reason that any termination or modification of a unilateral employment contract requires additional consideration and acceptance by the affected employees, because their only choices in light of a pending termination would be to resign or to continue working. (See, e.g., *Demasse v. ITT Corp.* (1999) 194 Ariz. 500, 984 P.2d 1138, 1145 (*Demasse*).)

Most recently, in *Demasse*, the Ninth Circuit certified a question to the Arizona Supreme Court whether a layoff seniority provision (stating that the company will lay off junior employees ahead of senior employees) may be unilaterally modified to permit the employer to lay off employees without regard to seniority status. (*Demasse*, supra, 984 P.2d at p. 1140.) The employee handbook reserved the employer's right to amend, modify, or cancel it. When the employees received the handbook, they signed an acknowledgement that they understood and would comply with its provisions. (Id. at p. 1141.) Four years later, the employer modified the layoff policy to base it not on seniority status, but on employee " 'abilities and documentation of performance.' " (Ibid.) The plaintiffs were employees whom the company laid off 10 days after the new policy took effect. They sued in federal district court, alleging they were laid off in breach of an implied-in-fact contract. (Ibid.)

After the district court found that the employer unilaterally could alter its handbook, the Ninth Circuit certified the question to the Arizona Supreme Court. That court concluded that, although most handbook terms are merely descriptions of the employer's present policies, some could create implied-in-fact contracts, depending on the parties' intent. (*Demasse*, supra, 984 P.2d at p. 1143.) The court adopted the minority rule, holding that once a handbook policy becomes an implied-in-fact contract, the employer cannot unilaterally modify it. (Id. at p. 1144.) Any change requires mutual assent, with continued employment inadequate consideration for the change. (Id. at p. 1145.) The court was concerned the employer could alter the contract terms and, on the same day, fire the employee, rendering the original contract illusory. (Id. at p. 1147.) It rejected Arizona precedent holding that the employer provided consideration for the change by continuing to provide jobs, and the employees manifested their assent by continuing to work. (Ibid.)

Vice Chief Justice Jones's dissent aptly rejected the notion that in order to free itself of future obligations, the company would be required to provide employees with a wage increase or other bonus amounting to new consideration. To do so, the dissent reasoned, would incorrectly impose a bilateral principle on the unilateral relationship, leaving the employer unable to manage its business, impairing essential managerial flexibility, and causing undue deterioration of traditional employment principles. (*Demasse*, supra, 984 P.2d at p. 1156 (dis. opn. of Jones, V.C.J.); see also *Fleming*, supra, 450 S.E.2d at p. 595.)

In preferring the more reasonable majority rule, the dissent also found unsatisfactory the *Demasse* majority's reasoning that employers not wanting to be bound by a handbook's terms are simply free never to issue one in the first place. As the dissent observed, "employers may be unilaterally forced by economic circumstance to curtail or shut down an operation, something employers have the absolute right to do. When the employer chooses in good faith, in pursuit of legitimate business objectives, to eliminate an employee policy as an alternative to curtailment or total shutdown, there has been forbearance by the employer. Such forbearance constitutes a benefit to the employee in the form of an offer of continuing employment. The employer who provides continuing employment, albeit under newly modified contract terms, also provides consideration to support the amended policy manual." (*Demasse*, supra, 984 P.2d at p. 1155 (dis. opn. of Jones, V.C.J.).) We agree with the *Demasse* dissent's thoughtful analysis and find its application of contract principles to the question before it reflected in our own state's developing case law and scholarly treatises....

We turn now to plaintiffs' several arguments that would restrict Pacific Bell's right to terminate or modify its MESP.

C. Application of Legal Principles

1. Consideration

Plaintiffs contend that Pacific Bell gave no valid consideration to bind the proposed MESP termination and subsequent modification. According to plaintiffs, when Pacific Bell unilaterally terminated the contract to create a new contract with different terms, it left its employees with no opportunity to bargain for additional benefits or other consideration. The parties' obligations were unequal, and hence, there was no mutuality of obligation for the change.

We disagree. The general rule governing the proper termination of unilateral contracts is that once the promisor determines after a reasonable time that it will terminate or modify the contract, and provides employees with reasonable notice of the change, additional consideration is not required.... The mutuality of obligation principle requiring new consideration for contract termination applies to bilateral contracts only.... In the unilateral contract context, there is no mutuality of obligation.... For an effective modification, there is consideration in the form of continued employee services.... The majority rule correctly recognizes and applies this principle[26].... Here, Pacific Bell replaced its

26. Curiously, the dissent sides with the minority of jurisdictions that chose to ignore these traditional rules governing unilateral contract termination or modification.

MESP with a subsequent layoff policy. Plaintiffs' continued employment constituted acceptance of the offer of the modified unilateral contract. As we have observed, a rule requiring separate consideration in addition to continued employment as a limitation on the ability to terminate or modify an employee security agreement would contradict the general principle that the law will not concern itself with the adequacy of consideration. (*Foley*, supra, 47 Cal.3d at p. 679, 254 Cal.Rptr. 211, 765 P.2d 373.)

The corollary is also true. Just as employers must accept the employees' continued employment as consideration for the original contract terms, employees must be bound by amendments to those terms, with the availability of continuing employment serving as adequate consideration from the employer. When Pacific Bell terminated its original MESP and then offered continuing employment to employees who received notice and signed an acknowledgment to that effect, the employees accepted the new terms, and the subsequent modified contract, by continuing to work. Continuing to work after the policy termination and subsequent modification constituted acceptance of the new employment terms. (See *Pine River State Bank v. Mettille* (Minn.1983) 333 N.W.2d 622, 626–627 [continued employment is sufficient consideration for employment contract modification].)

2. *Illusoriness*

Plaintiffs alternatively claim that Pacific Bell's MESP would be an illusory contract if Pacific Bell could unilaterally modify it. Plaintiffs rely on the rule that when a party to a contract retains the unfettered right to terminate or modify the agreement, the contract is deemed to be illusory. . . .

Plaintiffs are only partly correct. Scholars define illusory contracts by what they are not. As Corbin observes, "if a promise is expressly made conditional on something that the parties know cannot occur, no real promise has been made. Similarly, one who states 'I promise to render a future performance, if I want to when the time arrives,' has made no promise at all. It has been thought, also, that promissory words are illusory if they are conditional on some fact or event that is wholly under the promisor's control and bringing it about is left wholly to the promisor's own will and discretion. This is not true, however, if the words used do not leave an unlimited option to the one using them. It is true only if the words used do not in fact purport to limit future action in any way." (2 Corbin on Contracts, supra, § 5.32, pp. 175–176, fns. omitted.) Thus, an unqualified right to modify or terminate the contract is not enforceable. But the fact that one party reserves the implied power to terminate or modify a unilateral contract is not fatal to its enforcement, if the exercise of the power is subject to limitations, such as fairness and reasonable notice. . . .

As Pacific Bell observes, the MESP was not illusory because plaintiffs obtained the benefits of the policy while it was operable. In other words, Pacific Bell was obligated to follow it as long as the MESP remained in effect. Although a permanent no-layoff policy would be highly prized in the modern workforce, it does not follow that anything less is without significant value to the employee or is an illusory promise. (See *Bankey*, supra, 443 N.W.2d at pp. 119–120.) As long as the MESP remained in force, Pacific Bell could not treat the contract as illusory by refusing to adhere to its terms; the promise was not optional with the employer and was fully enforceable until terminated or modified. (2 Corbin on Contracts, supra, § 5.32, p. 177.)

3. Vested Benefits

Plaintiffs next allege that the MESP conferred a vested benefit on employees, like an accrued bonus or a pension. But as Pacific Bell observes, no court has treated an employment security policy as a vested interest for private sector employees.... In addition, plaintiffs do not allege that Pacific Bell terminated its MESP in bad faith. Although we agree with plaintiffs that an employer may not generally interfere with an employee's vested benefits, we do not find that the MESP gave rise to, or created, any vested benefits in plaintiffs' favor.

4. Condition as Definite Duration Clause

Plaintiffs alternatively contend that a contract specifying termination on the occurrence (or nonoccurrence) of a future happening, in lieu of a specific date, is one of definite duration that cannot be terminated or modified until the event occurs. (See *Wittmann v. Whittingham* (1927) 85 Cal.App. 140, 145, 259 P. 63 [contract to deliver shares of stock when stock dividends or profits had paid note is contract of definite duration]; *La Jolla Casa deManana v. Hopkins* (1950) 98 Cal.App.2d 339, 348, 219 P.2d 871 [contracts specified to last until " 'termination of the present war' " and until plaintiff " 'can reasonably build a home for herself' " are contracts for definite duration].) Because Pacific Bell declared that it would maintain its MESP "so long as" its business conditions did not substantially change, plaintiffs, like the dissent, assert that the specified condition is automatically one for a definite duration that Pacific Bell is obliged to honor until the condition occurs.

Contrary to plaintiffs and the dissent, a "specified condition" may be one for either definite or indefinite duration. Indeed, both plaintiffs and the dissent fail to recognize that courts have interpreted a contract that conditions termination on the happening of a future event as one for a definite duration or time period only when "there is an ascertainable event which necessarily implies termination." (*Lura v. Multaplex, Inc.* (1982) 129 Cal.App.3d 410, 414–415, 179 Cal.Rptr. 847; ...) As Pacific Bell observes, even though its MESP contained language specifying that the company would continue the policy "so long as" it did not undergo changes materially affecting its business plan achievement, the condition did not state an ascertainable event that could be measured in any reasonable manner. As Pacific Bell explains, when it created its MESP, the document referred to changes that would have a significant negative effect on the company's rate of return, earnings and, "ultimately the viability of [its] business." The company noted that if the change were to occur, it would result from forces beyond Pacific Bell's control, and would include "major changes in the economy or the public policy arena." These changes would have nothing to do with a fixed or ascertainable event that would govern plaintiffs' or Pacific Bell's obligations to each other under the policy. Therefore, the condition in the MESP did not restrict Pacific Bell's ability to terminate or modify it, as long as the company made the change after a reasonable time, on reasonable notice, and in a manner that did not interfere with employees' vested benefits. (See, e.g., *Consolidated Theatres, Inc. v. Theatrical Stage Employees Union* (1968) 69 Cal.2d 713, 731, 73 Cal.Rptr. 213, 447 P.2d 325 [contract for indefinite duration terminable after a reasonable time on reasonable notice].)

The facts show that those conditions were met here. Pacific Bell implemented the MESP in 1986, and it remained in effect until 1992, when the company determined that maintaining the policy was incompatible with its need for flexibility in the marketplace. The company then implemented a new Management Force Adjustment Program in which employees whose positions were eliminated would be given 60 days to either find another job within the company, leave the company with severance benefits after signing a release of any claims, or leave the company without severance benefits. The employees were provided with a booklet entitled Voluntary Force Management Programs detailing the new benefits the company provided following the MESP cancellation.

Thus, the MESP was in place for a reasonable time and was effectively terminated after Pacific Bell determined that it was no longer a sound policy for the company. Contrary to the dissent, Pacific Bell did not engage in behavior that one could characterize as "manipulative" or "oppressive." ... Employees were provided ample advance notice of the termination, and the present plaintiffs even enjoyed at least two more years of employment and corresponding benefits under a modified policy before they were eventually laid off. In sum, Pacific Bell maintained the MESP for a reasonable time, it provided more than reasonable notice to the affected employees that it was terminating the policy, and it did not interfere with employees' vested benefits. The law requires nothing more.

III. Conclusion

As discussed, our employment cases support application of contract principles in the decision whether an employer may unilaterally terminate an employment security policy that has become an implied in-fact unilateral contract. (See, e.g., *Foley*, supra, 47 Cal.3d at pp. 678–679, 254 Cal.Rptr. 211, 765 P.2d 373.) Under contract theory, an employer may terminate a unilateral contract of indefinite duration, as long as its action occurs after a reasonable time, and is subject to prescribed or implied limitations, including reasonable notice and preservation of vested benefits.... The facts clearly show that employees enjoyed the benefits of the MESP for a reasonable time period, and that Pacific Bell gave its employees reasonable and ample notice of its intent to terminate the MESP. The company also did not at any time interfere with employees' vested benefits in effecting the MESP termination. In addition, the employees accepted the company's modified policy by continuing to work in light of the modification. Therefore, in response to the Ninth Circuit's certification request, we conclude that we should answer as follows: An employer may terminate a written employment security policy that contains a specified condition, if the condition is one of indefinite duration and the employer makes the change after a reasonable time, on reasonable notice, and without interfering with the employees' vested benefits.

GEORGE, C.J. (DISSENTING). I respectfully dissent.

We granted the request of the United States Court of Appeals for the Ninth Circuit to answer the following certified question of law: "Once an employer's unilaterally adopted policy—which requires employees to be retained *so long as a specified condition does not occur*—has become a part of the employment contract, may the employer thereafter unilaterally rescind the policy, even though the specified condition *has not occurred?*"(Italics added.) The majority, however, inexplicably answers a different question—one in which it is assumed by the majority that the employer's policy requires employees to be retained *indefinitely*, because the condition assertedly is unascertainable and thus *may or may not have occurred.*

The entire analysis of the majority opinion rests upon the single false premise that the specified contractual condition permitting Pacific Bell to terminate its "Management Employment Security Policy" (MESP)—the occurrence of a "change that will materially affect Pacific Bell's business plan achievement" ("a serious financial situation")—does not describe "an ascertainable event that could be measured in any reasonable manner." ... This premise (1) conflicts with the language of the certified question, (2) contradicts the record, (3) is inconsistent with Pacific Bell's own briefing and explicit concessions, and (4) is refuted by established contract law. As explained below, the condition allowing termination of the MESP is ascertainable and specifies a definite duration for the MESP. Contrary to the majority's assertion, not even Pacific Bell contends that such a change cannot be measured in a reasonable manner. Indeed, Pacific Bell repeatedly has conceded that the condition has not occurred. Because a contract setting forth an express condition for its termination may not be terminated unilaterally before the condition occurs, Pacific Bell may not terminate the MESP.

The majority incorrectly determines—in a single paragraph at the end of its opinion—that the MESP specifies an unascertainable event for its termination and therefore is a contract term of indefinite duration. Because it mischaracterizes the contractual condition in this manner, the majority erroneously and unnecessarily decides a much broader issue that is not within the scope of the certified question, not properly before this court, and not properly before the Ninth Circuit. The majority thus provides no assistance to the Ninth Circuit in resolving the pending appeal and subverts the certification process. It is particularly unfortunate that the majority reaches out to address a broad issue that is not presented by this case, when the court is so closely divided and lacks the participation of all of its permanent members.

Rather than responding to a question different from that certified to us by the Ninth Circuit and presented by the record, I would answer the certified question with a simple "no." Once an employer's unilaterally adopted policy—which requires employees to be retained so long as a specified condition does not occur—has become a part of the employment contract, the employer may not rescind the policy unilaterally if the specified condition has not occurred. To the extent the majority addresses a different issue regarding the termination of an employment security policy that does not contain such a condition, its discussion is unnecessary to the proper resolution of this matter and, in any event, is contrary to established principles of contract law....

[Eds.: The bulk of the dissenting opinion is given over to arguing that the specified condition had not been met. The end of the dissent discusses the modification issue.]

IV.

... The parties agree that the MESP was an offer for a unilateral contract that plaintiffs accepted by continuing employment. The issue addressed in the majority opinion is whether an employer may modify an implied-in-fact employment security agreement lacking an express duration provision, simply by announcing a different policy.

"Modification is a change in the obligation by a modifying agreement, which requires mutual assent, and must ordinarily be supported by consideration. [Citations]." (1 Witkin, Summary of Cal. Law (9th ed.1987) Contracts, § 909, p. 814.) "[U]nder the traditional view, a promise by an employer or an employee under a subsisting contract to do more or take less than that contract requires is invalid unless the other party gives or promises to give something capable of serving as consideration." (3 Williston on Contracts (4th ed.1992) § 7:37, pp. 604–605, fn. omitted.) Consideration may be either a benefit conferred upon the promisor or a detriment suffered by the promisee. (1 Witkin, supra, Contracts, § 208, p. 217.) Doing or promising to do what one already is legally bound to do cannot be consideration for a promise. (Id., § 221, p. 227.)

Under these principles, Pacific Bell's modification of the employment contract to eliminate the MESP requires the assent of plaintiffs to take less under the contract. Plaintiffs' mere continued performance under the original agreement does not indicate assent to the modification. To be supported by consideration, an agreement by plaintiffs to forgo the benefits of the established security agreement must include some additional benefit to the plaintiffs. Continued employment under less favorable conditions was not a benefit to plaintiffs. Instead, Pacific Bell obtained the benefit of removing the restriction upon its continuing obligation to employ plaintiffs under the preexisting unilateral contract.

As one commentator has noted, the fallacy underlying decisions upholding unilateral modification in this context is that the modification of a contract is completely analogous to its formation. (Sullivan, Unilateral Modification of Employee Handbooks: A Contractual Analysis (1995) 5 Regent U. L.Rev. 261, 288–293.) The general rule that the act of continuing employment with knowledge of new or changed conditions may create binding obligations was framed initially in decisions in which the courts considered the formation of a unilateral contract. Continuing to perform and insisting upon one's rights under an existing contract, however, are not proper grounds from which to imply a party's assent to a subsequent modification of that contract. In addition, as with all contracts, in order to modify an employment security agreement, the employer must provide some new term or benefit that inures to the advantage of all affected employees. "A promise to do less than one is legally obligated to do cannot constitute consideration." (Id. at p. 292, fn. omitted.) "To argue that a contract is effectively modified simply because the same transactions which led to its formation have again occurred is an overly simplistic and incorrect axiom." (Id. at p. 293.)

The majority endorses this overly simplistic and incorrect view of the modification of contracts. It relies upon the so-called majority approach in other jurisdictions that permits employers to terminate benefits unilaterally under implied-in-fact employment agreements merely by giving reasonable notice. As I shall explain, however, the opinions adopting such a rule either expressly reject traditional principles of contract law or contain no independent contract analysis of the issue. Of those decisions resolving the issue by examining the law governing modification of ordinary contracts, all such decisions hold that, in order for the modification to be binding, the employer must provide additional consideration and the employee must assent to the modification. Because it is beyond question that under California law we must apply traditional principles of contract law in resolving this issue (*Foley*, supra, 47 Cal.3d at pp. 677–681, 254 Cal.Rptr. 211, 765 P.2d 373), I conclude, consistent with all courts that have engaged in a traditional contract analysis of this issue, that an employer may not modify an employment security agreement unilaterally, simply by maintaining the policy for a reasonable time and giving reasonable notice of the proposed modification.

The leading case adopting the so-called majority rule determined that unilateral contract analysis was insufficient to resolve the issue, and thus decided the question based upon public policy considerations—that the employer has a legitimate expectation that it may modify employment policies for economic and business reasons. (*In re Certified Question* (1989) 432 Mich. 438, 443 N.W.2d 112, 119–120 (*Bankey*).) In a subsequent decision addressing whether an employer unilaterally could modify an express contract term in an employment agreement, however, an intermediate appellate court in the same jurisdiction held that continued employment alone was insufficient to indicate the employee assented to the modification: "[A]cceptance cannot be presumed from the mere fact of continued employment; otherwise, how would such an offer ever be rejected, absent one leaving employment?" (*Farrell v. Automobile Club of Michigan* (1990) 187 Mich.App. 220, 466 N.W.2d 298, 301 [distinguishing *Bankey*]; . . .)

Because under California law implied-in-fact employee agreements stand on equal footing with express contracts, *Bankey*'s analysis and conclusions are not persuasive for our purposes. Contrary to the majority's suggestion that most of the courts adopting the so-called majority approach rely upon contract law because they refer to contract law . . ., actually most of these decisions simply rely upon *Bankey* and/or asserted public policy considerations to justify their conclusions.

Courts adopting the so-called minority rule, however, engage in an analysis of traditional principles of contract law and conclude that under such an analysis, an employer may not modify an existing contract unilaterally. They reject the policy-based approach of *Bankey* and its progeny. For example, in *Brodie v. General Chemical Corp.* (Wyo.1997) 934 P.2d 1263, 1267–1268 (Brodie), the Wyoming Supreme Court stated: "Employer contends that finding an implied-in-fact contract by recognition of handbook provisions involves an analysis which does not apply the normal contract law principles afforded to express contracts and further asserts that the distinction of express versus implied permits our applying different rules for modifying a handbook contract. The Michigan Supreme Court utilized an interpretation similar to Employer's argument in [*Bankey,* supra, 443 N.W.2d 112, 116]. . . . In *Bankey*, the Michigan Supreme Court . . . permit[ted] unilateral modifications because handbook promises were not enforceable under a contract theory, but rather under broad public policy considerations. [Citation.] [&] The *Bankey* rationale is inapposite for our purposes because, as explained above, our handbook decisions hold that an implied employment contract does arise from established contract law principles and our contract law concerning modification is well settled that an agreement altering a written contract, to be binding, must be based on consideration. [Citation.] . . . [E]stablished contract law principles apply to the employment contract whether express or implied. [Citation.]" . . .

Under contract law, we cannot simply ignore the original agreement and find that the employer has offered a new agreement that is accepted by continued performance, as was the original agreement. When the employment relationship begins, or when the employer confers additional benefits upon the employee such as a job security policy, it is reasonable to conclude that the employee accepts the unilateral offer by continuing employment. The employee provides services and forgoes the right to obtain employment elsewhere as consideration for the employer's promises, while the employer enjoys the extra productivity and loyalty conferred by the job security term. When the employee already is employed under an enforceable agreement, however, the employer is the party that must provide new consideration in exchange for the employee's agreement to forgo the valuable right to job security. This right is vested in the sense that, once the contract giving rise to the right has been created, Pacific Bell must honor its contractual commitment. (See *Hunter v. Sparling* (1948) 87 Cal.App.2d 711, 722–725, 197 P.2d 807.) . . .

Rejecting the employer's public policy argument, also advanced by Pacific Bell in the present case, that it would be undesirable to have different employees governed by different policies, and that an employer must be free to alter employment policies, the opinion in *Doyle*, supra, 237 Ill.Dec. 100, 708 N.E.2d 1140, further states: "Although we are aware of these potential drawbacks, we note that this is a matter of contract and see no compelling reason here to relieve the defendant of the obligations it has voluntarily incurred. Employers who choose to set forth policies in employee handbooks and manuals as an inducement to attracting and retaining a skilled and loyal work force cannot disregard those obligations at a later time, simply because the employer later perceives them to be inconvenient or burdensome." (Id. 237 Ill.Dec. 100, 708 N.E.2d at p. 1147.) Indeed, in the present case Pacific Bell obtained the advantages of offering the policy in order to retain qualified managers during good economic times, when these employees otherwise might have obtained jobs elsewhere, and then chose to disregard that policy when the marketplace changed and the employees could have benefited most from the policy. . . .

Because the majority concludes that plaintiffs provided the necessary consideration for cancellation of the MESP by continuing their employment, it does not reach Pacific Bell's contention that it provided its own consideration by conferring increased pension benefits upon plaintiffs. As explained above, I disagree that plaintiffs' continued employment provided consideration supporting the modification. The additional pension benefits provided by Pacific Bell to plaintiffs conceivably could constitute consideration given by Pacific Bell. A question of fact also remains whether plaintiffs, by continuing to work, accepted the offer of modification accompanied by these increased pension benefits. Those issues are not encompassed by the certified question, however. . . .

V.

The majority opinion is unsupportable in two fundamental respects: first, in purporting to decide an issue that is neither presented on this record nor encompassed by the certified question; and second, in providing an answer that conflicts with the basic precepts of controlling contract law. The majority endorses a patently unfair, indeed unconscionable, result—permitting an employer that made a promise of continuing job security to its employees in order to retain their services during a period of good job prospects, to repudiate that promise with impunity several years later when the employer determined that it was no longer in its interest to honor its earlier commitment.

I dissent.

Notes and Discussion

1. Adding Benefits. The 60 Pacific Bell ex-managers who brought this lawsuit had all, it seems, been working for Pacific Bell as "at will" employees when, in 1986, Pacific Bell issued its MES policy, which effectively offered them a new benefit: subject to some conditions, they would no longer be fired if their positions were eliminated, but instead retrained for other positions. How did this promised benefit become part of their employment contract? The usual legal analysis is that the issuance of the benefit (often through a pamphlet or a description in an employee handbook) constitutes an offer to modify the contract, which the employee accepts by continuing to work. *Pine River*, a 1983 Minnesota decision cited by the majority, is the leading case. In *Asmus*, the Court uses this theory, which it describes as a unilateral contract (an offer that is accepted by performance). Does the theory strike you as plausible in light of usual offer-and-acceptance theory?

Suppose that the employee failed to read the handbook "offer." Could the employer argue that the employee's continuing performance did not constitute acceptance? Most courts have rejected this argument; see, e.g., *Anderson v. Douglas & Lomason Co.*, 540 N.W.2d 277, 284 (Iowa 1995). Compare Restatement 2d § 211(2): A standardized agreement "is interpreted wherever reasonable as treating alike all those similarly situated, without regard to their knowledge or understanding of the standard terms of the writing."

The MES policy, obviously intended to boost employee morale, might have been substantially less effective had the policy come with an express disclaimer ("be warned: this benefit is revocable at any time"). Could Pacific Bell have protected itself by inserting a more general notice that the handbook was not intended to create contractual rights? Would such a notice have to be conspicuous? *Anderson v. Douglas & Lomason Co.*, supra, at 287–288, reviews the case law, which generally requires some visibility.

2. Subtracting Benefits. The real issue in *Asmus* is this: When an employer has not reserved the right to revoke the benefit, can it still do so? Here we can distinguish two classes of Pacific Bell employees. After Pacific Bell announced its termination of the MES policy, 52 of the original plaintiffs signed waivers accepting the policy's termination in exchange for enhanced benefits in other areas. They lost on summary judgment below.

The eight remaining plaintiffs did not accept the termination, evidently defying their employer. How do the following factors influence the majority's decision: 1) the MES policy had only a vaguely defined expiration point ("so long as there is no change that will materially affect Pacific Bell's business plan achievement"); 2) the MES policy was revoked only after it had been in force for several years; 3) Pacific Bell gave two years' notice before terminating the MES policy; 4) Pacific Bell encouraged employees to accept in writing the change in policy; 5) the employees did not have a vested interest in the benefit, "like an accrued bonus or a pension." Meeting all these conditions is potentially rather difficult; which ones are crucial?

Does the majority deal fairly with the plaintiff's objections to its position? Should Pacific Bell have been required to present evidence that the MES policy had harmful financial effects?

3. Criticism. The decision in the California Supreme Court, which was 4–3, has attracted considerable criticism. See, e.g., W. David Slawson, *Unilateral Contracts of Employment: Does Contract Law Conflict with Public Policy?*, 10 Tex. Wesleyan L.Rev. 9, at 28, 30 (2003) (footnotes omitted): "The new law [in decisions like *Bankey* and *Asmus*] allows an employer to change its employment practices any time it likes, without having to obtain its employees' agreements, provided only that it gives them reasonable notice of the intended changes. But existing contract law would allow an employer to do the same, provided only that it had the foresight to reserve the right to do so when it gave the employment rights initially.... In *Bankey*, the employment security rights that the employer unilaterally revoked two months before discharging the plaintiff in violation of them had apparently been in effect for at least thirteen years. In *Asmus*, the employer induced sixty of its management employees not to resign to take higher paying positions elsewhere in the then-booming high technology industries by promising them, in writing, that it would continue to employ them until retirement age so long as they did their jobs competently and undertook any necessary retraining. None of these employers could have used these assurances or promises to attract new employees or keep old ones if the new law had been in effect because the new law would have made them unenforceable."

Do you agree with Prof. Slawson?

WONG v. PAISNER

Appeals Court of Massachusetts, 1982.
14 Mass.App.Ct. 923, 436 N.E.2d 990.

A jury returned a verdict in favor of the plaintiff in his action to recover $4,400 which he claimed was owed under a contract with the defendant. We agree with the defendant that the judge committed reversible error in failing to instruct the jury on the defense of accord and satisfaction.

The jury could have found that the plaintiff agreed to prepare certain mechanical drawings for the defendant for a lump sum payment of $1,000. The plaintiff claimed, however, that there was a modification of the agreement by which an hourly rate payment was substituted for the lump sum payment. The defendant denied any such modification but testified that he agreed to an additional lump sum payment of $500. The plaintiff sent the defendant a bill in the amount of $5,400, representing 235 hours of work at $25 per hour, less the $500 that had already been paid. The defendant testified that before he received the bill, he sent to the plaintiff a cover letter and a check for $1,000 bearing the notation "payment in full for services rendered." The cover letter stated the defendant's position that their "original deal was for one time work." The letter reiterated that the defendant's check for $1,000 represented payment in full and that the defendant had tendered an additional $500 in an attempt to "appease" the plaintiff in light of their "misunderstanding" over the terms of the contract. The plaintiff deleted the "payment in full" from the check and deposited it in his account. The defendant requested an instruction on accord and satisfaction, the judge refused and the defendant seasonably objected to the action of the judge.

It is settled that acceptance and deposit of a check offered in full payment of a disputed claim constituted an accord and satisfaction and bars an attempt to collect any balance outstanding under a contract.... Whether an accord and satisfaction has been proved is a question of fact on which the defendant has the burden of proof.... There was evidence that the parties had a disagreement as to the amount owed by the defendant and that the dispute arose before the defendant sent the $1,000 check.... The notation on the check and the contents of the letter were evidence that the check was being offered in full settlement of the disputed claim.... The additional payment of $500 could have been found to constitute consideration supporting the condition imposed by the defendant; i.e. that the plaintiff's acceptance of the payment fully discharged the debt.... The action of the plaintiff in deleting the words, "payment in full" did not establish, as a matter of law, that there was no accord and satisfaction. See 15 Williston, Contracts § 1854 (3d ed. 1972). Therefore the defendant adequately raised the issue of accord and satisfaction, and the matter should have been dealt with by the judge in his instructions to the jury....

Notes and Discussion

1. **Take the Money and Run?** In this case there is an underlying dispute about whether the parties had modified their contract. The plaintiff, who had evidently been obliged to do substantially more work on the drawings than he had originally anticipated, would have been benefitted by an hourly rate rather than the lump sum payment. The jury clearly determined that the modification had occurred. So why may the plaintiff not be entitled to the full amount?

Two theories are relevant. The first is in Restatement 2d § 278(1): "If an obligee [here, the plaintiff] accepts in satisfaction of the obligor's duty a performance offered by the obligor that differs from what is due, the duty is discharged." Suppose, for instance, that a debtor owes her creditor $1,000, and offers in full satisfaction a machine instead; and the creditor accepts the machine. The debt is discharged by this substituted performance. (Illustration 1 to § 278).

Closely related to substituted performance, but not quite the same thing, is an accord, defined in § 281(1) as "a contract under which an obligee *promises to accept* a stated performance in satisfaction of the obligor's existing duty." (Emphasis added.) As the Restatement continues, "Performance of the accord discharges the original duty"—in which case, we speak of an accord and satisfaction. However, if the debtor breaches the contract by not rendering the performance agreed upon in the accord, then the original duty is reinstated. Id. (2). Illustration 1 to this section shows how this works: "A owes B $10,000. They make a contract under which A promises to deliver to B a specific machine within 30 days and B promises to accept it in satisfaction of the debt. The contract is an accord. A's debt is suspended and is discharged if A delivers the machine within 30 days."

In *Wong v. Paisner*, the Massachusetts Court holds that the jury should have been instructed on accord and satisfaction. That is, the Court interprets the defendant's check, with the notation "payment in full," as the offer of an accord, which was possibly followed by the plaintiff simultaneously accepting the offer (thus forming an accord) and accepting the performance in satisfaction. Is this the best way to interpret these facts? Does it really matter?

In any case, no matter how the transaction is described, can the plaintiff accept the defendant's proffered payment while rejecting the offeror's limitation that this was "payment in full"? Would it have helped his case any if the plaintiff had specifically added his rejection of the defendant's terms, for instance by writing "under protest" on the check?

2. The UCC. Had this contract been under the UCC, would the plaintiff's position have been improved? See § 1–207(1) (in the revised version, § 1–308(a)). Judicial holdings on the issue had varied; subsection (2) was added in order to settle the issue. Compare also § 3–311, which governs when accord and satisfaction is attempted (as in *Wong v. Paisner*) by a negotiable instrument such as a check; this section was added in 1990.

It is generally held that the offer of an accord must be "conspicuous." See, e.g., *New Hampshire Boring, Inc. v. Adirondack Envtl. Assocs., Inc.*, 145 N.H. 397, 762 A.2d 1036 (2000) (a letter stating that an enclosed check is payment in full is conspicuous). Is it sufficient simply to place a notation on the check?

3. Liquidated vs. Unliquidated Debts. Because of the dispute over how to calculate what the plaintiff in *Wong* was owed, this debt is "unliquidated," i.e., not clearly determined in dollars. Why is this important to the outcome?

Suppose the following situation (Illustration 3 to Restatement 2d § 278): "A owes B a liquidated and undisputed matured debt of $1,000. A offers B $500 in full satisfaction of the debt, and B accepts the $500." The outcome may surprise you: "A's debt is discharged only to the extent of $500." That is, A still owes the remaining $500. Why on earth should this be so? The reason is that B's promise to discharge the remainder of the debt lacks consideration (see § 273), and so is ineffective.

This outcome dates back to early modern Common Law and remains the law generally in the United States; e.g., *Employers Workers' Compensation Ass'n v. W.P. Indus.*, 925 P.2d 1225, 1229 (Okla. Civ. App. 1996) ("An essential element of the accord and satisfaction defense is a good faith dispute."). The rule, which has often been criticized, leads to paradox. For instance, in the illustration above, suppose that, by pre-arrangement, A gives B $1,000 as full payment, and that B then says, "Okay, your debt to me is now paid in full. Now take $500 as a gift.'' Is there any reason why such a transaction should be questioned?

4. **Should the Pre-Existing Duty Rule Be Abolished?** Consider this nuanced appraisal: ''Even where the pre-existing duty rule is abolished in connection with discharge of a duty, there remain the restraints imposed by the rules on duress and undue influence, along with the duty to act in good faith. Lest the reader's sympathy for 'poor' and 'weak' debtors, such as tenants paying rent and consumers paying for goods, obscure the full dimensions of the problem, it should be recalled that there are also 'over-reaching' debtors, such as tortfeasors and insurance companies settling claims and employers paying wages. Viewed from this perspective, the possibility of discharge by the creditor's oral statement, without more, poses obvious perils not unlike those inherent in the enforcement of gift promises. The compromise adopted by statutes that give effect to a written discharge may thus be justified if the required formality is thought to have a sufficient evidentiary and cautionary effect.'' E. A. Farnsworth, Contracts § 4.25 at 284 (4th student ed. 2004) (footnotes omitted).

Was the defendant in *Wong v. Paisner* an ''overreaching'' debtor?

Chapter 5

LEGAL REGULATION OF CONTRACTS

Here remember that you are looking at contract law rather like someone observing the universe through a telescope. In contracts courses the telescope focuses on the cases that your editors put before you. You cannot tell whether these cases fairly represent a Milky Way of similar cases or whether the few cases before you are the universe. Chapter 5 earns this warning because it deals with fascinating questions that, we suspect, recur only seldom in the law. Freeing a needy client from an onerous form contract because the contract is unconscionable is the mirage; but enforcing form contracts is the reality.

If you have talked to your classmates in sections that use other casebooks, you are now aware of a second license freely taken by casebook editors—to classify doctrines as they wish. For example, Professor Farnsworth's treatise inserts "Unenforceability on the Ground of Public Policy" between "Consideration" on the one hand and the "Statute of Frauds" on the other. So what we offer as "Legal Regulation of Contracts," he treats as merely another aspect of the "Enforceability of Contracts." The topics in this chapter could have been inserted separately or together in several other places. You should view our classification of the legal doctrines, here and elsewhere, with a skeptical eye. We encourage you to draw your own conclusions about our ordering of these topics and about their proper relation to other contract doctrines.

The person asserting "mistake" is almost always a defendant who is trying to get out of a contract that was properly formed and documented. A moment's thought will tell you that most "mistakes" do not let one off. Virtually every aggrieved party can plausibly assert that he was "mistaken" about the nature of the goods, services or real estate contracted for, or that he was "mistaken" about his need for or the utility of the goods or services. If such a plausible claim let one escape his contract duty, contract law would be a joke. So the mistake has to be something big; it must be a mistake of "fact," not of prediction, expectation or hope, and, usually, it has to be "mutual"—both parties must have suffered the same mistake. And, as you will see, the claim is destroyed if the risk of mistake was specifically or impliedly allocated to one or the other. When one is finished whittling away, there is only a little left. It is your now and future task to figure out what is left and what has been whittled away.

In life (when clients present their sad stream of consciousness about their contract problems), you will find that s client's story may call up several contract doctrines alongside mistake. First is "misunderstanding." How does mistake differ from misunderstanding and how are the consequences of a finding on one doctrine different from the consequences of a finding on the other? Mostly the consequences of a finding on one are the same as the other—the party who misunderstood or who suffered the mistake, if he satisfies all of the conditions, does not have to perform. In law school maybe we can distinguish the doctrines. A misunderstanding occurs when the offeror means one thing and the offeree understands another or vice versa. So when a buyer agrees to purchase cotton arriving on the ship Peerless (that he thinks will arrive in October) but the seller intends to sell cotton arriving on a ship of the same name to arrive in December, there is a misunderstanding. Without fault of either, each believes something different and the law says that there has been no agreement. But arguably there is no mutual mistake since both do not suffer the same mistake—as they might if each thought a pregnant cow was sterile. Still, confidence in our ability to distinguish these doctrines not only in law school but also in life might be undermined by the fact that the Restatement cites and discusses the Peerless case not only in Section 20 (on misunderstanding) but also in Section 153 (on mistake).

In life, yet other doctrines will compete with mistake. Consider misrepresentation and warranty. Where one's mistaken belief was intentionally fostered by another, the tort of fraudulent misrepresentation may have occurred, and where the mistake is fostered by the honest and good faith assurances of another, a warranty may have been given and broken. Surely the client will have much to say about the inaccurate and dishonest assertions of his seller, and if those can be proven, the road will be easier than the road to mistake. But there are some differences in remedy. Mistake and misunderstanding usually lead to a finding that there is no binding contract and so no damage recovery; misrepresentation and breach of warranty usually result in a damage recovery.

The doctrine of unconscionability is the most open and notorious of court regulation of contract. It comes close to inviting courts to strike down contracts that they find to be "unfair," without resort to other standard and more quantifiable measures. Professor Llewellyn, the father of the Uniform Commercial Code, railed against "covert remedies" on the ground that they were not reliable. For example a court, motivated by sympathy for an impecunious defendant who had signed an improvident form contract, might stretch the doctrine of consideration to free the defendant or the court might "interpret" the terms of the contract to the same result. In Llewellyn's view these remedies were unreliable both because some judges would not feel free to use them and because later courts might follow these earlier judgments even in cases where outrage over a plaintiff's unfair behavior did not demand it. So Llewellyn put section 2–302 into Article 2 of the UCC with the hope that it would permit courts to do openly what they had formerly done secretly and to authorize non-activist judges to act where they would otherwise have acted.

The cases in this Chapter (all chosen by the left leaning member of our team) might lead you to conclude that Llewellyn succeeded. The right wing member of the team is doubtful. He believes that there are much smaller number of findings of unconscionability than anyone would have predicted when the UCC was drafted in the 1960's, and he finds courts slow to abandon their comfortable, covert tools.

The third topic in this chapter, invalidation because of public policy, is *sui generis*. These cases are even more scarce than unconscionability cases. Some arise from the same source that brought federal anti-trust statutes in the early twentieth century—contracts that unduly inhibit commerce are anathema to a capitalist economy. (But don't all contracts limit competition?) And, of course, contracts to engage in illegal activities—gambling, sale of illicit substances, prostitution etc. are often thought to be against public policy. With these, one needs to be careful, for society's uncertainty about these laws sometimes leaks out into civil law. For example, in some places unexecuted gambling contracts will not be enforced, but a loser who has paid an illegal debt may not be able to get his money back. The case arising from Missouri's liquor license laws shows the state protecting its revenues (and maybe even guarding vestigial, puritanical virtues).

Perhaps you should regard this chapter as a hotchpot of doctrines and cases that do not fit comfortably anywhere else. You need to know these doctrines and cases for the unusual case that might walk into your firm someday.

A. MISREPRESENTATION AND MISTAKE OF FACT

As we saw in Chapter 2, American law generally lets parties arrive at their own individual assessments of how much their promises are worth. Although, in the judgment of an external observer, one party may seem to be giving away too much, courts are usually reluctant to intervene and set things right. This is true even when the party's viewpoint is clouded by a mistake about the factual basis on which the deal is being constructed. The underlying thought is apparently that parties will do better in the long run if they individually bear the responsibility of ferreting out the truth, even where the truth may be difficult to determine.

A good illustration of this principle is the antediluvian case of *Wood v. Boynton*, 64 Wis. 265, 25 N.W. 42 (1885), in which a woman sold a small stone (about as big as a canary's egg) to a jeweler for $1. The stone later turned out to be an uncut diamond worth about $700. The plaintiff sued to undo the sale, but was rebuffed. As the Supreme Court of Wisconsin argued, "In this case, upon the plaintiff's own evidence, there can be no just ground for alleging that she was induced to make the sale she did by any fraud or unfair dealings on the part of Mr. Boynton. Both were entirely ignorant at the time of the character of the stone and of its intrinsic value. Mr. Boynton was not an expert in uncut diamonds, and had made no examination of the stone ..." (Emphasis omitted.) 24 N.W. at 44. But if Boynton is entirely faultless, the same cannot necessarily be said of Wood, who "had the stone in her possession for a long time, and ... had made some inquiry as to its nature and qualities. If she chose to sell it without further investigation as to its intrinsic value to a person who was guilty of no fraud or unfairness which induced her to sell t for a small sum, she cannot repudiate the sale because it is afterwards ascertained that she made a bad bargain." Id. (citation omitted).

Nonetheless, this hard-nosed principle can run up against some very difficult situations in which the judicial enforcement of a contract comes to seem counterproductive. The modern legal doctrine of mistake is developed in Restatement 2d §§ 151–154. Mistake is defined in § 151 as "a belief that is not in accord with the facts." The next two sections distinguish two types of mistake: a "mutual" or "bilateral mistake" in which both parties enter a contract under the same mistaken belief (§ 152), and a "unilateral mistake" in which only one party does so (§ 153); as might be anticipated, courts handle the first type more generously than the second. But both sections make it clear that not just any mistake is germane, but only one that goes "to a basic assumption on which the contract was made [and] has a material effect on the agreed exchange of performances" (§ 152(1); the same language is lightly adapted in § 153(1)). Further, modern law is much more concerned than older law was with whether the party who is adversely affected by the mistake bore the risk of its occurrence, a concept that is developed in § 154.[1]

Successful pleas of mistake are fairly rare in modern law, doubtless because of the limits just described. Nonetheless mistake doctrine is interesting particularly in helping to clarify the nature of the agreement that is required to make a valid contract. We begin, however, with a case that illustrates the related problem of "induced mistake"—misrepresentation in the formation of contract—and the possibility of contractual relief when it occurs.

WEINTRAUB v. KROBATSCH

Supreme Court of New Jersey, 1974.
64 N.J. 445, 317 A.2d 68.

JACOBS, J. The judgment entered in the Law Division, as modified in an unreported opinion of the Appellate Division, directed that the

1. See also Melvin A. Eisenberg, *Mistake in Contract Law*, 91 Calif. L. Rev. 1573 (2003), and *Disclosure in Contract Law*, 91 Calif. L. Rev. 1645 (2003).

appellants Donald P. Krobatsch and Estella Krobatsch, his wife, pay the sum of $4,250 to the plaintiff Natalie Weintraub and the sum of $2,550 to the defendant The Serafin Agency, Inc. We granted certification on the application of the appellants. 63 N.J. 498 (1973).

The procedural steps below need not be dealt with at this point, other than to note that oral testimony was never taken and the matter was disposed of by summary judgment on the basis of meagre pleadings and conclusory affidavits. For present purposes we must resolve doubts in favor of the appellants and must accept their factual allegations, along with the inferences most favorable to them.... On that approach the following appears:

Mrs. Weintraub owned and occupied a six-year-old English-town home which she placed in the hands of a real estate broker (The Serafin Agency, Inc.) for sale. The Krobatsches were interested in purchasing the home, examined it while it was illuminated and found it suitable. On June 30, 1971 Mrs. Weintraub, as seller, and the Krobatsches, as purchasers, entered into a contract for the sale of the property for $42,500. The contract provided that the purchasers had inspected the property and were fully satisfied with its physical condition, that no representations had been made and that no responsibility was assumed by the seller as to the present or future condition of the premises. A deposit of $4,250 was sent by the purchasers to the broker to be held in escrow pending the closing of the transaction. The purchasers requested that the seller have the house fumigated and that was done. A fire after the signing of the contract caused damage but the purchasers indicated readiness that there be adjustment at closing.

During the evening of August 25, 1971, prior to closing, the purchasers entered the house, then unoccupied, and as they turned the lights on they were, as described in their petition for certification, "astonished to see roaches literally running in all directions, up the walls, drapes, etc." On the following day their attorney wrote a letter to Mrs. Weintraub, care of her New York law firm, advising that on the previous day "it was discovered that the house is infested with vermin despite the fact that an exterminator has only recently serviced the house" and asserting that "the presence of vermin in such great quantities, particularly after the exterminator was done, rendered the house as unfit for human habitation at this time and therefore, the contract is rescinded." On September 2, 1971 an exterminator wrote to Mr. Krobatsch advising that he had examined the premises and that "cockroaches were found to have infested the entire house." He said he could eliminate them for a relatively modest charge by two treatments with a twenty-one day interval but that it would be necessary to remove the carpeting "to properly treat all the infested areas."

Mrs. Weintraub rejected the rescission by the purchasers and filed an action in the Law Division joining them and the broker as defendants. Though she originally sought specific performance she later confined her claim to damages in the sum of $4,250, representing the deposit held in escrow by the broker. The broker filed an answer and counterclaim seeking payment of its commission in the sum of $2,550. There were opposing motions for summary judgment by the purchasers and Mrs. Weintraub, along with a motion for summary judgment by the broker for its commission. At the argument on the motions it was evident that the purchasers were claiming fraudulent concealment or nondisclosure by the seller as the basis for their rescission. Thus at one point their attorney said: "Your honor, I would point out, and it is in my clients' affidavit, every time that they inspected this house prior to this time every light in the place was illuminated. Now, these insects are nocturnal by nature and that is not a point I think I have to prove through someone. I think Webster's dictionary is sufficient. By keeping the lights on it keeps them out of sight. These sellers had to know they had this problem. You could not live in a house this infested without knowing about it."

The Law Division denied the motion by the purchasers for summary judgment but granted Mrs. Weintraub's motion and directed that the purchasers pay her the sum of $4,250. It further directed that the deposit monies held in escrow by the broker be paid to Mrs. Weintraub in satisfaction of her judgment against the purchasers. See *Oliver v. Lawson*, 92 N.J. Super. 331, 333 (App. Div. 1966), certif. denied, 48 N.J. 574 (1967). It denied the broker's summary judgment motion for its commission but held that matter for trial. On appeal, the Appellate Division sustained the summary judgment in Mrs. Weintraub's favor but disagreed with the Law Division's holding that the broker's claim must await trial. It considered that since the purchasers were summarily held to have been in default in rescinding rather than in proceeding with the closing, they were responsible for the commission. See *Ellsworth Dobbs, Inc. v. Johnson*, 50 N.J. 528, 558–62 (1967). Accordingly, it modified the Law Division's judgment to the end that the purchasers were directed to pay not only the sum of $4,250 to Mrs. Weintraub but also the sum of $2,550 to the broker.

Before us the purchasers contend that they were entitled to a trial on the issue of whether there was fraudulent concealment or nondisclosure entitling them to rescind; if there was then clearly they were under no liability to either the seller or the broker and would be entitled to the return of their deposit held by the broker in escrow. See *Keen v. James*, 39 N.J. Eq. 527, 540 (E. & A. 1885), where Justice Dixon, speaking for the then Court of last resort, pointed out that "silence may be fraudulent" and that relief may be granted to one contractual party where the other suppresses facts which he, " 'under the circumstances, is bound in conscience and duty to disclose to the other party, and in respect to which he cannot, innocently, be silent.' " 39 N.J. Eq. at 540–41. See also Goldfarb, "Fraud and Nondisclosure in the Vendor–Purchaser Relation," *8 Wes. Res. L. Rev.* 5 (1956).

Mrs. Weintraub asserts that she was unaware of the infestation and the Krobatsches acknowledge that, if that was so, then there was no fraudulent concealment or nondisclosure on her part and their claim must fall. But the purchasers allege that she was in fact aware of the infestation and at this stage of the proceedings we must assume that to be true. She contends, however, that even if she were fully aware she would have been under no duty to speak and that consequently no complaint by the purchasers may legally be grounded on her silence. She relies primarily on cases such as *Swinton v. Whitinsville Sav. Bank*, 311 Mass. 677, 42 N.E.2d 808, 141 A.L.R. 965 (1942), and *Taylor v. Heisinger*, 39 Misc. 2d 955, 242 N.Y.S.2d 281 (Sup. Ct. 1963). *Taylor* is not really pertinent since there the court found that the seller had "no demonstrated nor inferable knowledge of the condition complained of." 242 N.Y.S.2d at 286. *Swinton* is pertinent but, as Dean Prosser has noted (Prosser, supra at 696), it is one of a line of "singularly unappetizing cases" which are surely out of tune with our times.

In *Swinton* the plaintiff purchased a house from the defendant and after he occupied it he found it to be infested with termites. The defendant had made no verbal or written representations but the plaintiff, asserting that the defendant knew of the termites and was under a duty to speak, filed a complaint for damages grounded on fraudulent concealment. The Supreme Judicial Court of Massachusetts sustained a demurrer to the complaint and entered judgment for the defendant. In the course of its opinion the court acknowledged that "the plaintiff possesses a certain appeal to the moral sense" but concluded that the law has not "reached the point of imposing upon the frailties of human nature a standard so idealistic as this." 42 N.E. 2d at 808–809. That was written several decades ago and we are far from certain that it represents views held by the current members of the Massachusetts court. See *Kannavos v. Annino*, 356 Mass. 42, 247 N.E.2d 708, 711 (1969). In any event we are certain that it does not represent our sense of justice or fair dealing and it has understandably been rejected in persuasive opinions elsewhere. See *Obde v. Schlemeyer*, 56 Wash. 2d 449, 353 P.2d 672 (1960); ... See also Restatement 2d, Torts § 551 (Tent. Draft No. 12 (1966)); ...

In *Obde v. Schlemeyer*, supra, 56 Wash. 2d 449, 353 P. 2d 672, the defendants sold an apartment house to the plaintiffs. The house was termite infested but that fact was not disclosed by the sellers to the purchasers who later sued for damages alleging fraudulent concealment. The sellers contended that they were under no obligation whatever to speak out and they relied heavily on the decision of the Massachusetts court in *Swinton* (311 Mass. 677, 42 N.E.2d 808, 141 A.L.R. 965). The Supreme Court of Washington flatly rejected their contention, holding that though the parties had dealt at arms length the sellers were under "a duty to inform the plaintiffs of the termite condition" of which they were fully aware. 353 P.2d at 674; cf. *Hughes v. Stusser*, 68 Wash. 2d 707, 415 P.2d 89, 92 (1966). In the course of its opinion the court quoted approvingly from Dean Keeton's article supra, in 15 Tex. L. Rev. 1. There the author first expressed his thought that when Lord Cairns suggested in *Peek v. Gurney*, L.R. 6 H.L. 377 (1873), that there was no duty to disclose facts, no matter how "morally censurable" (at 403), he

was expressing nineteenth century law as shaped by an individualistic philosophy based on freedom of contracts and unconcerned with morals. He then made the following comments which fairly embody a currently acceptable principle on which the holding in Obde may be said to be grounded:

> In the present stage of the law, the decisions show a drawing away from this idea, and there can be seen an attempt by many courts to reach a just result in so far as possible, but yet maintaining the degree of certainty which the law must have. The statement may often be found that if either party to a contract of sale conceals or suppresses a material fact which he is in good faith bound to disclose then his silence is fraudulent.
>
> The attitude of the courts toward nondisclosure is undergoing a change and contrary to Lord Cairns' famous remark it would seem that the object of the law in these cases should be to impose on parties to the transaction a duty to speak whenever justice, equity, and fair dealing demand it. This statement is made only with reference to instances where the party to be charged is an actor in the transaction. This duty to speak does not result from an implied representation by silence, but exists because a refusal to speak constitutes unfair conduct. 15 Tex. L. Rev. at 31....

In *Saporta v. Barbagelata*, 33 Cal. Rptr. 661 (1963), the plaintiffs sought to rescind their purchase of a house on the ground that they were defrauded by the seller's real estate agent or broker, "by reason of the concealment and nondisclosure that said house contained an extensive termite and fungus infestation, and by certain representations that said house was not so infested." A summary judgment against the plaintiffs was granted by the trial judge but was reversed on appeal in an opinion which set forth the following which we consider of particular pertinence to the present stage of litigation in the matter before us:

> The principles controlling the conduct of a real estate agent or broker in the sale of real estate are well established in this state. He is not only liable to a buyer for his affirmative and intentional misrepresentations to a buyer, but he is also liable for mere nondisclosure to the buyer of defects known to him and unknown and unobservable by the buyer. (*Lingsch v. Savage*, 213 Cal. App. 2d 729, 29 Cal. Rptr. 201; ...) The underlying settled rule is that every person connected with a fraud is liable for the full amount of the damages and the wrongdoers, if any, are jointly and severally liable.... Whether a matter not disclosed by a real estate broker or agent is of sufficient materiality to affect the desirability or value of the property sold, and thus make him liable for fraudulent nondisclosure, depends upon the facts of each case. (*Lingsch v. Savage*, supra, 213 Cal. App. 2d 729, 29 Cal. Rptr. p. 205.) In the case at bench we have allegations which present triable issues of fact tendered not only on the basis of positive misstatements and misrepresentations of fact allegedly made by Dolman, but also the alleged

suppression and nondisclosure of facts known to him and unknown and unobservable by plaintiffs. 33 Cal. Rptr. at 667.

As in *Saporta*, supra, the purchasers here were entitled to withstand the seller's motion for summary judgment. They should have been permitted to proceed with their efforts to establish by testimony that they were equitably entitled to rescind because the house was extensively infested in the manner described by them, the seller was well aware of the infestation, and the seller deliberately concealed or failed to disclose the condition because of the likelihood that it would defeat the transaction. The seller may of course defend factually as well as legally and since the matter is primarily equitable in nature the factual as well as legal disputes will be for the trial judge alone. . . .

If the trial judge finds such deliberate concealment or nondisclosure of the latent infestation not observable by the purchasers on their inspection, he will still be called upon to determine whether, in the light of the full presentation before him, the concealment or nondisclosure was of such significant nature as to justify rescission. Minor conditions which ordinary sellers and purchasers would reasonably disregard as of little or no materiality in the transaction would clearly not call for judicial intervention. While the described condition may not have been quite as major as in the termite cases which were concerned with structural impairments, to the purchasers here it apparently was of such magnitude and was so repulsive as to cause them to rescind immediately though they had earlier indicated readiness that there be adjustment at closing for damage resulting from a fire which occurred after the contract was signed. We are not prepared at his time to say that on their showing they acted either unreasonably or without equitable justification.

Our courts have come a long way since the days when the judicial emphasis was on formal rules and ancient precedents rather than on modern concepts of justice and fair dealing. While admittedly our law has progressed more slowly in the real property field than in other fields, there have been notable stirrings even there. See *Schipper v. Levitt & Sons, Inc.*, 44 N.J. 70 (1965); *Reste Realty Corporation v. Cooper*, 53 N.J. 444 (1969); . . . In *Schipper* we elevated the duties of the builder-vendor in the sale of its homes and in the course of our opinion we repeatedly stressed that our law should be based on current notions of what is "right and just." 44 N.J. at 90. In *Reste* we expressed similar thoughts in connection with the lease of real property. We there noted that despite the lessee's acceptance of the premises in their "present condition" (a stipulation comparable to that of the purchasers in their contract here), the landlord was under a duty to disclose a material latent condition, known to him but unobservable by the tenant; we pointed out that in the circumstances "it would be a wholly inequitable application of caveat emptor to charge her with knowledge of it." 53 N.J. at 453–454. Both *Schipper* and *Reste* were departures from earlier decisions which are nonetheless still relied on by the seller here. No purpose would now be served by pursuing any discussion of those earlier decisions since we are satisfied that current principles grounded on justice and fair dealing, embraced throughout this opinion, clearly call for a full trial below; to that end the judgment entered in the Appellate Division is:

Reversed and remanded.

Notes and Discussion

1. **Contract and Tort.** Common law frequently provides tort "liability for commercial harm caused by the plaintiff's justifiable reliance upon material misrepresentations of fact that lead to contracts, transfers of property or other bargains." Dan B. Dobbs, The Law of Torts 1343 (2000). In order to prove misrepresentation, the plaintiff must show "(1) an intentional misrepresentation (2) of fact or opinion (as distinct from a promise) (3) that is material and (4) intended to induce and (5) does induce reasonable reliance by the plaintiff, (6) proximately causing pecuniary harm to the plaintiff." Id. at 1345. See also the discussion after the *New England Insulation Co.* decision in Chapter 3.D above.

There are two problems here for buyers like the Krobatsches. First, it is often difficult to prove this tort, particularly where, as here, the seller has been careful to say nothing on the point at issue (leaving the lights on to keep the roaches at bay). Second, in any case the Krobatsches were probably not interested in tort damages as a remedy. Rather, they simply wanted out of the contract altogether. The New Jersey Supreme Court's opinion (written at a time when this court was rapidly emerging as a preeminent protector of consumers) wrestles chiefly with the issue of whether, against older law, rescission and restitution are available to the Krobatsches as contractual remedies.

In a contract case such as this one, where the issue is not damages but rescission, should a plaintiff be required to show "*deliberate* concealment or nondisclosure [of a latent defect] not observable by the purchasers on their inspection"? (Emphasis added.) Should it be enough if concealment is reasonably likely?

2. ***Caveat Emptor.*** "Let the buyer beware." It's Latin, so it looks both venerable and authoritative. Not true. "It is one of that tribe of anonymous Latin maxims that infest our law. None of them have any real authority, some of them no real meaning; and there is scarce one, where the exceptions are not nearly as broad as the rule. But they are phrases 'of exceeding good command,' for they fill the ear and sound like sense, and to the eye look like learning; while their main use is to supply the place of either or both." Gulian C. Verplanck, An Essay on the Doctrine of Contracts 218 (1825). The maxim is not Roman, indeed only barely medieval; it did not become a central precept of our contract law until the free-wheeling individualism of the nineteenth century. Walton H. Hamilton, *The Ancient Maxim Caveat Emptor*, 40 Yale L. J. 1133 (1931); P. S. Atiyah, The Rise and Fall of Freedom of Contract 178–180, 464–479 (1979).

Still, the underlying intuition still has some teeth. In 1993, a New Jersey Superior Court was confronted with a case in which the plaintiff had purchased real estate at a foreclosure sale initiated by a second mortgagee. In believing the property to be unencumbered, plaintiff relied on the second mortgagee's title report, prepared by a title insurance company, that failed to include the existence of an open first mortgage on the property. Plaintiff brought suit against both the second mortgagee's attorney and the insurance company. Does *Weintraub* control? The judge thought not: "[P]laintiff was afforded the ability to protect himself by obtaining a title search and rescinding the bid if that search disclosed a defect for which the statute permitted rescission. In this situation, there is no unequal position: the equality is obvious. Plaintiff could have protected himself by a title search, just as he says that defendant Chicago [Title Insurance] is liable to him for not having properly reported the state of title to the foreclosing mortgagee. I therefore find that it *is* appropriate to apply the principle of *caveat emptor* to the circumstances presented here." *Smith v. Boyd*, 272 N.J.Super. 186, 194, 639 A.2d 413, 418 (1993).

3. **Breach of Warranty.** Misrepresentation also raises issues we have seen in looking at warranties (Chapter 4.D above). If Weintraub had been a merchant selling goods and not real estate, she would have been liable for any undisclosed material defect. Whether a seller's silence is permissible in other circumstances is much debated. Implied warranties in real estate transactions are not imposed on sellers in some states, but these rules have not grown out of a uniform statute, nor have they been adopted everywhere.

How would you draw the line between the cases where a seller of goods or services must make disclosures or be liable, and the cases where there should be no liability for silence? Ignoring rules that might be imposed under federal law, could United Technologies safely sell a division to General Electric without disclosing a problem the division was experiencing? How would you protect General Electric against such a failure to disclose?

4. **The Effect of Disclaimers.** "The contract provided that the purchasers had inspected the property and were fully satisfied with its physical condition, that no representations had been made and that no responsibility was assumed by the seller as to the present or future condition of the premises." Why didn't this affect the outcome? Before you commit yourself to an answer, read the cases below on mistake. Can they be distinguished?

LENAWEE COUNTY BOARD OF HEALTH v. MESSERLY

Supreme Court of Michigan, 1982.
417 Mich. 17, 331 N.W.2d 203.

RYAN, J. In March of 1977, Carl and Nancy Pickles, appellees, purchased from appellants, William and Martha Messerly, a 600–square-foot tract of land upon which is located a three-unit apartment building. Shortly after the transaction was closed, the Lenawee County Board of Health condemned the property and obtained a permanent injunction which prohibits human habitation on the premises until the defective sewage system is brought into conformance with the Lenawee County sanitation code.

We are required to determine whether appellees should prevail in their attempt to avoid this land contract on the basis of mutual mistake and failure of consideration. We conclude that the parties did entertain a mutual misapprehension of fact, but that the circumstances of this case do not warrant rescission.

The facts of the case are not seriously in dispute. In 1971, the Messerlys acquired approximately one acre plus 600 square feet of land. A three-unit apartment building was situated upon the 600–square-foot portion. The trial court found that, prior to this transfer, the Messerlys' predecessor in title, Mr. Bloom, had installed a septic tank on the property without a permit and in violation of the applicable health code. The Messerlys used the building as an income investment property until 1973 when they sold it, upon land contract, to James Barnes who likewise used it primarily as an income-producing investment.

Mr. and Mrs. Barnes, with the permission of the Messerlys, sold approximately one acre of the property in 1976, and the remaining 600 square feet and building were offered for sale soon thereafter when Mr. and Mrs. Barnes defaulted on their land contract. Mr. and Mrs. Pickles evidenced an interest in the property, but were dissatisfied with the terms of the Barnes–Messerly land contract. Consequently, to accommodate the Pickleses' preference to enter into a land contract directly with the Messerlys, Mr. and Mrs. Barnes executed a quitclaim deed which conveyed their interest in the property back to the Messerlys. After inspecting the property, Mr. and Mrs. Pickles executed a new land contract with the Messerlys on March 21, 1977. It provided for a purchase price of $25,500. A clause was added to the end of the land contract form which provides: "17. Purchaser has examined this property and agrees to accept same in its present condition. There are no other or additional written or oral understandings."

Five or six days later, when the Pickleses went to introduce themselves to the tenants, they discovered raw sewage seeping out of the ground. Tests conducted by a sanitation expert indicated the inadequacy of the sewage system. The Lenawee County Board of Health subsequently condemned the property and initiated this lawsuit in the Lenawee Circuit Court against the Messerlys as land contract vendors, and the Pickleses, as vendees, to obtain a permanent injunction proscribing human habitation of the premises until the property was brought into conformance with the Lenawee County sanitation code. The injunction was granted, and the Lenawee County Board of Health was permitted to withdraw from the lawsuit by stipulation of the parties.

When no payments were made on the land contract, the Messerlys filed a cross-complaint against the Pickleses seeking foreclosure, sale of the property, and a deficiency judgment. Mr. and Mrs. Pickles then counterclaimed for rescission against the Messerlys, and filed a third-party complaint against the Barneses, which incorporated, by reference, the allegations of the counterclaim against the Messerlys. In count one, Mr. and Mrs. Pickles alleged failure of consideration. Count two charged Mr. and Mrs. Barnes with wilful concealment and misrepresentation as a result of their failure to disclose the condition of the sanitation system.

Additionally, Mr. and Mrs. Pickles sought to hold the Messerlys liable in equity for the Barneses' alleged misrepresentation. The Pickleses prayed that the land contract be rescinded.

After a bench trial, the court concluded that the Pickleses had no cause of action against either the Messerlys or the Barneses as there was no fraud or misrepresentation. This ruling was predicated on the trial judge's conclusion that none of the parties knew of Mr. Bloom's earlier transgression or of the resultant problem with the septic system until it was discovered by the Pickleses, and that the sanitation problem was not caused by any of the parties. The trial court held that the property was purchased "as is", after inspection and, accordingly, its "negative * * * value cannot be blamed upon an innocent seller". Foreclosure was ordered against the Pickleses, together with a judgment against them in the amount of $25,943.09.

Mr. and Mrs. Pickles appealed from the adverse judgment. The Court of Appeals unanimously affirmed the trial court's ruling with respect to Mr. and Mrs. Barnes but, in a two-to-one decision, reversed the finding of no cause of action on the Pickleses' claims against the Messerlys.... It concluded that the mutual mistake between the Messerlys and the Pickleses went to a basic, as opposed to a collateral, element of the contract,[2] and that the parties intended to transfer income-producing rental property but, in actuality, the vendees paid $25,500 for an asset without value.

We granted the Messerlys' application for leave to appeal....

II.

We must decide initially whether there was a mistaken belief entertained by one or both parties to the contract in dispute and, if so, the resultant legal significance.

A contractual mistake "is a belief that is not in accord with the facts". 1 Restatement Contracts, 2d, § 151, p 383. The erroneous belief of one or both of the parties must relate to a fact in existence at the time the contract is executed. *Richardson Lumber Co. v. Hoey*, 219 Mich. 643, 189 N.W. 923 (1922); *Sherwood v. Walker*, 66 Mich. 568, 580, 33 N.W. 919 (1887) (Sherwood, J., dissenting). That is to say, the belief which is found to be in error may not be, in substance, a prediction as to a future occurrence or non-occurrence....

The Court of Appeals concluded, after a *de novo* review of the record, that the parties were mistaken as to the income-producing capacity of the property in question.... We agree. The vendors and the

2. The trial court found that the only way that the property could be put to residential use would be to pump and haul the sewage, a method which is economically unfeasible, as the cost of such a disposal system amounts to double the income generated by the property. There was speculation by the trial court that the adjoining land might be utilized to make the property suitable for residential use, but, in the absence of testimony directed at that point, the court refused to draw any conclusions. The trial court and the Court of Appeals both found that the property was valueless, or had a negative value.

vendees each believed that the property transferred could be utilized as income-generating rental property. All of the parties subsequently learned that, in fact, the property was unsuitable for any residential use.

Appellants assert that there was no mistake in the contractual sense because the defect in the sewage system did not arise until after the contract was executed. The appellees respond that the Messerlys are confusing the date of the inception of the defect with the date upon which the defect was discovered.

This is essentially a factual dispute which the trial court failed to resolve directly. Nevertheless, we are empowered to draw factual inferences from the facts found by the trial court. GCR 1963, 865.1(6).

An examination of the record reveals that the septic system was defective prior to the date on which the land contract was executed. The Messerlys' grantor installed a nonconforming septic system without a permit prior to the transfer of the property to the Messerlys in 1971. Moreover, virtually undisputed testimony indicates that, assuming ideal soil conditions, 2,500 square feet of property is necessary to support a sewage system adequate to serve a three-family dwelling. Likewise, 750 square feet is mandated for a one-family home. Thus, the division of the parcel and sale of one acre of the property by Mr. and Mrs. Barnes in 1976 made it impossible to remedy the already illegal septic system within the confines of the 600–square-foot parcel.[3]

Appellants do not dispute these underlying facts which give rise to an inference contrary to their contentions.

Having determined that when these parties entered into the land contract they were laboring under a mutual mistake of fact, we now direct our attention to a determination of the legal significance of that finding.

A contract may be rescinded because of a mutual misapprehension of the parties, but this remedy is granted only in the sound discretion of the court.... Appellants argue that the parties' mistake relates only to the quality or value of the real estate transferred, and that such mistakes are collateral to the agreement and do not justify rescission, citing *A & M Land Development Co. v. Miller*, 354 Mich. 681, 94 N.W.2d 197 (1959).

In that case, the plaintiff was the purchaser of 91 lots of real property. It sought partial rescission of the land contract when it was frustrated in its attempts to develop 42 of the lots because it could not obtain permits from the county health department to install septic tanks

3. It is crucial to distinguish between the date on which a belief relating to a particular fact or set of facts becomes erroneous due to a change in the fact, and the date on which the mistaken nature of the belief is discovered. By definition, a mistake cannot be discovered until after the contract is executed. If the parties were aware, prior to the execution of a contract, that they were in error concerning a particular fact, there would be no misapprehension in signing the contract. Thus stated, it becomes obvious that the date on which a mistaken fact manifests itself is irrelevant to the determination whether or not there was a mistake.

on these lots. This Court refused to allow rescission because the mistake, whether mutual or unilateral, related only to the value of the property. "There was here no mistake as to the form or substance of the contract between the parties, or the description of the property constituting the subject matter.... In the case at bar plaintiff received the property for which it contracted. The fact that it may be of less value than the purchaser expected at the time of the transaction is not a sufficient basis for the granting of equitable relief, neither fraud nor reliance on misrepresentation of material facts having been established." 354 Mich. 693–694.

Appellees contend, on the other hand, that in this case the parties were mistaken as to the very nature of the character of the consideration and claim that the pervasive and essential quality of this mistake renders rescission appropriate. They cite in support of that view *Sherwood v. Walker*, 66 Mich. 568, 33 N.W. 919 (1887), the famous "barren cow" case. In that case, the parties agreed to the sale and purchase of a cow which was thought to be barren, but which was, in reality, with calf. When the seller discovered the fertile condition of his cow, he refused to deliver her. In permitting rescission, the Court stated: "It seems to me, however, in the case made by this record, that the mistake or misapprehension of the parties went to the whole substance of the agreement. If the cow was a breeder, she was worth at least $750; if barren, she was worth not over $80. The parties would not have made the contract of sale except upon the understanding and belief that she was incapable of breeding, and of no use as a cow. It is true she is now the identical animal that they thought her to be when the contract was made; there is no mistake as to the identity of the creature. Yet the mistake was not of the mere quality of the animal, but went to the very nature of the thing. A barren cow is substantially a different creature than a breeding one. There is as much difference between them for all purposes of use as there is between an ox and a cow that is capable of breeding and giving milk. If the mutual mistake had simply related to the fact whether she was with calf or not for one season, then it might have been a good sale; but the mistake affected the character of the animal for all time, and for her present and ultimate use. She was not in fact the animal, or the kind of animal, the defendants intended to sell or the plaintiff to buy. She was not a barren cow, and, if this fact had been known, there would have been no contract. The mistake affected the substance of the whole consideration, and it must be considered that there was no contract to sell or sale of the cow as she actually was. The thing sold and bought had in fact no existence. She was sold as a beef creature would be sold; she is in fact a breeding cow, and a valuable one.

"The court should have instructed the jury that if they found that the cow was sold, or contracted to be sold, upon the understanding of both parties that she was barren, and useless for the purpose of breeding, and that in fact she was not barren, but capable of breeding, then the defendants had a right to rescind, and to refuse to deliver, and the verdict should be in their favor." 66 Mich. 577–578.

As the parties suggest, the foregoing precedent arguably distinguishes mistakes affecting the essence of the consideration from those which go to its quality or value, affording relief on a per se basis for the former but not the latter....

However, the distinctions which may be drawn from *Sherwood* and *A & M Land Development Co.* do not provide a satisfactory analysis of the nature of a mistake sufficient to invalidate a contract. Often, a mistake relates to an underlying factual assumption which, when discovered, directly affects value, but simultaneously and materially affects the essence of the contractual consideration. It is disingenuous to label such a mistake collateral.... Corbin, Contracts (one vol. ed.), § 605, p 551.

Appellant and appellee both mistakenly believed that the property which was the subject of their land contract would generate income as rental property. The fact that it could not be used for human habitation deprived the property of its income-earning potential and rendered it less valuable. However, this mistake, while directly and dramatically affecting the property's value, cannot accurately be characterized as collateral because it also affects the very essence of the consideration. "The thing sold and bought [income-generating rental property] had in fact no existence." *Sherwood v. Walker*, 66 Mich. 578.

We find that the inexact and confusing distinction between contractual mistakes running to value and those touching the substance of the consideration serves only as an impediment to a clear and helpful analysis for the equitable resolution of cases in which mistake is alleged and proven. Accordingly, the holdings of *A & M Land Development Co.* and *Sherwood* with respect to the material or collateral nature of a mistake are limited to the facts of those cases.

Instead, we think the better-reasoned approach is a case-by-case analysis whereby rescission is indicated when the mistaken belief relates to a basic assumption of the parties upon which the contract is made, and which materially affects the agreed performances of the parties.... Restatement Contracts, 2d, § 152, pp. 385–386. Rescission is not available, however, to relieve a party who has assumed the risk of loss in connection with the mistake.... Corbin, Contracts (one vol ed), § 605, p 552; 1 Restatement Contracts, 2d, §§ 152, 154, pp 385–386, 402–406.

All of the parties to this contract erroneously assumed that the property transferred by the vendors to the vendees was suitable for human habitation and could be utilized to generate rental income. The fundamental nature of these assumptions is indicated by the fact that their invalidity changed the character of the property transferred, thereby frustrating, indeed precluding, Mr. and Mrs. Pickles' intended use of the real estate. Although the Pickleses are disadvantaged by enforcement of the contract, performance is advantageous to the Messerlys, as the property at issue is less valuable absent its income-earning potential. Nothing short of rescission can remedy the mistake. Thus, the parties' mistake as to a basic assumption materially affects the agreed performances of the parties.

Despite the significance of the mistake made by the parties, we reverse the Court of Appeals because we conclude that equity does not justify the remedy sought by Mr. and Mrs. Pickles.

Rescission is an equitable remedy which is granted only in the sound discretion of the court.... A court need not grant rescission in every case in which the mutual mistake relates to a basic assumption and materially affects the agreed performance of the parties.

In cases of mistake by two equally innocent parties, we are required, in the exercise of our equitable powers, to determine which blameless party should assume the loss resulting from the misapprehension they shared.[4] Normally that can only be done by drawing upon our "own notions of what is reasonable and just under all the surrounding circumstances."

Equity suggests that, in this case, the risk should be allocated to the purchasers. We are guided to that conclusion, in part, by the standards announced in § 154 of the Restatement of Contracts, 2d, for determining when a party bears the risk of mistake.... Section 154(a) suggests that the court should look first to whether the parties have agreed to the allocation of the risk between themselves. While there is no express assumption in the contract by either party of the risk of the property becoming uninhabitable, there was indeed some agreed allocation of the risk to the vendees by the incorporation of an "as is" clause into the contract which, we repeat, provided: "Purchaser has examined this property and agrees to accept same in its present condition. There are no other or additional written or oral understandings." That is a persuasive indication that the parties considered that, as between them, such risk as related to the "present condition" of the property should lie with the purchaser. If the "as is" clause is to have any meaning at all, it must be interpreted to refer to those defects which were unknown at the time that the contract was executed.[5] Thus, the parties themselves assigned the risk of loss to Mr. and Mrs. Pickles.[6]

4. This risk-of-loss analysis is absent in both *A & M Land Development Co.* and *Sherwood*, and this omission helps to explain, in part, the disparate treatment in the two cases. Had such an inquiry been undertaken in *Sherwood*, we believe that the result might have been different. Moreover, a determination as to which party assumed the risk in *A & M Land Development Co.* would have alleviated the need to characterize the mistake as collateral so as to justify the result denying rescission. Despite the absence of any inquiry as to the assumption of risk in those two leading cases, we find that there exists sufficient precedent to warrant such an analysis in future cases of mistake.

5. An "as is" clause waives those implied warranties which accompany the sale of a new home, *Tibbitts v. Openshaw*, 18 Utah 2d 442, 425 P.2d 160 (1967), or the sale of goods. MCL 440.2316(3)(a); MSA 19.2316(3)(a). Since implied warranties protect against latent defects, an "as is" clause will impose upon the purchaser the assumption of the risk of latent defects, such as an inadequate sanitation system, even when there are no implied warranties.

6. An "as is" clause does not preclude a purchaser from alleging fraud or misrepresentation as a basis for rescission. See 97 A.L.R.2d 849. However, Mr. and Mrs. Pickles did not appeal the trial court's finding that there was no fraud or misrepresentation, so we are bound thereby.

We conclude that Mr. and Mrs. Pickles are not entitled to the equitable remedy of rescission and, accordingly, reverse the decision of the Court of Appeals.

Notes and Discussion

1. ***Sherwood v. Walker*: Two Cows?** In *Lenawee County*, the Michigan Supreme Court repudiates a view of mistake that it had previously taken in a classic case, *Sherwood v. Walker*. In that case the plaintiff, a banker, had purchased from Hiram Walker (the whiskey magnate) a cow that was thought to be barren; the price was $80. Before the cow was delivered, the seller discovered that it was pregnant, and hence (as a fertile cow) worth about ten times the purchase price. The seller refused to deliver, and the buyer brought suit.

The *Sherwood* court, following theories loosely derived from Roman and Civil Law, held that there was no valid agreement between the parties: "[A] party who has given an apparent consent to a contract of sale may refuse to execute it, or he may avoid it after it has been completed, if the assent was founded, or the contract made, upon the mistake of a material fact,—such as the subject-matter of the sale, the price, or some collateral fact materially inducing the agreement; and this can be done when the mistake is mutual." 33 N.W. at 923. In the portion of the opinion that the *Lenawee County* court quotes, the opinion acknowledges that there was "no mistake as to the identity of the creature"—i.e., both parties meant the same object. But the judge insists that: "A barren cow is substantially a different creature than a breeding one.... She was not in fact the animal, or the kind of animal, the defendants intended to sell or the plaintiff to buy." Id. In what sense is this true? Maybe the court is making a metaphysical point. Can anything intelligible be made of the "distinction between contractual mistakes running to value and those touching the substance of the consideration"?

Distinguish *Sherwood* from *Wood v. Boynton* (the uncut diamond case)? How is the theory in *Sherwood* different from *Merced County Sheriff's Employees' Ass'n.*, the misunderstanding case in Chapter 3?

2. ***Sherwood* Rejected.** In *Lenawee County*, the Court firmly limits *Sherwood* to its facts, preferring instead an analysis drawn from the Second Restatement that the outcome in *Lenawee County* would not necessarily have been different if the *Sherwood* test had been employed; true? The Court asserts in a note that: "Had [a *Lenawee County* type] inquiry been undertaken in *Sherwood*, ... the result might have been different." We wonder whether the modern analysis is just a new version of the traditional test, or something more.

Problem 5–1

A part-time coin dealer sold for $500 a dime purportedly minted in 1916 at Denver; the buyer was a retail dealer in coins. The dime turned out to be a fake, but when the sale was made, both parties were certain that the coin was genuine. Can the buyer rescind the sale? How would the case be different if the buyer was certain but the seller was unsure or unaware of the value issue?

If the buyer in this case loses on the ground of mistake, would he still have a claim on the implied warranty of merchantability? The two claims are functional equivalents. How do they differ?

LANCI v. METROPOLITAN INSURANCE CO.

Superior Court of Pennsylvania, 1989.
388 Pa.Super. 1, 564 A.2d 972.

MELINSON, J. This is an appeal from an order denying Metropolitan Insurance Co.'s ["Metropolitan"] motion to compel enforcement of a settlement agreement. Metropolitan contends that the trial court erred in voiding a release provision in the agreement after finding that it was based on a mutual mistake. . . .

The facts of this case are simple. Lanci was involved in an automobile accident with an uninsured motorist. Lanci and Metropolitan entered settlement negotiations and ultimately agreed to settle all claims for fifteen thousand dollars ($15,000.00). On or about October 17, 1986, Lanci signed a Release and Trust Agreement. Thereafter, he refused to accept the settlement proceeds asserting that Metropolitan had fraudulently or incorrectly represented that the policy limits were $15,000.00 rather than two hundred fifty thousand dollars ($250,000.00), the correct amount. Thus, Lanci argued, the release and trust agreements were signed as the result of a misrepresentation or mutual mistake and were therefore a nullity. The trial court agreed, relying on correspondence from Lanci's attorney to Metropolitan dated October 12, 1986, which stated: "This will confirm and memorialize our telephone conversation of October 10, 1986 during which it was agreed that you on behalf of your principal shall tender the sum of $15,000.00 in settlement of this claim which sum you have represented to be the straight and/or stacked policy limits applicable to this claim."

The trial court held that this correspondence evidenced a mutual mistake concerning the policy limits of the insured and denied Metropolitan's motion to enforce the settlement agreement.

Metropolitan argues that the record does not support the trial court's factual finding that there was a mutual mistake. Metropolitan relies on the deposition testimony of its claims adjuster, John Pellock, who refutes Lanci's assertion that the policy limits were discussed during settlement negotiations. Pellock testified that he did not discuss the limits with Lanci's attorney, nor did counsel for Lanci indicate that he was unaware of the policy limits, until after the settlement had been reached and the draft transmitted. He further testified that Lanci's attorney initiated the settlement negotiations with a demand for $15,000.00 and never asked for more.[7] We agree that this testimony, if

7. The record indicates that counsel for Lanci did not appear at the deposition despite receiving notice. As a result, there was no cross-examination of Pellock, and no explanation for his failure to respond to Lanci's letter accepting the settlement offer and specifying Lanci's understanding that the limit of the policy was $15,000.00. It is also unclear whether Pellock was aware of the correct amount of the policy limits during negotiations.

credited, does not support a finding of mutual mistake. However, we can affirm the decision of the trial court on any basis even if the reasons given by the trial court are incorrect....

A release is binding on the parties thereto, unless executed under fraud, duress or mutual mistake.... Whether relief should be granted to a party who is adversely affected by a mistake in a written contract depends upon the nature and effect of that mistake; the mistake must relate to the basis of the bargain, must materially affect the parties' performance, and must not be one as to which the injured party bears the risk before the party will be entitled to relief.... However, irrespective of actual fraud, if the other party knows or has reason to know of the unilateral mistake, and the mistake, as well as the actual intent of the parties is clearly shown, relief will be granted to the same extent as a mutual mistake. *Hassler v. Mummert*, 242 Pa.Super. 536, 364 A.2d 402 (1976). See also, *Com. Dept. of Educ. v. Miller*, 78 Pa.Cmwlth. 1, 466 A.2d 791 (1983) (where a mistake made in contracting is not mutual, but unilateral, and is not due to the fault of the party not mistaken, but rather to the negligence of one who acted under the mistake, it affords no basis for relief unless the party not mistaken has good reason to know of the mistake).

The Restatement (Second) of Contracts § 153 provides that a contract is voidable due to unilateral mistake under certain circumstances. "Where a mistake of one party at the time a contract was made as to a basic assumption on which he made the contract has a material effect on the agreed exchange of performances that is adverse to him, the contract is voidable by him if he does not bear the risk of the mistake..., and (a) the effect of the mistake is such that enforcement would be unconscionable, or (b) the other party had reason to know of the mistake or his fault caused the mistake."

In the instant case, the record reveals that Lanci did not have a copy of his policy and that Metropolitan was advised of that fact in Lanci's Petition to Appoint Arbitrators and to Compel Arbitration Hearing. Lanci's correspondence accepting the settlement offer clearly indicates his understanding that his policy limit is $15,000.00. We find, therefore, that Metropolitan knew, or should have known, that Lanci accepted the terms of this settlement offer under the mistaken belief that it was the limit of his coverage. Thus, Lanci is entitled to void the contract and the trial court did not err in denying Metropolitan's petition to enforce the settlement agreement.

Order affirmed.

Notes and Discussion

1. **Mutual versus Unilateral Mistake.** The trial court found that both parties had been mistaken as to the limit of Lanci's insurance. Why does the Superior Court reject this? What legal consequences flow from the Court's decision to treat this as an instance of unilateral mistake?

This case illustrates how difficult it can sometimes be to determine how mistakes occur in the course of negotiations. If Lanci and his attorney believed that the policy limit was $15,000, where did their view come from? The attorney's letter of October 12 (confirming the phone call of October 10) is not conclusive evidence of misrepresentation by Metropolitan's claims adjuster. What do you make of the incomplete deposition of Pellock?

2. Criteria for Rescission. What was Lanci's "mistake ... as to a basic assumption on which he made the contract," and how did it have "a material effect on the agreed exchange of performances that is adverse to him"? We wonder if it would matter if his actual losses because of the injury had been $22,000, or $220,000. What do you think?

Lanci evidently proceeded without obtaining and reading his policy. Does the Court hold, in effect, that the consequence of the attorney's letter of October 12 was that Metropolitan had an affirmative duty to notify Lanci about his mistake?

Because the Court holds that Metropolitan "knew, or should have known," of Lanci's mistake, it does not discuss the possibility of unconscionability. Should courts treat with suspicion agreements limiting the liability of insurance companies?

B. PUBLIC POLICY AND ILLEGALITY

Courts have long reserved to themselves the prerogative to limit enforcement of contracts that transgress the boundaries of "public policy." As Restatement 2d § 178(1) puts it, "A promise or other term of an agreement is unenforceable on grounds of public policy if legislation provides that it is unenforceable or the interest in its enforcement is clearly outweighed in the circumstances by a public policy against the enforcement of such terms." The easy case, of course, is when a statute directly prohibits enforcement, but few statutes are so direct. By easy extension, contracts that further illegal activities are also unenforceable; for example, if it is a crime to be paid for sex, it stands to reason that an agreement to do this is also unenforceable. *State v. Grimes*, 85 Or.App. 159, 735 P.2d 1277, 1278 (Ct. App. 1987).

But courts have traditionally extended their reach beyond direct enforcement of statutes, into areas of public policy that judges develop themselves. The doctrines in this area are inevitably contingent on context; what counts as policy today may seem intolerably dated tomorrow. And courts need also to face the real danger of treading where they are not welcome, even though they walk with the best intentions. Generally speaking, statutes and other clear expressions of public policy serve as safer signposts. As one early commentator observed, "The obvious criticism of any suggestion that the validity of contracts should depend upon an independent judicial answer to the question whether they comport with public policy, is that too much uncertainty would thus be injected into contractual relationships. If 'public policy' should be defined as something having no relationship to the judgments formulated by Constitutions, statutes, and prior judicial and non-judicial investigations, but as being ascertainable only by an unassisted judicial discovery of 'what is naturally and inherently just and right between man and man,' there would be much to be said in favor of the criticism. But if a determination of the relevant public policy rests upon authoritative legislative pronouncement and upon intelligent effort to procure informative data, the criticism loses force." Walter Gellhorn, *Contracts and Public Policy*, 35 Colum. L. Rev. 679, 695 (1935).

There are two areas in which courts have felt particularly free to maneuver. First, contracts in restraint of free trade have long been treated with suspicion: not just direct cartels (which are usually outright criminal), but also, for instance, contracts that restrain individuals from entering competition with one another. Second, courts also accord special protection to the family, marriage, and sexuality generally, although in this area decisions recognize the dramatically changed social conditions of the modern world.

Beyond the issue of what contracts will be subjected to suspicion on policy grounds, there is also the vexed question of what should be done when a contract is deemed wholly or partially unenforceable.

CLOUSE v. MYERS

Missouri Court of Appeals, 1988.
753 S.W.2d 316.

GREENE, J. Defendants Patricia Myers and her husband, Jerry Myers, (the Myers) appeal from a judgment in a court-tried breach of contract case. The judgment awarded plaintiff J. Todd Clouse (Clouse) $7,500 on his claim for damages, and denied relief to the Myers on their counterclaim.

No findings of fact and conclusions of law were requested or made by the trial court; therefore, all fact issues will be considered found in accordance with the result reached....

Relevant facts are as follows. In January 1987, Patricia Myers was operating the Green Door tavern in Granby, Newton County, Missouri. Mrs. Myers had a three-year lease, beginning on April 15, 1986, on the premises from owner John Hurn, Jr., for $500 a month. She had a sole owner, 5 percent beer by-the-drink license issued by the Missouri Division of Liquor Control.

In addition to the lease, the assets of the business consisted of the stock of beer on hand, glassware, an air conditioner and a beer box.

Clouse was a patron of the Green Door. During one of his visits to the tavern, Jerry Myers asked Clouse if he would be interested in purchasing an interest in the business. Negotiations followed which ultimately led to the signing of an agreement between Clouse and the Myers. The agreement, titled "Employment/Management Contract," was executed on January 28, 1987. In the contract, the Myers are referred to as "Employers" and Clouse as "Employee." It recited that (1) the Myers operated the Green Door pursuant to a contract with John Hurn "which provides a four year lease with option to purchase," (2) the Myers agreed to hire Clouse to manage the business for a four-year period, with Clouse to receive 60 percent of the net profit of the business as salary, and (3) Clouse pay to the Myers $15,000, with $7,500 to be paid at the time of the signing of the contract and the remainder at a later date. In return for fulfillment of the contract, Clouse was to receive, at the termination of the agreement or upon the exercise of the lease option to purchase, whichever came first, a 60 percent ownership interest in the Green Door, with the Myers agreeing to exercise their option to purchase the property from John Hurn within the lifetime of their lease with him. The agreement further provided that upon purchase of the property from Hurn, the Myers and Clouse were each to pay 50 percent of the purchase price.

After execution of the contract, Clouse paid $7,500, by check made payable to Patricia Myers, and began operating the tavern. Approximately two weeks later, Clouse received a telephone call from Larry Fuhr, an agent with the Missouri Division of Liquor Control, and was told to bring his contract with the Myers and the liquor license (Patricia Myers') to the Joplin Police Station where Fuhr's office was located. Clouse complied....

At trial, Clouse admitted that he knew that the liquor license was in Patricia Myers' name alone before he signed the agreement, and that the contract was an agreement for him to purchase 60 percent of the business, and was not an employment/management contract.

Fuhr was called as a witness by Clouse. He testified that after he became aware that the ownership of the Green Door had changed, he phoned Mrs. Myers and told her that if she sold part of the business, she would have to form a partnership and apply for a new license in the names of the partners. During the meeting in his office, Fuhr told Mrs. Myers that she could be "cited" for failure to comply with his instructions, and that such action might interfere with her getting a liquor license to operate a bar which she was planning to open in Carthage, Missouri. He said that Mrs. Myers then voluntarily relinquished her liquor license to Fuhr.

Clouse later applied for and received a liquor license to operate the tavern in his own name, and renegotiated the lease of the premises with Hurn, retaining the inventory that he had obtained from the Myers. Clouse requested that the Myers return his $7,500. When they refused to do so, he filed a lawsuit against them, claiming that he had been induced to enter into the "Employment/Management" contract by the false representations of Jerry Myers "that he was a partner in the business which formed the subject matter in said contract and held a leasehold interest in the business property," when in fact neither representation was so. The petition further alleged that as a direct result of such false representations, the Missouri Division of Liquor Control withdrew the

Green Door liquor license, thus triggering that portion of paragraph 12 of the contract which provided that should the Myers engage in any act

which would have the direct result of the loss of the liquor license, any monies paid by Clouse to the Myers would be refunded.

The Myers filed a counterclaim, denying they had breached the contract, and claiming that Clouse still owed them $7,500 on the contract.

The trial court entered judgment for Clouse on his petition and against the Myers on their counterclaim. This appeal followed.

In their first point relied on, the Myers contend the trial court erred in granting judgment for Clouse because he failed to prove that Jerry Myers made any misrepresentations with the intent or purpose to deceive Clouse, on which Clouse relied, which misrepresentations induced him to sign the agreement in question. We are inclined to agree, and reverse the judgment entered in favor of Clouse on his petition.

The essential elements of actionable fraud are (1) that a representation was made as a statement of fact, which was untrue and known to be untrue by the party making it, or else recklessly made, (2) that the representation was made with intent to deceive and for the purpose of inducing the other party to act upon it, (3) that the other party relied on the statement and was induced to act by it, and (4) was damaged thereby. Existence of fraud is never presumed, and each of its essential elements must be proven by the party asserting it. Failure to prove all of the essential elements is fatal. *Kreutz v. Wolff*, 560 S.W.2d 271, 277–78 (Mo.App.1977).

There is nothing in the record, other than representations in the contract language itself, indicating that Jerry Myers induced Clouse to do anything, or that he misrepresented anything to Clouse. While the contract language leaves the impression that Patricia Myers and Jerry Myers were partners in the Green Door operation, Clouse knew that the liquor license for the Green Door was issued solely in Patricia Myers' name. He further testified that at the time he signed the contract he knew it was not an "Employment/Management Contract," but was, in fact, a partnership agreement, and the reason that the agreement was labeled an employment/management contract "was so we could still operate under Patricia's license."

There is nothing in the record relative to the lease of the premises relevant to the issues here. While the lease agreement was between Hurn and Patricia Myers, and the agreement between the parties states that employers (the Myers) operated the business "pursuant to a contract entered into between themselves and one Johnny Hurn which provides a four year lease with option to purchase," there is nothing in the record to show that Clouse relied on such representation to his detriment. The reason Fuhr questioned the agreement was not because of the lease, but because an unlicensed person (Clouse) had entered into partnership agreement with a licensed person (Patricia Myers) to operate a tavern.

It is unlawful for any person, firm, partnership or corporation to sell or expose for sale in this state any intoxicating liquor without first obtaining a license.... Five percent beer is intoxicating liquor.... Clouse, as well as Patricia Myers, was violating the law when he knowingly entered into the subterfuge of calling the partnership agreement an employment/management contract so that they could operate the business on Patricia's license, without an attempt being made to secure a new partnership license, which the record indicates could have been done. There is lack of proof on the issues of reliance and damages, which of itself would defeat the attempt of Clouse to recover on the ground of fraud. Additionally, neither law nor equity can be invoked to redress a wrong that has resulted from the injured party's own wrongful and illegal conduct. *De Mayo v. Lyons*, 358 Mo. 646, 216 S.W.2d 436, 439 (1948). This principle of law also applies to the counterclaim of the Myers, as they should not be able to get another $7,500 from Clouse through reliance on an illegal agreement which they knew, or should have known, was illegal at the time they entered into it.

The judgment in favor of Clouse and against Patricia Myers and Jerry Myers in the sum of $7,500 plus interest is reversed. The judgment in favor of Clouse and against Patricia Myers and Jerry Myers on the Myers' counterclaim is affirmed.

Notes and Discussion

1. **An Illegal Contract.** Why was the contract between Clouse and the Myers illegal? Is it that the parties were deliberately aiming to flout the law, or that they concealed their intention? What are the larger issues of public policy that underlie this case, and how does the result serve to reinforce that public policy? Would the outcome have been different if Clouse could have shown that he did not realize there was anything irregular about the contract?

2. **Penalizing Todd Clouse.** Clouse eventually received a liquor license in his own name, and he took up the Myers's lease. What remained outstanding for him was the $7,500 he had paid to the Myers, for which, because the contract was illegal and unenforceable, he received nothing. Why should the Myers be able to keep the money? They are equally guilty, but perhaps the aim of this decision is not to punish Clouse but to insulate the judicial system from the "corruption" of illegal contracts. Rules governing restitution when contracts are unenforceable on public policy grounds are in Restatement 2d §§ 197–199.

Problem 5–2

Oliver was employed as a lumber trader for the North Pacific Lumber Co. His contract contained a non-competition clause preventing him from competing with North Pacific for two years after his employment ended. After Oliver quit and went to work for a competitor, North Pacific sought an injunction. At trial it emerged that while Oliver was working for North Pacific, it had engaged in various work-related illegal activities (such as secretly recording telephone conversations and personal conversations involving both plaintiff's customers and plaintiff's employees), and that Oliver had profited from some of these illegal activities. Will North Pacific get its injunction? Arguably, both parties came into court with "unclean hands." Does that necessarily mean that equitable relief should not be available?

HOPPER v. ALL PET ANIMAL CLINIC, INC.

Supreme Court of Wyoming, 1993.
861 P.2d 531.

TAYLOR, J. These consolidated appeals test the enforceability of a covenant not to compete which was included in an employment contract. The district court found that the covenant imposed reasonable geographic and durational limits necessary to protect the employers' businesses and enjoined a veterinarian from practicing small animal medicine for three years within a five mile radius of the city limits of Laramie, Wyoming. The district court denied a damage claim for breach of the employment agreement brought by the veterinarian's two corporate employers because it was speculative. The veterinarian appeals from the decision to enforce the terms of the covenant. In the companion case, the corporate employers appeal the decision to deny damages.

We hold that the covenant's three year duration imposed an unreasonable restraint of trade permitting only partial enforcement of a portion of that term of the covenant. We affirm the district court's conclusions of law that the remaining terms of the covenant were reasonable. We also affirm the district court's judgment refusing damages because the finding that damages were unproven is not clearly erroneous....

II. Facts

Following her graduation from Colorado State University, Dr. Glenna Hopper (Dr. Hopper) began working part-time as a veterinarian at the All Pet Animal Clinic, Inc. (All Pet) in July of 1988. All Pet specialized in the care of small animals; mostly domesticated dogs and cats, and those exotic animals maintained as household pets. Dr. Hopper practiced under the guidance and direction of the President of All Pet, Dr. Robert Bruce Johnson (Dr. Johnson).

Dr. Johnson, on behalf of All Pet, offered Dr. Hopper full-time employment in February of 1989. The oral offer included a specified salary and potential for bonus earnings as well as other terms of employment. According to Dr. Johnson, he conditioned the offer on Dr. Hopper's acceptance of a covenant not to compete, the specific details of which were not discussed at the time. Dr. Hopper commenced full-time employment with All Pet under the oral agreement in March of 1989 and relocated to Laramie, discontinuing her commute from her former residence in Colorado.

A written Employment Agreement incorporating the terms of the oral agreement was finally executed by the parties on December 11,

1989. Ancillary to the provisions for employment, the agreement detailed the terms of a covenant not to compete: "12. This agreement may be terminated by either party upon 30 days' notice to the other party. Upon termination, Dr. Hopper agrees that she will not practice small animal medicine for a period of three years from the date of termination within 5 miles of the corporate limits of the City of Laramie, Wyoming. Dr. Hopper agrees that the duration and geographic scope of that limitation is reasonable." The agreement was antedated to be effective to March 3, 1989.

The parties executed an Addendum To Agreement on June 1, 1990. The addendum provided that All Pet and a newly acquired corporate entity, Alpine Animal Hospital, Inc. (Alpine), also located in Laramie, would share in Dr. Hopper's professional services. As the President of All Pet and Alpine, Dr. Johnson agreed, in the addendum, to raise Dr. Hopper's salary. The bonus provision of the original agreement was eliminated. Except as modified, the other terms of the March 3, 1989 employment agreement, including the covenant not to compete, were reaffirmed and Dr. Hopper continued her employment.

One year later, reacting to a rumor that Dr. Hopper was investigating the purchase of a veterinary practice in Laramie, Dr. Johnson asked his attorney to prepare a letter which was presented to Dr. Hopper. The letter, dated June 17, 1991, stated:

> "I have learned that you are considering leaving us to take over the small animal part of Dr. Meeboer's practice in Laramie.
>
> "When we negotiated the terms of your employment, we agreed that you could leave upon 30 days' notice, but that you would not practice small animal medicine within five miles of Laramie for a three-year period. We do not have any non-competition agreement for large-animal medicine, which therefore does not enter into the picture.
>
> "I am willing to release you from the non-competition agreement in return for a cash buy-out. I have worked back from the proportion of the income of All–Pet and Alpine which you contribute and have decided that a reasonable figure would be $40,000.00, to compensate the practice for the loss of business which will happen if you practice small-animal medicine elsewhere in Laramie.
>
> "If you are willing to approach the problem in the way I suggest, please let me know and I will have the appropriate paperwork taken care of.
>
> "Sincerely,
>
> "[Signed] R. Bruce Johnson, D.V.M."

Dr. Hopper responded to the letter by denying that she was going to purchase Dr. Meeboer's practice. Dr. Hopper told Dr. Johnson that the Employment Agreement was not worth the paper it was written on and that she could do anything she wanted to do. Dr. Johnson terminated Dr. Hopper's employment and informed her to consider the 30–day notice as having been given. An unsigned, handwritten note from Dr. Johnson to Dr. Hopper, dated June 18, 1991, affirmed the termination and notice providing, in part: "Per your request to abide by your employment agreement with All Pet and Alpine as regards termination: Be advised that your last day of employment is July 18, 1991 for reasons that we are both aware of and have discussed previously."

Subsequently, Dr. Hopper purchased Gem City Veterinary Clinic (Gem City), the practice of Dr. Melanie Manning. Beginning on July 15, 1991, Dr. Hopper operated Gem City, in violation of the covenant not to compete, within the City of Laramie and with a practice including large and small animals. Under Dr. Hopper's guidance, Gem City's client list grew from 368 at the time she purchased the practice to approximately 950 at the time of trial. A comparison of client lists disclosed that 187 clients served by Dr. Hopper at Gem City were also clients of All Pet or Alpine. Some of these shared clients received permissible large animal services from Dr. Hopper. Overall, the small animal work contributed from fifty-one to fifty-two percent of Dr. Hopper's gross income at Gem City.

All Pet and Alpine filed a complaint against Dr. Hopper on November 15, 1991 seeking injunctive relief and damages for breach of the covenant not to compete contained in the Employment Agreement. Notably, All Pet and Alpine did not seek a temporary injunction to restrict Dr. Hopper's practice and possibly mitigate damages during the pendency of the proceeding. Trial was conducted on September 28, 1992.

The district court, in its Findings of Fact, Conclusions of law and Judgment, determined that the covenant not to compete was enforceable as a matter of law and contained reasonable durational and geographic limits necessary to protect All Pet's and Alpine's special interests. The special interests found by the district court included: special influence over and direct contact with All Pet's and Alpine's clients; access to client files; access to pricing policies; and instruction in practice development. Dr. Hopper was enjoined from practicing small animal medicine within five miles of the corporate limits of the City of Laramie for a period of three years from July 18, 1991. The district court found that the amount of damages suffered by All Pet and Alpine was speculative and not proven by a preponderance of the evidence....

IV. Discussion

A. *The Enforceability of a Covenant Not to Compete*

The common law policy against contracts in restraint of trade is one of the oldest and most firmly established. Restatement (Second) of Contracts §§ 185–188 (1981) (Introductory Note at 35). The traditional disfavor of such restraints means covenants not to compete are construed against the party seeking to enforce them.... The initial burden is on the employer to prove the covenant is reasonable and has a fair relation to, and is necessary for, the business interests for which protection is sought....

Two principles, the freedom to contract and the freedom to work, conflict when courts test the enforceability of covenants not to compete.... There is general recognition that while an employer may seek protection from improper and unfair competition of a former employee, the employer is not entitled to protection against ordinary competition.... The enforceability of a covenant not to compete depends upon a finding that the proper balance exists between the competing interests of the employer and the employee. See Restatement (Second) of Agency § 393 cmt. e (1958) (noting that without a covenant not to compete, an agent, employee, can compete with a principal despite past employment and can begin preparations for future competition, such as purchasing a competitive business, before leaving present employment).

Wyoming adopted a rule of reason inquiry from the Restatement of Contracts ... §§ 513–515 (1932) ... The present formulation of the rule of reason is contained in Restatement (Second) of Contracts, § 188 ... An often quoted reformulation of the rule of reason inquiry states that "[a] restraint is reasonable only if it (1) is no greater than is required for the protection of the employer, (2) does not impose undue hardship on the employee, and (3) is not injurious to the public." Harlan M. Blake, Employee Agreements Not to Compete, 73 Harv. L. Rev. 625, 648–49 (1960)....

Employers are entitled to protect their business from the detrimental impact of competition by employees who, but for their employment, would not have had the ability to gain a special influence over clients or customers.... *Beckman v. Cox Broadcasting Corp.*, 250 Ga. 127, 296 S.E.2d 566 (1982) illustrates the principle in the broadcast industry where the clients are the viewers of a particular station. Beckman was a television weather forecaster whose contributions to the "Action News Team" had been extensively promoted by Cox during his employment. Id. at 567. The promotion and Beckman's personality succeeded in attracting viewers to watch the television station. When his contract with Cox expired, Beckman accepted employment with a competitive television station in the same city and sought a declaratory judgment to determine the validity of a restrictive covenant which prevented him from appearing on television for six months within a radius of thirty-five miles of Cox's Station offices. Id.

The Supreme Court of Georgia agreed that Beckman was entitled to take to a new employer his assets as an employee which he had contributed to his former employer. Id. at 569. "It is true that an employee's aptitude, skill, dexterity, manual and mental ability and other subjective knowledge obtained in the course of employment are not property of the employer which the employer can, in absence of a contractual right, prohibit the employee from taking with him at the termination of employment." Id. The covenant permitted Cox to recover from the loss of Beckman's services by implementing a transition plan while still permitting Beckman to work as a meteorologist, but not to the extent of appearing on air with a competitive television station. Id. The *Beckman* court determined that the business interests of Cox required protection which enforcement of the reasonable terms of the covenant provided. Id.

The special interests of All Pet and Alpine identified by the district court as findings of fact are not clearly erroneous. Dr. Hopper moved to Laramie upon completion of her degree prior to any significant professional contract with the community. Her introduction to All Pet's and Alpine's clients, client files, pricing policies, and practice development techniques provided information which exceeded the skills she brought to her employment. While she was a licensed and trained veterinarian when she accepted employment, the additional exposure to clients and knowledge of clinic operations her employers shared with her had a monetary value for which the employers are entitled to reasonable protection from irreparable harm.... The proven loss of 187 of All Pet's and Alpine's clients to Dr. Hopper's new practice sufficiently demonstrated actual harm from unfair competition.

The reasonableness, in a given fact situation, of the limitations placed on a former employee by a covenant not to compete are determinations made by the court as a matter of law.... Therefore, the district court's conclusions of law about the reasonableness of the type of activity, geographic, and durational limits contained in the covenant are subject to *de novo* review.

All parties to this litigation devoted extensive research to evaluations of the reasonableness of various covenants not to compete from different authorities. However, we find precedent from our own or from other jurisdictions to be of limited value in considering the reasonableness of limits contained in a specific covenant not to compete.... We believe the reasonableness of individual limitations contained in a specific covenant not to compete must be assessed based upon the facts of that proceeding....

Useful legal principles do emerge from a survey of relevant authorities and may certainly be applied to decisions about the reasonableness of the type of activity, geographic, and durational limitations. Testing the reasonableness of the type of activity limitation provides an opportunity for the court to consider the broader public policy implications of a covenant not to compete.... The decision of the Court of Appeals of Ohio in *Williams v. Hobbs*, 9 Ohio App.3d 331, 460 N.E.2d 287 (1983) explains. The *Williams* court determined that enforcing a covenant not to compete restricting a radiologist's uncommon specialty practice would violate public policy because the community would be deprived of a unique skill. Id. at 290. In addition, the court held the type of activity limitation was unreasonable because it created an undue hardship on the physician where there were only a limited number of osteopathic hospitals available to practice his specialty. Id....

Enforcement of the practice restrictions Dr. Hopper accepted as part of her covenant not to compete does not create an unreasonable restraint of trade. While the specific terms of the covenant failed to define the practice of small animal medicine, the parties' trade usage provided a conforming standard of domesticated dogs and cats along with exotic animals maintained as household pets. As a veterinarian licensed to practice in Wyoming, Dr. Hopper was therefore permitted to earn a living in her chosen profession without relocating by practicing large animal medicine, a significant area of practice in this state. The restriction on the type of activity contained in the covenant was sufficiently limited to avoid undue hardship to Dr. Hopper while protecting the special interests of All Pet and Alpine.

In addition, as a professional, Dr. Hopper certainly realized the implications of agreeing to the terms of the covenant. While she may have doubted either her employers desires to enforce the terms or the legality of the covenant, her actions in establishing a small animal practice violated the promise she made. In equity, she comes before the court with unclean hands.... If Dr. Hopper sought to challenge the enforceability of the covenant, her proper remedy was to seek a declaratory judgment....

The public will not suffer injury from enforcement of the covenant. Dr. Hopper's services at All Pet and Alpine were primarily to provide relief for the full-time veterinarians at those clinics. In addition to dividing her time between the clinics, she covered when others had days off or, on a rotating basis, on weekends. While Dr. Hopper provided competent care to All Pet's and Alpine's clients, her services there were neither unique nor uncommon. Furthermore, the services which Dr. Hopper provided in her new practice to small animal clients were available at several other veterinary clinics within Laramie. Evidence did not challenge the public's ability to receive complete and satisfactory service from these other sources. Dr. Hopper's short term unavailability resulting from enforcement of a reasonable restraint against unfair competition is unlikely, as a matter of law, to produce injury to the public.

Reasonable geographic restraints are generally limited to the area in which the former employee actually worked or from which clients were drawn.... When the business serves a limited geographic area, as opposed to statewide or nationwide, courts have upheld geographic limits which are coextensive with the area in which the employer conducts business.... A broad geographic restriction may be reasonable when it is coupled with a specific activity restriction within an industry or business which has an inherently limited client base....

The geographical limit contained in the covenant not to compete restricts Dr. Hopper from practicing within a five mile radius of the corporate limits of Laramie. As a matter of law, this limit is reasonable in this circumstance. The evidence presented at trial indicated that the clients of All Pet and Alpine were located throughout the county. Despite Wyoming's rural character, the five mile restriction effectively limited unfair competition without presenting an undue hardship. Dr. Hopper could, for example, have opened a practice at other locations within the county.

A durational limitation should be reasonably related to the legitimate interest which the employer is seeking to protect. Restatement (Second) of Contracts, supra, § 188 cmt. b. "In determining whether a restraint extends for a longer period of time than necessary to protect the employer, the court must determine how much time is needed for the risk of injury to be reasonably moderated. When the restraint is for the purpose of protecting customer relationships, its duration is reasonable only if it is no longer than necessary for the employer to put a new [individual] on the job and for the new employee to have a reasonable opportunity to demonstrate his [or her] effectiveness to the customers. If a restraint on this ground is justifiable at all, it seems that a period of several months would usually be reasonable. If the selling or servicing relationship is relatively complex, a longer period may be called for. Courts seldom criticize restraints of six months or a year on the grounds of duration as such, and even longer restraints are often enforced." Blake, 73 Harv. L. Rev. at 677 (footnote omitted)....

The evidence at trial focused on the durational requirement in attempting to establish the three year term as being necessary to diffuse the potential loss of clients from All Pet and Alpine to Dr. Hopper. Dr. Charles Sink, a licensed veterinarian, testified as an expert on behalf of All Pet and Alpine and indicated that in Wyoming, his experience correlated with national studies that disclosed about 70% of clients visit a clinic more than once per year. The remaining 30% of the clients use the clinic at least one time per year. Dr. Johnson estimated that at All Pet and Alpine, the average client seeks veterinarian services one and one-half times a year. Apart from this data about average client visits, other support for the three year durational requirement was derived from opinion testimony. Dr. Johnson admitted that influence over a client disappears in an unspecified "short period of time," but expressed a view that three years was "safe." He also agreed that the number of clients possibly transferring from All Pet or Alpine to Dr. Hopper would be greatest in the first year and diminish in the second year.

We are unable to find a reasonable relationship between the three year durational requirement and the protection of All Pet's and Alpine's special interests. Therefore, enforcement of the entire durational term contained in the covenant not to compete violates public policy as an unreasonable restraint of trade. Restatement (Second) of Contracts, supra, § 188. Based on figures of client visits, a replacement veterinarian at All Pet and Alpine would be able to effectively demonstrate his or her own professionalism to virtually all of the clinics' clients within a one year durational limit. Since no credible evidence was presented supporting the need for multiple visits to establish special influence over clients, a one year limit is sufficient to moderate the risk of injury to All Pet and Alpine from unfair competition by Dr. Hopper.

A one year durational limit sufficiently secures All Pet's and Alpine's interests in pricing policies and practice development information. Pricing policies at All Pet and Alpine were changed yearly, according to Dr. Johnson, to reflect changes in material and service costs provided by the clinics as well as new procedures. Practice development information, especially in a learned profession, loses its value quickly as technological change occurs and new reference material become available. We hold, as a matter of law, that enforcement of a one year durational limit is reasonable and sufficiently protects the interests of All Pet and Alpine without violating public policy.

Under the formulation of the rule of reason inquiry adopted by Wyoming from the first Restatement of Contracts, the unreasonableness of any non-divisible term of a covenant not to compete made the entire covenant unenforceable. Restatement of Contracts, supra, § 518. It is perhaps due to the arbitrary nature of this rule that no previous decision of this court has permitted enforcement of a covenant not to compete.... The conceptual difficulty of the position taken in the former Restatement of Contracts, supra, § 518 leads to strong criticism by noted authors and the rejection of this so-called "blue pencil rule" by many courts....

Restatement (Second) of Contracts, supra, § 184, which we now adopt, accepts the Corbin view permitting enforcement of a narrower term which is reasonable in a covenant not to compete:

> "(1) If less than all of an agreement is unenforceable under the rule stated in '178 [dealing with restraints in violation of public policy in general], a court may nevertheless enforce the rest of the agreement in favor of a party who did not engage in serious misconduct if the performance as to which the agreement is unenforceable is not an essential part of the agreed exchange.
>
> "(2) A court may treat only part of a term as unenforceable under the rule stated in Subsection (1) if the party who seeks to enforce the term obtained it in good faith and in accordance with reasonable standards of fair dealing."

The position adopted in Restatement (Second) of Contracts, supra, § 184 does not permit the court to add to the terms of the covenant. "Sometimes a term is unenforceable on grounds of public policy because it is too broad, even though a narrower term would be enforceable. In such a situation, under Subsection (2), the court may refuse to enforce only part of the term, while enforcing the other part of the term as well as the rest of the agreement. The court's power in such a case is not a power of reformation, however, and it will not, in the course of determining what part of the term to enforce, add to the scope of the term in any way." Id. at § 184 cmt. b.

We believe the ability to narrow the term of a covenant not to compete and enforce a reasonable restraint permits public policy to be served in the most effective manner. Businesses function through the efforts of dedicated employees who provide the services and build the products desired by customers. Both the employer and the employee invest in success by expressing a commitment to one another in the form of a reasonable covenant not to compete. For the employer, this commitment may mean providing the employee with access to trade secrets, customer contacts or special training. These assets of the business are entitled to protection. For the employee, who covenants as part of a bargained for exchange, the covenant provides notice of the limits both parties have accepted in their relationship. The employee benefits during his tenure with the employer by his or her greater importance to the organization as a result of the exposure to the trade secrets, customer contacts or special training. When the employer-employee relationship terminates, a reasonable covenant not to compete then avoids unfair competition by the employee against the former employer and the specter, which no court would enforce, of specific performance of the employment agreement. When the parties agree to terms of a covenant, one of which is too broad, the court is permitted to enforce a narrower term which effectuates these public policy goals without arbitrarily invalidating the entire agreement between the parties and creating an uncertain business environment. In those instances where a truly unreasonable covenant operates as a restraint of trade, it will not be enforced....

Enforcement of a one year durational term, along with the other terms of the covenant not to compete, is reasonable in light of the circumstances of this case. Public policy is fairly served by this restraint on unfair competition by Dr. Hopper. All Pet and Alpine established irreparable harm from the loss of clients to unfair competition which entitled them to injunctive relief. While the terms of the covenant, as enforced, restrict Dr. Hopper's practice for a limited time, she will suffer no undue hardship from compliance with her bargained for promise. We, therefore, affirm the district court's conclusions of law that the type of activity and geographic limitations contained in the covenant not to compete were reasonable and enforceable as a matter of law. Because we hold that the covenant's three year durational term imposed a partially unreasonable restraint of trade, we remand for a modification of the judgment to enjoin Dr. Hopper from unfair competition for a duration of one year from the date of termination.

B. *Damages for Violation of a Covenant Not to Compete*

Wyoming's general rules of damage recovery are well established. "Damages must be proven with a reasonable degree of certainty; however, proof of exact damages is not required." *Coulthard v. Cossairt,* 803 P.2d 86, 92 (Wyo.1990). In awarding damages, a court may not speculate or conjecture about the proper amount.... A fundamental principle of damage assessment declares that a person injured receives only compensation for his loss and no more....

No previous decision of this court has considered the proper measure of damages for a breach of a covenant not to compete which is ancillary to a valid employment contract. However, consistent with our general principles of damage recovery, we accept the view that "lost profits are generally recognized as a proper element of recovery for breach of a covenant not to compete." *Matter of Isbell,* 27 B.R. 926, 930 (Bankr. W.D. Wis. 1983).... The lost profits are calculated based on a "net" figure requiring proof that: "(1) net profits were lost; (2) the amount of those profits can be determined with a reasonable degree of certainty; and (3) the defendant's breach was the proximate cause of the lost profits." Jeffrey L. Liddle & William F. Gray, Jr., Proof of Damages for Breach of a Restrictive Covenant or Noncompetition Agreement, 9 Employee Relations L.J. 455, 460 (1983). . . .

All Pet and Alpine presented three approaches to computing a damage figure. The first system considered an average fee charged for veterinarian services at All Pet and Alpine which was multiplied by the number of clients believed lost to Dr. Hopper. The second method considered the amount of profit realized by Dr. Hopper on the services she provided to former clients of All Pet and Alpine. The third approach calculated a loss of profits at All Pet and Alpine from a reduction in the total number of client visits in the year following Dr. Hopper's departure.

All three of All Pet's and Alpine's methods of damage calculation were based on figures for gross profits. In his testimony, Dr. Johnson speculated that his net profits from the lost clients would be ninety percent of the gross. He based this figure on the incredible assumption that his only costs for servicing these clients would be drugs. Dr. Johnson testified that his other fixed costs, including mortgage and receptionist, were paid for by the first clients who come in to the clinics. He assumed that the profit margin from all clients lost to Dr. Hopper would be at a higher rate because the lost clients would be served at the clinics after all fixed costs were paid.

The finding of the district court that the amount of damages suffered was speculative and unproven by a preponderance of the evidence is not clearly erroneous. The ninety percent net profit assumption defies logic and does not represent any attempt to apply common accounting principles, such as prorating of expenses. The necessary costs of doing business, such as costs of drugs dispensed, accounting charges, staff wages and depreciation on the value of equipment, were never established. Calculating the cost and expense of operation is an essential item in the proof of damages in a suit seeking net lost profits for violation of a covenant not to compete. . . . Without these calculations, All Pet's and Alpine's damage claims fail.

V. Conclusion

A well-drafted covenant not to compete preserves a careful and necessary economic balance in our society. While there are many layers to the employer-employee relationship, preventing unfair competition from employees who misuse trade secrets or special influence over customers serves public policy. Tempering the balance is the need to protect employees from unfair restraints on competition which defeat broad policy goals in favor of small business and individual advancement. Courts, in reviewing covenants not to compete, must consider these policy implications in assessing the reasonableness of the restraint as it applies to both employer and employee.

Affirmed as modified and remanded for issuance of a judgment in conformity herewith.

CARDINE, J., DISSENTING. Glenna Hopper has beaten the system. Just prior to being terminated, Dr. Hopper informed Dr. Johnson that "the [covenant] isn't worth the paper it's written on." And she was right. Upon termination, she went into the veterinary business in violation of her covenant not to compete. From July 15, 1991, until October 6, 1992, Dr. Hopper practiced small animal medicine in violation of her solemn promise in her employment agreement not to compete.

Whether she continued to practice small animal veterinary medicine after October 6, 1992, in violation of the covenant is not disclosed by the record on appeal.

The court has now decided as a matter of law that a one-year non-competition restriction is reasonable, and a longer period is unreasonable. This pronouncement establishes for the future the period during which competition can be restricted. In this case. appellant may have continued violating the covenant during her appeal—or she may have complied. We do not know. The trial court, on remand, should determine this question, and appellant ought to at least satisfy the one-year non-compete now imposed by this court.

I would hold, therefore, that the covenant was supported by consideration from the beginning and was lawful and enforceable, and I would require that appellant be enjoined from that part of the practice of veterinary medicine specified in the covenant not to compete from the date the trial court, on remand, enters its modified judgment for at least the one year period which this court now finds reasonable.

Notes and Discussion

1. Consideration. When a non-competition agreement is entered into after employment begins, the Wyoming court requires a separate consideration in order for it to be binding. This position is said to be supported by strong arguments of public policy. What are those arguments?

How does the court find consideration in this case? What if Hopper's pay raise had not incorporated the non-competition agreement?

This requirement of separate consideration is a bit odd because the Court also observes that the non-competition agreement was "ancillary to a valid employment contract"; that is, it was not a free-standing agreement. Suppose, by contrast, that Johnson had originally heard Hopper was thinking of setting up a business in Laramie and had promised her $5,000 if she did not do so; would that promise be enforceable? See Restatement 2d §§ 187–188.

2. Restricting the Agreement. The majority employ "trade usage" in order to establish the activities from which Hopper is restricted by the agreement, and they also accept the geographical restriction it contains, but they narrow the time restriction. How clear are the criteria that they use in making these judgments? Why does the dissent feel Hopper got away with breaking her contract?

The majority uses a common legal standard called the "Rule of Reason" which requires weighing all the facts and circumstances of a case to decide whether a restriction unreasonably restrains competition. This standard derives from *Mitchel v. Reynolds*, 24 Eng. Rep. 347 (Ch. 1711), as later reformulated in *Horner v. Graves*, 131 Eng. Rep. 284, 287 (C.P. 1831) ("whether the restraint is such only as to afford a fair protection to the interests of the party in favour of whom it is given, and not so large as to interfere with the interests of the public"). Restatement 2d § 188(1) holds that an ancillary non-competition promise "is unreasonably in restraint of trade if (a) the restraint is greater than is needed to protect the promisee's legitimate interest, or (b) the promisee's need is outweighed by the hardship to the promisor and the likely injury to the public." Would Hopper have been able to escape her promise if she could show that she needed to support a sick and unmoveable parent in Laramie? If Laramie was suffering from an acute shortage of pet hospitals?

The majority notes three different ways that courts have dealt with overreaching non-competition agreements: (1) they have declared the entire agreement unenforceable if any element of it was objectionable; (2) they have tried to "blue pencil" out the offending words and then enforce the remaining words; or (3) they have limited the scope of the agreement. The Wyoming court takes the third course, as do most (but not all) modern courts. Which of these three courses do you favor, and why?

3. Sale of Businesses. Suppose that Hopper had not been an employee at All Pet, but rather a partner, and that she had sold her interest to the other partners, who insisted, as part of the sale, that she sign a non-competition clause similar to the one in the principal case. Would the outcome be the same? For a good discussion, see *Weaver v. Ritchie*, 197 W.Va. 690, 478 S.E.2d 363 (1996), in which Ritchie, an optometrist, sold his practice subject to a condition to "refrain from the practice of optometry, or in any manner participating in the delivery of eye care services" for fifteen years; in return, the Weavers, as buyers, agreed to employ him for five years. The sales contract listed a separate consideration of $175,000 for this condition. When, after five years, the parties were unable to reach an agreement on his continued employment, Ritchie tried to set up a practice nearby that of the Weavers. Will the Weavers succeed in obtaining an ten-year injunction? The West Virginia court used the following test: "a restrictive covenant is reasonable only if it (1) is no greater than required for the protection of the employer, (2) does not impose undue hardship on the employee, and (3) is not injurious to the public." Id. at 369.

A.Z. v. B.Z.

Supreme Judicial Court of Massachusetts, 2000.
431 Mass. 150, 725 N.E.2d 1051.

COWIN, J. We transferred this case to this court on our own motion to consider for the first time the effect of a consent form between a married couple and an in vitro fertilization (IVF) clinic (clinic) concerning disposition of frozen preembryos.[8] B.Z., the former wife (wife) of A.Z. (husband), appeals from a judgment of the Probate and Family Court that included, inter alia, a permanent injunction in favor of the husband, prohibiting the wife from "utilizing" the frozen preembryos held in cryopreservation at the clinic. The probate judge bifurcated the issue concerning the disposition of the frozen preembryos from the then-pending divorce action.[9] The wife appeals only from the issuance of the permanent injunction. On February 8, 2000, we issued an order affirming the judgment of the Probate and Family Court. The order stated: "It is ordered that the permanent injunction entered on the docket on March 25, 1996 in Suffolk County Probate Court (Docket No. 95 D 1683 DV) be, and the same hereby is, affirmed. Opinion or opinions to follow." This opinion states the reasons for that order.

1. Factual Background

We recite the relevant background facts as determined by the probate judge in his detailed findings of fact after a hearing concerning disposition of the preembryos at which both the husband and wife were separately represented by counsel. The probate judge's findings are supplemented by the record where necessary.

a. History of the Couple

The husband and wife were married in 1977. . . . [Eds.: During their marriage they encountered considerable difficulties conceiving a child; they then went to an IVF clinic for help. The IVF procedure takes eggs from the mother and combines them with sperm produced by the father. If fertilization occurs, the resulting preembryos can be frozen and stored for later use. In this case, after protracted IVF treatment, the wife bore twin daughters in 1992. In spring of 1995, before their separation, she tried to become pregnant again without informing her husband. Relations between the couple deteriorated, and ultimately they separated and the husband filed for divorce. At that date, one vial containing four frozen preembryos remained in storage at the clinic.]

b. The IVF Clinic and the Consent Forms

In order to participate in fertility treatment, including . . . IVF, the clinic required egg and sperm donors (donors) to sign certain consent

8. We use the term "preembryo" to refer to the four-to-eight cell stage of a developing fertilized egg. . . .

9. The husband and wife separated in August, 1995, and later that month the husband filed for divorce. In September, 1995, the husband filed a motion for an ex parte temporary restraining order regarding a vial of frozen preembryos stored at the IVF clinic. The judge did not act on the motion, but ordered a hearing at which counsel for both the husband and the wife stipulated to a "standstill order." The judge then bifurcated the issue presented here from the pending divorce action, but stated that the disposition of the issue concerning the frozen preembryos would be a final determination incorporated into the final divorce judgment. The probate judge's order granting the husband a permanent injunction in this case was subsequently incorporated in the final divorce decree.

forms for the relevant procedures. Each time before removal of the eggs from the wife, the clinic required the husband and wife in this case to sign a preprinted consent form concerning ultimate disposition of the frozen preembryos. The wife signed a number of forms on which the husband's signature was not required. The only forms that both the husband and the wife were required to sign were those entitled "Consent Form for Freezing (Cryopreservation) of Embryos" (consent form), one of which is the form at issue here.

Each consent form explains the general nature of the IVF procedure and outlines the freezing process, including the financial cost and the potential benefits and risks of that process. The consent form also requires the donors to decide the disposition of the frozen preembryos on certain listed contingencies: "wife or donor" reaching normal menopause or age forty-five years; preembryos no longer being healthy; "one of us dying;" "should we become separated"; "should we both die." Under each contingency the consent form provides the following as options for disposition of the preembryos: "donated or destroyed—choose one or both." A blank line beneath these choices permits the donors to write in additional alternatives not listed as options on the form, and the form notifies the donors that they may do so. The consent form also informs the donors that they may change their minds as to any disposition, provided that both donors convey that fact in writing to the clinic....

c. *The Execution of the Forms*

Every time before eggs were retrieved from the wife and combined with sperm from the husband, they each signed a consent form. The husband was present when the first form was completed by the wife in October, 1988. They both signed that consent form after it was finished. The form, as filled out by the wife, stated, inter alia, that if they "should become separated, [they] both agree[d] to have the embryo(s) ... re-turn[ed] to [the] wife for implant." The husband and wife thereafter underwent six additional egg retrievals for freezing and signed six additional consent forms, one each in June, 1989, and February, 1989, two forms in December, 1989, and one each in August, 1990, and August, 1991. The August, 1991, consent form governs the vial of frozen preembryos now stored at the clinic.

Each time after signing the first consent form in October, 1988, the husband always signed a blank consent form. Sometimes a consent form was signed by the husband while he and his wife were traveling to the IVF clinic; other forms were signed before the two went to the IVF clinic. Each time, after the husband signed the form, the wife filled in the disposition and other information, and then signed the form herself. All the words she wrote in the later forms were substantially similar to the words she inserted in the first October, 1988, form. In each instance the wife specified in the option for "should we become separated," that the preembryos were to be returned to the wife for implantation.

2. The Probate Court's Decision

The probate judge concluded that, while donors are generally free to agree as to the ultimate disposition of frozen preembryos, the agreement at issue was unenforceable because of a "change in circumstances" occurring during the four years after the husband and wife signed the last, and governing, consent form in 1991: the birth of the twins as a result of the IVF procedure, the wife's obtaining a protective order against the husband, the husband's filing for a divorce, and the wife's then seeking "to thaw the preembryos for implantation in the hopes of having additional children." The probate judge concluded that "no agreement should be enforced in equity when intervening events have changed the circumstances such that the agreement which was originally signed did not contemplate the actual situation now facing the parties." In the absence of a binding agreement, the judge determined that the "best solution" was to balance the wife's interest in procreation against the husband's interest in avoiding procreation. Based on his findings, the judge determined that the husband's interest in avoiding procreation outweighed the wife's interest in having additional children and granted the permanent injunction in favor of the husband....

4. Legal Analysis

This is the first reported case involving the disposition of frozen preembryos in which a consent form signed between the donors on the one hand and the clinic on the other provided that, on the donors' separation, the preembryos were to be given to one of the donors for implantation. In view of the purpose of the form (drafted by and to give assistance to the clinic) and the circumstances of execution, we are dubious at best that it represents the intent of the husband and the wife regarding disposition of the preembryos in the case of a dispute between them. In any event, for several independent reasons, we conclude that the form should not be enforced in the circumstances of this case.

First, the consent form's primary purpose is to explain to the donors the benefits and risks of freezing, and to record the donors' desires for disposition of the frozen preembryos at the time the form is executed in order to provide the clinic with guidance if the donors (as a unit) no longer wish to use the frozen preembryos. The form does not state, and the record does not indicate, that the husband and wife intended the consent form to act as a binding agreement between them should they later disagree as to the disposition. Rather, it appears that it was intended only to define the donors' relationship as a unit with the clinic.

Second, the consent form does not contain a duration provision. The wife sought to enforce this particular form four years after it was signed by the husband in significantly changed circumstances and over the husband's objection. In the absence of any evidence that the donors agreed on the time period during which the consent form was to govern their conduct, we cannot assume that the donors intended the consent form to govern the disposition of the frozen preembryos four years after it was executed, especially in light of the fundamental change in their relationship (i.e., divorce).

Third, the form uses the term "should we become separated" in referring to the disposition of the frozen preembryos without defining "become separated." Because this dispute arose in the context of a divorce, we cannot conclude that the consent form was intended to govern in these circumstances. Separation and divorce have distinct legal meanings. Legal changes occur by operation of law when a couple divorces that do not occur when a couple separates. Because divorce legally ends a couple's marriage, we shall not assume, in the absence of any evidence to the contrary, that an agreement on this issue providing for separation was meant to govern in the event of a divorce.

The donors' conduct in connection with the execution of the consent forms also creates doubt whether the consent form at issue here represents the clear intentions of both donors. The probate judge found that, prior to the signing of the first consent form, the wife called the IVF clinic to inquire about the section of the form regarding disposition "upon separation": that section of the preprinted form that asked the donors to specify either "donated" or "destroyed" or "both." A clinic representative told her that "she could cross out any of the language on the form and fill in her own [language] to fit her wishes." Further, although the wife used language in each subsequent form similar to the language used in the first form that she and her husband signed together, the consent form at issue here was signed in blank by the husband, before the wife filled in the language indicating that she would use the preembryos for implantation on separation. We therefore cannot conclude that the consent form represents the true intention of the husband for the disposition of the preembryos.

Finally, the consent form is not a separation agreement that is binding on the couple in a divorce proceeding pursuant to G. L. c. 208, § 34. The consent form does not contain provisions for custody, support, and maintenance, in the event that the wife conceives and gives birth to a child. See G. L. c. 208, § 1A; C.P. Kindregan, Jr. & M.L. Inker, Family Law and Practice § 50.3 (2d ed. 1996). In summary, the consent form is legally insufficient in several important respects and does not approach the minimum level of completeness needed to denominate it as an enforceable contract in a dispute between the husband and the wife.

With this said, we conclude that, even had the husband and the wife entered into an unambiguous agreement between themselves regarding the disposition of the frozen preembryos, we would not enforce an agreement that would compel one donor to become a parent against his or her will. As a matter of public policy, we conclude that forced procreation is not an area amenable to judicial enforcement. It is well-established that courts will not enforce contracts that violate public policy.[10] ... While courts are hesitant to invalidate contracts on these

10. That is the relief sought by the wife in this case. We express no view regarding whether an unambiguous agreement between two donors concerning the disposi-

public policy grounds, the public interest in freedom of contract is sometimes outweighed by other public policy considerations; in those cases the contract will not be enforced.... To determine public policy, we look to the expressions of the Legislature and to those of this court....

The Legislature has already determined by statute that individuals should not be bound by certain agreements binding them to enter or not enter into familial relationships. In G. L. c. 207, § 47A, the Legislature abolished the cause of action for the breach of a promise to marry. In G. L. c. 210, § 2, the Legislature provided that no mother may agree to surrender her child "sooner than the fourth calendar day after the date of birth of the child to be adopted" regardless of any prior agreement.

Similarly, this court has expressed its hesitancy to become involved in intimate questions inherent in the marriage relationship. *Doe v. Doe*, 365 Mass. 556, 563, 314 N.E.2d 128 (1974). "Except in cases involving divorce or separation, our law has not in general undertaken to resolve the many delicate questions inherent in the marriage relationship. We would not order either a husband or a wife to do what is necessary to conceive a child or to prevent conception, any more than we would order either party to do what is necessary to make the other happy." Id.

In our decisions, we have also indicated a reluctance to enforce prior agreements that bind individuals to future family relationships. In *R. R. v. M. H.*, 426 Mass. 501, 689 N.E.2d 790 (1998), we held that a surrogacy agreement in which the surrogate mother agreed to give up the child on its birth is unenforceable unless the agreement contained, inter alia, a "reasonable" waiting period during which the mother could change her mind. Id. at 510.... And, in the same spirit, we stated in *Gleason v. Mann*, 312 Mass. 420, 425, 45 N.E.2d 280 (1942), that agreements providing for a general restraint against marriage are unenforceable.

We glean from these statutes and judicial decisions that prior agreements to enter into familial relationships (marriage or parenthood) should not be enforced against individuals who subsequently reconsider their decisions. This enhances the "freedom of personal choice in matters of marriage and family life." *Moore v. East Cleveland*, 431 U.S. 494, 499, 52 L. Ed. 2d 531, 97 S. Ct. 1932 (1977), quoting *Cleveland Bd. of Educ. v. LaFleur*, 414 U.S. 632, 639–640, 39 L. Ed. 2d 52, 94 S. Ct. 791 (1974).

We derive from existing State laws and judicial precedent a public policy in this Commonwealth that individuals shall not be compelled to enter into intimate family relationships, and that the law shall not be

tion of frozen preembryos could be enforced over the contemporaneous objection of one of the donors, when such agreement contemplated destruction or donation of the preembryos either for research or implantation in a surrogate.

We also recognize that agreements among donors and IVF clinics are essential to clinic operations. There is no impediment to the enforcement of such contracts by the clinics or by the donors against the clinics, consistent with the principles of this opinion.

used as a mechanism for forcing such relationships when they are not desired. This policy is grounded in the notion that respect for liberty and privacy requires that individuals be accorded the freedom to decide whether to enter into a family relationship. See *Commonwealth v. Stowell*, 389 Mass. 171, 173, 449 N.E.2d 357 (1983). "There are 'personal rights of such delicate and intimate character that direct enforcement of them by any process of the court should never be attempted.' " *Doe v. Doe*, supra at 559, quoting *Kenyon v. Chicopee*, 320 Mass. 528, 534, 70 N.E.2d 241 (1946).

In this case, we are asked to decide whether the law of the Commonwealth may compel an individual to become a parent over his or her contemporaneous objection. The husband signed this consent form in 1991. Enforcing the form against him would require him to become a parent over his present objection to such an undertaking. We decline to do so.

Notes and Discussion

1. Considering a Problem for the First Time. This case is an excellent example of a court's wrestling with a novel and troubling issue, one that arises out of the profound impact of modern medical methods on fertility and childbirth. Examine how the Court goes about creating public policy. What legislative and judicial materials does it rely on?

Numerous parallel cases have come up in recent years. The archetype, in many ways, is *In Re Baby M*, 109 N.J. 396, 537 A.2d 1227 (1988), in which the issue was a child surrogacy contract. Mary Beth Whitehead had been artificially inseminated with sperm from William Stern. She had agreed that, for $10,000, she would bear the child and hand it over to Stern and his wife, waiving all parental rights. After the child was born, Whitehead changed her mind, and the Sterns sued for specific performance. This case raises an important side issue, in that the judicial decision has since been supplanted by legislation; cf. *In re Adoption of Children by G.P.B.*, 161 N.J. 396, 736 A.2d 1277 (1999), citing N.J.S.A. 9:3–46, which emphasizes that the dominant consideration is the best interest of the child rather than the rights of their biological parents. Are courts better advised to wait for legislatures to act?

With the *A.Z. v. B.Z.* decision, compare *Davis v. Davis*, 842 S.W.2d 588 (Tenn. 1992) (in a divorce proceeding, awarding a husband custody of frozen embryos).

Problem 5–3

Terri and Beth lived together in Massachusetts from 1996 to 2000 (before the legal recognition of same-sex marriage in that State). In 1999, the couple decided to have a child through artificial insemination from an anonymous donor. Both parties were involved in the planning and expenditures associated with the process. Terri became pregnant and gave birth in July, 2000, but in the meantime the two had separated. Beth never sought visitation rights, and she gave Terri money for the child only once. Terri is now seeking child support from Beth.

Two questions: Is there an implied contract between Terri and Beth that Beth will support the child? And, if so, is that contract enforceable in light of *A.Z. v. B.Z.*?

Problem 5–4

Bill and Jane, who are cohabiting, have agreed that Jane will take birth control pills to ensure that she does not become pregnant. Jane wants to marry, but Bill has resisted the idea. In an effort to obtain his agreement, she stops taking the pills and becomes pregnant. However, Bill, instead of now agreeing to marriage, insists that she have an abortion. When Jane refuses, he brings suit for breach of contract. Will he prevail? If he does, what remedy? An order for an abortion? Damages equal to the amount of support he must contribute to the child?

One version of these facts arose when Frank Serpico (a retired policeman who had famously gone undercover to expose corruption) claimed in a paternity suit that the mother of his child had deceived him by pretending to be on contraceptives when she was actually highly fertile. A friend of the mother testified that she had boasted of her plot to seduce Serpico and force him to father her child. Nonetheless, he lost and was forced to pay child support. The general issue of fraudulently induced paternity remains hotly contested. See Sydney Morning Herald, Saturday, February 17, 2001: http://www.fact.on.ca/news/news0102/sm010217.htm.

C. UNCONSCIONABILITY

The opinion in *Lucy v. Zehmer*, as you will recall, notes in passing that the agreed-upon price was fair in relation to the value of the farm. This point was relevant because the plaintiffs were asking the court for specific performance, that the Zehmers be compelled to complete the sale. As you will see in Chapter 6, specific performance, an uncommon remedy in Common Law except for land transactions, is granted in equity, and equity courts traditionally declined to grant specific performance if they regarded an agreement as grossly unfair, particularly because of inequality of exchange. This conventional criterion was called unconscionability.

Although specific performance was not usually available in sale of goods cases, there were a few precedents in which unconscionability had also been used for them. A good example was *Campbell Soup Co. v. Wentz*, 172 F.2d 80 (3d Cir. 1948). In June, 1947, Campbell purchased carrots from several farmers for prices ranging from $23 to $30 per ton, depending on date of delivery. After the sale, the price of carrots shot upward to about $90 per ton in January, 1948. The farmers, seeking to profit, sold their carrots elsewhere and terminated their contracts with Campbell, which then sought specific performance. The decision rejects this remedy because Campbell's contracts were excessively one-sided. As the Court says, "We are not suggesting that the contract is illegal. Nor are we suggesting any excuse for the grower in this case who has deliberately broken an agreement entered into with Campbell. We do think, however, that a party who has offered and succeeded in getting an agreement as tough as this one is, should not come to a chancellor and ask court help in the enforcement of its terms. That equity does not enforce unconscionable bargains is too well established to require elaborate citation." Id. at 83 (citation omitted).

In cases like this one, unconscionability served mainly as a gatekeeper doctrine limiting access to a particular remedy; Campbell Soup could still sue the Wentzes for ordinary damages. But the authors of the UCC seized on such cases and, for sales of goods, greatly extended their underlying logic. A substantial part of the impetus for § 2–302 came, in particular, from Karl Llewellyn's recognition that the increasing salience of standardized form contracts necessitated widening the traditional concept of unconscionability. As Llewellyn argues, "Why, then, can we not face the fact where boiler-plate is present? There has been an arm's-length deal, with dickered terms. There has been accompanying that basic deal another which, if not on any fiduciary basis, at least involves a plain expression of confidence, asked and accepted, with a corresponding limit on the powers granted: the boiler-plate is assented to en bloc, 'unsight, unseen,' on the implicit assumption and to the full extent that (1) it does not alter or impair the fair meaning of the dickered terms when read alone, and (2) that its terms are neither in the particular nor in the net manifestly unreasonable and unfair." Karl N. Llewellyn, The Common Law Tradition: Deciding Appeals 370–371 (1960). The UCC's unconscionability provision was a novel legal means for dealing with cases where this assumption—usually one made by consumers—turned out to be highly improvident.

UCC § 2–302 gives courts sweeping statutory authorization to refuse to enforce all or parts of contracts for the sale of goods if "the court as a matter of law finds the contract or any clause of the contract to have been unconscionable at the time it was made." As in the older cases, the determination of unconscionability is made by judges (in equity), not by juries. The time frame is also explicit: the unconscionability must be present when the contract is made, and not simply arise because an initially fair contract turns out to be oppressive because of unexpected circumstances. Beyond that, however, the statutory language itself gives little assistance to courts. The Comment, however, is a bit more helpful: "The basic test is whether, in the light of the general commercial background and the commercial needs of the particular trade or case, the clauses involved are so one-sided as to be unconscionable under the circumstances existing at the time of the making of the contract.... The principle is one of the prevention of oppression and unfair surprise (Cf. *Campbell Soup Co. v. Wentz*, 172 F.2d 80, 3d Cir. 1948) and not of disturbance of allocations of risks because of superior bargaining power." UCC § 2–302 cmt. 1.

This language remains cryptic, though. Part of the task, for courts and commentators alike, was to tame this extraordinary grant of power by giving it clear limits. By and large, this effort has been successful, and unconscionability was subsequently accepted as a general contractual doctrine in Restatement 2d § 208. We begin this section with what is undoubtedly the most important early case on unconscionability—a case that, it should be noted, applies the rule to a transaction that occurred before the enactment of the UCC for the jurisdiction.

WILLIAMS v. WALKER–THOMAS FURNITURE CO.

United States Court of Appeals for the District of Columbia Circuit, 1965.
121 U.S. App. D.C. 315, 350 F.2d 445.

WRIGHT, J. Appellee, Walker–Thomas Furniture Company, operates a retail furniture store in the District of Columbia. During the period from 1957 to 1962 each appellant in these cases purchased a number of household items from Walker–Thomas, for which payment was to be made in installments. The terms of each purchase were contained in a printed form contract which set forth the value of the purchased item and purported to lease the item to appellant for a stipulated monthly rent payment. The contract then provided, in substance, that title would remain in Walker–Thomas until the total of all the monthly payments made equaled the stated value of the item, at which time appellants could take title. In the event of a default in the payment of any monthly installment, Walker–Thomas could repossess the item.

The contract further provided that "the amount of each periodical installment payment to be made by [purchaser] to the Company under this present lease shall be inclusive of and not in addition to the amount of each installment payment to be made by [purchaser] under such prior leases, bills or accounts; and *all payments now and hereafter made by [purchaser] shall be credited pro rata on all outstanding leases, bills and accounts* due the Company by [purchaser] at the time each such payment is made." (Emphasis added.) The effect of this rather obscure provision was to keep a balance due on every item purchased until the balance due on all items, whenever purchased, was liquidated. As a result, the debt incurred at the time of purchase of each item was secured by the right to repossess all the items previously purchased by the same purchaser, and each new item purchased automatically became subject to a security interest arising out of the previous dealings.

On May 12, 1962, appellant Thorne purchased an item described as a Daveno, three tables, and two lamps, having total stated value of $391.10. Shortly thereafter, he defaulted on his monthly payments and appellee sought to replevy all the items purchased since the first transaction in 1958. Similarly, on April 17, 1962, appellant Williams bought a stereo set of stated value of $514.95.[11] She too defaulted shortly thereafter, and appellee sought to replevy all the items purchased since December, 1957. The Court of General Sessions granted judgment for appellee.

11. At the time of this purchase her account showed a balance of $164 still owing from her prior purchases. The total of all the purchases made over the years in question came to $1,800. The total payments amounted to $1,400.

The District of Columbia Court of Appeals affirmed, and we granted appellants' motion for leave to appeal to this court.

Appellants' principal contention, rejected by both the trial and the appellate courts below, is that these contracts, or at least some of them, are unconscionable and, hence, not enforceable. In its opinion in *Williams v. Walker–Thomas Furniture Company*, 198 A.2d 914, 916 (1964), the District of Columbia Court of Appeals explained its rejection of this contention as follows: "Appellant's second argument presents a more serious question. The record reveals that prior to the last purchase appellant had reduced the balance in her account to $164. The last purchase, a stereo set, raised the balance due to $678. Significantly, at the time of this and the preceding purchases, appellee was aware of appellant's financial position. The reverse side of the stereo contract listed the name of appellant's social worker and her $218 monthly stipend from the government. Nevertheless, with full knowledge that appellant had to feed, clothe and support both herself and seven children on this amount, appellee sold her a $514 stereo set.

"We cannot condemn too strongly appellee's conduct. It raises serious questions of sharp practice and irresponsible business dealings. A review of the legislation in the District of Columbia affecting retail sales and the pertinent decisions of the highest court in this jurisdiction disclose, however, no ground upon which this court can declare the contracts in question contrary to public policy. We note that were the Maryland Retail Installment Sales Act, Art. 83 §§ 128–153, or its equivalent, in force in the District of Columbia, we could grant appellant appropriate relief. We think Congress should consider corrective legislation to protect the public from such exploitive contracts as were utilized in the case at bar."

We do not agree that the court lacked the power to refuse enforcement to contracts found to be unconscionable. In other jurisdictions, it has been held as a matter of common law that unconscionable contracts are not enforceable.[12] While no decision of this court so holding has been found, the notion that an unconscionable bargain should not be given full enforcement is by no means novel. In *Scott v. United States*, 79 U.S. (12 Wall.) 443, 445, 20 L. Ed. 438 (1870), the Supreme Court stated: "* * * If a contract be unreasonable and unconscionable, but not void for fraud, a court of law will give to the party who sues for its breach damages, not according to its letter, but only such as he is equitably entitled to. * * *"

Since we have never adopted or rejected such a rule, the question here presented is actually one of first impression.

Congress has recently enacted the Uniform Commercial Code, which specifically provides that the court may refuse to enforce a contract

12. *Campbell Soup Co. v. Wentz*, 3 Cir., 172 F.2d 80 (1948); *Indianapolis Morris Plan Corporation v. Sparks*, 132 Ind.App. 145, 172 N.E.2d 899 (1961); *Henningsen v. Bloomfield Motors, Inc.*, 32 N.J. 358, 161 A.2d 69, 84–96, 75 A.L.R.2d 1 (1960). Cf. 1 CORBIN, CONTRACTS § 128 (1963).

which it finds to be unconscionable at the time it was made. 28 D.C.CODE § 2–302 (Supp. IV 1965). The enactment of this section, which occurred subsequent to the contracts here in suit, does not mean that the common law of the District of Columbia was otherwise at the time of enactment, nor does it preclude the court from adopting a similar rule in the exercise of its powers to develop the common law for the District of Columbia. In fact, in view of the absence of prior authority on the point, we consider the congressional adoption of § 2–302 persuasive authority for following the rationale of the cases from which the section is explicitly derived. Accordingly, we hold that where the element of unconscionability is present at the time a contract is made, the contract should not be enforced.

Unconscionability has generally been recognized to include an absence of meaningful choice on the part of one of the parties together with contract terms which are unreasonably favorable to the other party. Whether a meaningful choice is present in a particular case can only be determined by consideration of all the circumstances surrounding the transaction. In many cases the meaningfulness of the choice is negated by a gross inequality of bargaining power.[13] The manner in which the contract was entered is also relevant to this consideration. Did each party to the contract, considering his obvious education or lack of it, have a reasonable opportunity to understand the terms of the contract, or were the important terms hidden in a maze of fine print and minimized by deceptive sales practices? Ordinarily, one who signs an agreement without full knowledge of its terms might be held to assume the risk that he has entered a one-sided bargain. But when a party of little bargaining power, and hence little real choice, signs a commercially unreasonable contract with little or no knowledge of its terms, it is hardly likely that his consent, or even an objective manifestation of his consent, was ever given to all the terms. In such a case the usual rule that the terms of the agreement are not to be questioned should be abandoned and the court should consider whether the terms of the contract are so unfair that enforcement should be withheld.

In determining reasonableness or fairness, the primary concern must be with the terms of the contract considered in light of the circumstances existing when the contract was made. The test is not simple, nor can it be mechanically applied. The terms are to be considered "in the light of the general commercial background and the commercial needs of the particular trade or case." Corbin suggests the test as being whether the terms are "so extreme as to appear unconscionable

13. . . . Inquiry into the relative bargaining power of the two parties is not an inquiry wholly divorced from the general question of unconscionability, since a one-sided bargain is itself evidence of the inequality of the bargaining parties. This fact was vaguely recognized in the common law doctrine of intrinsic fraud, that is, fraud which can be presumed from the grossly unfair nature of the terms of the contract. See the oft-quoted statement of Lord Hardwicke in *Earl of Chesterfield v. Janssen*, 28 Eng. Rep. 82, 100 (1751): "* * * [Fraud] may be apparent from the intrinsic nature and subject of the bargain itself; such as no man in his senses and not under delusion would make * * *." . . .

according to the mores and business practices of the time and place." 1 CORBIN, op. cit. supra Note 2.[14] We think this formulation correctly states the test to be applied in those cases where no meaningful choice was exercised upon entering the contract.

Because the trial court and the appellate court did not feel that enforcement could be refused, no findings were made on the possible unconscionability of the contracts in these cases. Since the record is not sufficient for our deciding the issue as a matter of law, the cases must be remanded to the trial court for further proceedings.

So ordered.

DANAHER, J., DISSENTING. The District of Columbia Court of Appeals obviously was as unhappy about the situation here presented as any of us can possibly be. Its opinion in the Williams case, quoted in the majority text, concludes: "We think Congress should consider corrective legislation to protect the public from such exploitive contracts as were utilized in the case at bar."

My view is thus summed up by an able court which made no finding that there had actually been sharp practice. Rather the appellant seems to have known precisely where she stood.

There are many aspects of public policy here involved. What is a luxury to some may seem an outright necessity to others. Is public oversight to be required of the expenditures of relief funds? A washing machine, e.g., in the hands of a relief client might become a fruitful source of income. Many relief clients may well need credit, and certain business establishments will take long chances on the sale of items, expecting their pricing policies will afford a degree of protection commensurate with the risk. Perhaps a remedy when necessary will be found within the provisions of the "Loan Shark" law, D.C.CODE §§ 26–601 et seq. (1961).

I mention such matters only to emphasize the desirability of a cautious approach to any such problem, particularly since the law for so long has allowed parties such great latitude in making their own contracts. I dare say there must annually be thousands upon thousands of installment credit transactions in this jurisdiction, and one can only speculate as to the effect the decision in these cases will have.

I join the District of Columbia Court of Appeals in its disposition of the issues.

Notes and Discussion

1. The Offending Clause. Read the language of the crucial clause carefully. What was the purpose of this clause? (The opinion describes it as "rather obscure," apparently implying that it was, at least, not totally

14. ... The traditional test as stated in *Greer v. Tweed*, [N.Y.C.P.] 13 Abb.Pr. N.S. [427 (1872)], at 429, is "such as no man in his senses and not under delusion would make on the one hand, and as no honest or fair man would accept, on the other."

unintelligible.) Surely most ordinary consumers would not have understood the clause, assuming that they read it. How did the clause operate in Ora Lee Williams's case?

This clause, which resembles a cross-collateral clause, is not atypical of the kinds of clauses that are used in standardized consumer contracts.

2. Some Background. Judge Wright quotes the lower court opinion noting that Williams was a welfare recipient with seven children. Why is this information relevant to the outcome? Would the case be substantially different if Williams had been a woman of means? What social assumptions underlie the decision in this lawsuit?

A detailed study of the facts leading up to this case showed that from 1957 to 1962 Williams had made sixteen purchases of furniture and household appliances from Walker–Thomas, and each time had signed a contract containing the same clause. In late 1962 Williams owed a total of $444 on her purchases, but, because of earlier payments, the *pro rata* amount owed on many of them was quite small: $0.25 on the first item purchased (price: $45.65), $0.03 on the second (price: $13.21), and so on. A significant balance was outstanding on only three of the sixteen items purchased. See Skilton and Helstad, Protection of the Installment Buyer of Goods under the Uniform Commercial Code, 65 Mich.L.Rev. 1465, 1477 (1967). For additional information on the case, see Colby, What Did the Doctrine of Unconscionability Do to the Walker–Thomas Furniture Co., 34 Conn.L.Rev. 625 (2002).

It is worth conjecturing about how Williams and others succeeded in bringing their cases to this level.

3. Applying § 2–302. How does Judge Wright escape the objection that the UCC was not in force at the time of this transaction?

Wright's formulation of the unconscionability doctrine ("an absence of meaningful choice on the part of one of the parties together with contract terms which are unreasonably favorable to the other party") has acquired classic status. Note that two elements are involved: first, a palpable defect in the bargaining process, such that one party is at a sharp disadvantage; second, evidence in the bargain itself of the consequences of that disadvantage. In later cases these two elements are referred to as procedural and substantive unconscionability, respectively. Wright further insists that the unconscionability must be present when the contract was made. Does he also recognize Walker–Thomas's right, under § 2–302(2), "to present evidence as to [the clause's] commercial setting, purpose and effect"?

The prevailing view today is that both procedural and substantive unconscionability must be present in order for a court to exercise its discretion to refuse to enforce a contract or clause under the doctrine of unconscionability. This distinction, which derives from Arthur Leff, Unconscionability and the Code—The Emperor's New Clause, 115 U. Pa. L. Rev. 485 (1967), is summed up by Prof. Murray: *Procedural* unconscionability ("bargaining naughtiness") is "the manner in which the contract was negotiated," while "*[s]ubstantive* unconscionability ... is concerned with whether the obligations assumed were unreasonably favorable to one of the parties." John Edward Murray, Jr., Murray on Contracts § 96 at 555–556

(4th ed. 2001). The distinction obviously resembles that drawn by Judge Wright in *Williams v. Walker–Thomas*: "an absence of meaningful choice on the part of one of the parties [' procedural unconscionability] together with contract terms which are unreasonably favorable to the other party [' substantive unconscionability]."

Surely no court would find a contract unconscionable because it was unfairly arrived at, even if its terms were completely fair. On the other hand, courts might find terms unconscionable because of their harshness, even though there is no detectable inequity in the process of formation, true?

But consider the following argument: "[T]he principle of freedom of contract ... demand[s] that the reasons invoked for not enforcing the contract be of one of two sorts. Either there must be proof of some defect in the process of contract formation (be it duress, fraud or undue influence); or there must be, but only within narrow limits, some incompetence of the party against whom the agreement is to be enforced.... Yet when the doctrine of unconscionability is used in its substantive dimension, be it in a commercial or consumer context, it serves only to undercut the private right of contract in a manner that is apt to do more social harm than good. The result of the analysis is the same even if we view the question of unconscionability from the lofty perspective of public policy...." Richard Epstein, *Unconscionability: A Critical Reappraisal*, 18 J. Law & Econ. 293, 315 (1975). Do you agree?

4. On Remand. If this case were to be retried, what is the likely outcome? It is not an inevitable conclusion that Walker–Thomas had engaged in what the Court of Appeals condemns as "sharp practice and irresponsible business dealings." Perhaps Walker–Thomas could show that, given Williams' general credit position, it was likely to lose money if it sold on terms less draconian than these. Would a finding of unconscionability then mean, in effect, that Walker–Thomas was legally prevented from selling stereos to poor customers?

Could Walker–Thomas show that other retailers in the same market resort to similar devices, and that almost all statutes regulating installment sales do not nullify a cross-collateral clause? (Both these propositions were apparently true at the time the *Williams* decision was made.) Would it help Walker–Thomas if it could show that its return on equity, in a lower-income market, is about the same as the return of more up-market retailers in Washington suburbs? (This is not unlikely.)

Is it possible that some contract terms could be so onerous that they cannot be regarded as voluntarily entered, no matter by whom? Would such terms be unconscionable *per se*?

In the fact, it appears that the parties settled before a re-trial: Walker–Thomas dropped its claims against Williams and paid her the fair value of what it had taken. Leon Dostert, *Appellate Restatement of Unconscionability: Civil Legal Aid at Work*, 54 A.B.A.J. 1183 (1968).

5. Legislation. Both the Court of Appeals and the dissenting judges favored corrective legislation rather than a judicial solution. What can be said pro and con about this view?

The Uniform Consumer Credit Code (UCCC), promulgated after the *Williams* decision, permitted cross-collateral clauses, but required that payments be "applied first to the payment of the debts arising from the sales first made." UCCC § 3–303(1). Is this a better way to deal with the problem in the present case? Versions of the UCCC were adopted in eleven states.

Many early cases of unconscionability had a strong "consumer protection" aspect, often arising from the desire of judges to lend a helping hand when the free market appeared to overwhelm the relatively defenseless. Well-known examples are *Jones v. Star Credit Corp.*, 298 N.Y.S.2d 264 (Sup. Ct. 1969) (under exceptionally adverse credit terms, welfare recipients buy home freezer from door-to-door salesman); *Weaver v. American Oil Co.*, 257 Ind. 458, 276 N.E.2d 144 (1971) (gas station operator with very limited education enters one-sided franchise contract); *Seabrook v. Commuter Housing Co.*, 72 Misc.2d 6, 338 N.Y.S.2d 67 (1972) (onerous lease clause). To a considerable extent, cases of this sort have been overtaken by the rise of statutory and administrative protections for consumers and other vulnerable parties, like franchisees.

6. Can Merchants be Victims? On the other hand, courts have generally been reluctant to accept pleas of unconscionability as between merchants. As one decision put it, "When the contract is between two commercial entities, unconscionability must be viewed 'in light of the general commercial background and the commercial needs of the particular trade or case,' and there is a presumption of conscionability when the contract is between businessmen in a commercial setting. Courts have rarely found a clause to be unconscionable in a commercial contract." *Imaging Fin. Serv. v. Graphic Arts Servs., Inc.*, 172 F.R.D. 322, 327 (N.D. Ill. 1997) (citation omitted). Exceptions have mainly come when inequity is particularly apparent. For instance, in *Moscatiello v. Pittsburgh Contractors Equipment Co.*, 407 Pa.Super. 363, 595 A.2d 1190 (1991), inconspicuous remedy-limiting clauses in a contract for the sale of a paving machine were held unconscionable because the buyer lacked experience with the industry and the seller's business practices, and the seller had not explained the limitations.

An interesting and important case that hovers right on the edge is *Graham v. Scissor–Tail, Inc.*, 28 Cal.3d 807, 623 P.2d 165, 171 Cal.Rptr. 604 (1981). Rock promoter Bill Graham entered a contract to present performances by Leon Russell. The contract, a standard one drafted by the American Federation of Musicians (AFM) and required of its members, dictated arbitration of any disputes by the International Executive Board of the AFM, "pursuant to and in accordance with the laws, rules and regulations of the said Federation." Graham, who had previously signed many such contracts, clearly knew the rules when he signed. When a dispute broke out, Graham sued, and the California Supreme Court held the arbitration agreement unconscionable, since "the agreement to *arbitrate* is essentially illusory.... [T]he 'minimum levels of integrity' which are requisite to a contractual arrangement for the nonjudicial resolution of disputes are not achieved by an arrangement which designates the union of one of the parties as the arbitrator of disputes arising out of employment—especially when, as here, the arrangement is the product of circumstances indicative of adhesion." 28 Cal.3d at 825.

7. Why Do Courts Care about Unconscionability? Most unconscionability cases involve "cognitive asymmetry" between two parties, arising "from circumstances peculiar to the contracting party (e.g., little education, low intelligence, lack of knowledge, lack of independence) or from circumstances peculiar to the contract (e.g., the contract was difficult to understand, was in fine print, or dealt with difficult-to-estimate probabilities)." Stephen A. Smith, Contract Theory 344 (2004). Smith argues that: "[T]he best explanation for why courts should care about the category of cognitive asymmetry unconscionability cases is that these are cases of presumed procedural defects. These are cases, in other words, in which courts have good reason to be concerned about fraud, undue influence, duress, or a simple failure to agree, but in which they lack direct evidence of the defect. Evidence of substantive unfairness provides indirect confirmation that the relevant risk materialized." Id. at 364.

Test this explanation against the facts in *Williams* and in the other cases below.

COOPER v. MRM INVESTMENT CO.

United States Court of Appeals, Sixth Circuit, 2004.
367 F.3d 493.

ALDRICH, J. This appeal concerns the validity and enforceability of an arbitration provision in an employment contract between plaintiff-appellee Tonya Cooper and defendant-appellant MRM Investment Company ("MRM"). Cooper alleges that while working as a manager at MRM's restaurant, she was sexually harassed and constructively discharged. She brought a Title VII action, and MRM moved to compel arbitration. The district court denied the motion, holding the arbitration agreement invalid or unenforceable on five grounds. The district court held that the arbitration provision is invalid as a matter of Tennessee law because it is an unconscionable contract of adhesion and is insufficiently bilateral, and invalid as a matter of federal law because it did not make clear that Cooper was waiving her right to a jury trial. The court also opined that as a matter of policy, Title VII claims belong in court, not in arbitration. For the reasons that follow, we reverse those portions of the district court's judgment.

The district court also held that the arbitration provision is unenforceable, as a matter of federal common law, because it incorporated American Arbitration Association ("AAA")[15] rules likely to impose undue costs on Cooper that she would not incur in court, rendering arbitration an ineffective forum to vindicate her rights. For the reasons that follow, we vacate this portion of the district court's judgment and remand for proceedings consistent with this opinion.

I. Background

Terry Rogers and Larry Mays are the sole shareholders of MRM, which owns and operates several Kentucky Fried Chicken/Taco Bell

15. The AAA, a non-profit public service organization, assists in the design and administration of dispute resolution systems for corporations, unions, government agencies, law firms and the courts....

("KFC") franchises. From January 3 through August 2000, Cooper worked as an assistant manager of MRM's KFC store in Waverly, Tennessee, at $400–450 per week plus possible bonuses.[16] On January 5, 2000, MRM required her to sign a document entitled "Arbitration of Employee Rights," which provides:

> Because of the delay and expense of the court systems, KFC and I agree to use confidential binding arbitration for any claims that arise between me and KFC, its related companies, and/or their current or former employees. Such claims would include any concerning compensation, employment (including, but not limited to any claims concerning sexual harassment), or termination of employment. Before arbitration, I agree: (i) first, to present any such claims in full written detail to KFC; (ii) next, to complete any KFC internal review process; and (iii) finally, to complete any external administrative remedy (such as with the Equal Employment Opportunity Commission). In any arbitration, the then prevailing rules of the American Arbitration Association (and, to the extent not inconsistent, the then prevailing rules of the [FAA]) will apply.

... The parties agree MRM did not separately advise Cooper that she was giving up her right to a jury trial, nor did they provide her with a copy of the AAA's rules.

As a result of sexual harassment, Cooper alleges, she was forced to quit in August 2000. She found a job at another restaurant, where she earned $7,200 in 2001, and tended bar part-time, earning an additional $300 to $500 per week as of early 2002. In January 2001, Cooper filed a Charge of Discrimination with the EEOC, which issued a Dismissal and Notice of Rights in September 2001. Cooper filed her complaint in December 2001. Following oral argument, the district court denied MRM's motion to compel arbitration on May 1, 2002. MRM appealed on May 28, 2002.

II. Analysis

A. *Standard of Review*

We review *de novo* the district court's holding that the arbitration agreement is invalid and unenforceable.... The court's factual findings, by contrast, will be set aside only if they are clearly erroneous ...

B. *Arbitration Agreements are Generally Enforceable and are Strongly Favored*

At common law, American courts were loathe to order specific enforcement of an agreement to arbitrate, adopting the "jealous notion held by the common law courts of England that arbitration agreements were nothing less than a drain on their own authority to settle disputes." *Raasch v. NCR Corp.*, 254 F. Supp. 2d 847, 853 (S.D. Ohio 2003) (citing *Dean Witter Reynolds, Inc. v. Byrd*, 470 U.S. 213, 219–20 n.6, 84

16. [Eds.: References to the trial records have been deleted throughout this opinion.]

L. Ed. 2d 158, 105 S. Ct. 1238 (1985)). In response, Congress enacted the Federal Arbitration Act, 9 U.S.C. § 1 et seq. ("the FAA"), "to place arbitration agreements upon the same footing as other contracts." *Gilmer v. Interstate/Johnson Lane Corp.*, 500 U.S. 20, 24, 114 L. Ed. 2d 26, 111 S. Ct. 1647 (1991). The FAA expresses a strong public policy favoring arbitration of a wide class of disputes. It provides, in part:

> A written provision in any maritime transaction or a contract evidencing a transaction involving commerce to settle by arbitration a controversy thereafter arising out of such contract or transaction ... shall be valid, irrevocable, and enforceable, *save upon such grounds as exist at law or in equity for the revocation of any contract.*

9 U.S.C. § 2 (emphasis added); see also 9 U.S.C. § 1 (excepting some disputes arising out of employment in interstate transportation). Thus, generally applicable state-law contract defenses like fraud, forgery, duress, mistake, lack of consideration or mutual obligation, or unconscionability, may invalidate arbitration agreements. See *Doctor's Assocs. v. Casarotto*, 517 U.S. 681, 687, 134 L. Ed. 2d 902, 116 S. Ct. 1652 (1996) (citations omitted); *Perry v. Thomas*, 482 U.S. 483, 492 n.9, 96 L. Ed. 2d 426, 107 S. Ct. 2520 (1987); *Fazio v. Lehman Bros.*, Inc., 340 F.3d 386, 393–94 (6th Cir. 2003). "The federal policy favoring arbitration, however, is taken into consideration even in applying ordinary state law." *Garrett v. Hooters–Toledo*, 295 F. Supp. 2d 774, 779 (N.D. Ohio 2003) (citing *Inland Bulk Transfer Co. v. Cummins Engine Co.*, 332 F.3d 1007, 1014 (6th Cir. 2003) (internal citation omitted)).

The Supreme Court has roundly endorsed arbitration and explained its benefits in the employment law context:

> We have been clear in rejecting the supposition that the advantages of the arbitration process somehow disappear when transferred to the employment context. Arbitration agreements allow parties to avoid the costs of litigation, a benefit that may be of particular importance in employment litigation, which often involves smaller sums of money than disputes concerning commercial contracts. These litigation costs to parties (and the accompanying burden to the Courts) would be compounded by the difficult choice-of-law questions that are often presented in disputes arising from the employment relationship ... and the necessity of bifurcation of proceedings in those cases where state law precludes arbitration of certain types of employment claims but not others. The considerable complexity and uncertainty that [a broader reading of § 1's exclusion] would introduce into the enforceability of arbitration agreements in employment contracts would call into doubt the efficacy of alternative dispute resolution procedures adopted by many of the Nation's employers, in the process undermining the FAA's proarbitration purposes and breeding litigation from a statute that seeks to avoid it. The Court has been quite specific in holding that arbitration agreements can be enforced under the FAA without contravening the policies of congressional enactments giving employees specif-

ic protection against discrimination prohibited by federal law; as we noted in *Gilmer*, 500 U.S. at 26, by agreeing to arbitrate a statutory claim, a party does not forgo the substantive rights afforded by the statute; it only submits to their resolution in an arbitral, rather than a judicial, forum.

Circuit City Stores v. Adams, 532 U.S. 105, 122–23, 149 L. Ed. 2d 234, 121 S. Ct. 1302 (2001) (citations and internal quotations omitted). Indeed, Title VII claims may be subjected to binding arbitration. See *Willis v. Dean Witter Reynolds, Inc.*, 948 F.2d 305, 310 (6th Cir. 1991); ... The question before the court, then, is whether there are "grounds ... at law or in equity" for the revocation or non-enforcement of the agreement. See 9 U.S.C. § 2.

C. Under Tennessee Law, the Arbitration Agreement was not a Contract of Adhesion

1. Tennessee Law on Contracts of Adhesion

... The district court held that the arbitration agreement is a contract of adhesion under Tennessee law. Tennessee defines a contract of adhesion as "a standardized contract form offered to consumers of goods and services on essentially a 'take it or leave it' basis, without affording the consumer a realistic opportunity to bargain and under such conditions that the consumer cannot obtain the desired product or service except by acquiescing to the form of the contract." *Buraczynski v. Eyring*, 919 S.W.2d 314, 320 (Tenn. 1996) (citations omitted). The essence of adhesion is that the parties' bargaining positions and leverage enable one party to "select and control risks assumed under the contract." See id.; see also BLACK'S LAW DICTIONARY 318 (7th ed. 1999). In *Buraczynski*, the state Supreme Court held that an arbitration agreement between a doctor and a patient was a contract of adhesion where it was presented to the patient well after her course of treatment had begun. Emphasizing the special doctor-patient relationship, the court noted that if the patient declined to sign, she would have suffered an interruption in care and lost the opportunity to continue treatment with the physician whom she had come to know and trust. See Buraczynski, 919 S.W.2d at 320.

A contract is not adhesive merely because it is a standardized form offered on a take-it-or-leave-it basis. Even after *Buraczynski*, Tennessee courts decline to find arbitration provisions adhesive where the consumer fails to prove that refusal to sign would cause some detriment other than not being able to buy from the particular merchant (such as not being able to obtain the goods or services elsewhere). *Pyburn v. Bill Heard Chevrolet*, 63 S.W.3d 351 (Tenn. Ct. App. 2001), held that an arbitration agreement between a car dealer and a buyer was not adhesive, as there was no proof that the buyer's refusal to agree would cause some detriment other than being unable to come to terms with the particular dealer. Id. at 359. The court reasoned, "if Defendant had refused to sell Plaintiff the van, Plaintiff could have gone to another

Chevrolet dealership (or any other type of dealership for that matter) and obtained a van elsewhere if he considered the Agreement unacceptable." Id. at 360....

2. *Analysis of Adhesion*

a. Agreement was "Take–It–Or–Leave–It" Standardized Form Prepared by MRM

The district court found that MRM prepared the agreement, a standardized form, with no negotiation or input from Cooper. See *Cooper v. MRM Inv. Co.*, 199 F. Supp. 2d 771, 778–79 (M.D. Tenn. 2002); ... The judge also did not err in finding that Cooper had to sign the agreement to get the job. Cooper's affidavit does not expressly allege that she was told she would not get the job if she did not sign the arbitration agreement; she says only that she "was presented with several documents and was told that [she] needed to sign the documents." But the packet of "several documents" which Cooper had to sign, clearly included the arbitration agreement. Attached to the brief MRM itself filed below, was a single-page photocopy containing the four short[17] documents MRM asked Cooper to sign, including the arbitration agreement and the sexual-harassment policy.

In addition, the district court recalled MRM's counsel conceding that MRM had presented the agreement as a "take-it-or-leave-it." See *Cooper*, 199 F. Supp. 2d at 778....

b. Cooper Failed to Show She Had No Alternatives to the KFC Job

The last element of adhesion is the absence of a meaningful choice for the party occupying the weaker bargaining position. The district court opined that "especially in today's economy, the choice to 'leave it' often amounts to no choice at all. Indeed, if she 'leaves it', she probably forgoes the opportunity for employment." *Cooper*, 199 F. Supp. 2d at 778 (citation omitted). The judge relied in part on an article which chronicled an increasing trend toward arbitration clauses in employment contracts: "Prospective employees often have no choice at all—that is, even if they decide to walk away from one mandatory arbitration contract, they will often have no choice but to accept another employment contract that mandates arbitration as well." Id. at 778 n.4 (citation omitted).

There was nothing wrong with referring to authorities for the proposition that, as a general matter, employers often condition employ-

17. The case for enforcing the agreement is strengthened by the fact that it is brief and embodied in a separate document. This court has already affirmed a district court's rejection of the argument that a merchant fraudulently induced consumers to sign an arbitration agreement, as "the contract language was clear and unambiguous. The defendants presented the arbitration agreements to the plaintiffs on a separate form. The contract terms were not hidden in boilerplate language or otherwise disguised." *Stout v. Byrider*, 50 F. Supp. 2d 733, 740 (N.D. Ohio 1999), aff'd, 228 F.3d 709 (6th Cir. 2000), cert. denied, 531 U.S. 1148, 148 L. Ed. 2d 963, 121 S. Ct. 1088 (2001). Compare *Howell v. NHC Healthcare–Fort Sanders*, 109 S.W.3d 731, 734 (Tenn. Ct. App. 2003) (arbitration clause in nursing home admission agreement was unenforceable where, *inter alia*, the clause was "buried" inconspicuously on page ten of eleven-page agreement), appeal denied (Tenn. June 30, 2003).

ment on a commitment to arbitration. Evidence that employers around the country require such agreements as a matter of course may provide context for an employee's claim that relevant employers in his locality also do so. To find this contract adhesive, however, there must be evidence that Cooper would be unable to find suitable employment if she refused to sign MRM's agreement. She presented no such evidence. For instance, she did not allege that she looked for comparable jobs but was unable to find one. Generalizations about employer practices in the modern economy cannot substitute for such evidence. See *Andersons, Inc. v. Horton Farms*, 166 F.3d 308, 324 (6th Cir. 1998) (no procedural unconscionability where grain seller "failed to present evidence that it searched for other alternatives and that there were none").

Recent Tennessee decisions on the enforceability of exculpatory clauses illustrate the need for such party-specific evidence in an unconscionability analysis....

Likewise, it was Cooper's burden to establish state law grounds for non-enforcement of her agreement with MRM; she failed to do so, leaving the record silent on whether other local employers might have hired her without a similar agreement....

D. Under Tennessee Law, the Arbitration Agreement Was Not Unconscionable

Even if the MRM arbitration agreement were adhesive, the agreement was enforceable under Tennessee law unless Cooper showed it was also unconscionable. "The common law ... subjects terms in contracts of adhesion to scrutiny for reasonableness." *Carnival Cruise Lines v. Shute*, 499 U.S. 585, 600, 113 L. Ed. 2d 622, 111 S. Ct. 1522 (1991) (Stevens, J., dissenting o.g.). Tennessee recognizes two types of unconscionability:

> Unconscionability may arise from a lack of a meaningful choice on the part of one party (procedural unconscionability) or from contract terms that are unreasonably harsh (substantive unconscionability). In Tennessee we have tended to lump the two together and speak of unconscionability resulting when the inequality of the bargain is so manifest as to shock the judgment of a person of common sense, and where the terms are so oppressive that no reasonable person would make them on one hand, and no honest and fair person would accept them on the other.

Trinity Indus., Inc. v. McKinnon Bridge Co., 77 S.W.3d 159, 170–71 (Tenn. Ct. App. 2001) (citations omitted). A contract is substantively unconscionable, then, when its terms "are beyond the reasonable expectations of an ordinary person, or oppressive...." *Buraczynski*, 919 S.W.2d at 320.

1. No Basis for Finding the Agreement Procedurally Unconscionable

The district court was troubled that MRM required an applicant to sign an arbitration agreement "precisely at the time that he or she is most willing to sign anything just to get a job." *Cooper*, 199 F. Supp. 2d at 780 and n.8. The judge found that people seeking jobs at a fast food restaurant have, on average, a weaker bargaining position than people seeking white-collar jobs at, for instance, a brokerage firm: "While this difference is not determinative, it certainly informs the Court's thinking." Id. at 778 n.3. The judge contrasted brokerages because several precedents holding that employment disputes may be subject to binding arbitration involved brokers....

The finding that an employee had less bargaining power is relevant to the procedural-unconscionability analysis. Moreover, as the district court judge implied, the disparity in bargaining power also informs the substantive-unconscionability analysis, because a job applicant who lacks "leverage" may be more likely to agree to unfair terms. In a close case, terms bordering on substantive unconscionability may look more unfair in light of circumstances suggesting that the stronger party pressed his advantage against the weaker party. In determining procedural unconscionability, however, the judge did not require the parties to present evidence on "factors bearing on the relative bargaining position of the contracting parties, including their age, education, intelligence, business acumen and experience, relative bargaining power, ... [and] whether the terms were explained to the weaker party...." See *Morrison v. Circuit City Stores*, Inc., 317 F.3d 646, 666 (6th Cir. 2003) (*en banc*) (citations omitted). As the record discloses, the judge made no findings on those factors. Absent such findings, there was no basis for a negative answer to "the crucial question ... [of] whether each party to the contract, considering his obvious education or lack of it, [had] a reasonable opportunity to understand the terms of the contract...." Morrison, 317 F.3d at 666 (citation and internal quotation omitted).

2. *No Basis for Finding the Agreement Substantively Unconscionable*

In turn, the district court's erroneous finding of procedural unconscionability contributed to its conclusion that the arbitration agreement's terms were unfair and the product of overreaching. Aside from the lack of support for the finding that Cooper had far inferior bargaining power, unequal bargaining power alone does not render a contract substantively unconscionable. The Supreme Court has cautioned, "mere inequality in bargaining power ... is not a sufficient reason to hold that arbitration agreements are never enforceable in the employment context." *Gilmer*, 500 U.S. at 33. As one court noted, "when a party ... voluntarily agrees to something in an attempt to obtain employment, they are not being 'forced' to do anything. ..." *EEOC v. Frank's Nursery & Crafts*, 966 F. Supp. 500, 504 (E.D. Mich. 1997), rev'd o.g., 177 F.3d 448 (6th Cir. 1999); ...

While the district court's compassion for job applicants is laudable, under its approach "practically every condition of employment would be an 'adhesion contract' which could not be enforced because it would have been presented to the employee by the employer in a situation of unequal bargaining power on a 'take it or leave it' basis." *Morrison v. Circuit City Stores, Inc.*, 70 F. Supp. 2d 815, 823 (quoting *Beauchamp*, 918 F. Supp. at 1098). Such a result would contravene Congress's intent that employment disputes be subject to valid arbitration agreements, unless excepted by FAA § 1 or rendered unenforceable under state contract law. For these reasons, the record does not support the conclusion that the arbitration agreement was procedurally and substantively unconscionable.

E. The District Court Erred in Finding the Agreement Lacked Sufficient Bilaterality

The district court also held that "there is an insufficient 'modicum of bilaterality' present in this case." *Cooper*, 199 F. Supp. 2d at 780. It reasoned that "the agreement was ... drafted by KFC, and imposed on a prospective employee precisely at the time that he or she is most willing to sign anything just to get a job. Although the KFC Arbitration Agreement binds both parties, only the Defendant is aware of the ramifications of the agreement." Id. (citation omitted). The court erred. The district court acknowledged that the MRM agreement "does contain a measure of what ... courts have termed a 'modicum of bilaterality,'" and, unlike the agreement held unconscionable in *Circuit City Stores, Inc. v. Adams*, 279 F.3d 889 (9th Cir.), cert. denied, 535 U.S. 1112, 153 L. Ed. 2d 160, 122 S. Ct. 2329 (2002), it requires both parties to arbitrate, not just the employee. See *Cooper*, 199 F. Supp. 2d at 780. Despite this, the judge found that the agreement lacked sufficient bilaterality because "there is an asymmetry born out of a difference in bargaining power that pervades the resulting arbitration agreement." Id. In so doing, the judge improperly conflated the procedural unconscionability and bilaterality analyses.

Even if Cooper had far less bargaining power, that would not detract from bilaterality, because MRM has the same duty to arbitrate as Cooper. See *Wilks v. Pep Boys*, 241 F. Supp. 2d 860, 863 (M.D. Tenn. 2003) ("the plaintiffs' claims that the Agreement is invalid for lack of consideration and because it constitutes an 'illusory promise' are without merit. Both parties are bound to arbitrate claims arising in their relationship. ...").

Moreover, the record does not support the supposition that only MRM knew the agreement's ramifications. Its defining ramification is that the parties will submit disputes to an arbitrator instead of a judge or jury. "The loss of the right to a jury trial is a necessary and fairly obvious consequence of an agreement to arbitrate." *Burden v. Check Into Cash of Kentucky*, LLC, 267 F.3d 483, 492 (6th Cir. 2001) (citation omitted). Absent evidence that MRM rushed Cooper or deceived her as to the agreement's consequences, *Burden* charges her with knowledge of that central consequence. Compare *Brennan v. Bally Total Fitness,* 198 F. Supp. 2d 377, 383 (S.D.N.Y. 2002) (arbitration agreement was unenforceable where employer gave employee only fifteen minutes to review sixteen-page document and used other high-pressure tactics).

F. *Lack of Express Waiver of Right to Jury Trial Did Not Render Agreement Invalid*

1. *Burden (6th Cir. 2001)*

The district court contrasted the MRM agreement, which said nothing about waiving the right to a jury trial, with the agreement enforced in *Buraczynski*. The latter alerted the weaker party, in ten-point capitals printed in red ink directly above the signature line, "BY SIGNING THIS CONTRACT YOU ARE GIVING UP YOUR RIGHT TO A JURY OR COURT TRIAL...." The district court held that the absence of such language in the MRM agreement rendered it unenforceable because "the waiver of any rights (substantive or procedural), must be both knowing and clear. * * * If the employee is not clearly made aware of the rights she is waiving, that waiver is not only invalid, but the entire agreement is rendered unduly oppressive." *Cooper*, 199 F. Supp. 2d at 775, 779.

This Court, however, has flatly rejected the claim that an arbitration agreement must contain a provision expressly waiving the employee's right to a jury trial. Without discussion, we stated, "As to the failure of the arbitration clause to include a jury waiver provision, 'the loss of the right to a jury trial is a necessary and fairly obvious consequence of an agreement to arbitrate.'" *Burden*, 267 F.3d at 492 (quoting *Sydnor v. Conseco Fin. Servs. Corp.*, 252 F.3d 302, 307 (4th Cir. 2001)); ... The Seventh Amendment confers not the right to a jury trial per se, but rather "only the right to have a jury hear the case once it is determined that the litigation should proceed before a court. If the claims are properly before an arbitral forum pursuant to an arbitration agreement, the jury trial right vanishes." *Bank One, N.A. v. Coates*, 125 F. Supp. 2d 819, 834 (S.D. Miss. 2001), aff'd, 34 Fed. Appx. 964 (5th Cir. 2002); accord *Marsh v. First USA Bank*, 103 F. Supp. 2d 909, 921 (N.D. Tex. 2000) (citing Geldermann, Inc. v. CFTC, 836 F.2d 310, 323 (7th Cir. 1987)).[18]

2. *KMC (6th Cir. 1985) is Distinguishable from Burden (6th Cir. 2001), Which Governs*

As discussed supra, Burden mandates reversal of the holding that the agreement is invalid because it did not contain an express waiver of Cooper's right to a jury trial. For that proposition, the district court relied on a pre-*Burden* panel decision: *K.M.C. Co. v. Irving Trust Co.*, 757 F.2d 752 (6th Cir. 1985). In *KMC*, the parties' contract contained a clause waiving the right to a jury trial. Nonetheless, when KMC sued for breach, the judge ordered a jury trial. He found that before the parties signed the contract, a representative of defendant told the plaintiff's president that "absent fraud, which was not present ..., the waiver provision would not be enforced." The defendant appealed, contending that the judge should have enforced the waiver of the right to a jury

18. Of the Circuits to squarely address the issue, all four share the view we expressed in Burden....

trial. We held that the waiver was unenforceable because it was not knowing and voluntary. See id. at 754–55.

[Eds.: The Court then distinguishes *KMC* on several grounds, essentially restricting it to its facts. On the issue of waiving the Seventh Amendment right to a jury trial, it observes:]

... As to the "clear" or "knowing and voluntary" character of the waiver of a judicial forum, the MRM agreement is short, clear and embodied in a separate document, not buried in a lengthy handbook which addresses issues not affecting Cooper's rights. Moreover, ... the MRM agreement specifically advised Cooper that she would be required to arbitrate sexual-harassment claims. Lastly, the MRM agreement does not restrict the arbitrator's authority to award punitive damages or any other remedy Cooper might obtain in court.

G. District Court's Statement that Title VII Claims Belong in Federal Court

The district court acknowledged that employers face many non-meritorious claims and that arbitration can offer greater efficiency and convenience than litigation. Without citing authority, however, the district court expressed hostility to the arbitration of employment discrimination claims:

> These cases do not 'clog' the federal docket—they belong in federal court. Employees must not be forced to either forgo employment or forgo their right to a day in court, and Courts must not use the perceived problems associated with employment discrimination [cases] to prevent employees, and society at large, from vindicating the rights that Congress enshrined in the Civil Rights Acts.

Cooper, 199 F. Supp. 2d at 779 n.7. Yet the Supreme Court holds that "having made the bargain to arbitrate, the party should be held to it unless Congress itself has evinced an intention to preclude a waiver of judicial remedies for the statutory rights at issue." *Gilmer*, 500 U.S. at 26 (citation omitted). The district court did not adduce evidence of a Congressional intent to prohibit employees from waiving a judicial forum for discrimination or harassment claims, and we find none.

On the contrary, the 1991 Amendments to Title VII "evince[] a clear congressional intent to make arbitration an alternative method of dispute resolution." ... Nonetheless, the district court indulged its belief that employers should not be allowed to require arbitration of statutory discrimination claims. That belief is incompatible with the strong congressional policy favoring arbitration. As this Court has held, "the fact that some of plaintiff's claims are based upon Title VII, a federal civil-rights statute, does not affect the enforceability of the arbitration agreement. It is well-settled that statutory claims may be the subject of an arbitration agreement enforceable under the FAA." ...

H. Was the Agreement Invalid Because Arbitration Would Be Prohibitively Expensive?

Unlike the findings that the agreement was adhesive, unconscionable, and insufficiently bilateral, the district court's other basis for finding the agreement unenforceable was potentially valid: under the AAA rules incorporated in the agreement, arbitration could be prohibitively expensive, deterring employees like Cooper from attempting to vindicate their rights. As a matter of public policy, the court rightly rejected MRM's argument that the agreement was enforceable because it is willing to pay Cooper's arbitration costs. An employee should not have to "jump through hoops" to show arbitration is too costly, only to have the employer jettison the unduly burdensome cost-splitting provision when it is challenged.

The AAA has since amended its rules, however, to hold employers responsible in the first instance for all expenses except a small filing fee and costs for the employee's witnesses. This may make it more difficult for Cooper to show her likely arbitration costs are prohibitively high, as she must to invalidate the agreement under *Green Tree Finance Corp. of Alabama v. Randolph*, 531 U.S. 79, 148 L. Ed. 2d 373, 121 S. Ct. 513 (2000) and *Morrison v. Circuit City*, 317 F.3d 646 (6th Cir. 2003) (*en banc*).

1. When Arbitration Costs Render an Arbitration Agreement Unenforceable

In *Green Tree Finance Corp. of Alabama v. Randolph*, 531 U.S. 79, 148 L. Ed. 2d 373, 121 S. Ct. 513 (2000), the Supreme Court adopted a case-by-case approach to determining whether an arbitration agreement's cost-splitting provision denies potential litigants the opportunity to vindicate their rights. "Where ... a party seeks to invalidate an arbitration agreement on the ground that arbitration would be prohibitively expensive, that party bears the burden of showing the likelihood of incurring such costs." Id. at 92. The agreement before the Court said nothing about arbitration costs, and the employee produced little evidence on the costs she was likely to incur and whether she could afford them. Accordingly, the Court found the plaintiff had not met her burden of proving she would actually bear prohibitive costs if required to arbitrate. The Court held,

> It may well be that the existence of large arbitration costs could preclude a litigant such as Randolph from effectively vindicating her federal statutory rights in the arbitral forum. But the record does not show that Randolph will bear such costs if she goes to arbitration. Indeed, [the record] contains hardly any information on the matter. * * * The record reveals only the arbitration agreement's silence on the subject, and that fact alone is plainly insufficient to render it unenforceable. The "risk" that Randolph will be saddled with prohibitive costs is too speculative to justify the invalidation of an arbitration agreement....

> To invalidate the agreement on that basis would undermine the "liberal federal policy favoring arbitration agreements." It would also conflict with our prior holdings that the party resisting arbitration bears the burden of proving that the claims at issue are unsuitable for arbitration.

Id. at 91–92 (citations omitted). Because the employee made no showing about his likely arbitration costs, the Court declined to specify "how detailed the showing of prohibitive expense must be before the party seeking arbitration must come forward with contrary evidence...." Id. at 92. Further guidance is available from our subsequent *en banc* decision in *Morrison v. Circuit City*, where we declared,

> We hold that potential litigants must be given an opportunity, prior to arbitration on the merits, to demonstrate that the potential costs of arbitration are enough to deter them and similarly situated individuals from seeking to vindicate their federal statutory rights in the arbitral forum. Our approach differs from the case-by-case approach advocated in *Bradford* [*v. Rockwell Semiconductor Systems*, 238 F.3d 549, 556 (4th Cir. 2001)] by looking to the possible "chilling effect" of the cost-splitting provision on similarly situated [potential] litigants, as opposed to its effect merely on the actual plaintiff in the given case. * * *
>
> A particular plaintiff may be determined to pursue his or her claims, regardless of costs. But a court considering whether a cost-splitting provision is enforceable should consider similarly situated potential litigants, for whom costs will loom as a larger concern, because it is, in large part, their presence in the system that will deter discriminatory practices. Nothing in *Green Tree* suggests that a case-by-case analysis should not treat similar cases similarly.
>
> For this reason, if the reviewing court finds that the cost-splitting provision would deter a substantial number of similarly situated potential litigants, it should refuse to enforce the cost-splitting provision in order to serve the underlying functions of the federal statute. I n conducting this analysis, the reviewing court should define the class of such similarly situated potential litigants by job description and socioeconomic background. It should take the actual plaintiff's income and resources as representative of this larger class's ability to shoulder the costs of arbitration.

Morrison, 317 F.3d at 663 (emphasis added); ...

The court must evaluate the likely cost of arbitration not in absolute terms, but relative to the likely costs of litigation. The up-front expense of litigation is often minimal, because many employee-plaintiffs can secure a contingency fee agreement where counsel advances discovery costs and defers collection of fees until judgment. See *Morrison*, 317 F.3d at 664. Conversely, a plaintiff "forced to arbitrate a typical $60,000 employment discrimination claim will incur costs ... that range from three to nearly fifty times the basic costs of litigating in a judicial, rather than arbitral, forum." Id. at 669 (citation omitted). Furthermore, because Title VII allows compensatory damage awards up to $300,000, the costs of arbitrating such a claim will range "higher and higher." Id.

Finally, the analysis of likely arbitration costs must consider only "up-front" costs, not the lower cost that may ultimately result if the arbitrator relieves the employee of costs presumptively imposed by AAA rules (e.g., if the employee prevails on the merits). See id. at 664. After all, it is the out-of-pocket costs an employee considers when deciding whether he can afford arbitration: "The issue is whether the terms of the arbitration agreement itself would deter a substantial number of similarly situated employees from bringing their claims in the arbitral forum, and thus the court must consider the decision-making process of these potential litigants. In many cases, if not most, employees considering the consequences of bringing their claims in the arbitral forum will be inclined to err on the side of caution, especially when the worst-case scenario would mean not only losing on their substantive claims but also the imposition of the costs of the arbitration." Id. at 664–65 (emphasis added) (citations omitted).

2. The Employee's Likely Up–Front Costs under the Former AAA Rules

The district court found that Cooper earned $7,253.74 in 2001 and that she "and others similarly situated, often cannot afford to pay the high costs of arbitration." See *Cooper*, 199 F. Supp. 2d at 781. There is no suggestion that Cooper has undisclosed assets or sources of income, or that her income has increased to a meaningful extent. Accordingly, the court did not err in determining that Cooper was likely to incur significant up-front costs under the then prevailing AAA rules which she would not incur in court. This comports with our comment that "many, if not most" employment plaintiffs who litigate their claims will be represented under contingency agreements, paying neither fees nor costs until and unless they secure judgment. See *Morrison*, 317 F.3d at 664.

Nor did the district court err in finding such costs would deter many employees in Cooper's circumstances from arbitrating their claims. We predicted, after all, that courts would regularly find arbitration costs too high to permit enforcement of a lower-or middle-income employee's duty to arbitrate. The courts "will find, in many cases, that high-level managerial employees and others with substantial means can afford the costs of arbitration, thus making cost-splitting provisions in such cases enforceable. In the case of other employees, however, this standard will render cost-splitting provisions unenforceable in many, if not most, cases." Id. at 665 (emphasis added and citations omitted).

3. District Court Properly Rejected MRM's Offer to Pay Cooper's Arbitration Costs

The Cooper–MRM agreement contained no provision stating that an invalid or unenforceable clause could be severed. The district court held that, in the absence of a severability provision, it could not enforce the clause requiring arbitration while simultaneously invalidating the cost-splitting provision (and allowing MRM to relieve Cooper of her contractual obligation to pay some arbitration costs would effectively treat the arbitration cost-splitting provision was invalid). The court's ruling on this issue was sound under both Tennessee law and federal common law.

Under Tennessee law, the court could not make a new contract for the parties by adding a term, such as a severability clause.... The Court could not invent a severability clause in order to "red-line" the cost-splitting provision while enforcing the clause requiring Cooper to arbitrate in the first place.

The district court's decision on this issue was also sound as a matter of federal public policy. As the Eleventh Circuit reasoned, "To sever the costs and fees provision and force the employee to arbitrate a Title VII claim despite the employer's attempt to limit the remedies available would reward the employer for its actions and fail to deter similar conduct by others." *Perez v. Globe Airport Sec. Servs.*, 253 F.3d 1280, 1287 (11th Cir. 2001), vac'd by 294 F.3d 1275 (11th Cir. 2002). But see *Gannon v. Circuit City Stores*, 262 F.3d 677, 683 n.8 (8th Cir. 2001) (questioning *Perez*). Under the contrary approach, an employer "will not be deterred from routinely inserting such a deliberately illegal clause into the arbitration agreement it mandates for its employees if it knows that the worst penalty for such illegality is the severance of the clause after the employee has litigated the matter." Brief of Amicus Curiae EEOC at 14–15 (citation omitted). Our *en banc* decision in *Morrison* made clear that the district court's decision to reject MRM's offer to pay was the proper course. See *Morrison*, 317 F.3d at 676–77; ...

Moreover, MRM's offer was an impermissible attempt to vary the terms of a contract. There was neither a meeting of the minds nor consideration to support such a post hoc unilateral amendment of the agreement. See *Popovich v. McDonald's Corp.*, 189 F. Supp. 2d 772, 779 (N.D. Ill. 2002) (accepting defendant's offer to pay all arbitration costs, contrary to contract, would effectively allow it to unilaterally modify contract).

III. Conclusion

For the foregoing reasons, we reverse on all issues except one: whether the likely costs of arbitration are so high that they will deter Cooper or similarly situated employees from exercising their right to arbitrate. On that issue we vacate and remand for the court to analyze the likely arbitration costs under the AAA's rules prevailing on the date that MRM filed its motion in district court to compel Cooper to arbitrate.[19]

19. Under our decision in *Morrison v. Circuit City Stores, Inc.*, 317 F.3d 646 (6th Cir. 2003) (*en banc*), the relevant costs are Cooper's out-of-pocket costs, without reference to the possibility that she may later recoup some of them. Hence the district court shall consider neither the arbitrator's possible award of fees and expenses to Cooper pursuant to the AAA Rules, nor MRM's offer to pay Cooper's arbitration costs.

Notes and Discussion

1. The Arbitration Revolution. In 1925, Congress enacted the Federal Arbitration Act (FAA), which allowed for contract-based compulsory arbitration of disputes. The first two sections of this act read, in part, as follows:

> *Section 1.* "[C]ommerce", as herein defined, means commerce among the several States or with foreign nations, or in any Territory of the United States or in the District of Columbia, or between any such Territory and another, or between any such Territory and any State or foreign nation, or between the District of Columbia and any State or Territory or foreign nation, but nothing herein contained shall apply to contracts of employment of seamen, railroad employees, or any other class of workers engaged in foreign or interstate commerce.
>
> *Section 2.* A written provision in any maritime transaction or a contract evidencing a transaction involving commerce to settle by arbitration a controversy thereafter arising out of such contract or transaction, or the refusal to perform the whole or any part thereof, or an agreement in writing to submit to arbitration an existing controversy arising out of such a contract, transaction, or refusal, shall be valid, irrevocable, and enforceable, save upon such grounds as exist at law or in equity for the revocation of any contract.

The FAA was probably intended fairly narrowly, to encourage arbitration in federal cases involving roughly co-equal commercial enterprises. However, in a series of decisions starting with *Prima Paint Corp. v. Flood & Conklin Mfg. Co.*, 388 U.S. 395, 87 S.Ct. 1801, 18 L.Ed.2d 1270 (1967), the Supreme Court, interested in promoting arbitration as an alternative to litigation, began systematically expanding the FAA's reach to many types of common contracts, including employment, commercial, and consumer contracts. They also held that the FAA widely preempts state law on arbitration agreements, although the exception in the last clause of Section 2 ("save upon such grounds as exist at law or in equity for the revocation of any contract") still allows state courts a degree of latitude. (But States cannot, for instance, require that contracts draw special attention to arbitration clauses: *Doctor's Associates v. Casarotto,* 517 U.S. 681, 116 S.Ct. 1652, 134 L.Ed.2d 902 (1996).) On this expansion, see Paul D. Carrington & Paul H. Haagen, *Contract and Jurisdiction*, 1996 Sup. Ct. Rev. 331 (1996). Since the mid–1990s, arbitration clauses have become extremely common in contracts; you've probably agreed to some yourselves. Look closely next time you buy a computer on-line, rent an apartment, apply for a job, get a credit card, and so on. They've spread like crabgrass.

The implications of the arbitration revolution are much disputed, but it is plain that consumers and employees are widely suspicious of them. Whether for just reason, remains in doubt; what is your gut feeling on this? See generally Thomas E. Carbonneau, The Law and Practice of Arbitration (2d ed. 2007); Edward Brunet, Richard E. Speidel, Jean E. Sternlight, and Stephen H. Ware, Arbitration Law in America: A Critical Assessment (2006).

2. *Armendariz* and *Circuit City*. In 1996, Marybeth Armendariz and Dolores Olague–Rodgers lost their jobs at Foundation Health Psychcare Services, a California firm. They then brought suit alleging that they, as heterosexuals, had been discriminated against by their gay supervisors (which was actionable under California nondiscrimination law). In applying for their jobs and again later, the two women had signed an arbitration clause requiring the arbitration of any future claim they might have of wrongful termination. Foundation accordingly filed a motion to compel arbitration.

The case presented several important issues. One was whether an employer could require employees to sign an arbitration agreement as a condition of employment. This question had long been controversial. In *Armendariz v. Foundation Health Psychcare Services, Inc.,* 24 Cal.4th 83, 6 P.3d 669, 99 Cal.Rptr.2d 745 (2000), the California Supreme Court decided that mandatory arbitration agreements in employment contracts were in principle acceptable under California law. The following year the U.S. Supreme Court, by a 5–4 majority, concluded they were legal also for most employment contracts under the FAA, since employment contracts are "commerce" as defined in Section 1 of that act. *Circuit City Stores v. Adams,* 532 U.S. 105, 121 S.Ct. 1302, 149 L.Ed.2d 234 (2001).

But for the California Supreme Court, this was not the end of the matter. Although a mandatory arbitration agreement might be acceptable in general, was the Foundation agreement in particular acceptable? The Justices held no, on two bases. First, a clause in the agreement limited recovery of damages to an amount below what was available in a trial; this was void on the basis of its illegality (a public policy argument). Second, the arbitration agreement in its entirety was also unconscionable because of lack of mutuality. "Given the disadvantages that may exist for plaintiffs arbitrating disputes, it is unfairly one-sided for an employer with superior bargaining power to impose arbitration on the employee as plaintiff but not to accept such limitations when it seeks to prosecute a claim against the employee, without at least some reasonable justification for such one-sidedness based on 'business realities.' " *Armendariz,* 24 Cal.4th at 117. In this case, no such justification was found, and, since the absence of mutuality could not be overcome by "severing" the offending clause, the agreement as a whole failed. When the *Circuit City* case was heard on remand. the Ninth Circuit came to the same conclusion regarding the arbitration clause in that case: acceptable in principle, but unconscionable either as a whole or in part because of its details. *Circuit City Stores, Inc., v. Adams,* 279 F.3d 889 (9th Cir. 2002).

Armendariz and *Circuit City,* taken together, serve to signal a new era for the doctrine of unconscionability, as you will (we trust) see below. *Cooper v. MRM* is a fairly good example of this era.

3. The Arbitration Agreement as a Whole: Procedurally Unconscionable? For our purposes, Judge Aldrich's opinion has two main parts. First of all, she argues in II.C. that the MRM arbitration agreement was not demonstrably a contract of adhesion; and in II.D., that even if it were, it was neither procedurally nor substantively unconscionable as an entirety. Follow her reasoning, particularly as she attempts to refute the trial judge's views. How does she understand the concept of procedural unconscionability?

You may find it helpful to compare her views with those in *Armendariz.* In that case, the California Supreme Court had no difficulty finding that the employment contract was adhesive, since: "It was imposed on employees as a condition of employment and there was no opportunity to negotiate.... [In] the case of preemployment arbitration contracts, the economic pressure exerted by employers on all but the most sought-after employees may be particularly acute, for the arbitration agreement stands between the employee and necessary employment, and few employees are in a position to refuse a job because of an arbitration requirement." 24 Cal.4th at 115. What's interesting about this analysis is that it is apparently considered sufficient to establish at least a strong presumption of procedural unconscionability as well; and many California decisions have explicitly taken this position. See, e.g., *Flores v. Transamerica Homefirst, Inc.*, 113 Cal.Rptr.2d 376, 382 (Ct. App. 2001) ("the undisputed facts indicate that the arbitration agreement was imposed upon plaintiffs on a 'take it or leave it' basis. The arbitration agreement was a contract of adhesion and thereby procedurally unconscionable"); *Gatton v. T-Mobile USA, Inc.*, 152 Cal.App.4th 571, 61 Cal.Rptr.3d 344, 355–356 (Ct. App. 2007) ("absent unusual circumstances, use of a contract of adhesion establishes a minimal degree of procedural unconscionability *notwithstanding the availability of market alternatives*"; footnote omitted, emphasis added). Cf. *Morris v. Redwood Empire Bancorp*, 128 Cal. App.4th 1305, 27 Cal.Rptr.3d 797, 807–808 (Ct. App. 2005) (with a good discussion of the ambiguous California law concerning this point).

Which of these two views seems to you preferable, at least in the ordinary employment or consumer context? Once "a minimal degree of procedural unconscionability" has been established, California courts use a "sliding scale" approach, which the *Armendariz* decision describes this way: "the more substantively oppressive the contract term, the less evidence of procedural unconscionability is required to come to the conclusion that the term is unenforceable, and vice versa." 24 Cal.4th at 114. Nonetheless, in practice procedural unconscionability usually just drops out of the picture altogether, and what remains is a court confronting its sense of whether the substantive terms of the contract are fair.

4. Prohibitively Expensive? Unconscionability in Part. In II.E–H of her opinion, Judge Aldrich examines a number of features of the MRM arbitration agreement. The only feature that disturbs her is that, in this case, arbitration could be prohibitively expensive for plaintiffs in Tonya Cooper's situation. On this point, the case is remanded for findings of fact, but with the caution that if, in actuality, arbitration would be too expensive for Cooper, the entire arbitration agreement would be invalid.

Granted her previous holding that the formation of this contract was not procedurally unconscionable, on what basis does Judge Aldrich then proceed to vet the contract for suspect elements? In addition to the provisions examined in this opinion (lack of bilaterality; lack of waiver of jury trial or of right to bring Title VII claims in federal court; the cost of arbitration), state and federal courts have found arbitration agreements entirely or partly unconscionable because they unduly restrict the statute of limitations, provide inadequate opportunities for discovery, select inconvenient forums for arbitration, limit damages, impose excessive confidentiality, and (most controversially) forbid classwide arbitration—the issue in the case that follows.

At what point does it seem reasonable to suggest that what many courts are now doing, in the wake of decisions like *Armendariz*, is really not traditional unconscionability analysis at all, but rather judicial regulation of the substance of contracts? If this diagnosis is correct, what new problems does such regulation introduce?

In any case, it is quite clear that, as a response to decisions such as these, drafters of arbitration clauses and other similar agreements have had to stay closely up-to-date with what is, or is not, acceptable by way of language. Here, for instance, is what Foley & Lardner, a California law firm, posted in 2003: "While crafting an arbitration agreement, employers should keep in mind that a court will review it. For arbitration agreements to be enforceable, they can't be one-sided. If employers use a 'take-it-or-leave-it' approach, courts won't hesitate to conclude that the employee executed the agreement involuntarily. In addition, if employers don't use plain language or properly explain the agreement, courts may find that workers didn't know the rights they relinquished—and, thus, conclude the agreement is unenforceable. When developing an alternative dispute resolution program, think about how your organization can prove that each employee voluntarily and knowingly agrees with the program." See http://www.foley.com/publications/pub_detail.aspx?pubid'1608. The firm goes on to list ten features that "maximize enforceability."

5. Severability. The MRM contract did not contain a provision allowing for the severability of any feature of the arbitration agreement found to be improper, and Judge Aldrich refuses to impose one, which means that MRM may lose arbitration altogether. The MRM drafters made a big mistake, didn't they?

Courts vary a good deal in their attitudes toward severability. For a lively and intelligent article on the subject, see Alan Scott Rau, *Everything You Really Need to Know About "Separability" in Seventeen Simple Propositions*, 14 Am. Rev. Int'l Arb. 1 (2003). How persuasive do you find Judge Aldrich's view?

6. The Progeny of *Armendariz*. Susan Randall, *Judicial Attitudes Toward Arbitration and the Resurgence of Unconscionability,* 52 Buffalo L. Rev. 185, 186–187 (2004), discusses recent trends in findings of unconscionability. In on-line judicial opinions for 1982–1983 there were 54 cases involving unconscionability, 9 of which (16.7%) were found unconscionable. Of those 54, 8 (14.8%) involved arbitration agreements, and only 1 of the 8 was found unconscionable. By contrast, in 2002–2003 there were 235 cases involving unconscionability, 100 of which (42.5%) were found unconscionable. Of these 235, 161 (68.5%) involved arbitration agreements. 50.3% of the arbitration agreements were found unconscionable, whereas 25.6% of other types of contracts were found unconscionable. Randall noted that: "Although federal and state courts in California decided a significant number of these cases, a total of 17 state courts [Alabama, California, Florida, Idaho, Kentucky, Louisiana, Massachusetts, Mississippi, Missouri, New Mexico, Nevada, Ohio, Pennsylvania, Tennessee, Texas, Washington, and West Virginia] and 15 federal courts [3rd Circuit, 4th Circuit, 9th Circuit, and district courts in Arkansas, California, Illinois, Iowa, Michigan, Minnesota, New York, Ohio, Oregon, Tennessee, Washington, and the Virgin Islands] found provisions in arbitration agreements unconscionable." She also notes a trend of courts upholding the same contract provisions in nonarbitration contracts that they find unconscionable in arbitration agreements. These include excessive costs that limit one party's access to arbitration; limitation of damages that may be awarded in arbitration; forum selection clauses; and confidentiality clauses.

Prof. Randall does not focus specifically either on *Armendariz* or on California law, but California is certainly not the only state holding certain arbitration clauses unconscionable, even though more of these cases have been found in California. Currently, states appear divided on the issue. For example, in *Lytle v. CitiFinancial Servs.* 810 A.2d 643 (Super. Ct. Pennsylvania 2002), the Court cites cases from the highest courts of Pennsylvania, West Virginia, Montana, and Ohio, all preceding *Armendariz* by several years, in which arbitration agreements were struck down as unconscionable. Interestingly, all these cases involved arbitration agreements which took place in a non-employment setting. The Court then remarks in a footnote that: "We are of course aware of a number of rulings to the contrary" and proceeds to list a number of cases from Texas, New Jersey, New York, and the 3rd Circuit.

So California has certainly not carried the day. *Armendariz* was rejected, for instance, by the Texas Supreme Court in a case involving a retail installment financing agreement that required the buyers to arbitrate all claims, but allowed the lenders to use the courts to "enforce its security interest, recover the buyers' loan obligation, and foreclose." *In re FirstMerit Bank, N.A.*, 52 S.W.3d 749, 752 (Tex. 2001). The decision observes: "The [plaintiffs] also argue that the agreement's terms are unconscionable because they force the weaker party to arbitrate their claims, while permitting the stronger party to litigate their claims. They point us to decisions in other jurisdictions that have found this type of clause to be unconscionable. Most federal courts, however, have rejected similar challenges on the grounds that an arbitration clause does not require mutuality of obligation, so long as the underlying contract is supported by adequate consideration. In any event, the basic test for unconscionability is whether, given the parties' general commercial background and the commercial needs of the particular trade or case, the clause involved is so one-sided that it is unconscionable under the circumstances existing when the parties made the contract. The principle is one of preventing oppression and unfair surprise and not of disturbing allocation of risks because of superior bargaining power. Here, the Arbitration Addendum allows the bank to seek judicial relief to enforce its security agreement, recover the buyers' monetary loan obligation, and foreclose. Given the weight of federal precedent and the routine nature of mobile home financing agreements, we find that the Arbitration Addendum in this case, by excepting claims essentially protecting the bank's security interest, is not unconscionable. We also recognize that the plaintiffs are free to pursue their unconscionability defense in the arbitral forum." Id. at 757 (citations omitted). Many jurisdictions are still of a similar opinion. Decide for yourself.

7. Preemption? Potentially serious, it seems, is the issue of FAA preemption: whether courts are applying unconscionability selectively to arbitration agreements. Susan Randall, *Judicial Attitudes toward Arbitration and the Resurgence of Unconscionability*, 52 Buffalo L. Rev. 185, 186–187

(2004), is convinced this objection has legs. She argues that: "[J]udges use an arbitration-specific version of the unconscionability doctrine to avoid the Federal Arbitration Act. First, judges currently find arbitration agreements unconscionable at twice the rate of nonarbitration agreements. ... Second, judges find unconscionable specific features of arbitration agreements, such as forum selection clauses and confidentiality requirements, which are routinely enforced as unobjectionable in nonarbitration agreements. Other features of arbitration agreements often found unconscionable in the arbitration context but not generally considered unconscionable are punitive damages limitations and cost-splitting provisions. ... Third, the statements of a few outspoken judges provide direct evidence that at least some judges dislike arbitration ... "

Prof. Randall continues: "Under the rule of *Armendariz*, parties to an arbitration contract cannot, unlike parties to other types of contracts or parties to arbitration contracts in other jurisdictions, expect judicial enforcement of their contract. California courts treat arbitration agreements differently precisely because they are arbitration agreements, in direct contradiction of the Federal Arbitration Act. Despite the California Supreme Court's protestations to the contrary, the Federal Arbitration Act in fact preempts *Armendariz* and its progeny." Id. at 209. Compare Stephen J. Burton, *The New Judicial Hostility to Arbitration: Federal Preemption, Contract Unconscionability, and Agreements to Arbitrate*, 2006 J. Disp. Resol. 469.

This logic is accepted by, e.g., Judge Easterbrook in *Oblix v. Winiecki*, 374 F.3d 488, 491–492 (7th Cir. 2004) ("no state can apply to arbitration (when governed by the Federal Arbitration Act) any novel rule" that would make the arbitration clause subject to a higher standard than other clauses of the contract). But California has stuck to its guns; see *Little v. Auto Stiegler, Inc.*, 29 Cal.4th 1064, 63 P.3d 979, 130 Cal.Rptr.2d 892 (2003) (*inter alia*, rejecting the preemption argument). Only the U.S. Supreme Court knows for certain the answer to this objection, and, so far anyway, they ain't saying.

THE NEW YORK TIMES **NATIONAL** *SUNDAY, NOVEMBER 21, 2004*

Fine Print

The detailed agreement that comes with a new credit card contains provisions that can add hefty fees, penalties and higher interest rates. A look at some of the important sections of a typical contract.

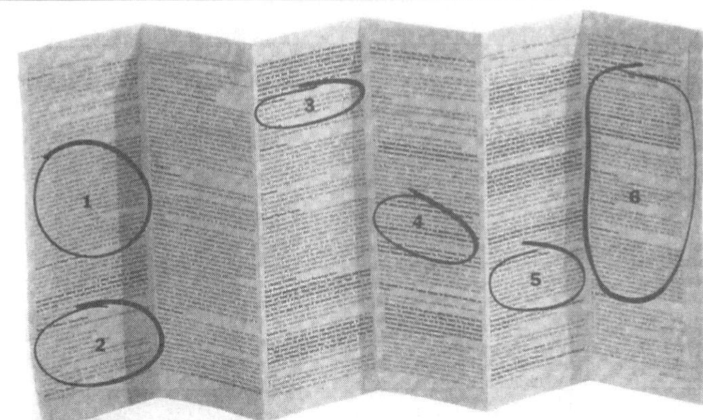

Both sides of a cardholder agreement from Chase Manhattan Bank, a unit of J. P. Morgan Chase, dated October 2004.

The New York Times/
Photograph by Tony Cenicola

1 SPENDING LIMITS AND CREDIT LINE There is no preset spending limit, but each charge will be evaluated based on the cardholder's credit history and the lender's understanding of the cardholder's current finances. The credit line may be increased, reduced or canceled at any time.

2 AUTHORIZING CHARGES Any request to use the card may be rejected for any reason, including:
- the account is in default.
- the company suspects fraud.

3 APPLYING PAYMENTS If there is more than one interest rate on the account, payments will go toward paying off the balance with the lowest rate first. Interest continues compounding on the balance with the higher rate.

4 DEFAULT RATES The highest rate *(28.49%)* may be charged if the cardholder is late making a payment to any creditor; this can include phone and utility bills, car payments and the like — even if credit card payments are made on time.

5 GRACE PERIOD If the balance is zero at the start of the billing period, the cardholder does not have to pay finance charges on purchases if the balance is paid in full again by the next due date. If not, interest accrues from the time of purchase.

6 FEES In addition to an annual fee, a fee may be charged for:
- late payment *($35)*.
- bounced or unsigned check *($35)*.
- copy of a statement *($5)*.
- payment by phone *($14.95)*.

7 RIGHT TO SUE Any dispute between the cardholder and the issuer may be resolved only by binding arbitration. The cardholder cannot take the issuer to court or be included in a class-action suit against the company.

8 TERMS OF AGREEMENT May be changed at any time for any reason. The cardholder will receive notice by mail. The changes will affect the current balance; use of the card constitutes acceptance of the new terms.

DISCOVER BANK v. BOEHR

Supreme Court of California, 2005.
36 Cal.4th 148, 113 P.3d 1100, 30 Cal.Rptr.3d 76.

MORENO, J. This case concerns the validity of a provision in an arbitration agreement between Discover Bank and a credit cardholder forbidding classwide arbitration. The credit cardholder, a California resident, alleges that Discover Bank had a practice of representing to cardholders that late payment fees would not be assessed if payment was received by a certain date, whereas in actuality they were assessed if payment was received after 1:00 p.m. on that date, thereby leading to damages that were small as to individual consumers but large in the aggregate. Plaintiff filed a complaint claiming damages for this alleged deceptive practice, and Discover Bank successfully moved to compel arbitration pursuant to its arbitration agreement with plaintiff.

Plaintiff now seeks to pursue a classwide arbitration, which is well accepted under California law. (See *Keating v. Superior Court* (1982) 31 Cal.3d 584, 613–614 [183 Cal. Rptr. 360, 645 P.2d 1192] (*Keating*), overruled on other grounds in *Southland Corp. v. Keating* (1984) 465 U.S. 1 [79 L. Ed. 2d 1, 104 S. Ct. 852] (*Southland*).) But plaintiff's arbitration agreement with Discover Bank has a clause forbidding classwide arbitration. Moreover, the agreement has a Delaware choice-of-law provision. Discover Bank argues that Delaware law allows contracting parties to waive class action remedies. The trial court ruled that the class arbitration waiver was unconscionable and enforced the arbitration agreement with the proviso that plaintiff could seek classwide arbitration. The Court of Appeal, without disputing that such class arbitration waivers may be unconscionable under California law and without addressing the choice-of-law issue, nonetheless held that the Federal Arbitration Act (FAA) (9 U.S.C. § 1 et seq.) preempts the state law rule that class arbitration waivers are unconscionable.

As explained below, we conclude that, at least under some circumstances, the law in California is that class action waivers in consumer contracts of adhesion are unenforceable, whether the consumer is being asked to waive the right to class action litigation or the right to classwide arbitration. We further conclude that the Court of Appeal is incorrect that the FAA preempts California law in this respect. Finally, we will remand to the Court of Appeal to decide the choice-of-law issue.

I. Factual And Procedural Background

The following undisputed facts are largely drawn from the Court of Appeal opinion. Plaintiff Christopher Boehr obtained a credit card from defendant Discover Bank in April 1986. The Discover Bank cardholder agreement (agreement) governing plaintiff's credit card account contained a choice-of-law clause providing for the application of Delaware and federal law.

When plaintiff's credit card was issued, the agreement did not contain an arbitration clause. Discover Bank subsequently added the arbitration clause in July 1999, pursuant to a change-of-terms provision in the agreement. Relying on the change-of-terms provision, Discover Bank added the arbitration clause by sending to its existing cardholders (including plaintiff) a notice that stated in relevant part: "NOTICE OF AMENDMENT ... WE ARE ADDING A NEW ARBITRATION SECTION WHICH PROVIDES THAT IN THE EVENT YOU OR WE

ELECT TO RESOLVE ANY CLAIM OR DISPUTE BETWEEN US BY ARBITRATION, NEITHER YOU NOR WE SHALL HAVE THE RIGHT TO LITIGATE THAT CLAIM IN COURT OR TO HAVE A JURY TRIAL ON THAT CLAIM. THIS ARBITRATION SECTION WILL NOT APPLY TO LAWSUITS FILED BEFORE THE EFFECTIVE DATE."

In addition, the arbitration clause precluded both sides from participating in classwide arbitration, consolidating claims, or arbitrating claims as a representative or in a private attorney general capacity: ". . . NEITHER YOU NOR WE SHALL BE ENTITLED TO JOIN OR CONSOLIDATE CLAIMS IN ARBITRATION BY OR AGAINST OTHER CARDMEMBERS WITH RESPECT TO OTHER ACCOUNTS, OR ARBITRATE ANY CLAIM AS A REPRESENTATIVE OR MEMBER OF A CLASS OR IN A PRIVATE ATTORNEY GENERAL CAPACITY."

The arbitration agreement also stated that the FAA would govern the agreement: "Your Account involves interstate commerce, and this provision shall be governed by the Federal Arbitration Act (FAA)." "The arbitrator shall follow applicable substantive law to the extent consistent with the FAA and applicable statutes of limitations and shall honor claims of privilege recognized at law." Existing cardholders were notified that if they did not wish to accept the new arbitration clause, they must notify Discover Bank of their objections and cease using their accounts. Their continued use of an account would be deemed to constitute acceptance of the new terms. Plaintiff did not notify Discover Bank of any objection to the arbitration clause or cease using his account before the stated deadline.

On August 15, 2001, Boehr filed a putative class action complaint in superior court against Discover Bank. Plaintiff alleged two causes of action B breach of contract and violation of the Delaware Consumer Fraud Act (Del. Code Ann., tit. 6, §§ 2511–2527). The latter act in part prohibits misrepresentations "of any material fact with intent that others rely upon such concealment, suppression or omission in connection with the sale, lease or advertisement of any merchandise." (Id., § 2513.) He alleged that Discover Bank breached its cardholder agreement by imposing a late fee of approximately $29 on payments that were received on the payment due date, but after Discover Bank's undisclosed 1:00 p.m. "cut-off time." Discover Bank also allegedly imposed a periodic finance charge (thereby disallowing a grace period) on new purchases when payments were received on the payment due date, but after 1:00 p.m. The complaint acknowledged that the contract with Discover Bank provided that the contract was "governed by federal law and the law of Delaware." Plaintiff alleged, however, that "this choice of law provision applies only to plaintiff's substantive claims and not to other issues related to the contract, which plaintiff contends are governed by California or other applicable law."

Discover Bank moved to compel arbitration of plaintiff's claim on an individual basis and to dismiss the class action pursuant to the arbitration agreement's class action waiver.

Plaintiff opposed the motion, contending among other things that the class action waiver was unconscionable and unenforceable under California law.[20] Discover Bank, on the other hand, argued that the FAA requires the enforcement of the express provisions of an arbitration clause, including class action waivers. Discover Bank contended that under section 2 of the FAA, arbitration agreements should not be singled out for suspect status under state laws applicable only to arbitration provisions.

The trial court initially granted Discover Bank's motion in its entirety under Delaware law. After Discover Bank's motion to compel arbitration was granted, the Fourth District Court of Appeal decided *Szetela v. Discover Bank* (2002) 97 Cal.App.4th 1094 [118 Cal. Rptr. 2d 862] (*Szetela*), which held, for reasons explained below, that a virtually identical class action waiver was unconscionable. Plaintiff, citing *Szetela*, moved for reconsideration of that portion of the order enforcing the class action waiver.

The lower court found *Szetela* constituted new and controlling authority for the proposition that, under California law, an arbitration class action waiver is unconscionable and, thus, unenforceable. The trial court further conducted a choice-of-law analysis and concluded that enforcing the class action waiver under Delaware law would violate a fundamental public policy under California law as articulated in *Szetela*. Upon determining it would be proper to sever the class action waiver clause from the rest of the arbitration agreement, the trial court struck the class action waiver clause from the agreement, ordered plaintiff to arbitrate his claims individually, and left open the possibility that plaintiff may succeed in certifying an arbitration class under California law.

After the lower court granted plaintiff's motion for reconsideration, Discover Bank filed a writ petition seeking reinstatement of the lower court's original order enforcing the arbitration clause in its entirety by compelling plaintiff to arbitrate on an individual basis and precluding him from participating in class litigation or class arbitration. The Court of Appeal issued an order to show cause.

The Court of Appeal granted Discover Bank's writ. It did not take issue with the premise that class action waivers are unenforceable, at least under some circumstances, under California law and that this rule could override the Delaware choice-of-law provision. But the Court of Appeal held, for reasons elaborated below, that any California rule prohibiting class action waivers was preempted by the FAA, and that *Szetela* had failed to adequately analyze the federal preemption issue. It

20. Plaintiff also contended below that the unilateral addition of the arbitration clause was unconscionable under California law. (See *Badie v. Bank of America* (1998) 67 Cal.App.4th 779 [79 Cal. Rptr. 2d 273].) That contention was rejected by the trial court and the Court of Appeal, and the issue was not raised in the petition for review. Accordingly, we do not address the issue and omit most of the discussion of the proceedings pertaining to the issue in the courts below from our statement of facts.

therefore upheld the Discover Bank class action waiver. We granted review.

II. Discussion

A. *Class Action Lawsuits and Class Action Arbitration*

Before addressing the questions at issue in this case, we first consider the justifications for class action lawsuits. These justifications were set forth in Justice Mosk's oft-quoted majority opinion in *Vasquez v. Superior Court* (1971) 4 Cal.3d 800, 808 [94 Cal. Rptr. 796, 484 P.2d 964] (Vasquez): "Frequently numerous consumers are exposed to the same dubious practice by the same seller so that proof of the prevalence of the practice as to one consumer would provide proof for all. Individual actions by each of the defrauded consumers is often impracticable because the amount of individual recovery would be insufficient to justify bringing a separate action; thus an unscrupulous seller retains the benefits of its wrongful conduct. A class action by consumers produces several salutary by-products, including a therapeutic effect upon those sellers who indulge in fraudulent practices, aid to legitimate business enterprises by curtailing illegitimate competition, and avoidance to the judicial process of the burden of multiple litigation involving identical claims. The benefit to the parties and the courts would, in many circumstances, be substantial." . . .

These same concerns were acknowledged by the United States Supreme Court: " 'The policy at the very core of the class action mechanism is to overcome the problem that small recoveries do not provide the incentive for any individual to bring a solo action prosecuting his or her rights. A class action solves this problem by aggregating the relatively paltry potential recoveries into something worth someone's (usually an attorney's) labor.' " (*Amchem Products, Inc. v. Windsor* (1997) 521 U.S. 591, 617 [138 L. Ed. 2d 689, 117 S. Ct. 2231].)

It is this important role of class action remedies in California law that led this court to devise the hybrid procedure of classwide arbitration in *Keating*, supra, 31 Cal.3d 584. In that case, plaintiff 7–Eleven franchisors sought to invalidate an arbitration agreement between them and Southland Corporation and proceed with class action litigation to redress Southland's alleged systemic misconduct. This court held that the arbitration agreement was enforceable for most of the claims. In considering the impact that enforcement of the arbitration agreement would have on class action claims, the Keating court stated: "This court has repeatedly emphasized the importance of the class action device for vindicating rights asserted by large groups of persons. We have observed that the class suit 'both eliminates the possibility of repetitious litigation and provides small claimants with a method of obtaining redress for claims which would otherwise be too small to warrant individual litigation. [Citation.]' [Citation.] Denial of a class action in cases where it is appropriate may have the effect of allowing an unscrupulous wrongdoer to 'retain[] the benefits of its wrongful conduct.' [Citation.] [Moreover,] '[c]ontroversies involving widely used contracts of adhesion present ideal cases for class adjudication; the contracts are uniform, the same principles of interpretation apply to each contract, and all members of the class will share a common interest in the interpretation of an agreement to which each is a party.' " (*Keating*, supra, 31 Cal.3d at p. 609, fn. omitted.)

The *Keating* court recognized that "[w]ithout doubt a judicially ordered classwide arbitration would entail a greater degree of judicial involvement than is normally associated with arbitration, ideally ' "a complete proceeding, without resort to court facilities." ' [Citation.] The court would have to make initial determinations regarding certification and notice to the class, and if classwide arbitration proceeds it may be called upon to exercise a measure of external supervision in order to safeguard the rights of absent class members to adequate representation and in the event of dismissal or settlement. A good deal of care, and ingenuity, would be required to avoid judicial intrusion upon the merits of the dispute, or upon the conduct of the proceedings themselves and to minimize complexity, costs, or delay. [Citation.] [¶] An adhesion contract is not a normal arbitration setting, however, and what is at stake is not some abstract institutional interest but the interests of the affected parties." (*Keating*, supra, 31 Cal.3d at p. 613.) *Keating*'s endorsement of classwide arbitration has been echoed by subsequent Court of Appeal decisions....

B. *The Enforceability of Class Action Waivers*

Keating judicially authorized classwide arbitration in a case in which the arbitration agreement at issue was silent on the matter. It did not answer directly the question whether a class action waiver may be unenforceable as contrary to public policy or unconscionable. Recent cases have addressed that question. [Eds.: The Court goes on to discuss recent California Court of Appeals cases, including *America Online, Inc. v. Superior Court* (2001) 90 Cal.App.4th 1, 108 Cal. Rptr. 2d 699 (*America Online*), and *Szetela*, supra.]

Turning to the present case, ... plaintiff contends that class action or arbitration waivers in consumer contracts, and in this particular contract, should be invalidated as unconscionable under California law.

"To briefly recapitulate the principles of unconscionability, the doctrine has ' "both a 'procedural' and a 'substantive' element," the former focusing on "oppression" or "surprise" due to unequal bargaining power, the latter on "overly harsh" ' 'or "one-sided" results.' [Citation.] The procedural element of an unconscionable contract generally takes the form of a contract of adhesion, 'which, imposed and drafted by the party of superior bargaining strength, relegates to the subscribing party only the opportunity to adhere to the contract or reject it.' ... [¶] Substantively unconscionable terms may take various forms, but may generally be described as unfairly one-sided." (*Little v. Auto Stiegler, Inc.* (2003) 29 Cal.4th 1064, 1071 [130 Cal. Rptr. 2d 892, 63 P.3d 979] (*Little*), cert. den. sub nom. *Auto Stiegler, Inc. v. Little* (2003) 540 U.S. 818 [157 L. Ed. 2d 35, 124 S. Ct. 83].)

We agree that at least some class action waivers in consumer contracts are unconscionable under California law. First, when a consumer is given an amendment to its cardholder agreement in the form of a "bill stuffer" that he would be deemed to accept if he did not close his account, an element of procedural unconscionability is present. (*Szetela*, supra, 97 Cal.App.4th at p. 1100.) Moreover, although adhesive contracts are generally enforced (*Graham v. Scissor–Tail, Inc.* (1981) 28 Cal.3d 807, 817–818 [171 Cal. Rptr. 604, 623 P.2d 165]), class action waivers found in such contracts may also be substantively unconscionable inasmuch as they may operate effectively as exculpatory contract clauses that are contrary to public policy. As stated in Civil Code section 1668: "All contracts *which have for their object, directly or indirectly, to exempt anyone from responsibility for his own fraud, or willful injury* to the person or property of another, or violation of law, whether willful or negligent, are against the policy of the law." (Italics added.)

Class action and arbitration waivers are not, in the abstract, exculpatory clauses. But because, as discussed above, damages in consumer cases are often small and because " '[a] company which wrongfully exacts a dollar from each of millions of customers will reap a handsome profit' " (*Linder*, supra, 23 Cal.4th at p. 446), " 'the class action is often the only effective way to halt and redress such exploitation.' " (Ibid.) Moreover, such class action or arbitration waivers are indisputably one-sided. "Although styled as a mutual prohibition on representative or class actions, it is difficult to envision the circumstances under which the provision might negatively impact Discover [Bank], because credit card companies typically do not sue their customers in class action lawsuits." (*Szetela*, supra, 97 Cal.App.4th at p. 1101.) Such one-sided, exculpatory contracts in a contract of adhesion, at least to the extent they operate to insulate a party from liability that otherwise would be imposed under California law, are generally unconscionable.

We acknowledge that other courts disagree. Some courts have viewed class actions or arbitrations as a merely procedural right, the waiver of which is not unconscionable. (See, e.g., *Strand v. U.S. Bank National Association* ND (2005) 2005 ND 68 [693 N.W.2d 918, 926] (*Strand*); *Blaz v. Belfer* (5th Cir. 2004) 368 F.3d 501, 504–505; *Johnson v. West Suburban Bank* (3d Cir. 2000) 225 F.3d 366, 369; *Champ v. Siegel Trading Co., Inc.* (7th Cir. 1995) 55 F.3d 269, 277; but see *Leonard v. Terminex Intern. Co. L.P.* (Ala. 2002) 854 So. 2d 529, 538 [class action waiver together with limitation of damages clause in adhesive consumer arbitration agreement deprives plaintiffs of a "meaningful remedy" and is therefore unconscionable]; *State v. Berger* (2002) 211 W. Va. 549 [567 S.E.2d 265, 278] [holding contract provision limiting class action rights unconscionable]; *Powertel v. Bexley* (Fla.Dist.Ct.App. 1999) 743 So. 2d 570, 576 [same].) But as the above cited cases of this court have continually affirmed, class actions and arbitrations are, particularly in the consumer context, often inextricably linked to the vindication of substantive rights. Affixing the "procedural" label on such devices understates their importance and is not helpful in resolving the unconscionability issue.

Nor are we persuaded by the rationale stated by some courts that the potential availability of attorney fees to the prevailing party in arbitration or litigation ameliorates the problem posed by such class action waivers. (*Strand*, supra, 693 N.W.2d at p. 926; *Snowden v. Checkpoint Check Cashing* (4th Cir. 2002) 290 F.3d 631, 638.) There is no indication other than these courts' unsupported assertions that, in the case of small individual recovery, attorney fees are an adequate substitute for the class action or arbitration mechanism. Nor do we agree with the concurring and dissenting opinion that small claims litigation, government prosecution, or informal resolution are adequate substitutes.

We do not hold that all class action waivers are necessarily unconscionable. But when the waiver is found in a consumer contract of adhesion in a setting in which disputes between the contracting parties predictably involve small amounts of damages, and when it is alleged that the party with the superior bargaining power has carried out a scheme to deliberately cheat large numbers of consumers out of individually small sums of money, then, at least to the extent the obligation at issue is governed by California law, the waiver becomes in practice the exemption of the party "from responsibility for [its] own fraud, or willful injury to the person or property of another." (Civ. Code, § 1668.) Under these circumstances, such waivers are unconscionable under California law and should not be enforced.

C. *FAA Preemption of California Rules Against Class Action Waivers*

1. *The Court of Appeal Opinion*

The Court of Appeal did not dispute the conclusions of *America Online* and *Szetela* that, at least under some circumstances, a class action waiver would be unconscionable or contrary to public policy. The court concluded, however, that when class action waivers are contained in arbitration agreements, California law prohibiting such waivers is preempted by section 2 of the FAA (9 U.S.C. § 2). We conclude the Court of Appeal erred.

We begin by reviewing some basic principles pertaining to the enforcement of arbitration agreements. "California law, like federal law, favors enforcement of valid arbitration agreements. [Citation.] ... Thus, under both federal and California law, arbitration agreements are valid, irrevocable, and enforceable, save upon such grounds as exist at law or in equity for the revocation of any contract." (*Armendariz*, supra, 24 Cal.4th at pp. 97–98, fn. omitted; see also 9 U.S.C. § 2; Code Civ. Proc., § 1281.) In other words, although under federal and California law, arbitration agreements are enforced "in accordance with their terms" (*Volt Info. Sciences v. Leland Stanford Jr. U.* (1989) 489 U.S. 468, 478 [103 L. Ed. 2d 488, 109 S. Ct. 1248] (*Volt*)), such enforcement is limited by certain general contract principles " 'at law or in equity for the revocation of any contract.' " (id. at p. 474.)

At the outset of our discussion, we note that the FAA is silent on the matter of class actions and class action arbitration. Indeed, not only is classwide arbitration a relatively recent development, but class action litigation for damages was for the most part unknown in federal jurisdictions at the time the FAA was enacted in 1925. (Act of Feb. 12, 1925, ch. 213, 43 Stat. 883.) The Congress that enacted the FAA therefore cannot be said to have contemplated the issues before us. Accordingly, our conclusions with respect to FAA preemption must come from the United States Supreme Court's articulation of general principles regarding such preemption....

"[U]nder section 2 of the FAA, a state court may refuse to enforce an arbitration agreement based on 'generally applicable contract defenses, such as fraud, duress, or unconscionability.' " (*Little*, supra, 29 Cal.4th at p. 1079, quoting *Doctor's Associates, Inc. v. Casarotto* (1996) 517 U.S. 681, 687 [134 L. Ed. 2d 902, 116 S. Ct. 1652].) In the present case, the principle that class action waivers are, under certain circumstances, unconscionable as unlawfully exculpatory is a principle of California law that does not specifically apply to arbitration agreements, but to contracts generally. In other words, it applies equally to class action litigation waivers in contracts without arbitration agreements as it does to class arbitration waivers in contracts with such agreements. (See *America Online*, supra, 90 Cal.App.4th at pp. 17–18.) ...

[Eds.: The Court reviews at length U.S. Supreme Court precedents and argues that none of them exclude California from applying its own standards of unconscionability.]

Nor did the court address the question whether that determination of unconscionability should be made by a court or an arbitrator. The court was in general agreement that courts should be left to decide certain "gateway matters" ... or "fundamental" matters such as the validity and scope of the arbitration agreement.... Under California law, the question whether "grounds exist for the revocation of the [arbitration] agreement" (Code Civ. Proc., § 1281.2) based on "grounds as exist for the revocation of any contract" (id., § 1281) is for the courts to decide, not an arbitrator.... This includes the determination of whether arbitration agreements or portions thereof are deemed to be unconscionable or contrary to public policy....

Nor are we directed to anything concrete that would cause us to reconsider *Keating*'s holding over 20 years ago that classwide arbitrations are workable and appropriate in some cases. (See Sternlight, As Mandatory Binding Arbitration Meets the Class Action, Will the Class-action Survive? (2000) 42 Wm. & Mary L.Rev. 1, 38–44 & fns. 148–151 [reporting, based on surveys of court decisions and discussions with attorneys, that class action arbitration is rare but viable, with trial courts acting to resolve class issues and other collateral matters]; ...)

We reiterate what this court said over 20 years ago in *Keating*: "Classwide arbitration, as Sir Winston Churchill said of democracy, must be evaluated, not in relation to some ideal but in relation to its alternatives." (*Keating*, 31 Cal.3d at p. 613.) We continue to believe that the alternatives—either not enforcing arbitration agreements and requiring class action litigation, or allowing arbitration agreements to be used as a means of completely inoculating parties against class liability—are unacceptable. Nothing in the FAA ... requires us to reconsider that assessment.

It may be the case that arbitration becomes a less desirable forum from Discover Bank's viewpoint if the arbitration must be conducted in a classwide manner. But the fact that a court's refusal to enforce an unconscionable term of an arbitration agreement makes that agreement less desirable to the party imposing the term does not argue in favor of its enforcement.[21]

D. Choice-of-law Issue

Our holding that the FAA does not prohibit a California court from refusing to enforce a class action waiver that is unconscionable does not bring a resolution to this case. The agreement between Discover Bank and plaintiff has a Delaware choice-of-law agreement and Discover Bank argues that under Delaware law, a class arbitration waiver is enforceable. Because the Court of Appeal concluded that any California rule against class arbitrations waivers was preempted by the FAA, it did not address the question whether the Delaware choice-of-law provision requires the enforcement of the class arbitration waiver. It must do so on remand. For the Court of Appeal's guidance on remand, we offer these comments.

We have summarized California's choice-of-law provisions as follows: "If the trial court finds that the ... claims [at issue] fall within the scope of a choice-of-law clause, it must next evaluate the clause's enforceability pursuant to the analytical approach reflected in section 187, subdivision (2) of the Restatement Second of Conflict of Laws (Restatement). Under that approach, the court must first determine: '(1) whether the chosen state has a substantial relationship to the parties or their transaction, or (2) whether there is any other reasonable basis for the parties' choice of law. If neither of these tests is met, that is the end of the inquiry, and the court need not enforce the parties' choice of law. If, however, either test is met, the court must next determine whether the chosen state's law is contrary to a fundamental policy of California. If there is no such conflict, the court shall enforce the parties' choice of law. If, however, there is a fundamental conflict with California law, the court must then determine whether California has a 'materially greater interest than the chosen state in the determination of the particular issue ...' (Rest., § 187, subd. (2).) If California has a materially greater

21. We note both parties agree that, in the event a classwide arbitration is compelled, Discover Bank may waive the arbitration agreement and have the matter brought in court.

interest than the chosen state, the choice of law shall not be enforced, for the obvious reason that in such circumstance we will decline to enforce a law contrary to this state's fundamental policy." A (*Washington Mutual Bank*, supra, 24 Cal.4th at pp. 916–917, fns. and italics omitted.)

Assuming that Discover Bank establishes the "substantial relationship" and "reasonable basis" prongs of the choice-of-law analysis, and assuming that Delaware law regarding class arbitration waivers is contrary to California law, the court must then resolve whether and to what extent Delaware law should apply. As reviewed above, in *America Online* the court concluded that a Virginia choice-of-law provision that would have compelled waiver of the plaintiff's right to bring a class action lawsuit under the CLRA would not be enforced against a California resident, concluding that the CLRA class action remedy furthered a "strong public policy of this state." (*America Online*, supra, 90 Cal. App.4th at p. 15.) The present case differs from *America Online* in that plaintiff is not invoking the antiwaiver provision of the CLRA, nor is he seeking to enforce an obligation imposed by the CLRA or any other California statute. Instead, he has brought this action under the Delaware Consumer Fraud Act and Delaware contract law, but seeks to enforce those Delaware laws in a California court with a California unconscionability rule against class action waivers that arguably is not found under Delaware law. Whether he may do so remains to be determined on remand. Also to be addressed is plaintiffs' argument that class arbitration rules are procedural rules that California courts are to apply even when the substantive law dictated by contract is from another state (see Rest.2d Conf. of Laws, supra, § 122), as well as any other choice-of-law arguments appropriately raised.

III. DISPOSITION

The judgment of the Court of Appeal is reversed, and the cause is remanded for proceedings consistent with this opinion.

BAXTER, J., CONCURRING AND DISSENTING. I concur in part and dissent in part. I agree with the majority that federal law does not compel enforcement of contractual class action waivers simply because they are contained in arbitration agreements. But I lament the majority's determination to use this case as a vehicle to resolve the issue of California's policy on class action waivers. For two reasons, we need not, and should not, confront that question here.

First, because the Court of Appeal upheld the instant waiver solely by finding federal preemption of any California antiwaiver policy, that court did not decide whether such a policy exists. Ordinarily, we do not address, on review, issues that were not decided by the Court of Appeal.

Second, the majority's questionable decision to deem the class action waiver in this contract unconscionable by California standards—a determination at odds with the vast weight of authority elsewhere (see discussion, post)—is simply moot under the particular circumstances. The parties reasonably agreed that Delaware law would govern all aspects of their contractual relationship, and plaintiff has asserted only Delaware causes of action. Thus, regardless of California's position on class waivers, California has a manifest obligation to evaluate the waiver under Delaware law alone. Because Delaware, like most other jurisdictions, would uphold the waiver, California—the fortuitous venue for this "nationwide" class action—must honor it....

[Eds.: Justice Baxter reviews the choice of law issues at length. In the course of his dissent, he makes the following argument:]

I cannot accept the facile premise that lack of a class remedy is equivalent to exculpation of an alleged wrongdoer. Class treatment, in whatever forum, is a relatively recent invention, designed to encourage and facilitate the resolution of certain kinds of disputes. It may provide valuable procedural leverage to one side. But as we noted in *Washington Mutual*, supra, 24 Cal.4th 906, " '[c]lass actions are provided only as a means to enforce substantive law.' " (id., at p. 918, quoting *City of San Jose v. Superior Court* (1974) 12 Cal.3d 447, 462 [115 Cal. Rptr. 797, 525 P.2d 701], fn. omitted, italics added.) They must not be confused with the substantive law to be enforced. (Ibid.) Even if the unavailability of class relief makes a plaintiff's pursuit of a particular claim "less convenient" (*Moses H. Cone Hospital v. Mercury Constr. Corp.* (1983) 460 U.S. 1, 19 [74 L. Ed. 2d 765, 103 S. Ct. 927]; see also *Gilmer v. Interstate/Johnson Lane Corp.* (1991) 500 U.S. 20, 32 [114 L. Ed. 2d 26, 111 S. Ct. 1647]), such claims may nonetheless be pursued on an individual basis.

Moreover, the majority exaggerates the difficulty of pursuing modest claims where class treatment is unavailable and overlooks the many other means by which Discover Bank could be called to account for the mischarges plaintiff alleges. For example:

(1) The cardholder may contact the bank and attempt to resolve the matter informally. Discover Bank's cardholder agreement specifically provides a 60–day period in which to contact the company with billing questions and disputes. Plaintiff's complaint does not state that he pursued this avenue. (Indeed, though the complaint asserts widespread improper billing practices by Discover Bank, it does not allege that the bank has ever mischarged plaintiff himself. Plaintiff admitted in his deposition that he does not know whether Discover Bank has ever done so.)

(2) Pursuant to the agreement, the cardholder may pursue one-on-one arbitration of Delaware state law claims, including those under the Delaware Consumer Fraud Act (Del. Code Ann., tit. 6, § 2511 et seq.). The agreement includes several provisions designed to make the individual arbitration process fair and accessible. Under the agreement's terms, Discover Bank will arbitrate in the federal judicial district where the cardholder resides. Further, the cardholder may obtain an advance of all forum costs and will never pay forum costs exceeding those he or she would have had to pay in court litigation.

(3) For claims under $5,000, the cardholder may proceed in small claims court. (See Code Civ. Proc., § 116.210 et seq.) In the cardholder agreement, Discover Bank promises that it "will not invoke [its] right to arbitrate an individual claim," involving less than $5,000, which is pending only in a small claims court. The only mandatory expense of a small claims action is a modest filing fee plus the actual cost of any mail service by the court clerk. (Id., §§ 116.230, subds. (a), (c), 116.910.) The claim is pled by filling out a standard form. (Id., §§ 116.310, subd. (a), 116.320.) No formal discovery is permitted (id., § 116.310, subd. (b)), and neither party may be represented by a lawyer (id., § 116.530, subd. (a)), though free advisory assistance is available to the claimant (id., § 116.260).

(4) The cardholder may arbitrate, pursuant to the terms of the cardholder agreement, his rights under such federal statutes as TILA. (15 U.S.C. § 1601 et seq.)[22] This statute imposes mandatory disclosure requirements for consumer credit transactions, including those arising on credit card accounts. As to the latter, the statute provides for detailed disclosure of the terms on which credit is being extended, including annual percentage rates, methods of computing outstanding balances, finance charges, grace periods, and late fees. (15 U.S.C. § 1637.) The cardholder, if he or she prevails, may recover actual damages, twice the finance charge imposed in connection with each violative transaction, and attorney fees and costs. (Id., § 1640(a)(1), (2)(A), (3).)

(5) If Discover Bank's conduct violates California's unfair competition statutes (Bus. & Prof. Code, § 17200 et seq.), which broadly prohibit "any unlawful, unfair or fraudulent business act or practice" (id., § 17200), the Attorney General and designated local law enforcement officials (who are not bound by the cardholder agreement) may sue on the People's behalf for injunctive relief and for mandatory civil penalties of up to $2,500 for each violation (id., §§ 17203, 17204, 17206). The amount of a civil penalty shall be calculated in accordance with "any one or more of the relevant circumstances ... including, but not limited to ... the nature and seriousness of the misconduct, the number of violations, the persistence of the misconduct, the length of time over which the misconduct occurred, the willfulness of the defendant's misconduct, and the defendant's assets, liabilities, and net worth." (Id., § 17206, subd. (b).)

(6) Finally, in the highly regulated banking and credit industry, other means of sanctioning and remediating illegal conduct are available at the behest of both federal and Delaware law. (See, e.g., 12 U.S.C. § 1818 (b) [Federal Deposit Insurance Corporation may issue cease-and-desist orders and order corrective measures including restitution]; Del.

22. ... [F]ederal circuits addressing the issue have uniformly held that claimants must arbitrate TILA claims pursuant to agreement, that arbitration precludes class relief under TILA, that arbitration agreements containing express waivers of class treatment, even for small individual amounts in dispute, are not unconscionable with respect to TILA claims, and that, although TILA contemplates class actions, it includes no "unwaivable" right to class relief....

Code Ann., tit. 5, § 121 et seq. [investigative and enforcement powers of Delaware State Banking Commissioner]; Del. Code Ann., tit. 29, § 2504 [investigative and enforcement powers of Delaware Attorney General].)

Under these circumstances, it cannot be said that, by upholding cardholders' contractual waiver of a class remedy under Delaware law, we would effectively absolve Discover Bank of its objectionable conduct. Thus, there is no basis to conclude that enforcement of the class waiver pursuant to the parties' choice of Delaware law would contravene a fundamental California statutory policy against exculpatory agreements....

I would hold the parties to their agreement, expressly governed by Delaware law, which calls for individual arbitration of disputes arising between Discover Bank and its cardholders. Accordingly, I would affirm the judgment of the Court of Appeal, which directed the issuance of a petition for mandate requiring the trial court to (1) compel arbitration of plaintiff's complaint and (2) reinstate the waiver of class treatment.

Notes and Discussion

1. **Four Things You Need to Know.** First, the Superior Court is the respondent in this case because Discover (petitioner) had appealed the Superior Court's granting of Boehr's motion for reconsideration of the court's previous grant of Discover's motion to compel arbitration. Second, the California Supreme Court decision was 4–3, which is the equivalent of saying that the minority may well be right. Third, Christopher Boehr, who was the real plaintiff in this lawsuit, was apparently something of an anti-credit card gadfly. He also brought a class-action suit, on the identical issue, against Centurion Bank, a subsidiary of American Express; that suit was settled, with resulting checks to class members on the order of 41 cents. Steve Duin, *Class-Action Suits: Pennies from Heaven*, The Oregonian (Portland), July 31, 2005, at B1.

Fourth, although the majority opinion in this case settled some issues of California law, the real remaining issue was the applicability of Delaware law. On remand, the California Court of Appeals held the Delaware choice of law provision valid and enforceable, because Discover Bank is headquartered in Delaware, and because Delaware has a greater interest in the case than California since the sole defendant is from Delaware whereas only some of the class of plaintiffs are from California. *Discover Bank v. Superior Court*, 134 Cal.App.4th 886, 36 Cal.Rptr.3d 456 (2005). Since Delaware law permits contractual exclusion of class-wide arbitration, Boehr's case presumably stalled out. There is no record of an appeal.

2. **Avoiding Classes.** Although the main reason why business prefer arbitration is undoubtedly their desire to escape the vagaries of jury trials, a close second is the avoidance of class actions with their prospect of high damage awards (particularly if punitive damages are assessed). At present, "many consumer financial services (including the ten largest credit-card issuers), most telecommunications companies (including all the major cellular service providers), and even the majority of car dealerships" use clauses barring classwide arbitration. John W. Hanson, Discover Bank *and Its*

Aftermath: What's Left of "No Class Action Arbitration Clauses" in Consumer Contracts? 12 Ass'n of Bus. Trial Lawyers Rept. 3, 3–4 (November 2005); see also Linda J. Demaine & Deborah R. Hensler, *"Volunteering" to Arbitrate Through Predispute Arbitration Clauses: The Average Consumer's Experience*, 67 Law & Contemp. Probs. 55, 65 (2004) (in an unscientific study, more than 30% of arbitration clauses in consumer or employee contracts bar classwide arbitration). So this case was a big deal.

On what basis does the California Supreme Court find such clauses unconscionable? As to procedure, is adhesiveness the only problem, or does the court also object to the use of "bill stuffers" that consumers are unlikely to notice? That is, would the clause be less objectionable if it were an initial term in the credit card contract? As to substance, does the court observe the requirement that a provision be oppressive as of the time the contract is made, and not just as a result of subsequent events? Would the outcome be any different if, for instance, Discover Bank offered to pay the arbitration fees for its consumers, provided they did not bring classwide claims? If the underlying problem is that large players like Discover Bank may, in effect, cheat many consumers out of amounts too small to merit litigation individually, then how do we determine what "small" means?

California is certainly not alone in moving to permit classwide arbitration at least when small claims are involved. See, for instance, *Leonard v. Terminex Intern. Co. L.P.*, 854 So.2d 529 (Ala. 2002); *Bellsouth Mobility LLC v. Christopher*, 819 So.2d 171 (Fla. App. 2002); *State ex rel. Dunlap v. Berger*, 211 W.Va. 549, 567 S.E.2d 265 (2002); *Whitney v. Alltel Communications, Inc.*, 173 S.W.3d 300 (Mo. App. 2005); *Muhammad v. County Bank of Rehoboth Beach*, 189 N.J. 1, 912 A.2d 88 (2006). On the other hand, contract prohibitions of classwide arbitration have also been upheld, e.g., in *Strand v. U.S. Bank National Ass'n ND*, 2005 ND 68, 693 N.W.2d 918.

Recently, the Illinois Supreme Court examined these and other decisions in *Kinkel v. Cingular Wireless, LLC*, 223 Ill.2d 1, 857 N.E.2d 250 (Ill. 2006); it concluded: "If there is a pattern in these cases it is this: a class action waiver will not be found unconscionable if the plaintiff had a meaningful opportunity to reject the contract term or if the agreement containing the waiver is not burdened by other features limiting the ability of the plaintiff to obtain a remedy for the particular claim being asserted in a cost-effective manner. If the agreement is so burdened, the 'right to seek classwide redress is more than a mere procedural device.' " 223 Ill.2d at 41. In that case, a Cingular customer brought suit over a $150 early termination fee. The court held that a mandatory arbitration term was unconscionable because it was contained in an adhesion contract that failed to inform the customer of the cost to her of arbitration and did not provide a cost-effective mechanism for individual customers to obtain a remedy for the specific injury alleged in either a judicial or an arbitral forum. But the court also held that the offending clause was severable from the arbitration clause. In *Hubbert v. Dell Corp.*, 359 Ill.App.3d 976, 988–9, 296 Ill.Dec. 258, 835 N.E.2d 113, 125–6 (Ill. Ct. App. 2005), however, a plaintiff lost because it failed to prove that it could not collect punitive damages owing to the size of arbitration filing fees.

3. Should Congress Act? "Companies are increasingly using arbitral class action prohibitions to insulate themselves from class action liability.

These prohibitions are detrimental not only to potential class members but to the public at large in that they are preventing the law from being adequately enforced. In essence, by precluding class actions, companies are engaging in 'do-it-yourself tort reform,' freeing themselves from liability without having to convince legislatures to change the substantive law. The unconscionability defense, while sometimes successful, is itself too expensive and unwieldy to adequately regulate companies' attempts to elude class action liability. Thus, as a matter of fairness, efficiency, and justice, Congress should prevent companies from exempting themselves from class action liability." Jean R. Sternlight & Elizabeth J. Jensen, *Using Arbitration to Eliminate Consumer Class Actions: Efficient Business Practice or Unconscionable Abuse?* 67 Law & Contemp. Probs. 75, 103 (2004). Is this a better suggestion?

As you would guess, Congressional attempts to revise the antiquated FAA have met with a buzzsaw of special interest lobbying.

4. A Word of Warning. Contracts casebooks, written by professors who have a keen interest in developing legal doctrine, sometimes give the misleading impression that modern contract law has departed radically from the principle of fidelity to the original agreement of the parties. In reality, nothing could be further from the truth. "We spend so much time on the unusual cases where courts find a way to let people out of their bad deals that students begin to think these cases are the norm. Students are amazed when I tell them that it is virtually unheard of for a sophisticated party, or even a party only moderately sophisticated, to prevail on an unconscionability argument. Yes, you can win an unconscionability case if your client is poor and uneducated, and if the other party is a sleazy organization that preys on poor people, and if you're able to afford an appeal, and if you get Skelly Wright on the bench. But absent these circumstances, the client is going to be stuck with the documents she signs." Robert M. Lloyd, *Making Contracts Relevant: Thirteen Lessons for the First–Year Contracts Course*, 36 Ariz. St. L.J. 257, 267 (2004).

BATFILM PRODUCTIONS, INC. v. WARNER BROS. INC.

Superior Court of California, 1994.
Consolidated Cases No. BC 051653 and No. BC 051654.

YAFFE, J.

PHASE I

Statement of Decision

The Court divided the trial of this case into two phases. Phase I consisted of a bench trial of plaintiffs' non-jury claims. Those claims primarily concern plaintiffs' "Net Profits" participation in the *Batman* motion pictures.

The plaintiffs are two individuals, Benjamin Melniker and Michael Uslan, and the two corporations that furnish their services, Batfilm Productions, Inc., and Franklin Enterprises, Ltd. The defendants are

Warner Bros. and Polygram Pictures, Inc. (The Court previously granted the summary judgment motion of defendants Peter Guber, Jon Peters, and the GuberBPeters Entertainment Co.) Polygram Pictures did not participate in the bench trial.

In 1979, Mr. Melniker and Mr. Uslan obtained an option on the motion picture rights to the Batman comic book characters. In November 1979, they made a deal with Casablanca Productions (Polygram's predecessor) the development and production of a motion picture to be based on those characters (the "Casablanca Agreement"). Under the Casablanca Agreement, Mr. Melniker and Mr. Uslan were entitled to receive certain fixed and contingent compensation if a *Batman* motion picture were produced.

In 1981, Polygram assigned to Warner Bros. its rights and obligations under the Casablanca Agreement. In 1988, Mr. Melniker and Mr. Uslan and Warner Bros. signed a written amendment to the Casablanca Agreement (the "Warner Agreement"). Under the Warner Agreement, Mr. Melniker and Mr. Uslan were entitled to receive $300,000 in fixed compensation for *Batman*, plus a $100,000 "deferment" once the film generated a certain level of receipts, plus 13% of the so-called "Net Profits," as defined in an attachment to the Warner Agreement.

Warner Bros. has paid Messrs. Melniker and Uslan the $300,000 fixed fee and $100,000 deferment. Under the Warner Agreement, Warner Bros. has also paid Melniker and Uslan an additional $700,000 in fixed fees on two additional motion pictures (*Batman Returns* and *Batman: Mask of the Phantasm*). Warner Bros. will have similar financial obligations to plaintiffs on each additional *Batman* motion picture. Although *Batman* has generated more revenue than any other Warner Bros. film, it has not generated any "Net Profits" under plaintiffs' contract. Melniker and Uslan filed suit in 1992 claiming, *inter alia*, they were denied their fair "Net Profits" compensation.

The primary claims originally to be tried to the Court were the Tenth Cause of Action for an accounting of the revenues and expenses of *Batman* and the Eleventh Cause of Action for a declaration that plaintiffs' "Net Profits" definition is unconscionable and, thus, unenforceable. On the first day of trial, however, plaintiffs dismissed their accounting claims. Warner Bros. is therefore entitled to prevail on that cause of action.

At the close of plaintiffs' case, Warner Bros. moved for judgment pursuant to section 631.8 of the Code of Civil Procedure. In reviewing the evidence, the Court believed that Mr. Melniker and Mr. Uslan had offered evidence to prove that the Warner Agreement was contract of adhesion that should be strictly interpreted in a way that would be contrary to plaintiffs' reasonable expectations.

But a contract of adhesion is not the same as an unconscionable contract, which is no contract at all. "Unconscionability" requires a far different level of proof. The plaintiffs' did not prove that they are to be relieved of their contract with Warner Bros. on the ground of unconscionability.

Mr. Melniker negotiated the Warner Agreement in his and Mr. Uslan's behalf. No one is less likely to have been coerced against his will into signing a contract like the Warner Agreement than Mr. Melniker. This former general counsel and senior executive of a major motion picture studio (Metro–Goldwyn–Mayer) knew all the tricks of the trade; he knew inside and out how these contracts work, what they mean, and how they are negotiated.

Even with Mr. Melniker's knowledge and experience, plaintiffs complain that Warner Bros. knew when the parties signed the Warner Agreement in 1988 that *Batman* would not generate "Net Profits." Plaintiffs did not explain the relevance of this to the issue of whether their contract is unconscionable. Even if they had, however, they failed to prove that Warner Bros. knew in 1988 that *Batman* would not generate any "Net Profits."

At the core of plaintiffs' case is their argument that the contract was not fair to them because Warner Bros. and others earned millions of dollars on *Batman* and plaintiffs did not. The answer to that argument is that ever since the King's Bench decided *Slade's Case* in 1602, right down to today, courts do not refuse to enforce contracts or remake contracts for the parties because the court or the jury thinks that the contract is not fair.

That principle is not some medieval anachronism. This society, this country, this culture operates on the basis of billions of bargains struck willingly every day by people all across the country in all walks of life. And if any one of those people could have their bargain reexamined after the fact on the ground that it was not fair, we would have a far different type of society than we have now; we would have one that none of the parties to this case would like very much.

When one talks about a motion picture and the claims of this type that are made, they all have one thing in common: the plaintiff comes in and says, "Without me, they would have had nothing, and look how they treated me." But the process of making a motion picture consists of the process of bargaining with many talented people on many different and inconsistent bases, and making bargains with them that cannot rationally be compared one to another. It would not be good for the motion picture business or for the parties to this case if any one of those people on any motion picture could come back and ask a court to remake the bargain that he made on the ground that he now asserts, after the fact and in light of the success of the picture, that he was not fairly treated in comparison with others. Whether a contract is fair is not the issue. A contract is not unconscionable simply because it is not fair. Plaintiffs claim that the Warner Agreement is unconscionable within the meaning of Civil Code section 1670.5. To be unconscionable, a contract must "shock the conscience" or, as plaintiffs alleged in paragraph 139(b) of their complaint, it must be "harsh, oppressive, and unduly one-sided."

After considering all the evidence, the Court finds that the plaintiffs have failed to prove that the Warner Agreement, taken as a whole, is unconscionable.

That, however, is not the end of the inquiry that the Court must make. Under Civil Code section 1670.5, if the evidence shows that any part of a contract is unconscionable, the Court may refuse to enforce that part of the contract.

During the trial, plaintiffs claimed that eight elements of the Warner Agreement's "Net Profits" definition were unconscionable: (1) the 10% advertising overhead charge; (2) Warner Bros.' retention of any economic value of United States tax credits created by the payment of taxes in the foreign territories where *Batman* was distributed; (3) application of the 15% production overhead charge on participation payments to third parties; (4) application of the 15% production overhead charge on the $100,000 deferment; (5) all of the interest charges; (6) the costs charged by Pinewood Studios in England for holding sets and stages after completion of photography; (7) application of the 15% production overhead charge to the costs incurred at the Pinewood Studio lot; and (8) the inclusion in "gross receipts" of only 20% of the revenue from videocassettes, less a distribution fee. (These items, and the dollar amounts associated with them, are listed on Exhibit B9.)

In considering Warner Bros. motion for judgment under Code of Civil Procedure section 631,8, the Court had little difficulty in rejecting seven of the plaintiffs' claims.

As to all of the items relating to overhead charges (Items One, Three, Four, and Seven), the Court granted Warner Bros. motion for judgment because the plaintiffs failed to prove that historically Warner Bros. indirect general administrative expenses for motion picture production and advertising—"overhead"—do not equal or exceed the amount charged under the "Net Profits" definition, namely, 15 percent of production costs and 10 percent of advertising expenditures. As a matter of fact, plaintiffs conceded that they could not show that overhead charges under the "Net Profits" definition exceeded Warner Bros.' actual overhead costs, taken as a whole.

Plaintiffs argued that charging overhead on certain production costs, advertising expenses, gross participations, deferred payments, and payments paid to foreign studios was unconscionable because the administrative cost of providing those goods or services was less than the contractual 10 or 15 percent overhead surcharge. Plaintiffs did not prove that allegation. And, more important, the test is not whether Warner Bros. overhead charge on a particular direct cost item exceeded the "actual" administrative or other indirect expenses associated with providing that one item or service to the production or advertising of a movie. As the accounting experts for both sides testified, overhead cannot be assessed with such precision. Under the circumstances, the test must be whether the production and advertising overheads charged by using the percentage allocations are, in total, unconscionably higher than Warner Bros.' actual production and advertising overhead costs on a motion picture. Plaintiffs offered no evidence to support such a finding.

Plaintiffs also failed to show that the advertising costs, gross participations, deferred payments, and payments paid to foreign studios were not historically included in the pool of costs that were compared to Warner Bros. general and administrative expenses to estimate its rate of overhead. In sum, plaintiffs simply failed to prove that any of the overhead charges are unconscionable.

The Court also granted Warner Bros. motion for judgment as to Item Two, the foreign tax credit. According to plaintiffs, when a motion picture is distributed overseas, many countries impose a tax on the receipts generated. That tax payment gives rise to a credit that can be used under certain circumstances to offset United States tax obligations. Plaintiffs claimed that, in calculating their "Net Profits," it is unconscionable for Warner Bros. to deduct foreign taxes as a distribution expense without adding something for the value of foreign tax credits. The plaintiffs failed to prove, however, that Warner Bros. received any foreign tax credits on *Batman*, or the amounts thereof, or that Warner Bros. received any actual financial benefit from those tax credits when calculating and paying its United States obligations. Even if such a credit had not been received, the plaintiffs failed to prove that they ever asked Warner Bros. to agree that, in computing "Net Profits," Warner Bros. would augment the gross receipts of the picture by the amount of the tax credits. No such provision is contained in plaintiffs' contract and there is no evidence that they ever expected such treatment of the tax credits.

The Court also granted the motion for judgment as to Item Six, the Pinewood Studios sound stage holdover costs, because there was no evidence that the holdover charge is not properly a cost of the first *Batman* movie.

The Court granted the motion for judgment as to Item Eight, videocassette distribution, on the ground that Mr. Melniker knew that a 20 percent royalty was standard in the industry. He never questioned it. He never asked that it be changed. The plaintiffs did not prove that the 20 percent royalty unconscionably exceeded the actual revenues, less expenses, from videocassette distribution. They also offered no evidence that a "distribution fee" on the distribution of videocassettes was unconscionable. Nor did they prove that they could have negotiated a better deal elsewhere at the time this deal was made, in which a higher percentage of video revenue, without deduction of a distribution fee, would be credited to the picture in calculating "Net Profits."

Item Five concerned the "interest" charge on production costs. Under Paragraph 2A of plaintiffs' contract, "Net Profits" become payable once the picture generates enough gross receipts to cover the specified distribution fees, distribution expenses, and production costs. Until then, under paragraphs 2A and 9 of plaintiffs' "Net Profits" definition, the production costs bear an interest charge. Under the contract, Warner Bros. reduces the interest-bearing balance of production costs with only those gross receipts that remain after deducting the distribution fees and expenses. Plaintiffs claim that is unconscionable for Warner Bros. to not credit the interest-bearing production cost balance with all the gross receipts of the picture. They also claim that because the distribution fee represents a source of "profit" for Warner Bros., this method of calculating interest in unconscionable because it allows Warner Bros. to charge interest on the cost of production after the picture has generated revenues in excess of that amount.

Plaintiffs did present sufficient evidence to require Warner Bros. to defend its method of computing interest under the contract.

After listening to the evidence presented by Warner Bros, and the arguments of counsel, however, the Court finds that Warner Bros. met its burden of showing that the method of calculating interest provided in their contract is not unconscionable. Warner Bros. met its burden in a number of ways.

Warner Bros. showed that the interest provision in the Warner Agreement is really the same provision found in the 1979 Casablanca Agreement that Warner Bros. did not have anything to do with. Plaintiffs were bound by that contract before they ever dealt with Warner Bros. They cannot complain that they were harmed by being required to abide by a similar provision with the same effect.

Warner Bros. also showed that plaintiffs would not have gotten any better deal on the calculation of interest it they had borrowed the production costs from a third party lender, had produced *Batman* themselves as independent producers, and had hired Warner Bros (or presumably anybody else) just to distribute it for them. In that case, plaintiffs would not have been able to use all of the gross receipts generated by the film to repay their lender. Just as in their contract with Warner Bros., they would have been able to repay the production financier only with the gross receipts left over after the distributor retained enough to cover the distribution fees and expenses.

And, if there is a "profit" embedded within Warner Bros.' distribution fee, plaintiffs did not prove the amount of it or that it prevented the picture from showing a net profit.

All of that evidence is sufficient to overcome the plaintiffs' evidence as to the unconscionability of the method of calculating interest under their "Net Profits" contract.

Separately, plaintiffs argued that the language of their "Net Profits" contract did not permit Warner Bros. to continue charging interest once the gross receipts of the picture—prior to the deduction of distribution fees and expenses—exceed the total production costs. The duty of the Court is to find out what the parties meant by the language of their contract. If the contract is one of adhesion, the Court interprets it so that it does not defeat the reasonable expectations of the party who was forced to adhere to it. But the Court will not substitute its own interpretation of the contract if that is not what the evidence shows that the parties intended.

The Court rejects plaintiffs' argument because there was no evidence that plaintiffs ever interpreted the language of the interest provisions in the manner claimed at trial. Mr. Melniker was an old hand at motion picture agreements of this type and had negotiated other "Net Profits" contracts like this himself. He had experience with similar provisions yet he never mentioned the interest issue with anyone at Warner Bros. Plaintiffs offered no evidence that they expected Warner Bros. to compute interest in any other manner. They have thus failed to prove that the contract defeated their reasonable expectations.

Given the Court's decision in favor of Warner Bros. on plaintiffs' unconscionability claim, Warner Bros. is entitled to prevail on plaintiffs' Thirteenth Cause of Action for "unfair competition" because that claim was dependent on a finding that their "Net Profits contract was unconscionable."

Finally, Warner Bros. is entitled to prevail on plaintiffs' Fourteenth Cause of Action arising from the exhibition of the animated *Batman* television series. Plaintiffs presented no evidence on this cause of action at trial.

Notes and Discussion

1. ***Buchwald v. Paramount Pictures.*** In 1982, the humorist Art Buchwald pitched a film idea to Paramount Studios, which then entered into an option contract with a standard term giving Buchwald a percentage of the "net profits" if a movie was developed "based upon" Buchwald's idea. The studio abandoned the project in 1985, but in 1987 began work on a different project that resulted in "Coming to America," a highly successful Eddie Murphy vehicle. This film gave story credit to Murphy, but not to Buchwald, who was also not paid. Buchwald sued, and the California Superior Court, in an unpublished decision of 1990, supported his contention that the film was in fact "based upon" Buchwald's idea.

Subsequently the Court turned to examine Paramount's alleged breach of the option contract. Here the case centered on the "net profits" clause. Paramount claimed that although the film had racked up $350 million in ticket sales, it had never made "net profits" because of its development and marketing costs. Creative "Hollywood accounting" had long been ridiculed as a ruse intended to cheat authors of their royalties. The Court found that the clause in Buchwald's contract was unconscionable and that Buchwald was therefore entitled to pursue a separate tort claim against Paramount. The studio appealed, but, evidently fearing the outcome, it settled with Buchwald before the appeal could be argued and decided; as part of the settlement, the unconscionability decision was vacated. For a lively account of this lawsuit, see Pierce O'Donnell and Dennis McDougal, Fatal Subtraction: The Inside Story of Buchwald v. Paramount (2nd ed. 1996), which also reproduces the unpublished Superior Court opinions.

On the face of it, is *Buchwald* distinguishable from *Batfilm*?

2. The Standard Profit Definition. This rather strange concept is investigated in Joseph F. Hart and Philip J. Hacker, *Less Than Zero: Studio Accounting Practices in Hollywood*, available on-line at http://hollywood network.com/Law/Hart/columns/ (footnotes omitted).

"At the heart of these legal disputes is the very meaning of the term *net profit*. Most accountants and business people would define *net profit* as revenue less expenses. Beyond this simple statement, the complexities of certain businesses and the unique nature of various industries demand a special language to explain when revenue is recognized and expenses are incurred. These definitions have been codified by the accounting profession in an information database called *Generally Accepted Accounting Principles* (GAAP).

"In addition to GAAP, the accounting profession has developed unique accounting guidelines dealing with standards for particular industries. One such guideline produced for the motion picture industry is entitled *Financial Accounting Standards Bulletin 53* (FASB 53). This guideline discusses when income from the exploitation of a motion picture is to be recognized as earned and when the cost of producing and distributing a motion picture is recognized as incurred.

"It is somewhat surprising to the layperson, then, to learn that the reports to net-profit participants by studios do *not* follow GAAP or FASB 53. Instead, these rules are disregarded, and the reported net profit follows a complex document which explains the accounting methodology employed by the studio.

"This document generally surfaces as a schedule to the participant's employment agreement containing the studio's *Standard Profit Definition* (SPD)....

"The accounting provisions which are contained in the studios' SPDs make it difficult, if not mathematically impossible in many cases, for net profits ever to be achieved. It may be said in jest, although there is a great deal of truth in the statement, that the studios' SPDs are designed *not* to achieve net profits, and therefore, not to pay any share to profit participants, even though the motion picture may have achieved an economic net profit according to GAAP.

"The fundamental foundation of GAAP is the accrual method of accounting. The accrual method provides that revenue is recognized when it is earned and expenses are recognized when they are incurred. In an SPD, the contract language invariably states that revenue will be recognized when the cash is received and expenses will be recognized when they are incurred. This mismatching of revenue and expenses will delay, possibly forever, the reporting of profits, and will also have a significant impact on the computation of interest, an important element in determining net profit."

What other theories, beyond unconscionability, might a lawyer conceivably employ in attacking a "net profits" clause?

To date, there has been no conclusive appellate decision. Hart and Hacker conclude (footnote omitted): "Whether an appellate court will ever be asked to sort out these issues remains to be seen. As in the Buchwald case, the studios seem intent on settling any dispute out of court before precedent-making law can be issued, and the talent, for the most part, seems willing to go along. So, absent specific direction by an appellate court, disputes over net profits will continue to be resolved between studios and the participants by strenuous and protracted negotiations, and costly and time-consuming litigation."

3. The Net Profits Puzzle. Why have "net profits" clauses been so common in the movie industry despite what might seem to be their palpable absurdity? In *Batfilm*, the Court argues that the plaintiffs should have protected themselves during the contract negotiations. Why wouldn't experienced producers have insisted on a more favorable formula?

An answer is suggested by Victor P. Goldberg, *The Net Profits Puzzle*, 97 Colum. L. Rev. 524, 524 (1997). Goldberg argues: "[A] successful movie will fail to yield net profits only if a 'gross participant' (a major star whose compensation is in part a function of the film's gross receipts) becomes associated with the film. Since the net profits participants typically are associated with the project first, the question becomes: Why would they be willing to sacrifice some (or all) of their contingent compensation when a gross participant is added to the project? The answer is that the net participants are made better off, ex ante, both directly by increasing their expected earnings, and indirectly because the studio is willing to pay for the increased flexibility. Contingent compensation is endemic in the movie industry. Because the inputs for the commercial success of a movie are not all supplied simultaneously, the compensations schemes will be tailored to induce effort at the appropriate time. If the studio-distributor gives up too much of the back-end, it waters down its incentives to market the film effectively. At the same time, giving the net profits participants a share of the back-end sharpens their incentives, both before and after the completion of production. The net profits clause nicely balances these two effects." See now also Victor P. Goldberg, Framing Contract Law: An Economic Perspective 13–36 (2006).

Assuming that Goldberg's explanation is approximately correct, what light does it shed on the unconscionability discussion in *Batfilm*? Would testimony of this type be admissible at trial in order to explain to a judge "the commercial setting, purpose and effect" (§ 2–302(2)) of the Warner Bros. contract with Batfilm?

Chapter 6

REMEDIES

The conventional remedy for breach of contract is damages. In almost all contract cases the damages awarded are called **expectation damages**. This label means that the plaintiffs recover enough money to fulfill their economic expectations for the contract. Put differently, the court is like a genie with the power and intention to carry the plaintiff to the economic place where he would have been had the contract been performed. Now, like almost everything in contract law, that simple statement is not precisely true, for the plaintiff will not usually recover the cost of this trip (his lawyers' fees), and, of course, the genie can lose its way and carry the plaintiff to a place quite unlike the one that he had contracted for.

Understand what is not expectation damages. Expectation damages do not carry the plaintiff back to the starting point—like a tort recovery should. Expectation damages do not give to the plaintiff the money that the defendant was able to earn because he broke the contract. And, by hypothesis, damages are not an order to the defendant to perform the contract—damages are to be contrasted with an order of "specific performance."

The contract literature and the Uniform Commercial Code have formulas to measure expectation damages. For example Professor Farnsworth gives the following general formula: *general measure = loss in value + other loss − cost avoided − loss avoided.* E. Allan Farnsworth, Contracts § 12.9 at 764–768 (4th student ed. 2004). "Loss in value" is the difference in value between what the injured party would have received under the contract and what the party has received. "Other loss" is the injured party's costs arising from the breach, such as costs previously incurred in justified reliance on the contract, or costs associated with arranging substitute performance. "Cost avoided" is what the injured party does not have to pay out as a result of the breach. "Loss avoided" is any savings the injured party may make after the breach.

Consider a variation on Farnsworth's example in which an owner breaches a contract to build a house for $100,000. Assume that the owner breaches after the contractor has purchased $20,000 of materials but has done no other work. Assume that the materials can be returned for $18,000 and that the total cost of the builder's performance would have been $85,000. Here the builder needs $17,000 ($100,000 + $20,-000 − $85,000 − $18,000 = $17,000) to be in the economic position where performance would have put him.

One may find other formulas buried in the UCC text. For example the standard formula for breach of warranty as to goods that the buyer has accepted is: *damage = value as warranted − value as delivered.* If one bought goods for $1,500 and they were worth only $1,200 because of a defect, the formula yields $300. This formula comes from § 2–714; look at it.

The usual damages for buyers of goods or sellers of goods are found in §§ 2–713 and 2–708(1) respectively. In general these formulas direct one to subtract market price from contract price (or vice versa).

Of course all of these formulas obscure many complex issues. What, for example, is the builder's cost of completing of the contract? Just because he says that it would cost him $85,000 to perform the contract does not mean that is so. There may be costs that he did not foresee; there might be labor problems; his foreman might quit or the shingles that he plans to use might not work. And what is the "market" to which 2–708(1) and 2–713 refer? Is it some local retail market or is it wholesale? How does one prove this market when it is not thick and well defined? We should be skeptical of the formulas; they help but not as much as we would like. A formula that one of us uses to test his legal conclusion about damages is to ask the question: If the contract had been performed and not broken, and if all other things are unchanged, how much larger or smaller would plaintiff's wealth be? That difference is the plaintiff's damages.

In rare cases where a plaintiff cannot show what his expectation damages would be, he may recover **reliance damages**. These are the return to the plaintiff of his outlay in performing the contract. Even more rarely a plaintiff might recover **restitution damages**. These are the part of the plaintiff's outlay that actually benefitted the defendant. So a plaintiff's cost of lumber purchased but never used for a contract to build a house could be recovered as reliance damages, and plaintiff's cost of lumber that was installed in defendant's house before defendant broke the contract could be recovered as restitution damages. Since expectation damages include the plaintiff's profit but reliance and restitution damages do not, the plaintiff normally seeks expectation damages, not reliance and not restitution.

Equally rare are contract cases where the court orders the defendant to perform the contract. The general principle of American contract law is stated in § 359(1) of the Restatement 2d (Contracts): "**Specific performance or an injunction** will not be ordered if damages would be adequate to protect the expectation interest of the injured party." (Emphasis added.) Since damages are usually "adequate" at least to approximate plaintiff's loss, this rule bars specific performance in almost all cases. In many contract cases the contract is not like Humpty

Dumpty, it can be put back together; often a contract can still be performed even after it has been breached. Then why not order that performance? Why not give the buyer exactly what he contracted for instead of a money substitute? In many cases even delayed performance might be better than a money substitute. The cases and discussion below give some answers, but at least one of us does not find the arguments against specific performance particularly persuasive.

The cases and the UCC refer to certain subcategories of expectation damages. For example, § 2–715 of the UCC and the famous *Hadley v. Baxendale* case deal with **consequential damages** and the foreseeability requirement. These damages are to be distinguished from an unnamed form of damages that sometimes are called **direct damages**. If, for example, a seller delivered a car that failed to conform to the contract, the buyer could recover the difference in the value of the car as delivered and the value that it would have had if it had been as promised, see § 2–714. These would be direct damages. If the defect in the car caused it to run through the buyer's garage door and destroy the car and the garage, the damage to the car and the garage would be consequential damages and could only be recovered if the plaintiff met the additional test in § 2–715 and *Hadley v. Baxendale*. Why "consequential"? Presumably because these damages are the "consequence" of the breach and not its "direct" result.

This Chapter also deals with the **duty to mitigate**, a byproduct of cancellation. Even an aggrieved party who has properly cancelled because of another's breach, should not sit on his thumbs and so increase the loss that he has suffered. If a seller of natural gas broke its contract with a utility, we expect the utility to find alternative fuel. If it does not make reasonable efforts to find replacement fuel, its damage recovery is reduced by the amount that it would have saved by diligent mitigation. The rule minimizes waste and promotes efficiency.

An important part of the sport in this Chapter is to ask why we find 21st century American law as we do. Why, for example, is specific performance more prevalent in Civil Law than in the Common Law? Why are we hesitant to award consequential damages in contract when they are the fuel that drives the American tort system? Does some unseen law of economics command that a plaintiff get no more than his expectation so that efficient breaches are encouraged?

A. EXPECTATION DAMAGES

The general rule—putting the plaintiff in the same position as if the contract had been performed—is easy to state and, usually, easy to apply. Assume a lawyer with a contract to work for one year for $100,000. If her employer fires her without cause and if she finds work elsewhere for $60,000, her expectation damage is $40,000. Easy. If a seller has a contract to sell oil for $12 million and if the buyer breaches when the available market is $10 million, the seller's loss is $2 million.

And if the buyer of a computer for $4,000 gets a computer that needs a $300 patch to perform as promised, $300 is the appropriate expectation recovery.

One should never dive into the formulas in UCC Article 2 or in the Restatement without first surveying the water. One should always ask first, "How much would performance of the contract increase (or decrease) the plaintiff's wealth?" If the answer to that question is not consistent with the formula, you probably have the wrong formula.

Consider some complications. Sometimes the plaintiff, as in *Freund* below, will not be able to prove that the contract would have increased his wealth by as much as he thinks. If so, he gets only what he can prove, or maybe some less satisfactory proxy.

By contrast, we must respect idiosyncratic tastes, or deviant contracts could never be enforced. Assume that an author of considerable wealth has an eccentric attraction to lavender and that he makes a contract to have his house painted in lavender; assume that painting the house so will reduce its value by $10,000. When the painter who was engaged to paint the house for $8,000 breaks the contract and is replaced with another at $12,000, the author should recover $4,000. Even though the lavender paint will decrease his measurable wealth, the author's contract and his follow through with the subsequent contract tells us that the author's subjective happiness is increased by having a lavender house, and it tells us that he was injured by having to pay $12,000 instead of $8,000.

Assume a lawyer with a one-year employment contract for $100,000 is fired without cause and finds other work right away that pays $60,000. If our lawyer's new job were in an exciting entertainment practice where she had always wanted to be, can we reduce her recovery from $40,000 on the ground that her new psychic wealth offsets some of her economic loss? Having read the author's case, the defendant here can certainly argue that what is good for the goose is good for the gander. But that argument stinks in the mouth of the person who fired her, doesn't it?

And there is trouble in the formulas too. Assume that buyer breaches its contract to buy a 747 from Boeing; Boeing then sells the 747 to another with whom it had a preexisting contract. When Boeing sues, the breaching buyer argues that the damages are zero, namely $200 million (the contract price on the broken contract) minus $210 million (the contract price on the second contract). When you get to the *El Paso Refinery* case, you will see why Boeing should recover its profit despite the formula's answer of zero damages.

In the special case of "consequential" damages, Anglo-American law imposes additional requirements. We see those in *Hadley v. Baxendale* and in Section 2–715 of Article 2. They too are expectation damages.

Note: Expectation Damages and Efficient Breach of Contract

Tom Clancy's first novel, *The Hunt for the Red October*, was originally published by the United States Naval Institute, a non-governmental organization with a relatively small press publishing mainly scholarly books related to naval history and warfare. Of course, the book was a runaway bestseller. In September, 1984, the Naval Institute arranged with Berkley Publishing Group for a mass paperback edition to be issued "not sooner than October 1985." In clear breach of its contract, Berkley brought out the paperback two weeks early, and it immediately shot to the top of the paperback bestseller list. The consequence, of course, was a steep drop in sales of the Naval Institute's hardbound edition. The Naval Institute then brought suit seeking disgorgement of "all of Berkley's profits from pre-October 1985 sales of the Book; it estimated those profits at $724,300." *United States Naval Inst. v. Charter Communications, Inc.,* 936 F.2d 692, 693–694 (2nd Cir. 1991).

What the Naval Institute eventually received was a much lower amount: $35,380.50, its estimated loss in profits from hardbound sales—that is, its actual damages as a consequence of the breach. As the Court comments, "While on occasion the defendant's profits are used as the measure of damages ... , this generally occurs when those profits tend to define the plaintiff's loss, for an award of the defendant's profits where they greatly exceed the plaintiff's loss and there has been no tortious conduct on the part of the defendant would tend to be punitive, and punitive awards are not part of the law of contract damages. See generally Restatement (Second) of Contracts § 356 comment a ('The central objective behind the system of contract remedies is compensatory, not punitive.'); id. comment b (agreement attempting to fix damages in amount vastly greater than what approximates actual loss would be unenforceable as imposing a penalty); id. § 355 (punitive damages not recoverable for breach of contract unless conduct constituting the breach is also a tort for which such damages are recoverable)." Id. at 696–697 (some citations omitted).[1]

Now imagine that you are Berkley's lawyer in mid-Summer, 1985, advising your client on the implications of breaching its contract by issuing the paperback early. Contract law gives you a basis for estimating the cost of breaching: the damages payable to the Naval Institute. Shouldn't you advise Berkley that if their anticipated financial gain from the breach is greater than the damages payable (including possible litigation costs), then the law not only enables them to breach but in effect actually encourages them to do so? That is, despite all the pious words with which judges praise the sanctity of solemn agreements, the law ignores these high moral considerations when it comes to evaluating actual contract breaches.

Although, as we shall see, contract law's position is more nuanced than this, there is a considerable element of truth in the view just stated. What explains why our law is not more assertive in deterring breaches of contract?

The leading modern explanation passes under the rubric "efficient breach of contract," a term that became popular through the writings of Professor (now Judge) Richard Posner. He sets out the basic idea by means

1. For a good study of the limited exceptions to the rule preventing contract plaintiffs from obtaining disgorgement, see E. Allan Farnsworth, *Your Loss or My Gain? The Dilemma of the Disgorgement Principle in Breach of Contract Cases*, 94 Yale L.J. 1339 (1985). See also Melvin A. Eisenberg, *The Disgorgement Interest in Contract Law*, 105 Michigan L.R. 559 (2006).

of an example: "In many cases it is uneconomical to induce completion of performance of a contract after it has been broken. I agree to purchase 100,000 widgets custom-ground for use as components in a machine that I manufacture. After I have taken delivery of 10,000, the market for my machine collapses. I promptly notify my supplier that I am terminating the contract, and admit that my termination is a breach. When notified of the termination he has not yet begun the custom grinding of the other 90,000 widgets, but he informs me that he intends to complete his performance under the contract and bill me accordingly. The custom-ground widgets have no use other than in my machine, and a negligible scrap value. To give the supplier a remedy that induced him to complete the contract after the breach would waste resources. The law is alert to this danger and, under the doctrine of mitigation of damages, would not give the supplier damages for any costs he incurred in continuing production after notice of termination....

"In [this example] the breach was committed only to avert a larger loss. But in some cases a party is tempted to break his contract simply because his profit from breach would exceed his profit from completing performance. He will do so if the profit would also exceed the expected profit to the other party from completion of the contract, and hence the damages from breach. So in this case awarding damages will not deter a breach of contract. It should not. It is an efficient breach. Suppose I sign a contract to deliver 100,000 custom-ground widgets at 10¢ apiece to A for use in his boiler factory. After I have delivered 10,000, B comes to me, explains that he desperately needs 25,000 custom-ground widgets at once since otherwise he will be forced to close his pianola factory at great cost, and offers me 15¢ apiece for them. I sell him the widgets and as a result do not complete timely delivery to A, causing him to lose $1,000 in profits. Having obtained an additional profit of $1,250 on the sale to B, I am better off even after reimbursing A for his loss, and B is also better off. The breach is therefore Pareto superior.[2] True, had I refused to sell to B he could have gone to A and negotiated an assignment to him of part of A's contract with me. But this would have introduced an additional step, with additional transaction costs—and high ones, because it would be a bilateral-monopoly negotiation." Richard A. Posner, Economic Analysis of Law 119–120 (7th ed. 2007).

This is the theory of efficient breach. The underlying thought is that when a breach of contract is truly efficient, law should not discourage the breach. Although judges today occasionally refer to efficient breach theory, it is not actually a legal doctrine, nor part of our law.[3] The law of contract damages does not try to distinguish between breaches that are thought to be

2. [Eds.: A allocation or reallocation of resources is "Pareto superior" if achieving it means that at least one person is made better off and no one is made worse off. In Posner's hypothetical, I (as the seller) and B are both better off as a result of the breach, and A is not worse off after he receives compensatory damages. The concept of Pareto superiority comes from Vilfredo Pareto, an Italian political economist (1848–1923) best known for applying mathematics to economic analysis.]

3. See, as to this, Craig S. Warkol, *Resolving the Paradox Between Legal Theory and Legal Fact: The Judicial Rejection of the Theory of Efficient Breach*, 20 Cardozo L. Rev. 321 (1998). More optimistic is Nathan B. Oman, *The Failure of Economic Interpretations of the Law of Contract Damages,* 64 Washington & Lee L. Rev. (forthcoming, 2007).

efficient and those that are not. Rather, the theory of efficient breach is intended to provide a broad intellectual justification for why our law takes the position that it does regarding the consequences of a breach of contract.

As we will see in this chapter, there are many reasons to be doubtful about the theory of efficient breach, both in general and as it applies to individual cases. For present purposes, however, it suffices to keep in mind three broad issues:

First, the theory points up the importance of a potential breacher being able to calculate, with considerable accuracy, the profit that would stem from a breach; for only then can the breacher know whether the breach will, in fact, be efficient. But to the extent that legal rules make such an estimate difficult—for example, by providing alternative measures of relief that the injured party can choose among—efficient breaches may be deterred.

Second, the theory assumes that the injured party can be fully compensated for the breach, and hence is held harmless by the law; otherwise, the outcome will not be Pareto superior because the injured party will be worse off. This assumption is, however, questionable. To give just one example, if because of the breach the injured party is obliged to sue, it will normally have to pay its own legal expenses—often, a "transaction cost" that may substantially undermine the worth of the eventual award.

Third, the real crux of the theory is that, as between the breaching party and the victim, the breaching party gets to keep the entire gain from the more efficient allocation of resources. Posner makes an attempt to justify this outcome at the end of the quoted passage, arguing, in brief, that the breaching party will then have the maximum incentive to breach efficiently. But this issue requires some additional thought, particularly in relation to the alternative remedy of specific performance.

There are many other subtleties, but for now keep your eye on these three central issues: whether contract damages can be precisely estimated in advance of a breach; whether our law fully compensates the victim of a breach; and whether the breaching party should receive the entire profit from the breach. At the end of the day, it is hard to tell whether efficient breach theory has much real practical value. For instance, it is hard even to know whether, if contract law operated exactly as Posner wants it to, the real economic gains in efficiency would be meaningful. But efficient breach theory does at least have the virtue of bringing certain crucial issues into the center of our discussion.

On efficient breach theory, see recently Stephen A. Smith, Contract Theory 108–136 (2004), summarizing earlier debate.

FREUND v. WASHINGTON SQUARE PRESS, INC.

Court of Appeals of New York, 1974.
34 N.Y.2d 379, 314 N.E.2d 419, 357 N.Y.S.2d 857.

RABIN, J. In this action for breach of a publishing contract, we must decide what damages are recoverable for defendant's failure to publish plaintiff's manuscript. In 1965, plaintiff, an author and a college teacher, and defendant, Washington Square Press, Inc., entered into a written agreement which, in relevant part, provided as follows. Plaintiff ("author") granted defendant ("publisher") exclusive rights to publish and sell in book form plaintiff's work on modern drama. Upon plaintiff's delivery of the manuscript, defendant agreed to complete payment of a nonreturnable $2,000 "advance." Thereafter, if defendant deemed the manuscript not "suitable for publication", it had the right to terminate the agreement by written notice within 60 days of delivery. Unless so terminated, defendant agreed to publish the work in hardbound edition within 18 months and afterwards in paperbound edition. The contract further provided that defendant would pay royalties to plaintiff, based upon specified percentages of sales. (For example, plaintiff was to receive 10% of the retail price of the first 10,000 copies sold in the continental United States.) If defendant failed to publish within 18 months, the contract provided that "this agreement shall terminate and the rights herein granted to the Publisher shall revert to the Author. In such event all payments theretofore made to the Author shall belong to the Author without prejudice to any other remedies which the Author may have." . . .

Plaintiff performed by delivering his manuscript to defendant and was paid his $2,000 advance. Defendant thereafter merged with another publisher and ceased publishing in hardbound. Although defendant did not exercise its 60-day right to terminate, it has refused to publish the manuscript in any form.

Plaintiff ... initially sought specific performance of the contract. The Trial Term Justice denied specific performance but, finding a valid contract and a breach by defendant, set the matter down for trial on the issue of monetary damages, if any, sustained by the plaintiff. At trial, plaintiff sought to prove: (1) delay of his academic promotion; (2) loss of royalties which would have been earned; and (3) the cost of publication if plaintiff had made his own arrangements to publish. The trial court found that plaintiff had been promoted despite defendant's failure to publish, and that there was no evidence that the breach had caused any delay. Recovery of lost royalties was denied without discussion. The court found, however, that the cost of hardcover publication to plaintiff was the natural and probable consequence of the breach and, based upon expert testimony, awarded $10,000 to cover this cost. It denied recovery of the expenses of paperbound publication on the ground that plaintiff's proof was conjectural. The Appellate Division, (3 to 2) affirmed, finding that the cost of publication was the proper measure of damages. In support of its conclusion, the majority analogized to the construction contract situation where the cost of completion may be the proper measure of damages for a builder's failure to complete a house or for use of wrong materials. The dissent concluded that the cost of publication is not an appropriate measure of damages and consequently, that plaintiff may recover nominal damages only.[4] We agree with the dissent. In so

4. Plaintiff does not challenge the trial court's denial of damages for delay in promotion or for anticipated royalties.

concluding, we look to the basic purpose of damage recovery and the nature and effect of the parties' contract.

It is axiomatic that, except where punitive damages are allowable, the law awards damages for breach of contract to compensate for injury caused by the breach—injury which was foreseeable, i.e., reasonably within the contemplation of the parties, at the time the contract was entered into. *Swain v. Schieffelin*, 134 N.Y. 471, 473 (1892). Money damages are substitutional relief designed in theory "to put the injured party in as good a position as he would have been put by full performance of the contract, at the least cost to the defendant and without charging him with harms that he had no sufficient reason to foresee when he made the contract." (5 Corbin, Contracts, § 1002, pp. 31–32; 11 Williston, Contracts [3d ed.], § 1338, p. 198.) In other words, so far as possible, the law attempts to secure to the injured party the benefit of his bargain, subject to the limitations that the injury—whether it be losses suffered or gains prevented—was foreseeable, and that the amount of damages claimed be measurable with a reasonable degree of certainty and, of course, adequately proven. (See, generally, Dobbs, Law of Remedies, p. 148; see, also, Farnsworth, Legal Remedies for Breach of Contract, 70 Col. L. Rev. 1145, 1159.) But it is equally fundamental that the injured party should not recover more from the breach than he would have gained had the contract been fully performed. (*Baker v. Drake*, 53 N.Y. 211, 217 (1873); see, generally, Dobbs, Law of Remedies, p. 810.)

Measurement of damages in this case according to the cost of publication to the plaintiff would confer greater advantage than performance of the contract would have entailed to plaintiff and would place him in a far better position than he would have occupied had the defendant fully performed. Such measurement bears no relation to compensation for plaintiff's actual loss or anticipated profit. Far beyond compensating plaintiff for the interests he had in the defendant's performance of the contract—whether restitution, reliance or expectation (see Fuller & Perdue, Reliance Interest in Contract Damages, 46 Yale L.J. 52, 53–56) an award of the cost of publication would enrich plaintiff at defendant's expense.

Pursuant to the contract, plaintiff delivered his manuscript to the defendant. In doing so, he conferred a value on the defendant which, upon defendant's breach, was required to be restored to him. Special Term, in addition to ordering a trial on the issue of damages, ordered defendant to return the manuscript to plaintiff and plaintiff's restitution interest in the contract was thereby protected. (Cf. 5 Corbin, Contracts, § 996, p. 15.)

[Eds.: Plaintiff made no claim for reliance damages, and thus none are awarded.]

As for plaintiff's expectation interest in the contract, it was basically two-fold—the "advance" and the royalties. (To be sure, plaintiff may have expected to enjoy whatever notoriety, prestige or other benefits that might have attended publication, but even if these expectations were compensable, plaintiff did not attempt at trial to place a monetary value on them.) There is no dispute that plaintiff's expectancy in the "advance" was fulfilled—he has received his $2,000. His expectancy interest in the royalties—the profit he stood to gain from sale of the published book—while theoretically compensable, was speculative. Although this work is not plaintiff's first, at trial he provided no stable foundation for a reasonable estimate of royalties he would have earned had defendant not breached its promise to publish. In these circumstances, his claim for royalties falls for uncertainty. (*Cf. Broadway Photoplay Co. v. World Film Corp.*, 225 N.Y. 104 (1919); *Hewlett v. Caplin*, 275 App. Div. 797 (S.C. N.Y. 1949).)

Since the damages which would have compensated plaintiff for anticipated royalties were not proved with the required certainty, we agree with the dissent in the Appellate Division that nominal damages alone are recoverable. (*Cf. Manhattan Sav. Inst. v. Gottfried Baking Co.*, 286 N.Y. 398 (1941).) Though these are damages in name only and not at all compensatory, they are nevertheless awarded as a formal vindication of plaintiff's legal right to compensation which has not been given a sufficiently certain monetary valuation. (*Cf. Baker v. Hart*, 123 N.Y. 470, 474 (1890); *see, generally*, Dobbs, Law of Remedies, p. 191; 11 Williston, Contracts [3d ed.], § 1339A, pp. 206–208.)

In our view, the analogy by the majority in the Appellate Division to the construction contract situation was inapposite. In the typical construction contract, the owner agrees to pay money or other consideration to a builder and expects, under the contract, to receive a completed building in return. The value of the promised performance to the owner is the properly constructed building. In this case, unlike the typical construction contract, the value to plaintiff of the promised performance—publication—was a percentage of sales of the books published and not the books themselves. Had the plaintiff contracted for the printing, binding and delivery of a number of hardbound copies of his manuscript, to be sold or disposed of as he wished, then perhaps the construction analogy, and measurement of damages by the cost of replacement or completion, would have some application.

Here, however, the specific value to plaintiff of the promised publication was the royalties he stood to receive from defendant's sales of the published book. Essentially, publication represented what it would have cost the defendant to confer that value upon the plaintiff, and, by its breach defendant saved that cost. The error by the courts below was in measuring damages not by the value to plaintiff of the promised performance but by the cost of that performance to defendant. Damages are not measured, however, by what the defaulting party saved by the breach, but by the natural and probable consequences of the breach *to the plaintiff*. In this case, the consequence to plaintiff of defendant's failure to publish is that he is prevented from realizing the gains promised by the contract—the royalties. But, as we have stated, the amount of royalties plaintiff would have realized was not ascertained with adequate certainty and, as a consequence, plaintiff may recover nominal damages only.

Accordingly, the order of the Appellate Division should be modified to the extent of reducing the damage award of $10,000 for the cost of publication to six cents, but with costs and disbursements to the plaintiff.

Order modified, with costs and disbursements to plaintiff-respondent, in accordance with opinion herein and, as so modified, affirmed.

Notes and Discussion

1. **The Lower Court's Reasoning.** The majority below had decided in favor of Freund on the following reasoning: "Is a nonrefundable advance plus nominal damages all that the author may be entitled to or may an author claim an ascertainable aspect of damage for a breach as any other breach in any other field of law would entail?

"There may be an 'impossibility of determining a work's value until it has been exploited.' ... However, here the publisher by the terms of the agreement has acknowledged the possibility of a claim ... which should at least put the author in the position, similar to that of any other business contractee, that he would have been in had the defendant abided by its agreement ...

"Assume this was a construction contract and the defendant builder failed to complete the house or used the wrong materials. 'It is true that in most cases the cost of replacement is the measure ... The owner is entitled to the money which will permit him to complete, unless the cost of completion is grossly and unfairly out of proportion to the good to be attained. When that is true, the measure is the difference in value.' (*Jacob & Youngs v. Kent*, 230 N.Y. 239, 244 [Cardozo, J., 1921]). . . .

"It is contended that the author by this decision is more than made whole, because he keeps his advance against royalties and receives the cost of publishing and then, if he does publish, and owns the books, he can sell them and gain an additional profit. This is not a valid argument.

" 'Under statutory sales law, however, the reseller need not account to the defaulting buyer for any profits over and above the seller's claim.' (The Manufacturer's Right to Resell Patented and Copyrighted Goods by John A. Friedman, 38 N. Y. U. Law Rev. 948, 966 [1963].)" *Freund v. Washington Square Press, Inc.*, 41 A.D.2d 371, 343 N.Y.S.2d 401, 403–404 (App. Div. 1973).

2. **Certainty.** The Court holds that Freund's expected royalties from sale of the book are "speculative" since "at trial he provided no stable foundation for a reasonable estimate" of them. As a general rule, "Damages are not recoverable for loss beyond an amount that the evidence permits to be established with reasonable certainty": Restatement 2d § 352. However, courts today enforce this rule with some leniency. For example, in the *Hunt for the Red October* case discussed above, the Naval Institute would have had a hard time determining exactly its lost sales for September, but the trial court had allowed it to project from August sales. In upholding this projec-

tion, the Second Circuit observes: "Though there was no proof as to precisely what the unimpeded volume of hardcover sales would have been for the entire month of September, any such evidence would necessarily have been hypothetical. But it is not error to lay the normal uncertainty in such hypotheses at the door of the wrongdoer who altered the proper course of events, instead of at the door of the injured party." *United States Naval Inst.*, 936 F.2d at 697. The *Freund* decision may be too demanding in this respect, especially granted the plaintiff's prior publications and the press's likely experience with other scholarly books. Numerous cases hold that the certainty requirement is relaxed if a breach is "willful." See, for instance, *Locke v. United States*, 283 F.2d 521, 524 (Ct. Cl. 1960) ("The defendant who has wrongfully broken a contract should not be permitted to reap advantage from his own wrong by insisting on proof which by reason of his breach is unobtainable.").

Assuming that Freund's damages are too indefinite, that fact should possibly influence his ability to obtain specific performance or cost of performance. See below, *Walgreen Co. v. Sara Creek Property Co.*, for a discussion. The certainty rule can cut especially sharply in the case of new businesses that do not have a track record as to profits, although courts often find ingenious ways to estimate profits indirectly. Can you think of some such ways?

Had Freund foreseen the possibility that he might receive only nominal damages for a breach, how might he better have protected himself in the contract?

3. An Efficient Breach? Washington Square Press evidently made a business decision to stop publishing hardbound books, with Freund's book one casualty of the decision. The Court declines to use the publisher's saved cost (by not printing the book) to measure the damages. The case thus illustrates one of the standard rules about contract damages, namely they are not to be measured by the gain that the breacher enjoyed. If the breacher's gain were the measure, the law would foreclose efficient breaches. Do you see why?

Suppose that, after the original publisher had broken its contract, Freund had paid another publisher $11,000 to do a private printing of the book, and that he had then sued to recover this amount. Would the outcome be different? (It should be noted that Philip Freund, a distinguished author and literary critic, eventually decided not to publish this book elsewhere, since another book on the subject had appeared in the interim.)

Problem 6–1

Contractor agrees to build a house on plaintiffs' lot for a total price of $250,000. After contractor has completed about one fifth of the work but before buyer has paid anything, contractor defaults. Buyer hires another contractor who completes the work for $300,000. Buyer sues the first contractor for $50,000.

Defendant contractor makes the following arguments:

1. I get a credit, or about $50,000, for the work I did, and so no damages are due.

2. When completed, the house enhanced the value of the lot by $450,000, therefore I owe no damages.

3. The proper measure of damages is Market Price less Contract Price, not Replacement Contract Price less Contract Price. Since the going market for the contracted work (after I had done one fifth) would have been only $210,000, I owe no damages and, in fact, the buyer owes me about $40,000 in restitution for work I did for which I was never paid.

Which of these arguments may work?

PEEVYHOUSE v. GARLAND COAL MINING CO.

Supreme Court of Oklahoma, 1962.
382 P.2d 109.

JACKSON, Justice. In the trial court, plaintiffs Willie and Lucille Peevyhouse sued the defendant, Garland Coal and Mining Company, for damages for breach of contract. Judgment was for plaintiffs in an amount considerably less than was sued for. Plaintiffs appeal and defendant cross-appeals. . . .

Briefly stated, the facts are as follows: plaintiffs owned a farm containing coal deposits, and in November, 1954, leased the premises to defendant for a period of five years for coal mining purposes. A 'strip-mining' operation was contemplated in which the coal would be taken from pits on the surface of the ground, instead of from underground mine shafts. In addition to the usual covenants found in a coal-mining lease, defendant specifically agreed to perform certain restorative and remedial work at the end of the lease period. It is unnecessary to set out the details of the work to be done, other than to say that it would involve the moving of many thousands of cubic yards of dirt, at a cost estimated by expert witnesses at about $29,000.00. However, plaintiffs sued for only $25,000.00.

During the trial, it was stipulated that all covenants and agreements in the lease contract had been fully carried out by both parties, except the remedial work mentioned above; defendant conceded that this work had not been done.

Plaintiffs introduced expert testimony as to the amount and nature of the work to be done, and its estimated cost. Over plaintiffs' objections, defendant thereafter introduced expert testimony as to the "diminution in value" of plaintiffs' farm resulting from the failure of defendant to render performance as agreed in the contract—that is, the difference between the present value of the farm, and what its value would have been if defendant had done what it agreed to do.

At the conclusion of the trial, the court instructed the jury that it must return a verdict for plaintiffs, and left the amount of damages for jury determination. On the measure of damages, the court instructed the jury that it might consider the cost of performance of the work defendant agreed to do, "together with all of the evidence offered on behalf of either party".

It thus appears that the jury was at liberty to consider the "diminution in value" of plaintiffs' farm as well as the cost of "repair work" in determining the amount of damages.

It returned a verdict for plaintiffs for $5,000.00—only a fraction of the "cost of performance", *but more than the total value of the farm even after the remedial work is done.*

On appeal, the issue is sharply drawn. Plaintiffs contend that the true measure of damages in this case is what it will cost plaintiffs to obtain performance of the work that was not done because of defendant's default. Defendant argues that the measure of damages is the cost of performance "limited, however, to the total difference in the market value before and after the work was performed".

It appears that this precise question has not heretofore been presented to this court. In *Ardizonne v. Archer*, 72 Okl. 70, 178 P. 263, this court held that the measure of damages for breach of a contract to drill an oil well was the reasonable cost of drilling the well, but here a slightly different factual situation exists. The drilling of an oil well will yield valuable geological information, even if no oil or gas is found, and of course if the well is a producer, the value of the premises increases. In the case before us, it is argued by defendant with some force that the performance of the remedial work defendant agreed to do will add at the most only a few hundred dollars to the value of plaintiffs' farm, and that the damages should be limited to that amount because that is all plaintiffs have lost.

Plaintiffs rely on *Groves v. John Wunder Co.*, 205 Minn. 163, 286 N.W. 235, 123 A.L.R. 502. In that case, the Minnesota court, in a substantially similar situation, adopted the "cost of performance" rule as-opposed to the "value" rule. The result was to authorize a jury to give plaintiff damages in the amount of $60,000, where the real estate concerned would have been worth only $12,160, even if the work contracted for had been done.

It may be observed that *Groves v. John Wunder Co.*, supra, is the only case which has come to our attention in which the cost of performance rule has been followed under circumstances where the cost of performance greatly exceeded the diminution in value resulting from the breach of contract. Incidentally, it appears that this case was decided by a plurality rather than a majority of the members of the court.

Defendant relies principally upon *Sandy Valley & E. R. Co. v. Hughes*, 175 Ky. 320, 194 S.W. 344; *Bigham v. Wabash-Pittsburg Terminal Ry. Co.*, 223 Pa. 106, 72 A. 318; and *Sweeney v. Lewis Const. Co.*, 66 Wash. 490, 119 P. 1108. These were all cases in which, under similar circumstances, the appellate courts followed the "value" rule instead of the "cost of performance" rule. Plaintiff points out that in the earliest of these cases (*Bigham*) the court cites as authority on the measure of damages an earlier Pennsylvania tort case, and that the other two cases follow the first, with no explanation as to why a measure of damages ordinarily followed in cases sounding in tort should be used in contract cases. Nevertheless, it is of some significance that three out of four appellate courts have followed the diminution in value rule under circumstances where, as here, the cost of performance greatly exceeds the diminution in value.

The explanation may be found in the fact that the situations presented are artificial ones. It is highly unlikely that the ordinary property owner would agree to pay $29,000 (or its equivalent) for the construction of "improvements" upon his property that would increase its value only about ($300) three hundred dollars. The result is that we are called upon to apply principles of law theoretically based upon reason and reality to a situation which is basically unreasonable and unrealistic.

In *Groves v. John Wunder Co.,* supra, in arriving at its conclusions, the Minnesota court apparently considered the contract involved to be analogous to a building and construction contract, and cited authority for the proposition that the cost of performance or completion of the building as contracted is ordinarily the measure of damages in actions for damages for the breach of such a contract.

In an annotation following the Minnesota case beginning at 123 A.L.R. 515, the annotator places the three cases relied on by defendant (*Sandy Valley*, *Bigham* and *Sweeney*) under the classification of cases involving "grading and excavation contracts".

We do not think either analogy is strictly applicable to the case now before us. The primary purpose of the lease contract between plaintiffs and defendant was neither "building and construction" nor "grading and excavation". It was merely to accomplish the economical recovery and marketing of coal from the premises, to the profit of all parties. The special provisions of the lease contract pertaining to remedial work were incidental to the main object involved.

Even in the case of contracts that are unquestionably building and construction contracts, the authorities are not in agreement as to the factors to be considered in determining whether the cost of performance rule or the value rule should be applied. The American Law Institute's Restatement of the Law, Contracts, Volume 1, Sections 346(1)(a)(i) and (ii) submits the proposition that the cost of performance is the proper measure of damages "if this is possible and does not involve unreasonable economic waste"; and that the diminution in value caused by the breach is the proper measure "if construction and completion in accordance with the contract would involve *unreasonable economic waste*". (Emphasis supplied.) In an explanatory comment immediately following the text, the Restatement makes it clear that the "economic waste" referred to consists of the destruction of a substantially completed building or other structure. Of course no such destruction is involved in the case now before us.

On the other hand, in McCormick, Damages, Section 168, it is said with regard to building and construction contracts that "... in cases where the defect is one that can be repaired or cured without *undue expense*" the cost of performance is the proper measure of damages, but where "... the defect in material or construction is one that cannot be remedied without *an expenditure for reconstruction disproportionate to the end to be attained*" (emphasis supplied) the value rule should be followed. The same idea was expressed in *Jacob & Youngs, Inc. v. Kent,* 230 N.Y. 239, 129 N.E. 889, 23 A.L.R. 1429, as follows: "The owner is entitled to the money which will permit him to complete, unless the cost of completion is grossly and unfairly out of proportion to the good to be attained. When that is true, the measure is the difference in value."

It thus appears that the prime consideration in the Restatement was "economic waste"; and that the prime consideration in McCormick, Damages, and in *Jacob & Youngs, Inc. v. Kent*, supra, was the relationship between the expense involved and the "end to be attained"—in other words, the "relative economic benefit".

In view of the unrealistic fact situation in the instant case, and certain Oklahoma statutes to be hereinafter noted, we are of the opinion that the 'relative economic benefit' is a proper consideration here. This is in accord with the recent case of where, in applying the cost rule, the Virginia court specifically noted *Mann v. Clowser*, 190 Va. 887, 59 S.E.2d 78, that "... the defects are remediable from a practical standpoint and the costs *are not grossly disproportionate to the results to be obtained*" (Emphasis supplied)

23 O.S.1961 §§ 96 and 97 provide as follows:

> § 96. ... Notwithstanding the provisions of this chapter, no person can recover a greater amount in damages for the breach of an obligation, than he would have gained by the full performance thereof on both sides....
>
> § 97. ... Damages must, in all cases, be reasonable, and where an obligation of any kind appears to create a right to unconscionable and grossly oppressive damages, contrary to substantial justice no more than reasonable damages can be recovered.

Although it is true that the above sections of the statute are applied most often in tort cases, they are by their own terms, and the decisions of this court, also applicable in actions for damages for breach of contract. It would seem that they are peculiarly applicable here where, under the "cost of performance" rule, plaintiffs might recover an amount about nine times the total value of their farm. Such would seem to be "unconscionable and grossly oppressive damages, contrary to substantial justice" within the meaning of the statute. Also, it can hardly be denied that if plaintiffs here are permitted to recover under the "cost of performance" rule, they will receive a greater benefit from the breach than could be gained from full performance, contrary to the provisions of Sec. 96.

An analogy may be drawn between the cited sections, and the provisions of 15 O.S. 1961 §§ 214 and 215. These sections tend to render void any provisions of a contract which attempt to fix the amount of stipulated damages to be paid in case of a breach, except where it is impracticable or extremely difficult to determine the actual damages. This results in spite of the agreement of the parties, and the obvious and well known rationale is that insofar as they exceed the actual damages suffered, the stipulated damages amount to a penalty or forfeiture which the law does not favor.

23 O.S.1961 §§ 96 and 97 have the same effect in the case now before us. *In spite of the agreement of the parties*, these sections limit the damages recoverable to a reasonable amount not "contrary to substantial justice"; they prevent plaintiffs from recovering a "greater amount in damages for the breach of an obligation" than they would have "gained by the full performance thereof".

We therefore hold that where, in a coal mining lease, lessee agrees to perform certain remedial work on the premises concerned at the end of the lease period, and thereafter the contract is fully performed by both parties except that the remedial work is not done, the measure of damages in an action by lessor against lessee for damages for breach of contract is ordinarily the reasonable cost of performance of the work; however, where the contract provision breached was merely incidental to the main purpose in view, and where the economic benefit which would result to lessor by full performance of the work is grossly disproportionate to the cost of performance, the damages which lessor may recover are limited to the diminution in value resulting to the premises because of the non-performance.

We believe the above holding is in conformity with the intention of the Legislature as expressed in the statutes mentioned, and in harmony with the better-reasoned cases from the other jurisdictions where analogous fact situations have been considered. It should be noted that the rule as stated does not interfere with the property owner's right to "do what he will with his own" (*Chamberlain v. Parker*, 45 N.Y. 569), or his right, if he chooses, to contract for "improvements" which will actually have the effect of reducing his property's value. Where such result is in fact contemplated by the parties, and is a main or principal purpose of those contracting, it would seem that the measure of damages for breach would ordinarily be the cost of performance.

The above holding disposes of all of the arguments raised by the parties on appeal.

Under the most liberal view of the evidence herein, the diminution in value resulting to the premises because of non-performance of the remedial work was $300.00. After a careful search of the record, we have found no evidence of a higher figure, and plaintiffs do not argue in their briefs that a greater diminution in value was sustained. It thus appears that the judgment was clearly excessive, and that the amount for which judgment should have been rendered is definitely and satisfactorily shown by the record.

We are asked by each party to modify the judgment in accordance with the respective theories advanced, and it is conceded that we have authority to do so. 12 O.S.1961 § 952; *Busboom v. Smith*, 199 Okl. 688, 191 P.2d 198; *Stumpf v. Stumpf*, 173 Okl. 1, 46 P.2d 315.

We are of the opinion that the judgment of the trial court for plaintiffs should be, and it is hereby, modified and reduced to the sum of $300.00, and as so modified it is affirmed.

IRWIN, J. (DISSENTING). By the specific provisions in the coal mining lease under consideration, the defendant agreed as follows:

> '7b Lessee agrees to make fills in the pits dug on said premises on the property line in such manner that fences can be placed thereon and access had to opposite sides of the pits.
>
> '7c Lessee agrees to smooth off the top of the spoil banks on the above premises.
>
> '7d Lessee agrees to leave the creek crossing the above premises in such a condition that it will not interfere with the crossings to be made in pits as set out in 7b.
>
> '7f Lessee further agrees to leave no shale or dirt on the high wall of said pits. * * * '

Following the expiration of the lease, plaintiffs made demand upon defendant that it carry out the provisions of the contract and to perform those covenants contained therein.

Defendant admits that it failed to perform its obligations that it agreed and contracted to perform under the lease contract and there is nothing in the record which indicates that defendant could not perform its obligations. Therefore, in my opinion defendant's breach of the contract was willful and not in good faith.

Although the contract speaks for itself, there were several negotiations between the plaintiffs and defendant before the contract was executed. Defendant admitted in the trial of the action, that plaintiffs insisted that the above provisions be included in the contract and that they would not agree to the coal mining lease unless the above provisions were included.

In consideration for the lease contract, plaintiffs were to receive a certain amount as royalty for the coal produced and marketed and in addition thereto their land was to be restored as provided in the contract.

Defendant received as consideration for the contract, its proportionate share of the coal produced and marketed and in addition thereto, the *right to use* plaintiffs' land in the furtherance of its mining operations.

The cost for performing the contract in question could have been reasonably approximated when the contract was negotiated and executed and there are no conditions now existing which could not have been reasonably anticipated by the parties. Therefore, defendant had knowledge, when it prevailed upon the plaintiffs to execute the lease, that the cost of performance might be disproportionate to the value or benefits received by plaintiff for the performance.

Defendant has received its benefits under the contract and now urges, in substance, that plaintiffs' measure of damages for its failure to perform should be the economic value of performance to the plaintiffs and not the cost of performance.

If a peculiar set of facts should exist where the above rule should be applied as the proper measure of damages, (and in my judgment those facts do not exist in the instant case) before such rule should be applied, consideration should be given to the benefits received or contracted for by the party who asserts the application of the rule.

Defendant did not have the right to mine plaintiffs' coal or to use plaintiffs' property for its mining operations without the consent of plaintiffs. Defendant had knowledge of the benefits that it would receive under the contract and the approximate cost of performing the contract. With this knowledge, it must be presumed that defendant thought that it would be to its economic advantage to enter into the contract with plaintiffs and that it would reap benefits from the contract, or it would have not entered into the contract.

Therefore, if the value of the performance of a contract should be considered in determining the measure of damages for breach of a contract, the value of the benefits received under the contract by a party who breaches a contract should also be considered. However, in my judgment, to give consideration to either in the instant action, completely rescinds and holds for naught the solemnity of the contract before us and makes an entirely new contract for the parties.

In *Goble v. Bell Oil & Gas Co.*, 97 Okl. 261, 223 P. 371, we held: "Even though the contract contains harsh and burdensome terms which the court does not in all respects approve, it is the province of the parties in relation to lawful subject matter to fix their rights and obligations, and the court will give the contract effect according to its expressed provisions, unless it be shown by competent evidence proof that the written agreement as executed is the result of fraud, mistake, or accident."

In *Cities Service Oil Co. v. Geolograph Co.*, Inc., 208 Okl. 179, 254 P.2d 775, we said: "While we do not agree that the contract as presently written is an onerous one, we think the short answer is that the folly or wisdom of a contract is not for the court to pass on."

In *Great Western Oil & Gas Company v. Mitchell*, Okl., 326 P.2d 794, we held: "The law will not make a better contract for parties than they themselves have seen fit to enter into, or alter it for the benefit of one party and to the detriment of the others; the judicial function of a court of law is to enforce a contract as it is written."

I am mindful of Title 23 O.S.1961 § 96, which provides that no person can recover a greater amount in damages for the breach of an obligation than he could have gained by the full performance thereof on both sides, except in cases not applicable herein. However, in my judgment, the above statutory provision is not applicable here.

In my judgment, we should follow the case of *Groves v. John Wunder Company*, 205 Minn. 163, 286 N.W. 235, 123 A.L.R. 502, which defendant agrees "that the fact situation is apparently similar to the one in the case at bar", and where the Supreme Court of Minnesota held: "The owner's or employer's damages for such a breach (i. e. breach hypothesized in 2d syllabus) are to be measured, not in respect to the value of the land to be improved, but by the reasonable cost of doing that which the contractor promised to do and which he left undone."

The hypothesized breach referred to states that where the contractor's breach of a contract is willful, that is, in bad faith, he is not entitled to any benefit of the equitable doctrine of substantial performance.

In the instant action defendant has made no attempt to even substantially perform. The contract in question is not immoral, is not tainted with fraud, and was not entered into through mistake or accident and is not contrary to public policy. It is clear and unambiguous and the parties understood the terms thereof, and the approximate cost of fulfilling the obligations could have been approximately ascertained. There are no conditions existing now which could not have been reasonably anticipated when the contract was negotiated and executed. The defendant could have performed the contract if it desired. It has accepted and reaped the benefits of its contract and now urges that plaintiffs' benefits under the contract be denied. If plaintiffs' benefits are denied, such benefits would inure to the direct benefit of the defendant.

Therefore, in my opinion, the plaintiffs were entitled to specific performance of the contract and since defendant has failed to perform, the proper measure of damages should be the cost of performance. Any other measure of damage would be holding for naught the express provisions of the contract; would be taking from the plaintiffs the benefits of the contract and placing those benefits in defendant which has failed to perform its obligations; would be granting benefits to defendant without a resulting obligation; and would be completely rescinding the solemn obligation of the contract for the benefit of the defendant to the detriment of the plaintiffs by making an entirely new contract for the parties.

I therefore respectfully dissent to the opinion promulgated by a majority of my associates.

Notes and Discussion

1. A Very Close Decision. The Oklahoma Supreme Court split 5–4. What made the decision so hard? The background of the case is explored in Judith L. Maute, *Peevyhouse v. Garland Coal Co. Revisited: The Ballad of*

Willie and Lucille, 89 Nw. U. L. Rev. 1341 (1995). Which of the following additional facts (all from Maute's article) might have swayed the court in one direction or the other:

- The Peevyhouses were not "country bumpkins," but skillful negotiators who rejected many of the contract's standard form provisions.
- The sixty acres leased to Garland was not their entire farm, but only half of it, and the damage to the sixty acres probably affected the remainder.
- The Peevyhouses were initially offered $3,000 ($50 per acre) for return of their land in unreclaimed state; but because they did not feel it was right to leave the land useless, the Peevyhouses rejected this offer in favor of the remedial provisions. (The parol evidence rule kept this information from the jury.)
- Garland found much less coal than it had anticipated. It made about $30,000 on what it extracted, and paid the Peevyhouses about $2,500 for the coal; the contract had no minimum royalty clause.
- Remedial steps were hampered by Garland's decision to abandon mining before the site had been fully exploited, as well as by severe weather.
- After the breach, Willie Peevyhouse repeatedly requested Garland to lease a bulldozer to him (for up to $3,000) so he could grade the land himself. Garland refused, but counteroffered $3,000 on condition that he sign a release that, *inter alia*, required him to take responsibility for any injuries to third parties resulting from a creek diversion Garland had made. Peevyhouse refused to sign.
- Garland considered the $5,000 jury award a victory. The Peevyhouses initially appealed, and Garland's cross-appeal was merely retaliatory.
- Today the land is a mess, littered with water-filled pits in one of which a teenage boy drowned in 1974.
- Some evidence suggests bribery in the case. The following year one justice, who broke a tie at the last minute, was implicated, along with several other justices, in a bribery scandal involving another case.

2. **The Choice of Remedies.** After rejecting the jury award of $5,000, the Oklahoma Supreme Court confronted a stark choice between two competing damage measures: the difference in value of the land ($300) as against the cost of performance ($25,000 or more). Restatement 2d § 348(2) covers situations where "a breach results in defective or unfinished construction and the loss in value to the injured party is not proved with sufficient certainty"; here damages can be either "(a) the diminution in the market price of the property caused by the breach, or (b) the reasonable cost of completing performance ... if that cost is not clearly disproportionate to the probable loss in value to" the injured party. This formulation suggests that in *Peevyhouse* a third measure of damages should have been at stake, beyond difference in value and cost of performance: namely, the actual value to the Peevyhouses of having their land restored. Of course, this will usually be hard to determine.

Why might the outcome of this case have been different if the Peevyhouses had hired a third party to re-grade their land (say, for $30,000), and then sued Gardner for this amount?

If the actual value of the reclamation to the Peevyhouses was in fact substantially higher than $300, how could they have better protected themselves when negotiating the contract?

3. "Economic Waste" and Efficient Breach. To the reasonable observer, spending $25,000 to achieve a $300 difference in value will doubtless seem senseless. Is it also therefore necessarily wasteful? The majority seems to think so; but, as they admit, "economic waste" is a technical legal concept that refers to "the destruction of a substantially completed building or other structure," not to an individual decision to do something the world deems foolish. Indeed, the majority readily concedes that the outcome would probably have been different if reclamation had been "a main or principal purpose" of this contract. Why should this be so?

By breaching, Garland hoped to save at least $25,000. If it only has to pay the Peevyhouses $300 for the breach, isn't this a substantial windfall to Garland? Why is such an outcome more desirable than an exactly complementary windfall to the Peevyhouses?

Remember that finding an efficient breach always involves comparing the cost of performance relative to breach with the value of performance relative to breach. So we necessarily compare the economic state of each party in two states: performance and breach. When the cost of performance exceeds its value, breach is efficient. Note that whenever breach is efficient, both parties can be made better off under breach than under performance, if the breaching party were to compensate the other (thus, resulting in a Pareto improvement). The majority in Peevyhouse is sniffing around the edges of the doctrine, but we do not think that they fully appreciate the complexities of applying the doctrine here.

Assume that the cost of reclamation is $25,000, and that the value of reclamation to the Peevyhouses is either $25,000 or $300. If the Peevyhouses' value is $25,000 and, as a result of the verdict, Garland pays them only $300, the breach cannot be described as efficient because the gain from it no longer exceeds the loss (the Peevyhouses are $24,700 worse off than they would have been if the contract had been performed, while Garland is $24,700 richer). On the other hand, society as a whole is not poorer—the coal company is richer by the exact amount of the Peevyhouses' loss. In that sense, this case is different from Judge Posner's example where the seller escapes costly production of something that no one wants—and so prevents not only a loss to the seller but also a loss to society (waste). We would argue therefore that this breach is not inefficient; it simply causes an improper wealth transfer from the Peevyhouses to Garland. We describe the wealth transfer as "improper" because we are assuming that the Peevyhouses valued the reclamation at $25,000 (here we ignore the possibility that the outcome might be "improper" for the additional reason that the Peevyhouses might have bargained for all or much of the surplus by insisting on the reclamation term in the lease), and therefore the proper damages to measure these plaintiffs' subjective loss are $25,000, not $300. As economists observe, "Economic efficiency is concerned with the *production* of wealth, not the *transfer* of it.'' Robert Cooter and Thomas Ulen, Law and Economics 121 (3rd ed. 2000).

On the other hand, if the Peevyhouses' value is $300 for the reclamation, we believe that the breach is efficient because performance would have required the expenditure of $25,000 to produce a $300 benefit. Neither the Peevyhouses nor society (represented by the market price) valued the $25,000 of work at more than $300, and $24,700 was saved for some other productive use by the breach. Since this outcome leaves the Peevyhouses exactly where they would have been from performance ($300 richer), there is no ''wealth transfer,'' but there is a gain from non-performance to Garland (and thus to society). Should we make Garland share that gain with the Peevyhouses? At least in theory, making Garland share will lower its incentive to commit efficient breaches; is that a bad thing?

And what if the Peevyhouses, valuing the reclamation at $300, strike a lucky chord with the jury and recover $25,000? There is still an efficient breach (no wasted money spent leveling the barren back sixty), but now we have a wealth transfer from the coal company to the Peevyhouses.[5] They ''deserved'' only $300 but recovered $25,000, which they can use to move to California and leave the old $300 scar on the back sixty to their successors.

As a final complication, consider what might happen if American law allowed any plaintiff the remedy of specific performance. Presumably the Peevyhouses would ask for that remedy—at least at the outset of the suit—but they might not really want it, true? Assume again that the Peevyhouses could care less about the back sixty; they are soon to be off for Long Beach. Now they would like the $25,000, or, indeed, any amount over $300, rather than performance. A moment's thought will tell you why they will ask for specific performance, yet eventually retreat from that position in the settlement negotiations. What posture might you take in response if you were Garland's lawyer?

4. ***Groves v. John Wunder Co.*** This is the leading case in opposition to *Peevyhouse. Groves* involved a contract whereby Wunder would extract gravel from a 24-acre industrial tract and then leave the property at a uniform grade; Wunder failed to grade, and Groves sued. As in *Peevyhouse*, the contract did not give a separate price for the grading. The cost of performance was $60,000; the reasonable value of the land in its smoothed-over state would have been only just over $12,000, largely because of sinking land prices during the Depression.

The Minnesota Supreme Court, by a 3–2 vote, favored giving Groves the full $60,000. The majority emphasizes the ''willfulness'' of Wunder's breach, and holds: ''The objective of this contract of present importance was the improvement of real estate.... [T]here can be no unconscionable enrichment, no advantage upon which the law will frown, when the result is but to give one party to a contract only what the other has promised; particularly

5. Of course, if Garland anticipated that the judgment would be $25,000 then Garland would not gain anything from breach, and it might as well perform. At the very least, it can make a credible threat to perform! Now the Peevyhouses will get, not the $25K, but only the $300 worth of performance. If they are smart, they will offer to sell Garland a release from the $25K remedy, to convince Garland not to perform the inefficient reclamation.

where, as here, the delinquent has had full payment for the promised performance." *Groves v. John Wunder Co.*, 205 Minn. 163, 286 N.W. 235, 238 (1939).

Can this case be distinguished from *Peevyhouse*? (For instance, was Garland's breach "willful"?) Would it matter to you if you learned that Groves did not use its $60,000 award to finish the grading, and that the tract lay idle for decades? In deciding on a remedy, how should we factor in the effect that the Depression had on land prices?

Andrew Kull has argued that breaching parties can legitimately be required to disgorge their gains if their breach is both profitable and "opportunistic"—that is, if the defendant breaches in order to improve on the terms of the contractual exchange, and does in fact do so; disgorgement is then "justified by reference to the familiar restitutionary goal of denying a profit from conscious wrongdoing—treating the breach of contract as an intentional wrong." In all other circumstances, normal contract damages should be sufficient to deter breach. Andrew Kull, *Disgorgement for Breach, the "Restitution Interest," and the Restatement of Contracts*, 79 Tex. L. Rev. 2021, 2021 (2001). Although this does not appear to be our law in fact, do you think that it should be? What would be the result in *Peeveyhouse* and *Groves*?

5. Environmental Legislation. In 1963 the Oklahoma court paid scant attention to the public policy issue of environmental restoration. Since then, of course, the situation has changed dramatically. If a case substantially identical to *Peevyhouse* were to arise today, would the salience of environmentalism be enough to change the outcome? In *Rock Island Improvement Co. v. Helmerich & Payne, Inc.*, 698 F.2d 1075 (10th Cir. 1983), a federal court using Oklahoma law declined to apply *Peevyhouse* in a somewhat similar case. Citing Oklahoma legislation on land reclamation, it concluded: "We are convinced that the Oklahoma Supreme Court would no longer apply the rule it established in *Peevyhouse* in 1963 if it had the instant dispute before it. *Peevyhouse* was a 5–4 decision with a strong dissent. More importantly, the public policy of the state has changed, as expressed in its statutes. Although we are bound by decisions of a state supreme court in diversity cases, we need not adhere to a decision if we think it no longer would be followed." Id at 1078 (footnote omitted).

Nonetheless, in *Schneberger v. Apache Corp.*, 890 P.2d 847 (Okla. 1994), the Oklahoma Supreme Court stayed with *Peevyhouse*. It noted: "Likewise, Oklahoma case law from statehood to the present, including cases resolved under the Act as of 1986, have interpreted the proper measure of damages to be diminution in value. And although *Peevyhouse* interpreted the application of the diminution in value rule to where the lease provision breached was incidental to the main purpose of the contract, certainly later cases make no such distinction. Whatever the rationale, the essence of the *Peevyhouse* holding—to award diminution in value rather than cost of performance—has been consistently adhered to in cases giving rise to temporary and permanent injuries to property. This approach attempts to resolve in as fair a manner as possible the inequities inherent in a situation regarding two competing interests and it still represents the majority view." Id. at 852 (footnote omitted). Still wrong after all these years?

Problem 6–2

The City of New Orleans entered into a five-year contract with a private organization that was to provide services for extinguishing fires. The contract required the contractor to keep 124 employees in its service and to maintain a certain length of hose. During the contract, the contractor, at considerable savings to itself, employed no more than 70 firefighters and had much less than the required amount of hose. However, because no emergency arose, New Orleans suffered no perceptible loss as a result of the breach. If New Orleans sues, can it force the organization to disgorge its profits from the breach? Can the city obtain any other damages?

KRAFSUR v. UOP (IN RE EL PASO REFINERY, L.P.)

U.S. Bankruptcy Court, Western District of Texas, 1996.
196 B.R. 58.

[Eds.: This action was brought by Krafsur, the bankruptcy trustee for El Paso Refinery, L.P. ("L.P."), objecting to a claim by UOP for the sum of $4,019,028.86. L.P. owned and operated a petroleum refinery under a licensing contract to use refining technology developed by defendant UOP. UOP claimed that L.P. owed the above sum in unpaid royalties, and pre-petition goods and services, essentially as a remedy for the breach of the licensing contract. In October, 1992, L.P. filed for Chapter 11 bankruptcy relief. In May, 1993, L.P.'s creditors foreclosed on the refinery and conveyed its ownership to a newly formed holding company, Refinery Holding Company ("RHC"). RHC contracted with Chevron USA ("Chevron") to run the refinery, and RHC/Chevron continued to operate the refinery using UOP technology. After UOP claimed that RHC/Chevron lacked a license to do so, the parties eventually entered into a new contract that required RHC/Chevron to pay $3.7 million in royalties. The trustee asserts that UOP's claim against L.P. should be mitigated by this payment. UOP responds that they were under no duty to mitigate their damages, and that they had an unlimited supply of licenses, so they were a lost volume seller.]

CLARK, J. . . . In the instant case though, whether UOP had a *duty* to mitigate its damages is not the question before the court. The question rather is whether the sale of licenses to RHC in fact *did* mitigate UOP's damages. This is really just another way of asking whether UOP is a lost volume seller. If UOP is a lost volume seller, then the sale to RHC did nothing to mitigate UOP's losses from L.P.'s breach. On the other hand, If UOP is not a lost volume seller, then the court must determine to what extent UOP has already recouped the loss it suffered due to L.P.'s breach.

The normal measure of damages for breach of contract is the contract price minus the resale price. The idea is that the seller is made whole or has received the benefit of his bargain if the breaching party simply makes up the difference in price between what the seller expected to receive from the breaching party, and what the seller actually received from the new buyer.

A lost volume seller is not bound by the traditional damage calculation of contract price minus resale price because such a calculation would not adequately recompense it for its true loss. That is, it would not give the non-breaching party the benefit of his bargain, since, absent the buyer's breach, a lost volume seller would have earned profits from *two* sales rather than just one. The parties cite different cases which have announced varying tests for determining whether a given seller is a lost volume seller. The essential point of all the tests, however, is the same: a damage award for breach of contract, whether lost volume seller or otherwise, is intended to put the non-breaching party in as good a position as it would have been in had the breach never occurred. As an Illinois appellate court put it, "the guiding rule and basic principle is that *compensation* is the general purpose of the law in fixing the measure of damages." *Wired Music, Inc. v. Clark,* 26 Ill. App. 2d 413, 168 N.E.2d 736, 739 (Ill. App. Ct. 1960) (emphasis added)

In *Wired Music,* the plaintiff provided a service whereby it would deliver music via the telephone lines to area businesses. The defendant was one such customer. Seventeen months into a three year contract with the plaintiff, the defendant moved his business and discontinued the plaintiff's music service. A new tenant moved into the office space abandoned by the defendant and began its own separate contract for the plaintiff's services. When the plaintiff sued to recover from the defendant the remaining amount due on the contract (nineteen months), the defendant asserted that the plaintiff's damages should be lessened by the amount received from its new client at the defendant's old address. The court held for the plaintiff, finding that the plaintiff had been damaged in an amount equal to the profit it would have received had the defendant not breached.

UOP insists that *Wired Music* is controlling, and mandates that no mitigation occurred as a result of the sale of a license to RHC/Chevron. The Trustee counters that, because *Wired Music* was decided before the formal development of the lost volume seller doctrine in Illinois, reliance on it by this court would be misplaced. The Trustee argues that *Wired Music* only applied "the first prong of what would later become the lost volume seller analysis under Illinois law, as set out by the Seventh Circuit." Trustee's Post-trial Brief at 7 (underscoring in original); see *R.E. Davis Chemical Corp. v. Diasonics, Inc.,* 924 F.2d 709 (7th Cir. 1991). UOP responds by questioning the propriety of a federal court defining the "lost volume seller analysis under Illinois law." As UOP correctly points out, a federal court should follow an intermediate appellate level state court's judgment on an issue of state law unless the federal court is persuaded that the state's highest court would find otherwise. *See West v. American Telephone and Telegraph Co.,* 311 U.S. 223, 237, 85 L.Ed. 139, 61 S.Ct. 179 (1940). *Wired Music,* even though it is now well over thirty years old, is still reproduced in many casebooks used to teach the law of contracts to law students. It is very likely that the Illinois Supreme Court will follow *Wired Music* in future cases, and unlikely that that court would overturn it. Therefore, *Wired Music* should be accorded precedential value by the court in this case.

Although *Wired Music* does not use the term "lost volume seller" it does detail the essential rationale behind the doctrine. Simply put, even though a lost volume seller resells the same "car," the lost volume seller has not recouped his losses from the earlier breach. But for the breach, the lost volume seller would have earned profits from two sales instead of just one. The notion behind the *Wired Music* case, and all other lost volume cases, is that the non-breaching party is entitled to the benefit of his bargain.[6]

By the same token, the lost volume doctrine cannot be construed so broadly as to swallow up all other theories of contract remedies. *See* Alex Devience, Jr., *An Analysis of the Lost Volume Seller Doctrine under Article 2 of the Uniform Commercial Code,* 97 Com. L.J. 198, 198 (Summer 1992); Comment, *Finding the Lost Volume Seller: Two Independent Sales Deserve Two Profits Under Illinois Law,* 22. J. Marshall L. Rev. 363, 387 (Winter, 1988). To quote from the comment: "If Illinois courts agree with the seventh circuit that lost-volume sellers are entitled to a profit remedy under Uniform Commercial Code section 2–708(2), they will face the difficult but necessary task of deciding which sellers are entitled to the remedy. Courts in other jurisdictions have too frequently permitted a profit remedy to undeserving sellers because previous lost-volume seller definitions were either inadequate or poorly applied. Because it comports with the general damages philosophy of the U.C.C. and produces results consistent with the general common law theory of contract damages, Illinois courts should adopt the two-step analysis of 'capacity' and 'wholly independent sales event' to ensure that the section 2–708(2) profit remedy is only available to true lost-volume sellers." Comment, *supra.* The author of the comment cogently spells out a sensible decisional matrix for applying the lost-volume seller doctrine. He explains that a court ought first to ask about the capacity of the seller to demonstrate that it had excess manufacturing capacity or present ready access to additional inventory at the time of the repudiation or breach. This prong of the inquiry simply demands that the seller be able to demonstrate that it could have made a "second sale."

The second prong requires the court to answer this question: "Would the plaintiff have made a sale to the ultimate resale purchaser even if there had been no repudiation by the original buyer of the goods?" Comment, *supra* at 382. In other words, the original sale and the resale after breach must be wholly independent events, as opposed to

6. "If Defendant's contention were adopted by this court, it would have the effect of denying to the plaintiff the benefit of his bargain. This case is not at all like the situation where a plaintiff has one house to rent or one car to sell or a fixed quantity of personal property or real estate. Here, plaintiff has so far as the evidence shows, an unlimited supply of music limited in its distributions only by the number of contracts which plaintiff can secure." *Id.* at 738–39.

the second sale being a mere replacement for the first sale. To make this determination, three important variables should be examined.

First, as to the seller, the court ought to determine that the breach of the original sale did not provide the opportunity to make the resale (establishing that the resale is not merely a replacement sale). Second, the court ought to examine the resale buyer's particular needs, in order to determine whether the resale buyer would have bought from the seller even if the original buyer had not breached. *See* Sebert, *Remedies Under Article Two of the Uniform Commercial Code: An Agenda for Review,* 130 U. PA. L. REV. 360, 388 (1981). Finally, the trier of fact ought to examine the characteristics of the particular goods involved in the breach and that the resale buyer ultimately purchased, keeping in mind that the more specialized the particular item, the more likely it is that its subsequent sale is merely a replacement sale. Comment, *supra* at 385.

In Wired Music, the "plaintiff [had] so far as the evidence showed, an unlimited supply of music *limited in its distributions only by the number of contracts which plaintiff can secure." Id.* at 738–39. (emphasis added). UOP wishes to analogize themselves to the plaintiff in *Wired Music,* and concentrates on the fact that they, like that plaintiff, have an unlimited amount of "product" to sell, *i.e.,* technology licenses. The difference is of course that the list of potential customers from whom UOP can secure contracts is significantly more limited than was the plaintiff's list of potential customers in *Wired Music.* UOP's capacity for resale is limited not only by the number of licenses it can grant but also by whether a given potential buyer has a refinery, and more specifically a refinery that needs this process in order to operate. The universe of refinery operators is considerably more circumscribed than is the universe of potential users of piped-in music.

The service provided by the *Wired Music* plaintiff was not only of unlimited supply, but also had a value to and could be marketed to practically anyone. The plaintiff's list of possible customers included every business connected to a telephone line. The new tenant would have been a likely customer even if the defendant had not moved, because whatever location the new tenant ultimately rented would likely have been connected to a telephone line. The plaintiff therefore was deprived of the opportunity to provide service to, and obtain profits from contracts with *both* the defendant and the tenant. Petroleum refining technology, unlike music piped in over telephone lines, is not particularly useful to anyone without a refinery. In order to be a potential customer of UOP, one must either own, operate, or soon plan to own or operate a refinery. *Wired Music* did not "explicitly reject[] any requirement that a party in UOP's position be required to grant a credit for the revenue from a subsequent transaction to the debt on a breached contract." UOP's Post-Trial Brief at 5. UOP is not in the same position as was the plaintiff in *Wired Music,* in terms of its capacity.

The essence of the *Wired Music* holding was that a non-breaching party deserves to be compensated for losses incurred attributable to another party's breach. This is not a new theory; it is the essential purpose of contract damages in all cases. All that *Wired Music* adds is that the usual rule used by courts to measure damages *(i.e.,* contract price minus resale price) would have been inadequate to compensate a true lost volume seller for its loss. *Wired Music* teaches that a court must look at the totality of the facts in a given case to determine whether, despite a subsequent sale, a plaintiff has still been damaged. To make this determination a court must analyze what would likely have happened had the breaching party not breached. As discussed above, if the defendant in *Wired Music* had not breached and abandoned the location, the plaintiff could have had contracts with both the defendant and the tenant at different locations. As that court put it, "we are unable to say that the music sold in the location that defendant abandoned could not have been sold but for the breach of the defendant." *Id.* at 739.

In the instant case, by contrast, the RHC licenses could not have been sold *but for* L.P.'s breach. If L.P. had not breached and vacated the refinery, RHC would not even exist let alone own a refinery. The court is likewise unconvinced that UOP has been deprived of a second profit through the sale to some entity other than RHC. Unlike music traveling over telephone lines, the Licenses are unit-specific. UOP attempted to argue that, even if L.P. had not breached and was still operating the refinery, UOP could sell additional licenses to a second operator on the same units. The evidence in support of this point was, however, somewhere between thin and nonsensical. Although it may be theoretically possible to sell additional licenses on an El Paso unit that is already being operated, in reality it has not and would not happen, as UOP's representative himself acknowledged in his testimony.[7] The inescapable conclusion is that, if L.P. were still operating the El Paso refinery, UOP would not and could not have made an additional sale. L.P.'s breach eliminated one customer and created another. If L.P. had never breached, UOP would have received $1,970,037.38 in royalty payments from L.P. Instead, thanks to L.P.'s breach it has received $3,600,000 in royalty payments from RHC. Any loss UOP may have suffered because of L.P.'s breach has been more than mitigated by the sale to RHC: a sale UOP would not have made if L.P. had still been operating the refinery. UOP has thus not suffered a loss from L.P.'s breach of its duty to pay UOP for the L.P. Licenses and is therefore not entitled to maintain its claim against L.P. for unpaid royalties. To do so, would amount to a double recovery for UOP.

7. The best UOP's witness could muster in support of the argument was the situation in which a license on a given unit was still *in force* but was not actually being used (perhaps because the operator had gone out of business or abandoned operations at the refinery). A subsequent operator of the refinery might then be sold a new license, resulting in two licenses being in place on the same refinery. To be a true loss volume seller, however, one would have to postulate *two* operators *both* operating the *same refinery* under different licenses *at the same time.* No operator with any common sense would ever permit another entity to operate its refinery at the same time, given the extensive risks and liability that would be involved. Indeed, UOP's witness knew of no such situation anywhere in the nation, either now or at any time in the past.

This analysis conforms as well to the decisional matrix suggested in the Comment alluded to earlier. UOP's capacity is significantly delimited by its universe of buyers with refineries. Indeed, given that the licenses are unit-specific, the "second sale" of this license was limited to the El Paso Refinery itself. The resale to RHC fails to qualify as an "independent event" as well. But for the breach, RHC would not have existed and there would not have been a "second sale" to RHC. The opportunity to sell a new license to RHC was presented by L.P.'s breach of the original license (and subsequent bankruptcy which led to the foreclosure by the Term Lenders). The resale buyer had a particular need for a license on the El Paso Refinery, and did not need a license on any other refinery. Finally, the item "resold" was highly specialized—identified to the El Paso Refinery itself. Thus, the resale was not truly an independent event but rather a mere replacement of the prior sale to L.P.

The court is satisfied that the foregoing analysis is sufficient to explain why UOP's claim for unpaid royalties should be disallowed. However, the parties also cite to *R.E. Davis Chemical Corp. v. Diasonics, Inc.,* 924 F.2d 709 (7th.Cir. 1991), as an alternative analytical matrix. The *R.E. Davis* court held that, in Illinois: "in order to qualify as a lost volume seller, a plaintiff must establish the following three factors: (1) that it possessed the *capacity* to make an additional sale, (2) that it would have been *profitable* for it to make an additional sale, and (3) that it *probably would have made* an additional sale absent the buyer's breach." *Id.* at 711. (emphasis added).

Davis is not controlling precedent, given that it is but an attempt at extrapolation of Illinois law by a federal court. This court's discussion *supra,* examining the instant facts under the *Wired Music* analysis is nonetheless equally applicable under the *Davis* three part test.[8] This is so because that test in fact merely tracks the decisional matrix already laid out *supra.*

UOP's "product" is a license to use its technology, and at least theoretically, UOP has an unlimited supply of such licenses. Yet, as explained above, the supply is not unlimited in fact. UOP *did not* have an unlimited supply of site-specific licenses.[9] On the second element of *Davis,* UOP has an easier time of it, as the major costs associated with technology licenses all are derived from the initial development of the technology. After the technology has been developed and patented the marginal cost of each new sale is negligible. Thus, any additional sale will likely be profitable.

8. The parties seem to be under the misconception that the *Wired Music* court's analysis concentrated solely on the sellers capacity for additional sales (*i.e. Davis's* first prong). As discussed *supra,* upon a careful reading of *Wired Music* it is apparent that the court's analysis incorporated all of the factors enunciated in the three-part *R.E. Davis* test.

9. True, a license is just an agreement not to sue for infringement and UOP could agree not to sue an unlimited amount of entities for infringement. Still, the reality is that each license is tied to a specific unit, and each unit can produce only a finite amount of product. Therefore, there is a finite amount of licensing purchasers would be willing to buy.

UOP is unable to overcome the third prong of the *Davis* test—the *probability* that it would have made an additional sale but for L.P.'s breach. As noted in the discussion earlier under *Wired Music,* UOP was not deprived of an additional sale, and so has not been damaged. Similarly, under the *Davis* analysis, it cannot be said that UOP would probably have made an additional sale but for L.P.'s breach. Without a breach, RHC would not even have existed.

UOP attempted to argue that the "second sale" that it lost as a result of the breach was the sale of a license to Chevron on *its* refinery next door to the El Paso Refinery. But that is not the "second sale" on which a court ought properly to focus when applying the lost volume analysis. Rather, the question is whether had there not been a breach, would UOP have sold a license to *RHC,* the resale buyer in this case. Chevron was a subsidiary licensee under RHC's license, with the consent of UOP, but was not the purchaser of the license.[10]

Moreover, a presumed "lost sale" to Chevron would not be a lost sale of the very license resold to RHC. The licenses sold by UOP were a unit-specific licenses on the El Paso Refinery. Such licenses would not have "worked" on Chevron's own plant. Indeed, Chevron already *owns* licenses on its own plant—from UOP. It would not have been a potential purchaser of a new license from UOP in any event.[11]

Even if the court were to hold that an additional sale to Chevron was likely, UOP still would not be entitled to maintain its claim against L.P. for unpaid royalties as a lost volume seller. An aggrieved party is given lost volume status because, even after a subsequent sale, the party is still damaged and has not received the benefit of its bargain. The seller would be better off if the buyer had not breached. In the instant case UOP is better off *because* of L.P.'s breach. If L.P. had not breached, UOP would only have received the $1,970,037.38 remaining to be paid on

10. UOP attempted to prove that, in fact, Chevron was also a "purchaser" of a license, but the totality of the facts demonstrate that Chevron instead made certain financial accommodations to UOP and RHC in order to "make the deal work." Its involvement in the transaction arose only from the serendipitous decision of RHC to hire Chevron to operate the refinery on its behalf. The licenses themselves were issued to RHC. UOP also relies on a "side letter" agreement between it and Chevron, which it maintains establishes that the "true sale" was to Chevron. But the most that can be said for the letter agreement was that it might make it easier for RHC to transfer the licenses without further concern that it a subsequent purchaser would have to go through with UOP what *it* did when it took over the refinery after the foreclosure.

11. The most that UOP can argue here is that Chevron might, at some point in the future, have elected to expand its volume under its license, requiring perhaps an "upgrade" of its existing license. There is no probative evidence in the record to determine what such an upgrade might cost, or whether Chevron would ever want to put such an upgrade into place. Chevron's refinery is fairly old, compared to El Paso Refinery, and an upgrade of capacity would cost more to Chevron than simply acquiring expanded licensing from UOP. Chevron would in all likelihood have to engage in an overall refinery modernization project costing tens of millions of dollars before it would ever be in a position to ask for any substantial increase in licensing capacity. Above and beyond the unlikelihood of Chevron's engaging in such a project any time soon, the evidence on the point is speculative at best. Moreover, given the way in which the lost volume doctrine operates, there is considerable doubt that such evidence would even be relevant.

the L.P. Licenses. Instead, because L.P. breached, they were able to negotiate a deal with RHC worth $3,700,000. Therefore, because of L.P's breach, UOP is $1,729,962.62 better off. Even were the court to find that, but for the breach, Chevron would have purchased additional licenses, there was no evidence whatsoever that Chevron would have purchased in excess of $1,729,962.62 worth of licenses.

The simple answer to this difficult question is that UOP is better off now than they would have been absent a breach by L.P. UOP has received the benefit of its bargain and more. That portion of UOP's claim consisting of past due royalties is accordingly disallowed....

Notes and Discussion

1. **Defining the Lost Volume Seller.** *Neri v. Retail Marine Corp.*, 30 N.Y.2d 393, 334 N.Y.S.2d 165, 285 N.E.2d 311 (1972), is the leading case concerning lost volume sellers. Retail Marine sold Anthony Neri a boat of a specified model for $12,587.40, on which Neri paid a deposit of $4,290. Six days later he unjustifiably repudiated the contract. Retail Marine, which in the meantime had received the boat from the manufacturer, declined to refund his deposit, but later resold the boat to a second customer for the same price. Neri sued to recover most of his deposit (see UCC § 2–718(2)(b)), and Retail Marine countersued for damages because of the breach.

How should Retail Marine's damages be determined under UCC §§ 2–706 and 708(1)? Since Retail Marine was able to resell the boat for the exact same price, isn't it already (at least if we ignore incidental damages arising from storing the boat between the two sales, etc.; cf. § 2–710) "in as good a position as if the other party had fully performed"? UCC § 1–106(1); cf. revised UCC § 1–305(a). The short answer is no, if (and only if) we can assume that but for Neri's breach, Retail Marine could have sold two boats, one to Neri and the other to the second buyer. If Retail Marine cannot recover its profit on the Neri sale, then it ends up in a worse position because of the breach. Therefore Retail Marine is entitled to its lost profits, as mandated in § 2–708(2)—which you should read closely.[12]

As the New York Court of Appeals explains, "Closely parallel to the factual situation now before us is that hypothesized by Dean Hawkland as illustrative of the operation of the rules: 'Thus, if a private party agrees to sell his automobile to a buyer for $2000, a breach by the buyer would cause the seller no loss (except incidental damages, i.e., expense of a new sale) if the seller was able to sell the automobile to another buyer for $2000. But the situation is different with dealers having an unlimited supply of standard-priced goods. Thus, if an automobile dealer agrees to sell a car to a buyer at the standard price of $2000, a breach by the buyer injures the dealer, even though he is able to sell the automobile to another for $2000. If the dealer

12. Note particularly the final phrase of § 2–708(2), which gives the buyer "due credit for ... proceeds of resale." On its face, this language seems to mean that Retail Marine must offset the second purchase price—which would make the alternative remedy useless in this case. The *Neri* court follows the consensus of opinion in ignoring this final clause except when the object of sale is scrapped. *Neri*, 285 N.E.2d at 313 n.2.

has an inexhaustible supply of cars, the resale to replace the breaching buyer costs the dealer a sale, because, had the breaching buyer performed, the dealer would have made two sales instead of one. The buyer's breach, in such a case, depletes the dealer's sales to the extent of one, and the measure of damages should be the dealer's profit on one sale. Section 2–708 recognizes this, and it rejects the rules developed under the Uniform Sales Act by many courts that the profit cannot be recovered in this case.' (Hawkland, Sales and Bulk Sales (1958 ed.), pp. 153–154; and see Comment, 31 Fordham L.Rev. 749, 755–756.)" *Neri*, 285 N.E.2d at 314.

In what respects are the *Wired Music* and *In re El Paso Refinery* cases more difficult?

2. Is Caution Warranted? Economists have expressed qualms about the award of lost profits in some situations. Charles J. Goetz and Robert E. Scott, *Measuring Seller's Damages: The Lost Profits Puzzle,* 31 Stan. L. Rev. 323, 332 (1979), argue that granting lost profits under § 2–708(2) may give the plaintiff more than he should get. They suggest that while the seller's ability to produce more goods may be unbounded, its ability to sell them *at a profit* may not be.

Imagine a perfectly competitive market, in which many suppliers produce essentially the same product and an individual supplier has little or no control over the market price of a product. Certain commodities markets may approximately meet these criteria. Suppose that steel is one such market, and that the market price is $11 per ton, but the supplier's marginal cost gradually rises as more steel is produced, and rises above $11 per ton after the first 100,000 tons have been produced. Finally, suppose that the producer had a contract for 100,000 tons of steel at $12 per ton, which the buyer then breached. In this case, the producer could then sell the steel on the market for $11 per ton; but would not find it profitable to produce more steel whether or not a breach occurred. Therefore the best measure of damages would be the difference between $11 per ton and $12 per ton, exactly as under § 2–708(1). Id. at 333–335.

But most markets are not perfectly competitive, and each individual producer has at least some control over the price. In such a case, a producer cannot keep producing more product indefinitely, since this could lower the market price below the marginal cost. Id. at 335–341. If marginal costs of production increase, then a breach lowers the cost of the last item produced, and the seller may find it profitable to expand output for other sales. Although this might not seem to be the case if marginal costs are constant, the breach could still result in additional sales if the buyer of a product (for instance, a Boeing 747), should it not need the plane, can decide to resell it on the market. In that case, Boeing may lose the second sale or alternatively have to sell all its remaining 747s at a lower price. Id. at 341–346.

Robert Cooter and Melvin Aron Eisenberg, *Damages for Breach of Contract*, 73 Cal. L. Rev. 1432, 1455–1459 (1985), examine these economic models, and also the "fishing model" of business conduct, generally involving pre-existing contracts. Under this model, the seller "fishes" for buyers, using the product as "bait." If a buyer "gets away" by breaching a contract, it has no effect on other sales the seller makes. Therefore damages from the breach should be calculated as the price minus marginal cost of the last item sold.

For example, suppose that the seller has 10 contracts, and that the marginal cost of its goods declines over the first eight contracts but rises for the last two. If the second contract is broken, the seller uses goods that would have been used for the second contract to fulfill contract 10, for which no goods need to be produced. So the seller's lost profit is not the loss on the second contract but rather the profit it would have earned on contract 10 if all ten contracts had been fulfilled. Do you see why? If one assumes that the last sale in a particular period is close to the break-even sale (because seller's costs of production are rising), this loss might be small.

For a more extensive discussion of these issues, see James J. White and Robert S. Summers, Uniform Commercial Code, supra, § 7–14 at 293–294 (5th student ed., 2000).

Problem 6–3

Assume that Seller has contracts to sell 10 modular homes in 2009 for $200,000 each. Its direct costs of manufacture are as follows on each of the ten contracts: 1–2, $150,000; 3–7, $120,000; 8–9, $130,000; 10, $170,000. (Seller's costs fall at first, but then rise again as it has to use less efficient workers and machines—a common pattern.)

1. If Buyer on contract #2 breaches and his modular home is delivered to Buyer #10, and if Seller makes only nine sales in 2009, Seller's damages are:

 a. 50,000

 b. 30,000

 c. other

2. Assume that Seller had a grossly bloated overhead and large interest costs—totaling together more than $900,000 and not included in the "direct costs"—so that its net income for 2009 would have been negative $100,000. In that case Buyer claims to owe no damages because Seller lost money on every sale and Buyer claims that his breach actually saved Seller money. Will that argument work?

Problem 6–4

Assume an oligopolistic industry for the manufacture and sale of a vinyl monomer that is the base stock for PVC plastic. Two companies, Scipio and Fabius, control 80% of the market, with the remaining 20% divided among small producers. Hannibal is a purchaser of the monomer and is a large producer of PVC pipe. One of the two large producers of the monomer, Scipio Chemicals, has constructed a plant adjoining Hannibal's Missouri production facility and has a ten year contract to deliver the monomer across the fence in a pipe to Hannibal. In the fifth year of the contract, Hannibal repudiates. After an unsuccessful attempt to find buyers for the output of its plant, Scipio closes the Missouri plant. Hannibal has found a cheaper source of the monomer from Fabius Chemical, the other large American producer.

Scipio sues Hannibal under 2–708(2) for lost profits. Assume that Scipio shows that its average annual profit in the first 5 years of the contract was $20 million and gives credible evidence that those profits would have continued for the last 5 years of the contract had it not been cancelled.

Hannibal defends the 2–708(2) action on several grounds. First, Hannibal argues that Scipio should not have closed the plant, and that it had a duty to mitigate by selling the plant's output to others. Any profits it could have earned by selling to others should be set off. Scipio responds that it has a right to stop performance under 2–704, and that its plant could not have been moth-balled because it was old and the monomer was corrosive. Had the plant been shut down even for a limited period of time, it could not have been re-opened because of corrosion.

Second, Hannibal argues that any damages must be reduced by the gains that Scipio enjoyed through sales to third parties who formerly would have been served by Fabius. You should assume that the market for the monomer is stable and that Scipio's agreement to provide the requirements of Hannibal would have left it without the capacity to serve many other people in the market that it had formerly served. Some of those old customers will buy from other plants that Scipio continues to operate. In addition Hannibal argues that the closing of Scipio's plant and the reduction in industry capacity has caused a nationwide increase in the spot and contract market for the monomer. It claims the additional profits earned from that change should also be subtracted from its damages.

How would you respond on behalf of Scipio?

KGM HARVESTING COMPANY v. FRESH NETWORK

Court of Appeal, 6th District California, 1995.
36 Cal.App.4th 376, 42 Cal.Rptr.2d 286.

COTTLE, J. Seller sued buyer for balance allegedly due on invoices and buyer filed cross-complaint for alleged breach of contract. The Superior Court, Monterey County, No. 92248, Robert O'Farrell, J., entered verdict determining that seller breached contract and thus buyer was entitled to cover damages and prejudgment interest commencing 30 days before trial. Both buyer and seller appealed. The Court of Appeal, Cottle, P.J., held that: (1) buyer could recover from seller as damages difference between cost of cover and contract price, and (2) error in original calculation of damages was minor and did not make damage sum uncertain for determination of prejudgment interest.

Affirmed in part, reversed and remanded in part.

California lettuce grower and distributor KGM Harvesting Company (hereafter seller) had a contract to deliver 14 loads of lettuce each week to Ohio lettuce broker Fresh Network (hereafter buyer). When the price of lettuce rose dramatically in May and June 1991, seller refused to deliver the required quantity of lettuce to buyer. Buyer then purchased lettuce on the open market in order to fulfill its contractual obligations to third parties. After a trial, the jury awarded buyer damages in an amount equal to the difference between the contract price and the price buyer was forced to pay for substitute lettuce on the open market. On appeal, seller argues that the damage award is excessive. We disagree and shall affirm the judgment. In a cross-appeal, buyer argues it was entitled to prejudgment interest from August 1, 1991, as its damages were readily ascertainable from that date. We agree and reverse the trial court's order awarding prejudgment interest from 30 days prior to trial.

FACTS

In July 1989 buyer and seller entered into an agreement for the sale and purchase of lettuce. Over the years, the terms of the agreement were modified. By May 1991 the terms were that seller would sell to buyer 14 loads of lettuce each week and that buyer would pay seller 9 cents a pound for the lettuce. (A load of lettuce consists of 40 bins, each of which weighs 1,000 to 1,200 pounds. Assuming an average bin weight of 1,100 pounds, one load would equal 44,000 pounds, and the 14 loads called for in the contract would weigh 616,000 pounds. At 9 cents per pound, the cost would approximate $55,440 per week.)

Buyer sold all of the lettuce it received from seller to a lettuce broker named Castellini Company who in turn sold it to Club Chef, a company that chops and shreds lettuce for the fast food industry (specifically, Burger King, Taco Bell, and Pizza Hut). Castellini Company bought lettuce from buyer on a "cost plus" basis, meaning it would pay buyer its actual cost plus a small commission. Club Chef, in turn, bought lettuce from Castellini Company on a cost plus basis.

Seller had numerous lettuce customers other than buyer, including seller's subsidiaries Coronet East and West. Coronet East supplied all the lettuce for the McDonald's fast food chain.

In May and June 1991, when the price of lettuce went up dramatically, seller refused to supply buyer with lettuce at the contract price of nine cents per pound. Instead, it sold the lettuce to others at a profit of between $800,000 and $1,100,000. Buyer, angry at seller's breach, refused to pay seller for lettuce it had already received. Buyer then went out on the open market and purchased lettuce to satisfy its obligations to Castellini Company. Castellini covered all of buyer's extra expense except for $70,000. Castellini in turn passed on its extra costs to Club Chef which passed on at least part of its additional costs to its fast food customers.

In July 1991 buyer and seller each filed complaints under the Perishable Agricultural Commodities Act (PACA). Seller sought the balance due on its outstanding invoices ($233,000), while buyer sought damages for the difference between what it was forced to spend to buy replacement lettuce and the contract price of nine cents a pound (approximately $700,000).

Subsequently, seller filed suit for the balance due on its invoices, and buyer cross-complained for the additional cost it incurred to obtain substitute lettuce after seller's breach. At trial, the parties stipulated that seller was entitled to a directed verdict on its complaint for

$233,000, the amount owing on the invoices. Accordingly, only the cross-complaint went to the jury, whose task was to determine whether buyer was entitled to damages from seller for the cost of obtaining substitute lettuce and, if so, in what amount. The jury determined that seller breached the contract, that its performance was not excused, and that buyer was entitled to $655,960.22, which represented the difference between the contract price of nine cents a pound and what it cost buyer to cover by purchasing lettuce in substitution in May and June 1991. It also determined that such an award would not result in a windfall to buyer and that buyer was obligated to the Castellini Company for the additional costs. The court subtracted from buyer's award of $655,960.22 the $233,000 buyer owed to seller on its invoices, leaving a net award in favor of buyer in the amount of $422,960.22. The court also awarded buyer prejudgment interest commencing 30 days before trial.

DISCUSSION

A. Seller's Appeal

Section 2–711 of the California Uniform Commercial Code provides a buyer with several alternative remedies for a seller's breach of contract. The buyer can " 'cover' by making in good faith and without unreasonable delay any reasonable purchase of . . . goods in substitution for those due from the seller." (§ 2–712, subd. (1).) In that case, the buyer "may recover from the seller as damages the difference between the cost of cover and the contract price. . . ." (§ 2–712, subd. (2).) If the buyer is unable to cover or chooses not to cover, the measure of damages is the difference between the market price and the contract price. (§ 2–713.) Under either alternative, the buyer may also recover incidental and consequential damages. (§§ 2–711, 2–715.) In addition, in certain cases the buyer may secure specific performance or replevin "where the goods are unique" (§ 2–716) or may recover goods identified to a contract (§ 2–502).

In the instant case, buyer "covered" as defined in Section 2–712 in order to fulfill its own contractual obligations to the Castellini Company. Accordingly, it was awarded the damages called for in cover cases—the difference between the contract price and the cover price. (§ 2–712.)

In appeals from judgments rendered pursuant to Section 2–712, the dispute typically centers on whether the buyer acted in "good faith," whether the "goods in substitution" differed substantially from the contracted for goods, whether the buyer unreasonably delayed in purchasing substitute goods in the mistaken belief that the price would go down, or whether the buyer paid too much for the substitute goods. (See generally White & Summers, Uniform Commercial Code (3d ed. 1988) Buyer's Remedies, Cover, § 6–3, pp. 284–292 [hereafter White & Summers], and cases cited therein.)

In this case, however, none of these typical issues is in dispute. Seller does not contend that buyer paid too much for the substitute lettuce or that buyer was guilty of "unreasonable delay" or a lack of "good faith" in its attempt to obtain substitute lettuce. Nor does seller contend that the lettuce purchased was of a higher quality or grade and therefore not a reasonable substitute.

Instead, seller takes issue with Section 2–712 itself, contending that despite the unequivocal language of Section 2–712, a buyer who covers should not necessarily recover the difference between the cover price and the contract price. Seller points out that because of buyer's "cost plus" contract with Castellini Company, buyer was eventually able to pass on the extra expenses (except for $70,000) occasioned by seller's breach and buyer's consequent purchase of substitute lettuce on the open market. It urges this court under these circumstances not to allow buyer to obtain a "windfall."

The basic premise of contract law is to effectuate the expectations of the parties to the agreement, to give them the "benefit of the bargain" they struck when they entered into the agreement. In its basic premise, contract law therefore differs significantly from tort law. As the California Supreme Court explained in *Foley v. Interactive Data Corp.* (1988) 47 Cal.3d 654, 254 Cal.Rptr. 211, 765 P.2d 373, "contract actions are created to enforce the intentions of the parties to the agreement [while] tort law is primarily designed to vindicate 'social policy.' " (Id. at p. 683, 254 Cal.Rptr. 211, 765 P.2d 373, citing Prosser, Law of Torts (4th ed. 1971) p. 613.)

" 'The basic object of damages is compensation, and in the law of contracts the theory is that the party injured by breach should receive as nearly as possible the equivalent of the benefits of performance. [Citations.]' " (*Lisec v. United Airlines, Inc.* (1992) 10 Cal.App.4th 1500, 1503, 11 Cal.Rptr.2d 689.) A compensation system that gives the aggrieved party the benefit of the bargain, and no more, furthers the goal of "predictability about the cost of contractual relationships ... in our commercial system." (*Foley v. Interactive Data Corp.*, supra, 47 Cal.3d at p. 683, 254 Cal.Rptr. 211, 765 P.2d 373; Putz & Klippen, Commercial Bad Faith: Attorney Fees–Not Tort Liability–Is the Remedy for "Stonewalling" (1987) 21 U.S.F.L.Rev. 419, 432.)

With these rules in mind, we examine the contract at issue in this case to ascertain the reasonable expectations of the parties. The contract recited that its purpose was "to supply [buyer] with a consistent quality raw product at a fair price to [seller], which also allows [buyer] profitability for his finished product." Seller promised to supply the designated quantity even if the price of lettuce went up ("We agree to supply said product and amount at stated price regardless of the market price or conditions") and buyer promised to purchase the designated quantity even if the price went down ("[Buyer] agrees to purchase said product and amounts at stated price regardless of the market price or conditions, provided quality requirements are met"). The possibility that the price of lettuce would fluctuate was consequently foreseeable to both parties.

Although the contract does not recite this fact, seller was aware of buyer's contract with the Castellini Company and with the Castellini

Company's contract with Club Chef. This knowledge was admitted at trial and can be inferred from the fact that seller shipped the contracted for 14 loads of lettuce directly to Club Chef each week. Thus, seller was well aware that if it failed to provide buyer with the required 14 loads of lettuce, buyer would have to obtain replacement lettuce elsewhere or would itself be in breach of contract. This was within the contemplation of the parties when they entered into their agreement.

As noted earlier, the object of contract damages is to give the aggrieved party " 'as nearly as possible the equivalent of the benefits of performance.' " (*Lisec v. United Airlines, Inc.*, supra, 10 Cal.App.4th at p. 1503, 11 Cal.Rptr.2d 689; see also § 1–106 ["The remedies provided by this code shall be liberally administered to the end that the aggrieved party may be put in as good a position as if the other party had fully performed.... "].) In the instant case, buyer contracted for 14 loads of lettuce each week at 9 cents per pound. When seller breached its contract to provide that lettuce, buyer went out on the open market and purchased substitute lettuce to fulfill its contractual obligations to third parties. However, purchasing replacement lettuce to continue its business did not place buyer "in as good a position as if the other party had fully performed." This was because buyer paid more than nine cents per pound for the replacement lettuce. Only by reimbursing buyer for the additional costs above nine cents a pound could buyer truly receive the benefit of the bargain. This is the measure of damages set forth in Section 2–712.

As White and Summers point out, "Since 2–712 measures buyer's damages by the difference between his actual cover purchase and the contract price, the formula will often put buyer in the identical economic position that performance would have." (White & Summers, supra, § 6–3, p. 285.) Therefore, "[i]n the typical case a timely 'cover' purchase by an aggrieved buyer will preclude any 2–715 [incidental and consequential] damages." (Ibid.) "Not only does the damage formula in 2–712 come close to putting the aggrieved buyer in the same economic position as actual performance would have," White and Summers conclude, "but it also enables him to achieve his prime objective, namely that of acquiring his needed goods." (Id. at p. 292.)

In this case, the damage formula of Section 2–712 put buyer in the identical position performance would have: it gave buyer the contracted for 14 loads of lettuce with which to carry on its business at the contracted for price of 9 cents per pound.

Despite the obvious applicability and appropriateness of Section 2–712, seller argues in this appeal that the contract-cover differential of Section 2–712 is inappropriate in cases, as here, where the aggrieved buyer is ultimately able to pass on its additional costs to other parties. Seller contends that Section 1–106's remedial injunction to put the aggrieved party "in as good a position as if the other party had fully performed" demands that all subsequent events impacting on buyer's ultimate profit or loss be taken into consideration (specifically, that buyer passed on all but $70,000 of its loss to Castellini Company, which passed on all of its loss to Club Chef, which passed on most of its loss to its fast food customers). For this proposition, seller relies on two cases limiting a buyer's damages under a different provision of the Commercial Code, Section 2–713 (*Allied Canners & Packers, Inc. v. Victor Packing Co.* (1984) 162 Cal.App.3d 905, 209 Cal.Rptr. 60; HBWBH Cattle Co., Inc. v. Schroeder (8th Cir. 1985) 767 F.2d 437), and on one Section 2–712 cover case in which damages were apparently limited (*Sun Maid Raisin Growers v. Victor Packing Co.* (1983) 146 Cal.App.3d 787, 194 Cal.Rptr. 612).

We begin with the cover case. In *Sun Maid Raisin Growers v. Victor Packing Co.*, supra, 146 Cal.App.3d 787, 194 Cal.Rptr. 612, the seller (Victor) repudiated a contract to sell 610 tons of raisins to Sun-Maid after "disastrous" rains damaged the raisin crop and the price of raisins nearly doubled. Sun-Maid attempted to cover but was only partially successful. It was able to obtain only 200 tons of comparable raisins. For the remaining 410 tons, it had to purchase inferior raisins that had to be reconditioned at a substantial cost. Apparently the total cost of purchasing the 200 tons of high quality raisins and of purchasing and reconditioning the remaining 410 tons was $377,720 over the contract price.

The trial court awarded Sun-Maid, as consequential damages under Section 2–715, $295,339.40 for its lost profits. Victor appealed, arguing that the amount of lost profits was unforeseeable by either party when the contracts were formed. The Court of Appeal affirmed, noting that the evidence established that Victor knew Sun-Maid was purchasing the raisins for resale.

In its discussion, the court recounted the various measures of damages available to an aggrieved buyer under the Uniform Commercial Code for a seller's nondelivery of goods or repudiation of contract, citing Sections 2–712, 2–713, 2–715 and 2–723. The court seemed to wonder why the trial court had chosen lost profits rather than the cost of cover as damages, noting that the court did not specify why it had determined damages in that manner and that neither party had requested findings. However, as neither Sun-Maid nor Victor was contesting that measure of damages on appeal (the only issue was whether lost profits were foreseeable consequential damages), the court observed that the trial court "probably found that damages should be limited to the amount that would have put Sun-Maid in 'as good a position as if the other party had fully performed.' (§1–106.)" (Id. at p. 792, 194 Cal.Rptr. 612.)

From this simple observation, seller claims that "[i]n cases, like the instant case, involving forward contracts, *California courts hold that Section 1–106 limits the damages to be awarded under Section 2–712* (i.e., the cover damages statute) and Section 2–713 (i.e., the market damages statute) for the very reason that the non-breaching party is entitled to nothing more than to be placed in the position which would result from the breaching party's full performance of the agreement. See *Sun Maid Raisin Growers v. Victor Packing Co.* (1983) 146 Cal.App.3d

787, 792, [194 Cal.Rptr. 612] (cover case); *Allied Canners & Packers, Inc. v. Victor Packing Co.* (1984) 162 Cal.App.3d 905, 915 [209 Cal.Rptr. 60] (non-cover case)." (Emphasis added.)

In fact, the *Sun Maid* court held no such thing. It simply offered one possible explanation for the trial court's award, which no one was contesting. Under the facts of that case, the cost of cover might have been unduly difficult to calculate. Sun Maid was able to purchase only 200 tons of comparable raisins in a timely manner. There were no other Thompson seedless free tonnage raisins available within a reasonable time after seller's breach (August 1976). It was considerably later before buyer could find another 410 tons to purchase, and those raisins were damaged in part because of rains occurring after the breach, in September 1976. Under these circumstances, the trial court and the parties may simply have chosen to focus on the easily calculable consequential damages (which buyer claimed were foreseeable and seller denied were foreseeable) and to ignore the difficult to calculate cover damages.

We now look to the "non-cover" case relied upon by seller, *Allied Canners & Packers, Inc. v. Victor Packing Co.*, supra, 162 Cal.App.3d at 915, 209 Cal.Rptr. 60, which in fact does hold that Section 1–106 acts as a limitation on the amount of damages otherwise recoverable under Section 2–713. Before discussing the *Allied Canners* case, however, a few observations on the differences between the contract-cover differential of Section 2–712 and the contract-market differential of Section 2–713 are called for.

As noted earlier, Section 2–712 "will often put buyer in the identical economic position that performance would have." (White & Summers, supra, § 6–3, p. 285.) In contrast, the contract-market differential of Section 2–713 "bears no necessary relation to the change in the buyer's economic status that the breach causes. It is possible that this differential might yield the buyer a handsome sum even though the breach actually saved him money in the long run (as for example when a middleman buyer's resale markets dry up after the breach). It is also quite possible that the buyer's lost profit from resale or consumption would be greater than the contract-market difference." (Id., § 6–4, at p. 294.)

White and Summers argue that the drafters of Section 2–713 could not have intended to put the buyer in the same position as performance since "[p]erformance would have given the buyer certain goods for consumption or resale" (White & Summers, supra, at p. 294) which would have resulted in "either a net economic gain for the buyer or a net economic loss." (Ibid.) The best explanation of Section 2–713, they suggest, is that it is a "statutory liquidated damage clause, a breach inhibitor the payout of which need bear no close relation to the plaintiff's actual loss." (Id. at p. 295; accord Peters, *Remedies for Breach of Contracts Relating to the Sale of Goods Under the Uniform Commercial Code: A Roadmap for Article Two* (1963) 73 Yale L.J. 199, 259.) In discussing the "problem of a buyer who has covered but who seeks to ignore 2–712 and sue for a larger contract-market differential under 2–713," the authors suggest: "If the Code's goal is to put the buyer in the same position as though there had been no breach, and if 2–712 will accomplish that goal but 2–713 will do so only by coincidence, why not force the covering buyer to use 2–712?" (Id. at p. 304.) Professor Robert Childres has actually called for the repeal of Section 2–713 and the requirement of compulsory cover. (Childres, Buyer's Remedies: The Danger of Section 2–713 (1978) 72 NW. U. L. Rev. 837.)

With these prefatory comments in mind, we look to the *Allied Canners* case. In *Allied Canners*, the same raisin supplier (Victor Packing Company) involved in the Sun Maid case breached another contract to sell raisins in 1976. The buyer, Allied Canners, had contracts to resell the raisins it bought from Victor to two Japanese companies for its cost plus 4 percent. Such a resale would have resulted in a profit of $4,462.50 to Allied. When Victor breached the contract, Allied sued for the difference between the market price and the contract price as authorized by Section 2–713. As the market price of raisins had soared due to the disastrous 1976 rains, the market-contract price formula would have yielded damages of approximately $150,000. Allied did not purchase substitute raisins and did not make any deliveries under its resale contracts to the Japanese buyers. One of the Japanese buyers simply released Allied from its contract because of the general unavailability of raisins. The other buyer did not release Allied, but it did not sue Allied either. By the time Allied's case against Victor went to trial, the statute of limitations on the Japanese buyer's claim had run.

Under these circumstances, the court held that the policy of Section 1–106 (that the aggrieved party be put in as good a position as if the other party had performed) required that the award of damages to Allied be limited to its actual loss. It noted that for this limitation to apply, three conditions must be met: (1) "the seller knew that the buyer had a resale contract"; (2) "the buyer has not been able to show that it will be liable in damages to the buyer on its forward contract"; and (3) "there has been no finding of bad faith on the part of the seller. . . ." (*Allied Canners & Packers v. Victor Packing Co.,* supra, 162 Cal.App.3d at p. 915, 209 Cal.Rptr. 60.)

The result in *Allied Canners* seems to have derived in large part from the court's finding that Victor had not acted in bad faith in breaching the contract. The court noted, "It does appear clear, however, that, as the trial court found, the rains caused a severe problem, and Victor made substantial efforts [to procure the raisins for Allied]. We do not deem this record one to support an inference that windfall damages must be awarded the buyer to prevent unjust enrichment to a deliberately breaching seller. (Compare *Sun Maid Raisin Growers v. Victor Packing Co.*, supra, 146 Cal.App.3d 787, 194 Cal.Rptr. 612 [where, in a case coincidentally involving Victor, Victor was expressly found by the trial court to have engaged in bad faith by gambling on the market price of raisins in deciding whether to perform its contracts to sell raisins to Sun Maid].)" (162 Cal.App.3d at p. 916, 209 Cal.Rptr. 60.)

We believe that this focus on the good or bad faith of the breaching party is inappropriate in a commercial sales case. As our California Supreme Court recently explained, courts should not differentiate between good and bad motives for breaching a contract in assessing the measure of the non-breaching party's damages. (*Applied Equipment Corp. v. Litton Saudi Arabia Ltd.* (1994) 7 Cal.4th 503, 513–515, 28 Cal.Rptr.2d 475, 869 P.2d 454.) Such a focus is inconsistent with the policy "to encourage contractual relations and commercial activity by enabling parties to estimate in advance the financial risks of their enterprise." (Id. at p. 515, 28 Cal.Rptr.2d 475, 869 P.2d 454.) " 'Courts traditionally have awarded damages for breach of contract to compensate the aggrieved party rather than to punish the breaching party.' [Citations.]" (*Foley v. Interactive Data Corp.*, supra, 47 Cal.3d at p. 683, 254 Cal.Rptr. 211, 765 P.2d 373.)

The *Allied Canners* opinion has been sharply criticized in numerous law review articles and in at least one sister-state opinion. In *Tongish v. Thomas* (1992) 251 Kan. 728, 840 P.2d 471, the Kansas Supreme Court rejected the Allied Canners approach and instead applied the "majority view [which] would award market damages even though in excess of plaintiff's loss." (Id., 840 P.2d at p. 475.) Relying on an article by Professors Simon and Novack, Limiting the Buyer's Market Damages to Lost Profits: A Challenge to the Enforceability of Market Contracts (1979) 92 Harv.L.Rev. 1395, the *Tongish* court explained that use of the market price/contract price damage scheme of Section 2–713 " 'encourages a more efficient market and discourages the breach of contracts.' " (*Tongish v. Thomas*, supra, 840 P.2d at p. 476.)

Similarly, in Schneider, UCC Section 2–713: A Defense of Buyers' Expectancy Damages (1986) 22 Cal.W.L.Rev. 233, 264, the author states that "[b]y limiting buyer to lost resale profits, the [Allied Canners] court ignored the clear language of section 2–713's compensation scheme to award expectation damages in accordance with the parties' allocation of risk as measured by the difference between contract price and market price on the date set for performance. If the court wanted to avoid giving greater damages, it would have been better for it to view what occurred to the availability and price of raisins as being beyond the risks contemplated by the parties and thus to have ruled under the doctrine of commercial impracticability as provided in section 2–615(a)."

In addition numerous New York courts have chosen not to limit a buyer's damages to actual losses. (See e.g., *Fertico Belgium v. Phosphate Chem. Export* (1987) 70 N.Y.2d 76, 517 N.Y.S.2d 465, 510 N.E.2d 334; *Apex Oil Co. v. Vanguard Oil & Service Co.* (2d Cir. 1985) 760 F.2d 417; *G.A. Thompson & Co. v. Wendell J. Miller, Etc.* (S.D.N.Y.1978) 457 F.Supp. 996.)

As the foregoing discussion makes clear, we have serious reservations about whether the result in *Allied Canners*, with its emphasis on the good faith of the breaching party, is appropriate in an action seeking damages under section 2–713. We have no reservations, however, in not extending the *Allied Canners* rationale to a section 2–712 case. As noted earlier, no section 2712 case, including *Sun Maid Growers v. Victor Packing Co.*, supra, 146 Cal.App.3d 787, 194 Cal.Rptr. 612, has ever held that cover damages must be limited by section 1–106. The obvious reason is that the cover-contract differential puts a buyer who covers in the exact same position as performance would have done. This is the precisely what is called for in section 1–106. In this respect, the cover/contract differential of section 2–712 is very different than the market/contract differential of section 2–713, which "need bear no close relation to the plaintiff's actual loss." (White & Summers, supra, at p. 295.)

In summary, we hold that where a buyer " 'cover[s]' by making in good faith and without unreasonable delay any reasonable purchase of ... goods in substitution for those due from the seller, ... [that buyer] may recover from the seller as damages the difference between the cost of cover and the contract price...." (§ 2–712). This gives the buyer the benefit of its bargain. What the buyer chooses to do with that bargain is not relevant to the determination of damages under section 2–712.

B. Buyer's Cross-Appeal

Buyer contends it should receive prejudgment interest from July or August 1991 rather than from 30 days before the start of trial as awarded by the trial court. We agree.

The facts relevant to this claim are as follows: On July 26, 1991, buyer filed a complaint under PACA with the Department of Agriculture in Washington, D.C. The complaint stated, in pertinent part: "8. On or about May 13, 1991, Respondent breached the October 1990 contract by failing to provide to Complainant the required quantity of lettuce. Complainant notified Respondent of its breach on May 16, 1991 by a letter, a copy of which is attached hereto as Exhibit E, and began to purchase open market lettuce against Respondent's account to meet its requirements. [¶] 9. As a consequence of Respondent's breach of contract, Complainant has been required to purchase lettuce from other sources, for which it has paid the amount of $704,895.71 more than it would have had there been no breach of contract. The determination of said sum is more fully set forth in Exhibit F, attached hereto, as a description of the sources and prices which Complainant was charged." Exhibit F was a detailed schedule listing on a week-by-week basis the identity of the supplier, the purchase order number, the date of the purchase, the number of bins, the price actually paid to the supplier, and the price that would have been paid under the contract. The total sum paid for replacement lettuce was $966,908.30, which was $704,895.71 more than the contract price.

When buyer filed its cross-complaint in February 1992, it sought damages of $704,895.71, together with interest from June 16, 1991. Seller never challenged buyer's figures. Instead, its argument was that buyer was not entitled to damages (except for $70,000) because buyer had passed on all of its losses except $70,000 to the Castellini Company.

In preparation for trial, buyer's controller reviewed his calculations and discovered that a few of the purchases listed in Exhibit F of the PACA complaint were not in substitution for lettuce due from seller. He revised his calculations eliminating these purchases. The revised figures showed the cost of cover to be $908,564.94, the cost of lettuce had it been purchased at nine cents per pound to be $252,604.72, and the consequent cover damages to be $665,960.22. The jury accepted his figures to the penny.

Subsequently, the trial court awarded buyer prejudgment interest commencing 30 days before trial.

Civil Code section 3287, subdivision (a) provides: "Every person who is entitled to recover damages certain, or capable of being made certain by calculation, and the right to recover which is vested in him upon a particular day, is entitled to also recover interest thereon from that day, except during such time as the debtor is prevented by law, or by the act of the creditor from paying the debt." As the facts are not in dispute, we independently review whether and when buyer's damages were certain or capable of being made certain by calculation. It is from that day that buyer's entitlement to prejudgment interest commences.

The test for recovery of prejudgment interest under section 3287, subdivision (a) is whether defendant (1) actually knows the amount of damages owed plaintiff, or (2) could have computed that amount from reasonably available information. (*Chesapeake Industries, Inc. v. Togova Enterprises, Inc.* (1983) 149 Cal.App.3d 901, 907, 197 Cal.Rptr. 348.) "If the defendant does not know or cannot readily compute the damages, the plaintiff must supply him with a statement and supporting data so that defendant can ascertain the damages. [Citation.]" (*Polster, Inc. v. Swing* (1985) 164 Cal.App.3d 427, 435, 210 Cal.Rptr. 567.)

In the instant case, that is exactly what buyer did when it supplied seller with Exhibit F, listing all lettuce purchases, purchase order numbers, bin number, and price information. The fact that an error of approximately 5.5 percent was made in the original calculations does not make the damages uncertain. Several cases are instructive.

In *Marine Terminals Corp. v. Paceco, Inc.* (1983) 145 Cal.App.3d 991, 193 Cal.Rptr. 687, for example, the plaintiff sent various invoices to the defendant demanding that defendant reimburse it for costs associated with defendant's faulty repair work. At trial, it emerged that not all of the $38,918.71 charged by the repair facility was for work done on the left gear. In fact, five work orders totaling $2,461.80 were for inspections and work done on the right gear. This 6.3 percent discrepancy did not make the damages uncertain. "The errors ... were minor and could have been easily corrected at the time the demand for payment was made. Defendant Paceco disputed its liability but at no time prior to trial disputed the amount or method of calculating plaintiff's damages. Those damages were readily ascertainable and capable of being made certain from the data furnished to defendant in 1977. Plaintiff is entitled to prejudgment interest." (Id. at pp. 997–998, 193 Cal.Rptr. 687.)

Likewise in *Esgro Central, Inc. v. General Ins. Co.* (1971) 20 Cal. App.3d 1054, 1062, 98 Cal.Rptr. 153, the court held that the insured's damages for loss of a business during a riot were ascertainable even though the jury's award was greater that the amount sought in the proof of loss statement. The discrepancy did not "detract from the proposition that the damages [were] fixed or determinable." (See also *Coleman Engineering Co. v. North American Aviation, Inc.* (1966) 65 Cal.2d 396, 408–409, 55 Cal.Rptr. 1, 420 P.2d 713, disapproved on another ground in *Earhart v. William Low Co.* (1979) 25 Cal.3d 503, 513, 158 Cal.Rptr. 887, 600 P.2d 1344 [plaintiff's original demand was $7,000 too high due to an error in the pricing formula; court explained that "the erroneous omission of a few matters from the account or erroneous calculation of the costs do not mean that the damages are not capable of being made certain by calculation." (Id. at p. 409, 55 Cal.Rptr. 1, 420 P.2d 713.)].)

Similarly in the instant case, buyer's controller's minor error did not make buyer's damages uncertain. Accordingly, buyer was entitled to prejudgment interest from Aug 1, 1991.

DISPOSITION

The order of the trial court awarding prejudgment interest from 30 days before trial is reversed and the cause is remanded. The trial court is directed to enter a new order awarding buyer prejudgment interest from August 1, 1991. In all other respects, the judgment is affirmed. Costs on appeal to buyer.

Notes and Discussion

1. **Questions, Questions.** The damages provisions of the UCC have raised problems that go to the very heart of how we should conceive of damages in contract law. In *Allied Canners & Packers, Inc. v. Victor Packing Co.*, 162 Cal.App.3d 905, 209 Cal.Rptr. 60 (1984), Allied purchased raisins from Victor and then promptly resold them to two Japanese importers, for a total anticipated profit of about $4,500. Victor failed to deliver, but since (for various reasons) the Japanese firms did not enforce their contracts, Allied basically lost only its anticipated profit from the deals. Nonetheless it sued Victor under § 2–713(1) for "the difference between the market price at the time when the buyer learned of the breach and the contract price," about $150,000.

In *KGM Harvesting*, a seller defaulted on delivery of lettuce, and the buyer then purchased substitute lettuce on the open market, at a much higher price. The buyer was able to pass on most of this higher cost to its ultimate customers. Nonetheless it sued under § 2–712 for "the difference between the cost of cover and the contract price." UCC § 2–712(2). The seller wanted damages limited to the buyer's actual losses.

The underlying issues here are profound. We can concentrate first on some problems in *KGM Harvesting*.

(1) What if Burger King, Taco Bell and Pizza Hut had intervened in this case? Could they have asked that the buyer, Fresh Network, share its recovery with them? How should Fresh Network respond, and how should the law respond?

(2) The plaintiffs in this case exercised self help by "setting off" (refusing to pay some of the amounts that they acknowledge to be due). Section 2–717 authorizes such behavior but, of course, anyone using 2–717 needs to be sure that it is due "damages" or its set off will put it in breach.

(3) If Fresh Network had discovered that its cover price was an unusually good one and that the general market price for lettuce was actually higher than its cover price, could it have brought suit under § 2–713 for the larger difference (between market and contract) despite the fact it had replaced the lettuce by purchasing below that market price? Put otherwise, does the act of cover foreclose suit under § 2–713? In answering this question, consider Comments 1 and 5 to 2–713. These comments seem to suggest that a buyer who covers is foreclosed from using 2–713.

(4) Do not ignore the discussion of the plaintiff's right to interest. In law school we often overlook a plaintiff's right to interest and to lawyer's fees, but, in life, interest and fees can be a big thing. The court deals with a common distinction, namely that interest often accrues before the time of judgment on "liquidated" amounts but not for "unliquidated" amounts. Rights to interest vary substantially from state to state and—depending upon the particular cause of action and the kind of damages—within a state. Under American law, one gets lawyer's fees from the other side only in unusual cases (mostly where statutes so provide).

2. Windfall? It may seem intuitively obvious to you that when the injured party's actual expectation damages are less than the "abstract" market differential (as measured under §§ 2–708(1) or 2–713), the injured party needs recompense for no more than its actual damages in order to be restored into "as good a position as if the other party had fully performed." UCC § 1–106(1) (revised § 1–305(a)). What argument does the *KGM Harvesting* decision use in rejecting the intuitive view? According to the Court, the *Tongish* court, relying on a scholarly article, has "explained that use of the market price/contract price damage scheme of Section [2–713] 'encourages a more efficient market and discourages the breach of contracts.' " Really?

Victor Goldberg, Framing Contract Law: An Economic Perspective 232 (2006), suggests that: "There are three easy paths to the proper outcome in these [middleman] cases. . . . The first is to respect privity and the allocation of counterparty risk. There is no reason for the court to treat the middleman as a broker when the contractual arrangement specifically rejects that. How, or whether, parties deal with the price risks of a particular contract in the remainder of their business is irrelevant. The second, as the *Tongish* court put it, is to encourage a more efficient market. Allowing sellers to back out of forward contracts when the market price exceeds the contract price discourages contracting. Finally, the *Allied* court could have considered the nature of the contract it was constructing if it granted the commission-only damage remedy. The seller receives a 'put option' (the right, but not the obligation, to sell) with the contract price being the exercise price and the price of that option being the middleman's commission. Middlemen who willingly write such contracts do not survive long. There is no good reason to impose such a contract on them." All three paths lead to the outcome in *KGM Harvesting*; do you see why?

Problem 6–5

Tesoro Petroleum Corporation contracted to sell ten million gallons of gasoline to Holborn Oil Company in New York, at a price of $1.30 per gallon. Shortly before making this contract, Tesoro had purchased the gasoline for $1.26. After the price at the delivery point plunged to about 75 cents per gallon, Holborn repudiated while Tesoro's ship was at sea. Tesoro then arranged to sell the gasoline in Argentina, where the price was $1.10. Tesoro has now brought suit against Holborn under § 2–708 for the market differential, about fifty-five cents per gallon. Holborn counters that damages should be limited to twenty cents per gallon, reflecting the re-sale price.

What outcome? Read closely §§ 2–703, 2–706, and 2–708; and make sure that your solution takes account of the arguments in *KGM Harvesting.*

FERTICO BELGIUM v. PHOSPHATE CHEMICALS EXPORT ASS'N, INC.

New York Court of Appeals, 1987.
517 N.Y.S.2d 465, 70 N.Y.2d 76, 510 N.E.2d 334.

BELLACOSA, J. A seller (Phoschem) breached its contract to timely deliver goods to a buyer-trader (Fertico) who properly sought cover (under the Uniform Commercial Code that means acquiring substitute goods) from another source (Unifert) in order to avoid breaching that buyer-trader's obligation to a third-party buyer (Altawreed). The sole issue involves the applicable principles and computation of damages for breach of the Phoschem-to-Fertico contract.

We hold that under the exceptional circumstances of this case plaintiff Fertico, as a buyer-trader, is entitled to damages from seller Phoschem equal to the increased cost of cover plus consequential and incidental damages minus expenses saved (UCC 2–712[2]). In this case, expenses saved as a result of the breach are limited to costs or expenditures which would have arisen had there been no breach. Thus, the seller Phoschem is not entitled to a credit from the profits of a subsequent sale by the first buyer-trader Fertico to a fourth party (Janssens) of nonconforming goods from Phoschem. Fertico's letter of credit had been presented by Phoschem and honored so, under the specific facts of this case, Fertico had no commercially reasonable alternative but to retain and resell the fertilizer. This is so despite Fertico's exercise of cover in connection with the first set of transactions, i.e., Phoschem to Fertico to Altawreed. The covering buyer-trader may not, however, as in this case, recover other consequential damages when the third party to which it made its sale provides increased compensation to offset additional costs arising as a consequence of the breach.

In October 1978 appellant Fertico Belgium S.A. (Fertico), an international trader of fertilizer, contracted with Phosphate Chemicals Export Association, Inc. (Phoschem), a corporation engaged in exporting phosphate fertilizer, to purchase two separate shipments of fertilizer for delivery to Antwerp, Belgium. The first shipment was to be 15,000 tons delivered no later than November 20, 1978 and the second was to be 20,000 tons delivered by November 30, 1978. Phoschem knew that Fertico required delivery on the specified dates so that the fertilizer could be bagged and shipped in satisfaction of a secondary contract Fertico had with Altawreed, Iraq's agricultural ministry. Fertico secured a letter of credit in a timely manner with respect to the first shipment. After Phoschem projected a first shipment delivery date of December 4, 1978, Fertico advised Phoschem, on November 13, 1978, that the breach as to the first shipment presented "huge problems" and canceled the second shipment which had not as of that date been loaded, thus ensuring its late delivery. The first shipment did not actually arrive in Antwerp until December 17 and was not off-loaded until December 21, 1978. Despite the breach as to the first shipment, Fertico retained custody and indeed acquired title over that first shipment because, as its president testified "[w]e had no other choice" (Rec on app, at 597–598) as defendant seller Phoschem had presented Fertico's $1.7 million letter of credit as of November 17, 1978, and the same had been honored by the issuer (see, UCC 5–114).

Fertico's predicament from the breach by delay of even the first shipment, a breach which Phoschem does not deny, was that it, in turn, would breach its contract to sell to Altawreed unless it acquired substitute goods. In an effort to avoid that secondary breach, Fertico took steps in mid-November to cover (UCC 2–712) the goods by purchasing 35,000 tons of the same type fertilizer from Unifert, a Lebanese concern. The cost of the fertilizer itself under the Phoschem-to-Fertico contract was $4,025,000, and under the Unifert-to-Fertico contract $4,725,000, a differential of $700,000. On the same day Fertico acquired cover, November 15, 1978, Fertico's president traveled to Baghdad, Iraq, to renegotiate its contract with Altawreed. In return for a postponed delivery date and an additional payment of $20.50 per ton, Fertico agreed to make direct inland delivery rather than delivery to the seaport of Basra. Fertico fulfilled its renegotiated Altawreed contract with the substitute fertilizer purchased as cover from Unifert.

In addition to the problems related to its Altawreed contract, Fertico was left with 15,000 tons of late-delivered fertilizer which it did not require but which it had been compelled to take because Phoschem had received payment on Fertico's letter of credit. This aggrieved international buyer-seller was required to store the product and seek out a new purchaser. Fertico sold the 15,000 tons of the belatedly delivered Phoschem fertilizer to another buyer, Janssens, on March 19, 1979, some three months after the nonconforming delivery, and earned a profit of $454,000 based on the cost to it from Phoschem and its sale price to Janssens.

In 1981 Fertico commenced this action against Phoschem seeking $1.25 million in damages for Phoschem's breach of the October 1978 agreement. A jury returned a verdict of $1.07 million which the trial court refused to overturn on a motion for judgment notwithstanding the verdict. The Appellate Division vacated the damage award, ordered a new trial on the damages issue only and ruled, as a matter of law, (1) that the increased transportation costs on the Altawreed contract were not consequential damages; (2) that the higher purchase price paid by Altawreed to Fertico was an expense saved as a consequence of the Phoschem breach; and (3) that the Fertico damages had to be reduced by the profits from the Janssens' sale (*Fertico Belgium v. Phosphate Chems. Export Assn.*, 120 A.D.2d 401, 501 N.Y.S.2d 867). Fertico appealed to this court on a stipulation for judgment absolute. We disagree with propositions (2) and (3) in the Appellate Division ruling, and conclude that the Uniform Commercial Code and our analysis support a modification and reinstatement of $700,000 of the damage award in a final judgment resolving this litigation between the parties.

Failure by Phoschem to make delivery on the contract dates concededly constituted a breach of the contract (White and Summers, Uniform Commercial Code § 6–2, at 207 [2d ed]). The Uniform Commercial Code § 2–711 gives the nonbreaching party the alternative of either seeking the partial self-help of cover along with recovery of damages (UCC 2–712), or of recovering damages only for the differential between the market price and the contract price, together with incidental and consequential damages less expenses saved (UCC 2–713; see also, *Productora e Importadora de Papel, S.A. de C.V. v. Fleming*, 376 Mass. 826, 383 N.E.2d 1129). Fertico exercised its right as the wronged buyer-trader to cover in order to obtain the substitute fertilizer it required to meet its obligation under its Altawreed contract (see, UCC 2–712, comment 1).

A covering buyer's damages are equal to the difference between the presumably higher cost of cover and the contract price, plus incidental or consequential damages suffered on account of the breach, less expenses saved (UCC 2–712[2]). Fertico is thus entitled to a damage remedy under this section because its cover purchase was made in good faith, without unreasonable delay, and the Unifert fertilizer was a reasonable substitute for the Phoschem fertilizer (UCC 2–712[1]; *Reynolds Sec. v. Underwriters Bank & Trust Co.*, 44 N.Y.2d 568, 572–573, 406 N.Y.S.2d 743, 378 N.E.2d 106).

Fertico's additional costs for delivering the fertilizer inland rather than at a seaport would usually constitute consequential damages because they resulted from Phoschem's breach, because Phoschem knew that Fertico would incur damages under its separate contract obligation and because the damages were not prevented by the cover (UCC 2–715[2]). The increased costs attendant to the Altawreed contract are consequential damages because they did not "arise within the scope of the immediate [Phoschem-Fertico] transaction, but rather stem from losses incurred by [Fertico] in its dealings [with Altawreed] which were a proximate result of the breach, and which were reasonably foreseeable by the breaching party at the time of contracting" (Petroleo Brasileiro, S.A. Petrobras v. Ameropan Oil Corp., 372 F.Supp. 503, 508). Ordinarily, an award for consequential damages occasioned by the seller's breach would be necessary to put a buyer like Fertico in as good a position as it would have been had there been no breach (UCC 1–106; see, Neri v. Retail Mar. Corp., 30 N.Y.2d 393, 334 N.Y.S.2d 165, 285 N.E.2d 311; 3 Hawkland, Uniform Commercial Code Series § 2–715:01, at 389). Inasmuch as Altawreed compensated Fertico for the additional delivery costs, Fertico was insulated from any loss in that respect as a result of Phoschem's breach, thereby eliminating this category of potential damages. On this question of consequential damages, the Appellate Division was correct.

The additional compensation to Fertico, an international trader, from Altawreed is not, however, an expense saved as a consequence of the seller Phoschem's breach for which Phoschem is entitled to any credit (UCC 2–712 [2]). In most instances, and particularly in this case, saved expenses must be costs or expenditures which would be anticipated had there been no breach (see, Productora e Importadora de Papel, S.A. de C.V. v. Fleming, 376 Mass. 826, 839, 383 N.E.2d 1129, 1137, supra). For example, if a seller were to breach a contract to deliver an unpackaged product to the buyer and the buyer were to cover with the same product prepackaged, the cost of packaging which the buyer would have had to perform is an expense saved as a consequence of the breach (see, 3 Hawkland, Uniform Commercial Code Series § 2–712:02, at 362). The increased remuneration from Altawreed was compensation for the additional shipment responsibilities incurred by Fertico, not a cost or expenditure anticipated in the absence of a breach, and therefore was erroneously analyzed and credited in Phoschem's favor by the Appellate Division.

The third prong of the damages analysis relates to the profit made from the independent sale of the Phoschem fertilizer to Janssens. The Appellate Division erred in offsetting this profit against the damages otherwise suffered since that court mistakenly concluded that the sale stemmed from and was dependent upon Phoschem's breach. This offset, on these peculiar facts, would severely disadvantage Fertico, a trader in fertilizer who both buys and sells, and who would have pursued such commercial transactions had there been no breach by Phoschem. It would be anomalous to conclude that had it not been for Phoschem's breach Fertico would not have continued its trade and upon such reasoning to counterpoise the profits from the Janssens' sale against the damages arising from Phoschem's breach. Inasmuch as the facts here are exceptional because Fertico met its subsale obligations with the cover fertilizer and yet acquired title and control over the late-delivered fertilizer from Phoschem, our decision does not fit squarely within the available Uniform Commercial Code remedies urged by the dissent. Thus, strict reliance on *Neri v. Retail Mar. Corp.*, 30 N.Y.2d 393, 334 N.Y.S.2d 165, 285 N.E.2d 311 (supra) and on Hawkland's commentary (3 Hawkland, Uniform Commercial Code Series § 2–714:05, at 384), as undertaken by the dissent, does not provide an adequate resolution to the particular problem presented in this case.

Fertico learned of Phoschem's breach after Phoschem had negotiated Fertico's $1.7 million letter of credit, which constituted complete payment for the first shipment. With no commercially reasonable alternative, Fertico took custody of the first shipment but canceled the second (UCC 2–601[c]), having previously notified Phoschem of its breach (UCC 2–607). The loss resulting to Fertico by having to acquire cover, even in the face of its acceptance of a late-delivered portion of the fertilizer, is properly recoverable under section 2–714(1) (3 Hawkland, Uniform Commercial Code Series § 2–714:05, at 384–385). At the same time, Uniform Commercial Code § 1–106 directs that the remedies provided by the Uniform Commercial Code should be liberally administered so as to put the aggrieved party in as good a position as if the other party had fully performed. Had Phoschem fully performed, Fertico would have had the benefit of the Altawreed transaction and, as a trader of fertilizer, the profits from the Janssens' sale as well. "Gains made by the injured party on other transactions after the breach are never to be deducted from the damages that are otherwise recoverable, unless such gains could not have been made, had there been no breach" (5 Corbin, Contracts § 1041, at 256; see also, *Steen Indus. v. Richer Communications*, 226 Pa.Super.Ct. 219, 314 A.2d 319). Fertico's profit made on the sale of a nonspecific article such as fertilizer, of which the supply in the market is not limited, should not therefore be deducted from the damages recoverable from Phoschem (5 Corbin, Contracts § 1041, at 258–260; see also, *Neri v. Retail Mar. Corp.*, 30 N.Y.2d 393, 401, 334 N.Y.S.2d 165, 285 N.E.2d 311, supra).

Fertico was concededly wronged by Phoschem's breach and Fertico resorted to Uniform Commercial Code remedies which are rooted in what we perceive to be the realities of the marketplace. Fertico did what reasonable traders would do and would like to do in mitigating risks inflicted in this case by Phoschem and in exerting its commercial resourcefulness. That is, it took steps to save its business, its customers, its good will and its deals and ultimately to also recover appropriate damages from a wrongdoer. That did not produce a "windfall" or a "double benefit" to the aggrieved party as the dissenting opinion asserts. The result we reach today countenances no such thing. On the contrary, to deprive the buyer-trader Fertico of its rightful differential damages of $700,000 and to credit this transactionally independent profit to Phoschem would perversely enrich the wrongdoer at the expense of the wronged party, a result those in the marketplace would find perplexing and a result which the generous remedial purpose of the Uniform Commercial Code does not compel or authorize. The dissent's characterization of the recovery by an injured party of damages for a breach of contract as a "benefit" is wrong, since that functionally attributes a kind of lien against the independently pursued benefit derived out of that separate transaction.

Accordingly, the order of the Appellate Division affirming liability but vacating, on the law, the damage award and remanding the matter for a new trial on the issue of damages, as appealed to this court on a stipulation for judgment absolute, should be modified and damages awarded to Fertico in the amount of $700,000 in accordance with this opinion.

TITONE, J. (DISSENTING). At issue in this appeal is the relationship among the various remedies that article 2 of the Uniform Commercial Code provides for buyers aggrieved by sellers' defaults. Central to the analysis is the principle that the Code's remedies "shall be liberally administered to the end that the aggrieved party may be put in *as good a position* as if the other party had fully performed" (UCC 1–106[1] [emphasis supplied]). Here, the majority has concluded that the aggrieved buyer may retain both cover damages and the profit from the resale of the late-delivered goods, in effect, securing the benefit of its bargain twice. Since that result is not required by, and indeed is not even consistent with, the purpose of Code's generous remedial provisions, I must respectfully dissent.

I begin with the premise that an aggrieved buyer who has purchased substitute goods and sued for "cover" damages under UCC 2–712 has impliedly rejected the seller's nonconforming performance and, consequently, holds the seller's goods only as security for any prepayments made to the seller (see, UCC 2–706[6]; 2–711[3]). I find the contrary position—that an aggrieved buyer may compatibly resort to cover and also retain and resell the nonconforming goods for its own account—to be legally insupportable and economically unsound. The "cover" remedy represents a recognition by the Code's drafters that a buyer aggrieved by a breach or repudiation "may not be made whole by the mere recovery of damages, because he is left, thereby, in a position in which he does not have the goods he wants" (3 Hawkland, Uniform Commercial Code Series § 2–712:01, at 360). The Code's "cover" provision, which authorizes the buyer to purchase equivalent goods in the open market and then sue the breaching seller for any price differential (see, UCC 2–712), was intended as a practical method of furnishing the buyer with a fair substitute for the goods it bargained for but did not receive. Thus, from an economic standpoint, the buyer receives the full benefit of his bargain when he obtains cover damages under UCC 2–712. Allowing the buyer to retain and resell the goods in addition obviously leads to a windfall, since the buyer is receiving more than the benefit of the transaction it bargained for.

Moreover, the language of the Code makes clear that the buyer cannot both sue for cover and accept the goods. UCC 2–712(1) defines "cover" as a purchase of goods "*in substitution for* those due from the seller" (emphasis supplied) and authorizes an aggrieved buyer to resort to cover only "[a]fter a breach within [UCC 2–711(1)]," which specifically states that cover "under [UCC 2–712(1)]" is available when "the seller fails to make delivery * * * or the buyer rightfully rejects or justifiably revokes acceptance" (UCC 2–711 [1]). Finally, any doubt about the applicability of the cover remedy referred to in UCC 2–711 is dispelled by comment 1: "The remedies listed here are those available to a buyer *who has not accepted the goods or who has justifiably revoked his acceptance*" (emphasis supplied).

In short, consistent with its purpose, the cover remedy is, by its terms, available only in situations where the buyer either does not have the needed goods because of nondelivery or cannot use the goods that were delivered because of a defect in the seller's performance. In all other situations, the aggrieved buyer must resort to the remedies provided in UCC 2–714, which concerns nonconforming goods that have been accepted (see, UCC 2–711, comment 1). While there are instances in which an accepting buyer may also seek cover damages under UCC 2–714(1), even the commentary the majority cites makes clear that the cover remedy is not intended to be used with respect to those nonconforming goods that the buyer has received and accepted; rather, the remedy is properly used only to replace the portion of needed goods the buyer either does not have or does not take (3 Hawkland, op. cit. § 2–714:05, at 384–385).

Viewed within the framework of these basic principles, cases such as this one involving late delivery are not difficult to resolve. As in cases where there has been a total failure to deliver, the buyer in late-delivery cases may reject the untimely performance and cover with substitute goods. Additionally, unlike the buyer aggrieved by a total failure to deliver, the buyer aggrieved by a late delivery has the alternative option of accepting the belatedly delivered goods and retaining for itself any profit realized on resale. However, contrary to Fertico's claims, the aggrieved buyer may not pursue both courses simultaneously, since it would then benefit twice from what was a single bargain—a result that is unacceptable under UCC 1–106 (see, *Melby v. Hawkins Pontiac*, 13 Wash.App. 745, 537 P.2d 807 [alternative remedies may be pursued under UCC, but not where double recovery would result]).

The majority has attempted to rationalize that result here by relying on a damages rule that has previously been applied only to aggrieved sellers. The rule permits a seller who regularly deals in goods of a particular type to sue the breaching buyer for lost profit even though the wrongfully rejected goods have been sold to another buyer without loss. The rule applies only where the seller has an unlimited supply of standard-price goods (see, *Neri v. Retail Mar. Corp.*, 30 N.Y.2d 393, 399–400, 334 N.Y.S.2d 165, 285 N.E.2d 311; 3 Hawkland, op. cit. § 2–708:04, at 331–332). In those situations, "it may safely be assumed that" the seller would have made two sales instead of one if the buyer had not breached, and, consequently, it can fairly be said that the buyer's breach deprived the seller of an opportunity for additional profit (3 Hawkland, op. cit., at 332). Thus, traditional remedies such as resale or market price differential are "inadequate to put the seller in as good a position as performance would have done", and the seller may sue for the lost profit (UCC 2–708[2]).

The Code, however, does not contain an analogous provision allowing aggrieved buyers to recover profits from lost sales, and there is good reason for that omission, since neither of the conditions necessary for application of the sellers' lost-profit remedy may be satisfied in the case of an aggrieved buyer. First, a party in the position of a buyer cannot, by definition, be said to have an unlimited supply of the goods at his disposal for resale; even where the goods are fungible, the buyer who intends to resell must go into the marketplace to acquire the goods in the first instance.[13] Second, a buyer who must go into the market to obtain goods will ordinarily not be able to rely on the availability of a "standard price"; rather, unlike the seller who has an unlimited supply of standard-price goods in its inventory, the reselling buyer remains at the mercy of the wholesale market's price fluctuations. Because of these differences, it cannot "be safely assumed" that the aggrieved buyer-dealer would have made a second sale at a particular profit were it not for the seller's breach. To the contrary, the occurrence of and profit on a second transaction would depend on such other, unrelated variables as the availability and wholesale market price of the goods at the time the buyer-dealer went into the market to acquire them. Thus, the rationale for the seller-dealer's lost-profit remedy is simply inapplicable to buyer-dealers.

Indeed, this case illustrates the difficulty of applying the seller's lost-profit remedy to aggrieved buyers. Were it not for Phoschem's breach, Fertico would have delivered the 15,000 tons of fertilizer it had purchased from Phoschem to Altawreed and would have had to go into the marketplace again to acquire an additional 15,000 tons if it wished to make a second sale to Janssens. In this respect, Fertico's position here is really no different in principle from that of an aggrieved seller which had only one set of goods at its immediate disposal. In both instances, the breach of a prior agreement is what has made the goods available for a second sale (cf., 5 *89 Corbin, Contracts § 1041, at 256). And, while a second sale may have been theoretically possible even without the breach, the uncertainties occasioned by the buyer/seller's need to return to the marketplace for more goods of the same kind preclude the assumption, implicit in the majority's holding (see also, *Neri v. Retail Mar. Corp.*, supra), that the second sale and its accompanying profit would have been made on the same terms even if no breach had occurred.

Finally, I cannot agree with the majority's reliance on the supposedly "exceptional" circumstance that Fertico both "met its subsale obligations with the cover fertilizer and * * * acquired title and control over the late-delivered fertilizer".... First, the basis for and significance of the majority's conclusion that Fertico acquired title to the goods is left unclear. Certainly, the fact that Fertico had already paid for the goods

13. Indeed, it seems somewhat ironic to recognize, on the one hand, the buyer's right to go into the marketplace and acquire "cover" goods at an increased cost and, on the other hand, treat the buyer as a party in the position of a seller with an unlimited supply of goods at its disposal.

cannot be controlling, since the Code clearly does not equate payment and receipt of the goods with passage of title. To the contrary, the Code expressly contemplates and accounts for these situations by permitting a wronged buyer who has rejected to retain and resell the goods in its possession to recover any down payment (UCC 2–706[6]; 2–711[3]). The Code also requires in these situations, however, that the buyer account to the breaching seller for any additional profit it has made on the resale (UCC 2–706[6]). Nothing in the majority opinion satisfactorily explains why this remedy is insufficient.[14]

Furthermore, the majority's emphasis on the asserted "exceptional facts" is unpersuasive because under the terms of the majority's holding the outcome in a given case would turn, in large measure, on the fortuity of which party had possession of the goods after the breach. In the case of a simple late delivery the buyer will ordinarily have possession after the breach. Under the majority's holding, that buyer may both obtain cover damages and resell the seller's goods, retaining any profit for itself. In the case of a complete failure to deliver, however, the seller will ordinarily have possession of the goods after the breach. Under the Code, the buyer in such a case may obtain either cover damages or the goods (if they have been specifically identified to the contract, but not both UCC 2–716[3]). Thus, the buyer aggrieved by a late delivery is placed in a substantially better position than a buyer aggrieved by a complete failure to deliver, although there is no apparent legal or commercial justification for the distinction. Even more seriously, a seller who completely repudiates is placed in a more advantageous position than one who merely delivers late. While both must pay cover damages, the repudiating seller may resell the undelivered goods in its possession for its own account—an option unavailable to the seller who has delivered, albeit late. Since I cannot agree with a rule of law that ultimately imposes a greater penalty on the less serious of two similar breaches, I dissent and vote to affirm.

Notes and Discussion

1. **The Letter of Credit.** The buyer had to give the seller a "letter of credit." Letters of credit are very common particularly in international commerce. The letter of credit might provide that the seller Phoschem would present invoices, bills of lading, perhaps insurance certificates and other documents, together with a draft to an American bank, and receive payment of the agreed amount from that bank before the goods were actually delivered. It is easy to see why a seller who is shipping to another country would like a letter of credit. Do you see the practical consequences of the letter? For example, the presence of the letter and the ability of the beneficiary/seller to get payment in the United States may mean that the seller will wind up as the defendant, not the plaintiff, in a lawsuit. It may

14. That retention and resale of Phoschem's goods was the most "commercially reasonable alternative" ... does not alter Fertico's obligation under the Code to hold any profits made on the resale for Phoschem's account (UCC 2–706[6]; 2–711[3]).

also mean that jurisdiction will be proper only in the United States and not in Belgium or some other place. For more on the meaning and significance of letters of credit take a look at § 5–108 of the UCC.

2. Reasonability in Covering. Examine closely how Fertico behaved in handling the late shipment of fertilizer. The UCC's cover provision, § 2–712(1), allows the buyer to cover "by making in good faith and without unreasonable delay any reasonable purchase of or contract to purchase goods in substitution for those due from the seller." Comment 2 adds: "[I]t is immaterial that hindsight may later prove that the method of cover used was not the cheapest or most effective." This provision resembles many in the UCC in measuring conduct by a standard of "reasonability" or "commercial reasonability." There seems to be no question that Fertico meets this test, but many other cases have befuddled judges. As White and Summers observe, "The drafters have hardly left us with a solid basis to predict whether a given act was or was not 'reasonable'; each addition in the Comment is like an additional bucket of muck thrown into a quagmire." James J. White & Robert S. Summers, Uniform Commercial Code § 6–3 at 206 (5th student ed. 2000). In the *Fertico* case, for instance, problems might arise if the fertilizer had not been of equivalent character—if, for instance, the only fertilizer available on the spot market had been of higher quality and at a much higher price.

It should also be noted that cover is optional; a buyer who fails to cover still has all other remedies available (§ 2–712(3)), meaning, above all, that a buyer who no longer wants the goods can still seek market-differential damages under § 2–713.

3. Offset. Section 2–712(2) provides that the buyer can recover any increased cost from cover, "but less expenses saved in consequence of the seller's breach." The main issue dividing the Court is how to interpret this clause. Who seems to have the better of the argument?

White and Summers comment that: "*Fertico* is a close case and we are not sure about the proper outcome. The real question for us is to compare the plaintiff's economic status at the end of all the relevant transactions with the economic status that the plaintiff would have enjoyed had the defendant not breached the contract. In *Fertico* the majority assumes that if the contract had been performed, the plaintiff would have made the intended resale to the Iraqi buyer, and also a second resale to the other buyer. The dissent suggests that is only speculation. The dissent indicates that it is likely that if the American seller had not breached, the European buyer would not have sought substitute goods in Lebanon to fulfill its contract with the Iraqis and in fact would only have had one sale. If that is what would have happened, the dissent is correct. If, on the other hand, the European reseller would have had both resales, then the majority seems correct." White & Summers, supra at 205.

4. **The CISG.** Why wasn't this case brought under the CISG? If it had been, would the outcome have been different? See CISG art. 75.

Note: The Effect of Post Breach Events on Damage Recoveries

Busy modern courts hear complicated cases that involve extensive discovery and elaborate motion practice, and so it is common for a contract lawsuit to come to trial several years after the breach. In such circumstances, events that occur between breach and trial will often suggest that the damages that would have been awarded on the date of breach are no longer the appropriate damages.

Consider the cases that you have seen already in this chapter. Fertico–Belgium is complicated by the buyer's resale of the delivered 15,000 tons to a third party. KGM Harvesting and the Victor Packing cases cited there all involve post breach events. By hypothesis, every defendant who argues that the plaintiff should be foreclosed from contract market damages because the plaintiff has covered is invoking post breach events. These and other cases are not in agreement and, in fact, seldom acknowledge the conflict and confusion about a court's duty or right to consider post breach events in establishing damages.

David Simon and Gerald A. Novack, *Limiting the Buyer's Market Damages To Lost Profits: A Challenge to the Enforceability a Market Contracts*, 92 Harvard Law Review 1395 (1979), argue that a contract is a bet and that the payoff should be made on the basis of knowledge available at the breach despite the fact that other knowledge later gained might show different damage to be appropriate. The Simon and Novack argument arguably conflicts with the instruction in section 1–106 to award only the damages actually suffered and with the suggestion in comment 5 to section 2–713 that a contract market recovery "applies only when and to the extent that the buyer has not covered."

Problem 6–6

In July 1998 the owner of an oil tanker chartered the tanker to YK at a very favorable rate for seven years. The charter ran from July 1998 through July 2005. The charter contract had the following provision about war:

> 33. If war or hostilities break out between any two or more of the following countries: U.S.A., former USSR, PRC, UK, Netherlands, Liberia Japan, Iran, Kuwait, Saudi Arabia, Qatar, Iraq, both owners and charters have the right to cancel this charter.

In December 2001 YK repudiated the charter, and the owners took the ship back. In 2003 the Second Gulf War started; had the charter still been in place, YK could and would have invoked clause 33 to cancel the contract at that time.

Assume that the damages between 2001 and 2003 would have been $5 million and that the damages for the period between 2001 and 2005 would have been $15 million. Does the charter recover 5 or 15?

Problem 6–7

In problem 6–6 assume that the original contract ran from 1999 to 2003 and that YK had an option to extend the charter for two years (from 2003 to

2005). Now no one will award more than 5 million, correct? But how is this situation different from 6–6?

HADLEY v. BAXENDALE[15]

In the Court of Exchequer, 1854.
9 Exch. 341, 156 Eng. Rep. 145.

[General report of the case and its outcome on appeal.] Where two parties have made a contract, which one of them has broken, the damages which the other party ought to receive in respect of such breach of contract should be such as may fairly and reasonably be considered either arising naturally, i.e. according to the usual course of things, from such breach of contract itself, or such as may reasonably be supposed to have been in the contemplation of both parties at the time they made the contract, as the probable result of the breach of it. Where the plaintiffs, the owners of a flour mill, sent a broken iron shaft to an office of the defendants, who were common carriers, to be conveyed by them, and the defendants' clerk, who attended at the office, was told that the mill was stopped, that the shaft must be delivered immediately, and that a special entry, if necessary, must be made to hasten its delivery; and the delivery of the broken shaft to the consignee, to whom it had been sent by the plaintiffs as a pattern, by which to make a new shaft, was delayed for an unreasonable time; in consequence of which, the plaintiffs did not receive the new shaft for some days after the time they ought to have received it, and they were consequently unable to work their mill from want of the new shaft, and thereby incurred a loss of profits: Held, that, under the circumstances, such loss could not be recovered in an action against the defendants as common carriers.

[The declaration of the plaintiffs.] The first count of the declaration stated, that, before and at the time of the making by the defendants of the promises hereinafter mentioned, the plaintiffs carried on the business of millers and mealmen in copartnership, and were proprietors and occupiers of the City Steam-Mills, in the city of Gloucester, and were possessed of a steam-engine, by means of which they worked the said mills, and therein cleaned corn, and ground the same into meal, and dressed the same into flour, sharps, and bran, and a certain portion of the said steam-engine, to wit, the crank shaft of the said steam-engine, was broken and out of repair, whereby the said

15. [Eds: This unusually full report of a classic case comes from Floyd R. Mechem and Barry Gilbert, Mechem's Cases on Damages 170 (3d ed. 1902), published by the West Publishing Company. (The book was used in 1902 by White's grandfather at the University of Michigan, where Mechem was the Tappan Professor of Law. In his note to the second edition Professor Mechem states the classic casebook editor's lament and makes a sly bow to the West Publishing Company: "Arbitrary, but inexorable, considerations of size and price have determined the scope of the selection; and, for reasons perhaps sufficiently obvious, preference has been given, when possible, to cases which have appeared in the National Reporter System.") We have inserted section markers so that you can keep track of where you are in the report. We have also used bold face for judicial interventions during the oral arguments; these interventions are important for the decision.]

steam-engine was prevented from working, and the plaintiffs were desirous of having a new crank shaft made for the said mill, and had ordered the same of certain persons trading under the name of W. Joyce & Co., at Greenwich, in the county of Kent, who had contracted to make the said new shaft for the plaintiffs; but before they could complete the said new shaft it was necessary that the said broken shaft should be forwarded to their works at Greenwich, in order that the said new shaft might be made so as to fit the other parts of the said engine which were not injured, and so that it might be substituted for the said broken shaft; and the plaintiffs were desirous of sending the said broken shaft to the said W. Joyce & Co. for the purpose aforesaid; and the defendants, before and at the time of the making of the said promises, were common carriers of goods and chattels for hire from Gloucester to Greenwich, and carried on such business of common carriers, under the name of Pickford & Co.; and the plaintiffs, at the request of the defendants, delivered to them as such carriers the said broken shaft, to be conveyed by the defendants as such carriers from Gloucester to the said W. Joyce & Co., at Greenwich, and there to be delivered for the plaintiffs on the second day after the day of such delivery, for reward to the defendants; and in consideration thereof the defendants then promised the plaintiffs to convey the said broken shaft from Gloucester to Greenwich, and there on the said second day to deliver the same to the said W. Joyce & Co. for the plaintiffs. And although such second day elapsed before the commencement of this suit, yet the defendants did not nor would deliver the said broken shaft at Greenwich on the said second day, or to the said W. Joyce & Co. on the said second day, but wholly neglected and refused so to do for the space of seven days after the said shaft was so delivered to them as aforesaid.

The second count stated, that, the defendants being such carriers as aforesaid, the plaintiffs, at the request of the defendants, caused to be delivered to them as such carriers the said broken shaft, to be conveyed by the defendants from Gloucester aforesaid to the said W. Joyce & Co., at Greenwich, and there to be delivered by the defendants for the plaintiffs, within a reasonable time in that behalf, for reward to the defendants; and in consideration of the premises in this count mentioned, the defendants promised the plaintiffs to use due and proper care and diligence in and about the carrying and conveying the said broken shaft from Gloucester aforesaid to the said W. Joyce & Co., at Greenwich, and there delivering the same for the plaintiffs in a reasonable time then following for the carriage, conveyance, and delivery of the said broken shaft as aforesaid; and although such reasonable time elapsed long before the commencement of this suit, yet the defendants did not nor would use due or proper care or diligence in or about the carrying or conveying or delivering the said broken shaft as aforesaid, within such reasonable time as aforesaid, but wholly neglected and refused so to do; and by reason of the carelessness, negligence, and improper conduct of the defendants, the said. broken shaft was not delivered for the plaintiffs to the said W. Joyce & Co., or at Greenwich, until the expiration of a long and unreasonable time after the defendants received the same as aforesaid, and after the time when the same should have been delivered for the plaintiffs; and by reason of the several premises, the completing of the said new shaft was delayed for five days, and the plaintiffs were prevented from working their said steam-mills, and from cleaning corn, and grinding the same into meal, and dressing the meal into flour, sharps, or bran, and from carrying on their said business as millers and mealmen for the space of five days beyond the time that they otherwise would have been prevented from so doing, and they thereby were unable to supply many of their customers with flour, sharps, and bran during that period, and were obliged to buy flour to supply some of their other customers, and lost the means and opportunity of selling flour, sharps, and bran, and were deprived of gains and profits which otherwise would have accrued to them, and were unable to employ their workmen, to whom they were compelled to pay wages during that period, and were otherwise injured, and the plaintiffs claim 300l.

[The defendants' plea.] The defendants pleaded *non assumpserunt* to the first-count; and to the second payment of 25l. into Court in satisfaction of the plaintiffs' claim under that count. The plaintiffs entered a *nolle prosequi* as to the first count; and as to the second plea, they replied that the sum paid into Court was not enough to satisfy the plaintiffs' claim in respect thereof; upon which replication issue was joined.

[The trial court proceedings.] At the trial before Crompton, J., at the last Gloucester Assizes, it appeared that the plaintiffs carried on an extensive business as millers at Gloucester; and that, on the 11th of May, their mill was stopped by a breakage of the crank shaft by which the mill was worked. The steam-engine was manufactured by Messrs. Joyce & Co., the engineers, at Greenwich, and it became necessary to send the shaft as a pattern for a new one to Greenwich. The fracture was discovered on the 12th, and on the 13th the plaintiffs sent one of their servants to the office of the defendants, who are the well-known carriers trading under the name of Pickford & Co., for the purpose of having the shaft carried to Greenwich. The plaintiffs' servant told the clerk that the mill was stopped, and that the shaft must be sent immediately; and in answer to the inquiry when the shaft would be taken, the answer was, that if it was sent up by twelve o'clock any day, it would be delivered at Greenwich on the following day. On the following day the shaft was taken by the defendants, before noon, for the purpose of being conveyed to Greenwich, and the sum of 2l. 4s. was paid for its carriage for the whole distance; at the same time the defendants' clerk was told that a special entry, if required, should be made to hasten its delivery. The delivery of the shaft at Greenwich was delayed by some neglect; and the consequence was, that the plaintiffs did not receive the new shaft for several days after they would otherwise have done, and the working of their mill was thereby delayed, and they thereby lost the profits they would otherwise have received.

On the part of the defendants, it was objected that these damages were too remote, and that the defendants were not liable with respect to them. The learned Judge left the case generally to the jury, who found a verdict with 25l. damages beyond the amount paid into Court.

[The appeal.] Whateley, in last Michaelmas Term, obtained a rule nisi for a new trial, on the ground of misdirection.

[Argument on appeal for the plaintiffs, with judicial interventions in brackets.] Keating and Dowdeswell (Feb. 1) shewed cause. The plaintiffs are entitled to the amount awarded by the jury as damages. These damages are not too remote, for they are not only the natural and necessary consequence of the defendants' default, but they are the only loss which the plaintiffs have actually sustained. The principle upon which damages are assessed is founded upon that of rendering compensation to the injured party. This important subject is ably treated in Sedgwick on the Measure of Damages. And this particular branch of it is discussed in the third chapter, where, after pointing out the distinction between the civil and the French law, he says (page 64), "It its sometimes said, in regard to contracts, that the defendant shall be held liable for those damages only which both parties may fairly be supposed to have at the time contemplated as likely to result from the nature of the agreement, and this appears to be the rule adopted by the writers upon the civil law." In a subsequent passage he says, "In cases of fraud the civil law made a broad distinction" (page 66); and he adds, that "in such cases the debtor was liable for all the consequences." It is difficult, however, to see what the ground of such principle is, and how the ingredient of fraud can affect the question. For instance, if the defendants had maliciously and fraudulently kept the shaft, it is not easy to see why they should have been liable for these damages, if they are not to be held so where the delay is occasioned by their negligence only In speaking of the rule respecting the breach of a contract to transport goods to a particular place, and in actions brought on agreements for the sale and delivery of chattels, the learned author lays it down, that, "In the former case, the difference in value between the price at the point where the goods are, and the place where they were to be delivered, is taken as the measure of damages which, in fact, amounts to an allowance of profits; and in the latter case, a similar result is had by the application of the rule, which gives the vendee the benefit of the rise of the market price" (page 80). The several cases, English as well as American, are there collected and reviewed. **[Parke, B. The sensible rule appears to be that which has been laid down in France, and which is declared in their code—Code Civil, liv. iii. tit. iii. ss. 1149, 1150, 1151, and which is thus translated in Sedgwick (page 67.): "The damages due to the creditor consist in general of the loss that he has sustained, and the profit which he has been prevented from acquiring, subject to the modifications hereinafter contained. The debtor is only liable for the damages foreseen, or which might have been foreseen, at the time of the execution of the contract, when it is not owing to his fraud that**

the agreement has been violated. Even in the case of non-performance of the contract, resulting from the fraud of the debtor, the damages only comprise so much of the loss sustained by the creditor, and so much of the profit which he has been prevented from acquiring, as directly and immediately results from the non-performance of the contract."] If that rule is to be adopted, there was ample evidence in the present case of the defendants' knowledge of such a state of things as would necessarily result in the damage the plaintiffs suffered through the defendants' default. The authorities are in the plaintiffs' favour upon the general ground. In *Nurse v. Barns* (1 Sir T. Raym. 77), which was an action for the breach of an agreement for the letting of certain iron mills, the plaintiff was held entitled to a sum of 500l., awarded by reason of loss of stock laid in, although be had only paid 10l. by way of consideration. In *Borradaile v. Brunton* (8 Taunt. 535, 2 B. Moo. 582), which was an action for the breach of the warranty of a chain cable that it should last two years as a substitute for a rope cable of sixteen inches, the plaintiff was held entitled to recover for the loss of the anchor, which was occasioned by the breaking of the cable within the specified time. **[Alderson, B. Why should not the defendant have been liable for the loss of the ship? Parke, B. Sedgwick doubts the correctness of that report.[16] Martin, B. Take the case of the non-delivery by a carrier of a delicate piece of machinery, whereby the whole of an extensive mill is thrown out of work for a considerable time; if the carrier is to be liable for the loss in that case, he might incur damages to the extent of 10,0001. Parke, B., referred to *Everard v. Hopkins* (2 Bulst. 332).]** These extreme cases, and the difficulty which consequently exists in the estimation of the true amount of damages, supports the view for which the plaintiffs contend, that the question is properly for the decision of a jury, and therefore that this matter could not properly have been withdrawn from their consideration. In *Ingram v. Lawson* (6 Bing. N. C. 212) the true principle was acted upon. That was an action for a libel upon the plaintiff, who was the owner and master of a ship, which he advertised to take passengers to the East Indies; and the libel imputed that the vessel was not seaworthy, and that Jews had purchased her to take out convicts. The Court held, that evidence shewing that the plaintiff's profits after the publication of the libel were 1500l. below the usual average, was admissible, to enable the jury to form an opinion as to the nature of the plaintiff's business, and of his general rate of profit. Here, also, the plaintiffs have not sustained any loss beyond that which was submitted to the jury. *Bodley v. Reynolds* (8 Q. B. 779) and *Kettle v. Hunt* (Bull. N. P. 77) are similar in principle. In the latter, it was held that the loss of the benefit of trade, which a man suffers by the detention of his tools, is recoverable as special damage. **[Parke, B. Suppose, in the present case, that the**

16. The learned Judge has frequently observed of late that the 8th Taunton is of but doubtful authority, as the cases were not reported by Mr. Taunton himself.

shaft had been lost, what would have been the damage to which the plaintiffs would have been entitled?] The loss they had sustained during the time they were so deprived of their shaft, or until they could have obtained a new one. In *Black v. Baxendale* (1 Exch. 410), by reason of the defendant's omission to deliver the goods within a reasonable time at Belford, the plaintiff's agent, who had been sent there to meet the goods, was put to certain additional expenses, and this Court held that such expenses might be given by the jury as damages. In *Brandt v. Bowlby* (2 B. & Ald. 932), which was an action of assumpsit against the defendants, as owners of a certain vessel, for not delivering a cargo of wheat shipped to the plaintiffs, the cargo reached the port of discharge but was not delivered; the price of the cargo at the time it reached the port of destination was held to be the true rule of damages. "As between the parties in this cause," said Parke, J., "the plaintiffs are entitled to be put in the same situation as they would have been in, if the cargo had been delivered to their order at the time when it was delivered to the wrong party; and the sum it would have fetched at that time is the amount of the loss sustained by the non-performance of the defendants' contract." The recent decision of this Court, in *Waters v. Towers* (8 Ex. 401), seems to be strongly in the plaintiffs' favour. The defendants there had agreed to fit up the plaintiffs' mill within a reasonable time, but had not completed their contract within such time; and it was held that the plaintiffs were entitled to recover, by way of damages, the loss of profit upon a contract they had entered into with third parties, and which they were unable to fulfil by reason of the defendants' breach of contract. **[Parke, B. The defendants there must of necessity have known that the consequence of their not completing their contract would be to stop the working of the mill. But how could the defendants here know that any such result would follow?]** There was ample evidence that the defendants knew the purpose for which this shaft was sent, and that the result of its non-delivery in due time would be the stoppage of the mill; for the defendants' agent, at their place of business, was told that the mill was then stopped, that the shaft must be delivered immediately, and that if a special entry was necessary to hasten its delivery, such an entry should be made. The defendants must, therefore, be held to have contemplated at the time what in fact did follow, as the necessary and natural result of their wrongful act. They also cited *Ward v. Smith* (11 Price, 19); and Parke, B., referred to *Levy v. Langridge* (4 M. & W. 337).

[Argument on appeal for the defendant.] Whateley, Willes, and Phipson, in support of the rule (Feb. 2). It has been contended, on the part of the plaintiffs, that the damages found by the jury are a matter fit for their consideration; but still the question remains, in what way ought the jury to have been directed? It has been also urged, that, in awarding damages, the law gives compensation to the injured individual. But it is clear that complete compensation is not to be awarded; for instance, the non-payment of a bill of exchange might lead to the utter ruin of the holder, and yet such damage could not be considered as necessarily resulting from the breach of contract, so as to entitle the party aggrieved to recover in respect of it. Take the case of the breach of a contract to supply a rick-cloth, whereby and in consequence of bad weather the hay, being unprotected, is spoiled, that damage could not be recoverable. Many similar cases might be added. The true principle to be deduced from the authorities upon this subject is that which is embodied in the maxim: "*In jure non remota causa sed proxima spectatur.*"[17] Sedgwick says (page 38), "In regard to the quantum of damages, instead of adhering to the term compensation, it would be far more accurate to say, in the language of Domat, which we have cited above, 'that the object is to discriminate between that portion of the loss which must be borne by the offending party and that which must be borne by the sufferer.' The law in fact aims not at the satisfaction but at a division of the loss." And the learned author also cites the following passage from Broom's Legal Maxims: "Every defendant," says Mr. Broom, "against whom an action is brought experiences some injury or inconvenience beyond what the costs will compensate him for."[18] Again, at page 78, after referring to the case of *Flureau v. Thornhill* (2 W. Blac. 1078), he says, "Both the English and American Courts have generally adhered to this denial of profits as any part of the damages to be compensated and that whether in cases of contract or of tort. So, in a case of illegal capture, Mr. Justice Story rejected the item of profits on the voyage, and held this general language: 'Independent, however, of all authority, I am satisfied upon principle, that an allowance of damages upon the basis of a calculation of profits is inadmissible. The rule would be in the highest degree unfavourable to the interests of the community. The subject would be involved in utter uncertainty. The calculation would proceed upon contingencies, and would require a knowledge of foreign markets to an exactness, in point of time and value, which would sometimes present embarrassing obstacles; much would depend upon the length of the voyage, and the season of arrival, much upon the vigilance and activity of the master, and much upon the momentary demand. After all, it would be a calculation upon conjectures, and not upon facts; such a rule therefore has been rejected by Courts of law in ordinary cases, and instead of deciding upon the gains or losses of parties in particular cases, a uniform interest has been applied as the measure of damages for the detention of property.' " There is much force in that admirably constructed passage. We ought to pay all due homage in this country to the decisions of the American Courts upon this important subject, to which they appear to have given much careful consideration. The damages here are too remote. Several of the cases which were principally relied upon by the plaintiffs are distinguishable. In *Waters v. Towers* (1 Exch. 401) there was a special contract to do the work in a particular time, and the damage occasioned by the non-completion of the contract was that to which the plaintiff's were held to be entitled. In *Borradale v. Brunton* (8 Taunt. 535) there was a direct engagement that the cable should hold

17. [Eds.: "In law, not the remote but the proximate cause is observed."]

18. Broom's Legal Maxims, p. 95; *Davies v. Jenkins,* 11 M. & W. 755.

the anchor. So, in the case of taking away a workman's tools, the natural and necessary consequence is the loss of employment: *Bodley v. Reynolds* (8 Q. B. 779). The following cases may be referred to as decisions upon the principle within which the defendants contend that the present case falls: *Jones v. Gooday* (8 M. & W. 146), *Walton v. Fothergill,* (7 Car. & P. 392), *Boyce v. Bayliffe* (1 Camp. 58) and *Archer v. Williams* (2 C. & K. 26). The rule, therefore, that the immediate cause is to be regarded in considering the loss, is applicable here. There was no special contract between these parties. A carrier has a certain duty cast upon him by law, and that duty is not to be enlarged to an indefinite extent in the absence of a special contract, or of fraud or malice. The maxim "*dolus circuitu non purgatur,*"[19] does not apply. The question as to how far liability may be affected by reason of malice forming one of the elements to be taken into consideration, was treated of by the Court of Queen's Bench in *Lumley v. Gye* (2 E. & B. 216). Here the declaration is founded upon the defendants' duty as common carriers, and indeed there is no pretence for saying that they entered into a special contract to bear all the consequences of the non-delivery of the article in question. They were merely bound to carry it safely, and to deliver it within a reasonable time. The duty of the clerk, who was in attendance at the defendants' office, was to enter the article, and to take the amount of the carriage; but a mere notice to him, such as was here given, could not make the defendants, as carriers, liable as upon a special contract. Such matters, therefore, must be rejected from the consideration of the question. If carriers are to be liable in such a case as this, the exercise of a sound judgment would not suffice, but they ought to be gifted also with a spirit of prophecy. "I have always understood," said Patteson, J., in *Kelly v. Partington* (5 B. & Ad. 651), "that the special damage must be the natural result of the thing done." That sentence presents the true test. The Court of Queen's Bench acted upon that rule in *Foxall v. Barnett* (2 E. & B. 928). This therefore is a question of law, and the jury ought to have been told that these damages were too remote; and that, in the absence of the proof of any other damage, the plaintiffs were entitled to nominal damages only *Tindall v. Bell* (11 M. & W. 232). *Siordet v. Hall* (4 Bing. 607) and *De Vaux* v. *Salvador* (4 A. & E. 420) are instances of cases where the Courts appear to have gone into the opposite extremes—in the one case of unduly favouring the carrier, in the other of holding them liable for results which would appear too remote. If the defendants should be held responsible for the damages awarded by the jury, they would be in a better position if they confined their business to the conveyance of gold. They cannot be responsible for results which, at the time the goods are delivered for carriage, are beyond all human foresight. Suppose a manufacturer were to contract with a coal merchant or mine owner for the delivery of a boat load of coals, no intimation being given that the coals were required for immediate use, the vendor in that case would not be liable for the stoppage of the vendee's business for want of the article which he had failed to deliver: for the vendor has no knowledge that the

19. [Eds.: "Fraud is not purged by evasion."]

goods are not to go to the vendee's general stock. Where the contracting party is shewn to be acquainted with all the consequences that must of necessity follow from a breach on his part of the contract, it may be reasonable to say that he takes the risk of such consequences. If, as between vendor and vendee, this species of liability has no existence, a fortiori the carrier is not to be burthened with it. In cases of personal injury to passengers, the damage to which the sufferer has been held entitled is the direct and immediate consequence of the wrongful act.

Cur. adv. vult.[20]

[The verdict is announced.] The judgment of the Court was now delivered by—

ALDERSON, B. We think that there ought to be a new trial in this case; but, in so doing, we deem it to be expedient and necessary to state explicitly the rule which the Judge, at the next trial, ought, in our opinion, to direct the jury to be governed by when they estimate the damages.

It is, indeed, of the last importance that we should do this; for, if the jury are left without any definite rule to guide them, it will, in such cases as these, manifestly lead to the greatest injustice. The Courts have done this on several occasions; and, in *Blake v. Midland Railway Company* (18 Q. B. 93), the Court granted a new trial on this very ground, that the rule had not been definitely laid down to the jury by the learned Judge at Nisi Prius. "There are certain established rules," this Court says, in *Alder v. Keighley (15 M.* & W. 117), "according to which the jury ought to find." And the Court, in that case, adds: "and here there is a clear rule, that the amount which would have been received if the contract bad been kept, is the measure of damages if the contract is broken."

Now we think the proper rule in such a case as the present is this: Where two parties have made a contract which one of them has broken, the damages which the other party ought to receive in respect of such breach of contract should be such as may fairly and reasonably be considered either arising naturally, i.e., according to the usual course of things, from such breach of contract itself, or such as may reasonably be supposed to have been in the contemplation of both parties, at the time they made the contract, as the probable result of the breach of it. Now, if the special circumstances under which the contract was actually made were communicated by the plaintiffs to the defendants, and thus known to both parties, the damages resulting from the breach of such a contract, which they would reasonably contemplate, would be the amount of injury which would ordinarily follow from a breach of contract under these special circumstances so known and communicated. But, on the other hand, if these special circumstances were wholly unknown to the party breaking the contract, he, at the most, could only be supposed to have had in his contemplation the amount of injury which would arise generally, and in the great multitude of cases not affected by any special

20. *Curia advisari vult*: the judges withdraw to consider their verdict.

circumstances, from such a breach of contract. For, had the special circumstances been known, the parties might have specially provided for the breach of contract by special terms as to the damages in that case; and of this advantage it would be very unjust to deprive them. Now the above principles are those by which we think the jury ought to be guided in estimating the damages arising out of any breach of contract. It is said, that other cases such as breaches of contract in the non-payment of money, or in the not making a good title to land, are to be treated as exceptions from this, and as governed by a conventional rule. But as, in such cases, both parties must be supposed to be cognisant of that well-known rule, these cases may, we think, be more properly classed under the rule above enunciated as to cases under known special circumstances, because there both parties may reasonably be presumed to contemplate the estimation of the amount of damages according to the conventional rule. Now, in the present case, if we are to apply the principles above laid down, we find that the only circumstances here communicated by the plaintiffs to the defendants at the time the contract was made, were, that the article to be carried was the broken shaft of a mill, and that the plaintiffs were the millers of that mill. But how do these circumstances shew reasonably that the profits of the mill must be stopped by an unreasonable delay in the delivery of the broken shaft by the carrier to the third person? Suppose the plaintiffs had another shaft in their possession put up or putting up at the time, and that they only wished to send back the broken shaft to the engineer who made it; it is clear that this would be quite consistent with the above circumstances, and yet the unreasonable delay in the delivery would have no effect upon the intermediate profits of the mill. Or, again, suppose that, at the time of the delivery to the carrier, the machinery of the mill had been in other respects defective, then, also, the same results would follow. Here it is true that the shaft was actually sent back to serve as a model for a new one, and that the want of a new one was the only cause of the stoppage of the mill, and that the loss of profits really arose from not sending down the new shaft in proper time, and that this arose from the delay in delivering the broken one to serve as a model. But it is obvious that, in the great multitude of cases of millers sending off broken shafts to third persons by a carrier under ordinary circumstances, such consequences would not, in all probability, have occurred; and these special circumstances were here never communicated by the plaintiffs to the defendants. It follows, therefore, that the loss of profits here cannot reasonably be considered such a consequence of the breach of contract as could have been fairly and reasonably contemplated by both the parties when they made this contract. For such loss would neither have flowed naturally from the breach of this contract in the great multitude of such cases occurring under ordinary circumstances, nor were the special circumstances, which, perhaps; would have made it a reasonable and natural consequence of such breach of contract, communicated to or known by the defendants. The Judge ought, therefore, to have told the jury, that, upon the facts then before them, they ought not to take to the loss of profits into consideration at all in estimating the damages. There must therefore be a new trial in this case.

Rule absolute.

Notes and Discussion

1. The Case's Background and Importance. The background to this case is examined by Richard Danzig, *Hadley v. Baxendale: A Study in the Industrialization of the Law*, 4 J. Legal Stud. 249 (1975), largely reprinted in Richard Danzig and Geoffrey R. Watson, The Capability Problem in Contract Law 57–91 (2nd ed. 2004). Joseph and Johan Hadley operated a huge mill in Gloucester, England; their mill, now restored as an apartment building (for a picture: http://home.freeuk.net/gdsc2/furinfo/studies/pridaysmill.htm), was brought to a halt when the engine shaft broke on May 12, 1853. According to Danzig, on May 13 the Hadleys sent an employee to Baxendale's firm "to inquire as to the fastest means of conveying the shaft to ... Greenwich, where it would serve as a model for the crafting of a new shaft." The Baxendale employee represented to them that it would be delivered "on the second day after the day of ... delivery" to Baxendale's firm, which was May 14; but the shaft was not delivered until May 21. Danzig, supra at 77.

On June 7-8, 2004, an academic conference was held in Gloucester to celebrate the sesquicentennial of the decision. The conference attracted scholars from the United Kingdom, the United States, Canada, Australia, Germany and elsewhere. The conference theme was "The Common Law of Contracts as a World Force in Two Ages of Revolution"; it featured papers not only on the history of the English common law in the 19th century, but also on the role contract law plays today and will play in the future in a world of increasing global commercial relationships. The conference's organizer, Prof. Franklin G. Snyder from Texas Wesleyan University, observed: "No case better exemplifies the international reach of the common law of contracts than *Hadley v. Baxendale*, a simple dispute over the shipment of a mill shaft that for a century and a half has been studied by law students and relied on by courts in places as diverse and distant as distant as Texas and Tanzania, Brisbane and Bombay."

According to an on-line address finder, there are 24 people in the United States with the name Hadley V. Baxendale.

2. Where Did the Holding Come From? Read closely the final opinion by Baron Alderson. The Baron holds that: "Where two parties have made a contract which one of them has broken, the damages which the other party ought to receive in respect of such breach of contract should be such as may fairly and reasonably be considered either arising naturally, i.e., according to the usual course of things, from such breach of contract itself, or such as may reasonably be supposed to have been in the contemplation of both parties, at the time they made the contract, as the probable result of the breach of it." In the Baron's view, how does this rule affect the Hadleys' claim for damages?

Now look at the statement of facts by the court reporter at the outset of the case. There is an important discrepancy between these facts and what

Baron Alderson believes to be the case. This discrepancy and its legal significance have led to enduring debates among scholars. How plausible are the Baron's speculations about what the Baxendale firm is likely to have known about the Hadley mill at the time the contract was made?

Now look closely, first at the initial declaration of the Hadleys' claim, and then at the course of the pleadings. Examine how the Hadleys state their claim, and the difference between their two theories of the case. In oral argument, how do the barristers on either side frame the issue of damages? To what extent do the judicial interventions (which we have highlighted so that you can spot them more easily) take the case in a different direction?

3. How Wide is the Rule? One of the most important difficulties in applying the rule in *Hadley v. Baxendale* is to determine its scope. What exactly does it mean to insist that the resulting damages "may reasonably be supposed to have been in the contemplation of both parties, at the time they made the contract, as the probable result of the breach of it"? In the first place, it is not required that "both parties" must foresee the damages; legal interest is only in whether the breaching party would foresee these damages.

But the greater difficulty centers on the meaning of foreseeability ("contemplation"). Consider first this view, from Oliver Wendell Holmes: "If a breach of contract were regarded in the same light as a tort, it would seem that if, in the course of performance of the contract the promisor should be notified of any particular consequence which would result from its not being performed, he should be held liable for that consequence in the event of non-performance. Such a suggestion has been made. But it has not been accepted as the law. On the contrary, according to the opinion of a very able judge, which seems to be generally followed, notice, even at the time of making the contract, of special circumstances out of which special damages would arise in case of breach, is not sufficient unless the assumption of that risk is to be taken as having fairly entered into the contract. If a carrier should undertake to carry the machinery of a saw-mill from Liverpool to Vancouver's Island, and should fail to do so, he probably would not be held liable for the rate of hire of such machinery during the necessary delay, although he might know that it could not be replaced without sending to England, unless he was fairly understood to accept 'the contract with the special condition attached to it.' " O.W. Holmes, *Lecture VIII: The Elements of Contract, in* The Common Law 289, 301–302 (Boston, Little Brown & Co. 1881) (citations omitted.). On this view, Baxendale would not be liable for stoppage of the Hadley's mill unless this condition had been specially "attached" to the contract, i.e., the parties had more or less explicitly distributed the risk to his firm.

Today, most contract scholars reject this constricted view. But where then should the boundary be drawn? A leading English case formulates the rule in this way: "Everyone, as a reasonable person, is taken to know the 'ordinary course of things' and consequently what loss is liable to result from breach of contract in that ordinary course. This is the subject matter of the 'first rule' in *Hadley v. Baxendale*. But to this knowledge, which a contract-breaker is assumed to possess whether he actually possesses it or not, there may have to be added in a particular case knowledge which he actually possesses, of special circumstances outside the 'ordinary course of things,' of such a kind that a breach in those special circumstances would be liable to cause more loss. Such a case attracts the operation of the 'second rule' so as to make additional loss also recoverable." *Victoria Laundry (Windsor) Ltd. v. Newman Indus. Ltd.* [1949] 2 K.B. 528, 529 (Eng. C.A.). This softens Holmes's position; do you see how?

Although the exact formulation varies, modern American decisions tend to this second view. The Restatement 2d § 351(1) states the rule as follows: "Damages are not recoverable for loss that the party in breach did not have reason to foresee as a probable result of the breach when the contract was made." Subsection (2) divides foreseeable damages into two groups, as in *Hadley*: those that follow "in the ordinary course of events," and those that arise "as a result of special circumstances, beyond the ordinary course of events, that the party in breach had reason to know."

The UCC does not give consequential damages to a seller (cf. §§ 2–703, 710 in its present version), but, except for sales to consumers, the amended version (§ 2–710(2)-(3)) reverses this position. On the other hand, a buyer can recover as consequential damages "(a) any loss resulting from general or particular requirements and needs of which the seller at the time of contracting had reason to know and which could not reasonably be prevented by cover or otherwise; and (b) injury to person or property proximately resulting from any breach of warranty." UCC § 2–715(2). Comment 2 to that section rejects Holmes' "tacit agreement" test.

Restatement 2d § 351(3) also allows a court to limit damages for foreseeable loss "if it concludes that in the circumstances justice so requires in order to avoid disproportionate compensation." The Restatement gives this illustration: "A, a plastic surgeon, makes a contract with B, a professional entertainer, to perform plastic surgery on her face in order to improve her appearance. The result of the surgery is, however, to disfigure her face and to require a second operation. In an action by B against A for breach of contract, the court may limit damages by allowing recovery only for loss incurred by B in reliance on the contract, including the fees paid by B and expenses for hospitalization, nursing care and medicine for both operations, together with any damages for the worsening of B's appearance if these can be proved with reasonable certainty, but not including any loss resulting from the failure to improve her appearance." § 351 illus. 19. This example is drawn from the well known case of *Sullivan v. O'Connor*, 363 Mass. 579, 296 N.E.2d 183 (1973). For a good commentary on the case, see John Kidwell, *Sullivan v. O'Connor: Supplementary Comments*, in Danzig, supra, 15–43.

4. The Economics of *Hadley*. "The court's resolution [in *Hadley v. Baxendale*] is an ingenious one. The mill will receive these damages only if, at the time of contracting, it explained to the railroad the magnitude of risk that was at stake. This result effectively avoids the question of allocating a realized risk and replaces it by one of allocating efforts to avoid the realization of the risk. More explicitly, the resolution assumes that certain risks are borne by each party as a 'normal form' of the transaction. If any other risks are to be transferred, they must be considered explicitly during the negotiation. It can be assumed—if the negotiation operates as the rule anticipates—that the party undertaking to bear such atypical risks will charge an appropriate insurance premium and exercise appropriate extraordinary care in the execution of the transaction.

"What is most interesting about this resolution is that in effect it ... says, 'If you are *really* concerned that the other party may dishonor the contract, you may have to pay him extra!' ... Its result is exactly the duty to inform required to give the seller guidance when the negotiation is indeterminate...." John H. Barton, *The Economic Basis of Damages for Breach of Contract*, 1 J. Legal Stud. 277, 295–296 (1972). See also Ian Ayres & Robert Gertner, *Filling Gaps in Incomplete Contracts: An Economic Theory of Default Rules*, 99 Yale L.J. 87, 99 (1989), arguing that: "By setting the default rule in favor of the uninformed party, the courts induce the informed party to reveal information, and, consequently, the efficient contract results."

Are you persuaded? Can you imagine situations in which disclosure and subsequent negotiation might be more costly than the gain resulting from them? A common carrier like Fed-Ex, in any case, is unlikely to negotiate more than perfunctorily over potential damages if a shipment goes missing. See Melvin Aron Eisenberg, *The Principle of Hadley v. Baxendale*, 80 Cal. L. Rev. 563, 593–596 (1992).

5. The Civil Law Position. During the argument on appeal, the *Hadley* court discussed French law (as mediated through Theodore Sedgwick's A Treatise on the Measure of Damages, published in 1847, one of the earliest major American treatises on private law). But the actual Civil Law position is different, at any rate when the breaching party is held at fault for the breach. In French law, for instance, a contract breacher whose breach is deliberate or grossly negligent (and this would include an efficient breach of contract, no?) "is liable for all direct damage [to the victim], whether foreseeable or not." Barry Nicholas, French Law of Contract 229 (2nd ed. 1992).

In German law, "[L]iability for irregularity in performance very generally depends on the debtor's responsibility for it. The irregularity must have been due to his behaviour, and his behaviour must have been culpable. ... So far as *causal connection* is concerned, the criterion of adequate cause is employed. Rather like proximate cause in Anglo-American law, this criterion is very extensible and hardly leads to any genuine limitation of liability. Nor does German law have a rule like that of *Hadley v. Baxendale*, which limits liability in damages to the risks that were foreseeable to the debtor at the time the contract was formed. Contractual liability therefore goes very far." Norbert Horn et al., German Private and Commercial Law: An Introduction 112–113 (trans. Tony Weir, 1982).

Generally speaking, international contract conventions have adopted the Common Law rule. E.g., CISG Article 74 ("the loss which the party in breach foresaw or ought to have foreseen at the time of the conclusion of the contract, in the light of the facts and matters of which he then knew or ought to have known, as a possible consequence of the breach of contract"). See generally G. H. Treitel, Remedies for Breach of Contract: A Comparative Account 150–162 (1988).

6. Reform? Melvin Eisenberg, a central figure in modern contract law, has argued vigorously that the *Hadley* rule should be altered. "[C]on-tract law is now ready to substitute for the regime of *Hadley v. Baxendale* a regime in which liability, to the extent not controlled by contractual allocations of loss and the principle of fair disclosure, would fall within the general principle of proximate cause. Under this regime, the standard of feasibility required should vary according to the nature of the interest invaded and the wrong involved; when lost profits or forgone opportunities are involved, the baseline standard of reasonable foreseeability should be applied; and the relevant standard should be applied at the time of the breach. If adoption of a proximate-cause regime seems too radical to the courts, they should at least follow the trend of the case law ... and reinterpret the principle of *Hadley v. Baxendale* so that it requires only that a loss be reasonably foreseeable, not that it be the probable result of the breach." Eisenberg, supra, at 613 (footnote omitted). What do you think?

Problem 6–8

Armstrong operated a lath mill in Vanceboro, Maine. When the mill's crankshaft broke, he sent it for repair to the Bangor Mill Supply Corporation, a machine shop in Bangor. The shop did a poor job, and because of its failure Armstrong's mill was shut down for six days, with a resulting loss of earnings and of fixed expenses for wages, fuel, board of men and horses, and so on. On these facts, can Armstrong recover his consequential damages? See *Armstrong v. Bangor Mill Supply Corp.*, 128 Me. 75, 145 A. 741 (1929) (awarding the consequential damages). The *Armstrong* Court ignored *Hadley v. Baxendale*. Is it likely that the owner of a machine shop would be in a better position than a shipper to anticipate the consequential damages to the mill?

SIMEONE v. FIRST BANK NATIONAL ASS'N

United States Court of Appeals, Eighth Circuit, 1996.
73 F.3d 184.

ROSS, J. Prospective buyer of classic automobiles that had been repossessed by bank brought action against bank for breach of contract, breach of fiduciary duty, conspiracy and tortious interference with contract. The United States District Court for the District of Minnesota, Harry H. McLaughlin, Chief Judge, granted bank's motion for summary judgment and awarded expenses incurred in buyer's prior state court action, and buyer appealed. The Court of Appeals vacated and remanded, 971 F.2d 103. On remand, the District Court, James M. Rosenbaum, J., entered judgment in favor of buyer, and bank appealed. The Court of Appeals, Ross, Circuit Judge, held that: (1) collector automobile market, rather than market of repossessed goods in bank foreclosure sales, was relevant market in determining compensatory damages; (2) evidence was sufficient to establish it was foreseeable that buyer would seek to further his collection by engaging in sale or trade, as required to support award of increase in value of automobiles as element of consequential damages; (3) under Minnesota law, difference between buyer's cost of cover in purchasing classic automobile and contract price was not element of incidental damages; (4) contract was enforceable with regard to vehicle that was claimed by estate; and (5) value of automobiles was readily ascertainable, as required to support award of prejudgment interest.

Affirmed in part, reversed in part and remanded.

Appellant, Frederick Simeone, sought damages against appellee First Bank National Association (First Bank) and others for breach of contract and fraud stemming from an agreement by First Bank to sell Simeone 1920–1930 era vintage Mercedes-Benz automobiles and parts which had been repossessed from a defaulting loan customer, Leland Gohlike. We affirm in part and reverse in part.

I.

The vehicles in question included a one-of-a-kind 1929 Mercedes Benz SS Roadster, two 1930 era Mercedes Benz Roadsters (of which a total of 114 were ever manufactured), and a 1928 Mercedes Benz SSK (one of only 39 ever manufactured), which had been owned by the son of Sir Arthur Conan-Doyle, the creator of Sherlock Holmes. Additionally, there were thousands of loose parts, including shock absorbers, fenders, seat cushions and wheels, which were no longer manufactured and which were themselves extraordinarily rare. One of the automobiles and some of the parts repossessed from Gohlike were allegedly owned by the Estate of Herman Quante (Quante Estate). While First Bank never acknowledged the Estate's claim of ownership, it nonetheless agreed to pay the Estate $50,000 for its interest, if any.

On October 26, 1985, after receiving inquiries from several other potential purchasers, First Bank entered into an agreement to sell the repossessed automobiles and parts for $400,000 to Simeone, a self-described collector of vintage automobiles. In the same agreement, Simeone agreed to purchase the Quante Estate car and parts for $50,000. Simeone paid 10% of the contract price as a downpayment.

On November 4, 1985, the date set for the conveyance of title to Simeone, Leland Gohlike, the debtor, obtained a temporary restraining order (TRO) to prevent the sale of the collateral. Thereafter, First Bank refused Simeone's proffered tender of the balance of the purchase price. Prior to obtaining the TRO, Gohlike instituted a civil action against First Bank and its officers claiming a violation of due process and seeking $13,000,000 in damages.

Sometime on or before November 4, 1985, First Bank entered into negotiations with Gohlike and James Torseth, Gohlike's neighbor, to sell the automobiles and parts to Torseth in exchange for Gohlike's dismissal of his suit against the bank and a purchase price slightly in excess of Simeone's. Believing that it no longer had an obligation to sell the property to Simeone because of a condition in the agreement, First Bank subsequently sold the cars and parts to SMB, Inc., a corporation created by Torseth for the purchase and resale of the automobiles and parts, and Gohlike dismissed his suit against First Bank. SMB, Inc. later sold all of the cars and parts for $1,114,960, including $470,000 that Simeone himself paid for the purchase of the 1929 Mercedes Benz SS Roadster. Two experts at trial testified that, because of their rarity, by late 1987 or early 1988 the vehicles and parts were worth over three million dollars.

First Bank returned Simeone's downpayment with interest and Simeone filed suit alleging breach of contract and fraud. The district court granted summary judgment in favor of First Bank, finding that because a condition precedent was not satisfied, the sellers were not obligated by the contract. The Eighth Circuit subsequently vacated the summary judgment ruling, concluding that First Bank and the Estate had breached the contract by failing to convey the property to Simeone. *Simeone v. First Bank Nat'l Ass'n*, 971 F.2d 103, 106–07 (8th Cir. 1992). This court remanded the case to the district court for rulings on the other claims raised by Simeone, as well as an assessment of damages. Id. at 108.

Prior to trial on remand, Simeone agreed to dismiss the Quante Estate from the case with prejudice. The trial was conducted from February 28, 1994, through March 8, 1994. At the close of the breach of contract phase of the trial, the district court ruled as a matter of law that the Bank's conduct did not constitute fraud. However, the court permitted the fraud claim to be tried to the jury to forestall the necessity for a later trial in the event the fraud dismissal was reversed on appeal. The jury awarded Simeone $2,405,000 for breach of contract, including $585,000 in compensatory damages, $225,000 in incidental damages, and $1,595,000 in consequential damages, plus prejudgment interest. The jury also awarded $1.00 on the court-dismissed fraud claim. The district court denied First Bank's motion for a new trial or, in the alternative, amendment of the judgment or remittitur pursuant to Fed.R.Civ.P. 59.

II.

In its challenge to the compensatory damages award, First Bank argues the district court erroneously allowed Simeone's experts to rely on the collector automobile market as the relevant market in appraising the fair market value of the vehicles and parts at the time of the breach. Instead, First Bank contends the relevant market was the market of "repossessed goods in bank foreclosure sales."

Minn.Stat. § 336.2–713(1) provides the proper measure of damages for a seller's breach of contract: "[T]he difference between the market price at the time when the buyer learned of the breach and the contract price together with any incidental and consequential damages...."

"Market price" "is the price for goods of the same kind and in the same branch of trade." Minn.Stat. § 336.2–713, U.C.C. Comment 2. According to First Bank, the "branch of trade" in this case was the resale market of repossessed goods, not a collector automobile market. The Uniform Commercial Code, as adopted in Minnesota, permits opinion evidence as to the value of the goods in question: "Where the unavailability of a market price is caused by a scarcity of goods of the type involved ... [s]uch scarcity conditions ... indicate that the price has risen and under the section providing for liberal administration of remedies, *opinion evidence as to the value of the goods would be admissible in the absence of a market price* and a liberal construction of allowable consequential damages should also result." Minn.Stat. § 336.2–713, U.C.C. Comment 3 (emphasis added).

At trial, the evidence showed that the vehicles were rare, and in some cases unique, classic automobiles of historic significance. The disassembled parts, as well, were scarce commodities. At trial an expert in vintage automobiles valued the cars and parts at $1,355,000 at the time of the breach. Based on the evidence presented at trial, the jury concluded that, at the time of the breach, the value of the property owned by First Bank was $885,000 and the value of the property owned by the Quante Estate was $150,000, or a total market value of $1,035,000. The difference between this fair market value and the $450,000 contract price is $585,000, the amount of compensatory damages awarded.

The district court did not abuse its discretion in permitting the valuation of the automobiles and parts based on a collector's market. The evidence clearly supports the jury's determination and the award of compensatory damages is affirmed.

III.

First Bank next raises several challenges to the consequential damages assessed against it. The jury awarded $1,595,000 in consequential damages, which was derived from expert testimony as to what the automobiles and parts were worth in late 1987, two years after the breach of contract, minus the market price of the property at the time of the breach. First Bank now argues the evidence is insufficient to establish the foreseeability requirement to support the $1,595,000 consequential damages award.

Under Minnesota law, recoverable consequential damages include: "[A]ny loss resulting from general or particular requirements and needs of which the seller at the time of contracting had reason to know and which could not reasonably be prevented by cover or otherwise." Minn. Stat. § 336.2–715(2)(a). Under this section, consequential damages are not available in every case, but instead are only proper if the seller had reason to foresee the particular requirements of the buyer, and even then only if such loss could not be prevented. The focus is on what the seller had reason to know. Minn.Stat. § 336.2–715; U.C.C. Comment 3.

According to First Bank, Simeone repeatedly stated prior to contract formation that he was not in the business of selling automobiles and parts and therefore First Bank neither knew nor had reason to know that Simeone intended to trade or resell the automobiles and parts at any profit, let alone a profit of $1,595,000. First Bank contends the award of consequential damages erroneously treats the agreement as one for the purchase of goods for resale when that was clearly not the case.

The question of whether the buyer's consequential damages were foreseeable by the seller is one of fact to be determined by the trier of fact. *Franklin Mfg. Co. v. Union Pacific R.R.*, 311 Minn. 296, 248 N.W.2d 324, 326 (1976). First Bank asks that this court conclude as a matter of law that the consequential damages were not foreseeable. We decline to so hold. Mr. Garretson, commercial banking officer of First Bank and acting on behalf of the Bank during the relevant negotiations with Simeone, testified that he was aware that collectors may trade vehicles in order to enhance their collection. Further, Simeone testified he told First Bank's broker that he intended to use the cars and parts for trading or possible resale to obtain additional cars. Finally, Simeone contracted to purchase hundreds of automotive parts that the jury would reasonably presume would have to be either resold or assembled into something of increased value. The jury's determination that it was foreseeable that Simeone would seek to further his collection by engaging in sale or trade was not clearly erroneous.

Also with respect to consequential damages, First Bank argues the court erred in failing to adequately apply the doctrine of cover or mitigation of damages. First Bank claims that even if sufficient evidence existed to support an award of consequential damages under Minn.Stat. § 336.2–715(2)(a), such damages are only allowed to the extent that they "could not reasonably be prevented by cover or otherwise." This provision incorporates the common law policy that an aggrieved party has a duty to mitigate damages. See *Barry & Sewall Indus. Supply Co. v. Metal-Prep of Houston, Inc.*, 912 F.2d 252, 259 (8th Cir. 1990).

"The test of proper cover is whether at the time and place the buyer acted in good faith and in a reasonable manner, and it is immaterial that hindsight may later prove that the method of cover used was not the cheapest or most effective." Minn.Stat. § 336.2–712; U.C.C. Comment 2. The burden of proof rests with the seller to establish that the buyer acted unreasonably in failing to prevent his own loss. See *Bemidji Sales Barn, Inc. v. Chatfield*, 312 Minn. 11, 250 N.W.2d 185, 189 (1977). Further, the duty to cover "does not require an injured party to take measures which are unreasonable or impractical or which require expenditures disproportionate to the loss sought to be avoided or which are beyond his financial means." Gerwin v. Southeastern Calif. Ass'n of Seventh Day Adventists, 14 Cal.App.3d 209 (1971).

SMB, Inc. ultimately sold the automobiles and parts for $1,114,960. First Bank now contends that Simeone's consequential damages should be limited because he could have mitigated his damages by purchasing the vehicles and parts from SMB, Inc. at the increased price. The jury, however, rejected this argument. Although the evidence at trial showed that the automobiles and parts were for sale to the general public as soon as SMB, Inc. purchased them from First Bank, it is unreasonable to require that Simeone expend over $1,000,000, almost $700,000 more than the contract obligated him to pay, to purchase the cars and parts in order to effect cover and mitigate his loss. Indeed, First Bank made no showing at trial that Simeone even had such resources available to him or that it would be reasonable to require such cover. It is noteworthy that Simeone did, in fact, undertake efforts to effect cover when he ultimately purchased the 1929 SS Roadster from SMB, Inc. The purchase price of the Roadster exceeded that which Simeone had initially contracted to pay for all of the vehicles and parts. The suggestion that Simeone should have purchased the entire lot of automobiles and parts as a matter of law is not supported by the evidence.

Finally, First Bank contends the consequential damages award is too speculative as a matter of law to be the basis for recovery. Under Minnesota law, "[t]he controlling principle governing actions for damages is that damages which are speculative, remote, or conjectural are not recoverable." *Leoni v. Bemis Co., Inc.*, 255 N.W.2d 824, 826 (Minn. 1977) (quotation omitted). However, a plaintiff's losses need not be proven with mathematical precision. "Once the fact of loss has been shown, the difficulty of proving its amount will not preclude recovery so long as there is proof of a reasonable basis upon which to approximate the amount." Id.

Here, two experts in antique and classic cars testified as to the value of the vehicles and parts at the time of the breach as well as their appreciated value two years after the breach. This testimony was based on the expert's knowledge of the available market, the rate at which such unique cars appreciate in value because of their scarcity and desirability among collectors, as well as the prices commanded by comparable vehicles. This testimony provides a reasonable basis upon which to support the jury's determination of consequential damages.

IV.

First Bank next claims the district court erred in refusing to grant its motion for a new trial or in the alternative a remittitur because the evidence does not support the jury's award of incidental damages. Because we are reviewing state court claims, the appropriate standard for review is that applied by Minnesota appellate courts.... Thus, this court should uphold the trial court's denial of First Bank's new trial motion or motion for remittitur unless there has been a clear abuse of discretion....

Under Minnesota law, incidental damages resulting from a seller's breach are defined as: "[E]xpenses reasonably incurred in inspection, receipt, transportation and care and custody of goods rightfully rejected, any commercially reasonable charges, expenses or commissions in connection with effecting cover and any other reasonable expense incident to the delay or other breach." Minn.Stat. § 336.2–715(1). See also *Mattson v. Rochester Silo, Inc.*, 397 N.W.2d 909, 915 (Minn.Ct.App.1987). In contrast to incidental damages, Minnesota law also provides that "the buyer may 'cover' by making in good faith and without unreasonable delay any reasonable purchase of ... goods in substitution for those due from the seller." Minn.Stat. § 336.2–712(1). The buyer may recover from the seller as "cover damages" "the difference between the cost of cover and the contract price together with any incidental or consequential damages." Minn.Stat. § 336.2–712(2); *Barbarossa & Sons v. Iten Chevrolet, Inc.*, 265 N.W.2d 655, 661 (Minn.1978).

Here, the jury awarded Simeone $225,000 in incidental damages. Simeone speculates that this amount represents his cost of cover in purchasing the 1929 SS Roadster ($470,000 purchase price minus $250,000 contract price, plus $5,000 for dismissal of SMB, Inc. from a civil action). Appellee's Brief at 31. However, the difference between the cost of cover and the contract price is not properly characterized as incidental damages. Rather, incidental damages are, among other things, the "charges," "expenses" and "commissions" incurred in effecting cover. Minn.Stat. § 336.2–715(1). In contrast, the award of damages for the difference between Simeone's purchase price of the Roadster and the contract price falls under Minn.Stat. § 336.2–712 as "cover" damages. The jury's award of incidental damages in this case represents a double recovery to the extent that it compensates Simeone for the difference between the contract price and the price he actually paid for the Roadster. Simeone was compensated for the difference between the contract price and the purchase price through both the compensatory and consequential damages awards. Since there is no other evidence of incidental damages, the award of incidental damages must be reversed.

V.

First Bank argues it should not be held accountable for the failure to convey the vehicle that had been claimed by the Quante Estate, the Conan-Doyle car. We do not agree. The contract, drafted by First Bank, specifically provides that "this Agreement shall constitute a binding contract for the disposition of the Conveyed Assets enforceable as *between the Bank and the Purchaser* upon execution of this Agreement by the Bank and the Purchaser...." (Emphasis added). Under the express terms of the contract, the phrase "Conveyed Assets" includes the assets claimed by the Quante Estate. The contract, therefore, provides that the agreed upon disposition of the Conan-Doyle car is enforceable as between the Bank and Simeone. Thus, under the express terms of the contract, Simeone can enforce his claim with respect to all the vehicles against First Bank.

Moreover, the contract provides that the automobiles and parts, including the Conan-Doyle car, would be conveyed to Simeone "unless ... the Bank determines that it is precluded from performing." Under the express terms of the contract, the Estate could play no role in the decision to refrain from conveying the automobiles to Simeone.

It was First Bank that made the decision not to accept Simeone's wire transfer of the balance due under the contract on November 4, 1985. Further, it was First Bank that entered into negotiations with Gohlike and Torseth and ultimately agreed to sell the automobiles and parts to Torseth rather than Simeone in exchange for Gohlike's agreement to dismiss his suit against First Bank.

The district court properly held First Bank accountable for the breach of contract with respect to the Conan-Doyle car.

VI.

A trial court's authority to award prejudgment interest is governed by statute. See Minn.Stat. § 549.09. Prejudgment interest is an element of damages awarded to provide full compensation by converting time-of-demand damages into time-of-verdict damages. It is designed to compensate the plaintiff for the loss of the use of the money owed. *Johnson v. Kromhout,* 444 N.W.2d 569, 571 (Minn.Ct.App.1989). Prior to 1984, prejudgment interest was allowed on an unliquidated claim only where the damages were readily ascertainable by computation or reference to generally recognized standards such as market value. *Solid Gold Realty, Inc. v. J.B. Mondry*, 399 N.W.2d 681, 684 (Minn.Ct.App.1987). In 1984, however, § 549.09 was amended to provide that "[t]he prevailing party shall receive interest on any judgment or award." Minn.Stat. § 549.09. The amended statute allows prejudgment interest "irrespective of a defendant's ability to ascertain the amount of damages for which he might be held liable." *Lienhard v. State,* 431 N.W.2d 861, 865 (Minn. 1988). Further, the expert's valuations based on the fair market value of the vehicles and parts, as well as First Bank's own assessment of the value of the property in 1985, satisfies the readily ascertainable standard. The "[m]ere difference of opinion as to the exact amount of damages [is] not sufficient to excuse the defendant from compensating the plaintiff for loss of the use of [his] money." *Solid Gold Realty, Inc.*, 399 N.W.2d at 684 (quotation omitted).

We conclude that Simeone is entitled to prejudgment interest on the revised damages award.

VII.

Based on the foregoing, the judgment of the district court is affirmed in part, reversed in part and remanded for further proceedings consistent with the views expressed in this opinion.

Notes and Discussion

1. **Compensatory Damages.** The Court upholds the jury award of $585,000 in compensatory (i.e., direct) damages, on a sale of $450,000. So the court holds, in effect, that Simeone had purchased the cars for less than half of their true value. This seems a straightforward application of UCC § 2–713(1), but the difference between the negotiated contract price and the market price is startling. Comment 2 to that section states that "The market or current price . . . is the price for goods of the same kind *and in the same branch of trade.*" (Emphasis added.) Comment 3 discusses instances when market price is difficult to determine because a good is scarce: "Such scarcity conditions . . . indicate that the price has risen and under the section providing for liberal administration of remedies, opinion evidence as to the value of the goods would be admissible in the absence of a market price and

a liberal construction of allowable consequential damages should also result.''

Simeone (and presumably First Bank as well) had ''experts'' who gave their opinions about the value of the automobiles and parts. Does it seem strange to you that someone's ''opinion'' is accepted as evidence of a fact? There has, of course, been much debate about the kinds of opinions to which the court should listen, particularly in the case of those who present ''scientific'' evidence.

To understand better what is going on in this portion of the decision, imagine that you purchase, in an on-line auction, a used Jaguar for $30,000. Its regular market value at the time of the purchase is $40,000. If the seller repudiates, what damages are you entitled to?

2. Cover? The contract evidently specified that the price for the 1929 Mercedes Roadster was $250,000, i.e., more than fifty percent of the total contract price. Simeone subsequently purchased this same Roadster at auction for $470,000. Isn't this cover? Shouldn't his damages have been limited, as to the Roadster, by the cover price difference ($220,000)?

3. Consequential Damages. The award of compensatory damages (plus pre-judgment interest) should have restored Simeone to the position he would have been in had First Bank performed. We are not sure how he deserved an additional $1.6 million dollars based on the escalating price of the cars in the years after the breach. Assume, for instance, that the cars had declined in value by $200,000 in the intervening years; would we subtract this amount from the award? No. So the court's award in this case is wrong, no?

To continue the Jaguar example from above, should it matter that, two years later when your lawsuit comes to trial, the market value for the Jaguar is now $150,000?

4. Emotional Distress. The law of contracts is a hard-nosed law, and recovery for emotional disturbance is ordinarily not allowed; victims of breach are expected to suck it up and get on with their lives. See Restatement 2d § 353, which, however, makes exceptions when a breach causes bodily harm or when emotional disturbance is a particularly likely result of breach. Illustration 3: ''A makes a contract with B to conduct the funeral for B's husband and to provide a suitable casket and vault for his burial. Shortly thereafter, B discovers that, because A knowingly failed to provide a vault with a suitable lock, water has entered it and reinternment is necessary. B suffers shock, anguish and illness as a result.'' Any guesses as to whether B can recover, in contract, for emotional distress? The illustration is based on *Hirst v. Elgin Metal Casket Co.*, 438 F.Supp. 906 (D. Mont. 1977)

Explaining the usual exclusion is more difficult. Does it seem plausible to you to argue that emotional distress over a breach usually cannot be foreseen when a contract is made, and hence that such damages are excluded under *Hadley v. Baxendale*? Suppose, for instance, that an employee is unjustifiably discharged and then ''claims that, under the contract, she was entitled to job security and the peace of mind that is associated with job security. Because an employment contract providing for job security has a personal element, and breach of such a contract can be expected to result in mental distress, . . . she should be able to recover mental distress damages." This was the situation in *Valentine v. General American Credit*, 420 Mich. 256, 362 N.W.2d 628, 628 (1984). The Court concedes that emotional distress is "foreseeable within the rule of *Hadley v. Baxendale*," but nonetheless concludes, as "a gloss on the generality of the rule," that: "because an employment contract is not entered into primarily to secure the protection of personal interests and pecuniary damages can be estimated with reasonable certainty, . . . a person discharged in breach of an employment contract may not recover mental distress damages." Id. at 630–631. Can you think of a better explanation?

B. MITIGATION

In the leading case, a man named Clark had arranged with Marsiglia for restoration of some paintings, and Marsiglia began the job; but Clark changed his mind and ordered Marsiglia to stop. Instead of doing so, Marsiglia completed the restoration and then sued to get the agreed-upon payment for the job. He won at trial but lost on appeal. As the decision explains, "The defendant, by requiring the plaintiff to stop work upon the paintings, violated his contract, and thereby incurred a liability to pay such damages as the plaintiff should sustain. Such damages would include a recompense for the labor done and materials used, and such further sum in damages as might, upon legal principles, be assessed for the breach of the contract; but the plaintiff had no right, by obstinately persisting in the work, to make the penalty upon the defendant greater than it would otherwise have been." *Clark v. Marsiglia*, 1 Denio 317, 318 (N.Y. Sup. Ct. 1845).

The principle here is easy to state: When one party breaks a contract, the other may not take action that would increase the damage. In many cases, indeed, the injured party may have an affirmative obligation to "mitigate" its damages by making substitute arrangements. This rule cuts especially hard in the case of employment contracts. For instance, an employee who is unjustifiably fired can frequently find another job, the wages from which will serve to alleviate whatever losses she sustained by being fired; and further, she will even have an obligation to make reasonable efforts in obtaining another job.

Here, however, the problems begin, for this "duty to mitigate" is slippery. In one particularly famous case, the actress Shirley MacLaine had a contract with Twentieth-Century Fox to play a leading role in a musical called "Bloomer Girl," for compensation of $750,000. The studio cancelled "Bloomer Girl" and breached her contract, but offered her another role in a "western-type" film called "Big Country, Big Man." MacLaine turned up her nose at the offer and sued for her three-quarter million. The defendant studio argued that her recovery should be reduced by the amount that she would have earned by acting in the western. The California courts sided with MacLaine and held—over a strongly worded dissent—that the proffered role was not, as a matter of law, a substitute. *Parker v. Twentieth Century-Fox Film Corp.*, 3 Cal.3d

176, 89 Cal.Rptr. 737, 474 P.2d 689 (1970). For a lively analysis, see Victor P. Goldberg, Framing Contract Law 279–312 (2006).

Many difficulties lurk here. The two roles were not completely equivalent: a musical that would have made use of her dancing talent, versus a western; "Bloomer Girl" to be filmed in California, and "Big Country, Big Man" in Australia, with MacLaine having appreciably less artistic control. If MacLaine had a legal "option to reject, or fail to seek, different or inferior employment" (id. at 693), were such disparities enough to signify? Did it matter that the alternative offer came from the same studio that had failed to carry through on its promise to produce "Bloomer Girl"? And how responsive should the court be to MacLaine's personal sensitivities? For instance, "Bloomer Girl" was a Hollywood version of the life of the nineteenth-century feminist Amelia Bloomer. MacLaine, a noted social activist, might well feel passionately about such a film, but rather less so about a "western-type" film set in an Australian opal mine. On the other side, does it matter that she had expressed some interest in "Big Country"? And, in the last analysis, how should we feel about "permitting the employee simply to remain idle during the balance of the contract period"? (474 P.2d at 695.)

How and when the aggrieved party must mitigate in more conventional commercial contracts needs study too. In general there is no duty to mitigate where damages will be measured by the formulas in 2–708(1) or 2–713(1) because those formulas *assume* mitigation. The subtrahend in the formula is the "market" when the seller is suing and, in effect, treats the seller as though he has already sold on the market at the appropriate date. For buyer/plaintiffs the use of the market as the minuend comes from the same assumption. Note that 2–715(2) also has a mitigation condition although it is not so labeled: one can get consequential damages only if they could not have been "reasonably . . . prevented by cover or otherwise." Recall First Bank's argument that Simeone should have mitigated by buying the Mercedes from SMB.

MADSEN v. MURREY & SONS CO.

Supreme Court of Utah, 1987.
743 P.2d 1212.

HOWE, J. Appellant Murrey & Sons Company, Inc. (seller), seeks reversal of the trial court's judgment ordering it to return $21,250 to respondent Erik H. Madsen (buyer) in partial restitution of $42,500 paid by him on a contract between the parties which the buyer subsequently breached. Utah Code Ann. § 70A–2–718(2), (3) (1980).

Seller is a corporation located in Los Angeles, California, and engaged in the business of manufacturing and selling pool tables. In early 1978, buyer, a resident of Salt Lake City, Utah, was working on an idea to develop a pool table which, through the use of electronic devices installed in the rails of the table, would produce lighting and sound effects in a fashion similar to a pinball machine. Buyer was experimenting with his idea on a used pool table in his home. This table had been modified to consist of ten pockets, rather than six as originally constructed, and buyer was attempting to design the electronics to be used in the table.

In late February 1978, Patrick W. Murrey, the general manager for seller, travelled to Salt Lake City to learn about buyer's idea, observe the pool table buyer had developed, determine the feasibility of constructing such a table, and discuss the possibility of manufacturing a large quantity of the unique tables for buyer. While in Salt Lake City, and through subsequent communications between the parties by means of telephone and mail, Mr. Murrey recommended that buyer abandon the idea of using a customized ten-pocket pool table and encouraged him to use seller's standard 4' x 8' six-pocket coin-operated pool table, with a customized rail. Buyer agreed.

Shortly thereafter, buyer and seller entered into a written agreement by means of a sales order signed by both parties. Seller agreed to manufacture 100 of its M1 4' x 8' six-pocket coin-operated pool tables, with customized rails capable of incorporating the electronic lighting and sound effects desired by buyer. Under the agreement, buyer was to design the rails and provide the drawings to seller, who would manufacture them according to buyer's specifications. Buyer was also to design, supply, and install all of the electronic components for the tables. Buyer agreed to pay seller $550 per pool table, or a total of $55,000 for the 100 tables.

On March 13, 1978, buyer paid $5,550 to seller, $550 of which went toward the purchase of a separately ordered and delivered pool table to be used as a prototype, leaving $5,000 as an advance on the purchase price for the 100 pool tables. In May and June 1978, buyer advanced another $25,000 and $12,500, respectively, totalling $42,500 in advance payments. During this time, seller commenced the manufacturing of the pool tables and buyer continued his efforts to develop a satisfactory design for the electronics and the customized rails. However, he encountered numerous problems with both. By the fall of 1978, the designs remained undeveloped, and buyer advised seller that he would be unable to take delivery of the 100 pool tables. Buyer then brought this action for restitution of the $42,500 he had paid.

Following buyer's repudiation of the contract, seller dismantled the pool tables and used the salvageable materials to manufacture other pool tables. A good portion of the material was simply used as firewood. As admitted by Patrick Murrey, seller did not attempt or make any effort to market or sell the 100 pool tables at a discount price or at any other price in order to mitigate or minimize its damages.

The trial court, sitting without a jury, found that buyer did not complete the design for the customized rails or the designs for the electronic components. Seller had already manufactured the 100 pool tables to the extent that it could do so and, the court found, "fully performed all of its obligations under the agreement." The court also found that had seller completed the tables, they would have had a value of at least $21,250 and could have been sold by seller for at least that amount following the repudiation of the contract. In turn, the court concluded that seller's action in dismantling the tables for salvage and for firewood, rather than attempting to sell or market them at a full or discounted price, was not commercially reasonable. The court fixed seller's damages at $21,250 and held that seller did not prove that it had been damaged any greater. Apparently in reliance on Utah Code Ann. § 70A–2–718(2), (3), judgment was entered that buyer recover from seller the $42,500 paid, less the $21,250 damages suffered by seller as a result of the repudiation, for a net recovery of $21,250.

I.

Seller first contends that the trial court erred in concluding that it had failed to mitigate or minimize its damages in a commercially reasonable manner by not attempting to sell the 100 pool tables on the open market. It is a well settled rule of the law of damages that "no party suffering a loss as the result of a breach of contract is entitled to any damages which could have been avoided if the aggrieved party had acted in a reasonably diligent manner in attempting to lessen his losses as a consequence of that breach." 3 Williston on Sales § 24–5, at 405 (4th ed. 1974). This doctrine is the mitigation of damages rule "that a party has the active duty of making reasonable exertions to render the injury as light as possible ... and that no recovery may be had for losses which the person injured might have prevented by reasonable efforts and expenditures." *Fairfield Lease Corp. v. 717 Pharmacy, Inc.*, 109 Misc.2d 1072, 1077, 441 N.Y.S.2d 621, 624 (N.Y.City Civ.Ct.1981) (citations omitted). We have held: "Where a contractual agreement has been breached by a party thereto, the aggrieved party is entitled to those damages that will put him in as good a position as he would have been had the other party performed pursuant to the agreement. A corollary to this rule is that the aggrieved party may not, either by action or inaction, aggravate the injury occasioned by the breach, but has a duty actively to mitigate his damages." *Utah Farm Production Credit Association v. Cox*, 627 P.2d 62, 64 (Utah 1981) (citations omitted).

Seller asserts that it sufficiently mitigated its damages by dismantling the pool tables and salvaging various components that could be used to manufacture other pool tables. The salvage value to seller was claimed to be $7,448. It presented testimony that selling the tables as "seconds" would damage its reputation for quality and that the various holes, notches, and routings placed in the tables to accommodate the electrical components to be installed by buyer weakened the structure of the tables so as to submit seller to potential liability if they were sold on the market.

On the other hand, Ronald Baker, who had been involved with the manufacturing and marketing of pool tables for 25 years, testified on behalf of the buyer that the notches, holes, and routings made in the frame to accommodate electrical wiring would not adversely affect the quality or marketability of the 100 pool tables. According to Baker, the tables could have been sold at full value or at a discounted price. In addition to this testimony, the trial court had the opportunity to view the experimental table developed by buyer and his associates and observe the holes, notches, and routings necessary for the electrical components.

The trial court found that seller's action in dismantling the tables and using the materials for salvage and firewood, rather than attempting to sell or market the tables at full or a discounted price, was not commercially reasonable. The court then concluded that seller had a duty to mitigate its damages and failed to do so. The finding is supported by competent evidence. We find no clear error. Utah R.Civ.P. 52.

II.

Seller next contends that the trial court erred in finding that the 100 pool tables, before being disassembled by seller, had a value of at least $21,250 and could have been sold by seller for at least that amount following the repudiation of the contract. Again, we do not retry the facts and will sustain findings supported by evidence in the record unless clearly erroneous.

At trial, substantial evidence was presented concerning the value of the pool tables at the time of buyer's repudiation and refusal to accept delivery upon tender. This evidence varied from Mr. Murrey's testimony that the tables had no value because they were not marketable to Mr. Baker's testimony that the tables could have been sold for full value or a discounted value because the integrity and marketability of the tables were not impaired. Murrey partially disputed his own testimony by admitting that the tables could have been sold at a discount. The evidence presented a broad range from which the trial court could determine the value of the 100 pool tables. The trial court's finding that the tables had a value of at least $21,250 was within the range of the evidence presented at trial. We will not overturn that finding.

III.

The trial court found that seller suffered damages as a result of buyer's repudiation of the agreement in the amount of $21,250 and that it did not prove that it had been damaged any greater. The court offset the amount of seller's damages against the amount buyer paid on the contract ($42,500) and awarded buyer a judgment of $21,250. Seller contends that the trial court erred in assessing its damages at $21,250 by failing to consider loss of expected profit, together with any incidental damages and costs incurred. Utah Code Ann. § 70A–2–708(2) (1980).

Buyer's right to recover any amount of the $42,500 paid on the contract arises under section 70A–2–718(2), (3), which provides in pertinent part:

(2) Where the seller justifiably withholds a delivery of goods because of the buyer's breach, the buyer is entitled to restitution of any amount by which the sum of his payments exceeds . . .

(b) . . . twenty per cent of the value of the total performance for which the buyer is obligated under the contract or $500, whichever is smaller.

(3) The buyer's right to restitution under subsection (2) is subject to offset to the extent that the seller establishes

(a) a right to recover damages under the provisions of this chapter . . . and,

(b) the amount or value of any benefits received by the buyer directly or indirectly by reason of the contract.

As a result of buyer's breach, seller justifiably withheld delivery of the 100 pool tables. Still, buyer is entitled to recover the $42,500 paid on the contract less the damages suffered by seller. We recently held that "in fixing damages, the trial court is vested with broad discretion, and the award will not be set aside unless it is manifestly unjust or indicates that the trial court neglected pertinent elements, or was unduly influenced by prejudice or other extraneous circumstances." *Mabey v. Kay Petersen Construction Co.*, 682 P.2d 287, 291 (Utah 1984). Our review of the record reveals that the trial court neglected pertinent elements of Utah's commercial code in assessing seller's damages.

The applicable statute to be used in determining seller's damages for nonacceptance or repudiation is Utah Code Ann. § 70A–2–708 (1980) . . .

Seller argues that section 70A–2–708(2) is the proper formula for assessing its damages. That, however, would be inconsistent with the general rule that requires application of section 70A–2–708(1) where the trial court finds that a reasonably accessible market exists wherein the aggrieved seller can market its goods. See *Detroit Power Screwdriver Co. v. Ladney,* 25 Mich.App. 478, 181 N.W.2d 828 (1970); *Anchorage Centennial Development Co. v. Van Wormer & Rodrigues, Inc.*, 443 P.2d 596, 599 (Alaska 1968). "By market, we mean a market which, if availed of, would have substantially mitigated [seller's] damages." *Timber Access Industries Co. v. U.S. Plywood-Champion Papers, Inc.*, 263 Or. 509, 525, 503 P.2d 482, 490 (1972). The trial court concluded that seller failed to perform its duty to mitigate its damages by not marketing or attempting to sell the pool tables on the open market. Having found that a market existed, seller's damages must be determined under section 70A–2–708(1).

Applying the trial court's finding that the pool tables if completed could have been sold for at least $21,250, seller's damages are the difference between the market price ($21,250) and the contract price ($55,000), or $33,750. The trial court found that seller was not entitled to any incidental damages. Buyer is not entitled to any further credit for expenses saved by seller in consequence of buyer's breach. Since the

$21,250 which the trial court charged seller with was for completed tables, no savings would have occurred. Under section 70A–2–718(2), (3), buyer's right to restitution of advance payments on the contract ($42,-500) is subject to offset to the extent that seller establishes damages ($33,750), for a total recovery of $8,750.

Buyer contends that seller failed to carry its burden of proving the amount of offset as required by section 70A–2–718(3). The findings and conclusions of the trial court, however, show otherwise. The agreement between the parties, as evidenced by the signed sales order, was a valid and enforceable contract. As a result of buyer's repudiation, buyer breached the agreement. Seller fully performed all of its obligations under the agreement and was entitled to damages under section 70A–2–708(1).

IV.

Seller next contends that the trial court erred in finding that buyer made advance payments on the contract totalling $42,500 instead of $41,950. We will not overturn this finding as it is supported by substantial evidence.

Buyer is entitled to recover from seller the sum of $8,750. The judgment is affirmed as modified.

Notes and Discussion

1. Lost Volume Seller? Murrey contended that, as a lost volume seller, it was entitled to lost profits when Erik Madsen repudiated. Assume that in 1978 Murrey had ten customers, each of whom had ordered 100 pool tables, and that only Madsen's tables required extensive custom fittings. Because of their customization, the Madsen tables undoubtedly cost more to make (say, $40,000 total) than ordinary Murrey tables. Although the value of the custom tables was quite high to Madsen at the time the contract was made, on the general market they were presumably worth appreciably less than ordinary Murrey tables. (As Patrick Murrey testified, their sale would have been "at a discount.")

From this perspective, were Murrey's actions after the breach—essentially, reducing the tables to scrap—commercially unreasonable, particularly in relation to its probable market strategy? What might its motives have been for scrapping the Madsen tables? Why might Murrey have felt that it was entitled to damages under § 2–708(2)?

2. Mitigation and the Article 2 Remedies. The Court requires a seller, after a breach, to take steps to mitigate the damages that the buyer will have to pay. This duty is a general one in contract law, and does not derive specifically from the UCC. The UCC does state, however, that a buyer cannot recover consequential damages from a seller if these damages could "reasonably be prevented by cover or otherwise": § 2–715(2)(a). What were the implications for Murrey of, as the Court sees it, its failure to mitigate?

As we note in the introduction to this section, the direct damages provisions in the UCC do not mention any duty to mitigate when describing the market difference measure: §§ 2–708(1), 713(1). The reason is that the market difference measure tacitly presupposes mitigation: a seller who is a victim of a breach will typically re-sell on the market and can claim the difference as damages, and conversely for an aggrieved buyer. By contrast, mitigation is alluded to when the UCC describes the "lost volume seller" in § 2–708(1) and cover in § 2–712. Why do these latter sections raise mitigation problems?

Problem 6–9

Siemens, a manufacturer of electrical products, made a large sale to Coleman Electrical Supply, a wholesaler. Siemens delivered a substantial portion of the electrical supplies on credit to Coleman, which accepted delivery; but Coleman then encountered financial and management difficulties, as a consequence of which it was unable to pay for the supplies. When Siemens sued for the unpaid price, Coleman responded that Siemens had failed to mitigate damages when it turned down Coleman's offer to return some of the unpaid goods. Will this argument work?

Siemens's action was for the "price," not, strictly speaking, for seller's damages. Take a look at UCC § 2–709. The most common defendant under 2–709 is a buyer who has "accepted" the goods. Sellers, of course, would like the full contract price every time they could get it, but often there has been no acceptance by the buyer, so the seller cannot get the price, only damages. Read § 2–606, on "What Constitutes Acceptance of Goods." What policy justifies the law's refusal to give the seller the price when the buyer has not accepted?

Assume that Coleman had returned the goods soon after they had been delivered and despite the fact that they conformed to the contract. Presumably this would be an effective (if wrongful) rejection under UCC § 2–602 of the UCC. Presumably, too, that would have kept "acceptance" from occurring under § 2–606, and would therefore save Coleman from the obligation for the price because of §§ 2–607 and 2–709. If Siemens then came to you to ask your advice about what they should and could do with the goods that had been rejected, what would you tell them?

MANOUCHEHRI v. HEIM

Court of Appeals of New Mexico, 1997.
123 N.M. 439, 941 P.2d 978.

HARTZ, J. Jeff Heim sold Dr. A.H. Manouchehri a used x-ray machine. Manouchehri sued for breach of warranty and was awarded $4400 in damages after a bench trial. Heim appeals, claiming the following errors: (1) venue was improper; (2) direct damages based on the cost of repair should not have been awarded because there was no evidence of such cost; and (3) consequential damages should not have been awarded because (a) Manouchehri could have avoided them by obtaining a replacement machine; (b) they were not foreseeable, and (c) they were not proved with the required certainty. We affirm.

I. BACKGROUND

Manouchehri was the sole witness at trial. Heim presented no evidence other than through cross-examination of Manouchehri. We summarize Manouchehri's testimony.

Manouchehri is a physician in Cedar Crest, New Mexico. Heim, a sales representative of a medical supply company, had previously sold various items to Manouchehri. In December 1991 Heim learned that Manouchehri wanted to buy a used 100/100 x-ray machine. The two numbers refer to the rating of the machine in kilovolts and milliamps, respectively. The rating of the machine affects the quality of the image obtained. A weak machine often will not be able to produce adequate images.

On December 9 Manouchehri purchased a machine from Heim. He paid with a check for $1900 on which he wrote at the top "guaranteed to work (install Continental 100-100 x-ray) without limitation" and wrote on the memo line "purchase and installation of Continental 100-100 x-ray." Heim signed his name on the front of the check after Manouchehri read the notations to him.

During the following weeks Manouchehri realized that the machine was performing as a 100/60 machine. The power was sufficient only for x-rays of small children and thin people. Manouchehri notified Heim and asked him to repair it, offering to pay half the repair costs. Although Heim sent someone to inspect the machine, no repairs were made. Manouchehri continued to talk regularly with Heim about the problem until the lawsuit was filed in September 1994. Heim at first denied knowing that the x-ray machine was a 100/60 machine but later admitted that he knew. At that time he indicated that it was the sort of machine one can buy for only $1900.

Manouchehri initially obtained a default judgment, but it was later set aside. After trial on April 4, 1996 Manouchehri obtained judgment in the amount of $4400. Of the total, $1900 was for direct contract damages and $2500 was for consequential damages. The district court denied Heim's motion for reconsideration and Heim appealed....

B. Consequential Damages

The district court's judgment awarded "$2500 for incidental damages." Again, the judgment was not prepared with sufficient care. The damage award was clearly for consequential damages, not incidental damages. See § 55–2–715 (defining "incidental" and "consequential" damages). Finding No. 6 of the district court's decision states: "[Manouchehri] has suffered consequential damages in the form of loss of business of at least $2,500.00 during the time [Manouchehri] reasonably waited for [Heim] to repair the X-Ray machine or otherwise perform under the guarantee."

Manouchehri's testimony with respect to consequential damages was straightforward. He said that taking an x-ray would cost him from three to six dollars and he would charge "about $85 to $88" for taking and reading an x-ray. He also claimed that the inadequacy of the machine prevented him from taking at least 30 x-rays a month, although he had no documentation to support his estimate. Using the lowest possible profit per x-ray, Manouchehri contended in closing argument that the monthly loss would be $2370—computed by multiplying $79 net income per x-ray times 30 x-rays a month.

Heim contends that the award is improper for three reasons. First, he contends that Manouchehri failed to present evidence that he could not avoid the damages by renting or buying a substitute machine. Second, he contends that any lost profits were not reasonably foreseeable. Third, he contends that the proof of damages was too indefinite. Each of Heim's arguments has some force. But they must be examined in light of the district court's award of only $2500. It appears that the district court considered the three matters raised by Heim and adjusted the award accordingly. We now examine each of Heim's arguments.

1. Failure to Obtain Replacement Machine

Consequential damages are not recoverable if they could "reasonably be prevented by cover or otherwise." Section 55–2–715(2)(a). Heim argues that Manouchehri needed to present evidence that he could not avoid the damages by renting or buying a substitute machine. On the record before us, we reject the argument.

Manouchehri testified that he asked Heim to have someone repair the machine and that Heim responded that he would have someone come to the office for that purpose. Manouchehri further testified that he talked to Heim on a monthly basis regarding the problem and that until about a month before he filed the lawsuit he believed that Heim would fix the problem.

The UCC requirement to take reasonable steps to prevent consequential damages derives from standard contract law. In particular, guidance in interpreting Section 55–2–715(2)(a) can be found in the Restatement (Second) of Contracts § 350 (1981). See 1 White & Summers, supra, § 10–4, at 577 ("Restatement [§ 350] may be regarded as an articulation of the rules embodied in the adverb 'reasonably' in 2–715."). Restatement, supra, Section 350 reads: "Avoidability as a Limitation on Damages. (1) Except as stated in Subsection (2), damages are not recoverable for loss that the injured party could have avoided without undue risk, burden or humiliation. (2) The injured party is not precluded from recovery by the rule stated in Subsection (1) to the extent that he has made reasonable but unsuccessful efforts to avoid loss."

The comment to this section states that it may be reasonable to rely on a breaching party's assurances that the breach will be remedied. See id. cmt. g and illus. 19; *Steele v. J.I. Case Co.,* 197 Kan. 554, 419 P.2d 902, 911 (1966). See generally Gary D. Spivey, Annotation, *Seller's Promises or Attempts to Repair Article Sold as Affecting Buyer's Duty to Minimize Damages for Breach of Sale Contract or of Warranty,* 66 A.L.R.3d 1162, 1164 (1975) (courts generally recognize an excuse of mitigation duty when seller makes assurances regarding forthcoming performance, at least until it is no longer reasonable to rely on seller's assurances)....

We cannot say that it was unreasonable as a matter of law for Manouchehri to delay seeking a replacement machine for a few months. The district court found that Manouchehri "suffered consequential damages in the form of loss of business of at least $2,500.00 during the time [he] reasonably waited for [Heim] to repair the X-Ray machine or otherwise perform under the guarantee." The district court did not state how long it was reasonable for Manouchehri to wait, nor did it state how much business Manouchehri lost in any particular month. Nevertheless, we see no need for mathematical precision in the circumstances of this case. The question is only whether it was rational for the district court to find, on the basis of the evidence presented, that by the time Manouchehri should have stopped relying on Heim's promises, he had lost at least $2500 in profits. Our answer is yes.

2. *Foreseeability*

Heim next argues that the lost profits cannot be awarded because Manouchehri failed to present any evidence on the issue of foreseeability. He relies on the language in Section 55–2–715(2)(a) that restricts recovery for consequential damages to losses "resulting from general or particular requirements ... of which the seller at the time of contracting had reason to know...." We are not persuaded.

This was not a sale of a mass-produced item to an anonymous buyer. Heim knew his customer and knew how the x-ray machine was to be used. Any reasonable person in his position would assume that a doctor using such a machine would charge more for its use than the cost of operation and would earn income from it. Moreover, Manouchehri testified to conversations with Heim that at least touched on the economics of the machine. For example, Manouchehri related one occasion when parts from an old failed x-ray machine were in front of his office: "[Heim] asked that I had that x-ray and what to do with them and how come it was still sitting there. And I told him that this was a failed x-ray and I am stuck with the loss of this much money. And at that time he promised me, quoting from him, that 'I know a doctor that has just x-ray that you want. X-ray 100/100 is what you want, and I can get it for you and install in your office for this much money.' "

On the evidence at trial the district court could properly find that lost income would be a foreseeable consequence of an underpowered x-ray machine. Cf. *Camino Real Mobile Home Park Partnership v. Wolfe,* 119 N.M. 436, 446, 891 P.2d 1190, 1200 (1995) ("In cases where profit is an inducement to making a contract, loss of profits as a result of the breach is generally considered to be within the contemplation of the parties and recovery for lost profits will be allowed as damages if causation is proved with reasonable certainty."). Although Manouchehri did not tell Heim how much income he would earn from use of the machine, he did not need to do so in order to recover consequential damages so long as the consequence of lost income was reasonably foreseeable. The law does not require those who enter into contracts to disclose to other parties the profits they expect to make from the contracts. See Richard A. Posner, Economic Analysis of Law 115 (3d ed. 1986) ("Any other rule would make it difficult for a good bargainer to collect damages unless before the contract was signed he had made disclosures that would reduce the advantage of being a good bargainer—disclosures that would prevent the buyer from appropriating the gains from his efforts to identify a resource that was undervalued in its present use."); see generally Melvin Aron Eisenberg, *The Principle of Hadley v. Baxendale*, 80 Cal.L.Rev. 563, esp. 588–90 (1992). Perhaps some limit could be placed on recovery for particularly large lost profits, cf. Restatement, supra, § 351(3) (court may limit damages for foreseeable loss "in order to avoid disproportionate compensation"), but the award of $2500 in this case was within proper bounds.

3. Certainty of Proof of Damages

Finally, Heim argues that the evidence of lost profits was not certain enough. We disagree. We recognize that "when it is *possible* to present accurate evidence on the amount of damages, the party upon whom the burden rests to prove damages must present such evidence." *First Nat'l Bank v. Sanchez*, 112 N.M. 317, 323–24, 815 P.2d 613, 619–20 (1991) (emphasis added) (setting aside damage award of $1,053,000 for several reasons, including the fact that the award greatly exceeded the amount that the evidence could support). This requirement must be understood, however, in the context of the amount at stake. What it is "possible" to present in a suit for a million dollars may be an excessive burden for a small claim. Although Manouchehri's evidence was minimal, it was adequate in the circumstances. The absence of detail and documentary corroboration detracted from the weight of the testimony, but the district court could still find it sufficiently credible to support the $2500 award.

IV. Conclusion

We affirm the judgment below.

IT IS SO ORDERED.

Notes and Discussion

1. What Should the Doctor Do? After Dr. Manouchehri realized that the x-ray machine was inadequate, he first tried unsuccessfully to get Heim to repair it, and only then brought suit, even though he lost substantial business during the month. Was it wholly reasonable for him to rely on Jeff Heim's promises, especially if he suspected that Heim had deceived him about the power of the machine. The Court cites, but does not quote, Comment g on Restatement 2d § 350, which states that: "[I]f the breach is accompanied by assurances that performance will be forthcoming ... the injured party is not expected to arrange a substitute transaction although he may be expected to take some steps to avoid loss due to a delay in performance." The doctor's conduct doesn't meet this standard, does it?

2. Efficient Breach Revisited. Holmes once stated that "[t]he duty to keep a contract at common law means a prediction that you must pay damages if you do not keep it—and nothing else." Oliver Wendell Holmes, *The Path of the Law*, 10 Harv. L. Rev. 457, 462 (1897). This goes to the heart of expectation damages, but also allows for a breach that is voluntary, and sometimes also efficient. As you will recall from the beginning of this Chapter, Judge Posner argues that giving simple expectation damages gives the promisor an incentive to fulfill his promise unless the result would be an inefficient use of resources; thus, in the typical case, contracted-for goods or services are channeled to the user who values them more highly, while transaction costs are kept to a minimum.

The efficient breach theory has often been criticized; see, for a summary, Robert A. Hillman, The Richness of Contract Law 220–224 (1997). Perhaps the most trenchant critic is Daniel Friedmann, who suggests the following argument: "The 'right' to break a contract is not predicated on the nature of the contractual right, its relative 'weakness,' or its status as merely in personam, as opposed to the hardier rights in rem. Rather it is on the ground that the breach is supposed to lead to a better use of resources. The theory, therefore, is, in principle, equally applicable to property rights, where it leads to the adoption of a theory of 'efficient theft' or 'efficient conversion.' To see the point, observe how this account of efficiency plays out in two cases. In the first, A promises to sell a machine to B for $10,000 but then turns around and sells it instead to C for $18,000. In the second, B owns a machine for which he has paid $10,000, which A takes and sells to C for $18,000.

"To keep matters simple, assume that B values the machine at exactly $12,000 in both cases. If the willful contract breach is justified in the first case, then the willful conversion is justified in the second. In the first, B gets $2,000 in expectation damages and is released from paying the $10,000 purchase price. In the second, B obtains damages for conversion equal to $12,000 because he has already paid the $10,000 purchase price to his seller. The two cases thus look identical even though they derive from distinct substantive fields." Daniel Friedman, *The Efficient Breach Fallacy*, 18 J. Legal Stud. 1, 4 (1989).

Of course, this is a *reductio ad absurdum*. Whoever in their right mind would subscribe to the notion of "efficient theft"? But why do we treat breach of contract so differently from violation of a property right? This line of argument should get you thinking more deeply about the structure of contract damages in our law. Ward Farnsworth, The Legal Analyst: A Toolkit for Thinking about the Law 189 (2007), suggests, for instance, a fundamental distinction between property rules and liability rules: "If a right is protected by a property rule, invasions of it are punished, whether with jail, fines, or punitive damages. A liability rule requires only that the violator of a right pay for whatever damage he has caused. Nobody likes to do that, but it isn't considered *punishment.* Punishments try to force people to behave in a certain way, whereas holding people liable doesn't necessarily do that; it just puts them to a choice: respect the right or pay for the costs created by invading it."

Punitive damages are only rarely available in a contract action; see Restatement 2d § 355 ("unless the conduct constituting the breach is also a tort for which punitive damages are recoverable"). However, if Judge Posner's view is accepted, should there be a punishment for inefficient breachers, in order to deter such behavior? Punitive damages for deliberate inefficient breaches have been advocated. Richard Craswell, *Contract Remedies, Renegotiation, and the Theory of Efficient Breach*, 61 S. Cal. L. Rev. 629, 665–668 (1988), suggests a rule that a party committing a "willful and unjustified" contractual breach be subject to over-compensatory damages.

You have now looked closely at a fair number of damages cases. Are there any of them you would describe unqualifiedly as efficient breaches? How many are clearly inefficient, and how many are indeterminate?

Problem 6–10

Charles has a contract with Leo to sell an antique vase for $9,000. Before the sale is made, Charles learns that Fiona is interested in purchasing the same vase, and would be willing to pay $15,000 for it (because it matches a vase she already owns). Assume that Charles does not know Leo's value, nor does Leo know of the existence of Fiona or of her willingness to pay $15,000 for the very same vase. Also assume that there is no obvious market for this vase; only Leo and Fiona are known to prize it. What is the most economically efficient use of resources? Charles, of course, will want to breach the contract with Leo and sell to Fiona. Charles will gamble that Leo does not value (or at least cannot prove that he values) the vase at much more than $9,000, and would be willing to pay any small difference, say $1,500, in damages to Leo in order to make a large profit by selling to Fiona. Would the breach still be efficient if Leo values the vase at $13,000?

At first glance, it seems efficient to breach if Leo's value is $11,000. Charles would pay Leo $2,000, and sell the vase to Fiona for $15,000; there is still a $4,000 surplus. However there are still negotiation costs and, possibly, litigation costs. Why couldn't Charles approach Leo and propose that Leo sell to an unnamed buyer for $15,000? Charles would, of course, ask for a finder's fee.

Problem 6–11

Drew, a star college quarterback and also a star baseball player, signs with the Yankees for $12 million to be paid over three years. After the first year in the majors goes poorly for him, Drew decides to give up his baseball career and breaks his contract. He signs with the Chicago Bears for $15 million over three years.

Assume that Drew cannot hit major league curve balls and was never destined to make the Yankee roster. Is his breach efficient? What can the Yankees recover from the Bears?

C. RELIANCE DAMAGES

Though the normal measure of damages in contract is expectation, alternate measures of damages are available to the injured party. The Restatement (Second) of Contracts, § 349 illustrates this: "As an alternative to the measure of damages stated in § 347, the injured party has a right to damages based on his reliance interest, including expenditures made in preparation for performance or in performance, less any loss that the party in breach can prove with reasonable certainty the injured party would have suffered had the contract been performed."

Expectation damages give the profit that would have been expected under the contract, while reliance damages seek to put the plaintiffs back to where they would have been had the contract not been signed. Why would the plaintiff choose reliance damages instead of expectation damages? The first thought that may come to mind is that the plaintiff realizes that the contract would have been a losing contract anyway. The last clause in restatement § 349, however, invites the party in breach to subtract expectation losses from reliance damages. That caps reliance damages at plaintiff's expectation.

Reliance damages are worth the plaintiff's while if neither profits nor losses can be calculated with reasonable certainty. In this case, the plaintiff can ask for what was expended in reliance on the contract in return, and at least be put in as good a position as he would have been had the contract never come into existence. In *Security Stove & Manufacturing Co. v. American Railways Express Co.*, 227 Mo.App. 175, 51 S.W.2d 572 (1932), the defendant was to transport certain parts of a furnace equipped with a novel oil and gas burner to a convention in Atlantic City, N.J.; Security Stove was planning to show its furnace in hopes of eventual sales. All but one part of the furnace arrived in time, but the missing part made it impossible for the plaintiff properly to display the stove. Plaintiff sought damages for all expenses related to the convention, including hotel stays for those who would have displayed the stove. Recognizing that expectation damages are the norm, but holding that under peculiar circumstances that were known to the defendant (that the stove was to be exhibited at a convention for possible future sale), the court awarded the cost as reliance damages.

The plaintiff in *Security Stove* likely expected to make a profit on showing the stove at the convention. Remember, however, that one must prove expectation damages with reasonable certainty. Plaintiff may have realized that he could not prove any profits with reasonable certainty, and was better off making the argument that he should get his expenses back instead. The court is essentially saying that while the plaintiff may not be able to prove that it would have been profitable had the stove been displayed, it can at least claim that it would have broken even on their investment, and should be entitled to get its entire investment back. Restatement § 349 clearly allows the breaching party to submit evidence stating that the other side would not have broken even, but instead would have suffered a loss, but there was no such proof in this case.

Problem 6–12

Oregon Landmark-One leased a commercial space to Russell and Jean Sullivan, who wanted to operate a restaurant and bookstore. The Sullivans signed a lease with Oregon Landmark-One, both parties agreeing to make substantial improvements. The couple then spent many hours preparing to operate the restaurant. They studied books on how to operate a restaurant, tested recipes, obtained financing, purchased equipment, and performed myriad other tasks associated with the new business. They also spent numerous hours preparing to perform their remodeling obligations under the contract: speaking with designers, reviewing building code requirements, negotiating with contractors and suppliers of building materials, and performing various other tasks associated with all their contractual obligations. They incurred expenses associated with all the tasks, including bills for telephone, postage, license fees, legal fees, and interest on capital investment loans. They also purchased equipment and supplies and other miscellaneous items, such as plants and books.

The landlord ultimately failed both to make the improvements (which turned out to be much more expensive than anticipated) and to deliver the premises as promised. The Sullivans then sued for damages. Assume there is no way to estimate their expectation damages (since the restaurant never got started), nor did they confer any benefit on the landlord. Can they recover reliance damages? If so, are these confined to their out-of-pocket expenditures, or can they also recover for their labor expended? Should their own labor be treated differently from that of persons whom they hired? If they were both unemployed while preparing to perform, would they have to show that they would have been able to obtain work elsewhere? Can they recover for other lost opportunities?

D. RESTITUTION DAMAGES

A third measure of damages is sometimes called restitution damages. Beware the word "Restitution." In American law it is both the name of a cause of action and the label for certain damages. The goal of restitution as a claim is to restore to the injured party the benefit that was conferred by the injured party on the other. Like reliance damages, these are rarely sought, for the plaintiff does not recover any profit he would have received under the contract.

Of course, when these damages are awarded in restitution causes of action there is no actual contract, but instead a situation that smells like a contract, or was executed like a contract, and some benefit is conferred. This restitution cause of action is sometimes called "quasi-contract" or a contract implied in law.

In *Campbell v. Tennessee Valley Authority*, 421 F.2d 293 (5th Cir. 1969), we see an example of quasi-contract. Campbell had contracted

DISCUSSION

A. The Measure and Allocation of Damages

The question which faces us on this appeal is one of some jurisprudential complexity. It has engaged the attention of commentators for many years. As a matter of pure contract law it is generally true that if two individuals enter into a contract and one breaches, the breaching party cannot obtain a recovery from the innocent party. Rather, if the innocent party has suffered, a recovery against the party in breach is generally accorded. See, e.g., California Civil Code § 3300; *Bruckman v. Parliament Escrow Corp.*, 190 Cal.App.3d 1051, 235 Cal.Rptr. 813 (1987). In building contracts "[t]he measure of damages ... is the reasonable cost ... to finish the work in accordance with the contract." *Walker v. Signal Cos., Inc.*, 84 Cal.App.3d 982, 993, 149 Cal.Rptr. 119 (1978).

On the other hand, if the breaching party has conferred a benefit upon the innocent party rather than a detriment, it would unjustly enrich the innocent party and unduly punish the breaching party if the latter received nothing for its services. Quasi contract principles will supply the remedy for that. See 12 S. Williston, A Treatise on the Law of Contracts §§ 1479–84 (3rd ed. 1970) (Williston)....

These policies appear to conflict to some extent, so anyone who considers them must reconcile their opposing tendencies. When faced with these propositions, the commentators have resolved them by stating that the breaching party is entitled to the reasonable value of its services less any damages caused by the breach. See 5 A. Corbin, Corbin on Contracts § 1124 (1964). They have added that the breaching party should not, in any event, be able to recover more than the contract price, or perhaps even a ratable part of that contract price. Id. See also, 5 A. Corbin, Corbin on Contracts § 1113 at 606 (1964). Williston puts it as follows: "The true measure of quasi contractual recovery, where the performance is incomplete but readily remediable, is the unpaid contract price less the cost of completion and other additional harm to the defendant except that it must never exceed the benefit actually received by him. This is the net benefit by which the defendant is enriched." Williston § 1483 at 301.

While this phraseology is somewhat more complex, it can readily be seen that the effect is to preclude a recovery by the breaching party which will cause the innocent party to pay more than the contract price itself.[21] The Restatement is in accord with this approach, for while it, too, allows for recovery for part performance, it indicates that the amount of that recovery is not only limited to the extent that the innocent party's gain exceeded its loss, but is also limited to no more than a ratable portion of the total contract price. Restatement (Second) of Contracts § 374 comments a & b (1981).

21. In the case at hand, for example, the mathematics would come out as follows: (a) contract price–$235,137.00; (b) unpaid portion–$120,378.02; (c) cost of completion–$126,673.56; (b)-(c) =-$6,295.54, which is exactly the damage to CSE and which leaves no quasi contractual recovery for Palmer.

It is interesting to observe that treatise illustrations of the application of these principles demonstrate that the innocent party never winds up paying a total that is more than the contract price itself. See, e.g., Restatement (Second) of Contracts § 374 comment b, illustrations (1981). That is sensible. Were it otherwise, there would be a powerful inducement to breach rather than complete any contract which did not turn out to be profitable. By doing so, the ultimate loss of the bargain would be shifted from the breaching party to the innocent party, which is precisely what would occur in the case at hand if the district court's judgment stands.

Palmer has referred us to cases from our and other circuits but not one of them stands for the proposition that an innocent party must pay more than the contract price for the goods or services it sought. See *United States ex rel. C.J.C., Inc. v. Western States Mechanical Contractors, Inc.*, 834 F.2d 1533 (10th Cir. 1987) (breaching prime contractor had to pay quantum meruit charges to subcontractor); ... *American Surety Co. v. United States ex rel. B & B Drilling Co.*, 368 F.2d 475 (9th Cir. 1966) (breaching party could recover for what it did at the contract rate less setoffs for damages incurred on account of the breach).

Moreover, if the breaching party were permitted to recover an amount that leaves the innocent party paying more than the contract price for the goods and services contracted for, that would cause an increase in the loss to the innocent party on account of the breach and would offset the additional amount demanded by the breaching party. However, no such paraphrastic principles are needed if the cost to the innocent party for the goods and services contracted for is limited to the contract price itself. The breaching party would then be required to pay damages for excess costs imposed upon the innocent party.

California law is not to the contrary. In the leading case of *Roseleaf Corp. v. Radis*, 122 Cal.App.2d 196, 264 P.2d 964 (1953), the court dealt with a situation where a purchaser of property was to obtain a new refinancing loan in an amount not to exceed $75,000. Instead, the purchaser obtained a loan for $125,000. That loan was accepted by the seller. When the purchaser sought credit for the costs of obtaining the loan, the seller claimed that the purchaser had no entitlement whatever because the purchaser had breached. The court disagreed and, instead, awarded the purchaser a credit in the amount of the costs that would have been proper if a $75,000 loan had been obtained.

In reaching that unexceptional conclusion the court pointed to the fact that the case was one of "imperfect performance, accepted without waiver of a claim for damages...." 122 Cal.App.2d at 203–04, 264 P.2d 964. It went on to quote Williston to the effect that the issue of damages for a breaching party is one which has caused great difficulties and differences of opinion because there is a clash of fundamental policies. Those policies were identified as: "On the one hand, it seems a violation of the terms of a contract to allow a plaintiff in default to recover—to allow a party to stop when he pleases and sell his part performance at a value fixed by the jury to the defendant who has agreed only to pay for full performance. On the other hand, to deny recovery often gives the defendant more than fair compensation for the injury he has sustained and imposes a forfeiture on the plaintiff." Id. at 205, 264 P.2d 964.

The court stated that "[t]here is no hard and fast rule in cases of imperfect performance by which liability of the promisee to render compensation, and the amount of an allowable recovery can be judged." Id. at 204, 264 P.2d 964. It then went on to state that there had been no harm to the seller, so that the proper measure of damages would be the contract price, for "there was no difference in amount between the contract price, less damages, and the value of the financing" to the seller. Id. at 207, 264 P.2d 964. In other words, the seller simply paid the amount it contracted to pay, no more, no less. Similarly *Lacy Mfg. Co. v. Los Angeles Gas & Elec. Co.*, 12 Cal.App. 37, 106 P. 413 (1909), to which Palmer earnestly draws our attention, allowed a party whose performance was late to recover the value of his services, less damages for late performance. It contains no hint that the recovery could be more than the contract price. Palmer also presses *Castagnino v. Balletta*, 82 Cal. 250, 23 P. 127 (1889) upon us. It is no more to the purpose than the other cases brought to our attention. There the innocent subcontractor recovered the contract price plus agreed upon extras.

It is, therefore, apparent that the district court erred when it offset the damages to CSE against the raw value of the work done by Palmer, with the result that CSE was ordered to absorb the loss that Palmer incurred by entering into a contract which turned out to be unprofitable to it. Instead, when it became apparent that Palmer's breach actually cost CSE $6,295.54 more than the contract price, CSE should have been awarded its damages and Palmer should have recovered nothing.[22]

[Eds.: Other issues and a concurring opinion are omitted.]

CONCLUSION

It is possible to syncretize the principles which require people to carry out their contracts and those which prevent people from unjustly retaining benefits conferred upon them. In other words it is possible to reach a just result in cases which involve both principles. We hold that where, as here, the innocent party has paid more than the contract price for the goods and services ordered from the breaching party, the innocent party may recover the overage from the breaching party. The breaching party may not obtain a quasi contractual recovery from the innocent party. In short, the innocent party is not unjustly enriched when it receives what it bargained for and pays no more than the contract price.

22. Of course, if CSE had not previously paid out $114,758.98 to Palmer, there could have been some amount due to Palmer. That is the situation that has usually been illustrated by the commentators. But payment had been made. Far from being entitled to recover more, Palmer should have been ordered to disgorge part of what it already had received.

CSE is therefore entitled to recover the sum of $6,295.24 plus prejudgment interest of $1,478.88 from Palmer. CSE is also entitled to recover attorneys fees and costs for its litigation expenses in the district court, as well as its costs on appeal.

REVERSED AND REMANDED for entry of judgment in favor of CSE and for a determination of the amount of attorneys fees and costs to which CSE is entitled.

Problem 6–13

Betsy Bilder Enterprises contracted to build an elementary school for the Cook School Board; the contract price was $10,000,000. To date Bilder has spent $8,000,000 on the project, but has come to realize that the contract is a losing one; it will have to spend a total of $12,000,000 to complete the school. The value of its construction so far is $7,000,000; the remaining million went for materials it has purchased but not yet used, all of which can be diverted to other purposes or reused. It has been paid $5,000,000 for its performance so far.

Owing to an internal Board dispute about the need for a new school, the Cook School Board has unexpectedly repudiated. If Bilder sues, what will be its likely expectation damages? Can it sue instead for restitution damages, and, if so, what will they be? Should its restitution damages be limited by its expectation interest? See Restatement 2d § 373.

Where a party has entered into what turns out to be a losing contract, the likely effect of these legal rules may be that this party becomes super-vigilant in hunting for reasons to terminate justifiably. A classic case in this area is *United States ex rel. Coastal Steel Erectors, Inc. v. Algernon Blair, Inc.*, 479 F.2d 638 (4th Cir. 1973).

Problem 6–14

Power Generator and Utility sign a 20 year contract under which Generator will sell electrical power to Utility at a rate that escalates annually by two percent per year for the first 10 years and then remains flat for the last ten years. The contract is signed October 30 and ends in October 20 years hence. The contract has a schedule of rates for years one through twenty, but the contract nowhere states whether the rate changes on January 1 or on the anniversary of the signing, October 30. Each month Utility computes the amount due and remits that amount to Generator. The person at Utility who computes the amount due is a comparatively low level employee and is not a lawyer. Because he knows of other contracts whose prices change on January 1, he assumes that January 1 is the change date and pays accordingly. After three years of such payments, higher level managers look at the contract and conclude that the price should change in October, not January. If Utility had used the initial price until October of the first year and not raised the price in January, it would have paid $17 million less to Generator than it did.

(1) Can Utility recover the $17 million from Generator on a theory of restitution? (Here we are certainly talking about the cause of action, but maybe also about the damage theory.)

(2) Would it make any difference if it was discovered that the low level person's supervisor believed from the start that October was the change date (as proven by her notation on her copy of the contract)?

(3) Would it matter that one of Generator's managers had casually asked the low level Utility employee about the change date in circumstances that might lead one to conclude that Generator's employees suspected that October was the right date?

(4) How would any recovery be affected by the fact that Utility had passed some or all of the added cost on to its rate payers in the form of higher charges?

E. SPECIFIC PERFORMANCE

In general, specific performance (in the form of an order to do something or of an injunction against doing something) will only be ordered if monetary damages are inadequate to right the wrong. When is money not enough?

A contract to purchase something that has some sort of sentimental attachment might be an example. Assume a widow finds a deck of cards on eBay that are being sold with the claim that they were used by soldiers in France during World War II. Upon closer inspection, the widow realizes that this actual deck was found in an area near where her husband's platoon was attacked, and where her husband likely perished. Based on the likelihood that these actual cards were used by her husband during his last days, the widow bids on them, and wins the auction at the small amount of $20.00. The seller, however, breaches. In this case, it can be argued that monetary damages are inadequate. The cards are clearly worth much more to the buyer than the market value would indicate. No amount of damages could compensate, and the widow should get specific performance, true?

We suspect that most successful specific performance cases in American courts are to enforce contracts to sell land where a plaintiff/buyer is seeking an order directing the defendant/seller to convey. Perhaps relying too much on our English heritage, courts routinely indulge in the notion that no two pieces of land are alike. For example, the Arkansas Supreme Court observed in 1920: "Where land or any estate or interest in land is the subject-matter of the agreement, the jurisdiction to enforce specific performance is undisputed, and does not depend upon the inadequacy of the legal remedy in the particular case. It is as much a matter of course for courts of equity to decree a specific performance of a contract for the conveyance of real estate, which is in its nature unobjectionable, as it is for courts of law to give damages for its breach." *Dollar v. Knight*, 145 Ark. 522, 224 S.W. 983, 984–985 (1920) (citing 36 Cyc. p. 552). But this idea, though deeply lodged in courts of equity, has become particularly hard to justify in commercial real estate deals where the parties sometime deal with parcels of land like so many hogs or spark plugs.

The reasons commonly given for the Common Law courts' aversion to specific performance are not particularly persuasive. For example, it is sometimes said that courts will not order specific performance because such orders require court time and effort for their enforcement. Yet Civil Law courts do not seem to have such problems, and our own courts now routinely grant sweeping orders that involve far more supervision than the performance of a measly little contract.

WALGREEN CO. v. SARA CREEK PROPERTY CO.

United States Court of Appeals, Seventh Circuit, 1992.
966 F.2d 273.

POSNER, J. This appeal from the grant of a permanent injunction raises fundamental issues concerning the propriety of injunctive relief: 775 F.Supp. 1192 (E.D.Wis.1991). The essential facts are simple. Walgreen has operated a pharmacy in the Southgate Mall in Milwaukee since its opening in 1951. Its current lease, signed in 1971 and carrying a 30-year, 6-month term, contains, as had the only previous lease, a clause in which the landlord, Sara Creek, promises not to lease space in the mall to anyone else who wants to operate a pharmacy or a store containing a pharmacy. Such an exclusivity clause, common in shopping-center leases, is occasionally challenged on antitrust grounds, Milton Handler & Daniel E. Lazaroff, "Restraint of Trade and the Restatement (Second) of Contracts," 57 N.Y.U.L.Rev. 669, 683–708 (1982); Note, "The Antitrust Implications of Restrictive Covenants in Shopping Center Leases," 86 Harv.L.Rev. 1201 (1973)—implausibly enough, given the competition among malls; but that is an issue for another day, since in this appeal Sara Creek does not press the objection it made below to the clause on antitrust grounds.

In 1990, fearful that its largest tenant—what in real estate parlance is called the "anchor tenant"—having gone broke was about to close its store, Sara Creek informed Walgreen that it intended to buy out the anchor tenant and install in its place a discount store operated by Phar-Mor Corporation, a "deep discount" chain, rather than, like Walgreen, just a "discount" chain. Phar-Mor's store would occupy 100,000 square feet, of which 12,000 would be occupied by a pharmacy the same size as Walgreen's. The entrances to the two stores would be within a couple of hundred feet of each other.

Walgreen filed this diversity suit for breach of contract against Sara Creek and Phar-Mor and asked for an injunction against Sara Creek's letting the anchor premises to Phar-Mor. After an evidentiary hearing, the judge found a breach of Walgreen's lease and entered a permanent injunction against Sara Creek's letting the anchor tenant premises to Phar-Mor until the expiration of Walgreen's lease. He did this over the defendants' objection that Walgreen had failed to show that its remedy at law—damages—for the breach of the exclusivity clause was inadequate. Sara Creek had put on an expert witness who testified that Walgreen's damages could be readily estimated, and Walgreen had countered with evidence from its employees that its damages would be very difficult to compute, among other reasons because they included intangibles such as loss of goodwill.

Sara Creek reminds us that damages are the norm in breach of contract as in other cases. Many breaches, it points out, are "efficient" in the sense that they allow resources to be moved into a more valuable use. *Patton v. Mid-Continent Systems, Inc.*, 841 F.2d 742, 750–51 (7th Cir. 1988). Perhaps this is one—the value of Phar-Mor's occupancy of the anchor premises may exceed the cost to Walgreen of facing increased competition. If so, society will be better off if Walgreen is paid its damages, equal to that cost, and Phar-Mor is allowed to move in rather than being kept out by an injunction. That is why injunctions are not granted as a matter of course, but only when the plaintiff's damages remedy is inadequate. *Northern Indiana Public Service Co. v. Carbon County Coal Co.*, 799 F.2d 265, 279 (7th Cir. 1986). Walgreen's is not, Sara Creek argues; the projection of business losses due to increased competition is a routine exercise in calculation. Damages representing either the present value of lost future profits or (what should be the equivalent, *Carusos v. Briarcliff, Inc.*, 76 Ga.App. 346, 351–52, 45 S.E.2d 802, 806–07 (1947)) the diminution in the value of the leasehold have either been awarded or deemed the proper remedy in a number of reported cases for breach of an exclusivity clause in a shopping-center lease.... Why, Sara Creek asks, should they not be adequate here?

Sara Creek makes a beguiling argument that contains much truth, but we do not think it should carry the day. For if, as just noted, damages have been awarded in some cases of breach of an exclusivity clause in a shopping-center lease, injunctions have been issued in others.... The task of striking the balance is for the trial judge, subject to deferential appellate review in recognition of its particularistic, judgmental, fact-bound character. *K-Mart Corp. v. Oriental Plaza, Inc.*, 875 F.2d 907, 915 (1st Cir. 1989). As we said in an appeal from a grant of a preliminary injunction—but the point is applicable to review of a permanent injunction as well—"The question for us [appellate judges] is whether the [district] judge exceeded the bounds of permissible choice in the circumstances, not what we would have done if we had been in his shoes." *Roland Machinery Co. v. Dresser Industries, Inc.*, 749 F.2d 380, 390 (7th Cir. 1984).

The plaintiff who seeks an injunction has the burden of persuasion—damages are the norm, so the plaintiff must show why his case is abnormal. But when, as in this case, the issue is whether to grant a permanent injunction, not whether to grant a temporary one, the burden is to show that damages are inadequate, not that the denial of the injunction will work irreparable harm. "Irreparable" in the injunction context means not rectifiable by the entry of a final judgment. *Diginet, Inc. v. Western Union ATS, Inc.*, 958 F.2d 1388, 1393 (7th Cir. 1992); *Vogel v. American Society of Appraisers*, 744 F.2d 598, 599 (7th Cir. 1984). It has nothing to do with whether to grant a permanent injunction, which, in the usual case anyway, is the final judgment. The use of "irreparable harm" or "irreparable injury" as synonyms for inadequate remedy at law is a confusing usage. It should be avoided. Owen M. Fiss & Doug Rendleman, Injunctions 59 (2d ed. 1984).

The benefits of substituting an injunction for damages are twofold. First, it shifts the burden of determining the cost of the defendant's conduct from the court to the parties. If it is true that Walgreen's damages are smaller than the gain to Sara Creek from allowing a second pharmacy into the shopping mall, then there must be a price for dissolving the injunction that will make both parties better off. Thus, the effect of upholding the injunction would be to substitute for the costly processes of forensic fact determination the less costly processes of private negotiation. Second, a premise of our free-market system, and the lesson of experience here and abroad as well, is that prices and costs are more accurately determined by the market than by government. A battle of experts is a less reliable method of determining the actual cost to Walgreen of facing new competition than negotiations between Walgreen and Sara Creek over the price at which Walgreen would feel adequately compensated for having to face that competition.

That is the benefit side of injunctive relief but there is a cost side as well. Many injunctions require continuing supervision by the court, and that is costly. ...; *Bethlehem Engineering Export Co. v. Christie,* 105 F.2d 933, 935 (2d Cir. 1939) (L. Hand, J.). A request for specific performance (a form of mandatory injunction) of a franchise agreement was refused on this ground in *North American Financial Group, Ltd. v. S.M.R. Enterprises, Inc.*, 583 F.Supp. 691, 699 (N.D.Ill.1984); see Edward Yorio, Contract Enforcement: Specific Performance and Injunctions § 3.3.2 (1989). This ground was also stressed in *Rental Development Corp. v. Lavery,* 304 F.2d 839, 841–42 (9th Cir. 1962), a case involving a lease. Some injunctions are problematic because they impose costs on third parties. *Shondel v. McDermott*, 775 F.2d 859, 868 (7th Cir. 1985). A more subtle cost of injunctive relief arises from the situation that economists call "bilateral monopoly," in which two parties can deal only with each other: the situation that an injunction creates. ... The sole seller of widgets selling to the sole buyer of that product would be an example. But so will be the situation confronting Walgreen and Sara Creek if the injunction is upheld. Walgreen can "sell" its injunctive right only to Sara Creek, and Sara Creek can "buy" Walgreen's surrender of its right to enjoin the leasing of the anchor tenant's space to Phar-Mor only from Walgreen. The lack of alternatives in bilateral monopoly creates a bargaining range, and the costs of negotiating to a point within that range may be high. Suppose the cost to Walgreen of facing the competition of Phar-Mor at the Southgate Mall would be $1 million, and the benefit to Sara Creek of leasing to Phar-Mor would be $2 million. Then at any price between those figures for a waiver of Walgreen's injunctive right both parties would be better off, and we expect parties to bargain around a judicial assignment of legal rights if the assignment is inefficient. R.H. Coase, "The Problem of Social Cost," 3 J. Law & Econ. 1 (1960). But each of the parties would like to engross as much of the bargaining range as possible—Walgreen to press the price toward $2 million, Sara Creek to depress it toward $1 million. With so much at stake, both parties will have an incentive to devote substantial resources of time and money to the negotiation process. The process may even break down, if one or both parties want to create for future use a reputation as a hard bargainer; and if it does break down, the injunction will have brought about an inefficient result. All these are in one form or another costs of the injunctive process that can be avoided by substituting damages.

The costs and benefits of the damages remedy are the mirror of those of the injunctive remedy. The damages remedy avoids the cost of continuing supervision and third-party effects, and the cost of bilateral monopoly as well. It imposes costs of its own, however, in the form of diminished accuracy in the determination of value, on the one hand, and of the parties' expenditures on preparing and presenting evidence of damages, and the time of the court in evaluating the evidence, on the other.

The weighing up of all these costs and benefits is the analytical procedure that is or at least should be employed by a judge asked to enter a permanent injunction, with the understanding that if the balance is even the injunction should be withheld. The judge is not required to explicate every detail of the analysis and he did not do so here, but as long we are satisfied that his approach is broadly consistent with a proper analysis we shall affirm; and we are satisfied here. The determination of Walgreen's damages would have been costly in forensic resources and inescapably inaccurate. . . . The lease had ten years to run. So Walgreen would have had to project its sales revenues and costs over the next ten years, and then project the impact on those figures of Phar-Mor's competition, and then discount that impact to present value. All but the last step would have been fraught with uncertainty.

We may have given too little weight to such uncertainties in *American Dairy Queen Corp. v. Brown-Port Co.*, 621 F.2d 255, 257 n. 2 (7th Cir. 1980), but in that case the district judge had found that the remedy at law was adequate in the circumstances and the movant had failed to make its best argument for inadequacy in the district court. Id. at 259. It is difficult to forecast the profitability of a retail store over a decade, let alone to assess the impact of a particular competitor on that profitability over that period. Of course one can hire an expert to make such predictions, Glen A. Stankee, "Econometric Forecasting of Lost Profits: Using High Technology to Compute Commercial Damages," 61 Fla.B.J. 83 (1987), and if injunctive relief is infeasible the expert's testimony may provide a tolerable basis for an award of damages. We cited cases in which damages have been awarded for the breach of an exclusivity clause in a shopping-center lease. But they are awarded in such circumstances not because anyone thinks them a clairvoyant forecast but because it is better to give a wronged person a crude remedy than none at all. It is the same theory on which damages are awarded for a disfiguring injury. No one thinks such injuries readily monetizable, . . . but a crude estimate is better than letting the wrongdoer get off scot-free (which, not incidentally, would encourage more such injuries). Randall R. Bovbjerg et al., "Valuing Life and Limb in Tort: Scheduling 'Pain and Suffering,' " 83 Nw.U.L.Rev. 908 (1989). Sara Creek presented evidence of what happened (very little) to Walgreen when Phar-Mor moved into other shopping malls in which Walgreen has a pharmacy, and it was on the right track in putting in comparative evidence. But there was a serious question whether the other malls were actually comparable to the Southgate Mall, so we cannot conclude, in the face of the district judge's contrary conclusion, that the existence of comparative evidence dissolved the difficulties of computing damages in this case Sara Creek complains that the judge refused to compel Walgreen to produce all the data that Sara Creek needed to demonstrate the feasibility of forecasting Walgreen's damages. Walgreen resisted, on grounds of the confidentiality of the data and the cost of producing the massive data that Sara Creek sought. Those are legitimate grounds; and the cost (broadly conceived) they expose of pretrial discovery, in turn presaging complexity at trial, is itself a cost of the damages remedy that injunctive relief saves.

Damages are not always costly to compute, or difficult to compute accurately. In the standard case of a seller's breach of a contract for the sale of goods where the buyer covers by purchasing the same product in the market, damages are readily calculable by subtracting the contract price from the market price and multiplying by the quantity specified in the contract. But this is not such a case and here damages would be a costly and inaccurate remedy; and on the other side of the balance some of the costs of an injunction are absent and the cost that is present seems low. The injunction here, like one enforcing a covenant not to compete (standardly enforced by injunction, Yorio, supra, 401-08), is a simple negative injunction—Sara Creek is not to lease space in the Southgate Mall to Phar-Mor during the term of Walgreen's lease—and the costs of judicial supervision and enforcement should be negligible. There is no contention that the injunction will harm an unrepresented third party. It may harm Phar-Mor but that harm will be reflected in Sara Creek's offer to Walgreen to dissolve the injunction. (Anyway Phar-Mor is a party.) The injunction may also, it is true, harm potential customers of Phar-Mor—people who would prefer to shop at a deep-discount store than an ordinary discount store—but their preferences, too, are registered indirectly. The more business Phar-Mor would have, the more rent it will be willing to pay Sara Creek, and therefore the more Sara Creek will be willing to pay Walgreen to dissolve the injunction.

The only substantial cost of the injunction in this case is that it may set off a round of negotiations between the parties. In some cases, illustrated by *Boomer v. Atlantic Cement Co.,* 26 N.Y.2d 219, 309 N.Y.S.2d 312, 257 N.E.2d 870 (1970), this consideration alone would be enough to warrant the denial of injunctive relief. The defendant's factory was emitting cement dust that caused the plaintiffs harm monetized at less than $200,000, and the only way to abate the harm would have been to close down the factory, which had cost $45 million to build. An injunction against the nuisance could therefore have created a huge bargaining range (could, not would, because it is unclear what the current value of the factory was), and the costs of negotiating to a point within it might have been immense. If the market value of the factory was actually $45 million, the plaintiffs would be tempted to hold out for a price to dissolve the injunction in the tens of millions and the factory would be tempted to refuse to pay anything more than a few hundred thousand dollars. Negotiations would be unlikely to break down completely, given such a bargaining range, but they might well be protracted and costly. There is nothing so dramatic here. Sara Creek does not argue that it will have to close the mall if enjoined from leasing to Phar-Mor. Phar-Mor is not the only potential anchor tenant. *Liza Danielle, Inc. v. Jamko, Inc.*, 408 So.2d 735, 740 (Fla.App.1982), on which Sara Creek relies, presented the converse case where the grant of the injunction would have forced an existing tenant to close its store....

To summarize, the judge did not exceed the bounds of reasonable judgment in concluding that the costs (including forgone benefits) of the damages remedy would exceed the costs (including forgone benefits) of an injunction. We need not consider whether, as intimated by Walgreen, exclusivity clauses in shopping-center leases should be considered presumptively enforceable by injunctions. Although we have described the choice between legal and equitable remedies as one for case-by-case determination, the courts have sometimes picked out categories of case in which injunctive relief is made the norm. The best-known example is specific performance of contracts for the sale of real property.... The rule that specific performance will be ordered in such cases as a matter of course is a generalization of the considerations discussed above. Because of the absence of a fully liquid market in real property and the frequent presence of subjective values (many a homeowner, for example, would not sell his house for its market value), the calculation of damages is difficult; and since an order of specific performance to convey a piece of property does not create a continuing relation between the parties, the costs of supervision and enforcement if specific performance is ordered are slight. The exclusivity clause in Walgreen's lease relates to real estate, but we hesitate to suggest that every contract involving real estate should be enforceable as a matter of course by injunctions. Suppose Sara Creek had covenanted to keep the entrance to Walgreen's store free of ice and snow, and breached the covenant. An injunction would require continuing supervision, and it would be easy enough if the injunction were denied for Walgreen to hire its own ice and snow remover and charge the cost to Sara Creek. Cf. *City of Michigan City v. Lake Air Corp.*, 459 N.E.2d 760 (Ind.App.1984). On the other hand, injunctions to enforce exclusivity clauses are quite likely to be justifiable by just the considerations present here—damages are difficult to estimate with any accuracy and the injunction is a one-shot remedy requiring no continuing judicial involvement. So there is an argument for making injunctive relief presumptively appropriate in such cases, but we need not decide in this case how strong an argument.

AFFIRMED.

Notes and Discussion

1. A Blast of Undiluted Chicago. Judge Posner's thoughtful and well-reasoned opinion considers specific performance from the angle of law and economics. The general rules for granting specific performance or an injunction are stated (in more traditional form) in Restatement 2d §§ 357–360. Particularly important is § 359(1): "Specific performance or an injunction will not be ordered if damages would be adequate to protect the expectation interest of the injured party." Section 360 describes the circumstances that are "significant" in determining the adequacy of damages: "(a) the difficulty of proving damages with reasonable certainty, (b) the difficulty of procuring a suitable substitute performance by means of money awarded as damages, and (c) the likelihood that an award of damages could not be collected." Examine how these circumstances play out in *Walgreen*. To what extent does it seem probable that they would be more salient in land transactions than in deals involving goods and services?

The UCC attempted to expand the availability of specific performance in contracts for the sale of goods: § 2–716(1) ("Specific performance may be decreed where the goods are unique or in other proper circumstances.") Comment 1 notes that: "this Article seeks to further a more liberal attitude." An example of freer application is *Stephan's Machine & Tool, Inc. v. D & H Machinery Consultants, Inc.*, 65 Ohio App.2d 197, 417 N.E.2d 579 (1979), where the buyer of a machine received specific performance even though substitute goods were available on the market; the buyer's financial circumstances, however, did not permit it to purchase elsewhere. But such extensions are still exceptional, unless there is a clear public interest in enforcement.

2. Should Specific Performance Be Used More Widely? Advocates of specific performance argue that the grant of specific performance is the best remedy of all, for it gives the plaintiff exactly what he bargained for. It, so the argument goes, is therefore the most efficient of all remedies; it neither over nor under compensates the plaintiff. It avoids strategic behavior by a plaintiff who might exaggerate his damages by making untruthful claims about his preferences ("the back forty was the spot for my homestead, and where I hoped to bury my dog and my husband, and now it's ruined by a spoil bank").

Others argue that specific performance is less efficient than damages because it offers every plaintiff the hope of performance even when some other person values the performance more highly. Thus, the subject matter of the contract may wind up in the wrong hands or it may take another transaction (with its attendant costs) to get the goods into the hands of the one who values them most. What do you think? Consider the following excerpts.

The first is from Alan Schwarz, *The Case for Specific Performance*, 89 Yale L.J. 271. 275–277 (1979) (footnotes omitted): "[T]here are three reasons why [specific performance] should be routinely available. The first reason is that in many cases damages actually are undercompensatory. Although promisees are entitled to incidental damages, such damages are difficult to monetize. They consist primarily of the costs of finding and making a second deal, which generally involve the expenditure of time rather than cash; attaching a dollar value to such opportunity costs is quite difficult. Breach can also cause frustration and anger, especially in a consumer context, but these costs also are not recoverable....

"Second, promisees have economic incentives to sue for damages when damages are likely to be fully compensatory. A breaching promisor is reluctant to perform and may be hostile. This makes specific performance an unattractive remedy in cases in which the promisor's performance is complex, because the promisor is more likely to render a defective performance when that performance is coerced, and the defectiveness of complex performances is sometimes difficult to establish in court. Further, when the promisor's performance must be rendered over time, as in construction or requirements contracts, it is costly for the promisee to monitor a reluctant promisor's conduct. If the damage remedy is compensatory, the promisee would prefer it to incurring these monitoring costs. Finally, given the time necessary to resolve lawsuits, promisees would commonly prefer to make substitute transactions promptly and sue later for damages rather than hold their affairs in suspension while awaiting equitable relief. The very fact that a promisee requests specific performance thus implies that damages are an inadequate remedy.

"The third reason why courts should permit promisees to elect routinely the remedy of specific performance is that promisees possess better information than courts as to both the adequacy of damages and the difficulties of coercing performance. Promisees know better than courts whether the damages a court is likely to award would be adequate because promisees are more familiar with the costs that breach imposes on them. In addition, promisees generally know more about their promisors than do courts; thus they are in a better position to predict whether specific performance decrees would induce their promisors to render satisfactory performances.

"In sum, restrictions on the availability of specific performance cannot be justified on the basis that damage awards are usually compensatory. On the contrary, the compensation goal implies that specific performance should be routinely available. This is because damage awards actually are undercompensatory in more cases than is commonly supposed; the fact of a specific performance request is itself good evidence that damages would be inadequate; and courts should delegate to promisees the decision of which remedy best satisfies the compensation goal...."

And a counterpoint from Richard A. Posner, Economic Analysis of Law 131–132 (6th ed. 2003): " ... Suppose the promisee could obtain a decree ordering the promisor to complete the performance due under the contract. Although the promisor could pay the promisee to remove the injunction (as an alternative to suffering the penalties for disobeying it), the amount of the payment would bear no relation to the costs to the promisee of the promisor's failure to perform. Indeed, since an injunction could require the promisor to incur possibly unlimited costs (infinite, in a case of true physical impossibility) to comply with the contract, the promisor might, depending on the costs of defying an injunction, have to yield his entire wealth to the promisee in order to obtain a release from his obligation—and this even though nonperformance might have imposed only trivial costs on the promisee. The promisor is unlikely to have to pay *that* much; the lesser of his wealth and of the cost of defying the injunction would merely be the upper limit of the range within which bargaining would occur between the parties to the contract (what would be the lower limit?). But this just means that injunctive relief in this case creates a bilateral monopoly, one limited moreover by the fact that a court will not punish as contempt a flat inability to obey an injunction."

3. The Civil Law Position. The position of European Civil Law is very different from our own. An example is German law: "Owing to the influence of Roman law, the claim to performance (Erfüllungsanspruch) remains even where there is irregularity in performance. Except where performance is actually impossible, the creditor may choose to stand by his claim to performance and need not invoke the remedies that exist for dismantling the contract. This is seen most clearly in the case of delay, for a claim for damages for delay lies *in addition* to a claim for performance." Norbert Horn et al., German Private and Commercial Law: An Introduction 109 (Tony Weir trans., 1982).

In general, see G. H. Treitel, Remedies for Breach of Contract: A Comparative Account 47–74 (1988); Konrad Zweigert & Hein Kötz, Introduction to Comparative Law 470–485 (Tony Weir trans.; 3rd ed. 1996), who note that: "the actual contrast [between Civil Law systems and Common Law] is not quite so sharp. In Germany, ... where the claim to performance is regarded as the primary legal remedy, it does not in practice have anything like the significance originally attached to it, since whenever the failure to receive the promised performance can be made good by the payment of money commercial men prefer to claim damages rather than risk wasting time and money on a claim for performance whose execution may not produce satisfactory results." Id. at 484.

Although German victims of breaches often prefer damages, how does the freer availability of specific performance in German law alter the pretrial negotiating positions of the two parties?

In accord with Civil Law, the CISG encourages specific performance for the international sale of goods between merchants (cf. Art. 46(1) for buyers, Art. 62 for sellers). However, at the insistence of Common Law nations, Article 28 states that: "a court is not bound to enter a judgment for specific performance [under the CISG] unless the court would do so under its own law in respect of similar contracts of sale not governed by this Convention."

Problem 6–15

How would it have affected settlement negotiations in *Peevyhouse* if Willie and Lucille had had a realistic chance of specific performance under Oklahoma law?

F. LIQUIDATED DAMAGES AND AGREED REMEDIES

A liquidated damages clause is a contractual provision specifying the amount of damages to be awarded in the event of a breach. Clauses of this type represent an attempt by the parties to determine in advance the consequences of a breach, and, as such, they obviously aim in part to limit what courts can do if a breach occurs. Perhaps for this reason, courts have not traditionally favored such clauses except in special circumstances. Restatement 2d § 356(1) permits such clauses provided that they are "at an amount that is reasonable in the light of the anticipated or actual loss caused by the breach and the difficulties of proof of loss." Further, "A term fixing unreasonably large liquidated damages is unenforceable on grounds of public policy." Compare also UCC § 2–718(1), which you should examine as well in its amended version.

It is easy to understand why consumer advocates are not friends of liquidated damage clauses. Their clients never draft such clauses; they only sign them. And the ones that they sign are invariably drafted to favor the seller, not the consumer buyer. But beyond consumers, why do we see restrictions on liquidated damage clauses of the kind found in §§ 2–718 and 2A–504? Courts are especially cautious of what they see as penalty clauses providing a means of pressure on a party that is contemplating breach, so as to coerce it into performing its contractual duties.

Closely related to liquidated damages clauses are contractual clauses that prescribe remedies. Such clauses are authorized by § 2–719 and found in most commercial and many consumer contracts; they are a part of everyday commercial life. The most common form is the seller's restriction of a buyer to the remedy of repair or replacement. Commercial deals often have mediation or arbitration clauses and they frequently bar either party from consequential damages.

ePLUS GROUP, INC. v. PANORAMIC COMMUNICATIONS LLC

United States District Court, Southern District of New York, 2003.
50 UCC Rep. Serv. 2d 213.

COTE, J. This diversity action, which arises out of a default on an equipment lease agreement, was filed by plaintiff ePlus Group, Inc. ("ePlus") on October 8, 2002. The complaint alleges claims for breach of contract, negligence, breach of insurance contract, breach of warranty, breach of the covenant of good faith and fair dealing, interference with contractual relations, fraudulent conveyance and conspiracy to effect fraudulent conveyance. The plaintiff has moved for summary judgment on its claim of breach of contract against defendants Panoramic Communications LLC ("Panoramic") and epb.communications, inc. ("epb") (collectively "Defendants"), and seeks enforcement of the liquidated damages provision of the contract. The Defendants contend that genuine issues of material fact exist as to both liability and damages, and argue in the alternative that plaintiff's motion is premature as discovery has not yet been conducted in this action. For the reasons stated below, the plaintiff's motion for partial summary judgment is granted in part as to liability and denied as to damages.

BACKGROUND

The following facts are undisputed or as asserted by Defendants unless otherwise noted. ePlus is a commercial equipment leasing company. On May 24, 1999, ePlus and epb, then known as Earle Palmer Brown, entered into a lease agreement for computer equipment ("Master Lease"). The parties subsequently entered into twenty-five schedules ("the Schedules") which provided specific information, such as equipment lists, lease dates and rental amounts, for the individual leases covered by the Master Lease. (The Master Lease and the Schedules will be referred to collectively as the "Lease.") On April 26, 2001, the Master Lease was modified to make Panoramic a co-lessee. During the summer of 2002, the Defendants began to experience difficulty in making timely lease payments. According to a former vice president at epb, at a meeting on August 1 (the "August 2002 Meeting"), Panoramic and ePlus agreed that the purchasers of three Panoramic-related entities would retain certain of the leased equipment and that, once ePlus was able to complete new lease arrangements with these purchasers, ePlus would look exclusively to these purchasers for future rent payments.

On September 30, 2002, ePlus notified epb and Panoramic by letter that they were in default. In the letter, ePlus declared the Master Lease and the Schedules terminated as of September 1, and demanded payment of unpaid rent in the amount of $106,463.81, late fees in the amount of $3,285.73, and a casualty value payment in the amount of $1,088,445.33, for a total of $1,198,194. It is not disputed that the Defendants have not made any payments since receiving ePlus' written demand. The total amount that the plaintiff would have received had the Lease been fully performed from the date of default is $361,010.02.

LEASE TERMS

The Master Lease provides that the "nonpayment by Lessee of Rent or any other payable sum upon written notice by its due date" constitutes an event of default. Master Lease & 14(a). In the "event of default," ePlus has several nonexclusive remedies. Id. at & 14(b). ePlus may "terminate any or all Schedules," "[p]roceed by appropriate court action to enforce the performance of the Schedule and/or recover damages, including all of Lessor's economic loss for the breach," and "upon notice to Lessee, take possession of the Asset(s) wherever located." Id. Under & 14(b) of the Master Lease, the lessee, upon an event of default, agrees to return the equipment to ePlus. Id.

Under the liquidated damages clause, ePlus may also require the lessees, upon notice, to pay immediately: *"the sum of (a) the Casualty*

Value set forth on the Schedule as of the date of default, or if Casualty Values are not shown on such Schedule, all Rent due during the remainder of the Schedule Term; (b) *all Rent* and other amounts *due* and payable on or *before the date of default; and (c) costs*, fees (including all reasonable attorneys' fees and court costs), expenses and (d) interest on (a) and (b) from the date of default at 1 1/2% per month or portion thereof (or the highest rate allowable by law, if less) and, on (c) from the date the Lessor incurs such fees, costs or expenses." Id. (emphasis supplied).

The Master Lease explains that the Casualty Value is set forth in each of the respective Schedules. Id. In each Schedule the Casualty Value represents a percentage of the "Total Asset Unit Cost Value" of the leased asset. The Total Asset Unit Cost Value represents the original cost of the equipment to ePlus.

The Casualty Value varies according to the pay period in which the default occurs. For example, in one Schedule the Casualty Value rate varies from 109% of the Total Asset Unit Cost Value if a default occurs during the first pay period, to 79.6% if a default occurs during the thirty-sixth or final pay period. Thus, if a default occurs in the thirty-sixth pay period, the lessee would be obligated to pay 79.6% of the Total Asset Unit Cost as a Casualty Value. All of the Schedules have substantially the same provisions, differing only with respect to equipment specifications, length of term and amount of rent.

The Master Lease also provides an offset or credit to the lessee against the total amount of liquidated damages in certain circumstances. Id. at & 14(c). In the event of default, the lessee is obligated to return the leased assets or allow the lessor to repossess them. Id. at & 14(b). Upon the return or repossession of the equipment, ePlus is required to: "*[U]se reasonable efforts to sell, re-lease or otherwise dispose of such Asset(s)* in such manner and upon such terms as Lessor may determine in its sole discretion (the amount, if any, which Lessor certifies it obtained through remarketing shall be conclusively presumed to be the Asset(s) fair market value)." Id. at & 14(c) (emphasis supplied).

Upon the disposition of the equipment, the Master Lease provides a formula for crediting the "Net Proceeds" of any sale or re-lease against the liquidated damages paid or payable by the Defendants. Id. The Net Proceeds are the proceeds from a sale less the Casualty Value, or certain proceeds from a re-lease, after "all costs and reasonable expenses" have been deducted. Costs and expenses include costs for the repair, recovery, storage, remarketing and disposition of the equipment. Id. The relevant portion of the Master Lease provides: "Upon disposition of the Asset(s), *Lessor shall credit the Net Proceeds (as defined below)* to the damages paid or payable by Lessee. *Proceeds upon sale of the Asset(s) shall be the sale price paid to Lessor less the Casualty Value in effect as of the date of default. Proceeds upon a re-lease of the Asset(s) shall be all rents to be received for a term not to exceed the remaining Schedule Term*, discounted to present value as of the commencement date of the re-lease at the

Lessor's current applicable debt rate. *'Net Proceeds' shall be the proceeds of sale or re-lease as determined above, less all costs and reasonable expenses* incurred by Lessor in the recovery, storage and repair of the Asset(s), in the remarketing or disposition thereof, or otherwise as a result of Lessee's default, including any court costs and reasonable attorneys' fees and interest on the foregoing at eighteen percent (18%) per annum (or the highest rate allowable by law, if less), calculated from the dates such costs and expenses were incurred until received by Lessor. Lessee shall remain liable for the amount by which all sums, including liquidated damages, due from Lessee exceed the Net Proceeds. Net Proceeds in excess thereof are the property of and shall be retained by Lessor." Id. (emphasis supplied).

As this passage indicates, only that portion of the proceeds from a sale which exceeds the Casualty Value as of the date of default is used to offset the liquidated damages. In the case of a re-lease, the amount of credit is limited to the present value of the total amount of rents to be received under the new lease for the number of months that remained under the term of the defaulted lease.

In the event the lessee is not in default, the lessee had the option to purchase the equipment at its fair market value at the end of the Lease. Schedule No. 1 & 6. The relevant portion of the provision states: "*Provided Lessee is not in default* hereunder and Lessee gives Lessor written notice not less than ninety (90) days prior to the expiration of the Initial Lease Term, *Lessee may elect to purchase* all of the Asset(s) *at the then current fair market value*. The term 'fair market value' shall mean the fair market value price, in place, that would be obtained in an arm's-length transaction between an informed and willing buyer under no compulsion to buy and an informed and willing seller under no compulsion to sell." Id. (emphasis supplied).

Post-Default Disposition Of Assets

On October 7, ePlus entered into a leasing agreement with Creative Partners LLC to re-lease some of the equipment formerly leased by Panoramic. The present value for all rents under this agreement is $18,110.08. On October 10, ePlus entered into a leasing agreement with BEN Marketing Acquisition LLC to re-lease some equipment formerly leased by Panoramic. The present value for all rents under this agreement is $61,584.06. ePlus is currently in negotiations with another company, The Michael Allen Company, to lease equipment formerly leased by the Defendants. The anticipated present value for all rents under this agreement is $12,028.56. On November 25, 2002, Panoramic returned a substantial portion of the equipment to ePlus. ePlus sold equipment returned by Panoramic through a blind bid process for $34,100.

In its reply papers, ePlus reduced its requested damages by $113,794.14 from $1,198,194.40 to $1,084,400.30. This reduction reflects a $79,694.14 credit for the re-leases and a $34,100 credit for the sale of returned equipment. Crediting the $34,000 for the sale of leased equipment does not appear to follow the procedures outlined in & 14(c) of the Master Lease, which would have required this sum to exceed the Casualty Value before it could be used as a credit against the amount of liquidated damages owed by the lessee. Similarly, it is unclear if the credit given for the new leasing arrangements follows the formula in the Master Lease which would limit a credit to the present value of the payments to be made for only those months that remained under the Defendants' Lease. The parties have yet to conduct substantial discovery in this action.

Discussion

. . . The Master Lease contains a Virginia choice of law provision. A federal court sitting in diversity must apply the choice of law rules of the forum state. See *Klaxon Co. v. Stentor Elec. Mfg. Co.*, 313 U.S. 487, 496 (1941). Given that there are sufficient contacts between Virginia and the contract—ePlus is incorporated in Virginia and Virginia is its principal place of business—New York's choice of law rules require that the choice of law provision be enforced and that Virginia law be applied to the interpretation of the Lease. See *Hartford Fire Ins. Co. v. Orient Overseas Containers Lines (UK) Ltd.*, 230 F.3d 549, 556 (2d Cir. 2000).

A. *Breach of Contract*

The essential elements of a cause of action for breach of contract under Virginia law are: (1) a legal obligation of a defendant to the plaintiff, (2) a violation or breach of that obligation, and (3) a consequential injury or damage to the plaintiff. . . .

The plaintiff has established that no genuine issue of material fact exists as to its claim for breach of contract, except for those pieces of equipment re-leased as a result of the August 2002 Meeting. ePlus entered into a lease agreement with the Defendants. The terms of the Lease clearly indicated that the failure to make timely lease payments by the due date constitutes an event of default. The Defendants defaulted on their payments under the Lease—a fact not disputed by the Defendants. As a direct consequence of the Defendants' breach, ePlus suffered damage in the form of unpaid lease payments.

The Defendants have shown, through evidence that is undisputed by ePlus, that ePlus agreed at the August 2002 Meeting that certain of the Lease obligations could be transferred to entities that purchased Panoramic affiliates. The Defendants assert on informed belief, that those entities have made their required lease payments. ePlus does not dispute their assertion, and does not even address this issue in its reply brief. There is an issue of fact, therefore, as to whether a breach of contract can be found at this time as to the equipment that was re-leased as a result of the August 2002 Meeting. The motion for summary judgment on the breach of contract claim against Panoramic and epb is therefore granted to the extent it is addressed to equipment other than that re-leased pursuant to the agreement at the August 2002 Meeting.

B. The Liquidated Damages Clause

ePlus has also moved for a declaration that it is entitled to damages based upon the liquidated damages provision in the Master Lease in the amount of $1,084,400.30. The Defendants argue that the liquidated damages clause is an unenforceable penalty that seeks to recover approximately three times as much as the plaintiff would have received had there been no breach. The Defendants argue in the alternative that they are entitled to discovery on whether the clause is reasonable and whether the plaintiff has used reasonable efforts to mitigate its damages. The dispute between the parties on the issue of liquidated damages therefore involves two separate questions: (1) whether the liquidated damages clause is enforceable, and (2) whether the plaintiff has properly calculated the amount of damages given its obligation under the Master Lease to mitigate.

1. Virginia Law on Liquidated Damage Clauses in Commercial Leases

Under Virginia common law, which governed liquidated damage clauses in commercial leases until 1991, liquidated damage clauses were enforceable. *Perez v. Capital One Bank*, 258 Va. 612, 615 (1999). Where damages are hard to predict at the time a contract is entered, a liquidated damage clause was enforced if it was "not out of all proportion to the probable loss." Id. at 616. Where the amount of damages is predictable, such clauses were enforced when they did not "grossly exceed actual damages." Id.

In 1991, Virginia adopted Article 2A ("Article 2A") of the Uniform Commercial Code ("UCC"), which covers commercial lease agreements. 1991 Va. Acts ch. 536. Liquidated damages provisions in such leases are governed by Va.Code Ann. § 8.2A–504 (2002) ("Section 2A–504"). The relevant portion of Section 2A–504 provides: "Damages payable by either party for default, or any other act or omission, including indemnity for loss or diminution of anticipated tax benefits or loss or damage to lessor's residual interest, may be liquidated in the lease agreement but only at an amount or by a formula that is *reasonable in light of the then anticipated harm caused by the default* or other act or omission." Va.Code Ann. § 8.2A–504(1) (emphasis supplied).

The fact that a party enters into a contract containing a liquidated damages clause does not prevent that party from later litigating the validity of the clause. *O'Brian v. Langley School*, 256 Va. 547, 551 (1998). The party challenging the validity of the liquidated damages clause bears the burden of demonstrating its invalidity. Id. . . .

As the Official Comment explains, Section 2A–504 is intended to "invite the parties to liquidate damages." Va.Code Ann. § 8.2A–504, Official Comment ("Cmt."). Through a series of significant revisions to UCC Section 8.2–718 ("Section 2–718"), the section which governs liquidated damages in sales contracts, the drafters intended to introduce "greater flexibility" in lease agreements in recognition of the fact that the "ability to liquidate damages is critical to modern leasing practice."

Id.; see also 1A Thomas M. Quinn, Quinn's Uniform Commercial Code Commentary and Law Digest § 2A–504[A][2] (2d ed. 2002).

For example, Section 2A–504 does not condition the enforceability of liquidated damage provisions on the demonstration of the difficulty of proof of loss or nonfeasibility of obtaining an adequate remedy—two factors found in Section 2–718. The Section also removed the last sentence of Section 2–718 which prohibits "unreasonably large" liquidated damages so that leasing parties could liquidate damages regarding anticipated tax benefits from the contract. Cmt.

The freedom of parties to contract regarding liquidated damages is, however, still constrained by a "rule of reasonableness." Cmt. According to the Official Comment, whether a particular formula for liquidated damages is enforceable "will be determined in the context of each case by applying a standard of reasonableness in light of the harm anticipated when the formula was agreed to." Cmt. Thus, the overall effect of the revisions, as commentators have explained, is to create a standard which supports the "power of the parties to impose their own rules" and "tells the court not to substitute its judgment for the parties' agreed liquidated damages, which should be imposed unless they are unreasonable in light of the harm anticipated at signing." 2 James J. White & Robert S. Summers, Uniform Commercial Code § 14–4 (4th ed.1995); see also 5 Lary Lawrence, Lawrence's Anderson on the Uniform Commercial Code § 2A–504:3 (3d ed. 2001).

While the Official Comment does not explain how a court should determine whether a contract provision is reasonable in light of the anticipated harm, commentators have explained that "the theory of remedy [under Article 2A] is to place the lessor roughly in the same position the lessor would have been in had the first lease deal gone through." 2 James J. White & Robert S. Summers, Uniform Commercial Code § 14–3. This theory of recovery is evident in the list of examples provided in the Official Comment to Section 2A–504.

The Official Comment provides four examples of common formulas used to compute liquidated damages. One example requires that proceeds from a sale or re-lease be credited against the total amount of liquidated damages. Cmt. In this formula, the "sum of lease payments past due, accelerated future lease payments, and the lessor's estimated residual interest, less the net proceeds of disposition (whether by sale or re-lease) of the leased goods" constitutes the liquidated damage. Cmt. The other examples are a "periodic depreciation allocation as a credit" to mitigate damages, a fixed number of periodic payments, and stipulated loss and damages schedules. Cmt. Commentators have interpreted the listing of these formulas as an implicit endorsement of the formulas, constrained always by the rule of reasonableness embodied in the statute. 2 James J. White & Robert S. Summers, Uniform Commercial Code § 14–4.

Additional provisions of the UCC support the conclusion that the drafters of Section 2A–504 intended that a liquidated damage clause should not place a lessor in a better position than it would have been in had the lease been fully performed. The Official Comment to UCC Section 2A–523, the provision outlining generally what a lessor's remedies are in the event of breach by the lessee, explains: "Whether, in a particular case, one remedy bars another, is a function of *whether lessor has been put in as good a position as if the lessee had fully performed* the lease contract. Multiple remedies are barred only if the effect is to put the lessor in a better position than it would have been in had the lessee fully performed under the lease." Id. Va.Code Ann. § 8.2A–523, Official Comment & 4 (emphasis supplied); see also Va.Code Ann. § 8.2A–528(2) (providing that measure of damages should place lessor "in as good a position as performance would have").

In applying Section 2A–504, courts in other jurisdictions have found a liquidated damages clause to be reasonable if it "leaves [the lessor] in no better position than it would be in had the lease been fully performed." *Montgomery Ward & Co., Inc. v. Meridian Leasing Corp.*, 269 B.R. 1, 9 (D.Del.2001) (citing *Case Credit Corp. v. Baldwin Rental Centers, Inc.*, 228 B.R. 504, 509 (Bankr.S. D. Ga.1998)) (emphasis removed); *Coastal Leasing Corp. v. T-Bar S Corp.*, 128 N.C.App. 379, 385 [34 UCC Rep Serv 2d 694] (N.C.Ct.App.1998). Nonetheless, a reasonable liquidated damages agreement that has proved in hindsight to be an inaccurate estimation of loss is not invalid. *Coastal Leasing Corp.*, 128 N.C.App. at 383. '[T]he fact that there is a difference between the actual loss, as determined at or about the time of the default, and the anticipated loss or the stipulated amount or formula ... does not necessarily mean that the liquidated damages clause is unreasonable.' Id. (citation omitted).

A liquidated damages provision has been held to violate Section 2A–504 where it permitted the lessor to collect the present value of all future rent and the present value of the equipment's fair market value at the end of the lease, and permitted the lessor to sell the repossessed equipment immediately without providing the lessee with any credit for the proceeds of the sale. *Carter v. Tokai Fin. Services, Inc.*, 231 Ga.App. 755, 759 (Ga.Ct.App.1998). See also *Sun v. Mercedes Benz Credit Corp.*, 254 Ga.App. 463, 467 (Ga.Ct.App.2002). Such a provision allows the lessor to have "the benefit of both the property and the value of all future rent payments," placing it in a "superior position following default to that which it was in before" the default. Carter, 231 Ga.App. at 759; see also 2 James J. White & Robert S. Summers, Uniform Commercial Code § 14–4.

2. *Enforceability of the Liquidated Damages Clause in the Master Lease*

The plaintiff has failed to show in this motion that the liquidated damages clause in the Master Lease is reasonable under Section 2A–504. The Defendants have raised questions of fact as to whether the clause is in effect a penalty by placing ePlus in a far better position than it would have been had the lease been fully performed.

Had the Lease been fully performed, the plaintiff would have received the computer equipment back or, at the lessee's option, sold the equipment to the lessee for—according to the Lease—its fair market value. The plaintiff would also have been paid by that time the full amount due under the Lease, which in this case amounts to $361,010.02 in additional lease payments. Under the Lease, in the event of a default, the lessor receives the equipment back but has the responsibility to sell or re-lease it and provide a credit from that transaction's proceeds to the lessee under the formula set forth in the Lease. In addition, the lessor is due a Casualty Value. In this case, the Casualty Value amounts to $1,088,445.33. There are at least two ways in which the liquidated damages clause may be shown to be unreasonable. The first is the rate at which the Casualty Value is set.

In this case the Casualty Value is approximately three times the amount of the lease payments lost through the default. ePlus readily admits that the Casualty Value is also set "substantially" above the fair market value of the equipment. According to ePlus, the Casualty Value rate is based on its assumption that it can frequently sell or re-lease the equipment to the lessee for an amount above the equipment's fair market value. The defendants contend that, given the fact that three-year-old used computer equipment has a negligible sale or release value, the Casualty Value rate grossly overstates what a purchaser of the equipment—including a lessee in possession of the equipment—would be willing to pay for such equipment. ePlus has not submitted evidence to establish that it has historically been able to sell or re-lease equipment to a lessee at the expiration of the initial lease term, or that, when it has sold or re-leased equipment to the lessee, it has done so at the rate above fair market value. Moreover, the Lease itself permits the lessee to purchase the equipment at its fair market value as of the end of the Lease. Thus, based on plaintiff's own affidavits and the terms of the Lease, there are questions of fact regarding the reasonableness of the Casualty Value.

The second way in which the liquidated damages clause may be shown to be unreasonable concerns the formula for crediting the proceeds from the sale of repossessed equipment against the damages owed by the Defendants. The formula specifies that only that portion of the proceeds from a sale which exceeds the amount of the Casualty Value in effect as of the date of default will be credited against the damages payable under the clause. Since the sale of the equipment is unlikely to exceed the Casualty Value, because, as already discussed, it is undisputed that the Casualty Value exceeds the fair market value of the equipment, this formula means that in the ordinary course there would be no opportunity for the lessee to have the proceeds of a sale credited against the liquidated damages it owes.

Thus, the Defendants may be able to show that ePlus knew that in practice the liquidated damages formula would operate to provide it with a windfall by permitting it to receive substantially more than the lost lease payments and to keep the entire proceeds from an immediate sale of the repossessed equipment.

ePlus' argument that the "flexibility" and freedom to contract referred to in the Official Comment of Section 2A–504 support the enforceability of its liquidated damages clause is unpersuasive. The Official Comment and the text of Section 2A–504 itself require any such clause to be reasonable. The Defendants have raised questions of fact regarding the reasonableness of the Lease's clause which prevent summary judgment from being entered in favor of the plaintiff prior to discovery.

ePlus relies upon the decisions in *Sun* and *Case Credit Corp.* to support the enforceability of the liquidated damages clause in the Master Lease. This reliance is misplaced. Neither of these cases reviewed a liquidated damages clause that contained a provision equivalent to the Lease's Casualty Value, and each case endorsed a formula in which the lessee received a credit from the sale of repossessed goods. The court in *Sun* upheld a liquidated damages clause which permitted recovery on an accelerated basis of the future lease payments, with a deduction to account for the present value of the amount owed. *Sun*, 254 Ga.App. at 467. It rejected the argument that this formula was deficient because it did not account for unearned interest. Id. It cited with approval the decision in *Carter*, supra, that refused to enforce a clause in which the lessor was allowed to recover not only the present value of future rents, but also the proceeds from any sale of the repossessed equipment. Id. The liquidated damages clause in Case Credit Corp. required that the defaulting lessee be given a credit in the amount of the proceeds from a sale or re-lease of the returned goods. *Case Credit Corp.*, 228 B.R. at 509.

Finally, the plaintiff relies on *Gordonsville Energy, L.P. v. Virginia Electric & Power Co.*, 40 Va. Cir. 448 [29 UCC Rep Serv 2d 849] (Va.Cir.Ct.1996), in which the trial court applied Virginia common law to enforce a liquidated damages clause in an energy sales contract. Id. at 450. In *Gordonsville*, the court analyzed the liquidated damage provision on the basis of a developed record following trial. Id. at 453. At the very least, in this case, discovery will be necessary to determine whether the plaintiff is able to enforce this clause as one that meets the test set forth in Section 2A–504.

Conclusion

For the reasons stated, the plaintiff's motion for summary judgment is granted in part as to liability for its breach of contract claim against defendants Panoramic and epb.communications, inc. and denied as to its request for a declaration that the liquidated damages clause in the Master Lease is enforceable.

Notes and Discussion

1. Liquidated Damages in UCC Article 2A. This Article, adopted in 1987 and currently under review, "applies to any transaction, regardless of form, that creates a lease" (§ 2A–102): as the Comment puts it, "transactions as diverse as the lease of a hand tool to an individual for a few hours and the leveraged lease of a complex line of industrial equipment to a multinational organization for a number of years." Article 2A covers ePlus's lease of computer equipment to Panoramic and epb.

Section 2A–504(1) provides that: "Damages payable by either party for default, or any other act or omission, including indemnity for loss or diminution of anticipated tax benefits or loss or damage to lessor's residual interest, may be liquidated in the lease agreement but only at an amount or by a formula that is reasonable in light of the then anticipated harm caused by the default or other act or omission." How does the Court go about applying this section to the ePlus lease? Consider how the outcome changes if one applies either the present § 2–718(1) on sale of goods, or the amended version of § 2–718(1).

2. Penalty Clauses in Civil Law. As we have seen repeatedly in this Chapter, Civil Law typically accords greater respect to party autonomy in shaping their remedies. Penalty clauses are generally permissible provided that they do not grotesquely over-or undercompensate. For instance, the French Civil Code, Article 1152, allows the parties considerable latitude in defining "a fixed sum as damages," even where the intent is to exert pressure on one party; however, a 1975 amendment to this Article permits the judge to "diminish or increase the agreed penalty if it is manifestly excessive or derisory," and also removes the right of parties to limit this judicial power. See generally G. H. Treitel, Remedies, supra, 208–244.

3. What's So Evil about Penalties? The Common Law stance on penalty clauses has been widely criticized as incoherent. After all, as Victor Goldberg observes, "A penalty is just one element of the consideration for a contract. The party received something of value because it was willing to take the risk of having the penalty imposed upon it. Courts do not, in general, inquire into the adequacy of the consideration for a contract; yet if it is possible to characterize an element of a contract as a penalty, the court will scrutinize the adequacy of that element of the consideration more carefully. The judicial hostility to penalties goes too far." Victor P. Goldberg, *Further Thoughts on Penalty Clauses*, in Readings in the Economics of Contract Law 161, 161 (ed. Goldberg 1989).

The thought here is that if I value the other party's performance so highly that I am willing to give up something in order to get the other party to guarantee performance through a penalty clause, why should a court not respect the deal that we then strike? Think here particularly about the Peevyhouses; supposing that they had realized that their attachment to the farmland was idiosyncratic and hard to evaluate in cash, could they have negotiated for a liquidated damages clause (say, $25,000) to protect their interest in the event that Garland failed to restore the land? Could they have negotiated for a penalty clause (say, $40,000) in order to guarantee Garland's performance? What's the difference?

Problem 6–16

Contracts can prescribe "alternative performances" that allow a contract party to discharge its obligation in a number of ways. When they do, neither alternative needs to pass through § 2–718 (or the Common Law counterpart of 2–718) in order to be effective. By contrast, if a contract has a liquidated damages or penalty clause, it is not open to a party to discharge itself by paying the penalty instead of performing its principal contractual obligation.

But sometimes it is difficult to determine whether performances are "alternative" or whether one alternative is really liquidated damage for failed performance. Which of the following four cases are for alternative performance and which are for performance or liquidated damages?

1. Buyer agrees to purchase a thoroughbred racing horse for $150,000. If the seller delivers the horse, the price will be $154,000.

2. Construction Company undertakes to construct a library; it agrees that for every day after September 1, 2005, that work is not completed, $1,000 will be deducted from its contract price.

3. Construction Company shall receive a bonus of $1,000 per day for every day between the date of completion and October 1, 2005, if it completes the project before October 1, 2005.

4. A buyer of natural gas is obliged either to take all of the output of seller's well and pay $4.00 per million BTU or, alternatively, pay $4.00 on the seller's estimated potential output each year and have the right to take the gas in later years of the five-year contract. You should assume that, because of physical limitations on the amount of gas that can be brought out of the well in any year, it would be highly unlikely for the buyer to get more than two years of gas out of the well in a single year. If the buyer refuses to take the gas or to pay, is the contract payment equivalent to liquidated damages? And if not, what should the damages be: the full amount of the payment due, or the market differential in the gas to be sold?

Problem 6–17

UCC § 2–718(1): "Damages for breach by either party may be liquidated in the agreement but only at an amount which is reasonable in the light of the anticipated or actual harm caused by the breach, the difficulties of proof of loss, and the inconvenience or nonfeasibility of otherwise obtaining an adequate remedy. A term fixing unreasonably large liquidated damages is void as a penalty."

UCC § 2–718(1) as amended: "Damages for breach by either party may be liquidated in the agreement but only at an amount which is reasonable in the light of the anticipated or actual harm caused by the breach and, in a consumer contract, the difficulties of proof of ~~loss,~~ loss and the inconvenience or nonfeasibility of otherwise obtaining an adequate remedy. ~~A term fixing unreasonably large liquidated damages is void as a penalty.~~ Section 2–719 determines the enforceability of a term that limits but does not liquidate damages."

Compare the two statements of liquidated damages above. If you represented a buyer who wanted to overturn a liquidated damage clause, which Section 2–718 would you prefer?

Note: Limitation of Remedies

By far the most common agreed remedy in sale of goods contracts—particularly in contracts with consumers—is a term that makes the seller liable for repair or replacement but prohibits the recovery of damages. In general such terms do not have to meet any specific formal requirements; unlike disclaimers under § 2–316, they need not be conspicuous nor have any particular magic language. However, under 2–719(1)(b) they must be "exclusive." Woe to the lawyer who simply says "buyer's remedy is repair or replacement." Since the sentence doesn't say "buyer's *only* remedy is repair or replacement," Section 2–719(1)(b) makes the repair or replacement optional and leaves the seller open to a damage claim.

Repair and replacement promises are occasionally challenged under § 2–719(2) on the ground that they have failed of their "essential purpose." Commonly a remedy will be found to have failed of its essential purpose where the seller is either unwilling to repair or replace or incapable of doing so. A common case would arise when a buyer of a car has repeatedly taken his car to the shop of the seller and the seller has been unable to cure the problem. If the seller has restricted the buyer's remedies to repair or replace, the remedy fails of its "essential purpose," namely, to protect the buyer from lemons. In *Bishop Logging Co. v. John Deere Industrial Equipment Co.*, 317 S.C. 520, 455 S.E.2d 183 (App. 1995), logging equipment was sold for $608,899 with an exclusive remedy of repair or replacement; this remedy failed of its essential purpose when the seller spent over $110,000 in vain attempts to fix numerous equipment failures. The buyer was then allowed to recover economic losses of $723,323.

Section 2–719(3) has specific rules on limiting consequential damages. Those rules explicitly invoke unconscionability, and they have especially bad things to say about limitation of consequential damages where those damages are for personal injury.

We have seen other agreed remedies. For example, in Chapter 3.E, the *Gateway* case is a fight over the enforceability of an arbitration clause in Gateway's contract, and *Carnival Cruise* is a fight over a forum selection clause that named Florida as the only place where a suit could be brought. Both commercial and consumer contracts often have terms on arbitration, choice of law, and forum selection, but all of these, at least in the sale of goods, are far less frequent than repair and replacement terms.

Of course, a buyer is not restricted to § 2–719 in challenging the effectiveness of a seller's limitation on buyer's remedies. Although the buyers did not win at the Supreme Court in *Carnival Cruise Lines*, they did win in the lower court by arguing that the forum selection clause was unconscionable or unfair. And in a subsequent *Gateway* case from New York, the buyers of a Gateway computer successfully avoided an arbitration clause where the cost of the arbitration might have exceeded the value of the computer. *Brower v. Gateway 2000*, 676 N.Y.S.2d 569, 571, 246 A.D.2d 246, 250 (App. Div. 1998).

Because of the different rules that apply to disclaimers on the one hand, and other limitations on liability and to restrictions on remedies on the other, it is important both for the drafter and for the litigator to keep them separate and to understand that in the sale of goods one looks primarily at 2–719 with respect to remedies but to sections such as 2–316 for disclaimers.

Chapter 7

CONDITIONS AND SELF-HELP REMEDIES DURING PERFORMANCE

This Chapter deals with express and implied (or "constructive") conditions. A condition is defined by Restatement 2d § 224 as: "an event, not certain to occur, which must occur, unless its non-occurrence is excused, before performance under a contract becomes due." Although an entire contract can be made to depend on a condition (such that no rights and duties arise on either side unless the event occurs), here we are dealing chiefly with conditions that arise during the course of a contract's performance.

This chapter also deals with rights that we call self-help remedies. These rights arise on the failure of a condition to occur. As we note below, conditions are not promises, and one can never recover damages for the non-occurrence of a condition. On the other hand, the non-occurrence of the condition is important precisely and only because of the rights that it gives to the beneficiary of the condition. These rights, these self-help remedies, are present in every case involving conditions, but, since they are not often labeled as remedies, are easy to overlook. They include suspension of performance, cancellation of the contract, rejection of goods, and revocation of acceptance of goods. The materials that follow will reveal the difficulty in determining whether the non-occurrence of a condition has given rise merely to the right to suspend performance or is so serious and long lasting that it also has given the beneficiary of the condition the right to cancel the contract. Whether a buyer of goods has a right to reject or to revoke acceptance on the seller's failure to deliver conforming goods is determined by a set of complex rules in Sections 2–601 through 2–608 of the UCC.

So, this chapter does two things. First it gives you exercise in understanding what are conditions and how they differ from promises. Second it gives you an appreciation for the self-help remedies that become available to the beneficiary of a condition when the condition does not occur.

Conditions in contract law are both familiar and confusing. They serve up a handful of intellectual irritants. Consider a classic express condition: "It is a condition of the seller's obligation to pay on its warranty that the buyer give written notice of any claim within thirty days of the manifestation of the cause for the claim." The most direct legal significance of this term is plain: no notice, no payment from the seller. In the words of the Restatement, the contractual duty of the seller/warrantor to pay is "conditioned" on the buyer's giving notice. But understand what the condition is not: it is not a promise by the buyer to give notice. If the buyer fails to give notice, that is only his problem. He loses a claim, but neither the seller nor anyone else can sue him for breach of contract.

But what if the warranty provided that: "Buyer promises to give written notice of any claim within thirty days of the manifestation of the cause of the claim"? Now that sounds like a promise. If it is a promise and not a condition and the seller is injured because of lack of notice (for example because it was deprived of the opportunity to inspect the damaged goods to determine the cause of loss), seller can always counterclaim for breach of the promise to give notice for breach. But if the term were only a promise and not a condition, seller might still have to pay on the warranty (less an amount for its injury arising from the breach of the promise to give notice), in which case its promise on the warranty would not be subject to an express condition and would usually arise despite the buyer's breach of contract.

This simple example shows why sometimes persons argue that terms are promises, and sometimes that they are conditions. Because the failure of a condition to occur ordinarily keeps the duty from arising, insurance companies (who understand that they, not the insured, will have to perform upon the occurrence of the insured event) frequently state the insured's obligations—e.g., to pay the premium and to give notice and the like—as conditions. Construing such a term as a condition means that the insurance company avoids the messy argument that would occur if the term were a promise of the insured. If the term were a promise of the insured, there would be arguments about whether he breached and about the damages suffered by the insurance company that could be set off against its obligation to pay. As we see below in the discussion of implied conditions, the insurer might also argue that the insured's performance of its promise (to pay the premium or to give notice of its claim) was an implied condition to the insurer's promise to pay, but this argument runs uphill against various counter-arguments of the insured. Non-occurrence of an express condition on the other hand is a flat bar to the insurer's duty to pay, no questions asked and no messy argument about breach, setoff or the nature of any implied conditions.

Now consider the express condition's second cousin, implied or constructive conditions. You are so familiar with the idea that one can sue a contracting party for failure to perform (as opposed to failure to perform properly), it might surprise you to know that Anglo-American law was slow to recognize the right to sue someone in contract for failure to perform a promise. Where there was no suit for breach of an unperformed part of the contract, one had no need to worry about the right of one party to stop his performance on the failure of another to perform. If one could not be sued for an executory failure to perform a contract, then not performing could not expose an honest party to any liability if he stopped because his counterpart had already broken the contract.

But once suit for breach of the executory part of a contract became possible, there was a problem. When the owner fails to make a progress payment due to a contractor who is building the Brooklyn Bridge, what rights does the contractor have? May it suspend work? Can it even abandon the work? Now that question must be answered. The English courts' answer was to "construct"—to imply into the contract—a condition that any major failure by one party, any "material breach," gave the other the right to suspend and, eventually, to cancel. And while courts were at it, they found some other conditions by implication too, namely the right to stop performance without breaking the contract when its performance became "impossible" or "impracticable" or its purpose was "frustrated." We study all of these implied conditions here.

Note how these implied conditions differ from express conditions. Of course, they are not express but only implied ("constructed"), and so one judge might find a particular condition, and another judge a different one, buried at the same place in the same contract. They are the common law's expression of the presumed intention of contracting parties who never wrote down their own intention. And, at least to today's mind, most are so obvious that one wonders why they have to be stated. Who possibly would say that the contractor must trudge on brick by brick when the city has stopped paying for the work?

Still they hide dangerous legal problems. A party's immaterial breach does not entitle the other party to suspend performance. But when is a breach "material," so giving the right to suspend? And when has a material breach ripened into a "total" breach, so allowing cancellation? These are hard questions, often presented to the lawyer. They are the very questions that the insurance company hopes to avoid by using express conditions whose failure, however small and unimportant, bars its duty.

To get a better grip on implied conditions and their operation, consider Restatement § 237 and its first two illustrations:

> Except as stated in § 240, it is a condition of each party's remaining duties to render performances to be exchanged under an exchange of promises that there be no uncured material failure by the other party to render any such performance due at an earlier time.
>
> Illustration 1. A contracts to build a house for B for $50,000, progress payments to be made monthly in an amount equal to 85% of the price of the work performed during the preceding month, the balance to be paid on the architect's certificate of satisfactory

completion of the house. Without justification, B fails to make a $5,000 progress payment. A thereupon stops work on the house and a week goes by. A's failure to continue the work is not a breach and B has no claim against A. B's failure to make the progress payment is an uncured material failure of performance which operates as the non-occurrence of a condition of A's remaining duties of performance under the exchange. If B offers to make the delayed payment and in all the circumstances it is not too late to cure the material breach, A's duties to continue the work are not discharged. A has a claim against B for damages for partial breach because of the delay.

Illustration 2: The facts being otherwise as stated in illustration 1, B fails to make the progress payment or to give any explanation or assurances for one month. If, in all the circumstances, it is now too late for B to cure his material failure of performance by making the delayed payment, A's duties to continue the work are discharged. Because B's failure to make the progress payment was a breach, A also has a claim against B for total breach of contract (§ 243).

The rules in Article 2 of the UCC differ from the general rules stated in the Restatement. In contracts for the sale of goods there is no materiality requirement for rejection (except in installment contracts under § 2–612) or for cancellation thereafter (§§ 2–601, 2–711). If the buyer has accepted goods, he can revoke acceptance only if the defect "substantially impairs" them (i.e., if the goods are "materially" defective). The summary statements of the rights of buyers and sellers of goods in §§ 2–703 and 2–711 do not condition cancellation on the materiality of the breach (except with respect to installment contracts and revocation of acceptance, see §§ 2–608 and 2–612).

Parties also have the right to cancel contracts without liability when their performance is "frustrated" and when their performance has become "impossible" or "impracticable." The notion of frustration of purpose comes from a famous British case where a person had rented rooms on the coronation parade route at a dear price, only to learn that the King was sick and that the coronation would not take place during the term of his rental. Performance of this contract was not rendered impracticable or impossible. The renter could still pay and still look out the window; however, since he would not be looking at the King, his purpose was "frustrated." *Krell v. Henry*, [1903] 2 K.B. 740 (Eng. C. A.). Impracticability might arise under § 2–615 when a farmer promised to sell the corn crop to be grown in 2005 on his 640 acres and the crop was destroyed by drought.

When these doctrines apply, the promisor is discharged; he is not liable for damages. The first part of the previous sentence marks where the horse is buried; the doctrines are easy to state, hard to apply. If the farmer promised to sell 60,000 bushels of corn without mention of the land on which this corn was to be grown, is performance impracticable? The farmer could replace the corn on the market, true?

The big learning in this Chapter is to understand conditions, their operation, and how they differ from promises, and to understand the variety of self-help remedies that the non-occurrence of a condition gives to its beneficiary. The implied condition that a mature material breach discharges a party is particularly important. Many of you can look forward to your own frustration and to your clients' anger when you explain that you cannot tell them whether they can safely cancel an improvident long term contract they have made with a weasel who is performing, but just barely.

A. EXPRESS CONDITIONS

During the summer of 1979, a law student named Mark Dove worked at Rose Acre Farms, an Indiana egg factory producing over three million eggs per day. The factory's owner-operator, David Rust, was given to somewhat eccentric bonus programs that offered his employees money if, for instance, they kept their cars spotlessly clean or consistently showed up exactly on time for work. Under one such bonus program, Dove was to receive a $5,000 bonus if he worked on a construction project for five full days a week for ten weeks. Dove kept up the schedule until the tenth week, when on Thursday he came down with a high fever that prevented him from working the remainder of the week. Rust denied him the bonus because Dove had missed two days of work, and Dove sued. Then, when he lost at trial, Dove appealed.

The Indiana Court of Appeals affirmed. Dove had argued: "Rose Acre got what it bargained for, that is, the completion of the project.... [H]e was present on the job, including the hours he worked late, at least 750 hours during the ten weeks, while regular working hours would amount to only 500 hours. Therefore, ... there was substantial compliance with the agreement, and he should not be penalized because he failed to appear on the last two days because of illness." *Dove v. Rose Acre Farms, Inc.*, 434 N.E.2d 931, 933 (Ind. Ct. App. 1982).

But the Court rejected this argument. "[T]he bonus rules at Rose Acre were well known to Dove when he agreed to the disputed bonus contract. He certainly knew Rust's strict policies and knew that any absence for any cause whatever worked a forfeiture of the bonus. With this knowledge he willingly entered into this bonus arrangement, as he had done in the past, and ... he must be held to have agreed to all of the terms upon which the bonus was conditioned. If the conditions were unnecessarily harsh or eccentric, and the terms odious, he could have shown his disdain by simply declining to participate, for participation in the bonus program was not obligatory or job dependent. Contrary to Dove's assertion that completion of a task was the central element of the bonus program, we are of the opinion that the rules regarding tardiness and absenteeism were a central theme." Id. at 935.

This is the law of conditions working at its fiercest. Dove's "substantial compliance" was not enough; Dove had either to work to Rust's specifications, or forfeit his bonus entirely. But you will already notice certain boltholes that the Court has left itself. The condition was crystal clear, and also clearly comprehended. The money offered was a bonus, over and above Dove's usual salary. Dove's participation in the program was totally voluntary. Although the condition may have been strange, it had a discernible and legal aim, and Rust was entitled to enforce it to the letter. What will happen when one or more of these features is not present?

MERRITT HILL VINEYARDS, INC. v. WINDY HEIGHTS VINEYARD, INC.

Court of Appeals of New York, 1984.
61 N.Y.2d 106, 460 N.E.2d 1077, 472 N.Y.S.2d 592.

KAYE, J. In a contract for the sale of a controlling stock interest in a vineyard, the seller's undertaking to produce a title insurance policy and mortgage confirmation at closing constituted a condition and not a promise, the breach of which excused the buyer's performance and entitled it to the return of its deposit, but not to consequential damages. On the buyer's motion for summary judgment seeking recovery of both the deposit and consequential damages, the Appellate Division correctly awarded summary judgment to the buyer for its deposit and to the seller dismissing the cause of action for consequential damages, even though the seller had not sought this relief by cross appeal.

In September, 1981, plaintiff, Merritt Hill Vineyards, entered into a written agreement with defendants, Windy Heights Vineyard and its sole shareholder Leon Taylor, to purchase a majority stock interest in respondents' Yates County vineyard, and tendered a $15,000 deposit. The agreement provides that "[if] the sale contemplated hereby does not close, Taylor shall retain the deposit as liquidated damages unless Taylor or Windy Heights failed to satisfy the conditions specified in Section 3 thereof." Section 3, in turn, lists several "conditions precedent" to which the obligation of purchaser to pay the purchase price and to complete the purchase is subject. Among the conditions are that, by the time of the closing, Windy Heights shall have obtained a title insurance policy in a form satisfactory to Merritt Hill, and Windy Heights and Merritt Hill shall have received confirmation from the Farmers Home Administration that certain mortgages on the vineyard are in effect and that the proposed sale does not constitute a default.

In April, 1982, at the closing, plaintiff discovered that neither the policy nor the confirmation had been issued. Plaintiff thereupon refused to close and demanded return of its deposit. When defendants did not return the deposit, plaintiff instituted this action, asserting two causes of action, one for return of the deposit, and one for approximately $26,000 in consequential damages allegedly suffered as a result of defendants' failure to perform.

Special Term denied plaintiff's motion for summary judgment on both causes of action. The Appellate Division unanimously reversed

Special Term's order, granted plaintiff's motion for summary judgment as to the cause of action for return of the deposit, and upon searching the record pursuant to CPLR 3212 (subd [b]), granted summary judgment in favor of defendants, dismissing plaintiff's second cause of action for consequential damages. Both plaintiff and defendants appealed from that decision. This appeal raises two issues: first, whether as a matter of procedure, the Appellate Division could grant defendants summary judgment in the absence of a cross appeal, and second, if so, whether the Appellate Division, on the merits, correctly determined that the failure to supply the title insurance policy and mortgage confirmation obligated defendants to return plaintiff's deposit but did not subject them to liability for consequential damages. Because the Appellate Division was correct both as to procedure and as to substance, we affirm.

I. As Matter Of Procedure, The Appellate Division Had The Authority To Grant Summary Judgment To Defendants Even In The Absence Of A Cross Appeal By them.

On plaintiff's appeal from the denial of its motion for summary judgment, the Appellate Division was required to review the record to determine if any issues of fact existed as to either of plaintiff's causes of action which required a trial. After searching the record, the Appellate Division determined that no issue of triable fact existed as to either cause of action, that plaintiff was entitled to judgment as a matter of law on the first, but that defendants were entitled to judgment as a matter of law on the second. CPLR 3212 (subd [b]), provides that "[if] it shall appear that any party other than the moving party is entitled to a summary judgment, the court may grant such judgment without the necessity of a cross-motion." Pursuant to that rule, the Appellate Division properly entered summary judgment in favor of defendants and dismissed plaintiff's second cause of action.

The question that next arises, however, is whether the Appellate Division could grant such relief in the absence of a cross appeal by defendants. While it is clear that this court could not grant summary judgment to a nonappealing party . . . , the Appellate Division is not so precluded. . . . This court has consistently upheld the Appellate Division's authority to grant such relief pursuant to CPLR 3212 (subd [b]), even in the absence of an appeal by the nonmoving party. . . .

Unlike this court, which has no original jurisdiction over motions and limited authority to review facts, the Appellate Division is a division of the Supreme Court see NY Const, art VI, §§ 4, 7, and shares that court's power to search the record and award summary judgment to a nonmoving party even where, as here, the nonmovant did not appeal. As was aptly explained in language adopted by this court in *De Rosa v. Slattery Contr. Co.* (14 AD2d 278, 280–281, affd 12 NY2d 735):

> "Rule 113 of the Rules of Civil Practice [the predecessor of CPLR 3212] provides judgment may be awarded to the opposing party even in the absence of a cross motion. Defendant Slattery did

not ask for summary judgment either at Special Term or on appeal. It may be entitled to that relief, however, if it has a good defense to the action. The material facts are undisputed and mandate summary judgment dismissing the complaint * * *

"The Appellate Division, as the successor of the General Term, possesses all of the original jurisdiction of the Supreme Court, including the hearing and determination of motions * * * On an appeal from an intermediate order resulting in a reversal or modification, the Appellate Division generally entertains jurisdiction of and decides the underlying motion * * * The Court of Appeals, unlike the Appellate Division, has no original jurisdiction of a motion in an action or proceeding, and in the absence of an appeal therefrom it has held that it is without power to decide it." (Citations omitted.)

Ever since its first appearance in this State by legislative enactment in 1921, summary judgment has offered an effective means for resolving disputes which present only questions of law.... "[The] practicalities of frivolous litigation and court congestion mandate a summary procedure upon the ascertaining that there is no cause of action." (*Senrow Concessions v. Shelton Props.*, 10 NY2d 320, 326.) This is as true when the infirmity in a cause of action or defense is ascertained by the Appellate Division as it is when that decision is made at Special Term. Once it determined that no issue of material fact existed as to plaintiff's second cause of action and that defendants were entitled to judgment as a matter of law, the Appellate Division had the power and responsibility to award summary judgment.

Thus, the order below was correct as a matter of procedure.

II. On The Merits, Plaintiff's Right to Return of its Deposit or to Consequential Damages Depends Upon Whether The Undertaking to Produce the Policy and Mortgage Confirmation Is A Promise or a Condition.

2nd issue

A promise is "a manifestation of intention to act or refrain from acting in a specified way, so made as to justify a promisee in understanding that a commitment has been made." (Restatement, Contracts 2d, § 2, subd [1].) A condition, by comparison, is "an event, not certain to occur, which must occur, unless its non-occurrence is excused, before performance under a contract becomes due." (Restatement, Contracts 2d, § 224.) Here, the contract requirements of a title insurance policy and mortgage confirmation are expressed as conditions of plaintiff's performance rather than as promises by defendants. The requirements are contained in a section of the agreement entitled "Conditions Precedent to Purchaser's Obligation to Close," which provides that plaintiff's obligation to pay the purchase price and complete the purchase of the vineyard is "subject to" fulfillment of those requirements. No words of promise are employed.[1] Defendants' agreement to sell the stock of the

1. Plaintiff contends that the failure to produce the policy and confirmation is also a breach of section 5, entitled "Representations, Warranties and Agreements." A pro-

vineyard, not those conditions, was the promise by defendants for which plaintiff's promise to pay the purchase price was exchanged.

Defendants' failure to fulfill the conditions of section 3 entitles plaintiff to a return of its deposit but not to consequential damages. While a contracting party's failure to fulfill a condition excuses performance by the other party whose performance is so conditioned, it is not, without an independent promise to perform the condition, a breach of contract subjecting the nonfulfilling party to liability for damages (Restatement, Contracts 2d, § 225, subds [1], [3]; 3A Corbin, Contracts, § 663; 5 Williston, Contracts [Jaeger–3d ed], § 665). This is in accord with the parties' expressed intent, for section 1 of their agreement provides that if defendants fail to satisfy the conditions of section 3 plaintiff's deposit will be returned. It does not provide for payment of damages.

On the merits of this case the Appellate Division thus correctly determined that plaintiff was entitled to the return of its deposit but not to consequential damages.

Accordingly, the order of the Appellate Division should be affirmed. Order affirmed, without costs.

Notes and Discussion

1. A Promise or a Condition or Both? Section 3 of the contract contained what it describes as "conditions precedent" regarding a title insurance policy and a confirmation from the FHA about the mortgages. Judge Kaye reads the contract to say simply that if these conditions are not met, Merritt Hill is not obligated "to pay the purchase price and to complete the purchase." What are the consequences of this construction with regard to Merritt Hill's recovery both of its "liquidated damages" deposit and of consequential damages? Why is the outcome different?

Do you think that the contract could also be construed to mean that Windy Heights *additionally promised* to satisfy these two conditions? As the footnote to the opinion indicates, Merritt Hill tried to argue this by using other provisions in the contract. Judge Kaye's rejection of this view is not entirely convincing, right? On this alternative construction, how would the outcome differ? How would the parties have to have written their contract in order to satisfy Judge Kaye?

HOWARD v. FEDERAL CROP INSURANCE CORP.

United States Court of Appeals, Fourth Circuit, 1976.
540 F.2d 695.

WIDENER, J. Plaintiff-appellants sued to recover for losses to their 1973 tobacco crop due to alleged rain damage. The crops were insured by

vision may be both a condition and a promise, if the parties additionally promise to perform a condition as part of their bargain. Such a promise is not present here. The only provision of section 5 conceivably relevant is that "Windy Heights has good and marketable title to the Property and all other properties and assets * * * as of December 31, 1980." But this is quite different from the conditions of section 3 that a title insurance policy and mortgage confirmation be produced at the closing, which took place in April, 1982. Both the complaint and plaintiff's affidavits are premised on nonperformance of section 3 of the agreement, not section 5.

defendant-appellee, Federal Crop Insurance Corporation (FCIC). Suits were brought in a state court in North Carolina and removed to the United States District Court. The three suits are not distinguishable factually so far as we are concerned here and involve identical questions of law. They were combined for disposition in the district court and for appeal. The district court granted summary judgment for the defendant and dismissed all three actions. We remand for further proceedings. Since we find for the plaintiffs as to the construction of the policy, we express no opinion on the procedural questions.

Federal Crop Insurance Corporation, an agency of the United States, in 1973, issued three policies to the Howards, insuring their tobacco crops, to be grown on six farms, against weather damage and other hazards.

The Howards (plaintiffs) established production of tobacco on their acreage, and have alleged that their 1973 crop was extensively damaged by heavy rains, resulting in a gross loss to the three plaintiffs in excess of $35,000. The plaintiffs harvested and sold the depleted crop and timely filed notice and proof of loss with FCIC, but, prior to inspection by the adjuster for FCIC, the Howards had either plowed or disked under the tobacco fields in question to prepare the same for sowing a cover crop of rye to preserve the soil. When the FCIC adjuster later inspected the fields, he found the stalks had been largely obscured or obliterated by plowing or disking and denied the claims, apparently on the ground that the plaintiffs had violated a portion of the policy which provides that the stalks on any acreage with respect to which a loss is claimed shall not be destroyed until the corporation makes an inspection.

The holding of the district court is best capsuled in its own words: "The inquiry here is whether compliance by the insureds with this provision of the policy was a condition precedent to the recovery. The court concludes that it was and that the failure of the insureds to comply worked a forfeiture of benefits for the alleged loss."

There is no question but that apparently after notice of loss was given to defendant, but before inspection by the adjuster, plaintiffs plowed under the tobacco stalks and sowed some of the land with a cover crop, rye. The question is whether, under paragraph 5(f) of the tobacco endorsement to the policy of insurance, the act of plowing under the tobacco stalks forfeits the coverage of the policy. Paragraph 5 of the tobacco endorsement is entitled *Claims*. Pertinent to this case are subparagraphs 5(b) and 5(f), which are as follows:

> 5(b) *It shall be a condition precedent* to the payment of any loss that the insured establish the production of the insured crop on a unit and that such loss has been directly caused by one or more of the hazards insured against during the insurance period for the crop year for which the loss is claimed, and furnish any other information

regarding the manner and extent of loss as may be required by the Corporation. (Emphasis added)

5(f) The tobacco stalks on any acreage of tobacco of types 11a, 11b, 12, 13, or 14 with respect to which a loss is claimed *shall not be destroyed until the Corporation makes an inspection*. (Emphasis added)

The arguments of both parties are predicated upon the same two assumptions. First, if subparagraph 5(f) creates a condition precedent, its violation caused a forfeiture of plaintiffs' coverage. Second, if subparagraph 5(f) creates an obligation (variously called a promise or covenant) upon plaintiffs not to plow under the tobacco stalks, defendant may recover from plaintiffs (either in an original action, or, in this case, by a counterclaim, or as a matter of defense) for whatever damage it sustained because of the elimination of the stalks. However, a violation of subparagraph 5(f) would not, under the second premise, standing alone, cause a forfeiture of the policy.

Generally accepted law provides us with guidelines here. There is a general legal policy opposed to forfeitures. *United States v. One Ford Coach*, 307 U.S. 219, 226, 83 L.Ed. 1249, 59 S. Ct. 861 (1939); *Baca v. Commissioner of Internal Revenue*, 326 F.2d 189, 191 (5th Cir. 1963). Insurance policies are generally construed most strongly against the insurer. *Henderson v. Hartford Accident & Indemnity Co.*, 268 N.C. 129, 150 S.E.2d 17, 19 (1966). When it is doubtful whether words create a promise or a condition precedent, they will be construed as creating a promise. *Harris and Harris Const. Co. v. Crain and Denbo, Inc.*, 256 N.C. 110, 123 S.E.2d 590, 595 (1962). The provisions of a contract will not be construed as conditions precedent in the absence of language plainly requiring such construction. *Harris*, 123 S.E.2d at 596. ...

Plaintiffs rely most strongly upon the fact that the term "condition precedent" is included in subparagraph 5(b) but not in subparagraph 5(f). It is true that whether a contract provision is construed as a condition or an obligation does not depend entirely upon whether the word "condition" is expressly used. Appleman, Insurance Law and Practice, (1972), vol. 6A, § 4144. However, the persuasive force of plaintiffs' argument in this case is found in the use of the term "condition precedent" in subparagraph 5(b) but not in subparagraph 5(f). Thus, it is argued that the ancient maxim to be applied is that the expression of one thing is the exclusion of another.

The defendant places principal reliance upon the decision of this court in *Fidelity-Phenix Fire Insurance Company v. Pilot Freight Carriers*, 193 F.2d 812, 31 ALR 2d 839 (4th Cir. 1952). Suit there was predicated upon a loss resulting from theft out of a truck covered by defendant's policy protecting plaintiff from such a loss. The insurance company defended upon the grounds that the plaintiff had left the truck unattended without the alarm system being on. The policy contained six paragraphs limiting coverage. Two of those imposed what was called a "condition precedent." They largely related to the installation of specified safety equipment. Several others, including paragraph 5, pertinent in that case, started with the phrase, "It is further warranted." In paragraph 5, the insured warranted that the alarm system would be on whenever the vehicle was left unattended. Paragraph 6 starts with the language: "The assured agrees, by acceptance of this policy, that the foregoing conditions precedent relate to matters material to the acceptance of the risk by the insurer." Plaintiff recovered in the district court, but judgment on its behalf was reversed because of a breach of warranty of paragraph 5, the truck had been left unattended with the alarm off. In that case, plaintiff relied upon the fact that the words "condition precedent" were used in some of the paragraphs but the word "warranted" was used in the paragraph in issue. In rejecting that contention, this court said that "warranty" and "condition precedent" are often used interchangeably to create a condition of the insured's promise, and "manifestly the terms 'condition precedent' and 'warranty' were intended to have the same meaning and effect." 193 F.2d at 816.

Fidelity-Phenix thus does not support defendant's contention here. Although there is some resemblance between the two cases, analysis shows that the issues are actually entirely different. Unlike the case at bar, each paragraph in *Fidelity-Phenix* contained either the term "condition precedent" or the term "warranted." We held that, in that situation, the two terms had the same effect in that they both involved forfeiture. That is well established law. See Appleman, Insurance Law and Practice (1972), vol. 6A, § 4144. In the case at bar, the term "warranty" or "warranted" is in no way involved, either in terms or by way of like language, as it was in *Fidelity-Phenix*. The issue upon which this case turns, then, was not involved in *Fidelity-Phenix*.

The *Restatement of the Law of Contracts* states: " '261. Interpretation of Doubtful Words as Promise or Condition. Where it is doubtful whether words create a promise or an express condition, they are interpreted as creating a promise; but the same words may sometimes mean that one party promises a performance and that the other party's promise is conditional on that performance."

Two illustrations (one involving a promise, the other a condition) are used in the *Restatement*:

> 2. A, an insurance company, issues to B a policy of insurance containing promises by A that are in terms conditional on the happening of certain events. The policy contains this clause: 'provided, in case differences shall arise touching any loss, *the matter shall be submitted to impartial arbitrators*, whose award shall be binding on the parties.' This is a promise to arbitrate and does not make an award a condition precedent of the insurer's duty to pay.
>
> 3. A, an insurance company, issues to B an insurance policy in usual form containing this clause: 'In the event of disagreement as to the amount of loss it shall be ascertained by two appraisers and an umpire. The loss shall *not be payable until 60 days after the award of the appraisers when such an appraisal is required*.' This

> provision is not merely a promise to arbitrate differences but makes an award a condition of the insurer's duty to pay in case of disagreement. (Emphasis added)

We believe that subparagraph 5(f) in the policy here under consideration fits illustration 2 rather than illustration 3. Illustration 2 specifies something to be done, whereas subparagraph 5(f) specifies something not to be done. Unlike illustration 3, subparagraph 5(f) does not state any conditions under which the insurance shall "not be payable," or use any words of like import. We hold that the district court erroneously held, on the motion for summary judgment, that subparagraph 5(f) established a condition precedent to plaintiffs' recovery which forfeited the coverage.

From our holding that defendant's motion for summary judgment was improperly allowed, it does not follow the plaintiffs' motion for summary judgment should have been granted, for if subparagraph 5(f) be not construed as a condition precedent, there are other questions of fact to be determined. At this point, we merely hold that the district court erred in holding, on the motion for summary judgment, that subparagraph 5(f) constituted a condition precedent with resulting forfeiture.

The explanation defendant makes for including subparagraph 5(f) in the tobacco endorsement is that it is necessary that the stalks remain standing in order for the Corporation to evaluate the extent of loss and to determine whether loss resulted from some cause not covered by the policy. However, was subparagraph 5(f) inserted because without it the Corporation's opportunities for proof would be more difficult, or because they would be impossible? Plaintiffs point out that the Tobacco Endorsement, with subparagraph 5(f), was adopted in 1970, and crop insurance goes back long before that date. Nothing is shown as to the Corporation's prior 1970 practice of evaluating losses. Such a showing might have a bearing upon establishing defendant's intention in including 5(f). Plaintiffs state, and defendant does not deny, that another division of the Department of Agriculture, or the North Carolina Department, urged that tobacco stalks be cut as soon as possible after harvesting as a means of pest control. Such an explanation might refute the idea that plaintiffs plowed under the stalks for any fraudulent purpose. Could these conflicting directives affect the reasonableness of plaintiffs' interpretation of defendant's prohibition upon plowing under the stalks prior to adjustment?

We express no opinion on these questions because they were not before the district court and are mentioned to us largely by way of argument rather than from the record. No question of ambiguity was raised in the court below or here and no question of the applicability of paragraph 5(c) to this case was alluded to other than in the defendant's pleadings, so we also do not reach those questions. Nothing we say here should preclude FCIC from asserting as a defense that the plowing or disking under of the stalks caused damage to FCIC if, for example, the amount of the loss was thereby made more difficult or impossible to ascertain whether the plowing or disking under was done with bad purpose or innocently. To repeat, our narrow holding is that merely plowing or disking under the stalks does not of itself operate to forfeit coverage under the policy.

The case is remanded for further proceedings not inconsistent with this opinion.

Vacated and remanded.

Notes and Discussion

1. Language. The FCIC claimed that subparagraph 5(f) (tobacco stalks not to be destroyed prior to inspection) merely implemented 5(b) (Howard's duty to establish nature of loss as a condition precedent for recovery). Review the cases on interpretation in Chapter 4.B. The Court's interpretation may strike you as implausible on its face. How much does the Court rely purely upon plain meaning in distinguishing the *Fidelity-Phenix* case? What additional reasons does the Court have for favoring the view that 5(f) should not be construed as a condition? If 5(f) wasn't a condition, then what was it doing in the contract?

Restatement 2d § 227(1) states that: "In resolving doubts as to whether an event is made a condition of an obligor's duty, and as to the nature of such an event, an interpretation is preferred that will reduce the obligee's risk of forfeiture, unless the event is within the obligee's control or the circumstances indicate that he has assumed the risk." Subsection (2) goes on to indicate a general preference for interpreting ambiguous language as a promise, rather than as a condition or as both a condition and a promise. Illustration 1: "A, a general contractor, contracts with B, a sub-contractor, for the plumbing work on a construction project. B is to receive $100,000, 'no part of which shall be due until five days after Owner shall have paid Contractor therefor.' B does the plumbing work, but the owner becomes insolvent and fails to pay A." What outcome on the principles just stated? This hypothetical is based on *Thos. J. Dyer Co. v. Bishop Intern. Engineering Co.*, 303 F.2d 655 (6th Cir. 1962).

Re-draft the FCIC policy so that the term in 5(f) is a condition and not a promise.

2. Forfeiture. Comment b on § 227 states the policy argument behind the section: "The non-occurrence of a condition of an obligor's duty may cause the obligee to lose his right to the agreed exchange after he has relied substantially on the expectation of that exchange, as by preparation or performance.... Although the rule is consistent with a policy of avoiding forfeiture and unjust enrichment, it is not directed at the avoidance of actual forfeiture and unjust enrichment. Since the intentions of the parties must be taken as of the time the contract was made, the test is whether a particular interpretation would have avoided the risk of forfeiture viewed as of that time, not whether it will avoid actual forfeiture in the resolution of a dispute that has arisen later."

However, even if a contract term is clearly a condition, a court may still excuse it if its non-occurrence "would cause disproportionate forfeiture."

Restatement 2d § 229. This is a very important escape hatch, to which we will return below in *Jacob & Youngs, Inc. v. Kent.*

In *Howard*, the forfeiture is clearly that the farmer may not receive compensation for his crop loss. Would it matter if Howard had not yet relied substantially on the policy hitherto—e.g., if this was his first year growing tobacco, and to date he had made only one relatively small insurance payment?

3. Waiver. Suppose that, in *Howard*, subparagraph 5(f) had been clearly written as a condition, and that, after his crop was inundated, Howard was concerned about pest control and called his local FCIC agent, who said to him, "Go ahead and plow." This would be a waiver of the express condition. The general requirements for a valid waiver are described in *Wagner v. Wagner*, 95 Wash.2d 94, 621 P.2d 1279, 1283–1284 (1980) (citations omitted): "Waiver is the intentional relinquishment of a known right. It is necessary that the person against whom waiver is claimed have intended to relinquish the right, advantage, or benefit and his action must be inconsistent with any other intent than to waive it. Further, to constitute a waiver, other than by express agreement, there must be unequivocal acts or conduct evincing an intent to waive. Intent cannot be inferred from doubtful or ambiguous factors. Estoppel requires (1) an admission, statement, or act inconsistent with the claim afterwards asserted, (2) action by the other party on the faith of such admission, statement, or act, and (3) injury to such other party resulting from allowing the first party to contradict or repudiate such admission, statement or act." Note that the waiver of a condition does not have to be in writing, even when the contract itself is within the Statute of Frauds. Further, it can also arise from non-verbal conduct, as where the FCIC agent simply pays Howard without asking to see the crops.

On waivers, see generally Restatement 2d § 84(1), which permits waivers to work "unless (a) the occurrence of the condition was a material part of the agreed exchange for the performance of the duty and the promisee was under no duty that it occur; or (b) uncertainty of the occurrence of the condition was an element of the risk assumed by the promisor." Apply these restrictions to the hypothetical version of the *Howard* case given above. In form, a waiver can be construed as a promise ("I will pay you for your crop even though you plow it under before I can inspect it"), but it does not inherently require consideration in order to be valid.

One final wrinkle is stated in § 84(2): a condition that has been waived can be reinstated provided that reasonable notice is given to the other party and that party has not in the meantime materially changed position in reliance.

Problem 7–1

Roy Inman worked as a derrickman for Clyde Hall Drilling Company until he was fired on March 24. Inman, who believed his discharge was unjustified, on April 5 filed suit against Clyde Hall; and the company responded. Inman's contract, however, contained the following language: "You agree that you will, within thirty (30) days after any claim (other than a claim for compensation insurance) that arises out of or in connection with the employment provided for herein, give written notice to the Company for such claim, setting forth in detail the facts relating thereto and the basis for such claim; and that you will not institute any suit or action against the Company in any court or tribunal in any jurisdiction based on any such claim prior to six (6) months after the filing of the written notice of claim hereinabove provided for, or later than one (1) year after such filing.... It is agreed that in any such action or suit, proof by you of your compliance with the provisions of this paragraph shall be a condition precedent to any recovery."

If, on April 25, Inman has not yet given Clyde Hall a written notice of his claim, can it successfully seek summary judgment?

MORIN BUILDING PRODUCTS CO. v. BAYSTONE CONSTRUCTION, INC.

United States Court of Appeals, Seventh Circuit, 1983.
717 F.2d 413.

POSNER, J. This appeal from a judgment for the plaintiff in a diversity suit requires us to interpret Indiana's common law of contracts. General Motors, which is not a party to this case, hired Baystone Construction, Inc., the defendant, to build an addition to a Chevrolet plant in Muncie, Indiana. Baystone hired Morin Building Products Company, the plaintiff, to supply and erect the aluminum walls for the addition. The contract required that the exterior siding of the walls be of "aluminum type 3003, not less than 18 B & S gauge, with a mill finish and stucco embossed surface texture to match finish and texture of existing metal siding." The contract also provided "that all work shall be done subject to the final approval of the Architect or Owner's [General Motors'] authorized agent, and his decision in matters relating to artistic effect shall be final, if within the terms of the Contract Documents"; and that "should any dispute arise as to the quality or fitness of materials or workmanship, the decision as to acceptability shall rest strictly with the Owner, based on the requirement that all work done or materials furnished shall be first class in every respect. What is usual or customary in erecting other buildings shall in no wise enter into any consideration or decision."

Morin put up the walls. But viewed in bright sunlight from an acute angle the exterior siding did not give the impression of having a uniform finish, and General Motors' representative rejected it. Baystone removed Morin's siding and hired another subcontractor to replace it. General Motors approved the replacement siding. Baystone refused to pay Morin the balance of the contract price ($23,000) and Morin brought this suit for the balance, and won.

The only issue on appeal is the correctness of a jury instruction which, after quoting the contractual provisions requiring that the owner (General Motors) be satisfied with the contractor's (Morin's) work, states: "Notwithstanding the apparent finality of the foregoing language, however, the general rule applying to satisfaction in the case of contracts for the construction of commercial buildings is that the satisfaction clause must be determined by objective criteria. Under this standard, the question is not whether the owner was satisfied in fact, but whether the owner, as a reasonable person, should have been satisfied with the materials and workmanship in question." There was much evidence that General Motors' rejection of Morin's exterior siding had been totally unreasonable. Not only was the lack of absolute uniformity in the finish of the walls a seemingly trivial defect given the strictly utilitarian purpose of the building that they enclosed, but it may have been inevitable; "mill finish sheet" is defined in the trade as "sheet having a nonuniform finish which may vary from sheet to sheet and within a sheet, and may not be entirely free from stains or oil." If the instruction was correct, so was the judgment. But if the instruction was incorrect—if the proper standard is not whether a reasonable man would have been satisfied with Morin's exterior siding but whether General Motors' authorized representative in fact was—then there must be a new trial to determine whether he really was dissatisfied, or whether he was not and the rejection therefore was in bad faith.

Some cases hold that if the contract provides that the seller's performance must be to the buyer's satisfaction, his rejection—however unreasonable—of the seller's performance is not a breach of the contract unless the rejection is in bad faith. See, e.g., *Stone Mountain Properties, Ltd. v. Helmer*, 139 Ga.App. 865, 869, 229 S.E.2d 779, 783 (1976). But most cases conform to the position stated in section 228 of the Restatement (Second) of Contracts (1979): if "it is practicable to determine whether a reasonable person in the position of the obligor would be satisfied, an interpretation is preferred under which the condition [that the obligor be satisfied with the obligee's performance] occurs if such a reasonable person in the position of the obligor would be satisfied." See Farnsworth, Contracts 556–59 (1982); Annot., 44 A.L.R.2d 1114, 1117, 1119–20 (1955). *Indiana Tri-City Plaza Bowl, Inc. v. Estate of Glueck*, 422 N.E.2d 670, 675 (Ind.App.1981), . . . adopts the majority position as the law of Indiana.

We do not understand the majority position to be paternalistic; and paternalism would be out of place in a case such as this, where the subcontractor is a substantial multistate enterprise. The requirement of reasonableness is read into a contract not to protect the weaker party but to approximate what the parties would have expressly provided with respect to a contingency that they did not foresee, if they had foreseen it. Therefore the requirement is not read into every contract, because it is not always a reliable guide to the parties' intentions. In particular, the presumption that the performing party would not have wanted to put himself at the mercy of the paying party's whim is overcome when the nature of the performance contracted for is such that there are no objective standards to guide the court. It cannot be assumed in such a case that the parties would have wanted a court to second-guess the buyer's rejection. So "the reasonable person standard is employed when the contract involves commercial quality, operative fitness, or mechanical utility which other knowledgeable persons can judge.... The standard of good faith is employed when the contract involves personal aesthetics or fancy." *Indiana Tri-City Plaza Bowl, Inc. v. Estate of Glueck*, supra, 422 N.E.2d at 675; see also *Action Engineering v. Martin Marietta Aluminum,* 670 F.2d 456, 460–61 (3d Cir. 1982).

We have to decide which category the contract between Baystone and Morin belongs in. The particular in which Morin's aluminum siding was found wanting was its appearance, which may seem quintessentially a matter of "personal aesthetics," or as the contract put it, "artistic effect." But it is easy to imagine situations where this would not be so Suppose the manager of a steel plant rejected a shipment of pig iron because he did not think the pigs had a pretty shape. The reasonable-man standard would be applied even if the contract had an "acceptability shall rest strictly with the Owner" clause, for it would be fantastic to think that the iron supplier would have subjected his contract rights to the whimsy of the buyer's agent. At the other extreme would be a contract to paint a portrait, the buyer having reserved the right to reject the portrait if it did not satisfy him. Such a buyer wants a portrait that will please him rather than a jury, even a jury of connoisseurs, so the only question would be his good faith in rejecting the portrait. *Gibson v. Cranage*, 39 Mich. 49 (1878).

This case is closer to the first example than to the second. The building for which the aluminum siding was intended was a factory—not usually intended to be a thing of beauty. That aesthetic considerations were decidedly secondary to considerations of function and cost is suggested by the fact that the contract specified mill-finish aluminum, which is unpainted. There is much debate in the record over whether it is even possible to ensure a uniform finish within and among sheets, but it is at least clear that mill finish usually is not uniform. If General Motors and Baystone had wanted a uniform finish they would in all likelihood have ordered a painted siding. Whether Morin's siding achieved a reasonable uniformity amounting to satisfactory commercial quality was susceptible of objective judgment; in the language of the Restatement, a reasonableness standard was "practicable."

But this means only that a requirement of reasonableness would be read into this contract if it contained a standard owner's satisfaction clause, which it did not; and since the ultimate touchstone of decision must be the intent of the parties to the contract we must consider the actual language they used. The contract refers explicitly to "artistic effect," a choice of words that may seem deliberately designed to put the contract in the "personal aesthetics" category whatever an outside observer might think. But the reference appears as number 17 in a list of conditions in a general purpose form contract. And the words "artistic effect" are immediately followed by the qualifying phrase, "if within the terms of the Contract Documents," which suggests that the "artistic effect" clause is limited to contracts in which artistic effect is one of the things the buyer is aiming for; it is not clear that he was here. The other

this risk of extending credit. But when they fail to do so, judges have long been willing to step in and impose constructive conditions of exchange. Not surprisingly, for simple transactions such as cash sales where two promised performances can be rendered simultaneously, these performances are also due simultaneously; see Restatement 2d § 234(1). In the language of conditions, each party's performance is impliedly conditional on at least the tender of the other party's performance. Compare UCC §§ 2–507(1) and 2–511(1).

More complex contracts—say, a contract to build a new City Hall—cause greater trouble. Here, Restatement 2d § 234(2) gives the traditional rule: "where the performance of only one party under such an exchange requires a period of time, his performance is due at an earlier time than that of the other party, unless the language or the circumstances indicate the contrary." Suppose a construction contract in which the parties agree that the contractor will build according to certain specifications, and the owner will pay $250,000. In the absence of contract provisions or other indications of party intent, can the contractor demand progress payments as the work advances? No; the owner's duty to pay is impliedly conditional on the contractor's completion of the project. An example of a case where a contractor got caught by this rule is *Stewart v. Newbury*, 220 N.Y. 379, 115 N.E. 984 (1917), in which a contract did not provide for progress payments. Stewart, the contractor, apparently believed that these payments were customary and so part of the contract; he demanded payment from Newbury and ceased work when Newbury refused to pay. The Court of Appeals of New York held for Newbury: "Where a contract is made to perform work and no agreement is made as to payment, the work must be substantially performed before payment can be demanded." Id. at 985.[2] Since, at least for large projects, contractors are certain to want progress payments in order to maintain liquidity, they have a strong incentive to bargain for such payments when the contract is negotiated.

Almost infinite permutation of these simple scenarios is possible; for instance, there are distinct rules for installment contracts, see Restatement 2d § 233 (2). But the underlying issue is always the same: if the parties have not expressly agreed, when should law impose conditions that, in effect, require one to extend credit to the other?

Material Breach. Rules on constructive conditions have important implications. As the introduction to this Chapter suggests, the nature and seriousness of a breach can have a variety of effects upon the obligation of the other party to perform. If the breach is small, the other party must perform and cannot suspend performance. Thus, if I am doing a $200,000 renovation to your fancy house in Bel–Air and I fail to put the correct hardware on one window out of 50, you can deduct the cost of fixing that window, but you cannot put off your next payment. If, on the other hand, my breach is larger (material), you have the right to

2. Although the case is still valid law, a court today might well take greater notice of Stewart's argument that progress payments were trade usage.

stop payment. For example, if seven windows are supposed to go on the east side of the house and I put them on the west side, certainly you could suspend payments until I correct the error. Finally, if that material default goes on too long, it can amount to total breach and give you a right to cancel the contract and sue for breach. Additionally, under § 253(2) of the Restatement, a repudiation of the contract discharges the other party's duty to perform and gives him a right to commence suit for breach of the entire contract. This section reads in full as follows: "Where performances are to be exchanged under an exchange of promises, one party's repudiation of a duty to render performance discharges the other party's remaining duties to render performance."

Now apply this rule to *Stewart v. Newbury*. When Stewart ceased work in the honest but erroneous belief that he was entitled to progress payments, there can be no real doubt that he committed a material breach entitling Newbury to cease all payment under the contract. It makes no difference that in Stewart's view it was Newbury that had committed the material breach, because Stewart, as a court later determined, was wrong. Lesson: Carry a big stick, all right, but whack with circumspection.

Our present concern is with the right of a party to stop performance or to cancel the contract upon the other party's breach, not with the question whether the aggrieved party can only sue for particular breaches that have occurred or for breach of the entire contract. Whether or not there is a repudiation or total breach as opposed to something less also answers the second question, but we do not deal with it here.

K & G CONSTRUCTION CO. v. HARRIS

Court of Appeals of Maryland, 1960.
164 A.2d 451, 223 Md. 305.

PRESCOTT, J. Feeling aggrieved by the action of the trial judge of the Circuit Court for Prince George's County, sitting without a jury, in finding a judgment against it in favor of a subcontractor, the appellant, the general contractor on a construction project, appealed.

The principal question presented is: Does a contractor, damaged by a subcontractor's failure to perform a portion of his work in a workmanlike manner, have a right, under the circumstances of this case, to withhold, in partial satisfaction of said damages, an installment payment, which, under the terms of the contract, was due the subcontractor, unless the negligent performance of his work excused its payment?

The appeal is presented on a case stated in accordance with Maryland Rule 826 g. The statement, in relevant part, is as follows:

> ... K & G Construction Company, Inc. (hereinafter called Contractor), plaintiff and counter-defendant in the Circuit Court and appellant herein, was owner and general contractor of a housing subdivision project being constructed (herein called Project). Harris and Brooks (hereinafter called Subcontractor), defendants and coun-

ter-plaintiffs in the Circuit Court and appellees herein, entered into a contract with Contractor to do excavating and earth-moving work on the Project. Pertinent parts of the contract are set forth below:

Section 3. The Subcontractor agrees to complete the several portions and the whole of the work herein sublet by the time or times following:

(a) Without delay, as called for by the Contractor.

(b) It is expressly agreed that time is of the essence of this contract, and that the Contractor will have the right to terminate this contract and employ a substitute to perform the work in the event of delay on the part of Subcontractor, and Subcontractor agrees to indemnify the Contractor for any loss sustained thereby, provided, however, that nothing in this paragraph shall be construed to deprive Contractor of any rights or remedies it would otherwise have as to damage for delay.

Section 4. (b) Progress payments will be made each month during the performance of the work. Subcontractor will submit to Contractor, by the 25th of each month, a requisition for work performed during the preceding month. Contractor will pay these requisitions, less a retainer equal to ten per cent (10%), by the 10th of the months in which such requisitions are received.

(c) No payments will be made under this contract until the insurance requirements of Sec. 9 hereof have been complied with.

Section 5. The Contractor agrees—(1) That no claim for services rendered or materials furnished by the Contractor to the Subcontractor shall be valid unless written notice thereof is given by the Contractor to the Subcontractor during the first ten days of the calendar month following that in which the claim originated.

Section 8. ... All work shall be performed in a workmanlike manner, and in accordance with the best practices.

Section 9. Subcontractor agrees to carry, during the progress of the work, * * * liability insurance against * * * property damage, in such amounts and with such companies as may be satisfactory to Contractor and shall provide Contractor with certificates showing the same to be in force.

While in the course of his employment by the Subcontractor on the Project, a bulldozer operator drove his machine too close to Contractor's house while grading the yard, causing the immediate collapse of a wall and other damage to the house. The resulting damage to contractor's house was $3,400. Subcontractor had complied with the insurance provision (Sec. 9) of the aforesaid contract. Subcontractor reported said damages to their liability insurance carrier. The Subcontractor and its insurance carrier refused to repair damage or compensate Contractor for damage to the house, claiming that there was no liability on the part of the Subcontractor.

Contractor gave no written notice to Subcontractor for any services rendered or materials furnished by the Contractor to the Subcontractor....

Contractor was generally satisfied with Subcontractor's work and progress as required under Sections 3 and 8 of the contract until September 12, 1958, with the exception of the bulldozer accident of August 9, 1958.

Subcontractor performed work under the contract during July, 1958, for which it submitted a requisition by the 25th of July, as required by the contract, for work done prior to the 25th of July, payable under the terms of the contract by Contractor on or before August 10, 1958. Contractor was current as to payments due under all preceding monthly requisitions from Subcontractor. The aforesaid bulldozer accident damaging Contractor's house occurred on August 9, 1958. Contractor refused to pay Subcontractor's requisition due on August 10, 1958, because the bulldozer damage to Contractor's house had not been repaired or paid for. Subcontractor continued to work on the project until the 12th of September, 1958, at which time they discontinued working on the project because of Contractor's refusal to pay the said work requisition and notified Contractor by registered letters of their position and willingness to return to the job, but only upon payment. At that time, September 12, 1958, the value of the work completed by Subcontractor on the project for which they had not been paid was $1,484.50.

Contractor later requested Subcontractor to return and complete work on the Project which Subcontractor refused to do because of nonpayment of work requisitions of July 25 and thereafter. Contractor's house was not repaired by Subcontractor nor compensation paid for the damage.

It was stipulated that Subcontractor had completed work on the Project under the contract for which they had not been paid in the amount of $1,484.50 and that if they had completed the remaining work to be done under the contract, they would have made a profit of $1,340.00 on the remaining uncompleted portion of the contract. It was further stipulated that it cost the Contractor $450.00 above the contract price to have another excavating contractor complete the remaining work required under the contract. It was the opinion of the Court that if judgment were in favor of the Subcontractor, it should be for the total amount of $2,824.50.

... Contractor filed suit against the Subcontractor in two counts: (1), for the aforesaid bulldozer damage to Contractor's house, alleging negligence of the Subcontractor's bulldozer operator, and (2) for the $450 costs above the contract price in having another excavating subcontractor complete the uncompleted work in the contract. Subcontractor filed a counter-claim for recovery of work of the value of $1,484.50 for which they had not received payment and for loss of anticipated profits on uncompleted portion of work in the amount of $1,340. By agreement of the parties, the first count of Contractor's claim, i.e., for aforesaid bulldozer damage to Contractor's house, was submitted to jury who found in favor of Contractor in the amount of $3,400. Following the finding by the jury, the second count of the Contractor's claim and the counter-claims of the Subcontractor, by agreement of the parties, were submitted to the Court for determination, without jury. All of the facts recited herein above were stipulated to by the parties to the Court. Circuit Court Judge Fletcher found for counter-plaintiff Subcontractor in the amount of $2,824.50 from which Contractor has entered this appeal.'

The $3,400 judgment has been paid.

It is immediately apparent that our decision turns upon the respective rights and liabilities of the parties under that portion of their contract whereby the subcontractor agreed to do the excavating and earth-moving work in "a workmanlike manner, and in accordance with the best practices," with time being of the essence of the contract, and the contractor agreed to make progress payments therefore on the 10th day of the months following the performance of the work by the subcontractor. The subcontractor contends, of course, that when the contractor failed to make the payment due on August 10, 1958, he breached his contract and thereby released him (the subcontractor) from any further obligation to perform. The contractor, on the other hand, argues that the failure of the subcontractor to perform his work in a workmanlike manner constituted a material breach of the contract, which justified his refusal to make the August 10 payment; and, as there was no breach on his part, the subcontractor had no right to cease performance on September 12, and his refusal to continue work on the project constituted another breach, which rendered him liable to the contractor for damages. The vital question, more tersely stated, remains: Did the contractor have a right, under the circumstances, to refuse to make the progress payment due on August 10, 1958?

The answer involves interesting and important principles of contract law. Promises and counter-promises made by the respective parties to a contract have certain relations to one another, which determine many of the rights and liabilities of the parties. Broadly speaking, they are (1) independent of each other, or (2) mutually dependent, one upon the other. They are independent of each other if the parties intend that *performance* by each of them is in no way conditioned upon *performance* by the other. 5 Page, The Law of Contracts, ¶ 2971. In other words, the parties exchange promises for promises, not the *performance* of promises for the *performance* of promises. 3 Williston, Contracts (Rev. Ed.), ¶ 813, n. 6. A failure to perform an independent promise does not excuse non-performance on the part of the adversary party, but each is required to perform his promise, and, if one does not perform, he is liable to the adversary party for such non-performance. (Of course, if litigation ensues questions of set-off or recoupment frequently arise.) Promises are mutually dependent if the parties intend *performance* by one to be conditioned upon *performance* by the other, and, if they be mutually dependent, they may be (a) precedent, i.e., a promise that is to be performed before a corresponding promise on the part of the adversary party is to be performed, (b) subsequent, i.e., a corresponding promise that is not to be performed until the other party has performed a precedent covenant, or (c) concurrent, i.e., promises that are to be performed at the same time by each of the parties, who are respectively bound to perform each. Page, op. cit., ¶ ¶ 2941, 2951, 2961.

Professor Page, op. cit., ¶ 2971, says there are three classes of independent promises left: (1) those in which the acts to be performed by the respective parties are, by the terms of the contract, to be performed at fixed times or on the happening of certain events which do not bear any relation to one another; (2) those in which the covenant in question is independent because it does not form the entire consideration for the covenants on the part of the adversary party, and ordinarily forms but a minor part of such consideration; and (3) those in which the contract shows that the parties intended performance of their respective promises without regard to performance on the part of the adversary, thus relying upon the promises and not the performances (Cf. *Brown v. Fraley,* 222 Md. 480, 161 A.2d 128).

In the early days, it was settled law that covenants and mutual promises in a contract were *prima facie* independent, and that they were to be so construed in the absence of language in the contract clearly showing that they were intended to be dependent. Williston, op. cit., ¶ 816; Page, op. cit., ¶ ¶ 2944, 2945. In the case of *Kingston v. Preston*, 2 Doug. 689, decided in 1774, Lord Mansfield, contrary to three centuries of opposing precedents, changed the rule, and decided that performance of one covenant might be dependent on prior performance of another, although the contract contained no express condition to that effect. Page, op. cit., ¶ 2946; Williston, op. cit., ¶ 817. The modern rule, which seems to be of almost universal application, is that there is a presumption that mutual promises in a contract are dependent and are to be so regarded, whenever possible. Page, op. cit., ¶ 2946; Restatement, Contracts, ¶ 266. Cf. Williston, op. cit., ¶ 812.

While the courts assume, in deciding the relation of one or more promises in a contract to one or more counter-promises, that the promises are dependent rather than independent, the intention of the parties, as shown by the entire contract as construed in the light of the circumstances of the case, the nature of the contract, the relation of the parties thereto, and the other evidence which is admissible to assist the court in determining the intention of the parties, is the controlling factor in deciding whether the promises and counter-promises are dependent or independent. Page, op. cit., ¶ 2948; Williston, op. cit., ¶ 824. *Pollak v. Brush Electric Ass'n*, 128 U.S. 446, 9 S.Ct. 119, 32 L.Ed. 474; *Bryne v. Dorey*, 221 Mass. 399, 109 N.E. 146; Rosenthal *Paper Co. v. National Folding Box & Paper Co.*, 226 N.Y. 313, 123 N.E. 766. Restatement, Contracts, ¶ ¶ 258, 261.

Considering the presumption that promises and counter-promises are dependent and the statement of the case, we have no hesitation in holding that the promise and counter-promise under consideration here were mutually dependent, that is to say, the parties intended performance by one to be conditioned on performance by the other; and the subcontractor's promise was, by the explicit wording of the contract, precedent to the promise of payment, monthly, by the contractor. In *Shapiro Engineering Corp. v. Francis O. Day Co.*, 215 Md. 373, 380, 137 A.2d 695, we stated that it is the general rule that where a total price for work is fixed by a contract, the work is not rendered divisible by progress payments. It would, indeed present an unusual situation if we were to hold that a building contractor, who has obtained someone to do work for him and has agreed to pay each month for the work performed in the previous month, has to continue the monthly payments, irrespective of the degree of skill and care displayed in the performance of work, and his only recourse is by way of suit for ill-performance. If this were the law, it is conceivable, in fact, probable, that many contractors would become insolvent before they were able to complete their contracts. As was stated by the Court in *Measures Brothers Ltd. v. Measures*, 2 Ch. 248: "Covenants are to be construed as dependent or independent according to the intention of the parties and the good sense of the case."

We hold that when the subcontractor's employee negligently damaged the contractor's wall, this constituted a breach of the subcontractor's promise to perform his work in a "workmanlike manner, and in accordance with the best practices." And there can be little doubt that the breach was material: the damage to the wall amounted to more than double the payment due on August 10. 3A Corbin, Contracts, § 708, says: "The failure of a contractor's [in our case, the subcontractor's] performance to constitute 'substantial' performance may justify the owner [in our case, the contractor] in refusing to make a progress payment . . . If the refusal to pay an installment is justified on the owner's [contractor's] part, the contractor [subcontractor] is not justified in abandoning work by reason of that refusal. His abandonment of the work will itself be a wrongful repudiation that goes to the essence, even if the defects in performance did not.' See also Restatement, Contracts, § 274; Professor Corbin, in § 954, states further: 'The unexcused failure of a contractor to render a promised performance when it is due is always a breach of contract. . . . Such failure may be of such great importance as to constitute what has been called herein a 'total' breach. . . . For a failure of performance constituting such a 'total' breach, an action for remedies that are appropriate thereto is at once maintainable. Yet the injured party is not required to bring such action. He has the option of treating the non-performance as a 'partial' breach only. . . ." In permitting the subcontractor to proceed with work on the project after August 9, the contractor, obviously, treated the breach by the subcontractor as a partial one. As the promises were mutually dependent and the subcontractor had made a material breach in his performance, this justified the contractor in refusing to make the August 10 payment; hence, as the contractor was not in default, the subcontractor again breached the contract when he, on September 12, discontinued work on the project, which rendered him liable (by the express terms of the contract) to the contractor for his increased cost in having the excavating done—a stipulated amount of $450.

The appellees suggest two minor points that may be disposed of rather summarily. They argue that the contractor "gave no written notice to subcontractor for any services rendered or materials furnished by the contractor to the subcontractor," in accordance with the terms of the contract. It is apparent that the contractor's claim against the subcontractor for ill-performance did not involve, in any way, "services rendered or materials furnished" by the contractor; hence, the argument has no substance. They also contend that the contractor had no right to refuse the August 10 payment, because the subcontractor had furnished the insurance against property damage, as called for in the contract. There is little, or no, merit in this suggestion. The subcontractor and his insurance company denied liability. The furnishing of the insurance by him did not constitute a license to perform his work in a careless, negligence, or unworkmanlike manner; and its acceptance by the contractor did not preclude his assertion of a claim for unworkmanlike performance directly against the subcontractor.

Judgment against the appellant reversed; and judgment entered in favor of the appellant against the appellees for $450, the appellees to pay the costs.

Notes and Discussion

1. **A Contract Collapses.** K & G was "generally satisfied" with the performance by Harris and Brooks until the bulldozer incident, which caused $3,400 damage. Neither Harris, Brooks nor their insurer thought that the subcontractor was liable for the damage. That is, they did not believe there had been a breach. Had they been right, how would the legal interpretation of subsequent events have differed?

After the incident, K & G immediately ceased making progress payments, obviously as a means to put pressure on Harris and Brooks to repair or pay for the damage. The subcontractor initially continued working, and K & G allowed this; why, do you think? Only a month later, evidently after not receiving the second payment, did the sub finally refuse further performance.

At what point was this contract finally at an end, so that the only thing remaining was to determine who owed what?

2. **Recognizing a Material Breach.** Unfortunately, the court does not indicate the size of the entire project. Damage of $3,400 might seem minor if the building had cost, say, $7 million; but much more significant if the entire project is worth $20,000. This does not mean that K & G was not in any case entitled to claim damages (probably measured as the cost to repair, no?); but the severity of the breach may be important in determining whether it could go further—in particular, by terminating the contract or by suspending its own performance until Harris and Brooks gave satisfaction.

Take a close look at Restatement 2d § 241, which lists five factors that are germane in determining whether a party's failure can be described as "material." Which of these factors seem especially germane in the present case? As Comment a observes, the "standard of materiality . . . is necessarily imprecise and flexible." This can make for considerable difficulty as parties try to figure out how to interpret one another's behavior.

3. Reacting to a Material Breach: The Possibility of Cure. As the Court says, "In permitting the subcontractor to proceed with work on the project after August 9, the contractor, obviously, treated the breach by the subcontractor as a partial one." That is, K & G suspended its own performance, while reserving the right (under Restatement 2d § 236(2)) to seek damages for the breach.

Could K & G have gone further? Now look at Restatement 2d § 242, which describes the "Circumstances Significant in Determining When Remaining Duties Are Discharged." Harris and Brooks's breach was material, we can assume, and it remained "uncured"; indeed, the subcontractor refused to accept responsibility for the breach. But it did not necessarily follow that K & G could end the contract. Especially important here is Comment a, which states: "[A] party's uncured material failure to perform or to offer to perform . . ., when it is too late for the performance or the offer to perform to occur, . . . also has the effect of discharging [the other party's] duties (§ 225(2)). Ordinarily there is some period of time between suspen-sion and discharge, and during this period a party may cure his failure." The victim of the material breach may go further and immediately end the contract only when "timely performance is so essential that any delay immediately results in discharge."

All of this should help make it much clearer why K & G behaved as it did after the bulldozer damaged the house; more was at stake than just simply hoping Harris and Brooks could be browbeaten into taking responsibility for the damage. The underlying principle is stated thus by Allan Farnsworth: "Even though a breach is serious enough to justify the injured party's suspending performance, the party in breach often can 'cure' the breach by correcting the deficiency in performance. . . . In such cases, courts have often been willing to allow the party in breach some period of time to cure its breach. It would therefore seem that if cure is possible, notice of suspension, and perhaps of the breach relied on to justify it, ought to be required if the party in breach would not otherwise be aware of them." E. Allan Farnsworth, Contracts § 8.17 at 569 (4th student ed. 2004) (footnotes omitted). See also especially UCC § 2–508.

4. The Language of Conditions. Take a second look at the middle of the opinion, the three paragraphs starting with "The answer involves interesting and important principles of contract law." Here the Court attempts to restate the basic legal situation in the language of conditions. The most important point to draw from these paragraphs is that, for contracts involving an exchange of promises, independent promises are rare. The consequence of this judicial construction of conditions is the all-important rule in Restatement 2d § 237.

TAYLOR v. JOHNSTON

Supreme Court of California, 1975.
15 Cal.3d 130, 123 Cal.Rptr. 641, 539 P.2d 425.

SULLIVAN, J. In this action for damages for breach of contract defendants Elizabeth and Ellwood Johnston, individually and as copartners doing business as Old English Rancho, appeal from a judgment entered after a nonjury trial in favor of plaintiff H. B. Taylor and against them in the amount of $132,778.05 and costs.

Plaintiff was engaged in the business of owning, breeding, raising and racing thoroughbred horses in Los Angeles County. Defendants were engaged in a similar business, and operated a horse farm in Ontario, California, where they furnished stallion stud services. In January 1965 plaintiff sought to breed his two thoroughbred mares, Sunday Slippers and Sandy Fork to defendants' stallion Fleet Nasrullah. To that end, on January 19 plaintiff and defendants entered into two separate written contracts—one pertaining to Sunday Slippers and the other to Sandy Fork. Except for the mare involved the contracts were identical. We set forth in the margin the contract covering Sunday Slippers.[3]

The contract provided that Fleet Nasrullah was to perform breeding services upon the respective mares in the year 1966 for a fee of $3,500, payable on or before September 1, 1966. If the stud fee was paid in full and the mares failed to produce a live foal (one that stands and nurses without assistance) from the breeding a return breeding would be provided the following year without additional fee.

On October 4, 1965, defendants sold Fleet Nasrullah to Dr. A.G. Pessin and Leslie Combs II for $1,000,000 cash and shipped the stallion to Kentucky. Subsequently Combs and Pessin syndicated the sire by selling various individuals 36 or 38 shares, each share entitling the

3. "Original

Important Please Sign Original and Return As Quickly As Possible Retaining Duplicate For Your Own File.

January 8, 1965

"Old English Rancho

Route 1, Box 224-A

Ontario, California 91761

"Gentlemen:

"I hereby confirm my reservation for one services to the stallion Fleet Nasrullah for the year 1966.

"TERMS: $3,500.00—Guarantee Live Foal.

"FEE is due and payable on or before Sept. 1, 1966.

"If stud fee is paid in full, and mare fails to produce a live foal (one that stands and nurses without assistance) from this breeding, a return breeding the following year to said mare will be granted at no additional stallion fee.

"Fee is due and payable prior to sale of mare or prior to her departure from the state. If mare is sold or leaves the state, no return breeding will be granted.

"Stud Certificate to be given in exchange for fees paid.

"Veterinarian Certificate due in lieu of payment if mare is barren.

"I hereby agree that Old English Rancho shall in no way be held responsible for accidents of any kind or disease.

Mr. H. B. Taylor 112 North Evergreen Street Burbank, California 91505

"Mare: Sunday Slippers Roan filly 1959 Moolah Bux-Maoli-Ormesby" (Veterinary certificate must accompany all barren mares.) "Stakes winner of $64,000.00 last raced in 1962 /s/ H. B. Taylor"

holder to breed one mare each season to Fleet Nasrullah. Combs and Pessin each reserved three shares.

On the same day defendants wrote to plaintiff advising the latter of the sale and that he was "released" from his "reservations" for Fleet Nasrullah.[4] Unable to reach defendants by telephone, plaintiff had his attorney write to them on October 8, 1965, insisting on performance of the contracts. Receiving no answer, plaintiff's attorney on October 19 wrote a second letter threatening suit. On October 27, defendants advised plaintiff by letter that arrangements had been made to breed the two mares to Fleet Nasrullah in Kentucky[5]. However, plaintiff later learned that the mares could not be boarded at Spendthrift Farm where Fleet Nasrullah was standing stud and accordingly arranged with Clinton Frazier of Elmhurst Farm to board the mares and take care of the breeding.

In January 1966 plaintiff shipped Sunday Slippers and Sandy Fork to Elmhurst Farm. At that time, however, both mares were in foal and could not be bred, since this can occur only during the five-day period in which they are in heat. The first heat period normally occurs nine days (and the second heat period thirty days) after foaling. Succeeding heat periods occur every 21 days.

On April 17, 1966, Sunday Slippers foaled and Frazier immediately notified Dr. Pessin. The latter assured Frazier that he would make the necessary arrangements to breed the mare to Fleet Nasrullah. On April 26, the ninth day after the foaling, Frazier, upon further inquiry, was told by Dr. Pessin to contact Mrs. Judy who had charge of booking the breedings and had handled these matters with Frazier in the past. Mrs. Judy, however, informed Frazier that the stallion was booked for that day but would be available on any day not booked by a shareholder. She indicated that she was acting under instructions but suggested that he keep in touch with her while the mare was in heat.

Sunday Slippers came into heat again on May 13, 1966. Frazier telephoned Mrs. Judy and attempted to book the breeding for May 16.[6] She informed him that Fleet Nasrullah had been reserved by one of the shareholders for that day, but that Frazier should keep in touch with her in the event the reservation was cancelled. On May 14 and May 15 Frazier tried again but without success; on the latter date, Sunday Slippers went out of heat.

4. Defendants' letter stated in part: "We wish to inform you that Fleet Nasrullah has been sold and will stand the 1966 season in Kentucky. You are, therefore, released from your reservations made to the stallion."

5. Defendants' letter stated in part: "Mr. Johnston has made arrangements for you to breed Sandy Fork ... and Sunday Slippers ... to Fleet Nasrullah for the 1966 season. Therefore, you should communicate with Dr. A. G. Pessin of Spendthrift Farm, Lexington, Kentucky, to finalize breeding arrangements...."

6. Frazier did not seek to breed Sunday Slippers on May 13, 1966, because the mare's follicle had not yet ruptured; conception can occur up to 12 hours after rupture of the follicle. Accordingly, Frazier normally tried to book a breeding for three days after the onset of heat.

On June 4, the mare went into heat again. Frazier again tried to book a reservation with Fleet Nasrullah but was told that all dates during the heat period had been already booked. He made no further efforts but on June 7, on plaintiff's instructions, bred Sunday Slippers to a Kentucky Derby winner named Chateaugay for a stud fee of $10,000.

Sandy Fork, plaintiff's other mare awaiting the stud services of Fleet Nasrullah, foaled on June 5, 1966. Frazier telephoned Mrs. Judy the next day and received a booking to breed the mare on June 14, the ninth day after foaling. On June 13, 1966, however, she cancelled the reservation because of the prior claim of a shareholder. Frazier made no further attempts and on June 14 bred Sandy Fork to Chateaugay.

Shortly after their breeding, it was discovered that both mares were pregnant with twins. In thoroughbred racing twins are considered undesirable since they endanger the mare and are themselves seldom valuable for racing. Both mares were therefore aborted. However, plaintiff was not required to pay the $20,000 stud fees for Chateaugay's services because neither mare delivered a live foal.

The instant action for breach of contract proceeded to trial on plaintiff's fourth amended complaint, which alleged two causes of action, the first for breach of the two written contracts, the second for breach of an oral agreement. Defendants' cross-complained for the stud fees. The court found the facts to be substantially as stated above and further found and concluded that by selling Fleet Nasrullah defendants had "put it out of their power to perform properly their contracts," that the conduct of defendants and their agents Dr. Pessin and Mrs. Judy up to and including June 13, 1966, constituted a breach[7] and plaintiff "was then justified in treating it as a breach and repudiation of their contractual obligations to him," and that defendants unjustifiably breached the contracts but plaintiff did not.[8] The court awarded plaintiff damages for defendants' breach in the sum of $103,122.50 ($99,800 net damage directly sustained plus $3,322.50 for reasonable costs and expenses for mitigation of damages). "Because of defendants' wholly unwarranted, high-handed, and oppressive breach of their contractual obligation to plaintiff, the plaintiff is entitled to recover from the defendants pre-

7. We set forth the significant paragraph of the findings at length: "When defendants sold Fleet Nasrullah in 1965 to a purchaser who shipped him to Kentucky, defendants put it out of their power to perform properly their contracts with plaintiff. Those contracts did not require that plaintiff's rights to the breeding services of Fleet Nasrullah should be relegated to a secondary or subordinate position to that of any other person, whether he be a holder of shares in the stallion or not. No such conditions were stated in the contracts and none can be inferred therefrom. From the conduct of the defendants, their agent Dr. Pessin, and their subagent Mrs. Judy, plaintiff was justified in concluding that the defendants were just giving him the runaround and had no intention of performing their contract in the manner required by its terms and as required by the covenant of good faith and fair dealing. Their conduct and that of their agent Dr. Pessin, and their subagent Mrs. Judy up to and including June 13, 1966 constituted a breach of defendants' breeding contracts with plaintiff (plaintiff's Exhibits 8, 9 and 10) and plaintiff was then justified in treating it as a breach and repudiation of their contractual obligation to him."

8. The court concluded that "The defendants unjustifiably breached these contracts; the plaintiff did not breach these contracts.

judgment interest at the rate of 7% per annum on the sum of $99,800 from August 1, 1968. . . ." It was concluded that defendants should take nothing on their cross-complaint. Judgment was entered accordingly. This appeal followed.

Defendants' main attack on the judgment is two-pronged. They contend: first, that they did not at any time repudiate the contracts; and second, that they did not otherwise breach the contracts because performance was made impossible by plaintiff's own actions. To put it another way, defendants argue in effect that the finding that they breached the contracts is without any support in the evidence. Essentially they take the position that on the uncontradicted evidence in the record, as a matter of law there was neither anticipatory nor actual breach. As will appear, we conclude that the trial court's decision was based solely on findings of anticipatory breach and that we must determine whether such decision is supported by the evidence.

Nevertheless both aspects of defendants' argument require us at the outset to examine the specifications for performance contained in the contracts. . . . We note that the reservation for "one services" for Fleet Nasrullah was "for the year 1966." As the evidence showed, a breeding is biologically possible throughout the calendar year, since mares regularly come into heat every 21 days, unless they are pregnant. The contracts therefore appear to contemplate breeding with Fleet Nasrullah at any time during the calendar year 1966. The trial court made no finding as to the time of performance called for by the contracts.[9] There was testimony to the effect that by custom in the thoroughbred racing business the breeding is consummated in a "breeding season" which normally extends from January until early July, although some breeding continues through August. It is possible that the parties intended that the mares be bred to Fleet Nasrullah during the 1966 breeding season rather than the calendar year 1966.[10]

However, in our view, it is immaterial whether the contract phrase "for the year 1966" is taken to mean the above breeding season or the full calendar year since in either event the contract period had not expired by June 7 and June 14, 1966, the dates on which Sunday Slippers and Sandy Fork respectively were bred to Chateaugay[11] and by which time, according to the findings (see fn. 5, *ante*) defendants had repudiated the contracts. There can be no *actual* breach of a contract until the time specified therein for performance has arrived. See Rest. 2d Contracts (Tent. Draft No. 8, 1973) § 260. Although there may be a

9. The trial court was not compelled to specify the exact time for performance because it concluded that defendants had breached the contracts by anticipatory repudiation, i.e., a breach which occurs prior to the time for performance.

10. Perhaps the fact that the stud fees were due to be paid September 1, 1966, at the close of the breeding season supports such a conclusion. Moreover, defendants concede without argument that the trial court impliedly found the time of performance to be the breeding season.

11. Both Sunday Slippers and Sandy Fork would have had at least one more heat during the 1966 breeding season—that of Sunday Slippers commencing on June 26, 1966, and that of Sandy Fork commencing on July 7, 1966.

breach by anticipatory repudiation: "[by] its very name an essential element of a true anticipatory breach of a contract is that the repudiation by the promisor occur before his performance is due under the contract." (*Gold Min. & Water Co. v. Swinerton, supra*, 23 Cal.2d at p. 29.)

In the instant case, because under either of the above interpretations the time for performance had not yet arrived, defendants' breach as found by the trial court was of necessity an anticipatory breach and must be analyzed in accordance with the principles governing such type of breach. To these principles we now direct our attention.

Anticipatory breach occurs when one of the parties to a bilateral contract repudiates the contract. The repudiation may be express or implied. An express repudiation is a clear, positive, unequivocal refusal to perform; an implied repudiation results from conduct where the promisor puts it out of his power to perform so as to make substantial performance of his promise impossible (*Zogarts* v. *Smith* (1948) 86 Cal.App.2d 165 [194 P.2d 143]; 1 Witkin, Summary of Cal. Law (8th ed.) § 632, pp. 538–39; 4 Corbin, Contracts (1951) § 984, pp. 949–51).

When a promisor repudiates a contract, the injured party faces an election of remedies: he can treat the repudiation as an anticipatory breach and immediately seek damages for breach of contract, thereby terminating the contractual relation between the parties, or he can treat the repudiation as an empty threat, wait until the time for performance arrives and exercise his remedies for actual breach if a breach does in fact occur at such time. (*Guerrieri* v. *Severini, supra*, 51 Cal.2d 12, 18–19.) However, if the injured party disregards the repudiation and treats the contract as still in force, and the repudiation is retracted prior to the time of performance, then the repudiation is nullified and the injured party is left with his remedies, if any, invocable at the time of performance.

As we have pointed out, the trial court found that the whole course of conduct of defendants and their agents Dr. Pessin and Mrs. Judy from the time of the sale of Fleet Nasrullah up to and including June 13, 1966, amounted to a repudiation which plaintiff was justified in treating as an anticipatory breach.... However, when the principles of law governing repudiation just described are applied to the facts constituting this course of conduct as found by the trial court, it is manifest that such conduct cannot be treated as an undifferentiated continuum amounting to a single repudiation but must be divided into two separate repudiations.

First, defendants clearly repudiated the contracts when, after selling Fleet Nasrullah and shipping him to Kentucky, they informed plaintiff "[you] are, therefore, released from your reservations made to the stallion." However, the trial court additionally found that "[plaintiff] did not wish to be 'released' from his 'reservations' ... [insisted] on performance of the stud service agreements ... [and] [threatened] litigation if the contracts were not honored by defendants...." Accordingly defendants arranged for performance of the contracts by making Fleet Nasrullah available for stud service to plaintiff in Kentucky through their agents Dr. Pessin and Mrs. Judy. Plaintiff elected to treat the contracts as in force and shipped the mares to Kentucky to effect the desired performance. The foregoing facts lead us to conclude that the subsequent arrangements by defendants to make Fleet Nasrullah available to service plaintiff's mares in Kentucky constituted a retraction of the repudiation. Since at this time plaintiff had not elected to treat the repudiation as an anticipatory breach[12] and in fact had shipped the mares to Kentucky in reliance on defendants' arrangements, this retraction nullified the repudiation. Thus, plaintiff was then left with his remedies that might arise at the time of performance.

The trial court found that after the mares had arrived in Kentucky, had delivered the foals they were then carrying and were ready for servicing by Fleet Nasrullah, plaintiff was justified in concluding from the conduct of defendants, their agent Dr. Pessin, and their subagent Mrs. Judy, that "defendants were just giving him the runaround and had no intention of performing their contract in the manner required by its terms" and in treating such conduct "as a breach and repudiation of their contractual obligation to him." . . . Since, as we have explained, defendants retracted their original repudiation, this subsequent conduct amounts to a finding of a second repudiation.

There is no evidence in the record that defendants or their agents Dr. Pessin and Mrs. Judy ever stated that Sunday Slippers and Sandy Fork would not be serviced by Fleet Nasrullah during the 1966 breeding season or that they ever refused to perform. Frazier, plaintiff's agent who made arrangements for the breeding of the mares admitted that they had never made such a statement to him.[13] Accordingly, there was no *express* repudiation or unequivocal refusal to perform. (*Guerrieri* v. *Severini, supra,* 51 Cal.2d 12, 18; *Atkinson* v. *District Bond Co., supra,* 5 Cal.App.2d 738, 743–744.)

The trial court's finding of repudiation, expressly based on the "conduct of the defendants" and their agents suggests that the court found an implied repudiation. However, there is no implied repudiation, i.e., by conduct equivalent to unequivocal refusal to perform, unless "the promisor *puts it out of his power to perform.*" (*Zogarts* v. *Smith, supra,* 86 Cal.App.2d 165, 172–173; 1 Witkin, Summary of Cal. Law (8th ed.) § 632, p. 538; 4 Corbin, Contracts, *supra,* § 984, pp. 949–951; Rest. 2d Contracts (Tent. Draft No. 8, 1973) §§ 268, 274.) Once the mares arrived in Kentucky, defendants had the power to perform the contracts; Fleet Nasrullah could breed with the mares. No subsequent conduct occurred to render this performance impossible. Although plaintiff was subordinated to the shareholders with respect to the priority of reserving a

12. Plaintiff concedes that the repudiation was not "accepted by plaintiff."

13. "Q. . . . At any time, did Mrs. Judy or anyone else ever tell you that she could not or would not breed either mare to Fleet Nasrullah before the end of 1966? . . .

"The Witness: No."

breeding time with Fleet Nasrullah, there is no evidence in the record that this subordination of reservation rights rendered performance impossible. Rather it acted to postpone the time of performance, which still remained within the limits prescribed by the contracts. It rendered performance more difficult to achieve; it may even have cast doubt upon the eventual accomplishment of performance; it did not render performance impossible.[14]

Because there was no repudiation, express or implied, there was no anticipatory breach. Plaintiff contends that defendants' conduct, as found by the trial court, indicated that "defendants were just giving him the runaround and had no intention of performing their contract" and therefore that this conduct was the equivalent of an express and unequivocal refusal to perform. Plaintiff has not presented to the court any authority in California in support of his proposition that conduct which has not met the test for an implied repudiation, i.e. conduct which removed the power to perform, may nonetheless be held to amount to the equivalent of an express repudiation and thus constitute an anticipatory breach. Without addressing ourselves to the question whether some conduct could ever be found equal to an express repudiation, we hold that defendants' conduct in this case as a matter of law did not constitute an anticipatory breach.

To constitute an express repudiation, the promisor's statement, or in this case conduct, must amount to an unequivocal refusal to perform: "A mere declaration, however, of a party of an intention not to be bound will not of itself amount to a breach, so as to create an effectual renunciation of the contract; for one party cannot by any act or declaration destroy the binding force and efficacy of the contract. To justify the adverse party in treating the renunciation as a breach, the refusal to perform must be of the whole contract ... and must be distinct, unequivocal and absolute." (*Atkinson v. District Bond Co.*, supra, 5 Cal.App.2d 738, 743.)

To recapitulate, Sandy Fork was in foal in January 1966, the commencement of the 1966 breeding season, and remained so until June 5, 1966. Throughout this period Fleet Nasrullah could not perform his services as contracted due solely to the conduct of plaintiff in breeding Sandy Fork in 1965. Biologically the first opportunity to breed Sandy Fork was on June 14, 1966, nine days after foaling. Frazier telephoned Mrs. Judy on June 6, 1966, and received a booking with Fleet Nasrullah

14. Plaintiff suggests that this conduct, namely delaying plaintiff's breeding until a day not reserved by a shareholder, amounted to an anticipatory breach because Mrs. Judy inserted a condition to defendants' performance, which as the trial court found was not contemplated by the contracts. Assuming *arguendo* that this conduct might have amounted to a breach of contract by improperly delaying performance, at most it would have constituted only a partial breach—insufficiently material to terminate the contracts (see Rest. 2d Contracts (Tent. Draft No. 8, 1973) §§ 262, 266, 268, 274). It did not constitute a repudiation of the contracts which was the sole basis of the trial court's decision since "[to] justify the adverse party in treating the renunciation as a breach, the refusal to perform must be of the whole contract or of a covenant going to the whole consideration...." (*Atkinson* v. *District Bond Co.*, supra, 5 Cal.App.2d 738, 743.)

for June 14, 1966. On June 13 Mrs. Judy telephoned Frazier and informed him she would have to cancel Sandy Fork's reservation for the following day because one of the shareholders insisted on using that day. Mrs. Judy gave no indication whatsoever that she could not or would not breed Sandy Fork on any of the following days in that heat period or subsequent heat periods. Frazier made no further attempts to breed Sandy Fork with Fleet Nasrullah. Thus, plaintiff, who delayed the possibility of performance for five months, asserts that the delay of performance occasioned by defendants' cancellation of a reservation on the first day during the six-month period that plaintiff made performance possible amounts to an unequivocal refusal to perform, even though there was adequate opportunity for Fleet Nasrullah to perform within the period for performance specified in the contract and even though defendants never stated any intention not to perform. We conclude that as a matter of law this conduct did not amount to an unequivocal refusal to perform and therefore did not constitute an anticipatory breach of the contract covering Sandy Fork.

Sunday Slippers foaled on April 17, 1966, first came into heat on April 26 and then successively on May 13 and June 4, 1966. Mrs. Judy informed Frazier that she would breed Sunday Slippers on any day that one of the shareholders did not want to use the stallion. Frazier unsuccessfully sought to breed the mare on April 26, May 14, May 15 and June 4, 1966, Fleet Nasrullah being reserved on those dates. Mrs. Judy continued to assure Frazier that the breeding would occur. Sunday Slippers was due to come into heat again twice during the breeding season: June 25 and July 16, 1966. At most this conduct amounts to delay of performance and a warning that performance might altogether be precluded if a shareholder were to desire Fleet Nasrullah's services on all the remaining days within the period specified for performance in which Sunday Slippers was in heat. We conclude that as a matter of law this conduct did not amount to an unequivocal refusal to perform and therefore did not constitute an anticipatory breach of the contract covering Sunday Slippers.

In sum, we hold that there is no evidence in the record supportive of the trial court's finding and conclusion that defendants repudiated and therefore committed an anticipatory breach of the contracts.

In view of the foregoing conclusion we need not consider defendants' remaining contentions.

The judgment is reversed.

Notes and Discussion

1. Anticipatory Breach. On April 12, 1852, De La Tour arranged with Hochster to serve as his courier during a three-month tour of Continental Europe; the tour was to last from June 1 to the end of August. On May 11, De La Tour informed Hochster that the trip was off. Hochster then arranged for another client on equally good terms, but that engagement was not to start until July 4. On May 22—still before the start of his contract with De La Tour—Hochster also sued De La Tour for damages. *Hochster v. De La Tour*, 118 Eng. Rep. 922 (Q.B. 1853).

As you should be able to see, this case presents a number of issues. One is this: If the time for performance on either side is not yet due, can Hochster take De La Tour's repudiation (as we would call it) as final, rather than waiting until June 1 in the hope that De La Tour might still change his mind? The English court held that he could. De La Tour had committed an anticipatory breach of contract. As the Court observes, "But it is surely much more rational, and more for the benefit of both parties, that, after the renunciation of the agreement by the defendant, the plaintiff should be at liberty to consider himself absolved from any future performance of it, retaining his right to sue for any damage he has suffered from the breach of it. Thus, instead of remaining idle and laying out money in preparations which must be useless, he is at liberty to seek service under another employer, which would go in mitigation of the damages to which he would otherwise be entitled for a breach of the contract." Id. at 926. Note how the rule as to anticipatory repudiation links up with the mitigation principle we examined in Chapter 6.B.

The modern form of the rule is Restatement 2d § 250, which defines a repudiation as either "(a) a statement by the obligor to the obligee indicating that the obligor will commit a breach that would of itself give the obligee a claim for damages for total breach under § 243, or (b) a voluntary affirmative act which renders the obligor unable or apparently unable to perform without such a breach." Is this test objective: that a reasonable person would understand the other party as repudiating? Examine how the definition plays out in *Taylor v. Johnston*.

One problem that often arises is that a statement or act may not be a sufficiently definitive repudiation; the standard for a statement, for instance, is not whether the obligor "may commit" a breach, but that it "will commit a breach." What if you receive such a statement and are uncertain?

A second problem is whether the recipient of an anticipatory repudiation is obliged to consider it a final breach. In this case, plaintiffs continued to insist on performance. Can they continue to do so even when it becomes unreasonable? In any case, a party can retract if the other party has not yet relied upon it or given notice that it considers the repudiation to be final: Restatement 2d § 256. For this reason, the aggrieved party is well advised to notify the other that the repudiation is final.

2. Weasels. The world is sparsely populated with forthright repudiators; it is filled with weasels. We suspect that many long term contracts suffer from the kind of malaise that infected the contract in *Taylor v. Johnston*. In these contracts one party repeatedly fails to perform in a timely way but offers continued assurances about future performance and repeated excuses about past failures. It is possible, as the court found in *Taylor v. Johnston*, that the person who is making excuses has good reason and is not engaging in intentional delay or obfuscation.

Stalling behavior by one who is not eager to perform a contract (where, for example, the price has turned against him) or who is incapable of doing so (for want of money or, as in Taylor, because he promised too much to too many) presents two recurring legal issues. First is the question whether the other party to the contract may at least cease performance or, better, cancel the contract. If the other party's failure constitutes merely justifiable delay, the first party's cancellation may be a repudiation.

The second problem is to determine a time when the plaintiff's damages will be measured. If, for example, a seller of nuclear fuel, who has a contract to sell at $7/pound when the market has risen to nearly $40/pound, hems and haws for 18 months, and if, in retrospect, the breach occurred 12 months prior to the time that the potential buyer thought it had occurred, how does that person measure its damages? Assume a rising market for nuclear fuel over an 18 month period; assume further that throughout that period the seller does not perform but gives continued oral assurances that he will. If three years later the court determines that the breach occurred in the second of the 18 months at a time when the market price for the nuclear fuel was $20, the buyer must measure his damages at the time of repudiation (or repudiation plus a reasonable time), yet he may have to cover at $40/pound. Most of the decisions under 2–713 and the language of the amended statute choose the time of repudiation or a time shortly after that even when it might not have been obvious to the plaintiff when the repudiation had occurred.

To some extent these issues are solved by § 2–609 of the UCC and by the analogous § 251 of the Second Restatement. The next case and the problems that follow it show that those sections are merely palliatives not cures.

KOCH MATERIALS CO. v. SHORE SLURRY SEAL, INC.

United States District Court, District of New Jersey, 2002.
205 F.Supp.2d 324.

ORLOFSKY, J.

I. Introduction

A good relationship is built on good communication. As this case proves, that aphorism is no less true of long-term business dealings than it is of marriages. One of the Defendants, Shore Slurry Seal, Inc. ("Shore"), a construction company, entered into a long-term exclusive requirements contract with the Plaintiff, Koch Materials Company ("Koch"). Midway through the term of the contract, Shore informed the Plaintiff, in rather uncertain terms, that it planned to sell most or all of its assets to the second Defendant, Asphalt Paving Systems, Inc. ("Asphalt") which is now also in the construction business. Koch, through its attorney, sought assurances that any successor would be willing and able to continue the original deal. Apparently unhappy about dealing through attorneys, rather than as businessmen, Shore's response was to refuse to give any meaningful information about the sale.

The law of contract, however, is designed to increase certainty in our dealings with one another. Otherwise, few reasonable businesses would be willing to invest in long-term cooperative agreements which, by virtue of the deal-specific investment, expose each party to significant risks of hold-up by the other. Thus, when one's contractual partner has reasonable grounds to fear that the contract will not be performed, one must answer those fears at the risk of giving the counterparty license to terminate the contract. Nor does the law, understandably, contemplate "I don't like lawyers" as an excuse for refusing to give such vital assurances.

Thus, for the reasons set forth here, and in more detail throughout the Opinion to follow, I must grant the Motion of the Plaintiff for Summary Judgment, authorizing Plaintiff to treat Shore's silence as a repudiation of the contract. I also grant much of the Plaintiff's Motion for Summary Judgment on the question of remedies, concluding that the contracts between the Plaintiff and Shore permit the Plaintiff to terminate and seek such damages as are authorized by the UCC and the common law. With respect to Asphalt, Shore's putative successor, I find disputed questions of material fact related to the question whether or not Asphalt is, in fact, a successor, and therefore deny the Cross-Motions for Summary Judgment by both sides.

II. Facts And Procedural History

Koch Materials Company, the Plaintiff in this case, is a manufacturer of asphalt and other road surfacing materials. In February of 1998, Koch bought from the Defendant, Shore Slurry Seal, Inc., an asphalt plant in New Jersey, as well as the domestic license rights to a specialty road surfacing substance, known as "Novachip." Koch's purchase price was five million dollars, payable in three installments. The last and smallest of these installments, in the amount of $500,000, is not due until 2004.

As part of the sale, Shore entered into two side contracts with Koch. First, Shore and Koch signed an Exclusive Supply Agreement, under which Shore agreed that for the seven years following the sale it would purchase all of its asphalt requirements from Koch, and in any event at least two million gallons of asphalt per year. The Agreement provided that, in the event Shore purchased less than six million gallons over the last three years of the contract, the $500,000 installment payment would be reduced by the same percentage by which Shore missed the six million gallon mark. Second, Shore promised to utilize at least 2.5 million square yards of Novachip annually, either in its own business or through sublicense agreements in certain permitted regions, and to pay royalties to Koch accordingly.

For the first three years of the contract, Shore met or exceeded its two million gallon minimum under the Exclusive Supply contract, but sold somewhat less than the 7.5 million square yards of Novachip the Sublicense Agreement called for. As the contracts provided, the parties adjusted the third-year installment payment to account for the shortfall.

On March 16, 2001, Robert Capoferri ("Capoferri"), the President and sole shareholder of Shore, sent a letter to Koch's general manager. The letter provided in relevant part that: "I have decided to retire from the road construction business....

"The attorney for the buyer purchasing my assets has been in contact with our legal counsel, and they are close to having drafts prepared for the proposed purchase agreement. In addition to the sale of all balance sheet assets, it is also intended that 100% of any and all existing Shore Slurry Seal, Inc. contracts will be assigned and/or sold to the prospective buyer. Given that the Nova Chip Sublicense Agreement is not part of this proposed asset sale, Shore Slurry Seal, Inc. will continue to exist beyond the closing date in order to primarily collect and remit Nova Chip royalties on behalf of Koch Pavement Solutions." Pl.'s R. 56.1 Statement Exh. E.

Capoferri sent a courtesy copy of the letter to his attorney. Koch responded on April 3, 2001, with a letter from its attorney to the attorney for Shore. After referencing the Capoferri letter, Koch's missive stated:

> "We have concerns about the sale because, during the next four years, Koch is owed a substantial amount of money from Shore under the February, 1998, Sale and Purchase Agreement, namely under the two schedules providing for exclusive supply and for Novachip royalties. In particular, we are concerned as to Shore's continued capacity to live up to its two million gallon per year commitment to buy asphalt emulsions and cutbacks and to meet its minimum square yardage requirements for Novachip.
>
> "Mr. Capoferri's secrecy surrounding Shore's negotiations and the terms and conditions of sale are adding to our discomfort. We do not know the prospective purchaser, the closing date or what, if any, arrangements have been made to provide for an assignment of Shore's obligations to the new purchaser. Further, we have no indication that Shore is providing, or is willing to provide any type of security to satisfy its obligations to Koch. To date we know only that the sign in front of Shore's current offices has been changed to read 'Asphalt Paving Systems' and that several company vehicles are now bearing this new moniker....
>
> "Of course, once Shore has provided Koch with adequate assurance of performance of its obligations to Koch the process which we began with this letter can be terminated." Id. Exh. F.

Shore's answer, on April 6, 2001, was again a letter from Capoferri to Koch's general manager. Capoferri noted that he had conferred with his attorney, and argued that: "There has not been a failure to pay amounts due or to comply with requirements under any of the agreements we have with Koch. Nothing in any of the agreements drafted by Koch prohibit me from retiring business, nor do they require me to provide any type of security, collateral, or personal guarantee of payments similar to those we imposed upon our Nova Chip sublicensees.

Regarding the assertion of secrecy contained in Mr. Hull's letter of April 3, 2001, I am not aware of provisions within our agreements requiring me to notify Koch of any business negotiations that I may be involved in." Id. Exh. G.

Finding little comfort in Shore's response, Koch filed a Complaint in this Court seeking recognition of their right to treat Shore's failure to give adequate assurances as a repudiation of the contract, pursuant to New Jersey's Uniform Commercial Code, N.J. Stat. Ann. § 12A:2–609(1) (1962), and the common law of contracts. Koch's Complaint also alleged breach of the Exclusive Supply and Novachip Sublicense Agreements due to Shore's bad faith. On October 30, 2001, Koch amended its Complaint to add as a party a possible successor of Shore, Asphalt Paving Systems, Inc. ('Asphalt'). Koch alleges that Asphalt is liable as Shore's successor, and, alternatively, if Asphalt is not a party to the contracts between Koch and Shore, that Asphalt tortiously interfered with those contracts.

Throughout the pendency of this dispute, Shore has continued to purchase asphalt and other products covered by the Exclusive Supply Agreement ("ESA") from Koch, and to remit royalties under the Sublicense Agreement.

Koch now seeks partial summary judgment on the liability aspects of its various claims, as well as on the question of what remedies are available to it under the contracts. Shore and Asphalt have both cross-moved for summary judgment on all of Koch's claims.

As the parties are completely diverse, and the amount in controversy exceeds $75,000, exclusive of interest and costs, I have jurisdiction over Koch's claims pursuant to 28 U.S.C. § 1332. I have jurisdiction over Shore's Counterclaim pursuant to 28 U.S.C. § 1367(a).

III. Discussion

B. *Koch's Claims Against Shore*

1. *Repudiation*

When, in a contract for the sale of goods, one party has reasonable grounds to doubt that the other party will be able to perform, the doubting party may demand of its counterpart assurance that performance will occur. N.J. Stat. Ann. § 12A:2–609 (1). If no adequate assurance is forthcoming within a commercially reasonable time, or in any event within 30 days, the doubting party may treat its counterparty as having repudiated the contract. Id. § 609(3), (4). A party need not wait for an actual material breach to demand assurances; it need only show that it reasonably believed that such an event might be in the offing. See *Magnet Res., Inc. v. Summit MRI, Inc.*, 318 N.J.Super. 275, 289–90, 723 A.2d 976 (App.Div.1998) (citing *Carfield & Sons, Inc. v. Cowling*, 616 P.2d 1008, 1010 (Colo.Ct.App.1980)). "Any facts which should indicate to a reasonable merchant that the promised performance might not be forthcoming when due should be considered reasonable grounds for insecurity." *Diskmakers, Inc. v. DeWitt Equip. Corp.*, 555 F.2d 1177,

1179 [21 UCC Rep Serv 1016] (3d Cir. 1977) (quoting N.J. Stat. Ann. 12A:2–609 N.J. Study cmt. 1). Assurances are adequate where they 'would instill in a reasonable merchant a sense of reliance that the promised performance will be forthcoming when due.' N.J. Stat. Ann. 12A:2–609 N.J. Study cmt. 1. New Jersey applies the same standards to contracts that are not for the sale of goods, as well. See *Magnet Resources*, 318 N.J.Super. at 290, 723 A.2d 976.

As an initial matter, I note that the parties have indulged in an extended debate about whether a variety of circumstances arising more than 30 days after April 3, 2001 provide either reasonable grounds for seeking assurances or adequate assurance. The question, however, is whether, at the time it sent the April 3, 2001 letter, Koch had a reasonable basis for doing so, and whether Shore adequately assured it within 30 days. I therefore fail to see why it is relevant (at least for liability purposes) whether, for example, Shore continued to buy product from Koch after May of 2001. See *By-Lo Oil Co., Inc. v. Partech, Inc.*, 2001 WL 630050, at *7 (6th Cir. 2001) (unpublished) ("May of 1998 is of no consequence in evaluating whether By-Lo had reasonable grounds for insecurity in January of 1998....").

Turning then, to the pertinent facts, I conclude that no reasonable fact-finder could fail to conclude that Koch had a commercially reasonable basis for demanding assurances on both the Exclusive Supply and Sublicense Agreements. The Sublicense Agreement analysis is straightforward. Shore reported that it planned to sell all of its "balance-sheet assets," but retain, rather than assign, the Sublicense Agreement. Even assuming that historically, Shore had met most of its Novachip obligations by selling sublicenses to third parties, rather than laying its own road surfacing, any reasonable person would wonder how Shore planned to sell anything with no telephones, no computers, and no office furniture. That Shore might well have leased these items only prompts further questions: Would Shore have had the financial capacity to obtain leases and hire a sales staff? Or were the proceeds of the sale going directly to Capoferri?

The Exclusive Supply Agreement is a bit more complex, but no less certain. In entering the ESA, Shore promised Koch not only a minimum annual purchase, but also all of the potential upside of Shore's requirements over and above the minimum should Shore's demand for asphalt grow over time. See Pl.'s L. Civ. R. 56.1 Statement Exh. B at 1. Thus, the identity of the purchaser, its future business plans, and its anticipated need for Koch's product could all affect significantly the amount of money that Koch would realize under the ESA, not only from the two million gallon minimum, but also from the potential upside. Capoferri's letter, it is true, promised that Shore's contracts, presumably including the ESA, would be assigned to the purchaser. Start-up construction businesses, however, begin unbonded, unable to win any bid for their first year and unable to secure sufficient bonding for large construction bids for several years. See Pl.'s Reply Br. Exh. 1 at 133; Shore's Br.App. Exh. 6 at 222–23. Koch had no way of knowing whether Asphalt was already a going business, and, if not, whether it would be able to win sufficient sub-contracting bids even to meet the minimum requirements, let alone approach the potential upside of an established enterprise like Shore.

Even aside from the particular facts of the construction industry, counterparty risk is an important feature of any requirements contract. Courts have often refused to permit assignment or delegation of duties under requirements or "best efforts" contracts where the assignment or delegation would be contrary to the justified expectations of the opposite contracting party. See E. Allan Farnsworth, Contracts 714–16, 745–47 & n. 38 (3d ed. 1999). "[M]uch depends on the circumstances of the assignment: a court will react differently to an assignment to a similar operator. . . ." Id. at 716.

Indeed, the ESA protected Koch against the risk of assignment of contract rights to unknown third parties, by requiring Koch's "prior written consent" before assignment. Pl.'s R. 56.1 Statement Exh. B at ¶ 14 ("¶ 14"). At the time of the April 3 letter, Koch knew that some of Shore's offices and assets were now under the control of an unknown new party, Asphalt. Koch also knew that it had certainly never agreed to any assignment of the contract Koch could reasonably have believed that a sale had already happened, either with no assignment of the ESA, or with an assignment in violation of the ESA's terms. Given the importance of the identity of the counterparty to the contract, the possibility that ¶ 14 might have been in danger of breach would alone have been reasonable grounds at least to seek assurances otherwise.

Shore contends, however, and Koch does not dispute, that Koch knew when it entered into the two agreements that Capoferri was in poor health and intended to retire within three years. Shore's argument is that Koch should not be permitted to demand assurances for an event Koch should have anticipated. Cf. *By-Lo*, 2001 WL603050, at *5 ('The grounds that give rise to this feeling have to be something that occurred after the contract was in place.'). Koch's contract, however, was with Shore, not Capoferri. The contract between Koch and Shore expressly provided for a transfer of Shore's interests. See Pl.'s R. 56.1 Statement Exh. B ¶ 14. Whatever Capoferri's personal plans, Koch was entitled to assurances that its contractual partner, Shore, as well as any successors or assignees, would carry out the obligations of the Agreement.

Shore also argues that, regardless of whether Koch had reasonable grounds for doubt, the April 3, 2001 letter was insufficient, as a matter of law, to trigger any obligation on the part of Shore to respond. Koch's letter tracked closely the language of § 609, and was sent from one attorney to another. In Shore's view, Koch should have not only quoted from the UCC, but also actually cited § 609. Yet courts have routinely accepted as sufficient under § 609 requests for assurances of a far less formal nature. See, e.g., *C.L. Maddox, Inc. v. Coalfield Servs., Inc.*, 51 F.3d 76, 81 (7th Cir. 1995) (holding that requests to sign a proposal "were in effect reasonable requests for assurances, or close enough to be

Problem 7-2

A popular singer has contracted to perform a concert at a local arena. The contract has many terms, and among them are the amount being paid, arrangements for the performer, and numerous clauses about the performance itself. Name some conditions that probably would not be expressed in the contract. Would the fact that the singer is still alive at the time of performance be an implied condition? That the arena still exists?

Problem 7-3

Assume a person applies for and receives a job as a school bus driver. The job description has rigorous safety requirements, but is silent about the driver's having other employment. Would it be an implied condition that the school bus driver not also have employment as a bartender working late nights?

JACOB & YOUNGS, INC. v. KENT

Court of Appeals of New York, 1921.
230 N.Y. 239, 129 N.E. 889.

CARDOZO, J. The plaintiff built a country residence for the defendant at a cost of upwards of $77,000, and now sues to recover a balance of $3,483.46, remaining unpaid. The work of construction ceased in June, 1914, and the defendant then began to occupy the dwelling. There was no complaint of defective performance until March, 1915. One of the specifications for the plumbing work provides that "all wrought iron pipe must be well galvanized, lap welded pipe of the grade known as 'standard pipe' of Reading manufacture." The defendant learned in March, 1915, that some of the pipe, instead of being made in Reading, was the product of other factories. The plaintiff was accordingly directed by the architect to do the work anew. The plumbing was then encased within the walls except in a few places where it had to be exposed. Obedience to the order meant more than the substitution of other pipe. It meant the demolition at great expense of substantial parts of the completed structure. The plaintiff left the work untouched, and asked for a certificate that the final payment was due. Refusal of the certificate was followed by this suit.

The evidence sustains a finding that the omission of the prescribed brand of pipe was neither fraudulent nor willful. It was the result of the oversight and inattention of the plaintiff's subcontractor. Reading pipe is distinguished from Cohoes pipe and other brands only by the name of the manufacturer stamped upon it at intervals of between six and seven feet. Even the defendant's architect, though he inspected the pipe upon arrival, failed to notice the discrepancy. The plaintiff tried to show that the brands installed, though made by other manufacturers, were the same in quality, in appearance, in market value and in cost as the brand stated in the contract that they were, indeed, the same thing, though manufactured in another place. The evidence was excluded, and a verdict directed for the defendant. The Appellate Division reversed, and granted a new trial.

We think the evidence, if admitted, would have supplied some basis for the inference that the defect was insignificant in its relation to the project. The courts never say that one who makes a contract fills the measure of his duty by less than full performance. They do say, however, that an omission, both trivial and innocent, will sometimes be atoned for by allowance of the resulting damage, and will not always be the breach of a condition to be followed by a forfeiture (*Spence v. Ham*, 163 N.Y. 220; *Woodward v. Fuller*, 80 N.Y. 312; *Glacius v. Black*, 67 N.Y. 563, 566; *Bowen v. Kimbell*, 203 Mass. 364, 370). The distinction is akin to that between dependent and independent promises, or between promises and conditions (Anson on Contracts [Corbin's ed.], sec. 367; 2 Williston on Contracts, sec. 842). Some promises are so plainly independent that they can never by fair construction be conditions of one another. (*Rosenthal Paper Co. v. Nat. Folding Box & Paper Co.*, 226 N.Y. 313; *Bogardus v. N. Y. Life Ins. Co.*, 101 N.Y. 328). Others are so plainly dependent that they must always be conditions. Others, though dependent and thus conditions when there is departure in point of substance, will be viewed as independent and collateral when the departure is insignificant (2 Williston on Contracts, secs. 841, 842; *Eastern Forge Co. v. Corbin*, 182 Mass. 590, 592; *Robinson v. Mollett*, L. R., 7 Eng. & Ir. App. 802, 814; *Miller v. Benjamin*, 142 N.Y. 613). Considerations partly of justice and partly of presumable intention are to tell us whether this or that promise shall be placed in one class or in another. The simple and the uniform will call for different remedies from the multifarious and the intricate. The margin of departure within the range of normal expectation upon a sale of common chattels will vary from the margin to be expected upon a contract for the construction of a mansion or a "skyscraper." There will be harshness sometimes and oppression in the implication of a condition when the thing upon which labor has been expended is incapable of surrender because united to the land, and equity and reason in the implication of a like condition when the subject matter, if defective, is in shape to be returned. From the conclusion that promises may not be treated as dependent to the extent of their uttermost minutiae without a sacrifice of justice, the progress is a short one to the conclusion that they may not be so treated without a perversion of intention. Intention not otherwise revealed may be presumed to hold in contemplation the reasonable and probable. If something else is in view, it must not be left to implication. There will be no assumption of a purpose to visit venial faults with oppressive retribution.

Those who think more of symmetry and logic in the development of legal rules than of practical adaptation to the attainment of a just result will be troubled by a classification where the lines of division are so wavering and blurred. Something, doubtless, may be said on the score of consistency and certainty in favor of a stricter standard. The courts have balanced such considerations against those of equity and fairness, and found the latter to be the weightier. The decisions in this state commit us to the liberal view, which is making its way, nowadays, in jurisdictions slow to welcome it (*Dakin & Co. v. Lee*, 1916, 1 K. B. 566, 579). Where the line is to be drawn between the important and the trivial cannot be settled by a formula. "In the nature of the case precise boundaries are impossible" (2 Williston on Contracts, sec. 841). The same omission may take on one aspect or another according to its setting. Substitution of equivalents may not have the same significance in fields of art on the one side and in those of mere utility on the other. Nowhere will change be tolerated, however, if it is so dominant or pervasive as in any real or substantial measure to frustrate the purpose of the contract (*Crouch v. Gutmann*, 134 N.Y. 45, 51). There is no general license to install whatever, in the builder's judgment, may be regarded as "just as good" (*Easthampton L. & C. Co., Ltd. v. Worthington*, 186 N.Y. 407, 412). The question is one of degree, to be answered, if there is doubt, by the triers of the facts (*Crouch v. Gutmann*; *Woodward v. Fuller*, supra), and, if the inferences are certain, by the judges of the law (*Easthampton L. & C. Co., Ltd. v. Worthington*, supra). We must weigh the purpose to be served, the desire to be gratified, the excuse for deviation from the letter, the cruelty of enforced adherence. Then only can we tell whether literal fulfillment is to be implied by law as a condition. This is not to say that the parties are not free by apt and certain words to effectuate a purpose that performance of every term shall be a condition of recovery. That question is not here. This is merely to say that the law will be slow to impute the purpose, in the silence of the parties, where the significance of the default is grievously out of proportion to the oppression of the forfeiture. The willful transgressor must accept the penalty of his transgression (*Schultze v. Goodstein*, 180 N.Y. 248, 251; *Desmond Dunne Co. v. Friedman Doscher Co.*, 162 N.Y. 486, 490). For him there is no occasion to mitigate the rigor of implied conditions. The transgressor whose default is unintentional and trivial may hope for mercy if he will offer atonement for his wrong (*Spence v. Ham*, supra).

In the circumstances of this case, we think the measure of the allowance is not the cost of replacement, which would be great, but the difference in value, which would be either nominal or nothing. Some of the exposed sections might perhaps have been replaced at moderate expense. The defendant did not limit his demand to them, but treated the plumbing as a unit to be corrected from cellar to roof. In point of fact, the plaintiff never reached the stage at which evidence of the extent of the allowance became necessary. The trial court had excluded evidence that the defect was unsubstantial, and in view of that ruling there was no occasion for the plaintiff to go farther with an offer of proof. We think, however, that the offer, if it had been made, would not of necessity have been defective because directed to difference in value. It is true that in most cases the cost of replacement is the measure (*Spence v. Ham*, supra). The owner is entitled to the money which will permit him to complete, unless the cost of completion is grossly and unfairly out of proportion to the good to be attained. When that is true, the measure is the difference in value. Specifications call, let us say, for a foundation built of granite quarried in Vermont. On the completion of the building, the owner learns that through the blunder of a subcontractor part of the foundation has been built of granite of the same quality quarried in New Hampshire. The measure of allowance is not the cost of reconstruction. "There may be omissions of that which could not afterwards be supplied exactly as called for by the contract without taking down the building to its foundations, and at the same time the omission may not affect the value of the building for use or otherwise, except so slightly as to be hardly appreciable" (*Handy v. Bliss*, 204 Mass. 513, 519. Cf. *Foeller v. Heintz*, 137 Wis. 169, 178; *Oberlies v. Bullinger*, 132 N.Y. 598, 601; 2 Williston on Contracts, sec. 805, p. 1541). The rule that gives a remedy in cases of substantial performance with compensation for defects of trivial or inappreciable importance, has been developed by the courts as an instrument of justice. The measure of the allowance must be shaped to the same end.

The order should be affirmed, and judgment absolute directed in favor of the plaintiff upon the stipulation, with costs in all courts.

MCLAUGHLIN, J. (DISSENTING). I dissent. The plaintiff did not perform its contract. Its failure to do so was either intentional or due to gross neglect which, under the uncontradicted facts, amounted to the same thing, nor did it make any proof of the cost of compliance, where compliance was possible.

Under its contract it obligated itself to use in the plumbing only pipe (between 2,000 and 2,500 feet) made by the Reading Manufacturing Company. The first pipe delivered was about 1,000 feet and the plaintiff's superintendent then called the attention of the foreman of the subcontractor, who was doing the plumbing, to the fact that the specifications annexed to the contract required all pipe used in the plumbing to be of the Reading Manufacturing Company. They then examined it for the purpose of ascertaining whether this delivery was of that manufacture and found it was. Thereafter, as pipe was required in the progress of the work, the foreman of the subcontractor would leave word at its shop that he wanted a specified number of feet of pipe, without in any way indicating of what manufacture. Pipe would thereafter be delivered and installed in the building, without any examination whatever. Indeed, no examination, so far as appears, was made by the plaintiff, the subcontractor, defendant's architect, or any one else, of any of the pipe except the first delivery, until after the building had been completed. Plaintiff's architect then refused to give the certificate of completion, upon which the final payment depended, because all of the pipe used in the plumbing was not of the kind called for by the contract. After such refusal, the subcontractor removed the covering or insulation from about 900 feet of pipe which was exposed in the basement, cellar and attic, and all but 70 feet was found to have been manufactured, not by the Reading Company, but by other manufacturers, some by the Cohoes Rolling Mill Company, some by the National Steel Works, some by the South Chester

Tubing Company, and some which bore no manufacturer's mark at all. The balance of the pipe had been so installed in the building that an inspection of it could not be had without demolishing, in part at least, the building itself.

I am of the opinion the trial court was right in directing a verdict for the defendant. The plaintiff agreed that all the pipe used should be of the Reading Manufacturing Company. Only about two fifths of it, so far as appears, was of that kind. If more were used, then the burden of proving that fact was upon the plaintiff, which it could easily have done, since it knew where the pipe was obtained. The question of substantial performance of a contract of the character of the one under consideration depends in no small degree upon the good faith of the contractor. If the plaintiff had intended to, and had complied with the terms of the contract except as to minor omissions, due to inadvertence, then he might be allowed to recover the contract price, less the amount necessary to fully compensate the defendant for damages caused by such omissions. (*Woodward v. Fuller*, 80 N.Y. 312; *Nolan v. Whitney*, 88 N.Y. 648.) But that is not this case. It installed between 2,000 and 2,500 feet of pipe, of which only 1,000 feet at most complied with the contract. No explanation was given why pipe called for by the contract was not used, nor was any effort made to show what it would cost to remove the pipe of other manufacturers and install that of the Reading Manufacturing Company. The defendant had a right to contract for what he wanted. He had a right before making payment to get what the contract called for. It is no answer to this suggestion to say that the pipe put in was just as good as that made by the Reading Manufacturing Company, or that the difference in value between such pipe and the pipe made by the Reading Manufacturing Company would be either "nominal or nothing." Defendant contracted for pipe made by the Reading Manufacturing Company. What his reason was for requiring this kind of pipe is of no importance. He wanted that and was entitled to it. It may have been a mere whim on his part, but even so, he had a right to this kind of pipe, regardless of whether some other kind, according to the opinion of the contractor or experts, would have been "just as good, better, or done just as well." He agreed to pay only upon condition that the pipe installed were made by that company and he ought not to be compelled to pay unless that condition be performed. (*Schultze v. Goodstein*, 180 N.Y. 248; *Spence v. Ham*, supra; Steel S. & E. C. Co. v. Stock, 225 N.Y. 173; *Van Clief v. Van Vechten*, 130 N.Y. 571; *Glacius v. Black*, 50 N.Y. 145; *Smith v. Brady*, 17 N.Y. 173, and authorities cited on p. 185.) The rule, therefore, of substantial performance, with damages for unsubstantial omissions, has no application. (*Crouch v. Gutmann*, 134 N.Y. 45; *Spence v. Ham*, 163 N.Y. 220.)

What was said by this court in *Smith v. Brady* (supra) is quite applicable here: "I suppose it will be conceded that everyone has a right to build his house, his cottage or his store after such a model and in such style as shall best accord with his notions of utility or be most agreeable to his fancy. The specifications of the contract become the law between the parties until voluntarily changed. If the owner prefers a plain and simple Doric column, and has so provided in the agreement, the contractor has no right to put in its place the more costly and elegant Corinthian. If the owner, having regard to strength and durability, has contracted for walls of specified materials to be laid in a particular manner, or for a given number of joists and beams, the builder has no right to substitute his own judgment or that of others. Having departed from the agreement, if performance has not been waived by the other party, the law will not allow him to allege that he has made as good a building as the one he engaged to erect. He can demand payment only upon and according to the terms of his contract, and if the conditions on which payment is due have not been performed, then the right to demand it does not exist. To hold a different doctrine would be simply to make another contract, and would be giving to parties an encouragement to violate their engagements, which the just policy of the law does not permit." (p. 186.)

I am of the opinion the trial court did not err in ruling on the admission of evidence or in directing a verdict for the defendant. For the foregoing reasons I think the judgment of the Appellate Division should be reversed and the judgment of the Trial Term affirmed.

Notes and Discussion

1. The Terms of the Contract. This celebrated decision was by a bare 4-3 majority. Excerpts from the original contract that George Edward Kent made with Jacob and Youngs, as published by Richard Danzig and Geoffrey R. Watson, The Capability Problem in Contract Law 96–100 (2nd ed. 2004):

> Art. II. It is understood and agreed by and between the parties hereto that the work included in this contract is to be done under the direction of the said Architect, and that his decision as to the true construction and meaning of the drawing and specifications shall be final....
>
> Art. III. No alterations shall be made in the work except upon written order of the Architect; ...
>
> Art. IV. The Contractors ... shall, within twenty-four hours after receiving written notice from the Architect to that effect, proceed to remove from the grounds or buildings all materials condemned by him, whether worked or unworked, and to take down all portion of the work which the Architect shall by like written notice condemn as unsound or improper, or as in any way failing to conform to the drawings and specifications, and shall make good all work damaged or destroyed thereby.
>
> Art. IX. It is hereby mutually agreed between the parties hereto that the sum to be paid by the Owner to the Contractors for said work and materials shall be Seventy thousand five hundred ($70,500) dollars, subject to additions and deductions as hereinbefore provided, and that

such sum shall be paid by the Owner to the Contractors, in current funds, and only upon certificates of the Architect, as follows:

On or about the first day of each month a certificate will be given by the architect to the contractors for a payment on account of value of the work finished and erected at the site, which represents in his judgment a fair proportion to the whole of the contract price less a fifteen per cent (15%) margin which shall be withheld until after the completion and acceptance of the entire work. The final payment shall be made within thirty (30) days after the completion of the work included in this contract, and all payments shall be due when certificates for the same are issued....

GENERAL CONDITIONS

(19) The Contractor is responsible for, and must make good any defects arising or discovered in his work within two years after completion of work and acceptance, or faults in labor or material, unless hereinafter changed.

(22) Where any particular brand of manufactured article is specified, it is to be considered as a standard. Contractors desiring to use another shall first make application in writing to the Architect, stating the difference in cost, and obtain their written approval of the change.

Character of Work and Labor: (24) The decision of the Architect as to the character of any material or labor furnished by the Contractor is to be final and conclusive on both Contractor and Owner.

Approved material: (225) The approval of the quality of any material will not be considered as acceptance of the work when installed should such material or work prove defective.

Wrought iron pipe: (227) All wrought iron pipe must be well galvanized lap welded pipe of the grade known as "Standard Pipe" of Reading manufacture. Burrs formed in cutting must be reamed out. Fittings shall be extra heavy, galvanized, malleable iron fittings.

2. "Substantial Performance." According to the contract, the architect's approval was an express condition precedent to Kent's duty to make the final payment, right? Does Judge Cardozo give us any reason to believe that the architect's refusal to give a final certificate was inherently unreasonable or not permitted by the contract? Why doesn't this settle the matter? Follow Cardozo's reasoning, if you can. Note how he links his interpretation of the contract to the general theory of damages. How significant is the disagreement between the majority and dissent as to the importance of the contractor's deviation?

Of this decision, Cardozo says: "This is not to say that the parties are not free by apt and certain words to effectuate a purpose that performance of every term shall be a condition of recovery." What else should Kent have done, in negotiating the contract, to make certain that he got Reading Pipe and it alone? After the decision, Kent moved for re-argument, pointing out that the language of the contract required that any work "not fully in accordance with the drawings and specifications ... is to be immediately torn down, removed and remade or replaced in accordance with drawings and specifications, whenever discovered," and that it gave Kent "the option at all times to allow the defective or improper work to stand and to receive from the Contractor a sum of money equivalent to the difference in value of the work as performed and as herein specified." The Court of Appeals rejected this argument, stating that "The promise to replace, like the promise to install, is to be viewed, not as a condition, but as independent and collateral, when the defect is trivial and innocent." *Jacob & Youngs v. Kent*, 230 N.Y. 656, 130 N.E. 933 (1921) (*per curiam*); see also Robert E. Scott & Jody S. Kraus, Contract Law and Theory 74 (rev. 3rd ed. 2002), who quote this contractual language from the record on appeal. Redraft the contract language to make it Cardozo-proof (if you can).

3. **Willfulness.** Judge Cardozo states that: "The evidence sustains a finding that the omission of the prescribed brand of pipe was neither fraudulent nor willful." This is important because of a distinction he attempts to draw later: "The willful transgressor must accept the penalty of his transgression," while "[t]he transgressor whose default is unintentional and trivial may hope for mercy if he will offer atonement for his wrong . . . ." Why this sudden high moral tone? Don't we normally ignore fault when dealing with breach of contract?

In subsequent decisions, the materiality of a breach often hinges in part on "the extent to which the behavior of the party failing to perform or to offer to perform comports with standards of good faith and fair dealing": Restatement 2d § 241(e). The idea, presumably, is that a breacher who unscrupulously forces changes on a customer will not be saved by having substantially performed. But recent cases have been cautious about using willfulness too absolutely. *Vincenzi v. Cerro*, 186 Conn. 612, 442 A.2d 1352 (1982), was a fairly typical construction case in which a builder sued to recover the contract price for a completed house that had some defects. The defendants claimed that the builder had not substantially performed because its breach had been willful or intentional. The Connecticut Supreme Court rejected this argument: "The pertinent inquiry is not simply whether the breach was 'willful' but whether the behavior of the party in default 'comports with standards of good faith and fair dealing.' Even an adverse conclusion on this point is not decisive but is to be weighed with other factors, such as the extent to which the owner will be deprived of a reasonably expected benefit and the extent to which the builder may suffer forfeiture, in deciding whether there has been substantial performance." Id. at 1354 (citations omitted). What do you think?

4. **Some Additional Facts.** How is your understanding of this case affected by the following information (which is also drawn from Danzig and Watson, supra, pp. 109–116)?

- George Edward Kent, a successful New York lawyer (and the son-in-law of New York City's mayor), is not known to have had any professional or financial ties to the Reading Company.
- By its own account, the Reading Company was the largest American manufacturer of wrought iron pipe, which cost about thirty percent more than steel pipe.
- There were, in the period before World War I, only four American manufacturers of wrought iron pipe; their pipes were considered equal

in quality and price irrespective of the manufacturer's name, and prior to argument in the Court of Appeals both litigants stipulated to this.

- Normal practice among architects at this date was apparently to assure inclusion of wrought iron pipe by naming a manufacturer, since some steel pipe manufacturers sold their pipe under misleading names like "wrought pipe."
- Kent was reputedly someone who "would go all over town to save a buck."
- Some evidence suggests that before this dispute Kent was already dissatisfied with Jacob and Youngs on other grounds, notably because of delays in completion and the need for modifications.

5. **Material Breach Revisited.** Look again at the *K & G Construction* decision. In that case, a subcontractor's bulldozer negligently harmed a building. As Eric G. Andersen points out in *A New Look at Material Breach in the Law of Contracts*, 21 U.C. Davis L. Rev. 1073 (1988), this injury threatened the general contractor in two distinct ways. First, "the general contractor suffered an impairment of the interest in present performance and therefore became entitled to damages sufficient to repair the harm done to the building." Second, "the general contractor's interest in future performance also was impaired if the circumstances indicated that the subcontractor was likely to commit other breaches of contract in the future. The payment of compensatory damages does nothing to remedy the general contractor's loss of confidence in the subcontractor's ability or commitment to perform its executory duties properly. The remedy for that loss is cancellation, which is made available by a finding of material breach." Id. at 1102 (footnotes omitted).

This situation is very different from that in *Jacob & Youngs*. Here, as also in many construction cases, a builder had completed performance, but only imperfectly. In Andersen's terminology, Kent's interest in present performance is impaired, but there is no future performance in question. Should this difference affect the remedies that owners like Kent have upon discovery of the breach? Andersen argues that when the builder has no further executory duties, "the proper approach is simply to disregard the material breach doctrine and consider recovery to be 'on the contract.'" Id. at 1139. In other words, even in the event of a material breach, Kent could no longer refuse the final payment altogether; rather, he would be obliged to settle accounts with Jacob & Youngs, with due allowance being made for any damages owing to imperfect performance. Is this preferable to the current rule?

Economic analysis adds a little to the legal understanding of *Jacob & Youngs*. George M. Cohen, *The Negligence-Opportunism Tradeoff in Contract Law*, 20 Hofstra L. Rev. 941, 973–974 (1992), cautions especially against the potential for opportunistic behavior by owners (like Kent) if the escape of substantial performance is not available: "opportunistic behavior produces no social benefits; instead of adding to the net wealth of society it merely redistributes wealth from one party to another.... Investments in opportunistic behavior and in taking precautions against such behavior can therefore be viewed as 'deadweight losses,' that is, decreases in society's total wealth." Should we also fear opportunism by contractors?

Problem 7–4

Mrs. Fred Cope arranged with Grun Roofing & Construction to install a new roof on her house. After Grun had installed the new roof, she noticed that it had streaks, which she described as yellow, due to a difference in color or shade of some of the shingles. Grun agreed to remedy the situation and he removed the nonconforming shingles. However, the replacement shingles did not match the remainder, and photographs clearly showed that the roof was not of a uniform color. According to Mrs. Cope, her roof has the appearance of having been patched, rather than having been completely replaced. Otherwise the roof is entirely sound.

If Mrs. Cope refuses to pay Grun for the roof, can he successfully sue her on the contract?

WILSON v. SCAMPOLI

District of Columbia Court of Appeals, 1967.
228 A.2d 848.

MYERS, J. This is an appeal from an order of the trial court granting rescission of a sales contract for a color television set and directing the return of the purchase price plus interest and costs.

Appellee purchased the set in question on November 4, 1965, paying the total purchase price in cash. The transaction was evidenced by a sales ticket showing the price paid and guaranteeing ninety days' free service and replacement of any defective tube and parts for a period of one year. Two days after purchase the set was delivered and uncrated, the antennae adjusted and the set plugged into an electrical outlet to "cook out."[15] When the set was turned on however, it did not function properly, the picture having a reddish tinge. Appellant's delivery man advised the buyer's daughter, Mrs. Kolley, that it was not his duty to tune in or adjust the color but that a service representative would shortly call at her house for that purpose. After the departure of the delivery men, Mrs. Kolley unplugged the set and did not use it.[16]

On November 8, 1965, a service representative arrived, and after spending an hour in an effort to eliminate the red cast from the picture advised Mrs. Kolley that he would have to remove the chassis from the cabinet and take it to the shop as he could not determine the cause of the difficulty from his examination at the house. He also made a written memorandum of his service call, noting that the television "Needs Shop Work (Red Screen)." Mrs. Kolley refused to allow the chassis to be

15. Such a "cook out," usually over several days, allows the set to magnetize itself and to heat up the circuit in order to indicate faulty wiring.

16. Appellee, who made his home with Mrs. Kolley, had been hospitalized shortly before delivery of the set. The remaining negotiations were carried on by Mrs. Kolley, acting on behalf of her father.

removed, asserting she did not want a "repaired" set but another "brand new" set. Later she demanded the return of the purchase price, although retaining the set. Appellant refused to refund the purchase price, but renewed his offer to adjust, repair, or, if the set could not be made to function properly, to replace it. Ultimately, appellee instituted this suit against appellant seeking a refund of the purchase price. After a trial, the court ruled that "under the facts and circumstances the complaint is justified. Under the equity powers of the Court I will order the parties put back in their original status, let the $675 be returned, and the set returned to the defendant."

Appellant does not contest the jurisdiction of the trial court to order rescission in a proper case, but contends the trial judge erred in holding that rescission here was appropriate. He argues that he was always willing to comply with the terms of the sale either by correcting the malfunction by minor repairs or, in the event the set could not be made thereby properly operative, by replacement; that as he was denied the opportunity to try to correct the difficulty, he did not breach the contract of sale or any warranty thereunder, expressed or implied.[17]

D.C.Code § 28:2–508 (Supp.V, 1966) provide: "(1) Where any tender or delivery by the seller is rejected because non conforming and the time for performance has not yet expired, the seller may seasonably notify the buyer of his intention to cure and may then within the contract time make a conforming delivery.

"(2) Where the buyer rejects a nonconforming tender which the seller had reasonable grounds to believe would be acceptable with or without money allowance the seller may if he seasonably notifies the buyer have a further reasonable time to substitute a conforming tender."

A retail dealer would certainly expect and have reasonable grounds to believe that merchandise like color television sets, new and delivered as crated at the factory, would be acceptable as delivered and that, if defective in some way, he would have the right to substitute a conforming tender. The question then resolves itself to whether the dealer may conform his tender by adjustment or minor repair or whether he must conform by substituting brand new merchandise. The problem seems to be one of first impression in other jurisdictions adopting the Uniform Commercial Code as well as in the District of Columbia.

Although the Official Code Comments do not reach this precise issue, there are cases and comments under other provisions of the Code

17. Appellee maintains that the delivery of a color television set with a malfunctioning color control is a breach of both an implied warranty of merchantability (D.C. Code s 282 314 (Supp. V, 1966)) and of an implied warranty of fitness for a particular purpose (D.C. Code s 282 315 (Supp. V, 1966)) and as such is a basis for the right to rescission of the sale. We find it unnecessary to determine whether a set sold under the circumstances of this case gives rise to an implied warranty of fitness for a particular purpose or whether, as appellant contends, the remedial provisions of the express warranties bind the buyer to accept these same remedial provisions as sole remedies under an implied warranty.

which indicate that under certain circumstances repairs and adjustments are contemplated as remedies under implied warranties. In *L & L Sales Co. v. Little Brown Jug, Inc.*, 12 Pa.Dist. & Co.R.2d 469 (Phila.County Ct.1957), where the language of a disclaimer was found insufficient to defeat warranties under §§ 2–314 and 2–315, the court noted that the buyer had notified the seller of defects in the merchandise, and as the seller was unable to remedy them and later refused to accept return of the articles, it was held to be a breach of warranty. In *Hall v. Everett Motors, Inc.*, 340 Mass. 430, 165 N.E.2d 107 (1960), decided shortly before the effective date of the Code in Massachusetts, the court reluctantly found that a disclaimer of warranties was sufficient to insulate the seller. Several references were made in the ruling to the seller's unsuccessful attempts at repairs, the court indicating the result would have been different under the Code.

While these cases provide no mandate to require the buyer to accept patchwork goods or substantially repaired articles in lieu of flawless merchandise, they do indicate that minor repairs or reasonable adjustments are frequently the means by which an imperfect tender may be cured. In discussing the analogous question of defective title, it has been stated that: "The seller, then, should be able to cure (the defect) under subsection 2–508(2) in those cases in which he can do so without subjecting the buyer to any great inconvenience, risk or loss." Hawkland, *Curing an Improper Tender of Title to Chattels: Past, Present and Commercial Code*, 46 Minn.L.Rev. 697, 724 (1962). See also Willier & Hart, Forms and Procedures under the UCC, 24.07 (4); D.C.Code § 282 608(1)(a) (Supp. V, 1966).

Removal of a television chassis for a short period of time in order to determine the cause of color malfunction and ascertain the extent of adjustment or correction needed to effect full operational efficiency presents no great inconvenience to the buyer. In the instant case, appellant's expert witness testified that this was not infrequently necessary with new televisions. Should the set be defective in workmanship or parts, the loss would be upon the manufacturer who warranted it free from mechanical defect. Here the adamant refusal of Mrs. Kolley, acting on behalf of appellee, to allow inspection essential to the determination of the cause of the excessive red tinge to the picture defeated any effort by the seller to provide timely repair or even replacement of the set if the difficulty could not be corrected. The cause of the defect might have been minor and easily adjusted or it may have been substantial and required replacement by another new set B but the seller was never given an adequate opportunity to make a determination.

We do not hold that appellant has no liability to appellee,[18] but as he was denied access and a reasonable opportunity to repair, appellee has

18. Appellant on appeal has renewed his willingness to remedy any defect in the tender, and thus there is no problem of expiration of his warranties. He should be afforded the right to inspect and correct any malfunction. If appellee refuses to allow appellant an opportunity to do so, then no cause of action can lie for breach of warranty, express or implied, and the loss must be borne by appellee.

not shown a breach of warranty entitling him either to a brand new set or to rescission. We therefore reverse the judgment of the trial court granting rescission and directing the return of the purchase price of the set.

Notes and Discussion

1. Goods-Based Remedies under Article 2 of the UCC. Section 2–507 states the standard conditions in the typical sale of goods under the UCC: "[t]ender of delivery is a condition to the buyer's duty to accept the goods, unless otherwise agreed, to his duty to pay for them." For the other side of the contract, subsection 2 of § 2–507 states the buyer's duty: "[w]here payment is due and demanded on the delivery to the buyer of goods or documents of title, his right against the seller to retain or dispose of them is conditional upon his making the payment due."

Section 2–601 gives buyer the right to "reject" goods that "fail in any respect to conform to the contract." Sections 2–602 through 2–605 state buyer's rights and responsibilities when buyer seeks to reject goods. Sections 2–606 through 2–608 define the technical term "acceptance" and give the buyer a right to "revoke acceptance" in certain circumstances. In general the right to revoke acceptance is more limited than the right to reject. Since revocation is almost always more remote from seller's delivery than rejection, the law is more suspicious of the buyer's motives and more skeptical of claims that seller delivered non conforming goods in revocation than in rejection.

2. Perfect Tender. Look closely at UCC § 2–601. Subject to certain exceptions (which are important), "if the goods or the tender of delivery fail *in any respect* to conform to the contract, the buyer may (a) reject the whole; or (b) accept the whole; or (c) accept any commercial unit or units and reject the rest." (Emphasis added.) This language rejects substantial performance in the case of sale of goods. What reasons can be given for requiring perfect tender in the sale of goods, but only substantial performance for most other contracts?

How perfect is "perfect"? The "reddish tinge" on Mrs. Kolley's TV screen is enough to warrant rejection; but what if the only problem had been a minor scratch on a part of the TV cabinet not ordinarily visible? In *Mitsubishi Goshi Kaisha v. J. Aron & Co.*, 16 F.2d 185 (2d Cir. 1926), Judge Learned Hand dealt with a case in which a buyer of soya bean oil "f.o.b. * * * Pacific Coast" rejected oil labeled "f.o.b. Dallas" even though this difference was apparently trivial. Hand upheld the rejection, observing: "There is no room in commercial contracts for the doctrine of substantial performance." Id. at 186 (citation omitted). It made no difference that the buyer's real reason for rejecting the oil was that its resale contract had fallen through. (Today, however, a court might well find that such a buyer had not been acting in good faith.)

In any case, there are some significant exceptions to the perfect tender rule. The most pertinent for our purposes concerns installment contracts under the UCC, where § 2–612(2) permits a buyer to reject a non-conforming installment "if the non-conformity *substantially impairs* the value of that installment and cannot be cured"; in § 2–612(3) "a breach of the whole" occurs only if "non-conformity or default with respect to one or more installments *substantially impairs* the value of the whole contract." (Emphasis added.)

Further, under the CISG (which here follows Civil Law), international contracts for the sale of goods are not subject to the perfect tender rule. See CISG art. 25: "A breach of contract committed by one of the parties is fundamental if it results in such detriment to the other party as *substantially to deprive him of what he is entitled to expect under the contract*, unless the party in breach did not foresee and a reasonable person of the same kind in the same circumstances would not have foreseen such a result." (Emphasis added.)

At the insistence of consumer advocates, the perfect tender rule is largely preserved in amended UCC § 2–601. White & Summers, supra, § 8–3 at 314, observe, "Are consumers asking for the right to return the dress with a single stitch out of place because they have found the same dress elsewhere at a lower price? For shame."

3. Acceptance, Rejection, and Cure. In the UCC, the buyer's receipt of goods constitutes a critical moment in the execution of a sale. The buyer is confronted with an immediate decision either to accept or to reject the goods. *Wilson v. Scampoli* provides a good illustration of the process in a consumer contract, although the same rules are largely applicable to commercial sales as well. Mrs. Kolley clearly indicated her dissatisfaction to the delivery man, and she also stopped using it; does this constitute rejection under § 2–602? (Note also § 2–605, which requires a buyer to specify its objections in many circumstances.) The post-rejection position of the two parties is sketched in §§ 2–603 and 604, but the most important section for the present case is § 2–508, which gives the seller a right to "cure" the defect. How does this right play out in the present case?

What would have happened if Mrs. Kolley had continued watching the TV while the controversy simmered? See Comment 4 on § 2–606: "[A]ny action taken by the buyer, which is inconsistent with his claim that he has rejected the goods, constitutes an acceptance." Continued use is ambiguous on this point, is it not?

Acceptance of the goods (§ 2–606) substantially alters the position of the buyer. In particular, if a defect then emerges, the buyer can no longer reject the goods, but can only revoke its acceptance. Section 2–608 sets out the requirements: revocation must occur within a reasonable time after discovery of the defect, and is available only if the "non-conformity *substantially impairs* its value to him" (emphasis added; substantial performance *redivivus*?) and only under particular circumstances. If the buyer cannot revoke acceptance, it is left with seeking damages for the non-conformity. In the amended Article 2, cure remains a possibility after a successful revocation.

Taken in their sum, these rules place a considerable responsibility on the buyer—whether a consumer or a huge corporation—to inspect goods promptly for defects and to notify the seller forthwith if any are discovered.

Problem 7–5

George owes Harriet fifty heavy bags of flour. On the appointed day he drives to Harriet's business in order to deliver them. After he has unloaded the bags, it turns out that he has only brought forty-nine rather than fifty of them. If Harriet rejects the flour, will George be able to deliver the fiftieth bag later that day, or will he have to reload them and take back the forty-nine bags in order to deliver all fifty bags at one and the same time?

For a comparative law analysis of this problem, see Reinhard Zimmermann and Simon Whittaker, Good Faith in European Contract Law 292–304 (2000).

C. IMPOSSIBILITY, IMPRACTICABILITY, AND FRUSTRATION

One of the main purposes of a contract is, of course, to allocate future risk between two (or more) parties. As we have seen, often this is done through express terms; but much more frequently it is done only through implication. The terms themselves may suggest that the parties were distributing some risk, but it will then be up to the court to interpret the contract in order to determine the allocation. Finally, in many instances the parties may simply not allocate future risk at all—either because they do not perceive the risk, or because, although they do perceive it at least dimly, they cannot be bothered to provide for every remote contingency. When such an unallocated risk then does come to pass, one party can find a contract considerably more disadvantageous than it had anticipated. Under what circumstances can this party hope to obtain relief from the law?

Common Law has evolved a rather narrow set of doctrines that excuse performance. Discussion may begin with two classic English cases. The first is *Taylor v. Caldwell*, 122 Eng. Rep. 309 (Q.B. 1863). The defendants had leased to the plaintiffs the use of a music hall for four concerts during the summer of 1861; but before the first concert the hall burned down without the fault of either party. The court held that: "The parties when framing their agreement evidently had not present to their minds the possibility of such a disaster, and have made no express stipulation with reference to it." Id. at 312. In such contracts, "in which the performance depends on the continued existence of a given person or thing, a condition is implied that the impossibility of performance arising from the perishing of the person or thing shall excuse the performance." Id. at 314. This is the doctrine of impossibility which is recast in Restatement 2d §§ 262–264. These three sections give the principal situations when courts have commonly accepted the excuse of impossibility: when a person whose existence is necessary for a contract's performance dies or is incapacitated prior to performance (§ 262); when a specific object necessary for the performance is destroyed or fails to come into existence (§ 263); and when performance is prevented by a governmental regulation (§ 264). The contracting parties are usually presumed not to have foreseen such events, although the presumption is rebuttable in particular cases.

From impossibility it is but a short step to a second doctrine, that of frustration of purpose. The leading case is *Krell v. Henry*, [1903] 2 K.B. 740 (Eng. C. A.), the celebrated "coronation case" discussed in the introduction to this Chapter. At a dear price the defendant had contracted in order to view the coronation processions for Edward VII from the plaintiff's apartment, but the king's illness forced cancellation of the coronation. In principle, of course, this contract could still be executed (the flat was not physically destroyed), but from the defendant's viewpoint the contract had lost its entire point. The court held that: "it cannot reasonably be supposed to have been in the contemplation of the contracting parties, when the contract was made, that the coronation would not be held on the proclaimed days," and that since the coronation was evidently "the foundation of the contract . . . [the court] would discharge both parties from further performance of the contract." Id. at 750.

The doctrines of impossibility and frustration still remain analytically distinct, but today the impossibility excuse has largely evolved into the broader theory of impracticability, as embodied in UCC § 2–615 and then in Restatement 2d § 261 (Discharge by Supervening Impracticability). Two things should be noted: first, both impracticability and frustration of purpose are available only in cases where the parties have not themselves allocated a risk either expressly or by implication; and second, in any case courts are not usually eager to employ these theories in order to get one party out of a mess it has arguably created for itself.

This is not simply because judges are hard-hearted, however. "Moral hazard," a central theory in law and economics, observes that if you are insured against something bad occurring, your initial incentive to avoid its occurrence declines, with potentially adverse social consequences in the form of higher "hazard costs." Insurance of this type might also take the form of robust contract doctrines calling on courts to intervene and "save the day" when contracts go horribly astray. But by and large, our courts have preferred only sparing intervention.

KARL WENDT FARM EQUIPMENT CO. v. INTERNATIONAL HARVESTER CO.

United States Court of Appeals, Sixth Circuit, 1991.
931 F.2d 1112.

JONES, J. Plaintiff Karl Wendt Farm Equipment Company ("Wendt") appeals and defendants International Harvester Company and International Harvester Credit Corp. (collectively "IH") cross-appeal from a deficiency judgement and preceding trial verdicts in this contract action relating to a dealer sales and service agreement. For the reasons set forth below, we reverse and remand in part and affirm in part.

I.

This diversity action arises out of IH's decision to go out of the farm equipment business after a dramatic downturn in the market for farm equipment. In the fall of 1974, Wendt and IH entered into a "Dealer Sales and Service Agreement" ("agreement") which established Wendt as a dealer of IH goods in the area of Marlette, Michigan. The agreement set forth the required method of sale, provisions for the purchase and servicing of goods, as well as certain dealer operating requirements. The agreement also provided specific provisions for the termination of the contract upon the occurrence of certain specified conditions.

In light of a dramatic recession in the farm equipment market, and substantial losses on the part of IH, IH negotiated an agreement with J.I. Case Co. and Tenneco Inc. ("Case/Tenneco") to sell its farm equipment division to Case/Tenneco. The sale took the form of a sale of assets. The base purchase price was $246,700,000.00 in cash and $161,300,000.00 to be paid in participating preferred stock in Tenneco. While IH asserts that it lost $479,000,000.00 on the deal, it also noted that this was a "paper loss" which will result in a tax credit offsetting the loss. J.App. at 405.

In its purchase of IH's farm equipment division, Case/Tenneco did not acquire IH's existing franchise network. Rather, it received "access" to IH dealers, many of whom eventually received a Case franchise. However, there were some 400 "conflicted areas" in which both a Case and an IH dealership were located. In these areas Case offered only one franchise contract. In nearly two-thirds of the conflicted areas, the IH dealer received the franchise. However, Marlette, Michigan was such a "conflicted area" and Wendt was not offered a Case franchise.

Wendt filed this action alleging breach of IH's Dealer Agreement and several other causes of action, but all Wendt's allegations save the breach of contract action were disposed of before trial. IH filed a counter-claim against Wendt for debts arising out of farm equipment and parts advanced to Wendt on credit.

At trial, the court allowed IH's defense of impracticability of performance to go to the jury on the contract action. The jury returned a verdict of no cause of action on the contract and the district court denied Wendt's motion for J.N.O.V./new trial, which was based on the invalidity of the impracticability defense. These actions by the court form a substantial basis of Wendt's appeal. In addition, however, the court ordered a directed verdict for Wendt as to IH's defenses of frustration of purpose, an implied covenant limiting the duration of the contract and a defense relating to whether Section 2 of the agreement permitted IH to cease production of all its product lines. The court's directed verdict on the viability of these defenses forms the basis of IH's cross-appeal....

II.

... Wendt asserts a number of errors surrounding the district court's allowing the defense of impracticability of performance to go to the jury. Wendt first contends that the defense of impracticability due to extreme changes in market conditions is not a cognizable defense under Michigan law. In the alternative, Wendt argues that there was insufficient evidence to withstand Wendt's motion for a directed verdict on impracticability. The jury's verdict of no cause of action against IH based on the impracticability defense also forms the basis of Wendt's motions for J.N.O.V. and new trial.

To determine whether the doctrine of impracticability is applicable under Michigan law based on the circumstances presented in this case, the court must first look to any controlling decisions of the Michigan Supreme Court.... If the Supreme Court has not spoken on a particular issue, the court must "ascertain from all available data what the state law is and apply it." *Bailey v. V. & O. Press Co*, 770 F.2d 601, 604 (6th Cir. 1985) (citations omitted). As this court recognized in *Angelotta*, "the 'available data' to be considered if the highest court has not spoken include relevant dicta from the state supreme court, decisional law of the appellate courts, restatements of law, law review commentaries, and the 'majority rule' among other states." *Angelotta*, 820 F.2d at 807 (quoting *Bailey*, 770 F.2d at 604)....

Generally, under Michigan law, "[e]conomic unprofitableness [sic] is not the equivalent to impossibility of performance. Subsequent events which in the nature of things do not render performance impossible, but only render it more difficult, burdensome, or expensive, will not operate to relieve [a party of its contractual obligations]." *Chase* [*Chase v. Clinton Cty.*, 241 Mich. 478, 484, 217 N.W. 565 (1928)], 241 Mich. at 484, 217 N.W. at 567....

In *Bissell* [*Bissell v. L.W. Edison Co.*, 9 Mich.App. 276, 156 N.W.2d 623 (1967)], the Michigan Court of Appeals, relying on the Restatement of Contracts section 457, concluded that the doctrine of impossibility is a valid defense not only when performance is impossible, but also when supervening circumstances make performance impracticable. Section 457 of the Restatement of Contracts, now section 261 of the Restatement (Second) of Contracts (1981) provides: "Discharge by Supervening Impracticability. Where, after a contract is made, a party's performance is made impracticable without his fault by the occurrence of an event the non-occurrence of which was a basic assumption on which the contract was made, his duty to render that performance is discharged, unless the language or the circumstances indicate the contrary."

Although *Bissell* did not involve non-performance due to economic causes, the court relied extensively on section 457 which defines impossibility to include, "not only strict impossibility but impracticability because of extreme and unreasonable difficulty, expense, injury and loss involved." *Bissell*, 9 Mich.App. at 285, 156 N.W.2d at 626. In the instant case the district court relied heavily on the language of section 457 quoted in *Bissell* to conclude that the extreme downturn in the market for farm products was "unreasonable and extreme" enough to present a jury question as to the defense under Michigan law. See J.App. at 47.

Recognizing that *Bissell* suggests that an impracticability defense may be cognizable under Michigan law in some circumstances, we must turn to the question of whether under Michigan law, the defense of impracticability was appropriately presented to the jury under the circumstances involving a dramatic downturn in the market for farm equipment which led to the contract action before us in this case. The commentary to section 261 of the Restatement (Second) provides extensive guidance for determining when economic circumstances are sufficient to render performance impracticable. Comment d to section 261 makes clear that mere lack of profit under the contract is insufficient: " '[I]mpracticability' means more than 'impracticality.' A mere change in the degree of difficulty or expense due to such causes as increased wages, prices of raw materials or costs of construction, unless well beyond the normal range, does not amount to impracticability since it is this sort of risk that a fixed price contract is intended to cover." Comment d also provides: "A severe shortage of raw materials or of supplies due to war, embargo, local crop failure, unforeseen shutdown of major sources of supply, or the like, which either causes a marked increase in cost or prevents performance altogether may bring the case within the rule stated in this Section."

More guidance is provided in Comment b to section 261. Comment b states: "In order for a supervening event to discharge a duty under this Section, the non-occurrence of that event must have been a 'basic assumption' on which both parties made the contract." Comment b goes on to provide that the application of the "basic assumption" criteria is also simple enough in the cases of market shifts or the financial inability of one of the parties. "The continuation of existing market conditions and of the financial situation of one of the parties are ordinarily *not* such assumptions, so that mere market shifts or financial inability do not usually effect discharge under the rule stated in this Section." (Emphasis added). Comment b also provides two helpful examples. In Illustration 3 of comment b, A contracts to employ B for two years at a set salary. After one year a government regulation makes A's business unprofitable and he fires B. A's duty to employ B is not discharged due to impracticability and A is liable for breach. In Illustration 4, A contracts to sell B a machine to be delivered by a certain date. Due to a suit by a creditor, all of A's assets are placed in receivership. A is not excused for non-performance under the doctrine of impracticability.

In our view, section 261 requires a finding that impracticability is an inappropriate defense in this case. The fact that IH experienced a dramatic downturn in the farm equipment market and decided to go out of the business does not excuse its unilateral termination of its dealership agreements due to impracticability. IH argues that while mere unprofitability should not excuse performance, the substantial losses and dramatic market shift in the farm equipment market between 1980 and 1985 warrant the special application of the defense in this case. IH cites losses of over $2,000,000.00 per day and a drop in the company's standing on the Fortune 500 list from 27 to 104. IH Brief at 7 (citing trial record). IH also put on evidence that if it had not sold its farm equipment division, it might have had to declare bankruptcy. While the facts suggest that IH suffered severely from the downturn in the farm equipment market, neither market shifts nor the financial inability of one of the parties changes the basic assumptions of the contract such that it may be excused under the doctrine of impracticability. Restatement (Second) of Contracts, section 261, comment b. To hold otherwise would not fulfill the likely understanding of the parties as to the apportionment of risk under the contract. The agreement provides in some detail the procedure and conditions for termination. IH may not have been entirely responsible for the economic downturn in the company, but it was responsible for its chosen remedy: to sell its farm equipment assets. An alternative would have been to terminate its Dealer Agreements by mutual assent under the termination provisions of the contract and share the proceeds of the sale of assets to Case/Tenneco with its dealers. Thus, we find that IH had alternatives which could have precluded unilateral termination of the contract. Further, application of the impracticability defense in this case would allow IH to avoid its liability under franchise agreements, allow Case/Tenneco to pick up only those dealerships its sees fit and leave the remaining dealers bankrupt. In such circumstance, application of the doctrine of impracticability would not only be a misapplication of law, but a windfall for IH at the expense of the dealers.

We find this understanding of the doctrine of impracticability to be more consistent with Michigan law than the district court's interpretation. In applying the doctrine of impossibility, the Michigan Supreme Court has repeatedly held that economic loss or hardship was not enough to excuse performance.... The fact that IH's losses in this case involved millions of dollars does not change the scope of the doctrine as the proportional effect of those changes is equivalent to the hardship imposed on the small businesses in the impossibility cases just described.

In the end, IH simply asserts that it would have been unprofitable to terminate its agreements with its dealers by invoking the six-month notice and other termination procedures embodied in the Dealer Agreement, or by sharing the proceeds of its sale of its farm equipment assets with dealers. This assertion does not excuse IH's performance under the agreement.

As *Bissell* did not address the question of economic circumstances which excuse performance under the doctrine of impracticability and neither the case law of the Supreme Court of Michigan nor the Restatement (Second) of Contracts suggests that the economic circumstances in this case would be sufficient to excuse performance, we hold that while the Supreme Court of Michigan might recognize the defense of impracticability, it would not do so in the circumstances of this case as a matter of law. Accordingly, we find that the district court erred in permitting the defense of impracticability to go to the jury and that Wendt was entitled to a directed verdict on this issue as a matter of law.

III.

In its cross-appeal, IH asserts that the court improperly granted a directed verdict for Wendt on its other affirmative defenses. Specifically, IH objects to the court's grant of a directed verdict on IH's defense of frustration of purpose, its defense based upon Section 2 of the Dealer Agreement and its defense based upon an implied covenant that the contract was not perpetual. We will address IH's defenses seriatim.

A. *Frustration Of Purpose*

It is undisputed that Michigan law recognizes the defense of frustration of purpose. See *Molnar v. Molnar*, 110 Mich.App. 622, 625–26, 313 N.W.2d 171, 173 (1981) (allowing the defense of frustration of purpose in a suit to discontinue child support payments when the beneficiary child died). However, the district court in the instant case determined that the defense was unavailable. In making this determination, the court relied on section 265 of the Restatement (Second) of Contracts which provides: "Where, after a contract is made, a party's principal purpose is substantially frustrated without his fault by the occurrence of an event the non-occurrence of which was a basic assumption on which the contract was made, his remaining duties to render performance are discharged, unless the language or the circumstances indicate the contrary."

In interpreting this provision, the district court relied on the Supreme Court of South Dakota's analysis of this same defense when raised by IH in a suit by a dealer for breach of the same dealer agreement in *Groseth Int'l. v. Tenneco*, 410 N.W.2d 159 (S.D.1987).

In *Groseth*, the court found that under the Restatement (Second), the defense of frustration requires the establishment of three factors. The first is that the purpose frustrated by the supervening event must have been the "principal purpose" of the party making the contract. Quoting section 265, comment a, the court noted, " 'It is not enough that [the contracting party] had in mind a specific object without which he would not have made the contract. The object must be so completely the basis of the contract that, as both parties understand, without it the transaction would make little sense.' " Id. at 165. The court interpreted this passage to require an inquiry into the principal purpose of the contract and a finding that the frustrating event destroys the primary basis of the contract. Id.

According to the *Groseth* court, the second factor required under the Restatement is that the frustration be "substantial." Once again quoting comment a to section 265, the court stated: " 'It is not enough that the transaction has become less profitable for the affected party or even that he will sustain a loss. The frustration must be so severe that it is not fairly to be regarded as within the risks that he assumed under the contract.' " Id. The court added, "[t]he fact that performance has become economically burdensome or unattractive is not sufficient to excuse performance." Id. (citations omitted).

Finally, according to *Groseth*, the third factor required to make out a defense of frustration under the Restatement is that the frustrating event must have been a "basic assumption" of the contract. See Restatement (Second) of Contracts, section 265 comment a. In analyzing this element, comment a states that the analysis is the same as under the defense of impracticability. Id. (referencing section 261, comment b) (quoted at p. 1117, supra.).

Applying these three factors in the instant case, the district court found that the primary purpose of the Dealer Agreement was stated in section 1 of the agreement. Section 1 provides, "The general purposes of the agreement are to establish the dealer of goods covered by this agreement, and to govern the relations between the dealer and the company in promoting the sale of those goods and their purchase and sale by the dealer, and in providing warranty and other service for their users." J.App. 506 (quoting agreement). The court interpreted this language to mean that the primary purpose of the agreement was to establish the dealership and the terms of interaction and was not "mutual profitability" as asserted by IH. Therefore, the court reasoned that a dramatic down-turn in the farm equipment market resulting in reduced profitability did not frustrate the primary purpose of the agreement. Id. at 505–07. The court went on to suggest that continuity of market conditions or the financial situation of the parties were not basic assumptions or implied conditions to the enforcement of a contract. Id. at 507. Thus, following Groseth, it held that the doctrine of frustration was not applicable to this case. Id.

IH does not offer any arguments which challenge the correctness of the *Groseth* decision or the district court's analysis. Rather, IH challenges the court's finding that the primary purpose of the contract was not "mutual profitability." In our view, the district court had substantial grounds for so finding and we affirm the district court's grant of a directed verdict for Wendt on the frustration defense. If IH's argument were to be accepted, the "primary purpose" analysis under the Restatement would essentially be meaningless as "mutual profitability" would be implied as the primary purpose of every contract. Rather, like the doctrine of impracticability, the doctrine of frustration is an equitable doctrine which is meant to fairly apportion risks between the parties in light of unforeseen circumstances. It is essentially an implied term which is meant to apportion risk as the parties would have had the necessity occurred to them. See *Groseth*, 410 N.W.2d at 166.... In this case, the frustrating event was IH's decision to sell its farm equipment assets and go out of that line of business. While IH might have determined that such a move was economically required, it may not then assert that its obligation under existing agreements are discharged in light of its decision.[19] For these reasons, we affirm.

19. In addition to an examination of whether the "primary purpose" of the contract was frustrated, Section 265 of the Restatement also requires that the frustrating event occur without the "fault" of the party seeking discharge. It does not seem to us a stretch to conclude that since the frustrating event was IH's decision to sell its

B. *Section 2 Of The Dealer Agreement*

Section 2 of the Dealer Agreement provides, in relevant part: "The agreement shall cover all those items of agricultural tractors, machines, equipment and attachments, which appear in the agricultural equipment price list issued by the company, and service parts for such goods. The company reserves the right to make additions to and eliminations from such list, including but not limited to reductions resulting from the discontinued production of a line or lines of such tractors, machines, equipment and attachments, without incurring any responsibility to the dealer." J.App. at 545. IH asserts that this provision authorizes IH to completely withdraw from the market. The theory is that if IH may withdraw some of its product lines it may also withdraw all of them.

Authority is split as to whether IH's asserted interpretation is correct. In *J.I. Case Co. v. Berkshire Implement Co.*, No. S86–555, slip op. at 7-10 (N.D.Ind. March 3, 1987) (following *St. Joseph Equipment v. Massey-Ferguson, Inc.*, 546 F.Supp. 1245 (W.D.Wis.1982)), the court interpreted a provision very similar to section 2 of the Dealer Agreement as enabling the manufacturer to eliminate all its product lines and go out of business. In *Groseth*, 410 N.W.2d 159 (S.D.1987), however, the court read section 2 of the same Dealer Agreement to allow IH to eliminate or change certain products or product lines, but not to eliminate its farm products altogether.

In the instant case, the district court followed the *Groseth* view of section 2 of the Dealer Agreement and we find that interpretation to be the correct one. Section 2, by its terms, seems to be intended to allow IH to make shifts in its product lines and to discontinue product lines without changing the binding force of the agreement. We find it quite a stretch to believe that the parties intended this provision to function as an alternative means for termination of the contract. This interpretation is reenforced by the fact that the agreement provides specific conditions and provisions for termination. See J.App. 555–61 (Section of the contract entitled "Termination of the Agreement"). As we find the court's interpretation of section 2 of the agreement correct as a matter of law, we affirm.

C. *An Implied Term That The Agreement Was Of Limited Duration*

Finally, IH asserts that the district court erred in refusing to find that an implied term of every dealership agreement is the ability of the manufacturer to go out of business. For this position, IH relies on dicta from the Supreme Court of Michigan in *Lichnovsky v. Ziebart Int'l. Corp.*, 414 Mich. 228, 324 N.W.2d 732 (1982). The court in *Lichnovsky* held that while it might be appropriate to imply a term for termination of an agreement when no termination provisions existed in the contract,

farm equipment assets without following the termination provisions of the contract, the frustration of the contract was IH's fault. IH would of course assert that it had no choice but to sell the assets, but we have covered this ground before. Thus, IH's fault in the frustration of its dealer agreements provides an additional reason for the inapplicability of the doctrine.

it would not imply such a term in a contract which provided for termination of the agreement for cause. Id. at 414 Mich. at 242–43, 324 N.W.2d at 739–40. In response to the argument that the Court's holding would create a perpetual franchise agreement, the Court stated:

> "There are relatively few enterprises that last even fifty or a hundred years, let alone forever. Just as an agreement for life employment (terminable for cause) is subject to the vicissitudes of human mortality, so too a franchise agreement is subject to the vicissitudes of the market[.]
>
> "* * * * * *
>
> "At some point, that which Ziebart and Lichnovsky agreed upon may no longer be viable. The life of the subject matter of their agreement will be at an end."

414 Mich. at 243–44, 324 N.W.2d at 740. Using this language, IH urges this court to imply a term which would allow termination of a franchise agreement when the manufacturer goes out of business. IH cites as precedent for this proposition *Delta Truck & Tractor v. J.I. Case, Co.*, No. 85–2606, 1990 WL 294415, slip op. at 2-3 (W.D.La.1990), which, relying on *Lichnovsky*, holds that in the absence of a specified duration of performance in the contract a reasonable time will be implied. The court held that a reasonable time in the circumstance of the IH franchise agreement was the period in which IH manufactured farm equipment. Hence, the court implied a term that when IH ceased to manufacture such equipment, the agreement was terminated. We find the court's invocation of *Lichnovsky* in *Delta Truck* misplaced as the Dealer Agreement, like the contract in *Lichnovsky,* has provisions for its termination for cause. Following *Lichnovsky* would require that no term be implied when the contract itself provides the circumstances for its own termination in its termination provisions.

As noted above, courts will use their equitable power to imply terms into contracts in circumstances which would apportion the risk of loss as the parties would have had they thought to include such a provision. See, e.g, *Groseth*, 410 N.W.2d at 166; Patch, 149 F.2d at 560. In this case, the evidence supports the conclusion that while either party might have anticipated market shifts neither party anticipated that IH would go out of the farm equipment business completely. Implying a term which enables IH to terminate its franchise agreement unilaterally without following the termination conditions of the agreement and without incurring a breach places all the risk on the dealer. Rather, if economic circumstances require that IH leave the market for farm products, it should properly seek to terminate its agreement under the terms of the agreement. This is precisely the same conclusion the *Lichnovsky* court arrived at in determining that a franchise agreement was not terminable at will, but rather terminable only for cause by its terms. See *Lichnovsky*, 414 Mich. at 242–43, 324 N.W.2d at 739–40. As there is no evidence which suggests that IH sought to terminate its agreement with Wendt by mutual agreement under the terms of the agreement, the district court properly granted a directed verdict for Wendt on this defense.

[Eds.: Discussion of other issues is omitted.]

V.

As the district court erred in allowing the defense of impracticability of performance to go to the jury in this case under Michigan law, we REVERSE and REMAND for a new trial only on the question of damages for IH's breach of its Dealer Agreement with Wendt. With respect to all other assignments of error by the parties, we AFFIRM.

RYAN, J. (DISSENTING). The court has held that the district court erred in submitting the defendants' defense of impracticability of performance to the jury. I disagree. . . .

It appears that the majority opinion rejects the impracticability defense "in the circumstances of this case" because, in the court's view, the economic reverses confronted by International Harvester were not so "extreme and unreasonable," severe, or catastrophic as to excuse performance of the franchise agreement with the plaintiffs. Although claiming to recognize that whether impracticability of performance has been proved is a question of fact for the jury, *Michigan Bean Co. v. Senn*, 93 Mich.App. 440, 287 N.W.2d 257 (1979), the court appears to disagree with the jury that International Harvester was confronted with economic circumstances sufficiently disastrous to justify discharge for impracticability. There were "alternatives," the court says, "which might have precluded unilateral termination of the contract." One such alternative open to International Harvester, the court suggests, might have been "to terminate [the] Dealer Agreements by mutual assent under the termination provisions of the contract and share the proceeds of the sale of assets to Case/Tenneco with its dealers."

Whether the "alternative" the court suggests ever occurred to International Harvester's management, or, if considered, was a feasible business solution, is entirely irrelevant on this appeal because it is the jury, not this court, that is empowered to determine whether International Harvester proved impracticability of performance as that defense was defined by the trial court. . . .

When all facts and reasonable inferences therefrom are taken in a light most favorable to International Harvester, they reveal a sudden, unforeseen, nationwide collapse of the farm implement industry so severe and so widespread that International Harvester, after losing over $2 billion in four years, was faced, in its business judgment, with no alternative but bankruptcy or selling off its farm implement division. Those are the facts as we must view them for purposes of this appeal. The question for us, then, is whether "reasonable people could differ" that those facts amounted to "an event, the non-occurrence of which was a basic assumption on which the contract was made." Restatement

(Second) of Contracts, supra. Manifestly, they could. The majority opinion is an indication of that.

Since there is nothing in the jurisprudence of the impracticability defense to suggest that a market collapse of the kind shown by International Harvester is not, as a matter of law, within the doctrine, we are not free to disturb the jury's verdict.

Notes and Discussion

1. **Alternative Defenses.** International Harvester attempted to defend itself under two distinct theories: that its performance had become impracticable, and that the purpose of its contract with Wendt had been frustrated. How did its impracticability argument differ from its frustration argument?

The trial court rejected the frustration theory summarily, but permitted the impracticability theory to go to trial. This suggests that IH's case for impracticability was at least arguable. But the boundary between a performance being merely "more difficult, burdensome, or expensive," and its becoming impractical "because of extreme and unreasonable difficulty, expense, injury and loss involved," is indistinct. Is the Court more concerned with the general economics of IH's continued manufacture of farm equipment, or with the specific economics of its contract with Wendt?

Decisions on this matter have been all over the map. "Cases have held that increases of fourteen percent, thirty one and one-half percent, fifty percent, or even a doubling of the cost of performance would be insufficient to meet the requirement of a sufficient increase in cost even if that increase were caused by an unforeseen or unexpected contingency. On the other hand, a ninety-three percent increase, and a $75 million dollar out-of-pocket loss, have been held sufficient." John Edward Murray, Jr., Murray on Contracts § 112 at 732 (4th ed. 2001) (footnotes omitted). In general, though, companies have not found a sympathetic ear when their contracts go south.

After failing in its attempts to escape the Wendt contract through an express or implied provision allowing termination, IH then had to use theories of excuse because of its own failure to negotiate an adequate bolt hole. Have you any sympathy?

2. **The *ALCOA* Debacle.** One prominent, although isolated, exception to the general pattern involves a notorious long-term contract between ALCOA and the Essex Group. *Aluminum Co. of Am. v. Essex Group, Inc.*, 499 F.Supp. 53 (W.D. Pa. 1980). The facts are complicated, but basically ALCOA was to process aluminum for Essex in return for a fee that was calculated, in part, on the basis of the whole-sale price index (WPI). For the first six years of the contract the pricing formula worked well: ALCOA's profits were within the range forecast as desirable by the contract. But electricity costs are of great importance in processing aluminum, and the pricing formula had failed to anticipate their quickly rising cost during the early 1970s. By the tenth year of the contract ALCOA was set to lose more than $75 million dollars; its losses thereafter were projected as catastrophic.

ALCOA sued for reformation of the pricing formula, alleging impracticability and frustration of purpose among other claims. The district court, in a 40-page opinion, found for ALCOA on almost every point, supporting ALCOA's contention that: "the shared objectives of the parties with respect to the use of the WPI have been completely and totally frustrated." Id. at 56. On this basis the judge intervened and set a new price that allowed ALCOA to receive a small profit. Essex appealed, but the parties settled before an appellate decision.

The academic reaction to the trial decision was swift and merciless. Especially toxic was John P. Dawson, *Judicial Revision of Frustrated Contracts: The United States*, 64 B.U. L. Rev. 1 (1984). Dawson had two main bases of criticism: first, that judges are singularly unqualified "to invent new designs for disrupted enterprises, now gone awry, that the persons most concerned had tried to construct but without success"; second, that in any case "from what source does any court derive the power to impose on [parties] a new contract without the free assent of both?" Id. at 37–38. For a more sympathetic appraisal, see, e.g., Robert A. Hillman, *Court Adjustment of Long-Term Contracts: An Analysis Under Modern Contract Law*, 1987 Duke L.J. 1, 33 ("The 'relational' realities of modern-day, long-term contracting suggest that when an unanticipated disruption causes calamitous losses to a party, a duty to adjust may arise."). Russell J. Weintraub, *A Survey of Contract Practice and Policy*, 1992 Wis. L.Rev. 1, 41–45, found that a plurality of the corporate counsel he surveyed favored judicial intervention of the ALCOA kind, provided that the parties had exercised customary care in drafting their agreement, if performance would result in a promisor's liquidation.

The fundamental issue here is, it should be stressed, more than academic. Since long-term contracts bring with them risks that become rapidly more difficult to foresee as the term lengthens, we need to ask what general position the law should take concerning such contracts. If courts are unwilling to intervene when the truly unexpected and disastrous occurs, law will be, in effect, scaring off parties from entering long-term contracts in the first place. As the ALCOA decision observes, "At stake in this suit is the future of a commercially important device—the long term contract. Such contracts are common in many fields of commerce. Mineral leases, building and ground leases, and long term coal sales agreements are just three examples of such contracts. If the law refused an appropriate remedy when a prudently drafted long term contract goes badly awry, the risks attending such contracts would increase. Prudent business people would avoid using this sensible business tool. Or they would needlessly suffer the delay and expense of ever more detailed and sophisticated drafting in an attempt to approximate by agreement what the law could readily furnish by general rule." 499 F.Supp. at 89.

By way of counterpoint: *Printing Industries Ass'n of Northern Ohio, Inc. v. International Printing and Graphic Communications Union*, 584 F.Supp. 990, 998 (N.D. Ohio 1984): "Although an instance may indeed occur in which both parties mutually chose the use of a variable factor on a mistaken assumption that the factor would function in a specific manner and rested their entire agreement on that assumption, courts should be reluctant to grant reformation. The willingness of courts to reform contracts on the basis of subsequent knowledge may undermine the policy of finality which is so essential and revered in contract law."

Frier, in accord with his usual *dirigiste* sympathies, thinks courts should intervene more aggressively and inventively than they now do. White is, to say the very least, rather more reserved. What do you think?

ALABAMA FOOTBALL, INC. v. WRIGHT

United States District Court, Northern District of Texas, 1977.
452 F.Supp. 182.

HILL, J. The cross motions for summary judgment filed by both parties on the Original Complaint of Plaintiff Alabama Football, Inc. (hereinafter "Alabama") and the motion for summary judgment filed by Defendant and Cross-Plaintiff Larry Rayfield Wright (hereinafter "Wright") on his counterclaim came on for consideration before the Honorable Robert M. Hill, United States District Judge. The court has considered the motions, the supporting and opposing briefs for both sides, and the oral arguments made by counsel and enters the following ORDER:

Original Complaint. The initial controversy centers itself around the definition of the word "bonus." In April of 1974 the parties entered into a contract whereby Wright agreed to play professional football for Alabama for the years 1977, 1978 and 1979. As per the terms of such contract Alabama, a member of the World Football League, paid Wright a $75,000 bonus at the time of the execution of the agreement. Subsequent to the execution of this agreement Alabama and the World Football League ceased to exist, thus making the whole of the contract incapable of being performed.

Alabama now seeks the return of the $75,000 claiming a total failure of consideration for the contract and contending that unjust enrichment will result if Wright is allowed to keep such bonus amount. Alabama specifically argues that the term "bonus" in the context of the relevant contract means compensation paid for services which were to be performed in the future by Wright for the benefit of Alabama. Therefore, since the unavoidable demise of Alabama and consequently Wright's inability to perform the contemplated future services, the advanced bonus should be returned for failure of mutual exchange of consideration.

Wright denies this claim. He argues that the word "bonus" in the context of the relevant contract and in the world of professional football means simply the payment of money in consideration for signing the contract. It is argued that the act of signing itself is full consideration for the bonus paid. Wright also argues that in addition to signing the contract he gave other valuable consideration for the bonus payment made by Alabama. Such other consideration is described as forbearance in negotiating with the Dallas Cowboys, Wright's existing employer, and with all other professional football teams for the 1975-1977 football seasons and allowing Alabama to publicize his name in promotions for

Alabama's team. Accordingly, Wright asserts there has been due consideration given Alabama for its payment of the bonus.

In the court's opinion Wright's argument is most compelling. The contract between the two parties is unambiguous. Therefore, this court's responsibility is to construe the intent of the parties and the terms of the contract from the language of the document itself and the surrounding circumstances at its execution. In considering the word "bonus" in the context of the contract and the usage made of such word in professional football, the court finds that the parties intended Wright to be paid a $75,000 bonus upon his execution of a player's contract with Alabama and that no further services were contemplated by the parties as a condition to such payment or the retention of such payment by Wright. The bonus was not paid merely in anticipation of Wright's future services as a football player, but in exchange for a fully performed act, Wright's signing of the contract. The court finds such contractual provision to be reasonable and fair.

Additionally, the court finds that Alabama benefitted from the execution of Wright's player contract. Such benefit consisted of obtaining Wright's playing services by at the latest the 1977 football season and for subsequent playing seasons and obtaining an exclusive agreement prohibiting Wright from negotiating or executing any other contract with any other professional football club in any football league. Even assuming the contract required more than the execution of the contract, these benefits accruing to Alabama upon execution of the contract would provide ample consideration to support the bonus payment.

Having concluded that the bonus segment of Wright's players contract is supported by consideration, two issues remain: (1) whether the contract must be read together and treated in its entirety or whether the contract is in divisible segments each capable of standing alone, and (2) whether the entire contract or any of its segments has failed because of commercial frustration and impossibility of performance and therefore both parties are absolved from performance under the contract or its segments.

To determine whether this contract is severable or entire, the court must determine the intention of the parties and ascertain whether different performances were contemplated with each performance to receive an agreed compensation. *Pittsburgh Plate Glass Co. v. Jarrett*, 42 F. Supp. 723 (M.D. Georgia) modified 131 F.2d 674 (5th Cir. 1942). Additional considerations are the subject matter and the purpose of the contract, the circumstances of the parties and whether the consideration is apportioned. *MacArthur v. C.I.R.*, 168 F.2d 413 (8th Cir. 1948).

Following these guidelines, the court is of the opinion that Wright's contract although a single instrument contemplates five independent financial agreements each of which, in the circumstances of the unprovided for contingency of the financial failure of Alabama, is to be dealt with separately. Such agreements consist of payment of a bonus when the contract was executed, payment of an additional bonus when Wright first reported to Alabama's training camp, and salary payments for the first three years Wright played for Alabama in accordance with the agreed conditions in the contract. See *Sample v. Gotham Football Club, Inc.*, 59 F.R.D. 160 (S.D.N.Y.1973).

The Counterclaim. Finding that five distinct agreements exist in the parties' contract and recognizing that one of those agreements, the execution of the contract itself, has been validly concluded, the question becomes whether the four remaining agreements are viable, breached, and require the possible payment of damages, or whether performance of the remaining segments is impossible and thus four-fifths of the contract a nullity.

Wright contends that the remaining provisions of the contract have been breached by Alabama in failing to provide a forum where Wright could perform the agreed services and that such failure is not excused because Alabama assumed the risk that its football team might fail. Alabama asserts that because of financial circumstances beyond its control and for which it has never assumed the risk the remaining provisions of the contract are impossible to be performed.

Impossibility occurs where (1) an unexpected contingency occurs, (2) the risk of which was not allocated either by agreement or custom, and (3) the occurrence of the contingency has made performance impossible. *West Los Angeles Institute for Cancer v. Mayer*, 366 F.2d 220 (9th Cir. 1966), *certiorari denied* 385 U.S. 1010, 87 S. Ct. 718, 17 L. Ed. 2d 548 (1967).

In the present case the contingency of Alabama's financial failure does not seem to have been expected by either party. No clause is provided in the contract setting forth the parties' rights in the event Alabama or the World Football League failed and there is no evidence of discussion concerning this possibility between the parties at any time. Further, the risk of bankruptcy was not expressly or impliedly allocated to either party. Alabama could not have reasonably foreseen such sudden demise of its team and the World Football League. Finally, it is undisputed that the dissolve of Alabama's team and the World Football League has made performance of the remaining unexecuted four-fifths of the contract impossible. Accordingly, the parties are excused from further performance in compliance with the contract.

Wherefore, Alabama's motion for summary judgment is overruled; Wright's motion for summary judgment on the Original Complaint is sustained; and Wright's motion for summary judgment on his counterclaim is overruled.

It is so ORDERED.

Notes and Discussion

1. An Ill-Fated League. The World Football League was formed on August 2, 1973 and folded on October 22, 1975. It sought to survive through rule innovations, but also by recruiting some major talent such as Rayfield

Wright (tight end for the Dallas Cowboys, 1967-1979; six-time Pro-Bowler) at what were, for that time, elevated salaries. The WFL struggled through two years of direct competition with the NFL, finally collapsing under enormous debt thirteen weeks into its second season. So great were the WFL's financial struggles that some of its teams relocated during mid-season, and a couple of the teams disbanded altogether before the league as a whole did. Was the risk of the WFL's demise actually unforeseeable (if perhaps "unexpected") when Wright entered his contract with the Birmingham Americans in April, 1974? (The Birmingham Americans won the first and only World Bowl in 1974, some months after executing this contract; but then faced the indignity of having to hand over their equipment to Sheriff's deputies because of debt.) To the extent that the risk was foreseeable, which party should have borne it in the absence of an express contractual allocation? On the WFL, see http://wflfootball.tripod.com/.

Although courts vary somewhat in their attitudes, many have held that a party assumes a risk if an event is foreseeable and it fails to provide for the risk. Remember Judge Posner's words in the *NIPSCO* case: "[A] fixed-price contract is an explicit assignment of the risk of market price increases to the seller and the risk of market price decreases to the buyer, and the assignment of the latter risk to the buyer is even clearer where, as in this case, the contract places a floor under price but allows for escalation. If, as is also the case here, the buyer forecasts the market incorrectly and therefore finds himself locked into a disadvantageous contract, he has only himself to blame and so cannot shift the risk back to the seller by invoking impossibility or related doctrines." 799 F.2d at 278 (citation omitted).

Could the Court have taken the same position in the *Wright* case? If Wright had won on his counterclaim, what damages would he have received?

2. **Discharge of the Duty to Render Performance.** In the *Wright* case, Alabama Football wanted back its $75,000 signing bonus, while Wright (who had presumably long since spent the money) naturally wanted to avert this. The delicate issue here is what the consequences are when the principal purpose of a contract is held to have been frustrated, particularly when performance has already begun on one or both sides. Suppose that, in the coronation cases, the person who hired the apartment had made a down payment of twenty-five percent when the contract was made. If the coronation is subsequently cancelled, he is excused from further performance, but can he also get restitution? The usual American rule is that both parties can seek restitution of any benefits conferred: Restatement 2d § 272(1). How does the *Wright* court argue in denying restitution to Alabama?

Reliance is a different matter. In the coronation cases, suppose that the apartment's owner, in fulfillment of the contract, had spent a substantial amount on redecorating before the cancellation. This expense does not benefit the other party, and, despite the recommendation of § 272(2), few American courts have permitted recovery of any of it, even in situations where the hirer can recover his restitution interest. The British solved this problem in 1943 through law reform (the Frustrated Contracts Act, 6 & 7 Geo. 6, c. 40), which permits judicial limitation of restitution damages to reflect an offsetting reliance interest; but there is no comparable American legislation. Surely there should be, since early payments under contracts are often intended to facilitate the other party's preparation costs.

3. The Economics of Impracticability and Frustration. Since legal acceptance of excuses based on impracticability or frustration recognizes that the imperfect rationality of parties and the high transaction costs of negotiating contracts lead to less than optimal provision for future contingencies, economists have been keenly interested in these excuses, and particularly in how ready courts should be to admit them. A leading article is Richard A. Posner & Andrew M. Rosenfeld, *Impossibility and Related Doctrines in Contract Law: An Economic Analysis*, 6 J. Legal Stud. 83 (1977), who argue that expectation damages should be analogized to insurance; the promisor, by being forced to pay these damages, in effect insures the promisee against the risk of breach. But just as an ordinary insurance policy excludes certain risks, so too should the rules for expectation damages. In general, the superior risk-bearer should bear the risk; but risks that are unforeseen, uncontrollable by the parties, and large are best shared by the parties—an efficient outcome, so it is believed.

Problem 7–6

A shipping company was scheduled to carry goods from Texas to India. The typical route of travel is eastward, through the Mediterranean, the Suez Canal, the Red Sea, and southward to India. As the ship passed through the Strait of Gibraltar, the Suez Canal was closed because of fighting between Israel and Egypt. The ship then reversed course and went around the Cape of Good Hope, a much longer and more dangerous route. The extra expenses were $131,978.44. Under the contract, the shipping company was to be paid a fixed fee of about $417,000, not by the day or the mile. Can the shipping company recover the additional $131,978.44?

Chapter 8

THIRD-PARTY RIGHTS AND RESPONSIBILITIES

Rules about third-party beneficiaries, assignment, and delegation are usually at the tail end of a course on contracts. This nonverbal message is not lost on students who soon learn that many courses peter out before the end of the book, and that late semester coverage is likely to be hurried and superficial. Conceding all that, and admitting to having given the conventional nonverbal message, we argue for the importance of third-party rights and obligations in contracts.

To see a third-party beneficiary in the flesh, look at UCC § 2–318. In its various alternatives, the section tells when a member of the family might enjoy the benefit of the warranty that was given by the seller to its buyer. When little Phil breaks his tooth on a pebble in the soup that mother Lucille bought, Phil has a warranty claim if Lucille does. He is a third-party beneficiary of her contract with Kroger. And under alternative C of 2–318, Lucille, if she buys a H–P computer, might have a claim against Hewlett–Packard the manufacturer, even though she bought it at Circuit City and had no contract directly with H–P. She would be the third-party beneficiary of the warranty that H–P gave to Circuit City. A traditional but seldom seen case arises when A owes a debt to C and B promises A that he will pay the debt to C. C can enforce the contract between B and A.

The Restatement portrays a world of "intended" beneficiaries (who can enforce) and "incidental" beneficiaries (who cannot enforce). In law "intended" are few; "incidental," many. Service on the School Board in Ann Arbor showed one of us why courts are hesitant to recognize legal rights in persons who are clearly incidental beneficiaries of contracts between third parties. Not a meeting of the School Board passed without some articulate citizen explaining how things could be done better, how the school buses should run at different times, how the new school should be constructed a different way or how teachers could teach more or different math. Most of these citizens could claim to be beneficiaries of every school contract, from the teacher's collective bargaining agreement on down. All of these citizens were articulate and most were smart, but their ideas ranged from merely self-interested and impractical to loony. If each of these well intentioned but officious persons were recognized as a third-party beneficiary of every contract that the school board signed, the school district, the teachers, and every school contractor would have found themselves in court on citizens' claims daily. So third-party beneficiary law is important but narrow. Most beneficiaries are "incidental" and have no legal rights on contracts between third parties.

One party to a contract often creates rights in a third party by *assigning* his rights, less often one creates third-party duties by *delegating* his duties to others. Section 2–210 is a good summary of the law within and without the Code on these questions. Generally the law is receptive to payees who wish to assign their rights to payment. Normally the debtor has no reason to refuse the claim of an assignee of a right to payment (except to be sure that his payment to the assignee discharges the original liability).

The same is not true of delegation of a duty to perform. Consider the possibility that Leonardo da Vinci, having agreed to paint a portrait of a smiling young woman in a blue dress, should delegate the duty of painting to a friend; that a renowned brain surgeon should leave the carving to a raw resident; or that a handsome and engaging young man should transfer his marriage contract to his aged, irritable uncle. Of course, most cases are not like these extreme examples; most routine duties can be delegated. Considering the fact that the original obligor remains obligated to do the job if the delegatee does not, it is not surprising that delegation is often permitted.

Commercial deals abound with other, more complex third-party issues. If Brian contracts to buy a car from a local dealer and gives a cashier's check (a check drawn by a bank on itself and payable to the car dealer), can the bank, at Brian's request, refuse to pay its cashier's check—refuse to honor its separate contract—if Brian finds that the car is non-conforming before the check clears? If the dealer later sues the bank, can the bank assert Brian's defense? The answer should be no and no; do you see why? This goes well beyond assignment and delegation for a first year contracts course, but we think it fair to open the door here to the related issue: what defenses may one assert, his own or others' too? See UCC § 3–305. Normally an assignee takes subject to the defenses that could be asserted against the assignor, but the holder in due course doctrine says that is not true of certain special assignees.

Although they are not third-party beneficiaries or assignees, guarantors, like assignors, are directly interested in one contracting party's performance. If Brian's father guarantees Brian's promise to pay for his car in installments, may father assert all defenses that Brian has? Brian might want to stop paying because of a material breach by the dealer; the father should be able to assert that defense, shouldn't he? But if Brian takes bankruptcy and so discharges his liability to the car dealer that is different.

We suspect that these apparently complex rules on the rights and obligations of third parties rest on common sense expectations. One way to think about these issues is to ask, what would mother expect me to do? (Wouldn't she agree that the bankruptcy of Brian should not relieve father since the threat of Brian's bankruptcy is the very reason why the dealer made father sign?)

A. THIRD–PARTY BENEFICIARIES

My next-door neighbors spend their summers in Door County, Wisconsin. While they are away, they contract with a lawn care service to mow their lawn once a week. This summer I have noticed that the service was mowing very irregularly, so that my neighbors' lawn is often a mess. This is of great concern to me, since I am trying to sell my house and want prospective buyers to have a favorable impression of the neighborhood. Nonetheless, even though I have an obvious interest in the lawn service's performance, I have no standing to sue the service for breach of contract. The reason is, of course, that I lack **privity of contract**; even though I benefit from my neighbors' contract, I am not a party to it, and I cannot sue on it even if my neighbors knew of my interest when they made the contract, unless they specifically intended the contract to benefit me. In the language of the Second Restatement, §§ 302(2) and 315, I am only an "incidental beneficiary" who "acquires by virtue of the promise no right against the promisor or the promisee." This boundary is often somewhat arbitrary, however.

In the nineteenth century privity of contract was a strong doctrine, and it still has teeth in some instances. But today it is universal law that under many circumstances a contract can create contractual rights in a third party. The case usually taken as seminal is the following one.

LAWRENCE v. FOX

Court of Appeals of New York, 1859.
20 N.Y. 268.

APPEAL from the Superior Court of the city of Buffalo. On the trial before Mr. Justice MASTEN, it appeared by the evidence of a bystander, that one Holly, in November, 1857, at the request of the defendant [Fox], loaned and advanced to him $300, stating at the time that he owed that sum to the plaintiff [Lawrence] for money borrowed of him, and had agreed to pay it to him the then next day; that the defendant in consideration thereof, at the time of receiving the money, promised to pay it to the plaintiff the then next day. Upon this state of facts the defendant moved for a nonsuit, upon three several grounds, viz.: That there was no proof tending to show that Holly was indebted to the plaintiff; that the agreement by the defendant with Holly to pay the plaintiff was void for want of consideration, and that there was no privity between the plaintiff and defendant. The court overruled the motion, and the counsel for the defendant excepted. The cause was then submitted to the jury, and they found a verdict for the plaintiff for the amount of the loan and interest, $344.66, upon which judgment was entered; from which the defendant appealed to the Superior Court, at general term, where the judgment was affirmed, and the defendant appealed to this court. The cause was submitted on printed arguments.

GRAY, J. [Eds.: The Judge holds that there was sufficient evidence of Holly's debt to Lawrence.] But it is claimed that notwithstanding this promise was established by competent evidence, it was void for the want of consideration. It is now more than a quarter of a century since it was settled by the Supreme Court of this State—in an able and pains-taking opinion by the late Chief Justice SAVAGE, in which the authorities were fully examined and carefully analysed—that a promise in all material respects like the one under consideration was valid; and the judgment of that court was unanimously affirmed by the Court for the Correction of Errors. (*Farley v. Cleaveland*, 4 Cow., 432; same case in error, 9 id., 639.) In that case one Moon owed Farley and sold to Cleaveland a quantity of hay, in consideration of which Cleaveland promised to pay Moon's debt to Farley; and the decision in favor of Farley's right to recover was placed upon the ground that the hay received by Cleaveland from Moon was a valid consideration for Cleaveland's promise to pay Farley, and that the subsisting liability of Moon to pay Farley was no objection to the recovery.

The fact that the money advanced by Holly to the defendant was a loan to him for a day, and that it thereby became the property of the defendant, seemed to impress the defendant's counsel with the idea that because the defendant's promise was not a trust fund placed by the plaintiff in the defendant's hands, out of which he was to realize money as from the sale of a chattel or the collection of a debt, the promise although made for the benefit of the plaintiff could not inure to his benefit. The hay which [Moon] delivered to [Cleaveland][1] was not to be paid to Farley, but the debt incurred by Cleaveland for the purchase of the hay, like the debt incurred by the defendant for money borrowed, was what was to be paid.

That case has been often referred to by the courts of this State, and has never been doubted as sound authority for the principle upheld by it.... It puts to rest the objection that the defendant's promise was void for want of consideration. The report of that case shows that the promise was not only made to Moon but to the plaintiff Farley. In this case the promise was made to Holly and not expressly to the plaintiff; and this difference between the two cases presents the question, raised by the defendant's objection, as to the want of privity between the plaintiff and defendant. As early as 1806 it was announced by the Supreme Court of this State, upon what was then regarded as the settled law of England, "That where one person makes a promise to another for the benefit of a third person, that third person may maintain an action upon it."

1. [Eds.: The judge reversed the names.]

Schermerhorn v. *Vanderheyden* (1 John. R., 140), has often been re-asserted by our courts and never departed from....

The same principle is adjudged in several cases in Massachusetts. I will refer to but few of them. (*Arnold v. Lyman*, 17 Mass., 400; *Hall v. Marston*, Id., 575; *Brewer v. Dyer*, 7 Cush., 337, 340.) In *Hall v. Marston* the court say: "It seems to have been well settled that if A promises B for a valuable consideration to pay C, the latter may maintain *assumpsit* for the money;" and in *Brewer v. Dyer*, the recovery was upheld, as the court said, "upon the principle of law *long recognized and clearly established*, that when one person, for a valuable consideration, engages with another, by a simple contract, to do some act for the benefit of a third, the latter, who would enjoy the benefit of the act, may maintain an action for the breach of such engagement; that it does not rest upon the ground of any actual or supposed relationship between the parties as some of the earlier cases would seem to indicate, but upon the broader and more satisfactory basis, that the law operating on the act of the parties creates the duty, establishes a privity, and implies the promise and obligation on which the action is founded." ...

But it is urged that because the defendant was not in any sense a trustee of the property of Holly for the benefit of the plaintiff, the law will not imply a promise. I agree that many of the cases where a promise was implied were cases of trusts, created for the benefit of the promiser. The case of *Felton v. Dickinson* (10 Mass., 189, 190), and others that might be cited, are of that class; but concede them all to have been cases of trusts, and it proves nothing against the application of the rule to this case. The duty of the trustee to pay the *cestuis que trust*, according to the terms of the trust, implies his promise to the latter to do so. In this case the defendant, upon ample consideration received from Holly, promised Holly to pay his debt to the plaintiff; the consideration received and the promise to Holly made it as plainly his duty to pay the plaintiff as if the money had been remitted to him for that purpose, and as well implied a promise to do so as if he had been made a trustee of property to be converted into cash with which to pay. The fact that a breach of the duty imposed in the one case may be visited, and justly, with more serious consequences than in the other, by no means disproves the payment to be a duty in both. The principle illustrated by the example so frequently quoted (which concisely states the case in hand) "that a promise made to one for the benefit of another, he for whose benefit it is made may bring an action for its breach," has been applied to trust cases, not because it was exclusively applicable to those cases, but because it was a principle of law, and as such applicable to those cases.

It was also insisted that Holly could have discharged the defendant from his promise, though it was intended by both parties for the benefit of the plaintiff, and therefore the plaintiff was not entitled to maintain this suit for the recovery of a demand over which he had no control. It is enough that the plaintiff did not release the defendant from his promise, and whether he could or not is a question not now necessarily involved; but if it was, I think it would be found difficult to maintain the right of

Holly to discharge a judgment recovered by the plaintiff upon confession or otherwise, for the breach of the defendant's promise; and if he could not, how could he discharge the suit before judgment, or the promise before suit, made as it was for the plaintiff's benefit and in accordance with legal presumption accepted by him (*Berley v. Taylor,* 5 Hill, 577–584, et seq.), until his dissent was shown.

The cases cited, and especially that of *Farley v. Cleaveland*, establish the validity of a parol promise; it stands then upon the footing of a written one. Suppose the defendant had given his note in which, for value received of Holly, he had promised to pay the plaintiff and the plaintiff had accepted the promise, retaining Holly's liability. Very clearly Holly could not have discharged that promise, be the right to release the defendant as it may. No one can doubt that he owes the sum of money demanded of him, or that in accordance with his promise it was his duty to have paid it to the plaintiff; nor can it be doubted that whatever may be the diversity of opinion elsewhere, the adjudications in this State, from a very early period, approved by experience, have established the defendant's liability; if, therefore, it could be shown that a more strict and technically accurate application of the rules applied, would lead to a different result (which I by no means concede), the effort should not be made in the face of manifest justice.

The judgment should be affirmed.

JOHNSON, Ch. J., DENIO, SELDEN, ALLEN and STRONG, Js., concurred. JOHNSON, Ch. J., and DENIO, J., were of opinion that the promise was to be regarded as made to the plaintiff through the medium of his agent, whose action he could ratify when it came to his knowledge, though taken without his being privy thereto.

COMSTOCK, J. (DISSENTING.) The plaintiff had nothing to do with the promise on which he brought this action. It was not made to him, nor did the consideration proceed from him. If he can maintain the suit, it is because an anomaly has found its way into the law on this subject. In general, there must be privity of contract. The party who sues upon a promise must be the promisee, or he must have some legal interest in the undertaking. In this case, it is plain that Holly, who loaned the money to the defendant, and to whom the promise in question was made, could at any time have claimed that it should be performed to himself personally. He had lent the money to the defendant, and at the same time directed the latter to pay the sum to the plaintiff. This direction he could countermand, and if he had done so, manifestly the defendant's promise to pay according to the direction would have ceased to exist. The plaintiff would receive a benefit by a complete execution of the arrangement, but the arrangement itself was between other parties, and was under their exclusive control. If the defendant had paid the money to Holly, his debt would have been discharged thereby. So Holly might have released the demand or assigned it to another person, or the parties might have annulled the promise now in question, and designated some other creditor of Holly as the party to whom the money should be paid. It has never been claimed, that in a case thus situated, the right of a third person to sue upon the promise rested on any sound principle of law....

The cases in which some trust was involved are also frequently referred to as authority for the doctrine now in question, but they do not sustain it. If A delivers money or property to B, which the latter accepts upon a trust for the benefit of C, the latter can enforce the trust by an appropriate action for that purpose. (*Berly v. Taylor*, 5 Hill, 577.) If the trust be of money, I think the beneficiary may assent to it and bring the action for money had and received to his use. If it be of something else than money, the trustee must account for it according to the terms of the trust, and upon principles of equity. There is some authority even for saying that an express promise founded on the possession of a trust fund may be enforced by an action at law in the name of the beneficiary, although it was made to the creator of the trust.... But further than this we cannot go without violating plain rules of law. In the case before us there was nothing in the nature of a trust or agency. The defendant borrowed the money of Holly and received it as his own. The plaintiff had no right in the fund, legal or equitable. The promise to repay the money created an obligation in favor of the lender to whom it was made and not in favor of any one else....

The judgment of the court below should therefore be reversed, and a new trial granted.

Notes and Discussion

1. The Background. *Lawrence v. Fox* is discussed in Anthony Jon Waters, *The Property in the Promise: A Study of the Third Party Beneficiary Rule*, 98 Harv. L. Rev. 1109, 1116–1148 (1985), who sheds considerable light on the case. The promise that is the subject of the lawsuit was made by Fox to "Holly" (actually, Hawley), most probably as part of a gambling transaction in Buffalo, New York. Hawley gave Fox $300 (then a substantial sum of money), in return for Fox agreeing to repay this amount to Hawley's creditor, Lawrence, on the following day. Lawrence was not present when the promise was made, but learned of it later. Hawley then dropped out of the picture, for reasons that are unclear (a run to the border?); and Lawrence brought suit directly against Fox for the $300.

In modern terminology, Lawrence was a creditor beneficiary because "the performance of [Fox's] promise will satisfy an obligation of the promisee [Hawley] to pay money to the beneficiary": Restatement 2d § 302(1)(a). If Lawrence had not been a creditor and Hawley had only been aiming to bestow a gift upon him, he would be a donee beneficiary: § 302(1)(b). The distinction between these two categories is of minor significance today; what is crucial, in the Second Restatement, is that Lawrence was clearly an intended and not an incidental beneficiary.

2. Distinctions. The central problem that the Court has with *Lawrence v. Fox* is that it does not quite fit any of the pre-existing legal categories. Had Hawley given the $300 to Fox in exchange for Fox's promise to convey these exact bills to Lawrence, that would have been a trust (Fox would have legal title to the money but Lawrence would be its "equitable" owner); and all the judges agree that Lawrence would then have been entitled, as the beneficiary of the trust, to bring suit for payment against Fox. But that is not what had happened. Rather, Fox received ownership of the money (which he was then free to gamble away), and agreed only to pay the same amount to Lawrence. Is this a big difference, as Judge Comstock thinks? (Today trusts are a great deal more flexible than they were in the mid-nineteenth century, although the basic idea remains the same.)

A second theory is invoked by two judges who concur in the result. They use the theory of agency, holding that Hawley, in accepting Fox's promise to pay $300 to Lawrence, was acting as Lawrence's agent at least as of the moment when Lawrence ratified the transaction. This interpretation is not impossible, but seems very strained; Hawley scarcely seems to have intended to act as Lawrence's agent.

Other theories are also possible, but the majority opts to cut the Gordian knot and simply declare the contract enforceable by Lawrence. What problems does this potentially create? Is the majority opinion too broadly written to be persuasive?

3. **Revocability and Vesting.** One issue that the dissent raises is that Hawley, "who loaned the money to the defendant, and to whom the promise in question was made, could at any time have claimed that it should be performed to himself personally." His point appears to be that the agreement between Hawley and Fox did not create a right in Lawrence because Hawley could at any time have revoked Fox's duty to pay Lawrence. How does the majority seek to counter this point?

Restatement 2d § 311(1) permits the parties to make the right of a third-party beneficiary irrevocable if they wish. Where they do not do so, they "retain power to discharge or modify the duty by subsequent agreement," but this power ends when the beneficiary, before being notified of the discharge or modification, justifiably relies on the promise, brings suit on it, or upon request of promisor or promisee agrees to accept the benefit. Restatement 2d § 311(2)-(3). Comment g indicates that reliance is presumed to be justified absent "contrary indication." You can see in these rules the consequence of fairly elaborate balancing of interests; is everyone adequately protected? As the modern rule on discharge or modification makes clear, the third party's right is in principle contingent, not an immediately vested one.

4. **Defenses.** "A promise creates no duty to a beneficiary unless a contract is formed between the promisor and the promisee; and if a contract is voidable or unenforceable at the time of its formation the right of any beneficiary is subject to the infirmity." Restatement 2d § 309(1). This rule embraces all the usual requirements for a binding contract, including consideration between promisor and promisee, their agreement, and the rules concerning illegality and the Statute of Frauds. What was the consideration for Fox's promise to Hawley?

In accord with the contingent nature of a beneficiary's contractual right, the promisor can also defend against the beneficiary if the main contract later becomes unenforceable "because of impracticability, public policy, non-occurrence of a condition, or present or prospective failure of performance":

Restatement 2d § 309(2). *Rouse v. United States*, 215 F.2d 872 (D.C. Cir. 1954), illustrates this point. Bessie Winston had a furnace installed in her home, and gave a promissory note for about $1000 to pay for it; the note was guaranteed by the Federal Housing Authority (FHA). In time, Winston sold her house to John Rouse, who in the contract of sale assumed payments for the furnace. (Therefore, for purposes of this promise, Rouse is the promisor, Winston the promisee, and the FHA the third-party beneficiary.) After Rouse defaulted, the FHA paid off the note and brought suit. Rouse defended by asserting that Winston had fraudulently misrepresented the condition of the furnace. The Court permitted this defense, noting that: "one who promises to make a payment to the promisee's creditor can assert against the creditor any defense that the promisor could assert against the promisee." Id. at 874. This includes fraud, of course.

Problem 8–1

Exercycle sells exercise machines through a series of regional distributorships. Each contract confines the distributor to a specified territory. The Michigan distributor was given exclusive rights in Michigan and the area around Toledo, while the Chicago distributor had rights in the area around Chicago. When the Chicago distributor began selling Exercycles in Michigan, it was sued on contract by the Michigan distributor, which claimed that it was the third-party beneficiary of Exercycle's contract with the Chicago distributor. What outcome?

Problem 8–2

The city of Rensselaer, New York, contracted with a water company to supply water to its water system, including fire hydrants. This water was to be furnished to private users within the city at their homes and factories. While the contract was in force, a fire broke out in a building and spread to the H.R. Moch Co. warehouse, which was destroyed along with its contents. The company has brought suit against the water company claiming that the loss occurred because it failed to maintain adequate water pressure in the hydrants—a breach of the contract with the city, of which Moch was an intended third-party beneficiary. What outcome?

Think about the issues raised by this problem before you proceed to the following case.

MARTINEZ v. SOCOMA COMPANIES, INC.

Supreme Court of California, 1974.
11 Cal.3d 394, 113 Cal.Rptr. 585, 521 P.2d 841.

WRIGHT, J. Plaintiffs brought this class action on behalf of themselves and other disadvantaged unemployed persons, alleging that defendants failed to perform contracts with the United States government under which defendants agreed to provide job training and at least one year of employment to certain numbers of such persons. Plaintiffs claim that they and the other such persons are third-party beneficiaries of the contracts and as such are entitled to damages for defendants' nonperformance. General demurrers to the complaint were sustained without leave to amend, apparently on the ground that plaintiffs lacked standing to sue as third-party beneficiaries. Dismissals were entered as to the demurring defendants and plaintiffs appeal.

We affirm the judgments of dismissal. As will appear, the contracts nowhere state that either the government or defendants are to be liable to persons such as plaintiffs for damages resulting from the defendants' nonperformance. The benefits to be derived from defendants' performance were clearly intended not as gifts from the government to such persons but as a means of executing the public purposes stated in the contracts and in the underlying legislation. Accordingly, plaintiffs were only incidental beneficiaries and as such have no right of recovery....

The complaint alleges that under 1967 amendments to the Economic Opportunity Act of 1964 (81 Stat. 688–690, 42 U.S.C.A. §§ 2763–2768, repeal by 86 Stat. 703 (1972)) "the United States Congress instituted Special Impact Programs with the intent to benefit the residents of certain neighborhoods having especially large concentrations of low income persons and suffering from dependency, chronic unemployment and rising tensions." Funds to administer these programs were appropriated to the United States Department of Labor. The department subsequently designated the East Los Angeles neighborhood as a "Special Impact area" and made federal funds available for contracts with local private industry for the benefit of the "hard-core unemployed residents" of East Los Angeles.

On January 17, 1969, the corporate defendants allegedly entered into contracts with the Secretary of Labor, acting on behalf of the Manpower Administration, United States Department of Labor (hereinafter referred to as the "Government"). Each such defendant entered into a separate contract and all three contracts are made a part of the complaint as exhibits. Under each contract the contracting defendant agreed to lease space in the then vacant Lincoln Heights jail building owned by the City of Los Angeles, to invest at least $5,000,000 in renovating the leasehold and establishing a facility for the manufacture of certain articles, to train and employ in such facility for at least 12 months, at minimum wage rates, a specified number of East Los Angeles residents certified as disadvantaged by the Government, and to provide such employees with opportunities for promotion into available supervisor-managerial positions and with options to purchase stock in their employer corporation. Each contract provided for the manufacture of a different kind of product. As consideration, the Government agreed to pay each defendant a stated amount in installments. Socoma was to hire 650 persons and receive $950,000; Lady Fair was to hire 550 persons and receive $990,000; and Monarch was to hire 400 persons and receive $800,000. The hiring of these persons was to be completed by January 17, 1970.

Plaintiffs were allegedly members of a class of no more than 2,017 East Los Angeles residents who were certified as disadvantaged and were qualified for employment under the contracts. Although the Government paid $712,500 of the contractual consideration to Socoma, $299,700 to Lady Fair, and $240,000 to Monarch, all of these defendants failed to perform under their respective contracts, except that Socoma provided 186 jobs of which 139 were wrongfully terminated, and Lady Fair provided 90 jobs, of which all were wrongfully terminated.

The complaint contains 11 causes of action. The second, fourth and sixth causes of action seek damages of $3,607,500 against Socoma, $3,052,500 against Lady Fair, and $2,220,000 against Monarch, calculated on the basis of 12 months' wages at minimum rates and $1,000 for loss of training for each of the jobs the defendant contracted to provide. The third and fifth causes of action seek similar damages for the 139 persons whose jobs were terminated by Socoma and the 90 persons whose jobs were terminated by Lady Fair . . .

Each cause of action alleges that the "express purpose of the [Government] in entering into [each] contract was to benefit [the] certified disadvantaged hard-core unemployed residents of East Los Angeles [for whom defendants promised to provide training and jobs] and none other, and those residents are thus the express third-party beneficiaries of [each] contract." The general demurrers admitted the truth of all the material factual allegations of the complaint, regardless of any possible difficulty in proving them . . ., but did not admit allegations which constitute conclusions of law . . . or which are contrary to matters of which we must take judicial notice. . . .

Plaintiffs contend they are third-party beneficiaries under Civil Code section 1559, which provides: "A contract, made expressly for the benefit of a third person, may be enforced by him at any time before the parties thereto rescind it." This section excludes enforcement of a contract by persons who are only incidentally or remotely benefited by it. (*Lucas v. Hamm* (1961) 56 Cal.2d 583, 590, 15 Cal.Rptr. 821, 824, 364 P.2d 685, 688.) American law generally classifies persons having enforceable rights under contracts to which they are not parties as either creditor beneficiaries or donee beneficiaries. (Restatement, Contracts §§ 133, subds. (1), (2), 135, 136, 147; 2 Williston on Contracts (3d ed. 1959) § 356; 4 Corbin on Contracts (1951) § 774; see Restatement, Second, Contracts, [§ 302],[2] coms. b, c.) California decisions follow this classification. . . .

A person cannot be a creditor beneficiary unless the promisor's performance of the contract will discharge some form of legal duty owed to the beneficiary by the promisee. (*Hartman Ranch Co. v. Associated Oil Co.* (1937) 10 Cal.2d 232, 244, 73 P.2d 1163; Restatement, Contracts § 133, subd, (1)(b).) Clearly the Government (the promisee) at no time bore any legal duty toward plaintiffs to provide the benefits set forth in the contract and plaintiffs do not claim to be creditor beneficiaries.

2. [Eds.: The case quotes from a tentative draft with different section numbers. Here and below we have substituted the final numbers.]

A person is a donee beneficiary only if the promisee's contractual intent is either to make a gift to him or to confer on him a right against the promisor. (Restatement, Contracts § 133, subd. (1)(a).) If the promisee intends to make a gift, the donee beneficiary can recover if such donative intent must have been understood by the promisor from the nature of the contract and the circumstances accompanying its execution. (*Lucas v. Hamm*, supra, 56 Cal.2d at pp. 590–591, 15 Cal.Rptr. 821, 364 P.2d 685.) This rule does not aid plaintiffs, however, because, as will be seen, no intention to make a gift can be imputed to the Government as promisee.

Unquestionably plaintiffs were among those whom the Government intended to benefit through defendants' performance of the contracts, which recite that they are executed pursuant to a statute and a presidential directive calling for programs to furnish disadvantaged persons with training and employment opportunities. However, the fact that a Government program for social betterment confers benefits upon individuals who are not required to render contractual benefits in return does not necessarily imply that the benefits are intended as gifts. Congress' power to spend money in aid of the general welfare (U.S. Const., art. I, § 8) authorize federal programs to alleviate national unemployment. (*Helvering v. Davis* (1937) 301 U.S. 619, 640–645, 57 S.Ct. 904, 81 L.Ed. 1307.) The benefits of such programs are provided not simply as gifts to the recipients but as a means of accomplishing a larger public purpose. The furtherance of the public purpose is in the nature of consideration to the Government, displacing any governmental intent to furnish the benefits as gifts.

Even though a person is not the intended recipient of a gift, he may nevertheless be "a donee beneficiary if it appears from the terms of the promise in view of the accompanying circumstances that the purpose of the promisee in obtaining the promise . . . is . . . to *confer upon him a right against the promisor* to some performance neither due nor supposed or asserted to be due from the promisee to the beneficiary." (Restatement, Contracts § 133 subd. (1)(a) (italics supplied); *Gourmet Lane, Inc. v. Keller* (1963) 222 Cal.App.2d 701, 705, 35 Cal.Rptr. 398.) The Government may, of course, deliberately implement a public purpose by including provisions in its contracts which expressly confer on a specified class of third persons a direct right to benefits, or damages in lieu of benefits, against the private contractor. But a governmental intent to confer such a direct right cannot be inferred simply from the fact that third persons were intended to enjoy the benefits. The Restatement of Contracts makes this clear in dealing specifically with contractual promises to the Government to render services to members of the public: "A promisor bound to the United States or to a State or municipality by contract to do an act or render a service to some or all of the members of the public, is subject to no duty under the contract to such members to give compensation for the injurious consequences of performing or attempting to perform it, or of failing to do so, unless, . . . *an intention is manifested in the contract,* as interpreted in the light of the circumstances surrounding its formation, *that the promisor shall compensate members of the public for such injurious consequences....*" (Restatement, Contracts § 145 (italics supplied)).[3]

The present contracts manifest no intent that the defendants pay damages to compensate plaintiffs or other members of the public for their nonperformance. To the contrary, the contracts' provisions for retaining the Government's control over determination of contractual disputes and for limiting defendants' financial risks indicate a governmental purpose to exclude the direct rights against defendants claimed here.

Each contract provides that any dispute of fact arising there under is to be determined by written decision of the Government's contracting officer, subject to an appeal to the Secretary of Labor, whose decision shall be final unless determined by a competent court to have been fraudulent, capricious, arbitrary, in bad faith, or not supported by substantial evidence. These administrative decisions may include determinations of related questions of law although such determinations are not made final. The efficiency and uniformity of interpretation fostered by these administrative procedures would tend to be undermined if litigation such as the present action, to which the Government is a stranger, were permitted to proceed on the merits.

In addition to the provision on resolving disputes each contract contains a "liquidated damages" provision obligating the contractor to refund all amounts received from the Government, with interest, in the event of failure to acquire and equip the specified manufacturing facility, and, for each employment opportunity it fails to provide, to refund a stated dollar amount equivalent to the total contract compensation divided by the number of jobs agreed to be provided. This liquidated damages provision limits liability for the breaches alleged by plaintiffs to the refunding of amounts received and indicates an absence of any contractual intent to impose liability for the value of the promised performance. To allow plaintiffs' claim would nullify the limited liability for which defendants bargained and which the Government may well have held out as an inducement in negotiating the contracts.

It is this absence of any manifestation of intent that defendants should pay compensation for breach to persons in the position of plaintiffs that distinguishes this case from *Shell v. Schmidt* (1954) 126 Cal.App.2d 279, 272 P.2d 82, relied on by plaintiffs. The defendant in *Shell* was a building contractor who entered into an agreement with the

3. The corresponding language of ... the Restatement, Second, Contracts (1973), Section [313(2)], is: "[A] promisor who contracts with a government or governmental agency to do an act or render a service to the public is *not subject to contractual liability* to a member of the public for consequential damages resulting from performance or failure to perform unless ... the terms of the promise provide for such liability ..."

The language omitted in this quotation and the quotation in the accompanying text relates to the creditor beneficiary situation in which the government itself would be liable for nonperformance of the contract. As noted earlier, plaintiffs do not claim to be creditor beneficiaries.

federal government under which he received priorities for building materials and agreed in return to use the materials to build homes with required specifications for sale to war veterans at or below ceiling prices. Plaintiffs were 12 veterans, each of whom had purchased a home that failed to comply with the agreed specifications. They were held entitled to recover directly from the defendant contractor as third-party beneficiaries of his agreement with the government. The legislation under which the agreement was made included a provision empowering the government to obtain payment of monetary compensation by the contractor to the veteran purchasers for the purchasers for the deficiencies resulting from failure to comply with specifications. Thus, there was "an intention ... manifested in the contract ... that the promisor shall compensate members of the public for such injurious consequences [of nonperformance]."[4]

Plaintiffs contend that section 145 of the Restatement, Contracts, previously quoted does not preclude their recovery because it applies only to promises made to a governmental entity "to do an act or render a service to ... the public." Even if this contention were correct it would not follow that plaintiffs have standing as third-party beneficiaries under the Restatement. The quoted provision of Section 145 "is a special application of the principles stated in §§ 133(1a), 135 [on donee beneficiaries]" (Restatement, Contracts § 145, com. A), delineating certain circumstances which preclude government contractors' liability to third parties. Section 145 itself does not purport to confer standing to sue on persons who do not otherwise qualify under basic third-party beneficiary principles.[5] As pointed out above, plaintiffs are not donee beneficiaries under those basic principles because it does not appear from the terms and circumstances of the contract that the Government intended to make a gift to plaintiffs or to confer on them a legal right against the defendants.

Moreover, contrary to plaintiffs' contention, section 145 of the Restatement, Contracts does not preclude their recovery because the services which the contract required the defendants to perform were to be rendered to "members of the public" within the meaning of the section. Each contract recites it is made under the "Special Impact Programs" part of the Economic Opportunity Act of 1964 and pursuant

4. In contrast to *Shell*, supra, is *City & County of San Francisco v. Western Air Lines, Inc.*, supra, 204 Cal. App.2d 105, 22 Cal.Rptr. 216. There, Western Air Lines claimed to be a third-party beneficiary of agreements between the federal government and the City and County of San Francisco under which the City and County of San Francisco under which the city received federal funds for the development of its airport subject to a written condition that the airport "be available for public use on fair and reasonable terms and without unjust discrimination." Western Air Lines asserted that it had been charged for its use of the airport at a higher rate than some other air carriers in violation of the contract condition, and therefore was entitled to recover the excess charges from the city. One of the reasons given by the court on appeal rejecting this contention was the absence of any provision or indication of intent in the agreements between the governments and the city to compensate third parties for noncompliance ...

5. The same is true ... of Section [313] of the Restatement, Second, Contracts....

to a presidential directive for a test program of cooperation between the federal government and private industry in an effort to provide training and jobs for thousands of the hard-core unemployed or under-employed. The congressional declaration of purpose of the Economic Opportunity Act as a whole points up the public nature of its benefits on a national scale. Congress declared that that the purpose of the act was to "strengthen, supplement, and coordinate efforts in furtherance of [the] policy" of "opening to everyone the opportunity for education and training, the opportunity to work, and the opportunity to live in decency and dignity" so that the "United States can achieve its full economic and social potential as a nation." (42 U.S.C.A. § 2701.)

In providing for special impact programs, Congress declared that such programs were directed to the solution of critical problems that existed in particular neighborhoods having especially large concentrations of low-income persons, and that the programs were intended to be of sufficient size and scope to have an appreciable impact in such neighborhoods in arresting tendencies toward dependency, chronic unemployment, and rising community tensions. (42 U.S.C.A. former § 2763.) Thus the contracts here were designed not to benefit individuals as such but to utilize the training and employment of disadvantaged persons as a means of improving the East Los Angeles neighborhood. Moreover, the means by which the contracts were intended to accomplish this community improvement were not confined to provision of the particular benefits on which the plaintiffs base their claim to damages—one year's employment at minimum wage plus $1,000 worth of training to be provided to each of 650 persons by one defendant, 400 by another, and 550 by another. Rather the objective was to be achieved by establishing permanent industries in which local residents would be permanently employed and would have the opportunities to become supervisors, managers, and part owners. The required minimum capital investment of $5,000,000 by each defendant and the defendants' 22-year lease of the former Lincoln Heights jail building for conversion into an industrial facility also indicates the broad, long-range objective of the program. Presumably, as the planned enterprises prospered, the quantity and quality of employment and economic opportunity that they provided would increase and would benefit not only employees but also their families, other local enterprises and the government itself through reduction of law enforcement and welfare costs.

The fact that plaintiffs were in a position to benefit more directly than other certain members of the public from performance of the contract does not alter their status as incidental beneficiaries. (See Restatement, Contracts § 145, illus. 1: C, a member of the public cannot recover for injury from B's failure to perform a contract with the United States to carry mail over a certain route.)[6] For example in *City & County of San Francisco v. Western Air Lines, Inc.*, supra, 204 Cal.App.2d 105,

6. This illustration is repeated in ... Restatement, Second, Contracts, Section [313] illustration 1.

22 Cal.Rptr. 216, the agreement between the federal government and the city for improvement of the airport could be considered to be of greater benefit to air carriers using the airport than to other members of the public. Nevertheless, Western, as an air carrier, was but an incidental, not an express beneficiary of the agreement and therefore had no standing to enforce the contractual prohibition against discrimination in the airport's availability for public use. The court explains the distinction as follows: "None of the documents under consideration confer on Western the rights of a third-party beneficiary. The various contracts and assurances created benefits and detriments as between only two parties—the United States and the City. Nothing in them shows any intent of the contracting parties to confer any benefit directly and expressly upon air carriers such as the defendant. It is true that air carriers, including Western, may be incidentally benefited by the city's assurances in respect to nondiscriminatory treatment at the airport. They may also be incidentally benefited by the fact that, through federal aid, a public airport is improved with longer runways, brighter beacons, or larger loading ramps, or by the fact a new public airport is provided for a community without one. The various documents and agreements were part of a federal aid program directed to the promoting of a national transportation system. Provisions in such agreements, including the nondiscrimination clauses, were intended to advance such federal aims and not for the benefit of those who might be affected by the sponsor's failure to perform." (204 Cal. App.2d at p.120, 22 Cal.Rptr. at p. 225.)

For the reasons above stated we hold that plaintiffs and the class they represent have no standing as third-party beneficiaries to recover the damages sought in the complaint under either California law of the general contract principles which federal law applies to governmental contracts.

The judgments of dismissal are affirmed.

BURKE, J. (DISSENTING). I dissent. The certified hard-core unemployed of East Los Angeles were the express, not incidental, beneficiaries of the contracts in question and therefore, have standing to enforce those contracts. . . .

The majority errs . . . because the congressional purpose was to benefit both the communities in which the impact programs are established and the individual impoverished persons in such communities.[7]

7. Evidence of Congress' purpose to aid the *individual* impoverished person in such communities can be gleaned from 42 U.S.C.A. § 2701, wherein Congress declared that if our country is to achieve its full potential, "every individual" must be given "the opportunity for education and training, the opportunity to work, and the opportunity to live in decency and dignity." Congress implemented this general policy of assisting our impoverished citizens in various ways, including the Special Impact Program involved in this case. Yet, contrary to the majority, nothing indicates that Congress' exclusive purpose in doing so was to assist the neighborhoods and communities in which these persons live. It seems clear that Congress intended both the communities and the individuals to be direct beneficiaries of the program. It is incorrect to label one as an intended *direct* beneficiary and the other as merely *incidental*.

The benefits from the instant contracts were to accrue directly to the members of the plaintiffs' class, as a reading of the contracts clearly demonstrates.[8] These direct benefits to members of the plaintiffs' class were not merely the "*means* of executing the public purpose," as the majority contend ..., but were the *ends* in themselves and one of the public purposes to which the legislation and subsequent contracts were addressed. Accordingly, I cannot agree with the majority that "the contracts were designed not to benefit individuals as such but to utilize the training and employment of disadvantaged persons as a *means* of improving the East Los Angeles neighborhood." (... italics added.)

The intent of the contracts themselves is expressed in their preambles.... By these provisions, the contracting parties clearly state as one of their purposes their intent to find jobs for the hard-core unemployed.

In accord with this expressed intent, the substantive provisions of the contracts confer a direct benefit upon the class seeking to enforce them. The contracts call for the hiring of stated numbers of hard-core unemployed from the East Los Angeles Special Impact Area for a period of at least one year at a starting minimum wage of $2.00 per hour for the first 90 days and a minimum wage of $2.25 per hour thereafter, or for the prevailing wage for the area, whichever is higher. In addition to requiring appropriate job training for such employees, the contracts also require "That the Contractor will arrange for the orderly promotion of persons so employed into available supervisory-managerial and other positions, and will arrange for all contract employees to obtain a total ownership interest not exceeding thirty (30) percent in the Contractor through an appropriate stock purchase plan...." The scope of the stock purchase plans is detailed in each of the contracts....

The language of section 133 [of the Restatement],[9] standing alone, could reasonably suggest that members of the general public are "donee beneficiaries" under any contract whose purpose is to confer a "gift" upon them. Section 145 qualifies this broad language and treats the general public merely as incidental, not direct, beneficiaries under contracts made for the general public benefit, unless the contract manifests a clear intent to compensate such members of the public in the event of breach. Section 145 does not, however, entirely preclude application of the "donee beneficiary" concept to every governmental contract. Whenever, as in the instant case, such a contract expresses an intent to benefit directly a particular person or ascertainable class of persons,

8. In the contracts, the defendants agreed to provide training and jobs to a specified class of persons, whom plaintiffs represent. The government's express intent, therefore, was to confer a benefit, namely training and jobs, upon an ascertainable identifiable class and not simply the general public itself.

9. Comment (c) to Section 133 of the Restatement of Contracts states in part that "By gift is meant primarily some performance or right which is not paid for by the recipient and which is apparently designed to benefit him." Thus, Section 133 states essentially the same rule as that enunciated in *Shell v. Schmidt*, supra 126 Cal.App.2d 279, 290–291, 272 P.2d 82. Section 133 has been followed by the California courts. (*Hartman Ranch Co. v. Associated Oil Co.*, supra, 10 Cal.2d 232, 244, 73 P.2d 1163; *Southern Cal. Gas Co. v. ABC Construction Co.*, 204 Cal.App.2d 747, 752, 22 Cal.Rptr. 540.)

section 145 is, by its terms, inapplicable and the contract may be enforced by the beneficiaries pursuant to the general provisions of section 133. Thus, I would conclude that that section 145 is consistent with the holding of *Shell v. Schmidt*, supra, 126 Cal.App.2d 279, 272 P.2d 82, and the *City and County of San Francisco v. Western Air Lines, Inc.*, supra, 204 Cal.App.2d 105, 22 Cal.Rptr. 216.

The majority contends that the inclusions of liquidated damage clauses in each of the contracts limits defendants' financial risks and was intended to preclude the assertion of third-party claims.... Yet, these clauses simply provide for various refunds of monies advanced by the government in the event of default. These so-called "liquidated damages" clauses nowhere purport to limit damages to the specified refunds. Nothing in the contracts limits the rights of the government or, more importantly, plaintiffs' class, to seek additional relief....

The majority also rely on the fact that, "The present contracts manifest no intent that the defendants pay damages to compensate plaintiffs or other members of the public for nonperformance." ... Therefore, it assertedly follows that giving plaintiffs the right to monetary benefit in lieu of performance would give to plaintiffs and the class they represent benefits never contemplated nor intended under the contracts. This argument disregards both the fact that the class was to receive a direct monetary benefit under the contracts in the form of wages, and that under well settled contract law, an aggrieved party is entitled to be compensated for all the detriment proximately caused by a breach of contract. (Civ. Code, § 3300).

It is my conclusion, therefore, that the trial court erred in sustaining the demurrer without leave to amend. I would order the trial court to determine the propriety of the plaintiffs' class action prior to proceeding upon the merits of the complaint.

Notes and Discussion

1. **If Not Here, Then Where?** The court turns aside a last desperate attempt by the beneficiaries of a failed effort under the Economic Opportunity Act to benefit the poor in East Los Angeles. That the contract (and indeed the entire thrust of President Johnson's Economic Opportunity Act) was directly to aid the poor does not make them intended beneficiaries of the contract. If beneficiaries of government subsidy programs were found to have rights under the contracts issued as part of those programs, it might change the American landscape. You can imagine the reaction of government bureaucrats to that possibility. What should be the reaction of a dispassionate voter? And what would be the response of a potential contractor to the possibility that it could be sued by every beneficiary?

Unconvinced? Suppose that you are a lawyer for Consolidated Edison, which supplies New York City with electricity, and, as a result of a blackout caused by the negligence of your employees, six million people are plunged into darkness. A tenant in a NYC apartment house brings suit over injuries she sustained in a hallway as a result of the blackout; she claims to be a third-party beneficiary of your client's contract with her landlord. If she succeeds in this claim, Con Ed may face thousands of similar suits. How do you argue? A claim like this failed in *Shubitz v. Consolidated Edison Co. of N.Y.*, 59 Misc.2d 732, 301 N.Y.S.2d 926 (Sup. Ct. 1969).

2. So When Can a Beneficiary Win? Barksdale Air Force Base sits in the middle of Bossier Parish, Louisiana. Between 1951 and 1964, when segregation was still the norm in Louisiana, the Bossier Parish school system accepted nearly two million dollars of federal money, in return for which the school board gave various "assurances" to the United States that children of personnel stationed at Barksdale would be admitted to the schools "on the same terms, *in accordance with the laws of the State* in which the school district of such agency is situated, as they are available to other children in such school district." When Bossier schools excluded the children of Black military personnel, a number of parents brought a class action as third-party beneficiaries of the arrangement. *Bossier Parish Sch. Bd. v. Lemon*, 370 F.2d 847, 850 (5th Cir. 1967).

The District Court granted the plaintiffs' motion for summary judgment. The School Board appealed, arguing from the Fourteenth Amendment that: "since the children live at Barksdale, they are not persons within the jurisdiction of the state. As a corollary, Negro children of fathers stationed at Barksdale have no right to attend Bossier schools; they are merely permitted to attend schools (Negro schools) by sufferance, permission that may be withdrawn at any time." Id. at 849–850. In affirming, the Fifth Circuit quoted with approval the decision below: "Defendants by their contractual assurances have afforded rights to these federal children as third-party beneficiaries concerning the availability of public schools. Such rights are identical in weight and effect to those rights possessed by children who are entitled to attend Bossier Parish schools simply because of residence instead of by contract. Having thus obligated themselves defendants are now estopped by their contractual agreement, and their acceptance of federal funds paid pursuant thereto, to deny that plaintiffs are entitled to the same rights to school attendance as are resident children." Id. at 850.

How can this case be distinguished from *Martinez*? In *Bossier Parish*, the school district would have been unjustly enriched if it had been allowed to keep the money without educating the military children, but this element is not crucial, see *Holbrook v. Pitt*, 643 F.2d 1261, 1275 n.28 (7th Cir. 1981) (tenants are intended beneficiaries of a contract between the owners of their apartment buildings and the federal government, whereby the government will subsidize the tenants' rent).

The *Bossier Parish* case is of fundamental importance in establishing third-party beneficiary claims under federal law, and it has had great influence.

Problem 8–3

Assume that Sebastian, Raphael and one million others buy Hewlett–Packard computers from Best Buy, Circuit City and other retailers. In each case they find a warranty document of the type set out below in the box with their computers. Each of the computers has the same defect and Sebastian and Raphael on behalf of themselves and all others similarly situated sue H–P. They state two causes of action. The first cause of action is for breach of the express warranty that is set out in the warranty document. The second is for breach of the implied warranty of merchantability (§ 2–314). They do not sue the retailers from whom they bought their computers. They seek damages for the difference in value of the computers as warranted and as delivered under § 2–714 as well as "such other relief as the court may allow."

Iowa has alternative C of 2–318 and Illinois has alternative A.

1. Assume that Sebastian lives in Waterloo, IA, and Raphael lives in Cairo, IL, and that the law of the place of residence controls. Will defendant's motion to dismiss (or for summary judgment) be granted as to either plaintiff with respect to either cause of action?

2. If H–P effectively disclaimed its implied warranty of merchantability that it would otherwise have given to Circuit City as part of its obligation to its buyer, Circuit City, will that cut off either of the causes of action of Sebastian and Raphael?

3. Does the prohibition on recovery of damages foreclose the recovery of damages on either cause of action?

Customer Responsibilities

You may be required to run HP-supplied diagnostic programs before replacement component (e.g., keyboard, monitor, mouse, etc.) is dispatched, or a replacement computer is shipped.

In the event of any service needs, either Consumer Parts Replacement or Express Exchange, you are responsible for the security of your proprietary and confidential information and for maintaining a procedure external to the products for reconstruction of lost or altered files, data, or programs. Any transfer of personal data and files from the hard disk of the defective computer to the replacement computer is the responsibility of the consumer. You should back up all data on your system before calling the HP Customer Care Center

Obtaining Hardware Warranty Repair Service

For the duration of the hardware warranty period, hardware repair service includes Consumer Replaceable Service and Express Exchange Service as described below. To obtain hardware warranty service, call HP's Customer Care Center at 1-208-323-HOME (1-208-323-4663).

Consumer Replaceable Service

Components such as the keyboard, mouse, speakers, microphone & monitor, may be serviced through expedited part shipment. In this event, HP will send you the component. In some cases, HP will ask for a credit card as collateral for the part (such as monitors) and will charge you for the retail price of the part if the failed product is not returned within 7 days.

HP Express Exchange Service

In the event of a hardware failure in the computer itself, we will send you a new or refurbished replacement computer equivalent to or with higher performance than your original system. When it arrives, pack the defective computer in the replacement's box, and return it to HP using the enclosed prepaid mailer.

A credit card number will be required as deposit for the return of the original system including all parts and components. In the event that we do not receive the unit back within 7 working days, the credit card will be charged the full value of the replacement system. The returned system will be inspected and if any missing parts or components are found, the value of these items will be charged.

HP Software Product License Agreement

The following License Terms govern your use of the accompanying Software unless you have a separate signed agreement with HP.

License

GRANT — HP grants you a license to use one copy of the Software. "Use" means storing, loading, installing, executing, or displaying the Software. You may not modify the Software or disable any licensing or control features of the Software. If the Software is licensed for "concurrent use," you may not allow more than the maximum number of authorized users to use the Software concurrently.

OWNERSHIP — The Software is owned and copyrighted by HP or its third-party suppliers. Your license confers no title to or ownership in the Software and is not a sale of any rights in the Software. HP's third-party suppliers may protect their rights in the event of any violation of these License Terms.

Copies

ADAPTATIONS — You may make copies or adaptations of the Software only for archival purposes or when copying or adaptation is an essential step in the authorized Use of the Software. You must reproduce all copyright notices in the original Software on all copies or adaptations. You may not copy the Software onto any public network.

If your computer was shipped with a Recovery CD, (i) the Recovery CD and/or Support Utility software may be used only for restoring the hard disk of the HP computer system with which the Recovery CD originally was provided, and (ii) if separate EULA(s) are included with your computer for any other Microsoft products which are included on the Recovery CD, those Microsoft products are subject to the terms of their respective EULA(s).

No Disassembly

DECRYPTION — You may not disassemble or decompile the Software unless HP's prior written consent is obtained. In some jurisdictions, HP's consent may not be required for limited disassembly or decompilation. Upon request, you will provide HP with reasonably detailed information regarding any disassembly or decompilation. You may not decrypt the Software unless decryption is a necessary part of the operation of the Software.

TRANSFER — Your license will automatically terminate upon any transfer of the Software. Upon transfer, you must deliver the Software, including any copies and related documentation, to the transferee. The transferee must accept these License Terms as a condition to the transfer.

TERMINATION — HP may terminate your license upon notice for failure to comply with any of these License Terms. Upon termination, you must immediately destroy the Software, together with all copies, adaptations, and merged portions in any form.

EXPORT REQUIREMENTS — You may not export or re-export the Software or any copy or adaptation in violation of any applicable laws or regulations.

Restricted Rights

RIGHTS — The Software and any accompanying documentation have been developed entirely at private expense. They are delivered and licensed as "commercial computer software" as defined in DFARS 252.227-7013 (Oct 1988), DFARS 252.211-7015 (May 1991) or DFARS 252.227-7014 (Jun 1995), as a "commercial item" as defined in FAR 2.101(a), or as "Restricted computer software" as defined in FAR 52.227-19 (Jun 1987) (or any equivalent agency regulation or contract clause), whichever is applicable. You have only those rights provided for such Software and any accompanying documentation by the applicable FAR or DFARS clause or the HP standard software agreement for the product involved.

B. THE ASSIGNMENT OF RIGHTS AND DELEGATION OF RESPONSIBILITIES

Third-party beneficiaries acquire rights because of the intentions of parties in forming or modifying a contract. By contrast, the third parties that are discussed in this section arise when a contract (with reciprocal rights and duties) is already in existence, and one party then either assigns its rights under the contract, or delegates its duties, or both, to a third party. To the extent that assignment or delegation brings the third party into the contract, privity of contract is disrupted. For example, for one reason or another the other contractual partner may not wish to deal with the newcomer.

CONTEMPORARY MISSION, INC. v. FAMOUS MUSIC CORP.

United States Court of Appeals, Second Circuit, 1977.
557 F.2d 918.

MESKILL, J. This is an appeal by Famous Music Corporation ("Famous") from a verdict rendered against it in favor of Contemporary Mission, Inc. ("Contemporary"), in the United States District Court for the Southern District of New York, after a jury trial before Judge Richard Owen. Contemporary cross-appeals from a ruling that excluded testimony concerning its prospective damages. The dispute between the parties relates to Famous' alleged breach of two contracts.

Facts

Contemporary is a nonprofit charitable corporation organized under the laws of the State of Missouri with its principal place of business in Connecticut. It is composed of a small group of Roman Catholic priests who write, produce and publish musical compositions and recordings.[10] In 1972 the group owned all of the rights to a rock opera entitled VIRGIN, which was composed by Father John T. O'Reilly, a vice-president and member of the group. Contemporary first became involved with Famous in 1972 as a result of O'Reilly's efforts to market VIRGIN.

Famous is a Delaware corporation with its headquarters in the Gulf + Western Building in New York City. It is a wholly owned subsidiary of the Gulf Western Corporation,[11] and, until July 31, 1974, it was engaged in the business of producing musical recordings for distribution throughout the United States. Famous' president, Tony Martell, is generally regarded in the recording industry as the individual primarily responsi-

10. For a further description of the group see *Robert Stigwood Group, Ltd. v. O'Reilly*, 346 F.Supp. 376, 379 (D. Conn. 1972), rev'd, 530 F.2d 1096 (2nd Cir. 1976).

11. Gulf + Western and another of its wholly-owned subsidiaries, Paramount Pictures Corp., were originally named as co-defendants. All of the causes of action pleaded against these co-defendants were dismissed by the trial judge. Contemporary has not appealed form those rulings, and thus neither Gulf + Western nor Paramount are parties to this appeal. . . .

ble for the successful distribution of the well-known rock operas TOMMY and JESUS CHRIST SUPERSTAR....

The relationship between Famous and Contemporary was considerably more harmonious in 1972 than it is today. At that time, Martell thought that he had found, in VIRGIN, another TOMMY or JESUS CHRIST SUPERSTAR, and he was anxious to acquire rights to it. O'Reilly, who was encouraged by Martell's expertise and enthusiasm, had high hopes for the success of his composition. On August 16, 1972, they executed the so-called "VIRGIN Recording Agreement" ("VIRGIN agreement") on behalf of their respective organizations.

The terms of the VIRGIN agreement were relatively simple. Famous agreed to pay a royalty to Contemporary in return for the master tape recording of VIRGIN and the exclusive right to manufacture and sell records made from the master. The agreement also created certain "Additional Obligations of Famous" which included, *inter alia*: the obligation to select and appoint, within the first year of the agreement, at least one person to personally oversee the nationwide promotion of the sale of records, to maintain contact with Contemporary and to submit weekly reports to Contemporary; the obligation to spend, within the first year of the agreement, no less than $50,000 on the promotion of records; and the obligation to release, within the first two years of the agreement, at least four separate single records from VIRGIN. The agreement also contained a non-assignability clause which is set out in the margin.[12]

On May 8, 1973, the parties entered into a distribution contract which dealt with musical compositions other than VIRGIN. This, the so-called "Crunch agreement," granted to Famous the exclusive right to distribute Contemporary's records in the United States. Famous agreed to institute a new record label named "Crunch," and a number of records were to be released under it annually. Contemporary agreed to deliver ten long-playing records and fifteen single records during the first year of the contract. Famous undertook to use its "reasonable efforts" to promote and distribute the records. Paragraph 15 of the Crunch agreement stated that a breach by either party would not be deemed material unless the non-breaching party first gave written notice to the defaulting party and the defaulting party failed to cure the breach within thirty days. The notice was to specify the nature of the alleged material breach. The contract prohibited the assignment by Contemporary, but it contained no provision relating to Famous' right to assign.

12. Paragraph 29 of the VIRGIN agreement provides, in full, as follows: This Agreement shall not be assignable by FAMOUS, except in the voluntary sale of FAMOUS' entire business in which the present work is used, or in connection with a merger between FAMOUS and another business organization, or to a majority-owned subsidiary or division of FAMOUS engaged in the same business of FAMOUS, *all conditioned upon the execution and delivery to [Contemporary] of an agreement whereby the assignee agrees to be bound by the obligations of this agreement.* (emphasis added).

Although neither VIRGIN nor its progeny was ever as successful as the parties had originally hoped, the business relationship continued on an amicable basis until July 31, 1974. On that date, Famous' record division was sold to ABC Records, Inc. (ABC). When O'Reilly complained to Martell that Famous was breaking its promises, he was told that he would have to look to ABC for performance. O'Reilly met with one of ABC's lawyers and was told that ABC was not going to have any relationship with Contemporary. On August 21, 1974, Contemporary sent a letter to Famous pursuant to paragraph 15 of the Crunch agreement notifying Famous that it had "materially breached Paragraph 12,[13] among others, of [the Crunch] Agreement in that [it had] attempted to make a contract or other agreement with ABC–Dunhill Record Corporation (ABC Records) creating an obligation or responsibility in behalf of or in the name of the Contemporary Mission." This lawsuit followed.

THE JURY VERDICT

Contemporary brought this action against several defendants and asserted several causes of action. By the time the case was submitted to the jury the only remaining defendant was Famous and the only remaining claims were that (1) Famous had failed to adequately promote the VIRGIN and Crunch recordings prior to the sale to ABC, (2) Famous breached both the VIRGIN and Crunch agreements when it sold the record division to ABC, and (3) Famous breached an oral agreement to reimburse Contemporary for its promotional expenses. The latter claim has no relevance to this appeal.

The district judge submitted the case to the jury in two parts: the first portion as to liability and the second concerning damages. The court's questions and the jury's answers as to the liability and the damages are set forth below:

Liability Questions

1. Has plaintiff established by a fair preponderance of the credible evidence that Famous breached the Virgin agreement by failing to adequately promote Virgin in its various aspects as it had agreed? Yes.

2. If you find a failure to adequately promote, did that cause plaintiff any damage? Yes.

3. Did the assignment of the Virgin contract by Famous to ABC cause any damage to plaintiff? Yes.[14]

13. Paragraph 12 of the Crunch agreement provides, in full, as follows: This agreement shall not be construed as one of partnership or joint venture, nor shall it constitute either party as the agent or legal representative of the other. Neither party shall have the right, power or authority to make any contract or other agreement, or to assume or create any obligation or other responsibility, express or implied, in behalf of or in the name of the other party or to bind the other party in any manner for anything whatsoever.

14. Judge Owen charged the jury as a matter of law that the assignment to ABC constituted a breach of the VIRGIN agreement's non-assignability clause.

4. Did plaintiff establish by a fair preponderance of the credible evidence that Famous failed to use "its reasonable efforts consistent with the exercise of sound business judgment" to promote the records marketed under the Crunch label? No.

5. Did plaintiff establish by a fair preponderance of the credible evidence that there was a refusal by ABC to perform the Crunch contract and promote plaintiff's music after the assignment? Yes.

6. If your answer is "yes" to either 4 or 5 above, did such a breach or breaches of the Crunch agreement cause plaintiff any damage? Yes.

7. Did Tony Martell, on behalf of Famous, in talking to any members of plaintiff, make any agreement to reimburse plaintiff for the expense of its members promoting their music around the country? Yes.

Damage Questions

1. To what damages is plaintiff entitled under the Virgin Agreement? $68,773.

2. To what damages is plaintiff entitled under the Crunch Agreement? $104,751.

3. To what unallocated damages as between the Virgin and Crunch and oral agreements is plaintiff entitled if any? $21,000.[15]

4. To what damages, if any, is plaintiff entitled under the oral agreement? $16,500.

Discussion

On this appeal, Famous attacks the verdict on several grounds. Their first contention is that the evidence was insufficient to support the jury's response to liability question number 1. Their second contention is that the jury's response to liability question number 4 precludes a recovery for non-performance of the Crunch agreement. Their third contention is that Contemporary is estopped from suing for a breach of the Crunch agreement. We find none of these arguments persuasive.

The Virgin Agreement

Judge Owen charged the jury as a matter of law that Famous breached the VIRGIN agreement by assigning it to ABC without getting from ABC a written agreement to be bound by the terms of the VIRGIN agreement. A reading of paragraph 29 of the agreement reveals that that charge was entirely correct, and Famous does not challenge it on appeal. Famous vigorously contends, however, that the jury's conclusion, that it had failed to adequately promote VIRGIN prior to the Sale to ABC, is at

15. The parties agree that if Famous is entitled to a reversal of the verdict as to either of the two contracts, it will also be entitled to a reversal of this award. Because we affirm the verdict as to both contracts, we affirm the award of unallocated damages.

war with the undisputed facts and cannot be permitted to stand. *O'Connor v. Pennsylvania R.R. Co.*, 308 F.2d 911, 915 & n.5 (2d Cir. 1962). In particular they argue that they spent the required $50,000[16] and appointed the required overseer for the project[17]. The flaw in this argument is that its focus is too narrow. The obligations to which it refers are but two of many created by the VIRGIN agreement. Under the doctrine of *Wood v. Lucy, Lady Duff-Gordon*, 222 N.Y. 88, 118 N.E. 214 (1917), Famous had an obligation to use its reasonable efforts to *promote* VIRGIN on a nationwide basis. That obligation could not be satisfied merely by technical compliance with the spending and appointment requirements of paragraph 14 of the agreement. Even assuming that Famous complied fully with these requirements, there was evidence from which the jury could find that Famous failed to adequately promote VIRGIN. The question is a close one, particularly in light of Martell's obvious commitment to the success of VIRGIN and in light of the efforts that were in fact exerted and the lack of any serious dispute between the parties prior to the sale of ABC. However, there was evidence that Famous prematurely terminated the promotion of the first single record, "Got To Know," shortly after its release, and that Famous limited its promotion of the second record, "Kyrie," to a single city, rather than

16. Martell testified that he was certain that over $50,000 had been spent. Melvin Schlissel, Famous; Vice–President of Finance, testified that in early 1973 he prepared a report that indicated that approximately $50,000 had been spent on the promotion of VIRGIN as of the date of the report. The report itself would have been admissible under the business records exception to the hearsay rule, Fed.R.Evid. 803(6), but the report had been lost, so the trial judge admitted oral proof of its contents, Fed.R.Evid. 1004. None of the parties recognized that the result was an oral business record—an apparent contradiction in terms. We express no view on the admissibility of an oral business record, for its admission is not claimed as error on this appeal.

Although Famous' proof that it spent over $50,000 was uncontradicted, the proof itself was not particularly strong; indeed, it was rather imprecise and self-serving. The jury could quite properly have concluded that the proof was insufficient.

Famous contends that Contemporary waived the $50,000 spending requirement. In return for an advance of $7,500, Contemporary agreed that Famous Music Corporation shall be relieved of its obligations to expend a minimum of $50,000.00 in the promotion of "Virgin" record sales if, as and when, in the sole option of Famous Music Corporation, such promotion shall cease to be effective and profitable.

This agreement did not operate as a present waiver of the spending requirement, as Famous contends. It granted Famous an option not to spend "if, as and when, in the sole option of Famous," the promotion became ineffective and unprofitable. Famous' argument is premise upon the notion that it had "absolute discretion concerning how much, if any, of the $50,000 to spend, and in its opinion could not be challenged." This is not true. Under New York law there is implied in every contract a covenant of fair dealing and good faith. *Kirke La Shelle Co. v. Paul Armstrong Co.*, 263 N.Y. 79, 87, 188 N.E. 163, 167 (1933); e.g., *Van Valkenburgh, Nooger & Neville, Inc. v. Hayden Pub. Co., Inc.*, 30 N.Y.2d 34, 45, 330 N.Y.S.2d 329, 333, 281 N.E.2d 142, 144, cert. denied, 409 U.S. 875, 93 S.Ct. 125, 34 L.Ed.2d 128 (1972). Thus, Famous' determination of effectiveness or profitability of promotion would have to be made in good faith. There is no indication that such a good faith determination was in fact made.

17. It is clear that the personal overseer requirement was met. Martell himself was actively and extensively engaged in the promotional effort. In addition, Herb Gordon, was clearly put in charge of the day-to-day supervision of the promotion. This adequately complied with the provisions of paragraph 14.

promoting it nationwide.[18] Moreover, there was evidence that prior to the sale to ABC, Famous underwent a budget reduction and cut back its promotional staff. From this, the jury could infer that the promotional effort was reduced to a level that was less than adequate. On the whole, therefore, we are not persuaded that the jury's verdict should be disturbed.

THE CRUNCH AGREEMENT

There is no dispute that the sale of Famous record division to ABC constituted an assignment of the Crunch agreement to ABC. The assignment of a bilateral contract includes both an assignment of rights and a delegation of duties. See 3 Williston on Contracts § 418 (3d ed. 1960). The distinctions between the two are important.

"Perhaps more frequently than is the case with other terms of art, lawyers seem prone to use the word 'assignment' inartfully, frequently intending to encompass with the term the distinct [concept] of delegation.... An assignment involves the transfer of rights. A delegation involves the appointment of another to perform one's duties." J. Calamari & J. Perillo, Contracts § 254 (1970) (footnote omitted). Famous' arguments with respect to the Crunch agreement ignore this basic distinction, and the result is a distortion of several fundamental principles of contract law.

It is true, of course, as a general rule, that when rights are assigned, the assignor's interest in the rights comes to an end. When duties are delegated, however, the delegant's obligation does not end. "[O]ne who owes money or is bound to any performance whatever, cannot by any act of his own, or by any act in agreement with any other person, except his creditor, divest himself of the duty and substitute the duty of another. 'No one can assign his liabilities under a contract without the consent of the party to whom he is liable.' This is sufficiently obvious when attention is called to it, for otherwise obligors would find an easy practical way of escaping their obligations...." 3 Williston on Contracts § 411 (3d ed. 1960) (footnote omitted). This is not to say that one may not delegate his obligations. In fact, most obligations can be delegated as long as performance by the delegate will not vary materially from performance by the delegant. The act of delegation, however, does not relieve the delegant of the ultimate responsibility to see that the obligation is performed. If the delegate fails to perform, the delegant remains liable. *Davidson v. Madison Corp.*, 257 N.Y. 120, 125, 177 N.E. 393, 394 (1931); *Devlin v. Mayor*, 63 N.Y. 8, 16 (1875).

Although the matter is not without considerable doubt, we shall assume, *arguendo*, that the duty to promote Contemporary's records was not sufficiently personal to bar its delegation. The fact that Martell

18. We recognize that the limited promotion of "Kyrie" was a result of "test marketing," i.e., the concentration of promotional efforts in one area before expanding the efforts to the rest of the country. However, because the promotion of "Kyrie" was thus limited, Famous only marketed three single records on a nationwide basis, and the contract required the nationwide promotion of four.

worked for Famous rather than ABC, however, would appear to militate in favor of the opposite conclusion.

Judge Owen correctly charged the jury that "after the assignment of the contract by Famous to ABC, Famous remained liable for any obligation that was not fulfilled by ABC." This was a correct statement of the law, and Famous' assault upon it, while valiant, is without merit....

Famous' final contention is that Contemporary is estopped from suing for a breach of the Crunch agreement. According to Famous, because Contemporary has always claimed that the assignment was void *ab initio*, it is estopped to claim that Famous is vicariously liable for a breach by ABC, because if the assignment was void, ABC had no obligation which could have been breached. This argument is without merits because it is premised upon the mistaken notion that Famous is being held liable for a breach by ABC. Such is not the case. The basis of the recovery is not a breach by ABC, it is a breach by Famous after the sale to ABC.

[Eds.: Discussion of damages and evidence omitted.]

The judgment of the district court is affirmed in all respects except as to its ruling with regard to lost royalties, and the case is remanded to the district court for further proceedings in accordance with this opinion.

[Eds.: A concurring and dissenting opinion is omitted.]

Notes and Discussion

1. **Contractual Regulation.** The VIRGIN contract contained a "non-assignability" clause, which the Court quotes in a footnote. The clause set certain conditions on the assignment of "[t]his Agreement." The parties to a contract can limit both the assignment of rights and the delegation of duties under the contract: Restatement 2d §§ 317(2)(c), 318(1), 322. Particularly relevant here is § 322(1): "Unless the circumstances indicate the contrary, a contract term prohibiting assignment of 'the contract' bars only the delegation to an assignee of the performance by the assignor of a duty or condition." See also UCC § 2–210(4). Restatement 2d § 322 Cmt. a: "[A]s assignment has become a common practice, the policy which limits the validity of restraints on alienation has been applied to the construction of contractual terms open to two or more possible constructions." Was Contemporary Mission concerned about assignment or delegation? As the Court observes, "lawyers seem prone to use the word 'assignment' inartfully."

The Crunch agreement had no such non-assignability clause. Does this mean that Famous could delegate its duties to ABC? The Court expresses unease on this score. Delegation of duties is usually permissible unless "the obligee [here, Contemporary Mission] has a substantial interest in having [the original person] perform or control the acts promised": Restatement 2d § 318(2); see also UCC § 2–210(1). If you contract with a neighborhood teenager to shovel the snow off your driveway, you normally have little interest whether that particular person does the work, so long as the drive gets shoveled. What facts make the issue closer in this case?

2. **Effects of Delegation.** Famous appears to have believed that, having transferred its record division to ABC, it had no further obligation to Contemporary Mission. As the Court notes, this belief was mistaken. See Restatement § 318(3): "Unless the obligee agrees otherwise, neither delegation of performance nor a contract to assume the duty made with the obligor by the person delegated discharges any duty or liability of the delegating obligor." What is the explanation for this rule?

Where the obligee agrees to accept performance by the delegated person, the contract is said to be novated (Restatement 2d §§ 280, 328, and 329). The original obligor would then be relieved of liability for performance and drop out of the picture entirely.

One wrinkle that is worth noting is UCC § 2–210(6): "The other party may treat any assignment which delegates performance as creating reasonable grounds for insecurity and may without prejudice to his rights against the assignor demand assurances from the assignee (Section 2–609)." This resembles what happened when O'Reilly met with ABC's lawyers.

Problem 8–4

Gordon Peterson was a news anchorman for WDVM–TV (Channel 9) under a long-term contract with its owner Post–Newsweek. After Post–Newsweek sold the station to the Evening News Association, Peterson attempted to accept a job at another rival television station; but Evening News then sought injunctive relief to prevent Peterson from moving. Peterson contends, however, that his Post–Newsweek contract required him to perform unique and unusual services and because of the personal relationship he had with Post–Newsweek the contract was not assignable. Is he right?

Note: Delegation in Commercial Contracts

While delegation of duties is not as common as assignment of rights, delegation in commercial practice often must be done. Note that subsection (1) of 2–210 deals with delegation of duties and that subsection (2) deals with assignment of rights. Notwithstanding that division, courts sometimes say that a delegation must meet four tests in section 2–210 in order to be effective. Technically this is wrong because the first subsection has only two conditions and the second subsection does not apply to delegation.

The most common way to forestall delegation is to include a term that prohibits it. Note that the sentence in 2–210(1) includes the clause "unless otherwise agreed." But a prohibition on delegation or assignment can be overridden in bankruptcy, section 365(e)(1). Note too that section 9–406, 9–407, and 9–408 override restrictions on assignment of rights in certain circumstances.

Mergers of parties in the same or related industries have been a source of conflict about the right to delegate duties. Assume for example that companies A and B are competitors and that A has a contract under which it sells all of its goods of a certain kind through distributor C. If B buys C, B will be privy to all kinds of information about A's business; B will have access to A's terms, including price, A's list of customers and to all kinds of information about the customers' historic buying practices.

In *Sally Beauty Co. v. Nexxus Products Co.,* 801 F.2d 1001 (7th Cir. 1986), Nexxus had contracted with Best Barber & Beauty Supply Co. to distribute its hair care products in most of Texas. While this contract was still in force, Best was acquired by and merged into Sally Beauty, which was, in turn, a wholly-owned subsidiary of Alberto–Culver—a direct competitor of Nexxus, which then cancelled. When Sally Beauty then sued, Nexxus defended by claiming that the contract with Best was not assignable (better, that its duties could not be delegated) or, in the alternative, not assignable to Sally Beauty. The Seventh Circuit found that this contract could not be assigned to the wholly-owned subsidiary of a direct competitor.

The decision centered on UCC § 2–210(1), which states that: "A party may perform his duty through a delegate unless otherwise agreed or unless the other party has a substantial interest in having his original promisor perform or control the acts required by the contract." The majority held that Nexxus had such an interest in this case. "[I]t is undisputed that Sally Beauty is wholly owned by Alberto–Culver, which means that Sally Beauty's 'impartial' sales policy is at least acquiesced in by Alberto–Culver—but could change whenever Alberto–Culver's needs changed. Sally Beauty may be totally sincere in its belief that it can operate 'impartially' as a distributor, but who can guarantee the outcome when there is a clear choice between the demands of the parent-manufacturer, Alberto–Culver, and the competing needs of Nexxus? The risk of an unfavorable outcome is not one which the law can force Nexxus to take." *Sally Beauty*, 801 F.2d at 1008.

This line of argument attracted a vigorous dissent from Judge Posner, who thought it unlikely that Nexxus would be materially hurt by the merger. Posner argues that market forces would prevent this. "Suppose Alberto–Culver had ordered Sally Beauty to go slow in pushing Nexxus products, in the hope that sales of Albert–Culver 'hair care' products would rise. Even if they did, since the market is competitive Alberto–Culver would not reap monopoly profits. Moreover, what guarantee has Alberto–Culver that consumers would be diverted from Nexxus to it, rather than to products closer in price and quality to Nexxus products? In any event, any trivial gain in profits to Alberto–Culver would be offset by the loss of goodwill to Sally Beauty; and a cost to Sally Beauty is a cost to Alberto–Culver, its parent." Id. at 1010. The risk is therefore negligible. "And there is no principle of law that if something happens that trivially reduces the probability that a dealer will use his best efforts, the supplier can cancel the contract." Id. at 1011. For a similar case see *In re Nedwick Steel Co*., 289 B.R. 95 (Bankr. N.D. Ill. 2003).

Problem 8–5

Axle has a contract to sell to Ford 250,000 dash moldings for a new sedan, at $40 each. The contract is silent on rights to assign or delegate.

1. Axle assigns its rights to payment under the contract to Bank as security for a loan. Bank gives notice of the assignment and Axle directs

Ford to pay the invoiced amounts directly to Bank. Axle breaks the contract by delivering 30,000 defective moldings which Ford must repair at $10 each. Shortly after it delivers the defective moldings Axle declares bankruptcy. When Ford deducts $30,000 from its last payment to Bank, the Bank claims that it may not deduct that amount but must pay the Bank and then recover the amount from Axle. Advise the Bank. See UCC § 9–404 and Restatement 2d, § 336.

2. In the foregoing case assume that Ford refused to pay Bank directly and that, despite instructions to pay Bank, Ford continued to pay Axle. Shortly after the last $150,000 due on the contract was paid to Axle, Axle declared bankruptcy. Assume that the $150,000 cannot be traced and that it has probably been paid out during the pre-bankruptcy period to various hungry creditors. Has Ford discharged its debt or can Bank recover the $150,000 from Ford? See § 9–406.

3. Assume that the Ford–Axle contract was to run for a five-year term with payments made monthly. Ford agreed to give Axle twelve negotiable notes for $60,000 each for the first 12 months' payments. Each note is due on the last day of a month. Assume that Axle indorsed those notes to Bank in return for a payment of $700,000. In the 6th month Axle ceased manufacture and went into bankruptcy. By mistake Ford paid Axle for the first two months ($120,000). At the end of the year Bank presents the notes to Ford for payment. Ford asserts the defense of total breach by Axle and of discharge by payment for the first two months. Bank cites UCC § 3–305(b). Assume that Bank is a holder in due course. Does Ford have to pay any or all of the $720,000?

4. Halfway through the contract term Axle sells all of its assets to Hun, Inc., a well-known tier-one auto supplier. Assume alternatively that Hun defaults and that Ford sues Axle for breach, or that Ford cancels the contract on learning of the sale of the assets to Hun. In each ensuing dispute what are Ford's rights?

5. If you were a lawyer for Ford (or for Axle) what terms might you add to the agreement to solve the foregoing problems? See § 9–404.

Problem 8–6

A University of Michigan student with a rare heart condition seeks legal advice. This potential plaintiff purchased health insurance from an HMO, which recently assigned its coverage from University of Michigan Medical Centers (UMMed) to St. Joseph's Medical Center (St. Joe's). St. Joe's offers approximately the same care as UMMed. UMMed would have followed the same protocol in diagnosing plaintiff's condition, but would have prescribed different treatment. Plaintiff's rare condition can probably be corrected with an innovative new surgery, pioneered coincidentally by a surgeon at the University of Michigan. The surgery is experimental, but the risks are few, the chance of success is great, and the only issue is the cost. The surgery would have been covered by plaintiff's policy had the HMO not assigned her care from UMMed to St. Joe's. The policy that plaintiff signed did not contain a clause prohibiting the HMO from assigning her care, and the HMO is refusing to pay. The HMO says St. Joe's offers all the services UMMed does, and will not pay for "unproven investigative research." Advise the student.

Problem 8–7

Rubin and his buddies, Parmet and Merkow, brought a check for $1,900,000 drawn by a west Texas car dealer on a west Texas bank into Guaranty Federal, a Dallas branch of a savings and loan. They opened an account by depositing the check (doubtless making them the largest depositor at the bank and making the teller, who took it, the queen for the month). Thirty minutes after the deposit, Parmet returned to Guaranty to obtain $900,000 of the funds he had just deposited, claiming he had forgotten to make the withdrawal previously. Parmet filled out an application for an "official check" of Guaranty to be made payable to the order of "Binion & Co." Parmet left the bank with a check drawn by Guaranty on its account at Citibank and payable to Binion for $900,000.

The boys then called the Binion brothers (then owners of the Horseshoe Casino in Las Vegas) and said they were coming up for some serious gambling with a $900,000 check. Not born yesterday, the Binions made several calls to different persons at Guaranty to confirm that the check had been issued. When the boys arrived at the Horseshoe, they got $900,000 worth of chips. Betting an average of $80,000 on each hand dealt, they lost $890,000 in four hours. They then asked Binion to get them "some girls" and a ride to the Union Plaza Hotel, where they were staying. Binion went with them to the hotel, told the hotel to bill Horseshoe for their expenses, and also reimbursed them for the jet they had chartered to get to and from Las Vegas. Binion also arranged for a limousine, and gave them $5,000 for "some walking around money."

When Guaranty opened the next day Parmet was waiting at the door; he informed the teller that the check from west Texas for $1,900,000 was not good and would bounce when it was presented in west Texas. Whereupon Guaranty promptly directed Citibank to refuse payment on its "official check" for $900,000 when it was presented. Citibank dishonored the $900,000 "official check."

Now what does all of this have to do with contracts, and what does it have to do with third-party rights on contracts? The check drawn by Guaranty (called an official or teller's check) is like a cashier's check, it bears the contract of Guaranty as the drawer. Guaranty in this case (and, you, every time you draw a check) contracts to pay the payee (Binions) if the check bounces.

When the "official check" bounced, the Binions sued Guaranty on its drawer's contract. The "third-party" issue is whether Guaranty can assert the defense it has against one not a party to the contract (fraud by the boys) against the Binions with whom it contracted by check.

1. What is Guaranty's defense and can it assert that defense against Binion? Section 164(2) of the Second Restatement might give an answer: "(2) If a party's manifestation of assent is induced by either a fraudulent or a material misrepresentation by one who is not a party to the transaction upon which the recipient is justified in relying, the contract is voidable by

the recipient, unless the other party to the transaction in good faith and without reason to know of the misrepresentation either gives value or relies materially on the transaction."

2. If the Binions had been holders in due course, they would have taken free of Guaranty's defense for sure. Read UCC § 3–305 carefully to see why.

C. SURETYSHIP AND GUARANTY CONTRACTS

Suretyship contracts are always ancillary to other transactions, usually to contracts to pay money. A father guarantees his daughter's debt, a company guarantees its subsidiary's repayment, a principal shareholder guarantees the debt of his thinly capitalized corporation. Suretyship has nearly disappeared from American law school curriculums, and, since many of the interesting suretyship issues are related to the issues in this Chapter, we offer a tincture of suretyship here.

When the creditor (who is the beneficiary of the guarantee) tries to enforce the suretyship contract, what defenses may the surety raise? It is clear and right that the surety not assert all of the defenses of the debtor. For example, a principal purpose of many guarantees is to protect the creditor against the debtor's default when the debtor goes into bankruptcy. Bankruptcy may discharge the debtor, and if so, that discharge will be a defense of the debtor to any suit by the creditor, but it would be wrong to let the guarantor assert that defense when he is sued by the creditor, and the law does not allow him to assert that defense. The guarantor may assert most other defenses of the debtor. If, for example, the father guaranteed the son's promise to pay for the Ford F–150 pickup, and the pickup proves to have been defective when it was delivered to the son, the father can assert that defense when he is sued.

And what are the conditions to liability on this suretyship contract? Must the creditor sue the debtor before he proceeds against the surety? Not unless the contract says so or the guarantee is only of "collection," i.e., is a promise merely to pay a judgment that cannot be collected. Must separate consideration go to the surety to bind him? No; the loan to the debtor is sufficient consideration to bind the guarantor too. Must the surety sign a writing? Yes; no signature and no exception to the rule, not binding. Why do you think that the ancient English statute of frauds, copied so faithfully by our states, required a writing from a surety? Is it because a surety is a fool with a pen?

If you thought about it a little, you now recognize the duty of the assignor (specified in 2–210 and elsewhere) to perform if his assignee/delegee does not, is a form of statutory suretyship obligation. The assignor stands by and is liable if the assignee/delegee stumbles.

The possibility that a contractual or a statutory surety will have to perform the duty of the assignee/delegee or of the debtor raises the question whether the surety can himself then pursue the debtor after he has paid the creditor. Common sense tells you yes, and the law recognizes various claims by the surety who has paid against the debtor/assignee/delegee who was supposed to perform. And you do not have to be too cynical to consider the possibility that the debtor and creditor might conspire to cheat the surety.

The best source for American suretyship law is the Restatement 3d of Suretyship and Guaranty (1996). It is complex but modern and comprehensive. The opinion below in the *Hall* case and Problem 8–8 rely heavily on §§ 37–39 of the Third Restatement:

§ 37 Impairment of Suretyship Status

(4) If the obligee impairs the secondary obligor's suretyship status

(a) after the secondary obligor performs any portion of the secondary obligation; or

(b) before the secondary obligor performs a portion of the secondary obligation, if the secondary obligor then performs:

(i) without knowledge of such impairment;

(ii) for the benefit of an intended beneficiary who can enforce the secondary obligation notwithstanding such impairment; or

(iii) under business compulsion;

the secondary obligor has a claim against the obligee with respect to such performance to the extent that such impairment would have discharged the secondary obligor with respect to that performance.

§ 38 Preservation of Secondary Obligor's Recourse

(1) When an obligee releases the principal obligor from, or agrees to extend the time for performance of, a duty to pay money pursuant to the underlying obligation, the release or extension effects a "preservation of the secondary obligor's recourse" with respect to that duty if the express terms of the release or extension provide that:

(a) the obligee retains the right to seek performance of the secondary obligation by the secondary obligor; and

(b) the rights of the secondary obligor to recourse against the principal obligor (§ 21–28) continue as though the release or extension had not been granted.

(2) When the obligee effects a preservation of the secondary obligor's recourse in conjunction with a release or extension, the principal obligor's duties of performance and reimbursement and the secondary obligor's rights of restitution and subrogation continue as though the release or extension did not occur.

§ 39 Release of Underlying Obligation

To the extent that the obligee releases the principal obligor from its duties pursuant to the underlying obligation:

(a) the principal obligor is also discharged from any corresponding duties of performance and reimbursement owed to the secondary obligor unless the terms of the release effect a preservation of the secondary obligor's recourse (§ 38);

(b) the secondary obligor is discharged from any unperformed duties pursuant to the secondary obligation unless:

(i) the terms of the release effect a preservation of the secondary obligor's recourse (§ 38); or

(ii) the language or circumstances of the release otherwise show the obligee's intent to retain its claim against the secondary obligor;

(c) if the secondary obligor is not discharged from its unperformed duties pursuant to the secondary obligation by operation of paragraph (b), the secondary obligor is discharged from those duties to the extent:

(i) of the value of the consideration for the release;

(ii) that the release of a duty to pay money pursuant to the underlying obligation would otherwise cause the secondary obligor a loss; and

(iii) that the release discharges a duty of the principal obligor other than the payment of money;

(d) the secondary obligor has a claim against the obligee to the extent provided in § 37(4).

WILL H. HALL & SON v. CAPITOL INDEMNITY CORP.

Court of Appeals of Michigan, 2003.
260 Mich.App. 222, 677 N.W.2d 51.

MURPHY, P.J. Plaintiff appeals as of right from a judgment granting defendant Capitol Indemnity Corporation's motion for summary disposition, which was brought pursuant to MCR 2.116(C)(7)(release) and (10), in this action involving a construction project and a performance bond. We affirm.

Plaintiff was the general contractor for a government Job Corps construction project, and defendant Ace Masonry was a subcontractor providing cement and masonry work on the project. The construction project required that Ace furnish a performance bond intended to protect plaintiff, and one was issued by Capitol. Subsequently, a dispute arose between plaintiff and Ace concerning the masonry work, and the project was not fully completed.

The complaint filed by plaintiff alleged breach of contract, fraud, and misrepresentation with respect to Ace. The complaint also included a claim against Capitol seeking recovery on the performance bond. Ace filed a counterclaim against plaintiff alleging breach of contract, and a third-party complaint against plaintiff's surety United States Fidelity & Guaranty Company.

The trial court granted Capitol's motion for directed verdict during a jury trial in regard to the performance bond claim. The trial court granted the directed *225 verdict, finding a "failure of proof regarding compliance with conditions precedent, including failure to declare default." Immediately after the trial court granted the directed verdict, plaintiff requested and obtained a brief recess to discuss a possible settlement with Ace. Following the recess, and on the record, plaintiff and Ace stipulated the release and dismissal of any claims the parties had against each other. The following colloquy took place regarding the settlement:

> Plaintiff's Counsel: [W]e have had an opportunity to [discuss] this matter amongst ourselves, in light of the [court] ... granting Capitol Indemnity's motion for directed verdict, the remaining parties in the case have discussed this matter and they're willing to settle this case by mutual release of all claims against each other.
>
> Judge: All right, Mr. Schaffer [counsel for Ace], do you wish to be heard on this?
>
> Ace's Counsel: I would just concur in that settlement-my client is here I just would ask that, on the record, he indicate that is his wish to do that....

Ace's representative proceeded to approve the settlement and release. The record does not reflect any statements by counsel for Capitol during discussion of the settlement. Further, the record does not indicate whether Capitol's counsel remained in the courtroom after the directed verdict was granted and when the settlement and release were placed on the record. Subsequently, plaintiff pursued an appeal of the directed verdict to this Court.

This Court, in an unpublished per curiam opinion, reversed the trial court's order granting the directed verdict, holding:

> Viewing [the] evidence in a light most favorable to plaintiff, we conclude that a reasonable factfinder could find that defendant received notice that the subcontractor committed a material breach, that plaintiff regarded the subcontractor to have failed to meet its contractual duties, and that plaintiff was asking defendant to perform under the terms of the bond.
>
> To the extent the trial court found plaintiff's notice to defendant untimely, we note that the only time frame provided in the performance bond is the two-year limitations period for filing a lawsuit. Where the time of performance is indefinite, performance may be required to be rendered within a reasonable time. The question regarding the reasonableness of plaintiff's claim, which was filed less than three months after Ace walked off the job, should

have been submitted to the jury. [*Hall & Son, Inc. v. Capitol Indemnity Corp.*, unpublished opinion per curiam of the Court of Appeals, issued June 15, 2001 (Docket No. 222262, 2001 WL 685772) (citations omitted).]

On remand, Capitol filed a motion for summary disposition, arguing that, in light of plaintiff's decision to dismiss the action against Ace, an action on the performance bond could no longer be maintained. Capitol claimed that the release of the principal, Ace, by plaintiff, the obligee, acted as a discharge of Capitol, the surety. On the basis of Capitol's argument, the trial court granted the motion for summary disposition and dismissed the action. Plaintiff appealed....

Plaintiff ... argues that although the general rule in Michigan is that the discharge of the principal serves as a discharge of the surety, there is an exception where the surety consents to the release of the principal. Plaintiff further argues that there were genuine issues of material fact concerning whether Capitol consented to the release of Ace, where the parties placed the settlement on the record with Capitol's counsel present.

A suretyship contract requires three parties; a principal, an obligee, and a surety. *In re Forfeiture of United States Currency*, 172 Mich.App. 790, 792, 432 N.W.2d 442 (1988). A surety is one who undertakes to pay money or take any other action if the principal fails therein. Id. "The liability of a surety is limited by the scope of the liability of its principal and the precise terms of the surety agreement." *Bd. of Governors of Wayne State Univ. v. Building Systems Housing Corp.*, 62 Mich.App. 77, 85, 233 N.W.2d 195 (1975) (citation omitted). In general, a surety may plead any defense available to the principal, and the liability of the surety is coextensive with the liability of the principal in the bond and can be extended no further. *In re MacDonald's Estate*, 341 Mich. 382, 387, 67 N.W.2d 227 (1954).

Plaintiff relies on *Westveer v. Landwehr*, 276 Mich. 326, 267 N.W. 849 (1936), for its proposition that there is an exception to the general rule of discharge where the surety consents to the release of the principal. In Westveer, a bank loaned money to a country club on multiple occasions, and the club's directors acted as sureties to guarantee payments on the loan through the execution of two bonds; the bonds being continuing guarantees. Id. at 327–329, 267 N.W. 849. One of the sureties who executed the bonds died and additional promissory notes were issued after his death. Id. at 328, 267 N.W. 849. Our Supreme Court held that in regards to the renewal notes, issued by the bank after the surety's death and after notice of his death, the deceased's estate was discharged from any liability based on the bond or guaranty. Id. at 329, 267 N.W. 849. The Court also held, however, that the release of the deceased surety's estate did not discharge the surviving sureties on the renewal notes, where those sureties did not exercise the option to be released from further liability at the time of the deceased surety's death and thus acquiesced in remaining on the guaranty thereafter. Id. at 329–330, 267 N.W. 849.

Westveer did not involve the release of a principal by the obligee as occurred in the case at bar.[19] *Westveer* only dealt with a situation where sureties had the opportunity to be discharged on a debt pursuant to an agreement but failed to exercise the steps necessary to be discharged and acquiesced in continuing liability. Here, Capitol was not required by any agreement to take affirmative steps to be discharged; therefore, it cannot be said that Capitol acquiesced in being held liable on the performance bond. *Westveer* does not stand for the proposition, as argued by plaintiff, that surety liability is continuing where the surety consents to the release of the principal. Even in the context of the facts in *Westveer*, whether the surviving sureties consented to the release of the deceased surety was not an issue and did not play into the Supreme Court's analysis and holding.

Plaintiff also relies on *Greenlee v. Lowing*, 35 Mich. 63 (1876). In Greenlee, the plaintiff brought an action to recover on a replevin bond. A judgment in replevin had been previously entered against the principal obligor by the plaintiff; however, the plaintiff and the principal had a private arrangement whereby the principal was released for consideration with the plaintiff being left at liberty to recover what he could from the sureties. Our Supreme Court stated:

> If an agreement was made releasing Mrs. Ridell [principal obligor] from liability in the judgment rendered against her in the replevin suit, the effect thereof undoubtedly would be to discharge the sureties unless they consented to the agreement, which is not claimed. [Id. at 66.]

The above quote was part of the Court's discussion concerning the propriety of a jury charge, not a substantive discussion on suretyship. Regardless, the case does not support plaintiff's position because the release agreement there allowed the plaintiff to pursue sureties. Therefore, when the Court discussed the matter of the sureties' consent to the agreement, which was not claimed, the consent would necessarily relate to not only the release but also to the sureties continuing potential liability. Here, the record in regards to the settlement and release reveals no agreement by plaintiff and Ace that plaintiff could continue to pursue Capitol. Moreover, the record does not indicate that Capitol consented to the release and its own continuing liability.

Michigan case law is minimal concerning sureties, and there are no cases, of which we are aware, that directly, substantively, and fully address the effect on a surety's liability following the obligee's release of any and all claims against the principal. However, we find guidance in

19. The country club was the principal obligor in *Westveer*, with the bank being the obligee.

Restatement Suretyship and Guaranty, 3d, § 39 (Release of Underlying Obligation),[20] which provides in relevant part:

> To the extent that the obligee releases the principal obligor from its duties pursuant to the underlying obligation:
>
> * * *
>
> (b) the secondary obligor (surety) is discharged from any unperformed duties pursuant to the secondary obligation unless:
>
> (i) the terms of the release effect a preservation of the secondary obligor's recourse . . . ; or
>
> (ii) the language or circumstances of the release otherwise show the obligee's intent to retain its claim against the secondary obligor[.]

See also *Axess Int'l, Ltd. v. Intercargo Ins. Co.*, 183 F.3d 935, 939 (C.A.9, 1999); *Amtote Int'l, Inc. v. PNGI Charles Town Gaming Ltd. Liability Co.*, 66 F.Supp. 2d 782, 793–794 (N.D.W.Va., 1999).

In *Axess Int'l*, supra at 939–940, a case involving a $50,000 surety bond covering damages arising from transportation-related activities, the United States Ninth Circuit Court of Appeals held that, pursuant to § 39(b) of Restatement Suretyship and Guaranty, 3d, the surety was not discharged from liability where a clause in the release specifically reserved the obligee's right to claim or take any proceedings against any other party, which clearly reflected an intent to release only the principal. The federal court cited comment d to § 39 of the Restatement in support of the position that the surety is not discharged when the release is intended to only discharge the principal obligor, and this intent can be manifested by a provision in the release. *Axess Int'l*, supra at 939.[21] The Axess Int'l court cited several state and federal decisions that were consistent with its position and the Restatements. Id. at 938–939.

20. See also Restatement Security, § 122 (1941), wherein it is stated that "[w]here the creditor releases a principal, the surety is discharged, unless (a) the surety consents to remain liable notwithstanding the release, or (b) the creditor in the release reserves his rights against the surety." We note that this Restatement has now been superseded by Restatement Suretyship and Guaranty, 3d.

21. The Ninth Circuit Court also relied on Restatement Security, § 122 (1941) (cited by us above . . .). Axess Int'l, supra at 939 n. 3. Comment d to Restatement Suretyship and Guaranty, 3d, § 39, provides:

> An obligee may release the principal obligor from its duties pursuant to the underlying obligation in a number of different circumstances. In some cases, such as an accord and satisfaction, the release is intended to discharge all claims of the obligee (including claims against other obligors) with respect to those duties. In those cases, the secondary obligor is discharged by the release. In other cases, however, the release is intended to discharge only the obligee's claim against the principal obligor, leaving the obligee free to pursue the secondary obligor. Paragraph (b) [of § 39 of Restatement] does not discharge the secondary obligor when the release is intended to discharge only the principal obligor. This intent can be manifested in a provision of the release effecting a preservation of recourse of the secondary obligor or otherwise indicating that the secondary obligor remains liable, or inferred from circumstances that indicate such intent. In the absence of such a provision or such circumstances, of course, the secondary obligor is discharged. . . .

Here, there is no evidence indicating that Capitol consented to remain liable notwithstanding the release, no language or circumstances indicating that plaintiff reserved the right to pursue Capitol, and no release terms effecting a preservation of Capitol's recourse against Ace. Because the release was broad, open-ended, and all-encompassing, it cannot be said that plaintiff intended to retain a claim against Capitol. We note illustration 4 to Restatement Suretyship and Guaranty, 3d, § 39, which provides:

> D agrees to construct a building for C for $1,000,000. S issues a performance bond for D's obligation. Soon after starting construction, D abandons the project. Investigation reveals that D is insolvent and has essentially no assets other than equipment left at C's work site. Realizing the futility of pursuing D, C agrees to release D from its obligations pursuant to the construction contract in exchange for title to the abandoned equipment. The circumstances indicate that C intended to retain its claim against S. S is not discharged pursuant to paragraph (b), but is discharged to *234 the extent provided in paragraph (c)[value of the consideration for the release].

Here, there was no documentary evidence presented by plaintiff in response to Capitol's motion for summary disposition showing that plaintiff could not recover its damages from Ace, or that the reason for the settlement and release was the insolvency of Ace. It is just as likely that **58 plaintiff settled the case with Ace in order to avoid any potential liability on Ace's counterclaim. In fact, it is apparent that plaintiff was not focusing at all on the future liability of Capitol when placing the settlement on the record, considering that Capitol had already been relieved of liability on the basis of the directed verdict. We conclude that plaintiff has failed to submit documentary evidence sufficient to create an issue of fact with respect to, and in support of, plaintiff's proposition that it intended to retain its claim against Capitol. MCR 2.116(C)(10). In placing the settlement on the record, plaintiff failed to appreciate the possibility that an appeal and a reversal could reinstate its action against Capitol.

Plaintiff's assertion that Capitol implicitly agreed to remain liable where it did not object to the stipulated dismissal is without merit. Capitol, having been relieved of liability pursuant to the directed verdict and, assuming that Capitol's counsel was present when the settlement was placed on the record, having heard no statements on the record by counsel for plaintiff and Ace that Capitol would somehow remain liable, had no reason to object to the settlement and release. Once again, the consent of the surety regards consenting to remain liable notwithstanding the release. We will not presume Capitol's consent to remain liable from its silence, assuming that Capitol's counsel was present at the time of settlement.[22]

22. Any reliance on *The President, Directors & Co. of the Farmers & Mechanics' Bank of Michigan v. Kingsley*, 2 Doug 379 (Mich. 1846), is misplaced for the reason

In a recent legal article discussing the effect of a release on a surety under Restatement Suretyship and Guaranty, 3d, the authors stated that "[i]f the obligee [plaintiff] releases the principal [Ace] *without more*, (a) both the principal and surety [Capitol] are discharged from duties to the obligee, and (b) the principal is discharged from all duties to the surety." Mungall[23] & Arena, *Effect on surety of obligee's release of principal: A critical look at the rules in the restatement*, 70 Def. Couns. J. 328 (2003) (emphasis added). Capitol submitted the transcript of the settlement and the amended order of dismissal for consideration in its motion for summary disposition, and plaintiff failed to submit evidence showing anything to the contrary. Therefore, without more, Capitol and Ace were completely released.

The fact that Capitol was a paid or compensated surety does not alter our conclusion. In *Grinnell Realty Co. v. Gen. Cas. & Surety Co.*, 253 Mich. 16, 21–22, 234 N.W. 125 (1931), our Supreme Court, providing an in-depth discussion distinguishing gratuitous sureties and paid sureties, stated:

> [T]he liability of a gratuitous surety will not be extended to a contract which in the slightest degree varies from the one for the performance of which he became bound. The risk he runs will not be increased in any manner without his consent, nor will the possibility of his immediately protecting himself in the event of default be lessened. Strict rules of law, which sometimes almost seemed harsh, frequently relieved him from his obligation on account of some very slight deviation from the contract by the obligee. The surety's liability was limited in all cases to the strict letter of his bond. In time, however, sureties began to exact compensation, commensurate with the risk they assumed, and surety companies were organized for profit. They charged premiums so as to make their business a profitable one. They drafted their own bonds and inserted therein such conditions as they thought necessary to properly protect themselves. The law thereupon recognized the difference between gratuitous and paid sureties and required that paid sureties, in order to be released from the obligations of their bond must show that they were damaged by some slight deviation from the contract by the obligee. Their bond was looked upon as one of insurance or indemnity instead of one of suretyship. There is no presumption that a paid surety was harmed, nor is the suggestion of mere contingencies or possibilities sufficient. It is not relieved from its obligations except when it is shown that there is a material departure from the contract which resulted in some injury to the surety. [Citations omitted.][24]

Here, there is no dispute about deviations or changes in the underlying contract between plaintiff and Ace that might have affected Capitol's

that here, there was a lack of evidence establishing consent to continuing liability by Capitol.

23. Daniel Mungall, Jr., served as associate reporter on Restatement Suretyship and Guaranty, 3d.

24. A prejudicial change or modification in duties or obligations is necessary to discharge a paid surety from liability. Hunters Pointe Partners Ltd. Partnership v. United States Fidelity & Guaranty Co., 177 Mich. App. 745, 749, 442 N.W.2d 778 (1989).

obligations under the performance bond. The matter presented to us is merely whether plaintiff's unconditional and broad release, without limitation, and without any consent by Capitol to remain liable, relieves Capitol of liability. Moreover, under Restatement Suretyship and Guaranty, 3d, § 39(a), Capitol would be harmed or prejudiced if plaintiff were allowed to pursue its action on the performance bond because Capitol would have no recourse against Ace. Section 39(a) provides that "[t]o the extent that the obligee [plaintiff] releases the principal obligor [Ace] from its duties pursuant to the underlying obligation: the principal obligor is also discharged from any corresponding duties of performance and reimbursement owed to the secondary obligor [Capitol] unless the terms of the release effect a preservation of the secondary obligor's recourse[.]" Because the terms of the release here do not effect a preservation of Capitol's recourse, and because plaintiff presented no documentary evidence showing Ace to be insolvent or uncollectible, Capitol would be prejudiced and harmed should plaintiff be allowed to pursue the action and recover on the performance bond.

The dissent, quoting Restatement Suretyship and Guaranty, 3d, pp 157, 175, argues that, under the Restatement, a release discharges a secondary obligor, Capitol, only to the extent that it suffers a loss. The Restatement provision concerning the dissent's argument is found in § 39. We have already concluded, on the basis of the documentary evidence, that Capitol would suffer a loss if it became liable to plaintiff. Moreover, we disagree with the dissent's interpretation of the Restatement. Section 39 of the Restatement provides:

> (c) if the secondary obligor is not discharged from its unperformed duties pursuant to the secondary obligation by operation of paragraph (b) [quoted above], the secondary obligor is discharged from those duties to the extent:
>
> > (i) of the value of the consideration for the release;
> >
> > (ii) that the release of a duty to pay money pursuant to the underlying obligation would otherwise cause the secondary obligor a loss; and
> >
> > (iii) that the release discharges a duty of the principal obligor other than the payment of money[.]

Plaintiff failed to present documentary evidence showing that Capitol was not discharged under subsection b of § 39 (terms of the release effect a preservation of the secondary obligor's recourse, or language or circumstances of the release otherwise show the obligee's intent to retain its claim against the secondary obligor). Thus, subsection c was not triggered. Assuming subsection c was triggered, there still would be a discharge under the Restatement because Ace's duty or obligation was one other than the payment of money, i.e., providing cement and masonry work. The reason for this distinction is explained in comment g to § 39, pp 173–174:

When the underlying obligation is performance other than the payment of money, a release of the principal obligor has an effect on the secondary obligor that is particularly difficult to quantify. First, as in all releases, the ability of the principal obligor to perform had there been no release must be considered. Yet the ability of a principal obligor to perform a nonmonetary obligation is typically not susceptible of reliable determination. Second, a factor not present when the underlying obligation is the payment of money-the relative cost of performance by the principal obligor and secondary obligor-complicates matters further. The cost of performance by the secondary obligor may be different than it would have been for the principal obligor.... Third, a principal obligor who has been released from the underlying obligation may be uncooperative in assisting the secondary obligor to establish defenses to the secondary obligation. These factual difficulties, combined with the fact that the secondary obligor's bargain contemplated the existence of a continuing obligation of the principal obligor to perform, make it inequitable to place on the secondary obligor any burden of demonstrating the existence and amount of the loss resulting from the release of the principal obligor when the underlying obligation is not the payment of money. Accordingly, this section discharges the secondary obligor to the extent of a release of nonmonetary obligations of the principal obligor.

Because it is unnecessary to our resolution of this case, we decline to decide today whether to adopt the exception in § 39(c) regarding nonmonetary obligations.

Affirmed.

C. L. LEVIN, J. DISSENTING. I respectfully dissent.

Plaintiff, Will H. Hall & Son, Inc., was the general contractor for a construction project in Flint, Michigan. Ace Masonry Construction, Inc., was the masonry subcontractor for two buildings in the project. Capitol Indemnity Corporation provided a performance bond for Ace. United States Fidelity & Guaranty Company provided a performance bond for Hall.

After Ace ceased work on the project, Hall hired another subcontractor to finish the masonry work. This litigation followed. Hall commenced an action against Ace. Ace counterclaimed against Hall, and filed a third-party complaint against USF & G.

Hall presented proofs in a jury trial, and rested. The trial court granted Capitol's motion for a directed verdict on the ground that Hall had not timely declared or notified Capitol of default. Hall and Ace then stipulated to release all their claims against each other. Hall appealed the directed verdict to this Court, which reversed and remanded for trial.

On remand, Capitol moved for summary disposition on the ground that the release of Ace, the principal on the bond, also released the surety as a matter of law. The motion was granted.

A.

I agree with the majority that the record does not show any agreement between Hall and Ace that Hall could continue to pursue Capitol, and does not indicate that Capitol consented to the release and its own continuing liability.[25]

The majority continues that there is no "language or circumstances indicating that [Hall] reserved the right to pursue Capitol," and that because the release "was broad, open-ended, and all-encompassing, it cannot be said that [Hall] intended to retain a claim against Capitol." Ante, p. 57. The majority further continues that there is no evidence that "[Hall] could not recover its damages from Ace, or that the reason for the settlement and release was the insolvency of Ace. It is just as likely that Hall settled the case with Ace in order to avoid any potential liability on Ace's counterclaim." Ante, pp. 57–58. The majority concludes that Hall "failed to submit documentary evidence sufficient to create an issue of fact with respect to, and in support of, [Hall's] proposition that it intended to retain its claim against Capitol." Id.

B

The majority adverts to the absence of "language or circumstances" indicating that Hall had the right to pursue Capitol, and also to the absence of evidence that Hall could not recover its damages from Ace, or that Ace was insolvent. The words "language or circumstances" are found in the Third Restatement of Suretyship, which provides that when an obligee (Hall) releases the principal obligor (Ace), the secondary obligor (Capitol) is discharged from any unperformed duties unless the release preserves the secondary obligor's recourse against the principal obligor or the "language or circumstances" of the release otherwise show the obligee's intent to retain its claim against the secondary obligor, and which further provides that the secondary obligor, if not otherwise discharged from further liability, is so discharged to the extent it can show loss or prejudice.

I would reverse and remand for trial because Capitol–not Hall–had the burden of persuasion on the issues of whether the "language or circumstances of the release otherwise show [Hall's] intent to retain its claim against" Capitol, and of "loss or prejudice [to Capitol] caused by [Hall's] act" in releasing Ace.

Release is an affirmative defense. MCR 2.111(F)(3)(a). The affidavit, and other papers, filed in support of Capitol's motion for summary disposition, did not advert to those issues, and did not claim or show that there was no genuine issue of material fact concerning those issues. On the summary disposition record so far made, there are genuine issues of material fact regarding those issues.

25. The surety's consent is not a prerequisite to an effective reservation of rights. Notice thereof to the surety "may be advisable." Restatement Suretyship and Guaranty, 3d, § 38, comment b, 165–166.

On remand, Capitol would also have the burden of showing, if it were to so claim, that the amount of loss Capitol sustained as a result of the release of Ace is not reasonably susceptible of calculation or requires proof of facts that are not ascertainable, shifting then the burden of persuasion to Hall to show the amount of Capitol's liability.[26]

Sections 37–49 of the Third Restatement of Suretyship and Guaranty set forth the authoritative view of the American Law Institute concerning the law applicable when the "obligee" (Hall) of a surety bond does an act that "changes the risks that were the subject of the secondary obligor's [Capitol's] assessment." "In most cases, in the absence of the secondary obligor's agreement to the contrary, this Title discharges a secondary obligor to the extent that such acts would otherwise cause the secondary obligor to suffer a loss."[27] (Emphasis added.)

Hall's release of the principal obligor (Ace) constituted "an impairment of suretyship status"[28] that may have resulted in the discharge of the secondary obligation, as set forth in sections 38, 39, and 49 of the Restatement.

Sections 38 and 39 concern release of the underlying obligation.[29] The Restatement would eliminate the historic reservation of rights doctrine, and requires, for there to be an effective reservation of rights, an express statement that the secondary obligor's-the surety's-rights of recourse against the principal obligor continue as though the release did not occur. [§ 38.]

If the obligee releases the principal obligor, the secondary obligor is discharged from any unperformed duties unless either the terms of the release effect a preservation of the secondary obligor's recourse or "the language or circumstances of the release otherwise show the obligee's intent to retain its claim against the secondary obligor." [§ 39.]

The Reporter's notes to § 39 comment that an obligee's release of the principal obligor was traditionally regarded as a complete discharge of the secondary obligor. The Third Restatement, however, "adopts the more modern policy generally followed by the Uniform Commercial Code with respect to impairments of recourse by discharging the secondary obligor *only to the extent it would suffer loss as a result of the release.*" (Emphasis added.)

The same concept of discharging the secondary obligor only to the extent that the obligee's act "impairing suretyship status" causes loss to the secondary obligor is set forth in § 40 (Extensions of Time), § 41 (Modification of Underlying Obligation), and § 44 (Other Impairment of Recourse).

26. Id., § 49(3). See discussion in Part II, infra.

27. Id., p. 157.

28. Id., § 37.

29. [Eds.: See §§ 38–39, quoted above.]

II

Section 49 of the Third Restatement speaks of the "burden of persuasion with respect to impairment of recourse."[30] In general, the secondary obligor, the *246 surety, has the burden of persuasion with respect to the occurrence of the act constituting the impairment, and, if the secondary obligor is, as is Capitol, in the business of entering into secondary obligations, it also has the burden of persuasion with respect to loss or prejudice caused by an obligee's act impairing the secondary obligor's recourse against the principal obligor.

Although, as the majority states, the summary disposition record does not, indeed, show language or circumstances indicating that Hall had the right to pursue Capitol, or that Hall intended to retain its claim against Capitol, or that Ace was insolvent, Capitol did not, under § 49 of the Restatement (concerning allocation of the burden of persuasion), discharge its burden of persuasion on its motion for summary disposition by simply showing that Capitol had released Ace.

Capitol's motion for summary disposition did not frame all the pertinent issues that need to be addressed before it can be decided whether Capitol's discharge of Ace fully discharged Capitol from all liability.

III

It was open to Capitol, before moving for summary disposition, to have taken depositions of persons involved in the release, and otherwise knowledgeable regarding Ace and Hall, with a view to establishing that there was no language nor were there circumstances evidencing an

30. Section 49 provides:

(1) A secondary obligor asserting discharge from a secondary obligation due to the obligee's impairment of the secondary obligor's suretyship status (§ 37) has the burden of persuasion with respect to the occurrence of the act constituting the impairment.

(2) Except as provided in subsection (3), the burden of persuasion with respect to loss or prejudice caused by an obligee's act impairing the secondary obligor's recourse against the principal obligor is allocated as follows:

(a) the burden of persuasion is on the secondary obligor if:

(i) the secondary obligor is in the business of entering into secondary obligations, received a business benefit for entering into the secondary obligation, or otherwise was induced to enter into the secondary obligation by separate consideration that directly benefits the secondary obligor; or

(ii) the act impairing recourse is a modification of the underlying obligation, unless the secondary obligor establishes that the modification is material;

(b) otherwise, it is presumed that the act impairing recourse caused a loss of impairment equal to the secondary obligor's liability pursuant to the secondary obligation and the burden of persuasion as to the nonexistence or lesser amount of such loss is on the obligee.

(3) Notwithstanding subsection (2)(a), if:

(a) the secondary obligor demonstrates prejudice caused by the impairment of recourse; and

(b) the circumstances of the case indicate that the amount of loss is not reasonably susceptible of calculation or requires proof of facts that are not ascertainable.

It is presumed that the act impairing recourse caused a loss or impairment equal to the secondary obligor's liability pursuant to the secondary obligation, and the burden of persuasion as to any lesser amount of such loss is on the obligee.

intent by Hall to retain its claim against Capitol, and that Ace was solvent and that the release caused loss or prejudice to Capitol. Because Capitol did not so claim or show in moving for summary disposition, genuine issues of material fact remained unaddressed on the summary disposition record, and it was error to grant summary disposition.

A

While the stipulation read onto the record by Ace and Capitol's lawyers did not include a reservation by Hall of the right to continue this action against Capitol, the understanding, and possibly the agreement, as well, between Hall and Ace may have included a reservation of rights. Lawyers do not necessarily put everything on the record. See *Mikedis v. Perfection Heat Treating Co.*, 180 Mich.App. 189, 195, 446 N.W.2d 648 (1989). And then, again, there may not have been a reservation of rights.

B

Without regard to whether there was an express reservation of rights by Hall to continue this action against Capitol, it appears likely-having a mind that there was a settlement on the record with Ace and no *248 settlement with Capitol-that Hall expected and, indeed, intended to continue, as it did, to prosecute this action against Capitol.

C

The concept that a guarantor is not discharged by an act of the obligee, absent a showing of loss or prejudice, expressed in the Uniform Commercial Code, is, of course most authoritative, because a legislative enactment is an expression of public policy.

Extending that concept to compensated sureties finds support in the case law.[31]

D

An Internal Revenue Service tax lien filed against Ace, adverted to in a pretrial motion, is some indication that Ace may have been in financial difficulty.

E

The Third Restatement states, in respect to a release of the principal obligor, an exception-likely to be relied on by Capitol on a remand-to the general principle that the surety must show loss or prejudice. Subsection (c)(iii) of § 39 states that where the release discharges a duty of the principal obligor other than the payment of money, the secondary obligor is discharged without regard to whether the secondary obligor can show a loss.

31. See *Becker-Boter Oil & Gas Co. v. Massachusetts Bonding & Ins. Co.*, 254 Mich. 94, 96, 235 N.W. 869 (1931); *In re Landwehr's Estate*, 286 Mich. 698, 282 N.W. 873 (1938); *Ramada Development Co. v. United States Fidelity & Guaranty Co.*, 626 F.2d 517, 521 (C.A.6, 1980); 72 C.J.S., Principal and Surety, §§ 125, 146.

This somewhat strange exception to the general principle that a compensated surety must show loss or prejudice is explained in comment g as justified on the ground that where the unperformed obligation is other than the payment of money the "effect on the secondary obligor" "is particularly difficult to quantify". The comment does not explain why this is not covered adequately by § 49(3)(b), which imposes the burden of persuasion on the obligee where the circumstances of the case indicate that the amount of loss is not reasonably susceptible of calculation or requires proofs of facts that are not ascertainable.

A recent article explains how this exception came about.[32] It appears that industry advocates persuaded the governing body of the American Law Institute (ALI), the Council, and the membership of the ALI, to insert this exception. We have found no case law, before or after, that supports or challenges this exception to the general principle that a compensated surety is required to show loss or prejudice.

In the instant case, in contrast with the example hypothesized in the commentary, the masonry work had been completed by another subcontractor before this action was commenced by Hall against Ace and Capitol. There was pretrial discovery, and active participation by Ace in the trial of this action against Ace and Capitol, until the trial court directed a verdict after Hall rested.

It is noteworthy that the industry advocates would unravel the principle that the surety must show loss or prejudice even where a sale of goods is involved, and the surety guarantees payment of money, which would seem to put the Restatement at odds with the Uniform Commercial Code.

I would reverse and remand.

Notes and Discussion

1. **Suretyship and Construction Contracts.** In *National Surety Corp. v. United States*, 31 Fed. Cl. 565 (1994): "The United States Veteran's Administration (VA or government) entered into a construction contract with Dugdale Construction Company (Dugdale) on September 19, 1983. The VA promised to pay Dugdale $1,081,630 to complete a water distribution system at a VA facility in Fort Harrison, Montana. National acted as surety on performance and payment bonds for this contract. The performance bond guaranteed that the VA would receive the contract work for the contract price. The payment bond promises payment to those who have performed services or delivered goods but who have not been paid. The issuers of both bonds are classic sureties.

"Dugdale abandoned the contract on October 26, 1984. As a result, the government terminated the contract for default on November 28, 1984. Dugdale's default triggered National's obligation under the performance bond. National honored that obligation by entering into a takeover agree-

32. Mungall & Arena, Effect on surety of obligee's release of principal: A critical look at the rules in the restatement, 70 Def Couns J 328 (2003).

ment with the VA and Dugdale on January 15, 1985. National then arranged for completion by another contractor. The VA accepted the completed work on September 6, 1985. Before it defaulted, Dugdale had been paid $977,417. The takeover agreement provided that National would complete performance for the remaining $126,333 of the contract price. The VA paid this amount to National." Id. at 567 (footnotes omitted).[33]

The "retainage" is an amount that an owner, the VA in this case, holds back from its progress payments. The retainage might be 10 to 20% of the progress payment. Because of the large amount of capital necessary for a large construction contract and because contractors do not commonly have sufficient capital to do the entire job without help, it is common for owners to make "progress payments;" these are payments in return for the contractor reaching certain milestones in the work. In effect the owner finances the construction by making such advances. Under the terms of the usual retainage, the contracting party has a right to satisfy any damages it suffers from the contractor's breach by a setoff. In *Dugdale*, the VA had turned the retainage over to Dugdale despite its breach and national sued the VA, arguing that the VA should have held the retainage for it, the surety.

The appellate court found that National was entitled to be subrogated to the VA's claim to the retained amounts and that the VA was liable for paying over the retainage. In the words of the Court "the government must administer the contract, in a way that does not materially increase the risk that was assumed by the surety when the contract was bonded."

The Court however held that there must be a remand to determine National's damages. If the retainage that was released to the contractor was used to buy additional labor or materials that went into the project, the surety might not have been hurt by the release since it would have had to have purchased that labor or those materials from its own funds otherwise.

2. A Third-Party Beneficiary? Under the contract, Dugdale was obliged to provide a project arrow diagram (a graphic description of the sequential steps that must be completed before a project can be completed), and the VA had a ten percent retainage on progress payments until it had approved the diagram. Ordinarily, in contracts between two parties, such requirements can be waived, as we saw in Chapter 7.

The presence of the surety and of a duty to the surety complicates this process, for the trial court argued from the language of Clause G–7A (in particular, because the phrase "to protect the interests of the Government" was associated with retainage after the arrow diagram's approval, but not with retainage before approval) that the retainage was for both the VA's and National's benefit. Id. at 576–577. Further, "[a]n even stronger reason for treating National as a third-party beneficiary appears in the disparity between the government's promise to withhold retainage and the government's interest in having discretion to release retainage. The government agreed to withhold retainage until Dugdale submitted an acceptable arrow diagram. But as the government insists and Fireman's Fund bears out, the government would have been better served if it had retained discretion to

33. These figures do not add up. Apparently, prior to the trial, Dugdale and National had together been paid about $22,120 more than the contract price, but the discrepancy is not explained and does not figure in the outcome.

release retainage to help Dugdale. And if the government wanted to protect itself against Dugdale's default, the government could have done so under discretionary clause 7(c) by choosing to withhold retainage. Yet the government chose to be bound. The court finds that the government could not have intended to benefit itself when it surrendered its discretion to release retainage. Nor could the government have intended to benefit Dugdale, which retainage would have hurt; nor could it have intended to benefit the public, whose interests in flexible project management were identical with the government's.... Thus the court concludes that the government must have intended to benefit National." Id. at 577 (citation omitted).

On appeal, both the majority and the dissent reject the argument that National was a third-party beneficiary. What do you think?

Problem 8–8

Axle borrows $1 million from Citi for the capital necessary to perform its large contract for dashboard consoles with Ford. Because Axle is the only one with the current capacity and expertise to do the dash consoles, Ford agrees to guarantee Axle's debt to Citi.

1. Assume that Axle falls on hard times and offers to pay Citi $300,000 in full satisfaction of its $1 million liability (it has made only interest payments). Citi decides to take the money in full satisfaction. Citi asks your opinion whether it can go after Ford for the remaining $700,000. Does Citi's release of Axle also free Axle from any subrogation or other claim against it by Ford?

2. Assume that National Surety gives Ford a bond of $1 million that assures Ford that Axle will properly complete the contract. Ford and Axle agree to resolve a dispute about the quality of the consoles by Axle's agreement to take only $900,000 in full payment. Ford gives Axle a complete release in return for the settlement payment. May Ford recover the remaining $100,000 from National Surety?

In answering, consider §§ 37–39 of the Restatement (Third) of Suretyship and Guaranty, quoted at the outset of this Section.

*

Index

References are to Pages

References are to Pages

References are to Pages

References are to Pages

References are to Pages

†